THE OXFORD HANDBOOK OF
LYING

This handbook brings together past and current research on all aspects of lying and deception, with chapters contributed by leading international experts in the field. We are confronted daily with cases of lying, deception, bullshitting, and 'fake news', making it imperative to understand how lying works, how it can be defined, and whether it can be detected. A further important issue is whether lying should always be considered a bad thing or if, in some cases, it is simply a useful instrument of human cognition. This volume is the first to offer a comprehensive and up-to-date exploration of these and other issues from the combined perspectives of linguistics, philosophy, and psychology. Chapters offer precise definitions of lying and its subtypes, and outline the range of fields in which lying and deception play a role, from empirical lie-detection and the acquisition of lying to its role in fiction, metaphor, and humour. They also describe the tools and approaches that are used by scholars researching lying and deception, such as questionnaire studies, EEG, neuroimaging, and the polygraph.

The volume will be an essential reference for students and researchers in a range of fields who are looking to deepen their understanding of all aspects of lying and deception, and will contribute to establishing the vibrant new field of interdisciplinary lying research.

Jörg Meibauer is Professor emeritus of German Language and Linguistics at Johannes Gutenberg University Mainz. His research focuses on cognitive pragmatics, with an emphasis on the grammar-pragmatics interface. His many publications include *Lying at the Semantics-Pragmatics Interface* (De Gruyter Mouton 2014) and he is the editor of multiple volumes, such as *What is a Context? Linguistic Approaches and Challenges* (with R. Finkbeiner and P. B. Schumacher; Benjamins 2012) and *Pejoration* (with R. Finkbeiner; Benjamins 2016).

OXFORD HANDBOOKS IN LINGUISTICS

Recently published

THE OXFORD HANDBOOK OF CHINESE LINGUISTICS
Edited by William S-Y Wang and Chaofen Sun

THE OXFORD HANDBOOK OF THE WORD
Edited by John R. Taylor

THE OXFORD HANDBOOK OF AFRICAN AMERICAN LANGUAGE
Edited by Sonja Lanehart

THE OXFORD HANDBOOK OF INFLECTION
Edited by Matthew Baerman

THE OXFORD HANDBOOK OF HISTORICAL PHONOLOGY
Edited by Patrick Honeybone and Joseph Salmons

THE OXFORD HANDBOOK OF LEXICOGRAPHY
Edited by Philip Durkin

THE OXFORD HANDBOOK OF NAMES AND NAMING
Edited by Carole Hough

THE OXFORD HANDBOOK OF DEVELOPMENTAL LINGUISTICS
Edited by Jeffrey Lidz, William Snyder, and Joe Pater

THE OXFORD HANDBOOK OF INFORMATION STRUCTURE
Edited by Caroline Féry and Shinichiro Ishihara

THE OXFORD HANDBOOK OF MODALITY AND MOOD
Edited by Jan Nuyts and Johan van der Auwera

THE OXFORD HANDBOOK OF PRAGMATICS
Edited by Yan Huang

THE OXFORD HANDBOOK OF UNIVERSAL GRAMMAR
Edited by Ian Roberts

THE OXFORD HANDBOOK OF ERGATIVITY
Edited by Jessica Coon, Diane Massam, and Lisa deMena Travis

THE OXFORD HANDBOOK OF POLYSYNTHESIS
Edited by Michael Fortescue, Marianne Mithun, and Nicholas Evans

THE OXFORD HANDBOOK OF EVIDENTIALITY
Edited by Alexandra Y. Aikhenvald

THE OXFORD HANDBOOK OF PERSIAN LINGUISTICS
Edited by Anousha Sedighi and Pouneh Shabani-Jadidi

THE OXFORD HANDBOOK OF LYING
Edited by Jörg Meibauer

For a complete list of Oxford Handbooks in Linguistics please see pp. 661–3

THE OXFORD HANDBOOK OF
LYING

Edited by
JÖRG MEIBAUER

Great Clarendon Street, Oxford, OX2 6DP,
United Kingdom

Oxford University Press is a department of the University of Oxford.
It furthers the University's objective of excellence in research, scholarship,
and education by publishing worldwide. Oxford is a registered trade mark of
Oxford University Press in the UK and in certain other countries

© editorial matter and organization Jörg Meibauer 2019
© the chapters their several authors 2019

The moral rights of the authors have been asserted

First published 2019
First published in paperback 2022

All rights reserved. No part of this publication may be reproduced, stored in
a retrieval system, or transmitted, in any form or by any means, without the
prior permission in writing of Oxford University Press, or as expressly permitted
by law, by licence or under terms agreed with the appropriate reprographics
rights organization. Enquiries concerning reproduction outside the scope of the
above should be sent to the Rights Department, Oxford University Press, at the
address above

You must not circulate this work in any other form
and you must impose this same condition on any acquirer

Published in the United States of America by Oxford University Press
198 Madison Avenue, New York, NY 10016, United States of America

British Library Cataloguing in Publication Data
Data available

Library of Congress Cataloging in Publication Data
Data available

ISBN 978–0–19–873657–8 (Hbk.)
ISBN 978–0–19–286337–9 (Pbk.)

Printed and bound by
CPI Group (UK) Ltd, Croydon, CR0 4YY

Links to third party websites are provided by Oxford in good faith and
for information only. Oxford disclaims any responsibility for the materials
contained in any third party website referenced in this work.

Contents

Preface — ix
List of figures and tables — xiii
List of contributors — xv

1. Introduction: What is lying? Towards an integrative approach — 1
   JÖRG MEIBAUER

PART I TRADITIONS

2. Classic philosophical approaches to lying and deception — 13
   JAMES EDWIN MAHON

3. Contemporary approaches to the philosophy of lying — 32
   JAMES EDWIN MAHON

4. Linguistic approaches to lying and deception — 56
   KAROL J. HARDIN

5. Psycholinguistic approaches to lying and deception — 71
   LEWIS BOTT AND EMMA WILLIAMS

6. Lying, deception, and the brain — 83
   ALEXA DECKER, AMANDA DISNEY, BRIANNA D'ELIA, AND JULIAN PAUL KEENAN

PART II CONCEPTS

7. Lying and truth — 95
   STEPHEN WRIGHT

8. Lying and assertion — 109
   MARK JARY

9. Lying, belief, and knowledge — 120
   MATTHEW A. BENTON

10. Lying, sincerity, and quality — 134
    ANDREAS STOKKE

11. Lying and deception — 149
    ANDREW ORTONY AND SWATI GUPTA

12. Lying and certainty — 170
    NERI MARSILI

13. Lying and omissions — 183
    DON FALLIS

14. Lying, implicating, and presupposing — 193
    JÖRG MEIBAUER

15. Lying and self-deception — 203
    KATHI BEIER

16. Lying, testimony, and epistemic vigilance — 214
    ELIOT MICHAELSON

PART III TYPES OF LIES AND DECEPTION

17. Knowledge lies and group lies — 231
    JULIA STAFFEL

18. Selfless assertions — 244
    JENNIFER LACKEY

19. Bald-faced lies — 252
    JÖRG MEIBAUER

20. Bullshitting — 264
    ANDREAS STOKKE

21. Bluffing — 277
    JENNIFER PERILLO

22. White and prosocial lies — 288
    SIMONE DIETZ

PART IV DISTINCTIONS

23. Lying and fiction 303
    EMAR MAIER

24. Lying and quotation 315
    MATTHEW S. MCGLONE AND MAXIM BARYSHEVTSEV

25. Lying and humour 326
    MARTA DYNEL

26. Lying, irony, and default interpretation 340
    RACHEL GIORA

27. Lying and vagueness 354
    PAUL EGRÉ AND BENJAMIN ICARD

28. Lying, metaphor, and hyperbole 370
    CLAUDIA CLARIDGE

29. Lying and politeness 382
    MARINA TERKOURAFI

PART V DOMAINS

30. Development of lying and cognitive abilities 399
    VICTORIA TALWAR

31. Lying and lie detection 408
    SAMANTHA MANN

32. Lying and computational linguistics 420
    KEES VAN DEEMTER AND EHUD REITER

33. Lying in social psychology 436
    BELLA M. DEPAULO

34. Lying and psychology 446
    KRISTINA SUCHOTZKI AND MATTHIAS GAMER

35. Lying and neuroscience 456
    GIORGIO GANIS

36. Lying and ethics 469
    THOMAS L. CARSON

37. Lying and the law 483
    STUART P. GREEN

38. Lying in economics 495
    MARTA SERRA-GARCIA

39. Lying and education 506
    ANITA E. KELLY

40. Lying and discourse analysis 517
    DARIUSZ GALASIŃSKI

41. Lying and deception in politics 529
    VIAN BAKIR, ERIC HERRING, DAVID MILLER, AND PIERS ROBINSON

42. Lying and history 541
    THOMAS L. CARSON

43. Lying and the arts 553
    BETTINA KÜMMERLING-MEIBAUER

44. Lying in different cultures 565
    FUMIKO NISHIMURA

References 579
Index 651

Preface

This handbook is the first handbook to provide a collection of in-depth research surveys on lying and deception. Lying is a phenomenon that was already being researched in ancient Greece. Yet, despite the huge public interest in all matters concerning lying and deception, attempts at forming an integrated, comprehensive approach to lying have been lacking. While this handbook is truly multi- and interdisciplinary in nature, three disciplines stand out as core disciplines. The first discipline is linguistics, the study of languages and the use people make of them in communication. Lying is a verbal act, and therefore it is bound to the structure of languages. Lying is dependent on the intention of speakers who try to deceive their addressees. Therefore, lying can be located at the semantics–pragmatics interface. The second discipline is the philosophy of language and ethics. Since ancient times, philosophers have attempted to define lying in a proper way, focusing on more or less clear cases of lying. This tradition has lasted until today. Moreover, philosophers have dealt with the important ethical question of whether lying is bad. The third discipline is psychology, together with related disciplines such as language acquisition research, psycho- and neurolinguistics, and the neurosciences. All of these disciplines are represented in this handbook but there are far more that contribute to a deeper understanding of the theory and practice of lying.

The overall structure of the handbook is as follows. It is organized into five parts, each part comprising several chapters. It starts with a comprehensive introductory article by the editor that gives a general survey on lying and deception. The first part, "traditions," comprises a set of chapters which give an overview of the classic philosophical approaches by Plato, Aristotle, and Socrates and a number of contemporary approaches, linguistic approaches, and also psycholinguistic and neurolinguistic approaches. These seem to be the traditions that will most forcefully inform a future general theory of the language of lying. The second part, "concepts," is devoted to an in-depth conceptual analysis, leading to an adequate definition of lying. The focus is on notions that directly or indirectly go into that definition, i.e., the notions of deception, truth and truthfulness, assertion, belief and knowledge, sincerity and quality, certainty, misleading, implicating and presupposing, omission, self-deception, testimony, including the notion of epistemic vigilance that has recently attracted some attention. The important notion of intention has a role in all of these chapters. Throughout the chapters, theoretical approaches from the most advanced researchers of lying are discussed in detail, while the more classical analyses of lying are closely observed. The third part, "types of lies and deception," assembles up-to-date chapters on a range of deceptive actions, thus fostering future discussions on the proper definition of these types. In addition to the classical cases of lying, other types of lying-related acts have been studied, e.g., knowledge lies and group lies, selfless assertions, bald-faced lies, bullshitting, bluffing, as well as pro-social lies and white lies. The fourth part, "distinctions," discusses broader aspects related to a proper definition of lying. It contains chapters analyzing the relation between lying and fiction, deception in quotation, the relation between lying and humor, irony, vagueness and imprecision, metaphor and hyperbole, and politeness. The fifth and final part, "domains," portrays lying with the perspectives of different domains and disciplines. From a cognitive point of view, lying is quite a sophisticated enterprise that demands high cognitive activity and control. Therefore, it is worth pointing out that lying skills have to be acquired. Further chapters deal with lying in the perspective of psychology and social psychology, where much work on lying and deception has been done. Lie detection, for instance with the help of the polygraph, is important in a practical ("applied") as well as a theoretical perspective. Computational models about lying and deception are also relevant here. Another chapter concentrates on findings about the location and processing of lying in the brain, as measured, for instance, on the basis of fMRI-data or evoked brain potentials. From the point of view of ethics and moral philosophy, lying has mostly been treated as a dishonest behavior. However, there are also approaches that view lying as a cognitive ability that is neutral with respect to dishonest versus honest behavior. In most Western societies, the law prohibits lying by the defendant, yet allows it under specific circumstances. One chapter explores these conditions, including perjury. Since lying has to be acquired (yet is not always tolerated in society), it is also a topic in education (from kindergarten to university level). Not much is known about lying as part of a wider discourse; hence, another chapter focuses on lying within different types of discourse and the methods for documenting them. We are well aware of lying in politics and in history. Moreover, lying and liars are topics in the arts (e.g., from Shakespeare to *Mad Men*). Finally, it is explored whether there are different ways to lie or to evaluate lying with respect to different cultures, pointing out cross- and intercultural aspects of lying.

While the handbook collects a number of excellent surveys, it is by no means exhaustive. In some cases, suitable authors could not be found, or promised chapters were not delivered. I hope that there will be occasions to fill these loopholes in the future. Responsibility for the material lies with the authors of the individual, peer-reviewed chapters, who were given guidelines as to the type of chapter requested, but were also allowed substantial freedom to structure their chapters according to their respective topics and academic backgrounds. The resultant diversity in style makes for an accessible and engaging collection. The chapters should be appealing to a wide audience. The handbook aims at scholars, researchers, graduate and advanced undergraduate students with an interest in lying and deception and invites transgression of disciplinary boundaries.

This handbook has been long in the making. I thank all the contributors and reviewers, the excellent staff at Oxford University Press, and Marta Dynel, Bettina Kümmerling-Meibauer, Neri Marsili, Alexander Sommerburg, Björn Technau, and Alex Wiegmann for cooperation, advice, and help in the editing of the manuscript.

A grant by the Volkswagen Foundation made the Mainz conference on lying and deception (Johannes Gutenberg University, 2014) possible, an inspiring event during which some of the contributors to this handbook gathered and exchanged their ideas. I hope that there will be more such fruitful exchange in the future, and that this handbook will be useful in fostering that.

Jörg Meibauer
Mainz
January 2018

List of figures and tables

Figures

5.1	Speech production process (Levelt 1989)	72
11.1	The relations among the goals of prevention-motivated deception (by commission) from the perspective of a speaker, S, whose motivating goal is to PREVENT the hearer, H, from believing q_c. S achieves this by means of lower-level communicative goals, CONTINUE, ACQUIRE, and CEASE, whose conditions for activation are indicated. The action (goal) side of each condition-action pair is the belief about p--the believed false proposition which S believes does not suggest q_c--that S seeks to obtain in H.	154
12.1	A visual representation of the certainty–uncertainty continuum.	172
27.1	Varieties of linguistic vagueness.	356
32.1	Example time-series input data for Babytalk BT45 system (from Reiter 2007). HR is heart rate, SO is oxygen saturation, TC is core temperature, TP is peripheral (toe) temperature, BM is mean blood pressure.	422
35.1	Schematic illustration of the logic of forward and reverse inferences. A forward inference is the probability that a certain pattern of brain activation (e.g., A1) is elicited by a certain mental state (e.g., deception, D). This information can be obtained by carrying out brain-imaging studies in which the mental state of interest is manipulated, and measuring the brain-activation effects of the manipulation. A reverse inference, in contrast, is the probability that a certain mental state (e.g., deception, D), is present, given a certain pattern of activation in the brain (e.g., A1). Given that a certain pattern of activation can be produced by multiple mental states (e.g., A1 can be elicited by D and S2), it is necessary to use Bayes' rule to calculate probabilities in inverse inferences (see text).	463
35.2	Results of the overlap analysis. In green are voxels engaged by one or more of the control tasks ('working memory', 'inhibition', 'task switching', and 'theory of mind'), but not by deception; in yellow are voxels engaged in common by deception and by at least one of the control tasks; in red are	

	voxels engaged exclusively by deception. The patterns of activation are overlaid on horizontal slices through a normalized and deskulled brain.	465
39.1	Competing goals in the classroom (adapted from Kelly and Maxwell (2016)).	515

Tables

11.1	For the three communicative subgoals of prevention-motivated deception (by commission), the initial conditions for a speaker, S, and S's target belief state for a hearer, H, vis à vis an asserted proposition, q, a Gricean Cooperative proposition, qc, and (with the exception of CEASE) some qc-incompatible false proposition, p.	156
11.2	Three goals of prevention-motivated deception (by commission) and some strategies that can achieve them (indicated with ✓). Strategies marked * can often (and in some cases, only) achieve the associated goals when applied in conjunction with Acquire.	168
29.1	Categorization of lies (reproduced from Bryant 2008: 32).	390
32.1	Types of deviation from the truth.	424
38.1	Overview of experimental designs to measure lying aversion.	499
44.1	The first excuse that appeared in the data.	575
44.2	Role A's responses to Role B's excuses.	576

List of Contributors

Vian Bakir is Professor in Political Communication and Journalism at Bangor University, Wales. Her research examines the interplay among journalism, political communication, and the security state, focusing on agenda-building, persuasion, influence, and public accountability. Her books include *Intelligence Elites and Public Accountability* (Routledge, 2018), *Torture, Intelligence and Sousveillance in the War on Terror* (Routledge, 2013) and *Sousveillance, Media and Strategic Political Communication. Iraq, USA, UK* (Bloomsbury Academic, 2010). Recent grants from the Economic and Social Research Council (ESRC) include *DATA—PSST! Debating & Assessing Transparency Arrangements: Privacy, Security, Surveillance, Trust* (2015–17); and *Political-Intelligence Elites: Towards Better Public Accountability through a Co-created Benchmark for Civil Society* (2016–17).

Maxim Baryshevtsev is a doctoral student at the University of Texas at Austin in the Department of Communication Studies. He focuses his research on deception, persuasion, dark side communication, and cybercrime. His recent publications and in-development studies involve the language used by sexual predators, how people perceive deception, and the strategies identity thieves use to manipulate and deceive their targets. His future research will focus on how practitioners can better educate vulnerable populations and how law enforcement can better identify and stop cybercriminals.

Kathi Beier is COFUND-Fellow at the Max Weber Centre for Advanced Cultural and Social Studies at the University of Erfurt, Germany. She has been Assistant Professor at the Department of Philosophy at the University of Vienna, Austria, and guest researcher at KU Leuven, Belgium. She received her PhD in Philosophy, with a thesis about self-deception (published as *Selbsttäuschung* by Walter de Gruyter, 2010). Her research interests also include virtue ethics old and new.

Matthew A. Benton is an Assistant Professor of Philosophy at Seattle Pacific University. Prior to that he held postdoctoral research fellowships at the University of Notre Dame and the University of Oxford. He writes mainly in Epistemology, Philosophy of Language, and Philosophy of Religion. He has published articles in *The Philosophical Quarterly, Analysis, Noûs, Philosophy & Phenomenological Research, Synthese, Philosophical Studies, Philosophical Perspectives, Episteme, Oxford Studies in Philosophy of Religion*, and *Religious Studies*, among other journals. He is co-editor of *Knowledge, Belief, and God* (Oxford University Press, 2018) and has a monograph on *Knowledge and Language* in preparation.

Lewis Bott is a Reader at the School of Psychology, Cardiff University. His PhD on "Prior Knowledge and Statistical Models of Categorization" was completed at Warwick University and he undertook postdoctoral work at the Institut des Sciences Cognitives, Lyon, and New York University, New York. He works on psycholinguistics and (experimental) pragmatics, and specializes in implications.

Thomas L. Carson is Professor of Philosophy at Loyola University Chicago. He is the author of *The Status of Morality* (Reidel, 1984), *Value and the Good Life* (Notre Dame, 2000), *Lying and Deception: Theory and Practice* (Oxford University Press, 2010), and *Lincoln's Ethics* (Cambridge University Press, 2015). In addition, he has co-edited two other books, *Morality and the Good Life* (Oxford University Press, 1997) and *Moral Relativism* (Oxford University Press, 2001), and authored more than ninety articles and reviews. He has written on a wide range of topics in ethical theory and applied ethics.

Claudia Claridge is Professor of English Linguistics at the University of Augsburg, Germany. Her research interests include the history of English (with a focus on Early and Late Modern English), diachronic and synchronic pragmatics (in particular figurative language), historical text linguistics, as well as corpus linguistics. She is a co-compiler of the *Lampeter Corpus of Early Modern English* (1640–1740). She has authored two monographs: *Multi-word Verbs in Early Modern English* (Brill Rodopi, 2000) and *Hyperbole in English* (Cambridge University Press, 2011). Currently she is working on intensifiers in the historical courtroom and the development of the register of historiography.

Brianna D'Elia has published on auditory perception in Drosophila melanogaster, demonstrating discriminatory patterns based on Pavlovian conditioning. In this work she parsed out the dissonance and consonance of frequency in sound waves and has discovered that certain sound intervals are associated with certain primary food resources. She is currently at The University of New England College of Dental Medicine.

Alexa Decker is trained in both molecular biology and cognitive psychology. Her graduate work focused on behavior genetics and Pavlovian conditioning in Drosophila melanogaster. She has reported evolutionary choice strategies in Drosophila such that ovipositioning is influenced by available food resources for offspring. Her previous work involved Drosophila genetic transmission of auditory learning across multiple generations and she developed a force-choice paradigm in flies that serves as an analogue to similar devices in mammals. She is currently in the private sector.

Bella M. DePaulo, PhD (Harvard), is an Academic Affiliate, Psychological and Brain Sciences at the University of California, Santa Barbara. She has published extensively on deception and the psychology of single life and has received federal funding for her work. Dr. DePaulo has lectured nationally and internationally and has been honoured with a variety of awards, including a James McKeen Cattell Award and a Research Scientist Development Award. Her website is www.BellaDePaulo.com.

Simone Dietz is Professor of Philosophy at the Heinrich Heine University of Düsseldorf. Her research interest are in ethics and social and cultural philosophy.

Besides several papers on lying and deception, she has published two monographs on lying: *Der Wert der Lüge. Über das Verhältnis von Sprache und Moral* (The value of lying. On the relation between language and moral) (Mentis, 2003) and *Die Kunst des Lügens* (The art of lying) (Reclam, 2017).

Amanda Disney has focused on both humans and Drosophila. In humans, she is investigating the role peer-pressure plays on deception in the Medial Prefrontal Cortex. She has also worked on issues of choice using Transcranial Magnetic Stimulation testing Libet's notion of free will. In Drosophila, Amanda investigated auditory discrimination in adults and larvae. She is currently at Indiana University School of Dentistry.

Marta Dynel is Associate Professor in the Department of Pragmatics at the University of Łódź. Her research interests are primarily in pragmatic and cognitive mechanisms of humour, neo-Gricean pragmatics, the pragmatics of interaction, (im)politeness theory, the philosophy of irony and deception, as well as the methodology of research on film discourse. She has devoted to these topics over eighty papers, two monographs, as well as ten co-edited volumes and special issues in journals. Her latest monograph is *Irony, Deception and Humour: Seeking the Truth about Overt and Covert Untruthfulness* (De Gruyter Mouton, 2018).

Paul Egré is Directeur de recherche at CNRS, Institut Jean Nicod, and Associate Professor in the Department of Philosophy of Ecole Normale Supérieure in Paris. His work over the last decade has focused mostly on the phenomenon of vagueness in natural language, with contributions in logic, semantics, and cognitive psychology. Paul Egré is also Editor-in-Chief of the *Review of Philosophy and Psychology* (Springer), and co-leader of an ANR-funded project on applications of trivalent logics to natural language (with Benjamin Spector).

Don Fallis is a Professor in the School of Information and an adjunct professor in the Department of Philosophy at the University of Arizona. His research interests include epistemology, philosophy of information, and philosophy of mathematics. His articles on lying and deception have appeared in the *Journal of Philosophy*, *Philosophical Studies*, and the *Australasian Journal of Philosophy*. He has also discussed lying on Philosophy TV and in several volumes of the Philosophy and Popular Culture series.

Dariusz Galasiński is Professor of Discourse and Cultural Studies at the University of Wolverhampton, UK and Visiting Professor at the University of Social Sciences and Humanities, Warsaw, Poland. As a discourse analyst, he specializes in discursively constructed experience of mental illness, organ donation, suicide attempts, and suicide notes. He is the author of *The Language of Deception. A Discourse Analytic Study* (Sage, 2000). His latest book is *Discourses of Men's Suicide Notes* (Bloomsbury, 2017).

Matthias Gamer is a Professor in Experimental Clinical Psychology at the University of Würzburg, Germany. Using a variety of approaches ranging from behavioural and psychophysiological to neuroimaging methods, his research is devoted to basic as well as applied issues in deception detection. He has published numerous journal articles on deception and co-edited the eBook *Basic and Applied Research on Deception and its Detection* (2014) for Frontiers.

Giorgio Ganis is currently Associate Professor/Reader in Cognitive Neuroscience at the School of Psychology at Plymouth University (UK). His research interests include the neural basis of cognitive control processes in social and visual cognition, with an emphasis on deception production and perception processes. For nearly two decades, he has been pursuing these interests using the tools of psychology and cognitive neuroscience (behaviour, ERPs, TMS, fMRI, NIRS). His work has been published in several tens of international journals, book chapters, and media articles.

Rachel Giora is Professor of Linguistics at Tel Aviv University. Her research areas include cognitive aspects of coherence and women and language. As of 1997, her work has focused on experimentally testing the Graded Salience Hypothesis and the Defaultness Hypothesis (2017), featuring the psycholinguistics and neurolinguistics of non-/default, non-/figurative language, context effects, optimal innovations, aesthetic pleasure, and discourse negation. She has published over 130 articles, a book—*On Our Mind* (Oxford University Press, 2003)—co-edited a six-volume series with Patrick Hanks on figurative language (2011) and also co-edited a volume with Michael Haugh, entitled *Doing Intercultural Pragmatics: Cognitive, Linguistic, and Sociopragmatic Perspectives on Language Use* (De Gruyter Mouton, 2017). Her website is http://www.tau.ac.il/~giorar.

Stuart P. Green is Distinguished Professor of Law at Rutgers University. His books include *Lying, Cheating, and Stealing: A Moral Theory of White Collar Crime* (Oxford University Press, 2006); *Thirteen Ways to Steal a Bicycle: Theft Law in the Information Age* (Harvard University Press, 2012); *Philosophical Foundations of Criminal Law* (co-edited with Antony Duff) (Oxford University Press, 2011), and the forthcoming *Criminalizing Sex: A Unified Theory*. The recipient of fellowships from the Leverhulme Trust, the US-UK Fulbright Commission, and Corpus Christi College, Oxford, Green has served as visiting professor or fellow at the Universities of Glasgow, Melbourne, Michigan, Oxford, and Tel Aviv, the ANU, and the LSE.

Swati Gupta is a principal research scientist at Callaghan Innovation, New Zealand government's Crow Entity. She took her PhD at the University of Sheffield, UK, in Natural Language Generation for Spoken Dialogue Systems. Inspired by theories in Cognitive Science, Social Psychology, and Linguistics, her research focuses on Human–Computer Interaction, especially as it can be applied to the solution of social, environmental, and health problems. Before joining Callaghan Innovation, she worked as a Scientist at A*STAR in Singapore.

Karol J. Hardin is Associate Professor of Spanish at Baylor University, where she teaches linguistics and coordinates Spanish for Health Professions. Her PhD is in Hispanic Linguistics, from the University of Texas at Austin. Combining pragmatics as well as Spanish in health-care contexts, her recent publications include articles on the pragmatics of dialogue in a health setting, the pragmatics of persuasion in sermons, a critical review of medical Spanish programs in the US, and a co-authored textbook entitled *Español conversacional para profesiones médicas: Manual de actividades* (Stipes Publishing, 2016). Her current research interests include miscommunication between physicians and Spanish-speaking patients.

Eric Herring is Professor of World Politics in the School of Sociology, Politics and International Studies at the University of Bristol. His books include *Iraq in Fragments: The Occupation and its Legacy* (Cornell University Press, 2006) with Glen Rangwala; *The Arms Dynamic in World Politics* (Lynne Rienner Publishers, 1998) with Barry Buzan; and *Danger and Opportunity: Explaining International Crisis Outcomes* (Manchester University Press, 1995). His research has been published in journals such as *Political Science Quarterly, Review of International Studies, Millennium*, and *Globalizations*. His current research has two main strands: promoting locally led development in Somalia and organized persuasive communication, including propaganda.

Benjamin Icard is pursuing a PhD in Philosophy under the supervision of Prof. Paul Égré at Institut Jean Nicod in Paris. His research interests concern the definition and evaluation of information quality, using resources from epistemology, logic, and conversational pragmatics. His doctoral project, funded by the French Ministry of Defence, aims at understanding the dynamics of complex unreliable attitudes (such as lying, deceiving, misinforming), and at solving some of the issues they raise through conceptual and experimental investigations.

Mark Jary is Professor of Linguistics and Philosophy at the University of Roehampton, UK. He has a strong interest in sentence types and the speech acts they are used to perform. He is the author of *Assertion* (Palgrave, 2010) and, with Mikhail Kissine, *Imperatives* (Cambridge University Press, 2014). He has published a number of papers relating to linguistic mood and illocutionary force in journals such as *Linguistics and Philosophy, Mind and Language, Linguistics*, and *Journal of Pragmatics*.

Julian Paul Keenan, PhD is a Professor in the Department of Biology at Montclair State University. He previously worked at Harvard Medical School in the Department of Neurology, where he examined the neural and evolutionary correlates of self-awareness and deception. He co-edited the collection *The Lost Self. Pathologies of the Brain and Identity* (Oxford University Press, 2005). His current work is focused on the molecular and genetic factors related to deception, self-deception, and human cognition.

Anita E. Kelly, PhD is a Professor of Psychology at the University of Notre Dame. She is author of the books, *The Clever Student: A Guide to Getting the Most from Your Professor* (Corby Publication, 2010) and *The Psychology of Secrets* (Springer, 2002), and has written a number of scientific articles on secrecy, self-presentation, and self-concept change. Her work on secrecy has been featured in the *Chicago Tribune*,

New York Times, *Los Angeles Times*, *Newsday*, and *Glamour* and *Health* magazines. Professor Kelly became a licensed psychotherapist in 1993 while serving as an assistant professor at Iowa State University, where she was awarded Outstanding Faculty Member for teaching. She has taught at Notre Dame since 1994 and became a Kaneb Teaching Fellow in 2008.

Bettina Kümmerling-Meibauer is a Professor in the German Department at the University of Tübingen, Germany. She has been a guest professor at the University of Växjö, Sweden, and the University of Vienna. She is the author of four books, including an encyclopedia of international children's classics (Metzler, 1999) and a monograph on canon processes in children's literature (Metzler, 2003). Her recent co-edited books include *Children's Literature and the Avant-Garde* (John Benjamins, 2015), *Canon Constitution and Canon Change in Children's Literature* (Routledge, 2017), *Maps and Mapping in Children's Literature* (John Benjamins, 2017), and *The Routledge Companion to Picturebooks* (Routledge, 2018).

Jennifer Lackey is the Wayne and Elizabeth Jones Professor of Philosophy at Northwestern University. Most of her research is in social epistemology, where she focuses on testimony, disagreement, group states, credibility, and applied epistemology. She is the author of *Learning from Words: Testimony as a Source of Knowledge* (Oxford University Press, 2010) and the editor of several volumes, including *Essays in Collective Epistemology* (Oxford University Press, 2017) and *The Epistemology of Disagreement: New Essays* (Oxford University Press, 2016).

James Edwin Mahon is Professor of Philosophy and Chair of the Department of Philosophy at The City University of New York–Lehman College. He is the author of the entry *The Definition of Lies and Deception* for the *Stanford Encyclopedia of Philosophy*, as well as a number of articles and book chapters on Kant on lies. He regularly teaches an undergraduate seminar on lies and deception for the Program on Ethics, Politics and Economics at Yale Summer Session.

Emar Maier is Assistant Professor at the University of Groningen, The Netherlands, affiliated with both the Philosophy and Linguistics Departments. He received his PhD in Philosophy from the University of Nijmegen (2006), held several postdoctoral positions, and led an ERC Starting Grant project. He is currently leading an NWO VIDI project, investigating the semantics of imagination and fiction, combining insights from philosophy, linguistics, and literary studies. His research interests include: narrativity, quotation, indexicality, and attitudes. He has published on these topics in a range of journals including *Theoretical Linguistics, Linguistics and Philosophy, Journal of Philosophical Logic, Mind and Language*, and *Journal of Literary Semantics*.

Samantha Mann is a Senior Research Fellow at the University of Portsmouth, with over nineteen years of experience in researching lie detection. Since her PhD examining the behaviour of high-stakes, real-life liars in their police interviews and police officers' ability to detect those lies, she has conducted research into designing interview protocols to enhance ability to detect deceit in cooperation with governments and police, and has over eighty publications on the topic of deception. Recently, Samantha's deception research has focused on the behaviour of, and devising methods to detect, smugglers, or any person posing a threat in a crowd.

Neri Marsili is a Juan de la Cierva Postdoctoral Fellow at the University of Barcelona (Logos Research Group). He obtained his PhD at the University of Sheffield with a dissertation on lying, assertion, and insincerity. His publications include "Assertion and Truth: rules versus aims (*Analysis*), "Lying by promising," (*International Review of Pragmatics*) and "Lying as a scalar phenomenon" (in the volume *Certainty-Uncertainty—and the Attitudinal Space in Between* (John Benjamins)).

Matthew S. McGlone, PhD (Princeton University) is Professor of Communication Studies and Associate Director of the Center for Health Communication at The University of Texas at Austin. He has edited two books (*The Interplay of Truth and Deception,* Routledge 2010, with Mark Knapp; *Work Pressures,* Routledge 2016, with Dawna Ballard) and co-authored a textbook (*Lying and Deception in Human Interaction*, Kendall Hunt, 2nd edn 2015, with Mark Knapp, Darrin Griffin, and Billy Earnest). His research explores persuasion and social influence, deception, and communication technologies for promoting health and wellness.

Jörg Meibauer is Professor of German Language and Linguistics at the Johannes Gutenberg University of Mainz, Germany. He is the author of the monograph *Lying at the Semantics-Pragmatics Interface* (De Gruyter Mouton, 2014), as well as a number of articles and book chapters dealing with lying and deception. Other monographs concern rhetorical questions, modal particles, and pragmatics. He has co-edited several collections, e.g., *Understanding Quotation* (De Gruyter Mouton, 2011), *Experimental Semantics/Pragmatics* (John Benjamins, 2011), *What is a Context?* (John Benjamins, 2012), *Satztypen des Deutschen* [Sentence Types in German] (De Gruyter, 2013), *Pejoration* (John Benjamins, 2016), and *Satztypen und Konstruktionen im Deutschen* [Sentence Types and Constructions in German] (De Gruyter, 2016).

Eliot Michaelson is a Senior Lecturer in Philosophy at King's College London. He completed his PhD on "This and That: A Theory of Reference for Names Demonstratives and Things in Between" at UCLA in 2013, and was a Mellon Postdoctoral Fellow at McGill University before joining the department at King's. He works primarily in the philosophy of language and occasionally makes the mistake of trying to do public philosophy. Together with Andreas Stokke, he is the editor of the forthcoming collection "Lying: Language, Knowledge, Ethics, Politics" (Oxford University Press).

David Miller is Professor of Sociology in the Department of Social & Policy Sciences at the University of Bath in England. From 2013 to 2016 he was RCUK Global Uncertainties Leadership Fellow, leading a project on understanding and explaining terrorism expertise in practice. Amongst his recent publications is *What is Islamophobia? Racism, Social Movements and the State* (Pluto Press, 2017). He is also the co-editor of *Impact of*

Market Forces on Addictive Substances and Behaviours: The Web of Influence of Addictive Industries (Pluto Press, 2017) and co-author of *The Israel Lobby and the European Union* (Spinwatch & Europal, 2016) and *The New Governance of Addictive Substances and Behaviours* (Oxford University Press, 2017).

Fumiko Nishimura is the convener of the Japanese Programme in the Faculty of Arts and Social Sciences at the University of Waikato, New Zealand. Her main research interests include sociolinguistics, cross-cultural communication, and Japanese language pedagogy. She is interested in everyday communication from cross-cultural perspectives and has published some of her findings in *Ibunka to komyunikēshon* [Different cultures and communication] (Hituzi Shobo, 2005) and *Japanese-Language Education around the Globe* (2007). Her recent research on Japanese learners' communication can be found in *Creating New Synergies: Approaches of Tertiary Japanese Programmes in New Zealand* (Massey University Press, 2016).

Andrew Ortony Professor Emeritus at Northwestern University, is a cognitive scientist best known for his research on metaphor and on emotions. His edited volume, *Metaphor and Thought* (Cambridge University Press, 2nd edn 1993) is a landmark interdisciplinary work in the field of metaphor, and the analysis of emotions described in his co-authored book, *The Cognitive Structure of Emotions* (Cambridge University Press, 1990), is used as the basis for most emotion-modelling efforts in Artificial Intelligence. Ortony's current interests centre on emotions in relation to social and linguistic behaviour.

Jennifer Perillo is an Assistant Professor of Psychology at Indiana University of Pennsylvania. Among her research topics is the psychology of bluffing and false confessions. Previously, she was an assistant professor at Winston-Salem State University. She received her PhD in Forensic Psychology from the City University of New York and her MA in Forensic Psychology from John Jay College of Criminal Justice. She has a BA in Psychology and Political, Legal, & Economic Analysis from Mills College in Oakland, CA.

Ehud Reiter is a professor of Computing Science at the University of Aberdeen. He is one of the most respected and cited researchers in the world in Natural Language Generation (with a Google Scholar h-index of 37), and founded the NLG research group at the University of Aberdeen. He also co-authored what has become the standard NLG textbook, *Building Natural Language Generation Systems* (Cambridge University Press, 2003). He currently spends most of his time working in a spin-out company, Arria NLG, which he helped to found. Professor Reiter's core research interests are building real-world NLG systems (such as the Babytalk system described in the chapter), evaluation of NLG systems, narrative generation, and lexical (word) choice. Several of his projects have involved generating texts which potentially have an emotional impact on the recipient, and working on these projects has highlighted the fact that there are cases in real-world applied NLG systems where it may be in the user's interest for the NLG system to "be economical" with the truth.

Piers Robinson is Chair in Politics, Society and Political Journalism at the Department of Journalism Studies, University of Sheffield. He researches organized persuasive communication and contemporary propaganda and is co-director of the Organisation for Propaganda Studies. Recent publications include *The Routledge Handbook of Media, Conflict and Security* (co-editors Philip Seib and Romy Fröhlich, Routledge, 2017) and *Learning from the Chilcot Report: Propaganda, Deception and the "War on Terror"*, in *International Journal of Contemporary Iraqi Studies* 11(1–2).

Marta Serra-Garcia completed her PhD in 2011 at Tilburg University and is currently Assistant Professor in Economics at the Rady School of Management, University of California San Diego. Her main research interests lie in the areas of behavioural and experimental economics. She focuses on the importance of morals and social norms in economic decision-making. Among other methods, she uses theory and experiments to study morality, with a focus on deception and self-deception.

Julia Staffel is an Assistant Professor of Philosophy at the University of Colorado at Boulder. She received her PhD in philosophy from the University of Southern California in 2013. She mainly works in the areas of traditional and formal epistemology, with a focus on questions about rationality and reasoning. Her book *Unsettled Thoughts: A Theory of Degrees of Rationality* will appear at Oxford University Press.

Andreas Stokke is a Pro Futura Scientia fellow at the Swedish Collegium for Advanced Study and a senior lecturer in the Department of Philosophy at Uppsala University. His research is mainly in the fields of philosophy of language and epistemology, but he has also worked on ethics and philosophy of action. He has worked extensively on lying, deception, and insincere speech more generally. He is the author of *Lying and Insincerity* (Oxford University Press, 2018) and co-editor of the collection *Lying: Language, Knowledge, Ethics, Politics* (with Eliot Michaelson, at Oxford University Press).

Kristina Suchotzki completed her PhD in 2014 at Ghent University in Belgium and is currently a postdoctoral fellow at the University of Würzburg in Germany. Her main research interests include the psychological mechanisms underlying deception and information concealment and how those may be used to improve deception detection methods. She mainly uses different behavioural, autonomic, and neural measures and recently published a meta-analysis on the validity of reaction times as measures of deception.

Victoria Talwar is a Professor and a Canada Research Chair (II) in Forensic Developmental Psychology in the Department of Educational and Counselling Psychology at McGill University. Her research is in the area of developmental psychology, with an emphasis on social–cognitive development and the Theory of Mind. She has published numerous articles on the development of lying in children, children's honesty and lie-telling behaviour, as well as child witness testimony.

Marina Terkourafi is a Professor and Chair of sociolinguistics at Leiden University, the Netherlands. Her main research interests lie in socio-pragmatics, with a focus on im/politeness and indirect speech, pragmatic variation, and how language resources are used to constitute various (ethnic, gender, social) identities in discourse. She has published over fifty journal articles and book chapters on these topics and sits on various editorial boards, including serving as co-editor in chief of the *Journal of Pragmatics* (Elsevier).

Kees van Deemter a Professor in Computing Science at Utrecht University, works in Computational Linguistics, a research area that belongs to both Artificial Intelligence and Cognitive Science. Kees' main areas of expertise are Computational Semantics and Natural Language Generation. He has long taken an interest in logical and philosophical issues arising from this work, and he has collaborated extensively with psycholinguists interested in algorithmic models of human language production. His research centres around computational models of human communication, and around applications of these models to practical problems (e.g., automatically explaining "big data" in human language). He is intrigued by situations in which communication is or appears to be flawed, as when we use expressions that are ambiguous or vague. Ambiguity was the topic of the collection *Semantic Ambiguity and Underspecification* (CSLI Publications, 1996). Vagueness is the focus of the book *Not Exactly: In Praise of Vagueness* (Oxford University Press, 2010). His latest book is *Computational Models of Referring: A Study in Cognitive Science* (MIT Press, 2016).

Emma Williams (CPsychol, AFBPsS) is a research associate at the University of Bath. She completed her PhD at Cardiff University in the area of lie detection and undertakes research on deception and influence across a range of contexts, with a particular focus on the interaction among individual differences, situational constraints, and message-based factors. Her current research examines human aspects of cyber security, in both work and home contexts.

Stephen Wright received his PhD in Philosophy from the University of Sheffield and is currently a lecturer in Philosophy at Trinity College, Oxford. His book *Knowledge Transmission* (Routledge, 2018) investigates the role that the concept of transmission should play in the epistemology of testimony. More generally, he has research interests in various issues of epistemology as well as issues related to testimony in moral philosophy and the philosophy of language. His most recent work explores the relationship between testimony and memory as sources of knowledge.

CHAPTER 1

.....

INTRODUCTION

What is lying? Towards an integrative approach

.....

JÖRG MEIBAUER

1.1 INTRODUCTION

LYING is a topic everyone is interested in. Being a liar and being lied to are fundamental experiences in human life, and there are many works of art dealing with lying, ranging from Shakespeare's *Othello* to the TV Series *Mad Men*. A great tradition of analysing lying in philosophy and the philosophy of language ranges from Aquinas and Augustine to Kant, Schopenhauer, and Nietzsche, to name only the most famous thinkers. Lying may be approached from a number of academic angles: for instance, history (Zagorin 1990; Snyder 2009), jurisprudence (Green 2006; Tiersma and Solan 2012), communication theory (McGlone and Knapp 2010), political theory (Cliffe, Ramsay, and Bartlett 2000; Jay 2010), philosophy (Dietz 2002; Williams 2002; Martin 2009; Carson 2010; Saul 2012a), sociology (Barnes 1994), pathology (Hirstein 2005), and psychology (Ekman 2009; Vrij 2008). Very broadly conceived, lying is a kind of deception (Harrington 2009; Levine 2014).

Not surprisingly, many types of lying and deception have been identified, resulting in a number of taxonomies. The most influential are the taxonomies of deception proposed by Chisholm and Feehan (1977), Vincent and Castelfranchi (1981), and Bok (1999). Chisholm and Feehan (1977) draw a basic distinction between cases of commission—an agent L contributes causally to the belief of an agent D—and cases of omission—an agent L "has failed to do something he could have done with respect to D and the belief that p" (Chisholm and Feehan 1977: 144). Note that in all cases the propositional content p is considered as false. Vincent and Castelfranchi's (1981) sub-classification of deceiving, in contrast, contains a distinction between lying and pretending/faking. Lying, in turn, comprises direct lying and indirect lying (e.g., insinuation, obfuscation, half-truth). Bok (1999) portrays deceptive acts such as white lies, excuses, justifications, lying in a crisis, lying to liars, lying to enemies, lies protecting peers and clients, lies for the public good, deceptive social science research, paternalistic lies, and lies to the sick and dying. At the same time, this can be read as a taxonomy of standard situations in which more or less "prosocial" lying occurs.

Recently, more relatives within lying and deception have been described, for instance the bald-faced lie (Sorensen 2007; Carson 2010), the knowledge lie (Sorensen 2010), the cynical assertion (Kenyon 2003), the selfless assertion (Lackey 2008; Turri 2015), bullshitting (Frankfurt 2005; Hardcastle and Reisch 2006; Meibauer 2016b), and diverse strategies of manipulation and propaganda (McGinn 2008; Coons and Weber 2014; Stanley 2015). To discriminate these and further types of lying and deception is an important task for the future.

An integrative theory of lying and deception should at least comprise insights from the philosophy of language, psychology, and linguistics. Arguably, these are core disciplines in the theory of lying. In what follows, I will focus on five questions that an integrative theory of lying should be able to answer. I will point out major research questions and mention relevant literature.

1.2 How can lying be defined?

The most basic question in lying research is how to define lying. Numerous answers have been given and are indeed possible. A definition that is unanimously accepted by all researchers does not exist.

First, consider the philosophy of language. In this field, one can broadly distinguish between a speech-act approach and a speaker-meaning approach. The speech-act approach defines lying as a kind of speech act (or communicative act), typically an insincere assertion. Note that lying is usually not seen as having a separate illocutionary point. Since types of speech acts, such as the promise, are standardly defined by means of a set of conditions for their success, the task is to provide such a set for the assertion and then to relate a definition of lying to that definition. There are numerous proposals how to define assertion, for instance the ones by Searle (1969, 1979c), Bach and Harnish (1979), Brandom (1994), and Alston (2000). In addition, philosophers are now discussing assertion from a number of perspectives (Jary 2010a; Brown and Cappelen 2011; Goldberg 2015; McKinnon 2015).

In general, speech-act theoreticians construe lying as an act of assertion in which the liar violates the Sincerity Condition (Searle 1969), does not believe what he/she asserts (Bach and Harnish 1979), or does not take responsibility for p (Alston 2000). Searle (1979a: 62) proposes that the Sincerity Condition for assertions is related to the speaker's commitment: "The sincerity rule: the speaker commits himself to a belief in the truth of the expressed proposition." A commitment approach is endorsed by MacFarlane (2011). Stokke (2013a, 2014, 2018) provides a detailed discussion of the notions of assertion and insincerity, and Marsili (2014) discusses insincerity with respect to (un)certainty of p.

The speaker-meaning approach lies in the tradition of Grice's (1989c) theory of meaning, in particular his theory of conversational implicature. Most prominently, Fallis (2012) argues for "lying as a violation of Grice's first maxim of Quality" (see also Fallis 2010a; Dynel 2011a, 2016a; Meibauer 2017). While it is evident that the Sincerity Condition in Searle's theory of speech acts has similar effects to those of the maxim of Quality in Grice's theory of implicature, the relation of the two has never been worked out in detail.

As is well-known, Grice's (1989c) theory of implicature contains—besides the maxims of Quantity, Relation, and Manner—a maxim of Quality. This maxim of Quality consists of a supermaxim "Try to make your contribution one that is true" and two submaxims, namely "1. Do not say what you believe to be false" and "2. Do not say that for which you lack adequate evidence." (Grice 1989c: 27). The supermaxim reflects a rational presumption about cooperative behaviour. As results from the Cooperative Principle, there is, in every conversation, an "accepted purpose or direction of the talk exchange" in which speakers are engaged (Grice 1989c: 26). This purpose requires a certain make-up of conversational contributions. Making contributions that are false, or mixing up false and true contributions, is a sort of irrational behaviour.

Grice seems to accept that, very often, it is not an easy task to make true contributions—but one should at least "try" to do so. The first submaxim requires that speakers should not say what they believe to be false. This sounds like a rule not to lie, but there is no hint at the deceptive intent connected to lies. The second submaxim requires that speakers—as it may be supposed in the case of assertive acts—should provide "adequate evidence." This rule echoes Searle's First Preparatory Condition ("S has evidence (reasons etc.) for the truth of p"), while the first submaxim bears some relation to the Sincerity Condition.

Recently, Carson (2010) and Saul (2012a) developed important philosophical approaches to lying and deception. Carson (2010) attacks the idea that lying is always an attempt to deceive the hearer; instead, the liar is said to be in a "warranting context." This characterization is taken up by Saul (2012a) who discusses her notion of 'misleading' in the light of post-Gricean debates on the distinction between 'what is said' and 'what is implicated' (see also Stokke 2013b, 2016a). The attack on the traditional idea that liars have an intention to deceive (e.g., Williams 2002: 96) is supported by philosophers such as Fallis (2009, 2015) and Sorensen (2007), but there are opposing views, too (Lackey 2013; Meibauer 2014a, b; Mahon 2015). At the centre of these debates is the notion of the bald-faced lie which is conceived of as a lie without any intention on the part of the speaker to deceive the addressee (Sorensen 2007; Carson 2010; Meibauer 2016a). There are also approaches that hold that objective falsity is more important that subjective intent to deceive (Turri and Turri 2015; Wiegmann, Samland, and Waldmann 2016).

The philosophy of language steadily informs linguistic debates on the semantics–pragmatics divide, especially with respect to the exact definition of speech-act theoretical notions, the role of pragmatic inferencing, and the notion of context.

Second, in linguistics, broadly understood as the study of language and communication, lying is primarily seen as a speech act, i.e., an utterance with a certain grammatical structure used to convey the speaker's meaning, in the standard case an insincere assertion. However, one does not find many linguistic analyses of lying. Since Frege, there is an important semantic tradition dealing with truth and truth conditions, but there are only a few attempts at clarifying the speech act of lying on that background (e.g., Falkenberg 1982; Vincent Marrelli 2004; Meibauer 2014a, 2018).

Since lying is a special sort of a speech act, the most relevant linguistic domain is pragmatics (Allan and Jaszczolt 2012; Cummings 2012; Huang 2017). Pragmatics has intimate relations with semantics, so that the semantics–pragmatics interface is crucial. Drawing the boundary between pragmatics and semantics—both being disciplines that deal with linguistic meaning—belongs to the most basic problems of modern linguistics. In recent years, a lively debate has emerged on that problem (cf. Levinson 2000; Carston 2002; Recanati 2004; Ariel 2010; Borg 2012; Börjesson 2014). Most researchers engaged in the debate relate their approaches to the fundamental work of Paul Grice, who made the classical distinction between 'what is said' and 'what is implicated' (Grice 1989c; Terkourafi 2010). Roughly speaking, the latter marks the territory of pragmatics while the former relates to the semantic domain.

An integrative approach to lying should try to analyse lying by settling it within this broader debate and it should show how this debate might profit from an exact case study of lying. Lying is obviously a case suitable for that purpose, since lying has to do with truth and truth conditions, i.e., issues that traditionally are associated with truth-conditional semantics (cf. Künne 2003).

A lexical-semantic approach to lying was developed in Coleman and Kay's (1981) classical questionnaire-based study on the lexical semantics of the English verb *to lie*. There too, a prototypical lie is considered an utterance in which the speaker S asserts some proposition P to an addressee A, and which complies with the following conditions: (a) P is false; (b) S believes P to be false. (c) In uttering P, S intends to deceive A. Thus, lying can be generally characterized as a deliberate, false, and deceptive utterance.

Against this background, Coleman and Kay's basic aim was to explore how native speakers of American English actually perceive this prototypical meaning (see Hardin 2010). They tested the hypothesis that "semantic categories frequently have blurry edges and allow degrees of membership," and that "applicability of a word to a thing is in general *not* a matter of 'yes or no', but rather of 'more or less' " (Coleman and Kay 1981: 27). To this end, they ran an experiment: Eight stories, construed in such a way that they presented variations of the above parameters, were presented to seventy-one people who then had to mark on a seven-point rating scale the extent to which a certain target utterance in the respective story was to be seen as a lie. What the results of this study revealed was that lying "consists in a cognitive prototype to which real or imagined events may correspond in varying degrees" (Coleman and Kay 1981: 26).

Furthermore, lying is also a speech act that is deeply embedded in rich situational and discourse contexts (Galasiński 2000; Dynel 2018a). What a lie is cannot be detected when abstracting away from the cognitive and social goals the liar has in mind (Vincent and Castelfranchi 1981) and thus amounts to strategic communication (Asher and Lascarides 2013). A genuine linguistic analysis that brings together these aspects is still a task for the future.

1.3 How can lying be detected?

First, consider psychology. Psychology deals with lying-related topics such as the motivation for lying, the emotions accompanying lying, control and executive functioning of lying. Social psychology focuses on social conditions of lying as related to the social goals and interests of the liar and their targets. What makes psychology and related areas so important from a public point of view is their impact on lie detection (Granhag, Vrij, and Verschuere 2015; Vrij 2015). The basic question is whether there are cues to lying, be it from facial expression ('microexpression', see Ekman 2009), statistical generalizations on the grammatical and stylistic make-up of the liar's speech (Newman, Pennebaker, Berry, and Richards 2003; Van Swol, Braun, and Malhotra 2012), or electrophysiological indices, for instance the polygraph (Meijer and Verschuere 2015).

One basic idea informing psychological research is that lying is cognitively more demanding than saying the truth. Under the pressure of being detected, the liar has to solve several tasks, and thus has to make more cognitive effort. Vrij (2008: 39–41) lists several factors that contribute to an increased mental load for the liar. Most importantly, the formulating of the lie may be demanding. Moreover, liars cannot take their credibility for granted, so the attempt to avoid everything that could further reduce their credibility adds to the mental load. Because of this, they possibly tend to monitor the addressee's reactions more closely than the truth-teller. Finally, yet importantly, the concentration on their own acting and role-playing may add to cognitive effort, as well as the suppressing of the truth, and the strengthening of the intention to lie, since the truth is often activated automatically whereas sticking to the lie calls for a special activation of the mind.

Because of factors that might influence the overall performance of the liar, one might look for clear indicators of lying. Among the nonverbal cues for lying ranges that have been researched in the past are the following vocal cues, which we take from the synopsis of more than hundred studies reviewed by Vrij (2008: 90–9): hesitations, speech errors, high-pitched voice, speech rate, latency period, pause durations, pause frequency. In addition, visual cues have been researched, such as gaze, smile, self-adaptors, illustrators, positions or movements of hand/finger, leg/foot, trunk, and head, as well as shifting position, and eye blink. The evidence is far more complex than can be shown here.

Many psychological methods aim at detecting liars. Vrij (2008), in his excellent overview, mentions among these methods the Behaviour Analysis Interview, the Statement Validity Assessment, Reality Monitoring, Scientific Content Analysis, and the polygraph, as used in the Concern Approach and the Orienting Reflex Approach.

Second, consider linguistics. While lying can never happen by using an explicit performative *(*I hereby lie that p)*, there seem to be linguistic cues for lying, at least on a statistical (trend-based) perspective (Vrij 2008: 101–2). Such cues include negative statements, generalizing items, self-references, immediacy, response length, plausible answers, lexical diversity, consistency, and contradictions. In all these dimensions there may exist differences in comparison to the verbal behaviour of truth-tellers (see also DePaulo et al. 2003). Again, the results of studies dealing with these putative cues are that an individual verbal diagnostic cue does not exist (Vrij 2008: 106). This is not surprising from a linguistic point of view; were it otherwise, the liar would commit "illocutionary suicide," i.e., act in a paradoxical way.

For a linguistic perspective on lying, linguistic cues poses a challenge since they show that there is, in principle, a relation between the act of lying and the language system that serves the liar's enterprise. Speech-act theory and implicature theory both have interfaces to the language system, hence a systematic reconstruction of this relationship must be possible.

1.4 How is lying to be processed?

With respect to the processing of lying, the two basic questions are: First, is lying, as measured in reaction times, more costly than telling the truth? This is exactly what one would think with regard to the fundamental assumption that lying is more difficult than telling the truth. Second, can the act of lying be located somewhere in the brain while doing it? If so, one would have an insight into the most basic cognitive abilities necessary for successful lying.

The most basic approach of analysing lying in the laboratory is to give the participants a Guilty Knowledge Task (Concealed Information Test, see Verschuere, Suchotzki, and Debey 2015). The idea is that liars react with an orienting reflex when they become aware of a stimulus that is personally relevant for them. This orienting reflex is then measured by using either a polygraph or an EEG.

In ERP-studies, the typical approach is to measure electrophysiological signals related to the computation of texts. These wave patterns can be compared with wave patterns received in other studies, so that ultimately a fine-grained picture of the overall architecture of a text or an utterance may emerge. Wave patterns associated with lying have been found in a number of studies. In particular, the so-called P300 (positive waves 300 ms after presentation of a cue) was identified (Vrij 2008: 357–62). P300-effects are to be seen when participants show an orienting reflex towards personally relevant stimuli. Hence, it is plausible that these effects occur regularly in Guilty Knowledge Tests.

In their review of the neuroimaging of deception, Sip et al. (2008: 49) point out that interpersonal deception is a complex behaviour that has to do with (a) information management ("keeping track of beliefs and monitoring feedback to maintain deception"), (b) impression management ("building trust through pseudo-cooperation and control of non-verbal signals"), (c) risk management (estimating the gains and losses of the deception and its long-term consequences") and (d) reputation management ("justifying deception on the basis of the 'greater good' "). The respective operations are not deceptive in their nature but appear in processes of deception, and they are intertwined.

In the fMRI-studies reviewed by Sip et al. (2008), deception is associated with the dorsolateral prefrontal cortex (DLPFC), the medial prefrontal cortex (MPFC), and the adjacent anterior cingulated cortex (ACC). The DLPFC has to do with response inhibition and control, and this plays an important role when the liar monitors their responses. The MPFC is involved because mentalizing, understood as "the ability to read and manipulate the mental states of others" (Sip et al. 2008: 50), is also necessary for deceiving others. Finally, ACC is associated with risk management, decision-making, and reward processing; in addition, it has also to do with "relating actions to their consequences, representing the expected value of actions and likelihood of errors," but also "with problem solving, motivation and the anticipation of the consequences of action" (Sip et al. 2008: 50). While fMRI-studies certainly give evidence of these brain areas being active during deception and lying, there is no such thing as a certain place or region in the brain solely responsible for deceptive behaviour: "The problem is that deception involves many cognitive processes, none of which are unique to it" (Sip et al. 2008: 50).

1.5 How is lying acquired?

We can assume that lying is a property of the human species, on a par with other cognitive abilities. Since lying appears to be connected with higher centres of the brain, such as the prefrontal cortex, we may assume that the ability to lie emerged during evolution. It is of course hard to tell why such an evolutionary output came about.

The psycholinguistics of lying studies the computation of lying, i.e., the production and comprehension of lying, as well as the acquisition of lying. Since lying is a common human behaviour, children have to acquire the skill of lying (Talwar and Lee 2008). The ability to lie goes together with the acquisition of metalinguistic abilities; for instance, lies must be differentiated from ironies, metaphors, and jokes (cf. Leekam 1991), and this presupposes an ability to reflect upon language and its functions. A milestone for a child's acquisition of lying is the Theory of Mind, understood as the ability to consider the thoughts, imagination, and feelings of others and respect them when acting (Miller 2012). Experimental research has shown that these abilities are usually acquired by the age of four. Precursors of the Theory of Mind are the imitation of intended actions at the age of 1.6 years, the distinction between one's own and others' feelings or goals, and the onset of symbolic and fictional play. At the age of 2.0, the ability to ascribe feelings and wishes to others (independently of one's own feelings and wishes) develops.

Usually, a distinction between first-order beliefs and second-order beliefs is made. First-order belief is related to the understanding that one can have a false belief about reality (appearance-reality distinction) (3.6–4.0 years of age), while second-order belief is connected with the understanding that one can have a false belief about the belief of another person (6.0 years of age). The insight that different perspectives about a belief of another person are possible is a late achievement in the development of children and young adults (between 12.0 and 17.0 years of age).

A seminal methodological tool in the research of the Theory of Mind is the Sally-Anne Task. Sally hides a toy in a basket (x) and leaves the room. Anne enters the room, takes the toy out of the basket, and puts it into a box (y). The question is where Sally will look when re-entering the room: in the basket (x) or in the box (y)? Children aged 2.6 to 3.0 answer that Sally will look in the box (y). From 3.6 to 4.0, children answer (correctly) that Sally will look in the basket (x) because this is where she left the toy. The assumption with regard to the acquisition of lying is that children initially do not grasp the aspect of intentionality; instead, they consider only factual truth or falsity.

In a landmark study, Wimmer and Perner (1983) used the Sally-Anne Task for research on the acquisition of lying. Participants were asked to indicate where the protagonist would look upon re-entering. The results were as follows: "None of the 3-4-year old, 57% of the 4-6-year old and 86% of 6-9-year old children pointed correctly to location x in both sketches" (Wimmer and Perner 1983: 103). A further question, aiming at the stability of children's belief, was how children behaved when intending to deceive another person about the location of the toy, or with the intention to tell a friend the truth about the location of the toy. Here the result was: "Independent of age, of those children, who correctly thought that the protagonist would search in x, 85% of the time they also correctly thought that he would direct his antagonist to location y and his friend to location x" (Wimmer and Perner 1983: 104). This shows that children are able to relate their representations of another person's belief to successful acts of deception.

A further aspect directly related to children's actual lying behaviour is executive functioning, i.e., controlling one's own lying history within a discourse. Generally, it is difficult for the liar not to mix up conflicting alternatives, e.g., what they have really done/thought vis-à-vis what they have said they have done/thought. Higher mental and verbal abilities are demanded, for instance self-regulation, planning of the discourse, flexibility of attention, discourse strategies, etc. These abilities develop only slowly.

1.6 HOW IS LYING EVALUATED?

Most people would rate lying as morally bad behaviour. This view is also supported by long-standing traditions in ethics and theology. Famously, Augustine and Immanuel Kant condemned all kinds of lying, even if it were to a murderer at the door asking for their victim. Also, lying is still condemned in recent theological approaches, e.g., Griffiths (2004) and Tollefsen (2014). However, these approaches typically fail to acknowledge the everyday practice of white or prosocial lying. When these cases are systematically taken into account (Bok 1999; Dietz 2002; Talwar, Murphy, and Lee

2007; Erat and Gneezy 2012; Hornung 2016), a more open picture of lying emerges. Lying is seen as a cognitive ability of human beings that can be used for bad as well as for good purposes. It depends on a number of factors, such as the situational context and the liar's motivation and goals, how lying is morally evaluated. With respect to pragmatics, mendacious vs. prosocial lying can be seen in connection with politeness and impoliteness. It is understood that there are social systems in which actions of lying and deceiving play an important role. Consider politics and economy, both social systems in which bargaining is common practice. To a certain extent, the actors are untruthful, a fact that is presupposed and accepted by all parties. In addition, lying on the internet is widespread and fostered by the anonymity of some writers (Hancock 2007; Hancock, Curry, Goorha, and Woodworth 2008; Whitty and Joinson 2009; Toma and Hancock 2012). One can assume that users of dating sites know that many self-descriptions of other users are simply not true. While some acts of lying and deception are prohibited by law, others seem to be tolerated or even made possible by law (Green 2006). Moreover, it is argued that law itself may contain in-built lies (Sarat 2015).

1.7 CONCLUSIONS

There are numerous conceptions of how to understand lying, more or less sophisticated theoretical ones but also everyday concepts of lying, as entertained by speakers and hearers. While these concepts can be wildly different, most researchers would assume that theoretical concepts should reflect, at least to a certain degree, those everyday concepts. How can we have access to those everyday concepts? When trying to answer these questions, empirical approaches to lying come to the fore (Dynel and Meibauer 2016). In particular, disciplines such as psychology, linguistics, philosophy, and economics apply experimental methods in order to find out how lying is understood, how it is processed, how it is used, how it can be detected, etc. In principle, one can extend these methods to issues connected with ethics, religion, the law, or even literature. To yield further insights into the mystery of lying and to form a truly integrative view on lying, we need to focus on interfaces between disciplines as well as on interactions between different kinds of lying-related knowledge, as it shows up in the practice of lying. This handbook offers pieces and parcels of such an integrated theory of lying.

PART I
TRADITIONS

CHAPTER 2

CLASSIC PHILOSOPHICAL APPROACHES TO LYING AND DECEPTION

JAMES EDWIN MAHON

2.1 INTRODUCTION

In his Tanner Lectures on Human Values, "Truthfulness, Lies, and Moral Philosophy: What Can We Learn from Mill and Kant?," Alasdair MacIntyre claimed that there were two "two contrasting and generally rival traditions" on the morality of lying, one that could be traced back to Plato, and another that could be traced back to Aristotle (MacIntyre 1995: 316). The Platonic tradition sought to justify lying under certain circumstances. Its followers included John Milton, Jeremy Taylor, Samuel Johnson, and John Stuart Mill. The Aristotelian tradition condemned all lies. Its followers included Augustine of Hippo, Thomas Aquinas, Blaise Pascal, Immanuel Kant, and John Henry Newman (MacIntyre 1995: 310–11, 315). While MacIntyre was right that Plato was much more permissive than Aristotle when it came to justifying lying,[1] nevertheless the views of Plato and Aristotle on the morality of lying[2] were different from those of Augustine, Aquinas, and Kant. It may be said, unequivocally, that Augustine, Aquinas, and Kant held the moral absolutist view that lying is always wrong and never justified (see Mahon 2009). This cannot be said about Aristotle, who, for example, permitted self-deprecating

---

[1] MacIntyre does not say if Socrates belongs to the tradition of Plato or the tradition of Aristotle when it comes to lying. As I shall argue below, Socrates was opposed to all lying, and may be said to belong to the same tradition as Augustine, Aquinas, and Kant.

[2] Following MacIntyre's example, I shall talk about philosophers' views on the 'morality' of lying rather than the 'ethics' of lying. Nothing of importance hangs on using this terminology. I do not mean to claim that all of these philosophers were working with the (modern) concepts of moral obligation, moral duty, etc. For an argument as to why 'morality' and 'ethics' are importantly different, see Anscombe (1958).

lies told by the magnanimous person. A better prospect as a holder of a moral absolutist view among the Ancient Greeks was Socrates, the teacher of Plato. In addition, but relatedly, Augustine, Aquinas, and Kant were more concerned about the distinction between lying and non-mendacious linguistic deception than either Plato or Aristotle. Finally, but also relatedly, Augustine and Aquinas showed greater concern with the definition of lying than either Plato or Aristotle (see Mahon 2014b). This chapter will be concerned exclusively with the views of Socrates, Plato, and Aristotle on the morality of lying.

2.2 Lying and the ordinary morality of ancient Greece

Before considering the views of the ancient Greek philosophers on the morality of lying, it is necessary to say something about how lying was viewed in the ordinary morality of ancient Greece. Speaking very generally, while their ordinary morality opposed lying, it did not oppose all lying. The permissibility of lying to others depended, at least in part, on what kind of relation one had with the other person, in terms of class or status (e.g., a free person and a slave, or a master and a servant), sex or gender (men and women), position in the family or age (e.g., a parent and a child), and whether they were on opposing sides of a conflict (e.g., an ally versus an enemy in a war). Whether or not lying to someone else was permitted also depended on the mental state of the other person—whether the other person was sick, enraged, depressed, in severe pain, and so forth—as well as on whether telling the other person the truth would harm him/her in some way. It also depended on whether telling the other person the truth would lead to the other person harming himself/herself, and on whether lying to the other person would prevent some greater injustice.

In general, it was held that free men did not, and should not, lie. Lying was something done under compulsion rather than of one's own volition. The motives for lying were normally fear, need, and poverty. Those who lied under compulsion were not subject to the same moral opprobrium as those who had control over their own actions (Zembaty 1988: 527). In addition, lying and deceiving others could be judged as acting in a cowardly way: "Guile and deception, though often indispensable to victory in warfare, especially to offset numerical weakness, could arouse repugnance and guilt if used aggressively against a relatively weak adversary or one whose intentions are innocent; and, of course, those defeated by guile in war would vilify the successful enemy as cowardly, although they would not have hesitated to use the same degree of guile if the opportunity had presented itself" (Dover 1974: 170). Despite the possibility of lying being considered cowardly in war, lying to enemies, as opposed to lying to friends or allies, was permitted, or even required. In his *Memorabilia*, Xenophon has the character of Socrates—not the historical Socrates—say to the character of Euthydemus, about "deception," which is

① — 100% Yes
② — 100% Yes
③ — 50% Yes
   40% Most
   10% Some
④ — 100% Yes
⑤ 70% Yes No 30%
⑥ 90% Yes 10% No
⑦ 80% Yes 20% No
⑧ 90% Yes 10% No
⑨ 100% Yes
⑩ 80% Yes 20% No   /188

Diss
28/5/24
or ∴

By 19/6/24

Resub 5/8/24
By 28/8/24

Ivan 30
Me 30 + Moderation
Charlotte 23 prorata
Jane 30
Steph 30

Karen Green 15 prorata
Faye 30

Niki — 20 + mod
Lou — 20

CLM

Stef Churchill — EPL Doha security
PREM — DNA cannulation + I/V Practical 4/9/24
Mahek Harding — ? Cannulat I/V Practical ?
Sophie Mullard — rehiring Sept 24

"Wrong," that "So perhaps all the things that we have put under Wrong ought to be put under Right, too … it is right to do this sort of thing to enemies, but wrong to do it to friends" (Xenophon 1990: 183).

Servants could be prohibited from lying to masters and mistresses, because the truth was owed to their employer and superior (Zembaty 1988: 520). Adults were permitted to lie to children who were sick, however, in order to get them to take medicine. Similarly, although it was normally impermissible for offspring to lie to their parents, it was permitted if their parents were, say, ill, and unwilling to take medicine (Zembaty 1988: 524). In general, it was more permissible to lie to women and to young men than to adult men, especially to spare them from pain, although this was because women and young men were viewed as being weaker, mentally, than adult men (Zembaty 1988: 525).

Even adult men, however, could be lied to, if the altered mental state (rage, grief, etc.) of the adult man was such that telling him the truth would result in some harm to him, or would lead him to harm himself. In Xenophon's *Memorabilia*, the character of Socrates approved of a general lying to his troops when they are "disheartened" (Xenophon 1990: 183). It was much rarer to justify telling lies to adult men simply in order to prevent them from harming others (Zembaty 1988: 525 n. 22). Lying to adult men whose mental states were not altered, merely in order to spare them pain, was not considered morally acceptable (Zembaty 1988: 527). Finally, it was permissible to lie to prevent greater injustice, or to make possible "the performance of a morally required action which the deceived person intends to prevent" (Zembaty 1988: 532). Nevertheless, lying to others simply in order to benefit them—purely benevolent lies—seems to have not been seen as justified (Zembaty 1988: 528, 540).

This view of lying is captured at least in part in the early sections of Plato's *Republic*. The character of Cephalus, who may be said to represent ancient Greek ordinary morality, is initially prepared to agree that justice is "truthfulness and returning what one has received from someone" (Plato 2006: 5). However, as soon as it is suggested to him that "if one received weapons from a friend in his right mind who then went mad and demanded them back," then one should not "be willing to tell the whole truth to a person in that condition," he replies, "You're right" (Plato 2006: 5). His considered position, therefore, is that lying to people who are not in their right mind is justified. Later his son, Polemarchus, defends the position attributed to Simonides that "justice is treating friends well and enemies badly" (Plato 2006: 7). It can be assumed that treating enemies badly includes lying to them, and hence that his position incorporates a "rejection of the view that justice entails truth-telling" (Page 1991: 4). Both Cephalus and Polemarchus may be said to embody the ordinary morality of ancient Greece when it comes to the morality of lying: it is permissible, at the very least, to lie to enemies, and to those who are not in their right mind.

In different ways, Socrates, Plato, and Aristotle each rejected the ordinary morality of ancient Greece when it came to the morality of lying, although perhaps Aristotle's position was closest to it.

2.3 SOCRATES AND LIES

Socrates appears to have been opposed to all lying. Karl Popper, Plato's great critic, "emphatically contrasts Plato's views on lying with Socrates's strong commitment to truth" (Zembaty 1988: 517; see Popper 1971). As Socrates says in the *Apology*, in a speech that is supposed to be faithful to what he said at his actual trial in 399 BC, he is "the man who speaks the truth" (Plato 2002: 22). Socrates did not believe that it would be morally permissible for him to lie even to an enemy. As Socrates says in the *Crito*, another dialogue that is supposed to provide us with the views of the historical Socrates: "One should never ... do any man harm, no matter what he may have done to you" (Plato 2002: 52). Socrates's prohibition on lying even to enemies was a significant departure from ordinary Greek morality: "Greek thinking takes it for granted that while lies are ordinarily harmful to those deceived, harming enemies is not only morally acceptable but even morally required—a view rejected by Plato's Socrates" (Zembaty 1993: 25).

Socrates believed that the gods never lied. In the *Euthyphro*, another dialogue that is supposed to provide us with the views of the historical Socrates, the character of Socrates tells his interlocutor, the priest Euthyphro, that he finds it "hard to accept things ... said about the gods" by other Athenians, such as "there really is war among the gods, and terrible enmities and battles" (Plato 2002: 7) and that "different gods consider different things to be just, beautiful, ugly, good, and bad" (Plato 2002: 9). Socrates believed the gods were completely good and that they did not disagree about anything, a view of the gods which was highly unorthodox,[3] and which, some have argued, was the reason he was put on trial for impiety and executed.[4] In particular, he believed that the gods never lied. About the god that speaks through the oracle at Delphi he is reported as saying: "surely he [the god] does not lie; it is not legitimate for him to do so" (Plato 2002: 26). In holding that it is "not legitimate" for a god to lie, Socrates was rejecting the view of the relationship between the gods and lying found in ancient Greek theology.

In the dialogues that are supposed to provide us with his actual views, Socrates did not consider the question of lying to those whose mental states are altered. It is true that, as was mentioned above, in the early part of the *Republic* the character of Socrates argues, against Cephalus, that it would be just to lie to a friend who has gone mad, in order to prevent him from harming himself or others. However, this view cannot simply be attributed to Socrates, since the same character of Socrates, speaking for Plato, makes many claims in the *Republic* that Socrates would reject.

---

[3] As Thomas Brickhouse and Nicholas Smith have said, "To those of us raised in religions that affirm the omnibenevolence of God, Socrates' commitment to the complete goodness and benevolence of the gods does not seem at all strange. But in the context of ancient Greece, such beliefs appear not to have been the norm ... Socrates' conception of fully moral gods, then, is not consistent with much of Greek mythology" (Brickhouse and Smith 2000: 236).

[4] See Vlastos (1991) and Burnyeat (1997).

2.4 SOCRATES AND IRONY

Despite his stated opposition to lying, there remains the question of whether Socrates could have been in good faith opposed to all lying, since he was often accused of deceiving others. In his trial, as well as in dialogues which are believed to be historically accurate on this point, Socrates tells his interlocutors that he lacks ethical knowledge and that he is not a teacher. This would seem to have been deceptive self-deprecation or false modesty, since he agreed with the god (who spoke through the oracle at Delphi) that no-one was "wiser" than he was (Plato 2002: 26). In the *Republic*, the character of Thrasymachus reacts to what he takes to be the "irony" (*eirōneía*) displayed by the character of Socrates in his debate with the character of Polemarchus: "Heracles! he said. Here, is that accustomed irony [*eirōneía*] of Socrates. I knew it! I told these people in advance that you would refuse to answer, that you would play the sly fox and do anything rather than answer if someone asked you something" (Plato 2006: 14). Thrasymachus is here castigating Socrates as an *eirōn*, that is, someone who uses *eirōneía*: "*eirōneía* is the use of deception to profit at the expense of another by presenting oneself as benign in an effort to disarm the intended victim" (Wolfsdorf 2007: 175).

However, Socrates's defenders have insisted that Socrates did not engage in *eirōneía*. Although, as Gregory Vlastos has pointed out, "the intention to deceive, so alien to our word for irony, is normal in its Greek ancestor *eirōneía*," over time, "from Greece in the fourth century B.C. to Rome in the first ... the word has now lost its disagreeable overtones" (Vlastos 1991: 28; see also Weinrich 2005). Its connotation changed to "speech used to express a meaning that runs contrary to what is said" (Vlastos 1991: 28). According to Vlastos, it was Socrates himself who effected this change in its meaning, and removed the deceptive connotation: "What, I submit, we can say is *who* made it happen: Socrates" (Vlastos 1991: 29). If Socrates himself, by his example, changed the meaning of *eirōneía*, from a certain kind of deceptive behavior to modern, non-deceptive irony, he cannot have been guilty of deceiving his interlocutors.

For Vlastos, not only is Socrates not engaged in *eirōneía*, in the traditional deceptive sense, but Socrates's statements about his lacking ethical knowledge and not being a teacher are not even ironic, in the modern, non-deceptive sense. Socrates's 'false modesty' is actually sincere modesty. This is what Vlastos calls Socrates's "complex" irony: what he says is true in one sense, even if it is false in another:

> Here we see a new form of irony, unprecedented in Greek literature to my knowledge, which is peculiarly Socratic. For want of a better name, I shall call it "complex irony" ... In "simple" irony what is said just isn't what is meant: taken in its ordinary, commonly understood, sense the statement is simply false. In "complex' irony what is said both is and isn't what is meant: its surface content is meant to be true in one sense, false in another ... So too, I would argue, Socrates's parallel disavowal of teaching should be understood as complex irony. In the conventional sense, where to "teach" is simply to transfer knowledge from a teacher's to a learner's mind, Socrates

means what he says: that sort of teaching he does not do. But in the sense which *he* would give to "teaching"—engaging would-be learners in elenctic argument to make them aware of their own ignorance and enable them to discover for themselves the truth the teacher had held back—in that sense of "teaching" Socrates would want to say that he *is* a teacher.

(Vlastos 1991: 32; see also Brickhouse and Smith 2000)

Even if Socrates's defenders are correct in saying that Socrates did not engage in *eirōneía*, in the traditional deceptive sense, because he was sincere in his claims that he lacked ethical knowledge and was not a teacher, there however, the objection that Socrates was insincere with his interlocutors in a different way. Socrates often claimed that those he debated with were wise, when he believed no such thing. As Thomas Brickhouse and Nicholas Smith have said, Socrates does appear to have engaged in *deceptive false praise*:

> any time we find Socrates calling one of his interlocutors "wise," attributing knowledge to him, or saying that he hopes to become the other's "student," what we have called mocking irony is at work ... Those guilty of the most extreme or dangerous pretensions (such as Euthyphro and Hippias) are given the most lavish ironical praise ... Thus we have found at least one form of irony that Socrates commonly uses, which we have called mocking irony ... There does seem to be clear mocking irony when Socrates calls others wise or "recognizes" them as ones who have the knowledge that he, himself, claims to lack. But the mockery does not work by his own disclaimer of such things; the irony is in the mocking compliments and flattery Socrates lavishes on others. So Socrates is not guilty of mock-modesty; his modesty is genuine. His praise of others, however, is often mock-praise and not at all sincere— there is mockery in such praise.

(Brickhouse and Smith 2000: 63)

Their contention supports the argument of Jane Zembaty that "Putting aside the vexing question of the sincerity of Socrates's profession of ignorance, we can still find numerous examples of 'ironic' statements made by Socrates to an interlocutor, praising his knowledge and wisdom while leading him to a state of *aporia* and revealing his ignorance to his audience" (Zembaty 1988: 544). If Socrates did engage in such deceptive false praise, then it can be argued that he did engage in *eirōneía*, in the traditional deceptive sense.

Zembaty has considered the question of whether "Socrates would reject all lies as immoral," given his false praise of others, and has argued[5] that it is possible to understand Socrates's false praise as

> the use of falsity in words in order to prevent someone in a mad or anoetic state from harming himself or others. On Socrates [sic] view, after all, those with incorrect beliefs about virtue *are* in a defective cognitive state ... If "lies" told to them during the

---

[5] Zembaty credits Elinor J. M. West with this line of argument.

questioning process work to alleviate some of their ignorance or to lessen their potential to harm others, Socrates might see his "lies" as justified.

(Zembaty 1988: 544–5)

However, this is to make Socrates's false praise turn out to be regular deceptive lying, and not even merely *eirōneía*, in the traditional deceptive sense. If Socrates believed that he was justified in lying to those who have incorrect beliefs about virtue, in order to alleviate their ignorance or lessen their potential to harm others, then it seems that he would have believed that he was justified in lying to the jury at his trial, and to Meletus, since he believed that the jury, and certainly Meletus, had incorrect beliefs about virtue, and were harming others with their prosecution of him. This seems implausible.

The only way, it seems, to defend Socrates from the accusation that his false praise was *eirōneía*, in the traditional deceptive sense, is to argue that his false praise, while certainly false, was not deceptive at all, because it was ironic, in the modern, non-deceptive sense. This is to argue that his false praise was "simple" irony, in Vlastos's terminology. That is, Socrates was indeed mocking the pretensions of others with his false praise, but he was not deceiving them.

If it is granted that his use of irony to mock the pretensions of others was not deceptive, it follows that Socrates's use of irony to mock others was consistent with his opposition to all lying. Such an opposition to all lying, of course, would amount to a rejection of the ordinary morality of ancient Greece when it came to lying.

2.5 Plato on real falsehoods and falsehoods in words

In contrast to Socrates, Plato explicitly defended lying in his most important work of moral and political philosophy, the *Republic*. Plato's defense of lying went far beyond the defense of lying contained in the ordinary morality of ancient Greece.

Like Socrates, Plato held that gods were only "good," that they never "do harm," and that they were never "responsible for any evil" (Plato 2006: 64). Instead, the gods were "beneficial" and "responsible for things that are good" and not "for all things" (Plato 2006: 64–5). The gods, furthermore, did not alter in any way, since they were "most beautiful and as good as possible," and for a god to alter himself would have been to "willingly make himself worse" (Plato 2006: 66). The gods did not change their shape, they did not "take on all sorts of disguises" (Plato 2006: 65–7). Further, the gods did not "use deception and magic to make us think that they appear in many different forms," because a god would not have been "willing to deceive in word or deed by putting forth a false appearance" (Plato 2006: 67). According to Plato, the gods did not lie.

Plato distinguishes between two types of falsehood (the Greek term ψεύδω "can mean 'lie' or 'falsehood'" (Baima 2017: 2 n. 3)). The first kind of falsehood, a "real falsehood" (or a "true falsehood") (Plato 2006: 67, 68), is to be contrasted with what may be called a real truth. Real falsehoods are about "things which are," which Plato also says are "the most determinative things" (Plato 2006: 67). To say that real falsehoods are about the "most determinative things" means that they are about morality (see Baima 2017) or about moral reality—the eternal, immutable Forms, especially the Form of the Good and the Form of Justice (see Brickhouse and Smith 1983; Simpson 2007; Woolf 2009). Correspondingly, real truths are truths about morality or about moral reality. Real falsehoods would include 'unjust people can be happy', 'just people can be unhappy', 'injustice can be to one's own advantage', and 'justice can be contrary to one's own advantage'. Plato says that real falsehoods are "in the soul of him who is deceived" (Plato 2006: 67), which implies that they are believed, and not merely spoken. In the case of a real falsehood, the person believes the falsehood to be true, and is ignorant of the real truth (e.g., 'injustice is always to one's own advantage'). Real falsehoods are the very worst kind of falsehoods. They cannot be beneficial, either directly or indirectly. Everyone "especially fears" these falsehoods and everyone "refuses to be willingly deceived" in this way: "no one would choose to be deceived and in error in their soul about things which are, or be ignorant and have what is false there. They would least accept falsehood and especially hate it in that quarter" (Plato 2006: 67). Real falsehoods are "hated" by the gods (Plato 2006: 68). The gods never tell these 'pure' lies, as they may be called.[6]

In addition to a real falsehood, there is also a "falsehood in words" (Plato 2006: 68) or a "not quite falsehood unmixed" (Plato 2006: 68), that is, a mixed or impure falsehood. Falsehoods in words, or impure falsehoods, are not about "the most determinative things." They are not about or morality or moral reality. They are about things that are, as it were, not important: "A verbal falsehood misrepresents only unimportant things (unimportant in the scheme of Platonic things)" (Simpson 2007: 345). Falsehoods in words are about the non-moral, natural, facts.[7] Plato says that a falsehood in words is an "imitation ... in words," or "a mere image" (Plato 2006: 67). In the case of falsehoods in words, the person does not believe the falsehood in words to be true. The person either knows the truth, or knows that the falsehood is not true. The falsehood is in the words of the speaker, but not in the speaker's soul (Baima 2017: 7).

Falsehoods in words may be divided into myths and regular lies. *Mythoi*, or myths or false stories ("fiction"; see Page 1991: 8), are to be contrasted with true stories, or histories. True stories, or histories, are "accurate reports about matters (human affairs) concerning which factual knowledge is possible. Plato's concept of truth in this context is, then, close to our concept of factual truth" (Belfiore 1985: 49). By contrast, myths are false stories in which factual knowledge is not possible (at least for human beings), because they are about the distant past, or life after death, or about life from a divine perspective (Gill 1993: 56), and are about gods, heroes, the underworld, and so forth: "Plato's

---

[6] Although Plato never refers to real falsehoods or lies as 'pure' falsehoods or lies, they may be called pure falsehoods or lies for the purpose of contrasting them with impure falsehoods or lies.
[7] Baima says that Plato "does not specify the content of impure falsehoods" (Baima 2017: 3), but all the examples that Plato gives of impure falsehoods concern non-moral, natural, facts.

mythoi," "false stories," are, then, stories "about gods, heroes, and other matters about which we cannot ascertain the truth, told by those who pretend to know the truth about these things" (Belfiore 1985: 49).

Regular lies, unlike myths, are about human affairs, about which knowledge is possible and can be had by humans. They are deliberate falsehoods: "the deception woven in words or what might usually be thought of as a lie in the primary sense" (Page 1991: 16). These include lies told to deceive enemies, out of fear of being harmed, and lies told to friends who have become mad or foolish, in order to stop them from harming themselves or others. Regular lies are to be contrasted with regular truthful statements.

In addition to never telling real falsehoods, or pure lies, the gods also never tell falsehoods in words, or impure lies. That is, the gods never create myths, and they never tell regular lies. The gods have no need of myths, the first kind of impure lie, since the gods are never ignorant about factual knowledge, including the past, or about the afterlife, etc.: "How then is falsehood useful to the god? Would he make false likenesses through not knowing the past? That's ridiculous" (Plato 2006: 68). The gods also have no need of regular lies. The gods never need to lie to deceive their enemies out of fear of being harmed, since, as gods, they are never afraid. "But would he deceive his enemies out of fear? Of course not" (Plato 2006: 68). The gods also never need to lie to their friends when their friends become mad or act foolishly, since the gods do not have such friends: "No one foolish or mad is loved by the gods. So it's not possible to deceive for this reason" (Plato 2006: 68). In general, the gods do not tell falsehoods or lies of any kind—either pure or impure: "So what is spiritual and divine is in every way without falsehood" (Plato 2006: 68).

2.6 PLATO ON GOOD MYTHS AND BAD MYTHS

Like the gods, according to Plato, people should never tell real falsehoods, or pure lies, that is, falsehoods about morality or moral reality. Real falsehoods should be hated by people as much as by the gods: "real falsehood is hated not only by gods but also by men" (Plato 2006: 68). Pure lies are completely prohibited by Plato in his ideal state: "No one is to say this in his own city, if it is to be well governed, nor is anyone, young or old, to hear it in verse or prose" (Plato 2006: 65).

In contrast to the gods, however, people must and should tell both types of falsehoods in words—myths and regular lies. Nevertheless, in the *Republic*, only the rulers of the ideal state are allowed to engage in this falsehood-telling. Only the rulers may tell myths and regular lies, and only to non-rulers. Falsehoods in words may harm as well as benefit, and they may be used only by experts in morality, just as only doctors may use medicinal drugs, since they are knowledgeable of the craft (*technē*) of medicine: "Again, truth must be counted of the utmost importance. For if we were right just now, and falsehood really is useless to gods, and useful to men only as a form of medicine, it is clear that such a thing must be administered by physicians, and not touched by laymen ... Then it belongs to the rulers of the city—if indeed to anyone—to deceive enemies or citizens for the benefit of the city. No one else is to touch such a thing ... So if the ruler catches anyone else in the city lying, "among the craftsmen, prophet or physician or carpenter," he will punish him for introducing a practice as subversive and destructive to a city as it is to a ship" (Plato 2006: 74–5).

Plato divides both types of falsehoods told by rulers—myths and regular lies—into good and bad falsehoods, according to whether or not they benefit those non-rulers to whom they are told. Myths are divided into good myths and bad myths (Belfiore 1985: 50). Good myths are falsehoods in words that contain real truths for their listeners and that are as close to the truth as possible. They do not contain any falsehoods about the gods causing anything evil, or engaging in any lying or deceiving: "Good stories ... are those that make the young better, by conforming to two "patterns," *typoi*: (1) that the gods are the cause of good things only and not of evil, and (2) that the gods do not change shape or otherwise deceive humans. These patterns do not concern specific events and deeds, but deal with the nature of the gods" (Belfiore 1985: 50). Plato advocates telling these myths "concerning events about which we cannot know the truth but which are consistent with what we do know about the nature of the gods" (Belfiore 1985: 52).

Bad myths, by contrast, Plato condemns. These myths are falsehoods in words that contain real falsehoods: "falsehoods unlike what could happen in a world with truthful and good divinities" (Belfiore 1985: 50). Plato condemns Hesiod and Homer, not because they tell myths, but because they are in "error about the gods" (Plato 2006: 64). They "composed falsehoods" and "misrepresent[ed] the nature of gods and heroes in discourse"—for example, the falsehood about Uranos imprisoning his children, and the falsehood about his son Cronus castrating him at the request of his mother, Gaia (Plato 2006: 62), and that "Theseus son of Poseidon and Peirithus son of Zeus were thus moved to terrible rapes," and in general "that any other kind of hero and child of a god ventured to do terrible and impious deeds such as are now falsely told of them" (Plato 2006: 77). In addition to depicting the gods as warring with one another and being the cause of evil, they also depicted the gods as lying to and deceiving humans. Such "'false' representations of gods and heroes produces [sic] 'falsehood in the psyche'" (Gill 1993: 50). These writers are in error about morality and moral reality: "poets and prose writers therefore speak badly about what is most important for men, claiming that many men are happy but unjust, or just but wretched, and that the doing of injustice is profitable if it escapes detection, which justice is another's good and one's own loss" (Plato 2006: 78). Bad myths, "produced by people who are ignorant in their psyche 'about the most important things', instil falsehoods in the psyche of their audience" (Gill 1993: 45–6), and harm listeners.

In contrast to Hesiod, Homer, and others, "the mythographers of Plato's ideal state ... know the truth about the nature of the gods and can therefore tell stories like the truth" (Belfiore 1985: 51). Such good myths told by the rulers, which may be incorrect about non-moral, natural and historical facts, even as they are as close to the truth as possible, but which are correct about the moral nature of the gods and about morality, contain real truths, and will be of benefit to the other citizens. They will instil real truths in souls. Most important of all are the good myths told by the rulers to children in Plato's ideal state, as described early on in the *Republic*:

> You don't understand, I replied, that we first tell children stories? Taken as a whole they are surely false, but there is also truth in them ... then, it seems, we must supervise the storytellers, accepting what they do well and rejecting what they don't. We'll persuade nurses and mothers to tell the children only what is acceptable, and to shape their souls with their stories even more than their bodies with their hands. Most of what they tell now has to be discarded.
>
> (Plato 2006: 61–2)

Plato does not only defend telling good myths to children, however. He also defends telling good myths to adult citizens. The most famous good myth of the *Republic* is the *gennaion pseudos*, or "noble lie" (Plato 2006: 106). This myth or lie is "not 'noble' in the sense of *kalos*, which is to say aesthetically beautiful or fine," but rather "'noble' in the sense of 'well-born' or 'well-conceived' ... The noble lie will generate an ideal just state by falsifying the origin, or generation of the citizens" (Carmola 2003: 40).[8] There are three parts to this myth. The first part (Baima 2017: 15) consists of telling people that everything "they thought they experienced—namely, that we reared and educated them—all happened as it were in a dream" (Plato 2006: 107). The second part is the so-called "Myth of Autochthony" (Page 1991: 22) that all of the citizens were "beneath the earth, being formed and nurtured within it," and that "When they were once fully completed, Earth, who is their mother, brought them forth, and now they must take counsel for the defense of their country as for a mother and nurse, if anyone comes against it, and consider the rest of their fellow citizens as brothers born of Earth" (Plato 2006: 107). This chthonic myth binds the citizens together as siblings with a common parent, and motivates them to defend the state against enemies. However, the final and most important part of the myth is the so-called "Myth of the Metals" (Plato 2006: 106), where the citizens are told that each of them has had a metal mixed into their soul, which determines which class they will belong to in a strict caste system: gold for the ruling guardian class, silver for the army auxiliary class, and iron and bronze for the working craftsperson class: "the god, in fashioning those among you who are competent to rule, mixed gold into them at birth, whereby they are most precious, and silver into the auxiliaries, and iron and bronze into the farmers and the other craftsmen" (Plato 2006: 107). It is the job of the ruling guardian class to monitor this caste system and keep all but the gold-souled individuals out of the ruling class, as well as to make sure that those who are gold-souled get to join the ruling class:

> it is possible that a silver child should be born of gold, or a golden child born of silver, and so all the rest from one another ... If their own offspring are born alloyed with

---

[8] Karl Popper calls it a "lordly lie" (Popper 1971: 140). He also refers to the myths about the origins of the ideal state as the "Myth of Blood and Soil" (Popper 1971: 140).

bronze or iron, they will assign it the grade appropriate to its nature and thrust it out among craftsmen or farmers without pity. And again, if any born from the latter are alloyed with silver or gold, they will honor them and lead them up, some to guardianship, others as auxiliaries, because of a prophecy that the city will be destroyed when guarded by iron or bronze.

(Plato 2006: 107)

Whereas the Myth of Autochthony "unifies the city by making the citizens think that they are all related," which benefits the citizens by "facilitating harmonious relations among them," the Myth of the Metals "divides the city by putting the city into distinct classes," which "provides the members of the different classes with an explanation for why members of different classes have different lifestyles and different political obligations" (Baima 2017: 15). Since the real reason why people are rulers, auxiliaries, and craftspeople is their natural abilities, maintaining the class division through this myth will benefit all of the citizens.

2.7 Plato on good lies

Myths are not regular lies. As it has been said, "it is not obvious that the pious yet historically ill-informed stories are lies, since it would be peculiar to regard telling myths to children as lying. There might be an accompanying act that is a lie (if we said: and this is a true story). Nor is it obvious that the myth of the metals, as it is presented, is a lie" (Simpson 2007: 345). Plato also divides regular lies into good lies and bad lies, and defends the telling of good lies. Whereas bad lies harm people, good lies benefit people. Children are to be told good lies, such as that no citizen has ever quarreled with another citizen: "But if somehow we can persuade them that not a single citizen ever quarreled with another, nor is it pious, that's the sort of thing old men and women should tell to children from the very first" (Plato 2006: 63). Adults are to be told good lies, also. Plato defends lies told "against enemies" and to "so-called friends, when through madness or some folly they undertake to do something evil" (Plato 2006: 68). Although it is not a lie told by a ruler, in the early part of the *Republic*, the character of Socrates, in his debate with Cephalus about the nature of justice, defends lying to a friend who has gone mad and who will harm himself or others.

Nevertheless, Plato goes further than defending good regular lies told to children, to enemies, and to friends who have gone mad. In the *Republic* Plato says that "The rulers will need to use a quite considerable amount of falsehood and deception for the benefit of those ruled. But we said, I think, that all such things are useful only in the form of medicine" (Plato 2006: 161). The most important good regular lie in the *Republic* is the lie, or set of lies, told by the rulers to non-rulers about the ideal state's eugenic practices. In order "for the race of Guardians to be kept pure," the "best must be mated to best as often as possible, worst to worst oppositely, and the offspring of the one raised but not the other. And that all this is taking place must be unknown except to the rulers themselves, if, again, the herd of Guardians is to be kept as free as possible from internal strife" (Plato 2006: 161–2). The best way to ensure that the best citizens mate with the best citizens is to arrange marriages only between them. However, in order to avoid jealousy and fighting, it will be necessary to "devise a clever system of lots," so that "at each pairing, the inferior fellow we mentioned will blame chance, not the rulers" for not being married, just as the best citizens will believe that it was by means of a sexual lottery that they were married (Plato 2006: 162). In addition, to ensure the purity of the rulers, "as offspring continue to be born, officials appointed for this purpose will receive them," and "They will take the offspring of good parents, I think, and carry them to the nursery, to nurses who dwell separately in another part of the city. But the offspring of inferior parents, or any others who may perhaps be born defective, they will conceal in a secret and out-of-the-way place, as is proper" (Plato 2006: 162). Parents of inferior offspring will be lied to by the rulers about their children being communally raised with the other children, when in fact they will be left to die. Some parents will thus not have children among the younger generation, although they will look upon all of the younger generation as their children, and the younger generation will look upon all of the older generation as their parents. These lies about the city's eugenic practices will help keep the best people as rulers of the ideal city, and help to maintain solidarity and unity, for the benefit of all citizens.

2.8 Plato and paternalistic lies

In the *Republic* Plato says that rulers are justified in lying to non-rulers about matters such as the sexual lottery and infanticide "in order to benefit the *polis*" (Plato 2006: 536). As Zembaty points out, there is "shift here from talk about the prevention of harm to talk about benefit," a shift that "seems to widen the scope of justifiable lies," since "rulers are to tell medicinal lies whenever they are necessary to *benefit* the polis and not merely to prevent harm" (either to the person lied to or to others) (Zembaty 1988: 536, 540). Lying is now justified "to foster unity" (Zembaty 1988: 539), which will be beneficial to all. Ordinary Greek morality did not justify lying "to individuals simply in order to make them better or to make them as beneficial as possible to themselves and others" (Zembaty 1988: 543). This is an extreme form of paternalism[9] which would justify lying to people simply in order to benefit them, as opposed to lying to them to prevent them

---

[9] I say paternalism rather than beneficence since a beneficent lie does not necessarily benefit the person who is lied to, whereas a paternalistic lie necessarily benefits the person who is lied to, albeit without the person's consent.

from being harmed, or to prevent them from harming others.[10] Despite what Popper says about Plato being "utilitarian" (Popper 1971: 140), this "approach is not a utilitarian one," since "his main criterion for determining which beliefs should be possessed is the welfare of their possessor not society overall," and there is nothing that would support the idea that Plato "would countenance sacrificing the interest of a subject for the wider good of the city" (Woolf 2009: 24, 26 n. 32).[11] However, since Plato defends telling lies to enemies in the same way that he defends telling lies to friends who have gone mad, "Perhaps even the treatment of enemies with falsehood is thought of as bestowing benefit on them to the extent that it prevents bad behavior on their part" (Woolf 2009: 26).

Plato departed from the ordinary morality of ancient Greece when it came to the morality of lying insofar as he "greatly widened the scope of justified lies," with the proviso, of course, "that these lies can only be told by properly trained rulers" (Zembaty 1988: 543). Further, in what amounts to "an interesting reversal of one of the strands in Greek thinking about the morality of lying, it is the noblest and the freest for whom it is fitting to lie" (Zembaty 1988: 543). The freest person of all, the philosopher ruler with knowledge of the Forms, is the only person who may lie, on Plato's alternative morality of lying.

2.9 Aristotle and the Lover of Truth

Early on in the *Nicomachean Ethics*, Aristotle mentions three virtues that are "concerned with association in conversations and actions" (Aristotle 1985: 47–8). Virtues, for Aristotle, are mean or intermediate states of character between excessive and deficient states of character. About the first of these virtues, truthfulness, Aristotle says: "In truth-telling, then, let us call the intermediate person truthful, and the mean truthfulness; pretence that overstates will be boastfulness, and the person who has it boastful; pretence that understates will be self-deprecation, and the person who has it self-deprecating" (Aristotle 1985: 48). Truthfulness, therefore, is a virtue that is an intermediate or mean state of character between the vice that is the excessively truthful state of character (boastfulness) and the vice that is the deficiently truthful state of character (self-deprecatingness).

When Aristotle discusses the truthful person and being truthful later in the *Nicomachean Ethics*, he makes it clear that he is not discussing "someone who is truthful in agreements and in matters of justice and injustice" (Aristotle 1985: 11). A person who is truthful in agreements and matters of justice (justice is the whole of virtue in relation

---

[10] Xenophon's example of a general lying to troops when they are "disheartened" (Xenophon 1990: 183) is a possible case of this.

[11] As Raphael Woolf points out, "How exactly those who lose out in the rigged lotteries are supposed to benefit is unclear," but Plato "is justifying the falsehood by reference to those who are told" (Woolf 2009: 25).

to others and prescribed by correct laws, both written and unwritten, for the good of the political community) is a just person. Aristotle's concern is with someone "who is truthful both in what he says and in how he lives, when nothing about justice is at stake, simply because that is the state of his character" (Aristotle 1985: 11). Someone who is truthful when agreements or justice are not at stake is a lover of truth: "Someone with this character seems to be a decent person. For a lover of the truth who is truthful even when nothing is at stake will be still keener to tell the truth when something is at stake" (Aristotle 1985: 111). A lover of truth avoids lying "in itself" (Aristotle 1985: 111). With respect to talking about himself and his qualities, the lover of truth is "straightforward, truthful in what he says and does, since he acknowledges the qualities he has without belittling or exaggerating" (Aristotle 1985: 110). The truth, Aristotle says, "is fine and praiseworthy" and "the truthful person...is praiseworthy" (Aristotle 1985: 110).

By contrast, Aristotle says that "in itself, falsehood is base and blameworthy," and "the tellers of falsehood are blameworthy" (Aristotle 1985: 110). This might seem to place lying in the same category as "adultery, theft, murder," and other actions the names of which, Aristotle says, "automatically include baseness" because "they themselves, not their excesses or deficiencies, are base" (Aristotle 1985: 45) and which are "always wrong" (Zembaty 1993: 21). However, Aristotle makes distinctions between different kinds of lies, and he does not hold that lying is always base or wrong.

2.10 ARISTOTLE AND SHAMEFUL LIES

Certain lies, according to Aristotle, are lies told "when something is at stake" (Aristotle 1985: 111). These lies would include "false oaths, perjury, slander, and bringing false charges against others as well as lies which are part of dishonest business dealings" (Zembaty 1993: 9). Such lies are unjust lies. Their "badness lies in their serving as a means to an unfair gain of goods or an unfair diminution of burdens," at "the same time that another individual suffers a concomitant unfair loss of goods or an unfair increase in some burden" (Zembaty 1993: 9, 10). Hence, "the specific moral badness of those lies which are instances of injustice does not consist simply in their being lies" (Zembaty 1993: 10). These lies are unjust lies, and as a result they are "shameful" (Aristotle 1985: 111). The shamefulness of these unjust lies stems from "motives and character defects that result in acts that are detrimental to the well-being of the community" (Zembaty 1993: 10). Furthermore, those "whose character is such that they deliberately use lies of various sorts out of a fixed disposition characterized by pleasure in gain should be correctly described as unjust rather than as liars" (Zembaty 1993: 10). People who tell these unjust lies, therefore, should be characterized as unjust people rather than as liars.

The boastful person "appears to be opposed to the truthful person" (Aristotle 1985: 111). Not all boastful people have the same motivation, however. Boasters who have an "ulterior" motive tell lies about themselves for reputation or for monetary gain: "Boasters who aim at reputation, then, claim the qualities that win praise or win congratulation for happiness. Boasters who aim at profit claim the qualities that gratify other people and that allow someone to avoid detection when he claims to be what he is not, e.g., a wise diviner or doctor" (Aristotle 1985: 111). Boasters who lie about themselves "for money or for means to making money" are more "disgraceful," or shameful, and are to be blamed more, than boasters who lie about themselves "for reputation or honour" (Aristotle 1985: 111). However, both types of boasters are telling lies "whose aim is some unfair share of honors or financial gain" (Zembaty 1993: 17). Hence, "the badness of these boasters would seem to consist in their being unjust rather than in their being boasters" (Zembaty 1993: 13). That is, boasters who lie about themselves for monetary gain or even just for reputation would appear to be unjust: "the badness of these boasters would seem to consist in their being unjust rather than in their being boasters" (Zembaty 1993: 13). Hence, their lies are also shameful, "at least in part, for consequentialist reasons" (Zembaty 1993: 12).

2.11 Aristotle and the Lovers of Lies

There is also the boaster who does not have an ulterior motive for telling lies about himself. This is the boaster who tells lies "because he enjoys telling falsehoods in itself" (Aristotle 1985: 111). Such a boaster is a lover of lies. In the *Metaphysics*, Aristotle says that a liar is someone "who readily and by deliberate choice gives false accounts, not because of something else but because of itself" (Aristotle 1971: 95). Such a lover of lies claims qualities "when he either lacks them altogether or has less than he claims" (Aristotle 1985: 110). This boaster's lies "seem to fall into the nonshameful category" (Zembaty 1993: 13). Such lies Aristotle nevertheless considers to be base. The "baseness of lies does not lie simply in their consequences" (Zembaty 1993: 15).

The person who tells such a nonshameful but base lie would appear to be a bad person: "If someone claims to have more than he has, with no ulterior purpose, he certainly looks as though he is a base person, since otherwise he would not enjoy telling falsehoods" (Aristotle 1985: 111). However, Aristotle says that "apparently he is pointlessly foolish rather than bad" (Aristotle 1985: 111). These lies "do not issue in behavior which in any direct or obvious way is harmful to others or to the *polis*" (Zembaty 1993: 14). Hence, "the individual who boasts may not be bad even though the act is base" (Zembaty 1993: 14). These lies "are treated as less reprehensible than those of other boasters since their regular use seems to be insufficient to justify labeling the foolish boaster bad" (Zembaty 1993: 14).

The merely foolish lover of lies is potentially harmful only to himself, since he risks being exposed as a "'lover of lies,'" and he may forfeit "the trust which is essential to friendship which, in turn, is essential to human well-being or happiness" (Zembaty 1988: 115). This kind of liar "takes enjoyment in doing something which is apparently trivial but which potentially has very grave consequences" (Zembaty 1988: 16) for him. His lies, while base, are not shameful, and his "enjoyment in lying may not qualify as a "moral" fault, but it certainly shows some kind of lack of sense" (Zembaty 1993: 15). Although he is not bad, he chooses to do "what is said to be base in itself" (Zembaty 1993: 15), that is, to lie. This "would seem, to indicate a serious character flaw, even though the foolish boaster's love of lying manifests itself only in lies about himself, which are potentially harmful only to him insofar as he risks having his pretensions exposed" and hence reducing his "well-being or happiness" (Zembaty 1993: 15, 16).

Boasters are not the only lovers of lies, according to Aristotle. There are also self-deprecators. The "self-deprecator" is the liar who "denies or belittles his actual qualities" (Aristotle 1985: 110). Not all self-deprecation is the same. Some self-deprecators "disavow small and obvious qualities" (Aristotle 1985: 112). These self-deprecators are worse than other self-deprecators, and are more similar to boasters: they "are called humbugs, and are more readily despised; sometimes, indeed, this even appears a form of boastfulness, as the Spartans' dress does—for the extreme deficiency, as well as the excess, is boastful" (Aristotle 1985: 112). However, those self-deprecators "who are moderate in their self-deprecation and confine themselves to qualities that are not too commonplace or obvious appear sophisticated" (Aristotle 1985: 112). These self-deprecators "seem to be avoiding bombast, not looking for profit, in what they say; and the qualities that win reputation are the ones that these people especially disavow, as Socrates also used to do" (Aristotle 1985: 112).

2.12 ARISTOTLE AND THE LIES OF THE MAGNANIMOUS PERSON

Self-deprecators are not the only people who tell self-deprecating lies, according to Aristotle. The person who has the virtue of magnanimity also tells self-deprecating lies. As Aristotle says about him: "Moreover, he must be open in his hatreds and his friendships, since concealment is proper to a frightened person. He is concerned for the truth more than for people's opinion. He is open in his speech and actions, since his disdain makes him speak freely. And he speaks the truth, except to the many" (to whom he does not tell the truth) but "not because he is self-deprecating" but because he is a magnanimous person (Aristotle 1985: 102). Indeed, when Aristotle discusses the truthful person, the lover of truth, he says that "He inclines to tell less, rather than more, than the truth; for this appears more suitable, since excesses are oppressive" (Aristotle 1985: 111). Although Aristotle "does not explicitly label the magnanimous person's self-deprecating statements lies" and although it is possible that "Aristotle would not consider the magnanimous person's falsehoods lies" (Zembaty 1993: 22–3), because the motivation is not the love of lies, it is not incorrect to label these less-than-truthful statements lies. Since Aristotle "sees self-deprecating lying as appropriate behavior for the magnanimous person, their self-deprecating lies cannot fall in the shameful category" (Zembaty 1993: 18), since magnanimous people cannot engage in shameful acts.

Indeed, since magnanimous people "never choose to do anything base, even if it would not be shameful" to perform the action, it follows that a "self-deprecating lie told by a good person to the 'right people' (the many) for the 'right reason' is not base" (Zembaty 1993: 18), as well as not being shameful.

The magnanimous person does not tell self-deprecating lies for monetary gain, or out of fear of any harm that could be done to him, or out of a desire for the approval of others. Hence, "some lies about oneself are neither base nor reprehensible because they do not stem from some base or foolish motive but exemplify the virtuous individual's freedom from some of the needs, desires, or passions that result in shameful and base actions" (Zembaty 1993: 20). Here, Aristotle "advances an example of someone whose independence is consistent with, and perhaps even demands, lying" (Zembaty 1993: 21). The magnanimous man is an example of a "case where self-respect would be lessened if one insisted on being completely truthful" (Zembaty 1993: 21).

2.13 Aristotle and Lies That Are Not Base

There are at least two kinds of lies that, it seems, Aristotle does not consider to be base, or wrong. First, as Zembaty has pointed out, in the *Rhetoric*, Aristotle "expresses the Greek view that lying to others toward whom one lacks good will is consistent with being a good individual and that one is expected to have that attitude toward enemies" (Zembaty 1993: 25 n. 36). Although he does not mention it in the *Nicomachean Ethics*, therefore, it seems that Aristotle does not consider lies told to enemies to be base, or wrong. Second, Aristotle does not consider lies told by the magnanimous person to "the many" about his possession of admirable qualities to be base, or wrong.

If Aristotle holds that some lies are not base, or wrong, then his claims that "in itself, falsehood is base and blameworthy," and that "the tellers of falsehood are blameworthy," stand in need of interpretation. It is possible to interpret his claim that "in itself, falsehood is base and blameworthy" as "no more than the claim that lies are normally such when considered without regard to attendant circumstances" (Zembaty 1993: 23). Aristotle's claim can be interpreted as one "similar to the contemporary view which maintains that lies have an initial negative weight because in the absence of special considerations, truth is preferable to lies" (Zembaty 1993: 24), or the view that lying is *prima facie* wrong (see Mahon, 2018). In general, it is possible to interpret his claim as the claim lies are base and blameworthy except when "(a) the lie is primarily self-regarding and harms no-one and (b) telling the truth is an indication of some weakness rather than excellence of character" (Zembaty 1993: 24). Although the only lies in the *Nicomachean Ethics* that have been shown to be not base are the magnanimous person's lies about his possession of admirable qualities, it can be argued that Aristotle should find morally acceptable any lie that is "a necessary means to some good end, harms no one and is rooted in excellence of character and sound thinking rather than in badness of character and foolishness" (Zembaty 1993: 25–6). A possible example would be "a lie told by a physician, relative, or friend in order to get the deceived person to submit to treatment or to take a medicinal drug which is needed to restore health but which the latter would otherwise reject," although it is true that "Aristotle never uses this example" (Zembaty 1993: 27). Such a lie:

> might be seen as conditionally good when (1) one's ability to correctly evaluate the situation and thereby make the right choices in relation to one's own wished-for ends is detrimentally affected by illness; (2) the lie is necessary to regain an important natural good which is among one's wished-for ends; and (3) the loss of the good could adversely affect one's future ability to make rational choices as well as prevent or hinder a great deal of virtuous activity.
>
> (Zembaty 1993: 28)

According to Zembaty, "it seems as if Aristotle would agree that at least some benevolently motivated lies are nonreprehensible insofar as they are instrumental in restoring the deceived person's possession of a good essential to continuing self-sufficiency and virtuous activity" (Zembaty 1993: 28). Such non-reprehensible lies, if they are indeed such, would be examples of "weak or soft paternalism" (Zembaty 1993: 28), and would not include cases of lying to people simply in order to save them pain.

Even if Aristotle considered certain lies to be not base, such as lies told to enemies, and self-deprecating lies told to "the many" by the magnanimous person, as well as, perhaps, some benevolently motivated lies, his views on the morality of lying were not as permissive as that of the ordinary morality of ancient Greece. Among the three ancient Greek philosophers, however, his views were closest to the ordinary morality of ancient Greece when it came to lying.

CHAPTER 3

CONTEMPORARY APPROACHES TO THE PHILOSOPHY OF LYING

JAMES EDWIN MAHON

3.1 INTRODUCTION

As Sissela Bok pointed out in *Lying: Moral Choice in Public and Private Life* in 1978 (first edition, see Bok 1999), the "major works of moral philosophy of this century ... are silent" on the subject of "truth-telling and lying," with the eight-volume *Encyclopedia of Philosophy* (1967), edited by Paul Edwards, containing "not one reference to lying or to deception, much less an entire article devoted to such questions" (Bok 1999: xix). Bok's book was part a resurgence of interest in the subject of lying among philosophers in the late 1970s. Today, more philosophers than ever before are working on the subject of lying.

This chapter will examine the work of philosophers on the subject of lying over the last fifty years. It will focus on their answers to, first, the analytical questions of how lying is to be defined and whether lying involves an intent to deceive, and second, the moral questions of why is lying morally wrong and whether lying is morally worse than other forms of deception. Although their answers to these questions are closely related, it will treat them separately.

3.2 THE TRADITIONAL DEFINITION OF LYING

According to the traditional definition of lying, defended by philosophers in the 1960s and early 1970s, to lie was to make a statement that one believed to be false, with the intention that the statement be believed to be true (see Isenberg 1964; Siegler 1966;

Mannison 1969; Lindley 1971). This definition qualified as a deceptionist definition of lying, insofar it was a necessary condition of lying that the liar intended the victim to believe to be true a statement that the liar disbelieved. It was a simple deceptionist definition of lying, however, insofar as it did not matter *how* the liar intended the victim to believe the disbelieved statement to be true.[1] If the liar (somehow) intended the victim to believe the disbelieved statement to be true on the basis of distrusting the liar—as in the case of a triple-bluff, for example[2]—the liar was still lying.

In 1976, John Morris modified the traditional definition of lying by substituting 'assertion' for 'statement'. He claimed that lying involved three modes of discourse: the assertoric mode, the doxastic mode, and the volitional mode. As he explained these three modes: "The liar must assert something ... must believe something which contradicts his words ... [and] must actually want his listener to believe his words" (Morris 1976: 390–1). To lie, then, was to *assert* a proposition that one believes to be false, with the intention that the proposition be believed to be true. Although Morris could not have anticipated it, the substitution of 'assertion' for 'statement' in the traditional definition of lying led to a change in how philosophers understood lying and to the swift abandonment of his modified definition.

Starting in the late 1970s, a number of philosophers argued that the substitution of 'assertion' for 'statement' in the modified traditional definition of lying rendered the volitional mode of discourse in the definition redundant. These philosophers were complex deceptionists. They held that the liar intended to deceive on the basis of trust or faith in the truthfulness of the speaker. They also held that an invocation or assurance of trust in the truthfulness of the speaker was *built into* assertion. Assertions necessarily aimed at causing belief in listeners, on the basis of trust or faith in the truthfulness of the speaker, because an invocation or assurance of trust in the truthfulness of the speaker was built into assertion. Hence the volitional mode of discourse in the traditional definition of lying—the liar "must actually want his listener to believe his words"—was redundant. The most influential of these assertionist philosophers, as they may be called,[3] were Roderick Chisholm and Thomas Feehan, Charles Fried, and David Simpson.

---

[1] For more on the distinction between 'deceptionist' and 'non-deceptionist' definitions of lying, as well as the distinction between 'simple' and 'complex' deceptionist definitions of lying, see my 'The Definition of Lying and Deception', *The Stanford Encyclopedia of Philosophy* (2015).

[2] In the case of an ordinary bluff (or lie), the speaker believes that his audience trusts him, and he says what he believes to be false, in order to deceive. In a double bluff, the speaker believes that his audience secretly distrusts him, and so he says what he believes to be true, in order to deceive. In a triple bluff, there is open distrust. The speaker believes that his audience believes that he believes that his audience distrusts him, and so forth. Here, a speaker may say what he believes to be false, in order to deceive his audience, whom he believes are anticipating a double bluff. This is a triple bluff.

[3] It is useful to have a term to refer to the position that the intent to be believed, on the basis of an assurance or invocation of trust or faith in the truthfulness of the speaker, is built into assertion. In this chapter, I have coined the term 'assertionism' to refer to this position, and I call those philosophers who defend this position 'assertionist' philosophers.

3.3 Lies as Untruthful Assertions

In their seminal article "The Intent to Deceive," Chisholm and Feehan distinguished between making statements and making assertions. When I wink my eye, cross my fingers, etc., while declaring something, or when I declare something in an ironic tone, tell a joke, speak on stage, write a novel, test a microphone, etc., I am merely making statements.[4] I am not making any assertions. In these circumstances, I do not believe that my listener is epistemically justified in believing that I believe my statement to be true—that is, that I am being truthful—and I do not believe that my listener is epistemically justified in believing that I intend my listener to believe that I believe my statement to be true—that is, that I intend my listener to believe that I am being truthful. I also do not believe that my listener is epistemically justified in believing my statement to be true. I therefore do not anticipate that my listener will believe that I am being truthful or will believe that what I am saying is true. If my statements are untruthful, I do not anticipate that my listener will be deceived, either about my beliefs or about what my statement is about.[5] When television host and comedian David Letterman said, on his show, about fellow television host and comedian Jay Leno, "he is humanitarian and a man of the people," and "he will probably, if I had to bet, step aside and let Conan continue as the host of *The Tonight Show*,"[6] he was being untruthful, but he was not asserting anything.

By contrast, when I am not winking, crossing my fingers, etc., while I am speaking, and when I am not speaking in irony, telling a joke, speaking on stage, etc., I am asserting. When I am asserting, I believe that my listener is epistemically justified in believing that I am being truthful, and I believe that my listener is epistemically justified in believing that I intend my listener to believe that I am being truthful. And, normally, I believe that my listener is epistemically justified in believing that what I am saying is true. I therefore anticipate that my listener will believe that I am I being truthful. Normally, I also anticipate that my listener will believe that what I am saying is true.[7]

---

[4] Their definition of making a statement was as follows: "L states that p to $D =_{df}$ (1) L believes that there is an expression E and a language S such that one of the standard uses of E in S is that of expressing the proposition p; (2) L utters E with the intention of causing D to believe that he, L, intended to utter E in that standard use" (Chisholm and Feehan 1977: 150). Note that using expressions in a language may be interpreted broadly to include using American Sign Language, Morse code, semaphore flags, smoke signals, and so forth, as well as using specific bodily gestures whose meanings have been established by convention, such as nodding one's head, or raising one's hand, in answer to a yes/no question.

[5] If my statement is a statement about my beliefs (e.g., "I believe he is innocent"), then this comes to the same thing.

[6] David Letterman, *The Late Show with David Letterman*, January 14, 2010. Letterman was commenting on the plan by NBC to move *The Tonight Show*, hosted by Conan O'Brien, to a later time, in order to allow Jay Leno to host his own show at the traditional time for *The Tonight Show*, because O'Brien was losing viewers, and they believed that Leno would bring them back.

[7] This is not always the case: "The point of asserting a proposition p need not be that of causing belief in the *assertum*, i.e., in p. (I may assert p to you, knowing that you believe p and thus knowing that my assertion would have no effect upon your beliefs with respect to p)" (Chisholm and Feehan 1977: 151–2).

When David Profumo said, in an official 'personal statement' to the House of Commons on March 22, 1963, that "There was no impropriety whatsoever in my acquaintance with Miss Keeler" (Seymour-Ure 1968: 268), he was making an assertion. He anticipated that his listeners would believe that he was being truthful and would believe that what he was saying was true.

A lie, Chisholm and Feehan claimed, is simply an untruthful assertion, where to be 'untruthful' means to be believed false, or to be believed not true.[8] Here they claimed to be following Gottlob Frege, who defined a lie as an untruthful assertion.[9] Since lies are assertions, the liar "gives an indication that he is expressing his own opinion" (Chisholm and Feehan 1977: 149) when in fact he is not. The liar gets "his victim to place his faith in him," only to betray that faith. As they said, "Lying, unlike the other types of deception, is essentially a breach of faith" (Chisholm and Feehan 1977: 149, 153). Profumo's assertion that there was no impropriety in his relationship with Christine Keeler was untruthful, because he had had an affair with Keeler. He lied.

When I lie, I anticipate that my listener will be deceived into believing that I am being truthful, and, normally, I anticipate that my listener will be deceived into believing that what I am saying is true. To give their definitions of asserting and lying, respectively:

> L asserts p to $D = _{df} L$ states p to D and does so under conditions which, he believes, justify D in believing that he, L, not only accepts p, but also intends to contribute causally to D's believing that he, L, accepts p,
>
> (Chisholm and Feehan 1977: 152)

> L lies to $D = _{df}$ There is a proposition p such that (i) either L believes that p is not true or L believes that p is false and (ii) L asserts p to D.
>
> (Chisholm and Feehan 1977: 152)

Chisholm and Feehan said that "the intent to deceive is an essential mark of a lie" (Chisholm and Feehan 1977: 153). Their definition of lying went beyond the liar's merely intending to deceive his victim, however (the title of their article notwithstanding). Their definition implied that the liar *anticipates* deceiving his victim. As has been said: "Essentially, under this definition, you are only lying if you expect that you will be successful in deceiving someone about what you believe" (Fallis 2009: 45).

---

[8] Chisholm and Feehan distinguish between believing something to be *false* and believing something to be *not true* (Chisholm and Feehan 1977: 146). Nevertheless, this distinction between two forms of untruthfulness does not generate a distinction between two types of lies.

[9] Frege stated in his 1892 article "On Sense and Reference" that "In 'A lied in saying he had seen B,' the subordinate clause designates a thought which is said (1) to have been asserted by A (2) while A was convinced of its falsity" (Frege 1952: 66n, quoted in Chisholm and Feehan 1977: 66n). But Frege nowhere defines assertion. One of the tasks of their article was to provide a definition of assertion that would complete Frege's definition of lying.

Although Chisholm and Feehan did not go so far as to claim that 'lie' is an achievement or success verb,[10] such that a liar is not lying *unless* his victim believes him, they did build the liar's anticipation of his victim's deception (at least about his being truthful) into their definition of lying. Of course, even if a liar anticipates deceiving his listener, a liar may happen to fail to deceive. Unbeknownst to the liar, the would-be victim may have a reason for not believing that the liar is being truthful. Nevertheless, according to them, a liar necessarily anticipated deceiving his listener (at least about his being truthful). Profumo anticipated deceiving his listeners, and he did deceive them.

While Chisholm and Feehan's definition of lying was extremely influential, there were a number of problems with it. By far the most serious problem was that it was not possible for me to make an assertion—and hence, to lie—to someone if I did not believe that the person was epistemically *justified* in believing that I was being truthful. That is, I could not lie to someone whom I believed had reason to believe that I was being untruthful. To take one of their examples, found in Kant's lectures on ethics (see Kant 1997: 203), if a thief grabs me by the throat and asks me where I keep my money, and I reply, untruthfully, 'All my money is in the bank', this is *not* an assertion. As Chisholm and Feehan say: "*L* has not *asserted* a proposition he believes to be false, for his act does not satisfy the conditions of our definition of assertion … *L* does not believe that the conditions under which he has uttered these words ["All my money is in the bank"] justify *D* in believing that he, *L*, believes *p* [i.e., that all my money is in the bank]" (Chisholm and Feehan 1977: 154–5). Since this is not an assertion, I am not lying, even though my statement is untruthful: "since, therefore, *L* has not asserted anything to *D*, *L* cannot be said to have lied to *D*" (Chisholm and Feehan 1977: 154–5). In these circumstances, I can merely make an untruthful *statement* to the thief. I cannot lie to him. This conclusion seems implausible.

In the same year that they published their article, another philosopher also claimed that it was impossible to lie to the thief in Kant's example. In *The Theory of Morality*, Alan Donagan argued that a lie was "a free linguistic utterance expressing something contrary to the speaker's mind," and that my utterance to the thief in the example is not free, because a thief who is threatening me 'knows full well that [I] will not, if [I] can help it, tell him the truth and that he has no right to demand it of [me]' (Donagan 1977: 88–9). Donagan also argued that in the case of another much more famous example found in Kant's published writings, in which a (would-be) murderer at my door asks me if my friend is at home (see Kant 1996b: 611–15),[11] it was impossible to lie to the murderer. Since the murderer knows that he has no right to demand this information, and that

---

[10] 'Deceive' is an achievement or success verb (see Ryle 1949: 130). One does not deceive unless one succeeds in getting someone to have or maintain a false belief. By contrast, 'lie' is not an achievement or success verb. One lies even if one fails to get someone to have or maintain a belief that one believes to be false and/or is false.

[11] Note that in this published work Kant holds that it is possible to lie to the would-be murderer at the door, although it is morally wrong, and a crime, to do so (see Mahon 2009).

I will not tell him the truth if I can help it, I am not lying to the murderer if I say that my friend is not at home.[12] I am merely making an untruthful statement to him.

Chisholm and Feehan, it seems, would be forced to reach the same highly problematic conclusion about it being impossible to lie to the murderer at the door. This conclusion was embraced some years later by Kenneth Kemp and Thomas Sullivan, for similar reasons. They held that it is a condition upon assertion that there is "a reasonable expectation that the speaker is using speech to communicate his thoughts to us" (Kemp and Sullivan 1993: 161). In the "special case of protecting fugitives from murderers" they said, the "very act of inquiring" into the whereabouts of the fugitive "automatically undermines the conditions under which assertions can be made," with the result that it is one of those "situations in which nothing one says could be a lie" (Kemp and Sullivan 1993: 163, 160).[13,14]

3.4 LIES AS INSINCERE PROMISES

Charles Fried rejected Chisholm and Feehan's definition of lying at least in part because it had the result that it is not possible to tell lies in certain circumstances. In his book *Right and Wrong*, Fried said about their definition of lying that "they find a way to treat as not lying some cases which seem to me to be cases of justified lying" (Fried 1978: 55 n1). Nevertheless, Fried was also an assertionist. He agreed with them that a lie is simply an untruthful assertion, and that there is no need to add an intention to deceive to the definition of lying.

When I assert, Fried argued, I am "seeking to cause belief in a particular way," namely, by giving an implicit "warranty" as to the truth of my statement (Fried 1978: 56, 57). Specifically, when I assert, I am making an implicit "promise or assurance that the statement is true" (Fried 1978: 57). When I assert, I intend to "invite belief, and not belief based *on the evidence* of the statement so much as *on the faith* of the statement" (Fried 1978: 56). A person lies "when he asserts a proposition he believes to be false" (Fried

---

[12] Donagan assumes that the (would-be) murderer is open about his murderous intent, or at least, that the murderer knows that I know that he is a murderer. This is the normal interpretation of the example. For an alternative interpretation, in which the murderer is not open about his intent, and does not know that I know that he is a murderer, see Korsgaard (1986).

[13] They claim that this is case "in which saying what is false with the intent to deceive is not lying" (Kemp and Sullivan 1993: 159). This would make it similar to, or a case of, a triple bluff (see Faulkner 2013: 3102–3). It is not clear if Chisholm and Feehan would consider it to be possible to have an intent to deceive in these circumstances.

[14] Alan Strudler distinguishes between being credible and being trustworthy, and holds that someone who is being threatened with harm unless he tells the truth can be credible (see Strudler 2005). If this is correct, then it seems that someone who is being robbed at knifepoint, or who is being threatened with being killed if he does not reveal the whereabouts of his friend, can believe that the aggressor is justified in believing that he is being truthful, on the basis of being credible. Hence, it seems, he can make assertions, and lie.

1978: 55). When I lie, I intend to cause belief in a statement that I believe to be false. I intend to do so on the basis of my implicit promise or assurance that the statement is true: "Every lie necessarily implies—as does every assertion—an assurance, a warranty of its truth" (Fried 1978: 67). This promise or assurance is insincere. Hence, in the case of every lie, I am making, and breaking, a promise—the promise that I believe that what I am saying is true, the promise that I am being truthful: "in lying the promise is made and broken at the same moment" (Fried 1978: 67).

Fried's definition of lying nevertheless had its own problems. According to him, the deception that was intended in lying was deception about what the lie is about, and not deception about whether the liar believes it. Sometimes it is not possible to intend to deceive a listener about what a lie is about, however, because of what has been called the *"intentionality condition"* (Newey 1997: 96). If S and A are persons, and p is a proposition, then "S cannot intend to get A to believe that p if S knows, or believes, that it is impossible to get A to believe that p" (Newey 1997: 116 n. 12). For example, if a crime boss says to one of his underlings, whom he knows to be an FBI informant, "My organization has no informants," he cannot intend that the informant believe that his organization has no informants. His intent is merely to make the informant believe that the crime boss *believes* that his organization has no informants (see Mahon 2008b). Strictly speaking, according to Fried's definition, the crime boss is not lying to the informant.

At one point in his discussion of lying, Fried did allow for the possibility that "even though he [the listener] does not believe the truth of the speaker's statement, he may believe the truth of the speaker's sincerity" (Fried 1978: 58). Fried did seem open, then, to amending his definition of lying to include the intention to deceive merely about being truthful. Unfortunately, Fried also called a lie that fails to deceive either about what the lie is about or about the liar being truthful "an attempted lie" (Fried 1978: 59) rather than a lie. This would appear to make 'lie' an achievement or success verb. Fried provided no argument to support the counterintuitive claim that a liar who fails to deceive his listener about what he is talking about, or about his being truthful, is not lying, and is only attempting to lie.

3.5 LIES AS INSINCERE ASSERTIONS

The most sophisticated articulation of the position that a lie is simply an untruthful assertion was provided by David Simpson. In his article "Lying, Liars and Language," Simpson said that we had a choice: "We can say that in lying there is assertion plus the invocation of trust, or we can say that assertion itself involves this invocation of trust" (Simpson 1992: 627). Simpson, like other assertionists before him, preferred the latter option. According to Simpson, a lie is just an "insincere assertion" (Simpson 1992: 625). His refinement was to argue that a liar intends to deceive in two ways, not merely one, and intends to deceive in both of these ways by means of a betrayal of trust.

First, according to Simpson, there is the "primary deceptive intention," which is "the intention that someone be in error regarding some matter, as we see the fact of the matter" (Simpson 1992: 624). Second, there is the intent to deceive "regarding our belief regarding that matter... We don't lie *about* this belief, but we intend to deceive *regarding* it" (Simpson 1992: 624). That is, a liar intends to deceive his victim about some matter (what is the case), as well as what he believes about this matter (that he believes it to be the case). The claim that a liar aims to deceive in two ways was not original to Simpson. Joseph Kupfer had also said some years before that "lying always involves intending for the deceived to believe *two* propositions which are false: one pertaining to the specific matter at hand, the other pertaining to the liar's beliefs" (Kupfer 1982: 116). Harry Frankfurt had similarly said that a liar "necessarily misrepresents at least two things. He misrepresents whatever he is talking about—i.e., the state of affairs that is the topic or referent of his discourse—and in doing so cannot avoid misrepresenting his own mind as well," hence, "If the lie works, then its victim is twice deceived" (Frankfurt 1986: 85).

Simpson's first refinement of the claim that a liar has two deceptive intentions was that the liar intends to realize the first deceptive intention *by means of* the second deceptive intention. That is, the liar intends to deceive about "the state of affairs that is the topic or referent of his discourse" *by means of* deceiving about "his own mind." His second refinement was that in order to realize both deceptive intentions, and in particular, the deceptive intention about his own mind, the liar "insincerely invokes trust" (Simpson 1992: 625). The liar does this by *asserting*. In asserting, "we present ourselves as believing something while and through invoking (although not necessarily gaining) the trust of the one" to whom we assert (Simpson 1992: 625). This "invocation of trust occurs through an act of 'open sincerity,'" according to which "we attempt to establish ... both that we believe some proposition and that we intend them to realize that we believe it" (Simpson 1992: 625). But in the case of a lie, "the asserter's requisite belief is missing" (Simpson 1992: 625). Other forms of intended deception that are not lies do not attempt to deceive "by way of a trust invoked through an open sincerity" (Simpson 1992: 626) even if they also attempt to deceive in two ways. This is what makes a lie special: "it involves a certain sort of betrayal" (Simpson 1992: 626). Liars aim to deceive about some state of affairs, as well as about what they believe, by means of a betrayal of trust—which is what an untruthful assertion was.

Simpson granted that "'lie' sometimes appears to be applied to cases in which there could be no question of invocation or betrayal of trust," such as in "war or politics," and in "court rooms" (Simpson 1992: 631). However, he considered "this use of 'lie,'" according to which a lie is "the intentional utterance of an untruth, and need involve no deceptive intentions" to be a "distinct application of the term" (Simpson 1992: 631) rather than the regular use that his analysis was attempting to capture. In writing about uses of 'lie' in which attempted deception is entirely absent, Simpson anticipated the claim of later non-deceptionist philosophers that lying has nothing essentially to do with intending to deceive the listener.

3.6 THE NEO-TRADITIONAL DEFINITION OF LYING

Chisholm and Feehan, Fried, and Simpson all held that lies were simply untruthful or insincere assertions because they believed that assertions necessarily aim at causing belief in listeners on the basis of trust or faith in the truthfulness of the speaker, and that the invocation or assurance of trust in the truthfulness of the speaker was built into assertion. By contrast, a number of philosophers writing about lying in the 2000s had a very different understanding of assertion. Assertions, they held, were not always aimed at causing belief. They returned to the three modes of discourse analysis of lying of Morris, and argued that to lie is to assert a proposition that one believes to be false, with the intention that the disbelieved proposition be believed to be true. The most important of these philosophers were Bernard Williams and Paul Faulkner.

3.7 LIES AS UNTRUTHFUL ASSERTIONS WITH THE INTENT TO DECEIVE

In his book *Truth and Truthfulness: An Essay in Genealogy*, Bernard Williams claimed that "A speaker can sincerely assert that P, and to some purpose, without supposing that his hearer thinks that he is sincere, and without caring whether he thinks so or not" (Williams 2002: 74). The mistake made by many philosophers writing on lying was that they read "sincere assertion too much in the light of insincerity" and paid "too much attention to effects" (Williams 2002: 74). That is to say, previous assertionist philosophers—although none are mentioned, this would certainly include Chisholm and Feehan, Fried, and Simpson—defined assertion too much in the light of defining lying. Although he rejected the view that assertion necessarily aimed at causing belief, Williams did hold that *lying* necessarily aimed at causing belief: "I think it is clear that in giving an account of insincere assertion, we do have to put back the idea of a speaker's trying to affect the beliefs of the person he is addressing. I have made the point that sincere assertions do not necessarily have the aim of informing the hearer; but insincere assertions do have the aim of misinforming the hearer" (Williams 2002: 72). Williams's own definition of lying was very similar to that of Morris: "I take a lie to be an assertion, the content of which the speaker believes to be false, which is made with the intention to deceive the hearer with regard to that content" (Williams 2002: 96–7).

The condition in Williams's definition of lying that a liar intends to deceive the listener "with regard to that content" would appear to leave his definition open to the objection that sometimes a liar intends to deceive the listener only about what he believes (namely, that he believes that what he asserts is true). But Williams was aware that although a liar normally primarily intends to deceive about some matter (that it is the case), a liar may also secondarily intend to deceive about his belief about this matter (that he believes that it is the case): "In the primary case, they aim to misinform the hearer about the state of things, the truth of what the speaker asserts. Derivatively, they may aim to misinform the hearer merely about the speaker's beliefs: the speaker may know that the hearer will not believe what he falsely asserts, but he wants her to believe that he himself believes it" (Williams 2002: 73–4). Williams was fully aware that "the intention to deceive the hearer about these two things may come apart. In asserting that P, the deceitful speaker may not intend his hearer to believe that P at all; he may know that the hearer firmly believes the opposite, and his aim may be, for some reason, only to get her to think that he, the speaker, believes that P" (Williams 2002: 75). Indeed, Williams' definition of assertion[15]—"A utters a sentence, 'S', where 'S' means that P, in doing which either he expresses his belief that P, or he intends the person addressed to take it that he believes that P" (Williams 2002: 74)—allowed for a liar to *only* intend to deceive his listener that "he believes that" what he asserts is true. Suitably modified, therefore, Williams' definition of lying could be said to be the following: a lie is an assertion, the content of which the speaker believes to be false, which is made with the intention to deceive the hearer, either with regard to that content and the speaker's belief in that content, or simply with regard to that content,[16] or simply with regard to the speaker's belief in that content. This elaborately simple deceptionist definition of lying nevertheless proved to be too simple for those who followed him in abandoning assertionism.

3.8 Lies as Untruthful Assertions with the Intent to Deceive by Means of a Betrayal of Trust

Chisholm and Feehan, Fried, and Simpson were assertionists and complex deceptionists. They held that a liar intended to deceive, and intended to do so on the basis of trust or faith in the truthfulness of the speaker, the assurance or invocation of which was built into assertion. In his article "What is Wrong with Lying?," Paul Faulkner rejected the view that a lie is simply an untruthful assertion. Siding with Williams,

---

[15] About his definition of assertion Williams says: "This is not meant to be a strict statement of sufficient and necessary conditions: especially in this field, I take it that it is impossible to produce such a thing without circularity" (Williams 2002: 74).

[16] Taking "Derivatively, they may aim to misinform the hearer merely about the speaker's beliefs" to mean that it is possible for liars to *only* intend to deceive the hearer about the content of the assertion, and not about their belief in the truth of that content. For that reason, Williams does not count as a complex deceptionist, despite his requirement that a lie must be an assertion.

he argued that a lie is an untruthful assertion that is aimed at deception. To this he added the complex deceptionist condition, which he credited to Simpson, about "*how the liar intends his asserting to deceive the hearer*" (Faulkner 2007: 536). The "liar's primary intention is to deceive about some matter of fact," and the liar "intends to deceive as to this matter of fact by further deceiving as to his beliefs about it" (Faulkner 2007: 536). The liar "aims to accomplish this deception by asserting what he believes to be false" (Faulkner 2007: 536). This untruthful assertion must be the reason—the sole reason—for the hearer's being deceived about what the liar believes, and ultimately, for the hearer's being deceived about the matter of fact. The hearer must be deceived about what the liar believes simply "*because of his telling it*" (Faulkner 2007: 537), that is, *simply on his say-so*. The only way that the untruthful assertion can be the reason for this double deception is if the hearer trusts the liar. "The liar," therefore, "invokes the audience's trust" (Faulkner 2007: 539). Since the liar is being untruthful, it follows that this trust is being betrayed. According to Faulkner, therefore, a lie is an assertion, the content of which the speaker believes to be false, which is made with the intention to deceive the hearer with regard to that content, by means of deceiving the hearer about the speaker's belief in that content, on the basis of a betrayal of trust in the speaker's truthfulness.[17]

Despite their disagreement over the nature of assertion, therefore, Simpson and Faulkner arrived at a similar complex deceptionist account of lying.

3.9 Deceptionists and non-deceptionists about lying

All of the philosophers discussed so far had assumed, as Chisholm and Feehan had put it, that "the intent to deceive is an essential mark of a lie." Lies, they held, were necessarily deceptive in intent. That is, they were all deceptionists about lying. At about the same time that Faulkner elaborated the most sophisticated complex deceptionist account of lying, a number of other philosophers were rejecting the assumption that lies are necessarily deceptive in intent. David Simpson had said that the use of 'lie' according to which a lie is "the intentional utterance of an untruth, and need involve no deceptive intentions" is merely a "distinct application of the term." These philosophers begged to disagree. These non-deceptionist philosophers included Thomas Carson, Roy Sorenson, Don Fallis, Jennifer Saul, Andreas Stokke, and Seana Shiffrin.

---

[17] Faulkner does not consider a case of a liar only attempting to deceive about his belief in the content of his assertion, and not about the content of the assertion itself (as in the case of a crime boss saying to one of his underlings, whom he knows is an FBI informant, "My organization has no informants.") Presumably, he would modify his account of lying, so that the intent to deceive the hearer about his belief in the content of the assertion is sufficient for lying.

3.10 Lies as Warranted Untruthful Statements

In his article, "The Definition of Lying", and his subsequent book, *Lying and Deception: Theory and Practice*, Thomas Carson argued that it is possible to lie without intending to deceive anyone, and without anticipating deceiving anyone. Carson broke with most previous philosophers writing on lying by avoiding the use of the term 'assertion' in his analysis of lying, saying that this would require "a detailed account of what is meant by 'asserting a proposition'" (Carson 2010: 31). Instead of defining lying in terms of assertion, Carson defined lying in terms of warrant. "If one warrants the truth of a statement," he said, "one promises or guarantees, ether explicitly or implicitly, that what one says is true" (Carson 2010: 26). One warrants the truth of a statement, first, by making the statement in a certain context, namely, a context that makes it the case that one is promising or guaranteeing that what one says is true, and second, by not taking oneself to be not in that context.[18] Everyday discourse, for example, was such a warranting context. If one made a statement in the context of everyday discourse, and if one did not take oneself to not be in that context, then this made it the case that one was promising or guaranteeing that what one said was true.

To lie was to warrant the truth of a statement when one did not believe the statement to be true, because one believed it to be false, or probably false, or because one simply did not believe it to be true. That is, to lie was to make a statement that one did not believe to be true, in a context that made it the case that one was promising or guaranteeing that one's statement was true, where one did not take oneself to be not promising or guaranteeing that one's statement is true. As Carson defined lying:

> A person S tells a lie to another person S1 iff: 1. S makes a false statement X to S1, 2. S believes that X is false or probably false (or, alternatively, S does not believe that X is true), 3. S states X in a context in which S thereby warrants the truth of X to S1, and 4. S does not take herself to be not warranting the truth of what she says to S1.
>
> (Carson 2010: 30)

---

[18] Carson added this clause because he held that even if one is in a context that makes it the case that one is promising or guaranteeing that what one says is true (for example, being on stage at a political convention), if one takes it that one is not in such a context (for example, one mistakenly believes that one is on stage at a comedy festival), so that one takes it that one is not promising or guaranteeing that what one says is true, then one is not warranting that what one says is true. However, as Don Fallis has argued (Fallis 2009: 48), this condition makes the actual context irrelevant to whether or not one is warranting. It seems that so long as one takes oneself to be promising or guaranteeing that what one says is true, one is warranting the truth of one's statement. Even if one is on stage at a comedy festival, so long as one takes oneself to be on stage at a political convention, one warrants the truth of one's statement. Hence, one can lie in such a context.

Because, when one lies, one is promising or guaranteeing that what one says is true, while not believing that what one says is true, every lie is a betrayal of trust: "To lie, on my view, is to invite others to trust and rely on what one says by warranting its truth, but, at the same time, to betray that trust by making false statements that one does not believe" (Carson 2010: 34). In holding that liars betray trust when they lie, Carson agreed with Chisholm and Feehan, as well as Fried, Simpson, and Faulkner. In holding that not all liars aim to deceive, Carson broke with all of them.

Carson provided two examples of people lying—and hence betraying trust—without intending to deceive. The first example was that of a student, caught cheating on an examination, who is brought in for questioning by the dean. The student knows that the dean's policy is not to punish a student for cheating unless the student admits to cheating. The student makes the untruthful statement 'I did not cheat'. Nevertheless, he does not intend that the dean believe him. As Carson says, if "he is really hard-boiled, he may take pleasure in thinking that the Dean knows he is guilty" (Carson 2010: 21). The second example was that of a witness in a trial who knows that all of the evidence points to the defendant's having committed a murder, and to his having witnessed the murder. The witness believes that if he admits that he witnessed the murder, he will subsequently be killed by the defendant and/or his henchmen. The witness makes an untruthful statement, such as 'I didn't see Marco kill Max'. Nevertheless, he does not intend that anyone believe his testimony (not the jury, the judge, the lawyers, the journalists covering the trial, the people in the gallery, the readers of the newspaper reports, etc.). In both of these cases, according to Carson, the speaker was making an untruthful statement in a context that made it the case that he was promising or guaranteeing that what he said was true. Hence, in both of these cases, the speaker was lying, and hence betraying trust, even though he did not intend to deceive anyone.

Carson had objected that "Chisholm and Feehan's definition has the very odd and unacceptable result that a notoriously dishonest person cannot lie to people who he knows distrust him" (Carson 2010: 23). But his own definition of lying had the same result. "In the US," as he said, "it is common and often a matter of course for people to deliberately misstate their bargaining positions during negotiations ... Suppose that two 'hardened' cynical negotiators who routinely misstate their intentions, and do not object when others do this to them, negotiate with each other. Each person recognizes that the other party is a cynical negotiator, and each is aware of the fact that the other party knows this. In this sort of case, statements about one's minimum or maximum price are not warranted to be true" (Carson 2010: 191). In such a context, one negotiator cannot lie to the other negotiator, because he cannot warrant the truth of his statement. He cannot warrant the truth of his statement because he believes that the other negotiator believes that he is a "cynical negotiator" who "routinely misstate[s]" his intentions. As his example reveals, it is a condition for believing that one is in a warranting context—which is actually both necessary and sufficient for warranting the truth of one's statement[19]—that one

---

[19] See note 18.

does not believe that one's audience believes that one is making false statements. Hence, it is a condition for lying that one not believe that one's audience believes that one is making false statements.

Given that Carson's definition has the same result as Chisholm and Feehan's definition when it comes to distrustful audiences (which might be expected, given their influence on his own definition), it can be argued that both of Carson's examples of non-deceptive 'lies' are not lies, by his own definition. The student cannot warrant the truth of his statement, because he believes that the dean believes that he cheated. Similarly, the witness in the courtroom cannot warrant the truth of his statement, because he believes that the jury (etc.) believes that he witnessed the crime. Neither the student nor the witness is lying, by Carson's own definition.

In her book, *Lying, Misleading, and What is Said*, Jennifer Saul agreed with Carson that the student and the witness were lying in the two examples. She defended a modified version of Carson's definition of lying according to which one was lying when one made an untruthful statement in what one believed was a context that warranted the truth of one's statement:

> If the speaker is not the victim of linguistic error/malapropism or using metaphor, hyperbole, or irony, then they lie iff (1) they say that P; (2) they believe P to be false; (3) they take themselves to be in a warranting context.
>
> (Saul 2012a: 3)

Saul's definition of lying is essentially the same as Carson's, however, and has the same problem. Saul considered the case of speakers being required to make untruthful statements about supporting the government in a totalitarian state, and concluded that they were not lies: "This is the case of utterances demanded by a totalitarian state. These utterances of sentences supporting the state are made by people who don't believe them, to people who don't believe them. Everyone knows that false things are being said, and that they are being said only because they are required by the state ... It seems somewhat reasonable to suggest that, since everyone is forced to make these false utterances, and everyone knows they are false, they cease to be genuine lies" (Saul 2012a: 9). She later added about this case that such untruthful statements were not warranted: "The people living in a totalitarian state, making pro-state utterances, are a trickier case (which they should be). Whether or not their utterances are made in contexts where a warrant of truth is present is not at all clear" (Saul 2012a: 11). From what Saul says about this case, if a speaker is making an untruthful statement to a hearer, and the speaker believes that the hearer believes that the speaker is not making truthful statements ("Everyone knows that false things are being said"), then it follows that the speaker does not believe that she is in a context that warrants the truth of her statement. Since she does not believe that she is in a warranting context, she is not lying if she makes untruthful statements in such a context. But in the case of both the student and the witness, the statements are "made by people who don't believe them, to people who don't believe them," and "Everyone knows that false things are being said." Hence, neither is in a warranting context. It follows that neither is lying, according to her own definition. These results should not be surprising, given how indebted her definition was to Carson's definition of lying, which was indebted to Chisholm and Feehan's definition of lying, which had the same result.[20]

3.11 Non-deceptive untruthful assertions as lies

While the first group of non-deceptionists maintained some continuity with Chisholm and Feehan, the second group of non-deceptionist philosophers made a clean break. In addition to holding that liars did not necessarily intend to deceive, they held that liars did not necessarily betray trust, either. Although they considered lies to be, simply, untruthful assertions, they agreed with Williams that assertions did not necessarily aim at causing belief. These philosophers were the most extreme non-deceptionists about lying.

In his article "Bald-Faced Lies! Lying Without The Intent To Deceive", Roy Sorensen (2007) rejected Carson's definition of lying because it had the result that a speaker cannot lie when the falsity of what the speaker is stating is common knowledge to the speaker and the listener (as his own example of the cynical negotiators later revealed). According to Sorensen, a negotiator who has told "a falsehood that will lead to better coordination between buyer and seller" (Sorensen 2007: 262) has told a lie, even if he believed that his audience believed that he was being untruthful. This lie was a "bald-faced" lie.

According to Sorensen, "Lying is just asserting what one does not believe" (Sorensen 2007: 256). He differentiated between assertions and mere statements on the basis of what he called "narrow plausibility": "To qualify as an assertion, a lie must have narrow plausibility. Thus, someone who only had access to the assertion might believe it. This is the grain of truth behind 'Lying requires the intention to deceive.' Bald-faced lies show that assertions do not need to meet a requirement of wide plausibility, that is, credibility relative to one's total evidence" (Sorensen 2007: 255). It remains completely unclear what counts as an assertion having "narrow plausibility," however, such that "someone who only had access to the assertion might believe it." Sorensen provided, as examples of untruthful assertions, and hence lies, the servant of a maestro telling an unwanted female phone caller that the piano music she hears over the phone is not the sound of the maestro playing but merely the sound of the servant "dusting the piano keys," and a doctor in an Iraqi hospital during the Iraq war telling a journalist who can plainly

---

[20] Another objection that has been made is that "These cases involve speech acts which are to varying degrees coerced," and "Coerced speech acts are not genuinely assertoric" (Leland 2015: 552). Although Carson does not define lying in terms of assertion, it can be argued that when one is coerced into making a statement, one does not warrant the truth of one's statement. Even if this objection were successful, though, it would leave intact examples of putative non-deceptive lies that are not coerced speech acts.

see military uniforms in the hospital wards, "I see no uniforms" (Sorensen 2007: 253). The claim that these are assertions may be rejected, it seems. The first 'assertion' by the servant that the piano music is simply the sound of him dusting the piano keys could be understood as a statement politely conveying to the caller that the maestro does not want to talk to her (and requiring her to stop asking questions), and the second 'assertion' by the doctor that he sees no uniforms could be understood as a refusal by a doctor to go on record about there being any injured Iraqi troops in the hospital. It is hard to disagree with the objection that "Sorensen does not offer a definition of asserting a proposition (with necessary and sufficient conditions) ... To the extent that he does not fully analyze the concept of assertion, Sorensen's definition of lying is unclear" (Carson 2010: 36).

In his article "What is Lying?" Don Fallis also held that lies were simply untruthful assertions: "you lie when you *assert* something that you believe to be false" (Fallis 2009: 33). According to Fallis, you asserted something when you made a statement and you believed that you were in a context in which the Gricean norm of conversation, 'Do not say what you believe to be false', was in effect (see Grice 1989c). To lie was to make an untruthful statement when you believed that you were in such a context. In response to counterexamples to this definition (see Pruss 2012; Faulkner 2013; Stokke 2013a), Fallis revised his definition of lying, and defined lying as making an untruthful statement while believing that you were in a context in which there was a norm of conversation against communicating something that you believed to be false, where you intended to violate that norm by making your untruthful statement:

> You lie if and only if you say that p, you believe that p is false (or at least that p will be false if you succeed in communicating that p), and you intend to violate the norm of conversation against communicating something false by communicating that p.
>
> (Fallis 2012: 569)

To refer to one of his own examples, in the case of a guilty witness, Tony, against whom there is overwhelming evidence, and who says 'I did not do it', without the intention that anyone believe him, Tony does intend to violate the norm of conversation against communicating something that he believes to be false (i.e., that he did not do it) by saying 'I did not do it'. He intends to communicate something that he believes to be false with his untruthful statement. He lies. Nevertheless, he does not intend that anyone believe this. Hence, he does not intend to deceive anyone with his lie.

Against Fallis, it is possible to argue that Tony does not intend to communicate something that he believes to be false when he says on the witness stand, 'I did not do it'. If this is so, then Tony is not lying, by Fallis's own definition. Fallis has rejected the claim that non-deceptive liars do not intend to communicate what they believe to be false: "Bald-faced liars might want to communicate something true. For instance, Tony may be trying to communicate to the police that that they will never convict him. But that does not mean that he does not also intend to communicate something false in violation of the norm. He wants what he actually said to be understood and accepted for purposes of the conversation. It is not as if 'I did not do it' is simply a euphemism for 'You'll never take me alive, coppers!'" (Fallis 2012: 572 n. 24). But in the case of polite untruths, such as "Madam is not at home," it can be argued that the untruthful statement is simply a euphemism: "For example, the words 'She is not at home,' delivered by a servant or a relative at the door, have become a mere euphemism for indisposition or disinclination" (Isenberg 1964: 256). In the case of polite untruths, there is no intent to communicate something that is believed to be false. Indeed, there may well be an intention to communicate something that is believed to be true, as is the case with irony (see Dynel 2011a: 151). If this is correct, then it is possible that non-deceptive 'liars' like Tony do not intend to communicate anything that they believe to be false with their untruthful statements (and may even intend to communicate something believed true). If so, they are not lying, according to Fallis's definition.

In his article "Lying and Asserting," Andreas Stokke, like Sorensen and Fallis before him, defended the view that lies were simply untruthful assertions: "you lie when you assert something you believe to be false" (Stokke 2013a: 33). According to Stokke, to "assert that p is to say that p and thereby propose that p become common ground" (Stokke 2013a: 47). A proposition, p, becomes common ground in a group "if all members accept (for the purpose of the conversation) that p, and all believe that all believe that all accept that p, etc." (Stokke 2013a: 716).[21] Stokke thus defined lying as follows:

> S lies to X if and only if: ... S says that p to X, and ... S proposes that p become common ground, and ... S believes that p is false.
>
> (Stokke 2013a: 49)

In the case of a speaker who makes an ironic untruthful statement (e.g., Marc Antony saying, 'Brutus is an honorable man'), the speaker does not propose that the proposition that is disbelieved become common ground. In the case of a speaker who makes an untruthful assertion with the intent to deceive (a deceptive liar), the speaker does propose that the disbelieved proposition become common ground (e.g., a homeowner hiding an innocent friend at his house by saying, 'He is not at home right now'). However, in the case of a speaker who makes an untruthful assertion without the intent to deceive, the speaker also proposes that the disbelieved proposition become common ground (e.g., the student telling the dean, "I did not cheat" (Stokke 2013a: 52)). This person is therefore also a liar, albeit a non-deceptive one. The fact that in the case of a non-deceptive lie it is common knowledge that the speaker disbelieves what he is saying does not change the fact that the speaker is proposing that the disbelieved proposition become common ground. Even if the believed truth is common ground before the non-deceptive liar proposes that the believed falsehood become common ground, it is still the case that the non-deceptive liar is proposing to "update the common

---

[21] Stokke is here quoting Robert Stalnaker (see Stalnaker 2002: 716).

ground with her utterance" (Stokke 2013a: 54). For example, in the case of the student and the dean, "The student wants herself and the Dean to mutually accept that [she] did not plagiarize" (Stokke 2013a: 54).

It can be argued that Stokke's account of assertion as proposing that something become common ground is too weak to count as assertion, and that non-deceptive 'lies' fail to be assertions, and hence, fail to be lies, according to his own definition of lying. Stokke follows Robert Stalnaker in holding that "It is common ground that ϕ in a group if all members *accept* (for the purpose of the conversation) that ϕ, and all *believe* that all accept that ϕ, and all *believe* that all *believe* that all accept that p, etc." (Stalnaker 2002: 716). To propose that a proposition become common ground, therefore, is to propose that it be accepted, for the purpose of the conversation, where being accepted is weaker than being believed. What does it mean for someone to accept a proposition, for the purpose of the conversation, without believing that proposition? Stalnaker provides an example of someone, Bob, accepting a proposition, but not believing it, for the purpose of the conversation: "Alice, talking to Bob at a cocktail party, says, "the man drinking a martini is a philosopher," intending to refer to a man that Bob knows is in fact drinking Perrier from a cocktail glass.... How should he respond? The most straightforward response would be for Bob to correct Alice ... But if the false proposition is irrelevant to the purposes of the conversation (the man's drinking habits are not at issue—the reference to the alleged martini was just a way to identify him), Bob might decide to ignore the matter, tacitly *accepting* what Alice is manifestly presupposing for the purpose of facilitating communication without disrupting the conversation with a distracting correction." (Stalnaker 2002: 717–18). Stalnaker also imagines a case in which both Alice and Bob mutually recognize that the same proposition is false, and mutually recognize that they are accepting the falsehood, for the purpose of the conversation: "Or perhaps it is mutually recognized that it is not a martini, but mutually recognized that both parties are *accepting* that it is a martini. The pretense will be rational if accepting the false presupposition is an efficient way to communicate something true—information about the man who is falsely presupposed to be the man drinking a martini" (Stalnaker 2002: 718). Stalnaker's characterization of two people mutually accepting a proposition that they both believe to be false, for the purpose of the conversation, as a "pretense," would seem to entail that accepting a proposition can consist of pretending. If to propose that a proposition be accepted can consist of pretending, then proposing that a proposition be accepted is too weak to count as assertion. If a non-deceptive 'liar' is proposing that her disbelieved proposition become common ground, and if this means that she is proposing that it be accepted, for the purpose of the conversation, in the sense of *pretending*, then this falls short of asserting the proposition. If this is correct, then non-deceptive 'lies' fail to be assertions, and hence fail to be lies, according to Stokke's own definition of lying.[22]

---

[22] For another argument that bald-faced lies are not genuine instances of lying because they are not genuine instances of assertion, see Keiser (2016).

Non-deceptionists, despite agreeing that there can be non-deceptive lies, have continued to disagree with each other about how to define lying, and arguably have yet to come up with a satisfactory definition of lying. Even if there can be non-deceptive lies, their conflicting definitions of lying have failed to capture them, it seems.

3.12 LIES AS VIOLATIONS OF MORAL NORMS

Despite their many disagreements, philosophers writing on lying—both deceptionists and non-deceptionists—were united in providing purely *descriptive* accounts of lying. According to all of them, a person is lying purely in virtue of certain descriptive facts about the person, such as what the person states, believes, and intends. In his book *Speech and Morality*, Terence Cuneo rejected all descriptive accounts of lying. Instead, he argued in favor of a *normative* account of lying, derived from the normative theory of speech acts (see Searle 1969; Wolterstorff 1995; Alston 2000). According to Cuneo, a person is lying in virtue of certain normative facts, including certain moral facts. More specifically, a person is lying if and only if she is in violation of certain norms, including certain moral norms. A person is lying if and only if she is rightly subject to moral "admonishment, or blame," and not merely factual correction (as in the case of an honest mistake), when "things are not as [she] present[s] them" (Cuneo 2015: 222). Or, to be more precise, a person lies when she is subject to moral admonishment or blame for presenting things as other than she believes them to be. If a person presents things as other than she believes them to be, and she is not rightly subject to moral admonishment or blame, then she is not lying—perhaps she is telling a joke, or being ironic, or speaking on stage, or testing a microphone, or writing a novel, etc. But if a person presents things as other than she believes them to be, and she is rightly subject to moral admonishment or blame, then she is lying. On this account, if the student with the dean, or the witness in court, is rightly subject to moral admonishment or blame for presenting things as other than he believes them to be (as opposed to being rightly subject to blame for obstructing justice, etc.), then he is lying; but if he is not rightly subject to moral admonishment or blame for presenting things as other than he believes them to be, then he is not lying.

One problem with this account of lying is that it seems to rule out the possibility of what Fried considered "justified" (Fried 1978: 55n1) lying, that is, lying that is not subject to moral admonishment or blame because it is morally permissible (whether optional or even obligatory, as in the case of the murderer/Nazi at the door). A greater problem is that, in order to avoid circularity, it must provide a purely descriptive account of lying. On this account, one is lying if and only if one is rightly subject to moral admonishment or blame for presenting things as other than as one believes them to be. But 'presenting things as other than one believes them to be' needs to be spelled out. It does not mean telling jokes, writing novels, etc. A purely descriptive account of 'presenting things as other than one believes them to be' that rules out jokes, writing novels, etc., and that rules in "There was no impropriety whatsoever in my acquaintanceship with Miss Keeler," etc. is required. But a purely descriptive account of 'presenting things as other than one believes them to be' that rules out the wrong things and rules in the right things is precisely a purely descriptive account of what is a lie.

3.13 THE DOUBLE WRONG OF LYING

In addition to providing definitions of lying, philosophers have attempted to explain why lying is morally wrong. Traditionally, lying was viewed as morally wrong simply because it was considered a species of intended deception. The wrong of lying was the wrong of intending to deceive, that is, the wrong of intending to violate "a duty to take due care not to cause another to form false beliefs based on one's behavior, communication, or omission" (Shiffrin 2014: 22). This view did not seem to adequately differentiate between lying and other forms of intended deception. These included making truthful but intentionally misleading assertions (otherwise known as palters (see Schauer and Zeckhauser 2009)), such as President Bill Clinton's palter "There is no improper relationship" (Saul 2012a: 89), which was truthful, albeit misleading, since the improper relationship had ended, as well as non-linguistic deceptive acts, such as the example from Kant's lectures: "I may, for instance, wish people to think that I am off on a journey," when I am not, "and so I pack my luggage: people draw the conclusion I want them to draw" (see Chisholm and Feehan 1977: 149).

Chisholm and Feehan held that lying was morally wrong for a reason that was distinct from, and in addition to, its being a species of intended deception: "their view [is] that there is a *sui generis* wrongness in lying which consists in its abuse of assertion" (Newey 1997: 116 n. 12). Assertions work by getting people to believe things on the basis of trust or faith on the part of the listener that the speaker is being truthful. Since lies are assertions, the liar intends to deceive on the basis of this trust or faith on the part of the listener that the he is being truthful: "in telling the lie, the liar 'gives an indication that he is expressing his own opinion.'" And he does this in a special way—by getting his victim to place his faith in him" (Chisholm and Feehan 1997: 149). It follows that every lie was a breach or betrayal of this trust or faith on the part of the listener that the liar is being truthful: "Lying, unlike the other types of deception, is essentially a breach of faith" (Chisholm and Feehan 1997: 153). When I make an assertion to another person, as opposed to telling a joke or making an ironic statement, then, because I am making an assertion, the other person has the right to expect truthfulness from me. He has the right to expect me to say what I believe. Since lies were assertions, the liar knowingly violated this right of the listener:

> It is assumed that, if a person *L* asserts a proposition *p* to another person *D*, then *D* has the right to expect that *L* himself believes *p*. And it is assumed that *L* knows, or at

least that he ought to know, that, if he asserts p to D, while believing himself that p is not true, then he violates this right of D's.

(Chisholm and Feehan 1977: 153)

It followed from this that every lie, in addition to being an attempt (which may or may not succeed) at deceiving the listener about what the liar believes—and, normally, an attempt at deceiving the listener about some matter—was also an *actual* betrayal of trust. Every lie was an actual violation of the right of the listener to expect to get truthfulness from the speaker, given that the speaker was asserting. Even if the lie failed to deceive, because the listener saw through it, the lie was nevertheless a betrayal of trust, a violation of a listener's right.

In this respect, Chisholm and Feehan held a position on the moral wrongness of lying that was similar to that of W. D. Ross earlier in the century, who held that the prohibition against lying stems from both "considerations of fidelity and non-maleficence" (Stratton-Lake 2002: xxxvi).[23] According to Ross, in addition to being an attempt to deceive, "the telling of a lie is always a breach of promise" (Ross 1939: 113), specifically, the promise to be truthful, which is implicit in the act of making an assertion: "the implicit undertaking not to tell lies which seems to be implied in the act of entering into conversation (at any rate by civilized men)" (Ross 2002: 21). What has been said about Ross could just as well have been said about Chisholm and Feehan: "This nicely explains why lying is other things equal more seriously wrong than deception that does not involve lying, such as intentionally leaving misleading evidence for someone ... or making true but incomplete statements in the hope of inducing him to draw a false conclusion: to the prima facie wrong in deception it adds the further wrong [of betraying trust]" (Hurka 2015: 188). David Simpson's development of their view was simply to argue that in lying, the moral wrong of deception (both about what I believe and about some matter) was to be achieved by means of the moral wrong of betraying trust. One moral wrong was to be achieved by means of the other moral wrong. In this way, Faulkner can be said to have agreed with Simpson about the double moral wrongness of lying. In making an assertion that p to someone, "a speaker ... invites trust in the affective sense" (Faulkner 2007: 554). The "audience, who affectively trusts a speaker, comes to construe the speaker's intention that [the audience] believe that p as the assumption of a certain responsibility" (Faulkner 2007: 554). The audience's affective trust provides the speaker with an opportunity "of being trustworthy and demonstrating shared values, and it does so because acting otherwise will provoke that resentment characteristic of a let down in trust" (Faulkner 2007: 554). The presumption is that 'the trusted' (the speaker) will be moved

---

[23] As David McNaughton says, "Ross later gives a similar account of the duty not to lie. He claims that this duty ... stems from two of the basic duties on his list: those of non-maleficence and fidelity. To lie to someone is (normally) to do an injury to that person (and perhaps to others). In addition, Ross holds that communication standardly presupposes an implicit mutual undertaking by all parties that they will use language to convey their real opinions. In such cases, to lie is to breach this implicit promise" (McNaughton 1996: 436).

by this trust on the part of 'the trusting' (the audience). The liar "both invites the audience to make this presumption and threatens resentment if the audience does not do so. What explains the strength of an audience's resentment on discovering that he has been lied to is then that the lie denies a presumption of relationship with the speaker which the speaker invited the audience to make and would have seemingly resented if [the audience] had not done so" (Faulkner 2007: 556).

While complex deceptionists such as Chisholm and Feehan and Simpson and Faulkner were able to argue that all lying involves a double moral wrong, even non-deceptionists such as Carson were able to argue that all lying involves the single moral wrong of betraying trust. Only the extreme non-deceptionists, who denied that lying as such involved a betrayal a trust, were led to the conclusion that a certain subset of lies—non-deceptive lies—were "morally neutral" (Sorensen 2007: 263). Other non-deceptionists have rejected their position and argued that all lying, even non-deceptive lying, involves the moral wrong of depriving us of "a reliable access to a crucial set of truths and a reliable way to sort the true from the false" (Shiffrin 2014: 23), namely, assertion, or testimony. There are "no alternative, precise, and authoritative avenues into the contents of each other's minds; there is only testimony. To use this avenue of knowledge for a contrary purpose is to render it unreliable and to taint it" (Shiffrin 2014: 23).

3.14 THE MORAL ASYMMETRY BETWEEN LYING AND MISLEADING

Traditionally, philosophers accepted that, ceteris paribus, lying is morally worse than all other forms of intentional deception, including all other forms of linguistic deception (see Adler 1997). In particular, they held that intending to deceive by means of lying (Profumo's "There was no impropriety whatsoever in my acquaintance with Miss Keeler") was morally worse than intending to deceive by means of paltering, including making 'false implicatures,' that is, making truthful assertions that conversationally implicated believed untruths (Clinton's "There is no improper relationship"), at least on the assumption that the latter acts of intended linguistic deception were not lies.[24] Even those who believed in the existence of non-deceptive lies held that, ceteris paribus, deceptive lies were morally worse than all other forms of linguistic deception. Philosophers held this view at least in part because most accepted that that (deceptive) lying involved a double moral wrong of intending deception and betraying trust, whereas other forms of linguistic deception involved merely the moral wrong of intending deception.

---

[24] For an argument that false implicatures are lies, see Meibauer (2014a).

Recently, the assumption that there is a moral asymmetry between lying and intending to mislead by means of truthful assertion, and that lying is the morally worse of the two types of act, has come under attack. Jennifer Saul has argued that misleading is just as much a betrayal of trust as (deceptive) lying.[25] She "rejects a general moral preference for misleading over lying" (Saul 2012a: 86). Both lying and misleading aim at deception, and both, equally, betray trust, she argues. That is, both lying and misleading involve an equal double moral wrong.

Saul's argument for a moral symmetry between deceptive lying and misleading, due to the equal double moral wrong of both, has not found a supporter to date. Some have rejected the argument that both lying and misleading equally betray trust. Jonathan Webber has argued that "lying damages both credibility in assertion and credibility in implicature, whereas misleading damages only credibility in implicatures" (Webber 2013: 651). Someone who lies, and who (obviously) cannot be trusted not to lie, cannot be trusted not to mislead, either, and hence, cannot be trusted at all, but someone who (only) misleads can be trusted not to lie, and hence, can be trusted to some extent. This alone "justifies society in reserving a more severe opprobrium for lying than is to be employed in response to misleading. An act that damages an informant's credibility across the board is considerably more detrimental to our collective needs as an epistemic community than is an act that only damages the credibility of that informant's conversational implicatures" (Webber 2013: 654). Others have rejected the moral symmetry between deceptive lying and misleading for the opposite reason, arguing that misleading involves an even greater betrayal of trust than lying. Clea Rees has argued that "mere deliberate misleading is generally a more serious moral wrong than is lying" (Rees 2014: 64). The reason for this is that "Whereas the liar exploits only the minimal trust involved in assuming others' assertions to be honest," the misleader exploits the "goodwill" required on the part of her audience "that her deceiver is cooperating with her in furthering shared conversational ends," and that "her deceiver's false conversational implicatures are thus as trustworthy as her assertions" (Rees 2014: 62). The misleader "requires the deceived to participate more actively in her own deception and relies to a much greater extent on her willingness to cooperate with and trust her deceiver" (Rees 2014: 60). Hence, the misleader "uses the deceived in an epistemically and morally objectionable way that the liar does not" (Rees 2014: 62). While the liar and the misleader both aim to deceive, misleading is a greater betrayal of trust than lying, and hence, misleading is morally worse than lying.[26]

---

[25] Saul allows for the possibility of non-deceptive as well as deceptive lying, but her argument is for the moral parity between deceptive lying and misleading.

[26] Although she does not make the same argument as Rees, Seana Shiffrin has argued that "indirect deception may in some cases be more manipulative and disrespectful of another's will than the lie, because the indirect deceiver's effort to influence another's mind is opaque" (Shiffrin 2014: 22).

3.15 Conclusion

This chapter has focused on the analytical questions of how lying is to be defined and whether lying involves an intent to deceive, and the moral questions of why lying is morally wrong and whether lying is morally worse than other forms of deception. It has shown that over the last fifty years, and especially over the last fifteen years, philosophers have given different answers to all of these questions, and have come to disagree about the most fundamental issues concerning lying. These lines drawn in the sand seem to be in no danger of being erased anytime soon.

CHAPTER 4

LINGUISTIC APPROACHES TO LYING AND DECEPTION

KAROL J. HARDIN

4.1 INTRODUCTION

LYING is a linguistic question because it revolves around matters of truth and falsity, which are fundamental notions of language. Consequently, the partial synonyms of fabricating, fibbing, perjuring, and prevaricating (Fraser 1994), are also essentially linguistic concepts (Sing 2007: 115). Linguistic analysis clarifies our understanding of lying and deception by effecting examination of the forms of language (for example, in lie detection), the meanings of utterances (as in prototype and cognitive linguistics of lying), and the use of language in context (for instance, in discourse analysis and cross-linguistic studies). It allows us to move beyond anecdotes and isolated examples to untruths in natural language communication as a whole. Hence, what linguistics has to offer is a more profound analysis, beyond isolated forms, and with more than mere attention to words or assertions. Instead, implicit assumptions from social and cultural contexts are necessary determinants of both lying and deception, and it is for this reason that linguistic theory can help reveal the complex nature of lying in real life.

4.2 BRIEF DEFINITIONS OF LYING AND DECEPTION

Lying and deception have a long history of analysis in religion, philosophy, psychology, and other areas of study. Lying is a deceptive move obtained by means of a communicative goal (Vincent Marrelli 2004: 259) and is achieved in two primary ways: by *concealing* (omission) and by falsifying (commission) (Ekman 2009: 28). A standard dictionary definition of the verb *to lie* is (a) "to make an untrue statement with the intent to deceive" and (b) "to create a false or misleading impression" (Merriam-Webster Online Dictionary 2015). However, as Carson (2010: 17) points out, the standard definition overlooks an essential feature of belief; a lie may be a "believed-false statement" to another person, a definition entailing an utterance and disallowing lying by remaining silent (Shibles 1985: 215). In more formal notation, a standard definition for lying is as follows (Falkenberg 1982: 75, quoted in Meibauer 2014a).

S lied at t, if and only if

(a) S asserted at t that p,

(b) S actively believed at t that not p

Lies are statements that the speaker believes to be false (although the statement itself may be true) and that are intended to mislead the addressee (Bok 1999). The intention to mislead is important to exclude communicative acts such as irony, jokes, and teasing that are not intended as lying or deception. Note, however, that there is some disagreement about whether or not to require the intent to deceive to be part of a formal lie definition (Carson 2010; Arico and Fallis 2013). Lying can also involve pragmatic meaning beyond the level of what is stated. In other words, a speaker can falsely implicate something while at the same time uttering a true statement, which is why Meibauer (2014a), unlike Adler (1997), additionally argues that what is falsely implied should also be included in the definition of a lie. Perhaps most importantly when describing actual language, definitions should capture the folk conception of lying (rather than traditional definitions) by looking at ordinary usage and determining which aspects speakers react to in their moral evaluations of lies (Arico and Fallis 2013), which is precisely what linguistic approaches offer.

Lying is also related to deception, a "successful or unsuccessful deliberate attempt, without forewarning, to create in another a belief which the communicator considers to be untrue" (Vrij 2000: 6). Verbal deception can be divided into lying, or verbally deceiving without lying; that is, an utterance can be both complete and truthful, yet still be deceptive. So one can deceive without lying or "misleading" (Green 2001), and lying is just one type of deception. Unlike lying, however, deception does not require spoken communication; any action from a faked yawn to wearing a hairpiece might be considered a lie (Mahon 2008b: 214). Indeed, deception by omission is possible because withholding information is "the essence of deception in general" (Galasiński 2000: 22). As Castelfranchi and Poggi (1994: 283) noted, one condition for deception is to deceive another person so that she is lacking some beliefs that are useful or necessary to her. Consequently, deception is heavily dependent on a speaker's belief and not on what is objectively false (Dynel 2011a).

4.3 Linguistic approaches to the study of lying

The study of linguistics is often subdivided into six basic fields: phonetics (speech sounds), phonology (sound systems), morphology (word formation), syntax (word order in sentences), semantics (meaning), and pragmatics (use and context).

Until the 1980s, most research on lying and deception focused on cues at the nonverbal level (Dilmon 2009), at which point researchers began to emphasize the "prosody of speech": paralinguistic cues such as pauses, response duration, speech errors, and linguistic markers of deception (Shuy 1998). Phonetic/phonological research related to lying is mainly found in empirical studies in forensic linguistics and lie detection (see section 4.4.1). Very little research has been done at the morphological level (for example, see section 4.4.1 regarding articles, fillers, and verb tense). Instead, linguistic analysis has historically emphasized semantics.

4.3.1 Words and semantics

One semantic explanation for lying results from lexical studies such as Wierzbicka's (1985: 341–2) notion of discrete semantic primitives in the following definition of 'lie', which she claimed applies across languages and cultures.

X lied to Y
X said something to Y
X knew it was not true
X said it because X wanted Y to think it was true
[people would say: if someone does this, it is bad]

These "cultural scripts" can reveal expectations about truth-telling in a given language (Vincent Marrelli 2004). For example, Travis (2006: 209) discussed *mentiras piadosas* 'white/pious lies' in Colombian Spanish. She applied pragmatic notions of politeness to lying by adding a cultural script for sensitivity to the feelings of others and a script recognizing that, in some cases, saying things expressly to make others feel good or avoiding saying things that will hurt others can override the value of telling the truth.

Mentira piadosa
people think like this:
some things are true
it is good if people say things of this kind to other people

sometimes it can be good if someone does not say things of this kind to another person, if this other person can feel something bad because of it

sometimes it can be good if someone says things not of this kind to another person, if this person can feel something good because of it

Further research in lexical studies could follow Wierzbicka's and others' approaches to determining ways of expressing truth and deception in a particular language. Some suggestions for lexical analyses include examining culturally significant keywords, studying so-called weasel words such as "new" or "virtually" that produce vague or misleading meanings (Wrighter 1984), and analyzing metaphors and the origin of words to reveal specific and universal conceptualizations about lying (Vincent Marrelli 2004).

4.3.2 Sentences and semantics

Weinrich's (2005) essay on the linguistics of lying (written in 1965) argued that lies typically occur at the sentence rather than at the lexical level. In fact, historically, lying research has focused on the sentence level and on Truth-Conditional Semantics, a theory oriented toward truth and its consequential deduction of falsehood (Sing 2007: 118). One problem with this theory is that verbal deception is not bound to assertions and should instead be defined using the semantic notion of proposition or meaning (Sing 2007; Meibauer 2014a). Instead, there are several specific sentence types that can encode lies in addition to prototypical declarative sentences, among them exclamatives and embedded sentences containing relative clauses (Meibauer 2014a). The problem is how to distinguish speech-act types from sentence types and propositions. Lies are typically insincere assertions, and assertions are typically encoded by declarative sentences; however, if one acknowledges deceptive propositions, then other sentence types may be included as well.

Truth-Conditional Semantics also require a binary approach, focusing on deviation from true declarative statements. This method does not account, however, for the frequent lack of duality in lying. Utterances are not merely true or false. Instead, lying has scalar dimensions (Marsili 2014). Furthermore, Coleman and Kay (1981) attempted to explain the graded nature in their seminal linguistic article on the prototype definition of a lie. They proposed a definition of a *lie* in which a speaker (S) asserts some proposition (P) to an addressee (A) with the following conditions.

(1) P is false.
(2) S believes P to be false.
(3) In uttering P, S intends to deceive A.

This definition entailed that an utterance containing all three elements would be considered a "perfect" prototypical lie, and that an utterance lacking one or more of the elements would still be classified as a lie, but to a lesser degree. To test their hypothesis, the authors developed a questionnaire containing eight stories with different permutations of the three elements. Based on participants' responses, a mean scale score was calculated, indicating the degree to which the subjects considered each story to be a lie. The principal finding was that for English, falsity of belief, hereafter [+belief], was the most important element of the prototype of *lie*. Intended deception [+intent] was the next most important element, and factual falsity [+false] was the least important (Coleman and Kay 1981: 43). While the account is elegant in its simplicity and empirical basis, a few linguists have leveled critiques. For instance, Tsohatzidis (1990) criticized one of the study's vignettes where participants were unable to make a definitive selection because they were responding to two different propositions in the story, one literal and one implied. Meibauer (2014a: 47) also noted that they seemed to assume that the declarative sentence is the sentence type most suited for lying. Prototype theory therefore explains some of the variation between bald-faced lies (Sorenson 2007), fibs, social lies, and accidental untruths. However, a purely semantic theory does not seem to account for culturally justified or social lies. Other accounts place lying within pragmatics as a speech act of pretended information with the intent to deceive (Castelfranchi and Poggi 1994).

4.3.3 Semantics and pragmatics

Because of its focus on context and use, pragmatic theory is particularly suitable for unmasking the "sneaky practices," equivocations, evasions, misleading, and loaded uses of language (Vincent Marrelli 2004: 34). Indeed, it is likely that truthfulness has been a pragmatic question since the very beginning of the discipline (Vincent Marrelli 2004: 33). Truth is a pragmatic question in that it may be reflected in more than one type of speech act and depends on some built-in knowledge or common sense shared by the speaker and the hearer, whose positions are crucial to the meaning and interpretation of utterances (Sing 2007: 124–5). Lying is also typically associated with discourse in a communicative context rather than in individual sentences (Sing 2007: 126). Nevertheless, pragmatic theory has yet to be fully applied to lying and deception. Pragmatic accounts for lying focus on several overlapping foci: Grice's (1975) Cooperative Principle, maxims, and resulting implicatures, speech acts, and (im)politeness.

Grice (1975) proposed that conversation is based on a shared principle of cooperation, The Cooperative Principle, along with four conversational maxims of Quantity, Quality, Relation, and Manner. These maxims roughly equate to being appropriately informative, true, relevant, and clear. Failure to obey the maxims can result in what Grice called "implicatures," or implied meanings. He offered the following utterances as violating the maxim of Quality.

Violation of Quality

    a. Irony: *X is a fine friend.*
                          [implicates the opposite meaning.]
    b. Metaphor: *You are the cream in my coffee.*

c. Meiosis: Of a man known to have broken up all the furniture, one says, "*He was a little intoxicated.*"
d. Hyperbole: *Every nice girl loves a sailor.*

Since communication is not merely a matter of logic or truth, but of cooperation (Grice 1975; Mey 1985), deception is a deviation from the conventional rules of discourse. Hence lies can reside within implicatures when a speaker conversationally implicates a proposition while believing the proposition to be false, thereby violating the Quality maxim (Meibauer 2005: 1382). This can be done by falsely implicating while telling the truth or with a false utterance. Galasiński (2000: 115) viewed deception as being at the core of noncooperation; a person may ignore the Cooperative Principle for personal benefit. However, deception can also be an act of cooperation, since speakers can work together to misrepresent reality to serve their overall discursive goals; that is, "cooperating to be uncooperative." Violation of Grice's Quantity maxim may also be involved in lies such as half-truths, since a half-truth involves not giving the hearer all the information that would be important to the hearer. The speaker thus suppresses some information, thereby violating the Quantity maxim (Vincent and Castelfranchi 1981: 762). Grice's theory has been applied to linguistic research on lying in many ways, particularly to conversations and discourse analysis.

Speech-act theory offers another pragmatic approach for lying research. The theory focuses on knowledge of underlying conditions for production and interpretation of spoken acts. As defined by Goffman (1974), speech acts are associated with frames with a conventional meaning or intent, such as requests, orders, and apologies. The theory arose from Austin's (1962a) and Searle's (1969) observations that we perform acts with "illocutionary points," or our basic intended purpose as speakers. So speech acts can be classified into categories based on their intent (examples below from Searle 1969; Reiss 1985).

Assertives:	*say, insist, swear (that), complain*
Declarations:	*name, define, resign, nominate, bless*
Commissives:	*promise, offer, permit, deny, accept, threaten*
Directives:	*command, ask (for), suggest, ask, warn, advise*
Expressives:	*thank, congratulate, greet, apologize*

A key notion pertaining to lying is that a speech act should be sincere in order to achieve its purpose (Searle 1969). Lying is not a defective speech act, since a liar does not break any linguistic rules (Sing 2007: 125). Instead, lying and related phenomena make creative use of existing rules, and lying generally involves more than one speech act. The sincerity condition is not complied with, yet the speaker intends an addressee to believe that it is met. Since a lie depends on the speaker's intention (illocutionary act), what is actually said (locutionary act), and the hearer's interpretation (perlocutionary act), a speaker may use truthful deception to say something the speaker believes true, and in doing so, lead the hearer to believe something the speaker believes false (Reboul 1994: 64). Speech acts do not always correspond to particular forms. Whereas early speech-act theorists focused on a systematic correlation between forms and functions, more recent analyses emphasize philosophical and psychological facets of assertive meaning (Jary 2010a: 16–30). It is important to note that different cultures may have different assignments for truthfulness of certain types of speech acts (such as promising), to the illocutionary points, and to the default interpretations of the gravity of certain speech acts (Vincent Marrelli 2004: 100, 354–5). For this reason, speech-act theory has been used in cross-cultural lying research.

(Im)politeness theory is especially pertinent to pragmatics research on lying. Of particular interest are white lies and social lies. White lies are untruthful utterances told without malicious intent and are accepted when politeness conditions supersede constraints for truthfulness (Camden et al. 1984; Talwar and Lee 2002b; Bloomquist 2009). The differences between these acts are only social; they convey false information in order to mislead, but they are all justified to some degree by rules of politeness or the harmlessness of the message (Verschueren 1985; Galasiński 2000). (For further information, refer to Chapter 29 by Marina Terkourafi and Chapter 22 by Simone Dietz.)

Brown and Levinson (1978) described the telling of white lies as a positive politeness strategy to protect face (one's public self-image), maintain social relationships, and avoid disagreement. Indeed, the social lie is a statement that may be true or false, but it is used in situations where politeness requires some sort of comment. The intent to deceive is not present, but the speaker does not necessarily believe his statement, and the statement can be false. Consequently, people may disagree as to whether social lies are really lies or not (Coleman and Kay 1981), particularly within a given language. For instance, Sacks (1975) illustrated how English greetings and their responses often necessitate a lie in the strictest sense because language simply functions to convey true information without embellishment. He instead regarded polite, conventional exchanges as something speakers always have to do. Sweetser (1987) further argued that an utterance is only a lie if the information is not beneficial to the hearer. Since white lies and social lies do not really misinform others and therefore are still beneficial to the hearer, she considered the truth-value irrelevant and that social lies instead involve acts of politeness (see also Lee and Ross 1997).

In contrast, cross-cultural research, for example in Spanish, shows that speakers often categorize as lies both white and social lies (Hardin 2010; Eichelberger 2012). Studies of these pro-social lies illustrate the degrees of lying and the importance of pragmatics and culture when it comes to real-world use and interpretation. An understanding of marginal (non-prototypical) lies depends upon recognizing the social and interactional contexts in which they occur, since even slight modifications may change an utterance from an obvious lie to something far less obvious (Coleman 2007: 67–8). In marginal cases, such as collusion and evasion, responsibility for lying may be co-constructed by the speaker and the hearer; for example, to misinform a listening audience or to mislead one another.

Other pragmatic phenomena, including the role of deixis (lexical items such as *this, we,* or *now* that require context to be understood) and information structure (the way information is presented in sentences, for example to emphasize, link, or background information) have yet to be fully investigated with reference to lying.

4.4 Empirical linguistic research on lying

Empirical linguistic studies of lying and deception are limited both in scope and in number. Most such research falls into four primary areas: linguistic cues for lying, the emergence of lying in language acquisition, attitudes to lies in different cultures, and applied research in various discourse genres.

4.4.1 Linguistic cues for lying

Linguistic cues by which to recognize lies and deception have provided a substantial field of inquiry in psychology and in police, forensic, and legal contexts. In his extensive review, Vrij (2008) noted that it is remarkable how verbal cues are relatively consistent in contrast to what is being discovered through research into non-verbal indicators of deception, which have more conflicting reports. Text analysis further suggests that markers of linguistic style, such as articles, pronouns, prepositions, and fillers (*um*) are, in many respects, as meaningful as specific nouns and verbs in telling us what people are thinking and feeling (Newman et al. 2003; Arciuli et al. 2010). Unfortunately, observers tend to focus on non-verbal behavior to detect deceit, instead of paying more attention to the content of the speech. Police and other observers could improve their lie-detection skills by paying more attention to what speakers actually say.

Phonological cues for lying/non-lying include:

- Speech hesitations (*ah, um, er, uh, hmmm*)
- Speech errors
- Pitch of voice (changes in pitch)
- Speech rate (number of spoken words in a certain period of time)
- Latency period (period of silence between question and answer)
- Pause durations (length of silent periods during speech)
- Frequency of pauses (frequency of silent periods during speech)

(Vrij 2008: 54-5)

Morphosyntactic and morphosemantic cues indicate an association with negative statements, generalizing items, and self-references. Also, when statements from two different people are compared, a trend emerges where lying pairs are more consistent (express more of the same details) than truth-telling pairs (Vrij 2008: 106). Knapp, Hart, and Dennis (1974: 25–6) hypothesized that liars use first-person pronouns either to disassociate themselves or because they lack personal experience. Liars therefore may resort to ambiguity and prolixity (the "cuttlefish effect") or concise assertiveness and elliptical eluding strategies (the "chameleon effect") (Anolli et al. 2003).

For pragmatics, Vrij (2008: 228–9) noted that in all of the studies at that time, truth-tellers included significantly more details in their accounts than liars. On the other hand, liars tended to describe events more in chronological order and with fewer details than truth-tellers (Vrij 2008). The process of creating a false story consumes cognitive resources, leading liars to tell less complex stories (Richards and Gross 1999). Participants also often choose concise, partially incomplete assertions in order to strengthen their semantic value and to avoid further inquiry (Anolli et al. 2003). Cues to deceit are most likely when liars experience emotions or cognitive load, or when they attempt to control themselves (Vrij 2008: 396). Consequently, they may exhibit "leakage" in their lies through slips of the tongue, tirades, or convoluted responses (Ekman 2009). In general, verbal characteristics most frequently associated with deceptive speech in empirical studies included: negative statements, implausible answers, shorter responses, fewer self-references, and more indirect replies (see also Adams and Jarvis 2006). In their computerized text analysis of false versus true stories, Newman et al. (2003) similarly found three language dimensions that are associated with deception: more negative emotion words, fewer self-references, and fewer markers of cognitive complexity. Despite the numerous studies on cues to lying, "focusing on individual cues is not a good strategy to detect lies because it is the equivalent of searching for Pinocchio's growing nose" (Vrij 2008: 230). A combination of individual cues offers the most useful associations for lie detection. (For more on Forensic Linguistics, see Chapter 37 by Stuart P. Green as well as Solan and Tiersma 2005.)

Few non-English or cross-linguistic studies have examined linguistic cues for lying. One example is an analysis of English and French role-plays while lying under oath. Dyas (2002) found that a heightened occurrence of filled pauses lowered credibility judgments in both languages. For French (only), the strongest trend for lowering judgments of truthfulness corresponded to increased use of imperfective verbs. In a different study concerning fabricated stories in Hebrew, Dilmon (2009) examined linguistic criteria belonging to morphology, syntax, semantics, and discourse. The author found fewer words, fewer independent clauses (economy), more conjunctions, fewer past-tense verbs, and fewer specific words in invented discourse. Furthermore, speakers demonstrated persuasive techniques such as greater use of idioms, many repetitions of details, and an exaggerated number of emotive words. Overall, differences between true and fabricated discourse were seen in small details rather than in general parts of the discourse.

In sum, while the presence of particular verbal criteria does not necessarily indicate that a person is lying, they may make it more likely. Liars and truth-tellers communicate in qualitatively different ways (Undeutsch 1967). A remaining issue for research is the need for a comprehensive examination of a wide range of linguistic areas in a variety of discourse types, languages, and real situations.

4.4.2 Emergence of lying and deception

For more than 100 years, the inception of lying and deception in children has been a productive area of research (Meibauer 2014a: 17). Human development specialists have found that children begin to tell lies around age four, yet it is widely known that children are incompetent liars (Blum 2005). The emergence of white-lie telling occurs between ages three and seven (Lewis et al. 1989; Talwar and Lee 2002b), but children learn to categorize and evaluate different types of lies at various ages as their definition of lying changes during developmental stages up to adulthood (Peterson et al. 1983; Bussey 1999). Children of ages five and older judge selfishly motivated lies to be worse than unintentional ones (Peterson et al. 1983); however, children have varying degrees of difficulty comprehending different levels of deceit because of the degree of cognitive load in a particular situation (Sullivan et al. 1994; Russell et al. 1995). For example, research demonstrates that children as old as thirteen may still have difficulty distinguishing irony from lying (Bosco and Bucciarelli 2008). (For a detailed treatment of lying development, see Chapter 30 by Victoria Talwar.)

Unlike first-language acquisition, studies of lying in second-language (L2) or non-native-language learners are scarce. Da Silva et al. (2013) claimed the first study of lie-telling for L2 speakers. Their experiment involved students at a Canadian university who were videotaped in a naturalistic situation involving cheating in a test and whose responses were subsequently rated for truthfulness. Results showed that participants were unable to discriminate between truth- and lie-tellers if the videotaped students were speaking in their second language. In fact, raters indicated a lie bias toward non-native speakers in contrast to a truth bias when observing native-language speakers. The study has potential implications for law enforcement and potential biases associated with lie detection in second-language speakers, because even though L2 speakers may be telling the truth, native-speaker observers are more likely to think that L2 speakers are lying when compared to native speakers.

Second-language learners have also been found to rely on their first-language pragmatic system when identifying lies. They therefore interpret social lies differently, rating them with a lower lie score than native speakers do (Eichelberger 2012). Instead, when L2 Spanish learners recognized commonly occurring cultural situations, they were more reluctant to classify statements in such situations as lies at all. Second-language acquisition remains an open field for research into lying and deception.

4.4.3 Intercultural and cross-cultural pragmatics

Intercultural Pragmatics examines how languages are used in social encounters between speakers with different first languages and cultures who communicate in a common language, whereas cross-cultural pragmatics studies language users from different cultures and languages. Most empirical pragmatic studies are cross-cultural.

Recall Coleman and Kay's semantic prototype analysis for English, which found that lying is a graded phenomenon containing three semantic features (a false statement, belief that the statement is false, and intent to deceive). Empirical support for this basic prototype lie comes from several replications of the study in Makkan Arabic and two dialects of Spanish. Beginning with the cross-cultural accounts, Cole's (1996) study of Arabic found no significant differences in the prototype between American English and Makkan Arabic, although comments by respondents indicated some cultural nuances in acceptability, based on age and religion. Cole (1996: 481) included two additional stories to examine possible cultural differences for *kathaba* 'lie'. She found that lying is overtly permitted for the purpose of reconciliation and to save one's life, but she did not explain how these exceptions supported the prototype theory.

Hardin (2010) also translated Coleman and Kay's stories into Ecuadorian Spanish along with five additional stories in which a lie might commonly occur yet seem acceptable to Ecuadorian Spanish speakers, possibly owing to factors outside the realm of semantics. Like Cole's research, Hardin's study reflected the same prototypical elements, but speakers indicated a difference of interpretation for the intent to deceive. Participants instead viewed some situations with [-intent] as more prototypical lies than those with [+intent], a finding contrary to Coleman and Kay's higher ranking for [intent]. The study demonstrated that cultural or social factors were likely involved when interpreting lies, suggesting the need for a sociolinguistic account.

A final partial replication of Coleman and Kay comes from Danziger's (2010) study of the Mopan Maya of Belize. She offered three scenarios comparing lie judgments between a literal falsehood in which the speaker knows his utterance is false (a prototypical lie), a literal falsehood without the speaker's knowledge of falsehood (a mistake), and one where the speaker knows his statement to be false, but the knowledge turns out to be erroneous (literal truth/a surprise). Interpretations for *tus* 'lying' were opposite to those for 'lying' in English. To the Mopan it mattered far more whether the utterance was actually false than whether the speaker believed it to be false. She argued that blame is assessed by the amount of damage done rather than the perceived degree of intent and therefore that the speaker's intention must be culturally understood. She therefore derived a specific Mopan version of the maxim of Quality that eliminates belief and intent and instead depends upon veracity of the utterance itself (Danziger 2010: 211).

With few exceptions, cross-linguistic research on lying/deception has contrasted English with other languages, highlighting differences in acceptability. Blum (2005), for example, highlighted the contrast in Chinese between deception and reality as opposed to the American tendency to focus on a contrast between truth and lying. In another Chinese study applying McCornack et al.'s (1992) Information Manipulation Theory, Yeung et al. (1999) noted that respondents in Hong Kong Chinese had a higher threshold of tolerance for flouting Grice's (1975) conversational maxims than Americans. He argued that in Hong Kong, speakers may manipulate their messages to avoid hurting others' feelings or to fulfill social expectations, but that such violations may not be intended to be covert. Instead, things may be left unsaid, with the expectation that others will read between the lines. In contrast, Americans may view such violations of conversational maxims as constituting intentionally deceptive acts. On the other hand, Chinese speakers may be embarrassed by Americans' directness and their inattention to face.

Another experiment comparing English and Chinese tested lying via a survey with nine stories containing untruth as well as three elements on a continuum: concealment, self-benefit, and other-benefit (Chen et al. 2013). For Americans, the more similar an assertion was to a lie, the more they found it morally objectionable. Chinese participants were harsher judges of lie-like assertions but displayed more tolerance for untruth. While they did not claim universal application, the authors argued that their research highlighted the variety of intentions that speakers may have when lying.

In a rare study from Oceania, Aune and Walters (1994: 165) found that Samoans were more inclined to deceive when it would be beneficial to the participant's family or group or when necessary to please an authority figure. Since Samoan culture is more collectivistic than North American culture, Samoan motivations to deceive are heavily based on how an utterance might affect the larger group. Related to the concept of politeness and face (Brown and Levinson 1987), the study was viewed as an example of how lying can be used as a politeness strategy to avoid conflict and save face.

Face is important in other cross-linguistic studies. For example, in a survey of Euro-Americans and Ecuadorians, both groups found it more acceptable to lie to an out-group than to an in-group. Both groups also found it acceptable to lie to maintain positive relations with others, but Euro-Americans also accepted lies that would self-flatter and lead others to think well of them (Mealy et al. 2007). Another politeness study compared British and Thai subjects (Intachakra 2011), noting that the British preferred to tell the truth more than Thai participants did. Thai respondents instead believed it would be better to hide their displeasure and say something nice to the other party. Similarly, in comparing US and Korean participants, Hee et al. (2007) found that Korean production and judgments of truthfulness were related to how they thought others would produce or judge the message. All of these studies emphasize the acceptability of lies and various aspects of politeness.

Intercultural pragmatics research on lying is scarce, although as described in section 4.4.2, the second portion of Eichelberger's (2012) report found that advanced second-language speakers of Spanish drew from their first language (English) pragmatic system when interpreting Coleman and Kay's scenarios in Spanish, particularly for social lies, and they had difficulty identifying lies at all because of their prior experiences in Spanish.

4.4.4 Intralinguistic studies and variational pragmatics

For languages other than English, intralinguistic (single language) studies have focused on differences with regard to the interpretation, and to a lesser degree, the production of lies and deception in single-linguistic accounts. Of particular interest are white lies, so-called "blue lies" (for the collective good), and social or well-meant lies. As Blum (2005) explains, deception occurs throughout human societies but with varying degrees of concern and frequency. The notion of 'lie' is also tied to cultural views of information and to a culturally molded sense of self and individuality (Sweetser 1987). For example, Brown's (2002) intracultural analysis of the Tzeltal did not replicate Coleman and Kay, but she argued that for *lot* 'lie, non-truth, mistake', the falsehood of a statement [+false] was interpreted as the strongest prototype criterion, and the weakest was [+belief]. She stated that lying relates to the verbal practice of conventionalized irony as a polite way to share an attitude (Brown 2002: 263–4).

Although few in number, single-culture linguistic accounts of lying/deception unrelated to Coleman and Kay's study have found that (1) pitch, response latency, and speech rate were cues to deception in Italian speech (Spence et al. 2012); (2) attitudes to individual responsibility for the truth of statements may be collectivistic, as in Tzeltal (Brown 2002) and Malagasy (Ochs Keenan 1974); (3) gender differences occur among Lebanese men and women when producing white lies in service encounters (in which one person provides a service to the other) (El Nakkouzi 2011); and (4) the extent of damage (material and interpersonal) caused by a lie determines its acceptability in both the Mopan Maya of Belize and the Ceará of Brazil (Danziger 2010; Pennesi 2013).

Related to both intralinguistic and cross-cultural pragmatics, Variational Pragmatics is a field of research that examines varieties of the same language. Eichelberger's (2012) replication of Hardin's study (including the five additional scenarios) for Spanish in Madrid is an example of this type of inquiry. This portion of her research again generally supported Coleman and Kay's basic prototype, but the ordering of semantic elements aligned more closely with that shown in data from Ecuador, showing that the Spanish *mentira* 'lie' is a common cultural tool used for politeness in social contexts. The study was also cross-linguistic, demonstrating differences in the order of semantic elements compared to English and Arabic. She noted the conflict between definitions of lies and the context of real-world situations, arguing for both a pragmatic and cultural explanation.

Replication studies of Coleman and Kay (1981) have uncovered sociolinguistic differences both in the notion of a prototype lie and in the relative importance of semantic elements related to a lie in English as compared to Arabic, Ecuadorian and Madrileño Spanish, and Mopan Maya (Cole 1996; Danziger 2010; Hardin 2010; Eichelberger 2012, respectively). Thus, cross-linguistic analysis so far has yielded rich insights into some sociolinguistic complexities of lying/deception, yet much remains for future research. The diverse approaches found in most studies have yet to be replicated across languages, let alone within dialects. In summary, replications of Coleman and Kay's prototype analysis and empirical studies suggest that a solely semantic account cannot account for lying. Instead, pragmatic and cultural explanations are required.

4.4.5 Discourse types and applications

Linguistics plays a vital role when particular discourses are analyzed for lying and deception. Media language, for example, has had a long history of analysis, since its use of language is a "loaded weapon," with its emphasis on literalism, euphemism, economic metaphors, power, and nice-sounding illogic (Bolinger 1980). As Lakoff (1982) noted, the violation of Grice's (1975) maxims in persuasive discourse such as advertising is covert, and the audience is tricked into assuming that an act of information is occurring. Deception in media language often occurs via conversational implicatures, as shown by Geis (1982), who analyzed advertisements, arguing for a "pragmatist" theory of truth in advertising in which advertisers would be legally responsible for what they conversationally implicate. Similarly, in their discourse analysis of televangelism, Schmidt and Kess (1985) found many persuasive (and deceptive) strategies similar to those typically present in advertising, particularly with respect to conventional and conversational implicatures. Advertisers use their linguistic skills of persuasion to get their audience to act in accordance with their interests (Lakoff 1982). So persuasion is a subset of manipulation in that the targets are made to believe, both through truth and deception, a preferred version of reality (Galasiński 2000: 21).

Politics and propaganda offer another obvious discourse type involving lying. For example, falsifications, distortions, and taking words out of context are three types of misrepresentations found in political debates (Galasiński 2000: 38). Implicatures are also frequent in this type of discourse, since the speaker can then easily deny the message and the addressee will have difficulty rejecting it (Giora 1994). Politicians consequently make use of ambiguity by pretending not to assert (via analogies and metaphor), use of questions as "statements in disguise," pretending to deny, pretending to assert, and pretending to apologize. Most cases of political lying and deception occur to manipulate public opinion and generate support for particular causes or to promote personal interests (Carson 2010).

Besides advertising, politics, law, and religion, discourse genres involving an unequal distribution of power and manipulation include therapeutic and courtroom discourse, job interviews, examination situations, academic language, and adult speech directed at children (Lakoff 1982; Mey 1985). Analyses of lying and deception in varied forms of discourse have shown diverse results. For example, as expected, shorter messages were associated with deception in online dating profiles. More surprisingly, first-person-pronoun use and negative emotional terms were not associated with lying in online discourse even though they were reliable indicators for lying in previous forensic linguistic research (Toma and Hancock 2012). Linguistic features have also been analyzed with regard to nurses lying to patients (Tuckett 1998), academic writing and plagiarism (Pecorari 2008), Nigerian fraud emails (Schaffer 2012), lying on Facebook (Underwood et al. 2011), and deception in Enron emails (Kessler 2010), to name just a few examples. The current roles of both Conversational Analysis (transcription and analysis at the micro-level) and computer-generated linguistic analysis are likely to be maintained across discourse genres related to lying on the Internet and in other media.

4.5 Conclusion

"Not every lie is a total lie. The problem of lying would not be a *magna quaestio* if black and white were always so clearly distributed. There are half-lies, and there are those minor deviations from the truth that are perhaps so dangerous because they are so hard to recognize . . . " (Weinrich 2005: 56). Despite a rich history and breadth of discussion, empirical linguistic studies are limited in both scope and number, and studies in so-called "experimental pragmatics" are rare (Meibauer 2014a). Indeed, one discerns a gap between the social reality of lying and the research on lying (Chen et al. 2013). What does the concept of lying look like for real speakers and hearers within their particular discourse contexts, communities of practice (Lave and Wenger 1991), and broader cultures? Future research should include replication of existing studies across discourse genres, languages, and dialects. Despite centuries of analysis, universals of lying and deception are largely theoretical and do not necessarily hold across language and cultural boundaries, nor are they purely semantic in nature. Lying and deception are therefore pragma-linguistic and sociolinguistic questions; theory that does not stand up to empirical testing may not be relevant to real-life language containing lies and deception.

CHAPTER 5

PSYCHOLINGUISTIC APPROACHES TO LYING AND DECEPTION

LEWIS BOTT AND EMMA WILLIAMS

5.1 INTRODUCTION

PEOPLE tell the truth by default. Successful communication can arise only when all parties agree to cooperate and cooperation involves telling the truth (Grice 1989c). When people lie, they depart from this default, which likely imposes additional demands on the language system. This chapter is concerned with the nature of those additional demands, and more generally, with how telling a lie alters the normal functioning of the language system.

We start by introducing the language production system. Lying involves producing a message, rather than comprehending a message, and the effects of lying should consequently be observed on the production system. We then discuss how the different components of lying might influence this process, before concluding with a section on the effects of reducing the cognitive resources available to the language processor.

5.2 THE PRODUCTION PROCESS

When people hear an utterance they map sound features onto phonemes, phonemes onto words, words onto syntactic and semantic structures, and words and structures onto, ultimately, a conceptual message. Producing an utterance is the reverse process. The speaker conceives of a message, the message is formulated into semantic and syntactic components, and then articulated to produce a motor output. Lying might influence any of these production stages.

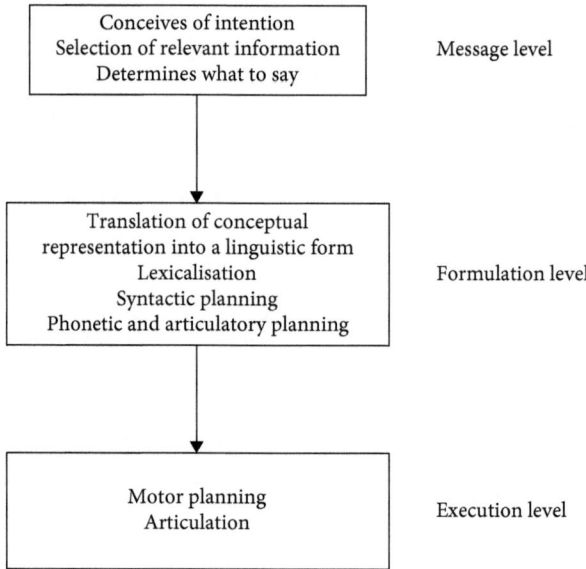

FIGURE 5.1 Speech production process (Levelt 1989).

Figure 5.1 illustrates the production stages in more detail. According to the classic model of Levelt (1989), production consists of three basic components: the message level; the formulation level; and the articulation level. While there have been considerable advances in our knowledge of the implementation of these stages since Levelt published the original model, e.g., Indefrey and Levelt (2000), the basic computational requirements of a production system, as shown in Figure 5.1, remain unchanged. At the message level, communicative intentions are conceived, such as a direct request for information, or a declaration of information that the listener wishes to counter by claiming it to be untrue. The intention to lie must also be conceived at this level, just like any other communicative intention. The speaker also selects the relevant information to be communicated, such as the propositional content of the declaration (what the message will be about), including the content of the lie. However, information is represented in a pre-verbal form, that is, it is not yet expressed as words and linguistic structures. The transformation from the pre-verbal to the verbal occurs at the formulation level. It is here that conceptual information is translated into linguistic form. Lexicalization of the concepts occurs (specific words are chosen), syntactic and semantic structures are selected, and detailed articulatory planning occurs, such as phonological encoding (e.g., specification of appropriate prosody). Finally, articulation takes place. This involves selecting the retrieval of chunks of internal speech from a buffer and execution of motor commands to pronounce the words.

Lying initially involves an intention different from truth-telling intentions, and hence at least some component of the lying process must occur at the message level. However, whether the intention is reflected at the message level or at later levels, or how it is realized, is an open empirical question and probably depends on the type of lie. For example, planning what information to use in a lie may be more difficult than planning the information to use in a truthful communication. Whether this difficulty is absorbed by parallel constraints at the message level, or is reflected in longer hesitations between clauses, or longer onset times in retrieving lexical information or syntactic frames, requires further consideration. Indeed, this question can be answered only by collecting data and considering the nature of the planning difference between lying and telling the truth. In the next section we summarize the available evidence.

5.3 Psychological components of lying

In this section, we map the psychological features that distinguish lying from truth-telling onto the different levels of the production process.

5.3.1 Suppression of relevant information

Lying involves suppressing information that the speaker believes to be relevant. This information is most likely to represent the truth.[1] For example, an errant husband, when asked for his whereabouts, would want to suppress the information that he was at his mistress's apartment. How would suppression affect the production of the upcoming utterance?

There are many studies claiming that suppression of truthful information contributes to a delay in the production of a deceptive utterance (Walczyk, Roper, Seemann, Humphrey et al. 2003; Vendemia, Buzan, and Simon-Dack 2005; Seymour and Kerlin 2008; Duran, Dale, and McNamara 2010; Williams, Bott, Patrick, and Lewis 2013). However, the majority of these studies do not distinguish between other potential processes required when people tell a lie, such as the activation and retrieval of relevant information from memory, the decision whether to lie or tell the truth, and the construction of an appropriate lie, including how much truthful information can be incorporated within this (Walczyk et al. 2003). Furthermore, most of this work has focused on moderating factors, such as the subject that an individual lies about (Gronau, Ben-Shakhar, and Cohen 2005), the relative frequency with which they lie (Verschuere, Spruyt, Meijer, and Otgaar 2011), and the degree of practice that they have had (Vendemia et al. 2005). Unambiguous evidence regarding the suppression of truthful information is provided by studies such as Duran et al. (2010) and Williams et al. (2013), which we discuss below.

Duran et al. (2010) used an innovative paradigm in which they asked participants to use a Nintendo Wii remote to respond honestly or deceptively (by clicking yes or no) in

---

[1] However, there may also be instances whereby the relevant information to be suppressed is false, for example, a pre-prepared lie that is no longer consistent with the knowledge of the receiver.

response to autobiographical information presented on a large projector screen. By analyzing the trajectories of the remote control across the screen as participants responded, the experimenters identified the presence of a dynamic curve towards the true response when participants responded deceptively. This curve was not present when participants responded truthfully, suggesting that the truthful information was considered and then overridden in order to produce a deceptive response.

Williams et al. (2013) focused explicitly on identifying the role and relative contribution of the suppression of truthful information when producing a lie. Using a simplified deception paradigm, participants were required to produce a deceptive or truthful vocal response about the colour of a square shown on a computer screen. In the most simple of these experiments, there were only two colours used throughout the experiment, red or blue, and participants had to lie with the colour not shown on the screen (e.g., if the square was red, they needed to say "blue" and vice versa). Participants were told when to lie and when to tell the truth. Williams et al. found that participants were slower to lie than to tell the truth. While this result is not particularly surprising, it is important to remember that there was no lie construction needed in this situation (participants had no choice about the content of the lie) and there was no decision needed about when to lie (they were told before the trial started how they would know whether to lie). There were consequently very few cognitive processes that could explain the lie response except for the need to suppress the truthful information.

Experiments by Williams et al. (2013) and others leave little doubt that suppressing relevant information delays speech production in scenarios where responding truthfully is the dominant response (for discussion of the impact of habitual lying on the lie response, see Verschuere et al. 2011). What is far less clear, however, is how and where the suppression occurs. Williams et al. suggest some possibilities. The first assumes that suppression of the truth is a serial process that must be completed before the remainder of the message is constructed. When a person lies, they initially activate the truth but then reject it in favour of an appropriate alternative. The delay is caused by an extra processing stage when lying compared to telling the truth. The second possibility assumes that truthful and other possible responses are activated to different degrees in memory. Making an utterance involves selecting one of those responses (normally the truthful one), and the time taken to respond depends on the difference in activation levels between the truth and other responses. When telling a lie, the activation of the truthful response is suppressed so that it becomes closer to the activation of the other responses. Since there is now less difference between the responses, choosing between them becomes more difficult and production time increases.

A final explanation for the findings of Williams et al. (2013) and others is that interference occurs between the truthful and the lie sentence. If people do not suppress the truthful message immediately they would need to simultaneously plan the truthful sentence and the lie sentence. The resulting interference would cause delays in production. Although there is no data that directly support this idea, evidence from tasks in which participants simultaneously listen and speak suggests that processing two similar messages impairs production (e.g., Glaser and Düngelhoff 1984; Cook and Meyer 2008). For example, Glaser and Düngelhoff found that when participants had to name a picture (e.g., a doll) at the same time as listening to a word ("TEDDY"), participants were slower when the word was related ("TEDDY") than when it was not ("HORSE"). Whether planning two messages at once is similar to planning one and listening to one remains to be seen, but it is quite possible that delays attributed to suppression of the truth might be due to the exact opposite: a failure to suppress the truth sufficiently early.

5.3.2 Lie construction

People need to construct a lie. In order to be successful, the lie must appear to adhere to the normal rules of conversational exchange (Grice 1989c). In other words, the response must be truthful (or apparently truthful), relevant, of sufficient quantity, and must be in an appropriate manner. For example, consider a husband asked about his whereabouts the previous evening. The response must, clearly, appear to be truthful, in that it has to be plausible. The husband cannot respond with the statement, "I was on the moon," because it is not plausible that he could have been there. It must also be relevant, otherwise he risks alerting his wife that he wishes to opt out of the topic of conversation. For example, he cannot say, "It's dark outside," without suggesting he wants to move the conversation on (even though the response might be truthful). It must also be of sufficient quantity to satisfy her request. For example, even though the statement, "I was on planet earth" is (a) true, and (b) relevant, it does not provide a sufficient quantity of information to be considered a normal conversational contribution. Finally, the lie must be expressed in a normal manner (style). For example, there must be an appropriate level of detail. In short, the content of the lie must satisfy all of the constraints of being cooperative, while avoiding the truth.

Unfortunately, there are very few studies that have directly addressed how people construct lies. We can find only two components of the lie construction process that have received any attention. The first is the process of making arbitrary choices in lie contexts and the second is the need to make the lie plausible.

5.3.2.1 *Choosing details*

People often provide arbitrary details when recounting a story ("And I remember he was wearing a red shirt," or "She had blond hair," or "It was a Volvo, just like mine"). People telling the truth can easily read off these details from memory, perhaps to give added interest to the story, or perhaps just because the details are salient to the storyteller. People engaged in lying must make up these details. What are the effects on the production system of having to do so?

Williams et al. (2013) investigated this question. As we described above, participants in this study either truthfully named the colour of a square on a screen, or lied about it. Voice onset times were the dependent measure. In Experiment 3, Williams et al. tested whether having to choose a lie was more difficult than having no choice about which lie to tell. There were two conditions. In the first, the coloured square could be blue or red (the two-colour condition). In the second, the coloured square could be blue, red, or green (the three-colour condition). This meant that in the two-colour condition, there was only one possible lie response (e.g., if the coloured square was blue, the lie had to be that it was red), whereas in the three-colour condition, there were two possible lie responses (e.g., if the coloured square was blue, the lie could be red or green). Williams et al. found that lies (but not truths) were more difficult in the three-colour condition than the two-colour condition. They concluded that making arbitrary choices requires an extra processing stage when lying compared to when telling the truth. People have to make a decision when they lie, but the truth arises automatically.

5.3.2.2 *Perspective-taking*

A liar tries to construct a message that convinces a listener of something other than the truth. This involves communicating a message that *appears* to be truthful. Or, in other words, the lie must be consistent with the knowledge of the addressee. For example, a husband asked about his whereabouts the previous evening could not successfully lie with the response, "I was bowling," when his wife was at the bowling alley, because this would not be consistent with his wife's representation of the people at the bowling alley. Ensuring that the intended message appears truthful means taking the perspective of the addressee when constructing the lie. Indeed, lying could be seen as perspective taking *par excellence*: its success necessarily depends on an accurate judgment of the listener's perspective.

Perspective taking has a long history in psycholinguistics (although very little has been directly concerned with lying). Much of the work relates to the *audience design hypothesis* (Clark and Murphy 1982). The basic idea is that successful communication can occur only when interlocutors have detailed models of each other's knowledge base, and moreover, that people use these models when constructing an utterance. Otherwise, so the argument goes, language would be excessively ambiguous. That people vary their language depending on the audience is not in dispute. For example, mothers address their children with a simplified vocabulary and syntax and with a high-pitched voice (child-directed speech, Snow 1972; Cameron-Faulkner, Lieven, and Tomasello 2003), speakers change their style depending on the social identity of their addressees (Dell 1984; Giles and Ogay 2007), and when speakers are asked to describe an abstract figure so that it can be recognized later on, they describe the figure differently if describing it for themselves than if describing it to someone else (e.g., Danks 1970). More pertinently, people tell minor 'white' lies all the time (DePaulo, Kashy, Kirkendol, Wyer, and Epstein 1996) and are often successful.

What is less clear is *when* and *how* people take into account the perspective of their audiences (Barr and Keysar 2006). For example, which levels of processing does audience design constrain? Do people take an audience perspective right from the message level of production, or do they start off being egocentric and adjust the message at a later stage? The reason that the answers to these questions are in doubt is that what appears to be low-level perspective-taking could be explained by later, higher-level processes such as *monitoring*. For example, an adult speaker who uses different vocabulary to speak to a child than they use to an adult could be either selecting different vocabulary automatically (at the functional stage), or they could initially select egocentric words and replace these after a perspective-taking monitor objected. Thus, the audience design component could be the result of later monitoring rather than early production. The same question arises with respect to lying. Some lie perspective-taking presumably occurs at the message level, since this is where propositions are formed, but whether the articulated sentence is an automatic consequence of the lie intention or follows from the action of a later, perspective-taking monitor is not clear. A monitor could constrain the range of lie choices considered, or it could filter out inappropriate choices after a selection of plausible propositions has already been selected.

The question of whether people hold an egocentric bias in language has received a lot of attention in psycholinguistics generally. The evidence is inconclusive, however. Some studies have favoured an egocentric account of perspective-taking (e.g., Horton and Keysar 1996; Rossnagel 2000; Barr and Keysar 2002). For example, Horton and Keysar found that utterances became more egocentric as participants were put under time pressure, suggesting that perspective-taking was a late process. Conversely, other work suggests that people are able to immediately make use of multiple probabilistic constraints, including the perspective of others (Hanna, Tanenhaus, and Trueswell 2003; Brown-Schmidt, Gunlogson, and Tanenhaus 2008; Heller, Grodner, and Tanenhaus 2008; Ferguson and Breheny 2011). For example, Ferguson and Breheny used a visual-world eye-tracking study to demonstrate that people could make complex, higher-order theory of mind inferences extremely rapidly. It appears, therefore, that the particular task used and the type of perspective-taking influence whether people are initially egocentric.

The only study that has used deceit to investigate perspective-taking (Lane, Groisman, and Ferreira 2006) was primarily interested in "ironic-processes effects" (Wegner 1994) and not lying, but the results are relevant here in that they suggest that lying involves a secondary, monitoring process. Lane et al. engaged participants in a dialogue task in which there was a speaker and a listener. On baseline trials, the speaker had to communicate the identity of a shape. In the experimental trials, there were always at least two objects of the same shape (e.g., two circles) but of different sizes (one small and one big) and two other shapes (e.g., a square and a diamond). This meant that to unambiguously refer to one of the circles, the director had to use a modifier (e.g., "small," as in "the small circle"). On conceal trials, the speakers were given additional instructions to hide the identity of a foil shape. Thus, in these trials, the speaker had to avoid using a modifier (otherwise the listener would become aware that the foil was of the same shape as the referent). Lane et al. found that participants used modifiers *more* often in the conceal trials than the baseline trials, even though this was contrary to their communicative intentions. Apparently, being instructed *not* to refer to something can make you more likely to refer to it. Lane et al. argued that the conceal instructions made the foil more salient and so participants were less able to suppress the associated modifier in the conceal condition. The implications of this finding are that because low-level factors such as salience can overcome perspective-taking, perspective-taking must be a secondary process, implemented after the primary egocentric sentence has been planned. Moreover, because the perspective-taking sentence was deceitful (omitting the modifier amounted to hiding the nature of the foil), the study suggests that lying is the late application of a secondary process that has edited the truthful sentence, rather than the result of constraints at the message level.

In summary, lying involves taking the perspective of others in order to construct a plausible sentence. This could either take place early at the message level, or later, using a secondary process. While there is some evidence for the latter (Lane et al. 2006), the deceit in Lane et al. was a very unusual form of deceit. Lying usually involves more planning than the omission of a modifier. It is, therefore, possible that more common forms of plausibility constraints arise at a much earlier stage than that observed in Lane et al.

5.3.3 Executing the lie

As well as suppressing the truth and constructing an appropriate lie (completed at the message level and the formulation level), the liar must execute the lie. This involves articulating the message and so occurs at the articulation level. Work in investigating the execution of the lie has been conducted from the lie-detection perspective and has focused on speech hesitations (frequency of using filler expressions, such as *ah* or *mm*, between words), speech errors (e.g., frequency of word repetition, sentence incompletion, slips of the tongue), and speech rate. The rationale for testing these areas has been that if lying is more difficult than telling the truth, then people should make more errors of articulation.

However, the evidence that lying affects any of these variables is mixed. Several studies have found differences between telling the truth and lying (e.g., Vrij and Mann 2001; DePaulo et al. 2003; Vrij et al. 2008). For example, Vrij et al. (2008) investigated whether lie detection was easier when people were under a high cognitive load. Participants witnessed a real-life event (a man stealing some money) and either recounted the events of the story in the order in which they experienced them, or in the reverse order. Half the participants were told to lie about the story and half were told to tell the truth. While the participants were recounting the story, Vrij et al. measured visual cues, such as finger movements, and more importantly for our purposes, speech hesitations, speech errors, and speech rate. Vrij et al. hypothesized that lie detection would be easier when liars were in the reverse-order condition than in the chronological condition, because they would be under a greater cognitive load. Their results showed that when participants recounted the story in the reverse condition, lying produced a greater proportion of speech errors, a lower speech rate, and a greater number of speech hesitations than telling the truth (although the statistical evidence that the speech cues in particular were affected by lying was weak in comparison to the evidence for non-vocal cues, such as eye-blinks).

Other studies have either not found differences in articulation parameters, or found effects in the opposite direction. For example, Porter, Doucette, Woodworth, Earle, and MacNeil (2008) analysed videotaped accounts of four autobiographical emotional events (two of which were true and two of which were fabricated) provided by a group of offenders and a group of university students. Although deceptive accounts were found to contain fewer details, the authors failed to find significant differences according to the presence of filled or unfilled pauses or speech rate. Similarly, Strömwall, Hartwig, and Granhag (2006) scored the nonverbal and verbal behaviours of thirty participants during long interrogations by police officers regarding their involvement in a mock crime. Despite finding the task more strenuous and being significantly more nervous than truth-tellers, liars failed to show any differences in speech rate, frequency of unfilled and filled pauses, or duration of unfilled pauses.

Why is it that there is such mixed evidence about the effects of lying on speech disturbances? One of the difficulties is that it is not clear which psycholinguistic factors cause many speech disturbances. Consequently, it is difficult to predict whether one would expect lying to have an effect. For example, while early evidence suggested that hesitations reflect the time needed for semantic planning (e.g., Goldman-Eisler 1968), more recent work concludes that hesitations also reflect syntactic planning (e.g., Petrie 1987). Now, while planning the semantics of lies is arguably more complex than planning the semantics of truths (e.g., lies might need to be checked for plausibility but truths would not), there is no reason to think that the same holds true for syntax (e.g., lies do not typically involve passive syntactic constructions any more than truths). Thus, hesitations may not reflect semantic planning, and even if they do, they may reflect a combination of syntactic with semantic planning. Under either of these conditions the effects of lying may be minimal. Another example is speech dysfluencies, such as *oh*, *uh*, and *um*. While these might reflect processing difficulties, there is evidence that they also convey information to the listener (Fox-Tree and Schrock 1999; Clark and Fox-Tree 2002). For example, *oh* indicates that the subsequent utterance is not connected to the immediately preceding information but to something earlier (Fox-Tree and Schrock 1999). If dysfluencies are not related to processing difficulty there is no reason why they should be influenced by lying. Clearly, a topic for future research is to identify which speech disturbances are likely to be affected by lying and to target those in particular.

A final point is that just because effects of lying are observed during the execution of the sentence, this does not mean that the effects are restricted to the execution mechanisms. Effects that arise earlier in the production process, for instance at the formulation level, could manifest themselves as greater speech dysfluencies, errors, or hesitations, and are not necessarily connected with the articulation stage per se. Indeed, none of the hypothesized reasons for speech effects have much to do with articulatory planning or execution. This raises the interesting question of whether there are effects of lying that are restricted to the articulation stage, for example, the motor programs that execute the articulators. However, the work so far on speech dysfluencies and lying has not been concerned with where in the production process the observed effects arise from and so at present, it is difficult to distinguish between effects restricted to the articulatory level and those caused by earlier affected processes.

5.4 Lying and central resources

Researchers involved in lie detection have often argued that lying is cognitively more demanding than telling the truth (e.g., Zuckerman et al. 1981; DePaulo et al. 2003; Vrij et al. 2008). The increased mental effort of lying is said to come about partly for the reasons suggested above, but also through a variety of nonlinguistic factors that might use up a general pool of central, cognitive resources. These factors are the following. First, liars are typically less likely than truth-tellers to take their credibility for granted (Gilovich, Savitsky, and Medvec 1998; DePaulo et al. 2003). This means they must monitor and control their own behaviour so that they will appear honest (DePaulo and Kirkendol 1989). Second, they must also monitor the behaviour of the listener to establish whether the listener believes them (Buller and Burgoon 1996). Third, liars have to remind themselves to act and role-play while truth-tellers do not (DePaulo et al. 2003), and fourth, lying is a more deliberate and intentional act than truth-telling, which requires mental effort (Walczyk et al. 2003; Walcczyk, Schwartz, Clifton, Adams, Wei, and Zha 2005). If lying uses up more central processing resources than telling the truth, how would this affect the language processor?

These questions relate to whether speech production is an autonomous, modular system that operates independently of a central processing resource. If it is, there is no reason to think that the language-independent components of lying should influence language production. Indeed, given that the language system is cognitively, anatomically, and genetically distinct from other, non-linguistic processes (e.g., Pinker 1994), and is a highly practised skill (e.g., Cohen, Dunbar, and McClelland 1990), there is a good case to be made for its modularity. However, there is now strong empirical evidence that at least some components of language production require central cognitive resources.

Ferreira and Pashler (2002) conducted the first detailed study into which components of the language-production process required central resources. Ferreira and Pashler used a dual-task paradigm to test whether lemma selection (word choice) and phonological word-form selection interfered with tone discrimination (a task known to use central resources). Participants were told to speak a sentence that ended with the participant naming a picture presented on the screen (Task 1). They manipulated whether the picture was high-frequency or low-frequency (a phonological manipulation) and whether the sentence was highly constrained or weakly constrained by the picture-naming. For example, if the picture was of a bed (a high-frequency word), the participant might have to read, "Bob was tired so he went to … ", in which the sentence severely constrains the picture, or "She saw a picture of a … ", in which the sentence does not. At various times after picture onset, participants had to discriminate among three tones (Task 2). Ferreira and Pashler found that both lemma selection and phonological word-form selection interfered with the tone-discrimination task. However, in a second, similar experiment, they found that phoneme selection did not interfere with the tone-discrimination task. They, therefore, concluded that while lemma selection and phonological word-form selection tapped central processing resources, phoneme selection did not.

Since Ferreira and Pashler (2002), there have been many studies that are consistent with the claim that at least some components of word planning require central processing resources (attention). For example, object-naming latencies are correlated with inhibitory control ability (Shao, Roelofs, and Meyer 2012) and with sustained attention ability (Jongman, Roelofs, and Meyer 2015), and gaze durations depend on the amount of conflict in the colour-word Stroop task (Lamers and Roelofs 2011). If lying requires more central resources than telling the truth, evidence suggests that word selection, at least, should be slower in lying.

5.5 Conclusion

This chapter has provided an overview of how lying might affect the cognitive processes of language production. We have discussed the cognitive components of lying, such as the suppression of the truth and the construction of a lie, as well as how lying might use up cognitive resources that indirectly influence the language system.

There are two points that stand out from this review. The first is that there are only a handful of studies that have directly investigated lying from a cognitive viewpoint. This is both bad news and good news for researchers interested in lying. The bad news is that the limited range of studies means that not much is known about how lying affects the language system. We have no idea, for example, what mechanisms are involved in the suppression of truthful information. The good news is that there are many interesting experiments still to conduct. The second is that psycholinguistic research on language production has provided a good framework on which to base further studies. Designing experiments to investigate where in the production process lying effects arise (at the message level, the formulation level, or the articulation level) would shed light on the sort of mechanisms that are responsible. For example, knowing whether people suppress truthful information at the message level or at the formulation level would tell us a great deal about how the suppression mechanism works.

We close by noting that researchers interested in lying and those interested in psycholinguistics, have much to gain from each other. The incentive for those interested in psycholinguistics to study lying is that lying engages many of the same processes as telling the truth, but at a more extreme level. For example, lying often involves the suppression of relevant material. Suppression is a domain-general mechanism that is used in a wide range of psycholinguistic processes, such as in the suppression of inappropriate meanings of homonyms (e.g., Swinney 1979) or inappropriate syntactic frames (e.g., McRae, Spivey-Knowlton, and Tanenhaus 1998). Suppression processes can be further extricated from message production in deception research by aligning with work conducted on lying by omission, as discussed in Chapter 13, whereby a lie response is not produced, but a truth may still be considered and suppressed. Understanding how people suppress the truth in these different contexts can help us understand the language architecture more generally. The incentive for those interested in lying should be clear from this chapter: understanding how people lie can only be understood with reference to how they tell the truth, that is, normal psycholinguistic processes.

CHAPTER 6

LYING, DECEPTION, AND THE BRAIN

ALEXA DECKER, AMANDA DISNEY,
BRIANNA D'ELIA, AND JULIAN PAUL KEENAN

6.1 INTRODUCTION

A complete understanding of any neurocognitive function lies in grasping its evolution. That stated, the three main constructs that we wish to explore (i.e., the brain, evolution, and deception) are so incredibly complex that a true, dare we say honest, understanding is in its infancy. Further, a full analysis of the evolution of the brain and deception across the phylogenetic spectrum would be beyond the scope of this volume, though we are aided by the fact that within this volume there is a related review (Ganis, Kosslyn, Stose, Thompson, and Yurgelin-Todd 2003; Ganis, Morris, and Kosslyn 2009; Ganis and Patnaik 2009; Ganis, Rosenfeld, Meixner, Kievit, and Schendan 2011). Chapter 35 by Giorgio Ganis is a thorough review of the relation between the brain and deception and we assume this chapter will be read in conjunction with that chapter, as well as Chapter 5 by Lewis Bott and Emma Williams.

Evolutionary biologists typically reconstruct the evolutionary history of *Homo sapiens* through the lens of social pressure and a reciprocating interplay among cognitive abilities, neural system expansions, and increased environmental manipulation, which all bought about advanced language, tool making, Theory of Mind, and self-awareness. Within this cycle, demands on cooperation were increased as the infant neural system needed a longer time to mature and this new advanced neural system needed increased caloric intake in order to feed its growing metabolic demands. Out of this system— which placed an extreme value on the quality of offspring rather than quantity—arose both a demand for knowing the hierarchies and other social nuances, and the abilities to manipulate social systems in order to mate, acquire resources, raise offspring, and pass on one's genes (Adenzato and Ardito 1999). It is intuitively natural to think that out of this system arose deception and that those individuals who deceived successfully left more descendants than those who did not. Understanding intentionality (i.e., self-awareness and Theory of Mind) aided in deception, as we think deception aided in increasing the depth of self-awareness and Theory of Mind (Keenan, Rubio, Racioppi, Johnson, and Barnacz 2005). Other factors, such as deontic reasoning, also favored those who were advanced deceivers. As foolish as it would be to ignore social pressures and advanced cognition in the evolution of *Homo sapiens*' deception, it would be equally foolish not to think that the evolved mechanisms of deception follow a linear trajectory.

6.2 You do not need a brain to deceive

Consider the family of Orchidaceae—a lovely, magnificent form of life, according to many humans. Yet, without a brain or even a hint of a central nervous system (CNS), the orchid is an incredible deceiver[1] (Gaskett 2011). Simply and typically, an orchid can mimic the female of a pollinator species, therefore achieving a basic life function, that is, successful pollination (Schiestl 2005; Jersáková, Johnson, and Kindlmann 2006; Waterman and Bidartondo 2008; Ayasse, Stökl, and Francke 2011). In other words, the orchid may send out visual signals that make it look like a female wasp, therefore attracting male wasps. And while the male wasp is duped, the orchid is pollinated. Incredibly, there is evidence that the mimicking of other species within Orchids has evolved independently (Ayasse et al. 2011), and that there is a tremendous interplay between how the Orchid mimics and what, and how other species are drawn to successfully pollinate (Gaskett 2011). By pretending to be (i.e., mimicking) another organism, the Orchid draws attention to itself and receives clear beneficial evolutionary advantages. It is worth pointing out immediately that the notion that deception can occur without a CNS, and that it evolved independently in a family of plants, indicates that the evolution story is a muddied one. Even at the flora level, there are pressures to deceive, thus if we even dare think we know what those pressures were for human deception to emerge, we are certainly speculating.

This deception is fairly typical in the multicellular domain. Making oneself out to be a 'thing' or a species or a sex one is not, to make oneself conspicuous is not uncommon. Batesian mimicry, for example, is the property of an animal that is itself quite palatable to predators making itself look like a different species that is highly unpalatable (Cheney and Côté 2005; Pfennig and Mullen 2010). Insects will look like other insects such that they look LESS like prey. This mimicry is often achieved through visual cuing (e.g.,

---

[1] Deception (Leal, Vrij, Fisher, and van Hooff 2008; Vrij 2008) here is seen as the nonintentional manipulation of facts, while lying is used to indicate an individual's knowledge of his/her deception. We have used this distinction because it is somewhat common in the literature, as well as in the vernacular, but also because it helps to identify the likelihood that humans add unique cognitive features and that self-deception is beyond the immediate purview of the deceiver.

spots, stripes, colors that match those of an unpalatable species). However, and remarkably, Batesian mimicry is not limited to physical signals, but to behavioral ones as well. Butterflies of one (palatable) species have a similar flight style when to that of another species of butterfly that is less palatable, thus decreasing the likelihood of their winding up as prey (Kitamura and Imafuku 2015).

Another example comes from the ant world, and here we can see a strategy of mimicry in which the deceiver hopes to NOT draw attention to itself by use of deception (Powell, Del-Claro, Feitosa, and Brandão 2014). And while, like the Orchid, there are many examples, ants are both great perpetrators (Powell, Del-Claro, Feitosa, and Brandão 2014; Wyatt 2014) and victims of deception (Uma, Durkee, Herzner, and Weiss 2013; Malcicka et al. 2015). Ants of one species can play 'Trojan Horse' by use of their own signaling with the intent of getting into the nest of another ant species. Ant nests are often rigorously defended, and species known as *Crematogaster ampla* are extremely aggressive. The deceptive species, *Cephalotes specularis,* uses mimicry to break through the defense. The perpetrators mimic the hosts to gain access to the massive home of the *Crematogaster ampla*. The mimics eat the food and follow the food trails of the hosts, thus giving themselves a tremendous advantage (Powell, Del-Claro, Feitosa, and Brandão 2014).

Being a flower, an ant, a butterfly, or even a protozoon (Cecílio et al. 2014) does not prohibit deception, but rather it is a mechanism that is so well-employed that it is a typical course of evolution. Deception and mimicry in organisms without complex central nervous systems has been observed for centuries (Kritsky 2008; Willer 2009). It is beyond question that other animals deceive, and it is observed with such regularity and commonness in both the laboratory and the natural world that we must concede that deceiving does not require an immense mammalian central nervous system. How is this possible? The answer is simple, as evolutionists even before Darwin had concluded, or at least suspected. Random mutations, or random traits generated via sexual reproduction may be selected for.[2] These mutations, be they a spot of blue in an orchid or a color that camouflages a snake, were and are[3] initially a random event. The deception does not occur in one generation, but rather gradually over time. The survival of the initial trait may in fact be random initially, such that a fish displaying a sandier color is randomly mated with for reasons that have nothing to do with coloration. However, over time, we might suspect the sandy-colored fishes living closer to the sea floor have a greater chance of successful reproduction than a sandy-colored fish that lives at the surface, therefore making this particular trait non-random.

---

[2] Randomness is a highly debated idea in evolution and is beyond discussion here. Passing on genetic material to the next generation is not via exclusively random attributes, but the appearance of a mutation or a novel trait through sexual reproduction is often (though not always) random. We wish to emphasize here that 'random' means that there is no planning involved. Simply, markings or pheromones can come to be, to appear in a new generation, or in a new environment, by way of a random event. Their sustained and long-term prognosis may not be random and in fact must provide some benefit for us to think that it belongs in the category of evolved deception.

[3] While it is potentially obvious to many reading this chapter, we wish to emphasize that evolution is not a long-gone phenomenon of the past, but rather a daily occurrence.

Because of the randomness of trait variation, a species can bypass a central nervous system or a complicated neural net and survive as a deceiver quite successfully. This being said, there are nuances that help create an understanding and subsequently build a theory.

6.3 A BRAIN CAN ASSIST IN MIMICRY AND DECEPTION

Having a brain can help in the deception of others and oddly enough, a healthy central nervous system allows for the deception of the possessing individual, which we often term self-deception (Trivers 2000; von Hippel and Trivers 2011). Even though not a requirement, evolved neural processes can assist in the production of deception, as well as numerous related processes (e.g., deception detection). In *Homo sapiens*, the CNS works to create deception in ways similar to those of many deceptive animals (e.g., changing our physical appearance to gain access to mates), as well as in novel ways that involve higher-order cognitive abilities possessed only by humans (Keenan 2002). For example:

A colleague of ours once showed one of us his fake ID. In the United States, the drinking age is 21 and has been for a number of decades. However, the college age of a typical freshman is about 18. Therefore, it is not uncommon for a college student to fake his/her age in order to drink alcohol. My friend had a ploy that involved digging deep into his mammalian central nervous system. He was to use his fake identification to gain access to alcohol. That fake identification was that of his brother. As such he planned his trip to the bar which involved pretending he was his brother. He memorized his brother's birthday, age, weight. He looked up events that his older brother might know that he did not. He found out where his brother drank, and avoided such bars so as to not be seen by his brother's friends.

This story is but a brief narrative that we are all familiar with. We tell a lie, act a lie, and become a lie. To tell an effective lie, we often employ many cognitive abilities that are uniquely human to advanced organisms such as Theory of Mind.

The ease with which humans deceive is so seamless that we take it for granted. While we should revel in the incredible cognitive gymnastics it takes to lie like a human (Byrne and Corp 2004), we think of it rarely, if ever. In the above 'fake ID' example, our friend is predicting the future, planning contingencies, and altering his own behavior and cognition in the hopes of altering others'. The best of what 'human' minds do, abstract thinking, planning, communication, meta-cognition, are all found in this example of a teenager trying to get drunk. Deception is aided by the primate CNS, but to what degree we do not know (Keenan et al. 2005). Teasing out what is only deception is nearly impossible, and it is not known if it is truly possible to do it.

It is not generally thought that this is how moths or protozoa deceive. They do not plot tomorrow's camouflage or wonder if their mothy noises are of a frequency outside of bat hearing. Most researchers think that they just do it (Keenan 2002), an idea nicely summarized under the construct of anoetic consciousness (Wheeler, Stuss, and Tulving 1995, 1997; Wheeler and Stuss 2003). They do not rehearse, or play "If the ant does this, I will do this" games in their minds. Unlike human deception, where we even tell the truth to deceive (i.e., 'bluffing'; Carrión, Keenan, and Sebanz 2010), it is thought to be unlikely that non-primate organisms play the advanced games that we do. And while it is impossible to prove the negative in this case, it is safe to suspect that human deception is entangled with cognitive features (de Waal and Ferrari 2010) not yet observed in other non-primate animals, and rarely exploited to such an extent in non-human primates (Povinelli 1993; Povinelli and Davis 1994; Penn and Povinelli 2007; Penn, Holyoak, and Povinelli 2012).

This makes a very simple question nearly impossible to answer. The question, typical in science, is, "Is it a difference of degree or of kind?" In this context we are simply asking if *Homo sapiens* deceives in a manner that is unique, with qualities that are not observed in the comparison group (i.e., all other organisms). While one member of the family of Orchids may differ in coloration in its mimicry from another, that difference is likely to be thought of only as a matter of degree, or in this case frequency. On the other hand, human deception is wholly different from Orchidaceae deception, an analysis that requires but the simplest of examples—such as the 'fake ID' example previously detailed. Human deception involves the complex cognitive abilities, from language to abstract thinking, which in turn makes the difference one of quality, not quantity. The Orchid's mimicking of an insect is not the same 'kind' of deception as our friend's mimicking his brother. The induced behavior of the deceived may be similar, but for the deceiver, there are immense differences.

6.4 WHEN DID THE FIRST HUMAN LIE?

Seen from an evolutionary perspective, if X falsely presents information to Y and X's fitness increases, all that matters is that fitness is increased. For the last 3.5 billion years, some genetic material has persisted and some has not. The countless examples of homologous traits and common descendants and shared nodes make many believe that all traits (behaviors and cognitions) are homologous, rather than analogous. This 'tree' thinking pervades the sciences and here we encounter an ultimately difficult case. Because deception has had multiple origins, tracing the evolution of *Homo sapiens* deception is very difficult. We have never encountered anyone who believes the protozoa passed the deception gene to the orchid, who passed it to the moth, and so on until we get to mammals and primates. A serious examination reveals that we do not know when hominid deception started, even to within millions of years.

This is highly unfortunate, because we suggest that no real understanding of any cognitive function can occur without a better picture of evolution. In terms of deception, we are in fact farther from a clear picture than we were twenty years ago.[4] That is to say, neuroimaging has truly achieved its scientific goal by generating more questions than it has answered. However, neuroscience and neuroimaging are not alone in making the picture difficult to clarify. The expansion of our understanding of the brain-cognition-evolution complication in the last two decades comes from incredible discoveries in physical anthropology, specifically neuroanthropology.[5] It is here that the confusion expands exponentially. As brains do not preserve, and endocasts are (as of this writing) our best tool in recreating evolved nervous systems, we have relied on a significant paucity of data. Furthermore, since behavior rarely fossilizes, we are again left with no direct evidence. In the last twenty years, we can think of examples that include the discovery of LB1 (*Homo floresiensis*) whose brain is, however you slice it (no pun intended), still challenging our ideas about the timeline of *Homo* brain expansion, the neural prerequisites for tool use, what it is about a brain (e.g., frontal gyri formation, overall volume) that allows for higher cognitive abilities (Brown et al. 2004; Morwood et al. 2004; Falk et al. 2005, 2009; Vannucci, Barron, and Holloway 2013). Within the time of this writing, the major discovery of *Homo naledi* with never-before-observed features carries drastic implications—from a potential new species to the possibility that our *Homo* ancestors were burying their dead[6] (Berger et al. 2015; Dirks et al. 2015). In other words, in terms of evolutionary cognitive neuroscience, we cannot answer the big questions yet and are still unearthing specimens that cloud rather than clear the goal of pinpointing "the first *Homo* or *Australopithecus* or primate" that ever told a lie. We do not even know, based on endocasts, whether early primates were or were not deceiving in the early or pre-Paleogene Period. Our common deceiving grancestor may in fact be a non-primate, but at least a (non-primate) terrestrial mammal. From fossils, we know little.

For example, it has been found that oxytocin facilitates deception in *Homo sapiens*, but amazingly only if the group is benefited. Lies that benefit the individual only are not influenced by oxytocin (Shalvi and De Dreu 2014). The evolution of oxytocin is such that it has existed for hundreds of millions of years, much longer than the primates. This

---

[4] Clear does not equal correct. Many of us were taught hypotheses in evolutionary cognitive neuroscience that are no longer thought to be valid, such as the direct connection between cortex/brain ratio and tool use.

[5] For one of the most fascinating discussions about LB1, taking the comic Hobbit tag to the extreme, see the esteemed journal *Nature* (Callaway et al. 2014).

[6] Burying the dead is a sign of altruism, and has been used as an indicator that Neanderthal man (*Homo sapiens neanderthalensis*) had Theory of Mind abilities, which are extremely intertwined with human deception (Keenan, Rubio, Racioppi, Johnson, and Barnacz, 2005) as both altruism and deception often tap into thinking about the thoughts of others. The idea that we had altruism two million years ago puts forward the possibility that early *Homo* or late *Austral* was capable of deceiving. This is a tenuous notion, but using indications of altruism gives us evidence of Theory of Mind which may be evidence that certain organisms had the potential to deceive.

leads to the quandary that prairie voles (*Microtus ochrogaster*) who have been examined ad infinitum in terms of oxytocin (Witt, Carter, and Walton 1990; Carter, Williams, Witt, and Insel 1992; Johnson et al. 2015; Shen 2015), may have some Theory of Mind and altruistic behavior components and those behavioral mechanisms are traced not only to oxytocin but to the anterior cingulate gyrus (Burkett et al. 2016). In other words, voles utilize components quite similar to those humans do, and it is not a stretch to think that the critical components to human deception and lying were in place long before there were humans.

Tracing our evolution through the 'next best' means maybe looking at our close ape and non-ape near relatives. Primatologists and evolutionary biologists have done much behavioral and neural work to determine human cognitive origins. Deception itself has received little attention, though there are some seminal pieces of research. Byrne and Corp (2004) used seventeen modern primates and discovered a relationship between neocortex and deception—reaching the conclusion that as neocortex size increases, so do rates of deception. This chapter is one of the only systematic approaches equating deception, cognition, and evolution. From the findings of a number of researchers, we know that our ape relatives can deceive, specifically in *Pan* (Hirata and Matsuzawa 2001; Hare, Call, and Tomasello 2006; Osvath and Karvonen 2012) with numerous experiments and case-study observations. However, if one were to categorize the cognitive deceptive abilities in non-human apes, most would suggest they are very limited abilities (Call and Tomasello 1999). Again, how humans deceive is likely very different from the way that a chimp does. Unfortunately, we do not know, and thus cannot paint much of an evolutionary picture based on non-human primates. We, however, like Byrne and Corp, suspect that even with relatives as close as monkeys and prosimians, deception does not include intention. We do not know (and may never know) if we had deception when we branched off from the monkeys, and then plopped our higher-order abilities on top, or if many primates developed deception independently, or both.

Our best chance for tracing the neurological evolution of deception will most likely come from contributions from molecular genetic studies (Ronan, Wu, and Crabtree 2013; Pulvermüller, Garagnani, and Wennekers 2014; Shibata, Gulden, and Sestan 2015). We are far from this, but the idea would be that once we have a map of RNA and DNA correlates of human cognition we could tease out what genes evolved and when they emerged. Until that point we must acknowledge that we do not know when, how, or why deception in *Homo* evolved. It is discouraging that major cognitive abilities are not mapped well in terms of evolution (Bolhuis 2015); for example, something as critical as knowing when humans started speaking or using Theory of Mind remains many steps beyond the 'just so story', but we have a long way to go.

To make a final point here, it is almost a certainty that social systems play a role in human deception (DePaulo, Kashy, Kirkendol, Wyer, and Epstein 1996; Vrij, Edward, and Bull 2001b; Morris et al. 2016). Many think our complex relationships rely upon deception (DePaulo and Kashy 1998). However, a species that we know to deceive, the ant, is also a highly social species. It is quite tempting to think humans are just big ants, and over the last 150 million years we have just been perfecting what has already been there. This may be true, but it is very unlikely and the truth is almost certainly more complex. We cannot say that humans gained their "enslaving others" instinct or "pretend to be someone I'm not" instinct from the ants, and that the neurons found in the ants that aid in complex social and deceptive behaviors are the same, homologous, neurons that *Homo sapiens* use for lying. The social system we employ is different from the very social ant systems, and even though there are commonalities it is highly unlikely that human deception has its origins in ant deception.

6.5 Humans' lies and self-deception

From a behavioral point of view, we can be guided by philosophers who have done an excellent job of explaining and describing differences between lying and deception, and may extract from this the idea that lying involves activities that 'only humans do'. Being somewhat brief, let us just say that humans lie and deceive, while most other animals just deceive. There is a huge grey area, and many things that humans do to lie (or lie well) are found in other animals, but this is described in section 6.4 (see Mahon 2015 for a full discussion).

Most think that intention is critical, and it is the ramping up, planning, sticking to it, and intentionally omitting that turns deception into lying. However, as Ganis indicates in Chapter 35, whichever direction we proceed in (i.e., from the brain to behavior or from behavior to the brain, using an additive or a subtractive process) we have yet to precisely tease out either the brain regions or any other physiological underpinnings that separate deception from anything else in a conclusive manner. Suspect regions such as Brodmann areas (BA) 24, 32, 44, 47–8, 9[7] (Abe 2009, 2011) still serve other functions which may or may not contribute to deception, and it remains unknown whether the brain considers deception a separate, independent process.

Self-deception (see Chapter 15 by Kathi Beier), employs similar regions in terms of the brain to those employed by the deception of others (Kwan et al. 2007; Barrios et al. 2008; Amati, Oh, Kwan, Jordan, and Keenan 2010; Farrow, Burgess, Wilkinson, and Hunter 2015). The area most associated with both intentional and non-intentional self-deception appears to be medial PFC (BA 9/10) as well as lateralized frontal regions including Right mPFC (BA 9, BA8) and Left lPFC. While it is not known if other animals self-deceive, it is certain that self-deception plays a role in human deception. Trivers has argued that one main reason we have seen the evolution of self-deception in *Homo* is that it allows us to be better deceivers of others (Trivers 2000; Byrne and Kurland 2001) as

---

[7] Brodmann areas (BA) are a way to communicate the particular region in the brain. For deception, we see mainly frontal and temporal lobe correlations, though there is also some parietal and motor strip activation during deceptive tasks.

well as providing an impetus to face challenges we might otherwise avoid (Lopez and Fuxjager 2012). Others have noted that self-deception appears to provide a social buffer and that depression may be associated with a lack of self-deception (Gil 2005). We have added to this theory suggesting a possible additional evolved mechanism by noting that deception detection rates fail to mimic deception rates, being typically at chance levels (DePaulo, Zuckerman, and Rosenthal 1980; Vrij 1993; Bond and DePaulo 2006; Vrij, Mann, Kristen, and Fisher 2007), which one would imagine would co-evolve at a greater pace. Why is this? One possible answer is that research on detecting deception uses non-natural scenarios and benchmarks that do not make ecological sense (i.e., in the real world we do not just respond 'he is lying' or 'he is telling the truth'—our real responses need to be much more subtle). A lively debate exists in the literature as to why experimental rates are low, and some have found that when certain controls are used, lie-detection experts do in fact emerge (Bond 2008). However, the point remains that deception remains highly effective and there are often times when people are duped.

Why would we not be better at deception detection? To answer this, we simply suggest this: It is possible that we cognitively lean toward a default state of truth. We assume our own cognitions are truthful, and thus assume that what others portray to us is also truthful (Guise et al. 2007). Over a lifetime, this of course changes, and enough dealings with deceptive individuals will change our outlook on others, just as a good psychotherapist can reveal our own self-deception. Yet, we may be born naïve and that naïve stance may serve us well in terms of self-deception, yet poorly in the detection of deception of others. We see this very speculative possibility as one potential line of future research. Even if this hypothesis fails to pan out it is important to acknowledge that self-deception has become a critical component of human existence and it is not by chance that Sigmund Freud based what was to become the most influential theory in psychology on self-deception (Freud 1938). It is not hyperbolic to suggest that tracing the origins of the brain's self-deception would unlock many mysteries about our existence.

Because we know so little of the evolution of deception and next to nothing of self-deception we are safe in saying that we are in the infancy of research with regard to tracing the evolution of deception and lying. As noted, microcellular techniques are currently promising, but that is not to suggest that out-of-the-ordinary experiments such as those by Libet (Libet, Wright, and Gleason 1983; Libet 1995; Libet 2006), which suggested that deception underlies all of our notions of intentionality, will not move the field in novel and fruitful directions. While the present is full of more questions than answers, we can take comfort in the irony that we are likely closer to the truth of deception.

6.6 Conclusion

In conclusion, we are far from knowing much about the evolution of deception. Research techniques and technological advances in the last three decades have now matured to the point where we can begin to systematically answer questions such as, "When did humans begin to deceive?" and "What are the necessary and sufficient brain regions involved in self-deception and when did these regions emerge?" A measured approach from molecular genetics and advanced neuroimaging will augment classic techniques from physical anthropology and psychology in detailing the account of how deception came to be in *Homo sapiens*.

PART II
CONCEPTS

PART 1

CONCEPTS

CHAPTER 7

LYING AND TRUTH

STEPHEN WRIGHT

> Pilate saith unto him, 'What is truth?' And when he had said this, he went out again unto the Jews...
>
> (John 18: 38; KJV)

7.1 TRUTH

IF the ensuing debate is anything to go by, Pilate may well have been right not to wait for an answer. Philosophers have disagreed over truth in various different ways. Not always about the same thing. Some argue about the *truth predicate*, a linguistic expression. Others consider the *concept of truth*, which is something like our idea of truth, and still others discuss the *property of truth*, which is what the concept in our heads latches onto in the world.

Philosophers have also disagreed about what sorts of things are true, at least in the most fundamental sense. According to some, the bearers of truth are non-linguistic entities, such as *propositions*. According to those who take this approach, linguistic entities, such as *sentences* or *utterances*, are true derivatively—in virtue of expression of certain (true) propositions. But propositions might seem like metaphysically strange objects. The fact that they are probably abstract makes it difficult to say too much about them. With this in mind, some treat linguistic entities, such as sentences or utterances, as the primary bearers of truth. There is, however, a case for thinking that we still need propositions to make sense of how two syntactically similar sentences can be semantically different, such as 'the bank is fifteen miles away' in different contexts.

A central disagreement in discussions of truth concerns the question of whether or not truth is something substantial. Amongst those who think that it is, there are *realist* theories, which claim that truth is a matter of a truth-bearer standing in a particular relation to something in the world, and *anti-realist* theories, which dispute this. On the realist side, there are *correspondence* theories and *truthmaker* theories. On the anti-realist side, there are coherence theories and *pragmatist* theories.

Correspondence theories claim that to say that something is true is to say that it corresponds to some fact. Austin (1950) and Russell (1967) offer classic accounts of correspondence theories. The challenge for correspondence theorists is to spell out exactly what it means to say that something *corresponds* to a fact. Correspondence theorists need to do this in such a way that it is both *informative* and *plausible*. This can be difficult to do.

Truthmaker theorists take it that, rather than something being true in virtue of its corresponding to a fact, something is true if there exists something else that makes it true. Whilst truthmaker theories do not talk about correspondence and thus have no need of spelling out what correspondence to a fact must amount to, they have the related challenge of attempting to spell out in virtue of what something makes something else true. There is also the question, for truthmaker theories, of what sorts of things make other things true. They might be facts, or they might be states of affairs, or individual objects, or properties. These are questions for truthmaker theorists.

On the anti-realist side, coherence theories, such as the one endorsed by Davidson (1989) claim that to say that something is true is just to say that it is part of a coherent set of beliefs. The question of what coherence amounts to is an obvious one, but it is also a difficult one for coherence theorists to find a convincing answer to. A set of beliefs being consistent is not enough for it to be coherent, but it is hard to see what other terms to put the notion of coherence in. One reason why consistency and coherence are not the same thing is that coherence admits degree, where consistency does not. Sets of beliefs are either consistent or they are not, but two sets of beliefs can both be coherent whilst one is more coherent than the other. The trouble is, it seems that truth is like consistency, in that it does not admit degree. This is a problem for the idea that truth and coherence go together.

Another anti-realist approach defines truth in pragmatist terms. What is true, according to this account, is what it is pragmatically good to believe. There are different accounts of what it might be pragmatically good for someone to believe, given by Peirce (1958), James (1975a, b), Putnam (1981), and Dummett (1978). But equally, there seem to be cases that are fairly uncontroversially *not* pragmatically good. There is presumably a truth about the number of grains of sand on Miami Beach, but it does not seem that it could be in any way pragmatically useful for anyone to know it.

On the other hand, there are those who do not think that there is anything substantive to be said about truth. These *deflationary* approaches hold that there is nothing more to understanding truth than recognising the truth of the assumption that, for any bearer of truth, the claim that it is true is equivalent to the claim itself. In other words, to say that 'x is true' is just to say that 'x' in some sense. Different deflationary ideas expand on this central theme in different ways.

For example, *redundancy* theories, of the type developed by Ramsey (1927) take it that a statement of the form 'x is true' simply means the same thing as 'x'. Equally, Strawson's (1950) *speech act* theory sought to align an utterance of the form 'x is true' with an endorsement of 'x'. An immediate worry with this kind of approach is that there seems to be more to truth than statements of the form 'x is true'. Statements such as 'what she says is true' or 'what he says is not true' do not appear to amount to the same thing as 'what she says' or 'not what he says'.

A more recent deflationary approach is given by Horwich (1998). According to the minimalist theory that Horwich advocates, all that there is to understanding truth is to be disposed to accept biconditional statements of the form ' "x" is true if and only if x'. In a similar spirit, Field (1994) claims that to understand truth is to treat statements of the form ' "x" is true' as intersubstitutable with statements of the form 'x'.

Whilst deflationary theories hold that statements of the form ' "x" is true if and only if x' are, in some sense, all there is to understanding truth, this is not always to say that truth cannot be useful for anything else. As we have already seen, it can be useful for making generalizations, by saying that everything that someone says is true. Nonetheless, deflationary theories think that substantive definitions of truth are wrongheaded. The claim that ' "x" is true if and only if x' is, of course, true for all truth theorists. But it is especially important for those who take deflationary approaches.

Pinning down a precise and specific theory of truth in the face of all of this is beyond the scope of this kind of discussion. But it seems that, for all of the argumentation over truth, we have some intuitive sense of truth that will suffice for a discussion of the relationship between lying and truth.

7.2 Lying

Lies come in different varieties. According to many, the most obvious type is encapsulated in the following example from Saul (2012):

> **Case 1:** Tony says that there are weapons of mass destruction in Iraq. Tony in fact believes that there are no weapons of mass destruction in Iraq, but wants to convince people that there are.
>
> (Saul 2012: 6)

This type of lying is fairly straightforward to understand. It is a case in which a speaker says something that she believes to be false to a listener with the intention of having the listener take her word for it and believe what she says because she said it. An obvious account of lying comes immediately out of this and takes it that all lies are statements where the speaker believes that what she says is false and seeks to have the listener take her word for it.[1] Unfortunately, however, not all lies are straightforwardly

---

[1] This account of lying or something like it is given by Bok (1999), Kupfer (1982), Primoratz (1984), Davidson (1985), Frankfurt (1988), and Williams (2002). The discussion is framed in terms of *statements* rather than *assertions* to avoid an unnecessary controversy over what is involved in asserting. See Stokke 2013a.

instances of this type. In particular, the following case from Carson (2006) does not have this structure:

> **Case 2**: A student is caught cheating on an exam and is brought before the Dean. The student knows that the Dean is fully aware that she was cheating on the exam and nothing that she can say will affect this. She also knows, however, that the Dean only punishes people when they confess to cheating. So the student says that she did not cheat on the exam.
>
> (Carson 2010: 21)

These two cases are both, it would seem intuitively, lies.[2] Whilst they are dissimilar in one important sense—the speaker in Case 1 seeks to be believed by his audience, whereas the speaker in **Case 2** does not seek to be believed by the listener—they are similar in another sense. Each case involves a statement of something believed by the speaker to be false. It seems obvious that there is a connection between lying and falsity. The question at the centre of this discussion concerns how to account for this connection. There are, as I see it, three obvious accounts of how to account for the connection between lying and truth:

(1)   A speaker's statement is a lie only if the speaker's statement is false.
(2)   A speaker's statement is a lie only if the speaker believes that her statement is false.
(3)   A speaker's statement is a lie only if the speaker does not believe what she says.

The first thing to note is that (1) gives an *objective* account of the connection between truth and falsity, where (2) and (3) respectively give *subjective* accounts of the connection. The idea is that (1) states that a speaker's statement is a lie only if what she says is *in fact* false. Regardless of whether or not the speaker believes that what she says is false, if what she says is *in fact* true, then the speaker's statement is not a lie. According to (2) and (3) respectively, the speaker's beliefs about whether or not what she says is false matter for the question of whether or not what she says is a lie. Specifically, if the speaker *believes* that what she says is true (even if she is wrong about this) then her statement is not a lie.[3]

It is important to note that (1), (2), and (3) are not all mutually exclusive. Firstly, one might conjoin (1) with (2) to get the following account of the connection between lying and falsity:

(4)   A speaker's statement is a lie only if the speaker's statement is false and the speaker believes that her statement is false.

According to this account, the connection between lying and falsity is such that the speaker's statement's being either true or believed by the speaker to be true prevents it

---

[2] Against the claim that the statement in **Case 2** is a lie, see Mahon (2008c) and Meibauer (2011).
[3] A recent defence of this is given in Turri and Turri (2015).

from being a lie. Equally, one might conjoin (1) with (3) to get the view that a speaker's statement is a lie only if the speaker's statement is false and the speaker does not believe what she says. Since I am not aware of anyone who endorses such an account, I will leave this view aside for the purposes of this discussion. It is also important to be clear that (2) implies (3). A speaker's believing that what she says is false implies that she does not believe what she says. In spite of this, however, (2) and (3) should be understood as competing accounts of the connection between lying and falsity. It is therefore worth making explicit the terms of the engagement here. Defending (3) as an account of the connection between lying and falsity involves claiming that there are instances of lying such that the speaker does not believe what she says, but equally does not believe that what she says is false. Endorsing (2) involves claiming that there are no such cases. Whilst it is strictly and literally true that (2) implies (3) and therefore that endorsing (2) involves endorsing (3), the theories for the purposes of this discussion should be understood as distinct and in competition with one another.

With an initial overview of the terrain in hand, I will turn to discuss each of the accounts of the connection between lying and falsity in turn. Rather than seeking to draw sharp conclusions about the viability of each of the above accounts, I will offer an overview of some of the considerations that might be brought to bear against each account and leave it to the reader to draw her own conclusions.

7.3 Saying what is false

First, consider the objective account of the connection between lying and falsity, encapsulated in the claim that:

(1)   A speaker's statement is a lie only if the speaker's statement is false.

The most prominent defence of (1) comes from Carson (2010). As observed in the introduction, however, the objective statement of the connection between lies and falsity given in (1) can be conjoined with either of the subjective accounts given in (2) and (3). And Carson seeks to conjoin (1) with (2), as described above, to give the following account:

(4)   A speaker's statement is a lie only if the speaker's statement is false and the speaker believes that her statement is false.

According to Carson "[a]ll lies are false statements, but not all false statements are lies" (Carson 2010: 17). In support of this, Carson gives the following case:

> **Case 3**: You and I go fishing and each of us catches a fish. I catch a big fish and you catch a smaller one. Unfortunately, our lines become crossed so that it appears that

you caught a big fish and I caught a smaller one. I therefore believe that I caught a small fish. When I go home, I decide to say that I caught a big fish, even though I don't believe this.

(Carson 2010: 16)

According to Carson, it is intuitive that the statement in this case is not a lie. Insofar as one shares this intuition, this seems to provide evidence for the objective connection between lying and falsity given in (4). It seems that the only reason that the above statement could fail to count as a lie is because of a problem with the connection between lying and falsity.

Carson offers a further observation in support of the objective connection between lying and falsity given in (4). Consider the following case:

Case 4: I tell you that Jesus College was founded in 1571 and you accuse me of lying. Later, you find out independently that Jesus College was in fact founded in 1571.

Carson notes that it seems that, in such a situation, you should withdraw your accusation that I was lying. But all that you find out in **Case 2** is that my statement is *in fact* true. You do not find out that I believed it to be true and you do not find out anything about what I believed.

This means that the intuition that you ought to withdraw your accusation that I was lying speaks in favour of an objective connection between lying and falsity. It is important that you find out about the truth of what I said by establishing it independently, rather than having me present you with the evidence for it. If I presented you with the evidence for the truth of what I said, one might think that this presents you with evidence for thinking that I did not say something that I do not believe. And this would diminish the force of the case in establishing an objective connection between lying and falsity, as Carson hopes to.

If your evidence that what I say is true comes from me, then the intuition that it is inappropriate to accuse me of lying can be explained away merely in terms of a subjective connection between lying and falsity. It becomes far from clear that I said something that I believed to be false and this by itself is enough to make it inappropriate for you to accuse me of lying. You finding out for yourself that what I said was true makes it harder for someone denying an objective connection between lying and falsity to characterize the situation.

Furthermore, it seems as though the observation here might well generalize. In Carson's words: "[s]howing that a statement is true is always sufficient to counter the accusation that one has told a lie" (Carson 2010: 16). This, I think, is the main case for thinking that there's an objective connection between lying and falsity. The case can be formulated into two arguments. The first argument goes as follows:

(1)   The statement in Case 3 is not a lie.

(ii)   If the statement in Case 3 is not a lie, then this is because saying something false is a necessary condition of lying.

Therefore

(iii) Saying something false is a necessary condition of lying.

The second argument can be summarized as follows:

(iv)   In **Case 4**, it is inappropriate to accuse the speaker of lying.
(v)   This inappropriateness can only be explained in terms of saying something false being a necessary condition of lying.

Therefore

(vi)   Saying something false is a necessary condition of lying.

Both arguments are intuition-driven. Premise (i) in the first argument and premise (iv) in the second argument rely on intuitions. And one might think that these intuitions are inconclusive at best. I myself do not feel the intuition supporting (i) particularly strongly. But more generally, one might think that there are equally intuitive cases that push in the opposite direction. Consider again **Case 1**, in which Tony intuitively lies about there being weapons of mass destruction in Iraq, by saying that there are such weapons whilst believing that there are not. Insofar as it is intuitively apparent that Tony's statement in **Case 1** is a lie, this exerts pressure on the connection between lying and falsity given in (4).

> **Case 1*:** Tony says that there are weapons of mass destruction in Iraq. Tony in fact believes that there are no weapons of mass destruction in Iraq, but wants to convince people that there are. Unbeknownst to Tony, however, there are weapons of mass destruction in Iraq.
>
> (Saul 2012: 6)

The fact that (4) is a conjunction of (1) and (2) can make things a little unclear. In arguing against (4) we need to be clear whether we think a reason for rejecting (4) is a reason for rejecting (1) only, or a reason for rejecting (2) only, or a reason for rejecting both. It is clear, however, that the situation in **Case 1** exerts pressure on (4) because it is an instance of lying that fails to be false. Whilst Tony *believes* that there are no weapons of mass destruction, there are *in fact* such weapons. Insofar as it is intuitively apparent that Tony's statement in **Case 1** is a lie, the situation in **Case 1** exerts pressure on the *objective* component of (4) rather than the *subjective* component.

The dialectic here becomes a dispute over intuitions and I do not have much to add. I leave it to the reader to assess for herself the case for an objective connection between lying and falsity in the form of a speaker's statement being false as a necessary condition of its being a lie. It is worth noting, however, that one fact that might be decisive is that, according to those who defend the indispensability of an objective connection, it is possible for a speaker to try, but fail, to lie. Insofar as this seems impossible, we might think that an objective connection between the speaker's statement and its falsity is unnecessary.

With this in hand, let us consider the second argument. The second argument is motivated by the observation that finding out that the speaker's statement is true makes it appropriate to withdraw the accusation that the speaker's statement is a lie. One might think, however, that the intuitions here need to be distilled more carefully before any substantive conclusions can be drawn from them. Once these are distilled further, I think that the argument faces a dilemma. The question is whether or not you have any special reason to believe that my statement in **Case 2** expresses something that I believe to be false.

If it is not the case that you have any such reason, then the intuition that you ought to withdraw the assertion that I was lying is evenly balanced between those who endorse an objective connection between lying and falsity and those who merely endorse a subjective connection. Finding out that what I said is true removes your evidence for thinking that I believed what I said to be false. As a result, those who endorse a subjective account of the connection between lying and falsity can claim that it seems that you ought to withdraw your accusation because you have no reason for thinking that I was lying. Specifically, you have no reason for thinking that I did not believe what I said and this is a necessary condition of lying. Your accusation is thus unsubstantiated and you ought to withdraw it.

On the other hand, if it is the case that you have some other reason for thinking that I did not believe what I said, then a defender of a merely subjective connection between lying and falsity cannot explain the idea that you ought to withdraw your claim that I was lying. However, if it is the case that you have some other reason for thinking that I did not believe what I said, then it is not as clear that you really ought to withdraw the claim. It might seem far less obvious that my statement was not a lie. If you have reason to think that, the truth of my statement notwithstanding, I did not believe it, then it becomes far less obvious that you ought to withdraw the accusation after all.

7.4 SAYING WHAT ONE BELIEVES TO BE FALSE

The second account of the connection between lying and falsity given above sought to characterize the connection between them in the following terms:

(2)   A speaker's statement is a lie only if the speaker believes that her statement is false.

This account is by far the most popular in the contemporary literature. It is endorsed by Fallis (2009), Saul (2012), Lackey (2013), and Stokke (2013a). Understanding what (2) amounts to involves understanding how it differs from various nearby propositions. A *locus classicus* in the philosophical literature on lying by Chisholm and Feehan (1977) helps bring out exactly what is meant by a speaker's saying something that she believes to be false.[4]

In a case where someone says that Jesus College is on fire, Chisholm and Feehan seek to distinguish between the following:

(i) The speaker not believing that Jesus College is on fire and also not believing that Jesus College is not on fire.
(ii) The speaker believing that Jesus College is not on fire.
(iii) The speaker believing that it is not true that Jesus College is on fire.
(iv) The speaker believing that it is false that Jesus College is on fire.

Possibly the most important distinction for understanding what the claim that a speaker's statement is a lie only if the speaker says something she believes to be false involves is the distinction between (ii) and (iv). The main difference that Chisholm and Feehan identify between (ii) and (iv) is that in the situation that (ii) describes, the speaker's statement expresses the negation of something that she believes, whereas in (iv), the speaker has what Chisholm and Feehan identify as a *second-level attitude* towards the proposition that Jesus College is on fire.

The central idea is that (iv) involves a level of cognitive sophistication that (ii) does not. For the truth of condition (ii) requires only the speaker's having a conception of Jesus College and what it would be for it to be on fire. By contrast, the truth of condition (iv) requires that the speaker have the additional concept of a proposition and of something *being false* (Chisholm and Feehan 1977: 147). The need to grasp the additional concept of something being false means that this requires an additional understanding, or level of cognitive sophistication.

Chisholm and Feehan ultimately endorse an account of the connection between lying and truth according to which a speaker's statement is a lie only if it is *either* a statement that the speaker believes to be not true, or else a statement that the speaker believes to be false (Chisholm and Feehan 1977: 152). This means that a speaker's statement can be a lie only if the speaker has a conception of truth and falsity and a conception of what a proposition is. The account of lying given by Fallis (2009) claims that a speaker lies to a

---

[4] Chisholm and Feehan do not themselves endorse (2) but endorse the related claim that:

(5) A speaker's statement is a lie only if the speaker believes what she says to not be true or she believes what she says to be false.

Since I think that the plausibility of (5) goes along with the plausibility of (2) for the purposes of this discussion, I will not discuss (5) separately.

listener only if the speaker believes that what she says is false. Likewise, Stokke (2013a) claims that a speaker's statement is a lie only if the speaker believes that it is false. And Lackey (2013) offers an account of lying according to which a speaker's believing that what she says is false is a necessary condition of the speaker's statement's being a lie.

Each of these accounts thus claims that lying requires a certain sophistication. It requires the speaker to have a concept of falsity (or, in the case of Chisholm and Feehan's theory, truth). Insofar as we can distinguish between someone saying that Jesus College is on fire whilst believing that Jesus College is not on fire and someone saying that Jesus College is on fire whilst believing that it is false that Jesus College is on fire, the kind of accounts under consideration here claim that the former does not exhibit the kind of connection between lying and falsity required for lying.

Against this view, one might think that it gives an overly intellectual account of what it is to lie to someone. More specifically, insofar as believing that Jesus College is not on fire and believing that it is false that Jesus College is on fire can come apart, one might wonder whether someone who believes the former but not the latter might be in a position to lie to a speaker. It would seem that a speaker who states that Jesus College is on fire whilst believing that it is not is being dishonest in the way that one might usually associate with lying. Consider again the situation in **Case 3**, which was supposed to be a straightforward instance of a lie. As it is currently set out, Tony says that there are weapons of mass destruction in Iraq whilst believing the negation of this—that there are no such weapons. Nothing in **Case 3** as it is currently set out claims that Tony believes that it is false that there are weapons of mass destruction in Iraq.

This means that, insofar as it is intuitively apparent that Tony's statement in **Case 3** is a lie, there is a reason for thinking that a speaker's testimony can be a lie even if it is not the case that the speaker believes that what she says is false. It seems that, as far as the connection between lying and falsity is concerned, the fact that Tony believes the negation of what he says is sufficient for his statement to be a lie (assuming the other conditions for lying are met). On the face of it, then, this kind of case makes trouble for the idea that a speaker's statement is a lie only if the speaker believes that what she says is false. Nothing in **Case 3** proves that Tony has the second-level attitude necessary for lying according to the popular account of the connection between lying and falsity.

By way of a response, one might suggest that, at least ordinarily, we assume that mature human adults *do* have a conception of truth and falsity and consequently, unless there is some reason to think that the speaker *does not* have such a conception, then it seems reasonable to move from the observation that the speaker believes the negation of what she says to the conclusion that the speaker believes that what she says is false. So the idea is that the fact that Tony believes that there are no weapons of mass destruction in Iraq is evidence that Tony believes that it is false that there are weapons of mass destruction in Iraq.

As a way of circumventing this kind of response, we might turn our attention to the following case:

Case 5: Alice believes that Jesus College is not on fire. She sees that there is smoke coming from the direction of Jesus College, but she also sees that the smoke is not coming from the college itself. As well as this, Alice lacks the second-level belief that *it is false that Jesus College is on fire*, but she does have the relevant conceptual sophistication to believe that Jesus College is not on fire. Upon being asked whether or not Jesus College is on fire, however, she says that it is.

This, I think, generates an intuitive difficulty for theories of lying that take it that the connection between lying and falsity involves the speaker believing that what she says is false, as described in (3). Insofar as the observation from Chisholm and Feehan that one might believe that Jesus College is not on fire whilst failing to believe that it is false that Jesus College is on fire is correct, the situation described in **Case 5** should represent a genuine possibility.

In such a situation, however, I think it is far from clear that Alice cannot be lying when she says that Jesus College is on fire. It certainly seems that Alice's testimony is deceptive, in that it expresses something that she believes the opposite of and furthermore, we might stipulate that Alice's testimony is intended to get the person asking her to believe that Jesus College is not on fire. The situation in **Case 5** seems to be clearly different from a case in which Alice *merely misleads* the listener by saying, for instance, that she saw smoke coming from the direction of Jesus College intending to induce the belief that Jesus College is on fire. Rather, she says that Jesus College is on fire with the intention of inducing that same belief. In other words, the situation in **Case 5** does not seem to clearly resemble a case of misleading more than a case of lying.

One suggestion might be that lying involves asserting, which requires an adequate grasp of truth and falsity. The idea that asserting requires this kind of sophistication is indicated in Dummett's (1978) discussion. This, however, is part of the reason that I have been trying to steer around discussions of assertion in this chapter and focus at the level of stating.

The distinction between believing that something is false and believing that its negation is true seems to indicate that someone can lie without saying something that she believes to be false. Assuming that Alice has a conception of what it would require for Jesus College to be on fire and a conception of what it would require for Jesus College to not be on fire, she can be aware that the latter is the case and aware that she says that the former is the case. Even without a second-level conception of what it is for something to be true, it seems that Alice can lie by believing that Jesus College is not on fire but saying that it is. This, I think, exerts intuitive force against the account of the connection between lying and falsity given in (2).

7.5 SAYING WHAT ONE DOES NOT BELIEVE

A final account of the connection between lying and falsity comes in the form of the view expressed in (3) according to which:

(3) A speaker's statement is a lie only if the speaker does not believe it.

The view expressed in (3) features in Sorensen's (2007) account of lying. According to Sorensen, to lie is to assert what one does not believe. It is immediately clear that the view given in (3) handles the considerations brought against the view given in (2) by **Case 5** relatively well. For in a case where Alice believes that Jesus College is on fire and says that Jesus College is not on fire, it is clear that Alice does not believe that Jesus College is not on fire. Hence the account in (3) coheres with the intuition that Alice's statement is a lie. Whilst she does not believe that what she says is false, she equally does not believe it.

Where the view given in (2) seemed restrictive, in that it leads to a very narrow account of which statements are lies, the view given in (3) is altogether more permissive. The worry, however, is that it might be altogether too permissive. Where (2) claims that statements that intuitively seem as if they might be lies are in fact not lies, one might think that (3) claims that statements that do not intuitively seem like lies are in fact lies.

An obvious case of this might seem to be where someone engages in metaphor or hyperbole. In saying *she's on fire today,* to make the point that the person in question is having a particularly successful day, one might not believe that the person in question is literally on fire, but nonetheless, it does not seem that someone who says *she's on fire today* is thereby *lying*. The reason that this kind of case does not count as lying, according to Sorensen's view, is that whilst it might meet the relevant untruthfulness condition, it does not meet the other conditions necessary for lying. According to Sorensen, statements of this kind lack the relevant sort of assertoric force (Sorensen 2007: 246).

This seems like the correct thing to say about metaphor and hyperbole. When they are used, the associated statements are not lies, but this is not necessarily because they fail the untruthfulness condition. Indeed, one might think of metaphor and hyperbole as a way of doing something very similar to lying, but without actually lying.[5] Nonetheless, even if metaphor and hyperbole, intuitively, should not be classified as lying, one might think that there are similar cases that are not so easily handled by the view that the connection between lying and truth is the one given in (3). We might consider the following case:

Case 6: Chloe thinks it is highly probable that the next flight to Oslo has a stopover in London. When asked by a friend whether or not the next flight to Oslo has a stopover in London, however, Chloe says that it does.

In **Case 6**, two things seem to be the case. The first is that Chloe does not believe that the flight in question will have a stopover. Rather, she believes that it is highly probable that it will have a stopover. To believe that something will probably happen is distinct

---

[5] On the possibility of metaphor and hyperbole being properly classified as lies, see Carson (2010) and Meibauer (2014a).

from believing that it will happen. And insofar as Chloe might believe that the flight will probably have a stopover rather than simply that the flight has a stopover, it seems that her saying that the flight has a stopover involves her expressing something that she does not believe.

Against this, one might note that, actually, it is not so much the case that Chloe does not believe that the flight has a stopover in London, but that she does not believe it strongly enough to justify asserting it. In this situation, it would seem that she is not lying, according to (3). This presents a challenge to this kind of view, though the exact strength of the challenge depends on exactly how far believing that something will happen can be differentiated from believing that something will probably happen.

The second thing to note is that, unlike cases of metaphor and hyperbole, it is far from clear that Chloe's assertion lacks the kind of assertoric force required to make it a lie. It might well be that her assertion is entirely serious and intended to induce the belief in her friend that the next flight to Oslo does have a stopover in London. It thus seems that, according to the account of the connection between lying and falsity given in (3), Chloe's statement might well be considered as a lie. At any rate, there seems to be no immediately obvious reason to discount its possibly being one.

One might think, however, that Chloe's statement in (3) is not a lie. This intuition can be brought out further by considering the fact that, whilst she is stating something that she does not believe and intending her friend to come to believe it, she is not seeking to deceive her friend into believing something that she thinks is false, since Chloe does not believe that it is *false* that the next flight to Oslo has a stopover in London. Nor is she seeking to be deceptive in saying that the next flight to Oslo has a stopover in London, since she is not obviously trying to withhold or conceal evidence relevant to the question of whether or not the next flight to London has a stopover in Oslo. In this way, Chloe's statement lacks the usual characteristics of a lie.

Furthermore, it seems that Chloe's statement lacks the usual characteristics of a lie in a way that cannot simply be explained in terms of the statement failing to have a certain kind of assertoric force. Insofar as it is intuitively apparent that Chloe's statement is not a lie even if she intends to have her friend take her word for it that the next flight to Oslo will have a stopover in London, her statement has all the assertoric force commonly associated with lies. Nonetheless, we might find it intuitively apparent that the statement is not a lie.

In any event, it seems relatively clear that Chloe's statement is different from ordinary instances of lies, such as the one given in **Case 1**. Ordinarily, as Lackey observes, lying is associated with seeking to deceive, or with otherwise being deceptive. The result is that, if Chloe's statement is a lie in virtue of the fact that she asserts it with the right force and does not believe it (rather than believing it to be false, or believing the opposite of it), then it is a lie of a different type to the paradigmatic cases of lying. Of course this is not, by itself, sufficient to make the case for the conclusion that Chloe's statement in **Case 6** is not a lie. Bald-faced lies, in which a speaker lies to a listener but without seeking to have the listener believe what she says are unlike paradigmatic cases of lying in important ways, but this does not in any sense make it intuitively apparent that they are not lies. But Chloe's statement in **Case 6** differs from a case of bald-faced lying because in the case of bald-faced lies, there is a strong intuition that such statements are in fact lies. Insofar as there is an intuition that Chloe's statement in **Case 6** is a lie, it is, I think, an altogether less strong one. And insofar as this is a less strong intuition, there is pressure to be exerted on the connection between lying and falsity given in (3).

CHAPTER 8

LYING AND ASSERTION

MARK JARY

8.1 INTRODUCTION

ATTEMPTS to define lying generally appeal to the notion of assertion. Lying is widely held to involve asserting something the speaker believes to be false, and this distinguishes it from other forms of verbal deception, such as falsely implicating. Once this is agreed upon, the competition between rival definitions of lying centres on who has the best account of assertion. Fallis (2009), for example, suggests that assertion should be analysed in terms of a Gricean maxim of Quality, according to which one should say only what she believes to be true (Grice 1989a: 27). Lying is then defined as a violation of that maxim. Stokke (2013a) objects that this definition wrongly treats ironical utterances as lies, and instead proposes Stalnaker's (1999) model of assertion as providing a better basis for the definition of lying. According to Stalnaker, an assertion is an attempt to modify the common ground shared by the participants in a conversation. Stokke argues that lying occurs when a speaker seeks to add to the common ground a proposition which she does not believe. Another assertion-based account is that of Chisholm and Feehan (1977). This has strong Gricean overtones, seeing as essential to assertion that the speaker justify the hearer in believing that the speaker believes the content of the utterance.[1]

---

[1] In this chapter, I focus on a narrow group of theories of assertion, primarily for the reason that they have been associated in some way with the analysis of lying. For an overview of theories of assertion, including those within the Searlean speech-act tradition, see Jary (2010a: ch. 1). Papers by a number of authors on various aspects of assertion can be found in Cappelen and Brown (2009). Pagin (2015) is a thorough review of philosophical accounts of assertion. Goldberg (2015) is a sophisticated defence of the view that assertion is constituted by a epistemic norm. Williamson (1996) defends the view that the norm that constitutes assertion is the knowledge rule. For an attempt to extend the definition of lying so that it goes beyond what is asserted and takes in what is implicated, see Meibauer (2014a).

The accounts of assertion that are called upon in these definitions of lying, although different, have in common that they take assertion not to be fundamental, but to be itself analysable in terms of other basic concepts such as belief, truth, and proposition: Grice's maxim of Quality enjoins the speaker to say only what he believes to be true; Stalnaker's model of assertion relies heavily on the notions of proposition and acceptance, with the latter defined as treating as true; and Chisholm and Feehan treat belief and its expression as essential to assertion. Such accounts can be contrasted with others that treat the notion of assertion as one which should be employed in the elucidation of concepts such as belief, truth, and proposition. The most well-known and developed of these is Brandom (1994), though Barker (2004) is also notable in this respect, and both are presaged by Dummett (1981).

Because they explicate the notions of belief, truth, and falsity in terms of assertion, theories that treat assertion as fundamental cannot simply define lying as asserting without the requisite belief, or as treating as true something which one believes to be false. It needs to be spelled out, therefore, how such accounts can accommodate the concept of lying as a means of verbal deception individuated by its assertoric nature. As we will see, doing so will bring out the tight relationship between the capacity to lie and the capacity to assert. Furthermore, the result will be a view of the relationship between the notions of assertion, lying, representation, and belief which, in terms of the relative conceptual priority it assigns each of these notions, appears to parallel the development in young children of these concepts and the abilities they underpin (see also Chapter 30, by Victoria Talwar).

8.2 Dummett

For Dummett (1981), lying plays an essential role in distinguishing assertions from other speech acts. Each of the accounts mentioned at the beginning of this chapter defines lying in terms of assertion without the requisite belief in what is asserted. On this approach, assertion has conceptual priority: it can be conceived of independently of lying, but the reverse is not the case. Dummett, by contrast, views the two notions as mutually necessary, so that lying and assertion are conceptual co-requisites:

> If a formulation of a principle for distinguishing assertions from other utterances is called for, it may be given as follows: assertions are those utterances which can be used to deceive, i.e., to lie, and which can also occur (perhaps deprived of some sign for assertoric force) as constituents of complex sentences.
>
> (Dummett 1981: 356)

> Before the child can be said to make assertions, he must learn to respond to the assertions of others. (Indeed, it must be proper to say of him that he says what he does in order to elicit the appropriate response from others. In this sense we might say

that the child cannot assert anything until he can lie. It is this insight which underlies Grice's account of meaning).

(Dummett 1981: 453)

So, while it is common among those who seek to define lying to hold the conditional (1), according to which the ability to assert is a necessary condition for the ability to lie:

(1)   You can lie → You can assert,

Dummett holds the stronger bi-conditional (2), so that those without the capacity to lie cannot be asserters:

(2)   You can lie ↔ You can assert.

Assertion, for Dummett, is a conventional practice: there is a convention such that declarative sentences are uttered with the intention of uttering only true ones (Dummett 1981: 354).[2] Thus, uttering a declarative sentence commits the speaker to the truth of the proposition thereby expressed, where this amounts to a commitment to act in accordance with the assertions one makes or assents to. The commitment to act in certain ways is the consequence of making or assenting to an assertion.

But asserting also requires knowing the conditions under which it is appropriate to do so. So becoming an asserter requires learning the conditions under which an assertion is justified. The conditions that justify the making of an assertion may also be those that determine its truth, but this need not be the case. We make many justified assertions even though the conditions for their truth do not obtain, predictions and expressions of intention being two cases in point (Dummett 1981: 355). Furthermore, the same conditions may justify assertions with different truth conditions. The conditions that justify the making of the assertions in (3) and (4) (from Brandom 1994: 121) are the truth conditions of (4) but not of (3). The same point can be made for (5) and (6) (from Barker 2004: 30–2) respectively.

(3)   I will write a book about Hegel
(4)   I foresee that I will write a book about Hegel
(5)   There is probably life on Mars
(6)   I believe that there is life on Mars

Hence, the conditions that justify the making of an assertion and the conditions for its truth need not be identical. A justified assertion is not necessarily one whose content is true.

---

[2] Unless there are further conventions, such as those governing theatrical performances, which inhibit the force conventionally associated with the declarative (Dummett 1981: 310–11).

Because assertions are distinguished by the conditions that justify them and the consequences they have both for the speaker and for those who assent to the assertion, treating an utterance as an assertion also requires recognizing that the act commits the speaker and any who assent to the assertion to a particular line of action.

> Learning to use a statement of a given form involves, then, learning two things: the conditions under which one is justified in making the statement; and what constitutes acceptance of it. Here 'consequences' must be taken to include both the inferential powers of the statement and anything that counts as acting on the truth of the statement.
>
> (Dummett 1981: 453)

Assertions thus constrain and guide behaviour, both linguistic and non-linguistic. To be sure, other speech acts, such as commands and questions, also direct behaviour, but they do so by virtue of being uttered to a specific addressee, so that he is now to comply with the command or answer the question. Assertions are different in that they affect behaviour in much the same way as perception: just as those who see the bears by the lake will generally seek to avoid the lake, so those who hear it asserted that there are bears by the lake will seek to avoid the lake, regardless of whether they are the addressees of the utterance. Assertions can thus serve as perception by proxy.

On Dummett's view, force relates to the point of an utterance and the point of assertions is that they constrain and guide behaviour by committing asserters and assenters to a line of action. Given this conception of assertion, an advantage to be had in lying becomes apparent: through lying we can guide the behaviour of others by having them assent to false assertions. As a consequence of such assent, their behaviour will be not as their senses and/or previous belief would guide it, but as the speaker would have it be.

But this position commits Dummett only to the conditional in (1). Why does he commit himself to the stronger bi-conditional (2)? In other words, why is the ability to lie a requisite for competence in assertion? To answer this question, we need to consider more carefully what grasping the distinction between the grounds for assertion and the consequences of acceptance amounts to.

We can imagine an individual who learns to utter declarative sentences only when the conditions that would justify asserting that sentence hold, but who has no conception of the consequences of doing so. Such utterances would have consequences for those who assented to them, but the speaker would be ignorant of these, and they would not motivate her decision to utter the sentence. She would be a reliable indicator that certain conditions obtained, but this is insufficient for her to count as an asserter: thermometers are reliable indicators of temperature, but they do not make assertions. Or to borrow an example from Dummett (1981: 354), a dog that barks when a stranger approaches a house is a reliable indicator that a stranger is approaching, but one would not want to say that the dog asserts that a stranger is approaching.

This is why consideration of the consequences of the utterance is crucial for Dummett's analysis of assertion. To count as an asserter, a speaker needs to be aware of (at least some of) the inferential and practical consequences of what she utters, and these need to motivate her utterance. But once this awareness is achieved, she becomes a potential liar, for she has the option of uttering a declarative sentence for the sake of the consequences of doing so rather than simply because the conditions for doing so obtain. That is to say, on Dummett's account, a competent asserter is able to perform these acts in order to guide the behaviour of others, owing to the awareness of the consequences of the act that is implicit in that competence. It is this awareness that gives her the capacity to lie.

So, according to Dummett, one cannot be capable of assertion without thereby being capable of lying. This is why he holds the bi-conditional (2): if we want to find individuals with the capacity to assert we must look for those with the capacity to lie. But lying is often defined, in part, in terms of the absence of belief in the proposition asserted. How does the notion of belief fit into this account of assertion?

Following Frege (1918–19/1997), it is common to think of assertion as the expression of belief. Frege saw assertion as the exteriorization of an internal act of judgement: one first grasps a thought, then judges it true, and finally makes manifest those internal acts by uttering a sentence that expresses the thought judged true. Dummett argues that this gets the order of explanation wrong. According to Dummett, because the notion of belief is reliant on the notion of truth, the explication of belief requires prior explication of the notion of truth. Truth, however, can only be explicated by considering what counts as treating as true, Dummett holds, and treating as true is best explained in terms of acting in accordance with the consequences of assertion (Dummett 1981: 453; see also the discussion in Jary 2010a: 33–8). On pain of circularity, then, assertion cannot be explained in terms of belief. Rather, belief must be explained in terms of a disposition to assert: to attribute the belief that P to an individual is to attribute to him the disposition to assert that P.

On this view, to grasp the nature of assertion is to grasp the concept of belief: once one is a competent asserter, in that one can make assertions and recognize assertions qua assertions when made by others, one thereby has the notion of belief. Armed with this notion, one is able to treat assertions as expressions of belief. This is why Dummett makes the comment relating the capacity to lie with Grice's account of meaning. According to Grice, the sort of meaning involved in assertion is dependent on the attribution of beliefs to others: in uttering a declarative sentence, the speaker seeks to convey that she believes that P (Grice 1989c: 123). Dummett's claim is that it is only by virtue of a conceptually prior capacity in assertion that such communication of attitudes is possible. On his account, we must view the attribution of a belief as an attribution of a disposition to assert. As for what it means to accuse someone of not acting in accordance with her beliefs, this is something that can best be articulated in the terms of Brandom's development of Dummett's conception of assertion, as we will see in the next section.

8.3 Brandom

While Dummett's account explains belief in terms of assertion, it nevertheless relies on the notion of truth: according to his account, the convention associated with declarative sentences is to utter only those that are true. The theory of assertion developed by Brandom (1994), although heavily influenced by Dummett's, has roles for neither truth nor belief: Brandom wants the notion of commitments, and the undertaking and attribution of these, to do all the work that the concepts of belief and truth do in other frameworks. Unlike Dummett, however, Brandom seems largely to ignore the issues presented by lying for an account of assertion. It will be instructive, therefore, to consider whether and, if so, how, his account can accommodate the view that lies are assertions made without the corresponding belief.[3]

For Brandom, assertions are individuated in relation to other speech acts by the fact that they can both require and stand as reasons. An assertion that John is in France can be challenged by asking 'How do you know?' and the challenge responded to by making a further assertion, perhaps to the effect that that he recently updated his Facebook status accordingly. A command can require a reason but cannot stand as one, and likewise a question.[4] Given an act that can both stand as and require a reason, the linguistic type whose tokening counts as performing this act is the declarative mood, on Brandom's account.

Like Dummett, Brandom stresses the distinction between the conditions for making an assertion and the consequences of doing so. However, he introduces, on the consequences side, a further distinction between commitments and entitlements. Commitments relate to what one *must* do as a result of making an assertion: asserting (7) commits one to assenting to (8). Entitlements are the moves that are left open by an assertion, what one *can* do: thus asserting (7) entitles one to assert (9). Incompatibility between assertions can be analysed in terms of entitlements that are removed as a result of an assertion: asserting (7) removes entitlement to (10).

(7) The dress is red.
(8) The dress is coloured.
(9) The dress is vermillion.
(10) The dress is green.

In Brandom's model, the commitments and entitlements undertaken by a speaker are kept track of by updating each speaker's scorecard. Each speaker keeps a scorecard for herself, and for the other participants in the conversation, on which she records the

---

[3] On the relationship between lying and belief, see Chapter 9 by Matthew Benton.
[4] Though there are some types of rhetorical question that can be judged true and hence can stand as reasons. It is not clear whether they can require reasons, though. Take, for example, Barker's (2004: 37) example: Jones, on observing someone trying to sell suntan lotion on a winter's day, asks rhetorically 'Who is going to buy 15 plus when it's 15 below?' Smith replies 'True. Who is going to?'

moves (i.e., assertions) made and the consequences for each participant. Consequences may be different for each speaker, depending on the prior commitments undertaken and recorded on their cards. For example, if speaker A has (11) on her score card but B does not, then adding (12) to each one's scorecard will result in (13) also being added to A's card but not to B's.[5]

(11) Philosophers are not to be trusted.
(12) John is a philosopher.
(13) John is not to be trusted.

As noted above, Brandom does not take the notions of belief and truth for granted, but rather seeks to explain them in terms of his scorekeeping model. On this account, to say of someone that she believes that P is to say that P is on her scorecard, which itself entails that she is committed to the inferential and practical commitments that follow from P (in combination with the other commitments on her scorecard). To say that P is true, according to Brandom's model, is to thereby acknowledge commitment to P in one's own case, i.e., to write it on one's own scorecard. Accordingly, to say that P is a false is to reject commitment to it in one's own case.

Making an assertion also results in the commitment to defend that assertion if challenged. One defends an assertion by giving reasons for it. These take the form of further assertions. An audience which accepts a response to a challenge that is defended by a further assertion in effect judges the inference from the defence of the challenged assertion to be a good one. Thus an assertion of (14), if challenged, might be defended by an assertion of (15), and acceptance of this defence would amount as judging the inference from (15) to (14) to be a good one.

(14) John is out.
(15) His car is not in the driveway.

The conditions for making an assertion are thus characterized, on Brandom's model, as further assertions which result in entitlement to that assertion.[6] An assertion, on this account, is part of an inferential chain which is justified by other assertions and itself justifies yet others. It is in this sense that an assertion can both be, and require, a reason.[7]

How is lying to be accounted for in such a framework? Recent work on the definition of lying leans towards the view that lying essentially involves asserting coupled with

---

[5] Brandom's notion of updating a scorecard differs from Stalnaker's (1999) notion of updating the common ground in a number of ways. To list a few: it does not take the notion of proposition as basic; it does not treat the conversational record as being held 'in common'; it does not rely on the notion of treating as true.

[6] Perceptual reports are an exception in that they do not require reasons (Brandom 1994: 199–229).

[7] For a partial endorsement of Brandom and a defence of a commitment-based approach to assertion, see MacFarlane (2011).

the absence of belief in the content of the assertion. The phenomenon of bald-faced lies (Sorensen 2007) has led many to conclude that the intention to deceive is not an essential condition (though see Lackey (2013), who holds that there must at least be an intent to be deceptive, where this is weaker than an intent to deceive). Explaining lying from a Brandomian perspective thus requires considering in greater detail how the notion of belief is to be cashed out in that model.

In Brandom's model, belief is a perspectival notion. As we have seen, to ascribe a belief to another, in his framework, is to ascribe to that person a commitment to defend an assertion, i.e., to write it on that person's scorecard. Lying involves assertion in the absence of belief. Because it rests on the absence of belief, lying must also be treated a perspectival notion in Brandom's framework. We need, therefore, to consider what it is to lie from two perspectives: that of a hearer and that of a speaker.

From a hearer's perspective, to accuse a speaker of lying is a special kind of challenge to her assertion: the challenge is not simply a request for justification, but an accusation that the speaker cannot provide acceptable reasons for the assertion she makes. The hearer may try to trap the alleged liar by repeated challenges of her assertion and the justifications she offers. In doing so, he in effect tries to demonstrate that she is seeking to engineer a disparity between the scorecard the hearer keeps of the speaker's commitments and the speaker's own scorecard of her commitments. In other words, the hearer accuses the speaker of keeping two scorecards for herself: a private one and another on which she writes the commitments she undertakes in the interaction that the hearer judges to be mendacious.

From a speaker's perspective, the decision to lie amounts to a decision to engage in double-entry scorekeeping. One scorecard has upon it the commitments she sees herself as committed to: these are the assertions she would make if the desirability, to her, of the consequences were not an issue for consideration. For some reason, however, the consequences of undertaking these commitments are undesirable and hence the liar seeks to avoid undertaking them, opting instead to undertake commitments whose consequences are more desirable. For example, a doctor living in an impoverished dictatorship might assert that there is no suffering in it because the consequences of asserting that suffering is rife in her country would have the consequence that she be subjected to torture. Absent these cruel consequences, she would not make this claim. In a case of deceptive, manipulative lying, the goal may be to have the hearer accept the assertion in order that he undertake the commitments that follow and behave as the speaker would have him do. Or, the goal may be to have the hearer update the scorecard he keeps of the speaker's commitments in such a way that he will ascribe to her commitments and entitlements distinct from those she ascribes herself. This in effect means that he will not predict her behaviour accurately.

In general, then, concerns about the consequences of assertion motivate lying, on the Brandom model. The liar either wishes to avoid undertaking certain commitments, to have the hearer undertake commitments that the liar presents herself as having on her own scorecard but does not in fact see as justified, or to have the hearer attribute to her commitments other than those she attributes to herself. This requires a grasp of the perspectival nature of the scorekeeping game, as presented by Brandom. On Brandom's account (and in contrast to that of Lewis 1979), there is no official scorekeeper: rather, each participant keeps a scorecard for himself and another for each of his interlocutors. It is a participant's awareness of the fact that the consequences of acceptance can differ for each participant, depending on their collateral commitments, that counts, on Brandom's model, as grasping the representational nature of assertion (Brandom 1994: ch. 8, Brandom 2000: ch. 5). Without such an awareness, lying would not be possible, as it is only with this grasp of the representational nature of assertion that the notion of falsity can also be grasped. As in Dummett's case, then, full competence in assertion, on Brandom's theory, amounts to the capacity to lie.

This view has the advantage of illuminating the view that lying involves not just the absence of belief in the proposition asserted, but the belief that that proposition is false (or that it is not true), as defended by Chisholm and Feehan (1977: 152). On Brandom's model of assertion, absence of the belief that P must be characterized as not having on one's scorecard the commitments that are undertaken by an assertion of P. But being in this state does not entail any concept of truth or falsity. To hold a proposition to be false, rather, entails viewing oneself as lacking entitlement to that proposition while nevertheless having a grasp of the consequences of acceptance for oneself and others: it requires the perspectival abilities that Brandom sees as foundational to a grasp of the representational nature of discourse. It is unclear what would motivate the assertion of a proposition that was merely absent from one's scorecard, but given a grasp of the consequences, for oneself and for others, of a proposition one takes oneself to be unentitled to assert, the motivation for lying becomes clear. In other words, the mere lack of entitlement to asserting that P provides no motivation for asserting that P, whereas the belief that P is false (or that it is not true) most certainly does, for it amounts to a grasp of the consequences of an assertion which one does not see oneself as entitled to make.

8.4 Assertion and sensitivity to lies in young children

According the Dummett–Brandom view, full competence in assertion amounts to a capacity to lie, and vice versa; competence in assertion is a prerequisite for a grasp of the notion of belief; and the practice of assertion involves the deployment of conventional signs, assertions being recognized as such by their form. This last point is stressed by Dummett, but it applies also to Brandom: making a move in the game of giving and requiring reasons is shown by the use of the right sort of counter, namely the declarative mood. If this philosophical stance towards assertion and lying is transposed to the empirical study of the development of assertion and lying in children, then certain predictions can be formulated (the ideas presented in this section are developed more fully in Jary 2010b, though not in relation to lying).

The first is that language, notably the use of declarative syntax, should be a precursor to the development of a notion of belief. This is because the notion of belief is grounded in competence in assertion, which requires being able to recognize an assertion by virtue of a form conventionally associated with this speech act. The second is that sensitivity to lies and the development of a conception belief should emerge in tandem, for they amount to a grasp of the representational nature of discourse: recall that on Brandom's story both lying and belief are to be explained in terms of an ability to adopt the scorekeeping perspective of another. This leads to a further prediction, namely that the development of a sensitivity to lying should be related to the development of perspective-taking abilities, for perspective taking is claimed to underlie the ability to attribute beliefs to others. In this section, we will see that there is evidence that supports each of these predictions.

There has been considerable research into the role of language in the development of the ability to pass classic false-belief tests, generally regarded as the acid test of possession of a full-fledged concept of belief.[8] Two findings stand out. First, it appears that language is a requirement for passing this test, as shown by data on normally developing children and data on children whose linguistic development is delayed or impaired (such as congenitally deaf children born to non-signing parents). Second, a particular aspect of linguistic construction is crucial, namely finite 'that' clauses such as are found in the complements of verbs reporting speech. Thus it appears that a full conception of belief cannot be acquired without prior competence in the syntax required for reporting assertive speech acts, and, furthermore, that training in this syntax, particularly in deceptive contexts, facilitates this acquisition (Astington and Jenkins 1999; de Villiers and de Villiers 2000; Lohmann and Tomasello 2003).

The second prediction is supported by research into the development of children's understanding of deceptive speech. This has found that their sensitivity to deception develops in line with their ability to pass the false-belief test. Mascaro and Sperber (2009) conducted a series of experiments looking at children's sensitivity to deceptive discourse and found that while children prefer information from benevolent interlocutors prior to the age of three, it is only after around age four that they are able to grasp the falsity of lies, this being followed by an understanding of an underlying intention to deceive between ages four and six. As noted by Sperber et al. (2010: 373), the first transition takes place around the same time that success in the false-belief tasks occurs, which, as we have seen, requires a prior competence in the syntax of reported speech.

The third prediction is that the development of a conception of belief should be found to be related to an ability to take the perspectives of others, for, as we saw, the sort of scorekeeping model proposed by Brandom (on which any account of lying on that model is dependent) relies on this ability. And perspective-taking has indeed been

---

[8] There is some evidence (Onishi and Baillargeon 2005; Surian et al. 2007; Southgate et al. 2010) that children can attribute false beliefs prior to passing classic tests of the type found in Baron-Cohen et al. (1985) and elsewhere. However, Butterfill and Apperly (2013) show that the capacity to pass the tests set for very young children can be modelled in non-representational terms.

shown to be related to the ability to pass the false-belief task. A studied carried out by Perner et al. (2002) showed how success in naming tasks which required the child to adopt the perspective of another correlated positively with success in false-belief tasks. Furthermore, work by Rubio-Fernández and Geurts (2013) indicates that false-belief tasks can be made easier for young children by reducing the perspective-taking demands, further suggesting a relationship between perspective-taking and possession of a concept of belief, as predicted by Brandom's theory of assertion.

8.5 Conclusion

While there is general agreement that the notion of assertion must be a part of the definition of lying, few authors consider the question of why this might be the case. Dummett is an exception, in that his conception of assertion equates the ability to assert with the ability to lie. According to Brandom's development of Dummett's account of assertion, the reason for this conceptual interdependence is that lying relies on exactly those capacities that constitute full competence in assertion: the ability to distinguish between the conditions for and the consequences of uttering a declarative sentence (under appropriate circumstances) and the ability to view those consequences both from one's own perspective and from the perspective of others, whose collateral commitments may be different from one's own. There is evidence to suggest that the order of conceptual priority in the Dummett–Brandom picture of assertion is reflected in the development of conceptual abilities in young children, and in their sensitivity to the possibility of deception through lying.

CHAPTER 9

LYING, BELIEF, AND KNOWLEDGE

MATTHEW A. BENTON

9.1 INTRODUCTION

WHAT is the relationship between lying, belief, and knowledge? One natural first-pass idea is to understand lying in terms of knowledge: to modify a line from Mark Twain, "Lying is telling someone something you know ain't so."[1] But many will regard this natural idea to be incorrect from the start, insofar as they judge that one can lie even when one simply believes, falsely, the negation of what one asserted: on their widely-accepted view one can lie even if one mistakenly tells another the truth. In what follows I shall proceed as if this widely held view should be respected as orthodoxy, though in section 9.5 I shall revisit a version of the Twain-style knowledge account of lying to explore how plausible it might actually be.

Several philosophers debate the exact conceptual analysis of lying. Many accept an analysis with the traditional three-clause structure:

(TRAD)   You lie to S just in case:
    (i) You assert that p to S;
    (ii) You believe that p is false; and
    (iii) By asserting p, you intend to deceive S (in some specified way).

Much of the debate over such an analysis concerns the exact nature of the third condition, in particular, whether the speaker intends for S to infer something false about the

---

[1] See the quote about faith from the school boy, in Twain's *Following the Equator*, ch. 12, "Pudd'nhead Wilson's New Calendar" (1898).

proposition asserted,[2] or about what the speaker herself believes, or perhaps that the former be inferred from an inference about the latter. However, many argue that a third such clause, requiring something about the speaker's intent to deceive, is not even necessary for an assertion to be a lie; for example, Sorensen (2007), Saul (2012), and Stokke (2013a) defend definitions of lying which retain the first two clauses above, but abandon any such third condition. Even if such a third condition is not necessary, most commentators are interested primarily in lies which are intended to deceive, and one might approach the project of analyzing what a lie is by focusing on deceptive lies (cf. Fallis 2010a: 4 ff.). While such lies are worthy of such interest, we shall see that an account of lying is available which can explain with other resources the deceptive intent typical of lies.[3]

The main focus of this chapter is the relationship, if any, between knowledge and belief, which figure in the epistemic norm of assertion, and the moral/social norms against lying. I develop a broad account of the injunction against lying according to which, roughly, lying involves intentionally misrepresenting oneself at the level of what one believes or knows, which in turn represents one's epistemic relationship to the proposition asserted. Two such accounts will be articulated, one in terms of belief, and one in terms of knowledge. Approaching the project in this way enables us to see how a norm against lying may be derived from the epistemic norm of assertion. And it opens up a new perspective on how to understand lying which mirrors the epistemic expectations which hearers have toward speakers who make assertions in testimonial exchanges.

9.2 THE NORM OF ASSERTION

First, some terminological preliminaries. *Assertion* is the linguistic act of committing outright to the truth of a proposition: by one's utterance one declares or claims or states[4] that something is so. As such, assertion is regarded as the default speech act for outright utterances made in the declarative or indicative mood. Speakers use assertions to make unhedged claims about the way things are, such as when one states *London is the capital of the UK*, or *Joanna is in her office*.[5] Amongst speech act theorists (e.g., Searle

---

[2] Different accounts specify the intent-to-deceive clause differently: see e.g., Mahon (2008a), and Lackey (2013). See Fallis (2010a) for an overview.

[3] For the purposes of this chapter, I shall largely set aside concerns about irony, hyperbole, or otherwise inaccurate claims involving scalar considerations: for example, when someone claims that he just swam a mile, or that it is 9 o'clock even though he knows that it is 8:59. Whether these ought to be classified as lies is a difficult question (though see Marsili 2014); but one might think that if so, this gives motivation for including a very specific clause about intent to deceive.

[4] Some theorists distinguish statements from assertions (Meibauer 2014a: 71), citing the German distinction between *Feststellungen* and *Behauptungen*. In English, however, there is little to distinguish them.

[5] For lengthy overviews, see Jary (2010a) and Pagin (2015); for shorter overviews, see MacFarlane (2011) and Goldberg (2015: ch. 1).

1979a: 2–5), it is common to distinguish assertion from other types of speech act (for example from interrogatives, imperatives, or performatives, among others) by noting, first, that the point of assertion is to represent the world as being a certain way, namely, the way represented by the proposition asserted; second, that assertion has a word-to-world direction of fit (the utterance is made true by being made to conform to the way the world is); and third, that assertion of a proposition expresses the psychological state of belief in that proposition. On this approach, assertion expresses belief even when the speaker asserts insincerely by not believing what she asserts.[6]

What is meant by an *epistemic norm* of assertion? Assertion's epistemic norm is a social linguistic rule that one satisfy some relationship to that proposition for properly asserting: typically, it specifies a necessary condition on (epistemically) proper assertion, such as that one must know it, or believe it, or have adequate evidence for believing it, or that it be true. Philosophers often think of belief as the mental correlate of assertion: it is the mental act of outright commitment to a proposition as true, which normally triggers dispositions to act on that belief. But beliefs, and assertions, can be false; whereas *knowledge*, though normally regarded as involving belief (one's belief can amount to knowledge), is distinguished from mere belief in that one can only know facts, that is, true propositions. Though one can hold a false belief, one can only know truths. Because of this, it is often said that knowledge is 'factive'.[7] (Moreover, knowledge requires some normative condition(s), for example that one's belief be well-formed, be the product of a safe method, or fit one's evidence, etc. Epistemologists disagree on the exact nature of these conditions, which typically fall under the label of '*epistemic justification*'; we shall not consider these issues here.)

Grice's maxim of Quality offers a candidate epistemic norm of assertion: its supermaxim is 'Try to make your contribution one that is true' and its two specific submaxims are

1. Do not say that which you believe to be false.
2. Do not say that for which you lack adequate evidence.[8]

Grice's first submaxim is sometimes called the *sincerity* condition, the second the *evidence* condition. Strictly speaking, Grice's Quality supermaxim does not require that one's assertion be true. But if we interpret it as being concerned with truth (and not merely *trying* to assert truths), we may understand its submaxims as corollaries the following of which will help one fulfil the supermaxim.

---

[6] Searle (1979a: 4). This importantly updates Searle's original position (Searle 1969: 64 ff.), on which sincerity was required in order even to make an assertion.
[7] For more on factivity, see Benton (draft, ch. 1).
[8] Grice (1989c: 27). Benton (2016) argues that Grice's maxim of Quality is best understood as the knowledge norm, 'KNA' in what follows.

Timothy Williamson (2000: ch. 11) and others[9] have defended knowledge as the epistemic norm of assertion (KNA), such that this norm is constitutively related to the speech act of assertion:

(KNA) One must: assert that *p* only if one knows that *p*.

The Knowledge Norm of Assertion imposes a strict duty, forbidding the combination that: one asserts *p* and one does not know that *p*. Because knowing involves believing, KNA forbids insincere assertions; and because knowing is factive, KNA forbids false assertions. On KNA, one does something epistemically improper when one asserts without knowing what one asserts, even if one thereby does something appropriate in, for example, the *prudential* or the *moral* sense. Much of what follows invokes KNA, but very little turns on this; many of the ideas developed here generalize to most rival accounts of the norm.

Lying is a category that most naturally applies to assertion, rather than to presupposition or conversational implicature, or to other speech acts, for example, to suggesting that a proposition is or might be true, or asking questions concerning whether a proposition is true.[10] Thus, a natural route into the connections between the communicative practice of assertion and the norms against lying is to consider the epistemic norm of assertion.

9.3 NORMS AND EVALUATIVE DIMENSIONS

We can gain some purchase on the relationship between KNA as the norm of assertion and lying by considering how KNA will affect conversational patterns, and how it will generate expectations of conversational participants who implicitly grasp the relationship of KNA to assertion. In particular, if KNA is correct, assertions will typically represent their speakers as knowing what they assert;[11] for by engaging in the practice of

---

[9] See especially Turri (2010, 2011, 2014a), Benton (2011, 2016, draft), and Buckwalter and Turri (2014), among many others. For an overview of this literature and its critics, see Benton (2014: §1), and Pagin (2015: §6.2).

[10] Does one do something akin to lying if one *predicts* that *p* when one knows that not-*p*? This will depend on whether one treats the force of predicting as on a par with asserting (e.g., for Stokke 2013a, who thinks of assertion along Stalnaker's lines of proposing that a proposition be added to the conversation's common ground, predicting might well have the same force as asserting). For an epistemic norm of the speech act of prediction in terms of proper expectation, see Benton and Turri (2014: esp. 1862 ff.).

[11] Moore (1962: 277) and Unger (1975: 251 ff.) endorse the thesis that asserting that *p* represents its speaker as knowing that *p*. The case for that thesis turns on conversational patterns and the kinds of criticism available, which any norm of assertion ought to well explain. Williamson notes that the KNA norm subsumes the assertions-represent-knowing thesis under more general principles: "In doing anything for which authority is required (for example, issuing orders), one represents oneself as having the authority to do it. To have the (epistemic) authority to assert *p* is to know *p*" (Williamson 2000: 252

assertion whose norm according to KNA its speakers implicitly grasp, a speaker would represent herself as conforming to KNA. Even if we allow that asserting instead represents something weaker about oneself—perhaps only representing oneself as believing, or as having some adequate evidence for, what one asserts—then still, asserting what one knows one does not believe will involve intentionally misrepresenting oneself in some way.[12] Does lying always involve misrepresenting what one believes? One gloss might be this:

(LIE) A lies to B if and only if:
  (i) A asserts that *p* to B,
  (ii) A believes that *p* is false (and does not believe, under the same guise, that *p* is true), and
  (iii) A intends by so asserting to represent herself as believing that *p* is true.[13]

The parenthetical clause of condition (ii) is needed to rule out as not being lies cases where one believes a proposition and its negation; this possibility, though typically overlooked, can occur (on a certain view of structured propositions) when one believes a proposition and its negation under different guises. Suppose I see the same object through two different windows, but do not realize that it is the same object. Through the right window, it looks gray, and through the left window it looks green. I come to believe both: *that object [seen through the right window] is gray*, and also *that object [seen through the left window] is not gray*. But if the object is in fact gray, and I tell someone (thinking of what I see through the left window) that the object is not gray, I have not lied. But without the parenthetical clarification in (ii), LIE would count this as lying.

More generally, it might be possible for someone to know a proposition but, perhaps by misremembering or by habit or by some irrational process which they do not recognize, they come to believe its negation. (My wife accidentally leaves her mobile phone behind, and I find it; it looks much like my own. Later I need to call her at a moment when I happen to be holding her phone, and out of habit, using her own mobile phone which looks like mine, I begin to try to call her mobile number. For that moment,

---

n. 6). Because the norm itself explains why asserters do represent this of themselves, the case for the representation thesis is also the case for the norm. Pagin (2016: §6 n. 20) disputes this by claiming that even here, 'authority' has a non-normative reading, namely "*satisfying of sufficient conditions*, which need not be related to any norms"; but sufficient for what? Presumably, an answer must be given in normative terms: that is, sufficient for *acceptable* or *appropriate* action undertaken as an authority.

[12] This is because people do typically believe what their evidence adequately supports; and plausibly in virtue of this, speakers express belief, or represent themselves as believing, when they assert. This creates a problem for Lackey's (2007a) alternative Reasonable-to-Believe Norm of Assertion (which does not even require belief for proper assertion), particularly because she also endorses a 'Not Misleading Norm of Assertion' (2007: 615–17). For criticism, see Benton (2016: esp. n. 27) and Turri (2014b).

[13] This gloss bears some resemblance to one considered by Davidson (1985: 88).

I plausibly believe that she has her phone, even though I know that she does not have it. If during that moment I tell someone that she has her phone, I am not lying.)

Some may suppose that LIE's condition (iii) is superfluous because they think of assertion as an intentional speech act requiring a speaker to intend to represent herself as being sincere, that is, as believing what she asserts. This way of thinking about assertion might well be correct; but it seems committed to the idea that one cannot ironically or metaphorically or playfully *assert* a falsehood so as to mean or convey instead its negation. On this view of assertion, irony involves cases where one *utters* that p, and 'makes as if to'[14] assert that p, but one is in fact asserting (roughly) that ¬p. Those who understand assertion in this way may leave off condition (iii), and insist that with ironic utterances a speaker does not lie, for she does not even fulfill condition (i).[15] But for those who prefer a thinner conception of assertion according to which one can assert something without intending to communicate it, or without intending to represent oneself as believing it, (iii) will be needed. On the thinner picture of assertion, (iii) can itself provide an interpretation of why standard cases of irony are not lies: for the hallmark of irony is that it typically does not involve the speaker's intending to represent herself as believing the falsehood uttered (*mutatis mutandis* for cases of metaphor, hyperbole, and so on).

Condition (iii) need not involve the intent to deceive B concerning either p or what A believes, because A might know that B knows what A believes. So this gloss properly counts many of Sorensen's bald-faced lies and 'knowledge-lies'[16] as lies. For bald-faced lies and knowledge lies are plausibly speech acts which are nevertheless used to represent oneself as believing what one asserts, even if everyone involved knows or thinks it likely that one does not believe it.[17] Clause (iii) also enables a satisfying pragmatic account of why, typically, lies do involve the intent to deceive: most scenarios in which one wants to misrepresent oneself are also occasions on which one does so for deceitful purposes. On those occasions, (i)–(iii) obtain because one endeavors to deceive someone into thinking that one believes p, and typically as a means to getting them to believe that p.[18] But because what is *typical* of lying may not be required for its definition, I suspect that a definition of lying need not include a clause concerning the intent to

---

[14] See Grice (1989c: 34, 53–4).

[15] See Stokke (2013a) and Chapter 10 by Andreas Stokke for helpful discussion.

[16] See Sorensen (2007, 2010; cf. also Staffel 2011). The above account will count such lies as knowledge-lies when they are uttered with the intent of preventing the addressee from knowing that what is asserted is untrue, but without the intent of deceiving them into believing it (see Sorensen 2010: 610).

[17] An example of a bald-faced lie: a student who is caught red-handed cheating on an exam nevertheless denies it to the headmaster in his office, because denying it results in a punishment that the student deems a preferable to what he would receive if he confessed to the cheating (for similar examples, see Carson 2006: 290 and Lackey 2013).

[18] One might think that one can lie while satisfying LIE's (i) and (ii) by asserting p whilst only intending to represent oneself as being in a good epistemic position with respect to p (that is, regardless of whether one believes p). I do not think that is a lie, but I do find something objectionable about it: I shall describe what is objectionable about it in section 9.4, under the notions of *negligent* and *vicious* assertion.

deceive. So I will proceed as if LIE is plausible enough to begin with as a general characterization of lying.[19]

Recall that KNA forbids the combination that one asserts a proposition but one does not know that proposition. That is, KNA is logically equivalent to: *One must not: (assert that p & not know that p)*. If KNA is the norm of assertion, then we can plausibly derive a secondary norm of assertion on which one *should* assert only if one reasonably takes oneself to know. This follows from a quite general schema connecting norms of a certain structure to the conditions under which one should do what the norm permits. The schema reads:

(1) If one must (φ only if C), then one should (φ only if one has evidence that C),

where the "transition from 'must' to 'should' represents the transition from what a rule forbids to what it provides a reason not to do" (Williamson 2000: 245). If we suppose (as seems plausible) that evidence is what makes belief reasonable,[20] and if we prefer talk of reasonable belief over merely one's having evidence, we may substitute these in thus:

(1*) If one must (φ only if C), then one should (φ only if one reasonably believes that C)

Substituting 'assert p' for 'φ' and 'one knows p' for 'C' yields the proposed derivation from KNA, which we may call KNA*:

(KNA*) If one must (assert p only if one knows p), then one should (assert p only if one reasonably believes that one knows p)

Given KNA, one may apply *modus ponens* to KNA* to derive the following norm (call it KNA**): one should assert a proposition only if one reasonably believes that one knows it.

Note that KNA**, derived in this way from KNA and KNA*, might seem to impose an extremely strong standard on what it takes to be in position to assert reasonably.[21]

---

[19] Fallis (2010a: 13 n. 43; 2013b) seems to agree, commenting on Davidson (1985).

[20] Epistemologists think of evidence in a variety of ways (some think of it as consisting of beliefs, or experiences, or propositions, or some collection of these; Williamson thinks of it as knowledge (Williamson 2000: ch. 11). But epistemologists tend to agree that however it is understood, evidence is the kind of thing (perhaps not the only thing) which somehow supports hypotheses (typically, by making them more probable). So they tend to agree that a belief that p is reasonable if p is supported by one's evidence.

[21] Though it is one which Williamson (2000: 256) seems to accept; how strong it actually is will depend on how hard it is to reasonably believe that one knows when one in fact knows; for example, it might be that knowledge that one knows is not that uncommon. Nevertheless, violating KNA** is presumably less important than violating KNA itself: one might develop virtuous cognitive habits such that one tends to assert only what one knows, even though one rarely forms a belief about whether one knows.

But KNA** is much stronger than what we need to generate a useful derivative norm. For given KNA, one who endorses it (tacitly or explicitly) will tend to accept the following:

(G) One must: refrain from asserting if one believes or accepts that one does not know that *p*.

Assuming normal cognitive agents who tend to believe or accept what their evidence suggests, (G) will serve as a guidance norm for one who aims to conform to KNA, because following (G) will make one less likely to violate KNA.[22] Agents who accept KNA will violate (G) on pain of either incoherence or *akrasia*: it would be incoherent if they accept KNA, prohibiting assertion of what one does not know, but also accept (against G) that they may on this occasion assert that which they believe they do not know; whereas it would be *akratic* if they accept KNA but owing to weakness of will, do anyway what they know that (G) forbids. Either way, they would be choosing to assert a proposition which they believe or accept to be in violation of a norm which they endorse.

9.4 LYING AND VICIOUS ASSERTION

One may distinguish evaluative dimensions of responsibility built up from any norm with a certain structure. Consider any moral, prudential (etc.) norm enjoining one to undertake an action φ only in circumstances C. If one endorses that norm on φ-ing, then one may be said to φ *reasonably* when one believes one is in C; one may be said to φ *negligently* when one does not even consider whether one is in C; and one may be said to φ *viciously* when one believes that one is *not* in C. For example, if a moral norm enjoins one to act only if one causes no one harm, then: one reasonably acts when one believes that by so acting one will cause no harm; one negligently acts when one acts without consideration of whether one's action will cause harm; and one acts viciously when one acts while believing that one's action will cause harm. Or for a legal example, suppose there is a legal rule enjoining one to send someone to prison only if they are guilty of breaking a law. A sentencer would thus act reasonably by sending someone to prison whom she believes to be guilty; she would act negligently by sending someone to prison when she does not consider whether or not they are guilty; and she would act viciously by sending someone to prison whom she believes is not guilty.

Given (G), and again on the simplifying assumption that a speaker grasps and endorses KNA, we can also distinguish between evaluative dimensions of responsibility

---

[22] I am also assuming that for such normal cognitive agents, their practice of believing what their evidence suggests makes the propositions believed objectively more likely to be true. For strange agents who (perhaps for some domain) constantly believe falsehoods more often than they believe truth, (G) will not help them much.

in the domain of assertion. These layers of responsibility turn on one's reflective stance toward one's epistemic position concerning the asserted proposition p:

(E1) One *reasonably* asserts that p when one believes that one knows p (that is, when one believes one conforms to KNA).

(E2) One *negligently* asserts that p when one does not consider whether one knows p.

(E3) One *viciously* asserts that p when one believes that one does not know p.[23]

These evaluative terms (*negligent, vicious*) aim to label the distinctively epistemic responsibility at play in assertion. For example, (E2) aptly captures something akin to Frankfurt's (2005) notion of bullshitting, that is, asserting without regard to whether one's claims are true.[24] Likewise, the viciousness of (E3) is primarily epistemic; so-called 'prosocial' lies, though undertaken with high moral or social aims, nevertheless exhibit epistemic vice.

According to (E1), one can reasonably assert even if one violates KNA (and thereby asserts improperly): by asserting when one believes that one knows, one is in some sense less subject to blame if one violates KNA, for one does something right by virtue of trying to conform to KNA.[25] According to (E2), one negligently asserts when one fails to evaluate one's epistemic position with respect to p but goes ahead and asserts p anyway; even if one in fact fulfills KNA, one has done something a bit irresponsible. Finally, given (E3), one viciously asserts when one also believes that one asserts in violation of KNA. In the case of vicious assertion where one asserts that p in order to express what one thinks that one does not know, because one knows that one believes the opposite, we plausibly have a lie. That is, where a speaker asserts that p in order to assert what she herself realizes that she does not believe (because she knows she instead believes that not-p)—and where she does not flag by any other means (such as by winking to her interlocutor) that something special is going on—she lies. Lying is then a special case of vicious assertion.[26]

---

[23] These distinctions owe much to Unger (1975: 260–2) and Williamson (2000: 245 and 255–6). Some, particularly those who think that KNA is too strong, will likely regard (E3), for example, as much too strong. Note however that (E3) fits well with our intuitive reaction to the knowledge version of Moore's paradox, namely assertions of the schema "p but I don't know that p." And (E2) fits well with our reaction to an assertion of "p but I haven't considered whether I know that p."

[24] For more, see Chapter 20 by Andreas Stokke.

[25] Compare Williamson's (2000: 256) distinction between reasonably asserting and permissibly asserting, and also DeRose's (2009: 93–5) distinction between "primary propriety" and "secondary propriety."

[26] Unger (1975: 260–2) gestures at such an idea, utilizing the asserting-represents-knowing thesis. Marsili (2014) claims that *graded-belief* lies, wherein one asserts that p but only believes that p is probably false, intuitively also count as lies. On the accounts developed here (LIE and LIE-K), they are not full lies, but they are still special cases of vicious assertion: one asserts the negation of what one thinks is probable, in order to assert what one realizes one does not (outright) believe.

9.5 KNOWLEDGE AND LYING

We have considered a subject who lies by asserting p while knowing that she believes that not-p. Because she knows that she does not believe p,[27] she thus knows that she does not know p. By asserting p, she misrepresents herself as believing p when she does not; and (E3) classified this as a vicious assertion, which our gloss LIE above counts as a lie.

LIE can seem plausible as a general characterization of lying, in part because its third clause invokes the intent to misrepresent oneself even though that intent may not extend to deceiving others. But perhaps the Twain-inspired knowledge slogan—that lying is telling someone something you know is not so—should be revisited, for it makes possible an attractive account of lying which parallels the knowledge norm of assertion:

(LIE-K) A lies to B if and only if:
   (i) A asserts that p to B,
   (ii) A knows that p is false (and does not believe, under the same guise, that p is true[28]), and
   (iii) A intends by so asserting to represent herself as knowing, or at least believing, that p is true.[29]

Like LIE from section 9.3, this knowledge account of lying counts bald-faced lies and 'knowledge-lies' as lies. LIE-K also makes good on the idea from section 9.4, that lying is a special case of vicious assertion. In fact, it makes characterizing that special case even easier: one viciously asserts p when one asserts it to express p when one also believes that one does not know that p. But when one knows that p is false it will typically be quite easy to form the belief that one does not know that p. So the special case of viciously asserting occurs when one believes that one does not know what one asserts because one knows its negation. Lying is thus the anti-paradigm of conforming to the norm of assertion: asserting what you know follows KNA; intentionally asserting the negation of what you know is lying.[30]

This mirroring relationship between lying and the KNA upholds the intuitive idea that lying involves violating a conversational norm (Fallis 2012: 577). It also suggests an elegant account of why it would be that lying is possible for assertion but not for

---

[27] We are assuming that she realizes that she does not believe both that p and that not-p.
[28] For reasons delineated in §3 above, discussing LIE.
[29] Turri (2016) considers a similar 'known-false' gloss on lying, but his does not include a third clause. Recall however that the third clause might be dropped on a thicker conception of what assertion is.
[30] Notice also that endorsing the derived KNA** from section 9.3 itself would provide a strong norm against lying in the sense given by LIE-K: for conforming to KNA** will ensure that one does not meet the conditions of LIE-K.

conversational implicatures or other non-explicit messaging, which themselves often depend on assertion.[31] If lying is conceptually related to the knowledge norm of assertion in the way envisioned above, it explains why one cannot lie that p by conversationally implicating that p: because conversationally implicating that p does not represent one as knowing that p, one does not undertake the same epistemic responsibility by conversationally implicating that p as when one asserts that p with full force. This is partly because conversational implicature and other implicit messages make possible denying what was conveyed, something which is not available with outright assertions. Claiming "I never said that p" when one has merely conversationally implicated that p can typically get one off the epistemic hook for having conveyed that p; but clearly, when what one said was that p, one cannot (truthfully!) deny that one said it.

LIE-K has the virtue of being more simple by dint of needing no intent to deceive clause, a clause invoked by many traditional accounts of lying (compare the third clause of the TRAD schema with which this chapter began). And when combined with KNA, it enables an account of why typical lies are misleading as well as epistemically problematic, even without an intent to deceive clause. Typical lies are misleading because, given KNA, they represent their speakers as knowing, and so believing, something which their speakers know to be false. And they are epistemically problematic because they frustrate hearers' cognitive efforts at gaining knowledge from others by way of testimony: indeed, when lies are taken up by hearers as the truth, they generate false beliefs which their hearers take on trust from their interlocutors to be knowledge. When testimonial uptake leads one to think that one knows something which is in fact false, and which one took on trust from someone else who was in fact the opposite of trustworthy, it is not just that one's epistemic position is compromised; the social goodwill we have toward others, especially those with whom we have ongoing relationships, is strained.

Notice that preface paradox scenarios can generate a case judged to be a lie by a belief account, but which is not judged a lie by the LIE-K account.[32] Think of a writer who has painstakingly researched and written a non-fiction book, in which she makes numerous claims. She accepts each claim as true, though she recognizes that given the book's length and her own fallibility, at least one of her claims is likely to be false; and in the preface she admits as much. She thus has asserted (by writing the whole book) a large series of claims, but has also claimed that (at least) one of them is false (cf. Makinson 1965). Similarly, suppose S believes each of a large set of propositions $p, q, r, \ldots n$, but which is a set such that S does not believe their conjunction. That is, S believes each of these propositions individually, but does not believe or assent to their conjunction: for S knows that one of the set's conjuncts is likely to be false, though S knows not which. For these reasons, S believes that the conjunction (call it 'CON') is false. And we shall stipulate that one of the conjuncts in that set is in fact false. If S asserts the conjunction CON

---

[31] See Fricker (2012) and Hawthorne (2012) for discussion. Adler (1997) argues that false conversational implicatures are not lies. Meibauer (2014a: 113 ff.) demurs, though he also allows that false implicatures could be called deceptive rather than lies (2014a: 135).

[32] Thanks to John Hawthorne for suggesting this case.

('*p* and *q* and *r* and ... *n*') to someone, S is asserting a proposition which S does not believe (though S believes each of its conjuncts); indeed, S believes that CON is false.

Let us suppose that the intuitive response to such a case is that S's conjunctive assertion of CON is not a lie. On many belief accounts of lying, such as LIE from section 9.3, the assertion of the conjunction CON will presumably, but counterintuitively, count as a lie. This is because S believes that CON is false. Even traditional schemas for defining lying, such as TRAD, will either have to deem it (counterintuitively) as a lie, or will have to explain the case as one in which S does not, by asserting the conjunction, intend to deceive the hearer into believing the conjunction. Yet the latter option seems a tall order, for asserting the conjunction looks like an act which is undertaken to put forth that conjunction to the hearer, even though the speaker believes that conjunction to be false.

LIE-K appears to have an advantage here: for LIE-K does not even count the assertion of CON as a lie. This is because S believes, but does not know, that CON is false. Now, S's asserting CON would count as a vicious assertion, because S regards herself as believing that she does not know CON. But it does not meet LIE-K, nor is S's asserting CON one of our special (lying) cases of vicious assertion. This is because S's assertion of CON is not undertaken in order to express what S knows that she does not believe (S would know this by knowing that she instead believes that CON is false). Rather, S undertook asserting CON merely by, and for the purpose of, asserting individually the conjuncts of CON, each of which S believes.

9.6 Objections

LIE-K will be opposed by those who insist that one can lie while (mistakenly) telling the truth.[33] These traditionalists always invoke belief rather than knowledge in the second clause of such accounts because they have the strong intuition that it is still a lie when one wrongly believes a falsehood, and tells someone its negation: if I really believe that the grocer is closed today, and I tell you it is open because I want to frustrate you by sending you to a closed shop (and you go and find it open and happily get on with your shopping), these traditionalists maintain that I have still told a lie. Some recent empirical studies suggest, however, that this intuition is wrong: results from Turri and Turri (2015) suggest that in fact, most people require falsity for a telling to be a lie.

Such findings are not the last word; indeed, the case developed for LIE-K above proceeded on independent grounds. But consistent with such findings, the proponent of LIE-K can claim that in the above case, when I told you the grocer was open, I merely tried (and failed) to tell a lie. To know whether you have lied, the LIE-K proponent will suggest, we must look not only at the speaker's inner mental life, but also at the way the world is.

---

[33] Contrast Carson (2006), who is rather exceptional in arguing that lies must have false subjects.

The LIE-K proponent can thus be concessive here to the traditionalist who prefers an account along the lines of (TRAD) or our (LIE) above: what traditionalists get right is that the attempted liar has done something wrong (and it might be that the traditionalist is conflating the judgment that the attempted liar has done something wrong with the judgment that she has lied). In particular, the attempted liar has engaged in vicious assertion, for he tells someone something which he himself believes he does not know, because he knows that he does not believe it (instead, the would-be liar believes its negation). That would be a vicious speech act the likes of which, when one chooses to engage in it, involves choosing to misrepresent one's own state of mind to someone else.[34] But it need not follow from this that the attempted liar has in fact lied.

Given the LIE-K account, is it possible to lie to someone even when one is not engaged in vicious assertion? If our claim above is correct, that lying is a special case of vicious assertion, then no, it would not seem possible. Suppose that Bill and Ashley are talking about France, where Bill would like to visit. And suppose that (i) Ashley asserts that *Lyon is the capital of France* to Bill, (ii) Ashley knows that this is false (and does not believe that it is true), and (iii) Ashley intends by so asserting to represent herself as knowing that it is true. For it to be plausible that Ashley is not engaging in vicious assertion, it would have to be the case that Ashley does not believe that she knows *Lyon is the capital of France* to be false. Now, it might be possible for Ashley to assert this to Bill without even forming a belief about what she knows concerning France's capital. She might be asserting this to Bill simply because it was the first proposition about France which, though false, popped into her head, and Ashley was just not reflective enough to assess her epistemic position with respect to *Lyon is the capital of France*. In our taxonomy of evaluative dimensions (E1)–(E3), Ashley here is asserting negligently (E2) rather than viciously. Note however that (E1)–(E3) are only sufficient conditions for reasonable, negligent, and vicious assertion, respectively; as such, some negligence might itself be vicious, particularly if one is intentionally acting recklessly. If one interprets the evaluative notions in this way, Ashley's lie might be merely negligent given (E2), but viciously so; and so the lie is still a case of vicious assertion, even though it may not be vicious in the sense given by (E3).

But even if we regard Ashley's assertion as negligent without being vicious, it is hard to see how Ashley could be unreflective about her epistemic position toward this proposition yet also (iii) intend by her assertion to represent herself as knowing that *Lyon is the capital of France*. For by intending through that assertion to represent herself as knowing this, it looks as if she at least has a cognitive perspective on it, which would involve enough reflection to see that she does not know it, and in fact knows its negation. More generally, I suspect that it will be hard to find cases in which a speaker does intend

---

[34] Notice that Lackey's (2007, 2013) (see also Chapter 18 by Jennifer Lackey) cases of "self-less assertions" are classified here as vicious assertions which are not in fact lies (on LIE-K) if they are true. I find this result satisfying, for selfless assertions are intuitively not epistemically appropriate assertions, even if they are in some respects admirable; for criticism of relying on such cases, see especially Turri (2015).

to represent herself as knowing something when she knows its negation, yet does not actually believe that she knows its negation. One reason why it will be hard to find such cases is that coming to form an intention to represent one's epistemic state as being a certain way plausibly engages one's reflective capacities on whether one's epistemic state is that way. This is plausible because cases of lying involve doing the opposite of what we normally do. Most of us assert knowledgeably, and thus truthfully, most of the time, and even when we do not, our default aim is truth rather than falsehood. Cases in which we opt against this habit and tell falsehoods require us to note mentally that we are telling someone something against what we believe, and such mental judgments will involve reflection on both what we think is true and why not to tell someone the truth.[35]

9.7 Conclusion

In this chapter, I have considered the relationship which belief and knowledge have to our understanding of lying. That relationship turns on the epistemic norm of assertion, and in particular, on the way in which belief and knowledge are required for proper assertion. Most of the results considered may be applied whatever is the correct epistemic norm of assertion, though the knowledge norm, KNA, has been widely defended. As such, I have used KNA to provide the background for articulating the normative epistemic dimensions to which we hold one another responsible in conversation. Epistemically reasonable, epistemically negligent, and epistemically vicious assertion provide a taxonomy for understanding the epistemic and social aspects of the wrongness of lying, as well as the wrongs of other speech which are not lying, but which are nonetheless misleadingly deceptive. The norms which may be derived from KNA offer a new perspective on how to understand lying: lying is knowingly doing, because one knows the opposite, that which the norm of assertion forbids. By intending one's assertion to represent one as knowing, or at least believing, the opposite of what one knows to be true, one lies. Lying is the inverse of an assertion which is beyond epistemic reproach; lying is as bad as knowingly asserting is good.

Acknowledgements

Thanks to Max Baker-Hytch, Rachel Fraser, John Hawthorne, Jörg Meibauer, John Turri, and Andreas Stokke for discussion and helpful comments. I am also grateful to two anonymous referees for useful feedback. This chapter was made possible through the support of a grant from the John Templeton Foundation. The opinions expressed in this publication are those of the author and do not necessarily reflect the views of the John Templeton Foundation.

---

[35] Lying engages more areas of the brain, including areas involved with suppressing the truth, and with anxiety. See Langleben, Schroeder, et al. (2002) and Langleben, Loughead, et al. (2005).

CHAPTER 10

LYING, SINCERITY, AND QUALITY

ANDREAS STOKKE

10.1 The Gricean category of Quality

PAUL Grice established an understanding of conversations as guided by a presumption of cooperation. Grice suggested that this kind of activity is governed by his Cooperative Principle and the maxims of conversation, which were to be thought of, roughly, as principles that rational creatures would (or should) follow given a mutual recognition of one or more purposes or directions for the talk exchange.[1]

Grice's Cooperative Principle is stated as follows:

> **Cooperative Principle**
> Make your contribution such as is required, at the stage at which it occurs, by the accepted purpose or direction of the talk exchange in which you are engaged.
>
> (Grice 1989c: 26)

In turn, the maxims were divided into four categories, Quantity, Quality, Relation, and Manner. Among these the category of Quality included a supermaxim and two specific maxims:

> **Supermaxim of Quality**: Try to make your contribution one that is true.
> **First maxim of Quality**: Do not say what you believe to be false.
> **Second maxim of Quality**: Do not say that for which you lack adequate evidence.
>
> (Grice 1989: 27)

---

[1] See in particular Grice (1989c: 26–9).

Lies are paradigmatic cases in which Quality maxims are violated. Most theorists of lying agree that when you lie you say something you believe to be false. Hence, a lie is a violation of, at least, the first maxim of Quality. But moreover, it is sometimes suggested (cf. e.g., Wilson 1995: 200; Wilson and Sperber 2002: 586; Fallis 2009: 33–4, 2012: 577; Dynel 2011a: 151) that lying—whether as a general phenomenon or at least with respect to a particular range of cases—can be understood in terms of violations of one or more of the Quality maxims.

This chapter first considers attempts to characterize lying in terms of the first maxim of Quality (sections 10.2–10.3). It then turns to attempts to characterize lying in terms of the supermaxim of Quality (sections 10.4–10.5). Finally, the common view that lies are insincere assertions is considered in relation to the Gricean view that the maxims of Quality have a special status in relation to the other maxims and the Cooperative Principle (sections 10.6–10.7). (The chapter does not consider lying in relation to the second maxim of Quality. For some relevant discussion, see Chapter 20 by Andreas Stokke.)

10.2 Covert and overt violations

Given that lying involves saying something one believes to be false, lies are violations of the first maxim of Quality. But moreover, a great many ordinary examples of lies are cases in which a speaker violates the first maxim of Quality *covertly*. Arguably, the most common type of lying is that in which the liar says something she believes to be false while hoping that the hearer will not detect that she is doing so. In particular, the typical purpose of lies is to deceive in the sense of making the hearer acquire a false belief. The success of this ordinarily depends on the hearer's being unaware that the speaker is relating disbelieved information.

Grice himself observed that covert violations of maxims often have deceptive effects. In distinguishing different ways in which a speaker can fail to fulfill the maxims, Grice wrote,

> He may quietly and unostentatiously *violate* a maxim; if so, in some cases he will be liable to mislead.
>
> (Grice 1989c: 30)

Hence, it is not unnatural to think that lying, in general, might be characterized in terms of such covert violations. For example, Deirdre Wilson and Dan Sperber (2002), who call the first maxim of Quality the *maxim of truthfulness*, suggest that

> Lies are examples of *covert violation*, where the hearer is meant to assume that the maxim of truthfulness is still in force and that the speaker believes what she has said.
>
> (Wilson and Sperber 2002: 586)

As we have said, many ordinary lies conform to this pattern. You tell me you have an important meeting across town and ask me when the bus leaves. Contriving to make you late for the meeting, I tell you that it leaves at 1 p.m., even though I know it leaves at 12.45 p.m. For my ruse to work, it is essential that you do not detect that I am saying something I believe to be false.

In this case, as in most other cases of deceptive lying, the liar not only tries to make her victim think she herself believes what she is saying, she also tries to make the victim believe what is said.[2] The point of my lying to you about when the bus leaves is for you to come to believe the falsehood I tell you. So, looking at such familiar examples of lying, one might think that to lie is to say something with the aim of getting one's listener to believe it, while one is covertly violating the first maxim of Quality, that is, one is hoping that the listener will think one is obeying the first maxim of Quality. One way to spell out this idea is as follows:

Lying as covertly violating the first maxim of Quality
A lies to B if and only if

(LC1) A says that p to B, and

(LC2) A believes that not-p, and

(LC3) By saying that p to B, A intends that B come to believe that p, and

(LC4) By saying that p to B, A intends that B come to believe that A believes that p.

This account of lying is a version of the traditional view that lying is a species of deception.[3] That is, when you lie, you intend to deceive your listener into believing something you believe to be false.

However, many theorists of lying reject the idea that lying necessarily involves intention to deceive.[4] That is, even if you do not aim at deceiving your listener, you might still be lying. One central type of counterexample to the traditional view involves so-called *bald-faced lies*. To a first approximation, a bald-faced lie is a consciously undisguised lie, i.e., a lie that is told despite the recognition that the relevant participants realize that it is a lie.

---

[2] There are also deceptive lies that have only the goal of making the hearer believe that the speaker believes what is said, without aiming to make the hearer believe what is said. Fallis (2010a: 9) gives the following example: "A crime boss, Tony, discovers that one of his henchmen, Sal, has become an FBI informant. But Tony does not want Sal to find out that his treachery has been uncovered. So, to keep his disloyal henchman at ease, Tony says with pride to Sal one day, 'I have a really good organization here. There are no rats in my organization.'" See also Chisholm and Feehan (1977: 153).

[3] See, e.g., Augustine (1952b); Isenberg (1964); Chisholm and Feehan (1977); Bok (1999); Kupfer (1982); Davidson (1985); Simpson (1992); Adler (1997); Williams (2002); Frankfurt (2005); Faulkner (2007); Dynel (2011a).

[4] E.g., Carson (2006); Sorensen (2007); Fallis (2009); Saul (2012a); Stokke (2013a). See also Chapter 19 by Jörg Meibauer.

Here is (a version of) an example that Thomas Carson gives:[5]

The Cheating Student

A student accused of cheating on an exam is called to the Dean's office. The student knows that the Dean knows that she did in fact cheat. But as it is also well known that the Dean will not punish someone unless they explicitly admit their guilt, the student says,

(1) I didn't cheat.

Many writers on lying think that, although the student says something she believes to be false, she does not intend to deceive the Dean.[6] More particularly, the student does not satisfy either (LC3) or (LC4). The student does not intend that the Dean come to believe that she did not cheat, nor does she intend that the Dean come to believe that she herself believes that. Even so, the student is lying. Hence, this is a bald-faced lie.

As this suggests, even though the bald-faced liar says something she believes to be false, bald-faced lies are not *covert* violations of the first maxim of Quality. That is, they are not cases in which the speaker violates the first maxim of Quality while "the hearer is meant to assume that the maxim of truthfulness is still in force and that the speaker believes what she has said" (Wilson and Sperber 2002: 586). In other words, if one thinks that bald-faced lies are genuine lies, then one cannot think that to lie, in general, is to covertly violate the first maxim of Quality.

Some writers on lying argue that bald-faced lies are not lies. For example, Meibauer (2014b) argues that bald-faced lies are not lies because the bald-faced liar

> does not really present p as true in the context since he *lets shine through* that p is false. He would not feel committed to the truth of p, and he would not be ready to provide further evidence.
>
> (Meibauer 2014b: 140)

However, this arguably runs contrary to the way most theorists and non-theorists will be inclined to think of the case of the cheating student.[7]

---

[5] See Carson (2006: 290, 2010: 21).
[6] Lackey (2013) disagrees. For a reply, see Fallis (2014).
[7] Meibauer (2014b) discusses a different example concerning a husband who denies being unfaithful even though both he and his wife know that he is being unfaithful, and both know that they know this. There may be cases in which the notion of letting one's untruthfulness "shine through" is applicable, and this may be one of them. (Indeed, it seems undeniable that something like this sometimes happens, whether in cases of bald-faced lying or not.) However, insofar as the suggestion is supposed to be illuminating of bald-faced lying in general, it should equally apply to the case of the cheating student.

First, there is no reason to think that the student "lets shine through" that her statement is false. Of course, the student knows that the Dean knows that what she is saying is false. But she is not indicating this in any way. For example, if one says something one believes to be false while winking at the speaker, this is naturally understood to be a way of "letting it shine through" that what one says is false, and many would take this kind of case as one in which no assertion has been made. But nothing of the sort is going on in Carson's example. There are undoubtedly also more subtle ways of "letting it shine through" that what one says is false. Yet there is no reason to think that something like this characterizes bald-faced lying in general.

Second, the student is clearly committed to her statement. There is no way for the student to defend herself later by claiming not to have been in earnest, or the like, as you can do if you are winking or making a joke.

Third, the student might not be ready to provide further evidence, simply because there is no further evidence, but that does not show that she is not committed to the statement. Indeed, if the student *could* produce evidence that would make it doubtful that she cheated, she would.

If one accepts that bald-faced lies are genuine lies, an alternative suggestion is to characterize lying simply in terms of violations of the first maxim of Quality, covert or overt. In a much discussed paper, Don Fallis (2009) suggested a definition of this kind:[8]

Lying as violating the first maxim of Quality

A lies to *B* if and only if

(LV1) *A* states that *p* to *B*, and

(LV2) *A* believes that the first maxim of Quality is in effect, and

(LV3) *A* believes that not-*p*.

According to this definition, lying is not a matter of covertly violating the first maxim of Quality. Rather, on this view, a lie is simply a statement that violates the first maxim of Quality, whether covertly or overtly. Bald-faced lies satisfy these conditions, i.e., they are statements of disbelieved information made while the speaker believes that the first maxim of Quality is in effect.

However, as we will see next, there are familiar ways of violating the first maxim of Quality without lying. In particular, standard cases of *irony* are counterexamples to (LV1)–(LV3).[9]

---

[8] In another paper Fallis (2010b) discusses various proposals on how to define the specific case of deceptive lying, i.e., the type of lying that bald-faced lying is not an instance of.

[9] Cf. Stokke (2013a). For similar arguments, see Pruss (2012) and Faulkner (2013). Among floutings of the first maxim of Quality, Grice (1989c: 34) included metaphor, meiosis, and hyperbole. If one thinks that, in these cases, the speaker says something false, they align with cases of irony in that they are not cases of lying. For discussion, see Saul (2012a). See also Chapter 28 by Claudia Claridge.

10.3 IRONY AND FLOUTING MAXIMS

Everyday examples of irony are cases in which someone says something while intending to convey the opposite. For example, suppose you ask me whether I enjoy talking to your friend, Allan, who I think is boring and uninteresting. I respond by (2).

(2) [Ironically] Yeah right, I really enjoy talking to Allan!

This is a straightforward example of the kind of irony in which what the speaker means is the negation of what is said. What I want to convey by uttering (2) is that I do not enjoy talking to Allan.

Although I did not lie, I said something I believe to be false, namely that I enjoy talking to Allan.[10] Fallis acknowledges that an ironic speaker of this kind "is certainly *saying* something that he believes to be false" (Fallis 2009: 53). In other words, (LV1) and (LV3) are both satisfied in this case. If (LV2) is also satisfied in cases of irony, then such cases are counterexamples to the suggestion that to lie is to violate the first maxim of Quality.

It is sometimes suggested that the first maxim of Quality is not in effect in these cases. For example, Wilson and Sperber (2002) write that

> Metaphor, irony and other tropes ... are *overt violations (floutings)* of the maxim of truthfulness, in which the hearer is meant to assume that the maxim of truthfulness is no longer operative, but that the supermaxim of Quality remains in force, so that some true proposition is still conveyed.
>
> (Wilson and Sperber 2002: 586)

Similarly, Fallis argues that the first maxim of Quality "is not in effect" in these cases and that "by flouting this norm of conversation, [the ironic speaker] turns it off" (Fallis, 2009, 53).

But although understanding irony as involving *flouting* the first maxim of Quality is in line with the Gricean analysis of this kind of speech act, the claim that when a speaker flouts a maxim, she does not believe it is in effect is in direct opposition to it.

According to the orthodox, Gricean conception, irony is an example of (particularized) conversational implicature (Grice 1989c: 34). That is, it is a speech act in which the speaker flouts a maxim of conversation, in this case the first maxim of Quality, in

---

[10] Grice himself held a particular, strong conception of the notion of *saying* something. According to this notion, that S said that p entails that S meant that p, and that S meant that p entails that S intended her audience to believe that p as a result of their recognizing this intention (see Neale 1992: 523). This chapter uses *say*, and cognates, in the less strict sense according to which one may say something without intending to communicate it.

order to trigger the kind of reasoning on the part of the audiences that Grice held was the source of such implicatures. Familiarly, the Gricean view is that an implicature of this kind arises when it is required in order to square the fact that the speaker said what she did with the presumption that she is observing the maxims and the Cooperative Principle.

For this reason, to flout a maxim, in the sense that is intended to trigger implicature, is to "blatantly fail to fulfill it" (Grice 1989c: 30). For Grice, "when a conversational implicature is generated in this way, ... a maxim is being *exploited*" (ibid.). That is, the speaker violates a maxim in a way that is obvious to everyone involved in order to get them thinking about what her intentions could be in doing so.

One cannot flout a rule (or a maxim), in this sense, if one does not believe that it is in effect. Suppose that it is a rule in our town that you cannot cross at a red light, except on Sundays where doing so is allowed because there is little or no traffic on those days. On days other than Sunday, I can flout this rule. That is, I can violate it in a way that calls attention to itself, and will most likely get people thinking about what my intentions could be in doing so. But I cannot do so on Sundays. Even if I cross at a red light in a way that calls attention to itself on a Sunday, I do not thereby flout the rule against crossing at a red light. No one will attempt to interpret my actions by trying to square my behavior with a presumption that I am obeying the rule against crossing at a red light. The reason is clear—the rule is not in effect on Sundays.

In order to flout a rule, I must assume the rule is in effect. And moreover, when flouting a rule, I do not intend for my audience to think the rule is "no longer in force" (Wilson and Sperber 2002: 586). Rather, my purpose is to trade on the fact that the rule is operative, and believed to be operative by everyone involved, so that my overtly violating it will trigger the intended inference.

Similarly, when someone is being ironic, on the Gricean view, their strategy is to violate the first maxim of Quality in a conspicuous way. This strategy depends on the belief that the first maxim of Quality is in effect. Consequently, when someone is being ironic in this way, they satisfy (LV2), in addition to (LV1) and (LV3). For example, when I utter (2) I am assuming that the first maxim of Quality is in effect. This is the reason I think I can succeed in communicating that I do not enjoy talking to Allan by saying that I do, given that it is obvious that I believe the former, and not the latter. However, given this, ironic utterances are incorrectly classified as lying, according to (LV1)–(LV3).

As we have seen, there are two ways of characterizing lying in terms of violations of the first maxim of Quality. According to one proposal, lies are covert violations of the first maxim of Quality. This position is committed to denying that bald-faced lies are genuine lies. If one wants to avoid that commitment, another proposal is that lies are violations (covert or overt) of the first maxim of Quality. However, this position is committed to the implausible claim that classic cases of ironic utterances are lies.

10.4 False Implicature

Lying is distinguished from irony in that, while both are instances of saying something believed to be false, the liar hopes to get this disbelieved information across to the listener, while the ironic speaker hopes to get across the opposite of what she says. Another way of putting this is to note that, while both liars and ironic speakers violate the first maxim of Quality, only the liar also violates the supermaxim of Quality. It is not unreasonable, therefore, to think that lying can be characterized in terms of violations of the supermaxim of Quality.

One proposal along these lines is that to lie is to contribute something one believes to be false. Assuming that this kind of view could be worked out satisfactorily, it would meet the challenge posed above. It would predict that ironic utterances, such as my utterance of (2), are not lies. Even though I said something I believe to be false, I did not violate the supermaxim of Quality because what I wanted to contribute to the conversation was something I believed to be true.

Given the Gricean understanding of irony as an instance of conversational implicature, these are cases in which what is implicated is something believed to be true. However, we also sometimes implicate things we believe to be false. In particular, saying something one believes to be true in order to implicate something one believes to be false is a familiar type of dissimulation. The suggestion that to lie is to violate the supermaxim of Quality amounts to the claim that cases of false implicature are cases of lying.

Such a view has been endorsed by a few writers on lying (e.g. Meibauer 2005; Dynel 2011a). Yet this view is rejected by the majority of theorists, and is arguably also counterintuitive.[11] Fallis writes,

> you are not lying if you make a statement that you believe to be true. In fact, you are not lying even if you intend to deceive someone by making this statement.
>
> (Fallis 2009: 38)

Similarly, Bernard Williams (2002) gives the following example:[12]

> "Someone has been opening your mail," she helpfully says, and you, trusting her, take it that it was not the speaker herself. If you discover that it was the speaker, you will

---

[11] See also Chapter 14 by Jörg Meibauer.

[12] Despite what might be inferred from this passage, Williams does not endorse the view that you lie only if you say something false, but rather agrees with the majority view that you lie only if you say something you believe to be false. See Williams (2002: 96).

> have to agree (if through clenched teeth) that what she said was true. So, you must also agree, she did not tell you a lie.
>
> (Williams 2002: 96)

The claim that saying something one believes to be true in order to implicate something one believes to be false is a way of lying thus rejects one of the most fundamental distinctions we make about verbal insincerity. This is the distinction between lying per se and other forms of linguistic deception and misleading.

Most of us are sensitive to this distinction in everyday matters. But the difference between lying and other forms of deception is also central to many systems of law and to a number of religious traditions. The enormous amount of attention paid to the difference between lying and misleading while not lying in everyday affairs, in legal practices (see, e.g., Solan and Tiersma 2005), and in religious contexts such as that of the medieval casuists (see, e.g., Williams 2002) will be seen as fundamentally misplaced by a view that insists on conflating lying and false implicature.

Moreover, even philosophers (e.g., Adler 1997; Williams 2002; Saul 2012a) who think that, in certain circumstances, lying and falsely implicating may be equally morally problematic, still take great care to distinguish the two phenomena. Jonathan Adler (1997) discusses the following biblical example:

> Abraham, venturing into a dangerous land and fearing for his life if Sarah is taken as his wife, tells Abimelech the king that she is his sister. God appears to Abimelech to warn him away from taking Sarah because "She is a married woman." Frightened, Abimelech confronts Abraham, who defends his obvious deception by denying that he lied:
> ... they will kill me for the sake of my wife. She is in fact my sister, she is my father's daughter though not by the same mother; and she became my wife...
>
> (Adler 1997: 435)

Most commentators, going back at least as far as Augustine (1952a), have defended Abraham as not having lied, although he was guilty of deception. Augustine wrote of Abraham,

> Thus, he concealed something of the truth, but did not say anything false in concealing the fact that she was his wife and in saying that she was his sister.
>
> (Augustine 1952a: 152)

The method of deception Abraham uses is that of implicating something he believes to be false. Suppose that Abraham's original utterance was:

(3) She is my sister.

The most obvious, Gricean way to explain this case is as exploiting Grice's (1989c: 26) first maxim of Quantity:

> **First maxim of Quantity**: Make your contribution as informative as is required (for the current purpose of the exchange).

The king will take Abraham as having implicated that Sarah is not his wife because that assumption is needed to make his uttering (3) consistent with the presumption that he is obeying the first maxim of Quantity.

But if to lie is to violate the supermaxim of Quality, Abraham counts as having lied, contrary to the judgments of most who have thought about this case. Abraham makes a statement that he believes to be true, namely that Sarah is his sister, while intending to deceive the king by implicating that she is not wife. But intuitively, he is not lying. While all lies violate the supermaxim of Quality, not all such violations are lies.

10.5 SAYING AND COMMUNICATING

In order to do justice to the difference between lying and other forms of linguistic insincerity, an account of lying must specify that lying involves saying disbelieved information, as opposed to contributing it in some other way, e.g., by conversational implicature. Responding to the kind of criticism rehearsed in section 10.3, Fallis (2012) has suggested an account of lying according to which

> you lie if and only if you intend to communicate something false by saying that thing.
> (Fallis 2012: 577)

Fallis argues that this proposal

> preserves the intuition that lying has to do with the violation of a norm of conversation. According to this definition, you lie if you intend to do something that would violate the norm against communicating something false if that norm were in effect.
> (Fallis 2012: 577)

As discussed earlier, given that bald-faced lies are lies, lying does not necessarily involve an aim of getting one's listener to believe what one says. Fallis therefore proposes to interpret "communicating something false" along the lines of contributing something false to the conversation. This account of lying, therefore, can be seen as a version of the claim that to lie is to violate the supermaxim of Quality. But moreover, it specifies that, in lying, the violation is perpetrated by saying something one believes to be false, as opposed to implicating it, or conveying it some other way.

My ironic utterance of (2) is a case of saying something I believe to be false. But I am not intending to violate the supermaxim of Quality, since what I say is not what I intend to contribute to the conversation. Rather, what I intend to contribute to the conversation is the opposite of what I say, i.e., something I believe to be true. So I am not lying, according to this proposal.

More generally, according to this account, anytime I say something I believe to be false, and thereby intend to contribute that thing to the conversation, I am lying. Correspondingly, even if I intend to contribute something I believe to be false to the conversation, as long as I do not say anything I believe to be false, I am not lying. This proposal therefore avoids counting ironic utterances and false implicatures as lies, while allowing that bald-faced lies are lies.

10.6 Sincerity and assertion

We have seen that while all lies are violations of the first maxim of Quality, the phenomenon of lying, in general, cannot be adequately understood in terms of violations of the first maxim of Quality, whether covert or overt. Moreover, we have seen that, while all lies are violations of the supermaxim of Quality, the phenomenon of lying, in general, cannot be adequately understood in terms of violations of the supermaxim of Quality.

Rather, as the proposal in Fallis (2012) indicates, to characterize satisfactorily what it is to lie, an account must focus on (i) what is said, (ii) what is believed, and (iii) what is communicated, or contributed to the conversation. Saying something and thereby proposing to contribute it to the conversation is a hallmark of *assertion*. Many writers on lying accordingly subscribe to the generic view that to lie is to assert something one believes to be false (e.g., Chisholm and Feehan 1977; Adler 1997; Williams 2002; Carson 2006, 2010; Sorensen 2007; Mahon 2008a; Fallis 2009, 2012; Saul 2012a; Stokke 2013a, 2014). On these views, lies are insincere assertions.

This approach assumes that lies, including bald-faced lies, are genuine assertions. That is, it is assumed that the fact that you believe that p is false does not make your saying that p fall short of being an assertion that p, provided that the further conditions on assertion are satisfied. This idea is rooted in classic speech-act theory. In John L. Austin's "doctrine of the Infelicities" (Austin 1962a: 14), insincere assertions were classified as *abuses*, that is, cases in which one performs a speech act while failing to have certain requisite thoughts or feelings. Crucially, for Austin, abuses of this kind were to be distinguishes from *misfires*, the latter being cases in which the act one purports to perform does not occur at all.[13] And similarly, according to John Searle's (1969) influential treatment, the sincerity condition on asserting that p is that the speaker believe that p, yet failing this condition does not prevent one's utterance from being an assertion.[14]

[13] See in particular Austin (1962a: 18).
[14] See in particular Searle (1969: 65).

But while traditional speech-act theory considers insincere assertions as genuine assertions, it is less clear that it is open to the Gricean to accept that an act of saying disbelieved information can be a genuine contribution to a conversation.

10.7 QUALITY AND INSINCERE ASSERTION

Fallis (2012) takes his Gricean account, according to which to lie is to violate the supermaxim of Quality by saying something one believes to be false, as an instance of the generic view that to lie is to assert disbelieved information. Hence, he takes contributing disbelieved information by saying it as instances of insincere assertion. This view suggests, then, that to assert sincerely is to obey both the first maxim of Quality and the supermaxim of Quality, that is, to contribute something one believes to be true by saying it. Conversely, violating either maxim (or both) would constitute insincere assertion.

On such a view, however, insincere assertion would cover both lies and cases of falsely implicating while not lying. Yet it is open to this kind of theorist to specify that lies are cases in which the assertion itself is insincere, that is, cases in which both the first maxim of Quality and the supermaxim of Quality are violated, whereas falsely implicating are cases of insincere assertion only in the sense that the supermaxim of Quality is violated, while the first maxim of Quality is observed.

However, the general proposal to characterize insincere assertion in terms of Quality maxims faces a more fundamental challenge. According to Gricean orthodoxy, the Quality maxims enjoy a special status in relation to the other maxims and the Cooperative Principle. First, in "Logic and Conversation", immediately after presenting his maxims, Grice comments,

> [G1] it might be felt that the importance of at least the first maxim of Quality is such that it should not be included in a scheme of the kind I am constructing; other maxims come into operation only on the assumption that this maxim of Quality is satisfied.
>
> (Grice 1989c: 27)

Second, in the "Retrospective Epilogue" to *Studies in the Way of Words*, Grice wrote,

> [G2] The maxim of Quality, enjoining the provision of contributions which are genuine rather than spurious (truthful rather than mendacious), does not seem to be just one among a number of recipes for producing contributions; it seems rather to spell out the difference between something's being and (strictly speaking) failing to be, any kind of contribution at all.
>
> (Grice 1989c: 371)

The first of these claims, G1, states that unless the speaker is obeying the first maxim of Quality, the other maxims do not apply. The second, G2, states that unless the speaker is obeying 'the maxim of Quality', by which Grice means the supermaxim of Quality, she is not making a contribution to the conversation at all. So, taken literally, since lies are violations of both the first maxim of Quality and the supermaxim of Quality, G1 and G2 together imply that the other maxims do not apply to lies and that lies are not contributions at all.

The first of these consequences is threatened by the fact that lies can trigger conversational implicatures, just like other assertions.[15] Consider, for example, the following dialogue.

Thelma has been drinking, but Louise is unaware of this.

(4) Louise. Are you OK to drive?
     Thelma. I haven't been drinking.

In this case Louise will take Thelma as having implicated that she is OK to drive. In turn, this implicature will be explained by appealing to the maxim of Relation, "Be Relevant" (Grice 1989c: 27). In other words, even though Thelma violates both the first maxim of Quality and the supermaxim of Quality, the maxim of Relation still applies to her utterance. In turn, given the Gricean account of the reasoning involved in figuring out implicatures, the Cooperative Principle is likewise in operation for Thelma's utterance.

The second consequence from above, i.e., that lies are not genuine contributions, likewise appears doubtful. First, the fact that the other maxims apply to lies is evidence that lies are contributions to the conversation on a par with truthful utterances. Second, as noted, many agree that lies are assertions, and at least one reason for this is that the liar is attempting to communicate what she says.

So, a quick conclusion is that the behavior of lies with respect to implicature generation shows that Grice was wrong about the special status of Quality. Yet this conclusion is arguably too quick. Matthew Benton (2016) has argued that Grice's remarks concerning the special status of Quality should be understood in a way that emphasizes the audience's presumptions about the speaker. In general, the Gricean explanation of communication, and in particular of implicature-generation, relies not on observations concerning when the maxims are *in fact* obeyed, but on those concerning when the speaker is presumed to be obeying the principles. Implicatures arise from the audience's attempt to make sense of what the speaker said given the presumption that she is obeying the Cooperative Principle and the maxims.

Along these lines, one way of understanding G1 is as follows:

[G1*] Unless the audience presumes that the speaker is obeying the First Maxim of Quality, the audience does not presume that the speaker is obeying the Cooperative Principle and the other maxims.

---

[15] For similar arguments, see Thomason (1990) and Davis (1998).

This restatement of G1 does not rule out an explanation of how Thelma's lie in (4) can give rise to the implicature. Since she is unaware of Thelma's insincerity, Louise is presuming that Thelma is obeying the first maxim of Quality. So, even if the first maxim of Quality has a special status among the maxims, since it is still presumed to be obeyed, the hearer's presumption that the other maxims apply is not blocked.

We can imagine a similar restatement of G2 as follows:

[G2*] Unless the audience presumes that the speaker is obeying the supermaxim of Quality, the audience does not presume that the speaker is making a contribution to the conversation.

Again, in the case of (4), Louise is clearly presuming that Thelma is obeying the supermaxim of Quality, and hence according to this way of interpreting Grice's claim about the centrality of the supermaxim of Quality, it does not rule out that lies such as Thelma's are genuine contributions.

Louise's utterance is an example of a deceptive lie told in order to implicate further disbelieved information. However, as we have seen, lying is not necessarily deceptive. Bald-faced lies are not cases in which the audience presumes the speaker is obeying either the first maxim of Quality or the supermaxim of Quality. Rather, they are cases in which the audience knows that both maxims are violated. For example, the Dean in the case of the cheating student knows that what the student says, and wants to contribute, is false, and that the student knows it is false. The phenomenon of bald-faced lying therefore casts doubts on the Gricean conception of the centrality of Quality.

To see that bald-faced lying is evidence against G1*, notice that bald-faced lies can trigger implicatures. Consider a non-deceptive variant of the example above, as in (5).[16]

Louise knows that Thelma is drunk. Thelma realizes that she knows this, and she realizes that Louise can see that she knows that Louise knows, etc.
(5) Louise. Are you OK to drive?
    Thelma. I haven't been drinking.

In this case Louise will understand Thelma's reply as providing an affirmative answer to the question. That is, she will take Thelma as having implicated that she is OK to drive. To be sure, Louise will not *believe* this implicature, anymore than she will believe what was said. But the fact that the reply is understood as conveying that Thelma is OK to drive shows that Thelma's utterance is interpreted according to the maxim of Relation. Yet Louise is not presuming that Thelma is obeying either the first maxim of Quality or the supermaxim of Quality. That bald-faced lies can trigger conversational implicatures, therefore, is evidence against G1*.

---

[16] Adapted from Bach and Harnish (1979: 58).

Further, G2* predicts that audiences of bald-faced lies do not take the bald-faced liar as making a genuine contribution to the conversation. So, both in the case of the cheating student and in the case of Thelma's bald-faced lie in (5), according to G2*, the hearer does not interpret the speaker as making a contribution to the conversation. However, as is often pointed out, bald-faced lies have all the characteristics of standard assertions, i.e., the bald-faced liar *warrants the truth* of what she says (Carson 2006; Carson 2010; Saul 2012a) and bald-faced lies are proposals for *changing the common ground* of the conversation (Stokke 2013a). For example, the student's lie about having cheated is the reason she escapes punishment, that is, the fact that she "goes on record" with this claim is the basis for the Dean's further actions.

The case of bald-faced lies shows that, contrary to the Gricean claim about the centrality of the first maxim of Quality and the supermaxim of Quality, it is not a condition on making a contribution to the conversation, and accordingly having one's utterance interpreted in accordance with the Cooperative Principle and the other maxims, that one's contribution is presumed to be a truthful one.

CHAPTER 11

LYING AND DECEPTION

ANDREW ORTONY AND SWATI GUPTA

11.1 THE GOALS OF DECEPTION

NORMALLY, when a speaker seeks to be deceptive, he or she neither wants nor expects the hearer to recognize that one or more maxims of Grice's (1975) Cooperative Principle have been violated. This means that an important difference between deceptive and other maxim-violating speech acts, such as those that arise in figurative language use, is that in deceptive speech acts (including some cases of politeness) the speaker hopes that the hearer will erroneously assume that the speaker is being conversationally cooperative.[1] In this chapter, we focus on another important feature of deceptive speech acts, namely the relation between an idealized Gricean cooperative proposition that the deceptive speaker would have expressed had he or she been complying with the Cooperative Principle, the proposition (whether true or false) that the speaker actually or implicitly asserts, and any false proposition that its assertion is intended to implicate.

There is much debate as to how exactly the concepts of lying and deception should be defined. As discussed in detail by Mahon (2015), most definitions of lying revolve around the idea that to lie is to make a believed-false statement with the intention that the addressee believe that statement to be true. Meanwhile, the standard account of verbal deception builds on the fact that "to deceive" is a success verb (Ryle 1949: 130) with its essence being only that the speaker causes someone to have a false belief. Accordingly, the main difference between the two is that in lying, the speaker makes an intentional believed-false statement, whereas in verbal deception the speaker can, intentionally or otherwise, say anything—something true or false, or in some cases even nothing—as

---

[1] Asher and Lascarides (2013) characterize Gricean cooperativity as "strong cooperativity," which they view as too constraining to explain many of the inferences that are made when the conversational goals of speakers and hearers are not aligned, as often happens in cases of verbal deception. They contrast strong cooperativity with a weaker condition that they refer to as "rhetorical cooperativity." However, for reasons of simplicity, we will continue to speak in terms of Gricean cooperativity.

long as it causes a hearer (not necessarily a specific target addressee) to have a false belief. In spite of the apparent plausibility of these definitions, philosophers ranging from Augustine to Thomas Aquinas and Kant and through to the modern day have adduced all manner of problematic examples, many purporting to show that proposed necessary conditions for lying and deception are in fact not necessary at all. Interestingly, in many cases, whether or not the alleged problems really are problems depends on whether a particular kind of deceptive speech act can properly be called a lie or deception, and this, we believe, is often as much a matter of linguistic taste as of anything else. Furthermore, the fact that successful challenges can be mounted against proposed necessary and sufficient conditions of lying and deception raises the possibility that such conditions do not exist and that different instances of these concepts are related by family resemblance rather than by strict criteria for category membership. To avoid becoming embroiled in these issues, we shall restrict our analysis to cases of verbal deception that are *intentional*, *oral*, and *interpersonal* (i.e., conversational).[2]

While traditional analyses of lying and verbal deception start by trying to clarify and define the concepts, we take as our starting point the prior question of why deceivers seek to be deceptive in the first place. To address this question, we draw upon the well-established principle in social psychology that the decisions people make are generally motivated by one of two goals—to attain a gain (referred to as *promotion focus*) or to avoid a loss (*prevention focus*). This aspect of motivation and decision-making is the purview of Regulatory Focus Theory (e.g., Higgins 1997), which along with its close relative, Prospect Theory (e.g., Kahneman and Tversky 1979), has been widely applied to explain and predict phenomena in domains as varied as economics, sports, education, and persuasion. For reasons of simplicity and to avoid confusion with the more nuanced meanings of promotion focus and prevention focus in Regulatory Focus Theory, we shall refer to these two motivational orientations as *promotion motivation* and *prevention motivation*. We believe that the distinction between them can help us better understand what goes on when people engage in verbal deception, the usual approach to which is that deceivers, because their goal is to instill a false belief in their addressees, are promotion-motivated. And to be sure, it is not difficult to find examples in which a speaker's motivation to deceive is unequivocally to attain some sort of direct gain. For example, the candidate who at his job interview volunteers that he has many contacts he would bring to the firm as new clients, when in fact he has none, is clearly promotion-motivated.

Notwithstanding the above, there is a large and important subset of lies and other verbal deceptions for which the speakers who issue them are prevention- rather than promotion-motivated—their main goal is to prevent hearers from having access to a presumed true belief rather than to instill a false belief.[3] And this claim is not mere

---

[2] In fact, we believe that much of what we say applies also to written forms of deception, including email and text message exchanges.

[3] This, as we shall see, even though they may instill a false belief in order to attain their real goal of concealing some truth. When deceivers *are* promotion-motivated—when their primary goal really is only to instill a false belief—their false claims are often rhetorical devices designed to impress, to

speculation. The results of a survey we collected from an internet sample of 101 (thirty-four females and sixty-seven males) individuals through the Mechanical Turk crowd-sourcing platform confirmed a strong prevention-motivation bias of just this kind. Respondents (whose average age was 32) were asked to recall the last time they had lied[4] and to indicate whether "your real, underlying, reason is better described [as having been] to prevent your audience from believing something you thought was true, or to get your audience to believe something you thought was false?" Seventy-four percent of respondents indicated that they had lied in order to prevent the other person from believing something they thought was true, with only twenty-six percent selecting the promotion-motivated false-belief option.[5] This unequivocal preponderance of prevention-motivated over promotion-motivated responses provides an empirical foundation for our starting point that *the underlying motive of deceivers is usually to prevent their addressees from believing some (presumed) truth rather than to get their addressees to believe something they (the deceivers) believe is false*. Stated more formally, when, in a conversational interaction, a speaker (henceforth, S) asserts some proposition, *q*, in order to deceive his or her hearer (henceforth, H), S's primary goal is usually that H should be prevented from believing that a Gricean cooperative proposition, *qc*, is true, rather than that H should believe some false proposition, *p*, which, if not the same as *q*, is likely to be suggested by *q*. So, for example, suppose a teenage boy has spent the evening at the movies, *qc*, and upon coming home is asked by his parents where he was. In response, he tells them that he had a homework assignment to finish (*q*). He says this because he believes that it will suggest that he had spent the evening doing schoolwork (*p*) and so prevent his parents from believing that he had gone to the movies, *qc*, which is the real motivation for his deceit.

Some of the examples we shall discuss are clearly cases of lying, and some less clearly so, but adjudicating such questions is not our main interest. Rather, our focus is on the basic goals and subgoals that underlie deceptive speech acts and the communicative strategies that speakers deploy in order to attain them. Given this perspective, the account in the literature that is most compatible with our own is that of Chisholm and Feehan (1977) who identified two sets of four types of deception characterized in terms of the intent of the deceiver to either *cause* (i.e., deception by commission) or *allow* (i.e., deception by omission) another person to (a) *acquire* a false belief, (b) *continue* to hold

---

persuade, or to inflame passions. Typically these arise in non-conversational contexts of the kind exemplified by political speeches, propaganda, and advertising. For example, an old advertisement for the "Belly Burner Belt" that made the blatantly false claim that it would "make you lose 60 pounds in 10 weeks" was surely not attempting to conceal a truth, except, perhaps, the truth that it was false!

[4] Most M-Turk respondents are probably not philosophers, so we did not expect them to be very sensitive to the difference between lying and other forms of verbal deception such as palter, misleading statements, and bald-faced lies. Given our purpose, we do not consider this to be problematic. In this respect, we share the "liberal" view of lying adopted by Meibauer (2014a).

[5] The effect was impressive for both females and males, but was particularly large for the (thirty-four) female as compared to the (sixty-seven) male respondents. For females the prevention-motivated advantage was 85 to 15% while for males it was 69 to 31%.

a false belief, (c) *cease* to hold a true belief, or (d) *be prevented* from acquiring a true belief. Because they represent more complex and interesting cases, we shall focus our discussion on Chisholm and Feehan's four types of deception by commission wherein S (intentionally) *contributes causally* to the desired belief state in H rather than on cases of deception by omission, in which S merely *allows* the establishment or maintenance of a false belief by, for example, failing to take an opportunity to correct a false belief.

While embracing Chisholm and Feehan's general view, we prefer to think of their *types* of deception in terms of *goals* (i.e., states that S seeks to obtain in H), because doing so enables us to see motivational aspects of deception that would otherwise go unnoticed. When we restate the four types of deception by commission as goals, we see that S can have (a) an Acquire goal: H should *acquire* a false belief; (b) a Prevent goal: H should *not acquire* a true belief; (c) a Continue goal: H should *continue* to hold a false belief; or (d) a Cease goal: H should *not continue* to hold a true belief. Analyzing lying and deception in terms of goals is by no means a new idea. Cristiano Castelfranchi and his colleagues were doing it four decades ago (e.g., Parisi and Castelfranchi 1977, 1981; Vincent and Castelfranchi 1981). However, their view was essentially a promotion-motivated view in that they thought of deceptive acts as having "the goal of getting the hearer to make a false assumption" (Vincent and Castelfranchi 1981: 753). It is true that they also recognized the importance of communicative moves designed to prevent someone from reaching a goal. For example, they viewed deception as hindering or preventing someone from reaching certain information (Vincent and Castelfranchi 1981: 752). However, while Castelfranchi and colleagues embraced, as do we, the basic distinctions proposed by Chisholm and Feehan, an elaboration of the interrelations between the different types (goals) of deception was not an issue with which they concerned themselves.

Characterizing lying and deception in terms of speaker goals moves the analysis beyond the purely communicative, speech-act, level to the deeper level of the psychological aspirations of the speaker, getting us closer to what Vincent and Castelfranchi (1981: 752 n. 14) referred to as the objective or top goal of deception, and closer to the causally important aspect of what Chisholm and Feehan (1977: 148) alluded to as some possible "further end" of a deceiver. Unfortunately, Chisholm and Feehan did not elaborate on what such an end might be, whereas for us in most cases it is the speaker's desire to prevent the hearer from believing the Gricean cooperative proposition, qc. It is this that is the real psychological driver of—the reason for—the deceptive act. Thus, whenever there is a qc (as there always is in prevention-motivated deception), S's overarching goal—S's reason for deceiving H in the first place—is to ensure that H does not end up believing qc, and this means that of the four goals, Acquire, Continue, Cease, and Prevent, *the dominant, motivating, goal is always the Prevent goal*, with the other goals being subgoals that are deployed in its service.

Before moving on, we need to briefly introduce a few observations about the notations we will be using. Much of what we have to say in the following sections will make use of a relation which, for want of a better term, we call *suggestion*. When a person entertains a proposition, as happens, for example, when a proposition is asserted, it is often the case that some other related proposition is brought to mind. Typically, this is because the one implicates the other (in the sense of Grice 1975), entails it, or presupposes it. It is this admittedly broad, vague notion that we refer to as *suggestion*. The reason for its importance is that in most cases deceivers believe (or at least, hope) that neither q, the asserted proposition, nor any proposition, p, that q might suggest, should suggest that the Gricean cooperative proposition, qc, is true.[6] Of course, it is not propositions that suggest propositions, but rather a person's asserting or entertaining a proposition, but for simplicity of exposition, we will often speak loosely of one proposition suggesting another. We represent this relation with the symbol => so that $p1$ => $p2$ should be interpreted as meaning that $p1$ is likely (or might be expected) to suggest $p2$.

The remaining aspects of the notation we use are straightforward. Because we need to contrast the beliefs of S and H with respect to the truth and falsity of various propositions, we adopt the somewhat unconventional practice of treating true and false as predicates that take a proposition as their arguments. Thus, for example, H's believing p we represent as bel(H, true(p)), and ($\neg$bel(H, true(p)) $\wedge$ $\neg$bel(H, false(p))) means that H has no prior belief pertaining to p. To indicate that p is not likely to suggest qc, it is usually sufficient to use $\neg(p$ => true(qc)) which, of course, is less restrictive than both p => $\neg$true(qc) and p => false(qc).[7] Thus, S's belief that asserting q will not suggest that qc is true is represented as bel(S, $\neg$[assert(S, q) => true(qc)]).

To summarize, in prevention-motivated cases of verbal deception, having H believe p is not an end in itself, and is not the purpose of S's deceit. Rather, it is a subgoal relative to the superordinate, or motivating, goal of preventing H from believing qc. This is in contrast to promotion-motivated cases, where having H believe the false proposition, p, *is* an end in itself and *is* the purpose of the deceit. As already indicated, these cases are relatively uncommon, which is one of the reasons why we shall concentrate on prevention-motivated cases. Furthermore, because deception by commission is generally more complicated and more interesting than deception by omission, our focus will be on prevention-motivated cases of deception by commission—cases in which S contributes causally to preventing H from believing something that S thinks is true.

In essence, what we are doing is distinguishing the *why* from the *how* of verbal deception: *why* does the deceiver choose to deceive, and *how* does the deceiver do it? This maps onto a distinction between psychological goals and communicative goals. S's goal of preventing H from believing qc—the Prevent goal—is a *psychological, motivating,*

---

[6] But see the discussions of Equivocation (section 11.3.4) and Pretending to Lie (section 11.4.8).
[7] Since we cannot know, given our level of analysis, exactly how the propositions p, q, and q_c are represented by S and by H, our regimentations usually do not need to distinguish between, for example, false(p) and $\neg$true(p). However, sometimes the distinction is important. For instance, in cases of Cease the goal is precisely bel(H, $\neg$true(q_c)) as opposed, for example, to $\neg$bel(H, true(q_c)), and Contrived Distraction for Continue depends on $\neg(q$ => false(p)) while other cases of Continue depend on q => true(p). We should also note that we think that our basic ideas can be characterized without using modal operators. It is true that although we often stipulate that H has no prior belief about p, H could perfectly well believe neither p nor not-p, while still believing that p is possible. However, we think that introducing modal operators would complicate our regimentations while yielding little real gain.

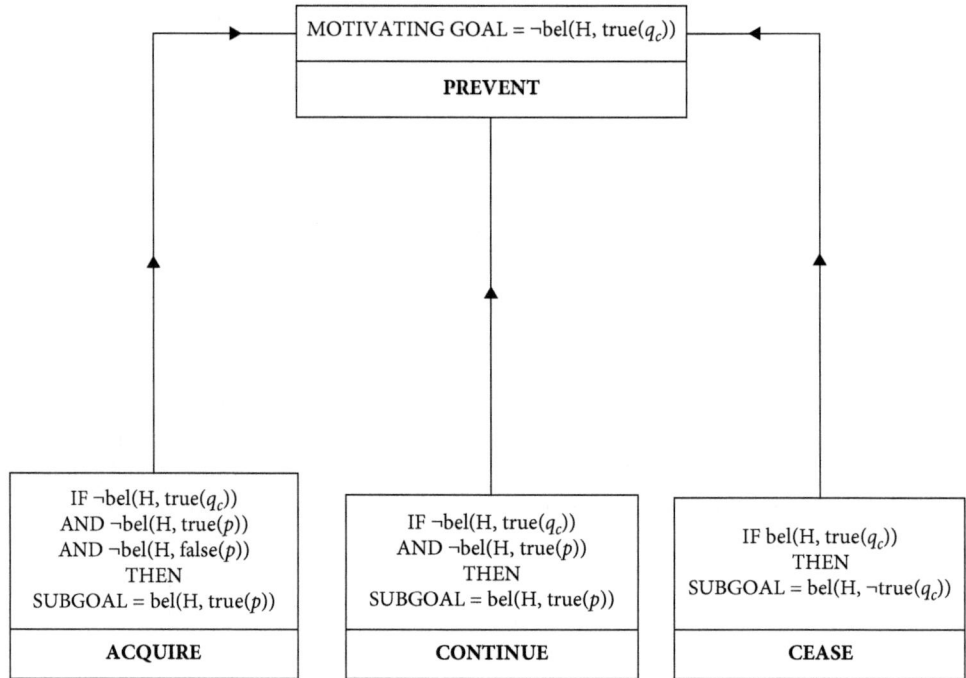

FIGURE 11.1 The relations among the goals of prevention-motivated deception (by commission) from the perspective of a speaker, S, whose motivating goal is to PREVENT the hearer, H, from believing q_c. S achieves this by means of lower-level communicative goals, CONTINUE, ACQUIRE, and CEASE, whose conditions for activation are indicated. The action (goal) side of each condition-action pair is the belief about p—the believed false proposition which S believes does not suggest q_c—that S seeks to obtain in H.

goal; it provides an answer to the question of why S is being deceitful. In contrast, the goal of ensuring that H believes the false proposition, p, by means of which S seeks to deceive H and which S believes is incompatible with qc,[8] is achieved through one or more of the *communicative* goals, Acquire, Continue, or Cease. In the context of deception by commission, these *communicative* goals—the subgoals of the Prevent goal—pertain to the question *how* S manages to deceive H, rather than to the question why.[9] Figure 11.1 shows, as condition-action pairs, the preconditions for each communicative subgoal in relation to the superordinate, motivating, Prevent, goal, all from the perspective of S. In the figure, the ACQUIRE box indicates that if (S believes that) H does not

---

[8] We are using "incompatible" in the sense that, *ceteris paribus*, the false proposition, p, is not likely to suggest the true proposition, q_c (i.e., bel(S, ¬($p => q_c$))). So, for example, claiming to have been at the library when in fact S had gone to a movie, would mean that S hoped that being at the library was not likely to suggest that S had gone to see a movie.

[9] Interestingly, in cases of deception by omission, the Prevent goal can function without a communicative subgoal, as when a question is simply ignored rather than answered, so as to avoid responding with the truth.

believe qc and has no prior belief about p, then S's action will be to cause H to come to believe p (in order to Prevent S believing qc). The CONTINUE box shows that if H does not believe qc but already believes some qc-incompatible proposition, p, then S will want H to continue to believe p. Finally, the condition-action pair shown in the CEASE box indicates that if H already believes qc, S will need to implement the Cease goal so that H comes to believe that qc is not true. All three of these (communicative) goals are shown as being subgoals of the motivating (psychological) PREVENT goal wherein H should not believe qc.

11.2 Some Strategies of Deception

While the communicative goals of Acquire, Continue, and Cease are subgoals of the superordinate, motivating goal of Prevent, as with all goal hierarchies, these communicative goals can have their own subgoals that allow them to be implemented in different ways. These different ways are the *strategies of deception* (see also, e.g., Turner, Edgley, and Olmstead 1975; Vincent and Castelfranchi 1981). We have selected eight such strategies to illustrate how different strategies can be used to attain the different goals.[10] There is nothing systematic about the way in which the strategies were chosen, and we readily admit that they might not all be distinct strategies. Indeed, strategies of deception can be grouped together (or broken apart) in different ways depending on the kind of analysis being undertaken (e.g., semantic-pragmatic, goal-based, information control, etc.). However, this does not compromise our immediate purpose of illustrating the relations between the various beliefs of S and H, and S's superordinate goal of preventing H from getting at what S considers to be the truth. The strategies that we shall use to illustrate these relations are:

- False Implicature: a conversational implicature (Grant 1958; Grice 1975) wherein what S says is true, but the implicature is false,
- Fabrication: a completely false, fabricated claim asserted by S,
- False Response: a response to a question (actual, implied, or potential) that S believes is in direct opposition to the truth,
- Half-truth: an assertion by S that masquerades as the whole truth by disclosing part of the truth but concealing another part,
- Contrived Distraction: a type of evasion wherein S finds an apparently important reason to change the subject,
- Overstatement: an exaggeration of something featured in the proposition about which S intends to deceive H,

---

[10] The ideas we are presenting here differ in important respects from our earlier proposals (Gupta, Sakamoto, and Ortony 2012) and the illustrative examples we use represent only some of the strategies discussed there.

Table 11.1 For the three communicative subgoals of prevention-motivated deception (by commission), the initial conditions for a speaker, S, and S's target belief state for a hearer, H, vis à vis an asserted proposition, q, a Gricean Cooperative proposition, qc, and (with the exception of CEASE) some qc-incompatible false proposition, p.

	Initial conditions for S	S's target belief for H
ACQUIRE	(1) bel(S, ¬bel(H, true(qc))) (2) bel(S, [¬bel(H, true(p)) ∧ ¬(bel (H, false(p))]) (3) bel(S, [assert(S, q) => true(p)] ∧ ¬[p => qc])	bel(H, true(p)) ∧ ¬(bel(H, true(qc)))
CONTINUE	(1) bel(S, ¬bel(H, true(qc))) (2) bel(S, bel(H, true(p))) (3) bel(S, [assert(S, q) => true(p)] ∧ ¬[p => qc])	bel(H, true(p)) ∧ ¬(bel(H, true(qc)))
CEASE	(1) bel(S, bel(H, true(qc))) (2) bel(S, [assert(S, q) => ¬true(qc)])	bel(H, ¬true(qc))

- Equivocation:[11] S says something ambiguous, perhaps to avoid being committed to the otherwise natural interpretation,
- Pretending to Lie: S says what S believes to be true, but hopes that H will think that it is false.

There certainly are strategies that we have not listed here. However, we are more concerned with representativeness than with completeness. Our purpose is to propose an approach to addressing the question of how people go about deceiving others, by offering a detailed discussion of the relation between the subgoals of deception and some of the strategies available to deceivers to attain them. Table 11.1 shows the regimentations for the general initial conditions for each goal together with the belief state that S seeks to obtain in H as a result of the deception. To reiterate, from the point of view of S, p is always false, while q is the proposition asserted by S in order to prevent H from believing the Gricean cooperative proposition qc.

11.3 STRATEGIES FOR ACQUIRE

The Acquire goal comes into play when S believes both that (1) H does not (already) believe qc and that (2) H has no prior belief about the believed-false proposition, p,

---

[11] Some authors (e.g., Vincent and Castelfranchi 1981) refer to this strategy as Deliberate Ambiguity.

by conveying which, S seeks to deceive H. The context is such that in order to prevent H from believing qc, S needs H to acquire p, a false proposition that is incompatible with and will not suggest qc. S communicates p to H by asserting (actually or implicitly) q, and believes that (3) (asserting) q is likely to suggest that p is true, but p does not suggest qc. Each particular strategy for Acquire has one or more conditions in addition to these three general ones, but because these general conditions apply to all cases, we will assume rather than re-specify them in our regimentations for each strategy, for which we will indicate only important additional conditions. To summarize: the conditions for all cases of Acquire are:

(1) $bel(S, \neg bel(H, true(q_c)))$
(2) $bel(S, [\neg bel(H, true(p)) \wedge \neg bel(H, false(p))])$
(3) $bel(S, [assert(S, q) => true(p)] \wedge \neg [p => q_c])$

11.3.1 False implicature for Acquire

S can cause H to acquire a false belief, p, through False Implicature alone by asserting q, which S believes to be true (see (1) below). As indicated in the general conditions for Acquire, S also believes that asserting q will suggest that p is true, and that p, which, as always, S actually believes is false, does not suggest qc. We say "False Implicature *alone*" because in False Implicature for Acquire it is the essential mechanism whereby H comes to believe p following S's assertion of q. In other strategies where it plays a role, it augments a different mechanism by providing one or more additional inferential steps. Apart from the general conditions for the Acquire goal, the only additional condition for False Implicature is

(1) $bel(S, true(q))$

Example: A gang member, H, is looking for Jones, who cheated him, so he asks a mutual acquaintance, S, where Jones is. But S is a friend of Jones, so he tells H that Jones has established a safe house in a nearby town, q, which is true. S believes that this will suggest that Jones can be found at the safe house, p, which is false, and thus prevent H from believing that Jones is actually at home, qc, which is S's underlying psychological motive for lying. Note that this does not preclude S from having superordinate motives for concealing the truth, such as a desire to protect Jones from harm. Motives and their associated goals come in hierarchies, so there could be a long chain of them, ultimately leading to a top goal such as self-preservation. What we are saying is that if we look *down* the hierarchy all the way from its ultimate reason—the *why* of deception—to the deceptive act itself, the lowest goal is a communicative goal—the *how* of deception.

11.3.2 Fabrication for Acquire

In the simplest case of the Fabrication strategy for the Acquire goal, S believes that (1) q is false and (2) that q and p are identical. Thus, substituting q for p in general condition (3) for Acquire shows that S believes that asserting q will not suggest qc. So the two additional conditions, over and above the general conditions, are:

(1) bel(S, false(q))
(2) $q = p$

Example: Using a similar scenario to that in the last example, we again have the gang member (H) looking for Jones. However, now, when H asks S where Jones is, S, wanting to conceal the fact that Jones is at home (qc), makes up the story that Jones has fled the country with his under-age girlfriend, q, which is pure fiction—false. S's intention might only be for q to be identical to p and to be incompatible with qc, but S might also imagine other ps for H—implicatures of q such as that Jones is reckless, that he is in love, and so on.

11.3.3 Overstatement for Acquire

When S uses Overstatement in order for H to acquire a false belief, S exaggerates the magnitude of some element of qc. The specific additional conditions are (1) that S believes that q is false, and (2) that q and p are identical. In addition, (3) q overstates qc, and does so to the extent that it does not suggest qc. Note that Overstatement is not the same as hyperbole because hyperbole is a figure of speech that is not intended to be taken literally, whereas in Overstatement, that the claim be taken as true is precisely the point. Not surprisingly, there is a parallel, Understatement, strategy (which we need not discuss) which differs from Overstatement only in the direction of the magnitude of misrepresentation. White lies—often well-intended politeness devices—tend to exploit these modulation strategies. In Overstatement, the additional conditions are:

(1) bel(S, false(q))
(2) $q = p$
(3) overstate(q, q_c)

Example: S is invited to a dinner party by his boss, H, who prides herself on her cooking. However, on eating the food, S, while not disliking it, thinks it quite unremarkable (qc). Needing to conceal this from H, S tells her that he very much likes it (q), believing that overstating his liking for the food will prevent S from recognizing his rather limited enthusiasm.

11.3.4 Equivocation for Acquire

When Equivocation is used as a strategy for getting H to Acquire a false belief, S formulates q, which S believes is true (1), in such a way that (2) q suggests both p, which is false, *and qc*. S also hopes that (3) asserting q will suggest to H either that p is true (which S would prefer H to believe) or that qc is true, but not both. The equivocation strategy is a counterexample to the general principle that S always wants to avoid saying anything that might suggest qc. Presumably, one purpose of Equivocation is plausible (?) deniability, in that it enables S, if necessary, to deny being deceptive by claiming that qc was not concealed. One might suppose that equivocation is a rather weak deceptive strategy. It has three additional conditions, although in this particular case, condition (3) is instead of, rather than in addition to the general condition (3) for Acquire as specified in section 11.3.1.

(1)   bel(S, true(q))
(2)   bel(S, [q => true(p)] ∧ [q => true(qc)])!
(3)   bel(S, [assert(S, q) => (true(p) ∨ true(qc))])

Example: A standard example is that of a request for a recommendation. H is a prospective employer who asks S, the current employer, to provide an evaluation of job candidate, Mr. Brown. S responds with the intentionally ambiguous assertion, q, "I can't recommend Mr. Brown highly enough," which either implicates qc, that Mr. Brown is so bad that S's recommendation could not be good enough to justify H's hiring him, or it implicates p, that Mr. Brown is so good that S's highest recommendation would fail to adequately reflect Mr. Brown's excellence. Let us assume that without explicitly disparaging Mr. Brown, S wants to prevent H from believing that she thinks Mr. Brown is a good candidate (qc). If S should subsequently feel the need to defend herself against the accusation that she gave a bad recommendation she could, technically speaking—although one might think somewhat implausibly—appeal to the positive interpretation that she thinks so highly of Mr. Brown that she had been unable to find a sufficiently strong way to intimate it.

The remaining four strategies, False Response, Half-truth, Contrived Distraction, and Pretending to Lie cannot be used to attain the Acquire goal, False Response because it violates the requirement that H has no initial belief pertaining to p, and the others because for them there is not, or need not be, a false belief to be acquired.

11.4 Strategies for Continue

As illustrated in Figure 11.1, the Continue goal is implemented when S believes that (1) H does not believe qc, but (2) already believes that p is true. Furthermore, (3) S believes that (asserting) q is likely to suggest that p is true, but that p does not suggest qc. Thus, S wants to prevent H from believing qc by having H continue to believe p because S believes that believing p is incompatible with believing qc. So, while each of the strategies for Continue has its own individual additional conditions, all strategies for Continue share the three general conditions:

(1) bel(S, ¬bel(H, true(qc)))
(2) bel(S, bel(H, true(p)))
(3) bel(S, [assert(S, q) => true(p)] ∧ ¬[p => qc])

11.4.1 False Implicature for Continue

In the case of False Implicature for Continue there is only one additional condition which is the same as for False Implicature for Acquire, namely, that (1) S believes that q is true. And as with False Implicature for Acquire, it is also true that S believes that q suggests p, which condition is implicit in the general condition bel(S, [assert(S, q) => true(p)] ∧ ¬[p => qc]).

(1) bel(S, true(q))

Example: In a variation of the gang-member scenario in which S is looking for Jones, S still knows that Jones is at his home (qc) but now he knows that H already believes (erroneously) that Jones is at the safe house (p). So, when S asks H where Jones is, S again tells H about the establishment of the safe house (q), expecting that H will continue to believe that that is where Jones is, thereby preventing H from believing that Jones is at home.

11.4.2 Fabrication for Continue

The only situation in which the Fabrication strategy can be used to achieve the Continue goal is if it is used in conjunction with Acquire. We start with the given—that S knows that H already believes the false proposition, p, which is incompatible with qc. The additional conditions for Fabrication for Continue are that S believes that (1) q is false, and (2) that H has no prior belief about the truth or falsity of q. As with all cases of Continue, S believes that asserting q will not suggest that p is false, thereby encouraging the maintenance of p by H. Thus the additional conditions are:

(1) bel(S, false(q))
(2) bel(S, [¬bel(H, true(q)) ∧ ¬bel(H, false(q))])

Example: A little boy, H, believes in the existence of the tooth fairy (p). One night his parents forget to replace with the expected reward his recently fallen-out tooth left under his pillow. When, in the morning, H complains that his tooth is still under his pillow, his mother, S, wants to prevent him from realizing that there really is no tooth fairy (*qc*), and so she wants him to continue believing that there is. Accordingly, she fabricates a story that the tooth fairy was sick and so could not visit in the night (*q*). Her implicit assumption is that if H acquires *q*, then because *q* presupposes the existence of the tooth fairy (*p*), *q* will not suggest to H that there is no tooth fairy.

11.4.3 False Response for Continue

False Response is a direct, typically yes or no, response to an actual or potential question. There are two types of False Response. Suppose a father asks his young teenage daughter if she had remembered to clean up her room. So as not to reveal that she did not (*qc*), she simply responds with "Yes." This, is a false affirmation. The second type is a false denial, which would be the case had the father posed the question by asking his daughter if she had *forgotten* to clean up her room, and she had responded "No" or "No. I didn't forget." In general, the response is to a direct, albeit sometimes implicit question, with *q* being either a simple affirmation, "yes," or a denial, "no," or an explicit false affirmation or denial that recapitulates the question (albeit with ellipsis, as in "No. I didn't . . .") while negating its propositional content. Thus the essential ingredient of the False Response strategy for Continue is that H has a question whose propositional content, *p*, H already erroneously believes to be true. Because (1) S believes that *q* is false, and because (2) the propositional content of *q* is identical to that of *p* and the negation of *qc*, S responds with *q* in the belief that it will result in H's continuing to believe *p*. So, the additional conditions are:

(1) bel(S, false(*q*))
(2) *q* = *p* = ¬*qc*

Example: H has few options for, and little experience of dressing up to go out on a date. He looks in the mirror with pride, mistakenly believing that he looks well dressed and nicely groomed. Seeking confirmation, he asks his roommate, S, "Don't I look great?"— a question whose propositional content, that H looks great (*p*), H believes to be true but S believes is false. In order to Prevent H from believing that he does not look good (*qc*), S wants H to Continue to believe that he looks great, and so falsely affirms that H looks good (*p*) by saying "Yes, you do," which is an implicit assertion of *q* and a negation of *qc*.

11.4.4 Half-truth for Continue

Whenever the Half-truth strategy is employed, *qc* is the conjunction of two (possibly complex) propositions, one of which, *qd*, S is willing to disclose, and one of which, *qh*, S seeks to hide. Crucially, S hides *qh* by simply not disclosing it, a fact which raises an important issue that warrants a short digression. We have indicated that our focus is on deception by commission rather than deception by omission, yet the Half-truth strategy appears to rely on S's *inaction*, which might be viewed as deception by omission because S *allows* H to believe *p* rather than *contributing causally* to H's believing *p*. For Chisholm and Feehan, deception by commission is associated with contributing causally, whereas deception by omission is associated with allowing H to believe *p*. But this association is in large part due to the fact that they opted for a narrow construal of *contributing causally* (Chisholm and Feehan 1977: 145–6), which ends up being their most prominent criterion for the distinction between deception by omission and deception by commission. The case of Half-truth raises the possibility that their commitment to a narrow sense of *contributing causally* is too restrictive because if S *intentionally* allows H to, for example, continue to believe *p*, then S's decision is an act—albeit a mental act—that S commits, and one that indisputably makes a causal contribution to (in this case, the perpetuation of) H's erroneous belief. Thus, we maintain that intentionally, as opposed to inadvertently, allowing H to harbor a false belief can in fact reasonably be viewed as deception by commission.[12]

Returning now to the question of how the Half-truth strategy enables S to attain the Continue goal, recall that (1) *qc* is the conjunction of *qd* and *qh*, and that (2) S believes that the disclosure of *qh* would lead H to doubt the truth of *p*, suggesting *qc* instead, while (3) disclosing *qd* will not have that effect. Because S is willing to disclose only *qd*, S assigns *qd* to *q* (4), which means that (5) S believes that *q* is true. So, the additional conditions are:

(1) $qc = qd \land qh$
(2) $bel(S, ([qh => false(p)] \land [qh => true(qc)]))$
(3) $bel(S, (\neg[qd => false(p)] \land \neg[qd => true(qc)]))$
(4) $q = qd$
(5) $bel(S, true(q))$

Example: Comfortable in the mistaken belief that their cheerful, teenage son, S, is an innocent and trustworthy paragon of virtue (*p*), S's parents leave him alone when they go away for a weekend. They could never have imagined that S would spend the Saturday evening with a friend watching movies and snorting cocaine (*qc*). Upon their return, his mother, H, asks S what he did on the Saturday night, and S replies that he watched movies *(qd)*, thereby allowing H to continue believing in the truth of *p* and preventing her access to *qh* and therefore to *qc*.

11.4.5 Contrived Distraction for Continue

Contrived Distraction is a form of evasion wherein S suddenly finds an apparently important reason to change the subject so as to avoid dealing with *qc*. In the case of

---

[12] This issue would seem to boil down to the question of whether the commission–omission distinction should be cast in terms of *contributing causally* versus *allowing*, or in terms of action versus inaction, and if the latter, whether actions should be restricted to physical acts (including saying and asserting) or whether they extend to mental acts, such as intending and deciding.

Contrived Distraction for Continue, the result of the distraction is simply that the false proposition, p, that H already believes, remains intact. The key feature of what S says, q, is not its truth value but its irrelevance to the context—its violation of the maxim of Relation. Particularly in Contrived Distraction, q need not be an assertion, it can be any speech act designed to intimate that something needs immediate and urgent attention with the result that S prevents H access to qc. However, the urgency needs to be contrived, not genuine, for otherwise the distraction would not be a deception. So, the propositional content of q can be true or false (1). It only needs to cause H to attend to something other than qc which then, by default, remains intact because (2) q does not suggest that p is false. Notice that this is a slight variation on general condition (3) for Continue (see also note 8). The structure of Contrived Distraction for Continue is as follows (where for simplicity, we assume that S asserts q, even though, as just discussed, speech acts other than assertion can achieve the same goal):

(1) $\text{true}(q) \underline{\vee} \text{false}(q)$
(2) $\text{bel}(S, \neg(q) => \text{false}(p))$

Example: We can use a slightly modified version of the tooth-fairy example that we used to illustrate Continue through Fabrication. In this variant, when H complains that his tooth is still under his pillow, his mother, still wanting to prevent him from realizing that there really is no tooth fairy (qc), changes the subject by suddenly complaining of an excruciating pain, q, which in fact she does not have, or by issuing an indirect request such as "I think the toast is burning in the kitchen," when the intention is not to solve the alleged toast problem but to change the subject. Thus, by distracting him, she causes her son to continue believing that the tooth fairy exists (p) so as to prevent him believing that it does not (q_c).

11.4.6 Overstatement for Continue

When S uses Overstatement to achieve the Continue goal, since H already holds the erroneous belief, p, S needs only to reiterate p. The specific conditions are the same as for Overstatement for Acquire, namely (1) that S believes that q is false, (2) that q and p are identical, and (3) that q overstates qc:

(1) $\text{bel}(S, \text{false}(q))$
(2) $q = p$
(3) $\text{overstate}(q, qc)$

Example: Modifying the example of Overstatement for Acquire, recall that S, while not disliking his hostess's food, thinks that it is merely average (qc), but he needs to prevent her from knowing this. If Overstatement is to result in H's continuing to believe p, S must believe that H already has an exaggerated estimation of S's liking for her food, which means that all S need do is reassert his feigned enthusiasm by asserting that the food is very good ($q = p$).

11.4.7 Equivocation for Continue

Except for the fact that the context differs in that S believes that H already believes p, Equivocation for Continue is the same as Equivocation for Acquire.

11.4.8 Pretending to Lie for Continue

When S pretends to lie in order that H should (continue to) believe p, (1) S believes that q is true, and (2) the propositional content of q is the same as that of qc. However, S knows that because of the common ground (e.g., Clark and Brennan 1991) shared with H, H will assume that S's assertion of q is not to be taken at face value. So, (3) S asserts q while believing that it cannot be the case that if q is asserted H will believe it, giving us the three additional conditions:

(1) bel(S, true(q))
(2) $q = qc$
(3) assert(S, q) ∧ bel(S, ¬ [assert(S, q) ∧ bel(H, true(q))])

Example: S is the same teenager as in the example for Half-truth for Continue (section 11.4.4). Again, his parents believe him to be a paragon of virtue (p) and leave him alone at home for the weekend. And again, S spends his Saturday evening with a friend, watching movies and snorting cocaine (qc). This time, however, when his mother, H, asks how his weekend was, S grins and replies, apparently in jest, that he spent the evening watching movies and snorting cocaine ($q = qc$). H buys into the joke and incorrectly assumes that what S said was not really true. In this way, her erroneous belief that p is true is maintained and she is prevented from believing qc.

11.5 STRATEGIES FOR CEASE

When H already believes qc, S has to implement a Cease strategy. In the simplest cases, if H asserts qc (either explicitly or implicitly) S merely contradicts it by asserting q which is the contrary of qc, giving us the basic condition (as shown in Table 11.1), bel(S, [assert(S, q) => ¬true(qc)]). In such cases, one could argue that S succeeds in getting H to stop believing qc without the involvement of any false belief, p, except, trivially, the negation of qc. These are all false denial cases of False Response for Cease, which is discussed in section 11.5.3.

That said, in general, it is not easy to make a person stop believing a proposition that he or she believes to be true, for which reason doing so often necessitates replacing the supposedly true belief with a different belief—and when it is done deceptively, replacing it with some incompatible, believed-false proposition, p. This means that preventing H from believing qc when H already believes it typically requires S to pursue the Cease goal in conjunction with Acquire—a conjunction that we might think of as a replace subgoal whereby S Prevents H from believing qc by causing H to Replace it with a newly acquired qc-incompatible p. Thus, apart from the defining requirement that (1) S believes that H already believes qc, in most cases of Cease, the basic condition, bel(S, [assert(S, q) => ¬true(qc)]), needs to be augmented to reflect the intervention of p, indicating that (2) S believes that asserting q will suggest that p is true, which in turn suggests that qc is not true.

(1) bel(S, bel(H, true(qc)))
(2) bel(S, [assert(S, q) => true(p) => ¬true(qc)])

11.5.1 False Implicature for Cease

False Implicature for Cease can be accomplished only if pursued in conjunction with Acquire (i.e., by Replacing qc with a qc-incompatible p). As is always the case with false implicature (therefore in both Acquire and Continue), S expects p to be erroneously inferred from q, even though (1) S believes that q is true. Also, because Acquire is involved, (2) S believes that H has no prior belief about p. Thus, S believes that the assertion of q suggests that the to-be-acquired false proposition, p, is true, which in turn suggests that qc is not true:

(1) bel(S, true(q))
(2) bel(S, ¬bel(H, true(p)) ∧ ¬bel(H, false(p)))

Example: Consider yet another variation of the gang-member scenario in which S is looking for Jones. Again, S knows that Jones is at his home (qc), but he also suspects that H believes this too. When H asks where Jones is, S tells him that Jones spends a lot of time at his girlfriend's place (q), implicating p, that Jones is at his girlfriend's place. S thus hopes that H will stop believing that Jones is at home.

11.5.2 Fabrication for Cease

Because the Fabrication strategy also can only accomplish the Cease goal through the use of Acquire, it too is a case of Replace. In Fabrication for Cease, (1) S believes that q is false, and (2) q and p are identical, and (3) S believes that H has no prior belief about p. Because q (i.e., p) is incompatible with qc, S expects that if H can Acquire p then H will no longer believe that qc is true. The three additional conditions for the Fabrication strategy for Cease are the same as those for Fabrication for Acquire:

(1) bel(S, false(q))
(2) $q = p$
(3) bel(S, ¬bel(H, true(p)) ∧ ¬bel(H, false(p)))

Example: S, a professional hit man, commits a murder in Detroit. He knows that the FBI believes he's the murderer (qc). When, a few days later, he is caught and arrested for the murder, he claims that he was in Los Angeles on the day of the murder, q (= p), implicating that he's not the murderer (¬qc).

11.5.3 False Response for Cease

Whereas in False Response for Continue S wants H to Continue believing p because p is the negation of qc, in False Response for Cease the propositional content of H's implicit question is qc. Again, S's response, q (which is identical to p), is the negation of qc. The additional conditions are the same as False Response for Continue, namely:

(1) bel(S, false(q))
(2) $q = p = ¬qc$

Example: Modifying the example we used in False Response for Continue (section 11.4.3), we now suppose that H, having dressed up to go out, looks in the mirror with disappointment rather than pride; he now believes that he looks awful (qc). When H asks his roommate, S, to confirm that he does not look good, S, wanting H to Cease feeling that he looks bad, responds with the false denial that H looks great (q), which is the contrary of qc.

11.5.4 Overstatement for Cease

In using the Overstatement strategy to cause H to stop believing qc, q, which is false (1) and is identical to p (2) is an exaggeration of qc (3) to the extent that it suggests that qc itself is false. The specific conditions are the same as for Overstatement for Acquire:

(1) bel(S, false(q))
(2) $q = p$
(3) overstate(q, qc)

Example: After his teacher has said that it would be helpful if each student in the class were to have a laptop, a young boy, S, wants to persuade his mother, H, to get him one.

However, H believes that the teacher has made clear that while having a laptop would be helpful it is certainly not necessary (qc), and S knows that H believes this. In order to stop H believing it, S tells H that the teacher said that it was very important (rather than merely helpful) that he have a laptop (q).

11.5.5 Equivocation for Cease

Equivocation for Cease is similar to that for Acquire and Continue. What S says suggests both qc and not-qc, in the unrealistic hope that if H already believes qc, the not-qc interpretation will prevail. This is a generally weak deception strategy, but it is particularly weak as a strategy to achieve the Cease goal.

The other three strategies—Half-truth, Contrived Distraction, and Pretending to Lie—are not applicable to the Cease goal. We do not see Contrived Distraction as a strategy because at best, H will forget qc, but there is no reason for H to reject it as false. For the same reason, we exclude Half-truth as a strategy for changing H's belief from (presumed true) qc to (presumed false) p. Finally, Pretending to Lie is not applicable because it violates the defining condition, namely that H already believes qc.

11.6 CONCLUSION

We have proposed an approach to analyzing lying and deception that emphasizes the speaker's psychological, motivating goal, which we have argued is usually to prevent the hearer from believing something that the speaker believes to be true. We suggested that in cases of prevention-motivated deception by commission (which most of the interesting and complex cases tend to be), the establishment or maintenance of a false belief or the cessation of an existing true belief are communicative subgoals that speakers establish in the service of their psychological, motivating, goals. We think that this approach has two interesting features. First, it takes as its starting point the fact that people have a *reason* for engaging in deception, and that the installation or maintenance of a false belief (the usual focus of most accounts of lying and deception) is unlikely to be that reason. Second, treating Chisholm and Feehan's (1977) four types of deception as goals opens the way to understanding the interrelationships between them and reveals the fact that they are not all of equal status. In particular, in most cases of lying and deception the Acquire, Continue, and Cease goals are all means of (i.e., subgoals for) attaining the fourth, the Prevention goal, and the Cease goal usually has to be implemented in conjunction with the Acquire goal whereby the speaker seeks to replace an existing believed-true belief with a believed-false one.

Whereas our way of conceptualizing deception enabled us to see how the goals of deception relate to one another, our second main aim was to show how different particular strategies relate to the different goals. Through examples we demonstrated, as

Table 11.2 Three goals of prevention-motivated deception (by commission) and some strategies that can achieve them (indicated with ✓). Strategies marked * can often (and in some cases, only) achieve the associated goals when applied in conjunction with Acquire.

	Goal		
Strategy	ACQUIRE	CONTINUE	CEASE
False Implicature	✓	✓	✓*
Fabrication	✓	✓*	✓*
False Response	n.a.	✓	✓
Half-truth	n.a.	✓	n.a.
Contrived Distraction	n.a.	✓	n.a.
Overstatement	✓	✓	✓*
Equivocation	✓	✓	✓*
Pretending to Lie	n.a.	✓	n.a.

summarized in Table 11.2, that not all strategies can be applied to all goals. Our attempt to show the relationships between different strategies and goals was intended to be illustrative rather than comprehensive; there surely are other strategies that we could have considered, possibly including ones that would call into question some of our putative generalizations about the underlying conditions of different strategies vis-à-vis different goals. Nevertheless, we think that our specification of some of the doxastic conditions under which different strategies can be used to realize different communicative goals is a useful first step.

Finally, we wish to return to the question of the motivation for deception and our distinction between *communicative* goals and *psychological* motives. When the gangster uses false implicature to get his hearer to acquire a false belief about the whereabouts of his friend, Jones, he uses a *communicative* strategy for achieving the Acquire goal, while the adoption of the Acquire goal itself is as a *communicative* subgoal established in order to achieve the gangster's motivating *psychological* goal. The reason that we are so comfortable with making the Prevent goal the superordinate, motivating, goal (relative to the communicative subgoals established to attain it) is that it gets us to the bedrock of the deceptive act—to the underlying psychological motivation. It highlights the connection between *why* the speaker seeks to be deceptive and *how* the speaker accomplishes the deception. The gangster's motive for trying to prevent the hearer from knowing Jones's whereabouts has nothing to do with communication; it is a *psychological* motive having to do with the state of affairs he wants to obtain, not with how he wants to bring about that state of affairs. Presumably, he wants to protect his friend from harm, which is why he wants to conceal his whereabouts, and that is why he thinks it will be beneficial to lie. The strategies and goals that we have discussed are nothing more than means to an end—they are communicative means of attaining personal, psychological, ends, which is the only reason anybody ever communicates anything to anyone in the first place.

Acknowledgements

We are grateful to Sanford Goldberg, Mitchell Green, Daniel O'Keefe, and Jelena Radulovic for helpful comments on various aspects of earlier drafts of this chapter.

CHAPTER 12

LYING AND CERTAINTY

NERI MARSILI

12.1 Drawing Boundaries

A prominent characteristic of lies is that they come in a variety of forms and kinds, and this is part of what makes them elusive and difficult to identify. As Montaigne nicely stated, while truth is unique, "the opposite of truth has many shapes, and an indefinite field" (Montaigne 1595: 1.IX). One of the ambitions of this book is to categorize these different shapes, and to provide systematic criteria to distinguish lies from other utterances.

This can be a hard challenge, and indeed for a theory of lying "the more difficult task [is] that of drawing lines" (Bok 1999: 46). There is a whole grey area of deceptive utterances that are difficult to classify (for instance, the so-called "half-truths") and, quite importantly, it is in this grey zone that liars strive. To shed some light in this obscure area, this chapter will consider the problem of classifying statements that are not fully believed to be false, but that are nevertheless not believed to be true. Are these statements lies? And how much confidence in their falsity is required for them to count as lies? We will focus on such questions, exploring the thin, elusive line that distinguishes a sincere assertion from an insincere one.

On a standard view, an utterance is a lie only if (1) it is an *assertion* and (2) the speaker believes it to be false.[1] However, the expression "believe to be false" is not really helpful in dealing with intermediate cases, as it does not specify which degree of confidence in the falsity of *p* counts as believing it to be false. As we analyse this issue, we will see that lies are difficult to categorize because lying is often a matter of degree (Isenberg 1964: 470; Bazzanella 2009). This is not because lying is a scalar predicate (one cannot say that *p* is more of a lie than *q*), but rather because being sincere is: a speaker can be more

---

[1] Some authors require a further condition: that the speaker intends to deceive the hearer (e.g., Mannison 1969: 132; Kupfer 1982: 134; Williams 2002: 96). For the purpose of this chapter, I will assume that while prototypical lies are intended to deceive, this intention is not a necessary condition for lying.

or less sincere—so that, indirectly, a lie can be a more or less severe violation of the linguistic (and moral) norm of sincerity.

12.2 SPEAKER CERTAINTY

12.2.1 Certainty, uncertainty, and graded beliefs

In this world nothing can be said to be certain, except death and taxes.
Benjamin Franklin (1789)

What is certainty? Most authors agree that it is a kind of attitude that a subject can have towards a proposition. More specifically, certainty (or what philosophers call 'psychological' certainty[2]) can be defined as the *highest degree of confidence* that a subject can have in the truth of a proposition. Thus understood, certainty is always relative to *someone's standpoint*: it does not matter if the subject has no ground (or bad grounds) for holding that belief, because certainty requires only that *the subject* be supremely convinced of its truth.

This conception of certainty, defined as the highest degree of belief a speaker can have in a proposition, presupposes that believing comes in degrees—and that there are degrees of belief lower than certainty. That beliefs can be graded is evident if one thinks about daily situations in which a subject lacks certainty in a proposition that he nonetheless, to some extent, believes. To see this, consider some examples: suppose Groucho believes that (i) he has a pair of moustaches, (ii) Bulgaria will beat Azerbaijan in their next football match, and (iii) there is life on some other planet in the universe. Groucho regards (i) as certain, (ii) as probable, (iii) as merely more likely true than not.

Groucho neither fully believes nor fully disbelieves (ii) or (iii). These intermediate, partial beliefs (believing to be probable, believing to be unlikely, etc.) are called in the literature "graded beliefs," because they can be ordered in a graded scale:[3] Groucho is more confident in the truth of (i) than he is in (ii), and in (ii) than he is in (iii). Formal accounts of degrees of belief (typically, Bayesian accounts) represent this scale with real numbers from 0 to 1, where 0 indicates certainty in the falsity of p, 1 indicates

---

[2] Philosophers often distinguish *psychological* certainty from *epistemic* certainty (Klein 1998; Reid 2008). Epistemic certainty refers to the *degree of epistemic warrant* that a proposition has, independently of the speaker's confidence in it (*i.e.*, independently of psychological certainty). While psychological certainty is purely 'subjective' (it depends only on the subject's confidence), epistemic certainty is in a sense 'objective' (it depends on the *actual solidity* of the subject's reasons to believe in that proposition). The literature on lying is generally concerned with *psychological certainty*, since the strength of the speaker's grounds for disbelieving an assertion is irrelevant to assessing whether he is insincere or not. Consequently, in this chapter, "certainty" (and "uncertainty") will refer to *psychological* certainty (and uncertainty).

[3] For a discussion of the mutual relations between flat-out beliefs and graded beliefs, see Jackson (forthcoming).

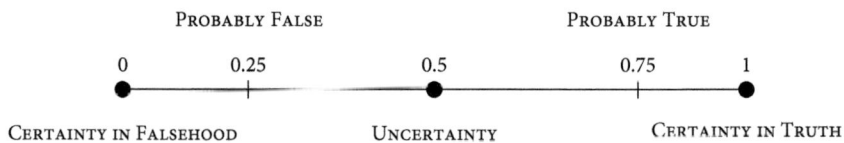

FIGURE 12.1 A visual representation of the certainty–uncertainty continuum.

certainty in the truth of *p*, and 0.5 indicates uncertainty (cases in which the subject regards *p* as just as likely to be true as to be false). On this view, uncertainty is the middle point (0.5) of a continuum of degrees of belief whose poles are certainty in falsity (0) and in truth (1) of the proposition (see Figure 12.1). To provide a formal account of the previous example, one could say that Groucho has degree of belief of 1 in (i), of 0.75 in (ii), of 0.51 in (iii).

Any account of sincerity that takes into consideration this wide array of graded beliefs will have to explain how they relate to the boundaries of the concept of lying. For instance, suppose that Groucho states that Bulgaria will beat Azerbaijan while believing that it is probably false, or as likely to be false as true. Would these utterances be sincere or insincere? And more generally, how are we to draw the boundary between sincere and insincere utterances, and (consequently) between lies and not lies?

12.2.2 Insincerity and (un)certainty

> *What constitutes the essence of lying,*
> *if not saying what you don't have in your heart?*
>
> Rosmini, Apologetica, 7–131

A necessary condition for lying is that the speaker utter an *insincere* statement. There are several ways to define insincerity. In a general sense, insincerity refers to a *discrepancy between the psychological state of the speaker* (e.g., believing, intending, desiring) *and the psychological state expressed by his linguistic action* (e.g., asserting, promising, requiring) (Falkenberg 1988: 94; Searle and Vanderveken 2005: 111). Defining 'insincerity' amounts to defining the nature of this discrepancy.

Limiting the present discussion to assertion,[4] and accepting the standard view that assertions express beliefs (Searle 1969: 65), this chapter will analyse insincerity as a discrepancy *between what is asserted* and *what is believed* by the speaker. Once graded

---

[4] Arguably, assertion is not the only speech act that can be used to lie. However, it seems that non-assertive speech acts can be used to lie only insofar as they *entail* an assertion (see Marsili 2016), so that an analysis of assertion is sufficient for our purposes. I am here referring to *illocutionary entailment* (Searle and Vanderveken 1985: 130), where F1 *illocutionary entails* F2 iff a speaker cannot perform F1 without also performing F2 (e.g., you cannot promise that you will *p* without also asserting that you will *p*).

beliefs are taken into account, the main challenge is to define how large this discrepancy has to be for a statement to count as insincere—and hence as a lie.

In the philosophical literature, this challenge is generally overlooked or ignored. It is taken as an uncontroversial claim that a statement is *sincere* when the speaker believes it to be *true*, and *insincere* when the speaker believes it to be *false*,[5] and that a more fine-grained analysis would be unnecessarily intricate (Saul 2012a: 5 n10). The standard "insincerity condition" for lying IC is generally phrased as follows:

IC = S believes *p* to be false

This condition correctly accounts for prototypical cases of lying, but is ill-suited to consider cases of uncertainty and graded beliefs. Since graded beliefs and uncertainty are ordinary psychological states, it seems that a theory of lying should account for them (D'Agostini 2012: 41; Meibauer 2014a: 223; Isenberg 1964: 468).

To see that the standard account of insincerity struggles to handle graded beliefs in a satisfactory way, consider the following example, inspired by historical events (cf. Carson 2010: 212–21): George is a political leader, and tells (1) to a journalist. Propositions (a), (b), and (c) indicate George's degree of confidence in his utterance, in three possible scenarios[6].

(1) Iraq has weapons of mass destruction
    (a)   (1/¬*p*)   [Iraq has *certainly no* weapons of mass destruction]
    (b)   (0.75/*p*)   [*Probably*, Iraq has weapons of mass destruction]
    (c)   (0.75/¬*p*) [*Probably*, Iraq *does not* have weapons of mass destruction]

Scenario (1a) is a clear-cut case of lying, since George believes (1) to be *certainly false*: the standard account correctly tracks the intuition that this is a lie. In (1b), by contrast, George believes the statement to be *probably true*: even if he is not completely confident that the statement is true, it seems that in this case he is not lying (Austin 1946: 65). The utterance is inaccurate, and perhaps misleading, because it misrepresents George's degree of belief in (1). However, being inaccurate or misleading is clearly not the same as lying (Saul 2012a; Stokke 2013b): condition IC is again on the right track, since it predicts that this utterance is not a lie.

Problems arise for scenario (1c), where George believes (1) to be *probably false*. It seems that condition IC does not count it as a lie, because George does not utterly

---

[5] A third option is that the speaker has *no opinion about p* (he *lacks a credal state about p*); I will come back on this in the next section.
[6] Assigning a defined, numeric degree of belief to these linguistic expressions (e.g., *probably, perhaps*) merely aims to indicate how these expressions can be ordered on a scale that goes from certainty to doubt (Holmes 1984; Levinson 1983: 134; Hoye 1997). Only their reciprocal relation in the scale matters to the present discussion—the accuracy of the numeric values is not important.

believe (1) to be false.[7] However, intuitively this is a case of lying, because George is saying something he believes to be very likely false. Since it excludes this sort of cases, IC is too narrow, and needs some refinement.

Cases like (1b, c) suggests that a more fine-grained account of lying is needed, one that appreciates how lying can involve graded beliefs. Such a definition of lying should offer an account of what we might call *'graded-belief lies'*: statements that are not outright believed to be false (or true), but are nonetheless lies. The next section will review a few attempts to revise the definition of lying in this direction.[8]

12.2.3 Degrees of (dis)believing

Carson (2006: 298) has offered a definition of lying that captures graded-belief lies. His proposal presents a strong and a weak version of the "insincerity condition" for lying. The first, "strong" version requires that the speaker believe his assertion to be "false or probably false." Let us call Carson's first condition the "strong insincerity condition" for lying:

SIC= S believes p to be at least *probably* false[9]

SIC correctly captures prototypical cases of lying like (1a). Unlike the traditional definition, it also includes lies that are not believed with certainty to be false, like (1c), that George believes to be *probably false*. This is an advantage of SIC over IC, since it seems intuitive that saying what you believe to be *probably* false counts as lying—even if it is arguably less insincere, and less deceptive, than a full-fledged lie.

However, it is not clear that the boundary between sincerity and insincerity lies exactly on the degree of confidence indicated by 'probably', and not on another. The term 'probably' indicates a degree of confidence in the truth (or falsity) of the proposition higher than uncertainty and lower than certainty: for the sake of the argument, let us assume it stands for a degree of belief of 0.75. If a degree of belief of 0.75 in the falsity of the proposition is enough for lying, there seems to be no reason to exclude

---

[7] To save IC against this objection, a partisan of the standard view might suggest interpreting IC in a non-literal sense, so that (2) counts as a case of believing p to be false, and hence as lying. However, this broad interpretation would open the problem of which intermediate credal states count as believing false and which do not. Since this is exactly the problem that the sincerity condition should solve, IC would still be an unattractive option for settling the issue.

[8] Further complications for a definition of insincerity, such as cases of *self-deception* (in which the speaker is mistaken about his own beliefs or mental states, cf. Moran 2005; Chan and Kakane 2011; Eriksson 2011; Stokke 2014) and *malapropism* (in which the speaker is mistaken about what he said, cf. Reimer 2004; Sorensen 2011; Saul 2012a: 15–19) will not be discussed here; for our purposes, to deal with these cases it is sufficient to require that the speaker satisfy (any version of) the insincerity conditions for lying *advertently*.

[9] I rephrased Carson's condition to avoid the counterintuitive consequence that degrees of belief included between "believing false" and "believing probably false" would not be counted as lies.

lower-graded beliefs such as 0.7, or 0.6, that are perceivably higher than uncertainty (0.5). To see this, consider the following scenarios:

(1) Iraq has weapons of mass destruction
    (c) (0.75/¬p) [*Probably* Iraq *does not* have weapons of mass destruction]
    (d) (0.6/¬p) [*Presumably* Iraq *does not* have weapons of mass destruction]

In (1d), George utters what he believes to be *more likely to be false than true*, so that it seems that he is lying. However, SIC does not capture (1d), because by hypothesis George's degree of confidence is higher than uncertainty but falls short of believing (1) to be probably false. Since it fails to account for the intuition that also (1d) is a lie (even if arguably less insincere than (1c)), SIC is too restrictive.

Carson's second, "weak" proposal avoids this problem. The "weak insincerity condition" posits that lying requires that the speaker "does not believe [the asserted proposition] to be true" (Carson 2006, cf. also Sorensen 2007: 256, 2011: 407).

WIC= S *does not* believe *p* to be true

Since it acknowledges that utterances like (1d) are lies, WIC is preferable to SIC. However, the WIC is too broad: it incorrectly captures cases in which the speaker has no idea whether what he says is true or false, but goes on saying it for some other reasons. These cases are classified in the literature as bullshit (Frankfurt 2005). The typical example of bullshitter is the politician who "never yet considered whether any proposition were true or false, but whether it were convenient for the present minute or company to affirm or deny it" (Swift 1710). Now, as long as the speaker has no opinion about the veracity of what he is saying, his utterance is better classified as a misleading utterance than as a lie (Saul 2012a: 20, Meibauer 2014a: 103, but cf. Falkenberg 1988: 93; Carson 2010: 61–2) and WIC is too broad to account for this intuition.

Given that SIC is too narrow and WIC is too broad, an ideal condition has to lie somewhere in the middle. Marsili (2014: 162) proposes a middle ground between these two proposals: his proposed view requires that the speaker believe *p more likely to be false than true*. Call this the *comparative insincerity condition*:

CIC= S believes *p* more likely to be false than true

Unlike WIC, CIC correctly rules out bullshit and statements uttered in cases of uncertainty. Unlike IC, it counts graded-belief lies as lies. And unlike SIC, it rules in the other cases in which the speaker does not believe the statement to be true—like (1c) and (1d).

A possible worry about the CIC is that it implicitly accepts that every belief can be represented as an assessment of probability and the speaker would take any such difference to be significant. To avoid this difficulty, CIC can be revised into CIC':

CIC'= S takes his degree of confidence in $\neg p$ to be stronger than his degree of confidence in p

Of course, it is possible to challenge the very assumption that there is a clear-cut boundary between insincerity and sincerity, so that we should allow for intermediate indeterminate cases (thereby treating insincerity and lying as vague predicates), see Isenberg (1964: 470). But this intuition can be accommodated by the CIC which, unlike the other accounts, allows for a progressive transition from sincerity to insincerity. At the same time, if a neat point of transition is to be individuated, the CIC is fine-grained enough to identify a boundary that meets our intuitions and avoids the counterexamples to which the alternative accounts fall victim.[10]

The proposed view correctly accounts for assertions that do not specify the speaker's degree of belief in the truth of the proposition (i.e., assertions that do not express graded beliefs): the next section will extend this view, and provide a broader framework to also treat assertions that express graded beliefs.

12.3 Insincerely expressing a graded belief

An assertion is insincere if there is a significant discrepancy between *the speaker's degree of belief* (henceforth BΨ) and *the degree of belief expressed by the sentence* (henceforth BΛ). The previous section has shown that this discrepancy can come in degrees, because of the graded nature of certainty—i.e., the graded nature of BΨ. A complete explanation of insincerity needs to account for the other side of the coin: the different degrees of belief that an assertion can express—the graded nature of BΛ.

Assertions that express graded beliefs are generally overlooked in the literature on lying. This is because, in standard cases, statements express a flat-out belief in the truth of the proposition, rather than a graded belief. For instance, (1) expresses a flat-out belief in the asserted proposition:

(1) Iraq has weapons of mass destruction

Not all statements, however, are as simple as (1), for some express graded beliefs. For instance, in (1e) the speaker believes that (1) is probably true, and in (1f) he expresses uncertainty in the truth of the proposition:

(1e)   (0.75/p)   *Probably* Iraq has weapons of mass destruction

(1f)   (0.5/p)   *Maybe* Iraq has weapons of mass destruction

---

[10] Note that this blocks counter examples based on borderline cases of uncertainty (see Krauss 2017). Krauss has proposed an alternative condition to CIC, that has been proven to be untenable by Benton (2018).

Now, the previous section has considered graded-belief lies, in which BΨ is graded. Graded assertions like (1e) and (1f), by contrast, are cases in which BΛ is graded. Three kinds of graded-belief lies are hence possible: (A) *BΨ-graded*: plain assertions like (1), uttered while holding a graded belief; (B) *BΛ-graded*: assertions expressing a graded belief, like (1e) and (1f), uttered while holding an outright belief; (C) *complex cases*, where both BΛ and BΨ are graded. In what follows, I will consider how the insincerity condition applies to cases (B) and (C), and discuss the difference between mitigating and reinforcing an assertion.

12.3.1 Two directions of belief misrepresentation

Few authors have raised the question how assertions that express graded beliefs are to be analysed within a theory of lying. Meibauer (2014a: 225) suggests that there are three kinds of BΛ-graded assertions that may qualify as lies: those "(i) expressing certainty when [you] are uncertain, those (ii) expressing uncertainty when [you] are certain, and those (iii) expressing certainty or uncertainty to a higher degree than being adequate with respect with [your] knowledge base." Since the third case seems to include the previous two, to simplify this taxonomy I will simply distinguish between two "directions" in misrepresenting your degree of belief: namely, pretending to have a *higher degree of belief* or a *lower degree of belief* than the one you have (cf. Falkenberg 1988: 93).

A first, tempting idea is to assume that these two directions are equivalent. This would mean that, from the point of view of the analysis of lying, "pretending to be more certain than you are" is *as insincere as* "pretending to be less certain than you are" (cf. Shiffrin 2014: 12 n15). A reason to make this assumption is that the "discrepancy" between your state of mind and the state of mind expressed by the statement is the same in both cases. However, at a closer look this assumption reveals it to be naïve, as the first case (overstating) is often perceived as being more insincere, or more misleading, than the second (understating). To see this, imagine two utterances:

(1g) (1/p) Certainly Iraq has weapons of mass destruction

(1h) (0.5/p) Perhaps Iraq has weapons of mass destruction

Imagine that in both cases George's mental state is in between certainty and uncertainty, so that he believes:

(0.75/p) [Probably Iraq has weapon of mass destruction]

According to the 'naïve' view, (1g) and (1h) are equally insincere, because the discrepancy between BΨ and BΛ is the same (0.25). These scenarios differ only in the direction of misrepresentation: (1g) represents the speaker as having a higher degree of belief than he has, while (1h) as having a lower degree of belief. Interestingly, however, it is natural to assess (1g) as more insincere than (1h). The reason is that we tend to judge (1h) as a prudent statement, that cooperatively avoids saying more than the speaker knows, while (1g) is perceived a misleading overstatement, that the speaker lacks sufficient knowledge to assert. In other words, *ceteris paribus*, understating your degree of belief is generally seen as a cooperative linguistic practice, while overstating it is generally regarded as uncooperative.

In line with this intuition, Falkenberg (1988: 94, 1990) proposes to distinguish between "hard lies" (overstatements, like (1g)) and "soft lies" (understatements, like (1h)). However, this taxonomy is misleading in two respects. First, not all overstatements and understatements are lies: if the CIC is a condition for lying, only statements displaying a certain level of discrepancy between BΨ and BΛ can be lies. Second, it is not clear if an *overstatement* (hard lie) is necessarily more of a lie than an *understatement* (soft lie): section 12.3.2 will show that the direction of misrepresentation is just one of the parameters of intensity that must be considered, another one being the discrepancy between BΨ and BΛ.

12.3.2 Epistemic modality markers and degrees of commitment

There is a vast literature exploring the various ways in which an assertion can be mitigated (expressing a lower degree of belief, as in (1g)) or reinforced (expressing a higher degree of belief, as in (1h)) (see Fraser 1980; Holmes 1984; Coates 1987; Bazzanella et al. 1991; Caffi 2007; Egan and Weatherson 2011). The most prominent linguistic devices used for these purposes (expressions such as 'certainly', 'probably', 'perhaps') are called *epistemic modals*. This section will explain their pragmatic function, and clarify why we generally assess *understatements* as more sincere (or more honest) than *overstatements*.

Epistemic modals both "indicate the *speaker's confidence* or lack of confidence in the truth of the proposition expressed" and "*qualify [his] commitment* to the truth of the proposition expressed in [his] utterance" (Coates 1987: 112, italic is mine). In other words, they act on two components of the assertion, altering both (1) the psychological state expressed by the speaker (the degree of belief), and (2) his degree of commitment to the truth of the proposition (the illocutionary strength[11]) (cf. Lyons 1977: 793–809; Holmes 1984: 349; Labinaz and Sbisà 2014: 52).

These two functions are distinct in nature, but are entangled: if a speaker S mitigates (or reinforces) the degree of belief conveyed by his assertion, then S automatically mitigates (or reinforces) the illocutionary force of his assertion (that is, the degree of his commitment to the truth of the proposition). For instance, if you state (2b) instead

---

[11] In speech-act theory, the illocutionary force is what characterizes the utterance of *p* as being the occurrence of a specific kind of illocutionary act (e.g., a question, an assertion, etc.). The illocutionary force of an assertion can be reinforced or mitigated (Searle and Vanderveken 1985: 99; Bazzanella, Caffi, and Sbisà 1991; Sbisà 2001), thus altering the speaker's degree of commitment to the truth of the proposition.

of plainly stating (2), you mitigate both the degree of belief expressed ((2b) expresses uncertainty in (2)) and the degree of your commitment to the truth of the asserted proposition (you are committed to the truth of (2) to a much lower degree if you utter (2b)).[12]

(2) Plato will quit smoking tomorrow
(2b) *Perhaps* Plato will quit smoking tomorrow

The role that epistemic modals play in reinforcing/weakening the illocutionary force of assertions explains why *understatements* are perceived as more honest than *overstatements*. *Ceteris paribus* (given the same degree of insincerity, as in (1g)–(1h)) a reinforced assertion has a stronger illocutionary force than a mitigated assertion, so that the speaker has a stronger commitment to its truth. And if the commitment to sincerity is stronger in reinforced statements, then violating that commitment is more serious in those statements than in mitigated ones.

Variations in illocutionary force induced by epistemic modals can also affect whether the speaker is asserting the proposition or not—and hence whether he is lying, because lying requires asserting. This is because epistemic modals can downgrade the degree of illocutionary force of a declarative sentence to such an extent that it no longer counts as an assertion, but rather as a supposition or an hypothesis (Labinaz and Sbisà 2014: 52–3). For instance, (2b) is a supposition rather than an assertion: its insincere utterance does not amount to lying, while insincerely uttering its unmitigated version (2) does. Carson (2010: 33, 38) shares this intuition: "there are weaker and stronger ways of warranting the truth of a statement. To count as a lie, a statement must be warranted to a certain minimum degree."

This is even more evident in other speech acts. For instance, if Matteo utters (3b) instead of (3), it is clear that he has not promised that he will buy you an elephant

---

[12] On this '*expressivist*' interpretation, epistemic modals are not part of the proposition asserted (at least not of the proposition against which speaker sincerity and commitment is assessed). A '*descriptivist*' might object that we should instead take them to be part of the content of the assertion (and hence of the proposition against which sincerity is measured). However, this would often yield counterintuitive predictions for the sincerity conditions of assertions. For instance, on a descriptive interpretation of "certainly p" as true iff (q): "the speaker is certain that p," a speaker that believes that there are 9/10 chances that p is true would counterintuitively be counted as insincere (as S would be certain that q is false). It should be noted that even if this section provides sincerity conditions for marked assertions interpreted in an expressivist fashion, it is not committed to expressivism: a descriptivist can still adopt the model proposed in section 1 (CIC). I follow Coates's (1987: 130) view that epistemic modals can be appropriately used and interpreted in both ways. When they are used 'literally' to assert the epistemic or psychological (un)certainty of a proposition (rather than *express* that the proposition asserted is (un)certain, the simple sincerity conditions provided by CIC will apply; in the other cases (that I take to be the prevalent uses), the expressivist explanation outlined in this section will apply instead. On the debate over the semantics of epistemic modals, cf. Kratzer (1981); DeRose (1991); Egan, Hawthorne and Weatherson (2005); Papafragou (2006); Yalcin (2007, 2011); Fintel and Gillies (2008); Swanson (2011).

(he is merely suggesting it), while he would be promising it if he uttered (3). It seems that an insincere utterance of the first amounts to lying, while this is not true for the second.[13]

(3)   Tomorrow I will buy you an elephant
(3b) *Perhaps* tomorrow I will buy you an elephant

To sum up, this section has considered how to account for assertions of type (ii), expressing graded beliefs (BΛ-graded lies), and (iii), complex cases where both BΛ and BΨ are graded. Both cases could have been dealt simply by appealing to condition CIC, but such an explanation would not have been able to account for differences determined by the direction of misrepresentation (overstatements versus understatements). This difficulty dissipates once it is understood that epistemic modals influence not only whether the sincerity condition is satisfied (by altering the degree of belief expressed), but also whether the assertion condition is satisfied (by altering the speaker's degree of commitment). This clarifies why Falkenberg's characterization of overstatements and understatements as "hard" and "soft" lies is misleading: first, assertions that represent the speaker as less certain than he is (understatements) can be "hard" (genuine) lies, if they achieve a sufficient degree of illocutionary force and insincerity; second, not all understatements and overstatements are lies, because they both may fail to achieve the sincerity and/or assertion condition for lying.

12.4 Lies that attack certainty

So far, this chapter has focused on speaker certainty. This last section will consider hearer certainty, and how lies can affect the hearer's degree of belief in the asserted proposition. The primary goal of lying is generally to attack a hearer's beliefs (or his grounds for believing): typically, to make the hearer believe that the asserted proposition is true, i.e., to *deceive* him. Traditionally, this intention to deceive was believed to be necessary for lying, but recently, on the grounds of several convincing arguments (e.g., Carson 2006; Sorensen 2007; Fallis 2010a, 2015) most authors believe that this intention is merely *frequently associated* with lying.

One prominent (but, we shall see, unsuccessful) argument against the idea that lying requires intending to deceive is the argument from *knowledge lies* (Sorensen 2010), or lies that attack certainty only. Knowledge lies aim to *prevent the hearer from being certain*

---

[13] One might wonder whether uttering (2b) or (3b) while being psychologically *certain* that the mitigated proposition is false would count as lying—i.e. whether a high degree of insincerity can compensate for a low degree of commitment. Marsili (2014: 166–8) argues against this view, claiming that these utterances are to be classified as misleading statements rather than lies.

of the truth of ¬*p* without *intending him to believe* that *p*.[14] Consider an example: Pietro has won a lottery and is ready to send his ticket to the address A1, to reclaim his prize. Luca wants to steal Pietro's ticket, so he tells him that he believes that the correct address is A2 instead. He knows that this way Pietro will have to go to an Internet café to be sure that the address is indeed A1, and plans to steal the ticket in the meanwhile. This is a knowledge lie because Luca has no intention to make Pietro believe that the address is A2 (otherwise Pietro would send it to A2, and the plan would fail): he merely aims to undermine Pietro's certainty (and knowledge) that the correct address is A1.

According to the argument from knowledge lies against the intention to deceive, (i) knowledge lies are not intended to deceive, but since (ii) knowledge lies are clearly lies, (iii) intending to deceive is not a necessary condition for lying. The problem with this argument is in premise (i), which holds only if one endorses a very narrow account of intended deception—one that includes attempts to make someone believe *p*, and excludes attempts to modify his degree of belief in *p*. However, it seems that intending to alter someone's degree of belief may count as intending to deceive him (Chisholm and Feehan 1977: 145; Fallis 2009: 45; but cf. Carson 2010: 181), and consequently that (i) is false. In fact, there is an obvious sense in which knowledge lies are intended to deceive (Fallis 2011; Staffel 2011): even if Luca does not intend to make Pietro believe that the address is A2, he aims to undermine Pietro's conviction that the address is not A2, thereby deceiving him.

The argument from knowledge lies hence fails to prove that lying does not require intending to deceive, but it should not be concluded that intending to deceive is a necessary condition for lying (other compelling counterexamples still hold), nor that knowledge lies are of no interest for theorizing about lying. On the contrary, knowledge-lies are remarkable in several respects. They effectively illustrate that manipulating the hearer can be more important than convincing him of the truth of the utterance, and that altering his degree of belief can be a powerful way to manipulate his behaviour: the lower somebody's confidence in a belief, the lower their disposition to act on its basis.

Knowledge lies help us to understand the essence of calumny, a common kind of political knowledge lie. Calumnies are lies that aim to undermine someone's reputation. Often, calumnies work like knowledge lies: this happens when they are merely aimed at calling someone's reputation into question, without aiming to convince anybody that the propositional content of the calumny is true. Here is an example from Italian politics: during the 2011 Milan mayoral elections, Letizia Moratti claimed that her opponent Giuliano Pisapia was sentenced for stealing a van used to kidnap and beat a young man. Pisapia had indeed been accused of the crime in 1985, but he was also acquitted of all

---

[14] Sorensen's original definition is slightly broader: it captures any believed-false statement that aims "to prevent the addressee from *knowing* that p is untrue" without intending him to believe that *p*, including statements that attack the hearer's ground for believing (i.e., epistemic certainty). However, since virtually every attack on epistemic certainty via lies is ultimately meant to attack psychological certainty (cf. Fallis 2011: 360–4), I will again restrict the discussion to lies that attack psychological certainty.

charges. This calumny can be read as a knowledge lie because it arguably did not aim to convince the electorate that Pisapia had committed the crime (a very difficult aim to achieve, given that all media quickly rectified Moratti's statement), but rather to publicly bring into question that Pisapia does not have a criminal record, thus undermining the electorate's certainty that Pisapia had never committed a crime.[15]

Finally, lies that alter hearer certainty are interesting as they represent a further parameter influencing the "intensity" of lies, that can be added to the ones considered in the previous sections: the higher the expected epistemic damage, the more reprehensible the lie.

This concludes the analysis of the concept of lying with respect to degrees of certainty, which has identified three dimensions of certainty that are relevant to lying: the speaker's degree of certainty, the degree of certainty expressed by the assertion, and the degree to which the speaker aims to modify hearer's certainty. Only the last two are relevant in defining lying, but all affect the relative 'strength' of the lie. Lying can thus be considered a scalar phenomenon (a phenomenon that comes in degrees), with three dimensions of gradability that are relevant to its evaluation from linguistic, epistemic, and ethical points of view.

---

[15] Cf. Poggi et al. (2011). Pisapia eventually won the elections.

CHAPTER 13

LYING AND OMISSIONS

DON FALLIS

13.1 INTRODUCTION

WORK in the philosophy of deception tends to focus on outright lying. According to the standard analysis, you *lie* if and only if you *say* something that you believe to be false with the intent to deceive your audience (see Mahon 2008a: §1).[1] For instance, the shepherd boy famously cried, "a wolf is chasing my sheep!" in order to trick the villagers and get them to come running. However, there are many other ways to intentionally cause people to have false beliefs. This chapter focuses on deceiving people by *not saying* things. It looks at what *deceptive omissions* are, why they are important, how they work, and how bad they are.

13.2 DECEPTIVE OMISSIONS

As with any form of deception, lying always involves omissions. After all, it does not do much good to convincingly tell someone something false if you immediately turn around and reveal the truth. Omissions themselves, however, can sometimes be deceptive. Admittedly, failing to tell someone something usually just leaves that person in a state of ignorance on the topic.[2] But as several philosophers (e.g., Bacon 2015 [1612]; Kant 1949 [1797]: 426; Chisholm and Feehan 1977: 144–45; Langton

---

[1] There is some philosophical controversy about whether lies have to be intended to deceive (see Carson 2010: 20–2; Fallis 2012: 565; Lackey 2013). But this chapter focuses on utterances and omissions that are intended to deceive.

[2] Some philosophers (e.g., Chisholm and Feehan 1977: 144; Skyrms 2010: 81–2) count merely leaving someone without a true belief as deception. But most philosophers (e.g., Mahon 2007: 187; Dynel 2011a: 154) do not.

1992: 489–90; Nyberg 1993: 74; Barnes 1994: 40; Ekman 2009: 28; Mahon 2007: 188; Carson 2010: 56) have noted, we can also cause a person to have a *false belief* by withholding information.

According to Thomas Carson (2010: 56), "if a tax adviser is aware of a legitimate tax exemption her client can claim that would allow the client to achieve considerable tax savings, her failure to inform the client about it constitutes deception. She thereby intentionally causes her client to believe falsely that there is no way for him to save more money on his taxes". Rae Langton (1992: 489–90) describes a (hypothetical) case of deceiving her friend Dora by asking her to help bake a cake while keeping quiet that her "secret plan is to use the delectable cake as the *pièce de résistance*" in an attempt to seduce Dora's boyfriend Otto. Indeed, according to the psychologist Paul Ekman (2009: 28), "if the doctor does not tell the patient that the illness is terminal, if the husband does not mention that he spent his lunch hour at a motel with his wife's best friend, if the policeman doesn't tell the suspect that a 'bug' is recording the conversation with his lawyer," they are engaged in deception.

Such deceptive omissions are also referred to as *dissimulation* (see Bacon 2015 [1612]; Snyder 2009).[3] This is in contrast with *simulation*, which is deception via active pretense, such as outright lying. But sometimes, deceptive omissions are called "*lies* of omission" or "concealment *lies*."[4] Strictly speaking though, deceptive omissions are not lies, because they do not involve using language to make a statement (see Mahon 2008a: §1.1; Dynel 2011a: 153–4). While the doctor, the husband, and the policeman do intend to deceive someone, they do not actually say anything that they believe to be false, which the standard analysis of lying requires.

A few researchers (e.g., Vincent and Castelfranchi 1981: 762; Ekman 2009: 28) do refer to deceptive omissions as lies (see also Vrij 2008: 16). Indeed, there is a sense in which we might say of anyone who is trying to deceive that she is "lying" (see Saul 2012a: 1). For instance, Mark Twain (1996 [1899]: 168) claimed that "almost all lies are acts, and speech has no part in them." But this is just a loose way of speaking that collapses the epistemologically and ethically important distinction between lying and other forms of deception.

It should be noted, however, that there are rare circumstances where you can make a statement just by remaining silent. As Charles Fried (1978: 57) explains, "if you know that your silence will be taken as assent, and you know that the other person knows that you know this, and you intend your silence to be so understood, then your silence can be a lie." An episode from Bob Woodward and Carl Bernstein's investigation of Watergate comes very close to providing an example.

---

[3] This is especially the case when the deception is about oneself and one's intentions.

[4] The term "concealment lies" comes from Ekman (2009: 29). Most philosophers (e.g., Carson 2010: 57; Lackey 2013: 241) distinguish concealing information from merely withholding information, where concealment is an act of commission and withholding is an act of omission. However, according to Ekman (2009: 28–9), "in concealing, the liar withholds some information without actually saying anything untrue... It is passive, not active."

In an attempt to confirm that President Nixon's chief of staff controlled a secret fund, Bernstein spoke on the phone to a lawyer who did not want to go on the record. Bernstein and the lawyer came to an agreement that "Bernstein would count to 10. If there was any reason for the reporters to hold back on the story, the lawyer should hang up before 10. If he was on the line after 10, it would mean that the story was okay" (Woodward and Bernstein 1974: 180). Although the lawyer stayed on the line until Bernstein was done counting, it turned out that there was a problem with the story. In this case, Woodward and Bernstein's false belief (that the story way okay) was actually accidental rather than intentional because "the attorney had gotten the instructions backwards and had meant to warn them off the story" (Woodward and Bernstein 1974: 194). But we can easily imagine this lawyer intending to deceive with his silence and, thus, lying to the reporters.[5]

It should also be noted that deceptive omissions do not necessarily involve saying nothing at all. *Half-truths* are true statements that fall deceptively short of the whole truth (see Vincent and Castelfranchi 1981: 762; Carson 2010: 57–8; Skyrms 2010: 76–7; Dynel 2011a: 155–6).[6] As Carson (2010: 57–8) puts it, "half-truths are true statements or sets of true statements that selectively emphasize facts that tend to support a particular interpretation or assessment of an issue and *selectively ignore* or minimize other relevant facts that tend to support contrary assessments" (emphasis added). A standard example is when pursuers—who did not recognize him—asked Saint Athanasius, "Where is the traitor Athanasius?" and he replied, "Not far away" (see Saul 2012a: 2). Even though Athanasius's statement was perfectly accurate, it succeeded in misleading his pursuers about his identity (precisely as it was intended to do) because it omitted critical facts. Similarly, President Clinton did not lie when he said during the Lewinsky scandal, "There is no improper relationship," because it was true at the time that *presently* there was no such relationship (see Saul 2012a: vii). But his statement was deceptive because he omitted to say that there *had been* an improper relationship in the past (see Meibauer 2014a: 113).

13.3 THE IMPORTANCE OF DECEPTIVE OMISSIONS

Although work in the philosophy of deception tends to focus on outright lying, deceptive omissions are an important phenomenon that deserves attention. For the prospective deceiver, deceptive omissions have several advantages over lies. First of all, they

---

[5] Moreover, while this would be deceptive and an act of omission, it would not be deceptive by virtue of the fact that the lawyer fails to provide information.

[6] When politicians try to deceive the public without saying anything false, it is often referred to as *spin*. But spin can be accurate as well as inaccurate (see Carson 2010: 57–8). Another related concept is *paltering* (see Schauer and Zeckhauser 2009). But this can involve deceiving by saying too much as well as by saying too little.

tend to be easier to carry out (see Ekman 2009: 29). For instance, you do not have to remember a false story, which lying typically requires. In addition, deceptive omissions can be easier to get away with than lies (see Ekman 2009: 29–30). For instance, it can be harder to prove that you did it because you can just claim that you forgot to mention that thing that you omitted to say. Finally, deceptive acts of omission are typically thought to be less bad than deceptive acts of commission (see Barnes 1994: 40; Ekman 2009: 29). Thus, the consequences are not usually as great if you do get caught. Given all of these advantages, deceptive omissions may be a much more common form of deception than lies (see Schauer and Zeckhauser 2009: 44–6). Indeed, Twain (1996 [1899]: 179) joked that "the proportion of the spoken lie to the other varieties is as 1 to 22,894."

13.4 THE EPISTEMOLOGY OF DECEPTIVE OMISSIONS

The philosophical literature on deceptive omissions tends to focus on *ethical* issues. In particular, several philosophers (e.g., Kant 1949 [1797]: 426–8; Adler 1997; Mahon 2006; Saul 2012a: 69–99) have studied whether, all other things being equal, lying is worse than deceiving someone without lying. Much less attention has been paid to *how* deceptive omissions work. But if we want to avoid being deceived by them, it is helpful to understand the *epistemology* of deceptive omissions. Indeed, as the final section of this chapter illustrates, knowing how omissions deceive people can also help us to determine their moral status.

But first, there is actually some philosophical controversy about whether omissions can really deceive people (see Chisholm and Feehan 1977: 144–6; Mahon 2006: 24–7). According to the standard analysis, you *deceive* someone if and only if you intentionally *cause* her to have a false belief (see Mahon 2007: 189–90; Carson 2010: 50).[7] Many philosophers (e.g., Armstrong 2004; Beebee 2004; Dowe 2004) claim that omissions cannot cause things to happen. If they are right, you cannot deceive someone with an act of omission.

According to a fairly plausible theory, causation requires some sort of physical interaction between a cause and an effect. As Phil Dowe (2004: 189) puts it, "a *causal interaction* is an intersection of world-lines that involves exchange of a conserved quantity." According to this theory, the shepherd boy's cry causes the villagers to have a false belief about there being a wolf. Unfortunately, this theory of causation rules out the possibility of causation by omission and, thus, the possibility of deceptive omissions.[8] If we want

---

[7] It is probably possible to deceive someone even if she does not end up with *full* belief in a false proposition (see Chisholm and Feehan 1977: 145). Simply increasing her *degree of belief* in a false proposition is probably sufficient. But this complication does not matter for our purposes here.

[8] It also rules out the possibility of causation by prevention and, thus, the possibility of deceptive preventions. However, several philosophers (e.g., Chisholm and Feehan 1977: 144; Carson 2010: 56–7;

to count omissions as being deceptive, we need to adopt a broader view of causation (at least for purposes of the analysis of deception).

There are actually many omissions that look like causes. For instance, it seems quite appropriate to say that my neighbor's failing to water my plant as she promised to do caused it to die. To handle these sorts of cases, several philosophers (e.g., Lewis 2000) have suggested that causation by omission occurs whenever the right counterfactual dependence exists between the omission and the event in question. That is, an omission causes an event E whenever the omitted event would have prevented the event E. This *counterfactual dependence* theory of causation opens up the possibility of deceptive omissions, but how exactly do they cause false beliefs?

13.4.1 Omissions that violate conversational norms

Paul Grice's (1989c: 26–30) work on *conversational norms* (or "maxims") is a conceptual tool that can help us understand how omissions (as well as lies) can be used to deceive people. Conversational norms are rules that we expect people to obey—and that we think that people ought to obey—whenever we are having a conversation (or "talk exchange"). For instance, you should "not say what you believe to be false," you should "not say that for which you lack adequate evidence," you should "make your contribution as informative as is required (for the current purposes of the exchange)," you should "avoid ambiguity," you should "avoid obscurity of expression," etc.

Grice (1989c: 30) was primarily interested in how people are able to communicate things other than what they literally say by "blatantly fail[ing] to fulfill" these conversational norms. For instance, when Marc Antony said sarcastically to the Romans, "Brutus is an honorable man," he was not complying with the norm against saying what one believes to be false. But since it was clear to Antony's audience that he believed that what he was saying was false, they recognized that Antony really intended to communicate the opposite (viz., that Brutus was *not* an honorable man).

Grice (1989c: 30) also pointed out in passing that someone can "quietly and unostentatiously *violate* a maxim; if so, in some cases he will be liable to mislead." For instance, several philosophers (e.g., Wilson and Sperber 2002: 586; Meibauer 2005: 1396; Dynel 2011a: 147; Fallis 2012) have pointed out that liars deceive people by violating what is known as Grice's "first maxim of Quality." Like Antony, the shepherd boy did not comply with this norm against "say[ing] what you believe to be false." But unlike Antony's audience, it was *not* clear to the villagers (at least the first few times he cried wolf) that the shepherd boy believed that what he was saying was false. They made the default assumption that he was obeying these conversational norms and, in particular, that he did believe what he was saying. Moreover, since they had no reason to doubt the shepherd

---

Lackey 2013: 241) think that you can deceive someone simply by keeping her from getting evidence that would have led her to give up a false belief.

boy's ability to identify a wolf when he saw one, they concluded that there really was a wolf.

Half-truths deceive people by violating a different conversational norm known as Grice's "first maxim of Quantity" (see Vincent and Castelfranchi 1981: 762; Dynel 2011a: 153–56; Meibauer 2014a: 104).[9] Athanasius, for instance, did not obey this norm of "mak[ing] your contribution [to a conversation] as informative as is required." His pursuers made the default assumption that the person that they were questioning was obeying this conversational norm. Thus, when this person only reported that Athanasius was not far away, they concluded that this person did not know Athanasius's location any more precisely. Moreover, since people typically know exactly where they are, the pursuers inferred that this person was not Athanasius.[10]

13.4.2 Omissions that violate other norms

It is not clear that all deceptive omissions work by violating the first maxim of quantity, however. Deceptive omissions can deceive people even if no conversation is presently going on and, thus, no conversational norms appear to be in play. As the deceptive omissions described at the beginning of the chapter suggest, there are other reasons why we might have a legitimate expectation that certain information will be revealed to us.[11]

Even if you have not spoken to her for months, you expect your tax adviser to inform you about any tax exemptions that you are entitled to. This is because you know that your tax adviser has a professional duty to do this even if she does not have a conversational duty (see Carson 2010: 56). Similarly, when you are buying a house, you expect the seller to disclose information about any repairs that are needed. This is because you know that the seller is under a legal obligation to do so (see Porat and Yadlin 2014). Whenever you have these sorts of expectations, it is possible for someone to deceive you by withholding information. As Carson (2010: 56) puts it, "withholding information can constitute deception if there is a clear expectation, promise, and/or professional obligation that such information will be provided."[12]

---

[9] Other conversational norms, such as manner and relevance, can also play a role in the deceptiveness of omissions (see Meibauer 2014a: 113). For instance, if you say, "Amanda and Beau got married and had children," when they actually had children before they got married, you have violated Grice's maxim of Manner (because you failed to "be perspicuous") as well as the first maxim of Quantity (because you failed to explicitly say what the temporal order was). Also, as Carson suggests, half-truths can involve withholding relevant, and emphasizing irrelevant, information.

[10] It should be noted that this particular case might be analyzed in other ways. For instance, it is possible that Athanasius misled his pursuers by tacitly referring to himself in the third person.

[11] Thus, intentionally violating the first maxim of Quantity is not a necessary component of deceptive omissions. Similarly, intentionally violating the first maxim of Quality is not constitutive of lying (see Fallis 2012: 575–7).

[12] If a client draws an inference about the *current* availability of tax breaks when she has not talked to her tax adviser for months, it is not very plausible that the inference could have anything to do with conversational norms. Indeed, someone who has never spoken to me at all might deceive me with an

The obligation in question need not be officially written down in the law or in a code of conduct. For instance, we have a right to expect the local newspaper to report on important current events simply because this is the social role that newspapers play (see Goldberg 2011: 93). Indeed, the obligation need not even be professional. For instance, Langton arguably has an obligation to tell her friend Dora why she is baking the cake. In all of these cases, someone might decide that a proposition is false—for instance, that Langton is interested in Otto—because "if that were true I would have heard about it by now" (Goldberg 2011: 92).

13.4.3 Omissions that do not violate any norm

When you conclude that P is false because someone has an obligation to tell you if P is true and she does not, you are forming what Sandy Goldberg (2011: 93) calls a "coverage-supported belief."[13] This obligation could be the result of a conversational norm (as in the Athanasius case) or of some other social norm (as in the tax adviser case). Through this mechanism of coverage-support, deceptive omissions can lead to brand new false beliefs or they can strengthen existing false beliefs. But there is yet another way that someone might end up holding a false belief as a result of a deceptive omission.

Someone might start out holding a false belief and continue to hold that false belief simply because someone else withholds information that would have enlightened her on the topic. For instance, suppose that it is my neighbor (rather than my tax adviser) who is aware that I am eligible for a tax break, but (because he does not like me very much) he does not say anything about it. In this case, my neighbor does not violate any norm (conversational or otherwise). Nevertheless, as a result of his omission, I continue to hold the false belief that there is no way for me to save more money on my taxes.

If we adopt the counterfactual dependence theory of causation, my neighbor's omission counts as being deceptive. I would not hold the false belief that I am not eligible for a tax break if he had told me about the tax break. (In other words, the omitted event would have prevented my false belief.) However, since my neighbor has no obligation to alert me to potential tax savings, I do not infer anything from his silence on the topic.

---

omission. For instance, I might conclude that my government has not engaged in certain nefarious activities because journalists have agreed to kill (i.e., not publish) the story at the request of the government.

[13] Epistemologists typically focus on how people form the belief that P when someone testifies that P (and on the conditions under which they are justified in forming such a belief). By contrast, here we are concerned with how people form the belief that not-P when someone fails to testify that P (see Goldberg 2011: 94–5). People form coverage-supported beliefs whenever they expect a particular source to have a particular topic *covered* (in the same sense that we expect reporters to cover certain sorts of stories). Strictly speaking, people can form such beliefs even when the source does not actually have an obligation to cover the topic.

I just continue to hold the false belief that I already held. Thus, it seems somewhat more appropriate to say that my neighbor has simply *left me in the dark* about the tax break than that he has *deceived* me.[14]

If we want to say that my neighbor's omission is not deceptive, we need a more restrictive theory of causation by omission. Fortuitously, Sarah McGrath (2005: 138–44) puts forward a theory that comes very close to doing the job. A simplified version of her theory says that an omission causes an event E whenever the omitted event would have prevented the event E *and* it would have been *normal* for the omitted event to have occurred.[15]

This *normality* theory allows us to count omissions that lead to coverage-supported (false) beliefs as being deceptive. For instance, if my tax adviser had told me about the tax break, I would not hold the false belief. But in addition, tax advisers normally advise their clients about important tax information.[16] So, it follows that the tax adviser caused my false belief by withholding the information. By contrast, my neighbor's omission does not count as being deceptive. Even though the right counterfactual dependence exists, it is not normal for neighbors to offer unsolicited tax advice.

But it may be that the normality theory of causation by omission is still too broad. For instance, suppose that my neighbor has a contract with the Internal Revenue Service to keep his neighbors informed about available tax exemptions. In that case, it would be normal for *this neighbor* to offer unsolicited tax advice and, thus, his omission would count as being deceptive. However, if I am completely unaware of his deal with the government (being new to the neighborhood), I will not infer anything from his silence on the topic. As in the original neighbor case, my false belief that I am not eligible for a tax break is not a coverage-supported belief. Thus, it still seems as if I am simply being intentionally left with a false belief rather than that I am being deceived. Admittedly, my neighbor's omission is morally worse if he actually has an obligation to inform me about tax breaks. But this case is *epistemologically* equivalent to the case given where he has no such obligation.

---

[14] It is possible to leave someone in the dark by causing her to acquire a new false belief (see Carson 2010: 54–5). But this case does not involve this sort of deception. Like the omissions that go along with any lie, my neighbor's omission merely leaves in place a false belief that already exists. Chisholm and Feehan (1977: 144–5) would count such an omission as being deceptive. But they have an extremely broad notion of deception (see note 2). It should also be noted that the counterfactual dependence theory of causation has other counterintuitive consequences. For instance, if we simply require that the right counterfactual dependence exists between the omission and the event in question, then the Queen of England caused my plant to die just as much as the neighbor who actually promised to water it (see McGrath 2005: 132–3).

[15] It can be normal in the sense that this sort of event regularly occurs or in the sense that there is a norm that obligates someone to bring about this sort of event. It should also be noted that McGrath's (2005: 141–2) theory is somewhat more complicated than I suggest in the text. For instance, it only requires that, *if* the event E had been prevented, it would have been normal for an event of this type to have prevented it. But these complications will not matter for our purposes here.

[16] Similarly, it is normal for people to make their contribution to a conversation as informative as is required.

13.5 THE ETHICS OF DECEPTIVE OMISSIONS

According to John Parkhurst (1825: 210), "when a man professes, or means to be understood, to tell the whole truth on any subject, the intentional concealment of any part, involves all the guilt of direct lying." However, many notable philosophers (e.g., Bacon 2015 [1612]; Kant 1949 [1797]: 426; Chisholm and Feehan 1977: 153) have claimed that, all other things being equal, lies are worse than deceptive omissions. But if what makes lying and deceptive omissions (*prima facie*) wrong is that they are forms of deception, why does the method that is used to deceive matter? (See Saul 2012a: 85). In general, it is not clear that *doing* something bad is morally worse than merely *allowing* it to happen (see Howard-Snyder 2011).

One reason why lying is supposedly worse than other forms of deception is that it involves a *betrayal of trust*. As Chisholm and Feehan (1977: 153) put it, "lying, unlike other types of intended deception, is essentially a breach of faith." There are certainly instances of deception that do not involve a betrayal of trust. For instance, even if you make a production out of packing your bags so that your neighbors will falsely conclude that you are leaving on a trip, you have not invited them to trust that you are leaving on a trip (see Kant 1949 [1797]). But deceptive omissions often do involve a breach of faith.

As Grice points out, in order to grasp what people are trying to communicate, we have to assume that they are being cooperative and obeying the conversational norms (that is, unless they *overtly* disobey a norm in order to communicate something other than what they literally say). And someone who tells a half-truth violates the first maxim of Quantity, just as the liar violates the first maxim of Quality. As noted above, deceptive omissions do not always involve the violation of a *conversational* norm. But they typically do involve the violation of some social norm (as in the tax adviser case). So, whenever people form coverage-supported (false) beliefs, there typically is a breach of faith.

Another reason why lying is supposedly worse than other forms of deception is that you bear *less responsibility* for your audience ending up with a false belief if you do not actually lie. If you outright lie to someone (e.g., about a wolf chasing your sheep), she has very little choice but to believe what you have said.[17] Thus, it is pretty much your responsibility that she is misled. By contrast, victims of deceptive omissions, such as Athanasius's pursuers, draw a conclusion on their own that goes beyond what was literally said. As Adler (1997: 444) explains the idea, "each individual is a rational, autonomous being and so fully responsible for the inferences he draws, just as he is for his acts. It is deception, but not lies, that requires mistaken inferences and so the hearer's responsibility."

However, even if the audience arrives at a false belief as a result of drawing an inference, the audience need not bear any responsibility for being misled (see Saul

---

[17] If someone is sufficiently skeptical, she could question your sincerity. But because it is such a serious allegation, most people are loath to call someone a liar unless they are absolutely sure.

2012a: 81–3; Meibauer 2014a: 109). In order to grasp what people are trying to communicate, we have to assume that they are being cooperative. Thus, victims of deceptive omissions, such as Athanasius's pursuers and the client of a deceptive tax adviser, also have very little choice but to draw the conclusion that they do.

But even if the victims do bear some responsibility for their being misled, this does not necessarily lessen the moral responsibility of the deceivers. Saul (2012a: 83–4) asks us to consider the following analogous case: Suppose that you walk around the bad part of town wearing expensive clothes and with a bulging wallet. If you are mugged and your wallet is stolen, there is a sense in which you are partly to blame. The theft would have been much less likely to have occurred if you had been more careful (e.g., by sticking to safer parts of town). But this does not lessen the thief's responsibility at all. Presumably, he deserves to be sent to jail as much as a thief that steals from more cautious citizens.

Of course, this is not an exhaustive list. There may be other reasons why lies really are morally worse than deceptive omissions. In any event, it should be noted that the distinction between lying and withholding information is certainly important *legally*. There are many circumstances in which the law allows people not to disclose information, but there are almost no circumstances in which the law allows people to lie (see Porat and Yadlin 2014).

Acknowledgements

I would like to thank Sara Bernstein, Tom Carson, Tony Doyle, Jerry Dworkin, Marta Dynel, Sandy Goldberg, Terry Horgan, Marc Johansen, Peter Lewis, Christian Loew, Kay Mathiesen, Sarah McGrath, Jörg Meibauer, Carolina Sartorio, Jennifer Saul, and Andreas Stokke for helpful feedback on earlier versions of this chapter. The writing of this chapter was facilitated by a visiting fellowship at the Tanner Humanities Center at the University of Utah.

CHAPTER 14

LYING, IMPLICATING, AND PRESUPPOSING

JÖRG MEIBAUER

14.1 Background

SEVERAL linguistic notions have been applied to the phenomenon that is the object of this chapter. First, consider 'indirect lying'. This notion is modelled after the notion of an 'indirect speech act' developed in Searle (1979b). For instance, the utterance *Can you pass the salt?* has the primary illocution of a request, while its secondary illocution, as indicated by the interrogative sentence type, is a question. Falkenberg (1982: 137) tentatively proposed the following definition of 'indirect lying': "A lied indirectly, iff (a) A asserted that p and thereby implicated that q, (b) A believed that not q" [my translation, J. M.]. However, he dismissed this definition because of its inconsistency with the logical principles of double negation, bivalency, and the excluded third. Note that there is a shift from speech act to implicature.

Indirect lying is also mentioned in Vincent and Castelfranchi (1981: 758) who call indirect lies "that sub-set of deceptive moves whose first communicative goal may be either truthful or deceptive, but at least one of whose super-goals is deceptive and achieved by communicative means." A case in point is a scenario "where a speaker asserts or directly expresses a proposition he assents to while having the super-goal that B infer from it a further proposition which A does not assent to, or actively dissents from." This is the classical scenario of 'lying while saying the truth' (see also Sutter 2009).

Second, consider 'falsely implicating', as explicated in Adler (1997: 437–8) (see also Pepp, 2020). He constructs the example of the murderer at the door who wants to know where Joe is. The addressee knows that the man wants to kill Joe. Thus, the addressee answers: "He's hanging around at the Nevada a lot" (the Nevada is the local diner). The murderer will take the addressee as having conversationally implicated that Joe is at the Nevada. In case Joe is not in fact there, as the addressee supposes, this relevance-based implicature may help serving Joe's life. Basically, Adler (1997) deals with the question whether lying is worse than merely falsely implicating.

The third notion is 'misleading', as explicated in Saul (2012a) (see also Stokke 2013a, b). She argues that misleading is distinct from lying or accidental falsehoods. Since misleading is a success predicate, a speaker can be said to mislead the hearer only when the deception is successful. In contrast, the speaker has successfully lied even when the hearer does not believe what the speaker untruthfully asserted. In addition, whereas lying always happens intentionally, misleading can happen accidentally, i.e., the speaker has no intention to mislead (Saul 2012a: 71). The case of misleading is discussed with respect to cases like Bill Clinton's infamous utterance *There is no improper relationship* during the Lewinsky trial and *Billy went to the top of the Empire State Building and jumped* (see also Carston 2002: 128) where additional information is triggered. Arguably, this information may be construed as a misunderstanding or as an untruthful implicature (Meibauer 2014a, b).

The fourth notion is 'insinuation' or 'insinuating'. Vincent and Castelfranchi (1981: 760) defined this communicative act as follows: "Insinuation is a communicative act with a communicative goal which consists of an implied assumption deliberately involving a negative value-judgment of the relevant referent, fact, or effect on the hearer." More recently, Fricker (2012: 64) uses 'insinuating' as a cover term for "various inexplicit mechanisms including the much-studied one of conversational implicature." In her epistemological approach, she emphasizes certain distinctions between so-called 'inexplicit primary messages' and 'implicit secondary messages' (alias conversational implicatures), both belonging to the realm of non-explicit communication (Fricker 2012: 70–2). In Fricker's approach, the evaluative component of Vincent and Castelfranchi's definition is absent. (See also Bertucelli Papi 2014.)

Finally, consider the notion 'paltering'. According to Schauer and Zeckhauser (2009: 43), a successful palter is a statement "in which the speaker intends for the listener to have a misimpression, and in which the listener does wind up with a misimpression as a result of the speaker's statement, but in which the connection between the speaker's intent to deceive and the listener's state of having a misimpression is not the literal falsehood, as in the true lie, but something short of literal or exact falsity." (See also Kelley 2014.)

From this survey it follows that untruthful implicating is a core instance of indirect lying. I will go into untruthful implicating in section 14.2. To this, untruthful presupposing is added in section 14.3. In section 14.4, I will go into the notion of misleading and deception. Finally, I will consider the Gricean notion of 'speaker meaning' or the 'total signification of an utterance' (TSU) with respect to untruthful implicature and untruthful presupposition.

14.2 UNTRUTHFUL IMPLICATING

Falsely implicating or untruthful implicating (Dynel 2011a) is connected to the speaker's intention, as Adler (1997: 446) correctly observes: "In falsely implicating, rather than lying, the outcome is still directly intended, not merely a foreseen consequence. Additionally, the deceiver performs an act that originates the deception, rather than merely allowing it to befall the victim." Taking up this insight, Meibauer (2005, 2011, 2014a, b) develops an extended notion of lying that includes untruthful implicature and untruthful presupposition (see Dynel 2015; Horn 2017a).

Meibauer holds that lying while saying the truth happens by conveying untruthful implicatures, according to the following definition (with S = speaker, p = propositional content, q = conversational implicature). Note that this definition presupposes that lies are insincere assertions:

(1) Lying with implicatures
A speaker S lies iff
(a) she or he asserts that p while not believing that p, or
(b) she or he conversationally implicates on the basis of her/his assertion that q while not believing that q.

Hence, implicit content, i.e., a conversational implicature, is included in the total speaker meaning which is a lie. Note in addition that (1) allows for double lying, namely via (1a) *and* (1b).

Consider the following classical example drawn from Grice (1989a: 37): If the speaker Ken utters *X is meeting a woman this evening* [= p], thereby conversationally implicating that 'The person to be met was someone other than X's wife' [= q], yet knows for sure that the person to be met is X's wife, then, according to definition (1), Ken is lying. Obviously, Ken leads his addressee Barbie into the false belief that the person to be met was someone other than X's wife.

There is an initial theoretical motivation and empirical evidence that supports an extended notion of lying as in (1). The theoretical motivation is to take Grice's (1989b: 41 ff.) notion of the "total signification of an utterance" seriously. Conversational implicatures have a propositional status, hence they are true or false; they are always *bound* to utterances; and they are intended. Therefore, if they are used for deceptive purposes, an extended notion of lying along the lines of (1) seems plausible. Initial empirical evidence stems from those studies, in the tradition of Coleman and Kay's (1981) questionnaire study, that probe into the applicability of verbs of lying to the following scenario):

(2) *Ex-boyfriend*
John and Mary have recently started going together. Valentino is Mary's *ex-boyfriend*. One evening John asks Mary, 'Have you seen Valentino this week?' Mary answers, 'Valentino's been sick with mononucleosis for the past two weeks.' Valentino has in fact been sick with mononucleosis for the past two weeks, but it is also the case that Mary had a date with Valentino the night before. Did Mary lie?

(Coleman and Kay 1981)

With respect to a 7-point Likert scale (7 points = lie, 1 point = no lie) participants judged as follows. Spanish Ecuador speakers (Hardin 2010): 4.84; American English speakers (Coleman and Kay 1981): 3.48. Interpreted cautiously, this shows that at least some speakers are willing to judge that Mary's utterance was a lie. It also suggests cultural and social variation.

Recent experimental research shows that the assessment of a deceptive target utterance is subject to variation. Weissman and Terkourafi (2016) asked subjects with respect to several cases of false implicature (eleven generalized conversational implicatures and four particularized conversational implicatures), following the design of Doran et al. (2012). Participants were asked whether a certain utterance in the respective vignette was a lie. Three conditions were used, namely true utterance, false implicature, and lie. Like Coleman and Kay (1981) and Arico and Fallis (2013), they used a 7-point rating scale.

Weissman and Terkourafi found that in most cases, subjects were not willing to count false implicatures as lies. Exceptions were false implicatures based on cardinals, N- and V-repetitions. For instance, when Ken is being asked where the missing five cupcakes are (one is left) and he answers that he ate three of them while he ate five then he deceptively implicates (= lies) that he did eat exactly three cupcakes (logically speaking it is true that he ate three cupcakes when he ate five cupcakes). The repetition cases included utterances such as *There were boxes and boxes* (when there were in fact two boxes) and *Ken drank and drank* (when he only drank two beverages).

In contrast, a study by Wiegmann and Willemsen (2017) shows that deceptive implicatures are considered as lies when the deceptive intent of the speaker is made clear. In their first experiment, concerning the violation of the maxim of Quantity (lies by omission), subjects were asked whether presenting half-truths (i.e., leaving out relevant information in order to avoid truthfully answering the question under discussion) was a lie. In this condition, 65% of the 451 subjects agreed. Two further experiments, dealing with the maxim of Relation and the maxim of Manner, also supported the claim "that lying occurs at the level of pragmatics, by deceiving others through falsely implicating" (Wiegmann and Willemsen 2017: 4).

Several cases can be added to conversational implicatures such as that in (2): the case of the mate and the captain (Meibauer 2005, 2014a); the case of the *community week* provided by Stokke (2013c: 3), and the case of the car borrower in Green (2006: 146). All of these cases involve conversational implicatures that are considered as lies by the respective authors. Consider the latter two cases:

(3) *Community Week*
     Jasper's neighborhood recently put on a *Community Week*. People helped the neighbors out with various chores and tasks that needed doing. Selfishly, however, Jasper used Community Week to fix the roof on his own house, ignoring the neighbors. The following week Jasper is having dinner with Doris. Jasper is keen to give Doris a good impression of himself. [When Doris asked, "So how did you help out during Community week?", Jasper answered "I fixed a roof"].

Stokke (2013c: 3) says: "Jasper's reply is a lie". This analysis is easily captured when the untruthful implicature is considered, since Jasper exploited the maxim of Quantity.

Green (2006: 146) presents the following scenario:

(4) *How Many Cars?*
Imagine that A needs to borrow a car for the evening and asks B how many he owns. B, who in truth owns four cars, replies, 'I have one car, and I'm using it this evening.' Has B lied in saying that he owns 'one car'? Has B made an assertion that is literally false, or has he merely led A draw an improper inference from a misleading statement? It seems wrong to say that B has merely misled. After all, B told A that he owns 'one car'. Perhaps A could have asked the follow up question, 'are you saying that you own only one car and no more?,' but this seems to take the principle caveat auditor to extremes.

He concludes: "In terms of everyday morality, one who responds to a specific quantitative inquiry by baldly understating a numerical fact should be regarded as uttering a lie." Again, the maxim of Quantity is what matters.

Moreover, it is agreed that it is also possible to lie while using figurative language, e.g., metaphor and irony (Meibauer 2014a). Adler (1997: 444 n. 27) gives the following example: "Teaching a child history, I assert: Stalin was a pussycat. Understood as intended, it is a lie." (Adler 1997: 444 n. 27). Recall that metaphors are exploitations of the maxim of Quality according to Grice (1989a).

Dynel (2016a) holds that lying by using deceptive irony and metaphor should be acknowledged as genuine cases of lying (cf. Meibauer 2014a: 161–71; Viebahn 2017). She hypothesizes "that covertly untruthful implicatures in the rhetorical figures which revolve around the floutings of the first maxim of Quality can be conceived as lies" (Dynel 2016a: 201). Accordingly, she proposes: "A lie is what is said in the form of an assertion that violates the first maxim of Quality, or in the form of making as if to say that promotes an implicature that violates the first maxim of Quality" (Dynel 2016a: 202). This means that the concept of lying is detached from insincere assertion and the declarative sentence as its prototypical bearer.

14.3 UNTRUTHFUL PRESUPPOSING

Vincent and Castelfranchi (1981: 763) think of precondition or presupposition faking "as a sub-type of pretending, or behaving-as-if, for it involves doing an act or making an utterance which would require certain preconditions for its appropriate use; when, however, these conditions do not exist, the speaker knows they do not exist, and his goal is that the hearer assumes that they do."

They give the following example: At his daughter's wedding breakfast, the speaker remarks: *It is rather a pity that Anne and Mark had to be at Burleigh this weekend.* Here, the speaker may very well be liable to multiple presupposition fakings: "For instance, that the speaker knows the two illustrious personages in question well enough to be on first-name terms with them, that the speaker actually invited them to the wedding, that A. and M. would have come but just could not avoid the very important business that took them elsewhere, etc." (Vincent and Castelfranchi 1981: 763).

Presuppositions are propositions that are related to presupposition triggers and remain constant under negation. For example, in *Ken realized/did not realize that the car was stolen*, the presupposition that the car was stolen is active. This is not the case with a non-factive verb uch as *to assert*. Meibauer (2014a) proposes to extend the concept of lying so that it includes untruthful presupposing. This makes lying independent of assertions. Thus, it is possible to lie while, e.g., using interrogative or imperative sentences. For instance, the utterance *Who saw the red car?* presupposes that there is a red car. However, when the police officers know for sure that there is no red car involved in the crime, but nevertheless ask this question, they are liable to try to deceive their audience, and, according to a general definition including untruthful implicatures, are lying. The approach just sketched fits into the recent work of Zhang (2008) who develops the view that truthfulness of the participants with respect to presupposition is the most important parameter in face-to-face conversation (see Meibauer 2014a: 137–40).

Hence, when untruthful implicatures and untruthful presuppositions are taken into consideration, an utterance such as *I have seen the vice president with a woman last night* can be a lie on a number of counts: (a) the speaker has not seen anyone, (b) there is no vice president, (c) the woman was the wife of the person referred to by the expression *the vice president*.

14.4 MISLEADING AND DECEPTION

One might object that untruthful implicature is simply a case of deception or misleading. On this view, there is no need for a general definition of lying encompassing untruthful implicatures and presuppositions. Thus, Adler (1997: 452) draws an analogy between falsely implicating and deception: "A lies-deception distinction corresponding to an assertion-implicature one is rational for us to want (for purposes of social harmony, lessening the strains of commitment, and facilitating the exchange of information). For these goals a norm is needed, since knowledge in advance, rather than on-the-spot calculation, is the only feasible way that the distinction would accomplish its goals." Yet this conclusion is reached solely for ethical reasons and on the basis of the postulation of a 'lessened demand of truthfulness norm' for implicatures (Adler 1997: 451). In this section, several arguments bearing on this issue will be presented, before the ethical dimension driving Adler's argumentation is briefly considered.

First, restricting deception to implicature seems analytically wrong, since lying is deception, too (Chisholm and Feehan 1977). This holds at least for the so-called 'deceptionists', as Mahon (2015) calls them. 'Non-deceptionists', in contrast, hold that lying does not necessarily involve an intention to deceive (see Chapter 19 on bald-faced lies). In general, deception is any attempt at leading someone into a false belief (Mahon 2015).

Second, Saul (2012a) argues that misleading is distinct from lying or accidental falsehoods (see also Stokke 2016a). It is supposed that misleading is a success predicate. This means that a speaker can be said to mislead the hearer only when the deception is successful. In contrast, the speaker has successfully lied even when the hearer does not believe what the speaker untruthfully asserted. In addition, whereas lying always happens intentionally, misleading can happen accidentally (i.e., the speaker had no intention to mislead) (Saul 2012a: 71). Hence, one could propose the following definition of misleading:

(5) Misleading
A speaker S misleads iff
(a) she or he utters a sentence s meaning p, and thereby
(b) intentionally or unintentionally (accidentally)
(c) leads the hearer into a false belief.
(Meibauer 2014c)

This definition covers the general notion of deception with respect to (5c). Intentional misleading happens with lying and with falsely implicating. What remains is unintentional misleading. This can be reconstructed as 'misunderstanding' (Meibauer 2014c). Thus, it is questionable whether 'misleading' is an independent pragmatic notion.

Third, there is a tendency to think of implicature as something that goes together with (a) a 'lessened demand of truthfulness' (Adler 1997), (b) a weaker 'commitment' (Moeschler 2013), (c) or weaker 'certainty' (Morency, Oswald, and de Saussure 2008). Thus, even if it is simply an additional proposition that is pragmatically derived, it has special properties beyond the defining properties of cancelability, context-dependency, non-conventionality, reconstruability, non-detachability, and reinforceability.

Lessened demands for truthfulness: Adler (1997: 451) states: "Speakers often have information which they believe useful to hearers, but which they are reluctant to offer if placing themselves in a position to have defend it fully." For instance, compare utterances B and B' in the following exchange (based on Grice 1989a: 32):

(6) A: Smith doesn't seem to have a girlfriend these days.
B: He has been paying a lot of visits to New York lately.
B': Smith [probably] has a girlfriend in New York.

With respect to B', "you, as A, are more inclined to ask" *How do you know?* This means that potential doubts of A are becoming less salient with B. While Saul (2012b: 6) endorses this line of argument, she proposes another norm, dubbed "a lessened demand for truthfulness when one has legitimate reason to deceive." However, if B' amounts to the conversational implicature to be derived from B, conversational implicatures being true or false propositions, there should be no degree in saliency. (Arguably, conversational implicatures could be more salient because of the effort to derive them.)

What motivates Adler's approach is the ethical question whether lying is worse than mere misleading. Adler (1997: 446) states: "If you are going to mislead, just go ahead and lie. From another angle, the deceiver does manage to avoid a far worse wrong, even if his means are tainted." Saul (2012b) shows convincingly that with respect to morality, there is no difference between misleading (untruthful implicating) and lying.

Commitment: The notion of 'commitment' is usually applied to properties of speech acts. For instance, according to Searle (1979c: 12), the illocutionary point of an assertive speech act is "to commit the speaker (in varying degrees) to something's being the case, to the truth of the expressed proposition" (Searle 1979c: 12). However, there are further notions of 'commitment' available, as pointed out by De Brabanter and Dendale (2008). Moreover, there are related notions such as 'taking responsibility' (Alston 2000) or 'warranting the truth' (Carson 2010). Harnish (2005: 25–33) points out several difficulties with classical 'Austinian' speech-act approaches and supports a 'Gricean' approach focusing on propositional attitudes. Applying 'commitment' to conversational implicatures we can ask whether speakers are committed to their content. This seems indeed to be the case. For instance, it would make no sense when B simply denies that he has suggested that Smith has a girlfriend in New York. Note that commitment to q and cancelability/context-dependency are not to be confused.

Moeschler (2013: 88) assumes "that the speaker's degree of commitment vis-à-vis her utterance depends on the nature of the inference it gives rise to: a speaker is more committed to a semantic content than to a pragmatic one." In short, there is a scale of the "strength of the content" such that entailment > presupposition > explicature > (generalized conversational) implicature, with ">" meaning "stronger than." While this is an attractive proposal, it is not easy to see why a generalized conversational implicature should be "weak," at least in comparison to the other meaning entities.

Thus, the speaker seems committed to the truth of a conversational implicature in the same way as they are committed to the truth of an assertion. For instance, if someone utters *X is meeting a woman this evening* [= p], conversationally implicating 'The person to be met was someone other than X's wife' [= q], then the speaker is committed to their implicature.

Certainty: It could be argued that commitment in the case of assertion is different from commitment to a conversational implicature, since the hearer is more uncertain with respect to the latter. This is the view of Morency, Oswald, and de Saussure (2008: 210–15) who elaborate on this point: "… it is the hearer who is responsible for invoking the appropriate hypotheses, and in this sense there is always a degree of uncertainty (a hearer can never obtain formal proofs that the assumptions he considers in processing implicatures correspond to those the speaker has mobilized herself, unless he asks her, *a posteriori*)." This seems correct. Nevertheless, the speaker is responsible for her/his implicatures because the hearer is entitled to ascribe certain intentions to her/him. Commitment misattribution is only possible when the speaker's intention and the hearer's recognition of that intention do not match. The psychological uncertainty of the hearer should not be confused with the fact that it is certain that the speaker has an intention when conveying an implicature.

The aforementioned issues of lessened demands of truthfulness, commitment, and certainty are, of course, connected with the 'cancelability' of conversational implicatures. Grice (1989a: 39) points out that there is either explicit cancellability ("by the addition of a clause that states or implies that the speaker has opted out") or contextual cancelability ("if the form of utterance that usually carries it is used in a context that makes it clear that the speaker is opting out"). However, applying the criterion of explicit cancelability to certain cases of implicature will lead to implausible results, for instance in cases of irony or certain indirect directives. Observations such as this have led researchers to some skepticism with regard to explicit cancelability (Weiner 2006).

In particular, Burton-Roberts (2010: 146) argues that the notion of cancelation should be replaced by the notion of 'clarification'. This is because implicatures are intended while intentions can never be canceled: "EITHER the speaker intended by her utterance to implicate that P—in which case she cannot undo (or 'cancel') it, OR she did not so intend, in which case there is no implicature to cancel in the first place." In the case of lies, be they realized by untruthful assertion or by untruthful conversational implicature, Meibauer (2014c) assumes that they can never be canceled and never be clarified. All the speaker can do is deny that she or he lied or confess that she or he lied. Thus, if Ken knows that the person to be met is X's wife and says: *X is meeting a woman this evening*, thereby conversationally implicating 'The person to be met was someone other than X's wife', then it is implausible when he adds *This (= q) was a lie* (cancelation) or *However, I did not intend to convey q* (clarification). All he can do is deny that he lied (*I only said that X is meeting a woman this evening without implicating anything*) or admit that he lied (*Yes, it was a lie. I wanted to deceive you*).

Note that these issues have repercussions on juridical questions, as Solan and Tiersma (2005), Green (2006), Schauer and Zeckhauser (2009), and Porat and Yadlin (2014) make clear. For instance, in the case *Bronston v. United States*, the juridical question was "whether a witness may be convicted of perjury for an answer, under oath, that is literally true but not responsive to the question asked and arguably misleading by negative implication" (Solan and Tiersma 2005: 213). In (7), Bronston conversationally implicates that he had no personal account, which was false.

(7) *The Bronston Case*
    Lawyer: Do you have any bank account in Swiss banks, Mr. Bronston?
    Bronston: No, sir.
    Lawyer: Have you ever?
    Bronston: The company had an account there for about six months, in Zurich.

The question is whether the "literal truth defense," that the US Supreme Court had acknowledged, is adequate. Solan and Tiersma (2005: 215) point out that such a strategy would not be accepted in other cases of crimes of language.

14.5 Lying and speaker meaning

With respect to the distinction between 'lying and misleading', Bach (2013) states: "This distinction is often understood as the difference between, in meaning something, trying to deceive explicitly and merely inexplicitly or indirectly. However, that overlooks the fact that almost all the utterances we count as lies are at least partly inexplicit and that there is no difference in kind between the communicative intentions associated with fully explicit utterances and those associated with less explicit ones. Whether or not the speaker is being completely explicit, what the speaker means is a matter of his communicative intention, something the audience has to identify in any case. Trusting the speaker is another matter."

The Gricean notion of speaker meaning is apt to support this view. Speaker meaning comprises 'what is said' and 'what is implicated' (Grice 1989a, b). Note that this is also the view of Adler (1997: 445): "Since implicatures are required for the speaker not to violate the maxims of conversation, they are part of speaker's meaning (what the speaker means in saying what is said). Consequently, the invitation or communicative intent extends to implicatures."

Thus, conversational implicatures go into the "total signification of an utterance" (TSU), a notion originally proposed by Grice (1989b: 41 ff.) (see also Martinich 2010). Burton-Roberts (2013: 26) explains the notion like this: "The TSU consists of everything communicated by an utterance however it was communicated—i.e., everything the hearer has on his communicative plate at the end of the day." Grice makes it clear that the TSU includes what is said and what is implicated. And it must clearly include anything deductively/semantically derivable from (or equivalent to) the conjunction of what is said and what is implicated.

For instance, when what-is-said is *X is meeting a woman this evening.* [= p] and the implicature *The person to be met was someone other than X's wife* [= q], then the TSU is 'X is meeting a woman this evening [= p] & The person to be met was someone other than X's wife [= q]'. With respect to this notion, it is clear that a definition of lying along the lines of (1), as explicated in Meibauer (2005, 2011, 2014a, b), makes sense. Ultimately, indirect lying should be analyzed within a general theory of indirectness, as discussed in recent contributions by Pinker, Nowak, and Lee (2008), Lee and Pinker (2010), Pinker (2011), Terkourafi (2011a, 2011b, 2014).

CHAPTER 15

LYING AND SELF-DECEPTION

KATHI BEIER

15.1 THE DEFINITION OF LYING AND SELF-DECEPTION

LYING is the act of deceiving another person by making an insincere statement, i.e., by asserting something as true that one judges to be false. Ever since lying has been a theme of philosophical discourse, three conditions have been considered to constitute a lie: (i) the intention to deceive another person, (ii) the intention to make a false assertion, and (iii) the falsity of the assertion.

There is reason, however, to consider that the second condition alone is sufficient for an utterance to qualify as a lie; it designates what a lie is essentially, or—as Thomas Aquinas says—'formaliter'. To lie is to make a statement or an assertion with the intention of uttering an untruth (Aquinas 1897: 110: 1). This means that for someone to qualify as a liar, condition (iii) is not necessary; it is not necessary to assert or state something that is in fact, or 'materialiter', false. One's assertion may be false, but one may mistakenly take it to be true. Thus, the material side of an assertion, i.e., its being (objectively) true or false, need not enter into the definition of lying. Moreover, a lie need not be 'effective', i.e., need not result in the second person actually being deceived. A person who lies may know in advance that the addressee will not believe her, and may consequently not even intend to deceive; so condition (i) is not necessary either. However, in so far as she intends to state as true what she herself believes to be false, she is a liar. Thus, neither the intention to deceive nor the effect of the asserted untruth, i.e., the other person's being deceived, belong to the definition of lying. Lying, then, seems to be sufficiently determined by condition (ii).

While there is little agreement on which conditions need to be met (Mahon 2015), philosophers from different times and different schools tend to agree on at least the following point: the liar essentially has a 'double heart' or a 'double mind'. Lying involves a mismatch between thinking or judging, on the one hand, and saying or asserting, on the other (Augustine (1952b): 3; Aquinas (1897): 110: 1; Kant: MM, Doctrine of virtue (Kant 1996c): §9; Kupfer 1982; Dietz 2002; Williams 2002; Sartre 2003; Löhrer 2012).

Self-deception has some basic features in common with lying. It too, so it seems, is the act of deceiving a person, though not a second person but rather oneself. The deception is brought about by inducing a false belief. Like the liar, the self-deceiver must be conceived of as having a 'double mind'. Though she has strong reasons or at least indications for believing that *not-p*, or may even know that *not-p*, she nevertheless makes herself believe that *p*. Self-deception involves a mismatch between, on the one hand, a belief one should adopt but does not and, on the other, a belief one should not adopt but which one does. Thus, by its very nature, self-deception is a form of untruthfulness. And like lying, self-deception is intentional or at least motivated. In contrast to error, deception is sought actively and wilfully. Self-deception is something like 'wilful ignorance' or 'disavowal'.

It is clear from the examples used to illustrate self-deception that the matter of the deception may vary significantly. Yet in all examples the matter must be of importance to the self-deceiver. For example, the self-deception displayed by the cuckold Alexej Karenin in Tolstoy's novel *Anna Karenina* is self-deception about another person, i.e., his wife Anna. According to Mike W. Martin, Karenin, when thinking about his marriage, "is left with no basis for doubting that she loves Vronsky. Though he has no absolute proof, he knows 'deep inside him' that the couple are having an affair. But throughout the following year, he evades acknowledging to himself what he knows. He simply 'refused to recognize' and confront it" (Martin 1986: 10–11). Likewise, in Henrik Ibsen's play *The Wild Duck*, we find people deceiving themselves about others, for example, Gregers Wehrle, who deceives himself about the strength and nobility of mind of his former friend Hjalmar Ekdahl. Yet others, for example, Hjalmar Ekdahl himself, are engaged in self-deception about themselves.[1] Both kinds of self-deception seem more likely to be successful if reinforced by other people.[2] However, self-deception need not be about persons at all. It can also be exerted with respect to a state of affairs, for example, when a military general wilfully misconceives the situation of his regiment (Gardiner 1970). Moreover, self-deception can relate to something in the past, e.g., the doping before the race, or to something in the present, e.g., the loyalty of one's partner, or to something in the future, e.g., one's child's ability to become a famous musician. These examples show that self-deceivers all try to evade an unpleasant truth; otherwise they would not go to the trouble of maintaining a false belief.[3]

---

[1] For Ibsen, see Löw-Beer (1990) and Dietz (2003). Other philosophers illuminate the mechanism of self-deception by referring to novels and stories by Gustave Flaubert (Davidson 2004a), Henry James (Bittner 1988), Marcel Proust (Nussbaum 1988), and André Gide (Landweer 2001).

[2] Assisted individual self-deception is to be distinguished, however, from cases of collective self-deception, either as joint or summative self-deception across a collective (Ruddick 1988) or as non-summative self-deception of a collective entity (Fleck 1980; Trivers 2000).

[3] While these cases illustrate the common structure of self-deception, it also seems possible that by deceiving oneself a person comes to believe something unpleasant, i.e. by making oneself believe what one wishes to be false. Compared to 'straight' self-deception, these 'twisted' cases require a more complex explanation (for these cases, see Mele 2001: Ch. 5).

In the light of examples like these, two conditions have been considered to constitute self-deception: (i) the adherence to a belief one already knows or at least suspects to be false (*knowledge condition*), and (ii) the intention or motivation not to acknowledge the falsity of the belief (*intentionality condition*). While these conditions partly overlap with the suggested conditions constituting a lie, the main difference between lying and self-deceiving is that it takes two to lie but only one to deceive oneself. Jean-Paul Sartre, identifying self-deception with what he calls bad faith ('mauvaise foi'), summarizes this idea in the following way:

> To be sure, the one who practices bad faith is hiding a displeasing truth or presenting as truth a pleasing untruth. Bad faith then has in appearance the structure of lying. Only what changes everything is the fact that in bad faith it is from myself that I am hiding the truth. Thus the duality of the deceiver and the deceived does not exist here. Bad faith on the contrary implies in essence the unity of a single consciousness.
>
> (Sartre 2003: 72)

Because this is the most obvious difference between lying and self-deception, it is not surprising that many philosophers have considered self-deception to be nothing other than lying to oneself.

15.2 SELF-DECEPTION AS LYING TO ONESELF

In an influential paper from 1960, Raphael Demos analyses self-deception and compares it to lying. He is convinced that self-deception must be conceived of as lying to oneself: "I will say that 'B lies to (deceives) C' means: B intends to induce a mistaken belief in C, B succeeds in carrying out this intention, and finally B knows (and believes) that what he tells C is false. All three: intention, results, and knowledge are included... Self-deception exists, I will say, when a person lies to himself, that is to say, persuades himself to believe what he knows is not so" (Demos 1960: 588). This position initially appears reasonable. Both the liar and the self-deceiver know that the belief they want to induce is at odds with what they themselves believe at the bottom of their hearts (knowledge condition). Additionally, both of them do so intentionally (intentionality condition). Upon closer examination, however, the account proves to be flawed. Demos himself concedes that the identification holds only if the two concepts are restricted "to a special (their strongest) meaning" (Demos 1960: 588). Yet restricting the concepts in this way has serious consequences: neither the essence of lying nor the essence of self-deception is graspable.

Let us first consider lying. As we have already seen, it does not belong to the essence of lying that the liar knows about the falseness of the belief she wishes to induce in the listener, nor that the liar succeeds in deceiving the other person. Demos takes the first to be a necessary condition for lying in order to exclude the odd case in which a liar by chance induces a true belief. So if B lies to C, she is asserting something she herself takes to be false; yet she may be mistaken. Still B must be called a liar, even though she accidentally tells the truth. The definition of lying as such does not exclude such a case.

Demos believes the success condition is necessary for lying because he does not distinguish between lying and deceiving. However, whereas B is a deceiver only if she has in fact managed to make C believe her, B is a liar even if C does not believe her. Demos grants that this is possible: "I have lied to you although you have not believed me and so have not been misled by me" (Demos 1960: 588). Nonetheless, his definition of lying is based on the strongest possible case of lying as successful deception.

Let us now consider deception and self-deception. According to a particular reading of the knowledge condition and the intentionality condition, it makes sense to apply them to all three acts—namely, lying, deception, and self-deception—except that in lying and deception one deceives not oneself but a second person. Yet the knowledge condition contains three elements: (i) untruthfulness, i.e., that the deceiver does not take to be true what she wants the deceived person to believe; (ii) success, i.e., that the deceived person believes the deceiver; and (iii) a certain effect, i.e., that the deceived person in fact comes to believe something false. These three elements reveal how self-deception differs from deception and lying.

With regard to (i) the untruthfulness condition, there is no visible difference between lying, deception, and self-deception. Just as it is the case for lying and deception that the deceiver does not take to be true what she wants the deceived person to believe, so it is for self-deception. What is puzzling, however, is how it is possible for the same person to be both the deceiver and the deceived person at the same time, since this entails that the self-deceiver has conflicting epistemic states.

With regard to (ii) the success condition, there is an obvious difference between deception and self-deception, on the one hand, and lying on the other. While it makes good sense to say to a liar, "You have tried to make me believe something but I do not believe you," nothing like this applies to a deceiver, let alone to cases of self-deception. Deceiving presupposes success. I have deceived you only if you believe me. Since deceiving oneself is taken to be a form of deceiving, the same should be true for self-deception. The self-reference essential to self-deception is what makes it conceptually impossible to state, "I have deceived myself but I have not believed me," or as Demos would have it, "I have lied to myself but I have not believed me."

To illustrate (iii) the effect condition, we can refer again to Karenin. If this reading of the knowledge condition is true, then Karenin is deceiving himself only if Anna and Vronskij are in fact engaged in a love affair. Consider the following alternative scenario: Karenin has evidence to suspect Anna and Vronskij are having an affair; but the thought of Anna's disloyalty is so unpleasant to him and would be so detrimental to his reputation that he intends to ignore it; he avoids talking to Anna about his suspicion and even avoids thinking about it; although there is a nagging doubt, he still clings to the belief that she is loyal and that their marriage is as good as ever. So far, this does not differ from the story Tolstoy actually tells. However, let us imagine that Anna and Vronskij have not fallen in love with each other. They are good friends and meet often, which is enough to cause rumours about their relationship. Is Karenin a self-deceiver in this scenario? The similarity between the two scenarios in his thinking and behaviour suggests that he is. Karenin is deceiving himself in both scenarios because he wilfully ignores the evidence that points to Anna's disloyalty. He persuades himself to believe what he has reason to judge as false. But if we are compelled to say he is also deceiving himself in this alternative scenario, then the effect condition is not necessary for self-deception, just as it is not necessary for lying. In other words, the concept of self-deception is too restrictive if it forces us to say that Karenin is not deceiving himself in this alternative scenario.[4]

In summary, neither lying nor self-deception is comprehensible if one represents self-deception as nothing other than lying to oneself.

15.3 THE PARADOXICAL NATURE OF SELF-DECEPTION

Given the definition of self-deception, both the knowledge condition and the intentionality condition constitute what may be called the nested 'paradox of self-deception'. The knowledge condition seems to create a problem of epistemic rationality, for it raises the question of how it is possible to stick to a belief that one takes to be false. Does a self-deceiver really believe both p and not-p? If so, how is this possible? The intentionality condition seems to create a psychological problem, for it gives rise to the question concerning the possibility of making oneself believe an apparent untruth. Can there be something like a will to believe? If so, can this include a will to believe something false? It is worth elaborating the two problems in more detail and examining their philosophical presuppositions.

15.3.1 The static paradox

The self-deceiver's epistemic state seems fundamentally paradoxical. In the analytic tradition, this paradox is expressed as follows: "In short, self-deception entails that B believes both p and not-p at the same time" (Demos 1960: 588). The apparent impossibility of this situation is summarized well by Demos:

> Believing and disbelieving are pro and con attitudes; they are contraries and therefore it is logically impossible for them to exist at the same time in the same person

---

[4] For a different view, which is similar to Demos', see Mele: "A person is, by definition, deceived in believing that p only if p is false; the same is true of being self-deceived in believing that p." He nonetheless distinguishes "being deceived in believing something" from "being deceived into believing it" (see also Barnes 1997: 9). This allows him to concede the following: "Motivationally biased treatment of data may sometimes result in someone's believing an improbable proposition p, that, as it happens, is true. There may be self-deception in such a case, but the person is not self-deceived in believing that p, or in acquiring the belief that p" (Mele 2001: 51).

in the same respect. When B lies to himself he comes to believe what he knows to be false; to accept this as the description of a fact is to admit a violation of the law of contradiction.

(Demos 1960: 591)

The "law of contradiction" is a basic principle of thinking. In its classical formulation, as it is found, for example, in Aristotle's *Metaphysics*, it states that "the same attribute cannot both belong and not belong to the same subject at the same time and in the same respect" (Aristotle 1971: Book Γ 3). That is to say, if we assign two different truth values to one and the same thought or proposition at the same time and in the same respect, then we deprive it entirely of meaning. But the "law of contradiction" itself has an epistemic value. If this principle were not true, we would not be able to believe or to know something or to say something meaningful, for to believe or to know something is to take it as true. Yet the validity of the "law of contradiction" suggests that self-deception is impossible: it is impossible that a person believes both p and *not-p* at the same time and in the same respect. Yet this is precisely what appears to happen in self-deception. According to Alfred R. Mele, this may be called the "static puzzle" of self-deception, since being self-deceived "requires being in an impossible state of mind" (Mele 2001: 6–7; see also 1998: 37–8; 1987: 121).

In order to escape this puzzle, philosophers have called into question the alleged analogy between self-deception and other-deception that the puzzle seems to rest upon. What characterizes a self-deceiving person, it is claimed, is not that she believes p and *not-p* at the same time and in the same respect, but rather that she attempts to block a certain insight. Consider Karenin again. His self-deception does not consist in his believing that his wife is loyal (p), on the one hand, while knowing that she is not loyal (*not-p*), on the other. This would indeed violate the "law of contradiction." Instead, Karenin deceives himself by believing in Anna's loyalty (p) in spite of strong evidence speaking against it. Yet Karenin refuses to reflect on the evidence; instead of following his doubts, he evades them, such that the belief that Anna is disloyal (*not-p*) as such never enters his conscious thinking.[5]

While this seems to be a solution to the "static puzzle" of self-deception and thus a way to account for self-deceptive states of mind, it does so at the expense of characterizing self-deceivers as fundamentally irrational. Self-deception conceived in this manner does not violate the "law of contradiction," yet it nonetheless violates a basic principle of rationality which Carl Gustav Hempel calls the "requirement of total evidence for inductive reasoning."[6] The principle states that, given a situation in which one has to choose between two mutually exclusive hypotheses, one is rationally required (i) to take into consideration all the reasons and evidence available, and (ii) to accept

---

[5] This is the most common approach to elucidating self-deception (Martin 1986; Löw-Beer 1990; Fingarette 2000; Mele 2001; Davidson 2004b). Yet there are different accounts of how the supposed evasion is to be explained. For this, see Deweese-Boyd (2006) and section 15.4.

[6] Donald Davidson refers to this principle in his analysis of self-deception (2004b).

the hypothesis that is warranted by the strongest reasons or the most powerful evidence. Self-deceivers do not meet these requirements. Hence, self-deception, though logically possible, is still an irrational state of mind.

15.3.2 The dynamic paradox

Self-deception does not come about involuntarily. According to the intentionality condition, it is intended, or at least motivated. Unlike persons who are deceived by others or subject to error, self-deceivers prefer to believe something false instead of facing the truth. But this is odd, given that human beings are rational animals. It is natural to expect them to care about the difference between truth and falsity and to prefer truth. The opposite would be unusual. Hence self-deception is an unusual and unsettling phenomenon.

Moreover, the fact that some of us sometimes deceive ourselves shows that in principle we are able to adjust our beliefs to what we want or wish to be true rather than to what we recognize as true. Does this mean that there is a will to believe something false? Sartre declares outright that such a will is impossible: "We must agree in fact that if I deliberately and cynically attempt to lie to myself, I fail completely in this undertaking; the lie falls back and collapses beneath my look; it is ruined from behind by the very consciousness of lying to myself which pitilessly constitutes itself well within my project as its very condition" (Sartre 2003: 72–3). Sartre's comments touch upon a second puzzle. While self-deception, in contrast to mere error, must be characterized by the intention to dismiss truth, it seems that self-deception cannot be intentional if it is to be successful, since knowledge of this intention undermines the very processes necessary for self-deception. As Sartre makes clear, an intentional attempt to believe something normally ends in failure. Alfred R. Mele calls this the 'dynamic puzzle' of self-deception (Mele 2001: 8; 1998: 37–8; 1987: 138).

15.4 How is self-deception possible?

In response to these puzzles, some philosophers have declared that self-deception as such does not exist (Gur and Sackheim 1979; Borge 2003); others have tried to reduce it to forms of other-deception (Haight 1980; Kipp 1980). But there is a third group of philosophers who, in contrast to these reductive approaches, take self-deception to be a genuine phenomenon and have tried to overcome the puzzles. In order to solve the static puzzle, those defending a 'divisionist' account of self-deception follow a 'partitioning strategy'. They assume that the human mind is divided into several subsystems; while one of the mental systems may come to believe that *p*, the other might still believe that *not-p*. This is taken to be irrational but not impossible, since the self-deceiver is not aware of the contradiction, and the mental subsystems may be internally consistent.

Others claim that self-deception is not intentional but instead based on a 'motivational bias' that causes the self-deceiver to misrepresent and misinterpret the evidence. This is thought to solve the dynamic puzzle. Because of the serious difficulties both the divisionist and the non-intentional approaches face, a third possibility has emerged that accounts for self-deception in terms of virtue theory.

15.4.1 Deception by division

Donald Davidson has famously proposed to solve the puzzles connected to self-deception by focusing on non-logical causal relations between parts or subsystems of the human mind (Davidson 2004a, b, c). According to Davidson, self-deception is irrational in the sense that in the self-deceiver's mind there is one mental event (e.g., a desire) that causes another mental event (e.g., a belief or an intention) without being a reason for it. Thus, according to Davidson, three things are needed to explain irrational thinking: (i) the absence of a logical relation between the mental events involved, (ii) mental causality, and (iii) the possibility of causal relations between separate and autonomous mental subsystems. Davidson declares that his theory is meant to defend central claims of Sigmund Freud's psychoanalytical model of the human mind (Davidson 2004a). The pleasant but unjustified belief is part of the self-deceiver's consciousness, while the opposing unpleasant belief is eliminated from consciousness, or is 'repressed'. Applied to Karenin, this means that, on the one hand, he believes Anna is loyal (p) because of his desire to believe that she is. On the other hand, Karenin has reasons to believe that Anna is disloyal (*not-p*), even though these reasons do not cause the respective conscious belief. Thus, Karenin consciously believes that p while unconsciously believing that *not-p*, without believing the conjunction, p and *not-p*, consciously at the same time.

Two main objections have been raised against this explanation. First, if the human mind is divided into independent and separate subsystems, self-deception is no longer an actual phenomenon that needs to be accounted for. As Sartre argues against Freud, there are only two options for psychoanalysis with respect to self-deception. Either the mind's segmentation into the "Conscious" and the "Unconscious" entails a strict separation, or it does not. If it does, that is, if the "Conscious" does not know anything about the drives and dispositions that slumber in the "Unconscious," then Freud has no explanation for self-deception but only for the odd case of "a lie without a liar," for the "Unconscious" is taken to be entirely concealed from the "Conscious" (Sartre 2003: 74). Hence the knowledge condition of self-deception is not met. But if there is no strict separation between the subsystems, that is, if there is a passage from the "Unconscious" to the "Conscious," perhaps guarded by a "Censor" which determines which drives and unconscious beliefs are to be repressed and which are to be granted access to consciousness, then the problem is not solved but simply shifted to the human *psyche*, for the "Censor" must know about the repressed content of the "Unconscious" (Sartre 2003: 76). Thus, the static puzzle reappears unsolved.

The second objection is related to rationality and irrationality (Beier 2010: 63–5). Divisionists such as Davidson, Amelie Rorty, and David Pears divide the human mind in order to explain irrational behaviour. Yet it seems that once the human mind is divided into several subsystems that can be causally connected but which lack any rational relation, irrational behaviour becomes as normal as rational. As a consequence, we are faced with the question of why irrationality and not rationality needs to be explained. According to Davidson, irrationality deviates from rationality and must be conceived of as "a failure within the house of reason" (Davidson 2004a: 169). Yet this claim cannot be accounted for by the theory of the divided mind—so long as one does not simultaneously offer a theory of its unity.[7]

15.4.2 Motivationally biased beliefs

In order to solve the dynamic puzzle of self-deception, some philosophers have considered the possibility that self-deception is not intentional after all. According to Alfred R. Mele, self-deception occurs when particular motives influence the self-deceiver's evaluation of the pros and cons of her beliefs, without her being conscious of that influence. Hence all self-deception comes down to a "motivationally biased belief" (Mele 2001: 11). For Mele, any desire of the form 'I wish p to be true' can cause the motivated, though not intentional, false belief that p. The desire can trigger one of the following four mechanisms: It can be responsible for (i) negative misinterpretation (e.g., the author of a scientific paper accuses the reviewer, who voted against accepting the paper, of being stupid); (ii) positive misinterpretation (e.g., a person tries to flirt with another and interprets the latter's negative reactions as an attempt to test her seriousness); (iii) selective focus (e.g., a daughter ignores all evidence that she is not her father's favourite child); (iv) selective search for evidence (e.g., a volunteer in an election campaign looks only for those events and actions which confirm her conviction that the candidate she supports is not sexist) (Mele 2001: 25–7). Applied to Karenin, this would mean that his self-deception starts with his strong desire to believe that Anna is loyal (p); this desire leads to a motivationally biased treatment of evidence of Anna's disloyalty and finally to his motivated false belief that she is loyal. Thus, there is no point at which Karenin comes to believe both p and *not-p*; the thought that Anna is disloyal (*not-p*) is present to him only at the very beginning but does not find mental support later on and is no longer maintained once Karenin comes to believe that p. This also implies that the static puzzle has dissolved.

---

[7] Maybe this is the reason why Davidson later changes his picture of the supposed separate parts of the human mind slightly by interpreting it more dynamically and functionally (Davidson 2004b; also Pears 1984 and 1986). The parts or segments of the mind, he now claims, are not to be apprehended statically, as permanently separated from each other; the irrationality of self-deception consists rather in drawing a line that helps keep the contradictory beliefs apart from each other. This may help solve the dynamic puzzle too.

Mark Johnston and Annette Barnes have raised an objection to this account. While they basically support Mele's deflationary and non-intentional account, they claim that not just any desire can cause the bias responsible for self-deception, but instead only 'anxious desires' (Johnston 1988: 66; Barnes 1997: 35). But it cannot be that all anxious desires lead to self-deceptive beliefs. This is why W. J. Talbott and J. L. Bermúdez claim that non-intentional approaches to self-deception have a selection problem. Bermúdez expresses it as follows: "There are all sorts of situations in which, however strongly we desire it to be the case that *p*, we are not in any way biased in favour of the belief that *p*. How are we to distinguish these from situations in which our desires result in motivational bias?" (Bermúdez 2000: 317; see also Talbott 1995: 60–1). It seems it is only because he intends to overlook the evidence pointing to Anna's disloyalty that Karenin can come to believe she is loyal. An additional objection to this account is that self-deception does not appear as blameworthy, for it is non-intentional. Yet this is counter-intuitive.

One might object that there are different types of self-deception, which are in need of different explanations. While the so-called non-intentionalists can account for a type of self-deception "in which the believing and the disbelieving occur at different and successive times," the so-called divisionists are able to explain cases in which "the agreeable belief occupies the conscious mind while the unpleasant one is repressed into the unconscious."[8] Be that as it may, we still have no explanation for the supposed strongest case of self-deception, that is, self-deception where "the belief and the disbelief are simultaneous and both exist in the consciousness of the person" (Demos 1960: 592).

15.4.3 Self-deception and virtue theory

According to Bernard Williams, the self-deceiving person lacks a particular epistemic virtue, the virtue of truthfulness. Truthfulness itself may be divided into two distinct virtues: sincerity and accuracy (Williams 2002). Self-deception, he claims, is more the result of a lack of accuracy—"our passion for getting things right"—than a lack of sincerity. He elucidates this by comparing self-deception to cases of other-deception:

> [A]t the ordinary social, interpersonal level, when there are deceivers around, it is at least as important to improve the caution of the potentially deceived as it is to censure the motives of the deceivers. The virtue of accuracy in listeners is as important as sincerity in informants. If there is such a thing as self-deception, the same, surely, should apply to it: our failures as self-deceived are to be found more significantly, in fact, in our lack of epistemic prudence as victims than in our insincerity as perpetrators.
>
> (Williams 1996: 606)

---

[8] For this description, see Siegler (1962: 469), who refers to Demos.

The virtue-theoretical approach offers a different perspective from which to examine self-deception and the puzzles it seems to involve. It first helps explain why we as rational animals can be inclined to deceive ourselves at all: since some of what we recognize as true can be unpleasant to us and some of what we have reason to recognize as false can appear pleasant, we may feel tempted to accept a thought as true because it pleases or soothes us, and to ignore the reasons that speak against it. Yet it also sheds light on why some of us in these cases may really come to think irrationally: our rational capacities, even though in a sense inborn and natural, have to be developed and brought to perfection for us to become fully rational animals, and that means we have to acquire certain virtues. This holds for both ethical and epistemic virtues. As Linda Zagzebski emphasizes, one learns how to believe the way one should rather than the way one wants, in a similar way to how one learns how to act the way one should rather than the way one wants (Zagzebski 1996: 151). Seen in this light, self-deceivers have not yet succeeded in believing the way they should, i.e., in developing the virtue of accuracy—just as, for instance, akratic agents have not yet developed the virtue of temperance. This is why Raphael Demos comes to explain self-deception in parallel with Aristotle's explanation of weakness of will or *akrasia*: "As with *akrasia*, there is an impulse favoring one belief at the expense of its contradictory; and the person who lies to himself, because of yielding to impulse, fails to notice or ignores what he knows to be the case" (Demos 1960: 594). So self-deception amounts to something like knowing something without noticing it.

Of course, this account needs to be elaborated. It is nonetheless promising, since it helps elucidate the phenomenon of self-deception in at least three important respects: it reveals how it is possible to have contradictory beliefs in a certain, albeit deviant way; it thereby stresses that self-deception is essentially both irrational and intentional; and it reveals that the puzzles of self-deception simply mirror the fact that self-deceivers lack the appropriate epistemic virtue, for their rational desire to get things right is distorted by irrational desires and motives.[9]

---

[9] This, to be sure, does not mean that accuracy equals mistrust because the former is a virtue whereas the latter is a vice.

CHAPTER 16

LYING, TESTIMONY, AND EPISTEMIC VIGILANCE

ELIOT MICHAELSON

16.1 INTRODUCTION

THE thought that knowledge cannot be acquired accidentally has proven to be an enduring one in epistemology. Knowledge, the idea runs, is a particular sort of cognitive achievement, something incompatible with its being the sort of thing that can be acquired by mere accident. In practice, this thought has been taken to mean that knowing that *P* requires more than just believing that *P* where *P* happens to be true. Rather, in order to acquire knowledge that *P*, one must form the belief that *P* on the basis of *good reasons*—reasons to be acquired, presumably, via the good epistemic conduct of the agent.[1]

This basic line of thought can make the acquisition of knowledge via testimony, the acquisition of knowledge that *P* on the basis of having been told "*P*," appear particularly puzzling. In a nutshell, the problem is this: we know that human beings are only so reliable in the best of circumstances, and we also know that they are not always operating in the best of circumstances. People make mistakes. Often, they are lazy in their inquiries and biased in their conclusions. Sometimes, they just plain lie. Given all this, the fact that sometimes we are told that *P*, where *P* is true, by someone who is in the know, might not seem to be enough to make our resultant belief count as non-accidental. If we simply

---

[1] What exactly these 'good reasons' amount to is a matter of significant and enduring controversy. In classical epistemology, the thought was generally that these reasons needed to guarantee *certainty* about what is known (viz. Descartes 1984, Locke 1996). In more contemporary epistemology, the thought has instead been that these reasons must offer a particular kind of *justification* or *warrant* for what one knows (cf. Goldman 1979, Feldman and Conee 2001). The nature of this justification or warrant is in turn disputed, with *internalists* claiming that it must be accessible to the knower (at least in principle) and *externalists* claiming that it need not be so long as it is delivered by systems which are themselves sufficiently reliable (or which bear some other epistemic good-making features).

believe the speaker, then it looks as if we could have just as easily come to believe ¬P if that's what we had instead been told. Many have therefore concluded that something more needs to be said about how the true beliefs we acquire via testimony can count as non-accidental in the relevant sense, and might therefore turn out to be knowledge.

It is worth noting that a few philosophers have been inclined to reject this puzzle by insisting that we rarely, if ever, come to know things on the basis of others' testimony (cf. Plato 1997 and Locke 1996). But given how much of both our ordinary and our specialized knowledge seems to be obtained via testimony—from newspapers, textbooks, airplane blogs, etc.—this looks to be a fairly radical position.[2] Most philosophers have been reluctant to adopt this sort of radicalism, and have therefore sought to offer some more substantive explanation of how the true beliefs we acquire via testimony can count as non-accidental, and can thus count as knowledge.

One common strategy here has been to claim that listeners must exhibit at least some minimal level of sensitivity to the ways in which testimony can be misleading in order to acquire knowledge on the basis of that testimony (cf. Fricker 1994, 2006 and Lackey 1999, 2008). In other words, it will not be a speaker's testimony that *P alone* which provides a listener with knowledge that *P*; rather, what yields knowledge is the speaker's testimony that *P combined* with the fact that certain of the listener's epistemic capacities were functioning properly in the relevant circumstances.

This strategy would seem to have much to recommend it. Consider, for instance, the following example from Lackey (2008: 67). Bill is compulsively trusting of others. In particular, he believes everything that Jill, who happens to be trustworthy but could just as easily not have been, tells him. Here is Lackey's assessment of the case:

> Bill is simply *incapable* of being sensitive to the presence of defeaters regarding her reports. In this respect, he is no better epistemically than a subject who has been brainwashed or programmed to accept any report that Jill makes. For were Bill to be inundated with massive amounts of counterevidence, he would have accepted Jill's testimony just as readily as he did in the complete absence of such counterevidence. Indeed, Bill is such that he would have accepted Jill's testimony *under any circumstances*.
>
> (Lackey 2008: 67)

Lackey contends that Bill cannot come to know things on the basis of Jill's testimony. The problem is that Bill trusts Jill blindly; he believes anything she says, regardless of whether or not he ought to. This sort of blind trust, the idea seems to be, could just as easily have led Bill to believe false things—had Jill been less trustworthy—as to believe true ones. In other words, the process by which Bill comes to believe something true here is, according to Lackey, too accident-prone to count as acquiring knowledge.

---

[2] Interestingly, such negative attitudes toward knowledge via testimony are still relatively popular with respect to aesthetic and moral knowledge.

Let us suppose, therefore, that something more than blind trust is required to acquire knowledge on the basis of the testimony of others. Now we face a new, and possibly much harder, set of questions: just how much more is required? How much evidence must the listener have that her interlocutor is trustworthy on the topic at hand—or at least not untrustworthy? And what sorts of evidence are required? Is all such evidence to be weighted equally, or are certain sources of evidence to be privileged over others in this calculus of trust and trustworthiness? Without answers to each of these questions, our original answer to the question of how we acquire knowledge via others' testimony looks crucially incomplete.

To begin to get a handle on these questions, it might seem tempting to look at the mechanisms we *actually* use to assess the trustworthiness of others' testimony. If we do in fact commonly gain knowledge via testimony, and if we actually make use of only a certain range of mechanisms to assess the trustworthiness of others' testimony, then those mechanisms had better be good enough for acquiring knowledge. This, in rough outline, is the methodology that Sperber et al. (2010) have recently proposed to follow in their inquiry into the nature of knowledge transmission via testimony. Sperber et al. suggest that there is good evidence that listeners actively attend to the apparent trustworthiness of both the speaker and what she is saying via a variety of different mechanisms—some inferential, some social, and some directly observational. It is by using the tools of empirical psychology that we can hope to discover which of these mechanisms of what Sperber et al. term 'epistemic vigilance' actually help us to reliably assess the trustworthiness of others' testimony, and thus to answer the question of which sorts of mechanisms listeners must deploy in order to acquire knowledge via testimony.

While both the general thought that something more than blind trust is required in order to acquire knowledge via testimony and Sperber et al.'s more specific suggestions regarding what that something more amounts to are prima facie appealing, I shall argue here that there is reason to doubt both. In fact, I shall maintain that it is far from clear that there is anything very general to be said at all about just what sorts of vigilance are required of the listener in order for her to acquire knowledge from truthful, well-sourced testimony. What is clear, I think, is that sometimes we can acquire knowledge via testimony even though we are in a state analogous to that of Lackey's compulsively trusting Bill. That is, as I shall argue, sometimes at least we are capable of acquiring knowledge via testimony without exhibiting even the least degree of epistemic vigilance.

16.2 The Reidean view of testimony

Before turning to Sperber et al.'s (2010) discussion of the mechanisms of epistemic vigilance, it will help to get their preferred opponent more squarely in view. Sperber et al. (2010) cast their view in opposition to a sort of view of testimonial knowledge that can be traced back to the 18th-century philosopher Thomas Reid. According to Reid and his successors, we are in general entitled to trust in the testimony of others. For Reid, this was because we are endowed by God with reciprocal dispositions to speak truthfully to and to trust one another. Our entitlement to trust can then be grounded in the disposition to speak truthfully, since, so long as we as speakers are not consistently misinformed, that trust will prove a reliable guide to truth (Reid 2000: section 24).[3] More recent inheritors of the Reidean tradition have (understandably) tended to eschew this sort of appeal to God. Instead, they have suggested that a priori arguments can be offered to ground the basic Reidean thesis: either to the effect that we could not have a shared language at all if a norm of truth-telling were not to generally obtain (cf. Coady 1992, Burge 1993, and Millikan 1987) or to the effect that trust in ourselves rationally demands trust in others (cf. Foley 2001, 2005 and Zagzebski 2012).[4]

Regardless of what exactly explains our entitlement to trust one another's testimony, the Reidean picture of knowledge transmission is completed by positing that knowledge will be successfully transmitted via testimony so long as (i) the listener in fact trusts the speaker, and thus forms the relevant belief on the basis of her testimony, (ii) the speaker tells the listener something that she in fact knows, and (iii) the listener's default entitlement to trust the speaker is not overruled in the relevant circumstances. Reidean views of testimony are generally assumed to be relatively permissive, allowing that knowledge can be transmitted via testimony in a wide array of circumstances. It is worth noting, however, that the permissiveness of the view in fact hinges on when exactly the Reidean envisions condition (iii) coming into play.[5]

Sperber et al.'s (2010) first objection to the Reidean view of testimony is that it is built on some empirically questionable foundations. Human beings appear to be rather trusting in situations where the stakes are low (Gilbert, Krull, and Malone 1990), but there is evidence that they will generally refrain from trusting each other when there is more at stake (Hasson, Simmons, and Todorov 2005). What's more, Sperber et al. (2010: 370) claim, there are good evolutionary reasons to think that humans will often be disposed to lie, so long as they think they can get away with it. So perhaps, pace Reid, human beings lack any sort of innate disposition to tell the truth or to trust each other.[6]

---

[3] And assuming, of course, that humans acting in good faith are generally reliable.

[4] For precursors to the former sort of argument, see also Lewis (1969) and Davidson (1973). For critical discussion of the latter sort of argument, see Fricker (2014, 2016a).

[5] If, for example, the Reidean were to add that this default entitlement is overruled in exactly the circumstances where the listener fails to exhibit any sensitivity to the ways in which testimony may be misleading, then the distance between the Reidean and her opponents would shrink substantially. There would still be the issue of whether it is best to conceive of the justification one has for one's knowledge as a priori (though with an a posteriori defeater) or a posteriori, but at this point one might reasonably wonder whether this amounts to anything more than a mere verbal dispute. Note that this question of *aprioricity*—which defines the line between 'reductionists' and 'anti-reductionists'—is distinct from the question of whether justification must be transparent to the knower in order to count as such. This latter question defines the line between epistemic internalists and externalists, as mentioned in note 1. For discussion, see Gerken (2013).

[6] Of course, an alternative explanation is available for the Hasson data: we are naturally disposed to trust one another, but that disposition is overridden in certain circumstances. For more on the difficulty of adjudicating between these alternatives, see Johnston (1992). See also Michaelian (2013)

That would presumably serve to undermine Reid's original argument for our having a broad, default entitlement to trust each other.

The enduring philosophical importance of Reid's ideas, however, has rested on his basic claim that we are, by default, entitled to trust each other—that, aside from some special circumstances, we can come to know P merely by hearing "P" from a knowledgeable speaker and then trusting that speaker—not on Reid's particular explanation for *why* we have this default entitlement. I will therefore set this first worry to the side and focus on what I take to be the core Reidean claim: that the widespread success of knowledge transmission via testimony is to be explained via an appeal to a default entitlement to trust each other, regardless of what exactly it is that grounds that default entitlement. As a purely epistemic thesis—a thesis about when we bear the epistemic status *entitlement to believe P*, a status which itself serves to underwrite the acquisition of knowledge that P in the right circumstances—this thesis is naturally compatible with a wide range of actual human behaviors. In particular, it is fully compatible with human beings being distrustful in many circumstances, or even by default.

The pressing question therefore becomes: are we, as Reid claimed, entitled by default to trust each other? And, if so, what can serve to overrule this default entitlement? I shall suggest that, at least sometimes, we are entitled to trust each other even when there is overriding evidence that we should not. The problem for those who defend the need for epistemic vigilance runs parallel to a traditional problem for foundationalists in epistemology (i.e., those who think that most of our knowledge is built up, via inference, from a relatively small pool of basic, non-inferential knowledge): in order to make judgments about the plausibility of some bit of testimony, we need to have some previous evidence either about the speaker or pertinent to whatever she is telling us. At some point, it seems, we will need to be naively credulous in order to get any sort of vigilance mechanisms up and running. If this is right, then it simply cannot be the case that we are required to always be epistemically vigilant in order to acquire knowledge via testimony.

16.3 THE MECHANISMS OF VIGILANCE

Suppose, as certainly seems plausible, that we do at least sometimes attend to the quality of a speaker's testimony that P in the process of coming to believe P on the basis of that testimony—or refraining from doing so. Just what sorts of mechanisms are involved in the process? Lackey (2008: 66) suggests that we sometimes have independent reasons—that is, reasons independent from our assessment of the proposition P—to suspect that a speaker is lying to us. For instance, one might know the speaker to be an inveterate liar. Or one might suspect that the speaker would be well-served by getting the listener

for more extensive discussion of the empirical and evolutionary evidence regarding human beings' disposition to trust one another, and for arguments in favor of such a disposition on the basis of that evidence.

to believe *P* regardless of whether or not *P* is true. Beyond this, however, Lackey offers us little detail on the sorts of reasons we might have for rejecting some bit of testimony. Others have suggested that when we acquire knowledge via testimony we typically check to see whether we already possess independent, corroborating evidence for the truth of what we have been told (cf. Fricker 1994, 2016b and Graham 2006).

Sperber et al. (2010) hope to shed additional light on this question by cataloguing the mechanisms of epistemic vigilance that have been studied in the recent literature in empirical psychology. They note four such mechanisms: first, listeners may make use of their background knowledge to decide whether the proposition *P* is independently plausible or implausible (374–6). In other words, listeners may check to see whether the proffered testimony coheres with their other beliefs. Second, listeners may rely on their own knowledge of the speaker's reliability or unreliability in past exchanges (369–71). Third, listeners may rely on more social assessments of the speaker's reliability or unreliability (379–84). Fourth, listeners may attend to nonverbal cues that the speaker produces, cues which might serve to inform the listener whether the speaker is testifying in good faith (370).

Sperber et al. (2010: 370) almost immediately dismiss the relevance of this fourth mechanism—attending to nonverbal cues while hearing some bit of testimony—to the question of how we manage to acquire knowledge via testimony on the basis of the fact that human beings turn out to be horribly unreliable at identifying deceptive intent on the basis of physiological cues (cf. Vrij 2000, Malone and DePaulo 2001, and Bond and DePaulo 2006). In fact, human beings seem to be rather bad lie detectors—no better than chance—even when we are explicitly trained to detect lies. What generally increases with training is confidence, not accuracy (cf. DePaulo and Pfeifer 1986, Ekman and O'Sullivan 1991, and Mann, Vrij, and Bull 2004, and Vrij 2004).[7] Thus, if what we wanted was some mechanism that would help us explain how it is that we systematically discount unreliable testimony, this cannot be it.

The remaining three sorts of vigilance mechanisms, the ones that Sperber et al. take to be potentially relevant to the project of explaining how we acquire knowledge via testimony, vary on two dimensions: on the one hand, these mechanisms may be social or non-social. On the other hand, they can target either the content of the specific testimony under consideration or they can target past instances of that speaker's testimony. Strangely, Sperber et al. (2010) fail to identify a social, content-targeted mechanism of epistemic vigilance. It is relatively easy to see what such a mechanism might amount to, however: listeners might appeal to their knowledge of whether reliable sources find *P* plausible, regardless of whether or not they themselves have any independent evidence for or against *P*.

---

[7] Interestingly, it also doesn't seem to matter whether the liars in question are experts or inexperienced, e.g., three-year-olds (Lewis, Stanger, and Sullivan 1989 and Talwar and Lee 2002a). For more on our development of the ability to deceive each other, see Chapter 32. It is also worth noting that there do seem to be both physiological, and especially verbal, correlates of lying—even if most of us are ill-adapted to actually picking up on them.

The important thing to notice about the three proposed mechanisms of epistemic vigilance that Sperber et al. identify as potentially relevant to explaining how we sort good from bad testimony, in addition to the fourth that I have added, is that each relies crucially on one or another sort of background knowledge.[8] This background knowledge varies with regard to whether it is relevant to the plausibility of P itself or whether it has to do with the reliability of the speaker in general, but it is background knowledge all the same. In order to engage any of these proposed mechanisms of epistemic vigilance, the listener must therefore either (i) know some other things relevant to whether P is plausible, (ii) know whether the speaker has proven reliable in the past on the sorts of matters at hand, (iii) know whether others have, in the past, found the speaker to be a reliable guide to the sorts of matters at hand, or (iv) know whether others (preferably experts) find P to be plausible. The question is whether any of these sorts of background knowledge can themselves plausibly be acquired independently of testimony.

Let us briefly pause to take stock. We began with the plausible idea, pushed forcefully by Lackey (2008), that if listeners are to obtain knowledge via testimony, they bear at least some responsibility for checking the quality of the testimony they are hearing before coming to believe it. Then we asked just what sort of responsibility this is, what sorts of plausibility-checking mechanisms listeners are required to employ in order to obtain knowledge via testimony. Following Sperber et al. (2010), who have provided perhaps the most extensive reckoning of the possible mechanisms to date, we identified four mechanisms that human beings might in fact use to sort good testimony from bad. Finally, we have observed that each of these proposed mechanisms of epistemic vigilance presupposes the possession of one or another sort of background knowledge. I turn now to a two-stage argument to the effect that, at least sometimes, we are capable of acquiring knowledge without employing anything like these proposed mechanisms of epistemic vigilance.

16.4 Stage 1: Toward a regress

If Sperber et al. (2010) are right about the general shape of the mechanisms of epistemic vigilance, then we find ourselves facing a puzzle: we need some background knowledge to get these mechanisms of epistemic vigilance up and running. But it looks as if

---

[8] Sperber et al. (2010) tend to speak of the listener's background 'beliefs' instead of her background 'knowledge'. However, since Sperber et al. reject the epistemic relevance of our perception of trustworthiness (or lack thereof) based on physiological cues on account of the extreme unreliability of such mechanisms, they cannot consistently rely purely on background beliefs as opposed to background knowledge. The problem is that an individual listener's background beliefs could be systematically unreliable (as with paranoid schizophrenics). That would mean that epistemic vigilance mechanisms based on those background beliefs would, in such cases, fail to reliably lead the listener to acquiring knowledge, as opposed to false beliefs, via testimony. On the other hand, if these mechanisms rely on background knowledge, then unreliability should not prove to be a serious worry.

testimony is one of our main sources of knowledge, particularly general world knowledge. Is it plausible that we could somehow acquire enough knowledge independently of the knowledge we acquire via testimony to get at least one of these mechanisms up and running? Supposing we could get even a single mechanism up and running, we might then hope to use that mechanism to bootstrap the rest into action. As I shall argue, the prospects for such bootstrapping look dim.

To see this, begin by focusing on the *sorts* of knowledge required for each of the proposed vigilance mechanisms we have considered. The first mechanism, consideration of whether *P* is independently plausible, will generally have to rely on what we might think of as *general* or *broad* world knowledge. This won't be knowledge to the effect that *that's a red flower* or *this pot is heavy*, but rather of *how cars work*, or *that things tend to spoil if left out for too long*, or *that whales are mammals*. It is knowledge of this latter sort, knowledge of generalizations, which allows us to gauge the plausibility of more specific claims in particular circumstances. But while generalizations of this sort can in principle be acquired by a single investigator, it seems safe to say that most of us acquire the vast majority of our general knowledge via testimony. If that's right, then this first mechanism looks ill-suited to bootstrap the others; far from explaining how we might acquire our first bits of knowledge via testimony, the proper function of this mechanism presupposes our antecedent possession of a significant stock of testimonial knowledge.[9]

The second mechanism, considering the record of the speaker, might at first seem to fare slightly better. For example, the speaker in question might have already made a number of claims involving things which are easily verifiable by an independent investigator. In that case, and assuming that the listener has followed up and independently investigated some number of these claims, the listener would seem to have acquired a body of independent evidence for or against the reliability of the speaker. Thus, it looks as though the listener should be in a good position to trust or distrust the speaker going forward, on the basis of this independent evidence. When this evidence points toward the trustworthiness of the speaker, the listener would seem to be in a position to start acquiring knowledge via testimony, at least from this source.

In contrast, the third mechanism—considering what other people think of the reliability of the speaker—looks less promising. The reason is simple: the most direct way of coming to know what others think of the trustworthiness and reliability of the speaker is via the testimony of those third parties. Otherwise, one is left either (i) relying on the testimony of others still about the mental states of the relevant third parties, or (ii) inferring what these third parties think of the speaker based on their non-testimonial behavior. (i) clearly won't help, since it relies on yet another sort of knowledge acquired via testimony. And, in the absence of further evidence, I am highly skeptical that (ii) will

---

[9] This basic point about the importance of general world knowledge for assessing the plausibility of testimony is not new with me. See, for instance, Coady (1992), Stevenson (1993), and Sosa (1994), all of whom make closely related points.

prove to rate any better than chance.[10] This mechanism thus looks like a poor candidate on which to pin our hopes.

Lastly, there is my fourth proposed mechanism: considering whether others find P to be plausible, regardless of what one thinks oneself. But this faces much the same problem as the third mechanism, in that it is unclear how one might come to know what others think about such things except via their testimony. So this mechanism too looks like a poor choice.

We are left with the following situation: the last two mechanisms plausibly rely on knowledge that must be acquired via testimony to get up and running. The first mechanism might, on occasion, fail to require such knowledge. But in a huge number of interesting cases, cases where we acquire some bit of knowledge not easily available via our own perceptual experience, its proper function plausibly presupposes a stock of knowledge acquired via testimony. The second mechanism, considering the record of the speaker, thus looks to be our best bet for explaining how we start acquiring knowledge via testimony—and, thereby, how we acquire sufficient background knowledge to get the remaining mechanisms of epistemic vigilance up and running.

The question we now need to ask is: how plausible is it that, outside of a laboratory environment, listeners regularly investigate a series of claims by a single speaker and thereby generate an assessment of her trustworthiness? It seems to me that the answer is: not very plausible. There are two main reasons for this. First of all, many of the things that we learn via testimony are things that simply cannot be investigated by a single individual—e.g., *that the Earth is round* or *that London has over ten million inhabitants*— except perhaps in some very special circumstances. In other words, there are serious practical limitations on our ability to assess the reliability of speakers by first-personally investigating the quality of their testimony. Second of all, it seems implausible to think that human beings regularly conduct follow-up investigations with regard to the initial testimony we hear from the first few speakers in our lives. Rather, the second proposed mechanism plausibly serves to help us distinguish reliable from unreliable testifiers only once we already have a stock of knowledge against which we can immediately, not subsequently, check the speaker's previous testimony.

Of course, such a priori considerations are hardly decisive in the present context. What we really want is some empirical evidence about how young children actually act. Thankfully, we now know a fair bit about this; unfortunately, it looks to run contrary to Sperber et al.'s predictions regarding how children should behave, supposing that they are relying on the second mechanism of vigilance. Sperber et al. (2010: 372) rightly stress that children are sensitive to speakers' ability to make false statements by the time they are three or four (Koenig and Harris 2007, Corriveau and Harris 2009, 2010, and Birch, Akmal, and Frampton 2010). However, in spite of this sensitivity, children around this age tend to remain indiscriminately trusting of adult speakers (Koenig,

---

[10] Our unreliability in judging trustworthiness based on cues other than the plausibility and other than the content of the utterance (discussed briefly in section 16.3) should, I think, serve to support this skeptical attitude. Ultimately, however, this is an empirical question.

Clément, and Harris 2004). In fact, although three-year-olds do display some sensitivity to false testimony, they seem to be largely incapable of using that information to track a reporter's reliability (Clément, Koenig, and Harris 2004). It thus hardly looks plausible to posit that young children employ anything like Sperber et al.'s second mechanism of epistemic vigilance when they acquire their first bits of knowledge via testimony.

In fact, adults too seem capable of acquiring knowledge via testimony even when they lack the requisite background knowledge to employ any of the mechanisms of epistemic vigilance identified by Sperber et al. For example, one might come to know that the Sears Tower is two blocks to the east of Union Station in Chicago on the basis of the testimony of a complete stranger (cf. Lackey 2007b).[11] Or one might acquire some bit of mathematical knowledge by relying on the Wikipedia entry on harmonic functions.[12]

Perhaps Sperber et al. and others like them will be willing to bite this second bullet, but I doubt they will want to bite the first. Their basic proposal was to offer a psychologically plausible story about how we are capable of acquiring knowledge via testimony by looking at how we actually evaluate the testimony we hear. What we have been pushed to is a story on which it is sufficient to deploy just one of their mechanisms of epistemic vigilance—gauging the speaker's trustworthiness based on her past testimony—in order to acquire our first instances of knowledge via testimony. But this seems to entail that early-stage knowers should be distrustful by default if they are to start acquiring knowledge. And the claim that young children are distrustful by default is a claim that we have absolutely no evidence for.

16.5 STAGE 2: LEARNING FROM UNRELIABLE SOURCES

So far, I have argued that Sperber et al.'s (2010) second proposed mechanism of epistemic vigilance looks to be the one that might most plausibly be deployed in the absence of any background knowledge acquired on the basis of testimony. Thus, it looks to be the most plausible mechanism to bootstrap the rest into functionality. The only problem was that it relied on young children's being distrustful by default, which seems highly implausible. Suppose instead that young children are trusting by default. Just how damaging would this be for Sperber et al.'s general picture of knowledge acquisition?

---

[11] Lackey (2007b: 353) herself suggests that the listener's ability to acquire knowledge via testimony in this case can be explained in terms of her background beliefs about the general reliability of strangers at giving directions. Whether or not this is correct, it doesn't appear to conform to any of the mechanisms that Sperber et al. consider.

[12] There are worries about whether we should think that such knowledge is obtained in related cases complicated with Gettier-type background conditions (cf. Harman 1973 and Plantiga 1993). I am not primarily concerned with such situations here, however.

If adults regularly go out of their way to be extra reliable around children, then perhaps this default trust would not be so damaging. In that case, then Sperber et al. might well adopt a *limited Reidean* position of the sort sketched in Goldberg (2008): one according to which childhood is treated as the safe training environment that enables us to acquire our first bits of knowledge via testimony and to get the sorts of mechanisms of epistemic vigilance we rely on in adulthood up and running. Unfortunately, I think we have reason to suspect that children are regularly exposed to both insincerity and error. At the very least, I think that proponents of epistemic vigilance will have a hard time squaring the claim that children's epistemic environment is specially protected with some of their own basic motivations.

Recall the dialectical situation we find ourselves in: proponents of epistemic vigilance as a requirement on the acquisition of knowledge via testimony thought that error and lies are so common in our ordinary epistemic environment that any true beliefs we might acquire simply on the basis of believing one another would count as *accidental*. Now, perhaps we do endeavor to lie to children less often than we do to adults, but that still leaves us facing the problem of unreliability. The fact that we are talking to children hardly seems to make us more attuned to the way the world is. For instance, until quite recently we were teaching our children *that the world is flat, that women are naturally less logical than men, that there are ghosts*, etc. This hardly looks like a stock of background knowledge, but rather one of false beliefs. Institutional settings such as schools hardly look to be any better in this regard. Perhaps they (sometimes) teach science and mathematics better than many parents would, but the history they teach is very often grossly distorted by considerations of political expedience.

Nor do I really think that we should accept that we don't regularly lie to children. Perhaps we do generally refrain from lying to other people's children, and perhaps we try to avoid lying to children in ways that will cause them immediate harm. But none of that means that we don't lie to children. Like Bok (1999), I think we very often lie to children about things we'd prefer not to explain to them. A Calvin & Hobbes cartoon by Bill Watterson from April 18, 1987 will nicely illustrate my point. Here, I present its content in dialogue form, since OUP claims that it cannot be reproduced under fair use:

> CALVIN: Dad, how do people make babies?
> DAD: Most people just go to Sears, buy the kit, and follow the assembly instructions.
> CALVIN: I came from Sears??
> DAD: No, *you* were a blue light special at Kmart. Almost as good, and a lot cheaper.
> CALVIN: Aauughhh!
> MOM: Dear, what are you telling Calvin now?!

Perhaps, one might claim, this is a highly uncommon phenomenon. But I doubt that; there's a reason, after all, that the comic strip is funny.

We thus have little reason to think that childhood constitutes a special type of safe learning environment, one where adults neither intentionally nor unintentionally misinform children. But if young children are trusting by default, then these children start to look rather similar to Lackey's compulsively trusting Bill—at least with respect to their parents, caregivers, teachers, etc. And yet, in contrast to Bill, there is little temptation here to think that children cannot acquire knowledge via testimony. If we were so tempted, we would then have to explain how it is that we ever manage to acquire the first bits of general world knowledge that plausibly underlie so much of our ability to distinguish good from bad testimony later on in life. In other words, we'd be back to facing the regress introduced in the last section.[13]

We find ourselves facing a trilemma: either (i) mechanisms of epistemic vigilance aren't required to acquire knowledge via testimony, or (ii) there are some mechanisms of epistemic vigilance that children actually apply but which we have somehow failed to consider, or else (iii) children are incapable of acquiring knowledge via testimony. I take it that the third horn won't prove widely palatable. Perhaps the second horn can be made good on, but I am skeptical that it can be. Tentatively then, I conclude that epistemic vigilance mechanisms are not always required to acquire knowledge via testimony. Children can acquire knowledge via testimony despite being extremely credulous (at least in certain situations, with respect to certain individuals) and incapable of distrusting a speaker even when, in some sense, they really ought to. That is, children look capable of acquiring knowledge via testimony even when they fail to exhibit any significant degree of epistemic vigilance.[14]

16.6 SURVEYING THE LANDSCAPE

Supposing that we take the first horn, what then might we say about the role of epistemic vigilance in the acquisition of knowledge via testimony? As far as I can tell, there are three main options, which I order from least to most radical. First, we might posit that children and adults simply acquire knowledge via testimony *differently* from each other (cf. Fricker 1995). That is, children are subject to different norms from those to which

---

[13] The above argument substantially overlaps with what Lackey (2005) calls the 'Infant/Child Objection', and it is very much indebted to her discussion there. Unfortunately, a full comparison of our respective arguments would require a lengthier digression into the reductionist/anti-reductionist debate introduced in note 5 than space allows for here.

[14] Interestingly, in spite of the mixed quality of the testimony that they hear—and for some period of time at least, believe—children commonly prove to be capable, over time, of disregarding at least some of the false things they were previously told. This might suggest that children's epistemic lives should be thought to mirror their lives as language learners, where children quickly disregard mistaken rules they have internalized. In particular, we might think of children as retroactively applying a degree of epistemic vigilance to the beliefs they acquire early on via testimony, once they have obtained a sufficient base to work from. However, we would still lack an explanation of how children might be able to build up networks of coherence in the *right way*, so as to be able to retroactively screen this earlier testimony and sort good from bad testimony at a rate greater than chance. So this sort of suggestion, while perhaps *prima facie* appealing, is also highly incomplete.

adults are. Adults are required to exhibit a degree of vigilance in order to acquire knowledge via testimony, whereas children are subject to no such requirement.[15] Put slightly differently: knowing that *P* is itself a context-sensitive status, and children and adults differ in the sorts of standards they must live up to in order to count as knowing that *P* in otherwise identical situations.[16]

Second, we might posit a sort of particularism about the norms to which people must conform in order to acquire knowledge via testimony. Adults must, in general, exhibit some degree of vigilance whereas children needn't—but these are generalizations, not rules, and there will turn out to be exceptions on either end. If we can cook up convincing cases of such exceptions, and if we cannot capture those exceptions with any neat set of epistemic principles, then we may well be motivated to explore this sort of particularist option.

Third and finally, we might reject the thought with which we began this chapter: that epistemic vigilance is required to explain the non-accidentalness of knowledge acquired via testimony. Instead, when we judge that compulsively trusting adults like Bill cannot gain knowledge from Jill, what we are really doing is judging that Bill is doing something *bad*, epistemically speaking. We expect more from normal adults, though not from children. As philosophers, the idea runs, we have been all too ready to move from the thought that *A* has done something epistemically bad in context *C* to the thought that *A* has failed to acquire knowledge in *C*. But this just shows that we are apt to conflate two distinct notions—good epistemic practices and what is required for the acquisition of knowledge via testimony—that are best kept apart when we seek to uncover what knowledge is.

While I am sympathetic to the last, and most radical, of these options, I will not pretend to be able to muster a full defense of that position here. Instead, I will constrain myself to offering a few considerations in its favor.[17] As against the first option, the third option allows us to retain a unified set of conditions under which we can acquire knowledge via testimony. Assuming that the nature of knowledge reflects, at least in part, the conditions under which it can be obtained, this preserves the hope of ultimately offering a unified account of knowledge, a single answer to the question 'What is knowledge?' The second option might not force us to give up this unity—if, for instance, we were to adopt a particularist line on the basis of our epistemic limitations while remaining open to there being a unified, if inaccessible, metaphysical story about knowledge—but

---

[15] Or perhaps proponents of this option will want to appeal to some other measure of mental development. It is also worth noting that children and adults might not turn out to be the only relevant cuts. There might, for instance, turn out to be different norms governing *expert knowledge* from those governing *ordinary adult knowledge*.

[16] If I'm wrong about the degree to which children's epistemic environments are unprotected, then one might instead claim that children and adults are subject to the same, environmentally sensitive norms as adults. Effectively, the suggestion would be to deny that children and adults are generally found in 'otherwise identical situations'.

[17] For very different arguments in favor a view of knowledge along these lines, see Aarnio (2010) and Baker-Hytch and Benton (2015).

it does at least put pressure on the thought that knowledge is a unified kind. Why, once we have adopted a particularist framework on knowledge-acquisition, should we think that knowledge constitutes a single natural kind as opposed to a hodgepodge of different kinds cobbled together over the course of our conceptual history?

Rather than try to face down either of these worries, I would suggest that we consider rejecting our initial judgment that Bill cannot gain knowledge from Jill via her testimony in the case where Bill is compulsively trusting. The worry was that Bill was too lucky, that he effectively acquired his true belief by accident. But while there is certainly a way in which we can think of Bill's acquisition of knowledge as accidental—Jill could, after all, have lied to him and he would have believed her anyway—there is an important way in which Bill's acquisition of knowledge here is not accidental at all. Given that Bill learned that P on the basis of the sincere testimony of a *knower*, he could not easily have acquired a false belief in this manner.[18] Perhaps then whatever sort of luck Bill exhibits in trusting Jill is not the right sort of luck to make his acquisition of a true belief accidental, and hence is not the right sort of luck to undermine his claim to knowledge.[19]

16.7 Conclusion

In this chapter, I introduced the basic motivation for the claim that the listeners need to live up to a certain standard—that they must exhibit some degree of epistemic vigilance—in order to acquire knowledge via testimony. The worry was that, if we don't require listeners to exhibit some degree of epistemic vigilance, then it looks as if they will be able to acquire knowledge via testimony too easily. For instance, listeners will be able to acquire knowledge via testimony even in cases where they could have just as easily been given false information, and where they would have believed it anyway. By requiring that knowers exhibit some degree of epistemic vigilance in order to count as such, we seem to be well-positioned to explain how it is that the knowledge we acquire via testimony is non-accidental in an important sense, how the mechanisms through which we acquire knowledge via testimony do not leave us beholden to the whims of liars and charlatans.

I then went on to sketch the ways in which philosophers and cognitive scientists more generally have suggested we might in fact exhibit epistemic vigilance. Following Sperber

---

[18] This is closely related, though not quite equivalent, to Lackey's (2008) claim that if one knows that P on the basis of testimony, then one could not have come to believe P via the same *evidential source* without P's being true. This notion of an evidential source—roughly, the manner in which the warrant or justification for the belief in question was ultimately acquired—is to be contrasted with a *testimonial source*—that is, the speaker.

[19] For discussion of the complexities of the myriad phenomena that might be classified as 'epistemic luck', see Pritchard (2005, 2008).

et al. (2010), I assumed that if we are required to regulate our trust in testimony in order to acquire knowledge, then the mechanisms by which we regulate that trust had better be psychologically real. We clearly do acquire knowledge via testimony, so we do not want to impose requirements that would prove to be at odds with this.

Finally, I argued that there looks to be no easy way of squaring the claim that epistemic vigilance is required in order to acquire knowledge via testimony with (i) the fact that the mechanisms of vigilance we apparently employ all require prior knowledge of the sort that is itself most plausibly acquired via testimony, (ii) the fact that children seem to acquire knowledge via testimony while failing to employ anything like vigilance mechanisms, and (iii) the fact that children's learning environments appear to be riddled with error and falsehoods. On the basis of these considerations, I urged that we should consider rejecting the thought that listeners must live up to a certain epistemic standard in order to acquire knowledge via testimony. Knowledge acquired via testimony will count as non-accidental, I have suggested, not because of the proper function of some epistemic capacity of the listener, but because it is acquired on the basis of the sincere testimony of a knower.

Acknowledgements

For very helpful discussion and feedback, thanks to Maria Alvarez, Denis Bühler, Julien Dutant, Mikkel Gerken, Nat Hansen, Justin Jennings, Clayton Littlejohn, David Owens, Matthew Parrott, Jessica Pepp, Andrew Reisner, Andreas Stokke, Sarah Stroud, two anonymous referees for this volume, and the participants in the King's College London Normativity and Rationality Seminar.

PART III
TYPES OF LIES AND DECEPTION

CHAPTER 17

KNOWLEDGE LIES AND GROUP LIES

JULIA STAFFEL

17.1 INTRODUCTION

An important part of the philosophical debate about lying focuses on delineating particularly interesting kinds of lies, and explaining how they work. This article is about two kinds of lies, knowledge lies and group lies, which have been singled out in the literature as meriting their own discussion.

Typically, we think of lies as working in roughly the following way: a liar wants her addressee to come to believe some claim p that the liar believes to be false. So the liar tells the addressee that p, hoping that the addressee will be deceived into believing that p.[1] For example, a child might lie and say she did not break the vase, hoping that her parents will believe her and will not punish her.[2]

Knowledge lies are interestingly different from such garden-variety lies, because in telling a knowledge lie, the liar does not intend to deceive the addressee into believing a false claim. Instead, the liar intends to prevent the addressees from knowing, but not necessarily from believing, some true claim. A compelling example of a knowledge lie can be found in the movie *Spartacus* (directed by Stanley Kubrick, USA 1960). The Roman general Marcus Licinius Crassus is trying to find Spartacus among a group of slaves, and tells the group that if they identify him, their lives will be spared. Spartacus gets up to turn himself in, but as soon as he gets up, one slave after another rises and declares "I am Spartacus." All the slaves are lying, but when they repeat "I am Spartacus," their intention is not to convince the general of any particular false

---

[1] Throughout this chapter, I will use the letter "p" to denote statements, such as "I am Spartacus," "This dish contains peanuts," or "Dr. Appendix is a good researcher."

[2] To be clear, this is not intended as a rigorous definition of lying. Rather, it is intended as a characterization of a stereotypical case of lying.

claim. They simply want to prevent him from knowing which of them is Spartacus (Sorensen 2010).

Group lies are lies that are told by a group, such as a company, a government, or your knitting circle. Group lies are unlike typical lies, because they are not straightforwardly related to lies told by individuals who are members of the lying group. A famous group lie was told by the East German politician Walter Ulbricht at a press conference on 15 June 1961, two months before the Berlin Wall was erected. Responding to a question about whether there would be an inner-city border at the Brandenburg gate, he declared that nobody had any intention to build a wall. Ulbricht was of course speaking—and lying—on behalf of the East German government, which was very keen on building a wall.[3]

In what follows, I will characterize knowledge lies and group lies in more detail. For each type of lie, I will first give a more rigorous characterization, then discuss why this kind of lie deserves special philosophical attention, and lastly provide some critical discussion of the accounts of each type of lie that have been proposed in the philosophical literature.

17.2 Knowledge Lies

17.2.1 What are knowledge lies?

Knowledge lies were first systematically characterized by Sorensen (2010). Besides giving a wealth of examples, he offers the following definition of a knowledge lie:

Knowledge lie:

An assertion that p is a knowledge-lie exactly if intended to prevent the addressee from knowing that p is untrue but is not intended to deceive the addressee into believing p.

(Sorensen 2010: 610)

---

[3] By contrast, the Spartacus example is not a case of a group lie. When a group lies, there is one statement that the group jointly lies about (see my discussion in the second part of this chapter). But this is not the case here: the first-person pronoun *I* refers to a different slave in each utterance. Hence, the content of each slave's lie is different. There is not one proposition that is the content of each lie, which could be the content of a lie the group is telling jointly. Rather, each slave tells a different lie, and taken together, these lies achieve the effect of masking Spartacus.

One might also be tempted to think that the slaves are telling bald-faced lies. Someone is telling a bald-faced lie when it is common knowledge between the liar and her audience that she is lying. However, the individual slaves' lies here do not meet that condition. Of course the general knows that at most one slave is not lying, but for each slave, he does not know that this particular slave is lying. Hence, it is not common knowledge for any specific slave that this slave is lying, and thus these are not examples of bald-faced lies.

The feature that makes knowledge lies special, according to Sorensen, is the absence on the part of the liar of an intention to deceive. Deceiving is understood in this context as intentionally causing someone to adopt a false belief. The liar who tells a knowledge-lie specifically targets her addressee's knowledge, but does not aim to alter her beliefs. Consider the following example:

> Dr. Head is considering firing Dr. Appendix because of his weak research. Head will only fire Appendix if he knows that his research is bad. Head thus consults Dr. Heart for a recommendation. Head knows that if Appendix's research is good, then Heart will tell the truth and say it is good. If Appendix's work is bad, then Heart may or may not tell the truth. Hence, if Heart says that Appendix's work is bad, Head will know it is bad, and so he'll fire Appendix. Heart knows that Head will interpret her statements in this way, and crafts her letter accordingly. She thinks Appendix's work is bad, but she wants to prevent Appendix from being fired, and so she lies and says his work is good. Heart knows that, by doing so, she won't make Head believe that Appendix's work is good, but she will prevent him from knowing that it isn't, and so she'll prevent Head from firing Appendix.
>
> (Sorensen 2010: 611)

What makes this example a case of a knowledge lies is Heart's intention to prevent Head from knowing that Appendix is a weak researcher, rather than to make Head believe that he is a good researcher. In fact, Head believes throughout that Appendix's research is bad; Heart's lie is intended to prevent this belief from being knowledge.

17.2.2 What makes knowledge lies interesting as their own category?

Why should we care specifically about lies that target knowledge, rather than belief? There are two reasons: one has to do with the special normative role many philosophers take knowledge to have that is not shared by mere belief. The second has to do with the alleged deception-free nature of knowledge lies.

In the recent philosophical literature on knowledge, it has been argued that our everyday practices give us good evidence to think that whether or not someone can permissibly act on some claim p, or assert p, depends on whether or not she knows that p is true (Williamson 2000; Hawthorne 2004).[4] Philosophers who hold this view typically endorse versions of the following norms:

Knowledge-action norm:

Do not rely on p in your practical reasoning unless you know that p.

---

[4] An excellent overview of the debate about knowledge norms can be found in Benton's article on the topic in the Internet Encyclopedia of Philosophy (Benton 2014), which also contains further references to the relevant literature.

Knowledge-assertion norm:

Do not assert that p unless you know that p.

Defenders of knowledge norms argue that having a true and/or justified belief in p is not sufficient for being in a position to act on p or assert p, only knowledge will do. A liar might thus tell a knowledge lie to prevent someone from knowing that p, because this will thereby prevent the person from permissibly acting on p.[5] This is exactly what happens in the example of Dr. Appendix: Dr. Head needs to know, rather than merely believe, that Appendix is a weak researcher in order to be in a position to fire him. Thus, Dr. Heart can prevent Head from being in a position to act by just attacking his knowledge. She does not need to get Dr. Head to change his beliefs. Moreover, attacking someone's knowledge without attacking their beliefs can be useful in cases where it would be inconvenient if the addressee's beliefs changed. For example, Dr. Heart would not want her lies about Appendix' research being good to be believed, since this might lead to the unwanted consequence of Appendix getting undeserved rewards.

The second reason why lies that are intended to attack knowledge, but leave belief intact, are of philosophical interest relates to the moral wrongness of lying. Recall that according to Sorensen, knowledge lies are not intended to deceive their addressee, where this means that a lie about p is not intended to get the addressee to adopt a false belief about p. If knowledge lies are not meant to deceive their addressee, then this potentially has consequences for how morally objectionable they are. In looking for features that makes lying morally wrong, one feature people frequently point to is the deceptiveness of lying.[6] So, if I can lie without intending to deceive the addressee of the lie, then I can potentially avoid doing something wrong.[7]

---

[5] Though as Fallis (2010a, 2011) points out, this strategy does not work if the addressee of the lie falsely believes that she knows, for example if, unbeknownst to the addressee, the belief that she justifies happens to be false, or is true merely through a lucky coincidence. In these cases, the agent does not have knowledge, but is unaware of this, because she is in a state that is internally indistinguishable from knowledge.

Another important caveat was pointed out to me by Jon Kvanvig: some philosophers endorse a knowledge-belief norm, which says that you should only believe that p if you know that p. If this norm is correct, then it is not possible to attack a person's knowledge in a way that makes them aware that they do not know without attacking their beliefs. Undermining someone's knowledge without undermining their belief is only possible on this view if either the agent does not realize her lack of knowledge (in which case the knowledge lie would fail to prevent action), or irrationally sticks to her belief, even though she realizes her lack of knowledge.

[6] See, for example, Bok (1999); Dietz (2002); Faulkner (2013). Other candidates for wrong-making features of lying that are discussed by these authors are, e.g., that lying is manipulative, that it is a breach of someone's trust, and that it restricts someone's freedom of choice. Lies that are not deceptive may be able to escape these wrong-making features as well.

[7] Fallis (2013a) discusses whether knowledge lies might play a special role in protecting someone's privacy, but eventually rejects this idea.

In sum: if knowledge lies can prevent knowledge without being intended to deceive, then this makes them an interesting category of their own. This is because by preventing the addressee's knowledge, the liar can paralyze her by precluding her from complying with the knowledge-norms. Moreover, the liar can do so in a way that avoids the prima facie morally objectionable act of deception.

17.2.3 Critical discussion

While it is uncontroversial in the literature that lies can be used to prevent knowledge, it is debated whether knowledge lies really do not involve an intention to deceive the addressee. Lackey (2013), Staffel (2011), and Fallis (2010c, 2011) argue that, given the right understanding of deception, knowledge lies are typically intended to deceive.

Lackey (2013: 241) proposes that we should at least distinguish between two kinds of deception:

Deceiving:

A deceives B with respect to whether p if and only if A aims to bring about a false belief in B regarding whether p.

Being deceptive:

A is deceptive to B with respect to whether p if A aims to conceal information from B regarding whether p.

Lackey argues that knowledge lies do not involve an intention to *deceive*; however, they do involve an intention to *be deceptive*. This is because they are intended to conceal information, which is a way of being deceptive. In the Spartacus example, the slaves assert "I am Spartacus" to conceal from the general which one of them is Spartacus. Thus, the slaves are being deceptive, according to Lackey, but they are not deceiving the general, because they do not intend to bring about a false belief in the general about which of them is Spartacus. Similarly, in the example of Dr. Appendix, Heart carefully crafts her recommendation letter to conceal information about the bad quality of Appendix's research, but she does not intend to make Head believe that Appendix's research is good. Thus, Lackey agrees with Sorensen that knowledge lies are not intended to deceive, if we adopt the narrow definition of *deceiving* given above. However, the knowledge liar is still *being deceptive*. Thus, her action involves deception, widely construed, and is thereby potentially morally wrong.

Staffel (2011), and Fallis (2010c, 2011) also argue against Sorensen's claim that knowledge lies are not intended to deceive their addressee, but in a different way from Lackey. They argue that Sorensen is incorrect to assume that A deceives B if and only if B is brought to adopt an outright belief in a false proposition. Rather, A can deceive B by merely making B more confident in a false proposition (see also Krishna 1961; Chisholm and Feeham 1977; Fallis 2009). For example, suppose B already falsely believes that he will be promoted. Yet, A wants to increase B's confidence that he will be promoted to prevent him from considering other jobs. So, A lies to B, claiming that he will be promoted. If A is generally trustworthy and B rationally responds to A's testimony, then B will become extremely confident that he will be promoted. In this case, A intends to deceive, and succeeds in deceiving B about his being promoted, even though B does not come to believe that he will be promoted on the basis of A's lie. Merely increasing B's confidence in the false proposition suffices for deception.

Staffel and Fallis both point out that on this understanding of deception, knowledge-lies are typically intended to deceive their addressee. This is because, in order to prevent the addressee's knowledge, the lie must have at least some credibility. If the lie has at least some credibility, then the addressee should respond by increasing her confidence in the content of the lie at least slightly, assuming that she is rational. But if this is how knowledge lies work, then they aim at increasing the addressee's confidence in a falsehood, which counts as deception on this definition.

In the example of Dr. Appendix, Staffel argues, the reason why Dr. Heart's recommendation letter has any evidential value at all is because it is more likely that she will say that Appendix's work is good given that it really is good than given that it is not good. Hence, the letter provides at least weak evidence that Appendix's research is good, and if Head is rational, he should respond by slightly increasing his confidence. But that means he's been deceived, which is what Heart intended to accomplish.[8]

In the Spartacus example it is uncontroversial that Antoninus, the first slave who says "I am Spartacus," intends to deceive the general, because he tries to convince the general that he is Spartacus. The following slaves who say the same thing do not intend to deceive the general in Sorensen's sense, but they seem to still count as intending to deceive the general according to Staffel's and Fallis' notion of deception. To see why this is, let us assume that there are five slaves, Spartacus, Antoninus, and three others. In the movie scene, Spartacus and Antoninus get up at the same time, and Antoninus says "I am Spartacus," cutting off Spartacus. At this moment, it is reasonable for the general to become very confident that Antoninus is Spartacus. Let us assume, just to make things precise, that he becomes ninety-six percent confident in this claim, and that he is only one percent confident that each of the other slaves is Spartacus. Hence, Antoninus has deceived the general, because he has made him highly confident in a falsehood. Next, the third slave gets up and says "I am Spartacus." This will change the general's degrees of confidence in such a way that he is now still only one percent confident that Spartacus or slaves four and five are the person he is looking for, and he will now divide the rest of his confidence between Antoninus being Spartacus, and slave three being Spartacus. Again, slave three's lie makes the general more confident in a falsehood: his confidence that slave

---

[8] See Fallis (2010c, 2011) for some alternative ways of spelling out the Dr. Appendix case.

three is Spartacus rises from one percent to just under fifty percent. This is deceptive, by Staffel's and Fallis' definition. Then, slaves four and five tell their lies. The general now realizes that any of the slaves might be Spartacus, and he divides his confidence between them evenly, just as he did before any of them had said anything (we will assume that Spartacus gets the same amount of confidence as the others at this point). But this means, again, that the general's confidence that any one of the remaining slaves is Spartacus rises above one percent, which meets Staffel's and Fallis' definition of deception. Hence, while the slaves' lies, considered jointly, leave the general just as confident about which of them is Spartacus as he was at the outset, each individual lie counts as deceptive on Staffel's and Fallis' definition, because it raises the general's confidence about whether a particular slave is Spartacus.[9] Hence, Staffel's and Fallis' proposed understanding of deception calls into question Sorensen's claim that knowledge lies are not intended to deceive.[10]

Another worry about Sorensen's definition of a knowledge lie is that it might be too narrow. There are interesting ways in which a liar can prevent someone from knowing that not-p without intending to deceive the addressee about p that do not fit Sorensen's definition.[11] For example, a liar can exploit the phenomenon that whether or not someone knows something often depends on whether they are in a high-stakes or low-stakes environment, at least according to some theories of knowledge (Fallis 2010c, 2011). The amount of justification sufficient for knowledge in a low-stakes situation need not be sufficient for knowledge in a high-stakes scenario (DeRose 2002; Hawthorne 2004). Hence, if a liar can tell a lie to convince her addressee that she is in a high-stakes situation, the addressee might lose her knowledge of not-p, even though the liar never attempted to deceive her into believing that p. For example, suppose you are going to a potluck dinner, and you do not want your nemesis to show up with a better dish than you. So you call her right before the potluck, and ask her if she knows

---

[9] Staffel points out that there are cases of knowledge lies that are not deceptive on her definition of deception, but she argues that they are atypical. These are cases in which either the knowledge lie's addressee is irrational, or the lie does not function as evidence.

The former case obtains when A tells a knowledge lie that p to B, which is intended to prevent B from knowing that not-p. If B responds rationally, she should become slightly more confident in p. However, she might refuse to change her attitude about p in response to the lie. In this case, B has not been deceived, but she is still prevented from knowing that not-p, because she has ignored some available evidence for p. A may or may not have expected B to react irrationally, so it is possible that A did not intend to deceive B. However, A still had to provide evidence that would have deceived B if B had been rational in order to prevent her from knowing.

The latter case obtains in scenarios where a lie prevents knowledge via non-evidential means. Suppose A has stashed her jewels on a rooftop, which B is trying to reach via a tightrope. A wants to prevent B from knowing that the jewels are there, and shouts "The jewels are not on the roof." As intended, B is startled by the shouting and falls to his death. A's lie is a knowledge lie: it prevents B's knowledge without deceiving her. However, in this case it is inessential that B's knowledge is prevented by a lie, since any loud noise would have achieved the desired effect.

[10] For further discussion of different notions of deception, see also Meibauer (2014a, b).

[11] Sorensen (2010) discusses some versions of stakes-raising, but does not address the fact that some of these cases do not seem to fit his initial definition.

whether her dish contains peanuts. She says (accurately) that she knows it contains no peanuts. You lie to her and tell her that some people with deadly peanut allergies may be at the party, which would make it dangerous to bring anything that contains even traces of peanuts. Having become convinced that she is in a high-stakes situation, your nemesis responds that she cannot be sure her dish contains no trace amounts of peanuts. She admits she therefore does not know it is peanut-free, and will not bring it to the party.[12]

In this case, you have prevented your nemesis from knowing that her dish is peanut-free by convincing her that she is in a high-stakes situation. Cases like this, in which liars prevent someone from knowing by raising the stakes, do not precisely fit Sorensen's definition of a knowledge lie. This is because the proposition that the liar asserts in order to convince her addressee that she is in a high-stakes situation is typically not the proposition that the liar wants to prevent the addressee from knowing. In our example, the lie is that there may be people with deadly peanut allergies at the party, and the proposition of which knowledge is meant to be prevented is that the potluck dish contains no peanuts. It is an open question whether the definition of a knowledge-lie can and should be expanded to account for these types of cases while retaining the idea that knowledge lies are a unified subclass of lies.[13]

If the preceding arguments are successful, then knowledge lies are a less significant category than seemed at first to be the case. Knowledge lies are thought to be interesting, because they can prevent knowledge without involving deception, which make them appear prima facie less bad than ordinary lies. Moreover, the existence of lies that generally do not deceive would call into question traditional definitions of lying, which take all lies to be aimed at deception. Yet, if knowledge lies are typically deceptive after all, then we cannot point to their non-deceptiveness to explain their importance. We have also seen that there seem to be lies that are intended to prevent knowledge, but that do not exactly fit the definition offered by Sorensen. If those lies are properly categorized as knowledge lies, then we need a broader definition of what a knowledge lie is.

---

[12] The precise mechanics of this case depend on what theory of knowledge is endorsed, for example contextualism or subject-sensitive invariantism (see, e.g., Hawthorne 2004: ch. 2, 4).

[13] Sorensen (2010: 612) wonders whether the addressee is prevented from having first-order knowledge or second-order knowledge in cases like this. Maybe we should claim that your nemesis still knows that her dish is peanut-free, but she no longer knows that she knows, which is enough to prevent her from acting in a high-stakes situation.

Also, notice that cases in which knowledge is prevented by a stakes-raising lie seem to typically involve deception. The liar must craft her lie to create the impression that a high-stakes situation obtains. In the potluck example, the liar intends to accomplish this by telling her nemesis that there may be allergic people at the party. The liar intends her lie to make her nemesis at least somewhat more confident that this is true, which counts as deception on Staffel's view. The liar also counts as being deceptive to her nemesis in Lackey's sense here, because she is concealing information about who will be at the party.

17.3 GROUP LIES

17.3.1 What are group lies?

Group lies are lies that are told by a group of people, such as a government, a company, your knitting circle, or any other group. Jennifer Lackey (2015) offers a definition of a group lie, which is modeled on her account of an individual lie:

> *Lie:*
>
> A lies to B if and only if (1) A states that p to B, (2) A believes that p is false, and (3) A intends to be deceptive to B with respect to whether p in stating that p.
>
> (Lackey 2015: 3)

Applied to a group, this becomes:

> *Group lie:*
>
> Group G lies to B if and only if (1) G states that p to B, (2) G believes that p is false, and (3) G intends to be deceptive to B with respect to whether p in stating that p.

In order for a group to tell a lie, it is necessary that the group make an assertion, which can happen in various different ways. One way in which this can happen is if a spokesperson asserts something on behalf of the group. We see this in the case of Walter Ulbricht's claim that the East German government had no intention of building a wall. Ulbricht is giving a press conference, and it is understood that he is not speaking for himself as an individual, but as a representative of his government.[14]

A more unusual instance of a group lie obtains when all the members of the group are actively involved in telling the lie. For example, imagine that a small company wants to surprise its biggest client for his birthday. Everyone in the company is in mutual agreement that he is their least favorite client, and they dread that they have to rely on his business for the company to survive in the future. Yet, they decide to send him a birthday card, in which they write "We wish you, our favorite client, a happy birthday! We look forward to doing business with you in the future." Each employee writes one word of the message and also signs their name. Here, each member of the group contributes a constitutive part of the assertion that is a lie.[15]

---

[14] Of course, a group can also make assertions that are lies in official communication, such as press releases, advertising materials, or instruction manuals.

[15] Real-world examples of this type of group assertion, where all the members of the group contribute to the assertion, can be hard to find, but a particularly vivid example is a promotional recruitment video made by the company Ernst & Young, in which the employees sing a song together that talks about the

This list is not meant to be exhaustive—for any way in which a group can assert something as a group, the group can use it to assert something that is a lie.

17.3.2 What makes group lies interesting as their own category?

Group lies have received little attention in the literature on lies, possibly because it might initially seem that they are not interestingly different from individual lies, or that they can be easily explained in terms of them. Lackey (2015) contends that this is false, and that group lies deserve their own philosophical treatment. She argues for two theses: (i) group lies cannot be understood in terms of individual lies told by the group's members, and (ii) group lies do not require a joint agreement of the group's members to lie. In order to argue for her first thesis, she examines the following definition of a group lie, which attempts to understand group lies in terms of individual lies. She calls this view *Simple Summativism**:

> SS*:
>
> A group G lies to B in stating that p if and only if most of the operative members of G lie to B in stating that p.

Lackey points out that this definition cannot be correct, because it is neither necessary nor sufficient that most of the operative members of G lie in order for G to lie. The following kind of example shows that it is not sufficient: suppose that there are three people, A, B, and C, who count as operative members of a tobacco company. Each of them knows that smoking causes lung cancer. A lies to his wife, D, and tells her that smoking does not cause cancer, in order to alleviate her worries about her son C's smoking, which she cannot prevent. C also lies to his mother about this to avoid her nagging. And B also lies to D about whether smoking causes cancer in order to avoid causing arguments in A's family.

Lackey argues that this is not a case of a group lie, in which the tobacco company lies to D about whether smoking causes cancer. This is because all of the operative members of the tobacco company lie to D not in their role as members of the company, but as private individuals. They would lie to D in the exact same way if they were unaffiliated with the tobacco company. Hence, A, B, and C do not tell a group lie to D in this example. But since SS* classifies this case as a group lie, SS* must be incorrect.

---

virtues of teamwork to the tune of "Oh happy day". The video can be found here (thanks to Fay Edwards for pointing this out): https://www.youtube.com/watch?v=MaIq9o1H1y0.
   One might wonder whether the employees are asserting what they sing, but it seems that whoever came up with the idea of this video was at least hoping the employees would sincerely assert the lyrics.

There are also examples that show that it is not necessary for most of the operative members of a group G to lie in order for G to lie. Lackey provides the following case: suppose the tobacco company hires a naïve spokesperson S, whose job it is to attend the board meetings, and to report to the public about them. The board members set up a meeting in which they deliberately present only evidence that indicates that there is no link between smoking and cancer, even though they are aware that the total available evidence supports the opposite conclusion. As planned, S concludes that there is no link between smoking and cancer, and reports this to the public in his role as the tobacco company's spokesperson.

This is a case in which none of the operative members of the tobacco company have told a lie, and neither has the spokesperson. The operative members have not stated that there is no link between smoking and cancer, and the spokesperson believes that her statement is correct. The spokesperson does not tell an individual lie, yet she unknowingly lies on behalf of the group. Via the spokesperson's statement, the company has lied to the public about whether there is a link between smoking and cancer. The definition SS* incorrectly classifies this case as one in which the group has not lied.

Together, the examples are intended to show that individual lies by group members are neither necessary nor sufficient for a group to lie. If Lackey's arguments are successful, then it is clear that group lies cannot be explained straightforwardly in terms of individual lies.

Lackey then examines whether a joint acceptance account of group lies fares better than SS*. Lackey considers the following alternative definition of a group lie, which she labels *Joint Acceptance*:

JA:

A group, G, lies to B in stating that p if and only if most of the operative members of G jointly agree to lie to B (in the sense found in *Lie*) in stating that p.

This definition correctly counts the naïve spokesperson's lie about the link between smoking and cancer as a group lie, and it also correctly predicts that there is no group lie in the case where A, B, and C each individually lie to D.

However, Lackey argues that *JA* has counterexamples as well, because "jointly agreeing to lie does not make it the case that a group lies, and merely refusing to jointly agree to lie does not necessarily prevent a group from lying" (Lackey 2015: 12–13). The former case obtains, for example, if all the operative members of the tobacco company secretly believe that smoking is safe, but tell each other that they believe the opposite. They might form a joint agreement to lie to the public, and, as a group, make statements about the safety of smoking. Yet, Lackey argues, since all of the members of the group in fact believe that smoking is safe, the group has not lied, because the believing p to be false-condition is not satisfied.

The latter case can be argued for by pointing out that a group cannot exculpate itself from the accusation of having lied by claiming that the group never made a joint agreement to lie. We can stipulate that in the naïve spokesperson example above, there was never a joint agreement to lie by misleading the spokesperson with cherry-picked evidence. But, Lackey argues, this does not make it the case that the tobacco company has not lied to the public via their spokesperson's statement that smoking is safe.

Lackey's own definition of a group lie, which was given in the previous section, avoids the problems that befall SS* and JA. Unlike SS* and JA, it relies on the notions of group assertion, group belief, and group intention without already trying to analyze them. SS* and JA, by contrast, tried unsuccessfully to analyze group lies in terms of individual lies, or in terms of joint agreement of the group members to lie. Lackey's arguments against SS* and JA give us good reason to single out group lies as their own category of philosophical interest.

It must of course be noted that there are many alternatives to SS* and JA that Lackey does not consider, and it will be up to future research to examine alternative accounts. Lackey's own definition employs the notions of a group assertion, a group belief, and a group intention, and it is a topic of current debate how these notions should be analyzed. Hence, Lackey's definition leaves us with many open questions.

If Lackey is right that we cannot analyze group lies in terms of individual lies, or in terms of a joint agreement to lie, then this also has interesting consequences for our views of moral responsibility. Discussions of moral responsibility tend to focus on what it takes for an individual agent to be morally responsible. However, if we cannot offer a reductive analysis of group lies, this shows that we need to think about whether and how groups can be morally responsible (see Smiley 2010).

17.3.3 Critical discussion

Lackey's definition of a group lie invokes several concepts that are of independent philosophical interest: group assertion, group belief, and group intention. Just like the concept of a group lie, we have reason to think that these concepts cannot be straightforwardly analyzed in terms of individual assertions, beliefs, or intentions. Lackey makes some headway in her paper toward explaining how groups can make assertions via a spokesperson. Yet, in order to get a general understanding of the phenomenon of group lies, we need general accounts of group assertions, group beliefs, and group intentions. The best-case scenario would be if we could simply plug our preferred accounts of these group notions into Lackey's definition, and thereby get an explanation of group lies "for free." Unfortunately, as Lackey herself points out, her view of group lies is not compatible with some of the recently proposed accounts of group belief and group intention. Various authors have proposed joint-acceptance accounts of group belief, which would not give the desired verdicts in Lackey's examples (Gilbert 1989; Tuomela 1992; Schmitt 1994; Tollefsen 2007, 2009). Lackey also points out that Bratman's (1993) account of group intention relies on a concept of group knowledge that is incompatible with her view.

In addition to the controversies about how to analyze group attitudes, we can also expect some variation in judgment about particular examples, and whether or not they involve particular group attitudes. For example, Lackey argues that in the case where everyone in the tobacco company secretly believes that smoking is safe, but pretends to believe at work that smoking is harmful, the company does not lie in telling the public that smoking is safe. This is because it is not true that the company believes that smoking is unsafe, and hence condition (2) of the definition of a group lie is not met. However, one could reasonably hold the position that a group can believe a claim p, while none of the members of the group believe p. For example, suppose four members of an exam committee must decide what grade to give to a thesis. Two of the committee members think the thesis should receive an A, and the other two members believe that it should receive a C. The committee agrees to give the thesis a B. In this case, each of the following two verdicts seems defensible: (i) the committee believes that the thesis should get a B, even though none of the members believe this individually (Mathiesen 2006), or (ii) the group does not believe that the thesis should get a B, the group (and each of its members) merely believe that giving the thesis a B is the best compromise.

Another case in which one might disagree with Lackey's assessment is the example in which the operative members of the tobacco company present the naïve spokesperson only with evidence that does not support a link between smoking and cancer. According to Lackey, none of the operative members have lied, yet the company lies when the naïve spokesperson tells the public that there is no such link. One might suggest that the operative members' cherry-picking the evidence constitutes lying by omission, contrary to Lackey's analysis.

In sum, it seems that a better understanding of group assertions and group attitudes is needed in order to make progress in explaining how group lies work. At the same time, group lies are an important and overlooked phenomenon that can help us improve our accounts of group assertions and group attitudes.

Acknowledgements

I would like to thank Roshan Abraham, Fay Edwards, Jennifer Lackey, Jörg Meibauer, Ryan Platte, Roy Sorensen, and an anonymous referee for helpful comments and suggestions.

CHAPTER 18

SELFLESS ASSERTIONS

JENNIFER LACKEY

ACCORDING to the traditional view, lying involves stating what one does not believe oneself and doing so with the intention to deceive. More precisely:

LIE-T: A lies to B if and only if (1) A states that p to B, (2) A believes that p is false, and (3) A intends to deceive B by stating that p.[1]

LIE-T remained the generally accepted view of the nature of lying until recently, with condition (3) coming under repeated attack. The form of this challenge is to aim to produce clear instances of lying where there is no intention on the part of the speaker to deceive the hearer, thereby showing that (3) is not a necessary condition for lying. Three central kinds of lies are used as counterexamples here: (i) bald-faced lies, (ii) knowledge-lies, and (iii) coercion-lies.[2]

A bald-faced lie is an undisguised lie,[3] one where a speaker states that p, believes that p is false, and it is common knowledge that what is being stated does not reflect what the speaker actually believes. For instance, suppose that a student is caught flagrantly cheating on an exam, all of the conclusive evidence for which is passed on to the Dean of Academic Affairs. Both the student and the Dean know that he cheated on the exam, and they each know that the other knows this, but the student is also aware of the fact that the Dean punishes students for academic dishonesty only when there is a confession. Given this, when the student is called to the Dean's office, he states, "I did not cheat on the exam."[4] This is a classic bald-faced lie: the speaker states a proposition that he believes is false and both the speaker and the hearer not only know that this is the case, but also know that the other knows this. There is, then, no intention on the part of the

---

[1] Proponents of various versions of the traditional view include Isenberg (1964), Chisholm and Feehan (1977), Williams (2002), and Mahon (2008a).
[2] See Sorensen (2007, 2010), Fallis (2009), and Carson (2010).
[3] Quoted from *The American Heritage Dictionary* in Sorensen (2010).
[4] This is a slightly modified version of an example found in Carson (2010).

speaker to deceive the hearer, and yet the student is clearly lying. This shows that condition (3) of LIE-T is false.[5]

The second kind of counterexample to LIE-T involves what Sorensen (2010) calls "knowledge lies." "An assertion that p is a knowledge lies exactly if intended to prevent the addressee from knowing that p is untrue but is not intended to deceive the addressee into believing [that] p" (Sorensen 2010: 610). For instance:

> In *Spartacus* (Universal Pictures, 1960), the victorious Roman general, Marcus Licinius Crassus, asks the recaptured slaves to identify Spartacus in exchange for leniency. Spartacus ... rises to spare his comrades crucifixion. However, the slave on his right, Antoninus, springs to his feet and declares, 'I am Spartacus!' Then the slave on Spartacus' left also stands and declares 'I am Spartacus!', then another slave, and another until the whole army of slaves is on their feet shouting, 'I am Spartacus!'
>
> (Sorensen 2010: 608)

Each slave in this case is offering a knowledge lie; however, with the exception of Antoninus, none intends to deceive Crassus into believing that he is actually Spartacus. For once the second slave claims this identity, it is clear that he is instead aiming to prevent Crassus from *learning* who Spartacus is. Given that each slave seems to be lying, condition (3) of LIE-T is again shown to be false.

The third kind of counterexample to LIE-T involves what we might call coercion-lies. A coercion-lie occurs when a speaker believes that p is false, states that p, and does so, not with the intention to deceive, but because she is coerced or frightened into doing so. For instance, suppose that an innocent bystander witnesses the murder of a gang member by someone from a rival gang, but is threatened with death if she testifies against the murderer. Because of this, the bystander states on the stand at trial, "I did not witness the defendant murder the victim in question."[6] Here the intention of the bystander is not to deceive the court into believing that she did not witness the murder; instead, her aim is to avoid retaliation from the defendant's fellow gang members. Indeed, she may even desperately wish for the court to believe that she did witness the crime. That the court ends up being deceived by her statement is simply an unintended consequence of the action needed to achieve the aim of self-preservation. Despite this, the bystander clearly lies on the stand, evidenced at least in part by the fact that she could be found guilty of perjury. The intention to deceive is again shown not to be necessary for lying.

Together, (i) through (iii) are taken to show quite decisively that the traditional conception of lying has been radically misguided. It is then concluded not only that lying

---

[5] Though he calls them "cynical assertions," Kenyon (2003) also discusses bald-faced lies. However, because he assumes the truth of LIE-T, he concludes that such assertions are not lies. This seems problematic, not only because bald-faced lies are called lies in our ordinary talk, but also because our corresponding actions support this talk, e.g., we would charge someone with perjury for offering a bald-faced lie on the stand, we would regard someone as a liar who repeatedly made bald-faced lies, and so on.

[6] This is a modified version of a case found in Carson (2010).

does not require the intention to deceive, but also that deception is not a part of what it is to lie.[7]

LIE-T has thus been replaced with a variety of competing accounts, none of which makes mention of deception. The three most prominent ones, offered by Fallis (2009), Carson (2010), and Sorensen (2007), respectively, are:

> LIE-F: A lies to B if and only if (1) A states that p to B, (2) A believes that p is false, and (3) A believes that she makes this statement in a context where the following norm of conversation is in effect: *Do not make statements that you believe to be false.*
>
> (Fallis 2009: 34)

> LIE-C: A lies to B if and only if (1) A states that p to B, (2) A believes that p is false or probably false (or, alternatively, A does not believe that p is true), and (3) A intends to warrant the truth of that p to B.
>
> (Carson 2010: 37)[8]

> LIE-S: A lies to B if and only if (1) A asserts that p to B, and (2) A does not believe that p.
>
> (Sorensen 2007: 256)

LIE-F, LIE-C, and LIE-S are virtually identical in the first two conditions, with the latter accounts simply allowing classic cases of bullshit, where the speaker does not believe that p is false but also does not believe that p is true, to count as lies.[9] But merely stating what one believes to be false is not sufficient for lying, since speakers frequently say what they believe is false when being ironic, joking, or reciting lines in a play, and yet are not lying when they do so. For this reason, each proposal adds a further component to capture only those statements that are genuine lies. Fallis does so through requiring that the speaker believes that she is offering her statement in a context where the following norm of conversation is in effect: *Do not make statements that you believe to be false.* Since such a conversational norm is not believed to be in effect by a speaker who is being ironic, humorous, or acting, LIE-F successfully rules them out as instances of lying. So, too, do LIE-C and LIE-S, the former because Carson understands intending to warrant the truth of a proposition as being a promise or

---

[7] Such a move is made explicitly by Fallis: shortly after presenting counterexamples to the condition that lying requires the intention to deceive, he concludes, "These cases show that lying is not always about deception" (Fallis 2009: 43).

[8] Carson also includes a condition requiring the actual falsity of the proposition that is being stated. But to my mind, the necessity of this condition is decisively refuted by a case that he himself discusses at (Carson 2010: 16). On this point, then, I am in agreement with Augustine when he writes, "... a person is to be judged as lying or not lying according to the intention of his own mind, not according to the truth or falsity of the matter itself" (Augustine 1952b: 55).

[9] See Frankfurt (2005) and Chapter 20 by Andreas Stokke for a discussion of bullshit.

guarantee that what one says is true[10] and the latter because speakers typically do not offer flat-out assertions in cases of irony, jokes, and acting.[11]

In contrast, Lackey (2013) rejects the divorce between lies and deception, and instead argues on behalf of the following account:

> LIE-L: A lies to B if and only if (1) A states that p to B, (2) A believes that p is false, and (3) A intends to be deceptive to B with respect to whether p in stating that p.[12]

Lackey emphasizes that there is a range of ways of being deceptive, the most obvious being the one that is the focus of proponents of non-deception accounts of lying, where the aim is to bring about false beliefs in the victim of the deceit. But another, less explicit, form of deception is where the aim is to *conceal information*. According to the *Oxford English Dictionary*,[13] deceit is "the action or practice of deceiving someone by concealing or misrepresenting the truth." And Carson, despite endorsing a non-deception account of lying, claims that "[t]o conceal information is to do things to hide information from someone—to prevent someone from discovering it. Often, concealing information constitutes deception or attempted deception" (Carson 2010: 57).[14] Given this, Lackey proposes the following distinction, which is sufficient for distinguishing between competing accounts of lying even though it does not purport to fully capture all of the ways of being deceptive:

> Deceit: A deceives B with respect to whether p if and only if A aims to bring about a false belief in B regarding whether p.
> Deception: A is deceptive to B with respect to whether p if A aims to conceal information from B regarding whether p.

Concealing information regarding whether p can be understood broadly, so that it subsumes, among other phenomena, concealing *evidence* regarding whether p. Moreover, notice that concealing information is importantly different from

---

[10] According to Carson, one warrants the truth of a statement when one makes a statement in a context where "one promises or guarantees, either explicitly or implicitly, that what one says is true" (Carson 2010: 26). Moreover, whether one warrants the truth of a statement is independent of what one intends or believes.

[11] According to Sorensen, the only condition on assertion is that it must have "narrow plausibility," where this is understood as follows: "someone who only had access to the assertion might believe it." "Wide plausibility," in contrast, is "credibility relative to one's total evidence" (Sorensen 2007: 255). Moreover, "[m]uch of what we say does not constitute assertion. We signal a lack of assertive force by clear falsity (as with metaphor) or by implausibility" (Sorensen 2007: 256).

[12] I am grateful to Don Fallis for suggesting the addition of the clause "with respect to whether p" in condition (3) of my account.

[13] http://www.oxforddictionaries.com/us/definition/american_english/deceit.

[14] Carson (2010) is interested in both lying and deception, but is clear that he regards the latter as not necessary for the former.

withholding information. To withhold information is to fail to provide it, rather than to hide or keep it secret. If I am trying to find a home for my challenging puppy, I withhold information about her lack of being housebroken if you do not ask me anything about it and I do not mention it. But if I frantically discard all of the training pads lying throughout my house before you come over, then I am concealing the information that she is not trained.[15] Finally, notice that concealing information is sufficient, though not necessary, for being deceptive; thus, it is merely one instance of a more general phenomenon. Obviously, another way of being deceptive is to be deceitful, where one's aim is to bring about a false belief in one's hearer.

Lackey argues that a clear reason to prefer LIE-L, which secures a connection with deception, to rival accounts is because only her view delivers the correct verdict in cases of *selfless assertion*.[16] There are three central components to this phenomenon: first, a subject, for purely non-epistemic reasons, does not believe that p; second, despite this lack of belief, the subject is aware that p is very well supported by all of the available evidence; and, third, because of this, the subject asserts that p without believing that p. A classic instance of a selfless assertion is the following:

> CREATIONIST TEACHER: Stella is a devoutly Christian fourth-grade teacher, and her religious beliefs are based on a personal relationship with God that she takes herself to have had since she was a very young child. This relationship grounds her belief in the truth of creationism and, accordingly, a belief in the falsity of evolutionary theory. Despite this, Stella fully recognizes that there is an overwhelming amount of scientific evidence against both of these beliefs. Indeed, she readily admits that she is not basing her own commitment to creationism on evidence at all but, rather, on the personal faith that she has in an all-powerful Creator. Because of this, Stella thinks that her religious beliefs are irrelevant to her duties as a teacher; accordingly, she regards her obligation as a teacher to include presenting material that is best supported by the available evidence, which clearly includes the truth of evolutionary theory. As a result, while presenting her biology lesson today, Stella asserts to her students, "Modern day *Homo sapiens* evolved from *Homo erectus*," though she herself does not believe this proposition.[17]
>
> (Lackey 2008: 48)

---

[15] For further discussion of the distinction between withholding and concealing information, see Carson (2010: 56–7).

[16] See Lackey (2007a, 2008).

[17] An article in *The New York Times* (February 12, 2007, "Believing Scripture but Playing by Science's Rules") about Dr. Marcus R. Ross, a creationist who also completed a geosciences PhD in paleontology, makes clear that the situation described in CREATIONIST TEACHER is by no means merely a thought experiment. As the author of the article writes, "For him, Dr. Ross said, the methods and theories of paleontology are one 'paradigm' for studying the past, and Scripture is another. In the paleontological paradigm, he said, the dates in his dissertation are entirely appropriate. The fact that as a young earth creationist he has a different view just means, he said, 'that I am separating the different paradigms.'"

Stella, whose fourth-grade students depend on her for their education, is able to put aside her own purely faith-based religious beliefs and offer an assertion that is both true and evidentially well-grounded. Moreover, she offers the assertion in question precisely *because* she recognizes that it is supported by an overwhelming amount of excellent evidence, evidence that she either cannot or will not allow to govern her own beliefs. The combination of these general features of a selfless assertion has the following result: one offers an assertion in the absence of belief and is not properly subject to criticism in any relevant sense. Indeed, *qua* asserter, one is properly subject to epistemic praise, since one is being guided by the best available evidence rather than one's own personal beliefs and desires. This is precisely the sense in which the assertion is selfless.

Despite this, Stella's selfless assertion that *Homo sapiens* evolved from *Homo erectus* satisfies all three non-deception accounts above, and so counts as a straightforward lie. Lackey argues that this is the wrong result—Stella is not lying to her students—and this is the case precisely because she does not intend to be deceptive to them.[18]

The first point to notice here is that Stella's statement that *Homo sapiens* evolved from *Homo erectus* clearly satisfies the conditions put forth in LIE-F, LIE-C, and LIE-S. She offers this statement to her students, where she herself believes that it is false. Moreover, since she clearly does not regard the context of her classroom as an ironic, humorous, or theatrical one, she does so while believing that the following norm of conversation is in effect: *Do not make statements that you believe to be false*. The reason why she violates this norm is that she believes it is overridden or defeated by the duty to state what the scientific evidence best supports when teaching her biology lesson.[19] Stella also intends to warrant the truth of the proposition that *Homo sapiens* evolved from *Homo erectus*, since she is promising her students that what she says is true, just as she does when she states what she herself believes.[20] And, finally, there is nothing about her statement or the context that prevents her statement from qualifying as an assertion.

The second point to notice is that Stella does not in any way aim to be deceptive to her students in stating that *Homo sapiens* evolved from *Homo erectus*. For though she does not herself believe this, she regards her own personal beliefs regarding religion—particularly those that are grounded in her relationship with God—as *irrelevant* to the information she conveys during her biology lesson. Reporting to her students what her religious beliefs are about the origin of humans would, for Stella, be comparable to sharing with them what her favorite aspect of evolutionary theory is. Both are irrelevant

---

[18] For other cases of selfless assertion that pose a problem for LIE-F, LIE-C, and LIE-S, see Lackey (2007a).

[19] In Fallis (2009: 51–3), he discusses at length how this conversational norm can be overridden or defeated. This case can also be understood as Stella choosing to violate Grice's first norm of quality—Do not make statements that you believe to be false—in order to obey his second norm of quality—Do not say that for which you lack adequate evidence. For more on this, see Grice (1989) and note 21 below.

[20] It is important to keep in mind that Carson believes that one can intend to warrant the truth of a proposition even when one is lying, and thus one can promise one's hearer that what one says is true, even when one knows that it is false. It is comparable to making a promise that one knows one cannot keep.

to her biology lesson. Given this, when Stella states to her students a proposition that she believes is false, her aim is not to bring about a false belief in her students or to conceal her own beliefs on the matter. In fact, we can imagine that she would willingly share her own views about evolutionary theory with her students, were they to ask her. Instead, Stella's aim is to convey to her students the theories that are best supported by the current scientific evidence, which include evolutionary theory but not creationism.

The final point to note is that Stella is not lying to her students. This is evident by the fact that, in allowing her assertions to be guided by the best available evidence rather than her own personal preferences, she is doing something praiseworthy. Of course, lying itself might be the right thing to do in various respects: I might, for instance, lie about the whereabouts of my friend in order to prevent her abusive partner from harming her. Here, my assertion might be the grounds for my praiseworthiness as a friend, as a moral agent, and so on. But in my evaluation distinctively as an asserter, I am open to criticism, for deliberately leading others astray is clearly in violation of the norm governing assertion. In cases of selfless assertion, however, the praiseworthiness is specifically in one's capacity *as a speaker*, and thus reveals something important about the corresponding assertion—namely, that it is not a lie.

The conclusion that Stella is not lying can be further supported by considering a slightly modified version of CREATIONIST TEACHER: suppose that everything about the case remains the same, except that Stella states to her students that *Homo sapiens* evolved from *Homo erectus*, not because she regards her religious beliefs on the matter as irrelevant to her biology lesson, but because she will get fired from her teaching job if she reveals such beliefs to her students. In such a case, the aim of Stella reporting what she herself does not believe is to conceal her own religiously grounded beliefs on the topic, and thus she intends to be deceptive to her students. Corresponding to this, Stella's statement also seems straightforwardly to be a lie.[21]

Selfless assertions, then, are crucial to understanding lying in that they reveal the need for a connection between lies and deception. Non-deception accounts, such as LIE-F, LIE-C, and LIE-S, all incorrectly count as lies selfless assertions, while LIE-L, in requiring the intention to be deceptive, does not. Stella does not lie to her students in CREATIONIST TEACHER, for instance, because her aim is to report what current scientific

---

[21] Interestingly, Fallis considers a version of my CREATIONIST TEACHER (which was used for a different purpose in the paper that he cites), but does not seem to recognize the full force of the case. He writes:

> Norms of conversation can "clash" with each other as well as with other interests that we have (Grice *op. cit.* 30). For example, when a teacher who believes in creationism has to give a lesson on evolution, Grice's first maxim of Quality comes into conflict with Grice's second maxim of Quality. If the teacher violates the norms against saying what she believes to be false solely in order to obey the norm against saying that for which she lacks adequate evidence, some (for example, Lackey *op. cit.* 602) might want to say that she is not lying. In order to accommodate that intuition, my definition might be modified to include an exemption for such cases (Fallis 2009: 52 n. 74).

It is, however, unclear what sort of "exemption" could be added to Fallis's account of lying to respond to this *counterexample* that would not simply be ad hoc.

evidence supports regarding evolutionary theory, but she does lie in the modified version since her intention is to conceal her own religiously grounded beliefs about creationism in order to avoid termination. Thus, while there may be reason to sever the connection between lying and the intention to deceive, selfless assertions show that lying nonetheless remains fundamentally tied to the intention to be deceptive.

Acknowledgements

I am grateful to Jörg Meibauer, Eliot Michaelson, and Baron Reed for helpful comments on an earlier version of this chapter.

CHAPTER 19

BALD-FACED LIES

JÖRG MEIBAUER

19.1 Introduction

Imagine a situation in which young adults have smashed a window on purpose. When the police arrive and ask them about the broken window, they reply, "What do you mean? We do not see any broken window!" Intuitively, we would categorize this utterance as a bald-faced lie because it is evident that the adolescents lie and each party knows that this is the case. While the term 'bald-faced lie' suggests that the utterance in question is a lie, it suggests also that there are differences between bald-faced lies and prototypical lies. This chapter explores those differences. In particular, it deals with the status of bald-faced lies in recent debates between "deceptionists" (scholars who hold that lying entails an intention to deceive) and "non-deceptionists" (scholars who hold that lying does not necessarily entail an intention to deceive).

The deceptionist tradition assumes that lying involves the intention of the speaker to deceive the addressee. This is the classic approach going at least back to Augustine (Mahon 2014a, b). A definition of lying might equate lying with deceiving, i.e., leading the addressee into a false belief, but it does not need to. If we equate lying with deceiving in our definition of lying, we will end up with something along the following lines:

(1) Definition of lying including the intent to deceive (adapted from Stokke 2013b: 348)
S lies to H if and only if there is a proposition p such that
(a) S says that p to H, and
(b) S believes that p is false, and
(c) by saying that p to H, S intends to deceive H into believing that p.

From Carson's (2010) perspective, condition (c) would be superfluous because lying does not necessarily involve an intention to deceive on the part of the speaker. Several authors support this analysis. In section 19.2, we will review the non-deceptionist approaches by Carson (2010), Sorensen (2007), and Fallis (2009), and add empirical evidence. In section 19.3, we will turn to the deceptionist critics Lackey (2013), Meibauer (2011, 2014a, 2016a), and Dynel (2015, 2016a), add further theoretical challenges (Leland 2015; Keiser 2016) and empirical findings. Section 19.4 concludes.

19.2 THE NON-DECEPTIONIST VIEW

19.2.1 Warranting the Truth

Carson (2010) proposes the following definition of lying (see also Carson 2006):

(2) Lying
A person S tells a lie to another person S1 iff:
  (i) S makes a false statement X to S1,
  (ii) S believes that X is false or probably false (or, alternatively, S does not believe that X is true), and
  (iii) S intends to warrant the truth of X to S1.

(Carson 2010: 37)

This definition is intended to implement the following two basic tenets of Carson's approach: (i) lying does *not* require that the liar intends to deceive others, and (ii) lying requires making a statement that one warrants to be true (Carson 2010: 15). According to Carson, one warrants the truth of a statement if "one promises or guarantees, either explicitly or implicitly, that what one says is true" (Carson 2010: 26).

Requirement (ii) is connected with the basic assumption that lying is essentially a breach of trust. Most speech-act theoreticians would wholeheartedly agree with this assumption. But warranting the truth of p is, of course, built into standard definitions of assertion (or statement, the difference often being neglected), be it in the style of Searle (1969) (Constitutive Rule: "Counts as an undertaking to the effect that *p* represents an actual state of affairs") or as in (1b) above. Therefore, "warranting the truth" seems to follow from a reasonable taxonomy of speech acts. As for (i), one can agree that deception should not be part of definitions of lying because the deception follows from the liar's lack of truthfulness. But is it correct that lying does not require an intention to deceive on the part of the liar?

To support his claim that lying does not require the liar's intention to deceive others, Carson (2010: 20-3) comes up with three examples in which a person lies without intending to deceive anyone. Let us focus on his first example:

(3) *The witness*
Suppose that I witness a crime and clearly see that a particular individual committed the crime. Later, the same person is accused of the crime and, as a witness in court, I am asked whether or not I saw the defendant commit the crime. I make the false statement that I did not see the defendant commit the crime, for fear of being harmed or killed by him. However, I do not intend that my false statements deceive anyone. (I hope that no one believes my testimony and that he is convicted in spite of it.)

(Carson 2010: 20)

Carson (2010: 20) goes on to comment: "Deceiving the jury is not a means to preserving my life. Giving false testimony is necessary to save my life, but deceiving others is not; the deception is merely an unintended 'side effect'. I do not intend to deceive the jury in this case, but it seems clear that my false testimony would constitute a lie."

Meibauer (2014b) argues that the witness has deceived the jury because the witness asserts that he has a certain belief, which he actually has not. In his approach, hinting at the possible fact that the witness does not actually hold that belief and that he only pretends to have this belief, is not a "side effect," as Carson puts it. Instead, Meibauer (2014b) proposes to analyze this interpretation as a conversational implicature. This conversational implicature can be derived only if there is some contextual clue or background that gives rise to the suspicion that the witness cannot tell the truth.

According to Lackey's taxonomy (Lackey 2013: 237–9) that contains a distinction between (a) bald-faced lies, (b) knowledge lies, and (c) coercion-lies, this type of example is a so-called coercion-lie. So let us turn to Sorensen (2007, 2010) who introduced the notion of bald-faced lie into the discussion. (Note that Lackey 2013 features the case of the cheating student found by Carson 2010 as a prototypical case of a bald-faced lie.)

19.2.2 Bald-faced lie and knowledge lie

As his introductory example, Sorensen presents a short dialogue between the official guide Takhlef and the Norwegian reporter Asne Seierstad, which took place in Iraq under the dictatorship of Saddam Hussein:

(4) *Seierstad's interview, I*
Takhlef: Everything [President Saddam Hussein] did in the past was good and everything he will do in the future is good.

Seierstad: How can you be so sure about that?
Takhlef: I know it as a result of my belief in the party and his leadership.
(Sorensen 2007: 251)

Takhlef's utterances, Sorensen (2007: 252) points out, are "not merely pretending to assert that Saddam's leadership is perfect," "he wants to be on the record" and "defends the proposition by words and deeds." Yet his utterances are bald-faced lies because it is mutually known (or so assumes Seierstad) in the context that Takhlef does not believe the propositions of his utterances in (4).

In order to account for cases like (4), Sorensen (2007) proposes a substitute for the concept of the intent to deceive, namely a distinction between narrow and wide plausibility. Assuming that "lying is just asserting what one does not believe" (Sorensen 2007: 266), he distinguishes between assertions with narrow plausibility, in which "someone who only had access to the assertion might believe it" and wide plausibility, understood as "credibility relative to one's total evidence" (Sorensen 2007: 267). Bald-faced lies are then a case of narrow plausibility, as in the assertions of a lawyer defending a guilty client, which neither the lawyer nor the jury are supposed to believe in.

However, the point with the lawyer's assertions is that they describe possible or fictitious worlds (in which evidence shows the innocence of their client) in order to force the jury to provide evidence for something the client is supposed to have done. Therefore, Sorensen (2007: 255) seems to be mistaken when he argues that "when the lawyer does not believe the conclusions he is lying." After all, one need not believe the content of fictitious scenarios; all that is expected in rational discourse is a certain plausibility of these scenarios.

Similarly, Takhlef's utterances are not bald-faced lies, but assertions, since his propositions may be presented with narrow plausibility and are not, as Sorensen (2007) rightly observes, self-defeating: It is contradictory to say *Everything Saddam did is good but I don't believe it* or the like. Hence, Seierstad may be wondering to what extent her guide is truthful.

It can be concluded, then, that Takhlef's utterances are either a case of assertion with narrow plausibility, a case of self-deception, or a case of a cynical assertion (Sorensen 2007: 260–1, drawing on Kenyon 2003). Here, the speaker is said to be "manifestly insincere." I take it that his manifest insincerity triggers a conversational implicature. For instance, Takhlef wants Seierstad to understand that he is under pressure to assert that Saddam Hussein is a good leader, but in reality he does not believe this and may even be someone who opposes Saddam's dictatorship.

Carson (2010) defends his view that asserting amounts to warranting the truth of p against Sorensen. Both agree that the intent to deceive is not a necessary precondition for lying. However, warranting the truth is also in the scope of Sorensen's approach to bald-faced lies, since he defines lying simply as asserting what is false. Carson (2010) takes up Sorensen's example of an exchange in an Iraqi hospital reported by Seierstad.

The exchange occurs in a civilian hospital in which she sees a ward with wounded soldiers, which shows that the military hospitals are already overcrowded:

(5) *Seierstad's interview, II*
Seierstad: How many soldiers have you admitted today?
Doctor: There are no soldiers here.
Seierstad: But they are wearing uniforms?
Doctor: I see no uniforms. You must go now, do you hear?

Carson (2010: 35)

Carson (2010: 35) (cf. Sorenson 2007: 253) argues that "the doctor still warrants the truth of what he says since he invites Seierstad to trust and rely on the truth of what he says and guarantees the truth of what he says." If what he says is evidentially false, one could add that he infringes the maxim of Quality, thus inviting the pragmatic inference that he is not entitled to admit the over-crowdedness of the hospital.

In addition to bald-faced lies, Sorensen (2010) introduces the so-called knowledge lies as cases in which no intention to deceive is at play. He presents the following scenario as an example of a knowledge lies:

(6) *Knowledge lie*
In *Spartacus* (Universal Pictures, 1960), the victorious Roman general, Marcus Licinius Crassus, asks the recaptured slaves to identify Spartacus in exchange for leniency. Spartacus … rises to spare his comrades crucifixion. However, the slave on his right, Antoninus, springs to his feet and declares, 'I am Spartacus!' Then the slave on Spartacus' left also stands and declares 'I am Spartacus!', then another slave, and another until the whole army of slaves is on their feet shouting, 'I am Spartacus!'

(Sorensen 2010: 608)

Sorensen (2010: 608) comments that "with the exception of Antoninus, none intend to deceive Crassus about who they are." Instead, "the slaves are preventing Crassus from *learning* who Spartacus is."

However, it cannot be taken for granted that the series of outbursts *I am Spartacus* constitutes a series of lies. From the point of view of the Roman general Crassus, the slaves (except Antoninus) cannot give serious answers to his question, which presupposes that there is exactly one person called Spartacus in the audience. Hence, their answers violate the maxim of Quality because it cannot be true that every slave is Spartacus. Moreover, it is not clear how the series of answers can be relevant for his question aiming at the identification of Spartacus; thus, the maxim of Relation is infringed. Furthermore, the answers do not accord with the maxim of Manner since such iterative assertions of the slaves are quite obscure. Hence, it is natural for Crassus to assume that he shall be deceived insofar as the true answer is concealed. After all, it is clear that in his audience, including Spartacus, Antoninus and the rest, only one person can be Spartacus.

The information that the audience wants to conceal the true answer to Crassus's question is a conversational implicature. As a matter of fact, the audience makes it clear that they do definitely not want to give the true answer to Crassus' question (aiming at the identification of Spartacus). As we have seen, multiple exploitations of maxims clearly point in this direction.

Staffel (2011: 301) replies to Sorensen's approach. She ventures that "Sorensen's thesis that knowledge lies do not involve deception occurs only when someone is brought to flat-out believe a false proposition"; this, she argues, is an "implausibly narrow" conception of deception, "because it overlooks the possibility of deceiving someone by merely making them more confident in a falsehood." Typical knowledge lies are deceptive by the criterion of making someone more confident in a falsehood: "For in asserting the false proposition q, the liar will prevent the addressee from knowing that –q by providing evidence for q that will raise the addressee's credence in q, thereby deceiving her" (Staffel 2011: 301). While this argument seems convincing, it is not very strong: In the case of Spartacus, it is plausible that the Roman general might get sceptical right after the second slave (after Antoninus) utters his false assertion.

19.2.3 Checking quality

Fallis (2009) develops a Gricean approach to lying, and provides the following definition (which is adapted here to the format of the other definitions for the sake of comparison):

(7) *Lying*
A lies to B if and only if
(1) A states that p to B,
(2) A believes that p is false and
(3) A believes that she makes this statement in a context where the following norm of conversation is in effect: *Do not make statements that you believe to be false.*

(Fallis 2009: 34)

Fallis (2009) also assumes that bald-faced lies are lies. He couches his analysis in the framework of Grice (1989a), seeing lying as a violation of the maxim of Quality. Fallis assumes that the liar knows that the maxim of Quality is to be observed. Thus, bald-faced lies are genuine lies in his analysis.

19.2.4 Empirical evidence

In Arico and Fallis (2013), 216 students were asked whether they considered a certain utterance, conceived of by the authors as a bald-faced lie, as a genuine lie. After presenting the respective vignette, students were asked whether the person in the story had lied, and they had the opportunity to mark the degree of lying on a 7-point Likert scale. The story in question goes like this:

(8) *Charlie the gambler*
Charlie has a gambling addiction, so he often sneaks away from work to bet on horses. He has just come home after spending another thousand dollars at the racetrack. As he enters the house, his wife Natalie says to him, "I tried calling you at work today, but no one could find you. You didn't skip out of work to go gambling again, did you?" Charlie knows that this wife doesn't approve and will likely leave him if she finds out he's been betting again. Before Charlie can say anything, Natalie reaches into his coat pockets and pulls out betting tickets from that afternoon's races. Despite the evidence, Charlie responds, "No, Honey, I wasn't gambling."
(Arico and Fallis 2013: 814)

The result was that 93.98% of the students opted for 7 points on the Likert scale (= "Definitely a lie"). In their discussion, the authors concede "that some percentage of participants might have interpreted the cases as involving attempted deception," but "it is unlikely that the vast majority of participants interpreted them that way" (Arico and Fallis 2013: 802).

However, it is possible that the participants interpreted Charlie's utterance as a downright lie because he flatly denied having been at the races. Thus, it is not clear to the participants that Charlie knew that Natalie knew that his statement was false, and Natalie knew that Charlie knew this. To deny something, even when evidence speaks against it, is a clear-cut lie in which the speaker takes their remotest chance of deceiving the hearer. In contrast, in bald-faced lies it must be mutually crystal clear that p is not true.

Rutschmann and Wiegmann (2017) draw a distinction between three types of lies: conflicting bald-faced lies, consistent bald-faced lies, and indifferent lies. Conflicting bald-faced lies are cases in which the speaker hopes that his statement is not believed by the audience (as in the witness case). Consistent bald-faced lies are cases in which the speaker would profit from the audience's believing him/her (like Takhlef in Seierstad's interview I, see (4), or Charlie, the Gambler in (8)). To this, they add indifferent lies as a new category. These are lies in the context of games, for instance, on "Opposite Day," one has to tell the opposite of what is true. Participants were asked whether they attributed to target utterances the evaluations of being a lie and being deceptive. Rutschmann and Wiegmann found that all bald-faced lies are considered lies (this is consistent with the findings in Meibauer 2016), as the non-deceptionists assume. However, they found also that an intention to deceive was ascribed to the target utterances—although the results for the consistent bald-faced lies were stronger than for the conflicting bald-faced lies. This speaks against the non-deceptionists, in particular against Arico and

Fallis (2013), since their "Charlie the Gambler" case was among Rutschmann and Wiegmann's materials. Finally, indifferent lies were considered as lies with no intention to deceive. From this, the authors conclude that there are lies without an intention to deceive, as the non-deceptionists claim. However, the context of a game is a highly artificial one, so that participants were most likely identifying "lying" with deliberately saying the untruth. The victims of these lies, not knowing they were involved in a game, would certainly qualify these utterances as deceptive. (See also Keiser's 2016 review in section 19.3.3.)

19.3 THE DECEPTIONIST VIEW

19.3.1 Deceit, deception, and selfless assertion

Lackey (2013) has argued against the "unhappy divorce" of lying and deceit/deception, yet she takes it for granted that bald-faced lies are lies. Meibauer (2011, 2014a, b) sides with her in thinking that lies are deceiving (cf. Meibauer 2011, 2014a), yet argues that bald-faced lies are no genuine lies. Note that Kenyon (2003) holds a similar view with respect to what he calls "cynical assertion." This position is dismissed by Lackey (2013: 238 n. 7), largely for intuitive reasons, and she states that "bald-faced lies are called lies in our ordinary talk."

Lackey (2013) provides an analysis of bald-faced lies (as well as coercion-lies and knowledge lies) that considers them as lies, yet argues against the idea put forth by Carson, Sorensen, and Fallis that bald-faced lies constitute evidence against the intention to deceive involved in lying. Her proposal is shown in (9):

(9) *Lying*
A lies to B if and only if
   (a) A states that p to B,
   (b) A believes that p is false and
   (c) A intends to be deceptive to B in stating that p.
   (Lackey 2013: 236–7)

The innovation comes with condition (iii) in which "being deceptive" is introduced. The trick is to draw a distinction between deceit and deception:

(10) *Deceit versus deception*
   (a) Deceit: A deceives B with respect to whether p if and only if A aims to bring about a false belief in B regarding whether p.
   (b) Deception: A is deceptive to B with respect to whether p if A aims to conceal information from B regarding whether p.
   (Lackey 2013: 241)

While the definition of deceit in (10a) relates to the traditional idea of deception, the definition of deception in (10b) focuses on the concealment of information as another strategy to be deceptive. (Note that this move implies that normal lies also have to do with deception in this sense, otherwise condition (9 iii) would be ad hoc.)

The case Lackey (2013) considers as a prototypical bald-faced lie is the following (recall that it is modelled after one of Carson's 2010 scenarios):

(11) *Cheating student* (Lackey's version)
... suppose that a student is caught flagrantly cheating on an exam for the fourth time this term, all of the conclusive evidence for which is passed on to the Dean of Academic Affairs. Both the student and the Dean know that he cheated on the exam, and they each know that the other knows this, but the student is also aware of the fact that the Dean punishes students for academic dishonesty only when there is a confession. Given this, when the student is called to the Dean's office, he states, 'I did not cheat on the exam'.
(Lackey 2013: 238)

Applying condition (10b), Lackey argues that "concealment is the central aim of the student's statement" (Lackey 2013: 242). Hence "the student does not deceive the Dean, but he does intend to be deceptive to him" (Lackey 2013: 242). Fallis (2015a), in his reply to Lackey (2013), discusses the case of the cheating student at length and tries to show that Lackey's definition is too narrow as well as too broad. While it is useful to accept that there can be deception by omission, as Chisholm and Feehan (1977) put it, this requires specific contexts, e.g., an interrogation. Thus, it can be argued that the distinction between deceit and deception is not necessary, and that the "bringing about of a false belief in someone" (with the intention to deceive) is sufficient. As additional evidence, Lackey adds "that non-deception accounts of lying count as lies classic cases of what I have elsewhere called selfless assertions" (Lackey 2013: 237). Lackey (2008: 48, 2013: 243) presents the case of a so-called selfless assertion, in which a creationist teacher named Stella asserts to her students *Modern-day Homo sapiens evolved from Homo erectus*, although she neither believes nor knows this proposition to be the case.

By providing this case, Lackey (2008) aims at a special relation between reliability and knowledge: "What CREATIONIST TEACHER reveals is that an *unreliable believer* may nonetheless be a *reliable testifier*, and so may reliably convey knowledge (justified/warranted belief) to a hearer despite the fact that she fails to possess it herself" (Lackey 2008: 49). Because Stella presents something as true that she does not believe in, it seems that she simply lied. Lackey, however, dubs Stella's behaviour as a case of "selfless assertion."

There are several possibilities to do justice to Stella's "selflessness" or renunciation. One could argue that it is a case of self-deception, a prosocial lie, a case of bullshitting (because of an indifference to the truth of what-is-said), or even a case in which the content of the selfless assertion is merely quoted (Meibauer 2014a: 227–8, 2014b).

19.3.2 Bald-faced lies are no lies

In contrast to the aforementioned philosophers (Carson, Sorensen, Fallis, Lackey), Meibauer (2014a, b) and Dynel (2015) argue that so-called bald-faced lies are *not* lies. The reason is that in bald-faced lies, the intention to deceive is lacking. It follows that what is called bald-faced lies must be another kind of speech act.

Meibauer (2014b: 140) presents the following example situated in the fictional world of the TV series *Mad Men* (note that the male protagonist is a notorious liar):

(12)   *Don betrays Betty*
Betty Draper asks her husband Don Draper who is coming home in the morning where he was last night. He responds: "I have spent the night in the office, because I had a meeting late in the evening." However, this is not true, since he spent the night with his recent love interest Dr. Faye Miller. As a matter of fact, Betty Draper believes that Don's answer is not true (because he gave the same answer on another occasion when he was also caught in the act of lying), and that Don knows this. Moreover, Don Draper believes that Betty knows that his answer is not true.

Meibauer (2014b: 140)

Clearly, Don Draper actively believed at t that not p. However, he did not really assert p since this requires, according to the definition of assertion, that the speaker (i) presents p as true, and (ii) wants the addressee to actively believe that p. Yet, Don Draper does not really present p as true in the context since he *lets shine through* that p is false. He would not feel committed to the truth of p, and he would not be ready to provide further evidence. Consequently, he does not want Betty to believe that he is right. Since in this story, there is a mutual understanding of the fact that Don uttered something that is false, his utterance cannot count as a lie. Therefore, Meibauer argues that such cases of bald-faced lies are not proper lies.

It appears important to consider the degree to which the speaker lets shine through that they are insincere. While Don is blatantly insincere, the witness in (3) (let us assume that "I" refers to Tony) is not. Hence, Tony is lying and he *is deceiving* the jury and the whole audience. What might be the case, however, is that implicatures are triggered (presupposing relevant background knowledge) by the fact that Tony only falsely asserts what he does because he fears the mafioso's revenge. The very fact that there may be other contexts in which implicatures such as these do *not* arise shows that Tony's utterance has to count as a lie, including the attempt to deceive the jury.

Similarly, the cheating student in (8) is a liar. He cannot say something like **I did not cheat on the exam. We mutually know that this is a lie, but I don't want to deceive you*. If an utterance is an assertion, the utterer is committed to its truth.

The case of Don Draper and the cases Sorensen developed are different from the case of the witness (Tony) and the case of the cheating student. If the utterances of Draper and the Iraqi officers are no lies, they should constitute a distinct kind of speech act, and we have to ask which one. Meibauer (2014a, b) proposes that they are cases of verbal aggression (insults) because they ostensively violate the Cooperation Principle (Grice 1989a) and thus attack the addressee's face (Neu 2008, Mateo and Yus 2013, Meibauer 2014b).

Dynel (2015: 313–22) is also sceptical about the status of bald-faced lies as genuine lies. Her approach is to align bald-faced lies with the rhetorical figures in which untruthfulness is overt, such as irony, metaphor, and understatement. In a way, she takes Sorensen's (2007: 263) remark seriously: "Since no bald-faced lie involves the intent to deceive, I suspect Kant and Ross would regard the bald-faced lie as no more a lie than metaphor, hyperbole, and sarcasm." Consequently, Dynel (2015: 317) claims that "bald-faced lies cannot be considered lies on the grounds of their *overt untruthfulness*, i.e., untruthfulness available to the hearer, rather than *covert untruthfulness*, which is the essence of lying ..." Thus, bald-faced lies cannot be lies to the same extent as, for example, ironical utterances cannot be lies. This parallel holds also for metaphor, hyperbole, and meiosis. Consequently, bald-faced lies, displaying overt untruthfulness, are connected to conversational implicatures in the same way as ironical implicatures are (Dynel 2015: 317, 2016a).

19.3.3 Bald-faced lies have no illocutions

Keiser (2016) argues that bald-faced lies have no illocutions but merely locutions. They are not contributions to a conversation but simply contributions to a language game. Thus, they are similar to proofs or exam games. The witness, for instance, does only make a move in the courtroom game. Since bald-faced lies operate on the locutionary level, they are no counterevidence to the assumption that ordinary lying involves an intention to deceive. Lying requires that an assertion is made. Yet in the witness case (Keiser provides a story taken from the Godfather Part 2 fitting Carson's story) no assertion has been made. Therefore, bald-faced lies cannot constitute counterevidence to the assumption that lying includes an intention to deceive. There are two problems with this approach: First, while the distinction between ordinary conversation and "games" is straightforward, it is not clear whether perjury via bald-faced lying is simply of a locutionary kind. After all, it is a criminal speech act (Green 2006: 133–47). Second, while coerced bald-faced lies (in an institutional context) may be analyzed as mere moves in a language game, it is not clear whether this extends to other bald-faced lies that do not happen in special institutional contexts.

Leland (2015: 552), considering the cases of the citizen of a totalitarian state (cf. (4)) and the scared witness (cf. (3)), argues that these are cases of coerced lies: "These cases involve speech acts which are to varying degree coerced. Coerced speech acts are not genuinely assertoric. Like an actor's utterance on stage, they are meaningful speech acts which fall short of being genuine assertions." Therefore, he concludes, these cases cannot convince as cases of (bald-faced) lying when lying is understood as a kind of assertion. Kenyon (2010) also discusses the question whether coerced utterances can count as assertions. He proposes to speak of capitulations rather than assertions.

19.3.4 Experimental evidence

Meibauer (2016) asked 128 students with respect to eight target utterances embedded in stories about putative bald-faced lies. The students were asked if/how far they considered the utterances (a) as lies, (b) as being deceptive, and (c) as brazen (in the sense of rude or aggressive). The stories presented in the questionnaire were called: witness (Carson 2010), (cheating) student (Carson 2010), daughter (fraudulent uncle) (Carson 2010), spouse/Don Draper (Meibauer 2014b), gambler, (Arico and Fallis 2013), Spartacus (Sorensen 2010), guide/Takhlef (Sorensen 2007), and believer (Kenyon 2003; Lackey 2008). With the exception of the guide/Takhlef and the believer/Stella, these cases were all rated as lies (more than 3.5 on a 7-point rating scale). The same results were obtained for the question whether these utterances are deceptive. The first result speaks against those approaches that deny that bald-faced lies are lies (as some deceptionists do). The second result speaks against those approaches that deny that bald-faced lies come with an intention to deceive (as the non-deceptionists do). The deception scores were somewhat weaker than the lie scores, with the exception of Spartacus, the guide, and the believer (recall that the latter two are not considered as lies). This shows that subjects took the motives of the speakers into account. With respect to (c), subjects distinguished clearly between those utterances that are brazen (student, spouse, gambler) and those that are not. This shows that brazenness can be an important aspect of at least some bald-faced lies.

19.4 CONCLUSIONS

Bald-faced lies have been presented as decisive evidence against deceptionists' accounts of lying. Yet it remains a matter of dispute whether this is correct. Non-deceptionists' approaches hold that lying is connected to the intention to deceive, i.e., leading the hearer into a false belief. If lying is a case of insincere assertion, it is insincerity (or the violation of the maxim of Quality) that is deceptive. Thus, it could be argued that bald-faced lies are not real lies because, by definition, it is mutually known by the participants that what the speaker says is false. Hence, the category of 'bald-faced lie' remains a problematic one and is a promising candidate for more empirically oriented research.

CHAPTER 20

BULLSHITTING

ANDREAS STOKKE

20.1 Frankfurt on Bullshit

In his essay "On Bullshit," Harry Frankfurt identified the phenomenon of bullshit as a distinctive trait of modern societies:[1]

> One of the most salient features of our culture is that there is so much bullshit.
>
> (Frankfurt 2005: 1)

One of Frankfurt's main examples of bullshit was a certain kind of political speech-making, as in the following example:

> Consider a Fourth of July orator, who goes on bombastically about "our great and blessed country, whose Founding Fathers under divine guidance created a new beginning for mankind."
>
> (Frankfurt 2005: 16)

According to Frankfurt, the central characteristic of bullshit of this kind is that the bullshitter is indifferent toward the truth or falsity of what she says. In an often-quoted passage Frankfurt describes the bullshitter as follows:

> Her statement is grounded neither in a belief that it is true nor, as a lie must be, in a belief that it is not true. It is just this lack of connection to a concern with truth—this indifference to how things really are—that I regard as of the essence of bullshit.
>
> (Frankfurt 2005: 33–4)

---

[1] The essay first appeared in *Raritan* (vol. 6, no. 2) in 1986. It was reprinted in Frankfurt (1988), and later as the monograph Frankfurt (2005). Frankfurt's analysis of bullshit explicitly owed much to Max Black's (1983) ideas about what he called *humbug*.

There are three further important features of Frankfurt's analysis of bullshit. First, Frankfurt describes the bullshitter as not caring about her audience's beliefs about the subject matter of her discourse. For example, he says,

> the orator does not really care what his audience thinks about the Founding Fathers, or about the role of the deity in our country's history, or the like. At least, it is not an interest in what anyone thinks about these matters that motivates his speech.
>
> (Frankfurt 2005: 17)

Second, Frankfurt argues that bullshitting always involves an intention to deceive the audience. Even though, for Frankfurt, the bullshitter is indifferent toward her audience's beliefs about what she says, the bullshitter intends to deceive her audience about her aims:

> The bullshitter may not deceive us, or even intend to do so, either about the facts or about what he takes the facts to be. What he does necessarily attempt to deceive us about is his enterprise. His only indispensably distinctive characteristic is that in a certain way he misrepresents what he is up to.
>
> (Frankfurt 2005: 54)

Third, and finally, Frankfurt insisted on a sharp distinction between bullshitting and lying.[2] For Frankfurt, whereas the bullshitter is indifferent toward the truth or falsity of what she says, the liar is "inescapably concerned with truth-values" (Frankfurt 2005: 51). He writes,

> Telling a lie is an act with a sharp focus. It is designed to insert a particular falsehood at a specific point in a set or system of beliefs, in order to avoid the consequences of having that point occupied by the truth.
>
> (Frankfurt 2005: 51)

To summarize, the bullshitter, for Frankfurt, is characterized by four different features, as spelled out below.

F1. The bullshitter is indifferent toward whether what she says is true or false.
F2. The bullshitter is indifferent toward her audience's beliefs.
F3. The bullshitter intends to deceive her audience into thinking that she is not bullshitting.
F4. Bullshitting and lying are incompatible.

---

[2] In his reply to Cohen (2002), Frankfurt (2002) argued that his account allowed the two categories to overlap. See section 20.6.

This chapter first reviews a number of reactions to Frankfurt's analysis of bullshit (sections 20.2–20.3). It then considers a proposal to account for bullshitting in terms of Gricean maxims of conversation (section 20.4). Next, an alternative proposal to analyze bullshitting in terms of the speaker's attitudes toward *inquiry* is discussed (section 20.5). Finally, the chapter turns to the relation between bullshitting and lying (section 20.6).

20.2 Bullshit, bullshitting, and nonsense

One strand of commentary on Frankfurt's essay concerns its target, that is, what it should be seen as providing an account of. In his well-known rejoinder to Frankfurt's view, G. A. Cohen (2002) argued that one should distinguish between the *activity* of bullshitting and the *product* bullshit. According to Cohen, Frankfurt provided an account of the former but not of the latter.

The product Cohen is interested in is what he calls *nonsense*.[3] As he describes it, nonsense is what is found in

> discourse that is by nature *unclarifiable*, discourse, that is, that is not only obscure but which cannot be rendered unobscure, where any apparent success in rendering it unobscure creates something that isn't recognizable as a version of what was said.
>
> (Cohen 2002: 332)

Cohen distinguishes between different ways in which an utterance may be unclear in the sense he has in mind. One of these he characterizes as "unclarity of a sentence itself," and another as "unclarity as to why a certain (possibly perfectly clear) sentence is uttered in a given context" (Cohen 2002: 332). For Cohen, both these kinds of nonsense can be the product either of bullshitting or of not bullshitting. As he says, "One can "talk nonsense" with any intentions whatsoever..." (Cohen 2002: 324).

To illustrate, consider Scott Kimbrough's (2006: 12–13) example of "an avid fan of conservative talk radio" who claims "that the French are an irrational and ungrateful people, and that liberals have an anti-Christmas agenda." The radio fan's statements are naturally thought of as involving nonsense. For example, the notion of "an anti-Christmas agenda" might be thought to be an unclarity of the first kind that Cohen distinguishes. Furthermore, it might be argued that the radio fan's statements cannot intelligibly be seen as pertinent, and hence that they are also examples of the second kind of nonsense.

---

[3] Compare Daniel Dennett's (2013: 56–57) notion of a *deepity*.

Whether the radio fan is bullshitting arguably depends on different factors. On one reading of the example, the radio fan firmly believes what he says and he wants to enlighten everyone else. In that case the radio fan is naturally seen as not bullshitting. Similarly, Cohen says that

> an honest person might read some bullshit that a Frankfurt-bullshitter wrote, believe it to be the truth, and affirm it. When that honest person utters bullshit, *she*'s not showing a disregard for truth.
>
> (Cohen 2002: 332)

Yet, on another reading, the radio fan is bullshitting. He might say what he does not because he is concerned with the truth or falsity of his statements, but because he wants to present himself in a certain light. In that case, the radio fan would be bullshitting (at least) in the sense of F1.

Cohen concludes,

> So it is neither necessary nor sufficient for every kind of bullshit that it be produced by one who is informed by indifference to the truth, or, indeed, by any other distinctive intentional state.
>
> (Cohen 2002: 332)

However, as Cohen acknowledges, Frankfurt's account is an account of the activity of bullshitting. In particular, F1–F4 are traits that, according to Frankfurt, distinguish someone who is engaged in bullshitting. Yet even as characteristics of bullshitting, each of F1–F4 has been challenged.

20.3 Problems for Frankfurt's account of bullshitting

Against F1, i.e., the claim that the bullshitter is indifferent toward the truth or falsity of what she says, a number of writers (e.g. Cohen 2002; Kimbrough 2006; Carson 2010; Wreen 2013; Stokke and Fallis 2017; Fallis 2015b) have pointed to examples in which someone appears to be bullshitting while caring about the truth-value of what they say. The following kind of example is not unfamiliar from everyday life:

Lisa is discussing a fishing trip to Lake Mountain View that she has planned to go on with her friends, Vern and Sue. They are all big fans of fishing and have been looking forward to the trip a long time. "I really hope the fishing is good there," Sue says. Lisa has no real evidence about the fishing at Lake Mountain View, and she has no idea what it is like. Still, caught up in the excitement, she exclaims, "The fishing there is outstanding!"

Many will think that Lisa is bullshitting in this case. Yet she is clearly not indifferent toward the truth-value of what she is saying. She wants it to be true that the fishing is good at Lake Mountain View. So this example illustrates that one may be bullshitting even if one cares about whether what one says is true or false.

Here is a different kind of example that Thomas Carson gives:

> A student who gives a bullshit answer to a question in an exam might be concerned with the truth of what [s]he says. Suppose that she knows that the teacher will bend over backwards to give her partial credit if he thinks that she may have misunderstood the question, but she also knows that if the things she writes are false she will be marked down. In that case, she will be very careful to write only things that are true and accurate, although she knows that what she writes is not an answer to the question.
>
> (Carson 2010: 62)

While Lisa cares about the truth of the particular thing she is saying, the student, in Carson's example, just cares about saying things that are true. But neither of them says things without caring about their truth-value. Examples of this kind have therefore been taken as challenges to F1.

The second feature, F2, of Frankfurt's analysis of bullshitting, i.e., that the bullshitter is indifferent toward her audience's beliefs, has likewise been drawn into question. For example, Cohen points out that,

> the bullshitting orator, as Frankfurt describes him, might well care a lot about what the audience thinks about the Founding Fathers.
>
> (Cohen 2002: 330)

Familiar forms of propaganda have the characteristic that it is designed to make its audience believe particular things, even if the propagandist herself is indifferent toward them. In other words, the observation is that someone might be bullshitting even if they are not indifferent toward whether their audience come to believe what they say.

Further, against the third feature, F3, of Frankfurt's account, Carson points out that bullshitting does not necessarily involve intentions to deceive the audience about what one is up to. He considers the following case:

> I am a student who needs to receive a good grade in a class. I am assigned to write a short essay on a very clearly and precisely defined topic. I know nothing about the topic and cannot write on it at all. Despite this, I know that my instructor will give me partial credit for turning in something, however incompetent and far off the topic. The worst grade I can receive for writing something that is completely incompetent and off the topic is an F—60%. If I write nothing I will receive a zero—0%. In producing a bullshit answer, I am not attempting to mislead my teacher about my level of knowledge or about what I am up to (namely bullshitting her). I don't care

about any of these things; I just want to receive 60 points instead of zero points. I might even want my bullshitting to be transparent to the teacher in order to amuse or annoy her.

(Carson 2010: 60)

In this example the student is bullshitting but is not trying to hide this fact from the teacher. Hence, this kind of example is evidence against Frankfurt's suggestion that the bullshitter's "only indispensably distinctive characteristic is that in a certain way he misrepresents what he is up to" (Frankfurt 2005: 54).

Finally, Frankfurt's claim, F4, that bullshitting and lying are incompatible has been rejected by a number of philosophers. For example, Carson argues that "One can tell a lie as a part of an evasive bullshit answer to a question" (Carson 2010: 61). He gives the following example:

Suppose that I teach at a university that is very intolerant of atheists. I am asked by an administrator whether a friend and colleague is an atheist. I know that he is an atheist and that it will harm him if I reveal this. I do not want to harm my friend nor do I want to lie and say that he is not an atheist as I fear that I am likely to be found out if I lie about this. I give an evasive bullshit answer. I say "as a boy he always went to church and loved singing Christmas Carols" even though I know this to be false. (I am not worried that I will be caught or found out if I lie about this).

(Carson 2010: 61–2)

According to Carson, the answer, in this case, "is evasive bullshit, but because I say what I know to be false in a context in which I know that I am warranting the truth of what I say, my answer is also a lie" (Carson 2010: 62).

20.4 Bullshitting and Gricean Quality

Given these kinds of challenges to Frankfurt's description of bullshitting, alternative positive accounts have been proposed. One type of view involves seeing bullshitting in terms of conversational norms.

In particular, both bullshitting and lying are modes of speech that typically violate one or more of the Gricean maxims of Quality (see Grice 1989c: 27). Grice's category of Quality consisted of a supermaxim and two more specific maxims:

Supermaxim of Quality: Try to make your contribution one that is true.
First maxim of Quality: Do not say what you believe to be false.
Second maxim of Quality: Do not say that for which you lack adequate evidence.

There have been attempts to characterize lying in terms of maxims of Quality (see Chapter 10 by Andreas Stokke). Similarly, it has been suggested that bullshitting can be characterized in terms of Quality maxims.

Marta Dynel (2011a) and Don Fallis (2009, 2012) have proposed accounts of bullshitting in terms of (versions of) the second maxim of Quality. For example, Dynel claims that

> The violation of the second Quality maxim "Do not say that for which you lack adequate evidence"... gives rise to *bullshit*, which the hearer takes to be truthful.
>
> (Dynel 2011a: 152)

And according to Fallis,

> you bullshit if and only if you intend to violate the norm of conversation against communicating something for which you lack adequate evidence by saying that thing.
>
> (Fallis 2012: 575)

These views imply that someone is bullshitting if they say that p and thereby intend to communicate that p, while lacking adequate evidence for p.

Problems for this type of account arise owing to the fact that one may believe that one has adequate evidence for a proposition, even though one does not. Typically, if someone says what they believe they have adequate evidence for, they are not bullshitting. Here is an example:

Joan has read a science-fiction novel in which one of the characters states that there is life on Saturn. Joan thinks science-fiction novels are a reliable guide to facts about extraterrestrial life. So she comes to believe firmly that there is life on Saturn, and she also believes that she has adequate evidence for that claim, that is, the novel's say-so. Indeed, Joan thinks she knows there's life on Saturn. Sometime later, her younger brother asks her whether there's life anywhere else than on Earth. Joan replies, "Yes, there's life on Saturn."

Joan is not bullshitting. She is not engaged in the kind of irresponsible talk that arguably characterizes Frankfurt's orator, as well as Lisa and the careful exam taker in Carson's example. Joan's response is motivated by her wish to inform her brother of what she believes to be the truth. But in saying something for which she lacks adequate evidence, and thereby intending to communicate that thing, Joan is violating the second maxim of Quality, and likewise the slightly modified norm that Fallis appeals to.

In response to this, one may want to argue that the second maxim of Quality should be understood as prohibiting statements made while one *believes* that one lacks adequate evidence for them. This would make the norm parallel to the first maxim of Quality, which prohibits saying something one believes to be false. So one might propose that someone is bullshitting if and only if they say that *p* and thereby intend to communicate that *p*, while believing that they lack adequate evidence for *p*.

This proposal can likewise be seen to be inadequate. In particular, it can be rejected by considering the kind of speakers that have been described by Jennifer Lackey (2008) and others. Consider, for example, the case of Stella from Lackey's "Creationist Teacher" case:

> Stella is a devoutly Christian fourth-grade teacher, and her religious beliefs are grounded in a deep faith that she has had since she was a very young child. Part of this faith includes a belief in the truth of creationism and, accordingly, a belief in the falsity of evolutionary theory. Despite this, she fully recognizes that there is an overwhelming amount of scientific evidence against both of these beliefs. Indeed, she readily admits that she is not basing her own commitment to creationism on evidence at all but, rather, on the personal faith that she has in an all-powerful Creator.
>
> (Lackey 2008: 48)

Suppose that Stella is asked, in a private conversation, outside school, what she thinks about the origin of species. She replies, "God created the species."

In this example, despite the fact that Stella says and intends to communicate something for which she believes she lacks adequate evidence, she is surely not bullshitting. She says what she does because she is convinced of its truth, and she is motivated by a wish to convey that truth to her interlocutor. This clearly distinguishes her from speakers like the orator.

In other words, it seems doubtful that one can identify a sufficient condition for bullshitting in terms of (a version of) the second maxim of Quality. As argued below, the same applies to the other Quality maxims.

According to most theories of lying, you lie when you say something you believe to be false, and thereby try to communicate that thing to the audience.[4] Hence, when someone tells a lie, they violate both the supermaxim of Quality and the first maxim of Quality. Furthermore, even if critics of Frankfurt such as Carson (2010) are right that lying is not incompatible with bullshitting, it is reasonable to think that Frankfurt was correct in thinking that at least some lies are not instances of bullshitting.

Consider, for instance, the following example:

Parker wants to convince his parents that he's ready for his chemistry exam. Even though Parker hasn't studied, when asked by his parents, he tells them, "I have studied really hard, and I'm ready for the chemistry exam."

Most likely, cases of lying of this kind were the motivation for Frankfurt's claims concerning the distinction between bullshitting and lying. In particular, lies like Parker's

---

[4] See, e.g., Chisholm and Feehan (1977), Williams (2002), Fallis (2009, 2012), Saul (2012a), and Stokke (2013a, 2014).

are "designed to insert a particular falsehood at a specific point in a set or system of beliefs, in order to avoid the consequences of having that point occupied by the truth" (Frankfurt 2005: 54). Accordingly, many will want to say that, even though Parker is lying to his parents, he is not bullshitting. Yet lies like this one violate both the supermaxim of Quality and the first maxim of Quality.

Finally, there are reasons to think that one can engage in bullshitting without violating Quality maxims. Consider Carson's exam taker who gives bullshit answers while carefully selecting what to say in order to say only things she believes to be true, because that is how she knows she will get partial credit. Assuming the student has adequate evidence for what she says, she is bullshitting while obeying all the Quality maxims. She is trying to make true contributions, and she says what she believes to be true and has adequate evidence for.

20.5 Bullshitting and inquiry

Frankfurt's central insight was that bullshitting involves indifference toward one's speech. His suggestion was that the indifference that marks bullshitting concerns the truth-value of what is said. Yet, given that bullshitters may care about the truth-value of what they say, an alternative route is to look for another way of characterizing bullshitting in terms of indifference.

Fallis (2015b) and Stokke and Fallis (2017) have proposed accounts on which bullshitting is characterized by indifference toward *inquiry*.[5] In the tradition originating in the work of Robert Stalnaker (1978, 1984, 1998, 2002) a discourse is seen as a cooperative activity of information sharing, ultimately aimed at the goal of inquiry, the discovery of how things are, or what the actual world is like.[6] Following Craige Roberts (2004, 2012) inquiry in this overarching sense can be distinguished from particular *subinquiries* that discourse participants engage in as means toward the goal of inquiry itself.[7]

According to one version of this account, someone is bullshitting when they do not care whether their statement is a contribution to a subinquiry that they believe to be true or a contribution that they believe to be false.[8] That is, when they are indifferent toward whether their statement steers the relevant subinquiry toward (what she believes to be)

---

[5] See Stokke (2013a, 2014) for related accounts of lying and other forms of linguistic insincerity.

[6] It is not suggested that discourse does not serve other goals, or have other aims, as well as the pursuit of truth. For example, engaging in discourse may be undertaken for entertainment, for socializing purposes, or for other ends.

[7] In the model of discourse developed by Roberts (2004, 2012), such subinquiries are identified with *questions under discussion* that, formally, structure the set of possible worlds among which assertions distinguish. The details of this are left out here. In contrast to the account in Fallis (2015b), the proposal of Stokke and Fallis (2017) is explicitly couched in terms of questions under discussion.

[8] There are refinements to the proposal to be considered in light of complications. We ignore these here. See Stokke and Fallis (2017) for discussion. See also Carson (2016) for some criticism of this view.

truth or falsity. Hence, on this view, the indifference that marks bullshitting is not indifference toward whether what is said is true or false, but indifference toward the effect of one's statement on subinquiries.

This account allows that someone can be bullshitting even though they care about the truth or falsity of their statements. For example, consider Lisa's wishful claim about the fishing at Lake Mountain View. Lisa is not indifferent toward the truth-value of her statement. She cares very much about whether it is true or not. However, she is careless about making contributions to the subinquiry about the fishing at Lake Mountain View based on what she believes. She is not making her statement because she is interested in making progress on this subinquiry, nor because she wants it to deteriorate. So, on this view, Lisa is bullshitting because she lacks concern for how the subinquiry fares as a result of her statement. Her statement is not motivated by a wish to move the subinquiry about the fishing at Lake Mountain View either in the direction of truth or in the direction of falsity.

To be sure, there may be nearby versions of the example in which Lisa does believe what she says. In those cases, however, Lisa may be seen as paralleling Stella, the Creationist Teacher, who says something she believes to be true, even though she has no evidence for it, and knows she does not. Even though this kind of talk is criticizable, it may not be considered as bullshitting.

Next, consider Carson's careful exam taker. The student in this case differs from Lisa in that she is not interested in contributing particular propositions because she cares about *their* truth-values. Rather, she is merely concerned with contributing true propositions. However, she is not concerned with whether her statements are true or false contributions to the subinquiry she is engaged in, i.e., the exam. So, on this view, the exam taker can be seen as illustrating the fact that while one may be interested in contributing truths to the discourse or conversation, one may be indifferent toward the effect of one's statements on a particular subinquiry.

Further, bullshitters who are indifferent toward making true or false contributions to an ongoing subinquiry may or may not be indifferent toward their audience's beliefs and may or may not intend to deceive them about their intentions and motivations. For example, while Frankfurt's 4th of July orator can be seen as disregarding whether his statements are true or false contributions to subinquiries—e.g., about the role of the deity in the history of his country, the inspiration of the Founding Fathers, etc.—he may still be concerned with whether his audience comes to believe what he says. And similarly, he may be hoping to deceive them about his indifference toward making true or false conversational contributions. So, this view also accommodates the criticism of F2–F3.

20.6 BULLSHITTING AND LYING

As we have seen, Frankfurt's original claim, F4, about the incompatibility of bullshitting and lying has been challenged. Frankfurt later conceded that bullshitting, in the sense of

F1, i.e., indifference toward the truth-value of what one asserts, is not incompatible with lying. In his reply to Cohen (2002), Frankfurt argued that "The relationship between bullshit and lies is not as problematic on my account … " (Frankfurt 2002: 340). In particular, Frankfurt noted that some instances of bullshitting are also instances of lying:

> My presumption is that advertisers generally decide what they are going to say in their advertisements without caring what the truth is. Therefore, what they say in their advertisements is bullshit. Of course, they may also happen to know, or they may happen to subsequently discover, disadvantageous truths about their product. In that case what they choose to convey is something that they know to be false, and so they end up not merely bullshitting but telling lies as well.
>
> (Frankfurt 2002: 341)

In other words, Frankfurt acknowledges that someone might be bullshitting in the sense of F1—i.e., by being indifferent toward the truth-value of what they say—even when they are saying something they know to be false. For Frankfurt, such speakers are "liars only, as it were, incidentally or by accident" (Frankfurt 2002: 341).

Moreover, there is at least one kind of lying that is clearly not bullshitting, on Frankfurt's view. These are cases in which someone has the goal of asserting a false proposition p, not because she is particularly interested in asserting p but because she is interested in asserting something false. This is what Augustine (1952b: 87) called the "real" lie, i.e., "the lie which is told purely for the pleasure of lying and deceiving … ". Someone who tells you such a lie wants you to believe something false *because* it is false. For example, if you ask someone for directions to the railway station, they might point you in the wrong direction simply for the amusement of making you go the wrong way. This kind of liar, therefore, cannot be said to be indifferent toward the truth-value of what she asserts, and hence lies of this kind are not counted as instances of bullshitting by F1.

However, as Frankfurt himself notes, few liars are Augustinian real liars:

> Everyone lies from time to time, but there are very few people to whom it would often (or even ever) occur to lie exclusively from a love of falsity or of deception.
>
> (Frankfurt 2005: 59)

The more common kind of lie is the kind exemplified by Parker's lie to his parents about having prepared for the chemistry exam. Parker says what he does because he is interested in saying *that thing*. Had he studied, his purposes would have been served just as well by telling the truth.

A challenge for Frankfurt's view, therefore, is whether it can agree that ordinary lies of this kind are not instances of bullshitting. If so, it can preserve the spirit of the original proposal by maintaining that, even though some bullshitting is also lying, most lying is not bullshitting.

Can it be argued that ordinary liars, like Parker, care about the truth-value of what they are asserting? One reason to think not is the following. The fact that the ordinary liar believes that what she asserts is false does not play a role in why she asserts it. Such liars assert that p because they want to assert p, while disregarding the fact that they disbelieve p. Hence, it is natural to say that the truth-value of p is unimportant to the ordinary liar. She wants to assert p, regardless of whether p is true or false. This makes the ordinary liar appear to be bullshitting, on Frankfurt's view, and consequently, threatens to make most lies instances of bullshitting.

One potential way of avoiding this result is suggested in "On Bullshit," where Frankfurt writes,

> For most people, the fact that a statement is false constitutes in itself a reason, however weak and easily overridden, not to make the statement. For Saint Augustine's pure liar it is, on the contrary, a reason in favor of making it. For the bullshitter it is in itself neither a reason in favor nor a reason against.
>
> (Frankfurt 2005: 59)

So, according to this line of thought, the fact he has not prepared for the exam is a reason for Parker to not assert that he has, albeit it is a reason that is overridden—or that he takes to be overridden—by the urgency of convincing his parents. On the other hand, for bullshitters, neither the truth or falsity of what they assert is a reason for asserting or not asserting them, not even reasons that have been overridden.

This characterization of the ordinary liar will strike many as plausible. It is natural to say that all else being equal—in particular, had he not needed to convince his parents—Parker would take the fact that he has not studied as a reason not to say that he has. However, it is less clear whether this can sufficiently distinguish the ordinary liar from the bullshitter. Consider the 4th of July orator. It may strike one as true of the orator that all else being equal—in particular, had he not needed to present himself in a particular light, or convince his audience of certain claims, or the like—he would count the falsity of a proposition as a reason against asserting it. Similarly, the advertisers Frankfurt describes may be said to have reasons for saying what they do, which they have allowed to override the reasons provided by their beliefs concerning the truth-values of the relevant claims.

To be sure, there may be some particularly hardened bullshitters who are indifferent toward how they present themselves, as well as to what their audience believes, and in general do not have reasons that can be said to override those provided by the truth or falsity of what they say. Yet it is arguable that this is a marginal phenomenon, if it is one.

Another suggestion Frankfurt gives concerns the stances of the liar and the honest person regarding describing the world:

> Both in lying and in telling the truth people are guided by their beliefs concerning the way things are. These guide them as they endeavor either to describe the world correctly or to describe it deceitfully. For this reason, telling lies does not tend to unfit a person for telling the truth in the same way that bullshitting tends to.
>
> (Frankfurt 2005: 59-60)

The Augustinian real liar is plausibly described as guided by her beliefs about how things are. She asserts that *p* because she wants to deceive about *p* and believes not-*p*. However, it is not obvious that liars like Parker are guided by their beliefs concerning the way things are. Parker does not assert that he has studied because of his beliefs about whether he has or not, but because that assertion is the one he needs to make. Hence, at least ordinary liars are not guided by their beliefs concerning how things stand with regard to what they are asserting. Perhaps it can be said of Parker that he is guided by his beliefs concerning how things stand with regard to some other facts, e.g., his parents' likely reaction to the truth, or the like. But the orator may equally be said to be guided by his beliefs concerning how things stand with regard to his potentially benefitting from saying certain things, or with regard to what is expected of him, or the like.

Even though Frankfurt's account allows that some bullshitting is also lying, adequately distinguishing the two phenomena remains a challenge for a view that focuses on attitudes toward the truth-value of what is asserted in characterizing bullshitting.

CHAPTER 21

BLUFFING

JENNIFER PERILLO

21.1 Introduction

In November 1989, 15-year-old Angela Correa was found raped and murdered in Peekskill, NY. Police quickly suspected 16-year-old Jeffrey Deskovic, a classmate of Correa, of the crime. Deskovic had been absent from school during the estimated time of the murder, and investigators felt he appeared too emotional during Correa's wake. Investigators spoke with Deskovic multiple times over the next two months, leading him to believe he was helping with the investigation. Finally, investigators asked Deskovic to take a polygraph examination to rule himself out as a suspect. Deskovic agreed.

Investigators took Deskovic to a testing center at 11:00 a.m. on January 25, 1990. Over the next six hours, Deskovic was interrogated between polygraph sessions. Investigators told Deskovic he had failed the polygraph test and confronted Deskovic with the fact that they would be testing the DNA evidence found inside Correa. Around 5:00 p.m., Deskovic finally confessed to Correa's murder. He then broke down sobbing, curling into the fetal position on the floor. None of the interrogation was recorded. Deskovic was convicted of the crime in January 1991, and he was sentenced to 15 years to life.

In 2006, the DNA found inside Correa was matched to Steven Cunningham. After this discovery, Cunningham, who was serving time for another murder, confessed to the crime. Jeffrey Deskovic was exonerated in September 2006 and released from prison after serving 16 years for a crime he had not committed. When asked why he had confessed, Deskovic stated, "Believing in the criminal justice system and being fearful for myself, I told them what they wanted to hear." Deskovic explained that he had believed the DNA evidence would prove his innocence, so he "thought it was all going to be O.K. in the end" (Santos 2006; see also Snyder, McQuillan, Murphy, and Joselson 2007; Brown 2014).

The case of Jeffrey Deskovic represents an example of bluffing, as the police claimed to have DNA evidence to convince Deskovic that they had strong evidence of his guilt.[1] Bluffing is a deceptive negotiating tactic "in which one attempts to misrepresent one's intentions or overstate the strength of one's position" (Carson, Wokutch, and Murmann 1982: 14), through the use of "conscious misstatements, concealment of pertinent facts, or exaggeration" (Carr 1968: 144). Bluffing can be active, involving deliberate misrepresentation, such as lying about one's age on a résumé, to impress a potential employer, or passive, such as not responding fully by truthfully claiming to not have a personal financial stake in a company but failing to disclose the financial interest of a close family member (Beach 1985).

The purpose of bluffing is to gain advantage in the interaction by manipulating the other individual's expectations and subsequent behavior (Lewicki and Robinson 1998). This is a complex task, as it involves not only modeling behavior that will convince the other party that something is true, but also simultaneously holding the knowledge of what is actually true (Bhatt, Lohrenz, Camerer, and Montague 2010). As an example, one may bid high in poker despite a bad hand to signal to the other players that one's hand is stronger than it is. Likewise, one may bid low when one's hand is strong in order to create the impression that one's hand is weak and draw the other players into betting more than they would have otherwise. In both of these instances, the poker bid misinforms the opponent about the actual strength of one's hand and makes increasing the pot appear riskier or safer depending upon the strategy used, thereby reducing the number of attractive response options. At the same time, the bluffer must remain aware of the actual strength or his or her hand relative to the other players to know when it is appropriate to continue betting versus fold.

Bluffing arises when there is uncertainty in the situation and the parties involved must signal strength or weakness (Varelius 2006). For the signaling to be effective, the opposing party in the negotiation must have incomplete information (Gardner and Morris 1989). When there is complete information, bluffing will be unsuccessful. For example, consider a poker game where the opposing player knows the bluffer is holding a weak hand. Betting high will fail to convince the opposing player that the hand is actually strong, because he or she already knows the truth. In that situation, signaling strength would only lose the bluffer more money.

Clearly, bluffing must be used strategically during negotiations (Bhatt et al. 2010). Whenever one bluffs, there are multiple possible outcomes. Certainly, one may bluff successfully and convince the opposing party to behave in the desired manner. However, one can also be unsuccessful and suffer the consequences of being caught bluffing (Ross and Robertson 2000). In poker, being caught bluffing is relatively minor—losing the money one has bet on that particular hand. In other contexts, however, being caught can have far more serious consequences. For example, a police officer can bluff that he

---

[1] In this particular case, Deskovic was actually innocent, but that does not negate the purpose behind the police's use of the bluff. With a guilty perpetrator, the intent would have been the same—convince the individual that there is strong evidence to leverage a confession.

has strong evidence of a suspect's guilt, as occurred in the Deskovic case. If the bluff is believed, the police officer has a stronger likelihood of producing a confession. If a guilty suspect recognizes the police officer is bluffing, however, it could inform the suspect that the evidence in the case is actually weak and undermine the likelihood of obtaining a confession.

Research supports the idea that bluffing is used strategically by balancing the potential risks versus rewards. Sundali and Seale (2004) conducted a study in which participants engaged in an n-person market-entry game. In each round, the capacity of the market was announced and participants were asked to signal whether they intended to enter the market, not enter, or not give an indication of their decision. Afterward, the aggregate results were presented to the participants, and each participant was asked to make a private decision on whether they actually entered the market. Participants earned or lost money based on whether the market capacity was met or exceeded when they entered the market. Participants were then shown the results and the amount of money they won or lost with their decision. In one condition of the study, deviating from one's previous signal was costless. In the other condition of the study, deviating from one's previous signal led to a monetary penalty. Each group of participants completed fifty trials of the market-entry game. The results showed that when the cost of inaccurate signaling was high, participants were less likely to bluff compared to when there was no cost for inaccurate signaling. Likewise, other research suggests individuals are less likely to bluff those with whom they have strong relationships because the costs of damaging those relationships would be higher (Ross and Robertson 2000).

Neurological evidence has also lent support to the idea of bluffing as a social strategy. Participants played a modified domino game that required occasional bluffing (Kahn et al. 2010). If the bluff was unsuccessful, the participants suffered a loss. Results showed participants had higher amygdala activation while waiting to find out if they had been caught after bluffing than they did in trials in which they did not bluff. As the amygdala is associated with processing fear and maintaining vigilance (Lowenstein et al. 2001), these results suggest that participants are aware of the risks and focus upon them while waiting to see if the bluff is successful.

In another study, researchers had participants complete a sixty-round bargaining game (Bhatt, Lohrenz, Camerer, and Montague 2010). Participants completed the game in pairs, one acting as a buyer and one as a seller. In each round, the buyer was given a private value for the object to be purchased and asked to make an offer to the seller. The seller was instructed to then set a price for the object after receiving the offer. All prices in the game were constrained between one and ten. If the price was less than the buyer's value, the trade was successful. If the price was higher than the buyer's value, the trade was unsuccessful (though the participants were never informed if the trades were successful or not).

The researchers classified the buyers' strategies by regressing their offers onto the given values of the objects. The group classified as strategists were the ones likely to engage in bluffing and provide offers that were negatively correlated with the private values of the objects. By following this technique, strategists would make higher offers for low-value objects but low offers on high-value objects in order to maximize long-term profits. The results showed that the strategists engaging in bluffing had different neural activity from the other groups. Specifically, strategists showed higher activation in the dorsolateral prefrontal cortex (DLPFC), the rostral prefrontal cortex (Brodmann area 10; BA10), and the right temporoparietal junction (rTPJ; Bhatt et al. 2010).

The DLPFC has been linked to working memory, and some experts suggest it indicates that the strategists were keeping track of their offer activity to make sure it looked honest (Camerer, Cohen, Fehr, Glimcher, and Laibson 2016). BA10 is important in goal maintenance and prospective memory (Bhatt et al. 2010), so the results support the idea that successful bluffing depends on the ability to understand and manipulate others' beliefs according to one's goals and plan one's future actions. The rTPJ showed greater activation only when strategists bluffed on the high-value trials when their decisions actually had consequence (Bhatt et al. 2010). The rTPJ has been implicated in the understanding of others' beliefs and attentional reorienting, again suggesting that bluffing is an active social strategy that requires balancing one's own beliefs and behaviors to create the desired beliefs in others.

The purpose of the current chapter is to provide an overview of bluffing. The chapter will first discuss the difference between lying and bluffing (section 21.2) before exploring the morality of bluffing (section 21.3). Finally, the impact of bluffing will be reviewed (section 21.4), before the chapter concludes with a reexamination of the definition and efficacy of bluffing (section 21.5).

21.2 LYING VERSUS BLUFFING

It is important to differentiate bluffing from lying, as both are forms of deception and have similarities. Just as bluffing requires incomplete information to be successful, so does lying. Furthermore, lies and bluffs are both used to gain benefits. Lying is used to "gain self benefit ... such as maintaining a secret or reputation, protecting someone or something, or avoiding punishment" (Williams, Hernandez, Petrosky, and Page 2009: 2). Bluffing is used to gain strategic advantage during negotiations (Bhatt et al. 2010). The key distinctions between lying and bluffing are instead tied into how and when these actions are made.

Bluffing and lying are different actions. Bluffing operates specifically through misrepresentation, whereas lying can take many different forms (Mahon 2008b). According to Fallis (2009), lying involves asserting something you believe to be false to someone when you should not. The purpose is to make the receiver believe something false, believe the liar believes something false, or a combination of the two (Mahon 2008b). This broad definition clearly encompasses a number of actions. Reservation prices when negotiating the sale price of a home provide a common example. A seller can bluff about his reservation price by saying that he would take no less than x amount. In this instance, the seller is misrepresenting the price at which he would sell the house. Conversely, the seller could lie to the buyer that he had already received an offer for x on the house, and he could state that the buyer must meet or exceed that price in order to win the bid. In the first example, the seller does not outright fabricate facts to substantiate the need to sell the house at x price, but he does in the second example.

Frankfurt (2005) also draws a distinction between lying and bluffing on the basis of action:

> Lying and bluffing are both modes of misrepresentation or deception. Now the concept most central to the distinctive nature of a lie is that of falsity: the liar is essentially someone who deliberately promulgates a falsehood. Bluffing too is typically devoted to conveying something false. Unlike plain lying, however, it is more especially a matter not of falsity but of fakery. This is what accounts for its nearness to bullshit. For the essence of bullshit is not that it is *false* but that it is *phony*. In order to appreciate this distinction, one must recognize that a fake or a phony need not be in any respect (apart from authenticity itself) inferior to the real thing.
>
> (Frankfurt 2005: 46–47)

Essentially, Frankfurt agrees that whereas lying is a form of deliberate assertion, bluffing occurs through fakery; the bluff involves misrepresentation and misdirection but does not have to convey deliberately false information. In fact, the bluff itself does not even have to be false; rather, the representation of that information is performed in a way to mislead the receiver. In Jeffrey Deskovic's case, the police officers bluffed rather than lied about the DNA evidence in the case. The police did in fact have DNA evidence; therefore, they were not making a deliberately false statement to Deskovic. The police had not yet tested the DNA evidence, however, so they were unaware of the actual strength of the evidence. By bringing up the DNA, the police officers were bluffing that the strength of evidence against Deskovic was strong, which they had no way yet of knowing. In actuality, the DNA evidence turned out not to match Deskovic.

Moreover, bluffing removes the warranty of truth present in the lie. According to Carson (1993), lying invites an individual to trust and believe the liar whilst the liar betrays that trust by deliberately making false statements. Because the liar is certifying what they say is true, they warrant the truth of the statement. Carson contrasts this with bluffing by noting that people do not expect the truth to be spoken in the situations where bluffing arises. In the home-buying example above, both the buyer and the seller are trying to obtain the best price for the home and expect the other party to misrepresent his or her reservation price. Therefore, when the seller states that he will go no lower than x, the buyer does not take that reservation price to be the actual amount at which the seller will sell his home. In contrast, if the seller is stating that he has received an offer on the house that the buyer must match or beat, the seller is asserting something that is not true in a situation where the buyer would believe the seller is telling the truth.

Lying and bluffing can thus be distinguished from each other on the basis of practice, expectations, and purpose. Lying always involves deliberate falsity, whereas bluffing does not. On the one hand, lies are expected to be true, because the liar certifies them as such (Williams, Hernandez, Petrosky, and Page 2009). Bluffs, on the other hand, are not warranted to be true, because those involved know that strategic misrepresentation of one's negotiating position is part of the process. Although both lies and bluffs are used for gain, bluffs specifically arise as a strategy during negotiation between parties whose aims are in conflict (Allhoff 2003); lies can occur outside of the negotiation context. Bluffs can therefore be understood as a misleading strategic negotiating maneuver whereas lies are deliberately false statements that arise in a number of contexts.

21.3 THE MORALITY OF BLUFFING

Some have argued that another defining difference between lying and bluffing is the morality of these actions. According to Carson (1993), violating the trust of one's audience is what makes lying wrong (cf. Carson 2006). Because the warranty of truth is removed in bluffing, some have argued that it should not be considered immoral. Whether bluffing is appropriate in business negotiation has been thoroughly debated, however. In his seminal work on bluffing, Carr (1968) argued that bluffing was simply a type of game strategy used in business. According to Carr, the realm of business holds different standards of morality from those held by typical society, so bluffing could be considered morally permissible because it was just the way things were done. Carson (1993) further argued that bluffing was act-utilitarian to use against one's opponent. Therefore, he qualified the morality of bluffing, suggesting it was moral to use an act of self-defense against someone who has already misstated his or her position, but the initial use of bluffing would remain immoral.

Allhoff (2003) disagreed with the above justifications of bluffing, but he also argued that bluffing could be considered moral on the basis of role-differentiated morality. Essentially, Allhoff argued that certain roles have different conditions of morality attached to them, so the morality of certain behaviors must be viewed within the moral lens of the role engaging in the behavior. Allhoff argued that bluffing is one such action that remains moral in business, because business has conditions of morality that *endorse* the use of misrepresentation and bluffing. Using the example of car buying, Allhoff argued it is rational to endorse the practice of bluffing in order to get a better outcome than one could get by telling the truth about one's reservation price. Moreover, Allhoff argued that there was no other mechanism by which one could lower the sale price and that removal of bluffing would render negotiations incoherent. He pointed out that if the seller and buyer were both honest about their reservation prices, the only option to settle the difference would be an arbitrary action such as splitting the difference in half, which he argued is not utilitarian or fair and would actually increase the likelihood of bluffing.

Others argue that bluffing cannot be considered a moral or advisable action (Lewicki and Robinson 1998). Koehn (1997) rejected the defense of bluffing put forth by Carr (1968), noting that stakes are higher in business than in game playing and may involve risking others' resources rather than one's own. Furthermore, although not explicitly weighing in on whether bluffing is a moral practice, Varelius (2006) rejected Allhoff's claims that role-differentiated morality supports the practice of bluffing. Varelius noted that many individuals do not endorse the use of bluffing in business and pointed out that there are many ways to negotiate that do not involve misrepresentation. He criticized Allhoff's car-purchasing analogy, pointing out that many business transactions have much higher stakes that make it more attractive to behave openly and honestly. Varelius also pointed out that bluffing is not the only mechanism by which one can negotiate. He noted that one could make several reasonable arguments to otherwise reduce the cost of the car, such as identifying costly repairs the vehicle needed that should be accounted for in the sale price. He argued that it would be utilitarian to split the sale price, and he disagreed that morality need concern itself with what is fair to good negotiators. Varelius also claimed that adopting the moral stance that one should not bluff would not increase bluffing in moral individuals, and he argued that the fact that some people would still violate the moral doctrine against bluffing was not enough to consider it morally permissible.

Empirical studies concerning the ethicality or morality of bluffing in business are similarly mixed. According to Guidice et al. (2009), most research in this area has shown that individuals consider bluffing to be "an ethically gray issue" (Guidice et al. 2009: 538). Although some bluffing tactics were considered ethical, others were considered neutral or even outright unethical. Moreover, the identity of the recipient of the bluffing tactic also influenced perceptions of the ethicality of bluffing. Vitell et al. (2000) found that individuals rated bluffing as less ethical when directed toward one's own customers and employees than to business competitors. Likewise, Guidice and colleagues (2009) similarly found participants rated bluffing as more ethical when used against competitors than to their own company, distributors, or customers. Men also were more likely to rate bluffing as an ethical practice overall compared to women.

As opposed to business bluffing, legal scholars have been more forceful in rejecting the appropriateness of bluffing in the legal system (McDonald, Cramer, and Rossman, 1980), though prosecutors tend to favor and commonly use the practice (McDonald, 1985; Robison, 2005). The general focus of these discussions of bluffing has been in the realm of plea bargaining. Plea bargaining is a negotiation process in which the parties in a legal case negotiate the charges and penalties in the case to come to an agreement that removes the necessity for a trial (Bibas 2004). For a defendant to accept a plea, he or she must judge the stated consequences as better than the risk of suffering even harsher consequences at trial (Caldwell 2012). However, scholars have argued that bluffing in this process unfairly affects innocent defendants, because they are more likely to have incomplete information about the strength of the prosecution's evidence than guilty defendants (Bibas 2004; Douglass 2007; Caldwell 2012). Prosecutors inherently have greater power in this process because they have complete information about the strength of their cases, can choose to overcharge at the beginning of the process to control the negotiation, and face few consequences if the bluff is unsuccessful (Caldwell 2012). Owing to this imbalance of information and power, innocent defendants may be more likely to take the plea bargain rather than risk larger possible penalties at trial.

It thus appears that the ethicality of bluffing may be somewhat context-dependent. Clearly in games such as poker and Risk, bluffing is not only accepted but expected practice. In business negotiations, the ethicality of bluffing becomes more complex, partially depending on who is being bluffed. In the legal system, however, bluffing becomes a troublesome tactic, given that large imbalance in knowledge and power inherent in the plea-bargaining process.

21.4 The Impact of bluffing

Regardless of the morality of bluffing, the question remains of whether bluffing is effective. Although some have argued that bluffing is essential to the negotiating process (Allhoff 2003), research has suggested that bluffing may in fact undermine one's negotiating success. Guidice et al. (2009) conducted a study in which participants played a simulated market-entry game similar to the one used by Sundali and Seale (2004). First, the administrator announced the carrying capacity of the market, which was changed randomly for each round. Participants were then responsible for deciding if they wished to enter the market. After everyone had signaled their intentions, participants decided whether to actually enter the market. Participants who did not enter the market made no points. Players who entered the market could win or lose points; participants won points if the market's carrying capacity was not met, but they lost points when the market went over capacity. Participants completed thirty rounds. Results showed that bluffers performed significantly worse across the simulation than did those who were truthful about their intentions, earning about a third of the points earned per round by those who did not bluff. It is important to note, however, that participants held more complete information than is typically encountered in actual negotiations, which may have undermined the efficacy of bluffing in the study. Moreover, participants engaged in thirty rounds within the same group, so the current results may be more reflective of the consequences of bluffing in a long-term relationship. Other research has suggested that bluffing may damage credibility and hinder the formation of long-term relationships with other organizations (Robertson et al. 1995).

The negative consequences of the bluff may also depend on how the bluff is presented. Shapiro and Bies (1994) conducted a study in which participants engaged in a negotiating scenario with a confederate. Each participant was assigned to act as a buyer in the scenario and negotiate the terms of two contracts regarding the sale of refrigerators in terms of delivery time, discount terms, and financing terms. During the first negotiation scenario, the confederate used threats in two conditions. In the first condition, the confederate claimed to have an offer from another buyer and threatened to break off negotiations and deal with the other buyer unless a better offer was made. In the second condition, the confederate hedged this threat by adding the disclaimer that the offer from the other buyer was a rumor. In the third condition, the confederate did not present a threat. After the first negotiation, half of the participants who received threats from the seller were informed that the seller was bluffing. Participants than completed the second negotiation. After the second negotiation, participants were asked to rate how much money the seller should lose owing to their bargaining actions. The results showed that participants rated their partners much more harshly and punished them more severely after finding out they had presented a false threat when a disclaimer did not accompany it; however, when the false threat had been delivered with a disclaimer, the evaluations of the seller and punishments given were not affected. The results also showed that individuals reached less integrative agreements overall when threats were used, with or without a disclaimer, suggesting that the use of bluffs still has negative consequences even when softened. Moreover, as noted by the authors, the somewhat protective measure of hedging may lose effectiveness quickly, suggesting it is better used as a short-term business strategy.

Research on bluffing in the legal system has similarly found that its use can have unintended consequences. Just as occurred in the case of Jeffrey Deskovic, experimental research has shown that bluffing about evidence during a police interrogation can increase the likelihood of false confession. In a police interrogation, police officers bluff when they misrepresent the strength of the evidence they have in the case, typically by claiming some form of evidence will soon become available (e.g., DNA testing is currently being conducted). In this way, the interrogator falls short of the lie, because he or she does not falsely claim to have actual evidence already proving guilt. According to the original assumption of the bluff, employing such a tactic should still threaten guilty suspects, because they should believe that the forthcoming evidence (if it actually existed) would implicate them. In contrast, innocent suspects should not feel threatened, because they know they are innocent of the crime and should know the evidence would not implicate them.

Kassin (2005) argued, however, that innocent suspects are subject to the phenomenology of innocence, whereby innocent suspects believe their innocence is obvious to everyone. Kassin (2005) pointed out that this belief could have a number of unanticipated consequences for innocent suspects that increase their likelihood of wrongful conviction. In the context of bluffing, the belief can backfire if participants believe they can confess to escape a stressful interrogation situation, believing the bluffed evidence will later prove their innocence. If the evidence does not truly exist—as would be expected in a bluff about evidence—then there would be no forthcoming evidence to test that would show innocence. If the evidence does exist, it may never be tested, or, as in the case of Jeffrey Deskovic, exonerating evidence may be ignored in favor of the "stronger" evidence of the (false) confession.

In a series of three studies, Perillo and Kassin (2011) found that bluffing did indeed backfire when used on innocent suspects. In two studies, the researchers used the ALT-key paradigm (see Kassin and Kiechel 1996). Participants were warned prior to participating in a reaction-time task that they should not touch the ALT key because it would crash the computer. The program always crashed, however, and all participants were accused of hitting the forbidden key. All participants were actually innocent. In the control condition, there were no claims of evidence. In the false-evidence condition, the confederate lied about seeing the participant hit the ALT key. In the bluff condition, the experimenter bluffed that a program had recorded all of the keystrokes and the record could later be checked. The results showed that lying and bluffing about evidence both significantly increased the risk of false confession compared to the control condition.

In the third study, Perillo and Kassin (2011) also investigated whether bluffing impacted innocent participants differently than guilty participants using the cheating paradigm (see Russano et al. 2005). In this study, participants alternate between completing individual question series alone and group question series with a confederate. In half of the sessions, the partner requested help on an individual questionnaire, which violates the rules of the study. Regardless of actual guilt, all participants were accused of breaking the study rules and asked to sign a confession admitting to sharing answers on an individual question series. In the bluff condition, the experimenter bluffed that the session had been videotaped and the footage could be reviewed upon the return of the technician. As found in other two studies, bluffing significantly increased the rate of false confessions, though it did not affect the rate of true confessions. Participants also cited the bluff as the reason for their false-confession decisions, saying they believed the experimenter would realize they were innocent upon review of the tape.

Overall, the evidence seems to indicate the use of bluffing may lead to more undesirable consequences than rewards. Although the evidence suggests that bluffing can successfully be used to gain a strategic advantage over others, it may be so powerful in some contexts that the wrong people are being affected (e.g., innocent suspects being convinced to falsely plead guilty). Moreover, bluffing may be problematic as a long-term strategy, as it compromises credibility and may be linked with less success in negotiation. Although there may be ways of avoiding the consequences of bluffing in short-term negotiations, research suggests that even short-term negotiations result in less optimal agreements when bluffing is used as opposed to when negotiators are honest.

21.5 Conclusion

The issue of bluffing is complex, as form, morality, and efficacy vary widely depending on the context in which bluffing is employed. As a negotiating strategy in games, bluffing can be an effective method of gaining advantages over other players (Carr 1968). In business, bluffing can be seen as a necessary negotiating strategy (Allhoff 2003), or it can be seen as a strategy that undermines negotiating success for both parties (Guidice et al. 2009). In the legal system, bluffing has been widely denounced as coercive and dangerous for innocent suspects in both plea-bargaining and interrogation settings (e.g., Bibas 2004; Perillo and Kassin 2011).

The distinction between bluffing and lying is also not perfect. As noted before, bluffing and lying have similarities in terms of goals and when the tactics are most likely to be utilized successfully. Some have even characterized bluffing as a type of lie. According to Lewicki and Robinson, bluffing is a form of lying, because bluffing functions "to misinform the opponent, to eliminate or obscure the opponent's choice alternatives, or to manipulate the perceived costs and benefits of particular options that the opponent may wish to pursue" (Lewicki and Robinson 1998: 666). Even Carson (2006: 2) acknowledged that sometimes bluffs constitute "borderline cases" of lying.

Woody et al. (2014) also advanced a context-dependent definition of bluffing as a form of lying specifically in terms of police interrogations. Rather than characterizing a bluff as a form of deception distinct from the false-evidence ploy, the authors distinguished between *explicit* and *implicit* false-evidence ploys. Whereas explicit ploys involve direct claims of false evidence (consistent with the definitions of lying advanced by Fallis and Mahon), implicit ploys instead merely suggest the possibility that the false evidence may be real. Woody and colleagues asserted that the bluff is merely an implicit false-evidence ploy.

Woody and colleagues' (2014) characterization of the bluff as an implicit lie is problematic, as lying requires that the information being misrepresented must always be false (e.g., Fallis 2009). As noted in Frankfurt's (2005) construction of bluffing, however, bluffs can involve true or false information. Consider again the example of Jeffrey Deskovic. In his case, the DNA evidence actually existed; the bluff involved misrepresenting the certainty of the testing outcome rather than lying about the actual existence of the evidence.

Overall, the existing literature seems to distinguish lying and bluffing as separate, though related, constructs where information is misrepresented for gain. Whereas lies are widely employed in a multitude of contexts, bluffing is a specific negotiating strategy that may be employed when parties have competing goals. Although some research has suggested that bluffing can be effective, other research has suggested it can have unintended consequences for both the bluffer and the receiver. Further research is necessary to elucidate the contexts in which bluffing may be advisable versus those where it should be avoided.

CHAPTER 22

WHITE AND PROSOCIAL LIES

SIMONE DIETZ

22.1 Introduction

WHITE and prosocial lies are lies with socially harmless or benevolent motives or consequences. In ethical debate, these types of lie as ambivalent or even paradox concepts are controversial. The discussion of white and prosocial lies is based on the definition of lying in general, the status of untruthfulness, and the intent to deceive in particular. According to a restrictive moral understanding, lying as an untruthful and deceptive use of language is morally parasitic and antisocial per se, and therefore improper in principle. From this view, first taken by Augustine in his inquiry "On Lying" (Augustine 1952b [395]) and by Kant in his treatise "On a supposed right to lie from altruistic motives" (Kant 1949 [1797]), the possibility of white or prosocial lies is completely rejected. A more moderate viewpoint, taken by most utilitarians, holds that lying in general is improper because of its harmful effects, especially on social trust, but that it might be justified in some cases of conflicting obligations, rights, or interests or because of its overall better consequences. According to a third opinion, lying as such is a conventional and morally neutral speech act which works for different motives with different moral statuses—egoistic, antisocial, and socially harmless motives as well as benevolent or socially useful ones. In this regard, there might also be objections against lies, even benevolent lies, but directed against involved motives—for example, paternalism—and not deception as such. The different cases of socially harmless, justified, or useful lies can be named defensive, benevolent, altruistic, and collaborative lies.

In section 22.2, this chapter explicates the definition of lying in general, of white and prosocial lies in particular, and of their different cases. In section 22.3, normative implications of lying and fundamental objections against white and prosocial lies are discussed: the violation of the norm of truthfulness and the intention to deceive, which are supposed to harm the social institution of trust and to disrespect the autonomy of the individual addressee. In section 22.4, the focus will be on the various extrinsic motives of lying, the cases in which lying could be morally accepted, and a taxonomy of white and prosocial lies.

22.2 Definition of lying, white, and prosocial lies

22.2.1 Definition of lying

According to a classical definition by Augustine "that man lies, who has one thing in his mind and utters another in words, or by signs of whatever kind." Additionally, he states that "the fault of him who lies, is the desire of deceiving in the uttering of his mind" (Augustine 1952b [395]: ch. 3), and concludes therefore that "a false utterance put forth with will to deceive is manifestly a lie" (Augustine 1952b [395]: ch. 5). These remarks indicate the four essential conditions that even the contemporary discussion on lying refers to. If 'uttering' is designated more precisely as 'asserting', the first two conditions of the definition can be considered as widely accepted: (a) Speaker S asserts toward hearer H that p (is true) and (b) S does not believe, that p (is true). However, the other two conditions are controversial: (c) S intends to deceive H with p; (d) p is false. Some authors claim that an assertion counts as a lie only if p is not only subjectively intended by the liar to be false, but also is factually false (Rott 2003: 10; Carson 2010: 15), though most other authors reject this condition (Bok 1999: 6; Falkenberg 1980: 328; Barnes 1994: 12; Horn 2017b). As the question of factual falsehood does not affect the type of white or prosocial lie in particular, it will not be considered further. In contrast, many objections to white or prosocial lies rest on condition (c), the intent to deceive, and will be discussed in section 22.4.

22.2.2 White lie

A *white lie* is a normative concept used in colloquial language as well as in moral discourse, referring to the intentions of the liar, the social consequences, and the moral status of the lie as harmless, excusable, or even justified. White lies may be either self-serving or prosocial, and are in contrast to the morally unacceptable 'black lies' which are meant to harm the addressee or other people. The concept of white lies can be used in a narrower or a broader sense. In the narrow sense, it indicates an excusable "falsehood not meant to injure anyone and of little moral import," while lies in general are considered as being morally improper (Bok 1999: 58; Hill 1984: 253; Levine and Schweitzer 2014: 108). A popular example for this sense is a false excuse in favor of politeness. In the broader sense, the term 'white lies' functions as a comprehensive concept covering all lies which are morally allowed or even requested for different reasons, such as harmlessness, social benefit, or cases of defense (Isenberg 1964: 472; Kupfer 1982: 109; Barnes 1994: 14; Erat and Gneezy 2012). Different from the German 'Notlüge' or the Italian 'menzogna necessaria', the term 'white lie' (like the French 'pieux mensonge') indicates the taintless soul or intentions of the liar but no justifying reasons or circumstances. Therefore, it may be interpreted as a "protective coloring" of lying (Bok 1999: 58). For analytic purposes, "the distinction between benevolent and malicious lies, depending on whether the liar intends to enhance the interests of the dupe or to harm them," is considered to serve better (Barnes 1994: 13). However, since white lies have more than benevolent motives, the benevolent-malicious alternative is not sufficient to furnish a comprehensive concept of excusable and justified lies and has to be perfected. An important case of white lies in this context are justified self-serving lies. This term indicates instances in which the liar has to defend her or his right against an unjustified attack, either an attack of brute force, or other threats of physical integration, or pushy questions violating the private sphere. Lying in this sense counts as an act of self-defense and does not violate justified interests of the dupe (Schopenhauer 1903 [1840]: 192; Kupfer 1982: 110). In contrast, self-serving, egoistic lies at the expense of others are typical cases of 'black lies'. Even with respect to others, the concept of benevolent lies does not go far enough while 'prosocial lie' is a broader term to comprehend all kinds of morally acceptable lies motivated by social cosiderations.

22.2.3 Prosocial lie

The term *prosocial lie*, common in contexts of social psychology, refers to lies with benevolent motives or socially useful effects. The term 'social lie' is sometimes used (Barnes 1994: 14) but strictly speaking, as an act of communication all lying is social lying. Prosocial lies are only those which are oriented to the benefit of others or intended to protect or increase social collaboration. This type of lying can be directed either to the benefit of another single person, to the harmony of interaction in a social group, or to public interest in general. Moreover, considering the cost and benefit of the liar, one can distinguish altruistic from collaborative, mutually beneficial lies (Levine and Schweitzer 2015), or alternately 'Pareto white lies' (Erat and Gneezy 2012). Both types "are made with the intention of misleading and benefitting," but altruistic lies "are costly for the liar" (Levine and Schweitzer 2015: 89), while in case of collaborative, mutually beneficial, or 'Pareto white lies', "both sides earn more as a result of the lie" (Erat and Gneezy 2012: 724). The term refers to the economist Vilfredo Pareto, who pointed to improvements making at least one person better off without making another person worse off. Beside the different types of benevolent, altruistic, and collaborative lies, referring to the social context and social patterns of conventions, one can distinguish between cases of prosocially polite, entertaining, educational, and political lies.

22.3 OBJECTIONS AGAINST THE PROSOCIAL CHARACTER OF LYING

The definition 'asserting p and not believing p' seems insufficient to distinguish lying from irony, metaphor, joking, acting, or reciting. In all these cases, the speakers might say something they do not believe but they are still not lying. To draw a distinction, there are two main strategies: the standard strategy in the tradition of Augustine and the linguistic strategy. The standard strategy requires the intent to deceive as a central condition for lying (Jankélévitch 1942: 213; Bok 1999: 13; Barnes 1994: 12; Williams 2002: 97; Lackey 2013: 247). The assessment of prosocial lying then has to reflect the tension between two different intentions of the speaker: antisocial deception and prosocial benevolence. The linguistic strategy, brought into debate by the main representatives of speech-act theory, Austin, Grice, and Searle, looks more carefully at the conditions of assertive speech acts and claims truthfulness as a condition which is violated by the liar or at least contradicted by lying. Most proponents of such an asserting-condition agree that lying implicates deceiving (Chisholm and Feehan 1977: 148; Davidson 1985: 88; Meibauer 2014a: 102); therefore, their propositions are not strictly controversial as regards the standard strategy but they avoid postulating a direct intention to deceive as necessary for lying. Moreover, they focus on the linguistic character of lying and its semantic and pragmatic implications. Some authors (Fallis 2009: 41; Carson 2010: 20) turn explicitly against a definition of lying which includes an intention to deceive, but as they argue in respect of special cases such as bald-faced lies, this exclusion does not touch the question of white or prosocial lying. The following sections will discuss the main objections to the possibility or positive evaluation of white and prosocial lies: section 22.3.1 examines lying as a violation of the rule of truthfulness, section 22.3.2 as a breach of trust, and section 22.3.3 as a violation of freedom and autonomy of the addressee.

22.3.1 The condition of truthfulness

The condition of truthfulness, already concluded by Kant (1949 [1797]), is the most important reason for the evaluation of lying as an antisocial action, which cannot be justified under any circumstances. Remarkably, in his reply to Benjamin Constant, Kant does not explicitly mention the categorical imperative but leans on the grounding value of truthfulness for the possibility of social contract and law in general. Lying as an "intentional untruthful declaration to another person" causes harm to "mankind generally, for it vitiates the source of law itself" (Kant 1949 [1797]: 348). It is not the intent to deceive a particular addressee that gives reason for the moral inadmissibility of lying, but the misuse of the social institution of language. The binding nature of declarations rests on the unconditional duty of truthfulness. If a right to lie in certain cases were admitted, it would undermine the general law and the integrity of the social community.

In discussing the well-known case of the murderer at the door, Kant believes that even if it saved the life of an innocent victim of persecution, a moral *right* to lie could not be admitted because it would contradict the absolute duty of truthfulness.

Modern speech-act theorists agree on the importance of truthfulness for conventional communication, but its status vacillates between linguistic convention and moral duty. Moreover, speech-act theory draws a distinction between assertions and commissive speech acts, such as promises or contracts. In ethical debate, the conventional linguistic difference between assertions and promises is often overlooked, namely when an untruthful assertion is taken as a breach of an implicit promise (Hill 1984: 253; Ross 2002: 21). The rule of truthfulness functions as a condition of asserting, and lies violate this rule. Therefore, Austin (1962a: 16) claims that lying does not simply follow the conventions of asserting but "abuses" them. As the act of abusing social conventions clearly has an antisocial connotation, this definition of lying points to an intersection of linguistic and ethical norms (Meibauer 2014a: 14, 154). Searle (1969: 63 ff.) postulates a "sincerity rule" for assertions which claims that S has to commit to the truth of p, but the normative status of this rule remains unclear (Falkenberg 1990: 134; Dietz 2002: 82 ff.). On the one side, an assertion is not impaired by being untruthful, and thus the sincerity rule should be regulative, not constitutive. From this point of view, the liability of assertions is not grounded in constitutive language conventions but rests on additional reasons and may differ from one context to another. On the other side, the claim of truthfulness seems to be necessary in general to perform an assertion in a functioning manner of interaction.

In recent debate, several proposals for a more adequate version of the rule of sincerity or alternative conditions of assertions have been made. Grice (1989c: 26 f.) argues that language is ruled by a non-conventional principle of cooperation and several more specific maxims and submaxims. The "maxim of Quality" claims the effort of the speakers to make their "contribution one that is true" and the first submaxim calls for the speakers not to say what they believe to be false. Chisholm and Feehan (1977: 151 ff.) go further by explicating the "essential normative" concept of assertion "by reference to justification": in asserting p, S justifies H in believing that S believes p; H "has the right to expect" that S believes p so that the liar "violates the right" of the addressee. Unfortunately, they do not go into the question of how to recognize if the right is valid in a certain context, how to weigh the right relative to other rights, and if the concept sticks to Kant's evaluation of the murderer case. Fallis (2009: 52) states that every lie violates Grice's maxim of truthfulness, but in case of altruistic or white lies, this maxim might be "overridden by other interests." According to Carson (2010: 15), the act of assertion rests on "an implicit promise or guarantee, that what one says is true," which is violated by any lie and therefore lying "involves a breach of trust."

Meibauer's (2014a) linguistic analysis and definition of lying clearly avoid morally loaded concepts like the violation of an obligation of truthfulness or a right of the addressee to expect truthfulness. According to Meibauer, an assertion requires that S present p as true and intends that H "actively believes that p" (Meibauer 2014a: 102). Lying, then, is defined by two conditions: "S asserted at t that p" and "S actively believed at t that not p" (Meibauer 2014a: 103). The concept is considered to be neutral with respect to moral evaluation and to the difference between antisocial and prosocial lying (Meibauer 2014a: 152 f.). Moral evaluation has to analyze "the manifold reasons for lying" and has to take into account pragmatic implications "of the speaker's and hearer's knowledge about standard situations in which it is possible or even likely that a lie will be presented" (Meibauer 2014a: 153 f.).

22.3.2 Loss of social trust

The loss of social trust is one of the most important arguments against lying, in common sense as well as in utilitarian ethics. According to Mill (1987 [1861]: 295), lying means "to deprive mankind" because it damages the "reliance which they can place in each other's word." Therefore, harmful consequences are limiting the use of prosocial lies. Even possible exceptions to the rule of veracity, such as the withholding "of information from a malefactor or of bad news from a person dangerously ill," must compensate for the negative effect of "weakening reliance on veracity" (Mill 1987 [1861]: 295). Furthermore, Sidgwick (1907 [1847]) acknowledges the social use of trustworthiness but points out that the duty of veracity is not to be confused with the duty of keeping promises (Sidgwick 1907 [1847]: 449) and that "it is not necessarily an evil that men's confidence in each other's assertions should, *under certain peculiar circumstances*, be impaired or destroyed" (Sidgwick 1907 [1847]: 467). To liars and "those who ask questions which they have no right to ask," it means no social harm to disappoint their expectations of truthfulness (Sidgwick 1907 [1847]: 467 f.). Moreover, Sidgwick mentions the difference between the confidence that the other shall speak the truth and the confidence that he or she shall defend his or her life and honor (Sidgwick 1907 [1847]: 470).

Trust may be based on more different items than just the truthfulness of the speaker. Therefore, untruthfulness does not necessarily contradict or harm social trust—even if it often does. People may also trust in the benevolence of others in order not to be embarrassed, ashamed, or insulted by their truthful statements, and therefore rely on their ability to lie. As Baier (1986: 240) defines it, trust is "accepted vulnerability" while "letting other persons ... take care of something the truster cares about, where such 'caring for' involves some exercise of discretionary powers." Referring to a similar definition, Levine and Schweitzer (2015) differentiate between the distinct types of integrity- and benevolence-based trust. They claim to demonstrate these by trust-game experiments; "although prosocial lies harm integrity-based trust, prosocial lies *increase* benevolence-based trust. In many cases, intentions matter far more than veracity" (Levine and Schweitzer 2015: 103).

22.3.3 The violation of freedom and the autonomy of the addressee

The violation of freedom and the autonomy of the addressee constitute another serious reason for moral condemnation of lies in classical and recent debates. Schopenhauer

(1969 [1859]: 337 f.) evaluates lies as well as violence as morally reprehensible means to force a person to serve somebody else's will. While violence uses physical means, lying uses the deception of the addressee, namely "distortion of his cognition" (Schopenhauer 1969 [1859]: 337 ff.). As symptoms of weakness and "cunning, perfidity, and treachery," egoistic or evil lies are even more reprehensible than violence because they split the band of faithfulness and honesty which binds individuals together (Schopenhauer 1969 [1859]: 337 ff.). However, Schopenhauer also acknowledges cases of morally justified white lies, as well as meritorious and even morally demanded prosocial lies. Lies are justified if they are used to resist attacks on one's life and property and to refuse unwarranted curiosity, i.e., as a means to defend legitimate rights. Lies are meritorious "whenever a man wills to take on himself the guilt of another"; even a duty to lie is given, "especially for doctors" (Schopenhauer 1903 [1840]: 195). In both cases, the liar's motive of sympathy is crucial for the moral approval of lying.

From a deontological perspective, the moral conviction of lying substantially refers to the intent to deceive, which is interpreted as a violation of the right of autonomy of the addressee. To respect other persons as free to choose their own ends implies not to misinform them. Even if the liar follows benevolent motives, they prevent the addressee from knowing relevant aspects of the situation and therefore manipulate their decision. Every justification of lying has to consider this objection. "Benevolent lies do not necessarily or always violate the right of autonomy, but we should not be hasty in concluding that a particular lie does not concern any significant decisions" (Hill 1984: 262). In addition, Kupfer (1982: 103) states the "restriction of the deceived's freedom" as an "inherent negative component of all lies." The disrespect of the deceived's freedom functions as a criterion of moral evaluation. White lies are "not limiting the deceived's freedom seriously or for long" (Kupfer 1982: 109); the liar's disrespect might be "mitigated by the concern for the other's well-being" (Kupfer 1982: 113) or could even be the "appropriate response to a coercive situation" (Kupfer 1982: 110). Korsgaard (1996b: 350) points to a third case, stating that "we may lie to s.o. who lacks autonomy if our end is to restore or preserve her autonomy."

22.4 A TAXONOMY OF WHITE AND PROSOCIAL LIES AND THEIR ETHICAL JUSTIFICATIONS

Extrinsic motives for lying are the focus of the moral evaluation of white and prosocial lies. All concepts referring to a norm of truthfulness and the great significance of social trust and individual freedom define lying in a negative way as an abuse or violation of asserting conditions. None of them explicitly takes into account that lying as a concept of rational behavior has to follow certain positive intentions or motives. Even if these motives might generally not be fixed because they differ from one case to another, their existence is a necessary condition both for understanding what the liar is doing and for judging the moral harm or value of lying. Thomas Aquinas (1266/72: II II q 110) already distinguishes between the intrinsic and extrinsic qualities of lying. Interpreted with the Aristotelian categories of causation, in Aquinas' classification untruthfulness functions as *causa formalis,* deception as *causa efficiens,* and the further intention of the liar as *causa finalis* (Müller 1962: 170 f.). Aquinas' morally important difference between the inexcusable blame of cheating and the venial sin of entertaining or socially useful lies concentrates on the *causa finalis.*

In the modern debate, Isenberg (1964: 467) refers to the common mistake of taking production of a belief or a deception as the intention of the liar: "ordinarily, a lie will have a motive beyond the desire to make someone believe it." According to Isenberg, "the extrinsic motive... is much more closely interwoven with the lie itself than is usually supposed" (Isenberg 1964: 478). To concentrate moral evaluation on the extrinsic motive, Dietz (2002) explains lying as a morally neutral, conventional second-order speech act, similar to irony, quoting, metaphor, etc., which uses the first-order speech act of asserting untruthfully but according to conventions of rational behavior. In contrast to those performing other second-order speech acts, the liar does not signalize or declare her or his untruthfulness and particular intentions. As a "covered second order speech act" (Dietz 2002: 114), lying does not reveal itself as lying to the addressee but the context might be ruled by conventions which imply the possibility of or even the social request for not being truthful in some respect.

The relevant question which arises from this debate on the cases of white and prosocial lies is whether all lies in general violate intrinsic norms of communication and cooperation or if it is at least possible that lying itself follows particular social conventions and therefore does not harm social relations in general. To answer this question, not only are the particular rules of asserting and lying important. The normative status of these rules has to be clarified as well. If lying necessarily implies the violation of the rule or convention of truthfulness in a moral sense, prosocial lies will always harm social trust and individual autonomy and therefore imply ambivalent moral tendencies. However, if lying can be convincingly explained as a morally neutral speech act, its categorization as prosocial or antisocial will depend only on the liar's extrinsic motives and the context-norms in the particular case.

Different to the fundamental rejection of lying, the moral acceptance of white and prosocial lies will always be the result of a careful consideration of the prevailing situation. This consideration refers to the rights, interests, expectations, conventions, and norms involved. An important part of the discussion is directed to social conventions valid in certain contexts, another part to particular duties related to particular social and professional roles. As far as a moral evaluation of white and prosocial lies refers to the conditions of particular fields of action, it is part of applied ethics (Bok 1999).

Conventional norms of truthfulness differ from one context to another. Asserting in advertisement, negotiating processes, or relations of politeness does not require the same conventions of truthfulness as are required in court, scientific research, or close friendship. While in contexts of contracts or science, truthfulness is considered as an essential rule, in contexts of politeness or entertainment it is of secondary importance. The same is true with professional duties: while the Hippocratic Oath focuses on the life and benefit of the sick and does not even mention veracity (Bok 1999: 223), other ethical codes of professional practice, such as journalism or science, rank it as a central duty.

In philosophical inquiries on lying from ancient to contemporary debate, some examples treated frequently symbolize different cases of permissible lies: the innocent victim and the attacker, the doctor and the mortally ill, the invited guest and the host. As the four general types of permissible lies, we can distinguish self-serving defensive lies, benevolent lies, altruistic lies, and collaborative lies. In each constellation, there is a reversal of antisocial and impermissible, egoistic, or domineering lies.

22.4.1 Self-defending lie

The first type, the *self-defending lie*, is represented by the innocent victim lying in order to protect his or her physical integrity or private sphere. Schopenhauer (1903 [1840]: 194) gives two examples to illustrate this kind of justified lie:

> Suppose, for instance, such a one is returning from a remote spot, where he has raised a sum of money; and suppose an unknown traveler joins him, and after the customary 'whither' and 'whence' gradually proceeds to inquire what may have taken him to that place; the former will undoubtedly give a false answer in order to avoid the danger of robbery. Again: if a man be found in the house of another, whose daughter he is wooing; and he is asked the cause of his unexpected presence; unless he has entirely lost his head, he will not give the true reason, but unhesitatingly invent a pretext.

In both examples given by Schopenhauer, the questioners might neither have any bad motives nor know that they are affecting a sore point of the other, but they nevertheless have no right to be informed about the other's affairs. All participants of conversation have to be aware by social convention that small talk is not the right atmosphere for delicate confession. Therefore, they have to expect and agree to get a false answer if the bounds of the language game 'small talk' are touched, either intentionally or unintentionally. As Schopenhauer (1903 [1840]: 194) puts it: "'Ask me no questions, and I'll tell you no lies' is here the right maxim." However, between the protection of the private sphere and deceitful avoidance of social sanctions there is a gradual transition. By lying to someone waiting for me that my delay was caused by a traffic jam, while I really was dawdling around, am I protecting my private sphere or do I avoid fair social consequences of my careless behavior? The ethical risk of the everyday self-defending liar is the trap not only of self-deceit but also of misjudging factual threats of questioning, bounds of conventions, and the legitimate interests of the other, and therefore paradoxically creates consequences of distrust in aiming to avoid it.

22.4.2 Benevolent lie

Undoubtedly the most popular example of a *benevolent lie*, mentioned by most philosophers from ancient to present times, is the doctor's lie to protect the ill patient from shocking news. While Mill and others just take the doctor's lie to be the lesser evil, for Schopenhauer it is even a duty. At least questionable is the true motive of the benevolent liar and the correct assessment of the addressee's state of mind: is the liar guided by sympathy with the sick addressee or by her or his own weakness in not wanting to be the bringer of bad news? Is the claim to know what is good for the addressee better than he or she knows him- or herself arrogant and paternalistic or proof of sympathy and compassion? Even if the lie is truly motivated by benevolent concern, it might contradict the addressee's interest. Therefore, the benevolent liar bears heavy responsibility. Two strategies might limit this: first, benevolent lying might be used temporarily to get through the very moment of actual weakness but then revealed later by the liar; second, the addressee might explicitly exclude unwanted benevolent lies in demanding truthfulness. In some official contexts of medical treatment, the patient's right to be informed truthfully about their affairs is guaranteed by law. Furthermore, the use of placebos has to conform with the patients' rights and rules of information.

A further example of benevolent lies similar to the doctor's case are educational lies: helpful stories about guardian angels and the tooth fairy, or lies told to children in order to protect them from a truth they could not deal with (Sidgwick 1981 [1874]: 465; Bok 1999: 205 ff.). In both cases, the intention to encourage or preserve autonomy may either legitimate lying or give reason to refuse it owing to the disrespect it fosters for the factual ability. Moreover, especially with regard to children, the liars are responsible not to overrate their own ability to hide the truth and to avoid the trap of double-bind communication, thus causing more harm than telling the truth.

In the field of politics, the 'noble lie' of political leaders lying to protect public welfare (first mentioned in Plato's *Politeia*, Book 3: 414e–415c) is hardly acceptable as an appropriate case of benevolent lies. In contrast to the case of invalids or children, there is no evidence why and in which respect citizens should have limited capacity to bear the truthfulness of their representatives. In modern democratic systems, benevolent political lies contradict the idea of representation and sovereignty of the people. To avoid disastrous social dynamics, like panic reactions in economic crisis, mass hysteria against social minorities, or defense against an attack by external enemies, political lies might temporarily be legitimated under extraordinary circumstances, but if the acute danger has been averted, the benevolent political liar has to face public judgment. According to Arendt (1967), politics is always in conflict with truth, but a serious threat arises from an organized practice of lying, leading to collective self-deceit and loss of orientation. For Geuss (2014: 142 f.), in modern politics to worry about lying often directs the attention to the wrong item, "the individual psychology," while the context which is "deeply structured by the play of powerful agents" is much more relevant. For international politics, Mearsheimer (2011: 6 ff.) claims that lying is acceptable in cases of "good strategic reasons for leaders to lie to other countries and even to their own people." Strategic lies "aim to facilitate the general welfare and they usually have at least a modicum of legitimacy." As far as international lying operates "in an anarchic system," the moral ground for conviction is lacking.

22.4.3 Altruistic lie

Altruistic lies, costly or at least risky for the liar, require constellations of not only two but three instances: the liar, the dupe, and the protected. In the already-mentioned case of the murderer at the door, the murderer has no right to be informed of the victim's whereabouts. Thus, the moral status of the liar's willingness to help is beyond doubt, even if there were fundamental reservations against the means, of lying. But in other situations for altruistic lies, responsibilities might be different: the protected victim might be a murderer, or the deceived pursuer might represent law and justice. As far as the liar takes a serious risk in favor of another person, lying has to be classified as altruistic—from the perspective of the protected person. As far as the liar is led by a kind of outlaw-solidarity and undermines rules of justice, lying has to be classified as parasitic—from the perspective of the legal community. The same is true for lies in which the liars burden themselves with the guilt of someone else: for the guilty it might be meritorious, but for the system of justice it is destructive.

22.4.4 Collaborative lie

The mutually beneficial *collaborative lie* is the kind of prosocial lie most common in everyday life. It implies a broad spectrum, including especially entertaining and polite lies. Entertaining lies, like humorous stories, are evaluated as harmless not only because they are agreeable and pleasant but also because in the context of entertainment "truth is not of any importance" (Hume 1902 [1777]: 196). For Isenberg (1964: 474), the case of entertaining lies disproves the deontological position of the intrinsic or prima facie wrongness of lying: "The deception of the guest of honor is not an unfortunate condition for the surprise party but a part of the fun, which the victim himself will share."

Polite lies are used above all to avoid conflict. According to Sidgwick (1981 [1874]: 463), the use of current conventional expressions, such as accepting "with great pleasure" a vexatious invitation, in common sense does not count as lying because conventional phrases are not taken as truthful assertions. However, as soon as politeness requires more than obeying ritualized formula, it requires lying. In many social situations, a whole personal attitude of kindness and gratitude is expected and might conflict with truthfulness. To praise a delicious meal, an interesting presentation, a wonderful present, or a good-looking hairstyle might be a truthful assertive speech act as well as an expression of goodwill without reliable propositional content. If the speakers did not care whether they seem reliable or not, they would rather appear impolite. The general motive for such a convention of lying is to protect social harmony, "to avoid conflict and facilitate uncomfortable social situations" (Levine and Schweitzer 2015: 89). Different from benevolent lies, polite lies are motivated both by the consideration of the other's vulnerability and by self-interest. Contexts of politeness create a well-ordered but distant atmosphere of disguised actors, needed in the public sphere to protect individual freedom and to avoid the tyranny of forced intimacy and conformity (Plessner 1999 [1924]). On the other side, contexts of politeness taken as rigid conventions of lying might create empty talk, anxiety, and taboo. It is the choice between concealment and truthfulness, social taboo and social conflict, first afforded by the ability of lying, which functions as a basis of personal identity and liberal social communication.

The general argument against lying, stressed not only by Augustine and Kant but by most other philosophers as well as by common sense, evaluates lying as morally bad because of intrinsic antisocial qualities, especially untruthfulness and the intention to deceive, which imply disrespect for the other's trust and autonomy. However, this intrinsic moral disapproval of lying can be more or less restrictive with respect to white and prosocial lies. According to the general ethical approach, white lies can be excused as a lesser evil with respect to conflicting duties, rights, or interests, or justified because they are supposed to lead to the best consequences in the end. A clear moral acceptance of prosocial lies appears if lying in general is classified without intrinsic moral qualities. A neutral linguistic definition of lying, which does not focus on the intention to deceive or on a moral norm of truthfulness, but which describes lying as a special kind or use of speech act, will do more justice to the common social practice and conventions of prosocial lying. It opens the view for the different extrinsic motives and contexts which can be differentiated by the taxonomy of self-defending, benevolent, altruistic, or collaborative lies in contrast to egoistic, oppressing, parasitic, or truth-censoring lies.

PART IV
DISTINCTIONS

CHAPTER 23

LYING AND FICTION

EMAR MAIER

23.1 FICTION AND LIES

LIES and fictional statements[1] share an important characteristic that sets them apart from more pedestrian forms of communication: what they express is false, or rather, believed by the author to be false. When I utter (1a) I know this cannot literally be true, because Frodo, Sam, and Mount Doom are all made up, they never existed. Similarly, when I say (1b) to impress my colleagues at lunch, I am well aware that what I am saying is false.

(1) a. Sam carried Frodo from Mount Doom.
    b. I read *Sein und Zeit* last week.

Assuming that, as their surface form suggests, lies and fictional statements are simply instances of the speech act of assertion, we get that they are assertions of propositions believed to be false by the author. In section 23.3, I discuss some refinements of the traditional notion of assertion needed to work out this simple, uniform account.

Despite this crucial similarity, I want to highlight in the remainder of this section some essential differences between fiction and lies. A first, salient prima facie difference concerns the intended effects on the addressee. When I said (1b) I wanted to deceive my addressee: I knew that I did not read *Sein und Zeit*, yet I wanted my audience to believe that I did. The whole point of lying seems to be to create such an asymmetry between speaker's and hearer's beliefs. By contrast, when you read Tolkien's work, or listen to me talk about it, there is no deception—in fact, the fictionality of the

---

[1] What I call fictional statements here include statements taken directly from a work of fiction, e.g., the actual opening lines of *Lord of The Rings*, as well as statements like (1a), that are not lifted word-for-word from some canonical work of fiction, but nonetheless describe events or facts holding in some fictional world, i.e., they express things that are true in the fiction.

statements is presumed common knowledge in these cases. Whatever the intended effect of my utterance of (1a) is exactly, it is not that you come to believe stuff about hobbits that I do not believe.

We can bring out this difference in Gricean terms as follows.[2] If we analyze both lying and fiction as assertions, they would both constitute violations of the maxim of Quality. In the case of lying, the violation is necessarily covert, which explains why no implicatures are generated. But in the case of fiction the violation is overt—every reader is aware that dragons or hobbits do not exist. Since overt violations normally trigger implicatures (e.g., leading to ironic, metaphorical, or otherwise non-literal interpretations), it seems that upholding the claim that fiction involves assertion will require some careful maneuvering. We return to this task in section 23.4.

The seemingly clear distinction that emerges from the discussion above is somewhat blurred again by cases of so-called bald-faced lies, i.e., lies that do not involve deception. Carson's (2006) famous example involves a witness who, for fear of repercussions, testifies in court that he did not see a certain criminal commit a certain crime, knowing full well that the jury has just seen video evidence that puts him at the scene. The witness knows he is not going to convince anyone that he did not see the crime. His assertion is therefore not meant to deceive the members of the jury that he is addressing, but to demonstrate to relevant members of the criminal organization that he is no snitch. If we want to count the witness as lying, then deception cannot be a defining difference between fiction and lying.[3]

A clearer difference between fictional statements like (1a) and lies like (1b) is the fact that although (1b) is just plain false, many philosophers have argued that (1a) is not really false, or even that it is in some sense true—e.g., true relative to *The Lord of the Rings* saga, or fictionally true. If your high-school English teacher discusses Tolkien's writings and asks who carried Frodo from Mount Doom, the only right answer will be Sam. To bring out this intuition of fictional truth consider also the negation of (1a), *Sam did not carry Frodo*, which *is* quite clearly false. In sum, while neither fiction nor lies are intended as expressing facts about the real world, in many contexts we are inclined to count some fictional statements as true (*Harry Potter is a wizard*), or at least fictionally true, or more true than some others (*Sherlock Holmes is a hobbit*).

Another difference between fiction and lies that has received a lot of attention, this time from the area of philosophy of art and fiction, is known as the paradox of (the emotional response to) fiction (Radford 1975). The paradox starts from the observation that we can be moved by stories—whether fact or fiction. For instance, when I meet you in a bar and tell you in some detail about my dog Hector dying after he saves a child

---

[2] Thanks to Andreas Stokke for pointing out this angle. Cf. Stokke (2016b) for details on the relation between lying and the maxim of Quality.

[3] Unless we say that bald-faced lies are not really lies (Meibauer 2014b), or are in fact deceptive (Meibauer 2016a). See Chapter 19 by Jörg Meibauer.

from a burning house, you may be moved to tears. When I then proceed to tell you that in fact I never had a dog, that I made the whole thing up, your sadness will quickly evaporate (and make way for anger or embarrassment, perhaps). Yet, as Radford puts it, we weep for Anna Karenina, even though we know quite well, even in advance, that Tolstoy's novel is a fiction and Anna Karenina never existed. Somehow, fiction allows us to "suspend disbelief" and be emotionally engaged with known falsehoods. Lies, according to Radford, lack this property: once it comes out that the lie is a lie, suspension of disbelief and emotional engagement in accordance with the story's content become impossible.[4]

Summing up, at first sight lies and fiction seem rather similar, with bald-faced lies straddling the divide. On closer inspection, we find important differences. Only fiction has the peculiar property that it generates 'fictional truths', whose known literal falsity, with respect to the real world, does not hinder emotional involvement or judgments of truth. I conclude that, despite initial similarities, fiction and lies are distinct phenomena.[5] Still, rather than just defining two new primitive speech-act types, in addition to assertions, commands, etc., it is worth investigating if we can specify a linguistic framework to describe both their similarities to and differences from each other, and factual assertions.

23.2 A SEMANTIC ANALYSIS OF FICTION AND LIES?

When we are trying to characterize the nature of fiction and lies, it is fairly obvious that syntax will not help us much. Depending on the context, a single sentence, say (2) (based on the above illustration of Radford's paradox of fiction), can be an instance of a truthful assertion, a lie, or part of a fictional narrative.[6]

(2) Hector ran into the burning house

Since the peculiarities of lies and fiction seem intimately related to semantic notions such as truth and falsity, we might want to turn to semantics next. In this section I discuss whether semantics, more specifically formal, or truth-conditional semantics (as

---

[4] It would follow that one cannot be emotionally engaged (in accordance with the content of the lie) with a bald-faced lie at all, since by definition it is common ground at the outset that such a lie is a lie.

[5] See Chapter 43 by Bettina Kümmerling-Meibauer for more on the history of the debate about the relationship between lying and fiction.

[6] This is not to say that there are no syntactic differences whatsoever between fictional and non-fictional assertions, for instance. It may well be that certain syntactic constructions ('once upon a time', free indirect discourse) are characteristic of fiction.

opposed to cognitive semantics, cf. Fauconnier 1994), indeed constitutes the right level of analysis. The answer will be negative.

23.2.1 Truth-conditional semantics

Semantics starts from the idea that knowing the meaning of a sentence consists in knowing its truth conditions. In order to count as knowing the meaning of 'methane is poisonous' I do not need to know whether methane is in fact poisonous, but I would need to know what kind of states of affairs would make the sentence true. In terms of possible worlds, a familiar tool from modal logic: when presented with an arbitrary (complete description of a) possible world, I need to be able, in principle, to figure out whether in that world the sentence is true or false. This epistemological idea is cashed out semantically by equating sentence meaning with truth conditions, and then often further equating a sentence's truth conditions with the set of worlds that make it true, also known as the proposition expressed by the sentence.

At this point let me dispel a common confusion arising from the use of the term 'possible world' in formal semantics, as opposed to its use in literary studies. When talking about fiction we often talk more or less informally[7] about 'fictional worlds', such as 'the world of *Harry Potter*'. However, in the context of formal semantics, there is no single possible world of *Harry Potter*. Rather, like individual sentences, the Harry Potter books express propositions, and hence correspond to *sets of worlds*. Thus, we can talk about 'the worlds of *Harry Potter*', which—to a first approximation, see section 23.4.2—are the possible worlds compatible with all the information written in the books. Since, the books do not mention, say, the exact time of Dumbledore's birth, this set will include possible worlds where Dumbledore was born at noon, worlds where he was born at 12:34, at 17:30, etc.

Back to the task at hand. Truth-conditional semantics is ill-suited to distinguish among fact, fiction, and lies. Take our ambiguous example (2). The truth conditions of this sentence will correspond to the set of worlds in which there was a point in time before the utterance time where some Hector ran into some contextually salient burning house. This proposition is expressed independently of whether or not the sentence is intended or assumed to be true, false, or fictionally true. The aim of semantics is to specify a systematic theory that derives truth conditions (in the form of possible-worlds propositions) from the syntactic structure of sentences and the lexical meanings of the words in them. What speaker and hearer *do* with this set of worlds once it is derived is not part of the semantics proper. That is, whether the actual world is believed to be among those worlds, or whether the proposition is intended to update the hearer's beliefs, or to constrain her imagination, and/or to trigger some action or emotional response—all of this falls outside the scope of semantics proper and belongs to pragmatics.

---

[7] Cf. Werth's (1999) Text World Theory for a formal version of this usage.

23.2.2 Empty names and the limits of semantics

As a matter of fact, not only does semantics fail to usefully distinguish between fiction, lies, and factual assertions, it fails to even assign any meaning to some typical instances of lying and fiction (including (2)). Frege (1892), arguably the founder of modern semantics, already noted that the use of empty names in fictional statements could cause trouble. He considers the following fictional statement:

(3)   Odysseus was set ashore in Ithaca while fast asleep.

Since Odysseus never existed, the name *Odysseus* has no reference. By the principle of compositionality (roughly, the reference of a statement depends on the references of its constituents—a principle constitutive of most forms of truth-conditional semantics), it follows that the statement as a whole has no reference. This is problematic for semantic systems that equate meaning with reference.

Frege solves the problem of empty names by invoking the notion of *Sinn* ('sense') as a separate level of meaning. Although *Odysseus* has no reference, it does have a Sinn, a mode of presentation, so the sentence as a whole can have a well-defined meaning at the level of Sinn. However, Kripke (1980) has since convincingly argued that proper names do not actually have a Sinn, they just refer directly to the individual who bears the name. If Kripke is right, (3) cannot have either a truth value or a Sinn. Since lies and fiction are natural habitats for empty names (cf. the name *Hector* for my made-up dog in (2)), they pose severe challenges for semantics.[8]

I conclude that traditional, truth-conditional semantics is the wrong place to look for an informative analysis of fiction. Even if we can somehow get around the problems surrounding empty names, symptomatic of fiction and lies, we are not likely to capture the difference between uses of (2) as a lie, a sincere assertion, or a fictional statement merely in terms of truth conditions or propositions expressed. It follows that we will have to turn to pragmatics—what do we do with the meanings that syntax and semantics give us?

23.3 THE PRAGMATICS OF LYING

Pragmatics, the study of how humans use language to communicate, is a vast, heterogeneous field. In this chapter I want to stay close to the semantic side of pragmatics. More precisely, I will stick with the well-known analysis of the semantics/pragmatics

---

[8] Sure enough, logicians and philosophers of language have devised many work-arounds to solve the puzzle of empty names, such as using 'free logics', giving up direct reference for some or all names, or enriching our ontology with nonexistent entities. See, for instance, Braun (2005) or Sainsbury (2005) and references therein.

interface pioneered by Robert Stalnaker (1970, 1978). In this section, I introduce Stalnaker's framework and present Stokke's (2013a) application of it to lying.

23.3.1 Assertion as common-ground update

In brief, on Stalnaker's analysis what we do with assertions is to update the common ground, where the common ground is the shared body of information that the speaker and hearer take for granted. On the one hand, the common ground is useful for modeling linguistic context-dependence. Speaker and hearer rely on the common ground to choose efficient modes of expression, such as pronouns, names, and indexicals, to refer to salient entities already established in the common ground (rather than just using descriptions that uniquely identify their referents independently of context). On the other hand, the common ground is in turn affected by what is said. Every time a speaker makes an assertion (and no one objects) its informational content becomes part of the evolving common ground.

Stalnaker works out this general picture of context-dependence and context change in a traditional possible-worlds semantics. In the following I will skip over the context-dependence part (i.e., the theory of presupposition satisfaction, see Beaver and Geurts 2011) and focus on context change, i.e., the way assertions shape the common ground. First of all, the common ground at each point in time is a set of possible worlds—roughly, the worlds compatible with the shared beliefs of speaker and hearer, or, put differently, the information that the speaker and hearer together take for granted. Statements express propositions, which are likewise modeled as sets of worlds. The central definition of Stalnaker's pragmatics says that updating a common ground C with an assertion of proposition p means removing all non-p worlds from C. Let me illustrate this with an example.

I am talking to you over the phone. We start with a common ground C_0 where we both know, for instance, that my name is Emar, that the Earth is round, that we are both academics, etc., but let us say you do not know where I am calling from. C_0 then contains worlds where I am in Groningen on February 22, 2017, and worlds where I am in Göttingen, Leiden, Nijmegen, etc.. C_0 does not contain worlds where the Earth is flat, or I am on Jupiter. Then I say, "I'm at a conference in Leiden," thereby expressing the proposition that Emar is at a conference in Leiden on February 22, 2017. Updating C_0 with this information means we remove from C_0 all the worlds where I am not in Leiden at that time. The result will be a new common ground, C_1, which is more informative in the sense that it excludes some possibilities that were not yet excluded before my announcement. C_1 then serves as background for the interpretation of the next utterance, which will again remove some worlds, and thereby become more informative, and so on.

There are a number of refinements of this basic propositional update idea that feature prominently in recent debates. The first is that updating the common ground is not something that the speaker can accomplish single-handedly. As Stalnaker (2002) himself stresses, all that the speaker can realistically do is *propose* an update.[9] The proposal becomes an actual update only once it is accepted by all interlocutors. In a totally cooperative discourse, perhaps acceptance may be the default, i.e., proposals automatically become updates unless someone objects. But when we move to less ideal situations, involving potentially mendacious speakers, it becomes essential to distinguish proposal and update, so that we can model a hearer's rejection of a proposed update. I will not pursue this issue further here (cf. Asher and Lascarides 2013 on dealing with noncooperative discourse).

The second refinement relevant to the current endeavor concerns the exact definition of the common ground. Typically, the common ground is thought of as common knowledge or common belief, notions that are well-studied in epistemic logic (Fagin et al. 1995). A proposition p is a common belief among a group of agents iff all agents believe that p, all agents believe that all agents believe that p, all agents believe that all agents believe etc. The common ground in a two-person conversation is then the intersection of all propositions that are commonly believed by speaker and hearer. We will see in the next section that lying and fiction necessitate further refinement of this notion.

23.3.2 Lying, acceptance, and the common ground

Now that we have an analysis of the speech act of assertion, the question arises if we can perhaps apply it to lying and fiction. In the remainder of this section I present Stokke's (2013a) analysis of lying within Stalnaker's pragmatic framework of assertion.

The null hypothesis is that lying is a form of asserting, viz. asserting something one believes to be false. In Stalnakerian terms, a lie is a proposal to update the common ground with a proposition that one believes to be false. On our reconstruction of the notion of common ground in terms of common beliefs, this is a non-starter. If the speaker's proposal to add p to the common ground is successful, p will be commonly believed, so then both she and the hearer believe p. But surely, telling a successful lie should not affect the speaker's belief that p is false.

As Stokke observes, some of Stalnaker's more cautious remarks about the notion of common ground offer a potential solution. Stalnaker observes that when we communicate successfully we do not always believe what our interlocutor says. In some cases, my disbelief will be grounds for an objection, thereby blocking the information growth in our common ground. But in other cases, I might want to just go along, perhaps just to see where my interlocutor is going, or out of politeness or fear. In such cases we would be interpreting the discourse just as we would otherwise, by accepting the propositions expressed, and modifying the common ground accordingly, following the usual rules of presupposition satisfaction and information update. If indeed we want to model

---

[9] This insight is part and parcel of more fine-grained discourse models developed on the basis of Stalnaker's (e.g., Farkas and Bruce 2009; Roberts 2012).

such cases as cases of genuine communication and common-ground update, we have to weaken our definition of common ground as common belief. Stalnaker proposes to define the common ground in terms of an attitude of 'acceptance for the purpose of conversation', which he further characterizes by saying that "to accept a proposition is to treat it as a true proposition in one way or another—to ignore, for the moment at least, the possibility that it is false" (Stalnaker 1984: 79). Stokke then extracts the following precise acceptance-based definition from Stalnaker (2002: 79) a proposition p is common ground iff both speaker and hearer accept p, and believe that they accept p, and believe that they believe that they accept p, etc, (more compactly: common ground is common knowledge of universal acceptance).

With this weakened notion of common ground we can now maintain our null hypothesis, viz. that lying is simply the assertion of some proposition that the speaker believes to be false. By uttering the lie, the speaker indicates that she herself accepts its truth—in the Stalnakerian sense of 'treating it as true'—and wants the hearer to do the same. Neither interlocutor needs to believe what was said, either before or after the assertion, but by accepting it, both are able to continue interpreting subsequent sentences in the usual way. Both would become committed to treating it as if it were true, at least temporarily, for the purposes of the current conversation.

23.4 THE PRAGMATICS OF FICTION

Following the reasoning above, we run into the same problems when we treat fiction as assertion in a belief-based common-ground model. The successful assertion of *Frodo is a hobbit* should not lead to an updated common ground that entails that speaker and hearer believe in the existence of hobbits. We should be able to interpret a fictional statement without either hearer or speaker being committed to believing it to be true. In sections 23.4.1–23.4.3, I explore how to adapt the basic Stalnakerian common-ground conception so as to circumvent problems with fictional assertions. In section 23.4.4, I sketch some more radical pragmatic proposals that go beyond common-ground updating and involve notions such as pretense and imagination.

23.4.1 Fiction and the common ground

Sainsbury (2011), like Stokke also crediting some remarks from Stalnaker, argues that the key to making sense of fiction is to replace belief with acceptance. So-called fictional truths, like *Harry Potter lived under the stairs*, are true relative to the acceptance of the content of the Harry Potter novels. When we read these novels we choose to accept—but probably not believe—what the fiction tells us, thereby constructing an ever more informative common ground of shared acceptance between writer and reader, who each treat the Harry Potter propositions as true, exactly as in other forms of assertion.

One of the problems with this approach is that it does not separate a fiction-based common ground from other, truth-oriented common grounds. For instance, J. K. Rowling and I both know that the Earth is round, humans are mortal, brooms do not fly, and wizards do not exist. This type of information will be part of our common ground in any communicative exchange between us. But then how can we maintain consistency in our common ground when I start adding the propositions that make up *Harry Potter and the Sorcerer's Stone*? And in the other direction, when we have somehow updated the common ground with all the information from these novels, how come we can still confidently and sincerely assert that Harry Potter is a fictional character and wizards do not exist? Somehow, we need to keep the fictional common ground separate from other common grounds.

Eckardt (2014) takes the idea of quarantining the fictional common ground as the core of her semantics of narrative discourse. When I pick up my first Harry Potter book, I start a fresh common ground in which to keep track of just what is going on in the Harry Potter universe. When I close the book and talk to J. K. Rowling about the weather I somehow close the fictional common ground and start (or continue) updating a more realistic common ground, one in which we both accept that wizards do not exist, among other things. In this discussion of lying, Stokke (2013a) explores a similar idea: fictional statements function like assumptions in mathematical proofs or philosophical thought experiments in that they are used to create a temporary "unoffical" common ground. A crucial difference between fiction and lying is then that a lie is a proposal to update the official common ground, while a fictional statement is a proposal to update or create an unoffical common ground.[10]

23.4.2 Importing world knowledge into fictional common grounds

However the isolation of fictional or unofficial common grounds is formalized, total isolation is too strong. If we start our fictional common ground from scratch we effectively sever all ties with the world as we know it. When in our reading we then encounter a name like 'France' or 'Napoleon', we might accept that there are entities by these names,[11] and continue updating the fictional common ground with information about those. But this way we can never account for the obvious fact that the author is

---

[10] As an anonymous referee points out, lies and fictions can also be iterated and embedded in each other. This should not cause any trouble here: if we are reading about a fictional character lying to another fictional character we are creating (or updating) an unofficial/fictional common ground containing the information that the two characters are having a conversation and thereby updating the official common ground between them. A special case of lying in fiction is that of the so-called unreliable narrator, cf. Zipfel (2011).

[11] By a process that Lewis (1979) has called accommodation of the presuppositions triggered by the use of these names.

referring to France—a large European country, capital Paris, populated by French-speaking people—and Napoleon, the nineteenth-century French emperor. Can we really say that I understood *War and Peace* if I failed to connect it to any familiar historical facts, people, and places? And, more generally, how much are we even going to be able to understand of any novel if we start with a tabula rasa and cannot assume even some basic principles of physics and human nature?

Theories of fiction interpretation thus look for a middle ground: we need to separate fictional common grounds from non-fictional ones, but we still want to have access to at least some basic world-knowledge when constructing fictional common grounds. For instance, when I first picked up *War and Peace* I automatically included in the new fictional common ground the information that humans breathe oxygen, the earth is round, and Napoleon was that French emperor who failed to conquer Russia—I did not need the book to explicitly inform me of these facts. Although not directly formulated in terms of common grounds and updates, Lewis's (1978) influential 'Truth in Fiction' is the locus classicus for this issue. For Lewis, roughly, a statement is true in a fiction iff it is true in those worlds compatible with the text that are maximally close to the actual world (or, more precisely, to the author's overtly expressed beliefs about the actual world). In effect, knowledge of the actual world thus enters into our representation of a fictional world, unless the text explicitly contradicts it. Applied to our example, when constructing a possible-worlds representation of *War and Peace* we might be led to include worlds where Napoleon utters certain phrases we know he in fact did not utter, but we exclude outlandish possible worlds where gravitational acceleration at sea-level is $11 m/s^2$ or Napoleon secretly has a robotic arm grafted on by aliens, even though the text itself does not explicitly exclude these possibilities. See Bonomi and Zucchi (2003) for an adaptation of Lewis's ideas into the Stalnakerian framework.

23.4.3 ... and the other way around

Arguably, there is also a kind of knowledge transfer in the opposite direction, from the fictional to the nonfictional domain. We have seen how reading Sherlock Holmes stories leads to a fictional common ground in which there is a flesh-and-blood detective named Sherlock. But when I am no longer consuming or otherwise engaging with the fiction directly, I can still talk about the fictional people and events described in it.

(4) a. Sherlock is just a fictional character, invented by Conan Doyle. He never really existed.
b. I prefer the BBC's Sherlock, as played by Benedict Cumberbatch, to Conan Doyle's original character.

Such so-called metafictional statements can be literally true (but not fictionally true, because in the novels Sherlock is not fictional but real). I may sincerely assert these statements and thereby express facts about the actual world, i.e., propose to update the official common ground between me and my interlocutor. This suggests that, while the fictional, or unofficial, common ground contains a real-life Sherlock, the official common ground contains a corresponding fictional entity that serves as the referent of the name *Sherlock* in (4). The ontological and semantic issues raised by such talk about fictional characters is a topic of much philosophical debate, which I cannot go into here (cf., e.g. Zalta 1983; Walton 1990; Thomasson 1999; Friend 2007; Kripke 2011).

Another case of information flowing from the fictional to the nonfictional domain involves the observation that reading literary fiction not only offers us an entertaining glimpse of a different world, but also contributes to our understanding of the actual world, the 'human condition', applicable in real life.[12] For an exploration of this idea, exploiting the tools of possible-worlds semantics, I refer to Bauer and Beck (2014).

23.4.4 More radical pragmatic accounts of fiction

I end by sketching a more radical pragmatic approach to fiction interpretation, one where we let go of the assumption that a work of fiction can be understood as a series of assertions, in the sense of proposals to update the common ground. A large subclass of such pragmatic approaches is sometimes grouped together as 'pretense theories'. There are two main flavors. First, according to Searle (1975) or Kripke (2011) a typical fictional statement is not an assertion but a 'pretend assertion'—Tolkien and his readers merely pretend to refer to Frodo, who they pretend exists. Second, according to Walton (1990) or Currie (1990) we are dealing with a sui generis speech-act type. Since the latter approach is highly influential—at least in contemporary philosophy[13]—let me end this section, and this chapter, with a brief sketch.

In the terminology of Walton, assertions are prescriptions for the hearer to believe. By asserting that chlorine is dangerous, I intend for you to believe that it is. Note that this is really just a simplified version of the Stalnakerian definition given, in which by asserting something I propose to make it common ground. In the same traditional terminology, Walton then characterizes fictional statements as prescriptions for the reader to imagine. The intended effect of reading a fictional text, say, is not that I believe the text to be true or common ground (official or unofficial); it is that I engage in a certain type of act of imagining. In this characterization, imagination is typically thought of as an individual, psychological attitude, rather than a shared group attitude, as in the Stalnakerian framework for assertion. Fiction interpretation thus lends itself to a more fine-grained type of semantic/pragmatic analysis where we consider the effects of interpretation on the complex mental states of individual speech-act participants rather than just lumping everything together in a single, intersubjective common ground. See Maier (2017) for

---

[12] The relationship between fiction and literature is a thorny issue that I cannot go into here. Cf. e.g., Hempfer (2004).
[13] Narratologists meanwhile have developed different 'radical pragmatic accounts', like e.g., Walsh's (2007) rhetorical approach, which is inspired by Relevance Theory (Sperber and Wilson 1986).

a formal semantic proposal along these lines, and García-Carpintero (2015) for a more Stalnakerian analysis in terms of shared commitments.

23.5 Conclusion

Lies and fictional statements are similar in that neither obeys Grice's first maxim of Quality: do not say that which you believe to be false. They are also essentially dissimilar, in that only fiction allows for a suspension of disbelief that lets us express seemingly true(-ish) propositions about creatures, such as Sherlock Holmes or Harry Potter, that both speaker and hearer know never existed. Although the characteristic properties of lies and fiction are at least partly semantic in nature, I have shown that there is little to no hope for an insightful analysis within a traditional truth-conditional semantic framework; we need to turn to pragmatics.

My main aim in this chapter has been to show how Stalnaker's influential pragmasemantic account of assertions as proposals to update the common ground may be adjusted to incorporate both lies and fiction.

For lying, we first explored the idea of basing the definition of common ground on a notion of acceptance rather than belief and saw that with this rather minimal adjustment lies could be treated as genuine assertions.

For fiction we saw that more is required; we need to somehow isolate information gained by reading the fictional work from information gained through other types of discourse—but not too strictly, because information must be allowed to flow back and forth between these distinct information repositories. Much contemporary work in the semantics and philosophy of fiction can be understood as concerned with these information flows.

The general conclusion one may draw from this chapter is that the Stalnaker model of assertion as common-ground updates is a powerful and flexible formal tool that can be used to shed new light on the seemingly idiosyncratic speech acts involved in lies and fiction. And in the other direction, studying lies and fiction leads us to the very boundaries of truth-conditional semantics, and has prompted important refinements of the highly influential Stalnakerian notion of common ground.

Acknowledgements

I thank Jörg Meibauer and two anonymous referees for valuable feedback on the first draft. I thank Andreas Stokke for helpful discussion and feedback. This research is supported by NWO Vidi Grant 276-80-004.

CHAPTER 24

LYING AND QUOTATION

MATTHEW S. MCGLONE
AND MAXIM BARYSHEVTSEV

24.1 INTRODUCTION

QUOTATIONS often serve as the foundational evidence upon which journalists build stories about public figures, and readers in turn form impressions of these figures and the journalist writing the story. Their presumed status as fact is symbolized by separating them from other text constituents via inverted commas, a stylistic convention that originated to call attention to sententious remarks (Garber 1999), but is now universally recognized in nonfiction as signaling an exact replication of a speaker's words (Culbertson and Somerick 1976; Gibson and Zillman 1993). However, empirical analyses of direct quotations suggest they are often far from faithful reproductions. In conversation, quotations are less likely to duplicate speech word for word than to selectively depict certain speech aspects while omitting or distorting others (Clark and Gerrig 1990). For example, one might recount an ironic comment overheard about the weather (e.g., *Nothing but blue skies, just like the weatherman said* uttered in a downpour) by reconstructing the intonation and illocutionary force of the comment (e.g., *She said 'Um, isn't this great weather?' in this totally sarcastic tone...*), but not the exact wording nor the target of derisive intent. Such reconstructions fail to meet the strict verbatim criterion we expect of passages portrayed as direct quotations, but do succeed as demonstrations of a speaker's intentions (Wade and Clark 1993; Blackwell and Fox Tree 2012).

Although the standards of accuracy of reproduction are higher in journalism, academia, and jurisprudence than in casual conversation, it is not uncommon for the quotations in news stories to be at variance with what was actually said (Lehrer 1989; Harry 2014). The least objectionable modifications occur when writers merely fix incorrect grammar, replace unheralded pronouns with proper names, or remove expletives from a statement, all practices recommended by many journalism educators (Kovach and Rosenstiel 2007; Shapiro, Brin, Bédard-Brûlé, and Mychajlowycz 2013). Slightly more problematic are cases in which synonyms are substituted for words the author deems too obscure for the target audience to understand: for example, replacing an academic term from a research study (e.g., cognitive dissonance) with something more familiar (e.g., psychological conflict) in a news article. Revising words does increase the potential for semantic drift from the original testimony; however, writers can keep it in check if they obtain second opinions from their sources and peers regarding any differences in meaning between the original and revised statements. At the other extreme are cases in which authors attribute entirely fabricated quotes to sources that misrepresent their attitudes or beliefs. In one infamous case, psychoanalyst Jeffrey Masson accused reporter Janet Malcolm of concocting several quotes in a 1983 *New Yorker* profile in which he came across as crass and egotistical. Malcolm denied the charge, insisting that Masson had in fact used provocative phrases such as "intellectual gigolo" to describe himself, even though the disputed phrases did not appear in her audiotape or written records of their conversations. At the end of a drawn-out libel lawsuit, the US Supreme Court found in the reporter's favor, ruling that the quotes in her article were protected by the First Amendment even if they had been concocted. The *Masson v. Malcolm* ruling generated considerable debate among journalism and legal scholars about ethical standards in quotation. While most journalists agree that inventing quotes is an unacceptable practice, few endorse prepublication review or other measures that might reduce its occurrence at the expense of ceding creative control of their work.

In light of the potential for distortion, forgoing any alteration of a source's testimony might seem the only sure-fire way to avoid misrepresenting it. However, verbatim replication in no way guarantees that a quote is a fair representation of the speaker's intended meaning or beliefs. Consider the oft-heard complaint from public figures cited in news media that although their words were accurately reproduced in a story, the words were nonetheless quoted "out of context." Taken literally, the charge is absurd, because there is no contextual void in which a sound bite can exist in isolation. The article or broadcast in which a quote appears constitutes its current context, albeit one different from the context in which the words were originally uttered. If the charge is modified to reflect this fact—i.e., one instead says the words were "quoted out of their original context"—it becomes merely banal, in that all quotes entail excerpting some portion of a speaker's words from their original context.

The real objection is not to removing a quote from its original context (as all quotes are), but to truncating it in a way that distorts the meaning of the excerpted words. Historian Milton Mayer (1966) coined the term "contextomy" to describe "surgical textual excerpting" (Mayer 1966: 135) conducted by Julius Streicher, editor of the infamous Nazi broadsheet *Der Stürmer* in Weimar-era Germany. One of the early tactics Streicher used to arouse anti-Semitic sentiments among the weekly's working-class Christian readership was to publish truncated quotations from Talmudic texts that, in their shortened form, appear to advocate greed, slavery, and ritualistic murder. In a similar vein, US clergyman and radio propagandist Father Charles Coughlin cited highly circumscribed quotations from the New Testament to persuade American Catholics that the Bible endorsed persecution of the Jewish people. Coughlin often invited his radio audience to consult the verses he had so brazenly abridged in order to "prove" to them that Jews are held in divine contempt (Warren and Warren 1996; McCollam 2010). Although rarely employed to the malicious extremes of the Nazis or their sympathizers, contextomy is nonetheless a common mechanism of misrepresentation in contemporary mass media (McGlone 2005, 2010).

24.2 Types of Quotation and Selective Excerpts

There are several varieties of quotation that can be distinguished from one another (Cappelen and Lepore 1997) and used to manipulate an original utterance for deceptive purposes (Meibauer 2014a). In a direct quotation, the speaker repeats the utterance word for word. For example, Alexandra's original utterance is *I don't like this book*. Afterwards, Michael quotes her as follows: *Alexandra said "I don't like this book."* Deception can occur when words are portrayed as a direct quotation whereas in fact one or more were altered intentionally by the speaker. Additionally, the speaker may also attribute the quotation to someone other than the original utterer. For example, *Alexandra said "I really like this book"* or *Frank said "I don't like this book"* (assuming Frank had not actually said this) could be deceptive in this regard.

Now imagine Michael said *Alexandra said that she doesn't like that book*. This is an indirect quotation, because Michael commits only to conveying the gist of her comment about the book rather than the exact words she used. An indirect quotation can be deceptive when the alleged gist it conveys is at odds with the belief or attitude she originally expressed (*Alexandra said that she loves the book.*), or even the degree of belief or attitude (*Alexandra said that she absolutely hates the book*). If the original utterance is compared to the deceptive indirect quotation, any inconsistencies could be attributed to misinterpretation or misremembering the actual words, rather than deceptive intentions.

A mixed quotation, on the other hand, is one that contains properties of a direct and indirect quotation. For example, *Alexandra said that she doesn't like "this book"* attributes only a portion of the original utterance to Alexandra. This allows the speaker to emphasize one part of the original utterance without quoting it entirely. When selectively misquoting an individual, this type of technique might be common because it allows deceivers to reproduce only the portion of the utterance that is compatible with their misrepresentation goals. For example:

Alexandra's original utterance:	*The book may have been entertaining at times, but overall I thought it was horrible and should have never been published.*
Selective mixed quotation:	*Alexandra said "the book" was "entertaining."*

It is clear when looking at the original utterance that Alexandra dislikes the book, but the quotation paints a different picture, attributing only the positive portion of the utterance to her evaluation of the book and completely dismissing her overall judgment.

One of the most familiar examples of selective excerpting is the ubiquitous "review blurb" used in film advertising. To create these blurbs, studio promoters dissect multiple reviews of a film and then select the most positive comments for use in print and television advertisements (McGlone 2005; Tynan 2011). The lure of media exposure associated with being "blurbed" by a major studio undoubtedly encourages some critics to write positive reviews of mediocre movies. However, even when a review is negative overall, studios may excerpt it in a way that misrepresents the critic's opinion. For example, the ad copy for Dreamwork SKG's dud *Norbit* attributed to Michael Wilmington (2007), a critic for the *Chicago Tribune*, the comment *[Eddie] Murphy's comic skills are immense*. One might infer from the quote that Wilmington was delighted to see Murphy's sizable skills on display in this film. The words in the review following this selective excerpt suggest a very different impression:

> *Murphy's comic skills are immense,* and 'Dreamgirls' shows he's a fine straight dramatic actor too. So why does he want to make these huge, belching spectaculars, movies as swollen, monstrous and full of hot air as [lead character] Rasputia herself—here misdirected by Brian Robbins of 'Good Burger,' 'Varsity Blues' and that lousy 'Shaggy Dog' remake?
>
> (Wilmington 2007: p. D5, italics added)

Similarly, Disney/Pixar contextomized critic Joe Morgenstern's (2009) review of their animated feature *Up*, including just one word from it—"irresistible"—in the film's ad copy. Examining the sentential context of this quote leaves little doubt that Morgenstern found the film easy (and even advisable) to resist:

> I'm still left with an unshakable sense of 'Up' being rushed and sketchy, a collection of lovely storyboards that coalesced incompletely or not at all. The one exception, apart from that silent montage, is the movie's most ephemeral element, the music ... touching, lilting, swooping, stirring, heartbreakingly elegiac, with intimations of Scott Joplin, Randy Newman and even Charles Ives, yet altogether original, and *irresistible*. The music is what the movie wanted to be.
>
> (Morgenstern 2009: E4, italics added)

Many critics become so fed up with having their opinions misrepresented via selective quotation that they change the way they write reviews. Instead of producing the punchy, quotable prose that has long been characteristic of the genre, these critics deliberately avoid one-liners, colorful similes, and effusive adjectives to thwart promotional excerpting (Tynan 2011). Using this type of language can result in ambiguity exploitable by those who wish to twist the words of a credible source to their advantage. Howard Movshovitz, film critic for the *Denver Post*, succinctly described this logic when he quipped "If I ever write a line I think can be quoted, I change it" (Reiner 1996).

Contextomy is also a common spin tactic among unscrupulous political journalists. For example, consider the Yew tree controversy that plagued former Vice-President Al Gore in the late 1990s. The trouble began when David Ridenour (1998), a columnist for the conservative *Austin American-Statesman*, wrote a piece criticizing the Vice-President's environmental policy agenda. Ridenour specifically criticized Gore's willingness to put "environmental politics before people" (Ridenour 1998: A15) as a moral failure and cited a passage from his 1992 book *Earth in the Balance* as evidence of this willingness. In the passage, Gore describes his stance on the preservation of the Pacific Yew, a tree with potentially important medicinal uses:

> The Pacific Yew can be cut down and processed to produce a potent chemical, Taxol, which offers some promise of curing certain forms of lung, breast and ovarian cancer in patients who would otherwise quickly die. It seems an easy choice—sacrifice the tree for a human life—until one learns that three trees must be destroyed for each patient treated.
>
> (Gore 1992: 119)

Proceeding from this quotation, Ridenour argued that the Vice-President would rather sacrifice people than deplete the Yew population, and thus lacked "basic human compassion" (Ridenour 1998: A15). Following the publication of the article, numerous references to the quotation appeared in conservative op-ed columns, magazines, and in radio and television shows across the country.

A year later, it even surfaced in a discussion of environmental policy on the floor of the House of Representatives. After reading the excerpt to his House colleagues, Rep. David McIntosh (Republican—Indiana) took issue with the Vice-President's apparent preference for trees over human lives:

> Three trees versus a human life, three trees versus the ability to prolong someone's life who is suffering from cancer? I would pick the individual, the person, the human being who is a cancer patient and suffering from that dreaded disease and say it is clear three trees are worth it. We can sacrifice three trees to save one human life. But the Vice President apparently does not think that is so clear.
>
> (109th Congress, 2nd Session, 145 *Cong. Rec.* H3376 1999)

If it were merely the ratio of trees to human lives that had bothered the Vice President, Rep. McIntosh's outrage might be justified. However, a very different picture of Gore's concerns emerges when the excerpt is examined in the context of the words immediately preceding and following it in the book (Ridenour's excerpt appears in italics):

> Most of the species unique to the rain forests are in imminent danger, partly because there is no one to speak up for them. In contrast, consider the recent controversy

> over the yew tree, a temperate forest species, one variety of which now grows only in the Pacific Northwest. *The Pacific Yew can be cut down and processed to produce a potent chemical, Taxol, which offers some promise of curing certain forms of lung, breast and ovarian cancer in patients who would otherwise quickly die. It seems an easy choice—sacrifice the tree for a human life—until one learns that three trees must be destroyed for each patient treated*, that only specimens more than a hundred years old contain the potent chemical, and that there are very few of these Yews remaining on earth. Suddenly we must confront some very tough questions. How important are the medical needs of future generations? Are those of us alive today entitled to cut down all of those trees to extend the lives of a few of us, even if it means that this unique form of life will disappear forever, thus making it impossible to save human lives in the future?
>
> (Gore 1992: 119)

In its original context, Gore's expression of reluctance to cut down Pacific Yews does not, as his critics alleged, appear to be motivated by a fanatical pro-flora platform. Rather, it is based on the pro-person concern that toppling too many now would limit the supply available to benefit cancer patients of future generations. By strategically omitting from the excerpt this and other legitimate reasons Gore offered for preserving the Yew, Ridenour reduced the Vice-President's sober assessment of the dilemma to an embarrassing blurb confirming his reputation among conservatives as a "radical" environmentalist.

The Yew tree affair illustrates how susceptible statements are to contextomy when they articulate the complexities underlying one's position on a controversial topic. Even when one's reasons for holding this position would be most accurately rendered in a nuanced, discursive public statement, the potential for reporters or opponents to misrepresent such a statement makes it a risky venture. Media and public relations consultants advise their clients to reduce this potential by keeping public statements simple, concise, and thin on rationale in most circumstances (e.g., Kerchner 2001). However, even speakers who are savvy about quotation tactics can be caught off guard. At a panel discussion on environmental journalism, former *Washington Post* executive editor Ben Bradlee discussed the risks faced by reporters who become advocates for environmental causes. In response to *Time* science editor Charles Alexander's admission that certain stories compel him to negotiate the fuzzy boundary between reporting and advocacy, Bradlee remarked as follows (as quoted by Brooks 1989):

> I don't think there's any danger in doing what you suggest. There's a minor danger in saying it, because as soon as you say, "To hell with the news, I'm no longer interested in the news, I'm interested in causes," you've got a whole kooky constituency to respond to, which you can waste a lot of time on.
>
> (Brooks 1989: A28)

A portion of this quotation appeared several months later in Ray and Guzzo's (1990) *Trashing the Planet*, a scathing critique of the environmentalist movement. Ray scolded the movement's leaders for exaggerating the environmental impact of phenomena such as acid rain and the greenhouse effect, and accused the news media of sensationalizing these issues to advance a liberal political agenda. As evidence of reporters' political motives, Ray cited Bradlee's *WSJ* remarks, but reproduced only the words "To hell with the news, I'm no longer interested in the news, I'm interested in causes ... " (Ray and Guzzo 1990: 76). This truncated version of Bradlee's comments received far more notice than the original, especially among critics of the alleged liberal bias in media. Bradlee threatened to sue over the matter, leading Ray to omit the distorted quote from the book's second printing. However, by that time it had been reproduced in numerous newspapers, magazines, and TV shows, none of which ever acknowledged its contextomized status (Bradlee 1995). Thus the quotability that contextomy had conferred on Bradlee's words perpetuated its misrepresentation of his intentions even after it had been retracted.

Selective excerpting is also a common tactic of another wing of the anti-environmentalist movement, the climate-change skeptics. For the past 100 years or so global temperatures have been on a steep incline (Mann, Bradley, and Hughes 1998), which most climate scientists attribute to human industrial growth. Despite the overwhelming consistency on this issue among climate scientists, skeptics have been perennially successful in spreading doubt among the public about the integrity of the scientific consensus. As it happens, their chief source of ammunition comes from the scientists themselves, particularly those belonging to the International Panel on Climate Change (IPCC). The IPCC was created by the United Nations Environmental Programme and World Meteorological Organization to gather, review, and assess scientific evidence pertaining to climate change. The upside of such a group is a globally representative authority on climate research that reviews new findings and regularly summarizes its conclusions for world policymakers. Specifically, the IPCC creates a summary for policymakers (SPM) every year to aid in the development of policies and regulations regarding waste management, fossil-fuel consumption, and other activities that contribute to climate change.

Given the amount of research the IPCC reviews each year and its efforts to describe it in digest form for a lay audience, the opportunities for contextomy proliferate. Take, for example, a passage from Chapter 9 (Dasgupta et al. 2014: ch. 5) in the IPCC's "Fifth Assessment Report (AR5)," selected by the editorial board of the *Wall Street Journal* for an uncredited op-ed published in 2014. The piece treats AR5 as a vindication of the newspaper's consistent skepticism over the years about the negative consequences attributed to climate change that had been delineated in previous IPCC assessments. The authors commend the IPCC for "toning down the end-is-nigh rhetoric that typified its past climate warnings" (Dasgupta et al. 2014: 18) and describe omissions and additions that warrant this commendation:

> Absent, too, are claims such as the one made in 2005 that global warming would create 50 million 'climate refugees' by 2010 (later pushed back to 2020). In its place, we have the refreshingly honest admission that "current alarmist predictions of

massive flows of so-called 'environmental refugees' or 'environmental migrants' are not supported by past experiences of responses to droughts and extreme weather events and predictions for future migration flows are tentative at best."

(Wall Street Journal Editorial Board 2014: A18)

The excerpts drawn from AR5 are portrayed as representing a single viewpoint from the IPCC with a cautious new outlook on climate change that acknowledges previous missteps. However, the complete sentence in the report from which these quotations are taken does not speak with the single voice the quoters imply:

> It is difficult to establish a causal relationship between environmental degradation and migration. Many authors argue that migration will increase during times of environmental stress (e.g., Brown and Crawford, 2008; Afifi, 2011; Kniveton et al., 2011; Gray and Mueller, 2012), and will lead to an increase in abandonment of settlements (McLeman, 2011). Climate variability has been associated with rural–urban migration (Mertz et al., 2011; Parnell and Walawege, 2011). Another body of literature argues that migration rates are no higher under conditions of environmental or climate stress (Cohen, 2004; Brown, 2008; van der Geest and de Jeu, 2008; Tacoli, 2009; McLeman and Hunter, 2010; Black et al., 2011a,b; Foresight, 2011; Gemenne, 2011; van der Geest, 2011). For Tacoli (2009) the *current alarmist predictions of massive flows of so-called "environmental refugees" or "environmental migrants" are not supported by past experiences of responses to droughts and extreme weather events, and predictions for future migration flows are tentative at best.*
>
> (Dasgupta et al. 2014: 628, italics added)[1]

Here, the IPCC's efforts to be ecumenical in its coverage of majority and minority views among scientists about climate change trajectories are used against it. The WSJ authors' choice to quote a proponent (Tacoli in this case) of the minority view they had endorsed in the past misrepresents the report as chastened rather than comprehensive.

Contextomy also can occur in international communications. For example, on August 29, 2014, Russian President Vladimir Putin had a confidential phone conversation with the then-president of the European Commission, José Manuel Barroso. Afterwards, Mr. Barroso disclosed to EU leaders that President Putin said, "if I wanted to, I could take Kiev in two weeks," in reference to Russia's presence in Ukraine (Norman 2014). Several news outlets treated the quotation as representative of the president's intention to invade, but received instant blowback when Kremlin aides claimed it was taken out of context. When the *Wall Street Journal*'s Laurence Norman spoke with Pia Ahrenkilde-Hansen, a spokeswoman for Barroso, about this statement, she responded as follows:

---

[1] We have preserved the citations in this excerpt strictly for the purpose of accurately reproducing the textual context from which the WSJ editorial board extracted its quotation. These are citations to research on climate science rather than deception or quotation, and consequently do not appear in the reference section.

> I can only add that the president of the Commission informed his colleagues in the European Council in a restricted session of the conversations he had with President Putin. Unfortunately part of his intervention was made public out of context.
>
> (Norman 2014)

Vladimir Chizhov, Russian ambassador to the EU, also claimed that the transcripts of the conversation would be released if necessary, although they never were. In this situation the quotation in question made the Russian leader's intentions seem aggressive, confirming the assumption many had made when Russian troops entered Ukrainian territories. It is not uncommon for speeches and public statements to be edited to create a false impression of a public figure, and for misquotation to be used to attack an opponent in discourse (Walton and Macagno 2009; Loving and Teufel 2012). With the confidentiality that accompanies official international conversations it is hard to disprove such a statement, making any denial even less effective. It is also possible that the language barrier between officials from two different countries could exacerbate the misinterpretation of a particular statement.

24.3 REVERSING THE DAMAGE

As the preceding examples illustrate, contextomy can be used to create a false impression of a speaker's attitudes in the service of motives as harmless as selling movie tickets or as harmful as character assassination or rolling back environment-preserving legislation. Yet even when it is put to malicious extremes, repairing the attributional damage would seem a straightforward matter. If an audience forms a false impression based on a contextomized quote, then "recontextualizing" it—i.e., presenting the quote with enough of its original context to make the speaker's true intention transparent—should correct the error. There are, however, problems with this strategy. One serious problem is the paucity of means by which to bring the recontextualized quote to the attention of the audience that has been misled. It would be ideal to transmit the correction via the same media vehicles (newspapers, news broadcasts, etc.) by which the contextomized version was disseminated in the first place. But mainstream news media rarely own up to quotation distortions, and highly partisan vehicles almost never do. Moreover, the errors that are corrected are primarily "objective" errors such as misidentifying the source, not "subjective" errors like quoting out of context (Ryan and Owen 1977; Lehrer 1989; Shapiro et al. 2013). There are currently few incentives for journalists to come clean about committing misquotation, regardless of whether they did it accidentally or on purpose. A survey of senior journalists by the *Columbia Journalism Review* found that more than half think major news organizations lack proper internal guidelines for correcting errors, and almost four in ten believe that most reporting errors are never corrected because reporters and editors try to hide them (Hickey 1999). The organizational climate of news media is simply not conducive to correcting its mistakes, let alone giving them prominent display. Unfortunately, the handful of media publications and programs that do put a spotlight on journalistic mistakes—e.g., *EXTRA*, the magazine of the media watch group FAIR (Fairness and Accuracy In Reporting), CNN's *Reliable Sources*, NPR's *On the Media*—draw small audiences. Ironically, these "watchdog" vehicles tend to attract people who already have a deep distrust of news media and consequently are among those least likely to be misled by reporting inaccuracies in the first place.

Many media critics (as well as some crusading insiders) have called on news organizations to do a better job of informing the public about reporting errors (Christian 2013; Shapiro et al. 2013). If these calls are heeded, reporters might someday be required to routinely disclose cases in which a source accuses them of quoting out of context, and would also be obliged to provide audiences with enough of the quote's original context for them to judge for themselves whether the accusation is justified (Louise 2013). Would these optimal conditions enable recontextualization to dispel the false impression created by a contextomized quote? Even under these conditions, there is reason to be skeptical. People are quick to infer character traits from inadequate behavioral evidence, a bias so pervasive and misguided that social psychologists often refer to it as the "fundamental attribution error" (e.g., Ross 1977). These dispositional snap judgments not only discount the influence of context (social or otherwise) on behavior, but also persist when people are made aware of how poor an indicator of character or attitudes the behavioral evidence is. For example, Jones and Harris (1967) asked people to read an essay about Fidel Castro purportedly written by someone randomly assigned the position of defending him in a composition contest. Despite the ambiguity of the writer's motives for making positive remarks about the Cuban leader, many readers nonetheless inferred that he was a Castro supporter prior to writing the essay. Remarkably, similar effects have been observed in this experimental paradigm even when the readers *themselves* are in charge of randomly assigning writers to affirmative or negative positions (Gilbert and Jones 1986). A bias toward dispositional attributions works against the repair of contextomy, which entails revising a dispositional attribution of verbal behavior (e.g., "the quote from Al Gore *indicates that* he puts the environment before people") to yield a contextual attribution ("the quote from Al Gore *was edited by someone else in a way that makes it appear as if* he puts the environment before people"). While dispositional attributions are unmediated and simple, contextual attributions are effortful and complex (Gilbert and Malone 1995). People may be reluctant to exchange a straightforward (albeit erroneous) dispositional interpretation of a quote for a more complicated contextual interpretation, especially when the inferred disposition coheres with other characteristics attributed to the target individual (e.g., "Al Gore is a liberal"). When several related characteristics are inferred from the same contextomized quote, it is therefore possible that their internal consistency will enable them to persist even after the quote has been recontextualized (McGlone 2005).

The selective excerpting phenomenon reviewed here is an incarnation of a more general problem in interpersonal communication—i.e., how to determine the extent to which verbal behavior reflects speakers' enduring beliefs rather than variables operating in the communicative context (Brown 1958; Quine 1960). This determination is never trivial and people often err. Various cognitive, cultural, and motivational factors tilt people toward dispositional rather than contextual explanations of others' messages (Ross 1977; Sperber and Wilson 1986). Selective excerpting exploits this tendency in advertising, journalism, and political debate by violating an assumption of intertextual discourse few people question. Audiences typically assume that words portrayed as a direct quotation constitute both a verbatim replication of the speaker's comments and a faithful rendering of their beliefs or attitudes. Transcripts, recordings, and "earwitness" testimony enable us to confidently assess whether the former condition has been satisfied, but the latter is harder to evaluate. Even a seemingly transparent declaration (e.g., "I did not have sexual relations with that woman ... Miss Lewinsky") can permit a circuitous route between words and intentions (Is fellatio "sex"? Does it depend on what the meaning of "is" is?) when it is politically expedient. The degree to which we resonate with the new spin on an old quote may depend less on the supporting evidence than on our prior attributional investment in the quote. It also depends on our knowledge of the social, cultural, and historical context in which the words were spoken, not merely their linguistic context. In the absence of such knowledge, we may overlook the subtle shifts in meaning that can occur when comments in black ink are retraced in a paler shade.

CHAPTER 25

LYING AND HUMOUR

MARTA DYNEL

25.1 INTRODUCTION

AT first blush, the notions of *humour* and *deception* (together with *lying*,[1] its salient type) may be considered to be incompatible, if not mutually exclusive. Deception is no laughing matter, because it carries negative interpersonal repercussions (if it should be discovered) and is typically regarded as being immoral and manipulative (e.g., Barnes 1994; Saul 2012).[2] Humour, on the other hand, is frequently seen as a pro-social communicative phenomenon, which fosters solidarity and promotes interpersonal bonding, helps resolve conflicts, testifies to the speaker's wit, and performs a number of other beneficial functions in human interactions (see Attardo 1994; Martin 2007).[3] It is thus hardly surprising that humour and deception should be presented as markedly distinct phenomena in the literature. Moreover, humour is frequently juxtaposed with lying and deception, exemplifying what the latter two are not.

It was Augustine who first dissociated "joci" from deception (see Vincent and Castelfranchi 1981). Similarly, Saul (2012) and Mahon (2015) differentiate between telling jokes and lying, both of which rest on untruthful statements, but only joke-telling is devoid of the speaker's intent to deceive. For their part, Vincent and Castelfranchi (1981) claim that joking and some irony,[4] which should be understood as categories of

---

[1] There is an ongoing debate, in which I do not wish to engage here, on whether lies must necessarily deceive, and thus whether they can be regarded as a type of deception. Here, support is given to the classical definition, according to which a lie rests on an assertion which the speaker believes to be false and whose aim is to deceive. (e.g., Mannison 1969; Chisholm and Feehan 1977; Bok 1999; Kupfer 1982; Adler 1997; Williams 2002; Carson 2006; Sorensen 2007; Fallis 2009; Mahon 2015).

[2] However, the importance of prosocial/white lies cannot be discounted. Such lies are deployed out of politeness, i.e. not to offend others.

[3] However, this does not necessarily pertain to genuinely aggressive humour, which performs a *disaffiliative* function (see Dynel 2013b).

[4] It must be stressed that not all irony is humorous (see Dynel 2013c, 2014 and references therein).

humour, share the characteristics of "acting," which is not deceptive (see also Vincent Marrelli 2004). Acting involves "A communicating to B that A is pretending" in the real world, and it is also anchored in "a fictional or imaginary world, where x is true" (Vincent and Castelfranchi 1981: 755). The metaphorical label "acting" involves communicating as if a pretended world is the real world while interactants must be well aware that it is not the real world. In other words, the speaker who is acting or producing humour will make his/her *pretence* overt to the hearer, not intending to deceive him/her. Incidentally, pretence is a nebulous notion (see Dynel 2018b) and does not seem to have been consistently defined, although it serves as a basis for a number of proposals concerning the interpretation of irony and fiction, as well as deception (see e.g., Austin 1958; Nichols and Stich 2000). Pretence may also be understood in terms of the speaker's *untruthfulness*, i.e., expression of what he/she believes to be false (see Vincent Marrelli 2003, 2004; Dynel 2011a, 2018a), which may be *overt* or *covert*. Generally, some (but not all) humour may be seen as being hinged on overt untruthfulness (as are other phenomena, such as irony and metaphor, or games of make-believe), whilst deception is contingent on covert untruthfulness. Thus, the speaker expresses a belief which he/she does not honestly hold, either to amuse or to induce a false belief in the hearer, respectively. Nonetheless, some humour rests on covert untruthfulness. In other words, deception may display humorous potential, as several authors have observed.

In his seminal monograph, Goffman (1974) discusses *benign fabrications*, i.e., acts of deception which are beneficial for, or at least not harmful to, the deceived individual. *Playful deceit* is one of their subtypes and it involves deceiving an individual "for the avowed purpose of fun—harmless, unserious, typically brief entertainment" (Goffman 1974: 87). Goffman (1974) seems to list a number of manifestations of playful joking, which he differentiates from put-ons (a "less innocent" genre): kidding, leg-pulling, practical jokes, and corrective hoaxing, yet he does not define any of these notions very precisely. For their part, Hopper and Bell (1984) propose *playings*, manifest in joking, teasing, or kidding, as a blanket notion for forms of deception performed for the sake of amusement. From another angle, Morreall (1983) states that people are often amused by lies, owing to the incongruity between what is asserted and what is known to be the case (see section 25.4). This claim appears to be premised on the presupposition of the hearer's realization that the speaker is lying. This line of argument misses the point of the liar's pivotal goal: a lie should remain undisclosed to the deceived hearer. Whilst a discovery of a lie, and hence a liar's failure, may be a source of pleasurable or even humorous experience for a hearer (e.g. a small child's inept lying), this can hardly be seen as a typical case of humorous lying.

The topical literature does not do justice to the complex relationships between humour, pretence/untruthfulness, and deception/lying (but see Vincent Marrelli 2004). Firstly, humour need not be based on overt untruthfulness/pretence, and it may carry serious/truthful meanings outside the *humorous frame* (see Dynel 2011b, 2018a, and references therein). Secondly, and more importantly here, humour may be hinged on the mechanisms of deception, whereby the hearer is deceived only to discover this fact in the context of the speaker's intentional revelation, or humour may emerge as a result of genuine deception from the viewpoint of a hearer who knows that the speaker is deceiving another hearer, dubbed the *target of deception*. Hence, two distinct sources of amusement may be distinguished: taking pleasure in surprising recognition that one has been deceived, with no repercussions following; and/or vicarious pleasure derived from another individual's being genuinely deceived. On a different, yet compatible axis, a distinction may be drawn between categories of humour, notions studied by humour researchers, which deploy deception; and genuine deception, which is meant to deceive but may simultaneously carry humour typically for hearers other than the deceived individual.

The primary objective of this chapter is to elucidate a number of forms and characteristics of deception conducive to humour (i.e., stimuli causing amusement) and humour experience (i.e., an individual's amusement typically manifest in smiling and laughter), with attention being paid to lying. The discussion will be illustrated with examples culled from the scripted discourse of "House," the medical drama series presenting the lives and work of a maverick diagnostician and his colleagues. The series, whose creation is credited to Paul Attanasio and David Shore, originally ran on the Fox network for eight seasons (November 2004–May 2012). For over a decade, it has also been aired internationally on other channels, streamed via the Internet, and syndicated on DVDs around the world. The examples of fictional talk will represent a selection of phenomena that can occur in real language use, which the former imitates. Also, the "fictional reality" and speakers' (un)truthfulness therein lend themselves to analysis more easily than real-life data (Coupland 2004). The viewer's role as a recipient of humour will also be accounted for, whenever relevant.

25.2 Categories of humour involving lying (or other forms of deception)

A few of the wide spectrum of humour categories reside in deception, with lying as one of its forms. Such forms of humour may appear in film/mass-media interactions, thanks to which it is also the viewers that are deceived and experience humorous effects, similar to the deceived hearer(s) on screen. Essentially, the targets of deception may be amused at discovering that they have just been taken in by the speaker operating within the humorous frame.

25.2.1 Garden-path jokes and witticisms

Chisholm and Feehan (1977) argue that when the speaker equivocates, he/she lies. This happens when the speaker knows that the utterance is "true if taken in the one way and that it is false if taken in the other: he utters it in order to cause D to interpret it in the second way and thereby believe a proposition that is false" (Chisholm and

Feehan 1977: 156). On the other hand, Vincent and Castelfranchi (1981: 763) list deliberate ambiguity as one form of deception (yet not lying) whereby an utterance invites two alternative interpretations, one of which is "true," whilst the other one, presumably the salient one, is "false." They illustrate this claim with an example of an advertising slogan: *No heat costs less than oil heat* (cf. the salient but "false" reading: "Oil heat is the cheapest of all types of heat" versus the "true" reading: "One pays less for using no heat than for using oil heat") (see Vincent Marrelli 2004). This instance manifests a form of what is known as *doublespeak* in folk theory (Lutz 1987). This is an umbrella term for manipulative or deceptive language use, one of whose vehicles is syntactic or semantic ambiguity. The malevolent use of ambiguity giving rise to deception is orientated towards encouraging a permanent false belief in the hearer. This may be manifest also in *underdeterminacy*, which shows, for instance, in: missing constituents, comparatives, unspecified scope of negation, and weakness or narrowness of constituents (see Meibauer 2014a).

Whilst it can be used to take unfair advantage of punters in advertising and political talk, ambiguity may be a source of humorous deception, inclusive of humorous lying. An intrinsic characteristic feature of ambiguity-based humorous deception is the speaker's revelation of the alternative "correct" interpretation, soon after the hearer has made the "wrong" one. Importantly, the deception is purely benevolent, for the hearer is expected to experience humorous surprise and be amused upon discovering the presence of ambiguity and the alternative interpretation. This is known in humour studies as the *garden-path mechanism* (see Hockett 1972; Yamaguchi 1988; Attardo and Raskin 1991; Attardo 1994; Attardo 2001; Dynel 2009, 2012; cf. Ritchie 1999, 2004) underpinning *jokes* and *witticisms*, as well as spontaneous conversational turns. It constitutes the most salient category of deception-based humour, which is why it deserves to be addressed here, even though it does not appear to recruit lies per se (see Vincent and Castelfranchi 1981). One-line jokes, witticisms and conversational turns pivoting on the garden-path mechanism may be relevantly intertwined into non-humorous discourse, with hearers being unprepared for a jocular jolt, and thus applying the belief system and communicative norms typical of non-humorous talk. This differs from *canned jokes*, i.e., humorous narratives or dialogues ending with punchlines (see Dynel 2009 and references therein), which the speaker typically indicates in advance or which receivers quickly recognize as jocular texts, assuming that the speaker is not (typically) communicating his/her beliefs. However, not only (GP) witticisms but also canned jokes may (but do not need to) be produced in conversation for the sake of ultimately conveying truthful speaker meanings.

A garden-path text deceives the hearer into arriving at a default interpretation, which has to be ultimately cancelled on the strength of an incongruous punchline, which invites a concealed sense (in part) of the preceding text and thus reveals its hitherto hidden ambiguity. The prerequisite for a garden-path humorous text is thus twofold. Its first part must entail *covert ambiguity*, with only one meaning being effortlessly accessible to the hearer, and the second part of the text (the punchline) must invalidate the interpreter's previous inference and prompt him/her to backtrack and reprocess the initial part of the text to appreciate an alternative meaning, congruent with the import of the punchline, or the closing part of an utterance.

The covert ambiguity central to the garden-path mechanism may be of a *semantic* (specifically *lexical* and/or *syntactic*) kind (Example 1), or a *pragmatic* kind, which account for different categories of the deceptive meaning (see Dynel 2009). In the case of lexical ambiguity, the first salient interpretation arises as literal meaning, which is duly substituted for an alternative sense of the ambiguous chunk of text. In garden-path texts couched in pragmatic ambiguity, the initial interpretation coincides with *implicature* or *presupposition*, which is subsequently cancelled in the light of the closing part of the text.

(1) [Wilson, House's best friend, suspects that House is attracted to Cuddy]
    1. Wilson: If you want her… ask her out.
    2. House: My God, man! She's not some floozy in a bar. She's the floozy I work for. There's gotta be no radical steps here. Gotta be subtle. We happen to attend the same party, the chat happens to turn personal.
                                  (*House* Episode 7, Season 6)

House's reply (2) to Wilson's (1) encouragement opens with garden-path humour. Based on "She's not some floozy in a bar", House invites the salient interpretation: "Cuddy is not one of those promiscuous women one can meet in bars." However, as this turn unfolds, it turns out that the quoted chunk has an alternative interpretation, based on a different scope of negation, i.e.,: "Cuddy is a promiscuous woman I work for." This is the meaning that House prioritizes for humorous purposes.

It must again be emphasized that a garden-path humorous text's distinguishing feature is its reliance on covert ambiguity,[5] which cannot be found in other forms of humour that involve deception duly revealed to the hearer.

25.2.2 Put-ons and other lie-based teasing

Put-on humour comes into being when "an addressee in a conversational interchange or an audience is tricked into believing that something is the case that is actually not the case" (Sherzer 2002: 53). While it is difficult to decide based on Sherzer's list of examples of Native American humour whether or not the hearer is ultimately allowed to recognise that he/she has been deceived, the definition of put-on humour endorsed here is that this must be the case. Typically, put-ons rely on the speaker's lying, i.e., asserting what he/she believes to be false (not what is "not the case") only to reveal this fact to the hearer immediately afterwards. Incidentally, the hearer need not be successfully deceived, but can be reasonably expected to see through the deception, or at least to be sceptical about

---

[5] Nonetheless, one can conceive of put-on humour (see 25.2.2) centred on covert ambiguity that surfaces across turns, not within one turn.

the speaker's truthfulness. Frequently, the untruthful message sounds uncanny to the hearer but is very convincingly presented by the speaker, which boosts the surprise effect after the speaker has revealed its untruthfulness. The hearer is intended to hold a false belief only for a moment, with the speaker soon retracting his/her previous utterance. The humorous effect (admittedly, of moderate funniness for the deceived individual) originates in the hearer's recognizing the fact that the speaker has just deceived him/her or attempted to do so. In the case of multi-party interactions or media talk, humorous effects may also arise from the viewpoint of the non-targeted individual present or recipient in front of the screen, albeit also deceived. Here is an example from *House* to illustrate this phenomenon:

(2)   [Dr House and Dr Chase are in the house owned by Dean of Medicine, Dr Lisa Cuddy, looking for clues to solve a medical case. House is going through her dresser drawer, whose contents are not shown on the screen.]
1.   House: Oh my God. She's got pictures of you in here.
2.   [Chase's eyes widen.]
3.   House: Just you. It's like some kind of weird shrine.
4.   Chase: You're kidding. [Chase approaches the dresser.]
5.   House: Yeah.
6.   [Chase looks disgruntled].

(*House* Episode 3, Season 2)

While the two doctors are searching for clues, House produces an utterance (1) which the addressee is meant to and, as his non-verbal reaction (2) indicates, does take to be truthful. House makes another contribution in the same vein (3), but this time Chase questions its truthfulness, refusing to be deceived. Each of House's turns (1 and 3) coincides with a lie, of which the target (in tandem with the viewer) is made aware (5) instantly after he has been taken in. Although the target is not amused (6), the viewer may find this deception humorous.

Put-on humour may be thought of as a subcategory of friendly *teasing*, a very broad type of humour widely discussed in humour studies in the context of its capacity to carry (truthful) meanings outside the humorous frame and (im)politeness effects related to the speaker's malevolent or benevolent intentions (see e.g., Boxer and Cortés-Conde 1997; Keltner et al. 1998; Martin 2007; Geyer 2010; Haugh 2010; Dynel 2011b, 2016; Sinkeviciute 2013). A statement can be ventured that deception lying at the heart of teasing can serve humorous purposes and solidarity politeness. Besides put-ons, more sophisticated forms of friendly teasing can also revolve around blatant lies, as in this interaction between two friends:

(3)   [Dr Wilson is eating a sandwich in the hospital cafeteria. Dr House walks in and sits down at his table. They start talking about Dr Lisa Cuddy, Dean of Medicine. For all the viewers know, neither of them has had intercourse with her.]
1.   House: You're trying to have sex with Cuddy.
2.   Wilson: [Looks at House.] Fries?

3. House: You took her to a play. You only take women to plays because...
4. Wilson: No, YOU only take women to plays for that reason. That's your theory.
5. House: Ok, then why did you take her to a play?
6. Wilson: She's a friend.
7. House: A friend with a squish mitten.
8. Wilson: It is possible to have a friend of the opposite sex without...
9. House: Blasphemer! She's not a friend of the opposite sex, she's a different species. [Takes a fry.] She's an administrator. She's going to eat your head after she's done.
10. Wilson: [Guiltily.] Yes, I slept with her.
11. House: [Shocked.] Seriously?
12. Wilson: No.
13. House: [Not convinced.] Yes you did.
14. Wilson: [Quietly.] Yes I did.
15. House: [Shocked.] Seriously?
16. Wilson: No. You've got a problem House.

(*House* Episode 19, Season 3)

As the two friends are conversing about Wilson's relationship with Cuddy, House (jealous as he seems to be) is adamant that the former had sexual intercourse with her. Averse to this assumption, Wilson starts teasing House by producing a lie (10), whose untruthfulness he duly reveals (12). Since the interlocutor does not seem to have believed the sincerity of the backtracking (13), Wilson lies for the second time (14) only to backpedal again (16). In his consecutive turns, Wilson means to tease House by being covertly untruthful in confirming House's misguided belief only to immediately uncover his mendacity.

Whilst the two examples above rest on two interlocutors' multi-turn interactions, deceptive teasing may be enclosed within one utterance, not necessitating a verbal indication from the target that they have been deceived. Such humour centres on following a covertly untruthful assertion with a pause and a textual element, such as *not, just joking*, or *I don't think*, which negates the meaning of the untruthful assertion, thereby revealing its untruthfulness. A similar deceptive strategy involves developing an expectation of what is to follow only to thwart it, as in the following example:

(4) [House is talking to a teenage patient's parents.]
1. House: Does your son smoke?
2. Father: I'd kill him.
3. House: [Smiles.] So, he talks to you about sex, crack, anything except cigarettes. He has a cigarette burn on his wrist, also a fading nicotine stain between two fingers. Bad news, your son has a filthy, unhealthy habit. Good news, he's trying to quit. Bad news, the quitting is killing him. Good news, I can cure him. Bad news... nope, that's the end of it.

(*House* Episode 12, Season 2)

The deception in House's utterance (3) rests on a surprising violation of a verbal pattern which he has developed, namely intertwining "bad news" and "good news." When, after two sequences, he indicates that another item of bad news is to follow, he must be well aware that there is no further bad news to be mentioned. Thus, he deceives the hearers that another entity is to follow only to reveal that this is not the case, which he means to be humorous.

Overall, the central mechanism underlying all these forms of humour necessitates the cancellation of the previously communicated message, which the hearer (ideally) has taken as being truthful. In fictional talk, it is not only characters but also viewers who can be lied to.

25.2.3 Lying to or decieving recipients

Recipients/viewers of films and series (like readers of literature) are typically given all significant insight into the fictional interactions, inasmuch as their understanding of characters' activities is the priority of *production crews*, i.e., scriptwriters, directors, editors, actors, etc. (cf. Dynel 2011c; on lying to recipients, see Chapter 23 by Emar Maier). Nonetheless, the deception of the viewers is by no means infrequent in thrillers and comedies, fostering suspense and humour respectively. *Deception in fiction*, which does not appear to have been widely acknowledged as a category of humour (but see Dynel 2013a), consists in encouraging viewers' false beliefs concerning characters' utterances and actions, as well as plot development. Such deception may manifest itself in specific utterances produced by characters, usually to deceive other characters, or it may rely on complex multi-modal cinematographic ploys (which are hardly conducive to lies, though), sometimes spanning almost an entire film or episode (note films such as *Memento, The Machinist*, or *The Sixth Sense*), with the camera working as an *unreliable narrator* (on unreliability, see Shen 2011 and references therein). Given the "willing suspension of disbelief" and immersion in the *fictional reality*, the viewer rarely pays heed to the ploys used by the production crew or consciously holds them accountable for communicated meanings (see Dynel 2011c). The viewer is to be deceived either alone or in tandem with another character (see examples (2)–(4)). Importantly, the recipient must recognize this deception at some point, rather than being permanently deceived. Having believed something the deceiver (a character or production crew) believes to be false in the fictional reality, the recipient is invited to recognize the deception and hence experience humour. If it is a character that is responsible for this lie (or an otherwise deceptive utterance) that duly transpires, he/she cannot be considered to have meant to entertain the viewer, but only another character. Nevertheless, a character may not have any humour-orientated intentions at all (see section 25.4), while the production crew aims to achieve this goal. Essentially, the deception of viewers is reminiscent of joke-telling, where an individual is deceived into believing something to be true in the fictional world of a film or joke. This deception does not have much bearing on the deceived individual's belief system beyond the fictional reality, whilst its main aim is to give him/her the momentary feeling of pleasurable surprise.

    (5) [House has been trying to diagnose a patient by the name of Jeff, who cannot move. House ends a discussion with his team by saying, "I have always wanted to do this." He enters the patient's room, and injects something in the patient's thigh.]

1. House: You are healed! Rise and walk.
2. Jeff: Are you insane?
3. House: In the Bible, you just say "Yes Lord" and then, start right in on the praising.
4. Jeff: First you tell me I've got cancer, and then you tell me that my manager [starts making a hand gesture and realises he can actually move his hand] What did you do?
5. House: No, what did you, Lord. Thymoma is a tumour in the thymus gland. It's a bit of a wimp, but he hangs with the tough guys. PRCA and an auto-immune disease called myasthenia gravis. MG causes muscle fatigue, including respiratory problems and difficulty swallowing.

...

6. House: You don't need your thymus. Take it out, everything else is manageable.
7. Jeff: Manageable. I thought you just cured me.
8. House: Nuh uh, this is just diagnostic. This just erases the symptoms of MG for five or six minutes [Jeff suddenly starts wheezing again and drops on to the floor. House stands there without raising a hair] Sometimes less. This is exactly why I created nurses. [Calls out from the room] Clean up on aisle three!

(*House* Episode 6, Season 2)

Like House's interlocutor, the viewer is deceived by House's lie (1), believing that the patient has been healed thanks to one injection. Both hearers, the addressee and the recipient, take the speaker's turn as truthful. Moreover, House continues deceiving the patient that he is healed (3 and 5) by withholding the pertinent information, until later in the interaction (6). At this stage, both hearers have reasons to start believing that the speaker cannot have been truthful, if the illness is manageable, which the patient's answer indicates (7). This is followed by House's revelation (8), thanks to which both the patient and the viewer become fully aware that they have been deceived. The viewer realizes that he/she has been led up the garden path by House (whilst, technically, the production crew is responsible) and, as opposed to the deceived patient, finds this fact to be humorous. It seems, therefore, that a genuine lie targeted at one individual may simultaneously amuse another hearer, whether or not a (fictional) speaker intends to amuse any other hearer.

25.3 Deceptive autotelic overt untruthfulness

One of the vexing problems concerning conversational humour, such as teasing (see section 25.2.2.), is its potential to convey relevant truthful meanings outside the humorous frame (Dynel 2011b, 2018a), and this is also where its deceptive capacity resides. The speaker may convey his/her genuine belief, for instance critical of the hearer, in the guise of humorous untruthfulness, with the hearer not being meant to discover the speaker's underlying intention and superordinate communicative goal. Such "pretending to joke"[6] (Vincent and Castelfranchi 1981; Vincent Marrelli 2004) involves passing off a genuine belief the speaker nurtures as if he/she did not and as if he/she was being overtly untruthful. This communicative strategy may be captured under the label *deceptive autotelic overt untruthfulness*, insofar as the speaker covertly pretends to be untruthful for humorous purposes only (note the "autotelic" label), thereby deceiving the target with regard to his/her genuine beliefs and communicative intentions. Also, should the hearer discover this and express this inference, the deceitful speaker reserves the right to backtrack on the truthful assertion on account of the underpinning humorous intent, and hence tell another lie. Pretending to be overtly untruthful, the speaker may indeed induce a humorous response in the unknowing butt, simultaneously displaying his/her superiority over the latter. This is the main source of amusement for the speaker, as well as another hearer/other hearers, should they be involved (the recipient included).

(6) [The previous night, Dr Cuddy, Dean of Medicine, and House kissed passionately. They both deny the significance of this fact, even if their true feelings seem to be otherwise. Anxious, Cuddy has approached House and they are now talking in the hospital hallway, in front of the conference room, separated by a glass wall. Following Cuddy's suggestion, they agree that they want to keep this event secret, together with the topic of their current conversation. House goes back into the conference room, where his team members have been sitting.]
1. Thirteen: What did Cuddy want?
2. House: [in a superior tone] I kinda hit that last night, so now she's all on my jock.
3. Thirteen: Wow! She looks pretty good for someone on roofies.
(*House* Episode 7, season 5)

---

[6] Such lay use of "joke" should best be avoided. A distinction can be made between "canned jokes" and "conversational humour"/"humour in interaction," used as the blanket terms for a whole gamut of humorous verbalizations or interactions.

When Thirteen (Dr Hedley) asks about the rationale for Cuddy's conversation with House (1), he replies in a manner that seems to be deliberately deceptive, of which the viewer is cognizant. Whilst House's utterance essentially communicates his true belief (elucidating the slang expressions, he did kiss Cuddy passionately, and she does indeed need his attention because of this), he produces it in a manner that suggests he cannot possibly be truthful. Presumably, House performs this deception via a seemingly overtly untruthful assertion (technically, not tantamount to a lie) in order to act in accordance with his agreement with Cuddy. What facilitates this deception is the team's background knowledge about the Cuddy–House relationship, which is based on continual power struggle and animosity, even if coupled with intermittent tokens of friendship (yet no signals of mutual affection). Indeed, Thirteen's humorous response that Cuddy would have needed to be drugged to be attracted to House (3) indicates that she has taken House's utterance to be jocular and overtly untruthful, and only tacitly communicating an implicit message that House is unwilling to provide a relevant answer to her question. Therefore, she appears to have been deceived, possibly together with the other team members. (Incidentally, as it turns out later, House's ulterior motive behind his utterance might have been for the deception to be detected, so that he could brag about his conquest.) Irrespective of the humorous reaction House means to elicit in his team members, his utterance is humorous also from the vantage point of the viewers, who have insight into the (un)truthfulness on the characters' communicative level. Sometimes only the latter aspect may come into play, with no humorous intention on the speaker's part.

25.4 Genuine lies in multi-party interactions

Genuine lying (and other forms of deception) may engender humour in multi-party interactions, whether real or fictional. Humour arises typically at the expense of the deceived target, the *butt*, who is hardly ever (meant to be) amused. Humorous experience stems from the deceiver's and non-targeted individuals' feeling of superiority over the butt. Moreover, the speaker may intend to lie without attempting to be humorous, but his/her deceptive utterance may still promote humour when it is performed in a multi-party interaction and a non-deceived hearer recognizes the speaker's mendacity (see the viewer's perspective on example (6)). On the other hand, a speaker may lie to one interactant and simultaneously aim to amuse another individual who can see through the deceptive act, sharing with the speaker the common ground to which the deceived individual is not privy. In either case, a lie will bring about different communicative effects for the distinct hearers, being humorous to those who are not deceived targets but are dissociated hearers experiencing a feeling of superiority over the deceived hearer(s).

This may concern participants in real-life conversations and viewers, who derive humorous pleasure from one character's deceiving another. If the viewer is aware of the deception on screen, he/she takes pleasure in witnessing it materialize successfully. As already indicated, whilst characters, fictional individuals, cannot intend to induce humorous experience in viewers, this can be one of the goals production crews pursue when having their characters lie.

(7) [House has learnt that Mark, Stacey's husband (whom House hates, as Stacey is his ex-fiancée) is participating in therapy for people coping with disability. A group therapy session is in progress when House walks in.]
    1. Mark: … When can I safely book a game of squash? When am I going to stop being angry?
    2. House: Not today. I've come for the healing. Dr Harper, as you know, I err, I have a bum leg. What you don't know is I'm upset about it. I need to talk.
    3. Mark: You know House! You know we have a history!
    4. House: You've been telling me for years that I should come by. Here I am. [to the group] Hi guys!
    5. Dr Harper: Got a Thursday group.
    6. House: Poker night.[7]
    7. Dr Harper: Monday morning?
    8. House: Book club. Well look, if it's a problem, I'll just go deal with my rage privately.
    9. Dr Harper: Wait. If you two could resolve this tension, you could really help each other.
    10. House: [nods thoughtfully] I'm tired of fighting.
    11. Mark: [laughs] What? So either I say yes or I'm the jerk?
    12. House: Oh god, I know that feeling.
(*House* Episode 6, season 2)

In the course of this interaction, House produces a sequence of lies (2, 6, 8, and 10), to which the viewer is privy. Mark also suspects that House is untruthful, surmising what his objectives are. The blatant lies (that House needs psychotherapy, that he is upset about his ability and needs to talk, that he has poker night on Thursday and book club on Monday morning, and that he is tired of fighting) do not seem to be produced by the speaker with an intention to induce amusement in anybody. It is the viewer who may take pleasure in House's audacity and find the lies amusing, as envisaged by the production crew. Clearly, then, deception may bring about different communicative effects for different hearers. Some explanation of what facilitates humour originating from deception is in order.

---

[7] Technically, this utterance is not an assertion but it can be paraphrased as one ("I've got a poker night on Thursday"). The same obtains for the lie in line 8.

25.5 Factors determining and facilitating humour experience

Humour psychologists have listed a number of factors accounting for the experience of humour (see Martin 2007), which must hold also for humour categories dependent on deception. These criteria will also be applicable to genuine lies (and genuine deception, in general) which enjoy humorous capacity from the viewpoint of non-deceived hearers.

In the case of humorous or genuine deception which is duly revealed and induces a feeling of positive surprise in the target, two crucial factors come into play. Firstly, the derivation of pleasure from being deceived is predicated on the target's cognitive safety, typical of humour experience (as in jokes and films) (cf. Rothbart 1976; Morreall 1987). Secondly, whether or not the fictional frame of reference is involved, no serious consequences can ensue for the deceived target. When receivers of films, jokes, or conversational humour consciously acknowledge having been deceived, they will have suffered no losses and faced no repercussions (mental or otherwise), thanks to which they can appreciate the emerging humour. On the other hand, in the case of deception which is humorous to a non-targeted hearer, the amused individual takes vicarious pleasure in a target's being deceived (in fictional interactions, as well as real interactions). Hence, the receiver of humour must affiliate with the deceitful person, not the deceived individual, as stipulated by the *superiority theory of humour*, and in particular the *disposition theory of humour* (Zillmann and Cantor 1972, 1976; see Dynel 2013b). Privy to the deceiver's genuine beliefs and/or facts, and thus cognizant of the deception taking place, a non-targeted hearer derives pleasure from the speaker's intellectual victory over the deceived (naive) individual(s). Whether or not deceived themselves, amused individuals will typically appreciate the deceiver's wit and cunning, or the intricacy of the deceptive utterance as such (in the case of canned jokes). As most of the examples quoted in the course of this chapter indicate, humorous deception tends to rest on verbal dexterity and creativity, which contribute to humour experience.

Deception-based humour can be captured by the widely recognized *incongruity-resolution* theory of humour (see e.g., Attardo 1994; Martin 2007; Dynel 2009, 2013c). Generally, the incongruity-resolution model presents humour interpretation as a linear process in which the hearer encounters an incongruity, which he/she then resolves according to an adequate cognitive rule, thereby rendering the incongruous element somehow congruent (Suls 1972, 1983). The incongruity, cognitive mechanism, and incongruity resolution may display innumerable manifestations. In essence, incongruity may be understood either as a mismatch in the structural features of a stimulus or as a clash with expectations and mental schemata (Morreall 1989, 2009), both of which are applicable in the interpretation of deception-based humour. Incongruity may be detected between the alternative interpretations anchored in the false/genuine beliefs, as they emerge consecutively (but see Dynel 2009 for an analysis of garden-path humour).

Humour is appreciated by a hearer aware of a lie, either when it is produced (so that the target, privy to the false belief only, should be deceived), or with the advantage of hindsight.

In the case of humour stemming from deception which is duly revealed, the incongruity-resolution pattern will manifest itself in the following way: the hearer experiences incongruity upon discovering that a belief that has been encouraged is a false one, after the speaker has revealed his/her true belief. A revelation of a lie produces *surprise* and *novelty* in the hearer's mind (e.g., Suls 1972; Morreall 1983; Forabosco 1992, 2008; Martin 2007), which are typically regarded as concomitants of incongruity. On the other hand, in deception which gives rise to humorous effects from a non-targeted hearer's viewpoint, the same process may be involved if the latter discovers the speaker's true belief only later. Alternatively, if the entertained hearer is cognizant of a lie as it is being performed, the incongruity will arise between the true belief already held and the false belief now communicated to the target. In all the cases, the resolution will consist in understanding the speaker's deceptive goal and making sense of the communicated meanings. Finally, it must be stressed that any recognized lie and act of deception may be deemed a source of true versus false incongruity, whilst it is only some incongruity that promotes humour experience, depending on the factors elucidated earlier.

Acknowledgements

This work was supported by the Ministry of Science and Higher Education in Poland (Project number IP 2015 012874, Decision 0128/IP3/2016/74).

CHAPTER 26

LYING, IRONY, AND DEFAULT INTERPRETATION

RACHEL GIORA

Although most sarcastic ironies trick comprehenders into misapprehension (Giora 2003; Giora, Fein, Laadan, Wolfson, Zeituny, Kidron, Kaufman, and Shaham 2007; Fein, Yeari, and Giora 2015), irony is not lying.[1] Admittedly, some ironies do share some resemblance with lying. In most cases, when uttering, ironists do not explicitly say what they believe to be true or relevant to the issue at stake. But, then, they do not intend comprehenders to take "what is said" at face value, but instead to re-interpret it vis à vis contextual information. (On lying involving an intention to deceive, see e.g., Meibauer 2011, 2014c). And even if untrue, irony is not a lie but, for instance, an act of Joint Pretense—a mutual recognition of a pretense shared by speakers and addressees, albeit not necessarily by the uninitiated (Clark and Gerrig 1984; Clark 1996). Even by Grice (1975), according to which irony involves a breach of the Quality maxim, which on the face of it might entitle it to the label of "lying," it is not. Given that this breach of truthfulness is *overt*, it cues comprehenders as to the need to reinterpret what is explicitly communicated in keeping with contextual information and authorial intent. Indeed, if comprehenders could tap the ironic interpretation directly or, at least, instantly revise their initial misapprehension, it might not resemble lying. Most of the evidence, however, indicates that comprehenders do not fully understand irony initially, even when it is cued and even when they detect incompatibilities. Rather, irony interpretation is fallible, especially when in the affirmative, where it is most misleading. Hence the resemblance to lying.[2] However, when interpreted directly, as when it is in the negative, irony bears no resemblance to lying.

---

[1] Irony and sarcasm are used here interchangeably to refer to 'verbal irony'.
[2] On "lie" being the most common error among brain-damaged individuals who understand irony, see Giora, Zaidel, Soroker, Batori, and Kasher (2000); on the preference for the "lie" choice among children, see, e.g., Ackerman (1981).

In what follows, comprehenders' optional gullibility is considered, while weighing affirmative (section 26.1) and negative (section 26.2) sarcastic ironies against each other.

26.1 Affirmative irony—the Graded Salience Hypothesis

Generally speaking, (nonconventional, non-lexicalized) irony or sarcasm is viewed as conveying or implicating the opposite or near opposite of what is explicitly communicated (Giora 1995; Carston 2002). In this sense, irony is an implicit or "indirect" negation (Giora 1995). Most of the ironies tested so far are in the affirmative, implying, rather than making explicit, that the opposite is invited, whether via the speaker's dissociative, ridiculing attitude (Sperber and Wilson 1986; Carston 2002) or via contextual misfit (Grice 1975).[3] And although under such conditions irony should be easy to process, it seems that deriving the opposite of what is said when invited by implicit cues often eludes comprehenders. Having activated the default, compositionally derived, salience-based interpretation of the target utterance—the interpretation based on the salient (coded and prominent) meanings of the utterance components (Giora 2003)—moving beyond that to constructing the ironic interpretation proves difficult.[4] And the idea that interpreting (non-lexicalized) sarcastic remarks immediately and directly, without going through its salience-based yet incompatible interpretation first (Gibbs 2002), has hardly gained support (but see Gibbs 1986a).

26.1.1 Experimental evidence

In a recent study, Fein et al. (2015) aimed to replicate previous results (Giora et al. 2007) showing that irony is interpreted initially via its *default*, salience-based yet contextually inappropriate interpretation. Note that according to the Graded Salience Hypothesis (Giora 1997, 1999, 2003), salient meanings and hence salience-based interpretations (based on these meanings) are default responses. Therefore, they will get

---

[3] Although not in the affirmative, echoic negated utterances are processed along similar lines.
[4] See, for example, Dews and Winner (1999); Giora, Fein, and Schwartz (1998); Giora and Fein (1999b); Pexman, Ferretti, and Katz (2000); Schwoebel, Dews, Winner, and Srinivas (2000); Colston and Gibbs (2002); Tartter, Gomes, Dubrovsky, Molholm, and Stewart (2002); Ivanko and Pexman (2003: Exp. 1); Katz, Blasko, and Kazmerski (2004); Giora et al. (2007); Giora, Fein, Kaufman, Eisenberg, and Erez (2009); Filik and Moxey (2010); Filik, Leuthold, Wallinton, and Page (2014); Kaakinen, Olkoniemi, Kinnari, and Hyönä (2014); Fein et al. (2015); see also Akimoto, Miyazawa, and Muramoto (2012) on intentional irony.

activated unconditionally, regardless of contextual information, or degree of nonliteralness. In contrast, nonsalient interpretations—interpretations not based on the lexicalized meanings of their components, but mostly on contextual cues—are nondefault; they will therefore lag behind. Findings in Giora et al. (2007) indeed support this view. They show that default salience-based interpretations were made available early on in both salience-based biased contexts and in contexts biasing the same targets toward their nonsalient sarcastic interpretation. However, nondefault nonsalient albeit contextually appropriate interpretations were not facilitated.

To replicate these results under stricter context-strength conditions, Fein et al. (2015) used revised dialogues used in Giora et al. (2007). These dialogues were found to strongly support an ironic interpretation, since they induced an expectation of ironic utterances. This expectation was shown to be raised by featuring an ironic speaker in dialogue midposition who also uttered the ironic target in dialogue prefinal position. (On prior stimulus sequences building up expectancy for another such occurrence, see, e.g., Jentzsch and Sommer 2002).

In Fein et al. (2015), these contexts were reinforced even further in an attempt to make the anticipation of an ironic utterance stronger. To this end, speakers' ironic utterances were prefaced by explicit ironic cues (*winking, mocking*), as shown in (1); nonironic speakers' utterances, in the nonironic counterpart texts, were prefaced by nonironic explicit cues (*worrying, impressed*), as in (2):

(1) Dani (rubbing his stomach): Do you have anything to eat around here?
Iris: Want me to make you a sandwich?
Dani: I'd like a proper meal, I'm starving.
Iris: Haven't you eaten anything today?
Dani: I've had a couple of chocolate bars and two donuts.
Iris (winking): **I see you're on a strict diet.**
Dani: Since I quit smoking I'm gobbling sweets all the time.
Iris: I didn't even know you used to smoke.
Dani: Well, I started smoking so I could quit sniffing glue.
Iris (mocking): **I see you've developed some great habits.**

(2) Dani (rubbing his stomach): Do you have anything to eat around here?
Iris: Want me to make you a sandwich?
Dani: I'd like a proper meal, I'm starving.
Iris: Haven't you eaten anything today?
Dani: Not really. A few snacks.
Iris (worrying): **You really should be more careful about what you eat.**
Dani: Don't worry. Today was not a typical day. Usually I am very strict with myself.
Iris: I'm happy to hear that.
Dani: I go to the gym three times a week, and eat only low-fat foods.
Iris (impressed): **I see you've developed some great habits.**

Results from reading times and lexical decisions replicated previous findings. They show that strengthening the context did not affect the pattern of results. Rather, in spite of the fact that the addition of the explicit cues prompted a stronger expectation of another sarcastic utterance than was found in Giora et al. (2007), default salience-based biased targets were activated initially, faster than nondefault nonsalient (ironic) alternatives (see also note 4). Such results, demonstrating the priority of default salience-based yet incompatible interpretations over nondefault yet compatible alternatives, might account for irony's apparent "deceptiveness."

Still could an even stronger, more explicitly biasing context effect a significant change? In Fein et al. (2015), another attempt was made to raise an expectation of a sarcastic utterance in the hope that this explicit cuing will make a difference. Here, another set of contexts used in Giora et al. (2007) was employed, where expectancy of a sarcastic remark was built up by manipulating the experimental design. Specifically, two types of item sequences were designed. In one, participants were presented with texts, all of which ended in an ironic utterance (3) (the +Expectation condition). In the other, participants were presented with texts half of which ended in a sarcastic utterance and half—in a nonsarcastic alternative (4). However, diverging from the 2007 study, here, in the +Expectation condition, expectation of a sarcastic utterance was boosted further by the explicit informing of participants that interpretation of sarcasm was examined:

(3) John was a basketball coach. For a week he had been feeling restless, worrying about the upcoming game. It was yet unclear how the two teams matched up, and he was anxious even on the day of the game. When he got a call telling him that the three lead players on his team would not be able to play that night, John wiped the sweat from his forehead and said to his friend: "**This is terrific news!**"

(4) John was a basketball coach. For a week he had been feeling restless, worrying about the upcoming game. It was yet unclear how the two teams matched up, and he was anxious even on the day of the game. When he got a call telling him that the three lead players on the opposing team would not be able to play that night, John wiped the sweat from his forehead and said to his friend: "**This is terrific news!**"

Regardless, results from lexical decisions, collected at various delays, replicated previous patterns of behavior. In both (+/-Expectation) conditions, only the default salience-based interpretations were facilitated, despite their contextual inappropriateness. Explicit contextual cuing, then, did not allow comprehenders an access, let alone a direct access to the *nondefault* ironic interpretations. Nondefault, nonsalient affirmative irony, relying on (context-driven) implicit negation, involves a contextually inappropriate interpretation, which might make it associable with lying.

26.1.2 Corpus-based evidence

According to the Graded Salience Hypothesis, the involvement of salience-based albeit contextually inappropriate interpretations in processing affirmative irony should be reflected by the environment of such utterances when used in natural discourses. Previous evidence indeed supports this prediction. They show that neighboring utterances of such ironies bear similarities to the ironic utterances; they thus "resonate" (à la Du Bois 2014) with these interpretations, despite their contextual misfit (Giora 2003, 2011; Giora and Gur 2003; Kotthoff 2003).

In a recent study, Giora, Raphaely, Fein, and Livnat (2014) investigated the contexts of ironic utterances in newspaper articles. Findings show that the environment of such utterances indeed echoes their default, salience-based (often literal) interpretations rather than their nondefault, contextually appropriate, sarcastic alternatives. Of the 1,612 ironies inspected, 689 (42.7%) were not echoed by their environment; 64 (3.9%) were addressed by reference to both their ironic and salience-based interpretations; 160 (9.9%) were extended ironies—ironies extended on the basis of their salience-based interpretation; 589 (36.5%) were addressed only via their salience-based interpretations; 122 (7.5%) were echoed only via their nonsalient ironic interpretations. As predicted, neighboring utterances of nondefault affirmative irony resonate with their default salience-based yet incompatible interpretation to a significantly greater extent than their nondefault yet compatible alternative. Resonance with default interpretations is the norm even when misleading, which renders affirmative sarcasm comparable to lying.

26.2 NEGATIVE IRONY—THE DEFAULTNESS HYPOTHESIS

Will negative irony be understood directly and thus be dissociable from lying? According to the Defaultness Hypothesis (Giora, Givoni, and Fein 2015), the answer to this is in the affirmative. The Defaultness Hypothesis, encompassing the View of Default Nonliteral Interpretations (Giora, Fein, Metuki, and Stern 2010; Giora, Livnat, Fein, Barnea, Zeiman, and Berger 2013; Giora, Drucker, and Fein 2014; Giora, Drucker, Fein, and Mendelson 2015), proposes that some *nonsalient* interpretations, derivable from certain novel (here, negative) constructions (*Friendliness is not her best attribute*), are *default* interpretations. Such nonsalient yet default interpretations will be activated unconditionally—*initially* and *directly*—even though a salience-based interpretation might be available, which, however, will lag behind. In contrast to the Graded Salience Hypothesis, the Joint Pretense, and the Gricean model, then, the Defaultness Hypothesis does not assume an initial inappropriate, misleading phase. When *default* sarcasm is considered, the semblance, noted earlier between sarcasm and lying, is now rendered vacuous.

What, then, is a default nonliteral interpretation? To be considered nonliteral *by default*, an interpretation must be derived under conditions which guarantee that nonliteralness cues, whether utterance internal (26.2.1a–b) or external (26.2.1c) are excluded, so that a preference between alternatives, whether of literal or nonliteral, is allowed:

26.2.1 Conditions for default Non/literal interpretations

To be derived by default,

(a) Constituents (words, phrases, constructions, utterances) have to be unfamiliar, so that salient (coded) literal or nonliteral meanings of expressions and collocations would be avoided. Items should therefore exclude familiar idioms (*Blow his horn*), metaphors (*Heartless*), sarcasms (*Tell me about it*), mottos, slogans, or any conventional formulaic expression (*hang in there*) (Gibbs 1980, 1981, 1994; Giora 2003), prefabs (*I guess*) (Erman and Warren 2000), or conventionalized, ritualistic, situation-bound utterances, such as occur in standardized communicative situations (*Break a leg*; Kecskés 1999, 2000). And if negative utterances are considered, they should not be negative-polarity items (*no wonder*), but should have an *acceptable* affirmative *counterpart*, so that conventionality is avoided.

(b) Semantic anomaly, known to trigger metaphoricalness (Beardsley 1958), such as *Fishing for compliments*, or any kind of internal incongruency, any opposition between the components of a phrase or proposition (known to trigger a sarcastic reading, see Barbe 1993) such as *he has made such a good job of discrediting himself* (Partington 2011) should not be involved, so that both literal and nonliteral interpretations are permissible. As a result, "epitomizations"—negative object-subject-verb constructions ("X s/he is not")—in which the fronted constituent is a proper noun (*Elvis Presley he is not*)—must be excluded. Such constructions are primarily metaphorical, even in their affirmative version. (On "epitomization," see Ward 1984; Birner and Ward 1998; Ward and Birner 2006; on the pragmatic functions of such constructions, see Prince 1981).

(c) Explicit and informative contextual information must be excluded, so that pragmatic incongruity—any breach of pragmatic maxims or contextual misfit on the one hand (Grice 1975)—and supportive biasing information, on the other (Gibbs 1981, 1986a, b, 1994, 2002; Katz et al. 2004; Campbell and Katz 2012), may not invite or obstruct a nonliteral or literal interpretation. Contextual or pragmatic cues such as explicit discourse markers (*literally speaking, metaphorically speaking, sarcastically speaking, just kidding*; Katz and Ferretti 2003; Kovaz, Kreuz, and Riordan 2013; Ziv 2013), explicit interjections, such as *gee* or *gosh*, shown to cue sarcastic interpretation (Utsumi 2000; Kreuz and Caucci 2007; Kovaz et al. 2013), and marked intonation or prosodic cues, whether nonliteral, such as sarcastic, effective even outside of a specific context (Rockwell 2000, 2007; Bryant and Fox Tree 2002; Voyer and Techentin 2010), or corrective, such as assigned to metalinguistic negation (Horn 1985, 1989: 375; Chapman 1993, 1996; Carston 1996), or nonverbal (such as gestures or facial expressions Caucci and Kreuz 2012) should be avoided, so that (non-)literalness would be neither invited nor disinvited.

To qualify as default nonliteral interpretations, then, targets and alternative counterparts should prove to be novel (26.2.1a) and potentially ambiguous between literal and nonliteral interpretations (26.2.1b), when presented in isolation or in a neutral nonvocalized discourse (26.2.1c).

26.2.2 Predictions

According to the Defaultness Hypothesis, some constructions, modifying favorable concepts (often in the superlative), such as "X s/he is not" (*Friendly she is not*), "X is not his/her forte" (*Friendliness is not my forte*), "X is not his/her *best attribute*" (*Friendliness is not her best attribute*), "X is not particularly/the best/the most Y" (*She is not particularly friendly; He is not the friendliest neighbor*),[5] conforming to the conditions for default (non-)literal interpretations specified above (26.2.1a–c),

(a) will be interpreted sarcastically and rated as more sarcastic than affirmative counterparts (to be rated as literal) when presented in isolation, regardless of structural markedness;
(b) as a result, will be processed sarcastically directly, irrespective of contextual information to the contrary or its absence. They will, therefore, be activated faster in contexts biasing them toward their *default* nonsalient sarcastic interpretation than toward their *nondefault* (yet equally strongly biased) salience-based (literal) interpretation;
(c) notwithstanding, will also be processed faster than their affirmative counterparts, embedded in equally strong contexts, biasing them toward their *nondefault*, nonsalient, sarcastic interpretation;
(d) and when biased toward their *nondefault* salience-based, literal interpretation, will take longer to process compared to the salience-based, literal, but *default* interpretation of their affirmative counterpart (predicted also by negation theories);
(e) as a result, when in natural discourse, (i) they will be interpreted sarcastically, conveying their *default*, nonsalient rather than their *nondefault*, salience-based interpretation; their affirmative counterparts, however, will convey their *default*, salience-based interpretation; (ii) hence, more often than not, when echoed by their neighboring utterances, the latter will resonate with their *default* yet

---

[5] For constructions involving affirmative rhetorical questions and modifiers affecting sarcastic interpretations by default, see Paolazzi (2013), Zuanazzi (2013), and Giora, Jaffe, Becker, and Fein (2018).

nonsalient, sarcastic interpretation rather than with their *nondefault*, salience-based (e.g., literal) interpretation; their affirmative counterparts, however, will be referred to via their *default*, salience-based interpretation.

In sum, according to the Defaultness Hypothesis, some non-coded nonliteral interpretations of specific constructions will be generated by default. They will therefore supersede their literal yet nondefault negative alternatives alongside their nondefault, nonliteral, affirmative counterparts. Defaultness, then, reigns supreme: Default interpretations will spring to mind unconditionally, regardless of context strength, degree of negation, degree of nonliteralness, and degree of nonsalience (Giora et al. 2010, 2013; Giora 2015; Giora, Drucker et al., 2015; and Giora, Givoni et al., 2015; in the latter, negative constructions and their affirmative counterparts are compared directly).

26.2.3 Experimental evidence

The Defaultness Hypothesis (Giora, Givoni et al. 2015), then, allows us to test the predicted superiority of default interpretations over nondefault counterparts, whether affirmative or negative, literal or nonliteral, salience-based or nonsalient. In what follows, I review our studies comparing default sarcastic and default literal interpretations with their nondefault sarcastic and nondefault literal alternatives. The following comparisons are considered:

(i) *Default*, nonsalient, sarcastically biased **negative** constructions (5 below) vis à vis their *nondefault* salience-based, literally biased versions (6 below);
(ii) *Default*, nonsalient sarcastically biased **negative** constructions (5 below) vis à vis their *nondefault* nonsalient, sarcastically biased **affirmative** versions (7 below);
(iii) *Default* salience-based, literally biased **affirmative** utterances (8 below) vis à vis their *nondefault*, nonsalient, sarcastically biased versions (7 below);
(iv) *Default* salience-based, literally biased **affirmative** utterances (8 below) vis à vis their *nondefault* literally biased **negative** versions (6 below).

In our studies, Hebrew constructions (whose novelty was established by a pretest) were examined. For instance, Giora et al. (2013) tested the "X s/he is not" (*Friendly she is not*) construction; Giora, Drucker et al. (2015) tested the "X is not his/her forte" (*Friendliness is not my forte*) and "X is not his/her best attribute" (*Friendliness is not her best attribute*) constructions; in Giora, Givoni et al. (2015), we tested the "X is not particularly/the best/the most Y" (*He is not the friendliest neighbor*) construction.

As predicted by the Defaultness Hypothesis (26.2.2a–b), findings in Giora et al. (2013) show that, when presented in isolation, novel negative constructions of the form "X s/he is not" (*Supportive she is not*), controlled for novelty, involving no semantic anomaly or internal incongruency, were interpreted sarcastically by default and were further rated as more sarcastic than their similarly novel affirmative counterparts (*Supportive she is yes*)[6], which were rated as literal. Weighing degree of structural markedness (+/-fronting) against degree of negation (not/yes) revealed that structural markedness played a role in affecting sarcasm. However, it was negation that rendered negative constructions significantly more sarcastic than their affirmatives versions, regardless of structural markedness. Hence, when embedded in contexts biasing them toward their default nonsalient sarcastic interpretation, they were read faster than when embedded in contexts (equally strongly) biased toward their salience-based yet nondefault literal interpretation.

Similarly, as predicted by the Defaultness Hypothesis (26.2.2a–b), findings in Giora, Drucker et al. (2015) show that, when presented in isolation, novel negative constructions of the form "X is not his/her forte/best attribute" (*Friendliness is not my forte/best attribute*), controlled for novelty, involving no semantic anomaly or internal incongruency, were interpreted sarcastically by default and were also rated as more sarcastic than their similarly novel affirmative counterparts (*Friendliness is my forte/best attribute*), which were perceived as literal. Weighing degree of structural markedness (+/-fronting) against degree of negation (not/yes) revealed that structural markedness did not play a role at all. Instead, and regardless of markedness, it was negation that affected sarcasm significantly, rendering the negative constructions significantly more sarcastic than their affirmatives versions, which were rated as literal. Consequently, when embedded in contexts biasing them toward their default nonsalient sarcastic interpretation, they were processed faster than when embedded in contexts (equally strongly) biased toward their salience-based yet nondefault literal interpretation.

In Giora, Givoni et al. (2015), we tested predictions (26.2.2a-d). The construction examined was "X is not particularly/the best/the most Y" (*She is not particularly friendly/the friendliest neighbor*) and its affirmative counterpart (*She is particularly friendly/the friendliest neighbor*). As predicted by the Defaultness Hypothesis (26.2.2a–d), findings show that, when presented in isolation, the negative constructions, controlled for novelty, involving no semantic anomaly or internal incongruency, were interpreted sarcastically by default and were rated as more sarcastic than their similarly novel affirmative counterparts, which were rated as literal (26.2.2a). Consequently, when embedded in contexts biasing them toward their *default* nonsalient sarcastic interpretation (see (5); target in bold, the next two-word spillover section in italics[7]), they were read faster than when embedded in contexts, equally strongly biased toward their salience-based albeit *nondefault* literal interpretation (26.2.2b; see (6); target in bold, spillover section in italics). In addition, they were also processed faster than their affirmative counterparts, embedded in equally strong contexts, biasing them toward their *nondefault*, nonsalient, sarcastic interpretation

---

[6] In Hebrew, the affirmative version is obligatorily marked for affirmation by an explicit marker.
[7] Spillover sections allow difficulties spilling over from a target segment to the next segment to be measured.

(26.2.2c; see (7); target in bold, spillover section in italics). And when biased toward their *nondefault* salience-based, literal interpretation, they took longer to process than the *default* salience-based, literal interpretation of their equally strongly biased affirmative counterparts (26.2.2d; explainable also by negation theories; see (8); target in bold, spillover section in italics):

(5) During the Communications Department staff meeting, the professors are discussing their students' progress. One of the students has been doing very poorly. Professor A: "Yesterday he handed in an exercise and yet again I couldn't make any sense of the confused ideas presented in it. The answers were clumsy, not focused, and the whole paper was difficult to follow." Professor B nods in agreement and adds: "Unfortunately, the problem isn't only his assignments. He is also always late for class, and when it was his turn to present a paper in class he got confused and prepared the wrong essay! I was shocked. What can I say? **He isn't the most organized student.** *I'm surprised* he didn't learn a lesson from his freshman year experiences."

(6) The professors are talking about Omer, one of the department's most excellent students. Professor A: "He is a very efficient lad. Always comes to class on time with all of his papers in order and all his answers are eloquent, exhibiting a clearly structured argumentation. I think that explains his success." Professor B: "Yes, it's true. Omer is simply very consistent and almost never digresses from the heart of the matter. But there are two other students whose argumentation and focus surpass his, so that I'd say that, only in comparison to those two, **he isn't the most organized student.** *I'm surprised* he asked to sit the exam again."

(7) During the Communications Department staff meeting, the professors are discussing their students' progress. One of the students has been doing very poorly. Professor A: "Yesterday he handed in an exercise and yet again I couldn't make any sense of the confused ideas presented in it. The answers were clumsy, not focused, and the whole thing was difficult to follow." Professor B nods in agreement and adds: "Unfortunately, the problem isn't only his assignments. He is also always late for class, and when it was his turn to present a paper in class he got confused and prepared the wrong essay! Professor C (chuckles): In short, it sounds like he really has everything under control." Professor A: "What can I say? **He is the most organized student.** *I'm surprised* he didn't learn a lesson from his freshman year experiences."

(8) During the Communications Department staff meeting, the professors are discussing their students' progress. One of the student has been doing very well. Professor A: "He is the most committed student in the class. Always on time, always updated on everything." Professor B: "I also enjoy his answers in class. He always insists on a clear argumentation structure and is very eloquent. In his last exam, each answer was not only to the point but also very clear. In my opinion, **he is the most organized student.** *I'm surprised* he asked to sit the exam again."

Default interpretations, then, rule. Whether in the negative (where the default interpretation is sarcastic, superseding an equally strongly supported, nondefault ironic interpretation of an affirmative counterpart and a nondefault literal interpretation of a negative counterpart), or in the affirmative, (where the default interpretation is salience-based, here literal, superseding an equally strongly biased, nondefault sarcastic interpretation and the equally strongly biased nondefault literal interpretation of the negative counterpart), default interpretations prevail.

In sum, some constructions, hedging a favorable concept (often in the superlative) by means of explicit negation, which allows them to be interpreted sarcastically *by default* (see also Giora et al., 2018), do not resemble lying. Instead, they activate their default sarcastic interpretation immediately and directly. They therefore differ from affirmative sarcastic counterparts, which are interpreted vicariously, involving initially an incompatible misleading phase (26.1).

Given their defaultness, will natural discourse reflect these constructions' sarcastic interpretations rather than their nondefault salience-based literal alternatives, as predicted by the View of Default Nonliteral Interpretations (26.2.2e)?

26.2.4 Corpus-based evidence

Using Hebrew constructions, Giora et al. (2013) and Giora, Drucker, and Fein (2014) tested the predictions specified in (26.2.2e). Accordingly, when in natural discourse, (i) the negative constructions under scrutiny here are expected to be used sarcastically, communicating their *default* nonsalient sarcastic interpretation rather than their nondefault, salience-based, literal alternative; their affirmative counterparts, however, will communicate their *default*, salience-based, literal interpretation. As a result, (ii) their environment will resonate with their *default* sarcastic interpretations rather than with their nondefault, salience-based, literal alternatives; their affirmative counterparts, however, will be echoed via their *default*, salience-based interpretation.

Giora et al. (2013) examined constructions of the form "X s/he/it is not" and their affirmative counterparts "X s/he/it is yes." Findings from 281 naturally occurring negative utterances (*Smart he is not*), collected from Hebrew blogs, indeed reveal that, as predicted, most of them (95%) were intended sarcastically; the 77 affirmative counterparts found (*Smart he is yes*) communicated only their salience-based literal interpretation.

How would their neighboring utterances resonate with these interpretations? What might the various resonance options be? For an illustration of exclusive resonance with the default sarcastic interpretation, consider example (9) (sarcastic target in bold, resonance with this sarcastic interpretation in italics):

(9) *Dumb* he is **Smart he is not**.[8]

---

[8] http://www.quickmeme.com/meme/3p4faf. Retrieved on February 20, 2015.

For exclusive resonance with the nondefault salience-based literal interpretation of the construction, consider example (10) (target utterance in bold, resonance in italics):

(10) "*Intelligence*"[9]: **Smart it is not.**

(Levin 2014)

In (11), resonance with the nondefault salience-based literal interpretation of such a sarcastic construction (in bold) is exemplified (underlined), alongside resonance with the default sarcastic interpretation (in italics):

(11) Netanyahu – **smart he is not.**
Today the following news item has been published: Netanyahu announces that Turkel commission will prove that we have acted appropriately. It's really frustrating ... Any time you think he may this time act <u>sensibly</u>, again [he proves you wrong]. What an *idiotic* advisor allowed him to say that sentence? And if he came up with it on his own, how *stupid* can a prime-minister be?

(Schwartz 2010)

In (12), exclusive resonance with the default salience-based, literal interpretation of the affirmative counterpart is exemplified (target construction in bold, resonance in italics):

(12) **Smart she is (yes),** *cleverness* flows out of her mouth in all directions...

(Amir 2008)

In all, findings support the predictions of the Defaultness Hypothesis (Giora, Givoni, et al. 2015). They show that in 109 of the 169 naturally occurring instances examined, the environment resonates either with the sarcastic or with the literal interpretation. However, in 100 (92%) of these 109 cases, it resonates exclusively with their sarcastic interpretation; in 9 cases (8%), it resonates exclusively with their salience-based literal interpretation. Out of the remaining 60 cases, the environment of 37 utterances reflects both their sarcastic and literal interpretations, while, in 23 cases, the environment does not resonate with any of the interpretations. As shown in Giora et al. (2013), most of the findings attest that the environment of such negative constructions reflects their default sarcastic interpretation.

Giora et al. (2014a) examined constructions of the form "X is not his/her forte/most pronounced characteristic" (*Patience is not her forte/most pronounced characteristic*) and their affirmative counterparts "X is his/her forte/most pronounced characteristic" (*Patience is her forte/most pronounced characteristic*). Findings from 141 naturally occurring negative exemplars (*Humor is not his/her/my forte*), collected from Hebrew and English blogs, reveal that, as predicted, most of the naturally occurring negative items (90%), were intended sarcastically; by contrast, most of the 155 (~ 97%) affirmative items were intended literally.

---

[9] "Intelligence" is a TV series.

How would their neighboring utterances relate to these interpretations? For an illustration of exclusive resonance with the default sarcastic interpretation, consider the hotel review in example (13) (sarcastic target in bold, resonance with this sarcastic interpretation in italics):

(13) Far from the City Centre and restaurants, crappy area, by far the worst complaint would be the *unprofessional conduct* of the staff. They have *no concept on how to behave in front of their clients* for e.g. Such as *shouting* at each other from across the room, in the restaurant and lobby area. You ask for something, they *pretend* to know what you're asking for and bring you something completely different ... **Politeness is not their forte** ... [10]

For an illustration of exclusive resonance with the nondefault salience-based literal interpretation, consider example (14) (sarcastic target in bold, resonance with this literal interpretation in italics):

(14) I fumbled with my bag, phone and music. The vehicle parallel to mine moved ahead just a bit, stopped at an odd angle, and a man sitting in the front passenger seat *smiled* and the one driving said something. I didn't quite appreciate the *smile* but gave a *polite smile* [and] murmured, 'hello'. **Synthetic politeness is not my forte** but I live and work in an environment of 'oral and visual *civility*' so in order to be *culturally adaptable I try to conform*. Anybody with less air in the head can see through my *polite pleasantries* though.[11]

For an illustration of resonance with both the default nonsalient sarcastic interpretation and the nondefault salience-based literal interpretation, consider example (15) (sarcastic target in bold, resonance with its sarcastic interpretation in italics, and resonance with its literal interpretation underlined):

(15) ... what you said "they DESERVED" to die ... You are, in plain and simple language, WRONG ... Learn to accept the fact that what you said was *hurtful and very MEAN* (to put it <u>politely</u>). Because "YOU DON'T LIKE BUILDERS" doesn't entitle you to make a *mockery* out of someone's death ... If you still have some sense of <u>respect</u>, you will realize what you said was wrong in more ways than one ... I was being as <u>polite</u> as I could when I put my point across to you, but as evident, **POLITENESS is definitely not your forte.** :).[12]

Findings regarding discourse resonance reveal that, out of the 127 naturally occurring negative instances examined, the contexts of 83 cases either resonated with their default

---

[10] http://www.expedia.ca/Shanghai-Hotels-Radisson-Blu-Hotel-Shanghai-Hong-Quan.h2064105-p4.Hotel-Reviews Retrieved on February 4, 2015.
[11] http://chhayapath.blogspot.no/2010_12_05_archive.html Retrieved on February 4, 2015.
[12] http://timesofindia.indiatimes.com/city/nagpur/Builder-wife-die-in-ghastly-mishap/articleshow/7940306.cms. Retrieved on February 4, 2015.

nonsalient sarcastic interpretation (see example (13)) or with their nondefault salience-based literal alternative (see example (14)). Of these, the environment of 73 cases (88%) exhibited exclusive resonance with the default nonsalient sarcastic interpretation as opposed to 10 cases (12%) in which neighboring utterances resonated exclusively with the nondefault salience-based literal interpretation. For each of the constructions examined, then, resonance with the default nonsalient sarcastic interpretation was the rule, as predicted. In addition, of the remaining 44 cases, the environment of 35 constructions reflected both their default sarcastic interpretation and their nondefault literal interpretation (see example (15)). In 9 cases, the environment did not resonate with any of the interpretations. Such findings support the superiority of default, nonsalient, contextually compatible sarcastic interpretations of some negative constructions over their nondefault, salience-based, yet contextually incompatible alternatives. Natural uses of negative sarcasm, then, highlight the significant extent to which such ironies differ from lying.

26.3 Discussion and conclusion: Defaultness rules

Can irony, then, be somehow related to lying? The answer to this is both "yes" and "no," depending on whether we are dealing with default or nondefault irony. According to the Graded Salience Hypothesis (Giora 1997, 1999, 2003), nonsalient ironic interpretations are *nondefault*; instead, salience-based interpretations—interpretations derived compositionally, based on the lexicalized meanings of the utterance components—are generated *by default*. They are, therefore, activated unconditionally, immediately, and directly, irrespective of context, which allows them to be initially involved in processing nondefault counterparts, such as sarcastic irony. This initial processing phase might mislead sarcasm interpretation down the wrong garden path. Hence the resemblance to lying.

However, according to the Defaultness Hypothesis (Giora, Givoni, et al. 2015; see also Giora et al. 2010, 2013; Giora, Drucker, and Fein 2014; Giora 2015), some interpretations of, e.g., negative constructions, modifying favorable concepts (*Friendly he is not, Friendliness is not his forte, Friendliness is not her best attribute, She is not particularly friendly*), albeit nonsalient, are derived *by default*; they are interpreted sarcastically immediately and directly, regardless of contextual information to the contrary. In contrast to affirmative sarcasm, then, default sarcastic interpretations of some negative constructions will not be misled down a garden path; therefore, they will not bear any resemblance to lying.

It is not irony, then, that might be associable with lying but *nondefault* interpretations.

Acknowledgements

This study was supported by The Israel Science Foundation grant (no. 436/12). I am also very grateful to Shir Givoni, Ari Drucker, and two anonymous reviewers for all their help.

CHAPTER 27

LYING AND VAGUENESS

PAUL EGRÉ AND BENJAMIN ICARD

27.1 Introduction

LYING may be defined as the deliberate utterance of a false sentence (or thought to be false), generally with the aim of misleading the hearer into thinking that the sentence is true. Paradigmatic examples of lies involve sentences expressing *incontrovertibly false* propositions. For example, when former French Minister of Budget Jérôme Cahuzac solemnly declared on December 5, 2012: "I do not have, Mr Deputy, I never had, any account in a foreign country, neither now nor previously," he made an outright false assertion whose falsity he could no longer deny after investigations found evidence that he had held bank accounts in Switzerland, Singapore, and the Isle of Man. Those investigations quickly led to Cahuzac admitting his lie and resigning.

The Cahuzac scandal is the example of a *blatant lie*: an utterance whose falsity is clear and eventually beyond doubt, including to the speaker. For many of our utterances, however, it is not so clear-cut whether they should be considered a lie or not, even after all the evidence has been collected, and even to the speaker. This happens when utterances are vague. The point is that vague sentences have unclear truth-conditions, and cannot easily be nailed down as false, for that matter. Consider horoscopes, and the question of whether they are truthful or not. Suppose my horoscope tells me (an example found on the Internet):

(1) Overall, you will feel rather good, physically and morally. You won't be too inhibited this time and …

Is the sentence true or false? The answer is unclear. Characteristic of horoscopes is the exploitation of vagueness. In an expression like *overall*, it is left underspecified exactly what proportion of the time. Similarly, *feel good* is a qualitative predicate for which there is no absolute criterion of application, and likewise *inhibited*. Further exploitation of vagueness can be found in the use of degree modifiers such as *rather* or *too*, whose interpretation is characteristically speaker- and listener-dependent (see Lakoff 1973; Wright 1995). Moreover, the indexical *this time* leaves its temporal reference open, making simply unclear which context is targeted by the sentence to be counted as true or false.

To philosophers of science, horoscopes are deceitful precisely because they exploit vagueness on such a large scale (Popper 1963). To casual readers, on the other hand, they are often pleasant to read, because it is easy to find confirming instances of their truth (horoscopes can be thus argued to exploit a well-documented psychological phenomenon by means of semantic vagueness, the phenomenon of *confirmation bias*, see Wason 1966). Such ambivalence suggests that vagueness can be a convenient way of calibrating the truth of an assertion. There is a trade-off between informativeness and truth, or correlatively, between vagueness and falsity. That is, the more vague an utterance, the more likely it is to be true relative to some contexts of interpretation, and the less likely it is to be false as a result. The more precise an utterance, on the other hand, the narrower the range of contexts relative to which it can be true. By decreasing informativeness, a vague sentence thus increases its chances of being true (Russell 1923).[1]

This inverse relationship between informativeness and truth is exploited not just by horoscopes, it is a pervasive feature of everyday conversations and exchanges, and it concerns commercial, moral, and legal transactions. Consider sales and advertising: like horoscopes, ads generally use vague vocabulary to sell their products. A famous case concerns the firm Ferrero, which used to advertise its star product as *healthy*. The firm was sued by a Californian customer on the grounds of making a false claim, considering the high rate of sugar in its product, but the company retorted that "there are health benefits associated with eating chocolate" (more on such moves below). In ordinary exchanges, however, vagueness is not necessarily used to deceive, but simply to avoid making claims that are too committal. Vagueness in that sense is not confined to horoscopes, but concerns predictive utterances quite generally (as in medical communication, see van Deemter 2009 and section 27.3). Vagueness is a feature of language that is used to avoid flouting Grice's first maxim of Quality ("Do not say what you believe to be false / that for which you lack adequate evidence") while exploiting Grice's second maxim of Quantity ("Don't make your contribution more informative than is required," see Grice 1975: 45–6).

The goal of this chapter is to clarify the ways in which the use of vague language relates to both of those maxims. Vagueness is a multifaceted notion, however. In the first part of this chapter, we start out by distinguishing two main manifestations of vagueness in language: pragmatic *imprecision*, and semantic *indeterminacy*, with more specific varieties of each. We then go on to explain in what sense vague language is a double-edged sword in relation to lying and truthfulness. First, we show that in

---

[1] "A vague belief has a much better chance of being true than a precise one, because there are more possible facts that would verify it" (Russell 1923: 91).

situations in which a cooperative speaker wishes to give information about a state of affairs about which she is uncertain, vagueness offers a resource for truthfulness: it avoids making more precise utterances which may be either false or not justifiably true (section 27.3). In situations in which a non-cooperative speaker is perfectly informed about the world, on the other hand, vagueness can be a deception mechanism. We distinguish two cases of that sort: cases in which the speaker is deliberately imprecise in order to hide information from the hearer, but remains literally truthful (section 27.4); and cases in which the speaker exploits the semantic indeterminacy of vague predicates to make utterances that are true in one sense, but false in another, what we call half-truths (section 27.5). The question is whether such half-truths should be counted as lies. The answer, we suggest, depends on the context: the lack of unequivocal truth is not always sufficient to declare falsity (section 27.6).

27.2 Varieties of Vagueness

Russell (1923) offered as a general definition that "a representation is vague when the relation of the representing system to the represented system is not one-one, but one-many." In the linguistic case, an expression is vague according to him if "there is not only one object that a word means, and not only one possible fact that will verify a proposition" (Russell 1923: 89–90). That is, the same utterance is compatible with several distinct meanings. This one-many relationship can be realized in several ways, and a merit of Russell's definition is that it covers a range of phenomena associated with linguistic vagueness. In what follows we distinguish four main manifestations: *generality*, *approximation*, *degree-vagueness*, and *open-texture*. Following several authors (see Pinkal 1995; Kennedy 2007; Solt 2015), we argue that generality and approximation are fundamentally cases of pragmatic imprecision, whereas degree-vagueness and open-texture are semantic phenomena, directly affecting the truth-conditions of expressions (see Figure 27.1).

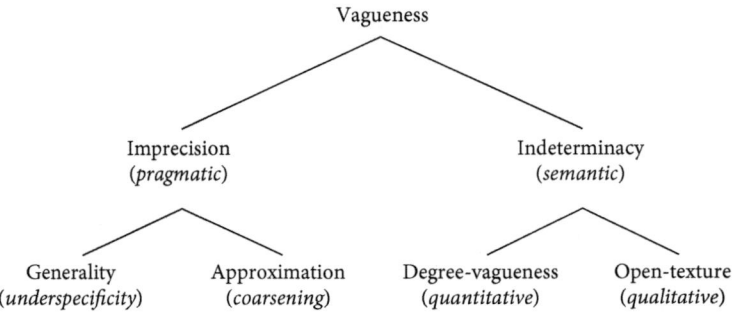

FIGURE 27.1 Varieties of linguistic vagueness.

27.2.1 Generality

A first instance of Russell's definition concerns the phenomenon of *generality* in language (being underspecific). Consider the following dialogue between a father and his son:

(2)   Q. Who did you see at the party?
      A. Some friends.

Let us assume that the son has ten friends, all known to the father. The son's answer is general in the sense that it is compatible with several more specific answers being true. The father cannot infer from the answer exactly which number of friends was seen. An answer like *two friends* would be more informative in that respect, but it would still be general, leaving the father uncertain as to which two-membered subset of the relevant set includes the friends seen by his son.

Important to note is that in this context a sentence like *I saw some friends* has completely clear truth-conditions, it simply means that the number of friends seen by the speaker is greater than zero. Vagueness in that case does not mean any indeterminacy in the statement of the truth-conditions of the sentence, but simply refers to the fact that the response to the question fails to be maximally informative.

Theorists of vagueness often dismiss generality as a central aspect for that matter (see Fine 1975; Keefe 2000). We find it important to keep it under consideration here, for the underspecificity of answers, although relative to the question under discussion, is a very common aspect of language use of particular relevance in relation to lying.

27.2.2 Approximation

A second illustration of Russell's definition of vagueness pertains to approximation. In cases of approximation an expression with precise truth-conditions is used to convey a meaning that differs from its literal meaning, but is close enough. As a result, the same expression is used with a coarser meaning (larger range of interpretations than its literal meaning). Consider the following dialogues:

(3)   Q. What do you make a month?
      A. 3,000 euros.

(4)   Q. What time did John arrive?
      A. He arrived at 3 o'clock.

(5)   Q. How old is she?
      A. She is 40.

In (3), the answer may be asserted by someone who knows the precise answer to actually be 3,287.23 euros. This is a case in which the speaker rounds off the actual number to a lower number, relying on the fact that it is more relevant to set the standard of precision to multiples of 1,000 euros than to a multiples of a single euro, let alone cents (see Krifka 2007). The same often happens with the other two examples: *3 o'clock* can be used when John in fact arrived at five past or five to (van der Henst et al. 2002), and *she is 40* could be used to refer to someone whose age is within a few months or even a few years of 40, depending on the context.

Approximation is not limited to numbering, but is also found in other domains, as exemplified in Austin's geometrical example (Austin 1962b; Lewis 1979):

(6) France is hexagonal.

The latter sentence would be false if taken to mean that France has precisely the shape of a hexagon, but we understand it to mean that it can be circumscribed to a reasonable approximation by a hexagon.

Cases of approximation are cases in which a semantically precise expression is used with slack (Lasersohn 1999). Importantly, there may not be an absolutely precise convention as to the range of meanings that are compatible with the use of an expression. When is it no longer fine to say *John is 40 years old*? What if John is 35 years old? Approximation is always relative to the context, to explicit or implicit standards of precision and to rounding rules, and how close a value needs to be to the literal meaning will often be at the speaker's discretion.

27.2.3 Degree-vagueness

The third aspect of vagueness we isolate concerns the quantitative indeterminacy attached to gradable expressions in particular (which we call degree-vagueness, following Alston 1964; Burks 1946 talks of linear vagueness). Consider the following variation on the dialogue between a father and his son:

(7) Q. How many people were at the party?
     A. Many people.

Here again, the answer is imprecise because compatible with a multiplicity of states of affairs obtaining (maybe 25 people were at the party, 50, or 100). Unlike *some*, however, *many* is not an expression for which we can state determinate truth conditions relative to a fixed countable domain. One way of viewing that phenomenon is as a form of context-dependence (see Sapir 1944; Partee 1989; Lappin 2000; Greer 2014; Egré and Cova 2015): whereas *some As are Bs* is true exactly if the number of As that are Bs is nonzero, *many As are Bs* would be true if the number of As that are Bs exceeds a context-sensitive number n (cardinal reading), or possibly if the number of As that are Bs exceeds a context-sensitive proportion α of the As or of some other comparison class (proportional reading). The setting of such parameters is problematic: assuming such threshold values, did the son intend *many* to mean *more than 5*, *more than a third*, or some other number? A remarkable fact about vague expressions such as *many* is that the speaker himself or herself need not have a precise idea of the values of such thresholds in order to apply the expression and to convey meaning.

Besides *many*, paradigmatic examples of vague expressions in that sense include gradable adjectives such as *tall, long, expensive, healthy*, etc., all of which accept degree-modification (as in *taller*) or modification by intensifiers (*very tall*) (see Kennedy 2007). Gradable adjectives give rise to familiar symptoms, in particular the admission of borderline cases of application and the susceptibility to sorites-reasoning (see Keefe 2000; Egré and Klinedinst 2011; Burnett 2016 for a more specific typology of gradable expressions). Borderline cases of application are cases for which it is unclear to the speaker whether the expression should apply or not: for example, it may be unclear whether a man 178 cm in height should be counted as *tall* or not. An important fact about borderline cases is, moreover, that they give rise to inconsistent verdicts both between and within subjects (see McCloskey and Glucksberg 1978). Cases of between-subject inconsistencies are often viewed as manifestations of the subjectivity and evaluativity of vague expressions: *many, tall, healthy, beautiful*, could mean different things without error depending on the speaker (Parikh 1994; Wright 1995; Kölbel 2004; Fara 2000; Raffman 2013; Kennedy 2013; Egré 2017; Verheyen et al. 2017). This subjectivity is important for an assessment of the falsity of vague sentences: the same vague sentence could be used truly relative to one speaker, but be viewed as false by another, depending on their context, interests, and evaluative standards (see in particular Kölbel 2004; McNally and Stojanovic 2017 on predicates of personal taste).

27.2.4 Open-texture

The fourth illustration of Russell's definition we single out concerns the openness of the respects constitutive of the meaning of an expression, what we call open-texture (following Waismann 1945; Burks 1946 talks of multidimensional vagueness, and Alston 1964 of combinatorial vagueness). This openness is found at different levels, and it has to do with polysemy and multidimensionality.

Already in the case of dimensional adjectives (such as *tall*), the selection of a comparison class is fundamental for the application of the adjective, but it can vary without limit, and it will impact the setting of a boundary between tall and not tall objects (*tall* for a building, for a basketball player, or for a fifth-grader, will mean different things, see Kamp 1975, Klein 1980).

For a number of gradable adjectives, moreover, several dimensions of comparison interact, and their number and structure is generally indeterminate, even when a comparison class has been fixed. Consider the adjective *healthy*. An indication that *healthy* is multidimensional is the occurrence of adjuncts such as *healthy in some respect, healthy in all respects* (Sassoon 2012). For example, *healthy* as applied to a meal could be predicated on whether it provides vitamins, or on whether it has a particular effect on blood pressure, or on some way of integrating those factors, and no definitive list of factors appears to be forthcoming.

The phenomenon of open texture is not limited to gradable adjectives, but it concerns the difficulty of providing necessary and sufficient conditions of applications for a vast number of expressions, including nominal expressions (Wittgenstein 1953 famously used the example of the word *game* to show the difficulty of providing a consistent and exhaustive list of defining criteria for that notion).

27.2.5 Representing vagueness

Degree-vagueness and open-texture can be thought of as forms of "referential multiplicity" (Raffman 2013). A convenient way of representing the meaning of a vague expression, following the supervaluationist tradition, is thus in terms of a set of admissible sharpenings or precisifications (Mehlberg 1958; Lewis 1970; Fine 1975; Kamp 1975). For an expression such as *tall*, for example, given a comparison class, the meaning can be represented by a set of precise intervals above a variable threshold; for an expression such as *healthy*, given a comparison class again, it may be thought of as a set of tuples consisting of variable respects and intervals on a common dimension set by those respects. Similarly for approximation: the meaning of *hundred* as used approximately can be represented by a set of numbers around 100 (Lasersohn 1999). Depending on the speaker, however, the range of such admissible sharpenings may differ.[2] Different speakers may also assign different weights to different sharpenings depending on the context (see Lassiter 2011; Lassiter and Goodman 2017 on probabilistic representations of vague meaning).

In this regard, the main difference between expressions such as *hundred* or *some students* on the one hand, and *tall* or *game* on the other, is that the former have determinate truth conditions. Because of that, generality and approximation are cases of *pragmatic vagueness*: by being general rather than more specific a speaker chooses to be less informative than she could be, and by being approximate she gives less information than what the expression literally means. Degree-vagueness and open-texture, on the other hand, are cases of *semantic vagueness*: the meaning of expressions such as *many, healthy,* or *game* is "intrinsically uncertain" (in the words of Peirce 1902: 748),

---

[2] This makes semantic vagueness close to lexical ambiguity, except that in the case of lexical ambiguity the meanings are supposed to be mentally far apart or disjoint (Keefe 2000; Pinkal 1995). Logically speaking, however, it is relevant to compare vagueness with ambiguity, since precisifications play the same role as disambiguations (see Lewis 1982). In the next section, we will see that vagueness, like ambiguity, can give rise to pragmatic equivocation.

that is, those expressions do not have constant truth-conditions across contexts and speakers.

With these distinctions in mind, we are now in a position to examine the ways in which vagueness interacts with the Gricean maxims. The Gricean maxims assume that conversation fundamentally rests on cooperation. As we know from game theory, however, speaker and hearer need not have their interests perfectly aligned, and sometimes they can diverge dramatically. It may be costly to reveal the truth, or to reveal the *whole* truth. Most of the time, however, making an assertion that the listener would recognize as false can be even more costly: if a false claim is exposed, the speaker incurs the risk of losing credibility, or greater costs (see Asher and Lascarides 2013). In the rest of this chapter, we distinguish two main classes of situations that motivate the use of vague language. On the one hand, there are situations where the speaker is *imperfectly informed* about the facts, and may simply wish to avoid speaking falsely by speaking too precisely. On the other hand, there are situations where the speaker is *perfectly informed* about the facts, but has an interest in hiding information from the hearer, and potentially to take advantage of the indeterminacy of vague expressions to bias or mislead.

27.3 AVOIDING ERROR

Grice's maxim of Quality enjoins one not to speak falsely, but also not to say things for which one lacks adequate evidence. One aspect in which the maxim of Quality justifies the use of vague language concerns cases where the speaker is uncertain about which precise state of affairs obtains (see Channell 1994; Frazee and Beaver 2010) or will obtain in the future (Channell 1985; van Deemter 2009).

Consider a situation in which you return from a party and are a fully cooperative speaker trying to convey maximum information. The party was attended by a group of people, but you do not know exactly how many there were, because you could not count them. Upon returning from the party, you are asked how many people were there. In this case, there is no number n for which you can truly and justifiably say: *there were exactly n people*. In order to respond truly and justifiably, the next option would be to specify an exact interval. Suppose you are sure that there were more than 20 people, and fewer than 200, but are uncertain of the point of fact in between. Then you may say:

(8) There were between 20 and 200 people.

The response is general in this case, but not very informative. It would be more informative to give your best estimate of a lower bound:

(9) At least 100 people.

But suppose there were in fact 93 people attending. The answer would be literally false, despite coming close to your assessment. On the other hand, you would not be wrong if you said:

(10)   a. About 100 people.
       b. Many people.

Semantic expressions such as *about* and *many* allow you to convey information truly in this case, compatibly with an indeterminate range of states of affairs obtaining. They allow you to avoid error, but also, somewhat surprisingly, to be more informative than you would if you tried to specify exact intervals without error.

Importantly, the hearer may have a different understanding of what to count as *many* from yours. Suppose you understand *many* to denote a range of sharp intervals (using the supervaluationist picture), with a probability distribution on them (some precisifications are more likely to you than other; see Lassiter 2011; Lassiter and Goodman 2017). The hearer may have a different probability distribution that rules out some of the intervals you consider possible, but you would still communicate successfully if the hearer ends up with a posterior distribution that includes the value you actually observed, and if it makes that value more likely than before you answered (see Parikh 1994; Lassiter 2011; Lassiter and Goodman 2017).

The point of the previous example is that vague language, in situations of uncertainty, may accomplish an optimal trade-off between the need to be truthful and the need to be informative (see Frazee and Beaver 2010). Use of vague language in situations of uncertainty is also modulated by the cost of speaking falsely, compared to the benefits of speaking accurately. An example discussed by van Deemter (2009) concerns cases of medical communication. Van Deemter points out that "a doctor who says 'These symptoms will disappear fairly soon' is less likely to get complaints, and to be sued, than one who says 'These symptoms will have disappeared by midnight'" (van Deemter 2009: 8).

Vague language, in summary, is a way of speaking truly and informatively in situations of uncertainty. This does not mean that vagueness is immune to falsity: suppose the symptoms disappear only after a month; then the patient may charge the doctor with incompetence, or even with having lied. The patient could complain that *fairly soon* was, in her perspective, incompatible with a time interval of a month. The doctor could deny having spoken falsely, on the other hand, by defending her own perspective. The relativity of vague interpretations to speakers makes charges of lies, as we will see, a delicate matter (see section 27.6).

27.4 HIDING INFORMATION

Let us now turn to cases where the speaker has no uncertainty about the world, but has an incentive to be noncooperative. Grice's Maxim of Quantity is twofold: it asks one to be as informative as required for the purpose of the conversation, but also to not be more informative than required. What counts as "required for the purpose of the conversation" is itself vague and heavily depends on the interests that speaker and hearer have in sharing information (Asher and Lascarides 2013). For a range of situations, a well-informed speaker can legitimately wish to retain information from the hearer, and so to be vague in order to limit cooperation.

Cases of what we called *generality* in the previous section are very common in that regard. Consider the dialogue in (2), repeated here.

(11) Q. Who did you see at the party?
      A. Some friends.

Let us assume that the father is actually interested in knowing whether his son saw a particular person, say Ann, whom he suspects his son of dating. The son, on the other hand, wishes to maintain his privacy. Assume the son saw Ann indeed, but also Don and Eli, two other friends known to the father. In this case, the son is giving a perfectly true answer, but he is not allowing the father to identify exactly whom he saw.

Compare with the example of the previous section. Assume you know this time that exactly sixty-three people attended the party, but have an interest not to reveal the exact number. You may choose to be underinformative by responding:

(12) Q. How many people were at the party?
      A. Fewer than a hundred.

The answer is literally true, but *partial* in the sense of Groenendijk and Stokhof (1982): it leaves possibilities open and fails to completely settle the question. Potentially, it is also misleading: for it triggers the implicature that it is compatible with your knowledge that there could have been ninety people or more attending (see Spector 2013). Such cases, in which a speaker is literally truthful but uses misleading implicatures, are called cases of misdirection by Asher and Lascarides (2013), who characterize them as instances of *rhetorical* as opposed to genuine Gricean cooperativity.[3]

Neither of the previous examples relies on utterances that are vague semantically, but we can find similar cases where a semantically vague expression is used to withhold information. Imagine nosey neighbors asking how much you paid for your apartment. Assume you know the exact price you paid, but do not want to reveal it:

(13) Q. How much did you buy your apartment?
      A. It was not too expensive.

---

[3] See in particular their discussion of *Bronston vs. United States* as an exploitation of literal truth to refute perjury, as well as the presentation of the case in Tiersma (2004). See Ransom et al. (2017) for a recent study comparing cases in which a truthful speaker may have an incentive to be completely uninformative to others where they may choose to be partially informative depending on the level of trust in the hearer.

An incentive to avoid being precise in this case is that you may want to avoid appearing either lucky (in case you paid less than your neighbors for the same size) or stupid (in case you paid more), or you may just want to give no indication of your assets. Use of a qualitative expression such as *expensive* is advantageous here because it avoids specifying a definite number, and it remains compatible with the preservation of truthfulness: we may assume that you are sincere in thinking that the price you paid was not expensive, even ahead of the dialogue (that assumption is not always warranted; see the next section).

Consider for comparison the following alternative answers, assuming the exact price you paid for your apartment is 220,000 euros:

(14) a. I paid 200,000 euros.
      b. I paid around 200,000 euros.
      c. I paid between 50,000 euros and 300,000 euros.

Answer (14a) is approximate in this case, but it does not signal that it is approximate. As pointed out by Meibauer (2014a), it may be truthfully asserted if the standard of precision in the context of the conversation is such that a difference of 20,000 euros would not be relevant. But the answer could be misleading, instead of just imprecise, if uttered with the intention of making your neighbors believe that you paid less than you actually did. For instance, it would count as false in a context in which the standard of precision needs to be maximal (say in the context of declaring taxes).

Answer (14b) makes the approximation explicit, and it is also semantically vague, owing to the use of the vague modifier *around*. Despite that, the answer remains more informative than the one in (13), for it lets your neighbors infer the actual price with less uncertainty than based on hearing *not too expensive*.

Answer (14c), finally, is neither approximate nor semantically vague: it states an exact interval but to create uncertainty. Like (13), it signals either that you do not know the price you paid, or that you do not want to answer the question precisely; however, the interval specified is so large here that the hearers would be better-founded in thinking that you do not want to answer the question. Also, the answer in (13) may end up being more informative than the one in (14c), despite relying on semantic vagueness, because upon hearing "not too expensive" the hearer is likely to narrow down the range of prices you potentially paid to a smaller interval than the one specified in (14c).[4]

27.5 MAKING HALF-TRUTHS

Besides cases in which a speaker is imprecise to hide information, there is a class of cases where the speaker can exploit the semantic indeterminacy of vague expressions

---

[4] This is because *I paid between 50,000 and 300,000 euros* scalarly implicates that it is possible you paid 51,000. With *not too expensive* this inference is not mandated at all. On the mechanism of such implicatures, see Fox (2014).

to produce utterances whose truth status is unclear: they are true under some way of resolving their vagueness, but that way can be tendentious or biased.[5]

Consider the following example (from C. List and L. Valentini, p.c.) where you receive an invitation for dinner. As a matter of fact, you would be free to go to that dinner, but have no inclination for it. Imagine the following dialogue:

(15) Q. Are you free to come for supper tomorrow?
A. Sorry, I have an engagement.

(16) Q. Are you free to come for supper tomorrow?
A. Sorry, I am busy.

In (15), your response ought to qualify as a lie. In the case of (16), the answer does not obviously count as a lie, but it does not clearly count as true either. One way of explaining the contrast is in terms of supervaluations (Fine 1975; Kamp 1975). On all admissible ways of sharpening the meaning of *I have an engagement*, the sentence would come out false (i.e., super-false). On the other hand, there are admissible ways of sharpening the meaning of *busy* for the sentence to count as true. *I am busy* may even be deemed super-true, that is true literally on all admissible ways of sharpening the meaning of *busy*, but this is moot: it depends on what is counted as an admissible precisification (see section 27.6). If you end up watching TV, you would obviously be *busy watching TV*, but at the time of utterance *busy* appears to convey that you have some obligation.

In our view, the answer in (16) is a half-truth, precisely because it is not clearly false, but not clearly true either. Concretely, *I am busy* offers a polite way of declining the invitation. A more informative alternative about the speaker's motives would be to say: *I am not very inclined*, but it would be clearly offensive. The intent of *I am busy* is partly to mislead, therefore, but consistent with satisfying a norm of politeness.[6]

A more extreme case of exploitation of semantic vagueness concerns President Bill Clinton's declarations about the nature of his relationship with Monica Lewinsky:

(17) I have never had sexual relations with Monica Lewinsky.

This case, importantly, is one where all parties had been fully informed of the relevant facts. To justify his claim without perjury, Bill Clinton took advantage of the open texture of the expression *sexual relations*, that is, of the lack of a clear definition. However, he did it not by making up a definition, but by exploiting an attempt made by his opponents to provide an explicit definition of the term "[engaging in]

---

[5] The term *half-truth* is used in a number of different senses in the literature. Our use is broadly compatible with Carson's (2010), who defines a half-truth to be a true statement that "selectively emphasize[s] facts that tend to support a particular interpretation or assessment of an issue" (57–8). We use *half-true* in the sense of *borderline true*.

[6] Thanks to C. List and L. Valentini for discussion of that aspect.

sexual relations" (see Tiersma 2004 for details).[7] Pressed to explain himself, Clinton's defense was:

(18) I thought the definition [of sexual relations, as read by Judge Wright] included any activity by the person being deposed, where the person was the actor and came in contact with those parts of the bodies with the purpose or intent of gratification, and excluded any other activity.

The way Bill Clinton defended himself can be put in supervaluationist terms again: it is not the case that on all ways of further precisifying the explicit definition proposed by his opponents, receiving oral sex counts as engaging in a sexual relation. Interestingly, in an earlier statement Bill Clinton commented about whether Monica Lewinsky had had "a sexual affair" with him as follows:

(19) Q. If she told someone that she had a sexual affair with you beginning in November of 1995, would that be a lie?
A. It's certainly not the truth. It would not be the truth.

In this occurrence, Clinton appeared to concede that the allegation would not necessarily be false, but without counting as true. In supervaluationist terms again, there are some admissible ways of precisifying *sexual affair* that would make Lewinsky's supposed statement true, yet *not all* ways of precisifying *sexual affair* would make it true. Overall, Bill Clinton was able to exploit the semantic indeterminacy of those expressions in order to avoid the charge of perjury. He would have been convicted if, from the jury's perspective, all admissible ways of precisifying the meaning had led to the sentence being false, but the jury in that case failed to rule out Clinton's way from being admissible.

27.6 Are half-truths lies?

Let us take stock. In section 27.4, we saw that in response to a question, a speaker can be underspecific without committing any lie. In section 27.5, however, we saw that semantic indeterminacy can be used to produce sentences whose truth status is unclear, what we called 'half-truths'. Should not half-truths be considered lies, however, given that those utterances fail to be clearly true?

---

[7] The explicit definition in question is: "A person engages in 'sexual relations' when the person knowingly engages in or causes contact with the genitalia, anus, groin, breast, inner thigh, or buttocks of any person with an intent to gratify or arouse the sexual desire of any person." "Contact" means "intentional touching, either directly or through clothing."

First of all, utterances like (16) or (17) may typically be uttered insincerely. In the case of (16), I may think to myself *in petto* "well, I am not really busy ... " or "well, I am busy watching TV," and Clinton may have silently thought to himself "well, except for an oral sexual relation." Those utterances then may be viewed as cases of *amphiboly* or *mental reservation* (Bok 1999; Mullaney 1980; Adler 1997), whereby the actual meaning that the speaker has in mind is in fact different from the meaning the hearer can reasonably infer.

To avoid that complication, let us assume that each utterance is made sincerely at the time it is uttered, and without mental reservation (without the speaker making any silent addition). In supervaluationist terms, the question we are asking is whether an utterance that fails to be super-true (true on all admissible precisifications) ought to be considered false on normative grounds. We think the answer to this question is nonobvious, for it depends on two parameters: the definition of what to count as an admissible precisification, and the choice of a standard for truth.

Regarding the first issue, most people would agree that Clinton's utterance is false *simpliciter*, despite being true under some very specific sharpening of the meaning of *sexual relation*, for they would deem that particular precisification to be inadmissible in an ordinary conversational context. In the legal context, however, Clinton was successful in making that sharpening relevant, and since it was incumbent on the jury to show that his statement was unequivocally false, it allowed for his sentence not to qualify as a lie, despite the sentence's not qualifying as a clear truth either.

This brings us to the second issue. Theories of vagueness differ on the standards whereby a sentence can be truthfully uttered. Supervaluationism treats sentences as true *simpliciter* if they are true on all admissible precisifications, but there is a dual theory, subvaluationism, which treats sentences as true *simpliciter* when true under some precisification (Hyde 1997). Subvaluationism is very liberal in that it predicts that a sentence and its negation can both be true then.[8]

In practice, the standards for truth and falsity appear to depend on the context. In the Clinton lawsuit, it was sufficient for the sentence to be true under some sharpening to not be considered a lie by the jury. In the class-action lawsuit that opposed Athena Hohenberg to the Ferrero company, on the other hand, the complaint was that *healthy* was used misleadingly for a product containing too much fat and sugar. Ferrero's defense was based on the fact that *healthy* is multidimensional, and that their product was at least healthy in the respects of bringing chocolate, having low sodium content, and so on.[9] Despite that, the court eventually forbade Ferrero from advertising the product as *healthy*. The court agreed that it is not enough for a sentence like *this product is healthy* to be true on just some ways of precisifying *healthy* in order for the sentence to avoid being misleading or to count as a lie, presumably in this case because the ways in which the

---

[8] This implies that *I am busy* and *I am not busy* would both be true in a context in which either is true under some admissible sharpening. But each of them would also be false, since false under some sharpening. The upshot would be that the sentence both is a lie, and fails to be a lie.

[9] See http://www.scpr.org/news/2011/02/10/23912/a-mom-sues-nutella-maker-for-deceptive-advertising/.

sentence is false outweigh those in which it is true (Ferrero's use would in fact violate the Gricean maxim of Relevance).

In general, however, the Ferrero example may be more emblematic of the ways in which vague language is interpreted. Grice's maxim of Manner recommends avoiding ambiguity (see Grice 1975: 46). There is evidence, however, that in cases in which a vague predicate is used without qualification, and where two interpretations are available for the predicate, a weak one and a strong one, the stronger interpretation will be the default (see Dalrymple et al. 1998). Upon hearing *this person is tall*, the default is to get that the person is clearly tall, rather than borderline tall (Alxatib and Pelletier 2011; Cobreros et al. 2012, 2015). Likewise, when saying *this product is healthy*, the default is probably to hear *this product is healthy in most respects*, rather than just ... *in some respects*. As a result, to say of a product that it is *healthy* without qualification would suggest that the product is more healthy than unhealthy: in the Ferrero case, this pragmatic enrichment is deceptive, and can legitimately be considered a lie.

We see, in summary, that often an utterance will be deemed a lie if it fails to be unambiguously true. But sometimes, as the Clinton case shows us, it might fail to be deemed a lie if it is not unambiguously false. Whichever of those two will prevail appears to depend not just on the *existence* of ways for a sentence to be true, but also on how *relevant* those ways are to the parties involved in the conversation.

27.7 CONCLUSIONS

Let us recapitulate the main lessons of our discussion of the relation between lying and vagueness. To begin with, we have seen that vagueness provides a way for a cooperative speaker to remain truthful in situations in which she is trying to communicate information about which she is uncertain. Vagueness may then be described as a way of avoiding error and therefore lies. This concerns all cases in which the use of qualitative but vague vocabulary (as in *many, long, expensive*) makes it unnecessary to commit oneself to precise quantitative expressions for which one fails to have adequate evidence. As opposed to that, we have highlighted two kinds of cases in which vagueness can be used deceptively. The first are cases in which a well-informed speaker has motives to hide or retain information. In such cases the speaker is deliberately imprecise and partial, but need not tell lies in the strict sense of the term. She may however be misleading if the partial information given triggers false implicatures. The second kind concerns what we have called half-truths, utterances whose status is borderline between true and false, depending on how vague expressions in them are interpreted. Such cases are more problematic. An utterance will be misleading if it is true only under some very peculiar precisification. On the other hand, the indeterminacy of vague expressions can make it difficult to prove that a vague utterance is a lie, as opposed to an expression whose intended meaning was misunderstood.

Acknowledgements

Thanks to Sam Alxatib, Nick Asher, Rae Langton, Christian List, Neri Marsili, Yael Sharvit, Stephanie Solt, Benjamin Spector, Laura Valentini, and Steven Verheyen for helpful conversations on the topics of this chapter, and to Jörg Meibauer for helpful comments and for his editorial assistance. We also thank Emar Maier for valuable advice regarding how to convert the chapter from Latex to MS Word, as well as the Lorentz Center and the organizers of the workshop "The Invention of Lying: Language, Logic, and Cognition", held in Leiden in January 2017, where Jörg Meibauer invited us to contribute this chapter. P.E. thanks the ANR Program TrilLogMean ANR-14-CE30-0010-01 for funding. B.I. thanks the Direction Générale de l'Armement for doctoral funding. Both researchers acknowledge grants ANR-10-LABX-0087 IEC and ANR-10-IDEX-0001-02 PSL* for research carried out at the Department of Cognitive Studies of ENS.

CHAPTER 28

LYING, METAPHOR, AND HYPERBOLE

CLAUDIA CLARIDGE

28.1 INTRODUCTION

"Honest deceptions" is what Leech (1969: 166 f.) labelled hyperbole, litotes, and irony, because "in a sense they misrepresent the truth" but do not deceive as long as the hearer is "aware of the true state of affairs." Metaphor he likens to "pretence—making believe that tenor and vehicle are identical" (Leech 1969: 151), but without mentioning any deceptive potential. Clark's (1996: 360–78) concept of "joint pretence" goes in a similar direction: "staged communicative acts" such as hyperbole, irony, and understatement (but apparently not metaphor) are not insincere, although they stand in salient contrast to the actual situation, because they are based on a pretence shared by both speaker and hearer. Treatments of hyperbole and metaphor in the literature thus commonly refer to the fact that 'what is said' is strictly speaking false (i.e., exhibits no world–word fit) but that nevertheless they are not meant as lies. Gibbs (1999: 155) lists overstatement (i.e., hyperbole) as one type of deceptive act, the others being lies, evasions, concealments, and collusions; whereas lies are intended "to create a belief in the receiver contrary to the truth or facts," hyperbole is intended to "magnify facts or data."

Closeness to or a potential for deception is therefore a possibility for both metaphor and hyperbole. The reasons for this are varied; they lie in the nature of the two devices as well as in the minds and actions of speaker and hearer.[1] It is in the nature of the devices that they are in some sense non-literal (inter alia figurative, context-dependent, non-automatic/marked),[2] providing no direct and simply decodable representation of

---

[1] Speaker and hearer stand equally for writer and reader.
[2] Cf. Ariel (2002) on the problems surrounding literal meaning, which cannot be treated here.

the state of affairs. Metaphors such as *he is a pig* or *biting cold* exhibit unusual (though not necessarily unconventional) reference and/or collocations based on processes such as similarity, analogy, and recategorization.[3] Hyperboles such as *be back in a second* and *a thousand phone calls to make this morning* contrast with more literal expressions (e.g., *in a few minutes, fifty/many calls*) by adding more semantic content within the same category (more time/speed, greater amount), which exceeds the limits of (extralinguistic) fact or appropriateness and often reaches extreme or absurd levels. Superficially, both devices are akin to lies in saying something that is not 'correct': for example, *I'll have to work till midnight / I'm a real slave to my company* may be (metaphorically) overstating the amount of time one has to work, perhaps in order to complain, or it may be a lie/evasion/deception so as to have an 'excuse' for not meeting somebody in the evening. One way to resolve such ambiguities is by getting to know the intentions of the speaker, i.e., whether she wanted to be hyperbolically/ metaphorically expressive or to actively mislead the hearer, the latter intent being a central component of deception/lying (Gibbs 1999: 155). Of course, the speaker's intentions can also include being purposefully ambiguous between the two options. In the mind of the speaker, at any rate, a question such as hyperbole *or* lie *or* both does not arise because it is clear. The difficulty lies with the hearer in inferring S's intentions and taking an utterance like the above either as an exaggeration or as a lie, for which she needs as much shared contextual knowledge as possible. The deceptive potential of metaphors and hyperbole is therefore 'positive' on the part of the speaker, in the sense that she can use it strategically and intentionally, but 'negative' on the side of the hearer, as she is left with the perhaps difficult task of inferring the one or the other and, if she chooses wrongly, being deceived.

This chapter deals with the issue in the following way. Section 28.2 presents selected theoretical approaches to highlight how closely or distantly the relationship 'metaphor/hyperbole versus lie' can be constructed. In section 28.3, the functional side is explored, especially as regards how far there is an overlap between the functions of deceiving and those typically attributed to metaphor and hyperbole respectively. The two parts of section 28.4 pick out certain types and uses of metaphor and hyperbole which either blur the distinction between them and lying or highlight/sharpen it.

28.2 THEORETICAL PERSPECTIVES

The relationship of metaphor or hyperbole to truth and falsehood, deception, and lying may depend on the theoretical approach taken to them. Some views from the fields of

---

[3] Defining metaphor and hyperbole in a nutshell and regardless of theoretical alignment is actually not possible. The brief characterizations here are simply guidelines for this chapter.

rhetoric, philosophy, Gricean pragmatics, relevance theory, and cognitive linguistics will be presented here in a selective and exemplary fashion.[4]

Classical rhetoric, for which Quintilian will serve as an example here, paid considerable attention to persuasive linguistic devices. Quintilian principally recognizes the role of falsehood and deception in oratory, which is legitimate in deceiving the audience but unproblematic as the orator himself is not deceived and the opinions expressed therefore not false (*Institutio Oratoria* II, 17). As to the deceptive potential of individual uses, he notes it for hyperbole but not for metaphors (*Institutio Oratoria* VIII, 6). He states that hyperbole lies (cf. *veri superiectio; ultra fidem*), but it is neither false in itself as the speaker does not assert by it (*non adfirmamus*) nor means to deceive. It is in fact proper (*decens*) and even a virtue (*virtus*) when what is being described is of an abnormal magnitude (*naturalem modum excessit*). With regard to metaphors he sees them as either a necessity (when no other word is available), as an ornament, or, crucially, as a means of making the message clearer. He only admits that an excessive use of metaphors may lead to obscurity of expression, thus causing comprehension problems—but apparently no deception (ibid.).

Philosophers have given ample attention to metaphor, but not to hyperbole, wherefore the latter will not be dealt with here. Also, we will concentrate on only one particular philosophical view, that by Davidson (1978), who explicitly picks up the issue metaphor—lying:

> ... lying, like making a metaphor, concerns not the meaning of words but their use. It is sometimes said that telling a lie entails saying what is false; but this is wrong. Telling a lie requires not that what you say be false but that you think it false. Since we usually believe true sentences and disbelieve false, most lies are falsehoods; but in any particular case this is an accident. The parallel between making a metaphor and telling a lie is emphasized by the fact that the same sentence can be *used,* with meaning unchanged, for either purpose. So a woman who believed in witches but did not think her neighbor a witch might say, "She's a witch," meaning it metaphorically; the same woman, still believing the same of witches and her neighbor but intending to deceive, might use the same words to very different effect.
>
> (Davidson 1978: 42–3)

His point is that there is no metaphorical meaning, but only the 'literal' one—and this is usually false. Nevertheless, deception does not necessarily follow, as Davidson admits a "metaphorical truth" (Davidson 1978: 41), i.e., what a metaphorical use makes us aware of, the "visions, thoughts, and feelings inspired" by it, which can be true (or also false).

---

[4] Needless to say, the almost infinite number of approaches to metaphor cannot be given adequate treatment; cf. for example Rolf (2005) for an overview. Hyperbole, in contrast, has not received as much attention.

Gricean pragmatics,[5] with its legs in both philosophy and linguistics, is ultimately based on the concept of conversational implicature linked to the cooperative principle and its associated maxims (cf. Grice 1989c). In the case of quiet and unostentatious violation of a maxim, the speaker is "liable to mislead" (Grice 1989c: 30), i.e., getting close to lying. This is particularly likely if the quality and quantity maxims are involved, which are exactly the two groups relevant for metaphor and hyperbole interpretation. Both such interpretations arise by way of implicature (and the hearer's inference thereof) via the flouting or exploitation of a maxim, i.e., the blatant failure to fulfil it. The difference between lying and metaphor/hyperbole is thus the manifestness to the hearer of the non-fulfilment of a maxim—but not the types of maxims infringed, as these can be identical. It is the first maxim of quality, "Do not say what you believe to be false," that is flouted in both metaphor and hyperbole according to Grice (metaphor: *you are the cream in my coffee*; hyperbole: *every nice girl loves a sailor*, Grice 1989c: 34); in hyperbole the second quantity maxim, "Do not make your contribution more informative than is required," may also be relevant (Claridge 2011: 135–8). In Grice's approach the words ('what is said') of a metaphor or hyperbole are usually false (i.e., in conflict with extralinguistic reality), but the implicature may be true (e.g., 'you are the best part of my life'). Recognizability (through blatant flouting) makes such uses undeceptive, but it is nevertheless possible to see them as lies owing to their counterfactuality (cf. Meibauer 2014a: 171). However, it may also be the case that the implicature is false (Grice 1989c: 39) or not something the speaker believes to be the case (Meibauer 2005: 1378, 1380). In the expressions *the world's worst [loud] speakers / the shittiest speakers on earth* (Santa Barbara Corpus of Spoken American English (2000ff), Text 2 (SBC2)) uttered in response to praise about the speakers' great live-like sound quality 'what is said' is false: the owner of the speakers is a middle-class Californian who can be assumed to possess reasonable speakers and the likelihood of the speakers being really the worst of the world is negligible. A possible implicature 'the speakers were cheap' (assumption: low price equals low quality) is almost certainly also false, given the usual consumer power and behaviour of the middle classes. In this case, this implicature would thus constitute a lie. However, this might not be the contextually most relevant implicature (jocularity and modesty issues are more relevant). Thus, while a number of hyperboles and metaphors may have (some) false implicatures, their lying potential will depend on their communicative relevance in the utterance situation (Meibauer 2005: 1391).

Relevance theory is a post-Gricean approach, which has abandoned both the maxim of truthfulness (i.e., quality) and the concept of overt violations. The former also severs the link between lies and tropes (which is at least implicit in Grice), as the literal-figurative distinction and thus the falsity of what is said are usually not an issue (but cf. Carston and Wearing 2011 on some metaphors). Wilson and Sperber (2004: 619–21) treat

---

[5] Neo-Griceans will be ignored here, although some conventionalized metaphors and hyperboles, treated in section 28.4.2 in respect of salience, can also be seen as working via generalized conversational implicatures (e.g., Levinson 2000).

metaphor, hyperbole, and (typically non-figurative) loose uses such as *a square face* in the same manner, all of them being subjected to the same comprehension process based on encyclopedic assumptions (but see Rubio-Fernández, Wearing, and Carston 2015 for further differentiation).[6] They are different but equal means of achieving optimal relevance, their explicit content is somewhat indeterminate, and they lead to a cluster of weak implicatures, i.e., implicatures that are not singly essential for arriving at an optimally relevant and satisfying interpretation but are equally possible, not individually necessary ones (e.g., for the metaphor *John has a square mind*: somewhat rigid in his thinking, does not easily change his mind, is a man of principle etc., Wilson and Sperber 2004: 620). Calculating implicatures stops as soon as optimal relevance is reached by the hearer. An irrelevant implicature like the one above in the loudspeaker example might therefore not be derived at all, thus also excluding or minimizing the possibility for false implicatures/lying by implicature.

With regard to cognitive linguistics, conceptual metaphor theory and psycholinguistic research on figurative language comprehension need to be mentioned. Conceptual metaphor theory, originating in Lakoff and Johnson (1980), crucially makes the point that metaphors are a way of thinking (not simply a matter of language), i.e., based on a whole system of conceptual associations, and deeply grounded in our embodied interaction with the world. Metaphors are often not optional, thus not based on speaker choice or intention, but unavoidable, e.g., the concept TIME being expressed by means of SPACE (*a long time*) and MOTION (*the time has come*) or thoroughly entrenched in a whole culture, e.g., TIME IS MONEY (*waste time*). The pervasiveness of metaphors and non-literalness in a strict sense has become obvious. In this approach the question of falsity, truthfulness, or deception does not arise, unless one wanted to say that our whole thinking, and even some of our experience, are false. Regarding the cultural and social embedding, Gibbs (1994: 393–4) also points out with regard to hyperbole that it need not violate truthfulness as the expressed beliefs of the speaker need not be (identical to) their own but somebody else's, society's, or reflecting a general cultural norm.

28.3 THE FUNCTIONAL PERSPECTIVE

This section deals with whether there is potential overlap in what the speaker wants to achieve when using either a metaphor, hyperbole, or a lie. The primary aim of lying is inducing a wrong belief in the hearer about the state of affairs and/or about the speaker's belief (misleading/deceiving the hearer), but this may be accompanied by or even serve

---

[6] Cf. also the example of *marathon* in Carston and Wearing (2011: 287), which can be used loosely, hyperbolically, or metaphorically. Also, many uses of *always, all, never*, etc. could be equally classified as simply loose or as hyperbolically loose.

other (persuasive) aims. Metaphor and hyperbole do not have such a clear core aim, but an array of different functions.

Of the various functions of hyperbole mentioned in Roberts and Kreuz (1994), Colston and Keller (1998), Colston and O'Brien (2000), McCarthy and Carter (2004), Cano Mora (2006), Claridge (2011), it is the one connected to politeness (Cano Mora 2006; Claridge 2011) that presents a potential link with lying. For example, hyperbolic expressions are used to express exaggerated praise of the addressee (e.g., in compliments), exaggerated reasons for non-compliance with the hearer's wishes (e.g., in refusals, apologies), and minimized cost to the addressee (e.g., in requests) as in (1 a–c) respectively.

(1)   a. You look <u>gorgeous</u> today!
       b. [on coming home late for dinner] There were <u>thousands of people</u> at Tesco.
       c. Can you lend me a hand for <u>just a minute</u>?

These may be linked to so-called white or prosocial lies (cf. Meibauer 2014a: 152–4), i.e., lies that have an underlying positive interactional intention.[7] (1a) is benevolent for the addressee as it is intended to make them feel good; as long as the speaker thinks the addressee looks 'nice' this is more of a hyperbole than a lie, but if the speaker thinks the hearer looks awful it turns into a lie. (1b) protects the speaker, but potentially also the hearer, because if the excuse is accepted it will prevent an argument. Again, if there were in fact many people or long queues the interpretation may be tilted towards a hyperbolic interpretation, but if the speaker is late because she went for a coffee with an acquaintance it is a lie. (1c) is somewhat more problematic, as superficially it profits only the speaker to downplay the time expense on the part of the addressee (whose potential for refusal is thus minimized). On a more general level, however, it fosters social goodwill, as it recognizes that imposition should be minimized, all other things being equal. It may be accepted as hyperbole,[8] as opposed to a lie, as long as the job really does not take more than, say, five minutes. In discussing these examples, the degree of difference between words and reality has been used to differentiate between hyperbole (smallish, reconcilable difference) and lying (large difference). Alternatively one might also regard all these cases as straightforward lies (simply because there is no complete world–word fit), or one might consider them all as ambivalent cases.

Roberts and Kreuz (1994) and Goatly (1997) list a number of metaphor functions, but only Goatly's functions of reconceptualization (Goatly 1997: 152), ideology (155), and disguise might be relevant for potential overlap. These have in common that they are used to instil a certain (new/changed) belief in the hearer—a belief (or

---

[7] Of the eight principal reasons for deceptions given by Gibbs (1999: 157), (b) manipulation of interaction, (c) protecting image, (d) avoiding confrontation, and (e) preventing discomfort for others potentially lead in the same direction.

[8] The hyperbole here is also linked to a common loose use of quantifiers, cf. Labov (1984).

implicature) which may of course be false or misleading. Political labels like those in (2) may be a case in point:

(2) a. States like these [North Korea, Iran, Iraq—CC], and their terrorist allies, constitute an <u>axis of evil</u>, arming to threaten the peace of the world (G. W. Bush, State of the Union Address, 2002).
b. The <u>Arab Spring</u> has become more a term of disillusionment than of hope (*Foreign Policy*, July 21, 2015).

The choice of *axis* in (2a) invites H to (re)conceptualize these three very different countries as a unified grouping with a common reductive political aim. Once reconceptualization has taken root it may influence actions. Political *spring* in (2b) with its origins in the liberal nineteenth-century European revolutions and echoes of the Prague Spring of 1968 carries ideological baggage: it reflects Western concepts regarding statehood, democracy, etc. and imposes these expectations on the Arab context. This may simply be an optimistic misapplication, but it may also be an intentional attempt at steering perceptions. The disguise function is connected by Goatly (1997: 158–60) to euphemism, among other things. The term *golden handshake* 'generous payment on leaving one's job', for example, hides the fact that the underlying message concerns lay-offs; it could be seen as a half-truth focusing on the more positive aspect of the matter. Such uses constitute covert (or indirect) communication, which shields the user from the full responsibility for what is said. Take the following advertising copy for sneakers:

(3) STRUT LIKE A FISH
Have you ever seen a trout cut through water? That fish has moves. Although he'll never know the pleasure of jumping from rock to rock ... But don't pity the trout. Get in there with it. Walk hand in fin. Because you're wearing the [Brandname]. And that means <u>your feet have gills</u> that breathe water in and drain it right back out again. We've evolved a lot in twenty years. Now get out there. Amphibiously yours, [Company name].

The metaphor implies that your feet will not get wet but as this is not stated directly the firm cannot be nailed down to this message. The metaphor thus navigates the middle ground between truth and falsehood.

28.4 METAPHOR AND HYPERBOLE IN USE

All kinds of non-literal speech, whether indirect, figurative, or vague, are pervasive in everyday conversation, and listeners usually seem to have no problems in inferring a reasonable message, close to the intended one (cf. Gibbs 1999: 145). Speakers can, however, help or hinder this process by choosing forms[9] that clear or muddy the waters, respectively. In the latter case figurative speech comes closer to lying, which is said to be amazingly common in everyday communication as well (Gibbs 1999: 157–8).

28.4.1 Blurring the distinction of lying

Hyperbole may be more prone than metaphors to be understood wrongly (and thus to be perceived as falsehood) because what is said does not constitute "a conceptual discrepancy with respect to the real world" but only offers a description "in terms of disproportionate dimensions" (Haverkate 1990: 103). The maxim flouting is thus per se more blatant in metaphors. Experimental results by Rubio-Fernández, Wearing, and Carston (2013: 62–3, 2015: 37–8) confirm this: hearers needed significantly more time to reject the literal and false interpretations of hyperboles than those of metaphors. The authors explain this by the "greater similarity between the (true) hyperbolic interpretation and the (false) literal meaning," as opposed to the clearer difference in metaphors. Not all hyperboles may be equal in this respect, however. Claridge (2011: 10) pointed to the degree of contrast between what is said and the actual state of affairs, which appears as a continuum in realizations of hyperbole; cf. also Colston and Keller (1998: 502, 510) mentioning such degrees as slight, moderate, extreme, and outlandish. Those with the greatest degree of contrast are hyperboles realized as metaphors (to a lesser degree also as metonymies), as well as absurd and extreme cases, which will not be in danger of being mistaken for lies (cf. section 28.4.2) because they represent "impossible" cases (Colston and Keller 1998: 507). It is "realistic" and "possible but not probable" instances (Colston and Keller 1998: 507) which can be tricky, as a fairly small contrast blurs the line to falsehood in the interpretation process. This can be illustrated with one of Colston and Keller's scenarios:

> (4) A married couple went on a vacation to a country where the climate was usually very cool. When the couple arrived, it was actually 80 degrees.
> a. impossible: It's a million degrees here.
> b. possible but improbable: *It's 120 degrees here.*
> c. realistic: It's 90 degrees here.
>
> (Colston and Keller 1998: 507)

(4a) is easy to identify as hyperbole (mainly through its conventionality, cf. section 28.4.2), for (4b) the hearer will need some amount of world knowledge about the country in question—whereas for (4c), the hearer will need very precise contextual knowledge in order to arrive at a hyperbolic identification and interpretation. If spoken

---

[9] The focus here lies on *linguistic* forms and cues, i.e., non-verbal behaviour, important though it can be for distinguishing deception and veracity, will be ignored.

directly in context, there is no problem with (4b, c), but if used later in telling the holiday story to a friend, there may be: she may take the 90 or even the 120 degrees at face value.

There are some registers and discourse domains in which figures of speech are pervasively used for persuasive purpose and in which therefore there might be a higher incidence of their use in ways indeterminate between metaphorical/hyperbolic implicatures and falsehoods. Hearers may thus have to be more careful in sorting out 'true' and 'false' in some texts than in others. Advertising and political discourse are the ones that come prominently to mind (cf. Goatly 1997; Charteris-Black 2005; Gibbs and Colston 2012), cf. examples (2) and (3) above. Metaphor in politics can be used to alter people's perceptions, attitudes, and especially emotions and as such they can be exploited for planting extralinguistically unwarranted ('false') conclusions. (5) comes from the context of political debate and a referendum concerning bilingual Spanish–English education in Arizona:

(5) They consider <u>English fluency the key to unlock the handcuff of poverty</u>, a key they themselves never possessed.
(quoted from Johnson 2005 in Gibbs and Colston 2012: 232)

Instead of seeing bilingualism as an asset and a chance in life, the quote construes it negatively, with Spanish as the language on the negative side. Hearers, here voters, are led to the conclusion that the state should not support such an apparently negative state of affairs. Equally, the use of metaphors such as *flood, avalanche* in the context of migrants and refugees makes a human plight sound like a natural catastrophe which countries need to be protected from. Hyperbolic *flood* used in the case of a few hundred or maybe thousand refugees may be taken as more 'false' than when applied to millions of them, but the implicated belief will be false in either case.

This leads us to another point, namely, the fact that human perception and memory can be influenced by word choice has been demonstrated by Loftus and Palmer (1974). They asked the question "About how fast were the cars going when they contacted / hit / bumped into / collided with / smashed into each other?" after showing films involving car accidents. Depending on which of the verbs forming a continuum of strength was used in the question, people estimated the speed of the cars from an average of 31.8 mph (for *hit*) to 40.8 mph (for *smash*). Verb choice and speed estimate also correlated with the presence of a 'false' memory, namely the presence of broken glass at the accident scene. This indicates that choice of, e.g., *smash*, led to an assessment of greater seriousness for the event and to the assumption of the presence of other elements in line with the assumed seriousness. As (hyperbolic) metaphors include such differences of degree they can also (be used to) create false impressions and conclusions.

28.4.2 Highlighting the distinction of lying

Lies are unobtrusive in order to fulfil their aim; they have no preferred form and are completely situation-dependent. Anything in hyperboles and metaphors that goes in the opposite direction thus highlights the distinction from lying and prevents their misinterpretation as falsehoods. Blatant flouts, metapragmatic marking, as well as common and conventional forms, are thus characteristics of interest here.

All those cases where speakers make their flouts absolutely obvious are well-distinguished from lying. Metaphors (including metaphorical hyperbole) with target and source domains semantically far apart, in particular when both are formally present in an utterance like *Chomskyan* (also a metonymy) and *steamroller* in (6a), are not likely to be mistaken. Similarly, hyperboles based on large contrast, i.e., often extreme and even potentially absurd ones like (6b), will be easily recognized for what they are:

(6) a. The <u>Chomskyan steamroller crushed</u> Sapir and Whorf and made sure they were <u>struck off the linguistics canon</u>.
(Blommaert 2005)
   b. So he got this super de-luxe model [car] <u>with 25 wheels</u> …
(Claridge 2011: 22)

The clearer the flout, the clearer the message to the hearer to look for the truly intended meaning.

It is useless and therefore impossible to metapragmatically indicate lying, insincerity, etc. while in the act of purposefully lying (cf. Haverkate 1990: 102 **I lie that I have seen John*). Both metaphors and hyperbole can be marked accordingly and still function more or less as expected, however. The examples in (7) and (8) label hyperbolic respectively metaphorical uses (in italics) with a term directly describing the figure of speech. While the labelling clarifies that no misinformation is intended, it also interestingly makes the hyperbole in (7) stronger and its author more trustworthy—the former especially through the accompanying concessions and contrasts (*though* …, *but* …), the latter by showing the writer to be aware of a potential problem and to be upfront about it.

(7) a. It is <u>perhaps overstating</u> the case to say that *motorists can speed with impunity in residential areas,* <u>but it is certainly true that the limit is widely disregarded and rarely enforced</u>.
(BNC (British National Corpus 2001) C8F 94)
   b. It would recognise, too, that industrial democracy cannot be conjured into being overnight, no more than was political democracy, no more than was the joint stock company as the common expression of industrial capitalism. <u>It may be an exaggeration—though not by much</u>—to observe that *industrial democracy stands now where political democracy did before the Great Reform Bill of 1832.*
(BNC EF4 986) (Claridge 2011: 119, 120)

(8) a. Roughly, and somewhat metaphorically, we can say that something of the following sort goes on when successful communication takes place. *The speaker ... chooses some message he wants to convey to his listeners: some thought he wants them to receive ... This message is encoded in the form of a phonetic representation ... This representation is decoded into a representation of the same message that the speaker originally chose to convey.*

(BNC CK1 811-817)

b. The immediacy of this world of conflict demands that regardless of his [= policeman's] proximity to the metaphorical *dirt* [= criminals] he is controlling, he needs to erect and maintain social and psychological barriers and separate himself conceptually from the 'prig'.

(BNC A0K 979)

Metalinguistic signalling can thus be a kind of honesty marker and, potentially more important, a safety net for the user. With the explicit uses of *metaphorical(ly)* in (8a, b), the writers distance themselves from the full literal import of their verbal choices. The marking indicates something like 'take my words with a pinch of salt' (8a) and 'this is perhaps not my own perspective/opinion' (8b). Such marking generally alerts addressees to alternative (usually less salient) meanings, as pointed out by Givoni, Giora, and Bergerbest (2013), which is not something one would want to do with lying. Metalinguistic reference to lying, if it occurs as in (9), is also different in so far as it functions within a repair mechanism, i.e., it cancels the earlier statement and corrects it (*half five > half six*); note also that it follows the statement referred to, unlike the labels in (7, 8). *Lie* itself is presumably here also used in a loose sense, not its strict meaning.

(9) Raymond ... I was up the park this morning Willy *at half five.*—Kylie: Yeah?—Raymond: It was, I tell a lie, *sorry half six.* Lovely it was.

(BNC KDN 3882-5)

A less direct signal than those in (7, 8) is *literally* in (10), which evokes figurativeness, and often has the somewhat paradoxical effect of intensifying and thus strongly asserting the hyperbole or metaphor.

(10) a. I will buy it because I have an addiction to the printed word. If I am caught without something to read *I will* literally *break out in a cold sweat.*

(Claridge 2011: 110)

b. It is the crowning folly of the Park, and *impregnates,* literally, *the whole district about the north end.*

(Goatly 1997: 173)

Other signals treated by Goatly (1997) or Claridge (2011), such as hedges of all types (*may, perhaps, in a way, kind of*), do not distinguish between figures of speech and lying, as they can occur in either case.

While metaphors and hyperbole have no fixed form by which they can be clearly recognized, repeated use and language change has produced a certain number of conventional uses. This concerns types which are still identifiable as non-literal but need no inferring effort, i.e., so-called tired metaphors in Goatly's (1997: 32) classification (e.g., *squeeze* 'financial borrowing restriction', *fox* 'cunning person') and hyperboles with an utterance-type meaning (Claridge 2011: 214), such as *age* 'too long a time', *dying to* 'wanting very very much to' and *starve* 'be very hungry'. Some of the latter are also supported by formal peculiarities such as phrasal frames (*for ages, take ages*; transitive *dying*), and morphosyntactic freezing (plural *ages*, participle). Hearers are the more likely to simply mentally access and decode such uses the more often they have encountered them and the more mentally entrenched they already are (i.e., roughly 'what is said' = 'what is meant'). The hyperbolic or metaphorical meaning here is the salient one (Giora 2003), which depends on the frequency, conventionality, and familiarity of an expression. In contrast, in novel metaphors and hyperboles it is the literal meaning that is salient. Only in the latter case is the addressee likely to pick the literal meaning and thus to be misled, completely or at least initially.

28.5 Conclusion

What can one say then about the closeness between lying on the one hand and metaphor and hyperbole on the other? First, that it depends on the theory used, with a greater potential affinity according to rhetorical and Gricean approaches than according to Relevance Theory or Cognitive Linguistics. Secondly, that it depends on whether one takes the speaker or the hearer perspective, the former but not the latter *knowing* the intention. Speakers can make their metaphorical or hyperbolic intentions abundantly clear by choosing unambiguous (blatant or conventional) forms, or they can exploit the closeness by using forms blurring the distinction, thus lying and protecting themselves in one move. Hearers, especially in the latter case, have the problem of inferring figurative intent as opposed to a literal (and false) interpretation, i.e., they can indeed be misled. Thirdly, when focusing on implicated beliefs instead of on what is said, there may in fact be considerable deceptive potential: the greater emotional impact of figurative speech may leave traces even when we reject the words used as false.

CHAPTER 29

LYING AND POLITENESS

MARINA TERKOURAFI

29.1 INTRODUCTION

GIVEN that lying is universally proscribed as morally reprehensible, it may seem odd to find lying discussed as anything but such in manuals about politeness and manners. However, as Bavelas has pithily remarked, "there are many situations requiring 'tact' when it would be unkind to be honest but dishonest to be kind" (Bavelas 1983: 132). The relationship between lying and politeness, that is, is more complex than a simple opposition between the two might suggest. The purpose of this chapter is to probe this complex relationship and explore how it may be cast in pragmatic and politeness theory terms.

Presaging Lakoff's (1973) setting up of an opposition between the Rules of clarity (captured in Grice's maxims; Grice 1975) and the Rules of politeness (proposed in her own work),[1] in the excerpt below English sociologist Harriet Martineau saw speaking the truth ("sincerity") and being "kind" as contrary ideals toward which different nations will gravitate.

> The conversation of almost every nation has its characteristics, like that of smaller societies... In one country, less regard is paid to truth in particulars, to circumstantial accuracy, than in another. One nation has more sincerity; another more kindliness in speech.
>
> Martineau (1989 [1838]: 224)

While Martineau's observation is best taken as a statement about cultural relativism than an endorsement of any inherent opposition between sincerity and

---

[1] Lakoff proposed three Rules of Politeness: 1) Don't impose; 2) Give options; and 3) Be friendly (Lakoff 1973: 298).

politeness—indeed, her own view was that "manners are inseparable from morals, or, at least, cease to have meaning when separated" (Martineau 1989: 222)—for the author of *L'art de plaire dans la conversation*, the 1688 treatise on civility that is the topic of the next excerpt, there is significant margin for various permutations between the two, even in one and the same culture.

> Words should please the ear, should conform to the ideas they express, and should be natural without baseness ... Lying is defined as speech which does not conform to the thought. The world hates liars as it hates tigers and panthers. This sounds uncompromising enough, but the author has some modifications to add. Captives in time of war, he declares, ambassadors in diplomatic negotiations, and lovers in praise of their mistresses need not always adhere to the truth ... Moreover, a man may be perfectly sincere without saying all he thinks ... Harmless exaggeration may be used to amuse the company, but there should be no real lies.
>
> Mason (1935: 264–5)

Identifying three phenomena that remain central to discussions of politeness and lying to this day—social or "white" lies, being economical with the truth, and banter—he allows that in these cases, one may depart from the truth; yet, "there should be no *real* lies" (Mason 1935: 265; emphasis added). In this way, the anonymous seventeenth-century author draws a distinction that can be as hard to defend in theory as it is common to implement in practice: that between "real lying," which is always morally reprehensible, and a host of neighboring notions that are viewed as more or less necessary to maintain a harmonious social existence.

29.2 "White" lies

As the two opening excerpts suggest, the prime example of lies told in the service of politeness are social or "white" lies.[2] When we tell a friend that we like her new haircut when in fact we do not, turn down an invitation falsely claiming to have a prior commitment, or tell our host that we like the food he cooked for us although in reality we find it barely palatable, we say something we do not believe to be true to avoid hurting our interlocutor's feelings and, potentially also in the long run, our relationship. We thus sacrifice truth in the name of interpersonal harmony; and while different cultures or people may vary in their degrees of engaging in this practice, equivalent terms can be found in many, if not most languages, testifying to the pervasiveness of this phenomenon.[3]

---

[2] On prosocial and white lies, see also Chapter 22 by Simone Dietz.

[3] An indicative list includes كذبة بيضا *kidba beːdˤa/* (= white lie) in (Egyptian) Arabic, 圆场谎 *yuánchǎng huǎng* (= lie smoothing over a situation) in Chinese, hvid løgn' (= white lie) in Danish, *Duruq- e- Maslahati* (= lie with good intentions) in Farsi, *pieux mensonge* (= pious lie) in French, *weiße Lüge* (= white lie) in German, κατά συνθήκην/αθώα ψέματα *kata sinθicin/aθoa psemata* (= lies by convention/

According to Bok's often-cited definition, white lies are falsehoods "not meant to injure anyone and of little moral import" (Bok 1999: 58). As Bok herself observed, the practice of sparing another's feelings is in some cases so routine that one who does not abide by it "might well give the impression of an indifference he [sic] did not possess" (Bok 1999: 58). Others have also noted that white lies are so pervasive as to potentially constitute a "particular sort of communicative competence" (Camden et al. 1984: 321) and Brown and Levinson incorporated them into their politeness model as a special case of the positive politeness strategy of avoiding disagreement in order to eschew damage to the hearer's positive face, i.e., his desire to be liked and approved of (Brown and Levinson 1987: 115–16). Quantitative measures support these claims: when Turner et al. (1975) asked subjects to rate the truthfulness of their own statements in casual conversation, only 38.5% of statements were rated as completely honest, suggesting that a good two thirds of everyday conversation consist of various degrees of falsehoods—a point masterfully driven home in the 2009 comedy *The Invention of Lying*.[4]

29.2.1 Are white lies lies?

But if white lies are so common, are they still lies? To answer this question, we must first define lying. Typically, definitions of lying have included some combination of the following: stating something which is false, stating something that the speaker believes to be false, having the intention of deceiving the hearer, or believing that the hearer will be deceived by the speaker's utterance (see Mahon 2015 and the references therein). However, there is no agreement as to whether all of these are required or equally important for lying. Moreover, rejecting the possibility of a checklist definition of lying, Coleman and Kay (1981) proposed to define lying as a prototypically structured category, a move also adopted by Sweetser (1987) and Chen et al. (2013).

While the possibility of gradations and cultural variability afforded by the latter type of definition is certainly welcome when discussing lies that may be acceptable, or even required socially, for the purposes of this chapter, the definition of Saul (2012: 29) seems more apt. According to this,

> If the speaker is not the victim of linguistic error/malapropism or using metaphor, or irony, then they lie iff (1) they say that P; (2) they believe P to be false; (3) they take themself to be in a warranting context

---

innocent lies) in Greek, *füllentés* (= white lie) in Hungarian, *bugie innocenti* (= innocent lies) in Italian, *hvite løgner* (= white lies) in Norwegian, невинная ложь *nevinnaia lozh* (= innocent lie) in Russian, *mentira* (or *mentirita*) *piadosa/ bianca* (= pious/ white (little) lie) in (Peninsular/ Latin American) Spanish, เกรงใจ /kreːŋ.tɕai/ (= to be (too) courteous) in Thai, *zararsız yalan* (= harmless lie) in Turkish, and سفید جھوٹ *Sufaid Jhoot* (= white lies) in Urdu.

[4] https://en.wikipedia.org/wiki/The_Invention_of_Lying; accessed June 23, 2015.

where a warranting context is one where sincerity is expected (as opposed to, e.g., being in a play, or telling a joke). This definition has the advantage of not only excluding floutings of Gricean Quality[5] such as metaphorical and ironic utterances that do not normally qualify as "lying" but of also managing to draw a fine line between lying and misleading, where only the former is tied to "what is said," that is, roughly, to the conventional meaning of the words uttered.[6]

This is of particular importance when discussing the relationship between lying and politeness because white lies *can* indeed be *recognized* as such, without that subtracting from their politeness (Coleman and Kay 1981: 29; Chen et al. 2013: 380). As one participant in Bryant's (2008) study noted, "it gets expected sometimes that you're gonna get lied to. Like sometimes you ask a question wanting one answer and when you get that answer you're happy. Even if it's completely wrong you're like, ok that's all I wanted to hear" (Bryant 2008: 36). In other words, to capture the 'lie' in white lie, what we need is a definition that makes lying a matter of what one says rather than what one means. Saul's definition offers precisely that.

That white lies are recognizable as being untrue without this being detrimental to their politeness is highlighted by the existence of conventionalized markers of their untruthfulness, such as the use of high pitch in Tzeltal described by Brown and Levinson (1978). Brown and Levinson (1978: 172) report that in this Mayan language,

> there is a highly conventionalized use of high pitch or falsetto, which marks polite or formal interchanges, operating as a kind of giant hedge on everything that is said ... Use of it seems to release the speaker from responsibility for believing the truth of what he utters so that the presence of this falsetto in an otherwise normal conversation may well mark the presence of a social lie.

Highlighting this highly conventional aspect of white lies, Bok also affirms that "the justification for continuing to use such accepted formulations is that they deceive no one, except possibly those unfamiliar with the language" (Bok 1999: 58).

At least some white lies, then, are lies only in name, without the speaker's having the intention of deceiving the addressee, or even expecting that the addressee will be deceived. Given this possibility, white lies do not qualify as lies under approaches that require that the speaker have the intention that the addressee believe the false statement (e.g., Isenberg 1964: 473); nor do they qualify as lies under a different set of approaches that require that lies be morally wrong (e.g., Grotius 1925 [1625]: §616–17).

---

[5] The maxim of Quality enjoins conversationalists to: "Do not say what you believe to be false. 2. Do not say that for which you lack adequate evidence" (Grice 1975: 46).

[6] The notion of "what is said" in (post-)Gricean pragmatics is notoriously thorny. While for Grice (1975), 'saying p' entailed 'meaning p', for Bach (2001) it is possible to 'say' something (in the locutionary sense of uttering the words) without meaning it (as in, for instance, slips of the tongue, or translating, reciting, and rehearsing). It is in the latter (Bach's) sense that the term "what is said" is used in this chapter. For a summary of current debates around this notion, see Terkourafi (2010) and the references therein.

In sum, whether white lies are considered to be lies or not depends on one's definition of lying. If we follow everyday usage and classify them as 'lies'—albeit 'white' ones—what we need is a definition such as the one by Saul (2012: 20) cited above, that ties lying to what is said by the speaker's utterance and not necessarily the intention behind it.

29.2.2 White lies as a type of speech act

Given the above discussion, it would seem that the politeness of a white lie emanates first and foremost from the speaker's willingness to utter it, rather than her intention to get the hearer to believe it—although if challenged, the speaker is, of course, supposed to insist that she meant it, thereby further strengthening the politeness of her remark. This strengthening effect is due to the fact that once the untruthfulness has been uncovered, politeness is the only possible basis left for the speaker's remark. The relevant reasoning by the addressee would seem to be as follows: "you are so kind to be willing to go out of your way to lie in order to make me feel good"—which, incidentally, builds the speaker's politeness out of her willingness to sacrifice truthfulness, thereby acknowledging truthfulness as a standard otherwise governing speech. This is in line with Lakoff's (1973) prediction that politeness and truthfulness stand in opposition to each other and that interactants will oscillate between the two, depending on the setting. As several researchers have pointed out, white lies are more acceptable in contexts where informativity expectations are low and an utterance that is a white lie in one type of setting may count as a real lie in another (Sweetser 1987; Walper and Valtin 1992; Lee and Ross 1997; Perkins and Turiel 2007).

If the above analysis is correct, we may distinguish between two types of intention that a potential lie comes with: the first, a classic Gricean reflexive intention (or r-intention for short; Grice 1957), is necessary to invest the speaker's utterance with meaning and is intended to be recognized and fulfilled in its recognition. Potential lies, however, come with a second 'lying' intention and that is not a Gricean r-intention at all but rather one that must remain hidden in order to be fulfilled. It is precisely in how they handle this second 'lying' intention that white lies differ from real lies: in real lies, this intention must not be recognized or it fails; but in white lies, it is permissible for it to be recognized and, in fact, the politeness of the speaker's utterance may be strengthened if it is.

In virtue of encompassing this second intention, lying cannot be a speech act on a par with promising, requesting, threatening, complaining, etc. In the cases of these acts, the speaker's intent to promise, request, threaten, complain, etc. *must* be recognized by the addressee for the act to count as a promise, a request, a threat, or a complaint, respectively.[7] However, in lying, the speaker's intent to lie must precisely *not* be

---

[7] This holds also in uptake/hearer-based accounts of speech acts, if this sentence is rephrased to read "uptake as a promise, request, threat, complaint, etc. must occur for the act to count as a promise, a request, a threat, or a complaint, respectively."

recognized for the lie to be successful.[8] On the other hand, white lies are potentially recognizable without this canceling out their point—to show consideration for the other's feelings. This means that, contrary to real lies, white lies *can* be a type of speech act, which agrees with the existence of conventionalized means for their performance (see Brown and Levinson's analysis of Tzeltal high pitch in 29.2.1, and the following example, of Persian taarof).

A highly ritualized use of white lies is the Persian practice of taarof. Miller et al. (2014) describe taarof as a linguistic practice involving "figurative language and extreme 'self-lowering' referring expressions" commenting that "these commonly used non-literal terms can make it seem that taarof comprises a collection of lies" (Miller et al. 2014: 15). However, they hasten to add, "the critically important level of meaning of taarof exchanges is not in the literal meanings of the words. It is rather in the nature of the conversational exchange, particularly how the interactants view their status in relation to each other and how this relates to the wants that drive the interaction" (Miller et al. 2014: 3). To native speakers, taarof functions as a token of goodwill and respect, a strategic move to achieve particular perlocutionary goals, or an indication of the speaker's good manners and upbringing (Miller et al. 2014: 19)—indeed, members of lower socioeconomic classes and villagers are thought not to be able to use taarof (Beeman 1986: 197).

Izadi (2015: 86) furnishes the following example of taarof. Two close friends in their late twenties, Ali and Reza, are returning home from an evening out.[9]

> Reza has given Ali a ride home and now they are at Ali's doorstep. Ali lives with his family, and the female members of the family generally cover up in front of a non-family member. It is almost midnight, and definitely not a proper time for receiving guests, especially if it is not prearranged. Both know that Ali's family is not prepared to receive a guest at this time ...

1 Ali: Come in.
2 Reza: Thanks a lot.
3 Ali: Come in.
4 Reza: Thanks. I've got to go. I have work.
5 Ali: Well, just come in for a minute then you can go.
6 Reza: ((extending hand)) May I sacrifice for you. Don't you need favor?
7 Ali: ((refuses to shake hands)) Are you doing taārof? (Are you standing on ceremonies?)
8 Reza: (1.0) No (I swear) by God, convey my hello.
9 Ali: ((extending hand)) I'm at your service.
10 Reza: I'm your slave.

---

[8] The argument that lies cannot be a type of illocutionary act is also defended by Reboul (1994) albeit on slightly different grounds.
[9] See Izadi (2015) for the original in Persian and English word-per-word rendition.

Ali's invitation in line 1 is clearly ostensible: it is not meant for Reza to accept, and both Ali and Reza know that. As Eslami (2005: 464) notes, such ostensible invitations are "solicited by context"; Ali is more or less obliged to issue this invitation and Reza to reject it. Nevertheless, this exchange is not pointless. As Koutlaki (1997: 119) points out, "the fact that a speaker takes the trouble to use a socially enjoined formula indicates her intention to accord respect to her interlocutor and takes on therefore a phatic function."

Taarof is a rather extreme example of a highly conventionalized use of white lies. As a widely recognized social practice, it involves the use of formulae such as "may I sacrifice for you" in line 6 and "I am your slave" in line 10 of the example above (but can also be realized in less conventionalized ways; Miller et al. 2014: 20), is frequent at particular moments during the interaction (especially with respect to offers/invitations, requests/orders, thanking, complimenting, greeting and leave-taking; Miller et al. 2014: 16) and shows gender and age stratification (Miller et al. 2014: 26 ff.). In all of these ways, taarof resembles more institutionalized types of speech acts found in a variety of cultures (see, e.g., Yang's 2008 discussion of ritual refusals in Chinese).

However, white lies are not always as clearly signposted in terms of where they occur in the exchange and the form that they take and a number of researchers have highlighted the existence of a continuum of cases from the most innocuous white lie to the most malicious black one. Indeed Bok's objection to white lies (or, at least, to their overuse) centers precisely upon the existence of this continuum, which she considers to be a slippery slope that threatens to erode "honesty and trust more generally" (1999: 60). While it may be up to the addressee to determine whether the speech act of social lying or, conversely, real lying has occurred, the acceptability of the recognition of the speaker's lying intention (i.e., the extent to which her goals would be served if her lying intention were recognized) furnishes an (additional) criterion by which to distinguish theoretically between the two types of situation.

29.2.3 Social motivations for white lies

Researchers who have investigated white lies have uncovered a range of motivations, some more harmful than others. According to Turner et al. (1975), the five major motivations for white lies in descending order of frequency are: (1) saving face; (2) avoiding tension or conflict; (3) guiding social interaction; (4) affecting interpersonal relationships; and (5) achieving interpersonal power. A different classification scheme is proposed by Hample (1980) who argued that motivations for social lies fall into four categories in descending order of frequency as follows: (1) those that benefit self, (2) those that benefit others in the interaction, (3) those that benefit the relationship, and (4) miscellaneous motivations. Combining these two classifications, Camden et al. (1984) proposed a 4x3 matrix with one dimension representing the motivation or expected reward from the lie and the other the intended beneficiary. The four major reward categories are (1) basic rewards (e.g., money, material goods), (2) affiliation rewards (e.g., interaction initiation, leave-taking), (3) self-esteem rewards (e.g., saving face), and (4) other rewards (e.g., dissonance reduction, humor), while intended beneficiaries may be (1) the liar, (2) the addressee, or (3) a third (potentially non-present) party (Camden et al. 1984: 312).

However, Bryant (2008) has argued that none of these schemes adequately capture the perspectives of the participants themselves. What is needed for that is an open-ended classification scheme, as afforded by a combined focus group and in-depth interview methodology, during which a series of themes emerging from the in-depth interviews are further probed through a semi-structured research protocol used to stimulate discussion among a group. Adopting such a methodology in her study, Bryant (2008) was led to propose the classification shown in Table 29.1.[10]

An important discovery enabled by Bryant's interview methodology is the existence of what her informants called "gray" lies (Bryant 2008: 36–7). These are lies in which the various factors (intention, consequences, beneficiary, etc.) are at odds with each other, making it impossible to classify them unambiguously as either "black" or "white." Take the case of a vegetarian asking her friend if the meal they just ate contained any meat products and the friend assuring her that it did not, despite knowing that it did. Since the question was asked after the fact when nothing could be done to repair the situation, a positive answer would have only saddened or angered the questioner. Hence the falsehood in this case can be said to benefit the addressee, yet the lie is more consequential than an innocuous, white one, making that label inappropriate in this case.

The existence of gray lies supports Bok's view that the line between real and white lies is not as clear-cut as some would have us believe. Several commentators have pointed out that, in the end, whether a lie is harmful or not depends on the recipient of the lie and how they feel about it. As Knapp and Comadena note, "what is a vicious, harmful lie for one person may be an act of loving concern for another ... Lies can only 'be' as they are perceived by specific involved people" (Knapp and Comadena 1979: 271). Bok (1999: 60) concurs: "what the liar perceives as harmless or even beneficial may not be so in the eyes of the deceived." A definition that does not advocate either way regarding the harmfulness or not of a lie, such as the one provided by Saul (2012: 29; see section 29.2.1) seems preferable in this respect.

29.2.4 The acquisition of white lies

An important area of research in recent years has been the acquisition of white lies by children. Studies have shown that children as young as three are capable of telling white lies (Talwar and Lee 2002b; Talwar et al. 2007), although they do so less frequently than older ones (Bussey 1999: 1343). Children's ability to tell white lies appears to develop parallel to their mastering an adult-like definition of lying. The earliest component of

---

[10] Since the table summarizes the perspectives of the participants themselves, the terms used are the participants' own and should rather be taken in their pre-theoretical sense.

Table 29.1 Categorization of lies (reproduced from Bryant 2008: 32)

		Factors				
		Intention	Consequences	Beneficiary	Truthfulness	Acceptability
Types of lies	Real lies	Malicious Deliberate Deceptive Deceitful	Serious Direct	Self-serving Egotistical	Complete fabrication Blatant untruth Zero truth	Unacceptable Not justified
	White lies	Benign Pure	Trivial Meaningless Harmless	Altruistic Other-focused Protecting Helpful	Partial truth Half truth Bending the truth Stretching the truth	Acceptable Justified Expected Common
	Gray lies					
	Ambiguous gray lies	Ambiguous intention	Ambiguous consequences	Ambiguous beneficiary	Ambiguous level of truth	Open to interpretation
	Justifiable gray lies	Malicious	Direct	Self-serving	Complete fabrication	Justified acceptable

this definition, already present in preschoolers, is factual falsity, followed by a grasp of the speaker's belief that they are making a false statement and their intention to deceive (Strichartz and Burton 1990; Lee and Ross 1997: 269–70). Mirroring this ability to think about the mental states of others, school-age children become increasingly able to infer and consider the needs and wants of others, enabling them to shift their focus from their own perspective to that of the addressee (Walper and Valtin 1992: 249). This ability develops rapidly as children enter school years (Talwar et al. 2007: 9). As Heyman and Lee remark, "by the time they reach age seven, [children] tend to view a concern for the feelings of others as a central factor that motivates lie telling in politeness situations" (Heyman and Lee 2012: 169).

Another impressive finding of this line of research is the context-dependence of white-lie-telling behavior. From a young age, children appear to be able to discriminate between situations that call for the truth and those that call for a white lie and favor prosocial lying over truth-telling in the latter (Walper and Valtin 1992; Bussey 1999). Finally, although white lies tend to be viewed more positively than other types of lies by children across the board, differences emerge cross-culturally in how the lies are justified. In Western contexts, white lies are justified primarily with respect to their effect on the recipient's emotional well-being, while in East Asian contexts emphasis is placed on the social implications for the recipient, which is consistent with the former cultures' greater emphasis on autonomy and the latter's on societal interdependence (Heyman and Lee 2012: 169). All in all, the results of research on the acquisition of white lies by children furnish a strong argument in support of the universality of this behavior, as well as the existence of a consistent developmental path for its acquisition.

29.3 Beyond Grayscale: Blue, Red, Yellow, and Green Lies

While the intersection of lying and politeness most readily calls to mind social/white lies, other types of lying behavior are also related to politeness and self-presentational concerns. A cursory look into the relevant literature reveals a whole 'rainbow' of lies, including "blue," "red," "yellow," and even "green" lies. Of these, blue lies are probably the best established. A blue lie is a lie told to benefit a collective (Fu et al. 2008), the term purportedly originating from the use of false statements by police to control a subject, protect the force, or ensure the success of the government's legal case against a defendant (Klockars 1984; Barnes 1994). The degree to which blue lies are condoned by society seems to be culturally determined. Research with children suggests that in societies where strong collectivist ideals are enshrined from an early age through both practice and moral education curricula, such as the People's Republic of China, children tend to favor lying to protect the group and may not even consider such statements to be lies (Fu et al. 2008).

The opposite tendency was observed among North American children, who not only eschewed lying for a collective but also endorsed lying to benefit an individual (a friend or oneself; Fu et al. 2007). As with white lies, these tendencies increase with age: by age eleven, nearly a third (29.7%) of Chinese children were prepared to lie to benefit the group. However, these tendencies were not unchecked: as Sweet et al. (2010) found, Chinese children judged lying to conceal their group's cheating against another group harshly, even more so than American children, suggesting that it is really only lying for the greater good that is culturally condoned.

Blue lies are akin to another type of lying behavior emanating from an emphasis on collectivist norms, modesty-related lying in public. This is common especially in East Asian contexts, possibly because in these contexts, "publicly calling attention to one's accomplishments violates norms about maintaining harmony within one's social group" (Heyman and Lee 2012: 170). Researchers found that Chinese and Japanese children judged lying in such cases more favorably than truthfully acknowledging one's prosocial acts. However, this behavior is again tempered by context: in contrast to American children, who thought of it as bragging, Chinese children did not find it inappropriate to disclose successful performance to poorly performing peers, since they viewed it as an implicit offer of help. This finding further highlights the context-dependence of cultural norms about lying.

According to the Urban Dictionary,[11] a "red lie" is "a statement told with complete awareness that the other person knows the statement to be false. This type of lie is often told and accepted to avoid the fallout that might occur from dealing with reality."[12] This definition is reminiscent of what are more often called bald-faced lies, that is, "lies that assert what is false while speaker and hearer both understand that the speaker does not believe what s/he asserts" (Meibauer 2014a: 127).[13] The existence of bald-faced lies has prompted some philosophers to remove deception from their definitions of lying, a result some (Fallis 2015a) are more happy with than others (Lackey 2013). On a different analysis, Meibauer (2014a) argues that bald-faced lies are not lies at all, but rather acts of verbal aggression since, by acting untruthfully and dishonestly, the speaker is blatantly opting out of the Cooperative Principle, thereby openly showing disrespect for the hearer. As Meibauer (2014a: 128) concludes, "the specific act involved is an insult, albeit of a special kind." Interestingly, this makes bald-faced lies as face-threatening as real lies (albeit for different reasons), while it simultaneously distinguishes them from white lies, which are used precisely to *avoid* face-threat or even to *enhance* the addressee's face (cf. Brown and Levinson's classifying white lies under positive politeness; section 29.2.1).

---

[11] Urban Dictionary is a crowd-sourced online dictionary of primarily slang words and phrases founded in 1999. At the start of 2014, it featured over seven million definitions. As with other crowd-sourced websites, definitions are submitted and rated by users, with minimal intervention by volunteer editors.

[12] http://www.urbandictionary.com/define.php?term=red+lie&defid=2174531; accessed June 23, 2015.

[13] On bald-faced lies, see Chapter 19 by Jörg Meibauer.

A "yellow lie", on the other hand, is "a cowardly lie told to cover up embarrassment."[14] Thus defined, yellow lies are a type of lie told to protect the speaker's, rather than the hearer's face, and are associated with self-politeness by Chen et al. (2013: 380). Contrary to the common perception that white lies are told to avoid hurting someone else's feelings, lies told to protect oneself were among the most common in Camden et al.'s study, accounting (on one understanding of self-interest) for some seventy-five percent of their corpus (Camden et al. 1984: 314).[15] Related to this, Camden et al. propose "psychological compensation" as one of four major rationales for white lies in their corpus. As they explain,

> Individuals occasionally struggle with their self-image, in the sense that they sometimes find themselves behaving or thinking in ways that are dissonant with the more positive aspects of their self image, or in ways which appear to reinforce the more negative aspects of their self image. Situations like these can instigate personal internal conflict for the individual ...which ... may be avoided or minimized by lying about the situation.
>
> (Camden et al. 1984: 320)

This explanation calls up another notion, that of verbal "accounts" as "specific types of exculpatory claims that people offer when they attempt to reconcile their actions with countervailing social expectations" (Shulman 2009: 120). Accounts include excuses and post-hoc lies that people use to justify their actions and are often told ostensibly for collective or self-protection. Protection is one of four social loopholes identified by Shulman that generally allow violations of social norms without threatening the stability of those norms. Nevertheless, despite allowing people "the illusion of legitimately departing from social expectations when economic and social demands may make such departures inevitable," social loopholes ultimately amount to "a form of social self-deception—a means by which social actors ignore that some cultural ideals are widely flouted" (Shulman 2009: 132–3).

The latest addition to the list of different colors of lies is "green lies." Typically, these are claims by manufacturers that their products are environmentally friendly when in fact there is no evidence supporting this. According to one website, "the biggest problem in the green marketplace is false labeling. Almost 70% of the products surveyed had labels boasting of endorsements that were never made. Lies. Teenie weenie greenie lies. Smaller than little white lies, but lies nevertheless."[16] Being designed to benefit manufacturers (the speaker) and potentially harmful to the consumer (the addressee), green lies come closest to real lies discussed earlier.

---

[14] http://www.urbandictionary.com/define.php?term=yellow+lie&defid=2063228, accessed June 23, 2015.

[15] Camden et al. (1984: 312) asked students to record the white lies they told over a period of two weeks. Twenty-four students participated in the study, contributing between nine and twenty white lies each for a total of 322 white lies analyzed.

[16] http://www.chuckroger.com/2010/11/12/greenwashing-green-lies/; accessed June 23, 2015.

29.4 OTHER FORMS OF SOCIALLY WARRANTED UNTRUTHS: EUPHEMISM AND BANTER

The final two phenomena considered in this chapter are euphemism and banter. Euphemisms are words or phrases used to avoid saying an unpleasant or offensive word in public and have been explicitly associated with politeness and saving the face of the speaker, the hearer, or a third party (Allan and Burridge 1991). Typical areas of euphemistic usage include death ("passing away"), lying ("not true," "tongue in cheek"), age ("mature"), illness or disease ("disturbed," "venereal diseases"), and bodily functions ("restroom")—although different topics can be taboo in different languages to different degrees (e.g., Rabab'ah and Al-Qarni 2012).

Euphemisms feature in all the classic politeness theories. According to Leech, euphemism is "the practice of referring to something offensive or delicate in terms that make it sound more pleasant or becoming than it really is" (Leech 1981: 45). This makes euphemisms compatible with Leech's Pollyanna Principle, namely the intuition "that participants in a conversation will prefer pleasant topics of conversation to unpleasant ones" (Leech 1983: 147). Lakoff (1973) mentions euphemisms as an example of her Rule 2 (Give Options), while Brown and Levinson classify them under off-record indirectness, noting at the same time the "constant pressure to create new euphemisms for truly taboo subjects, as by association the old euphemism becomes more and more polluted" (Brown and Levinson 1987: 216).

Yet, despite being sometimes slated as "the opposite of straight talk,"[17] euphemisms do not amount to lying; nor do the closely related phenomena of political correctness, which covers expressions used to avoid the negative connotations of alternative terms for what are often controversial topics (disability, sexual orientation, ethnicity, etc.), and 'unspeak' (Poole 2006), which refers to expressions that pack a whole worldview into them, rhetorically aiming to lure the addressee into agreeing with the speaker's point of view. Euphemism, political correctness, and unspeak *cannot* in fact constitute lying because, in all three cases, the referential meaning of the terms used is transparent, making their potential for deception nil. Nevertheless, the corresponding terms do shed a (positive or negative) light on their contents through connotation, and that is why they are often felt to be attempts to manipulate the belief state of the hearer, as real lies also do.

A more debatable case is that of withholding information or "being economical with the truth," which refers to stating something true, yet less informative than is required, while doing nothing to prevent the potential implicature from Quantity, that the more

---

[17] http://english.stackexchange.com/questions/96684/opposite-of-straight-talk; accessed June 23, 2015.

informative statement does not hold, from arising.[18] A prominent example of this is former US President Bill Clinton's statement that he "did not have sexual relations with that woman" referring to his association with White House aide Monica Lewinski—a statement that was true under a narrower definition of sexual relations than what is usually understood by that term—at the same time implying that the informationally stronger interpretation did not hold.[19] This type of scalar reasoning (Horn 1984) is felt to be closer to lying, since, although the speaker is not strictly speaking stating something false, she does seem to have an intention to mislead, and can indeed be successful in doing so. It is no wonder, then, that "being economical with the truth" has itself become a euphemism for "lying," and can, in this sense, be as face-threatening as the real thing.

Finally, *banter* is defined by Leech as saying something which is "(1) obviously untrue and (2) obviously impolite to [the] h[earer]" in order to show solidarity with him (Leech 1983:144). Banter can, in this sense, be considered the opposite of white lies: like white lies, it consists of saying something false but in contrast to them, its 'surface' goal is now to threaten rather than to enhance the hearer's face. Of course, ultimately, the goal is to show solidarity with the addressee, and in this sense, the goal is again an affiliative one. Moreover, in both cases, and unlike the case of real lies, the untruthfulness is potentially recognizable by the addressee. However, in the case of banter, the untruthfulness is not only potentially recognizable but *must* be recognized for the implicature of solidarity to be generated. Indeed, research shows that, the more likely a statement is to reflect reality, the less likely it is to be understood as banter, even between close friends (Vergis 2015; cf. Labov 1972 on factual falsity as a precondition for ritual insults). This is unlike white lies, which may well go undetected and still achieve the goal of showing consideration for the addressee. Both banter and white lies, then, adopt untruthfulness to get to affiliative goals, but they follow opposite paths getting there.

29.5 Conclusion

This chapter has presented a brief overview of different types of lying behavior in relation to politeness and face-threat/face-enhancement. Although white (or social) lies are the most frequently discussed aspect in this respect, a variety of behaviors, ranging from withholding information to outright malicious stating of falsehood, turned out to serve an equally wide variety of social goals. These goals include protecting one's own face and avoiding threat to, or even enhancing, another's face (all goals that are typically

---

[18] The implicature arises from flouting the first submaxim of Quantity ("Make your contribution as informative as is required (for the current purposes of the exchange)"; Grice (1975: 45).

[19] Scholars have defended different views on whether this example constitutes lying or not; see, e.g., Moore (2000), Saul (2000), and Meibauer (2014b: 156–8), among others.

associated with politeness) but also downright threatening another's face, resulting in intentional impoliteness or rudeness.

An important distinction has been drawn between white lies and real lies, arguing that the former's politeness lies in one's willingness to say (in the locutionary sense of 'saying') something untrue even though it may (but need not) be transparent to all that one does not mean it. The fact that one's insincerity may be transparent in the case of white lies (what I have called the recognizability of the speaker's lying intention), along with the existence of conventionalized linguistic markers of white lies, paves the way for analyzing white lies as a socially constituted type of speech act, unlike real lies, which cannot be so analyzed. Nevertheless, precisely because the speaker's lying intention is only potentially recognizable in white lies—that is, the speaker's intention to lie *may* but does not *need to* be recognized for a white lie to occur—white and real lies may be hard to distinguish in practice and whether a particular utterance is a white lie or not may remain debatable. In fact, a crucial claim made in this chapter is that the same behavior can have contrary connotations for different participants or in different contexts, making the association between lying and im/politeness context-dependent through and through.

The relationship between lying and im/politeness remains largely unexplored by politeness theorists to date—witness the fact that only euphemisms are mentioned by all three of the first wave of politeness theories (Lakoff 1973, Leech 1983, and Brown and Levinson 1987), with Leech additionally covering banter and Brown and Levinson social (white) lies, while none of the more recent frameworks addresses any type of lying behavior—possibly because of the intrinsically antisocial nature of real lying, which placed it outside of what Eelen (2001: 87) called politeness theorists' "focus on polite." As politeness studies are expanding their scope to take in impoliteness, verbal aggression, and conflict, becoming "im/politeness studies" in the process, and as research into lying reveals the ever finer shades of this complex phenomenon, the cross-fertilization of these two fields can be expected to yield fascinating results in the future.

PART V
DOMAINS

CHAPTER 30

DEVELOPMENT OF LYING AND COGNITIVE ABILITIES

VICTORIA TALWAR

30.1 INTRODUCTION

SINCE the emergence of developmental psychology, scientists and laypersons have been fascinated with children's lie-telling because it is a lens through which to view a multitude of behaviors, including children's developing cognitive, social, and moral abilities (Darwin 1877; Hall 1891; Stern, Stern, and Lamiell 1909; Hartshorne and May 1928). The scientific study of the development of lying began at the turn of the twentieth century, when the field of developmental psychology was just being established. However, a shift away from examining social influences and mental activity, and toward behaviorist principles meant that the investigation of deception lay dormant for nearly half a century. It is only during the last three decades, as cognitive and social explanations have regained acceptance among developmental scientists as playing a role in the development of intentional systems in children, that lying has become the focus of investigative efforts among researchers. The widespread prevalence of lying in everyday life (e.g., DePaulo et al. 1996) coupled with a strong emphasis on the promotion of children's truthful behaviors in society has also made the topic of interest to parents, educators, and professionals who work with children in clinical and forensic settings. Despite its ubiquity in everyday life, lying is considered a negative and reprehensible behavior (Bok 1999). Given the social interpersonal implications including loss of trust and credibility, and increased risk of antisocial behavior associated with chronic lying (Stouthamer-Loeber 1986; Gervais et al. 2000), researchers are interested in how this behavior emerges and develops in children and the factors that influence its manifestation as a social strategy.

Lying is commonly defined as a statement communicated with the intent to mislead another into believing something to be true that the lie-teller believes to be false. That is, there is a discrepancy between what is said by the lie-teller and what is known to be true.

In order to be a successful lie-teller and to effectively instill a false belief in the mind of the lie-recipient, the lie-teller must control their expressive behavior. This behavioral control must be exerted not only during the initial lie statement, but also throughout all related subsequent conservations about the topic. For instance, when lying about eating a forbidden cookie one has to make sure not to say anything that is not congruent with your assertion that you have not eaten a cookie (e.g., saying how good it tasted) or display any non-verbal cues (e.g., fidgeting, looking nervous) to arouse suspicion. Telling a lie involves complicated cognitive functions including theory–of-mind understanding and executive functioning abilities of self-regulation, planning, inhibitory control, and working memory. The current chapter reviews existing literature on the development of children's lie-telling behavior and its relation to various aspects of children's cognitive development.

30.2 The development of children's lie-telling

Previous research examining the development of children's lie-telling has tended to focus mostly on children's understanding and evaluations of lying (e.g., Piaget 1965 [1932]; Peterson et al. 1983; Strichartz and Burton 1990; Bussey 1992, 1999), while fewer studies have examined their actual lying behavior. Researchers on children's conceptual understanding of truth and lies have generally reported that children's knowledge of truth- and lie-telling emerges early in the preschool years. In terms of children's understanding of truths and lies, Bussey (1992, 1999) and Siegal and Peterson (1996) reported that young children (aged four years) were able to successfully identify lies and evaluated lies told with different intentions (e.g., to harm or protect another) differently. Children's conceptual and moral understanding of lies increases with age as they develop an appreciation for the intentionality component of a lie. Strichartz and Burton (1990) found that children as young as three years old defined a statement as a lie solely based on factuality. It was not until ages six to ten years that children tended to consider the speaker's beliefs when characterizing the honesty of their statements. Bussey (1992) also found that eight- and eleven-year-olds were more accurate at identifying lies than five-year-olds. Although these studies contribute to our understanding of the development of children's moral understanding about lies, they did not examine children's actual lying behavior.

Evidence of children's actual lie-telling behavior comes from observational and experimental studies. Anecdotal evidence and observational studies suggest that children become capable of deceiving others during the preschool years, with many children beginning to tell lies late in their second year (Newton et al. 2000; Wilson et al. 2003). While children have been observed telling lies as early as 2 ½ years of age, researchers have questioned the intentionality of very young children's lies; with some arguing the initial deceptions of the very young are mistaken utterances or momentary impulsive utterances rather than truly deliberate instances of deceit (e.g., Stern and Stern 1909; Ahern, Lyon, and Quas 2011). These impulsive false statements are founded on a desire, a type of wish-fulfillment (i.e., *I would like to not be the person who ate the cookies*), than on belief. However, it is from these desire-based statements, intentional first lies start to emerge. Children's first deliberate factually untrue statements tend to be about rule violations and to avoid getting into trouble. Given the fact that genuine lies told by children in later childhood tend to serve similar functions, it may be that children's earliest falsehoods in some instances are a rudimentary form of intentional verbal deception.

Lying is a difficult behavior to observe as by its very nature it is a behavior that is concealed and, if successful, difficult to detect. As a result, observational studies may not easily capture the behavior, especially if it is successful. Furthermore, researchers need to know the factual truth (i.e., who ate the cookie) to know if a statement (*No, I didn't eat it*) is true or false. To capture children's everyday lie-telling abilities, researchers cannot simply instruct a child to lie, as this does not create a natural situation in which the liar is trying to create a false belief in the listener's mind. When people lie they usually lie spontaneously without instruction to do so by the lie-recipient. Thus, researchers have created experimental paradigms to examine children's spontaneous lie-telling in the laboratory. To best observe lying as it exists in everyday situations, one must create naturalistic conditions in which an individual can spontaneously choose to lie or tell the truth (i.e., be self-motivated to lie) and where the truth is objectively verifiable. A common paradigm used to examine children's spontaneous lying is the modified temptation-resistance paradigm. In this paradigm children are given an opportunity to commit a transgression and are later asked about their behavior. For example, a common version used with preschool children involves children playing a guessing game in which they are instructed not to peek at a toy when an experimenter momentarily leaves the room. Upon the experimenters' return, children are asked about whether or not they did indeed peek at the toy. This situation is usually videotaped using a hidden camera so that children's true peeking behavior can be verified and compared with what they tell the experimenter. Children's behavior in this situation is spontaneous and self-motivated, as they are not prompted by anyone on how to behave if they chose to transgress and peek at the forbidden toy. Children who peek can then choose to confess or lie about their transgression. Researchers have thus been able to mimic the everyday settings in which children lie and examine children's lie-telling abilities.

Using a modified temptation-resistance paradigm, Lewis et al. (1989) found that thirty-eight percent of three-year-olds who peeked at the forbidden toy denied peeking, while thirty-eight percent confessed to peeking at the toy. In order to investigate whether children understood that they had committed a transgression by peeking at the toy, Polak and Harris (1999) replicated the procedure used by Lewis et al. with three- and five-year-olds, and included a control group of children who were permitted to look at the toy. They found that compared to children in the permission condition (allowed to look at the toy), children who were prohibited (told not to look at the toy) hesitated to look at the toy and actually peeked at the toy less often, as they viewed doing so as a transgression. In another study, Talwar and Lee

(2002a) investigated children's lie-telling behavior between three and seven years of age. They found that the majority of children of four years and older lied about their transgression, while more than half of the three-year-olds confessed. While approximately half of children between six and seven years of age were able to maintain their lies when asked follow-up questions about their behavior, younger children were poor at maintaining their lie and were more likely to let slip verbal cues to their deceit. Subsequent studies have found similar developmental patterns in terms of children's lie-telling to conceal a transgression and their ability to maintain those lies in subsequent statements (Talwar, Gordon, and Lee 2007; Talwar and Lee 2008; Evans and Lee 2011). These studies suggest that as children get older their lie-telling strategies become quite sophisticated, making it increasingly difficult for adults to detect children's truth- and lie-telling, even when children are asked follow-up questions intended to elicit the truth (e.g., Talwar and Lee 2002a). To better understand age-related differences in the complexity and sophistication of children's lie-telling, researchers have examined cognitive factors seemingly related to deception. In particular, two cognitive variables that have recently been discussed in relation to the development of lie-telling and lie maintenance are theory-of-mind understanding and executive functioning behaviors.

30.3 Cognitive abilities and lie-telling behavior

Although lying has traditionally been viewed as a negative behavior associated with a lack of moral understanding or behavioral control, recent research suggests it may be related to children's normal cognitive development and as such may be an adaptive behavior occurring as children develop the cognitive skills to strategically interact with their environment. The creation and maintenance of a lie is a relatively complex task that requires a sophisticated level of cognitive development. A successful liar must plan a story and remember it, take into account another individuals' knowledge, construct a false statement that differs from their own true beliefs, and readily adapt or manipulate their expressive behavior in order to remain convincing. Thus, deception is considered to be a hallmark of cognitive maturity that emerges once children begin to understand others' mental states and consciously control their own behaviors (Talwar and Crossman 2011). Children's lie-telling skills continue to evolve throughout their first decade of life and these improvements appear to coincide with significant advancements in cognition, specifically theory-of-mind understanding and executive functioning (Talwar and Lee 2008). However, only recently have researchers begun to empirically investigate the role that these specific cognitive factors play in children's abilities to lie successfully.

30.3.1 Theory-of-mind understanding and lying

Theory-of-mind (ToM) understanding is commonly defined as the ability to attribute mental states to oneself and others and to recognize that others' beliefs, desires, and intentions may differ from one's own (Baron-Cohen 1999). Closely related to this ability is the development of lying behavior, as by definition, telling a lie requires one to intentionally instill a false belief in the mind of another. To do so successfully necessitates an awareness that other people's knowledge of a situation may vary from one's own, and, moreover, an awareness that this knowledge can be manipulated through deceit (Talwar and Crossman 2011). That being said, lying is essentially ToM in action (Talwar and Lee 2008). Acts of deception such as lying have been identified as early indicators of at least a rudimentary understanding of belief and false belief (Hala et al. 1991; Sodian 1991; Sodian et al. 1991).

Previous research suggests that children's ToM understanding progresses through two developmental phases (Talwar and Lee 2008). Children acquire a basic awareness of others' mental states, or first-order belief understanding, around three to four years of age (e.g., Sodian 1991; Wellman et al. 2001). The development of this relatively simple insight corresponds with a significant shift in children's deceptive practices between three and four years of age (e.g., Lewis et al. 1989; Polak and Harris 1999; Talwar and Lee 2002a; Evans, Xu, and Lee 2011). Around four years of age, the majority of children will readily tell a lie to conceal their own transgression. More specifically, Polak and Harris (1999) reported that most children who chose to lie and deny a minor transgression (i.e., looked inside a forbidden toy house) had high ToM understanding scores. Thus, children's initial lies may reflect their ability to represent a false belief that is different from their belief about the true state of affairs. Talwar and Lee (2008) also found that children's performance on false-belief tasks predicted the false denials of their transgressive behavior. However, at this stage children appear to have difficulty maintaining their lies. Their subsequent statements following an initial false statement tend to be inconsistent with the initial lie and thus make their deception readily detected by naive adults (Talwar and Lee 2002a). Polak and Harris (1999) also reported in their study that the majority of children (sixty-three percent), including those with high ToM understanding scores, were unable to sustain their lies by appropriately responding to follow-up questions regarding their behavior. Evans et al. (2011) found that children were not able to tell intentional strategic lies until around four to five years of age. In light of this, researchers have suggested a developmental model of deception whereby the decision to tell a lie requires a relatively simple understanding of false beliefs, whereas the ability to maintain the lie during follow-up questioning requires a more advanced awareness of belief understanding (Polak and Harris 1999; Talwar and Lee 2002a, 2008).

At approximately six or seven years of age, children begin to develop a more advanced ToM, or second-order belief understanding (Perner and Wimmer 1985; Sullivan et al. 1995). It may be that this more sophisticated awareness is needed in order to sustain a false denial successfully and respond consistently to follow-up questions. This requires the liar to create a false belief and then infer what belief they ought to have given the false belief (Talwar and Lee 2008). In other words, one must be able to create a belief based on a false belief, or a second-order belief representation. At this stage, children gradually become more and more sophisticated at maintaining the plausibility of their lies. Children will tell a deliberate lie while ensuring that their subsequent statements do not contradict the initial lie, making their deceptive statements difficult to distinguish from statements made by a non-liar. For instance, Talwar, Gordon, and Lee (2007) investigated children's lie-telling practices and second-order belief understanding. Children, six to eleven years of age, participated in a modified temptation-resistance paradigm in which they were instructed not to peek at an answer to a trivia game question while left alone in a room. A series of follow-up questions assessed children's ability to sustain their initial false denial. As predicted, Talwar et al. (2007) discovered that children's ability to maintain consistency between their initial lie and subsequent verbal statements increased with age and was significantly related to their performance on second-order false-belief tasks. Children who had higher second-order belief scores were more likely to successfully conceal their lie when responding to follow-up questions by the experimenter. In another study, Talwar and Lee (2008) found a similar relationship among their sample of children aged three to eight years who were told not to peek at a forbidden toy. That is, they reported that children who performed better on first-order belief tasks were more likely to tell an initial lie, and those children who performed better on second-order belief tasks were more likely to provide plausible explanations for knowing the identity of a toy they should not have otherwise known. In a recent study, Williams, Moore, Crossman, and Talwar (2016) found that children's second-order belief understanding predicted children's ability to maintain a prosocial lie to be polite about a disappointing gift.

Further support for a link between children's ToM understanding and their lie-telling abilities comes from studies involving children with an Autism Spectrum Disorder (ASD). Autism Spectrum Disorder is commonly associated with deficits in ToM understanding (Baron-Cohen 1992). Two experimental studies have found that children with ASD not only lie at significantly lower rates than other children but they also have difficulty maintaining their lies and this is related to their ToM scores (Li et al. 2011; Talwar et al. 2012). Taken together, the evidence suggests there is a significant relationship between lie-telling and ToM understanding among both typically and nontypically developing children. While these studies show a seemingly consistent relationship pattern between lying, lie maintenance, and false-belief understanding, it is likely that other variables, such as executive functioning, facilitate and support the development of children's lie-telling capabilities.

30.3.2 Executive functioning and lying

Recent research suggests that children's lie-telling behaviors are related to their executive functioning abilities. 'Executive functioning' (EF) refers to a set of higher-order psychological processes that serve to monitor and control thought and action (Zelazo and Müller 2002; Carlson et al. 2004). Executive functioning encompasses a variety of cognitive skills, including self-regulation, inhibitory control, planning, attentional flexibility, and working memory. Executive functioning skills have been shown to emerge during late infancy and develop throughout childhood (Zelazo and Müller 2002), a time when researchers have also noted increases in lie-telling behavior. Thus, advances in EF are believed to be correspondingly associated with improvements in children's deceptive capabilities.

In particular, researchers have considered that inhibitory control and working memory are directly related to children's lying behaviors (Carlson et al. 1998; Hala and Russell, 2001; Talwar and Lee 2008). 'Inhibitory control' refers to the ability to suppress interfering thought processes or actions (Carlson et al. 1998), while working memory is a system for temporarily holding and processing information in the mind (Baddeley 1986). When choosing to tell a lie, children must suppress the truth (i.e., conceal the transgression or misdeed) while simultaneously representing and communicating false information that differs from reality in order to avoid being detected. To maintain their lies, liars must carefully inhibit any behaviors that may contradict their false statement while maintaining in their memory the contents of their lie. That is, a liar must hold in their mind conflicting alternatives regarding what they actually did and what they said they did in order to sustain their initial lie and remain undetected (Talwar and Crossman 2011).

Carlson and colleagues (1998) were among the first to examine the link between children's EF and their deceptive abilities. Carlson et al. (1998) reported that because it entailed overloading children's inhibitory control skills, children's ability to physically deceive a research assistant was less successful. Specifically, children who were told to deceive under conditions that required a high degree of inhibition (i.e., pointing to a misleading location to deceive a research assistant as to the whereabouts of a prize) were less successful than children in relatively low inhibitory control conditions (i.e., using a picture of an arrow to deceptively direct the researcher). Similar results were reported in a study by Hala and Russell (2001). Based on these findings, researchers concluded that young children's difficulties with deception may be related to their underdeveloped inhibitory control skills compared to older children in similar situations.

In fact, experimental studies examining children's verbal deception have found that children who perform better in tasks that require inhibitory control and working memory are more likely to lie and have better lie-telling abilities. For instance, Talwar and Lee (2008) investigated the roles of inhibition and working memory in the development of children's lying. Children ranging in age from three to eight years participated in a modified temptation-resistance paradigm. Children also completed several executive functioning tasks that examined their inhibitory control and working memory. Talwar and Lee (2008) found that children's false denials were related to their performance on a Stroop task; a test that measures both inhibition and working-memory skills. Specifically, children with higher Stroop task scores were more likely to lie about their transgression regarding peeking at a forbidden toy. Subsequent studies have also found that children's performance on the Stroop task predicts children's early emerging lying and the sophistication of older children's ability to maintain their lies (Evans and Lee 2011, 2013; Williams, Moore, Crossman, and Talwar 2016). Taken together, the evidence suggests it is the combined effect of both inhibitory control and working memory that predicts successful verbal deception. Thus, telling a convincing lie requires the dual ability to remember the rule that was violated while simultaneously inhibiting any mention of the wrongdoing. In addition to these abilities, there may be other EF abilities that play a significant role in the development and sophistication of children's lies. For instance, some preliminary evidence suggests children who take the time to plan a response tell more sophisticated lies (Evans and Lee 2011; Williams, Leduc, Crossman, and Talwar 2017). However, more research is needed to further investigate how these cognitive abilities play a role in the emergence and development of children's verbal deception.

30.4 THE DEVELOPMENT OF LYING AS A PROBLEM BEHAVIOR

Lie-telling appears to emerge initially in children as part of developing cognitive sophistication and to be a normative part of a child's development. Lying, in part, may be a sign of developing cognitive skills in young children. Nevertheless, over time, most children learn to effectively interact with and manage their social environments and relations in ways that do not require frequent lying. Children whose parents foster children's self-control, model honesty, and teach them the positive consequences of truth-telling will use lying only as an occasional strategy, while typically employing more effective cognitive and social skills to manage their social relationships. Indeed, evidence suggests that lying has an adaptive value as a social strategy only if it is used sparingly (Tyler et al. 2006). Thus, it may be that the developmental trajectory of lying as a normative behavior follows an inverted "u-shaped" function. That is, children's lie-telling may increase to a peak in elementary school, as their cognitive abilities develop, and then decrease thereafter owing to socialization processes of parents, peers, and others, to the level of occasional lie-telling found in adults (DePaulo et al. 1996; Evans and Lee 2011; Lavoie, Leduc, Crossman, and Talwar 2016).

However, for some children lie-telling can be a problem behavior. Children's chronic lie-telling, like other antisocial behaviors, may be a result of insufficient development of adaptive behavioral strategies (e.g., inhibitory control) and instead reflect reliance on immature strategies (e.g., impulsive behavior). Children who lack cognitive maturity may not learn to use this social strategy appropriately, leading to others having negative impressions of them, or may find that they need to use this strategy so often to cover their behavior that it becomes symptomatic of their maladjustment and conflicts with their environment (Talwar and Crossman 2011). For instance, one study with children with fetal alcohol syndrome, who commonly have aggressive and other behavior problems as well as low inhibitory control, found they were more likely than other children to tell lies to conceal misdeeds (Rasmussen et al. 2007). Thus, while on one hand EF skills appear to be related to the emergence and development of children's normative lie-telling, it may be that for some children that they use lying maladaptively to compensate for their poor EF skills, which leads them to engage in more impulsive behavior. Children with poor impulse control may be more likely to engage in problematic behaviors and use lying as an immature self-preservation strategy. While many children develop to tell lies only occasionally and in more socially accepted ways, other children use lying as a frequent strategy that becomes maladaptive and a chronic problem behavior. More research is needed to examine the relations among children's cognition, behavioral problems, and children's lie-telling behaviors. Future studies need to examine how lying first emerges as part of normative cognitive development but for some becomes a maladaptive strategy associated, at least for some, with lack of cognitive competence.

30.5 Conclusion

Overall, current and previous findings suggest that children's lie-telling emerges as a normative behavior in the preschool years and develops throughout the elementary-school years. Children's early lie-telling may develop as an adaptive strategy, as it protects the individual from negative or adverse environmental reactions, as well as serving self-interest. It appears to be related to children's growing cognitive sophistication; as they develop a better understanding of self and of others' mental states as well as increased inhibitory control and working memory, children's ability to tell convincing lies increases. Children with greater cognitive sophistication are better able to manipulate others, maintain their fabrication, and avoid negative consequences (e.g., being punished for breaking a vase). To the extent that lie-telling is related to the development of these skills, it is an adaptive behavior reflecting children's increasing ability to cope with the demands of their social environment. Thus, the emergence and initial development of lie-telling reflects children's acquisition of socially goal-directed strategies. In this sense, lie-telling may be seen as a result of a positive development in children's cognitive processing. Future researchers need to examine developmental trajectories of lie-telling behavior and how chronic lie-telling is related to children's cognitive abilities.

CHAPTER 31

LYING AND LIE DETECTION

SAMANTHA MANN

31.1 LYING

LYING, the act of deliberately attempting to mislead another, is a daily life event for most people (DePaulo, Kashy, Kirkendol, Wyer, and Epstein 1996). Situations where a person tells an untruth but believes it to be a truth are not considered herein to be a lie, since that person is not deliberately trying to mislead the other. Similarly, where a person does deliberately attempt to misinform another, but fails to convince them, this is still considered to be a lie, since mendacious intent is still present. Most lies are trivial 'white lies', and are often told as a social lubricant, e.g., for the benefit of others or to aid easy conversation, and the target may not be particularly motivated to detect such untruths. In turn, the consequences of such lies being detected are very low for the liar. These lies are known as *low-stakes* lies. Conversely, *high-stakes* lies are told when there is much at stake for the liar if he or she is caught out in the lie (Vrij 2008). Again, a target may not be motivated to detect such lies if the consequences of its discovery are likely to be painful. For example, a wife may choose to turn a blind eye to the philandering behaviour of her husband, opting to avoid questioning his excuses for his absences. However, other targets, such as a police officer investigating a crime, may be very motivated to determine when he or she is being lied to.

Broadly speaking, motivations to lie include: avoiding punishment or gaining advantage, for materialistic gain or for psychological reasons such as avoiding embarrassment or feeling bad. Each of these motivations may be self-oriented (to benefit ourselves) or other-oriented (to benefit others) and some lies may serve both ourselves and others (DePaulo et al. 1996). For example, if a friend asks for your opinion about a purchase she has made that she cannot return, and you feel compelled to lie and say that you really like the item, whereas in fact you really do not, this lie would be for psychological reasons, in part other-orientated to make your friend feel better, and in part self-orientated to avoid your embarrassment at making your friend feel bad about her purchase.

As mentioned above, most studies which have investigated the frequency with which we lie suggest that it is a daily event for more people, with many lying several times a day. Most of these have tended to be diary studies where people are asked to record how many of their interactions are deceptive (e.g., DePaulo et al. 1996). For more information about the frequency of lying see Chapter 33 by Bella DePaulo.

In psychology, lies take several different forms. These include outright lies, exaggerations, and subtle lies (DePaulo et al. 1996). An outright lie is a total fabrication, or where the content of the lie completely differs from the liar's belief of the truth. The exaggeration category includes both over- and understatements (Vrij 2008). For example, overembellishing one's achievements in a job interview, or underplaying how much time one spends on social media. Subtle lies include telling a literal truth but in such a manner that it is designed to mislead and lead the target to believe the opposite, or concealing information and failing to mention it at all.

Each liar is different, as is each lie and the circumstances in which it is told, and so detecting a lie is no easy task. Furthermore, a smart liar is unlikely to tell an outright lie, but instead build a lie around a truth (referred to as an *embedded lie*). Therefore, much of what is said may well be truthful (for example, the event itself may be something that the liar has actually experienced before), with the substitution of a few true details for false (e.g., the date and time at which that event occurred).

31.2 LIE-DETECTION RESEARCH

Research generally shows that lie-detection accuracy is in the range of forty-five to sixty percent with an average of around fifty-six percent. Furthermore, studies in which the lie-detection ability of professional lie detectors such as police and customs officers have been examined, have tended to result in similar accuracy rates to those of laypersons. It has been argued that this may be due to the fact that the lies being observed are condoned, low-stakes lies, since the majority of deception research has focused on laboratory studies where participants are asked to lie or tell the truth for the sake of the experiment. This is because it is impossible to ethically create a high-stakes lying situation. To find videotaped examples of liars in high-stake situations for whom the *ground truth* (i.e., knowing for sure what is a lie and what is a truth) is known, who lie (and tell the truth for comparison) spontaneously and of their own volition, and not because they have been asked to do so for the sake of an experiment, is rare, but has been achieved (see Mann, Vrij, and Bull 2002). In one series of studies (e.g., Mann, Vrij, and Bull 2004) where police officers were asked to make veracity judgements after watching video-clips of real-life suspects in their police interviews, accuracy ranged from sixty to seventy-three percent. This suggests that in such a contextually relevant situation, lie-detection rates may be higher than has been suggested in laboratory studies. More recently, lie-detection rates have been increased in studies that have focused on making an interview setting more difficult for liars, and focusing on differences between liars and truth-tellers in terms of speech content.

31.3 LIE DETECTION AND NONVERBAL BEHAVIOUR

Most people hold a stereotype of how a liar behaves. This typically consists of nervous behaviours, for example, avoiding eye contact and fidgeting. Indeed, it is likely that many people, when telling a serious lie, will feel nervous. There are several processes that may simultaneously take place within the liar (Vrij 2008). He or she may feel guilty about the lie, or fear being caught, and so this may lead to nervousness. Most lie-detection methods, particularly those involving any technology, for example, most (but not all) polygraph tests or voice analysers, actually measure signs of physiological arousal (more discussion of the polygraph follows). Hence, provided the liar is experiencing some form of emotion and/or anxiety which triggers an autonomic response, such devices may measure such changes.

However, at the same time the liar may experience increased cognitive load in order to fabricate a lie which will fit in with the evidence that the target potentially holds, whilst remembering to avoid revealing the truth and assessing the target's reaction. It is an established fact within cognitive psychology that increased cognitive load results in a decrease in (or neglect of) body language (Ekman 1997), including blinking (Bagley and Manelis 1979), as the brain attends to the mental problem it is attempting to solve. When thinking hard, most people will look away as they attempt to construct an answer (Doherty-Sneddon, Bruce, Bonner, Longbotham, and Doyle 2002).

Finally, the liar may try to control his or her behaviour in order to make a convincing impression (this is referred to as *impression management*). As mentioned above, most people expect a liar to display nervous behaviour, but what most people do not realize is that these behaviours, including eye gaze, are relatively easy to control. However, because most people are unaware of how much body language they normally display combined with a heightened awareness of their body language when they are engaging in deception, the result is often an unnatural stillness.

Several studies have shown that in terms of expressed behaviour, when the *cognitive load* and *attempted control* processes are dominant, they are likely to contradict any leakage of nervous behaviour. Another point to consider is that a truth-teller may also feel nervous, if he or she fears not being believed despite speaking the truth. This is referred to as the *Othello error* (Ekman 1985), an expression derived from the Shakespeare play where Othello accused his wife, Desdemona, of having an affair, and misread her nervous outburst when she realized she could not prove her innocence, as mendacious.

There are many myths within the area of deceptive behaviour. Some have even tried applying Neuro-Linguistic Programming (NLP) to deception, suggesting that certain eye movements correlate with mendacity. Neuro-Linguistic Programming was developed by Bandler and Grinder (1979) as a technique to develop rapport between therapist and client. The authors do not offer empirical evidence for their observations, neither do they mention deception, though others have extended these observations to suggest that there is a link between eye movements and lying (e.g., Gordon, Felisher, and Weinberg 2002). However, there is no theoretical basis for such claims, nor reliable research to back them up (see Mann et al. 2012). Deception research into nonverbal behaviour has repeatedly shown that, on the whole, liars tend to move less and blink less than truth-tellers, with no particular difference in the amount of time averting eye gaze. Eye contact is easier to control than most people would imagine, after all, we are social animals and are well practised in controlling it. Although most research shows no difference between liars and truth-tellers in terms of how much time is spent looking away from an interviewer, this is probably the result of different things simultaneously going on in the liar. He or she may feel an urge to avoid eye contact through nervousness whilst naturally looking away when experiencing an increase in cognitive load, yet at the same time face the conflict of deliberately attempting to maintain eye contact in order to make a convincing impression. Some recent research (Mann et al. 2012) suggests that liars exhibit more *deliberate* eye contact than truth-tellers, which is periods of engaging in unnaturally intent 'staring', combined with looking away, resulting in a normal overall amount of time making eye contact (which is about fifty percent of the time for most people). These differences, however, when they do exist are subtle, and at best unreliable. Studies examine large groups of people rather than focusing on one particular person, and people's behaviour varies. Research has shown that, if anything, concentrating on nonverbal behaviour will normally result in a decrease in deception-detection accuracy. In most people it is better to concentrate on what is said than on any accompanying nonverbal behaviour. There is no reliable cue to deceit akin to Pinocchio's nose. Hence, most deception researchers have long since moved away from studying nonverbal behaviour in the attempt to find more effective ways to catch out liars.

Of course, most people are familiar with the polygraph, and people commonly call it the 'lie detector'. In fact, the polygraph accurately measures physiological activity such as respiration and heart rate, electrodermal activity, and blood pressure. Polygraph examiners ask certain questions based on the assumption that truth-tellers and liars will respond differently in terms of such physiological activity. The most commonly used polygraph test is the Comparison Question Test, also known as the Control Question Test (CQT). This comprises five phases, of which in phase three the questions are devised. These questions should be answered with a 'yes' or a 'no', and fall into neutral (about non crime-related information), relevant (about the crime), and probable lie questions (in which a 'no' answer is likely to be, in the examiner's view, a lie). Responses to neutral questions are disregarded, and responses to probable lie and relevant questions are thought to provoke different physiological patterns in guilty and innocent examinees.

Another, less frequently used test is the Guilty Knowledge Test (GKT). Rather than being based on the assumption that certain questions create more anxiety in liars than in truth-tellers, the GKT is based on the orienting reflex, which occurs when someone is presented with a personally relevant stimulus. An often-used comparison is the 'cocktail party' phenomenon (Cherry 1953) when a person, unaware of the conversations of those around them, may notice if they hear their name mentioned. In a similar way, a murderer, for example, who denies any knowledge of the crime, may produce an orienting reflex when presented with the actual murder weapon, compared to several other weapons that were not used. However, for the GKT to work in such a situation, only the examinee should know what weapon was found at the crime scene, and so its utility is limited (see Chapter 34 by Matthias Gamer and Kristina Suchotzki for more information about the polygraph).

31.4 LIE DETECTION AND VERBAL BEHAVIOUR

Liars and truth-tellers, who both want to be believed, use similar strategies regarding nonverbal behaviour. However, their verbal strategies differ, and so verbal cues to deceit can be elicited by making the existing verbal differences between truth-tellers and liars more pronounced. Numerous methods have recently been developed to capitalize on verbal differences between truth-tellers and liars in an interview situation, and others are currently in development.

Various systems have been developed which involve coding the transcribed statement from an interviewee and analysing it, for detecting differences between liars and truth-tellers. Some systems involve the clustering together of certain individual verbal cues. For example, the computerized text analysis, *Linguistic Inquiry and Word Count* (LIWC) developed by Pennebaker and colleagues (Pennebaker, Francis, and Booth 2001) has shown high detection accuracy in some studies (see Chapter 4 for more information about linguistic cues). In particular, two which have been shown to be effective are *Criteria Based Content Analysis* (known as CBCA; see Vrij 2005 for a review) and *Reality Monitoring* (Sporer 2004). Criteria Based Content Analysis is actually a truth tool, developed by Steller and Köhnken (1989) to establish whether children are telling the truth in cases of alleged sexual abuse. A component of Statement Validity Analysis, CBCA has been shown to work well also with adults in deception studies by revealing differences in speech between truth-tellers and liars. Reality Monitoring works in a similar vein, and has also had success in deception studies, revealing differences between liars' and truth-tellers' accounts. For example, liars are less likely to include *spatial* (how objects relate to each other in space) and *temporal* (how events relate to each other in time) details than truth-tellers. However, whilst both techniques have been demonstrated to be highly effective in revealing differences between liars and truth-tellers, both have a number of drawbacks. These include (but are not limited to) the fact that both techniques require a transcript of the interview, which must be coded by a trained coder. This can be time-consuming and costly. In addition, the interviewee must give a reasonable amount of information in order for many of the coded criteria to be present. If an interviewee is not talkative, neither technique will be effective, and so both may be influenced by the age and personality of the person making the statement (for more information see Vrij 2008).

Recent methods to detect deceit have taken a more active approach in manipulating how much the interviewee says, or generally making life more difficult for a liar. Whereas previous research has generally involved asking the interviewee to 'give as much detail as possible', and then passively examining the result, recent research has started to follow a trend in exacerbating the differences in speech between liars and truth-tellers. This broadly falls into two categories: making an interview more difficult for a liar, and encouraging truth-tellers to say more. Whilst studies are still being developed to find ways that such techniques can be effectively integrated into, for example, police interviews, the results are promising.

31.5 MAKING LYING MORE DIFFICULT

Recently, much deception research has concentrated on developing methods that will make an interview situation harder for a liar than for a truth-teller, thereby increasing the chances of detecting the deceit. There are several ways of achieving this:

Imposing cognitive load: As mentioned above, lying is often more difficult than telling the truth. This is, of course, not always the case, but several studies suggest that in an interview situation, lying is normally more cognitively taxing than telling the truth. We know this because fMRI (functional magnetic resonance imaging) research has shown this to be the case. The fMRI scanner, a very expensive tool typically used in hospitals to detect disease or injury, has been used by some researchers to investigate the physiological brain processes involved during deception (e.g., Kozel et al. 2004; Spence et al. 2001); lying participants normally report that an interview is harder than their truth-telling counterparts find it; and liars tend to exhibit nonverbal signs of increased cognitive load (i.e., a reduction in movements).

There are several reasons for the increased cognitive burden on a liar. He or she has to make up a story that will not contradict what the interviewer may or may not know; remember what he or she has said and attempt to maintain consistency; withhold the truth; monitor the interviewer to see if the story appears to be accepted; and monitor his or her own behaviour in order to appear truthful. A truth-teller is unlikely to experience these burdens, or if he or she does then it will probably be to a lesser degree. For example, it is possible that a truth-teller, if worried about not being believed, may monitor the interviewer and so on, but most truth-tellers take their credibility for granted (this is referred to as the '*illusion of transparency*'). Therefore, when cognitive load is increased in all interviewees, liars are likely to struggle more than truth-tellers, as the lie is already compromising their cognitive capacity. This may then lead to verbal cues to the lie.

Several methods of increasing cognitive load have been investigated: Firstly, asking interviewees to recall an event in reverse chronological order. This does not bother truth-tellers as they are recalling an actual event from memory and can happily flit about to different parts of the event. Furthermore, asking a truth-teller to report an event in reverse order may well prompt more memories of the event as the interviewee alters the course of the recall. Liars however, tend to remember and rehearse their story in chronological order, and so to recall it in reverse order is more disconcerting and likely to result in less information, but more consistency. Secondly, asking participants to conduct a secondary task at the same time as recalling the event will make the process more difficult for liars, whose cognitive capacity is already compromised by the task of lying. Studies where this method has been effective have included asking participants to maintain eye contact with the interviewer, or to simultaneously take part in a secondary task, such as answering questions on a screen; or asking participants to operate a simulated driving game. Truth-tellers, who do not have to think so hard about what they say, can complete such secondary tasks with relative ease compared to the liar, who will normally suffer in terms of the story quality or ability in the secondary task. When clips or transcripts of interviews with liars and truth-tellers telling a story in chronological order, and reverse order, are shown to observers, detection accuracy increases in the reverse-order condition as discrepancies between the two become more obvious.

Unexpected questions: Asking questions that are not anticipated is likely to be more disconcerting for a liar than a truth-teller. A truth-teller can recall from memory the strange information, whereas a liar, who is likely to have prepared for expected questions (Granhag, Andersson, Strömwall, and Hartwig 2004) but unlikely to have prepared for unexpected questions, will have to improvise on the spot. Types of unexpected questions that have been investigated include those asking for temporal details or spatial details. To further the latter point, another technique that has been developed with some success is to ask participants to sketch a drawing, for example, of the location where the event took place. When describing a location verbally, liars are afforded some leeway into being vague about where objects and people are positioned. Drawing the location removes this opportunity to be vague. Furthermore, to first ask interviewees to discuss the location and to then ask them to draw it is likely to result in noticeable differences in a deceptive account.

Processes versus outcomes. Another focus of asking for unexpected information is known as *processes versus outcomes*. Asking interviewees to discuss the planning of an event, rather than the event itself, is likely to be unanticipated by a liar, and hence they will struggle more than truth-tellers to answer such questions, again, as on-the-spot improvisation is required (Warmelink, Vrij, Mann, Jundi, and Granhag 2012). For example, rather than simply ask a person who is entering a country what the purpose of their trip is (the outcome), to instead ask what planning they had to do to come on their trip, what they needed to pack, and what transport they will use to reach their destination (processes) is less expected.

Verifiable details: Another recent line of research is to ask interviewees to provide in their story details which can be verified by the interviewer. Obviously, since the liar's story is not true, he or she will struggle more to provide details which could be checked (such as including other people who could act as potential witnesses, the use of a mobile phone in a certain location, the GPS information, which will be checkable, and so on). Liars will be reluctant to include information which is likely to contradict their story, so instead provide details, but only those that cannot be verified (Nahari, Vrij, and Fisher 2014).

Strategic use of evidence: Typically in police interviews, the suspect is confronted with all the evidence against them at the start of the interview. This gives the suspect the opportunity to adapt their story in order to fit the existing evidence. A new line of research has involved investigating when the best time is to present evidence in order to better detect liars. If reseachers start with asking the interviewee to give their account of what happened, and then presenting them with any evidence once they have committed to the story, liars have a much more difficult job to then adapt and make their story fit the evidence. This is called the *Strategic Use of Evidence* (or SUE) technique (Hartwig, Granhag, and Strömwall 2007) and has been shown to be highly effective in detecting liars.

31.6 ENCOURAGING TRUTH-TELLERS TO SAY MORE

Recent research has identified another effective method of detecting deceit, by widening the gap between the speech of a liar and of a truth-teller. Liars will prefer not to talk too much, at least about details relating specifically to the event (though they may be very happy to talk extensively about things that do not specifically relate to the event about which they can be quite truthful, giving the impression of being relaxed and cooperative without actually providing any useful information). This is because by giving more information they may incriminate themselves, or lose track of what they have said, making it more difficult to be consistent. Furthermore, they may lack the imagination to invent extra details on the spot. Truth-tellers, however, are normally quite happy to talk, though people vary in the amount of information they consider to be appropriate and which they will spontaneously volunteer. Hence, methods of encouraging people to say more typically result in truth-tellers (but not liars) saying much more. Several lines of research have investigated methods of encouraging truth-tellers to say more:

Supportive interviewer: A supportive interviewer, who adopts a positive demeanour, smiles, and nods in response to what the interviewee says, has been demonstrated to encourage truth-tellers to say more (Mann et al. 2013). Conversely, a liar is likely to read these behavioural affirmations on the part of the interviewer as confirmation that they have said enough to satisfy any demands that they are required to meet, and this eliminates the likelihood of their adding any further information.

Mimicry: When conversation partners like and identify with each other, they typically (and unconsciously) mimic each other, using similar body language. Those with training in sales will be familiar with the concept of subtly mimicking the behaviour of a potential client to create a pleasant and supportive atmosphere. Research in which an interviewer mimicked the behaviour of liars and truth-tellers (Shaw et al. 2015) has demonstrated that (i) both truth-tellers and liars are very unlikely to notice they are being mimicked (so long as the mimicking is subtle, for example a mirrored seating position, rather than copying every movement) and (ii) truth-tellers are likely to add more details than when the behaviour is not mimicked. Again, liars will be more reluctant to add more detail for reasons listed above, such as not wanting to add incriminating or later to be forgotten details, and so mimicking does not have such an effect on liars.

Model statement: Recent research (Leal, Vrij, Warmelink, Vernham, and Fisher 2015) has investigated the utility of playing interviewees a 'model statement' (a pre-recorded statement which acts as a model of the amount of detail that is required of the interviewee). After asking interviewees to give their story, researchers played interviewees an audio-recording of a statement which was very rich in detail, but completely unrelated in terms of subject area to the event in question. This is because to give a statement which includes details that a liar may borrow to build his or her own story, or which may in any way contaminate the memories of a truth-teller, would be counter-productive. As mentioned above, many truth-tellers are not sure how much detail precisely is expected of them, even when specifically asked to 'give as much detail as they can possibly remember'. The playing of an example statement typically results in truth-tellers having a better idea of how much detail is required of them, and so they tend to add much more information. Again, liars will still be less keen to add more detail, as they feel it may result in their further incriminating themselves. Note, the playing of a standard and pre-recorded model statement has been shown to be considerably more effective than a similar technique whereby the interviewer gives the interviewee an example of how much detail they would like by, say, describing an object in great detail. The latter involves one item which is described in huge detail, whereas an effective model statement is a description, for example, of a whole event, whereby many different elements of the event are described in a lot more detail than most interviewees would spontaneously report. That said, a model statement audio-recording can last less than two minutes and still be highly effective.

Drawings: As mentioned briefly above in the *unexpected questions* section, drawings can be a useful interview tool to aid deception detection. When asked to sketch something related to the event, liars and truth-tellers tend to produce differing levels of detail in their drawings (Vrij, Leal, Mann, Warmelink, Granhag, and Fisher 2010). As mentioned above, liars have more difficulty in producing a fictitious drawing as this commits them to place items in space that may be referred to more vaguely when described verbally. In addition, liars are often more reluctant to include people in their drawings than truth-tellers, who automatically tend to include the people who were present at the event. This is logical for two reasons, because either to add people who were not there may lead to more difficult questions, or the liar may simply forget to add someone who, after all, was not actually there.

31.7 Alternative lines of research in detection of deceit

So far, only interviews with a seated, single interviewee have been discussed. Largely this is because deception research has predominantly investigated just this situation because, after all, it is typically the situation in a police interview. However, some professions require deceit detection in other contexts. For example, customs officers, border patrol guards, or security personnel may need to make judgements when dealing with groups of people. Recently, studies have been conducted into developing techniques that can be used to detect deceit collectively in pairs who are interviewed simultaneously. One advantage of interviewing two people together is that the interaction between the two can be observed. For example, lying pairs tend to spend more time trying to engage eye contact with the interviewer than with each other. Truth-tellers will happily interrupt each other, and generally communicate more with each other as they recall their story together. But furthermore, the interview can potentially be manipulated in order to elicit signs of deceit:

Collective Interviewing: Forced turn-taking: By asking one interviewee to commence describing the pair's activities, and then interrupting and asking the other member of the pair to continue, the interviewer can effectively distinguish differences between liars and truth-tellers (Vernham, Vrij, Mann, Leal, and Hillman 2014). Truth-tellers who have experienced an event together are recalling from memory and can quite happily continue each other's stories. Liars, however, who may have rehearsed an answer but do not have genuine experience to draw on, tend to find the request to continue each other's stories more cognitively demanding. As a result they will each be more inclined to start their 'turn' by repeating what the other pair member just said, and more inclined to pause before speaking, to the extent that observers can distinguish between truth-tellers and liars with high accuracy. It is not always possible to interview people together, but in some circumstances it is (for example, when unofficially questioning people or at border points), and the research conducted so far is promising in producing cues to deceit such as those mentioned above (e.g., see Vrij et al. 2012; and Vernham and Vrij 2015 for a review).

Nonverbal Deception: As mentioned above, most deception research has focused on seated participants. The trend in research has turned to verbal behaviour over nonverbal, so one may argue that there is little point in analysing the nonverbal behaviour of a walking person. A liar may exhibit signs of nervousness when walking as well as sitting, but then so may a truth-teller. For example, in an airport context, a person who is attempting to smuggle drugs through an airport may feel (and hence exhibit signs of being) nervous or emotional, but then so will many perfectly innocent travellers, depending on what awaits them at their destination, or through a fear of flying. However, one area where the examination of nonverbal differences between truth-tellers and liars is valuable is in the detection of differences between genuine and faked injuries. Some recent research (Hillman 2014) using point-light technology (the placing of balls on key joints of the body and specialized cameras resulting in video footage showing lights on those key joints only, whereby a person's movement can be easily observed and analysed) shows promise which may have huge potential for insurance companies and benefits agencies tasked with deciding who is genuinely injured and who is not, where diagnosis is not always objective and straightforward. Early results suggest that, as in a seated position, lying participants tend to 'overdo' the behaviour when attempting to demonstrate how they would walk with a foot injury compared to when they are actually experiencing a foot injury.

31.8 CONCLUSION

Lie detection is a difficult task, especially when taken at face value. Deception research has consistently shown that most people make poor lie detectors. There are many reasons for this, the primary one being that lying in itself is not a behaviour, but it may lead to various behaviours depending on (a) the liar, (b) the lie, and (c) the target. All of the different threads in deception research have one thing in common; there are large individual differences. A study with 100 participants may show that the majority will do one thing, but that 'thing' may be quite subtle, and there will always be people who will do the opposite. There are conflicting mechanisms that may be going on in a liar and again, these will vary depending on the person (their personality, how guilty they feel about lying, what their motivations for lying are) and on the lie (whether there is much at stake, who the lie is to, what the circumstances are). The liar may feel guilt and anxiety (which should lead to nervous behaviours) but conversely, he or she may control his or her behaviour in order to exhibit behaviours that appear credible (impression management) and also may experience cognitive load (that is, increased cognitive control, which may also reduce the appearance of behaviours typically associated with nervousness). Hence, deception researchers tasked with creating techniques to assist in the detection of deception have largely moved on to designing interview protocols that more reliably widen the gap between liars and truth-tellers, as well as attempting to dispel the myths that professional lie detectors, such as the police, may believe.

CHAPTER 32

LYING AND COMPUTATIONAL LINGUISTICS

KEES VAN DEEMTER AND EHUD REITER

32.1 INTRODUCTION

STUDIES of lying can take many shapes, from purely theoretical work to empirical studies and investigations into practical issues in law, medicine, and elsewhere. The present chapter takes a novel point of view that might be called the engineering perspective on lying. We show how departures from the truth can easily arise, either automatically or deliberately, when computers generate textual summaries of data. We shall explain how the processes of information selection and interpretation that are inherent in the presentation of data—whether this is done by computers or by people—can compromise the objectivity and truthfulness of the information presented; and also that sometimes falsehoods make sense because they are in the best interest of the hearer and/or speaker. The question which of all these deviations from the truth amount to lying will be briefly discussed, though we will not offer a definitive stand on this issue.

The plan for this chapter is as follows. First we explain briefly how Natural Language Generation (NLG) systems work when they talk about data. Then we present three types of deviations from the truth that NLG systems may indulge in. We then discuss each of these types of behaviour, illustrating our account through examples from practical NLG systems, focusing on a class of systems in which these issues come to the fore with particular force. We conclude by sketching a simple game-theoretical perspective that can help to explain our observations in the specific case when the NLG system is 'lying' because it believes this will help the hearer. We hope to shed light on a broad variety of deviations from the truth, whether it is people or computers that take the floor.

32.2 GENERATING TEXT FROM DATA

Natural Language Generation uses computational linguistics and artificial intelligence techniques to automatically generate texts in English (and other human languages) from non-linguistic input data (Reiter and Dale 2000). In this section we give a brief overview of how NLG systems work, using the Babytalk systems as examples.

Babytalk is a family of systems which generate summaries of clinical information, extracted from an electronic patient record (EPR), about a baby in a neonatal intensive care unit (NICU). There are four Babytalk systems:

- BT45 (Portet et al. 2009): summarizes 45 minutes of clinical data to help clinicians make real-time decisions about medical interventions.
- BT-Nurse (Hunter et al. 2012): summarizes events and observations over a 12-hour nursing shift, to assist in handover when a new shift starts.
- BT-Family (Mahamood and Reiter 2011): summarizes 24 hours' worth of data for the baby's parents.
- BT-Clan (Moncur et al. 2013): preliminary work was carried out on a system which summarized information for friends and relatives of the baby's parents.

The process of generating a text in Babytalk (and in other 'data-to-text' systems) involves five steps (Reiter 2007): signal analysis, data interpretation, document planning, microplanning, realization. We illustrate these using 3 minutes of example data input for BT45 (a full input data set is 45 minutes for BT45, 12 hours for BT-Nurse, and 24 hours for BT-Family and BT-Clan).

Signal analysis: Signal analysis looks for patterns, such as spikes or steps, in the input data. For example, in the example input in Figure 32.1, this module might identify the following patterns:

- Downward spike in HR (heart rate), just before 1040
- Downward step in SO (blood oxygen saturation), again just before 1040
- Upward spike in BM (blood pressure), at around 1040
- TC (core temperature) stable at 37.5
- TP (peripheral temperature) stable at 36.

Signal analysis would also determine parameters, such as when a spike occurred, how far it went, etc.

One of the challenges in signal analysis is distinguishing genuine patterns (i.e., actual changes in the baby's HR, etc.) from noise (e.g., the SO sensor is attached to the baby's foot, and if the baby kicks, the sensor can flap and measure air rather than the baby, which results in spurious values). It's not always easy to distinguish real patterns from noise, and signal analysis can return factually incorrect information about patterns if it makes mistakes in differentiating real patterns from noise.

Data interpretation: Data interpretation means interpreting and describing patterns using domain knowledge. For example, a clinically significant downward spike in heart rate (HR) is called a *bradycardia*; one simple rule is that a downward spike in HR in a NICU baby is a *bradycardia* if the change is at least 50 and the minimum value is below 100 (note that babies have much higher heart rates than adults). Similarly, a clinically significant downward step in blood oxygen saturation (SO) is called a *desaturation*; a simple rule is that a downward step in SO is a *desaturation* if the change is at least 10 and the value drops below 80. According to these rules, the change in HR in Figure 32.1 qualifies as a bradycardia, and the change in SO in Figure 32.1 qualifies as a desaturation. Bradycardias and desaturations are clinically significant events which should be reported to doctors and nurses. Of course the above rules

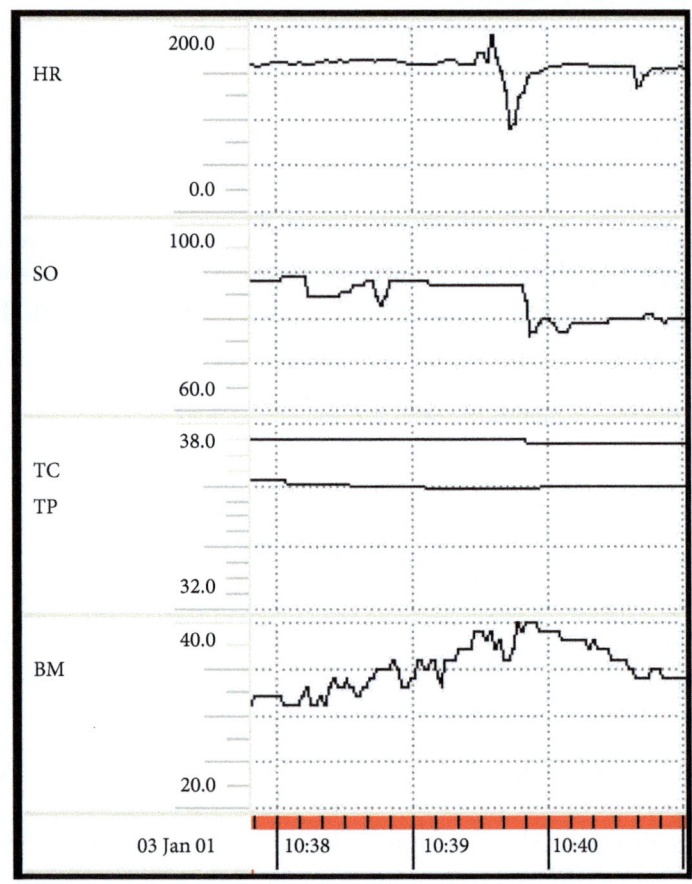

FIGURE 32.1 Example time-series input data for Babytalk BT45 system (from Reiter 2007). HR is heart rate, SO is oxygen saturation, TC is core temperature, TP is peripheral (toe) temperature, BM is mean blood pressure.

are very simple, and indeed an expert doctor who looked at this data described the HR change as a *bradycardia*, but did not describe the SO change as a *desaturation*. Mistakes in data interpretation due to over-simple rules can lead to incorrect assertions in texts, such as claiming that the baby had a desaturation when in fact this was not the case.

Data interpretation also links patterns and events. For example, this baby was given a morphine injection at 1039, and the system might link the changes in HR (bradycardia) and BM at 1040 to this event, using domain knowledge that injections are stressful to the baby and can cause spikes in HR and BM. Again, over-simplified rules (such as this one) can lead to incorrect inferences and hence mistakes in the generated text.

Document planning: The document planner decides which messages (information) to include in the text, what order the messages should occur in, and how messages are rhetorically linked. In this case, for example, the document planner might decide that it needed to mention the morphine injection and the bradycardia (change in HR), change in SO, and change in BM; but that it was not necessary to mention that TC and TP are stable. It might also decide on the order (Morphine, HR/bradycardia, BM, SO) (grouping HR and BM together because they both measure what the heart is doing, whereas SO is more about the lungs), and that the HR and SO events are rhetorically consequences of the morphine event.

Clearly document planning requires making decisions about what information should be in the generated text, which can lead to errors of omission. For instance, when the expert doctor looked at the above data, he thought that while it was correct not to mention changes in TC or TP on their own, the text should mention that the difference between TC and TP had increased (i.e., the baby's toes got colder compared to the baby's chest, which possibly indicated circulation problems).

Microplanning: The microplanner decides which words and syntactic structures should be used to express the information linguistically. For example, the microplanner would decide whether *BM*, *mean BP*, or *mean blood pressure* should be used to linguistically refer to the BM data channel. The microplanner might also decide to use passive constructs in order to avoid mentioning the doctor or nurse (e.g., "*an injection of morphine was given*" instead of "*the nurse gave an injection of morphine*"). As can be seen from these examples, the microplanner needs knowledge of the "genre" or "sublanguage" (Kittredge and Lehrberger 1982) used in the target texts.

The microplanner also has to decide how to express atomic pieces of information, including time, rhetorical relation, and size/duration of patterns. In some cases it may decide to use vague words (e.g., "*momentary*") instead of presenting specific numerical parameters (e.g., "*20 seconds*"). It may also decide not to explicitly express information. Rhetorical relations, for example, are often inferred by readers and hence do not need to be explicitly represented.

Microplanning can lead to misinterpreted texts when the microplanner does not use vague words, as expected by the reader. For example, if the microplanner used *momentary* to describe a bradycardia which lasts 10 seconds, whilst the doctor reading the text expects that *momentary* is only used for bradycardias which last 5 seconds or less.

Realization: The realizer uses the rules of grammar to generate texts in English or other human languages. For example, the realizer might produce the below text to express the above information:

An injection of morphine was given at 10.39. There was a momentary bradycardia and mean BP rose to 40. SO fell to 79.

If realization is done correctly, it is a mechanical process which should not lead to incorrect texts. Although even with realization, interpretation problems can arise if the generated text is syntactically ambiguous.

Summary: The above example is of course very simple, resulting in the production of just 23 words; a full Babytalk text is much longer (several pages in the case of BT-Nurse). But we can see that even just producing these 23 words is a complex process; and also that there is potential for introducing incorrect statements, and also errors of omission, because the algorithms used to perform signal analysis, data interpretation, etc. are not 100% correct.

32.3 Types of deviation from the truth

In this chapter, we distinguish between three types of behaviour (Table 32.1) which might be considered to be 'lying' (and for each type, we also distinguish between problems caused by partial information and problems caused by incorrect information). To avoid misunderstandings, we will speak about "deviations from the truth," rather than the morally loaded term 'lying', whose applicability is debatable in some of these cases. In presenting our distinctions we will take the point of view of

Table 32.1 Types of deviation from the truth

	Partial information	Incorrect information
Unavoidable or accidental	1. Filter information because you cannot communicate everything	2. Simplification and algorithmic errors
Avoidable, in hearer's interest	3. Do not say things which might hurt the hearer	4. Say incorrect things when one needs to say something, and truth might hurt the hearer
Avoidable, not in hearer's interest	5. Do not mention things which might dissuade the hearer from doing what the speaker wants her to do	6. Say things which cause the hearer to do what the speaker wants, even if they are incorrect

an NLG system but we shall argue that the same distinctions apply to human communication as well.

1. *Unavoidable or accidental*: The NLG system communicates incorrect and/or partial information, not because it intends to but because it is unable to communicate full correct information. In what follows, we shall not distinguish between cases in which a deviation from the truth is genuinely unavoidable and ones in which a deviation is merely accidental (e.g., a programming bug). For brevity, we shall use the term 'Unavoidable' whenever the system deviates from the truth without having an intention to do so.
2. *Avoidable, in hearer's interest*: The NLG system deliberately decides to communicate partial or incorrect information, because it believes this is better for the hearer.
3. *Avoidable, not in hearer's interest*: The NLG system deliberately decides to communicate partial or incorrect information, even though this is not in the hearer's interest, because it helps achieve a communicative goal held by the system.

We will discuss these types of behaviour next, focusing on the first two categories, because the third category is rare (there are very few NLG systems which deliberately communicate partial or incorrect information which is not in the hearer's interest). We also present a game-theoretic model of the second category, NLG systems which deliberately communicate partial or incorrect information because they think this helps the hearer.

32.3.1 Type 1: "The whole truth and nothing but the truth" is impossible: unavoidable partial or incorrect information

As we saw in the first section of this chapter, it is not generally possible for a data-to-text system to communicate all of its input data in its textual summary. For example, the twenty-three-word summary shown in the first section summarizes approximately 1000 data points (numbers); it is not generally possible for a twenty-three-word summary to precisely describe 1000 data points. And many data-to-text systems have much higher 'compression rates' than this; for example, RoadSafe (Turner et al. 2010) generates paragraphs which summarize tens of megabytes of data. Summarization at this level means the summary must both be very selective (and hence omit a lot of information), and also give high-level summaries of data instead of detailed descriptions.

Also as explained in the first section of this chapter, data-to-text systems make mistakes, because their algorithms are not perfect (e.g., for identifying bradycardias and desaturations), because of software bugs (which are unavoidable in real-world software), and because medical professionals can sometimes forget to enter information about medical interventions (e.g., when oxygen is administered to a baby) into the system by hand. Potentially, such an omission can even cause the system to misunderstand what caused a change in the baby's condition.

Most interesting from our perspective, selectivity, summarization, and mistakes can happen through the NLG process. For example,

Signal analysis: What patterns should the system look for? For example, the expert doctor thought changes in TC–TP (difference in temperature between chest and toe) in Figure 32.1 were important, because they give information about circulation. This pattern would not be detected by a system which only looked for patterns in the individual data channels (e.g., changes in TC and changes in TP, but not changes in TC–TP).

Data interpretation: Medically important downward spikes in HR (heart rate) are called *bradycardias*. But the rules used to identify which spikes are bradycardias may be too simplistic, for example just looking at changes in HR and ignoring important contextual factors such as the patient's age and health issues. This may result in false negatives (NLG system omitting a bradycardia which it should have mentioned), and false positives (NLG system incorrectly describing a pattern as a bradycardia). From the perspective of deviations from the truth, false negatives lead to partial information, and false positives lead to incorrect information.

Document planning: As mentioned above, document planners may make mistakes because they leave out medically important information. They can also make mistakes because they leave out information which is needed for narrative continuity; see sections 6.1 and 6.4 of Portet et al. (2009). It can also happen that causally unrelated events are accidentally juxtaposed, inviting a reader to mistakenly infer causality. For example, if a rise in oxygen saturation is reported immediately after a medical intervention, then a reader might understand the system to imply that the rise was caused by the intervention (as when we say "John's doctor asked him to lose weight. He went on a diet"; this can be taken to imply that the John went on a diet *because* his doctor asked him to lose weight).

Microplanning: Descriptions of data often use vague terms such as "*momentary*" or "*large*" instead of precise numbers such as "*19.456 seconds*" or "*34.865 bpm*." Vague terms are used because they speed up comprehension, and hence help busy domain experts quickly understand the situation. Unfortunately, human readers do not always interpret vague terms as expected, in part because there can be large differences between readers in how vague terms are interpreted (Toogood 1980; Berry et al. 2002; van Deemter 2010). Berry et al. (2002) point out that even numbers such as "25%" are interpreted differently by different people.

Realization: When information is finally expressed in sentences, there is a danger that syntactically ambiguous structures will be produced, as in "Brief coughing episodes and bradycardias were observed," where it is potentially unclear whether the adjective *brief* extends to *bradycardias* as well as *coughing episodes*. Avoiding *all* syntactic ambiguities is known to be a practical impossibility Abney (1996), so it has been argued that the best that NLG systems can do is avoid those ambiguous sentences that are likely to be misinterpreted (Khan et al. 2012). For example, if the intended meaning of the subject is (Brief (coughing episodes and bradycardias)), and this interpretation is in fact much more likely to be chosen by a reader than the competing interpretation ((Brief coughing episodes) and bradycardias)) then the sentence is not considered misleading.

A final point is that texts can also be factually incorrect because of over-simplification, especially when communicating complex technical information to non-technical audiences. For example, patient information leaflets must be short and easy to read, otherwise no one will read them, which means they will have no impact. But this means they are over-simplified. A dietary advice leaflet, for example, may say "avoid saturated fats," which is useful as a simple generic rule, but in detail is false, since some saturated fats (e.g., from nuts) are quite healthy.

In summary, it is often simply not possible for an NLG data-to-text system to create texts which are "the whole truth and nothing but the truth."

32.3.2 Type 2: Benign deceit: partial or incorrect information which is in the hearer's interest

Sometimes NLG systems deliberately omit information, for example when trying to persuade people to change their behaviour in desirable ways. For example, the STOP system (Reiter et al. 2003) generated personalized smoking-cessation letters, for people who wanted to stop smoking. STOP did not mention any information in its letters that might discourage smokers from trying to quit, such as low probability of success. Such information would perhaps be useful to a rational agent who is making a logical decision about whether to try to stop smoking. However, it was felt to be detrimental and discouraging to a human recipient who probably has tried to quit smoking before and failed, but who might be able to succeed now owing to changing circumstances.

The preferred strategy with information which is detrimental to the system and hearer is usually to omit it. However sometimes simple omission is not possible, because the system must say something, and in such cases NLG systems may deliberately say things which are not true.

Moncur et al. (2009, 2013) discusses a few cases of benign deceit. Moncur worked on Babytalk-Clan (discussed in section 32.2), which generated summaries of the status of a baby in neonatal intensive care for friends and relatives (the system was designed and partially evaluated, but not fully implemented). The content of the summary was controlled by the baby's parents (who received more complete information from a different system, Babytalk-Family), who could specify what information they wanted communicated to different recipients. Parents could also request that some recipients be told that the baby was doing well, even if in fact the baby was doing badly. This was typically because of privacy protection, impression management, and prevention of anxiety in the recipient. If we look for now just at the last of these, prevention of anxiety, one situation where this arose was when the recipient was herself in poor health (e.g., an elderly grandmother with a heart condition), and the parents did not want to risk adversely affecting the recipient (e.g., triggering a heart attack) by giving her distressing news. Because the recipient regularly received updates about the baby's states, it was necessary to send her something (a lack of an update would be very worrying), so the system told the recipient that the baby was doing well, even though this was factually incorrect.

Obviously there are deep ethical and moral questions here, which Babytalk-Clan ducked by leaving the choice to parents. But certainly one could imagine building a system which made such choices itself, in which case the decision logic (when to lie) would need to be explicitly programmed.

This sort of situation is unusual, but there are other situations where it is arguably in the recipient's interest to lie, at least in the short term, in order to reduce stress/distress. In particular, doctors sometimes lie to patients with psychological problems (Agronin 2011). However, we are not aware of any computational implementation of this behaviour.

A different reason for benign deceit is that it is the most efficient way to achieve a communicative goal. For example, Kutlak (2014) points out that this can be the case when referring to an object, if the user's knowledge is incomplete or incorrect. For instance, a system might refer to a dolphin using *"look at the big fish,"* if the hearer is not familiar with dolphins. This statement is factually incorrect, since a dolphin is not a fish, but it also may be the most efficient way to achieve the referential communicative goal. Another example is that a system might refer to Thomas Edison as *"the man who invented the light bulb."*. This is incorrect because Edison did not in fact invent the light bulb. However, most people believe Edison did invent the light bulb, and Kutlak's work shows that this phrase is the most effective way to identify Edison at least in some contexts.

Of course, in such cases it is often possible to be more precise and truthful, e.g., *"look at the thing which looks like a big fish"* instead of *"look at the big fish."* But in many communicative contexts the shorter expression is preferred and more appropriate, and indeed the longer, truthful expression may be perceived as pedantic.

32.3.3 Type 3: Taking advantage: partial or incorrect information which is not in the hearer's interest

In the above cases, the system is trying to do what is best for the hearer. However, there are also cases where the system may deliberately mislead or misinform the hearer because this helps the system achieve its goals. This happens especially in sales contexts. For example, Carenini and Moore (2006) describe an NLG real estate system which describes houses to interested buyers. It does not say anything which is factually incorrect, but it selects information which it believes will help convince the user to buy this property, and omits some information which might dissuade the user from buying this property. We are not, however, aware of any NLG systems used in sales contexts which utter deliberate falsehoods like the stereotypical used-car salesman.

Returning to Moncur et al.'s (2009, 2013) discussion of deceit in Babytalk-Clan, the other reasons mentioned here for deceit (in addition to anxiety reduction) were privacy protection and impression management. For example, if parents did not want a friend or relative to visit or telephone them, they might ask Babytalk-Clan to tell the relative that the baby was doing fine, even when this is false. Deception in this case is in the speaker's interest but arguably not in the hearer's interest; this is one of the very few cases we are aware of where an NLG system communicates false information which is not in the hearer's interest.

32.3.4 Caveat: what is a deviation from the truth?

Having discussed our classification of the different kinds of deviations from the truth, we need to add an important *caveat* that is sometimes overlooked: the inherent ambiguity and vagueness of human language means that it is sometimes debatable whether a given sentence (or a longer text, for that matter) constitutes a deviation from the truth.

One kind of example was mentioned before, where an NLG system juxtaposes two sentences (e.g., one describing a medical intervention and the other asserting a rise in oxygen saturation): it is debatable whether such a juxtaposition conveys a causal relation between the two events, so if this causal relation does not in fact exist, it is difficult to decide whether the system has lied. Other ambiguities can have a similar effect. For example, when we quantify, we often leave it unclear what we quantify over. Thus, we can say "The baby's temperature has consistently been below X," it may be unclear whether we talk about an entire day, about all the time since the last operation, or about all the time that the baby has been in hospital. Ambiguity complicates meaning, truth, and falsity.

Perhaps the most prolific source of 'debatable lying' arises from the fact that many of the words in every human language lack a precise definition: when we say it is nice weather, the word *nice* does not come with precise borderlines in terms of temperature, humidity, wind speed, and so on: it is *vague*, as linguists say. Despite efforts to 'precisify' medically relevant terms (e.g., defining obesity in terms of Body Mass Index), vagueness affects many of them (see van Deemter 2010 for discussion and analysis). Thus, for example, if an NLG system or a doctor asserts that a baby is 'stable', then a human reader may mistakenly conclude that all is well. Whether the system has deviated from the truth in such a case is, once again, debatable.

32.4 Lying?

Taking stock of our classification of deviations from the truth—which arose naturally from the engineering perspective, as we have seen—a natural question is: which of these constitute lying? At the heart of lying lies an intention to deceive (see Sakama et al. 2014 for an account in modal logic, with a role for half-truths, 'bullshitting', and withholding of information), and this rules out *unavoidable* deviations from the truth (the top cells of our table). But which of the remaining cells involve deception is difficult to say: both incomplete and incorrect information can cause false inferences in some cases, but whether such inferences are likely to be drawn in a particular situation depends on factors such as the hearer's background information; consequently, lying cuts across the cells of our table. Moreover, lying is usually associated with morally questionable motives. (Few people would speak of lying in connection with Kutlak's (2014) description of a dolphin as a *"big fish,"* for instance, where the motive is clarity; see section 32.3.2.) What is missing from our table is an analysis of the reasons why a speaker decides to deviate from the truth. These reasons will be addressed in the following section.

32.5 Towards a Game-Theoretic Model

Deceitful behaviour has been studied in game theory from von Neumann and Morgenstern's work onwards (von Neumann and Morgenstern 1944: section 19). At the time of writing, insights coming out of this tradition—which analyses social interactions in terms of their 'pay-offs' for participants—are frequently informing linguistic analyses of lying and other deceitful communicative actions (e.g., Franke et al. 2009; Asher and Lascarides 2013). The emphasis in the bulk of this work is on situations in which players have opposing interests; although we acknowledge the existence of such situations (bottom cells in our table), we focus here on 'benign deceit' situations where the NLG system is producing text with partial or incorrect information because it believes this is best for the hearer.

As argued in van Deemter (2009, 2010), the decisions of a human or artificial speaker can likewise be thought of in decision-theoretic or game-theoretic terms. Let us see how such a perspective might help to clarify the ways in which speakers deviate from the truth, bearing in mind the lessons from the previous sections. This is not to say that existing NLG systems perform game-theoretical reasoning yet, for although it is conceivable for deviations from the truth to be decided computationally, on the fly, existing systems do not work in this way. Babytalk-Clan, for example, leaves the decision on what information to omit (for a given audience) to the baby's parents. Other systems may be seen as hard-wired to "err on the side of caution": for example, the notion of a bradycardia will tend to be defined broadly enough that a borderline case (which may or may not be seen as a bradycardia) will still be flagged.

Our starting point is a simple game theory model (similar to Crawford and Sobel 1982), which was specifically designed for shedding light on communication. The model is agnostic about the details of linguistic theory and simply models information as a set of possible 'contents'. For our purposes, a content might be the diagnosis of a disease, for instance. Utterances are modelled as a set F of possible 'forms' (i.e., utterances) that the speaker can consider. A speaker S is modelled as mapping contents to forms, associating each content with a form that expresses the content. Furthermore, a hearer H maps forms to a set 'Actions', thereby associating each form with an 'action' undertaken by the hearer as a result of hearing the form in question. Schematically,

S: Contents → Forms
H: Forms → Actions

Each of these two mappings can be deterministic or stochastic, allowing that the same content may be expressed by means of different forms on different occasions. We are liberal about Actions: these may be states of mind (e.g., knowing something or not; being happy or depressed) as well as proper actions (e.g., changing one's diet). Crucially, the model lets the hearer (H) associate each action with a *utility* value between 0 and 1, saying how favourable the action is for H; the speaker (S) is modelled analogously, so this aspect of the model can be expressed schematically by means of two utility functions, where 0 is the lowest and 1 the highest utility:

Utility$_S$: Actions → [0, 1]
Utility$_H$: Actions → [0, 1]

Since an NLG system (S) is typically designed for the benefit of human users, let us start out assuming that the two utility functions are equal (that is, Utility$_S$ = Utility$_H$), so the interests of the user are perfectly aligned with those of the system and its human owners. For example, if S is a medical information system, we assume that S aims to maximize the utility for the user.

In earlier sections we saw that speakers may deviate from the truth by omitting information (Partial Information) or by adding (or inviting the hearer to infer) information that is false. To demonstrate the potential of a game-theoretical analysis, let us look at some different examples.

Consider a psychiatric patient in a crisis. The patient asks what is wrong with him and the psychiatrist, who knows that the patient suffers from condition C, can answer in two ways: either by giving the full name and prognosis of C (utterance F), or by sketching the nature of the illness in broad terms only (F'). The doctor faces a choice between F and F'. Suppose F will cause the patient to get more deeply depressed (A), whereas utterance F' will leave him much better off (A'):

S(C) = F or S(C) = F'
H(F) = A
H(F') = A'

$U_H(A) = 0.2$
$U_H(A') = 0.4$

In this situation, F′ would be preferable to F, from the perspective of both S and H. Of course in reality the hearer's response to an utterance is not known with certainty. A more realistic scenario might therefore associate each hearer's response with a probability (P). Suppose the doctor has a choice between an utterance F, which reliably leads to behaviour A1, and an utterance F′, whose consequences are associated with two possible outcomes A2 and A3, where one of these is better than A1, whereas the other is worse than A1:

$P(H(F)=A1) = 1$ (the effect of F on the patient is certain)
$P(H(F')=A2) = 0.6$
$P(H(F')=A3) = 0.4$
$U_H(A1) = 0.45$
$U_H(A2) = 0.7$
$U_H(A3) = 0.4$

Utterance F has an *expected utility* of 0.45; utterance, F′, has an expected utility of (0.6*0.7) + (0.4*0.4) = (0.42 + 0.16) = 0.58, suggesting that F′ might be preferable to F. A more refined analysis could go beyond expected utility. The procedure could be adapted in such a way that 'safe' utterances such as F are preferred over 'high-risk, high pay-off' ones such as F′. The difficult medical and moral question of what is the best procedure is not for us to answer. See, however, Porat and Yadlin (2016) for extensive discussion of these and related moral and legal issues.

More complex examples abound in the literature, and these can be analysed along similar lines. For instance, Agronin (2011) discusses an example of a dementia patient who asks about the availability of a car. A car is, in fact, available, and hence the doctor is faced with a choice between speaking the truth and producing a white lie ("We don't have a car here"). A game-theory analysis would assess the expected utility of each utterance by looking at all eventualities and their probabilities. In the case of speaking the truth ("We do have a car"), the probability of a car accident needs to be considered; in the case of a white lie, the question is whether the patient will find out that she has been told an untruth, and what the effect will be on her mood and her relationship with the doctor. As before, the most difficult part of the problem is to assess the utility of all possible outcomes.

So far we have focused on situations in which the interests of speakers and hearers coincide. In real life, different people have different needs, desires and interests. Suppose, for instance, a patient asks a doctor when he will be rid of his symptoms, and the doctor believes this will happen within two weeks. She could say "this will happen in two weeks' time" (F) or "perhaps a few weeks" (F′), avoiding loss of face (and perhaps a lawsuit) if her estimate proves to be too optimistic.

Speakers can also be tempted to offer incorrect information, of course, and game theory can shed light on these situations as well. A car salesman may lie about the mileage on a car, for example, in order to raise its price. Expected utility need not dictate directly what the speaker says: a salesman may well refrain from lying, in all or most cases. 'Lying as an exception' could be modelled by a utility function that takes into account the intrinsic value of speaking the truth, or the longer-term effect of lying: by lying, the salesman may destroy his reputation, in which case his business (and hence his expected utility) will suffer.

A model along the lines of this section could conceivably be built into future NLG systems. More immediately, the game-theory perspective suggests that there is no important difference between failing to speak the whole truth (i.e., offering partial information) and saying things that are false, consistent with the view that there is nothing morally wrong per se with deliberate deviations from the truth. It seems to us that what counts from a moral point of view is the intention behind the utterance: a doctor who withholds the truth from a patient because she believes this will benefit the patient (i.e., it will maximize U_H), perhaps even despite a risk to her own reputation (i.e., affecting U_S negatively), may be acting wrongly, but her failure was surely not a moral one.

Game-theory models are sometimes called "models by example" (Rasmussen 2001), because although they clarify how something *might* work, they do not necessarily tell us how things *actually* work. Who shall say what action will actually be triggered by an utterance, and how the utility of this action should be valued? The only things these models do is clarify how things work if a number of highly nontrivial assumptions are made.

32.6 Earlier accounts

Our account of deviations from the truth differs from that of most researchers, because we use an engineering perspective rather than a purely theoretical one. It may nonetheless be useful to indicate how our findings relate to those in the literature (e.g., Gupta et al. 2012 for a survey).

Our classification reflects several distinctions that are made in the literature on deception (e.g., Turner et al. 1975). Our classification chimes especially with Hopper and Bell (1984), who highlighted three dimensions, namely Premeditation (Is the deviation planned or unplanned?), Evaluation (Is it morally justified?), and Detectability (Is it easy to detect?). Broadly, our *unavoidable* deviations can be equated to Hopper and Bell's unpremeditated ones. Hopper and Bell's second dimension, Evaluation, calls to mind our game-theoretical account because, as we have argued, a comparison between speaker utility and hearer utility is highly relevant to this moral dimension. The third dimension, Detectability, highlights the question of whether readers have access to additional information: clinicians reading a machine-generated shift report of type BT-Nurse, for example, will typically have access to numerical data (as in Figure 32.1) in case any queries arise, but this information is not accessible to the beneficiaries of BT-Family.

In attempting to distinguish between lying and other deviations from the truth, some authors have argued that hearers are likely to draw false inferences from an utterance if the utterance violates Gricean Maxims (which ensure that utterances are always optimally cooperative, Grice 1975). Our account emphasizes how difficult it is to determine both whether an inference is likely, and whether an inference is incorrect. For example, if a medical report omits to mention a gradually quickening heartbeat, or if it loosely calls this quickening 'gradual', it is difficult to say whether a reader of the report is likely to draw incorrect inferences or to make clinical decisions that are incorrect; similarly, it is difficult to say whether any Gricean Maxims are violated. Only experimentation, addressing the inferences that readers actually make (see e.g., Khan et al. 2012 for experiments involving the likelihood of misunderstandings arising from ambiguous sentences) can hope to find answers.

32.7 Concluding remarks

Researchers in Artificial Intelligence are used to taking an engineering perspective on human abilities: by imitating what people do, we hope to understand better why and how they do it. The present chapter has applied this perspective to lying and other deviations from the truth.

We have seen how deviations from the truth arise almost unavoidably when computers present data in human-digestible form, because information needs to be selected, truncated, and interpreted to become optimally useful for human readers. Over and above this, we have seen how in practically deployed systems, the presumed effects on the reader have sometimes necessitated further deviations from the truth, with the ultimate purpose of promoting the well-being of the reader. We have also discussed deviations from the truth which are motivated by the well-being of someone other than the reader—e.g., the owner or maker of the system—and we have sketched a game-theory perspective that can help to make sense of these more deliberate deviations from the truth.

An interesting question that we have not touched upon so far is the question of *agency*: when an NLG system 'lies' (i.e., deviates from the truth), who is doing the lying? To see how difficult this question can be, consider once again the Babytalk-Clan system, focusing on a situation where—for the sake of this example—parents have specified that information about the baby's heart condition should never be divulged to the grandparents. Suppose, at some point, the baby's heart condition improves and, consistent with the parents' wish, the grandparents are not informed. The grandparents may well have noticed the baby's heart problems long before and might have been delighted to learn about the improvement. *Who* has been withholding information from them? The NLG system itself (which only carries out a deterministic computer program)? The parents (who do not produce any utterance themselves and, moreover, may not have anticipated the improvement of the baby's heart condition)? The programmer (who only implements what his employers ask him to)? Or the people who decided to deploy this system and to offer parents a choice as to what information everyone should receive? Perhaps it could be argued that agency, and hence responsibility, is shared between all of the above.

Even though we have gone into a certain (very modest) amount of technical detail to illustrate these issues, we believe that these may not be limited to computer-generated text: at least in broad outline, the steps performed by an NLG system are often thought to mirror those that are performed by a human speaker (see e.g., Levelt 1989 and many later models inspired by Levelt's). Moreover, the considerations taken into account by our game-theory model play the same role whether they are considered by a computer or by a person, or any other intelligent agent attempting to "do things with words," in the philosopher J. L. Austin's apt phrase (Austin 1976). For this reason, we believe they can shed a certain amount of light on the phenomenon of lying itself, and how difficult it is to avoid it.

Acknowledgements

We are grateful to Wendy Moncur, Graeme Ritchie, and two anonymous reviewers for useful comments on a draft of this chapter.

CHAPTER 33

LYING IN SOCIAL PSYCHOLOGY

BELLA M. DEPAULO

33.1 INTRODUCTION

IN the field of social psychology (the study of social interactions, including how people's thoughts and feelings and actions are influenced by others), scholars were slow to approach the study of lying. The first meta-analytic review article did not appear until 1981 (Zuckerman, DePaulo, and Rosenthal 1981). The number of studies grew after that, and exploded in the twenty-first century, especially in the US, perhaps because the terrorist attacks on September 11, 2011 greatly increased interest in deception-related topics.

The Zuckerman et al. review was titled 'Verbal and nonverbal communication of deception', reflecting the early interest in lying and detecting lies. A huge and still-growing literature has accumulated on cues to deception (DePaulo, Lindsay, Malone, Muhlenbruck, Charlton, and Cooper 2003) and the accuracy of people's attempts to detect deception (Bond and DePaulo 2006). That research is reviewed in Chapter 31 by Samantha Mann.

Social psychologists' study of cues to deception and success at deceiving and detecting deceit predated their research on more fundamental questions, such as: How often do people lie? Why do they lie? To whom do they tell their lies? What kinds of people are especially likely to lie frequently? Empirical answers to all of those questions are reviewed in this chapter.

As the field progressed, researchers wanted to know not just whether people were successful in their attempts to deceive other people, but also what strategies they used to try to fool others. They also examined the cognitive processes involved in lying. The interpersonal contexts of deception also attracted more research attention. Whereas early studies of cues to deception and accuracy of deception-detection were often conducted with liars and targets who were strangers to one another, subsequent studies of the psychology of lying focused more on the role of lying in different kinds of relationships, including very close ones. Social psychologists showed that the telling of lies instead of truths had implications for the way the liars viewed themselves as well as the people to whom they were telling their lies. Over time, certain kinds of deception can contribute to the deterioration, or even termination, of a relationship. In this chapter, separate sections on strategies for lying, cognitive factors in lying, and lying in relationships provide reviews of the relevant research.

33.2 How often do people lie?

Volumes had been written on lying, across many disciplines, before any systematic estimate of the frequency with which people lie had been available. Early studies were small, imprecise, and limited to college students. In 1996, DePaulo and her colleagues asked two groups of participants—seventy-seven college students and a more diverse group of seventy people from the community—to keep a diary of all of the lies that they told every day for a week (DePaulo, Kashy, Kirkendol, Wyer, and Epstein 1996). Significantly, they also asked participants to record all of their social interactions lasting at least ten minutes, regardless of whether they had told any lies during those interactions. That provided a measure of participants' opportunities to lie, which was missing from all previous research. They found that the college students told an average of one lie in every three of their social interactions (33%), and the people from the community told one lie in every five interactions (20%). Calculating the number of lies per day (rather than per social interaction), they found that the college students told an average of two lies a day and the people from the community told about one. Only one of the college students and six of the community members told no lies at all.

In studies in which participants report their own lies, how can we know whether participants are reporting their lies accurately? In the diary studies conducted by DePaulo and her colleagues, participants were encouraged to record their lies soon after they told them, to reduce issues of forgetting, and their diaries were collected several times a week. The diaries were anonymous, and that may have facilitated honest reporting. The two groups of participants were different in many ways, yet the psychology of lying was very similar for both. That, too, lends credibility to the findings.

In two small studies, George and Robb (2008) replicated the diary methodology of DePaulo et al. (1996), while examining additional different communication modalities—instant messaging, e-mail, phone, and face-to-face communications (as compared to written communications, telephone, and face-to-face in DePaulo et al.). Across all communication modalities, the rates of lying in the two studies, 25% and 22%, were comparable to the DePaulo et al. (1996) rates in their two studies of 33% and 20%. Taken together, the findings suggest that people lie in about one out of every four of their social interactions in their everyday lives.

Consistent with the DePaulo et al. (1996) results, George and Robb (2008) also found that rates of lying tended to be lowest in face-to-face communications. However, in the latter studies, individual comparisons between face-to-face and each of the other modalities were not significant.

Email communications and paper and pen messages are both text-based, but people feel more justified in lying by email, perhaps because it is viewed as less permanent and less personal. In a series of experiments, Naquin, Kurtzberg, and Belkin (2010) showed that people consistently tell more lies when emailing than when using pen and paper.

In a study focused specifically on lying in text messaging, college students provided the last fifteen text messages they had written to each of two people of their choosing (Smith, Hancock, Reynolds, and Birnholtz 2014). Then they indicated whether each message was a lie. Seventy-seven percent of the participants told at least one lie. An average of eleven percent of the messages were deceptive.

In an Internet survey, a national sample of 1,000 American adults reported the number of lies they had told in the previous 24 hours (Serota, Levine, and Boster 2010). No measure of social interactions was collected. On a per-day basis, though, the results were comparable to those of DePaulo et al. (1996), with participants telling an average of 1.65 lies per day. Sixty percent reported that they told no lies at all. Thus, the majority of lies were told by a minority of the participants.

Media accounts sometimes claim that people tell three lies every ten minutes. The finding comes from a study in which undergraduates had a ten-minute getting-acquainted conversation with another student (Feldman, Forrest, and Happ 2002). In a third of the conversations, one of the students was instructed to try to come across as very likable. In another third of the conversations, one of the students tried to come across as especially competent. In the rest, the students were given no particular instructions about what impression to convey. Of those trying to present themselves in particular ways, forty percent told no lies at all. The others told an average of three lies in the ten-minute conversation. Therefore, what the research really did show was that for undergraduates interacting with strangers and told to convey the impression of being extremely likable or competent, forty percent told no lies and the others told an average of three lies in the ten-minute conversations.

Other estimates of rates of lying come from more specific domains. For example, in a two-year study of applications to a psychiatry training program, applicants' reports of their publications were compared to their actual publications (Caplan, Borus, Chang, and Greenberg 2008). Nine percent of the applicants misrepresented their records. In research on a broader range of job applicants, investigating misrepresentations of employment history, educational history, and credentials, discrepancies were found in forty-one percent of the resumes (Levashina and Campion 2009).

33.3 PERSONALITY AND INDIVIDUAL DIFFERENCES IN LYING

Who lies? According to the research on the rate of lying in everyday life, the answer is probably everyone (DePaulo et al. 1996). With regard to the matter of personality and individual differences in lying, then, the question is whether particular types of people are especially more likely to lie than others.

In the diary studies of lying among college students and people in the community, participants completed a battery of personality tests in addition to recording their lies and their social interactions every day for a week (DePaulo et al. 1996; Kashy and DePaulo 1996). Most results were consistent across the two groups. As expected, more manipulative people (as measured by Machiavellianism and Social Adroitness scales) lie at a higher rate. So do people who care a lot about what others think of them and do a lot of impression management (as measured by Public Self-Consciousness and Other-Directed scales). People scoring higher on a scale measuring responsibility lied less often. Self-esteem and social anxiety did not predict rates of lying.

More extroverted people also lie more, and not because they are more sociable and therefore have more opportunities to lie; the rate of lying measure assesses the number of lies per social interaction (Kashy and DePaulo 1996). In a study based on a simulated job interview, Weiss and Feldman (2006) also found that more extroverted people lie more.

The link between Machiavellianism and the inclination to tell lies was further demonstrated in a study of the Dark Triad of traits, which also includes psychopathy (interpersonal antagonism, callous social attitudes, and impulsiveness) and narcissism (superiority, entitlement, and dominance). Participants recruited online filled out the relevant personality scales, and also described the lies they had told in the last seven days (Jonason, Lyons, Baughman, and Vernon 2014). People scoring higher on each of the three traits told more lies than those scoring lower. People scoring higher on Machiavellianism and psychopathy lied to more people. Narcissists were more likely to lie for self-serving reasons, and psychopaths more often admitted that they told lies for no reason at all.

Machiavellianism also predicts lying in sexual contexts (Brewer and Abell 2015). A wide range of adults recruited online completed a Machiavellianism scale, the Sexual Deception scale, and the Intentions Toward Infidelity Scale. People who scored higher on Machiavellianism said they were more willing to tell blatant lies in order to have sex with a partner, more willing to engage in sexual behavior to achieve some self-serving goal, more likely to lie to avoid confrontation with a partner, and more likely to be unfaithful to a partner.

In a study in which participants were interviewed by a skeptical police detective, college students who were not psychology majors were urged to claim that they were, and to continue to lie in response to every question (Vrij and Holland 1998). The students who persisted in telling the most lies were those who were more manipulative (as measured by the same Social Adroitness scale used by Kashy and DePaulo 1996) and more concerned with impression management (as measured by Other-Directedness, but not by Public Self-Consciousness). The more socially anxious the participants were, the less likely they were to persist in telling lies.

In an extension of the influential five-factor approach to personality, Ashton and Lee (2007) added to the factors of extroversion, agreeableness, conscientiousness, emotionality, and openness to experience a new factor of honesty-humility. The factor captures sincerity, fairness, modesty, and avoidance of greed. Hilbig, Moshagen, and Zettler (2015) predicted that people low in honesty-humility would be more likely to engage in morally questionable behavior such as infidelity in relationships, but less likely to admit it when asked directly. They found that such people admitted to more infidelity only when asked indirectly.

In their diary studies of lying in everyday life, DePaulo and her colleagues found no overall sex differences in rates of lying (DePaulo et al. 1996). They did, though, find sex differences in the telling of two different kinds of lies, self-serving lies (told in pursuit of the liars' interests, or to protect or enhance the liars in some psychological way) and other-oriented lies (told to advantage other people, or to protect or enhance them in some psychological way). Averaging across men and women, both the college students and the community members told about twice as many self-serving lies as other-oriented ones. The same disproportionate telling of self-serving lies characterized social interactions in which men were lying to women, women were lying to men, and especially when men were lying to other men. When women were lying to other women, though, they told just as many other-oriented lies as self-serving lies. People telling other-oriented lies are often trying to spare the feelings of the other person, as, for example, when they say that the other person looks great, prepared a great meal, or did the right thing, when they actually believe just the opposite. Women seem especially concerned with not hurting the feelings of other women.

33.4 MOTIVATIONS FOR LYING

Motivations for lying can be enumerated and classified in many different ways. Perhaps the most important distinction is between self-serving lies and other-oriented lies, with self-serving lies told far more often than other-oriented lies (DePaulo et al. 1996). In the diary studies of lying in everyday life, DePaulo and her colleagues also assessed whether each lie was told in the pursuit of materialistic versus psychological goals. Materialistic goals include the pursuit of money and other concrete benefits such as securing a job. Psychological goals include, for example, avoiding embarrassment or disapproval, creating a positive impression, and protecting other people from having their feelings hurt. Participants in both studies told more lies in the pursuit of psychological goals than materialistic ones.

In an experimental test of lying to get a job, Weiss and Feldman (2006) found that applicants described themselves in a job interview as having more technical skills than they really believed they had if the job was described as requiring such skills, and as having more interpersonal skills if the job instead required those skills. Material rewards do not undermine every person's honesty. In research in which participants are given a monetary incentive to lie, many refrained from lying (Lundquist, Ellingsen, Gribbe, and Johannesson 2009).

When people describe their own accomplishments more favorably than objective indicators warrant, how do we know they are deliberately lying and not just misremembering? The bias toward recounting in ways that are too generous rather than too harsh is one indication. Also, dispositionally, some people are even more inclined than others to self-enhance; those people have been shown to report even more exaggerated grade point averages than others. Furthermore, when people are given an opportunity to affirm their core values (for example, by writing about them), their need to self-enhance is satisfied, and they are then less likely to exaggerate their grades than people who did not get the self-affirmation opportunity (Gramzow and Willard 2006).

When people's self-esteem is threatened, they are more likely to lie in order to make themselves seem better than they really are. Tyler and Feldman (2005) demonstrated this in a study in which some participants were told that another student outperformed them, and that student would be evaluating them. The students who got the threatening feedback did indeed report lower self-esteem than those who were not told that the other student performed better, and then they lied more about their accomplishments and actions and personal attributes.

In addition to the categories of self-centered versus other-oriented lies, and lies told in the pursuit of materialistic versus psychological goals, Vrij (2008) suggests that another important distinction is between lies told to gain an advantage versus lies told to avoid a cost. Another typology adds conflict avoidance and social acceptance to the more commonly mentioned self-gain and altruistic motives (McLeod and Genereux 2008). Another approach (Gillath, Sesko, Shaver, and Chun 2010) acknowledges three motives identified as important across many domains, and applies them to the study of deception: power (lies told to control others), achievement (lies told to perform particularly well), and intimacy (lies told to increase closeness). A study of lies told by juvenile offenders (Spidel, Herve, Greaves, and Yuille 2011) underscored the significance of another motivation for lying—the thrill of fooling others, which Ekman (2009) calls duping delight. The broadest perspective on motivations for lying is the evolutionary one, which maintains that people lie because their attempted deceptions have resulted in selective advantages in reproduction and survival over evolutionary time (Smith 2004).

33.5 Strategies for Lying

In their research on suspects' strategies during police investigations, Hartwig and her colleagues (Hartwig, Granhag, and Stromwall 2007) found that innocent suspects typically do not strategize much—they simply tell the truth and expect to be believed. The same is likely to be true of truth-tellers in everyday life. Guilty suspects, in contrast, are more likely to strategize both before and during an interrogation. For example, they deliberately try not to seem nervous, and they try to avoid telling any outright lies while also denying any guilt or any admissions about incriminating evidence. They also try to offer detailed accounts and stay consistent.

Suspects who have prior criminal experiences are more likely to succeed in volunteering less incriminating information than those who have no criminal history. They are also unaffected by how suspicious the interrogators are of their guilt, whereas those new to the criminal justice system offer more information to the interrogators they believe to be more skeptical (Granhag, Clemens, and Stromwall 2009).

Outside of the legal system, people use a variety of strategies when accused of a serious offense. For example, they might deny the accusation completely, offer an explanation for their behavior, make a counter-accusation, admit to a relevant lesser offense, or admit to an irrelevant lesser offense. In experimental tests of the effectiveness of those strategies, Sternglanz (2009) found that people are more likely to be believed when they admit to a lesser relevant offense than when they completely deny that they did anything wrong. No strategy was significantly more effective than admitting to a lesser relevant offense.

Most of the lies of everyday life are not about serious offenses. Sometimes people lie when the truth would be hard to tell, as, for example, when answering a person's question honestly would hurt that person's feelings. Bavelas and her colleagues (Bavelas, Black, Chovil, and Mullett 1990) showed that in such challenging situations, people often equivocate—they try to avoid answering the question or giving their own opinion, they sometimes deliberately give unclear answers, and sometimes they avoid addressing the person who asked the question.

But what do they say? DePaulo and Bell (1996) created a paradigm in which participants indicated which of many paintings they liked the most and the least, and were subsequently introduced to an artist who pointed to one of their most disliked (or liked) paintings and said, "This is one that I did. What do you think of it?" As Bavelas et al. (1990) would have predicted, the participants often stonewalled when asked about the artist's own painting that they disliked the most. But they also amassed misleading evidence (mentioning more of what they liked about the painting than what they disliked) and implied a positive evaluation without saying explicitly that they liked the painting. They used strategies that they could defend as not technically a lie.

In online chat environments, liars are more likely than truth-tellers to choose avatars that are dissimilar from themselves (for example, in race, gender, or physical appearance). Perhaps, Galanxhi and Nah (2007) suggest, online participants believe that increasing their anonymity will improve their chances of getting away with their lies.

One of the most effective routes to deceptive success is not a strategy at all—it is an overall demeanor. People who have a truthful look about them will often be believed even when they are lying. Even trained and experienced government agents are routinely fooled by them (Levine et al. 2011).

33.6 COGNITIVE FACTORS IN LYING

Social psychologists interested in cognitive approaches to understanding deception have studied decisions about whether to deceive and the cognitive processes involved in lying and telling the truth. They have also examined ways in which lying instead of telling the truth changes self-perceptions, perceptions of the targets of the lies, and even perceptions of whether the untrue statements really were untrue.

From a self-control perspective, Mead et al. (2009) argued that situations in which people are tempted to lie often present a conflict between the inclination to lie or cheat and thereby reap an immediate reward versus choosing the more socially appropriate option of honesty. The latter requires more self-control. The authors showed that when people's capacity for self-control was already depleted by a previous task that used up some of their cognitive resources, they were less able to resist the temptation to behave dishonestly. They were also less inclined to avoid situations in which temptations to lie were more likely to be present.

In a review article, Vrij, Granhag, and Porter (2010) described six ways in which lying can be more cognitively demanding than telling the truth. First, formulating a lie may be more challenging than telling the truth, as, for example, when liars need to make up a story then remember what they said to whom. Second, because liars are less likely to expect to be believed than are truth-tellers, they use more cognitive resources monitoring and controlling their own behavior and (third) other people's reactions to their deceptions. Fourth, liars are more likely to expend cognitive resources reminding themselves to maintain the role they are playing. Fifth, truth comes to mind effortlessly, and liars need to use mental resources to suppress it. Finally, "activation of a lie is more intentional and deliberate, and thus it requires mental effort" (Vrij, Granhag, and Porter 2010: 109).

Lie-telling will not always be more cognitively demanding than telling the truth, though. Walczyk et al. (2014) formulated a model of answering questions deceptively that does not assume that the basic cognitive processes involved in lying are different from those involved in telling the truth. Their Activation-Decision-Construction-Action Theory (ADCAT) articulates key cognitive processes and predicts conditions under which lie-telling will be more or less cognitively demanding than truth-telling. For example, they argue that lying "will impose more cognitive load than truth telling ... the more complex, unfamiliar, or serious the truth-soliciting context is or the less rehearsed deceptive responding is. On the other hand, well rehearsed liars or those in highly familiar social contexts, for instance, are unlikely to need to monitor their own behavior [or] that of the targets ... " (Walczyk et al. 2014: 32). ADCAT incorporates key constructs from cognitive psychology such as theory of mind, working memory, and executive function.

The cognitive consequences of lying continue even after the lie has been told. For example, there is experimental evidence to indicate that liars can come to believe their lies

(Pickel 2004). In an example of moral disengagement, they also persuade themselves that their morally questionable behavior was really not so bad after all (Shu, Gino, and Bazerman 2011). In research in which people lie or tell the truth to another person, those who lie subsequently perceive the other person as more dishonest than those who told the truth (Sagarin, Rhoads, and Cialdini 1998). In sum, liars sometimes come to believe that what they said was not really a lie, that there was nothing wrong with what they did, and anyway, other people are also dishonest.

Many varieties of self-deception can facilitate deceptive success, argue von Hippel and Trivers (2011), by making people more confident, less burdened by the extra cognitive load that sometimes accompanies deceit, less likely to evince cues to deception, and less culpable if caught in the lies that they do not even believe they are telling. Moral disengagement after an initial but small transgression can lead the way to the commission of more serious transgressions that may have been inconceivable had the perpetrator not already committed lesser offenses, as Welsh et al. (2015) demonstrated in a series of studies of the slippery slope of ethical transgressions.

33.7 Lying in Relationships

In DePaulo and Kashy's (1998) diary studies of lying in everyday life, people told fewer lies (per social interaction) to the people with whom they had closer relationships. They also felt more uncomfortable lying to those people. With strangers and acquaintances, people told relatively more self-centered lies than other-oriented lies, but with friends, they told relatively more other-oriented lies. In research in which participants' liking for an art student was experimentally manipulated, people told more kind-hearted lies to the artists they were led to like than the ones they were induced to dislike, thereby protecting those artists from learning when the participants actually detested their work (Bell and DePaulo 1996).

People with an avoidant attachment style (who are fearful of intimacy) tend to lie more often, but only to their romantic partners. People with anxious attachment styles (who are preoccupied with issues of intimacy) lie more often to partners and others, including strangers, best friends, co-workers, bosses, and professors (Ennis, Vrij, and Chance 2008; Gillath et al. 2010). When people are prompted to think about a relationship that made them feel secure, they are less likely to lie to a current romantic partner and also less likely to lie in academic settings (Gillath et al. 2010).

Research on deception in relationships from an evolutionary perspective typically focuses on sex differences relevant to mating. For example, Marelich et al. (2008) found that men are more likely to tell blatant lies in order to have sex, whereas women are more likely to have sex to avoid confrontation. Tooke and Camire (1991) asked participants about the strategies they use to make themselves appear more desirable than they really are, both to other men and to other women. With both men and women,

women were more likely than men to lie about their appearance. With women, men more often faked commitment, sincerity, and skill at obtaining valuable resources such as money and career advancement; with other men, they exaggerated the frequency of their sexual behavior and depth of their relationships, as well as their popularity and general superiority.

The deceptive claims that men most often make in their interactions with their female partners are just the claims that upset women most when they discover the deceptions—claims about commitment, status, and resources. Women are especially more upset than men when their partners exaggerate their feelings in order to have sex. Men are more upset than women when their partners mislead them into believing that they are interested in having sex (Haselton et al. 2005).

When people discover that they have been deceived by a romantic partner, those with avoidant attachment styles are especially likely to avoid their partner and ultimately end the relationship. Anxiously attached people are more likely to talk around the issue but continue the relationship. Securely attached partners are especially likely to talk about the deception and stay together (Jang, Smith, and Levine 2002). The belief that a spouse may be concealing something is damaging to relationships. In a study of newlyweds, for example, those who thought their partners were hiding something felt excluded from their own relationship, and over time experienced less trust and engaged in more conflict (Finkenauer, Kerkhof, Righetti, and Branje 2009).

In their roles as targets of lies, both men and women evaluate lies more harshly than they do when they are the ones perpetrating the lies. As liars, people think their lies are more justifiable and more positively motivated, less damaging to the other person and more likely to have been provoked by the other person (Kaplar and Gordon 2004; DePaulo, Ansfield, Kirkendol, and Boden 2004).

A growing body of literature focuses on deception in online dating. Men who use online dating services admit that they misrepresent personal resources such as income and education more than women do; they also more often misrepresent their level of interest in a serious relationship and their personal attributes (such as politeness). Women more often admit that they misrepresent their weight (Hall et al. 2010). In another study (Toma, Hancock, and Ellison 2008), online daters reported to a laboratory where their characteristics could be measured objectively and compared to what was said in their profiles. Again, women lied about their weight more often than men did. Men more often lied about their height. In a similar study, online daters had their pictures taken in a lab and those pictures were then rated by other people (Toma and Hancock 2010). Daters whose lab pictures were rated as relatively unattractive were especially likely to post online photos that enhanced their attractiveness; they also lied more when verbally describing their attractiveness. The relatively more attractive daters posted more different photos of themselves than did the less attractive ones.

CHAPTER 34

LYING AND PSYCHOLOGY

KRISTINA SUCHOTZKI AND MATTHIAS GAMER

34.1 INTRODUCTION AND DEFINITION

LYING occurs in many different forms and contexts. There are the caring parents, who tell their children that the beloved dog went to an animal farm (instead of dying), or the shop assistant who tells you that the clothes you are trying on are fitting you just perfectly. But there is also the banker, who leaves out the risks when advising investment possibilities to a client, or the murderer who pretends not to have killed the victim. To describe these different types of lies, researchers have categorized them according to different dimensions. For instance, DePaulo, Kashy, Kirkendol, Wyer, and Epstein (1996) proposed that lies could be classified according to the reasons why people lie. According to these authors, lies can be classified as self- or other-oriented, as emitted to gain an advantage or to avoid costs, and as motivated by materialistic or psychological reasons. Clearly, many lies fall into several categories and the boundaries are not always strict. For instance, the parents lying to their children about the dog may do so to spare their children grief (i.e., other-oriented, avoiding costs, psychological reasons), but at the same time (secretly), the lie may also be self-oriented, as it spares the parents the difficult task of explaining the concept of death to their young children. Other classifications of lying refer to the degree to which a lie bends the truth: whether it is only a very subtle modification of the truth (e.g., "I did not have sex with that woman."), an exaggeration (e.g., "The fish I caught was soooo big."), or an outright lie (e.g., "I cannot come to work because I have a cold."). Finally, one can also distinguish the consequences that lies have if they were discovered, in which case lies are often referred to as low versus high-stake lies. This distinction is especially important in psychological research, as the severity of the consequences may affect many psychological and physiological correlates of lies.

Clearly, there is a great variety of lies. And although research shows that most people have a quite intuitive understanding of what they consider a lie and what not (Peterson 1995), finding a common definition of lying is not easy. One of the more recent attempts to such a definition is the one of Vrij (2008). He defines lying as "a successful or unsuccessful deliberate attempt, without forewarning, to create in another a belief which the communicator considers to be untrue" (Vrij 2008: 15). Importantly, Vrij (2008) thereby puts the emphasis on the fact that it is irrelevant whether the information that is communicated is actually false or not. What is important is that the deceiver considers it to be untrue. But although this aspect is shared by other definitions of deception, Turri and Turri (2015) recently showed that actual falsehood of a communicated fact may be more important to most people's concept of deception than previously assumed. Also central to Vrij's and other definitions of lying (e.g., Krauss 1981) is the intention to deceive. This serves to exclude for instance ironic or sarcastic remarks, in which the openly communicated fact is actually untrue, yet without any deceptive intention. In a similar vein, the specification "without forewarning" serves to exclude cases in which people expect to be misled, as for instance in the case of magicians or illusionists. Finally, Vrij's definition includes a social component: Another person has to be present. However, he also points out that for a communication to be defined as a lie, it is irrelevant whether the to-be-deceived person actually believes the information that is communicated.

As becomes evident from this and similar definitions, lying is a very complex social phenomenon and therefore a challenge to study in the laboratory. Also, it requires specific skills of the deceiver and it depends on certain characteristics of the social situation.

34.2 Relevant skills of the deceiver

In order to be able to intentionally deceive another individual, it is necessary to take the perspective of the interaction partner. Only when you can anticipate what a conspecific knows and thinks, can you use this information to dupe him or her successfully. This skill of mental perspective-taking is termed *Theory of Mind* (ToM). The development of ToM as well as impairments in ToM abilities have frequently been examined using the false-belief task (Premack and Woodruff 1978). In this task, the participant observes a protagonist who places an object at a certain location X. In the absence of the protagonist, a different individual transfers the object to location Y. Upon the return of the protagonist, the observer is asked where the protagonist will search for the object. Successful perspective-taking is indicated when the observer correctly infers that the protagonist will search at location X, because the protagonist did not observe the object transfer to Y. Such false-belief reasoning requires dissociating between the knowledge and beliefs of others and reality and it seems to be a skill that is confined to the human species. Although chimpanzees show evidence for other ToM aspects such as the understanding of goals and intentions, they fail on false-belief tasks (Call and Tomasello 2008). Whether they spontaneously show a simple form of deception or can mislead conspecifics in certain experimental situations is still debated in the literature (Hirata 2009).

Interestingly, children become able to correctly predict the behavior of the protagonist in the false-belief task around the age of four and at the same time, they also become capable of telling deliberate lies (Wimmer and Perner 1983; Sodian, Taylor, Harris, and Perne 1991). However, at even younger ages, children can deceive by misinforming others (Lewis, Stanger, and Sullivan 1989). These early lies are most often self-oriented, but there is also some evidence that young children can lie for prosocial reasons, for example not to affront others (Talwar, Murphy, and Lee 2007). Given that ToM abilities develop successively and seem to be present on a more implicit level at younger ages (Clements and Perner 1994), it seems likely that developments in ToM skills go hand in hand with improvements in children's ability to deceive. Such reasoning is also in line with empirical data showing impairments in ToM abilities in psychiatric disorders such as autism (Baron-Cohen, Leslie, and Frith 1985) that are paralleled by a reduced and suboptimal use of deception to reach individual goals (Sodian and Frith 1992; Li, Kelley, Evans, and Lee 2011).

34.3 Relevant aspects of the social situation

After learning that ToM is an essential precondition for being able to lie, we now turn to situations that trigger lies. What motivates us to lie? The most comprehensive examination of naturalistic situations that elicit lies has been conducted by DePaulo and colleagues (DePaulo et al. 1996). They asked two groups of seventy-seven students and seventy community members, respectively, to keep a diary for one week of all social interactions that lasted at least ten minutes. These diaries were analyzed to construct a taxonomy of lies and to identify situations and interaction partners that trigger lies. In general, people lied on an everyday basis with an average of one to two lies per day. Recently, it has been found that this average seems to result from a majority of people lying very infrequently (0–1 lies a day) and a small minority of people lying relatively frequently (more than four lies a day) (Serota, Levine, and Boster 2010). Lies primarily concerned feelings, achievements, actions, and plans. Most of them were told to serve the liar but interestingly, about one out of four lies was meant to benefit others. This indicates that contrary to the popular negative attitude toward deception (Backbier, Hoogstraten, and Terwogt-Kouwenhoven 1997), lying can also serve positive goals, by helping to establish and maintain social cohesion. The majority of lies were told to serve psychological goals. Thus, people lied because of self-presentational or emotional concerns rather than materialistic gains. Regarding the social context, the frequency of lies was found to decrease with social closeness and accordingly, feelings of discomfort before and after lying increased in emotionally closer relationships (DePaulo and

Kashy 1998). Also the motives to lie differed as a function of closeness. People seemed to be inclined to use more self-centered lies in casual relationships, whereas they used more altruistic lies that were meant to protect the interaction partner's feelings in close relationships.

Collectively, these studies show that lying occurs in a variety of situations, serves different goals, and concerns various topics. The common denominator of all lies seems to be the gaining of advantage or the avoidance of costs, either for the liar him/herself or for the interaction partner. According to this double-edged nature, lying can be both: a social lubricant or a selfish act (Vrij 2008: 34).

34.4 INVOLVED COGNITIVE FUNCTIONS

Compared to telling the truth, lying is a more complex task. When asked, people report that they experience lying as mentally more taxing than truth-telling (Caso, Gnisci, Vrij, and Mann 2005; Vrij, Semin, and Bull 1996). In computerized reaction-time paradigms, people usually make more errors and require a longer time for lying than for truth-telling (e.g., Spence et al. 2001; Fullam, McKie, and Dolan 2009; Verschuere, Spruyt, Meijer, and Otgaar 2011; Debey, Verschuere, and Crombez 2012; Van Bockstaele et al. 2012). Also, brain-imaging research shows that compared to truth-telling, lying results in greater neuronal activity in brain regions that are also active during complex cognitive tasks (i.e., the anterior cingulate, dorsolateral prefrontal, and inferior frontal regions; Christ, Van Essen, Watson, Brubaker, and McDermott 2009; Gamer 2011). Similar brain regions were also linked to response monitoring and behavioral control and some studies showed correlations between activity increases in these prefrontal brain regions and response times in deception paradigms (e.g., Gamer, Bauermann, Stoeter, and Vossel 2007).

These research findings have stimulated a more thorough and detailed investigation of the different cognitive functions that are necessary to lie successfully. First, it has been proposed that the formulation of a credible lie requires that the truth is retrieved and kept active in *working memory*. In support of this idea, it has been shown that facilitating the retrieval of a truthful response by presenting it next to a question enables people to lie faster and with fewer errors (Debey, De Houwer, and Verschuere 2014). Also, limiting working memory capacity with a concurrent task hinders lying in experimental deception paradigms (Ambach, Stark, and Vaitl 2011; Visu-Petra, Varga, Miclea, and Visu-Petra 2013; but see Morgan, LeSage, and Kosslyn 2009; Farrow, Hopwood, Parks, Hunter, and Spence 2010; Visu-Petra, Miclea, and Visu-Petra 2012 for conflicting results).

After being activated in working memory, it has been proposed that the truth would then *conflict* with the to-be-emitted lie and require *response inhibition* and *response monitoring* processes to prevent it from coming out. The conflict-inducing nature of the deceptive response has been demonstrated in research using event-related brain potentials (e.g., Johnson, Henkell, Simon, and Zhu 2008; Dong, Hu, Lu, and Wu 2010;

Suchotzki, Crombez, Smulders, Meijer, and Verschuere 2015) or by tracking arm-movement trajectories or muscle activity (Duran, Dale, and McNamara 2010; Hadar, Makris, and Yarrow 2012). For instance, tracking participants' arm movements while they moved a Nintendo Wii Remote to deceptive responses, Duran et al. (2010) observed an initial deviation of the trajectories toward the truthful response. In contrast, evidence for the involvement of response inhibition is more mixed. Increased neuronal activity during lying has repeatedly been found in the right inferior frontal gyrus (see two meta-analyses: Christ et al. 2009; Gamer 2011), a region hypothesized to be crucially involved in response-inhibition processes (Aron, Robbins, and Poldrack 2004, 2014). Also, performance of and involvement in other tasks that are hypothesized to require response inhibition have been found to correlate or interfere with lying, respectively (Visu-Petra et al. 2012; Hu, Evans, Wu, Lee, and Fu 2013). Yet, there are also studies that failed to find evidence for the role of response inhibition in lying. For instance, temporal disruption of the right inferior frontal gyrus by means of transcranial magnetic stimulation did not affect lying performance (Verschuere, Schuhmann, and Sack 2012). Also, alcohol consumption, which has been shown to hamper response inhibition, did not impact lying performance (Suchotzki, Crombez, Debey, van Oorsouw, and Verschuere 2015).

Finally, *task switching* has been proposed to be necessary to enable a liar to flexibly change between truthful and deceptive responses. Accordingly, in a study by Visu-Petra et al. (2013), a concurrent switching task hampered lying. Also, in two other studies, people with better task switching skills performed better in two different deception paradigms (Morgan et al. 2009; Visu-Petra et al. 2012).

The above-mentioned findings support the involvement of higher-order cognitive functions such as working memory, response inhibition, and task switching in lying, yet they are not entirely conclusive. Future research is necessary to explain some mixed findings and to integrate them in a more comprehensive cognitive theory of lying (see, e.g., Walczyk, Harris, Duck, and Mulay 2014). Recently, it has also been emphasized that there are situations in which truth-telling may be cognitively more demanding than lying (McCornack et al. 2014; Walczyk et al. 2014), for instance for well-rehearsed lies (see also DePaulo et al. 2003), or in cases in which a simple lie is more easy to convey than a complex truth. Identifying those situations is especially important as the observation that lying is cognitively more demanding than truth-telling also stimulated new approaches to deception detection. Recently, techniques have been developed that focus on indirectly inferring deception from measurements of cognitive load (e.g., Vrij, Edward, and Bull 2001a). Also, some techniques aim to exploit the finding that further enhancing cognitive load specifically burdens liars (e.g., Vrij et al. 2008; see section 34.6 and Chapter 31 by Samantha Mann). A thorough understanding of the exact processes underlying the enhanced cognitive load during lying is crucial in order to predict boundary conditions where such techniques work and—most importantly—to determine circumstances where they do not work (Walczyk, Igou, Dixon, and Tcholakian 2013).

34.5 Affective correlates

The idea that lying comes with altered or increased affect is widespread, both in popular belief as well as in psychological theories of lying. For instance, in Zuckerman, De Paulo, and Rosenthal's multifactor model (Zuckerman, DePaulo, and Rosenthal 1981), emotional reactions are, together with cognitive effort and attempted behavioral control, hypothesized to crucially underlie verbal and non-verbal cues to deceit. It is also reflected in Ekman's proposal to use very small and insuppressible expressions of emotions (i.e., microexpressions) to identify liars. Mostly, it has been proposed that lying, as distinct from truth-telling, evokes fear of getting caught and feelings of guilt in the liar. However, it has also been pointed out that lying may come with an increase in positive affect, as for instance reflected in the idea of a "duping delight" (Ekman 2009).

Empirical research investigating the affective correlates of lying is surprisingly scarce. It has been shown that regarding everyday lies, people report increased levels of distress during and after telling them (DePaulo et al. 1996). Also, in an experimental context in which people had to lie about the contents of a backpack, people reported being more tense during lying than during truth-telling (Caso et al. 2005). Interestingly, in this study, higher stakes, as operationalized by recording participants' interviews and announcing that they would be analyzed by police officers, did not selectively enhance tension during lying—it increased tension during truth-telling and lying to the same degree. Measuring physiological arousal during lying and truth-telling about two different, but well-matched sets of questions, Furedy and colleagues showed in a series of experiments that lying resulted in stronger physiological arousal than truth-telling (Furedy, Davis, and Gurevich 1988; Furedy, Posner, and Vincent 1991; Furedy, Gigliotti, and Ben-Shakhar 1994). Using functional magnetic resonance imaging (fMRI), Abe, Suzuki, Mori, Itoh, and Fujii (2007) observed an enhanced activation of the amygdala, an area involved in emotional processing, when participants were deceiving an interrogator compared to when they were not deceiving another person. This was accompanied by a higher rating of anxiety in the deceiving condition, which led the authors to interpret the higher amygdala activity as a result of either fear or threat during the deceit. Accordingly, Baumgartner, Fischbacher, Feierabend, Lutz, and Fehr (2009) found that breaking a promise was also associated with increased activation in the amygdala. In a similar study in which the authors looked at inter-individual differences, Baumgartner, Gianotti, and Knoch (2013) found that people with a higher baseline activation of the anterior insula, an area that has also been related to emotional arousal, were less prone to cheat and break their promises. As in this study participants also generally scored higher on a negative affect scale, the authors proposed that a higher negative baseline arousal may make deception more stressful and bothersome. Interestingly, however, most neuroimaging studies on deception failed to reveal consistent activity changes in neural circuits involved in emotional processing (Christ et al. 2009; Gamer 2011). It is currently unclear whether this is due to the predominant use of highly controlled laboratory tasks in the elicitation of deceit (Sip, Roepstorff, McGregor, and Frith 2008) or whether it provides genuine evidence for the negligible recruitment of emotional processes during lying (Gamer 2014).

Moreover, as mentioned above, some researchers have argued that lying may also cause positive emotions (e.g., Ekman's duping delight). The first empirical evidence on this has been found in a study by Ruedy, Moore, Gino, and Schweitzer (2013). In this study, in which cheating was not causing another person any disadvantage, the authors found that across several experiments, individuals who cheated on different problem-solving tasks consistently experienced more positive affect than those who did not cheat. Their findings suggested that this 'cheater's high' was caused by the thrill people felt at having gotten away with their cheating.

Evidently, the relation between affect and lying is a complex one. Contrary to popular belief, lying does not exclusively cause negative affect. And although basic deception research indicates that there is some relation between affect and lying, many researchers have warned against using this relationship for the applied purpose of lie detection (e.g., National Research Council 2003; Lykken 1998; Vrij 2008). These researchers have pointed out that the interrelation of lying and emotion is not strong and stable enough to reliably detect lies and most importantly, this relationship is not specific. As also suggested by the results of Caso et al. (2005), raising stakes will most likely also increase similar emotions in truth-tellers (e.g., fear and threat). A more elaborate critique of this approach to lie detection is presented in the following section.

34.6 Applied aspects: Lie detection

When talking about research on lying, one applied aspect that quickly comes to mind is lie detection. As introduced earlier, lies are employed in many areas of life and being able to specifically discover harmful lies would provide a big advantage for the one who is able to do so.

The most intuitive method of lie detection is the observation of a person's demeanor, for instance his/her verbal and non-verbal behavior. However, as numerous studies have shown, detecting deception from demeanor is no easy task. Contrary to what many people think, there are only very few verbal- and non-verbal cues that are actually indicative of deception. But although some produce significant effects on a group level, effects are usually too weak to be used for reliable individual classifications (DePaulo et al. 2003; Sporer and Schwandt 2007; Vrij 2008). Consequently, most people do not perform above chance when having to judge who is honest and who is deceptive (Bond and DePaulo 2006; Hartwig and Bond 2011). However, recently, with an increased attention on the cognitive mechanisms underlying deception, new methods have been developed that aim to specifically burden liars by enhancing cognitive load (e.g., Vrij, Granhag, Mann, and Leal 2011). Although their development is still in its infancy, first results indicate that such techniques may enhance verbal- and non-verbal cues to deception, thereby increasing the diagnostic value of such cues and the accuracy of observers. More information on such verbal- and non-verbal cues to deception and related lie-detection techniques can be found in Chapter 31 by Samantha Mann.

Another highly popular approach to lie detection relies on the use of psychophysiological measurements. Although often used as a synonym for the word 'lie detector', it seems noteworthy to point out here that the frequently used word 'polygraph' (translated from Greek: 'writing much') simply refers to the simultaneous measurement of several psychophysiological channels, such as skin conductance, heart rate, and respiration. Instead of focusing on the measure, in order to determine how valid a lie-detection technique can be, it is important to look at the questioning techniques that are used while someone is attached to the polygraph.

The questioning technique most frequently used in combination with the polygraph is the Control (or Comparison) Question Technique (CQT; Reid 1947). In the CQT, a suspect is interrogated with three different types of questions: relevant questions, irrelevant questions, and control questions. Imagine, for instance, that someone is suspected of having murdered Mr. X. In this case, a relevant question could be 'Did you murder Mr. X?', whereas an irrelevant question could be 'Is your name Y?'. Importantly, the crucial comparison is not between these two types of questions, but between the relevant and so-called control questions. Crucially, these control questions are designed to induce a differentially stronger arousal in innocent suspects, and a differentially weaker arousal in guilty suspects. The control questions are deliberately formulated vague and in a way that it is unlikely that anyone could honestly deny them (e.g., 'Have you ever in your life hurt someone?'). In a manipulative pretest interview, the examiner (incorrectly) explains to the suspect that answering these questions with 'yes' would be taken as an indication of guilt, and the suspect is lured into answering the control questions with 'no'. The rationale of the CQT is that guilty and innocent suspects differ with regard to which type of questions they experience as more stressful. It is reasoned that innocent suspects can truthfully answer the relevant questions, and the control questions pose the biggest threat to them. In contrast, the relevant questions are believed to be the most threatening for guilty suspects. Empirical laboratory studies looking at the accuracy of the CQT indicate between 8% and 10% of false classifications of liars (sensitivity = hit rate among guilty suspects: 90%–92%), and between 9% and 20% of false classifications of truth-tellers (specificity = hit rate among innocents: 80%–91%) (range of weighted accuracy estimates from mock crime studies excluding inconclusive cases; Kircher, Horowitz, and Raskin 1988; Ben-Shakhar and Furedy 1990; Raskin and Honts 2002). Yet, the CQT has been criticized on legal, ethical, theoretical, and empirical grounds. Both legally and ethically it is problematic that the CQT actually requires the examiner to lie to the suspect about the test principle. The most serious theoretical problem of the CQT is that there is no theoretical rationale for the expected differential response patterns of innocent and guilty suspects. In contrast, there are several reasons why such response patterns might not occur (e.g., greater emotional arousal for relevant questions owing to the accusatory nature of questions, or the fear of not being believed). Empirically, it is problematic that false classification rates are higher for innocent than for guilty examinees. Furthermore, it has been reasoned that the specificity of the CQT may be lower in real-life situations (compared to controlled laboratory environments), as stakes and emotional arousal levels are higher (Patrick and Iacono 1989). This also becomes apparent in a term used to describe one fundamental error that underlies the approach of inferring deception from emotional arousal. The so-called 'Othello error' refers to William Shakespeare's Othello, who failed to consider that Desdemona's stress might not be caused by her lying, but rather by her fear when she realized that she would be unable to prove her faithfulness (Ekman 2009: 170).

Not surprisingly, the National Research Council (2003) came to the conclusion that the CQT does not fulfill scientific standards. But despite these serious criticisms, the CQT is widely used in modern societies (e.g., in Canada, the USA, and Belgium). And many new methods that are used with similar questioning techniques are developed every year (e.g., voice stress analysis or thermal imaging; Pavlidis, Eberhardt, and Levine 2002). Yet, as pointed out by many scholars, none of these techniques can be expected to overcome the aforementioned limitations, unless they are based on more solid scientific principles (Meijer et al. 2009). In the same line of reasoning, the National Research Council (2003) put out an urgent call for more fundamental research on deception, to develop a better understanding of the phenomenon and to be able to develop lie-detection techniques that can be grounded on psychological, empirically tested theories.

One questioning technique that can also be used with the polygraph and that has the potential to overcome many of the above-mentioned shortcomings is the Concealed Information Test (CIT, previously referred to as Guilty Knowledge Test; Lykken 1959). Importantly, unlike the CQT, the CIT has been developed based on a psychological theory and has been empirically supported by a substantial amount of scientific research (Ben-Shakhar and Elaad 2003; Verschuere, Ben-Shakhar, and Meijer 2011; Meijer, Klein-Selle, Elber, and Ben-Shakhar 2014). Interestingly, the rationale of the CIT is not to measure deception directly, but rather to measure recognition of crucial, that is, crime-related information. During a CIT, a suspect is presented with questions referring to crime details that can be known only by the person who committed the crime. For instance, the question 'What was the murder weapon?' is presented with the alternatives 'Knife', 'Gun', 'Poison', 'Rope', and 'Hammer', presented one after the other. Whereas for an innocent suspect all alternatives are equally likely, only the guilty suspect recognizes the correct critical item. Recognition is measured as the average physiological response to the correct, compared to the incorrect, answers. Importantly, the increased responding to critical items has been theorized to be caused by the orienting response (Sokolov 1963), and this theory has been supported by a large body of empirical research (for a review see, e.g., Verschuere and Ben-Shakhar 2011). Validity studies on the CIT indicate between 16% and 24% false classifications of guilty/knowledgeable subjects (sensitivity: 76%–84%), and between 4% and 17% false classifications of innocent/unknowledgeable subjects (specificity: 83%–96%) (range of weighted accuracy estimates from mock crime studies; Ben-Shakhar and Furedy 1990; Elaad 1998; MacLaren 2001; Ben-Shakhar and Elaad

2003). Importantly, although accuracy estimates are roughly in the same range as for the CQT, false classifications especially concern guilty suspects, whereas the test is rather accurate in protecting innocent suspects. In fact, a large number of studies did not report any false positive result at all (Elaad 1998). But despite its advantages and its strong support by the scientific community (Iacono 2011), the CIT is applied only in Japan to date, with around 5,000 examinations per year (Osugi 2011; Matsuda, Nittono, and Allen 2012).

Unfortunately, recent discussions on developments in the field of lie detection strongly focused on measures (e.g., whether estimates of neural activity are more valid than autonomic measures, Greely and Illes 2007; Rusconi and Mitchener-Nissen 2013) instead of concentrating on the questioning techniques that are used to elicit cues to deceit. Given that verbal, non-verbal, and physiological responses are unlikely to be uniquely associated with deception, one needs elaborate techniques such as the CIT to become able to unequivocally interpret response patterns in such situations. Deception has a huge impact on society when being undetected in forensic and criminological domains and it therefore seems highly important to consider the above-mentioned issues in the development and use of lie-detection methods in the field (for further reading see also Granhag, Vrij, and Verschuere 2015).

34.7 Summary

This chapter set out to describe a psychological approach to deception. As discussed, lying is ubiquitous in all kinds of social relationships. It has a two-pronged nature as it serves to benefit the liar but might also satisfy prosocial motives. The ability to lie is strongly related to cognitive operations of mentalizing but also recruits executive functions to flexibly switch between lying and truth-telling. Lying might be accompanied by affective reactions but this relationship seems to be less reliable than is frequently supposed. Because of its dramatic impact in the forensic domain, the detection of deceit has been a major area of research in psychology and related disciplines. Based on substantial progress in recent years, it is hoped that a more thorough understanding of the psychological processes associated with lying might yield new insights and novel lie-detection applications in the near future.

CHAPTER 35

LYING AND NEUROSCIENCE

GIORGIO GANIS

35.1 INTRODUCTION

IN this chapter, the terms 'lying' and 'deception' will be used interchangeably. Deception can be defined as an attempt to convince someone to accept as true something the prevaricator believes to be untrue. This definition of 'deception' encompasses a broad range of behaviors from the omission of information to the generation of outright lies (Vrij 2008). Furthermore, this definition includes cases of concealed information, where one wants somebody else to incorrectly believe that one does not have certain information.

Humans have been interested in understanding and detecting deception for a long time, because deception is a pervasive social behavior (DePaulo, Kashy, Kirkendol, Wyer, and Epstein 1996) with potentially negative consequences for individuals and societies (Vrij 2008). The methods employed to investigate and detect deception have ranged from behavioral observation to psychophysiological monitoring, from text analysis to brain imaging (Raskin, Honts, and Kircher 2014). In spite of this variety of methods and paradigms, studies on deception can be organized on a continuum. At one end of the continuum there are more theoretical studies that focus on understanding deception by testing general theories, usually at the group level of analysis. Questions that might be examined at this level are whether lies about oneself are different from lies about other people (Ganis, Morris, and Kosslyn 2009), or whether certain cognitive control processes such as response inhibition are usually engaged during deception (Christ, Van Essen, Watson, Brubaker, and McDermott 2009). At the other end there are more applied studies that focus on methods of detecting deception in single subjects. Questions that are important at this level are whether it is possible to tell if a suspect is lying about having committed a specific crime. This chapter will review briefly some of the literature on the neuroscience of deception and deception-detection, and discuss some of the main issues in the field.

35.2 COGNITIVE NEUROSCIENCE APPROACH

Deception, like all other cognitive activities, is carried out by a set of brain processes, which is why the cognitive-neuroscience approach examines the brain to understand deception and to provide potential ways to detect it. For instance, since generating lies requires retrieving and manipulating memories stored in the brain, in order to study deception cognitive neuroscience attempts to leverage what the field already knows about the neuroscience of memory systems. The cognitive-neuroscience approach attempts to decompose deception into a number of neural subprocesses and draws heavily on psychological theories of deception, including Zuckerman's four-factor theory (Zuckerman, DePaulo, and Rosenthal 1981), information manipulation theory (McCornack 1992, 1997), and interpersonal deception theory (Buller and Burgoon 1996).

Within this approach, cognitive control, social cognitive processes, and memory processes are assumed to play key roles in deception. At minimum, producing a deceptive response typically (but not always) involves: i) Deciding to lie, although such a decision may not always be entirely explicit, possibly relying on complex moral and social computations, ii) retrieving or reactivating information from episodic and semantic memory; iii) maintaining and manipulating relevant retrieved information in working memory (at least until a response is made); iv) memory encoding of the response itself in order to be consistent in the future (especially in the case of a novel lie); v) inhibiting the corresponding honest response (which is coincidentally retrieved), as well as other potential deceptive responses; vi) managing the overall social interaction so as to come across as truthful. Since investigating all these processes at once with neuroscience-based methods would be unfeasibly complex, most studies have focused on a small subset of them, especially response monitoring and inhibition, and memory processes. One of the theoretically more important questions is whether deception engages any of these processes in a domain-specific manner, as will be discussed.

35.2.1 Deception paradigms

The vast majority of paradigms that have been used to investigate deception in cognitive neuroscience studies can be placed in one of two classes: differentiation of deception and concealed-information paradigms.

Differentiation of deception paradigms compare conditions that differ only in whether the responses to be made are truthful or deceptive (Furedy, Davis, and Gurevich 1988) and so they are especially useful for investigating deception per se. For example, participants could answer the same question truthfully or deceptively on different trials depending on a cue (Spence et al. 2001). Comparing deceptive and honest conditions in this paradigm should reflect neural processes that are uniquely engaged by deceptive responses, relative to honest responses, and so these paradigms have been typically used in theory development studies.

Concealed-information paradigms, on the other hand, are based on Lykken's original ideas on the orienting reflex (Lykken 1959) and attempt to determine if a person possesses memories about events or items of interest but deceptively claims not to possess such memories. In these paradigms, infrequently presented items of interest that only deceptive participants should be able to recognize (items relevant for a crime, for example, also referred to as 'probes') are compared with frequently presented control items (also referred to as 'irrelevants'), that is, items that neither deceptive nor honest participants should be able to recognize (e.g., a weapon that could have been plausibly used in the crime in question, but was not). Note that by definition probes and irrelevants differ from each other in many more ways than just deception (for example, they differ in saliency), which is why these paradigms are not well suited to investigate deception processes per se and they have been mostly used with applied goals in mind.

With a handful of exceptions (e.g., Carrión, Keenan, and Sebanz 2010; Sip et al. 2010; Yin, Reuter, and Weber 2015), participants in studies using both of these paradigms have been instructed to deceive at specific times. Even in the few studies in which deception was not instructed on specific trials, deception is sanctioned, in the sense that it is implicitly or explicitly an acceptable behavior within the study.

35.2.2 Cognitive neuroscience methods

The main cognitive neuroscience methods used to investigate and to detect deception have been brain sensing, mostly electroencephalography (EEG), and brain imaging, primarily functional magnetic resonance imaging (fMRI). Additional methods including magnetoencephalography (MEG), positron emission tomography (PET), near-infrared spectroscopy (NIRS), and brain stimulation techniques such as transcranial magnetic stimulation (TMS) and transcranial electrical stimulation (TES) have also been used, but only in a handful of studies and mostly with conflicting findings, and so they will not be discussed here (Seth, Iversen, and Edelman 2006; Priori et al. 2008; Mameli et al. 2010; Karton and Bachmann 2011; Verschuere, Schuhmann, and Sack 2012).

Electroencephalography methods for investigating the brain signatures of deception have been in use since the late 1980s (Fabiani, Karis, and Donchin 1986; Rosenfeld et al. 1988; Farwell and Donchin 1991). These methods provide a noninvasive measure of electrical brain activity obtained from electrodes placed on the scalp, with millisecond temporal precision. Electroencephalography methods have limited spatial resolution because EEG signals are the sum of a multitude of simultaneous neural processes unfolding in many brain regions. Thus, these methods are generally poor at addressing questions about the specific brain regions involved in complex cognitive processes and have focused on the time course of effects. A common way to extract meaningful measures of brain responses to events of interest, such as words or pictures, is to average the EEG data over many repetitions of the same event type (Luck 2014). Almost all electroencephalographic studies of deception have examined event-related potentials (ERPs), which are obtained by time-locking the EEG to the onset of the events of interest. Time-locked averaging decreases the influence of processes that are not related to the event of interest, and at the same time it increases the influence of processes that are in fact related to it. The resulting average shows a characteristic sequence of positive and negative deflections that unfold over time, referred to as ERP components (Luck 2014). Complementary EEG analysis methods such as examining features of the EEG frequency spectra and decomposing the EEG signals into independent components hold some promise (Delorme and Makeig 2004), but they have been used only sporadically in the deception literature (Matsuda, Nittono, and Allen 2013).

Although Positron Emission Tomography (PET) was first employed to study cognitive processes also in the late 1980s (Petersen, Fox, Posner, Mintun, and Raichle 1988), it was only after the advent of fMRI in the mid-1990s that neuroimaging methods began to be used to investigate deception. Unlike EEG, fMRI has excellent spatial resolution, and so it can localize brain processes with great precision. However, its temporal resolution is rather poor because it is based on detecting relatively slow changes in regional cerebral blood flow produced indirectly by neural activity (Logothetis and Wandell 2004). Although there are many ways to analyze fMRI data, most analyses also involve combining multiple trials of the same type to increase the signal to noise ratio of the results (Dale 1999). Functional magnetic resonance imaging has been used to study deception since 2001 (Spence et al. 2001), and tens of studies have been conducted on the topic since (Lisofsky, Kazzer, Heekeren, and Prehn 2014).

35.3 Overview of cognitive neuroscience findings

35.3.1 Electroencephalographic results

One of the most robust ERP components is the P300, a late positive peak with a parietal scalp distribution that occurs between 300 and 600 ms after the onset of a rare and meaningful stimulus (Chapman and Bragdon 1964; Sutton, Braren, Zubin, and John 1965). The P300 is the ERP component by far the most commonly examined in deception research, typically within concealed-information paradigms, since it is reliably larger for probes than irrelevants (Rosenfeld et al. 1988). These paradigms have focused on the applied issue of whether and to what extent it is possible to determine if a person is lying about knowing a certain item by trying to find evidence that one recognizes such an item. In addition to the P300, at least two other ERP components have been found to be modulated in these paradigms, though not always consistently. The first one is the anterior N2, which is an ERP component with a central or frontal scalp distribution occurring around 250 ms after stimulus onset and is thought to index cognitive control processes such as response conflict resolution (Folstein and Van Petten 2008). The anterior N2 has been found to be larger for probes than for irrelevants in some studies (Gamer and Berti 2010), but not in others (Ganis and Schendan 2012). The second one is the late positive potential (LPP), a positivity maximal at occipital sites occurring after 500 ms after stimulus onset, which is larger for probes than irrelevants when there is the intention to conceal information, rather than merely recognizing information (Matsuda et al. 2013).

Several concealed-information-paradigm variants have been designed over the years, in a process of progressive refinement. The original paradigm involved presenting only probes and irrelevants, and people would simply deny knowing all the items. Thus, individuals with no concealed information would truthfully deny knowledge of all items, whereas individuals with concealed information would lie when they denied knowledge of the probe. One problem with this version of the concealed-information paradigm is that there is no guarantee people will pay attention to any of the items to perform the task, since one can simply give the same mindless response to all stimuli without fully processing them. A paradigm that solves this problem is the three-stimulus variant (Rosenfeld et al. 1988; Farwell and Donchin 1991; Allen, Iacono, and Danielson 1992). In this paradigm, a third type of item, a target, is presented, together with the probes and the irrelevants. The instructions are to detect targets given to participants before the experimental session, which can be done only by fully processing all items in the stream. A drawback of these paradigms seems to be that they are vulnerable to simple cognitive countermeasures (Rosenfeld, Soskins, Bosh, and Ryan 2004) based on artificially increasing the saliency of the irrelevants. This led to the creation of a new variant of the paradigm, the Complex Trial Protocol (Rosenfeld et al. 2008), which appears to be resistant to saliency-based cognitive countermeasures. In this paradigm, the probe/irrelevant and target/no target categorization components of the task are separated in time and presented in rapid succession, making it very hard to implement saliency-based cognitive countermeasures.

A few ERP studies have used variants of differentiation-of-deception paradigms and have focused on response-monitoring and inhibition processes required to produce a deceptive response while at the same time inhibiting incompatible deceptive and honest responses (Johnson, Barnhardt, and Zhu 2004). These studies typically have found that deceptive responses elicit a larger medial frontal negativity (MFN) than honest responses when the ERPs are time-locked to the response. The MFN is an ERP component that peaks around 100 ms after a response and is typically larger in conditions that involve response conflict or ambiguity (Gehring and Knight, 2000; Ridderinkhof, Ullsperger, Crone, and Nieuwenhuis, 2004). The MFN usually localizes in portions of the anterior cingulate cortex (ACC), which has been implicated, among other things, in conflict monitoring and resolution (Ullsperger and von Cramon 2001; Gehring and Willoughby 2002; Johnson et al. 2004; Carter and van Veen 2007). Consistent with these findings, portions of the ACC and other parts of the medial prefrontal cortex are often found in neuroimaging studies of deception, as discussed later. In addition to the MFN, a late positive complex (LPC) following the MFN is usually smaller for deceptive than for honest responses. This is consistent with the idea that deception is a type of dual task that involves negotiating truthful and deceptive representations, and with the known inverse relationship between the LPC and cognitive load (Johnson, Barnhardt, and Zhu 2003).

There is no evidence that any of the ERP components just mentioned are specific for deception processes because they can also be elicited by perceptual and cognitive manipulations that have nothing to do with deception (Luck 2014). This lack of evidence for deception specificity is in part due to the limited spatial ability of the ERP data, in the sense that it is difficult to know whether two ERP effects have common neural generators. This is a key issue that will be discussed in some detail in the section on the neuroimaging results. Note, however, that this lack of specificity does not necessarily preclude using these methods in an applied way to try to detect deception in specific cases in which it is possible to rule out other processes.

35.3.2 Neuroimaging results

Rather than discussing a large set of neuroimaging studies individually, it is more efficient to focus on the results of recent quantitative meta-analyses of the literature. Specifically, three meta-analyses of neuroimaging studies of deception have been published over the last few years (Christ et al. 2009; Farah, Hutchinson, Phelps, and Wagner 2014; Lisofsky et al. 2014). The studies included in these meta-analyses used both variants of the differentiation of deception and concealed information paradigms. Although there is substantial variability in the pattern of activation from study to study, these meta-analyses converge in reporting a cluster of fronto-parietal regions that are more engaged by deceptive than by honest responses. Using the Brodmann area (BA) parcellation scheme of the human cortex, these regions include the anterior cingulate and surrounding medial prefrontal cortex (BA 24, 32, 8), the ventrolateral prefrontal and insular cortex, bilaterally (BA 44, 47, 48, and 13), portions of the left precentral, middle, and superior frontal gyrus (BA 6, 9, 46), and the inferior parietal lobular and supramarginal cortex, bilaterally (BA 39, 40, 7).

A key question is whether any of these results reflect patterns of activation due to unique deception-specific processes as opposed to general-purpose processes. This is primarily a theoretical question, but it has some consequences for potential applications as well. Indeed, the specificity of the findings has applied implications for our ability to infer deception from these patterns of activation. Furthermore, it has applied implications for the vulnerability of the methods to cognitive countermeasures (Ganis, Rosenfeld, Meixner, Kievit, and Schendan 2011) because nonspecific deception activations can be elicited by engaging in nondeceptive cognitive processes during the test (e.g., by intentionally altering the perceived salience of stimuli) and result in false positives.

This specificity question is an ontological one (Lenartowicz, Kalar, Congdon, and Poldrack 2010), that is, is deception an independent neurocognitive function with a unique neural substrate or rather a combination of other functions that have been studied classically by other subfields in cognitive psychology and neuroscience? This type of question is not unique to the field of deception research, of course. For example, a very similar question has been posed in the field of creativity research: is creative cognition unique or does it rely on the same processes that normative cognition relies on, perhaps just applied to a different context (Abraham 2013)? Addressing this question is easier, though not straightforward, for simple functions such as sensory processing. For instance, even though there are clear interactions between sensory modalities (Maunsell, Sclar, Nealey, and DePriest 1991), different modalities are supported by different neural pathways, at least in the early stages. However, for complex cognitive functions, it is much more complex to decide whether a certain function is unique.

The meta-analysis by Christ and collaborators (Christ et al. 2009) indicates that most of the regions engaged by deception are also engaged by general-purpose cognitive-control processes. This was demonstrated by overlapping the results of the deception meta-analysis with those of meta-analyses of three classes of cognitive-control processes that did not involve any deception: working memory, task switching, and inhibitory control. Specifically, the left IFG (BA 44), the left insula, the left precentral gyrus/middle frontal gyrus (BA 6), the right anterior cingulate (BA 24/32), parts of the inferior parietal lobule (BA 7/39), parts of the right IFG and insula (BA 6/44/45), and parts of the middle frontal gyrus (BA 9/10/46) were engaged not only by deception, but also by one or more of these cognitive-control tasks. Although these types of general-purpose processes are engaged during most types of deception (e.g., manipulating information in working memory while devising a lie), they are also engaged by many other cognitive functions that do not involve deception, and so these brain regions are not specific for deception. This aspect of the findings supports theoretical proposals suggesting that deception emerges out of more general problem-solving processes in which two or more agents are engaged in a communication interaction, and deception in some situations represents an optimal resolution strategy, given the ongoing constraints and capacity limitations (McCornack, Morrison, Paik, Wisner, and Zhu 2014). However, the meta-analysis also showed some regions engaged by deception that did not seem to be activated by any of the cognitive-control tasks. Such regions included the left inferior parietal lobule (BA 40), the right inferior parietal lobule/supramarginal gyrus (BA 39/40), parts of the right IFG and insula (BA 6/44/45), and parts of the right middle frontal gyrus (BA 9/10/46). This finding by itself does not provide strong evidence that these regions are unique to deception production because i) only a small subset of processes was investigated by the cognitive-control meta-analyses, and ii) only a few studies were included in each of these meta-analyses.

A more systematic approach to this issue involves using the concepts of forward and reverse inference, as well as employing large fMRI databases (Poldrack 2011; Yarkoni, Poldrack, Nichols, Van Essen, and Wager 2011). These concepts are important for understanding the mapping between cognitive and neuroscientific levels and taxonomies. A forward inference (Figure 35.1, top panel) involves going from the cognitive level (e.g., working memory) to the neuroscientific level (e.g., activation in dorsolateral

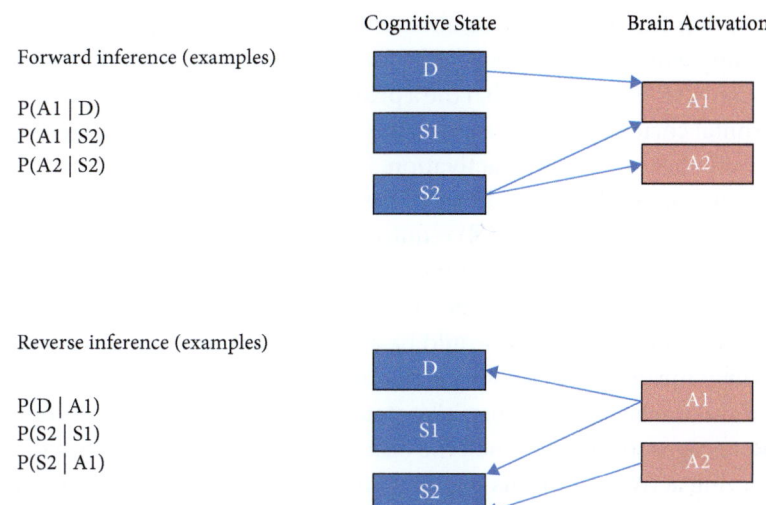

FIGURE 35.1 Schematic illustration of the logic of forward and reverse inferences. A forward inference is the probability that a certain pattern of brain activation (e.g., A1) is elicited by a certain mental state (e.g., deception, D). This information can be obtained by carrying out brain-imaging studies in which the mental state of interest is manipulated, and measuring the brain-activation effects of the manipulation. A reverse inference, in contrast, is the probability that a certain mental state (e.g., deception, D), is present, given a certain pattern of activation in the brain (e.g., A1). Given that a certain pattern of activation can be produced by multiple mental states (e.g., A1 can be elicited by D and S2), it is necessary to use Bayes' rule to calculate probabilities in inverse inferences (see text).

prefrontal cortex). Thus, a forward inference is the probability that a pattern of neural activation A (e.g., activation in dorsolateral prefrontal and posterior parietal cortex) is elicited by a certain mental state S (e.g., working memory). This is usually expressed as $P(A|S)$. This type of information can be provided by a neuroimaging study in which one manipulates, for example, working memory load and determines in which regions activation follows the manipulation. It is very easy to fall into the trap of reading a forward inference backward, and to infer incorrectly that a certain cognitive process is engaged by a certain pattern of brain activation just because this pattern of activation is typically elicited by that cognitive process. An example of this fallacy is inferring that working-memory processes are engaged from the finding that portions of the dorsolateral prefrontal cortex are activated. This logic is incorrect, however, because multiple cognitive states may actually generate that same pattern of brain activation (Figure 35.1, bottom panel): going from the neuroscientific to the cognitive level entails a reverse inference, calculating the probability that a certain mental state S is present, given that pattern of neural activation A is observed, $P(S|A)$. According to Bayes' rule (Lee 2012), a reverse inference requires knowledge of the corresponding forward inference, as well as of the base rates of engagement of the involved mental states and patterns of activation (Poldrack, 2011; Yarkoni et al., 2011): $P(S|A) = P(A|S)*P(S)/P(A)$. For example, let us assume that the probability of observing dorsolateral prefrontal cortex activation when using working memory (P(A|S) is .9, that the a priori probability of using working memory (P(S)) is .3, and that the a priori probability of activation in the dorsolateral prefrontal cortex (P(A)) is .5. Then, the probability of being engaged in working memory, given that we observe activation in the dorsolateral prefrontal cortex is. 9 * .3/.5 = .54. As mentioned, knowledge of the term P(A|S) is provided by neuroimaging data. However, knowledge of P(A) requires using information from large neuroimaging databases. The base rate of a brain region is the a priori probability of that region being active. If a brain region is activated by many different tasks, then the base rate for that region will be close to one (it would be exactly one if the region was activated by any task), which means that observing activation in this region conveys relatively little information about what specific cognitive state elicited it. At the other extreme, if only a single task engages this region, then the base rate for this region will be close to zero, and so observing activation in this region would reveal with very high probability the cognitive state that generated it. Estimates of base rates for the entire brain were calculated using NeuroSynth, which relies on a large and growing database with several thousand fMRI studies (Poldrack 2011; Yarkoni et al. 2011). Results show that most of the brain regions found in the deception meta-analyses described earlier coincide with regions with the highest base rates in the brain. These include the anterior cingulate and nearby medial prefrontal cortex, the anterior insula and parts of the ventrolateral prefrontal cortex, and large portions of the dorsolateral prefrontal cortex (Poldrack 2011; Yarkoni et al. 2011). This finding means that these regions tend to be engaged by a multitude of different mental states and so inferring selectivity for deception from their activation is problematic (see Figure 35.1).

The main regions found in deception meta-analyses that do not overlap with high base-rate regions are the inferior parietal and supramarginal foci mentioned earlier. Does this mean that these parietal regions are selective for deception? To address this question in more detail, the cognitive control meta-analysis carried out by Christ and collaborators was expanded by conducting an independent deception meta-analysis of thirty-five neuroimaging studies (resulting in 471 activation foci obtained from forty-eight individual experiments) and by comparing the results with those of control meta-analyses calculated using NeuroSynth. Next, forward inference maps for the terms 'working memory', 'inhibition', 'task switching', and 'theory of mind' were generated and then the regions that were activated selectively by deception were determined. The first three processes were also explored in the original meta-analysis by Christ and collaborators, using a much smaller set of studies, whereas the last process was included here because it is likely to be engaged, though not exclusively, during deception. The results are shown in Figure 35.2, and they can be described in terms of how many volume elements (voxels, in this case 2 x 2 x 2 mm cubes of brain tissue) were engaged in common or independently by the various tasks. Deception engaged a total of 2,345 voxels, but of these only 653 voxels were selectively engaged by deception, the other 1,692 were activated in common with one or more of the nondeceptive tasks. The deception-selective voxels (in red) were mostly located in portions of the

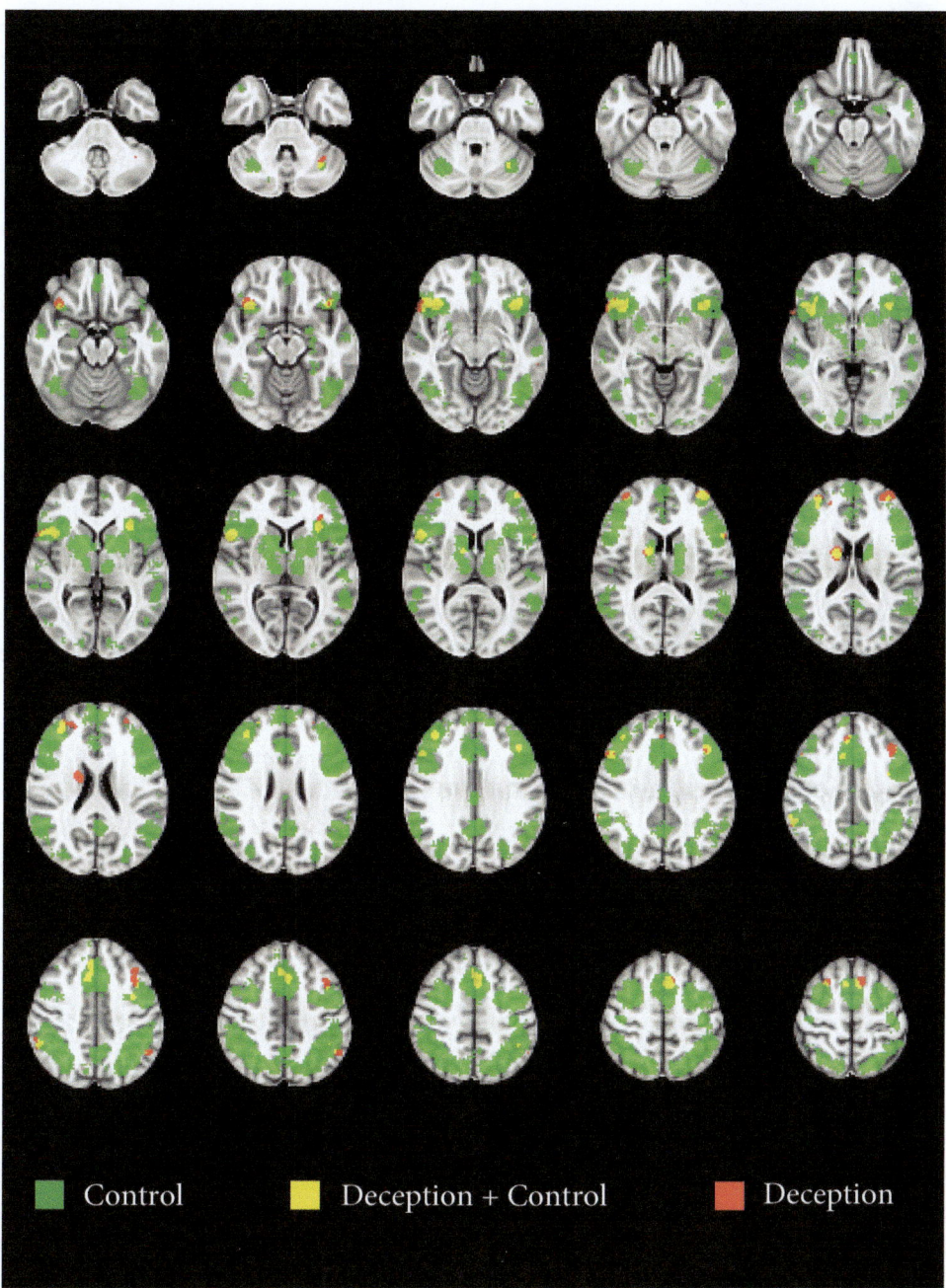

FIGURE 35.2 Results of the overlap analysis. In green are voxels engaged by one or more of the control tasks ('working memory', 'inhibition', 'task switching', and 'theory of mind'), but not by deception; in yellow are voxels engaged in common by deception and by at least one of the control tasks; in red are voxels engaged exclusively by deception. The patterns of activation are overlaid on horizontal slices through a normalized and deskulled brain.

superior frontal gyrus, bilaterally (BA 10), the left superior frontal gyrus (BA 6), the left middle frontal gyrus (BA 8), the left medial frontal gyrus (BA 6), the right inferior frontal gyrus (BA 47), the intraparietal lobule, bilaterally (BA 40), the left cerebellum, and parts of the right caudate. This overlap analysis suggests that some of these regions may be selective for deception, possibly reflecting domain specificity within these regions.

Overlap analyses based on univariate methods such as the ones discussed so far may ignore subtle details of the spatial patterns of neural activation as voxels are classified in a binary way, as active or not. It is possible that deception elicits unique spatial patterns of activation within regions that are shared with much more general functions. One way to investigate this issue would be by using multivoxel pattern analyses (MVPA), methods that provide more sensitive measures of spatial similarity useful to determine whether two conditions engage the same neural populations (Tong and Pratte 2012). Multivoxel pattern analysis methods assume that cognitive processes are carried out in a distributed fashion in the brain and so they examine and compare the distribution of brain activation across many voxels (Haxby et al. 2001). Although this type of analysis has been carried out in a handful of studies to try to discriminate between activation to deceptive and to honest responses (Davatzikos et al. 2005; Peth et al. 2015), it has not been carried out yet to address the issue of the uniqueness of deception as a cognitive function.

35.3.3 Accuracy of neurocognitive methods

With an applied focus, several ERP studies using concealed-information paradigms have quantified the accuracy of P300-based methods at discriminating between concealed-information cases and cases without concealed information using a receiver-operating characteristic (ROC) approach (Fawcett 2006). These studies were included in a recent meta-analysis (Meijer, Klein-Selle, Elber, and Ben-Shakhar 2014) that found an area under the curve of .88 (with 1 corresponding to perfect discrimination accuracy) and a mean effect size (d*) of 1.89. In other words, these paradigms are quite effective at detecting concealed information, at least in laboratory situations.

The extent to which the much smaller and variable N2 and LPP can be used for single individual classification is unknown, as not enough research has looked at these two components. Similarly, the MFN differences between deceptive and honest responses are much smaller and more variable than the P300 differences and so, to date, they have not been used to attempt to classify individual subjects as honest or deceptive.

A few neuroimaging studies have measured the accuracy of the methods (Davatzikos et al. 2005; Kozel et al. 2005; Langleben et al. 2005; Kozel, Johnson, et al. 2009; Kozel, Laken, et al. 2009; Monteleone et al. 2009; Nose, Murai, and Taira 2009; Ganis et al. 2011). Although there has not been a formal meta-analysis of the accuracy using ROC methods, the average accuracy rate for these studies is about

82% (Ganis 2015), which is comparable to that found in laboratory studies that have used standard autonomic nervous system variables such as skin conductance (Meijer et al. 2014).

An important question for potential applications is the extent to which the accuracy of these methods is affected by cognitive countermeasures. This topic has not been explored in detail, but both electrophysiological and hemodynamic methods are known to be highly affected by countermeasures (Rosenfeld et al. 2004; Ganis et al. 2011). Novel paradigms that appear to be insensitive to countermeasures, such as the CTP (Rosenfeld et al. 2008), hold promise, but the findings have not been replicated by independent laboratories yet.

35.4 Conclusions

This chapter provides a selective overview of the main ERP and fMRI paradigms and findings on the topic of deception and deception-detection. Although the results of several tens of studies indicate that deception manipulations are associated with replicable patterns of neural activation that can be used to better understand deception processes and potentially detect them, several issues remain.

First, from a theoretical perspective it is not clear that any of the observed patterns of neural activation are specific for deception production processes, as similar patterns can be elicited by manipulations that do not involve deception. Progress toward addressing this question may come from conducting systematic studies comparing deceptive and nondeceptive manipulations using multivariate analyses that can document subtle, but reliable, differences in the spatial patterns of activation.

Second, in applied terms, this apparent lack of specificity is one of the reasons why these methods tend to be vulnerable to countermeasures, which are typically based on producing patterns of activations that are incorrectly interpreted as reflecting deception by using nondeceptive means. Although there have been a few studies on the effects of countermeasures on both ERP and fMRI measures, more systematic investigations of this key limitation are required (Rosenfeld et al. 2004; Ganis et al. 2011).

Third, the vast majority of studies of deception have been conducted using highly nonecological laboratory paradigms, starting with instructing participants to lie. Results from the few studies that have given participants the free choice to lie are typically weakened by potential confounds, such as the different frequencies of deceptive and nondeceptive trials. Progress in this area will require the devising of new deception paradigms that are more ecologically valid, while retaining sufficient control over the relevant variables.

Fourth, the level of accuracy of these methods for potential forensic applications is still quite low, even in the laboratory. In fact, it is comparable to that of traditional psychophysiological methods that are much cheaper and easier to deploy. Although advances in machine learning and signal-processing may improve the accuracy of these methods, it is likely that parallel advances in the experimental paradigms will also be needed.

In sum, deception and deception-detection research should continue exploring the full potential of neurocognitive methods by devising novel paradigms and analysis techniques, and by devising ways to integrate them with more traditional methods.

CHAPTER 36

LYING AND ETHICS

THOMAS L. CARSON

THIS chapter surveys and assesses some important views about the morality of lying (absolutism, utilitarianism, and Ross's theory) and also discusses the moral relevance of the distinction between lying and deception.

36.1 ABSOLUTISM: AUGUSTINE

Augustine defends an absolute moral prohibition against lying.[1] In the "Enchiridion" he says that lying is always wrong because it involves using speech or language for something other than its intended purpose:

> Now it is evident that speech was given to man, not that men might therewith deceive one another, but that one man might make known his thoughts to another. To use speech, then, for the purpose of deception, and not for its appointed end is a sin. Nor are we to suppose that there is any lie that is not a sin, because it is sometimes possible by telling a lie, to do service to another.
>
> (Augustine 1961: 29)

We need to ask: what is the purpose of or "appointed end" of speech/language? and why is it always wrong to use something for a purpose other than that for which it was intended? Augustine's answer seems to be that "the appointed end" of speech is determined by God's purposes in creating creatures capable of using language and that all lying is contrary to God's will. Augustine quotes a number of Bible passages that he thinks support the view that God disapproves of all lies ("On Lying," 88–110, "Against

---

[1] In the "Enchiridion," he defines lying as follows: "every liar says the opposite of what he thinks in his heart, with purpose to deceive" (Augustine 1961: 29). He gives essentially the same definition in "On Lying," (54–6). In "Against Lying," he defines lying "as false signification told with desire to deceive" (160).

Lying", 126–7, 165–8). Among the passages he quotes are "Wisdom" 1.11: "The mouth that belieth, killeth the soul," "Psalms" 5:6 "Thou [God] will destroy all that speak a lie", and "Ephesians" 4:24 "Put away lying and speak the truth." He also argues that the Bible does not approve of any cases of lying ("Against Lying," 151–64). Abraham and Isaac concealed information from others and Jacob practiced deception, but their actions (which were approved of in the Bible) were not cases of lying ("Against Lying," 152). On several occasions, when Jesus was asked questions, he pretended not to know certain things which he actually knew. According to Augustine, in pretending not to know things that he actually knew, Jesus was not lying ("Against Lying," 160).

Augustine says that it would be wrong to tell a lie even to save the life of an innocent person. Using an example very similar to one that Mill later called an exception to the "sacred rule" that lying is wrong (see section 36.4), Augustine considers a case in which lying is necessary to prevent a gravely ill person from dying because of learning very bad news:

> a patient whose life is endangered by a serious illness and whose strength will not hold out any longer if he is told of the death of his beloved only son. He asks you whether the boy is still alive whose life you know is ended.
>
> ("Against Lying": 171)

If you do not answer the question, the patient will take this to mean that his son is dead—he will think that you are afraid to say so but do not want to lie. Augustine continues:

> of the three convincing answers, two are false: 'He is alive' and 'I don't know', and you cannot utter them without lying. But, if you make the one true answer, namely, that he is dead, and if the death of the anguished father falls hard upon it, people will cry that he was slain by you.
>
> ("Against Lying": 171)

Augustine says that he is moved by these arguments and sympathy for those involved but more greatly moved by "the radiance of truth" ("Against Lying": 171–2). He then argues that it would be wrong to lie in this case:

> if we grant that we ought to lie about the son's life for the sake of that patient's health, little by little and bit by bit this evil will grow and by gradual accessions this evil will slowly increase until it becomes such a mass of wicked lies that it will be utterly impossible to find any means to resist such a plague grown to huge proportions through small additions.
>
> ("Against Lying": 172)

This is clearly a bad argument. There is no reason to think that allowing for exceptions in cases in which lying is necessary to save someone's life opens the door to constant lying.

This line between permissible and impermissible lying is very clear and stark. Most of us have never told a single lie that was necessary to save someone's life.

36.2 ABSOLUTISM: KANT

Kant is generally regarded as an absolutist about lying. The *Metaphysics of Morals* (Kant 1996a) includes a dialogue between a teacher and pupil. Both the teacher and the pupil (and presumably Kant) endorse the view that lying is always wrong no matter what:

> Teacher: ... Suppose ... you could get a great benefit for yourself or your friend by making up a subtle *lie* that would harm no one ...
> Pupil: That I ought not lie, no matter how great the benefits to myself and my friend might be. Lying is *mean* and makes a man *unworthy* of happiness. Here is an unconditional necessitation through a command (or prohibition) of reason, which I must obey; and in the face of it all my inclinations must be silent.
>   (*Metaphysics of Morals* (hereafter "MM"; Kant 1996a: 481–2; all references to Kant include the page numbers from the Prussian Academy Edition.)

For other evidence that Kant endorses an absolute moral prohibition against lying in "MM" see "MM": 429–30).

In "On a Supposed Right to Lie," (hereafter "SR"; Kant 1993a) Kant presents a case in which lying seems to be necessary to protect someone from a would-be murderer and claims that it is morally wrong to lie in this case. Kant presents the following case. Someone who fears that he will be murdered has taken refuge in my home. The person he is hiding from comes to my door and asks me whether his intended victim is in the house. He demands to know whether his intended victim is in my house and I cannot avoid answering the question. Kant contends that it would be wrong for me to lie to him.

In this essay, Kant is largely concerned with the question of how the law should deal with people who lie from benevolent motives. He says that if the person who answers the door lies and, unbeknownst to him, the fugitive leaves the house and is later killed by the person who knocks on the door, the person who lies can be justly accused of having caused his death ("SR": 427).

But Kant also seems to say that it is morally wrong to lie in this case and some of the things he says seem to imply that all lies are wrong. Kant's essay replies to criticisms from Benjamin Constant. Constant says that the duty not to lie holds only for those who have a right to know the truth and that it is not wrong to lie to those who do not have that right ("SR": 425). Since the potential murderer does not have a right to know the information in question, Constant would say that it is not wrong to lie to him. Kant concedes that I would not wrong the would-be murderer by lying to him. However, he argues that in such cases lying is wrong because it wrongs and harms "humanity in general":

> That is, as far as in me lies, I bring it about that statements (declarations) in general find no credence, and hence also that all rights based on contracts become void and lose their force, and this is a wrong done to mankind in general ... For a lie always harms another; if not some other human being, then it nevertheless does harm to humanity in general, inasmuch as it vitiates the very source of right.
> ("On a Supposed Right to Lie Because of Philanthropic Concerns" (hereafter "SR"), Kant 1993a: 426)[2]

> To be truthful in all declarations is, therefore, a sacred and unconditionally commanding law of reason which admits of *no expediency whatever* [my emphasis].[3]
> ("SR": 427)

Kant also claims that the laws of duties of contracts (which he holds are founded in the duty of truthfulness) would be rendered uncertain and useless if even the "slightest exception" to them was permitted:

> ... truthfulness is a duty that must be regarded as the basis of all duties founded on contract, and the laws of such duties would be rendered uncertain and useless if even the slightest exception to them were admitted.
> ("SR": 427)

Kant's claim that by telling lies we bring it about that statements are given no credence so that all contracts become void and lose their force is patently false. He is also clearly mistaken in holding that contracts would be rendered useless if we allowed the slightest exceptions to the duties of contracts. Kant greatly overstates the bad consequences of individual lies (and the bad consequences of allowing exceptions to the moral prohibition against lying or to the laws of contracts) for the fabric of social trust. In our world, a very great number of lies are told, and most people endorse moral principles that sometimes permit lying and sometimes permit people to break contracts. However, the trust necessary for effective communication by means of language exists almost everywhere, and in many societies there exists a level of trust sufficient to sustain the viability of contracts and promise-keeping. One might object that Kant is merely claiming that telling lies weakens the trust and credence we give to statements. If that is all he is saying in the passages quoted above, it is no doubt true, but then what he says in "SR" is clearly not sufficient to show that lying is always wrong.

---

[2] Also see "Lectures on Ethics" (hereafter "LE"; Kant 1997), 434–5, where Kant also says that lying wrongs humanity, even if it does not wrong any particular person.

[3] I take this to mean that it is always wrong to lie (always wrong to make untruthful declarations).

It is at least debatable whether Kant claims that lying is always wrong in "SR" (see Varden 2010). But, in any case, it is clear that the arguments of "SR" do not provide good reasons for thinking that lying is always wrong. I will not insist on my interpretation of "SR." I only claim that the arguments of "SR" do not give us good reason for endorsing absolutism (my aim is to attack absolutism, not Kant).

Kant's argument about the murderer at the door is widely attacked and derided. Bernard Williams calls Kant's views "repellent" (Williams 2002: 106); Paton attributes them to Kant's "bad temper in his old age" (Paton 1954: 201). Allen Wood does not defend what Kant says about this case, but he claims that Kant is not really committed to the view that it would be wrong to lie to the would-be murderer at the door. According to Wood, Kant's definition of lying is inconsistent with his description of this case as one in which I would be lying if I told the would-be murderer that his intended victim is not in my house. In "SR," Kant defines lying as "an intentionally untruthful declaration to another man." According to Wood, Kant takes declarations to be statements that others are warranted or authorized to rely on (Wood 2008: 241–2). Since the person who answers the door in Kant's example is forced to answer the question, his statement cannot be a declaration (and thus cannot be a lie), because the would-be murderer would not be authorized to rely on the answer (Wood 2008: 241–2). So, Kant *could have said* that it would be right for me to speak falsely to the would-be murderer at the door if I am forced to answer, but that my doing so would not be a lie because it would not be a declaration (Wood 2008: 248).

In "SR" Kant makes no mention of the categorical imperative, nor does he mention or appeal to the categorical imperative in his discussion of lying in the "MM." We need to ask whether his moral theory (the categorical imperative) really commits him to the view that lying is always wrong no matter what. My answer is "no."

Kant states the first version of the categorical imperative as follows:

> Act only according to that maxim whereby you can at the same time will that it should become a universal law ... Act as if the maxim of your action were to become through your will a universal law of nature.
>
> (*Grounding for the Metaphysics of Morals*
> (hereafter "GMM"; Kant 1993b), Ellington translation, 421)

Maxims are general principles that prescribe or command actions, e.g., "never lie" or "never lie except to prevent grave harm to someone." A maxim can be a universal law of nature provided that it is possible that all rational beings always follow it or comply with it. The first version of the categorical imperative is roughly equivalent to the following:

Act only on maxims that you *can will* that every rational being in the universe follows, i.e., act only on maxims that it is possible for you to will that every rational being follows.

In "LE," Kant (1997: 496) asks us to consider the maxim "tell a lie or untruth whenever you can thereby gain a great advantage."[4] Arguably, it is impossible that everyone follows this maxim, since if *everyone* lied whenever she thought she could gain an advantage, dishonesty would be so widespread that people would not trust or rely on the assertions of others, and no one could gain an advantage by means of lying. But this does not show that the first version of the categorical imperative commits us to an absolute prohibition against lying, because this is not the only maxim that sometimes permits lying. Consider the following maxim:

Lie whenever lying is necessary in order to prevent an innocent person from being killed and lying does not produce any other consequences nearly as bad as the death of an innocent person.[5]

Universal adherence to this maxim would not make it impossible for people to communicate and advance their interests by using language. The great majority of people have never told a single lie permitted by this maxim during their entire lives. Further, many people *are willing* that everyone lie whenever lying is necessary in order to save the lives of innocent people, and, therefore, they *can will* that everyone makes it a policy to lie whenever lying is necessary to save the lives of innocent people.

Kant states the second version of the categorical imperative as follows:

> Act in such a way that you treat humanity, whether in your own person or in the person of another, always at the same time as an end and never *simply* [my emphasis] as a means.
>
> ("GMM," Ellington translation, Kant 1993b: 429)

Sometimes it is necessary to lie to others to protect them from grave harm (as in the case of lying to a dangerously ill person to prevent her from learning very bad news). It is unclear why this is inconsistent with treating him as an end in himself (respecting him as a rational person and treating him as someone who possesses intrinsic value and not using him "as a mere means" to one's own ends).

But Korsgaard claims that the second version of the categorical imperative implies that lying is always wrong. She appeals to a passage in which Kant derives moral duties from the second formulation of the categorical imperative (Korsgaard 1996a: 138):

> the man who intends to make a false promise will immediately see that he intends to make use of another man merely as a means to an end which the latter does not likewise hold. For the man whom I want to use for my own purposes by such a promise

---

[4] Kant writes "For suppose that someone were to have the maxim, that he might tell an untruth whenever he could thereby gain a great advantage...".

[5] Cf. Dietrichson (1969: 201), Herman (1993: 152), and Korsgaard (1996a: 136–7).

cannot possibly concur with my way of acting toward him and hence cannot hold himself the end of the action.

("GMM," 429–30, Kant 1993b, Beck translation)

Korsgaard argues that the second version of the categorical imperative requires that we never act toward others in ways that it is impossible for them to assent to.

Knowledge of what is going on and some power over the proceedings are the conditions of possible assent ... This gives us another way to formulate the test for treating someone as a mere means: suppose that it is the case that if the other person knows what you are trying to do and has the power to stop you, then what you are trying to do cannot be what is really happening. If this is the case, the action is one that by its very nature is impossible for the other to assent to.

(Korsgaard 1996a: 139)

The idea of it being possible for someone to assent to "another's mode of treating her" could mean either (i) it being possible for her to assent to a particular action with a particular end in particular circumstances, or alternatively, (ii) it being possible to assent to other people following general *policies or principles* that permit them to perform the particular action in question. Korsgaard clearly takes it to mean the former. I cannot both lie and deceive you about some particular matter at a particular time *and* at the same time obtain your assent to my deceiving you in that way. If you assent to what I am doing, then you will understand what I am trying to do and I will not be able to deceive you about the matter in question. However, you *can* assent to others acting on principles that sometimes permit them to lie and deceive you—you might assent to the idea that in the future physicians should lie to you to protect your health. For criticisms of Korsgaard that argue that (ii) rather than (i) is the correct interpretation of Kant, see Carson (2010: 81–5).

36.3 SOFTENING ABSOLUTISM

Most people find absolutism to be an untenable view in cases in which lying is necessary to protect others from death. Some absolutists try to deal with such cases by appealing to very narrow definitions of lying according to which many of the alleged cases of permissible lying are not genuine cases of lying (see Bok 1999: 14–15, 36–7). For instance, some hold that a necessary condition of one's lying is that the person to whom one's statement is directed has a right to know the truth, so that intentionally speaking falsely to someone who has no right to know the truth cannot be a lie.[6] However, endorsing

---

[6] Grotius holds that in order to tell a lie ("falsehood") the person(s) to who one's statement is directed must have a right to the truth (Grotius 1925, bk. 3, ch. 1; included as an appendix in Bok 1999: 263–4).

such a definition of lying does not save absolutists from being forced to say that lying is wrong in many cases in which lying is necessary to save someone's life. It might be permissible to lie to a gravely ill patient who has just undergone heart surgery to shield her from being shocked by learning about the death of her child, even though she surely has a right to know such information.

Some absolutists appeal to the doctrines of the mental reservation and equivocation to minimize the counterintuitive consequences of their view. According to the doctrine of "mental reservation," statements that would otherwise be lies are not lies provided that when one makes them one has an inner thought or "mental reservation," which when added to the statement makes it truthful (in accordance with one's beliefs) (Bok 1999: 35). For example, someone's deliberately false and misleading statement that he has never been unfaithful to his wife is not a lie if when he says it he inwardly adds the truthful thought "except once after the wild party during my business trip to Las Vegas in October 1979."

The doctrines of mental reservation and equivocation have been influential among those in the Roman Catholic tradition who want to defend absolutism about lying. In his book *Medical Ethics*, Father Charles McFadden says that lying is never morally permissible (McFadden 1967: 391). But he says that physicians can avoid conflicts of duties by use of "mental reservation":

> Mental reservation is the use of an expression which has two meanings; one meaning is the more obvious and usual interpretation of the word; the other meaning the less obvious and usual interpretation of the word; the more obvious interpretation of the word is the one the speaker believes the hearer will place upon the response; the less obvious interpretation of the words is the meaning which the speaker intends.
>
> (McFadden 1967: 391)

McFadden gives the following illustration. A patient has a medical condition which has produced a temperature of 102 F, which is normal *given his condition*. The patient asks "What is my temperature?" The doctor and nurse respond by saying "Your temperature is normal today" (McFadden 1967: 391–2). According to McFadden, they are not lying even though they deceive the patient and know that he will take their answer to mean that his temperature is 98.6 F.

Some versions of the doctrine of mental reservation are clearly absurd. It is absurd to say that the husband who denies his past martial infidelity is not lying. Whether or not one lies depends on what one says and communicates to others. Suppose that the unfaithful husband knows that his statement is false and that he says it with the intent to deceive others and does so in a context in which he warrants that what he says is true. Surely he is lying. His inner mental qualification does not negate the fact that he is lying unless he clearly communicates that qualification *as part of* his statement. McFadden's view makes use of the idea of equivocation and cannot be so easily dismissed. But his claim that nurses and physicians can *always* avoid conflicts of duties by withholding harmful information from patients by means of deceptive equivocal statements that fall short of lying is very doubtful. There is no reason to think that in the heat of the moment doctors and nurses can always quickly think of appropriate equivocations that are deceptive but fall short of lying when they need to protect patients from dangerous information.

36.4 ACT-UTILITARIANISM

Act-utilitarianism holds that one should always do whatever will have the best possible consequences, or more precisely:

An act is morally right if and only if there is no other possible alternative act open to the agent that would result in a better balance of good consequences relative to bad consequences.

I define act-utilitarianism broadly as any consequentialist theory of right and wrong according to which we should always act so as to bring about the best consequences. Mill and Sidgwick define (act)-utilitarianism more narrowly as a hedonistic consequentialism; they say that the good to be optimized is happiness or pleasure and the absence of pain (see Sidgwick 1966: 411, 413 and Mill 2001: 7).

Act-utilitarians hold that the rightness or wrongness of a particular action is determined solely by the consequences of *that particular action*. Rule-utilitarianism or rule-consequentialism (RC), holds that we should not judge the rightness or wrongness of individual actions directly by their consequences. Rather, it holds that the rightness or wrongness of an action depends on whether it is permitted by the ideal moral code, the moral code the general acceptance of which would produce better consequences than any other moral code.

Act-utilitarianism clearly implies that lying is sometimes morally permissible and that lying can be justified if it is necessary to avert extremely bad consequences. Few people object to this feature of the theory. However, many think that utilitarianism is too permissive about lying and permits lying in many cases in which it would be wrong to lie.

Mill addresses the objection that (act)-utilitarianism permits lying whenever it is "expedient" to lie. He grants that lying often has good consequences in the short run. For example, it can prevent quarrels or spare people from being embarrassed. But Mill claims that the short-term benefits of lying in such cases are usually outweighed by the long-term bad consequences of violating the very beneficial prohibition against lying. He says that lying has (or tends to have) two indirect bad consequences: 1. it weakens one's honesty or veracity, and 2. it diminishes the trust and reliance that we can have in each other's assertions (Mill 2001: 22–3). Mill calls the prohibition against lying "a sacred rule," but says that there are cases in which it is right to lie. He gives the example of lying to a gravely ill person in order to protect her from being shocked and perhaps even dying as a result of learning very bad news (Mill 2001: 23).

There are two other reasons why act-utilitarianism implies that there is a strong presumption against lying. First, lies often harm others by deceiving them. That creates a moral presumption against lying that is likely to deceive others. We are generally harmed when we are deceived because we cannot effectively pursue our ends and interests if we act on the basis of false beliefs. Being deceived about arcane facts that are not relevant to any of one's concerns or decisions seldom harms one. However, ordinarily, when we attempt to deceive others, we do so in order to influence their behavior. Thus, generally, when we deceive others, we deceive them about matters of interest and concern to *them*, and we try to influence them to do things that they would not do if they were not deceived and, thus, ordinarily, when we deceive others we *harm* them (make them worse off) or risk harming them.[7]

Second, several prudential considerations weigh strongly against lying. Most of us are such that it would be very harmful to our interests to be regarded as a dishonest person. For this reason, it is very detrimental to most people's interests to be caught in telling lies. Even when we succeed in concealing our lies, the price of maintaining the pretense of not having lied can be great. We need to be constantly on guard and remember what we said and to whom we said it. Sometimes, we need to suppress our spontaneous emotional reactions to events in order to maintain the pretense of not having lied. According to act-utilitarianism, all of these bad consequences of lying are morally relevant and weigh strongly against lying.

36.5 Ross's theory

Ross's theory is based on his concept of a "prima facie duty." A prima facie duty is one's actual duty (what one really ought to do on balance), other things being equal. Alternatively, a prima facie duty is one's actual duty on the condition that it does not conflict with another prima facie duty (or duties) of equal or greater importance (Ross 2002 [1930]: 19).

According to Ross, there are eight fundamental prima facie moral duties (Ross 2002 [1930]: 20–1):

1. The duty to keep promises.
2. The duty not to lie. This is a special case of the duty to keep promises, because one makes an implicit promise not to lie whenever one uses language to communicate with another person (Ross 2002 [1930]: 21). Telling a lie is tantamount to breaking a promise or making a promise in bad faith. There is a *negative* duty to refrain from lying but no *positive* duty to answer questions or reveal information.
3. The duty to make reparations to people one has harmed.

---

[7] Possible exceptions to this general rule arise when people lie to protect their own personal privacy.

4. The duty of gratitude.
5. The duty to distribute happiness according to merit, i.e., moral goodness. (Among other things this means that we have a stronger duty to benefit morally good people than morally bad people.)
6. The duty to do things that benefit others.
7. The duty to improve one's own intellect and moral character.
8. The duty not to harm others.

Ross does *not* say that there is a prima facie duty not to deceive others. He only says that there is a prima facie duty not to lie. He holds that lying is morally permissible when, and only when, the duty not to lie conflicts with a more important or equally important prima facie duty (or duties).

Ross gives two arguments against the utilitarian view about promise-keeping. First, utilitarians hold that, other things being equal, it does not matter whether one breaks a promise or keeps it. But if breaking a promise would have exactly the same consequences as keeping it and no other duties are involved, then it is clearly one's actual duty to keep the promise (Ross 2002 [1930]: 18). Second, utilitarianism implies that breaking a promise is morally right whenever breaking it produces slightly better consequences than keeping it. But it is *obvious* that I should not break my promise in such cases (Ross 2002 [1930]: 34–5, 38–9).

Since he regards lying as a case of promise-breaking, Ross would endorse the same objections to the utilitarian view about the morality of lying. His arguments can be reformulated as follows:

First, sometimes lying will result in *exactly* the same consequences (or *exactly* the same net amount of good and bad) as not lying. In such cases, utilitarians must say that it does not matter whether or not one lies. But surely this is unacceptable. *Other things being equal*, it is wrong to lie. Second, utilitarianism mistakenly implies that lying is morally justified whenever it has slightly better consequences than not lying.

Ross's theory is generally thought to be less permissive about lying than utilitarianism, but there are some cases in which Ross's theory permits lying and utilitarianism does not. Suppose that your telling a lie that causes slightly more harm than good is necessary for you to keep a promise and fulfill duties of gratitude and reparation. Ross's theory justifies lying in at least some such cases.

Ross's view about lying has been incorporated into standard versions of rule-utilitarianism/rule-consequentialism. Brad Hooker, arguably the most important contemporary defender of rule-utilitarianism/consequentialism, endorses the Rossian view that there is a prima facie duty not to lie (Hooker 2000: 126–8). He argues that the ideal moral code (the moral code whose general acceptance would have the best consequences) includes Rossian prima facie moral prohibitions, including a prohibition against lying. Hooker does not mention deception; he apparently agrees with Ross that there is a prima facie duty not to lie but no prima facie duty not to deceive others.

Another leading rule-utilitarian, Richard Brandt, also thinks that the ideal moral code includes prima facie moral prohibitions (Brandt 1979: 287).

36.6 Assessing the positions

As some of the earlier examples demonstrate, the duty not to lie can conflict with other moral duties such as the duty to help protect other people from grave harm. Therefore, if we say that lying is *always wrong* no matter what, we are claiming that the duty not to lie is *always* more important than any conflicting duties, even in cases in which lying is necessary to save the lives of many innocent people. In a similar vein Sidgwick writes:

> so if we may even kill in defense of ourselves and others, it seems strange if we may not lie, if lying will defend us better against a palpable invasion of our rights: and common sense does not seem to prohibit this decisively.
>
> (Sidgwick 1966: 315)

Anyone who is asked questions by a gravely ill person in cases like those described by Augustine and Mill clearly has prima facie duties that conflict with the duty not to lie.

Absolutism about lying is wildly counterintuitive and the arguments given by Augustine and Kant do not give us adequate reasons to accept absolutism about lying. Act-utilitarianism and Ross's theory are more promising theories about the morality of lying. But Ross's arguments for his view leave much to be desired. He says that it is self-evident that there is a prima facie duty not to lie and a prima facie duty to keep promises (Ross 2002 [1930]: 29–30). Moore, on the other hand, claims that it is self-evident that utilitarianism is true:

> It seems to me to be self-evident that knowingly to do an action which would make the world, on the whole, really and truly *worse* than if we had acted differently, must always be wrong.
>
> (Moore 1965: 77)

This is flatly inconsistent with Ross's view that lying can be wrong, even if it has slightly better consequences than not lying. In the following passage, Ross very explicitly rejects Moore's claim:

> It seems, on reflection, self-evident that a promise, simply as such, is something that *prima facie* ought to be kept, and it does *not,* on reflection, seem self-evident that production of maximum good is the only thing that makes an act obligatory.
>
> (Ross 2002 [1930]: 40)

Moral arguments that appeal solely to claims of self-evidence are unconvincing (see Carson 2010: ch. 5).

In an attempt to avoid relying on disputed moral intuitions, Carson defends a version of the golden rule that can be used to test moral principles. He argues that lying is morally wrong whenever it fails to produce the best consequences and that, at a minimum, there is a moral presumption against lying that is at least as strong as that endorsed by utilitarianism but not as strong as that endorsed by absolutism (Carson 2010: 129–66). He holds that, as far as the best available arguments can show, there is a range of different reasonable views about the morality of lying that includes both act-utilitarianism and Ross's theory (both theories pass golden-rule tests). He also argues that egoism[8] and absolutism both fail golden-rule tests and, therefore, are not reasonable views about the morality of lying.

36.7 THE MORAL RELEVANCE OF THE DISTINCTION BETWEEN LYING AND DECEPTION

Is there a morally relevant difference between lying and deception (or attempted deception) without lying? Many claim that, other things being equal, deception or attempted deception without lying is morally preferable to lying.

Augustine and McFadden hold that lying is always wrong but that deception is sometimes permissible. Kant says that it is sometimes permissible to deceive others without lying. He gives the example of a man who packs his bags with the intention of causing others to falsely believe that he is off on a journey. According to Kant, this action is morally permissible, but it would be wrong to tell a lie in order to bring about the same false belief ("LE," Kant 1997, 27: 446–8). He also thinks that some deceptive statements that fall short of lying are morally permissible (see MacIntyre 1995: 336–7).

Ross holds that there is a prima facie duty not to lie, but no prima facie duty not to deceive others short of lying. Utilitarianism implies that the difference between lying and deception is not morally relevant provided that they have the same consequences.[9]

Some philosophers hold that lying requires warranting the truth of statements that one believes to be false (or at least does not believe to be true).[10] This way of defining lying lends itself to the view that lying is worse than mere deception or attempted deception. According to this definition of lying, liars promise or give an assurance that

---

[8] The view that it is permissible to lie whenever lying best promotes one's own self-interest.
[9] Utilitarians would also say that lying and attempted deception that actually deceive others tend to be more harmful and thus morally worse than lying and attempted deception that does not cause others to have false beliefs.
[10] See Ross (2002 [1930]: 21), Fried (1978: 67), Carson (2010: 24–9), and Saul (2012a: 19).

what they say is true and invite trust and reliance on the truth of what they say. This implies that, at least typically, liars break a promise and hope/intend that others will trust them. By contrast, attempting to deceive others does not necessarily involve trying to get them to trust one. On the present view of the nature of lying, lying, unlike mere deception, involves breaking a promise and attempting to betray the trust of others and these are arguably morally relevant differences. If this is correct, then utilitarians might be able to say that this is a strong reason for thinking that lying *tends to be* morally worse than deception without lying (at least in cases where there exists or might develop a valuable kind of trust between people that is damaged or fails to develop on account of the lying).[11]

---

[11] It is not always a good thing if one person trusts another. It is not a bad thing if I come to distrust (or fail to develop trust for) someone who is unworthy of trust. For example, it is good if I am caused to distrust a con man.

CHAPTER 37

LYING AND THE LAW

STUART P. GREEN

37.1 INTRODUCTION

How should the law regulate lies and other forms of deception? Sometimes, as we shall see, it takes a hard line, subjecting those who engage in deception to serious criminal or disciplinary sanctions. Other times, it is quite tolerant, declining to impose sanctions, and even affording certain kinds of deception constitutional protection. This chapter offers a general survey of a very broad topic, focusing primarily on US law, but also attempting, in a selective manner, to contrast that law to the law of other jurisdictions.

Before we proceed, it will be helpful to distinguish between lies and other forms of deception. As I shall use the term here, *deception* refers to the communication of a message with which the communicator intends to mislead—that is, the communication of a message that is intended to cause a person to believe something that is untrue. I shall use the term *lying* to refer to a subset of deception in which the misleading message (1) comes in the form of a verifiable assertion, and (2) is literally false.[1]

The discussion that follows begins with a consideration of the various ways in which deception functions as an element in three very different sorts of criminal offenses: perjury, fraud, and rape by deception. We then look at how the law regulates deception by the police (during interrogations) and by lawyers (to courts and to their adversaries). Finally, we consider the possibility that deception used by the media and in the course of political campaigns might lie beyond the scope of permissible legal regulation.

The main point will be to show how the law's treatment of deception varies depending on the role of the person doing the deceiving (e.g., private individuals versus government officials) and the social context in which the deception occurs (such as a courtroom, the marketplace, a police station, or a sexual encounter). More generally, I hope

---

[1] The approach in this paragraph is borrowed from Green (2006: 76–7). For more on the distinction between lying and misleading, see Saul (2012a), passim.

to show the quite nuanced ways in which the law seeks to deter deceptive speech that is truly harmful without "chilling" deceptive speech that is harmless or even socially beneficial.

37.2 Lying and other forms of deception as an element in criminal offenses

Perhaps the most obvious way in which the law regulates deception is through criminal sanctions. Lying and other forms of deception constitute a key element in a collection of important criminal law offenses, though the precise form in which such deception occurs varies considerably from offense to offense. In this part, we consider three leading deception offenses: perjury, fraud, and rape by deception.

37.2.1 Perjury

The crime of perjury is typically defined as a false statement made under oath as to facts material to a given proceeding.[2] The harms of perjury are significant: Courts and other tribunals are deprived of accurate information material to the decision-making process. As a consequence, an innocent person might be unjustly convicted and imprisoned, while a guilty person might be acquitted and set free to commit other crimes. And even if, notwithstanding the witness's false testimony, the court's decision turns out to be the correct one, the potential for error has been increased and the integrity of the system undermined.

Perjury statutes have consistently been interpreted to require an assertion the truth or falsity of which can be ascertained with certainty. Thus, statements of belief or opinion cannot constitute perjury, except in those special cases in which the witness states that she holds an opinion or belief she does not in fact hold.[3] In such cases, the existence or nonexistence of the belief or opinion is itself a matter of material fact that is theoretically capable of verification.

A more complicated question is whether the government must prove that the witness made a statement that was literally false, or whether a statement that is "merely misleading" (even if literally true) is sufficient to support conviction. The answer varies from jurisdiction to jurisdiction. At common law, a witness could be prosecuted for perjury so long as he believed that his sworn statement was false, even if it later turned out to be

---

[2] 18 U.S.C. §1621. The discussion in this section is largely drawn from Green (2006: 133–47).
[3] e.g., *Sullivan* (1957). English law appears to follow a similar rule. See Smith and Hogan (1988: 746).

true (Smith and Hogan 1988: 746; Welling 1998: 215). This approach is still followed in Canada[4]. The prevailing rule in the US, England, and Australia, however, is now to the contrary.[5] For example, in *Bronston v. United States*, the Supreme Court made clear that the federal perjury statute does not apply to statements that are literally true, even if they are incomplete, misleading, or evasive.[6] As the Court explained, "[i]f a witness evades, it is the lawyer's responsibility to recognize the evasion and to bring the witness back to the mark, to flush out the whole truth with the tools of adversary examination" (*Trotchie* 1994: 358–9). To put it another way, the rule now followed in a majority of common-law jurisdictions requires that before a witness can be convicted of perjury, he must actually "lie" while under oath, rather than "merely mislead."

A leading example of what this rule mean in practice can be seen in the famous perjury case brought against President Bill Clinton. In testimony before a federal grand jury in 1998, Clinton was asked, among other things, whether he had ever been "alone" in the Oval Office with White House intern Monica Lewinsky.[7] He responded:

> [A]s I said, when she worked at the legislative affairs office, they always had somebody there on the weekends. Sometimes they'd bring me things on the weekends. She—it seems to me she brought things to me once or twice on the weekends. In that case, whatever time she would be in there, drop it off, exchange a few words and go, she was there. I don't have any specific recollections of what the issues were, what was going on, but when the Congress is there, we're working all the time, and typically I would do some work on one of the days of the weekends in the afternoon.[8]

According to the Independent Counsel seeking to remove Clinton from office, this response was perjurious because, in fact, Clinton *had* been alone with Lewinsky in the Oval Office on a number of occasions.[9]

In my view, the Independent Counsel was mistaken. While this statement of Clinton's was certainly misleading, it seems unlikely that it was perjurious. Note that Clinton never actually answered the question asked of him. He never said whether he and Lewinsky were alone together in the Oval Office. Instead, he offered a rambling explanation of the circumstances in which a legislative aide might have brought him materials in the Oval Office, an explanation that would appear to be accurate on its face. In other words, Clinton offered an evasive, non-responsive, and factually true reply to

---

[4] e.g., *Trotchie* (1994).
[5] On the rule in England, see Smith and Hogan (1998: 747). On the rule in Australia, see *Model Criminal Code Officers Committee* (1998: 13–15).
[6] *Bronston* (1973).
[7] Referral to United States House of Representatives Pursuant to Title 28 (1998: 126).
[8] Referral to United States House of Representatives Pursuant to Title 28 (1998: 126). For analytical clarity, I have omitted the words with which Clinton begins his response: "I don't recall." Because Clinton was almost certainly lying when he said he could not recall being alone together with Lewinsky in the Oval Office, this statement *should* be regarded as perjurious.
[9] Referral to United States House of Representatives Pursuant to Title 28 (1998): 126.

the question posed; but he did not actually lie. He evaded his interrogator's question by answering a different, relatively innocuous, question about White House procedures. Under clear US law, evasive answers of this sort are not perjurious: As the Court explained in *Bronston*, although a witness's testimony might be misleading, it is the responsibility of the questioning lawyer to probe until the truth can be uncovered; and this, Clinton's interrogator failed to do.

37.2.2 Fraud

Having considered the criminalization of lies made under oath in formal judicial proceedings, we now turn to deception that occurs in a range of commercial and regulatory settings, and which falls under the general umbrella of "fraud." Under American federal law, there are now dozens of specialized statutory provisions that criminalize offenses such as mail fraud, wire fraud, bank fraud, health care fraud, tax fraud, computer fraud, securities fraud, bankruptcy fraud, accounting fraud, and conspiracy to defraud the government (see Green 2006: 148–60). Although each offense provision has its own distinct elements, what they all have in common, roughly speaking, is a prohibition on the intentional use of deception to obtain money or property or impede government operations. The law in Canada and England is similar.[10] In this section, we explore several key ways in which the concept of deceit that helps define fraud differs from that which underlies perjury.

One way in which the deceit element in fraud differs from that in perjury is that fraud can be perpetrated in the absence of a factual assertion. A good example is the English case of *Barnard*, in which the defendant obtained credit from a shopkeeper by wearing an Oxford college cap and gown to create the false impression that he was an Oxford student.[11] Barnard was held guilty of false pretenses, and would have been so even if he had said nothing. By contrast, had Barnard taken the witness stand wearing clothes that created a similar false impression, it is clear that he would not have been committing perjury as such. Nor would he have committed perjury if, as a witness, he had made a false promise or prediction, or expressed a false opinion—even though any of these utterances could satisfy the requirement of deception that appears in fraud.[12]

A second way in which the deceit element in fraud differs from that in perjury is that fraud requires no showing of literal falsity; merely making a material statement that is misleading is enough.[13] For example, in the *Lucia* case, the defendants were charged with fraud after issuing a mutual-fund prospectus containing a ten-year profit comparison

---

[10] See Criminal Code (Canada) §380(1); Fraud Act 2006 (c 35) (UK).
[11] *Barnard* (1837).
[12] See, e.g., *Durland* (1896).
[13] In the commercial fraud context, the materiality requirement means that the deception must be "directed to the quality, adequacy or price of goods to be sold, or otherwise to the nature of the bargain." Deceptive "puffing" is not considered material. *Regent Office Supply* (1970), at 1182.

of junk bonds and United States Treasury notes.[14] Although the junk bonds had outperformed Treasury securities during the preceding ten-year period taken as a whole, the fact was that during the six years immediately preceding each fund's public offerings, their performance was worse. Despite the literal truth of the company's statement, the court concluded that a triable issue was presented as to whether the defendants had committed fraud. As the court put it, "[s]ome statements, although literally accurate, can become, through their context and manner of presentation, devices which mislead investors. For that reason, the disclosure required by the securities laws is measured not by literal truth, but by the ability of the material accurately to inform rather than mislead prospective buyers."[15] In short, a conviction for fraud requires a showing of mere deception, not an actual lie.

Why exactly should culpable deceit be easier to prove in cases of fraud than in cases of perjury? The distinct contexts in which the two crimes are committed suggest a possible answer: As noted above, perjury involves statements made under oath, often in a formal, adversarial setting where the truth of the witness's statement can be tested through probing cross-examination. Fraud, by contrast, typically occurs in a commercial or regulatory setting, where the deceiver and the deceived are engaged in an arm's-length, often one-shot transaction. In such circumstances, there is no opportunity for careful fact-finding or cross-examination. Likely for this reason, the courts have tended to define deception more broadly in the fraud context than in that of perjury.

37.2.3 Rape by deception

So far, we have considered how the criminal law applies to deception that occurs in formal legal proceedings and in the marketplace. Now we consider deception that occurs in connection with sexual matters.[16] For example, imagine a case in which a man obtained a woman's ostensible consent to sex by falsely claiming that he: loved her and would marry her, was a physician performing a medical procedure, was using birth control, was sterile, or did not have a venereal disease. In which, if any, of these cases should the man be prosecuted for rape or for some lesser sexual assault?

The law in this area is very much in flux. At common law, a successful prosecution for rape normally required proof not only that the victim did not consent to intercourse but also that such intercourse was obtained by "force." Indeed, the issues of non-consent and force were essentially merged: The only way to prove lack of consent was by presenting evidence of force. This meant that non-consensual sex obtained by means other than force, such as by deception or coercion, was not treated as rape. Sex induced by deception was treated, if at all, under the law governing the tort (and, later, the lesser crime) of seduction (see Larson 1993).

---

[14] *Lucia* (1994).
[15] *Lucia*, 36 F.3d at 175. See also Langevoort (1999).
[16] The discussion in this section relies on that contained in Green (2015); see also Falk (1998).

There were, however, two important exceptions to the general rule: Courts generally held that it *was* rape if the man obtained consent to sex by deceiving his victim into believing that she was (1) undergoing a medical procedure, rather than intercourse, or (2) having sex with her spouse. In the first instance, the courts reasoned that the victim was unaware that the act to which she was consenting was actually sexual intercourse.[17] In the second kind of case, the courts reasoned that the woman was being tricked not just into having sex but into committing what was then a crime—namely, adultery.[18]

This traditional common-law rule, with its two narrow exceptions, continues to be the law in most Anglo-American jurisdictions, including England and a majority of US states.[19] But the traditional rule has recently come under challenge. Rape is now widely conceptualized as a violation of a victim's right to sexual autonomy, regardless of whether any force is used.[20] And, assuming that a victim's sexual autonomy can be violated by deception just as thoroughly as it can be violated by force or coercion, it would seem to follow that deceit-induced sex should constitute rape in a much broader range of circumstances than it traditionally has.[21]

Perhaps the most prominent, and controversial, example of this broadened approach to rape by deception can be seen in the recent Israeli district court decision in *State of Israel v. Kashur*.[22] The defendant there misrepresented himself to a prospective sexual partner as unmarried, Jewish, and interested in a serious romantic relationship. Relying on these misrepresentations, the partner consented to sex. After his deceit was discovered, the defendant was charged with rape under Israeli Penal Law, which is defined to include "intercourse with a woman ... with the woman's consent, which was obtained by deceit in respect of the identity of the person or the nature of the act."[23] In affirming the conviction, the court stated that the "defendant interfered with [the victim's] ability to object by means of misrepresenting the facts of his personal situation—that he was a single man interested in a serious relationship. Consequently, the defendant exploited the accuser's desire for a deep emotional connection, for only on account of this did she agree to have intercourse with him."[24]

One of the reasons *Kashur* has engendered so much attention is that it constitutes a significant departure from the prevailing rule in Anglo-American jurisdictions. Various scholars and courts have continued to resist the notion that we should criminalize every case in which a defendant's deception of a victim is a but-for cause of the victim's consent, arguing instead for a more selective list of circumstances in which rape by deception (or perhaps a lesser form of sexual assault) is held to occur. These authorities have argued that almost everyone, at some point in their lives, has engaged in, or been the

---

[17] e.g., *Minkowski* (1962).
[18] e.g., *Dee* (1884).
[19] See, e.g., English Sexual Offences Act 2003 s. 76(2) (a).
[20] See, e.g., *M.T.S.* (1992).
[21] For a fuller articulation of this argument, see Estrich (1986); Herring (2005).
[22] *Kashur* (2012).
[23] Penal Law, 5737–1977, special volume LSI 1, §345(a)(2)(1977).
[24] *Kashur* (2012).

target of, some form of deception in the context of sex. As one commentator has put it, "[p]eople routinely wear perfume and deodorants that disguise their body odor; they wear makeup that disguises facial flaws or install hair plugs that disguise baldness; some color, straighten or curl their hair or undergo cosmetic surgery" (Colb 2013). Any of these deceptions could potentially serve as a but-for cause of the victim's consent to sex. But, the argument goes, to treat all such cases as rape would trivialize the offense, and chill private, socially positive or neutral behavior.

37.3 LAW'S TOLERANCE OF DECEPTION

In the discussion up to this point, we have considered three contexts in which deceitful speech or conduct is potentially treated by the law as a crime. In the next three sections, we turn to various contexts in which the law tends to take a more tolerant approach to deception: when police lie during an interrogation, when lawyers lie to the court or their adversaries, and when lies are told by the media or in the course of a political contest.

37.3.1 Deception by the police

As we saw above, when witnesses lie under oath in formal proceedings, they can potentially be subject to prosecution for perjury; and this is true regardless of whether the witness is an ordinary citizen, a police officer, or some other governmental official.[25] But what about police who use deceit when interrogating a suspect during the investigation of a crime? Imagine, for example, that a police officer falsely tells a suspect that his fingerprints have been found at the scene of the crime or that his alleged co-conspirator has just confessed and implicated him. Should the officer who engages in such deception be punished? Should a statement obtained pursuant to such misrepresentations be excluded from court?

The answer varies from jurisdiction to jurisdiction. German law reflects a demanding view of what constitutes a truly voluntary confession, prohibiting the admission not only of confessions obtained through coercion and force but also of those obtained by means of deception (Ross 2008: 447). An interrogator who uses such deceptive practices can be subject to disciplinary sanctions as well as a claim for damages. In part, the robustness of the German norm reflects an overarching reluctance to use the suspect as a source of evidence against himself.

---

[25] It should be noted, however, that the prosecution of police for lying under oath, at least in the American system, is extremely rare in practice, and many observers believe that the court system is all too tolerant of what has been called police "testilying." See generally the *Mollen Commission Report* (1994).

The rule in the USA is quite different. Not only is a police officer unlikely to face any sanctions for lying, but the confession obtained through such stratagems will not normally be excluded from evidence (so long as the suspect has been properly advised of his rights under *Miranda*). Ariel Porat and Omri Yadlin have referred to such lies as "truth-revealing" (Porat and Yadlin 2014). And, perhaps as a result, American law views confessions obtained through deception as much less troublesome than confessions obtained through coercion. As George Thomas has explained, "[t]he suspect who is told that he can be protected from a lynch mob only if he confesses feels far more pressure to confess than the suspect who is falsely told that his fingerprints were found at the scene of the crime (Thomas 2007). The American law of false confessions thus (loosely) parallels that of rape: when sex or a confession (as the case may be) is obtained through deceit, that is considered less problematic than when it is obtained through coercion.

37.3.2 Lawyer and client lies

What about lies told by lawyers and their clients? How does the law treat them? As we shall now see, the answer in common-law systems such as those in the United States and England varies depending on whether the lie is made to a court or to an adversary.

When an American lawyer is appearing before a tribunal, she must not only avoid making false statements but must also affirmatively "correct a false statement of material fact or law previously made to the tribunal by the lawyer."[26] English law is similar.[27] The duties with respect to opposing counsel are somewhat less demanding: Whereas the lawyer has a "duty of candor" to the court, her duty with respect to opposing counsel is merely to be "fair."[28] This means not "unlawfully obstruct[ing] another party's access to evidence or unlawfully alter[ing], destroy[ing] or conceal[ing] a document or other material having potential evidentiary value." In addition, the lawyer must not "falsify evidence, counsel or assist a witness to testify falsely, or offer an inducement to a witness that is prohibited by law."[29]

A particularly interesting problem arises in contexts in which a lawyer knows, or has good reason to believe, that her client wishes to take the stand and commit perjury. The lawyer in such cases is presented with a dilemma: On the one hand, she has a duty of candor to the tribunal. On the other hand, she has a duty of confidentiality to her client, which forbids her from revealing client confidences. Moreover, the client has a constitutional right to testify in her own defense. What should the lawyer do in such circumstances? (In inquisitorial systems such as France, the issue does not arise with the same frequency, since the defendant normally (1) does not testify under oath, (2) enjoys no

---

[26] *American Bar Association* (2013), rule 3.3.
[27] *Bar Standards Board* (2015) C6.2; *Solicitors Regulation Authority* (2011) IB(5.4).
[28] *American Bar Association* (2013), rule 3.4.
[29] Idem. A separate body of rules applies to cases in which lawyers lie to their adversaries in the course of negotiations. See Wetlaufer (1990).

privilege not to testify, and (3) will have already been questioned by an investigating magistrate.)

In the most egregious Anglo-American cases—say, where the lawyer has encouraged his client to testify falsely—the result could be a prosecution for subordination of perjury.[30] More commonly, however, the problem of client perjury is a matter for professional discipline, rather than the criminal law.[31] The prevailing (though not unanimous) American view, expressed in the ABA's Model Rules of Professional Conduct, is that a lawyer's duty of candor to the court should take precedence over his duty of confidentiality to his client. Thus, the Model Rules specifically provide that a "lawyer... who knows that a person intends to engage, is engaging, or has engaged in criminal or fraudulent conduct related to the proceeding shall take reasonable remedial measures."[32] And what do "reasonable remedial measures" consist of? The commentary to the rule states that the "the proper course is to remonstrate with the client confidentially, advise the client of the lawyer's duty of candor to the tribunal and seek the client's cooperation with respect to the withdrawal or correction of the false statement or evidence. If those procedures fail, the advocate must take further remedial action," such as seeking withdrawal from the representation.

37.3.3 Lies in politics and in the media

As we have seen so far in this chapter, there are some contexts in which the law condemns lying and treats it as an element in a crime, other contexts in which lying is prohibited as a matter of professional ethics, and yet more circumstances in which lying is essentially tolerated. In this final section, we consider several cases in which lying is not only permitted and tolerated, but potentially subject to constitutional protection—meaning that, even if a legislature wished to impose criminal sanctions on it, it would be barred from doing so.

Consider a 2005 US federal law that made it a crime for any person falsely to claim that he or she had received certain military honors.[33] Proponents in Congress argued that the law was needed to prevent impostors from "stealing the valor" of soldiers returning from engagements in Iraq and Afghanistan. Xavier Alvarez was prosecuted for misrepresenting himself as a Medal of Honor winner. In his defense, he argued that, even if he had done what was alleged, the law should be viewed as violative of his First Amendment right of free speech. A plurality of the US Supreme Court agreed; the mere fact that a statement is false, it said, does not mean that it is ineligible for First

---

[30] 18 U.S.C. §1622.
[31] The leading case is *Nix* (1986) (holding that client was not deprived of the right to counsel where his lawyer threatened to withdraw from representation if client insisted on taking the stand and perjuring himself).
[32] *American Bar Association* (2013) rule 3.3(b).
[33] Stolen Valor Act, 18 U.S.C. §§704(b) (c).

Amendment protection.³⁴ In doing so, the Court distinguished between false statements that are perjurious, fraudulent, or defamatory (and which *can* properly be prohibited) and the kinds of essentially harmless statements made here.

A second kind of false statement that may be constitutionally protected is one made in the course of a political campaign. A good example comes from Massachusetts, which enacted a law that made it a crime to publish any false statement about political candidates or political ballot initiatives "which is designed or tends to aid or injure or defeat such candidate ... [or] which is designed to affect the vote on such question."[35] Melissa Lucas was charged with violating the statute after her political action committee published brochures criticizing a candidate for public office.[36] In striking down the law, the Massachusetts Supreme Court reasoned that it was likely to "[chill] the very exchange of ideas that gives meaning to our electoral system" and as such violated Lucas' right to free speech.[37]

A final example comes from Canada. The Canadian Broadcasting Act of 1986 includes a provision stating that a "licensee shall not broadcast ... false or misleading news."[38] The provision has never been challenged in court, presumably because it has never actually been invoked against a broadcaster.[39] If this provision was challenged, however, it seems unlikely that it could survive scrutiny under Section 2(b) of the Canadian Charter of Rights and Freedoms. Under an earlier case, *R v. Zundel*, Holocaust denier Ernst Zundel was charged with "spreading false news" by publishing a pamphlet entitled "Did Six Million Really Die?" in violation of then-Section 181 of the Criminal Code, which made it a crime for one to "publish a statement, tale or news that he knows is false and causes or is likely to cause injury or mischief to a public interest."[40] The Canadian Supreme Court held that, while Zundel did violate the elements of Section 181, the provision could not survive scrutiny under Section 2(b). According to the Court, Section 2(b) protects all expression of a nonviolent form, even when it is demonstrably false. Under similar reasoning, I believe that the Broadcasting Act provision would also be struck down as a violation of free speech.[41]

---

[34] *United States v. Alvarez*, 132 S. Ct. 2537 (2012). For a more extensive discussion of *Alvarez*, see Norton (2013), passim; Shiffrin (2014): 120 et seq.

[35] Massachusetts G.L. c. 56, §42.

[36] *Commonwealth v. Lucas* (2015), 34 N.E.3d 1242 (Mass).

[37] Ibid. at 1257. Provisions similar to the Massachusetts law can be found in Ohio Rev. Code Ann. §3517.21(B) (criminalizing false statements made "during the course of any campaign for nomination or election to public office or office of a political party") and Minn. Stat. §211.B06, subd. 1 (making it a crime to "knowingly or with reckless disregard for the truth make a false statement about a proposed ballot initiative"). The Ohio law was challenged in *Susan B. Anthony List* (2014) and the Minnesota law in *Arneson* (2014), but neither case definitively resolves the constitutional issue raised. It seems likely that these questions will continue to be litigated in the lower courts and will eventually have to be resolved by the US Supreme Court.

[38] Canadian Broadcasting Act of 1986, Section 1.1, Subsection 3.

[39] 'False news proposal killed by CRTC' (2011).

[40] *Zundel* [1992] 2 S.C.R. 731.

[41] In 2011, apparently under pressure from a parliamentary committee, the Canadian Radio-television and Telecommunications Commission (CRTC) proposed an amendment that would have

37.4 Conclusion

Our legal system often speaks of its search for "the truth and nothing but the truth," but the reality is much more complex than this slogan would suggest. At almost every turn, the avoidance of deception must be weighed against other, potentially competing values—including the values of a free press, vigorous political debate, the energetic promotion of goods and services, the aggressive investigation of crime, a robust adjudicative process, and autonomy in sexual matters. Exactly how the balance will be achieved will differ significantly depending on the role of the actor doing the deceiving, the social context in which it occurs, and the background norms of the legal system in which it occurs.

References

'False news proposal killed by CRTC', CBC News (Feb. 25, 2011), [http://www.cbc.ca/news/politics/false-news-proposal-killed-by-crtc-1.1117504]
281 Care Committee v. Arneson (2014). 766 F.3d 774 (8th Cir.)
United States v. Alvarez (2012). 132 S. Ct. 2537
Commonwealth v. Lucas (2005), 34 N.E.3d 1242 (Mass.)
R. v. Barnard (1837). 173 Eng. Rep. 342
Bronston v. United States (1973). 409 U.S. 352
Durland v. United States (1896). 161 U.S. 306
State of Israel v. Kashur (2012). CrimA 5734/10 (English translation obtained from VolokhConspiracy blog, [http://volokh.com/2010/10/07/israeli-rape-by-fraud-cases/] (accessed 28 May 2018)
Lucia v. Prospect Street High Income Portfolio, Inc (1994). 36 F.3d 170 (1st Cir.)
In the Interest of M.T.S. (1992). 609 A.2d 1266, 1278 (N.J.)
People v. Minkowski (1962). 23 Cal. Rptr. 92, 105 (Cal. Ct. App.)
Nix v. Whiteside (1986). 475 U.S. 157
United States v. Regent Office Supply (1970). 421 F.2d 1174 (2d Cir.)
State v Sullivan (1957). 130 A.2d 610 (N.J.), cert denied, 355 U.S. 840
Susan B. Anthony List v. Ohio Elections Commission (2014). 2014 WL 4472634 (S.D.Ohio)
R. v. Trotchie (1994). 3 W.W.R. 201 (Saskatchewan Ct. App)
R. v. Zundel (1992). 2 S.C.R. 731
American Bar Association (2013). Model Rules of Professional Conduct
Bar Standards Board Handbook (9th ed. 2015). Code of Conduct (U.K.)
Solicitors Regulation Authority (2011). Code of Conduct (U.K.)

---

significantly narrowed the rule, to prohibit only "news that the licensee knows to be false or misleading and that endangers or is likely to endanger the lives, health or safety of the public." However, the CRTC subsequently withdrew the proposed amendment for reasons that are not entirely clear, and the law remains in its original expansive form. Whether this narrower version of the Act could survive scrutiny under the Charter seems to present a harder question.

Model Criminal Code Officers Committee (1998). Report on Administration of Justice Offences (Australia)

Commission Report (Milton Mollen, Chair): Commission to Investigate Allegations of Police Corruption and the Anti-Corruption Procedures of the Police Department, City of New York (1994)Referral to the United States House of Representatives Pursuant to Title 28, United States Code, §595(c) Submitted by the Office of the Independent Counsel, H.R. Doc. No. 105-310 (1998)

Massachusetts, G.L. c. 56, §42 (1964 [1946])

Minnesota Stat. §211.B06, subd. 1 (2008)

Ohio Rev. Code Ann. §3517.21(B)

Penal Law, 5737-1977, Special volume LSI 1, §345(a)(2) (1977) (Israel)

Perjury, 18 U.S.C. §1621

Sexual Offences Act (England and Wales) 2003 s.76(2)(a)

Stolen Valor Act, 18 U.S.C. §§704(b)(c)

CHAPTER 38

LYING IN ECONOMICS

MARTA SERRA-GARCIA

38.1 INTRODUCTION

LYING has become an increasingly important topic in economics in recent years. Until recently, the standard assumption in economics was that individuals would lie whenever there was a material incentive to do so (e.g., Holmstrom 1979; Crawford and Sobel 1982). For example, if the expected monetary gains from lying were to exceed the expected losses, *homo oeconomicus* would lie in his tax report and insurance claims.

Yet, many individuals file their insurance claims truthfully, despite incentives to report larger or nonexistent losses, which are difficult for insurance companies to verify. Every year many people also report their taxes truthfully, despite the low probability of inspection.[1]

Recent work in behavioral economics and psychology has shown that, in fact, many will not lie, even if there is a monetary incentive to do so. In other words, even in anonymous situations where lying can only be witnessed by the liar himself, a large share of individuals choose to be honest. At the same time, there is wide heterogeneity in the population in lying behavior. Some individuals will always lie, even if incentives are small. Others will not lie, even if the lie benefits its receiver.

Recent research has revealed rich patterns of individual morality. To understand how such patterns come about, a large body of work is currently studying the factors that govern moral norms in the context of lying. Such knowledge could lead to important changes in how we view human behavior in many economic transactions, including tax evasion, behavior in insurance markets and, more generally, markets in which private information is pervasive.

There are many studies in economics and psychology that examine dishonesty. In this chapter I will focus on some of the main findings on lying in behavioral economics to

---

[1] The overall audit rate for individuals is 1.03%, according to the IRS 2012 Data Book. For a recent press article on declining audit rates of the IRS, see http://blogs.wsj.com/totalreturn/2015/02/25/fewer-taxpayers-are-audited-amid-irs-budget-cuts/.

date. I start by reviewing the standard approach to information transmission in economics in section 38.2. The literature has generally studied two different scenarios: communication of private information and communication of intentions. The focus of this chapter will mainly be on the first type of communication, though the second will also be mentioned. Section 38.3 reviews studies that measure individuals' aversion to lying. Section 38.4 provides an overview of studies examining factors that influence lying.[2] Section 38.5 concludes.

38.2 THE STANDARD APPROACH

The classic theoretical framework for studying strategic information transmission in economics is the model by Crawford and Sobel (1982).[3] This model studies the interaction between a sender and a receiver. The sender is provided with private information, relevant to the transaction, which he can transmit to the receiver, who is uninformed and takes an action that affects the sender.

The model captures the essence of many important economic interactions in which one party is better informed than the other, such as buyer–seller interactions, bargaining among business partners, doctor–patient or lawyer–client interactions. Consider the purchase of a used car. The seller knows whether the car was involved in an accident or not and, if so, whether he repaired it at a friend's garage without reporting it to the insurance company and the police or not. This information is relevant to the buyer, since it determines the true value of the car. But, if the accident was not reported, the buyer cannot verify the car's true condition, unless the seller reveals this information. The question of interest is whether when prompted about the car's condition, the seller will report it truthfully or lie.

The model by Crawford and Sobel (1982) addresses this question as well as the more general one, namely how much information is transmitted when the sender and the receiver have conflicting interests regarding the action that the receiver should take. They show that, as the difference between the preferences of the sender and the receiver increases, less information will be transmitted. The receiver (buyer in the above example) is aware of the sender's (seller in the above example) material interests and interprets his message accordingly. At the same time, the sender anticipates the interpretation of the receiver and optimally adjusts his messages. If the conflict between the sender's and the receiver's interests is strong enough, communication will not be informative. In other words, if the seller can only sell the car and make profit at the expense of the buyer, he will lie. The buyer will therefore dismiss the seller's statements. Even though the transmission of information could be beneficial to each of the parties, the conflict

---

[2] A series of recent articles on deception can be found in Gneezy (2013).
[3] For early overviews of the literature on cheap talk, see Farrell and Rabin (1996) and Crawford (1998).

of interest is so large that no information will be transmitted. This provides a very pessimistic state of affairs. The important question is, will the predictions of the model be supported empirically?

Before examining existing evidence, let us mention that there are two potential interpretations of the messages sent by senders in the model of Crawford and Sobel (1982), depending on whether one only considers the messages within the particular interaction (voiding them of their literal meaning), or whether one considers the literal meaning of messages, as used outside of the given interaction. In the first interpretation messages do not have a meaning outside of the game. Hence, if the seller says, "the car had no accident," but it is commonly known and understood that this message means that the car *had* an accident, then the message would not be interpreted as a lie. Such interpretation raises questions about the emergence and evolution of language that have been studied in Blume et al. (1998).

The second, perhaps more natural, interpretation is that messages have a meaning outside the game, since as humans we already possess a language we communicate in.[4] In this case, if the seller says "the car had no accident," but it did, the message would be interpreted as a lie. The central assumption in economics, and in the work of Crawford and Sobel (1982) is that in one-shot interactions lying is costless, i.e., individuals do not experience any disutility (e.g., incur moral costs) when lying. This assumption greatly simplifies the analysis of such interactions, since the objective of each of the parties involved is only to maximize their own monetary gain, without considering whether this is achieved via lies or true messages. Yet, recent experimental evidence, to which we now turn, suggests that in many contexts such an assumption is wrong. Some individuals are willing to give up a personal (monetary) gain to be honest.

38.3 THE AVERSION TO LYING

A first step in understanding lying behavior is to understand the moral norms that guide an individual's decision to lie. There are two extremes on the spectrum of moral norms. The norm may be utilitarian, i.e., to always lie when there is a (monetary) benefit from doing so. This has been the standard assumption in economics, assuming that individuals do not experience disutility from lying or, in other words, do not incur costs from lying. Alternatively, the norm may be Kantian, i.e., to never lie under any circumstances. From the perspective of an individual's utility, this would imply that, should she lie, her disutility (or cost from doing so) would be infinite. In between, there may be norms such that lying is approved of when the consequences of the lie are benevolent, for example. An important empirical question is: What is the moral norm that most individuals follow. The studies reviewed below

---

[4] The importance of natural language was first highlighted by Farrell (1993).

have pursued this question, and an even simpler one—whether individuals experience a disutility from lying.

One of the first studies on lying in economics was conducted by Gneezy (2005). In a simplified sender–receiver game, there were two payoff distributions (labeled "options"). Option A yielded a higher monetary payoff than option B to the sender, while option B yielded a higher payoff than A to the receiver. The sender was asked to send a message to the receiver indicating which option yielded a higher payoff to the receiver, and the receiver chose an option after receiving the message. The receiver was uninformed about the incentives of the sender and any characteristics of the option. Senders, in this case students in an experiment, displayed an aversion to lying. A large portion chose to send a truthful message, "Option B will earn you more money than A," despite monetary incentives to do the opposite.

Gneezy (2005) investigated whether moral norms about lying were conditional on the consequences of the lie. In other words, whether individuals were willing to lie if the harm of the lie to the receiver was minor, but unwilling to do so when the harm inflicted on others by lying was large. To this end, he varied the monetary amount that the receiver and sender received when the sender lied (and was followed by the receiver) and when he was truthful. He found that fifty-two percent of the senders lied when the lie increased their payoff by $10, and harmed the receiver by $10. This share dropped to seventeen percent when the lie harmed the receiver by $10 but only increased the sender's payoff by $1.

Since then different experimental designs have been developed to measure the aversion to lying, as summarized in Table 38.1. First, the table defines whether the interaction in which lying occurs is part of a sender–receiver game or whether it corresponds to an individual decision, where the individual decides whether to lie or not, without affecting any other subject. In these cases, the only recipient of the message is the experimenter. The second column displays the information that was known (only) to the sender. The third column shows what the message was about. Then the receiver's identity is described, followed by the incentives of the parties involved and the main result, compared to the benchmark of no aversion to lying.

Contrary to standard economic assumptions, most individuals in Gneezy (2005) were willing to give up $1, and many individuals were willing to give up $10, when their lies harmed other individuals by $10. As displayed in Table 38.1, the frequency of lying was between seventeen percent and fifty-two percent, despite there being monetary incentives to lie 100% of the time. Additionally, their tendency to lie depended on the harm to others. If the harm to the receiver dropped from $10 to $1, significantly more lying was observed. This suggests that moral norms about lying may be conditional on the consequences of the lie.

Several papers have used a similar framework, with the aim of testing whether human behavior is in line with the predictions of the Crawford and Sobel (1982) model (Dickhaut et al. 1995; Blume et al. 1998, 2001; Cai and Wang 2006). In contrast to Gneezy (2005), in these studies receivers were aware of the opposed interest of the sender, leading them to be more suspicious about the sender's message. These papers

Table 38.1 Overview of experimental designs to measure lying aversion

Paper	Type of interaction	Information	Sender's message	Receiver	Incentives	Results (frequency of lying)
Gneezy (2005)	Sender–receiver game	Payoffs from choosing {A,B}	"Option X will earn you more money than Y"	Subject chooses {A,B}; not aware of sender's interests	Sender and receiver have completely opposed interests	17%–52% (benchmark = 100%)
Sánchez-Pagés and Vorsatz (2007)	Sender–receiver game	State of nature {A,B}	"The state of nature is X"	Subject chooses {A,B}; aware of sender's interest	Sender and receiver have completely opposed interests	45% (benchmark = 50%)
Mazar, Ariel and Amir (2008)	Individual decision	Performance in a task	"I have X correct answers"	Experimenter	Sender obtains a higher payoff when more correct answers are reported	7% (Experiment 1, benchmark = 100%)
Fischbacher and Heusi (2008)	Individual decision	Outcome of a die roll	"The outcome of the die roll is X"	Experimenter	Sender obtains a higher payoff when he reports a higher outcome, except 6	35% report 5 (benchmark = 100%, chance = 16.7%)
Gneezy, Rockenbach, and Serra-Garcia (2013)	Individual decision	State of nature (1 to 6)	"The state of nature is X"	Subject decides whether to follow message or not	Sender obtains a higher payoff when he reports a higher number	40%–65% (benchmark = 100%)

Note: This table provides a summary of several papers measuring the aversion to lying. The first column describes the type of interaction (whether the study used a sender–receiver game or an individual decision situation). The second column describes the information available to the sender, while the third column displays the message available to the sender. The fourth column describes the recipient of the lie, and the fifth column details the incentives of the sender. The sixth column provides a brief description of the results, comparing the frequency of lying to the benchmark of predicted lying if individuals do not exhibit costs from lying.

find that, even if there is a conflict of interests between the sender and the receiver, individuals are sometimes truthful, more so than the Crawford and Sobel (1982) model would predict. Sánchez-Pagés and Vorsatz (2007) also showed that, when receivers were given the opportunity to punish the sender—destroying the sender's payoff at a small cost to themselves—, punishing was most frequently observed after a receiver had been lied to. Interestingly, those receivers who were honest as senders were more likely to punish than individuals who were dishonest as senders. This suggests that individuals with higher moral costs of lying may also have a preference for preserving such a norm in society.[5]

A careful analysis of these first experiments, especially Gneezy (2005), raised a number of questions about the reasons why individuals chose not to lie. The first question is how important the expected reaction of the receiver is. Perhaps senders chose to be honest in Gneezy's experiment because they expected the receiver to choose the opposite of whatever they recommended. For example, if the sender recommended option B, the receiver could choose A. The importance of the expected action by the receiver was shown in Sutter (2009). While such strategic concerns were observed, for many senders this concern did not apply.

Another issue raised by the initial evidence was that the experimenter, who had invited and was going to pay the subjects for the study, observed the lie. If individuals wanted to look good in the eyes of the scientist, they may have been more honest than they would otherwise be. This would imply that moral norms about lying may not have been cleanly captured in the initial studies. To address this issue some researchers studied settings in which the individual decided on his own, without a receiver and without observation by the experimenter, whether to lie or not. For example, Mazar et al. (2008) asked students to complete several math exercises. After they finished, they were provided with the answer key. Students were then asked to grade their exercises and report the number of correct answers to the experimenter. Importantly, students were asked to destroy their answer sheets using a shredding machine available in the room before providing their report, so that the experimenter never found out whether they cheated. The higher the number of reported correct replies, the more the students got paid for the task. Mazar et al. (2008) found that only 0.6% of the students reported the maximum amount of correct answers. On average, comparing a condition in which cheating was not possible to one in which cheating was possible, students only lied about 7% of the possible amount.

Fischbacher and Heusi (2008) developed an even simpler task to measure the aversion to lying. They asked students to roll a six-sided die and report the outcome of the roll. They were paid the outcome of the die roll in dollars if the reported outcome was between 1 and 5, and received nothing if the reported outcome of the die roll was 6. Students rolled their die in private and no one other than the student could see the roll

---

[5] See also Gibson et al. (2013) who study heterogeneity in lying within an individual and across individuals.

of the die. Their results revealed that there is an overwhelming amount of honesty. The highest payoff, 5, was reported only 35% of the time. While this rate is higher than chance (16.7%), indicating that some individuals lied, it is much lower than 100%, the rate expected if there was no aversion to lying.

These two settings were so anonymous that the scientist cannot tell whether a particular individual was honest or not; there was always the possibility that he may have actually rolled a 5! In this simple task individual lying behavior—by design—cannot be observed. All tests compare the reporting behavior of a group of individuals to the distribution that would result from fully honest reporting, the null hypothesis. Nevertheless, there may still be a concern among individuals to appear honest. Reporting a 5 may look suspicious in the eyes of the experimenter, even if a 5 may have actually been the true outcome. In fact, many individuals in the die-roll experiment reported a 4, consistent with such a concern.

To examine lying behavior at the individual level, Gneezy et al. (2013) developed a paradigm that allows observation of each single individual as to their lying or not. In their setting senders received information about the "state," which is a number between 1 and 6. Each sender was asked to send a message to the receiver about the state, who then chose whether or not to follow that message. Importantly, the sender's payoff did not depend on whether the receiver followed the message; it only depended on the message he sent—his payoff increased with the state reported. The results revealed that a small fraction of individuals always lied and, similarly, a small fraction was always honest. A majority of individuals lied when the benefit to them was large and did not lie when the benefit was small. This suggests that individuals exhibit a cost of lying, but that this cost is moderate. This further supports the view that individuals follow a moral norm that is conditional on the consequences of the lie.

38.4 WHEN DO INDIVIDUALS LIE?

The evidence reviewed above suggests that individuals are not fully utilitarian about lying, as they will choose to be honest, despite monetary incentives to lie. However, many individuals will lie when the monetary gain is sufficiently large, suggesting that they weigh the moral costs of lying against its material benefits. An important question that arises is whether there are factors or interventions that can change lying behavior. In this section, we investigate four main factors: the consequences of lies, lies and promises, social interaction and simple interventions that can affect lying behavior.[6]

---

[6] See Cappelen et al. (2013) for an investigation of other factors that affect lying, such as individual characteristics and priming intuition or a market context. See also Dreber and Johannesson (2008) for gender differences in lying behavior.

38.4.1 The consequences of lies

In the studies reviewed above, lying was advantageous to the liar, often at the expense of the receiver of the lie. The strongest test for the existence of costs of lying is to examine whether individuals lie when the lie is advantageous to the receiver, as well as to the sender. Erat and Gneezy (2012) studied such lies, commonly known as white or paternalistic lies. Their results revealed that 35% of participants told the truth, instead of sending a lie that would benefit both the receiver and the sender. This shows that some individuals suffer a direct disutility from lying that is separate from the material consequences of the lie (see also Chapter 22 by Simone Dietz and Chapter 29 by Maria Terkourafi, in this volume).

38.4.2 Promises

Lying in everyday life may be about information we know, and others do not (private information), or about actions we are planning to take and others cannot observe (private actions). In parallel to the literature on lying aversion focused on private information, a large and growing literature has examined lying about actions. In a well-known study, Charness and Dufwenberg (2006) showed that individuals who promise to behave in a trustworthy manner are likely to keep their promises. In their study a principal could trust an agent to act in his benefit. The agent, however, had a monetary incentive to betray the principal. They found that, when agents were given the option of sending messages to principals, they often made promises. Promises increased trust by principals and agents often kept them. This finding is line with a large literature on pre-play communication in social dilemmas (see, e.g., Balliet 2010 for a meta-analysis), which has found that when individuals promised to cooperate with others in environments where cooperation is socially beneficial but individually costly, a substantial proportion kept their promises, which led to more efficient outcomes.

Breaking a promise can thus have moral costs, similar to lying in the studies previously reviewed. Yet, is there a difference between breaking a promise and lying about the information one holds? Serra-Garcia et al. (2013) conjectured that breaking a promise has a higher moral cost than lying about private information. One reason is that promises are directly tied to the sender's own actions, while lying about private information involves misreporting extraneous information that the sender holds. In their study, a leader and a follower could decide whether or not to contribute to a joint project. The leader knew the return of the joint project and also moved before the follower. The leader could send a message to the follower regarding the project's returns for both the follower and himself, e.g., "the project's return is high," or about his contribution, "I choose to contribute" to the project. The follower, who was uninformed, could not observe the actual return or the leader's decision before deciding whether to contribute or not. The question was whether the content of the leader's message, i.e., whether the message was about the return of the project or about his decision to contribute, matters. Both kinds of messages could achieve the same transmission of information. However, Serra-Garcia et al. (2013) found that individuals were more likely to lie about the return than about their contributions. These results suggest that sending a promise with the intention to break it has higher moral costs than lying about private information.

38.4.3 Social interaction

Moral norms about lying are often shaped by the society in which the individual lives. Observing the frequent dishonesty of others may change an individual's perspective on the moral norm to observe about lying. In markets, for example, sellers may observe how dishonest other sellers are. This may lead to contagion effects that generate widespread dishonest behavior.[7] Innes and Mitra (2013) study whether the contagion of lying behavior differs by society, by comparing undergraduate students' behavior in India and the US. In India students responded to a high level of dishonesty amongst others by behaving more dishonestly, and to a low level of dishonesty by behaving more honestly. Thus, not only "negative" norms (extensive dishonesty) generated imitation, but also "positive" norms did. Among US students, social information only spread dishonesty. When individuals were informed that a large majority of others are dishonest, they were more likely to behave dishonestly. Low levels of dishonesty did not lead to more honesty.

38.4.4 Ways to decrease dishonesty

A final question one may ask is whether there are the simple and costless ways—"nudges"—to increase honesty. Interventions that increase the moral saliency of honesty could ultimately increase individual honesty. One such intervention has been discussed above: promise-making. When individuals make promises, they are less likely to break them.

A well-known intervention to increase moral behavior involves the timing of honesty statements when filling taxes or insurance claims. In Shu et al. (2012) individuals were in one scenario asked to certify that the information they had provided was truthful *after* having completed all the information. In another scenario individuals were first asked to certify that the information they would provide in what followed was truthful. Does the timing of such a promise matter? The answer is yes. Shu et al.

---

[7] Social-interaction effects have been studied in a wide range of domains in economics, from labor (Mas and Moretti 2009), to education (Sacerdote 2001) and financial decision-making (Bursztyn et al. 2014). They have also been widely studied in psychology (see Cialdini and Goldstein 2004 for an overview).

(2012) showed that signing a form certifying the truthfulness of the statements in the beginning pushed the honesty of reports to 63%, compared to 21% when signing occurred at the end.[8]

Another costless manipulation involves the use of language. Individuals were asked to complete a simple task that involved reporting a number they had thought about. They were told "please don't cheat" in one condition and "please don't be a cheater" in another condition. The latter condition directly touches upon the individual's identity. By referring to the person as a cheater, an individual who wishes to cheat faces the cost of losing her identity as a good honorable person. Does this simple linguistic manipulation affect lying behavior? Bryan et al. (2013) showed that this simple wording change, evoking an individual's identity rather than simply referring to her behavior, decreased the extent of dishonesty significantly.

The results from these manipulations suggest that there are high moral costs to lying. More importantly, they suggest costless and simple ways in which dishonesty can be decreased, by making the moral costs of lying more salient to individuals. Such ideas have recently been tested within policy circles. In a recent experiment, the Social and Behavioral Sciences Team, a group of experts in behavioral science who work for the US Government, tested the timing manipulation among vendors of goods and services to the US Government and other administrations (SBST Report, 2015). Placing a signature box to confirm the accuracy of self-reported sales at the beginning led to an additional $1.59 million in fees collected within a single quarter.

38.5 Discussion and conclusion

The robust evidence of an aversion to lying, among some individuals and under some circumstances, has changed the perspective of economists regarding behavior in strategic information transmission settings and will likely bring about further new insights in the near future. A first impact of the research on lying aversion has been its influence on theoretical work. Several recent papers no longer assume that individuals have no disutility from lying, but rather incorporate this disutility into their models (e.g., Kartik et al. 2007; Kartik 2009).

Yet, there is an open discussion about the shape of lying costs. Existing work has assumed that the cost of lying depends on the size of the lie, i.e., the distance between the truth and the reported outcome. However, this may only hold if the distance between the truth and the reported outcome is directly related to the difference in material consequences for the parties involved. Further, lying costs potentially vary depending on multiple factors such as language and timing. More empirical and theoretical work is

---

[8] A related manipulation to increase honesty could involve limiting the time individuals have to report an event. Shalvi et al. (2014) show that under time pressure individuals are more likely to be honest.

needed to provide a systematic framework that guides our understanding of the moral costs of lying.

Inspiring new papers suggest that biology and dishonesty may be tightly linked. Wang et al. (2010), for example, show that pupil dilation increases among those individuals who lied. This suggests that such a biological marker could be used to detect dishonesty. Further, Belot and van de Ven (2017) show that when individuals interact face to face they are able to detect other's dishonesty.

Research in biology also suggests further interesting questions to be addressed. For example, Trivers (2010) argues that the best liars are those who deceive themselves into believing their own lies. The reason is that, if they themselves believe the lie, it will be harder for receivers to detect a lie, since the nervousness or facial expressions associated with lying will not be visible. In a recent experiment, Gneezy et al. (2015) find evidence consistent with self-deception. In their experiment, individuals are significantly more likely to behave unethically when there is scope for self-deception. Further work studying the origins of lying norms, including its evolutionary roots, could prove important to our understanding of morality in modern societies.

CHAPTER 39

LYING AND EDUCATION

ANITA E. KELLY

39.1 INTRODUCTION

EDUCATION, once valued as a pursuit of truth for its own sake, has come to be viewed as a means of obtaining status, influence, and/or employment. An increase in student lying and academic dishonesty has accompanied this historical shift toward viewing education in expedient terms. This chapter begins by describing this historical shift, efforts in higher education to contain the academic dishonesty, and developmental changes in children that allow them to become effective liars. The chapter then reviews education theories, practices, and definitions of lying. The chapter concludes with a brief proposal for a new didactic solution to lying.

39.2 EDUCATION FROM THE PURSUIT OF TRUTH TO THE PURSUIT OF STATUS

In ancient Greece, Plato (427–346 BCE) promoted the pursuit of truth through dialogue and critical analysis, viewing this pursuit as inherently good (see Kimball 1986, 1997). Learning was its own reward. For Plato's students, there was no need to justify their pursuit of knowledge or education with tangible outcomes.

In modern times, by comparison, forty-six percent of parents and thirty-five percent of college-bound high school students in a survey of Americans rated "learning for learning's sake" as the least important reason to attend college (Hersh 1997). Only six percent of each group rated that reason as most important. Even students seeking a liberal college education focus more on performing well on written examinations and term papers than on learning itself (see Jordan 2003). Jordan (2003) suggested that they are responding to pressure from parents and society to obtain the grades necessary to land a good job. Indeed, in the survey just mentioned, seventy-five percent of the parents and eighty-five percent of the students chose "prepares students to get a better job and/or increases their earning potential" (Hersh 1997: 20) as the most important reason to attend college.

Formal written examinations in college were originally instituted in England. Cambridge University began requiring formal examinations in the mid-1700s, with Oxford University following suit in 1800 (Judges 1969). This requirement was a response to a growing sentiment in society that higher education provided a way to achieve status and influence (Schwartz, Tatum, and Wells 2012). Ironically, given that the focus on exams today can detract from learning, the exams were designed to limit access to higher education to only those students interested in learning for its own sake. Students who were not sincerely committed to learning would at least have to demonstrate their knowledge by passing the challenging exams.

39.3 Historical efforts to contain academic dishonesty

Along with the examinations came the need for students to demonstrate academic integrity when completing them. The first honor system was instituted in 1736 at the College of William and Mary in Virginia. Its honor code stated that "special care must be taken of their morals, that none of the Scholars presume to tell a Lie" (College of William and Mary 1736). The honor codes that were developed during this seminal period included rules about classroom decorum and proper attire. In 1842, the University of Virginia instituted the first student-run honor system in the United States (Rudolph and Thelin 1990). Woodrow Wilson (1905), who was a professor before becoming president, lauded the honor system for the self-direction that students had over the completion of their examinations.

However, by the 1940s, the number of college students had grown, leading to an industry where writers would complete term papers for them (Gallant 2008). Naturally, this industry posed a threat to the honor system. Fearing a breakdown of academic integrity at their own colleges, administrators and faculty created honesty committees to enforce the honor codes (Schwartz et al. 2012). But these faculty-run committees defeated the very purpose of the honor system, that students could direct themselves. These committees widened the gap between students and professors, further compromising academic integrity. By the 1950s, honor codes had practically vanished from higher-education institutions (Schwartz et al. 2012).

It was not until the late 1990s that the Internet and accompanying term-paper sales prompted a return of honor codes in some form (Gallant 2008). These honor codes represented a way for colleges to contain the rise in academic dishonesty. Indeed, a meta-analysis at that time showed that just over seventy percent of the students surveyed did admit to having cheated in college (Whitley 1998).

Jordan (2003) proposed that the rise in academic dishonesty in college is rooted in a decreased connection to the rhetorical tradition of the pursuit of truth for its own sake, combined with the pressure to perform well on examinations. Implied in Jordan's analysis is that, in the absence of a reason to consider education inherently good, college students would be expected to engage in academic dishonesty. They would do so to ensure the good grades demanded of them. Jordan (2003) proposed a solution where professors would connect two specific questions to their course goals. The professors would regularly discuss these questions in lectures or small groups. The two questions are: "What in these courses is of intrinsic value to my intellectual well-being as a student?" and "How might my participation in these courses enable me to contribute to liberal society?" (Jordan 2003: 218).

39.4 Developmental changes in the capacity to lie effectively (ages 2–8)

According to DePaulo et al. (2004), studies of "both college students and adults from the community have shown that lies are a fact of everyday life" (DePaulo et al. 2004: 147). Studies of lying in children suggest that lying starts during the preschool years and increases as they mature (e.g., Lewis, Stanger, and Sullivan 1989; Peskin 1992; Polak and Harris 1999; Talwar and Lee 2002a, b; Talwar, Murphy, and Lee 2007; Evans and Lee 2013). In one study, for example, two- and three-year-old children had been asked not to peek at a toy (Evans and Lee 2013). Among the ones who peeked, most of the three-year-olds and one fourth of the two-year-olds lied (Evans and Lee 2013). Likewise, studies of children between the ages of three and twelve showed that the older, as compared to the younger, children told more lies (Talwar and Lee 2002b, 2008; Talwar et al. 2007).

Talwar and Lee (2008) studied three- to eight-year-olds to see whether the children's lie-telling abilities were related to the development of their *theory-of-mind* and *executive-functioning* skills. Theory of mind refers to the ability to see others as having thoughts, feelings, and motivations that are separate from one's own. 'Executive-functioning' skills refer to the abilities to self-regulate and marshal resources to achieve a goal.

Based on their findings, Talwar and Lee (2008) proposed that lying abilities in children develop in three levels from the ages of three to eight years. They suggested that, at the first level, children between the ages two and three years tell *primary lies*. For these lies, the children must simply be able to make untrue statements on purpose.

Talwar and Lee (2008) suggested that, at the second level, children between the ages of three and four years tell *secondary lies*. The researchers noted that these lies are related to the development of *first-order belief understanding*, or taking the perspective of the other person. As Talwar and Lee (2002a) had suggested earlier, this capacity to understand the perspective of others is what allows children to regulate their own nonverbal cues in order to appear honest.

At the third level, children at around the age of seven or eight years are able to tell what Talwar and Lee (2008) called *tertiary lies*. When telling these lies, these older children avoid making verbal statements that are inconsistent with their original lie, which is a mistake that is characteristic of secondary les. At the level of telling tertiary lies, the children can understand the complex interactions between their own and the other person's mental states. They are able to choose, through reasoning, the kinds of nonverbal and verbal behaviors that will sustain a lie (Talwar and Lee 2008).

39.5 MORAL EDUCATION ON LYING

The review offered in this chapter thus far implies that children can be expected to (a) lie to cover transgressions as kindergarteners and (b) develop the mental capacity to sustain their lies by the third grade. As adults, they can be expected to (a) seek a college education in order to land a good job and (b) engage in academic dishonesty once they attend college. Given these implied outcomes, what concepts and practices related to lying should their teachers consider and/or adopt?

39.6 MORAL JUDGMENTS ABOUT LYING

A key general principle in the literature on moral education is to teach children the importance of accuracy in observations and inferences (Scheffler 1973). Scheffler (1973) suggested that this accuracy includes offering rational justifications for the inferences that the children make. It also includes showing sensitivity toward the measured, rational arguments of others. The following paragraphs identify recommendations offered in the literature on moral education to address the problem of lying, along with the rationale behind these recommendations.

Developmental stages. In Kohlberg's (1971) well-known characterization, children's moral development progresses in stages. They come to understand increasingly complex moral judgments as a function of their progression through specific stages of cognitive development. According to this perspective, children should be taught not to lie according to what aspects of or ideas about lying they can comprehend at their own stage of cognitive development.

Recent discoveries about developmental changes in the capacity to lie effectively (outlined in the previous section) support this idea of tailoring education on lying to a child's stage of cognitive development. For instance, a way to stop lying that might be taught successfully to four-year-olds, but not to two-year-olds, is to appeal to the child's sense of compassion toward the recipient of the lie. This suggestion follows from Talwar and Lee's (2008) findings that two-year-olds lacked the perspective-taking capacity of the four-year-olds. Without taking the perspective of the recipient, it would be difficult for the two-year-olds to feel compassion toward that person.

An example of a lesson on not lying that might be successfully taught to seven—to-eight-year olds, but not to four-year-olds, is that keeping track of lies is mentally taxing. The older children, but not the younger children, would be expected to understand the complexity behind all that is required to maintain a lie. In particular, the child must understand and keep in mind who knows what about the truth, whether each party can believe the lie as a function of this knowledge, and whether the parties will talk to one another. Thus, only the older children would be expected to understand that being taxed could be avoided by not lying in the first place.

However, philosopher Ikuenobe (2002) took issue with this developmental approach to moral education on lying. He called into question whether different aspects of or ideas about lying could even be mapped onto these stages. Characterizing moral judgments on lying as multifaceted, he viewed the complex analysis of lies as not amenable to simplification, as explained in more detail later.

Practical wisdom. McDonough (1995) suggested that education on lying requires critical discussion and creative thinking. He recommended that children be asked to examine the essence of lying. They would then be asked to consider how those concepts about lying might be applied to a given case in a particular set of circumstances.

In particular, he recommended that children be taught to imagine various scenarios where an evaluation of lying would be relevant. They would be prompted to conjure up multiple, imaginative, detailed examples to help them learn the habit of making appropriate moral judgments. These examples would likewise serve to help them avoid making moral judgments that are unwarranted.

The rationale behind this approach is that moral education teaches children how to gain practical wisdom. Such wisdom becomes evident when they can apply a general rule to a given instance by attending to the nuances of each case. As McDonough (1995) put it, the use of examples teaches one to direct "attention to the connections and tensions between those principles, and the manner in which those principles must be applied in particular cases" (McDonough 1995: 81).

Meta-ethical analysis. Regarding all of the recommendations just reviewed, Ikuenobe (2002) argued that they do not provide adequate answers regarding what, how, and for what purpose children should be taught about lying. He suggested that one of the essential purposes of moral education is to develop children's capacity to reason. To this end, educators have a responsibility to clarify the issues pertaining to lying, justify their moral judgments, and be sensitive to the justifications offered by others (Ikuenobe 2002).

As mentioned earlier, Ikuenobe (2002) characterized moral judgments about lying as complex, with each judgment requiring rational discussion and conceptual analysis. He recommended that moral education on lying help a child engage in what he called a *meta-ethical analysis of lying*. This phrase refers to the simultaneous consideration of multiple, relevant ethical issues—with each instance of lying to be evaluated separately for all of these issues (Ikuenobe 2002). For a meta-ethical analysis, children would place actions related to lying in the appropriate conceptual categories. They would identify those actions to be avoided, features that are essential to these actions, and features that are similar across the actions.

Ikuenobe (2002) suggested that children be taught that "no one condition alone is necessary for one to make adequate moral judgments about lying" (Ikuenobe 2002: 61). He stated that the conditions for being called a liar would be met if a given person (a) uttered a falsehood, (b) intended to deceive, or (c) succeeded in deceiving. But to make that judgment, a child would need to assess the person's state of mind and intentions. The child would also evaluate that person's "moral principles about duty, cooperation, consequences, motives, and trust. These multiple considerations imply that we do not, from a set of facts, jump to a quick moral judgment: we need critical analysis and rational justification" (Ikuenobe 2002: 62).

39.7 Definitions of lies

As Ikuenobe (2002) compellingly argued, making moral judgments about whether a person can be called a liar is complex, is context-dependent, and requires critical analysis. A question his analysis raises is, "Does the complexity of moral judgments about lying imply that children should be taught nothing about lying until they are seven or eight years old?" A potential solution would be to separate teaching them how to identify lies, said to be part of everyday life (DePaulo et al. 2004), from teaching them how to make moral judgments about those lies.

Instruction on identifying lies could start in kindergarten with specification of the boundary between lies and non-lies. Then, if someone said, "You lied!" both the accuser and the accused could refer to that boundary to decide whether what was said qualified as a lie. Having this boundary as a reference is important because until students know how to identify lies, they have no reason to ask themselves, "Is what I am about to say a lie?" But what should this boundary be? In the paragraphs to follow, I answer this question by comparing definitions of lying from the moral philosophy literature.

Augustine's (400 AD) definition. Augustine (400 AD) defined a lie as "deliberately duplicitous speech, insincere speech that deliberately contradicts what the speaker takes to be true" (Griffiths 2004: 31). Whether the speech was, in fact, true was irrelevant. It was the contradiction between what was stated and what was believed that made it a lie. Augustine was careful to specify that the intention to mislead or deceive was not a defining ingredient of the lie (Griffiths 2004).

Augustine based his advice against lying on an individual's relationship with God. He stated that a person should never lie because even one lie puts that person's soul in jeopardy—it incurs the risk of the soul's condemnation to an eternity in hell. Even if a lie could save thousands of lives on earth, Augustine argued, it should still not be told

(Griffiths 2004). His rationale was that a lie is a sin because it goes against truth, and thus against God, who is Truth. Along these lines, the Book of Romans states, "God is true, but every man a liar" (Romans 3:4). And the Book of Leviticus advises, "Neither shall you deal falsely nor lie to one another" (19:11).

Bok's (1999) definition. The philosopher, Bok (1999), noted in her book that her purpose was to offer a usable definition of the lie. She defined the lie as an utterance that the speaker believes to be false and is intended to mislead the hearer. The simplicity of this definition makes it useful for helping young children identify lies. For example, "If you said something that is not true to trick Daddy, then you told a lie."

Regarding the negative impact of lying, Bok wrote that "some level of truthfulness has always been seen as essential to human society, no matter how deficient the observance of other moral principles" (Bok 1999: 18). She also stated that "trust in some degree of veracity functions as a foundation of relations among human beings" (Bok 1999: 31). She cautioned that trivial or "white lies" told for "our own good" (Bok 1999: 21) are problematic in relationships because the liar cannot be trusted to stick to just those lies.

Bok's use of the phrases "some level of truthfulness" and "some degree of veracity" is consistent with her premise that it is not possible to tell the whole truth. Thus, she claimed that the oath that witnesses take in legal proceedings to tell the whole truth is a misconception (Bok 1999). According to her analysis, at times lies are not only expected, but also required to prevent individuals from bodily harm (Bok 1999). She claimed that a person who cannot lie poses a threat to society, as in times of war. These arguments about the limits of truthfulness are consistent with cultural norms that require polite lying in order to protect the common good (Wang, Bernas, and Eberhard 2011).

Although Bok's definition would fall under Augustine's definition of the lie, there is a clear contradiction between how they characterize the lie. Whereas Augustine's definition classifies any insincere speech as a lie, Bok's definition requires the intention to mislead the hearer. Moreover, whereas Augustine depicted even one lie as jeopardizing a person's soul and advised against it, Bok suggested that telling lies is at times necessary for the good of society.

Williams's (2002) definition. Williams (2002) stated that a lie is "an assertion, the content of which the speaker believes to be false, which is made with the intention to deceive the hearer with respect to that content" (Williams 2002: 96). The key ingredients of the speaker's believing the statement to be false and their intending to mislead the hearer are the same as those in Bok's definition. What his definition adds is that the goal behind the deception pertains to the content of the statement itself.

Saul's (2012) definition. Saul (2012a) offered a definition of a lie that extends to examples left uncertain by Bok's definition. Saul's definition, which has essential features in common with Augustine's definition, is that a lie is a duplicitous statement made in a context to be taken seriously, where all acceptable interpretations of the statement are false (Saul 2012a). This definition builds on Bok's definition by clarifying that jokes, metaphors, and sarcasm are excluded as lies.

Whereas "technical truths" (see Rycyna, Champion, and Kelly 2009) might or might not qualify as lies in Bok's definition, in Saul's definition of the lie, technical truths are lies. For instance, a child who has not yet finished her homework says, "Yes, Mommy, I did all my homework" and then mentally adds, "last week." Even though she did finish her homework last week, what she said is a lie because no acceptable interpretation of it includes homework from last week.

Discerning between duplicitous and sincere statements is essential to Saul's definition. Consider the following example. Alex's mother tells his father that he is feeling sad. She explains that Alex did not qualify for the school's baseball team. The father calls Alex and says, "So what's up? Feel like chatting, Son?" Alex responds, "Not really ... Did you call for any particular reason?" The father responds with, "No. No reason." The father responds that way in order to avoid betraying the mother's confidence—not to mislead his son, who the father suspects already knows why he called. Thus, the example would not qualify as a lie in Bok's (or Williams') definition. But it would qualify as a lie in Saul's (and Augustine's) definition because the father's response is not sincere. It conflicts with a true statement that he is hiding from his son, "I did call for a reason."

Which is the better definition for educating students about lying? If the goal is to teach them not to lie, then Bok's definition works well. But if the goal is to teach them to communicate sincerely, then Saul's definition is better. A reason to teach them to communicate sincerely is that whereas avoiding lying serves as a foundation for justification, sincere communication provides a foundation for learning. This idea is unpacked in the next section.

39.8 A PROPOSED DIDACTIC SOLUTION TO LYING

This final section explains how and why (a) lies impair deductive reasoning and (b) justifications detract from learning. A didactic solution to lying is proposed that teaches students how to evaluate, rather than justify, empirical claims. This solution expressly encourages sincere speech in the classroom, potentially allowing students to enjoy learning for its own sake.

Popper (1959), the well-known philosopher of science and epistemology, argued that induction is not appropriate for empirical research because it is biased and serves the purpose of justification. He offered deductive methods of testing as an alternative, suggesting that they can always be used instead of induction. These nonbiased, deductive methods allow evaluation of the observations in an empirical study (Popper 1959). Namely, a *line of demarcation* is specified before testing, between all possible observations that confirm one prediction or an opposite, complementary prediction. An outcome confirming one prediction allows ruling out the opposite prediction (i.e., deduction).

The problems with induction are exemplified by a study of schizophrenics with delusional thinking who were asked to play a game of "Twenty Questions" (John and Dodgson 1994). Results showed that the schizophrenics, as compared with a control group, used induction to confirm a wrong conclusion to a greater extent. Moreover, the schizophrenics used deduction to rule out disconfirming evidence to a lesser extent (John and Dodgson 1994).

Problems tied to justifications are likewise exemplified in the psychological literature. *Justification* has been defined as an explanation for a questionable act, where the responsible party claims that the act was appropriate because it served some higher purpose (Shaw, Wild, and Colquitt 2003). In a review of the literature, De Witt Huberts, Evers, and De Ridder (2014) provided empirical evidence that justifications can contribute to failures in self-regulation, such as cheating on a romantic partner. De Witt Huberts et al. suggested that justifications can cause such failures through compromised reasoning, wherein a person inappropriately rules out alternative explanations for his or her questionable behaviors.

A recent in-the-field experiment sought to determine whether a business team leader's lying would hurt employees' ability to reason (Cialdini, Li, and Samper 2015). The employees were randomly assigned to one of two groups. The first, but not the second, group witnessed their team leader lie. Both groups then completed a standardized measure of deductive reasoning. It turns out that the employees who had seen their leader lie performed significantly worse. Cialdini and his colleagues (2015) suggested that this impaired reasoning was caused by the stress of being on a deceitful business team.

An alternative reading of why seeing their leader lie hurt the employees' deductive reasoning is as follows: Learning through deduction about one's job performance requires knowing where the leader draws the line between good and bad performance. This knowledge allows employees to evaluate their own conduct with respect to that line. But the employees in this study saw the leader lie. Therefore, they could no longer expect to know where the leader would draw this line, leaving them without a way to reach definitive conclusions about their performance. Thus, the employees might have given up on solving problems. They might have resorted to justifying conclusions instead, which compromised their deductive reasoning.

What follows is a proposed pedagogical solution that orients students away from engaging in justification and toward learning. See Figure 39.1. It is a solution based on my work with Scott Maxwell (Kelly and Maxwell 2016) that I have been implementing in my own college seminars for two years. The instructor begins the seminar by inviting students to always evaluate whether the opposite (i.e., the negation) of the instructor's claims can be ruled out (see Popper 1959). The students are encouraged to share their insights with the rest of the class whenever they cannot rule out the opposite of a given claim.

In essence, this pedagogical solution does not call upon students to offer rational justifications as in the philosophical tradition (Scheffler 1973). Rather, the students are

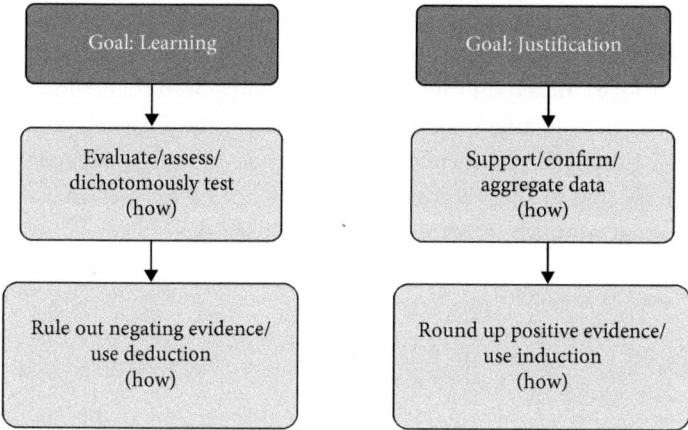

FIGURE 39.1 Competing goals in the classroom.

Adapted from Kelly and Maxwell (2016).

encouraged to learn through deduction. They are also called upon to specify for the rest of the class the logic and observations they used in learning. Instead of trying to persuade or win arguments, the goal of both teacher and pupil is to communicate sincerely. The students are expressly encouraged to speak sincerely in class, rather than to merely avoid lying (see Saul 2012a). Speaking sincerely, along with evaluating the teacher's claims, provides nonbiased means through which students can come to enjoy learning for its own sake.

By applying nonbiased methods for evaluating knowledge, this pedagogical solution orients students away from lying, exaggerating, or otherwise justifying claims that favor themselves in some way. These methods are expected to allow students to see that telling lies compromises their own capacity to evaluate and, thus to learn from, observations. In fact, this compromise to learning can explain why people often get very upset upon discovering a lie: All the previous conclusions that relied on the truthfulness of the liar's claims must now be re-evaluated in light of the discovered lie (see Scott 2010).

39.9 Conclusion

This chapter was on education, lying, and learning. It began with a description of the historical shift from valuing education for its own sake, to seeing it as a means to an end. This shift coincided with a rise in lying and academic dishonesty. The chapter then reviewed education theories, practices, and definitions of lying—along with the justifications behind them. Philosophy students have historically been taught to offer rational justifications for their position in an argument and to listen to the justifications of others (Scheffler 1973). However, rounding up evidence to justify a given claim does not serve the interests of learning in the way that ruling out contradictory evidence does (see Popper 1959). Based on this notion, it was proposed that students be taught to (a) evaluate, rather than justify, knowledge and (b) communicate sincerely, rather than merely avoid lying. Speaking sincerely in class and developing the capacity to evaluate knowledge are expected to allow students to enjoy learning for its own sake, as well as to avoid telling lies that could compromise their own learning.

CHAPTER 40

LYING AND DISCOURSE ANALYSIS

DARIUSZ GALASIŃSKI

40.1 INTRODUCTION

THE 'truth-bias', the expectation that, normally, one tells the truth is proposed to be the cornerstone of humanity (Bok 1999), it is the skill of displacement—speaking of things which are not present, and thus also the ability to deceive that is the basis of human language (Aitchison 1996). And yet, discourse analysis has been remarkably silent on such an important issue. This is because discourse-analytic pursuit of lying and deception in general is fraught with difficulties.

40.1.1 Discourse

Discourse is understood here as a form of social practice within a sociocultural context. That is to say, language users are engaged in meaning-making activities as members of social groups, organizations, institutions, cultures. It also means that to a considerable extent they speak the way one speaks, the way it is appropriate to speak. Moreover, language, discourse, communication (i.e., exchange of meaning) are rule-governed activities. They include both strict grammatical rules (what we say is either grammatical or not) and 'softer', more negotiable principles of interaction (Grice 1975), such as the one that, normally, people are truthful. Discourse analysts are interested not only in language users' following of such rules, but also in ways in which they interact with each other (for example, for stylistic effect), and how they are violated, ignored, or suspended (Grice 1975; Brown and Levinson 1987). Indeed, it is particularly these violations that are of interest to students of lying and deception.

Furthermore, discourse is socially constitutive. It enters into a 'dialectical' relationship with the contexts in which it occurs, so as much as it depends on its context, it also creates social and political 'realities' (Fairclough and Wodak 1997; van Leeuwen and Wodak 1999). Discourse is also a system of options from which language-users make their choices. Whatever can be said, can be said in a different way. But each option has consequences in that any representation of extralinguistic reality is necessarily selective, entailing decisions as to which aspects of that reality to include and how to arrange them. Each selection carries its share of socially ingrained values (Hodge and Kress 1993; Hall 1997) and alternative representations are not only always possible, but they carry different pictures of the world (physical and otherwise) as well as different significances (Fowler 1996). Texts seek to impose a 'preferred reading' (Hall 1981) or a 'structure of faith' (Menz 1989) upon the addressee. Finally, discourse is ideological. The selective character of representation leads to the view that it is through discourse and other semiotic practices that ideologies are formulated, reproduced, and reinforced. In a nutshell, discursive representations are organized into systems which are deployed by social classes and other groups 'in order to make sense of, figure out and render intelligible the way society works' (Hall 1996: 26), while at the same time they are capable of 'ironing out' the contradictions, dilemmas, and antagonisms of practices in ways which accord with the interests and projects of power (Chouliaraki and Fairclough 1999).

40.1.2 Discourse analysis

Discourse analysis here is regarded as a textually oriented analysis (Fairclough 1992). In contrast to the increasingly popular use of 'discourse' in the social sciences and beyond, discourse analysis is and should be a close analysis of texts—whether written, spoken, or indeed visual. A discourse analyst examines the content and particularly the form of stretches of discourse. The focus upon lexico-grammatical recourses of language, that is, upon the semantics and syntax of an utterance, is complemented by that upon the functions of what is said within the local context, and the social actions thus accomplished.

40.2 Discourse analysis and deception

Now, this account shows well why it is psychology (within communication studies) that has led empirical research into lying and deception. Discourse analysis deals with products of meaning-making—texts and not people who make them. And after all, deception is all about the deceiver, a person who wants us to believe something which is not the case (for a discussion of definitions of deception, see Galasiński 2000). There is, of course, a debate as to the need for the intention to deceive in lying, and this chapter takes the perspective of "deceptionists," as Meibauer (2014a) calls them (see also Meibauer 2011; Mahon 2008a; Lackey 2013).

The main problem with deception for discourse analysis is that it looks like something else. Indeed, the definition of lying and deception in language-based research always describes the text's relationship with reality (truth/falsehood) as, e.g., lies tend to be considered false. Some definitions, however, add the speaker's intention and goals (the intention to make the addressee believe something which is not the case), and accuracy of the speaker's beliefs (e.g., for some a mistaken liar who happens to make a true assertion is still lying, see Ng and Bradac 1993). In all cases, however, what is stressed is the covertness of the act (e.g., McCornack 1992; Galasiński 2000; Meibauer 2005; see, however, Carson 2010).

And indeed, in a recent account of lying, Meibauer (2005, 2011) proposes that a lie is an act of assertion which is defined by what the speaker believes in. The account encapsulates the perspective taken in this chapter, although with an addition of intentionality to deceive, mislead, or manipulate. And because of this addition, even though lying is a thoroughly linguistic affair, discourse analysis has very little to say about what lying is. As it focuses on the text, it simply analyses assertions—whether they are truthful or not, for a discourse analyst it is largely irrelevant.

Deception pretends to be something else—an assertion, a question, a promise, a prediction, or a declaration of love. This is why it is unlikely that there can be 'a speech act' of lying (see a discussion in Meibauer 2005). A lie is an assertion with an ulterior motive, but what is crucial is that it is an assertion and it must look like one and be accepted as one. Interestingly, the success of a lie is measurable in the same way as that of a truthful assertion. Similarly, an evasion is a covertly uncooperative answer, while pretending to be cooperative. This is why evasions are proposed to be (Galasiński 2000) metadiscursive acts of deception, with deception consisting in getting the addressee to think that the answer provided is cooperative. Consider, for example, the following exchange:

> Example 1.
> A: Where do you stand on gun control and what do you plan to do about it?
> B: I support the right to keep and bear arms. ... I believe we have to have is [sic] some way of checking handguns before they're sold, to check the criminal history, the mental health of people who're buying them.
> (Galasiński 2000: 73)

The questioner asks a US presidential candidate to focus on his views on gun control and the actions he plans to take in order to (or not to) enforce it. B does exactly what is, linguistically, demanded by the question—he focuses on himself, putting self-reference in the theme of the clause. In such a way he does pretend to answer the question. His answer is of course far too general to count as a cooperative one.

Essentially then, deception is an act of non-cooperation, while pretending to be the opposite. A deceptive speaker cooperates in that s/he participates in a communicative exchange, yet, s/he has goals to mislead her/his addressee. For example, misrepresentation of reality may manifest itself both as an active contribution to a conversation, and a more passive acceptance of the other contributor's actions. This is possible precisely because deception—in contrast to assertion, promises, questions, or apologies that are not associated with any conventional linguistic means carrying them—is a 'parasitic' form of communication. It is parasitic on other uses of language as speakers non-overtly use conventionally anchored forms of meaning exchange to further their deceptive goals.

40.2.1 Typologies

Deception can be achieved in a variety of ways and indeed there are many classifications of acts of deception. Acts of deception can be monologic or dialogic (as in covert evasion, where the speaker pretends to answer the question (e.g., A: *Do you want a tougher regime in these secure places?* B: *I want a regime that helps them* [inmates] *face up to their responsibilities . . .*, Galasiński 2000); can be active or passive (by withholding a message); can be done via explicit or implicit proposition (implicatures, presuppositions, e.g., the infamous: *Have you stopped beating your wife?*; e.g., Fricker 2012; Saul 2012a; Meibauer 2014a). Other important aspects of acts of deception are the relevance of the act and the accountability of the speaker (Bradac, Friedman, and Giles 1986). Finally, acts of deception can focus upon the extralinguistic reality or the message itself (see Galasiński 2000).

Now, the final classification to be presented here is the only one that focuses on the discursive aspects of deception (Galasiński 2000). There are three kinds of acts of deception: falsifications, distortions, and 'taking words out of context'. Falsifications are stereotypical lies; they consist in saying or writing something which is false. So, if a doctor writes in medical documentation *(She) has problems with sleeping*: "*I sleep better after (taking) a pill*," after the patient has said the opposite, i.e., that she has trouble falling asleep after taking sleeping pills, that is a falsification (an actual example from Galasiński and Ziółkowska 2013).

Distortions are based on assertions which are stronger/more general or weaker/more particular. For example, if one person says *We have no right to interfere in Russian internal politics* and another, referring to what that person said, says *In a narrow sense I agree with what the gentleman in the audience said. We cannot intervene. It's not our direct responsibility* (example from Galasiński 2000: 42), s/he distorts what the initial speaker said. The distortion consists in replacing 'interfere' with 'intervene' and in the process misrepresents what was initially said.

Finally, 'taking words out of context', ascribing to what was said a different function (e.g., different illocutionary force, Searle 1969) from the one it had had. For example, consider the following exchange:

> Example 2
> A: I don't think we will ever win with Saddam Hussein. I guess in the end, an assassin's bullet will get him.
> B: do I hear a churchwoman urging to go out and assassinate Saddam Hussein?
> A: I don't think I exactly said that.
>
> (Galasiński 2000: 49)

The initial speaker's statement is misrepresented as an act of urging. In other words, what is said initially has a goal of informing the audience of the person's opinion about the situation, the other utterance misrepresents it as aiming to get someone to do something. This type of deception and its analysis are particularly dependent on exploring and understanding the social context in which something is said. The types are not mutually exclusive and can and do occur together.

40.2.2 All-linguistic research

This typology calls for an 'all-linguistic' research into deception within discourse analysis. In other words, the typology assumes that both the deceptive communication (the 'lie') and the reality it misrepresents are linguistic. What is represented is an act of communication and it is misrepresented with regard to either its content or its function. Why is it necessary to do it in such a way? Below is a rationale behind the typology.

The main reason behind the postulate of 'all-linguistic' data is that it helps overcome the most acute problem discourse analysis faces when studying deception: real-life data. In other words, discourse analysts are interested in what 'real people' really say or write. Unfortunately, naturally occurring data are hugely difficult to come by in deception research. This is because deception is inextricably linked to the intention to mislead (as discussed earlier), which is covert, socially not accepted, and therefore empirically inaccessible. To put it simply: researchers have no access to the speaker's intention to lie or to deceive, and moreover, there is no way of verifying whether speakers tell the truth when asked or whether they told a lie, or perhaps merely made a mistake. After all, when asked about lying, speakers may well (continue to) lie. Of course, there is a very large body of research (together with a TV series—*Lie to Me*) into deception leakage, which claims to be able to establish the speaker's veracity. Yet, like any inductive (that is non-mathematical) research, this research cannot offer a guarantee of truthfulness and certainty. The intention to deceive remains and is likely to remain (one could add: thankfully) very much elusive.

And so, this is why most deception research is often based either on statements or on vignettes whose origin is the imagination of the researcher, or, as in social psychology, on researchers' instructions for the participants to lie or deceive. But then it is possible to argue that such research is based on constructions of deception rather than deception itself. Researchers make up scenarios they imagine reflect what happens in reality, and at the same time, research participants play liars and their actions are 'as if' they were lying. One could argue that such actions do not have to reflect actual communicative reality, where there might be high stakes associated both with deception and with being found out.

So, what is the way forward? Arguably, it is collection of data in which one has access both to the 'act of deception' and the reality it is designed to misrepresent. And it is precisely focusing on misrepresentation that is at least part of the solution (Miller and Stiff

1993; Galasiński 2000). The ideal data for the discourse analyst consist in two representations: First, the initial description of reality and then, second, the misrepresentation of that description. In other words, if we hear A say that her car is red and then hear B say that A had said her car was green, we know that we are dealing with a misrepresentation. Note that we do not have to have access, nor do we need it, to information about the actual car, which is often very difficult to obtain for the researcher, and it is even more difficult to ascertain whether B had access to it.

Of course, importantly, it needs to be stressed that the researcher still has no access to the speaker's intention to deceive, but on the assumption of the 'normality' of the world, one could argue that it is unlikely that person B would immediately forget what s/he had heard or that s/he would have misheard A, having heard everything else. It is perhaps likely, therefore, that the researcher could in fact assume that he or she is dealing with deception. Moreover, there is a plethora of discursive activities in both public and semi-public or private discourses in which deception can be expected. Discursive practices in politics, in advertising, in storytelling, or in contacts with, say, insurance companies are often assumed to be promote being economical with the truth. In such cases, it is the social context which makes it easier for the researcher to assume that even though he or she has no access to the speaker's intention to mislead, such an intention can be safely assumed to exist. For example, a politician who misrepresents his/her opponent's words to his/her advantage can quite safely be assumed not to have made an innocent mistake.

Yet, despite lack of insight into the deceptive intention, one has to solve two problems. First, access both to misrepresentation or deception and to the reality it misrepresents. Second, such data allow the discourse analyst to focus on what s/he can analyse—real-life discursive data that are amenable to analysis with discourse-analytic tools. It is such arguments that lay foundations for the typology of deceptive actions which was discussed earlier. The typology has another advantage. It focuses upon the crucial two aspects of any utterance: its (propositional) content and its function. Propositional content and in particular the truth relationship between what is said and what it represents is referred to in the first two types of deception, while the function is the focus in the third. In other words, the first two types are about what was said, the third about what it was said for.

There is a reservation to be made here, though. One of the chapters in this Handbook is devoted to media quotations. Even though the approach suggested here might appear simply to focus on quotations, the two should not be confused. Quotation is a specific journalistic practice whose point is, as McGlone and Baryshevtsev point out in Chapter 24, to build the evidence foundation upon which stories are built. Even though the data for discourse analysis proposed here are similar in that in both cases speakers refer to what has been said, yet such reference does not constitute quotation. However, if quotation is understood very broadly as everyday use of indirect speech, then instances of this could well be seen as constituting the data that are postulated here. Most generally, discourse-analytic deception research is necessarily metalinguistic, in that discourse analysts focus on utterances (or written texts) which refer to other utterances.

That said, of course, newspaper quotations also can be a rich source of deception data (Galasiński 2004).

Finally, because the classification is based on the basic aspects of what is communicated, it is probably exhaustive of all instances of linguistically rendered misrepresentations. In other words, each such misrepresentation can be seen in terms of what is said and how it is said and how these relate to the propositions accurately describing reality. Further research would be needed to see whether it could be used in the analysis of visual deception. Yet, given that some social semiotic analyses are based on the linguistic system (Kress and van Leeuwen 1996), such a possibility could be said to be likely.

40.3 Doctor–patient communication

Now, as might be expected, there is little discourse-analytic research based on naturally occurring data. Moreover, what little there is tends to focus upon the 'usual suspects'—politicians. In what follows I would like to discuss briefly a piece of recent discourse-analytic research which has been situated well outside the political scene and in a setting which, arguably, is significantly more important socially—medical practice.

In a recent study on information management in the patient's notes, Galasiński and Ziółkowska (2013) explore misrepresentations of clinical interviews in medical documentation. The two researchers had psychiatrists record their initial clinical interviews with patients diagnosed with depression and compared the transcripts of the interviews with the records the clinicians made in the patients' notes. Quite astonishingly, they found quite a lot of misrepresentations.

Using the above-discussed typology of deceptive actions, the study found all three types of deception. First, doctors recorded straight falsehoods. For example, a patient reporting no problems with sleep was recorded as saying (in quotation marks!) that she did have trouble sleeping (quoted above); patients reporting not being able to remember the names of their medications were reported to have suffered memory loss; difficulty concentrating was reported as difficulty doing things. Galasiński and Ziółkowska note that records with falsifications were far more numerous than they had expected and in fact, all notes which were examined contained some falsehoods.

Second, distortions (stronger/more general claims or their opposites) were found. Clinicians exaggerated or minimized what their patients said. For example, suicidal thoughts were recorded to be sporadic and, in fact, not suicidal. Consider these extracts:

Example 3
Doctor's notes:
> (1a)
> (She) feels resignation thoughts sporadically (without suicidal thoughts or suicide attempts).

Interview:
(1b)
Doctor: Have any thoughts of resignation appeared with you? That life has no sense, or even, I'd say, suicidal?
Patient: Indeed.
D: Hmm.
P: I am a believer so I try to pray not to do it. (They appear) obviously.
D: Have they appeared in the last few (unclear)
P: Yes, in the last few months.
D: and now, in the last days? After leaving the inpatient ward?
P: Maybe not.[1]

The doctor's notes contain a double distortion. First, to the (unfortunate) question of both suicidal and resignation thoughts the patient says she is a believer who prays 'not to do it', which is more than likely to imply suicidal thoughts. The doctor, however, records resignation thoughts, underscoring it by explicitly noting an absence of suicidal thoughts. No doubt this is a weaker statement than that made by the patient. But, second, the psychiatrist also makes a note that the thoughts are sporadic, even though nothing the patient said suggested their frequency.

Doctors also misrepresented the function of what was said. That is to say, they misrepresented that part of what is said which allows the speaker to perform a particular communicative action and attain her/his communicative goal. For example, an expression of despair is recorded as lack of cooperation with the clinician:

Example 4
Doctor's notes:
(2a)
Negatively predisposed towards treatment – "nothing can help me"
Interview:
(2b)
P: … there is no help for me. I am, so to speak, pushed aside. To take, kick and throw away, this is how I see myself, someone who cannot give anything more, because she cannot. I can't force myself to do anything. They tell me you must, you must. How am I supposed to have the strength? After all, this strength is in the head. Depression is in the head and perhaps the beginning of Alzheimer's.

---

[1] All the extracts we quote here are translation from the Polish originals. The translations are ours and we have done our best to render both what and how it was said or written. We realise that in attempting to render the 'flavour' of the originals, the result might seem bad or disjointed English.
Polish originals are presented in the Appendix.

Ascription of negativity to treatment in extract 10 has little to do with what the patient said. While the psychiatrist shows her as simply rejecting treatment, the patient shows resignation, despair. She might not believe in treatment, but that is quite different from having a negative attitude (with potentially significant connotations in psychiatry) towards it.

For a deception researcher, Galasiński and Ziółkowska's study offers at least three interesting points. First, it shows a methodologically ecological insight into misrepresentation practices and in a context where they are unlikely to be expected. In other words, the study shows doctors' practices of misrepresentation in a clinical context. Second, through this, it also positions research not only as pertinent in political or military contexts, but in the provision of mental health care, in both its quality and its safety. Indeed, it also offers insight into the workings of psychiatry and perhaps also medicine as a thoroughly communicative enterprise. This piece of misrepresentation research uncovered also a very clear need for further intensive training for clinical professionals. Language-oriented deception research is presented here as having direct application. Third, and final, it also shows deception, Galasiński and Ziółkowska argue, as resulting from the dominant discourses in which clinicians operate and espouse. Misrepresentation, and through this, deception become one of the embodiments of discursive power.

Yet, it must be emphasized, the main advantage of the study lies in its anchoring in real-life data. We get to know what really happens in the doctor's surgery and then what the doctor recorded as having happened. This is the most valuable aspect of discourse-analytic research into misrepresentation, deception, and lying. Moreover, while discourse analysis uncovers what deceivers really do, it also offers the opportunity for taking such research further.

40.4 FUTURE RESEARCH

The last point to be raised here is offering some indication as to avenues of future research. The greatest value that can be gained from discourse analysis' insights in misrepresentation/deception lies in its ability to probe actual communicative practices of social actors in a variety of contexts. While politics, media, perhaps the law are quite obvious choices, education or academic and commercial research are perhaps less obvious, but all the more more interesting areas to explore. To what extent do we teach children on the basis of misrepresented information, how do teachers deceive their pupils, how is research misrepresented in publications and reports? Answers to such questions are not only interesting in their own right, but they also offer tremendous insight into the fabric of social life. Such research is logistically fairly straightforward—actual deception in the family, in relationships, in school or the doctor's surgery would be perhaps even more fascinating, but extremely difficult to carry out. And indeed, while medicine acknowledges issues of lying and deception (Sokol 2006a, 2006b), we know little about deceptive practices in clinical settings.

Furthermore, deception strategies in various contexts could be criss-crossed with insight into the relationships of discursive aspects of deception to power relations as well as gender, ethnicity, age, ability, and social class. Significantly, research foundations set by discourse analysis can be used by sociology, social psychology, and other social sciences in their quantitative explorations of misrepresentation and deception. Galasiński and Ziółkowska's research could potentially be transformed into a study of the prevalence of deception in medical documentation, but also, in a more nuanced way, into a study of local contexts of its occurrence. For example, is suicide risk misrepresented more often than symptoms of an illness, or adherence to medication regimens? What kind of patients are misrepresented by what kind of doctors in the context of what kind of illness? Such research, once again, would not only be of intellectual value, but also would offer great opportunities to improve clinical care.

In addition to this, research into larger-scale discourses (such as medical discourse) or 'orders of discourse' and their relationship to deception would shed most interesting light into the workings of certain social contexts. If Galasiński and Ziółkowska (2013) are right in claiming that it is the characteristics of medical discourse with its underlying assumption of the doctor's (and particularly the psychiatrist's) being always right, one could assume that there are other such discourses. Their discovery and research into them is needed quite urgently.

However, this potentially very practical research should in my view be coupled with further conceptual and theoretical exploration of deception in discourse analysis. We still know relatively little about the relationship of deception with other strategic, non-overt acts of discourse. Manipulation and particularly persuasion have been researched quite extensively also in discourse analysis, and yet their relationship to deception has largely been ignored. Considerably more is needed in discourse analysis to complement social psychological work in the area (for an overview see, e.g., Simons and Jones 2011; Gass and Seiter 2014). However, very recently, Hansson (2015) has tried to combine issues of who discusses overcommunication and manipulation in a study of institutional communication.

Moreover, there is still a need to examine deception as a discursive act which is practiced by people with the use of linguistic and discursive means. Indeed, the relationship of deception to other acts of communication (perhaps speech acts), as well as other discourse practices is still worth exploring further.

At the end of this chapter, a declaration of omissions is necessary. There are three such areas which touch upon discourse analysis and have not been raised. First is the (potential) relevance of Conversation Analysis (see, e.g., Sidnell and Stivers 2012) in deception research. Its focus upon micro-analysis of turn-taking and the minutiae of discourse performance (hesitations, stops, overlaps) is potentially a fruitful way to underpin both discourse-analytic, but also psychological research into the language of deception (for a classical study see Kalbfleisch 1994).

Indeed, this is the second area of research that has not been touched upon in any detail. While for years deception leakage has mostly been studied in the area of non-verbal communication (some of the most notable research and writing has been authored by Paul Ekman, see Ekman 2009), more recently linguists also have taken to analysing deception leakage through language, following in the footsteps of classical studies by Shuy (1993), Picornell (2013), and Arciuli, Mallar, and Villar (2010).

The third area not touched upon in this chapter is the growing field of research into lying and deception on the Internet. With the famous adage "On the Internet, nobody knows that you're a dog," the Internet has been subject to research by scholars interested in deception. Psychological research (Whitty and Joinson 2009) is being complemented by linguistic analyses (e.g., Toma and Hancock 2012; Hancock and Gonzalez 2013).

Discourse analysis of deception is still one of those areas of study in which the researcher can be relatively safe in thinking that s/he will not be doing something that had been done before. The all-linguistic approach reported and advocated here helps with the task and makes such research empirically sounder. It also allows discourse analysis to move into research which can make significant difference.

Appendix

Example 3
Zapis lekarza w karcie:
 (1a) Sporadycznie odczuwa myśli rezygnacyjne (bez MS i PS).
Dane z wywiadu:
 (1b) L: yhm. czy pojawiały się u pani kiedykolwiek takie myśli rezygnacyjne? że życie nie ma sensu o czy nawet bym powiedziała samobójcze.
P: owszem
L: yhm.
P: proszę panią ja jestem wierząca to (.) staram się modlić żeby tego nie zrobić. (pojawiają się) oczywiście.
L: czy teraz też się pojawiają w ostatnich tych kilku (niejasne)
P: tak. w tych ostatnich kilku miesiącach.
L: a teraz dniach? już po wyjściu z oddziału stacjonarnego?
P: no może nie.

Example 4
Zapis lekarza w karcie:
   (2a) Negatywnie nastawiona do leczenia – „mnie się już nie pomoże".
Dane z wywiadu:
   (2b) P: na pewno … dla mnie już nie ma żadnego ratunku. ja jestem tak. że tak powiem zepchnięta na out. wziąć kopnąć wyrzucić. ja siebie tak widzę. takiego kogoś kto … nic już z siebie dać nie może bo: bo <u>nie może no.</u> no bo ja nie mogę się do niczego zmusić no. bo mi mówią musisz musisz musisz. skąd ja mam te siły? przecież te siły siedzą w głowie. w głowie jest depresja i nie wiadomo co jeszcze może początki Alzhemera.

CHAPTER 41

LYING AND DECEPTION IN POLITICS

VIAN BAKIR, ERIC HERRING, DAVID MILLER, AND PIERS ROBINSON

41.1 INTRODUCTION

FROM the sophists of ancient Greece, chastised by Plato (360 BC) for their specious rhetoric, through to the sixteenth-century *realpolitik* of Machiavelli and the twentieth-century advocacy of the necessity of deception in politics by thinkers such as Leo Strauss (1958, 1975), the issues of lying and deception have been perennials of politics. The twentieth and twenty-first centuries have witnessed numerous examples of political lying and deception: from the 'big lie' approach that Adolf Hitler (1939 [1924]: 184–5) attributed to the Jews but which is now seen as a staple of Nazi propaganda (Herf 2006); through to the *Pentagon Papers*, which exposed the secret enlargement of the US war in South-east Asia to Cambodia and Laos and the lies of US President Richard Nixon during the 1970s Watergate scandal (Sheehan 1971; Ellsberg 2003); and deception by US and UK political leaders about the certainty and threatening nature of the intelligence relating to Iraq and Weapons of Mass Destruction (WMD) in the period before the invasion in 2003 (Mearsheimer 2011; Herring and Robinson 2014: 2014–15). Indeed, according to some analysts, lying and deception are pervasive elements of politics (Jamieson 1992; Alterman 2004; Oborne 2005). It is therefore no surprise that we live in times of profound distrust of politics and politicians, at least in much of the Western world, as evidenced by opinion polls spanning from the 1950s to the present day in the US, Australia, and Europe (Bakir and Barlow 2007).

Drawing upon scholarship emerging in political communication studies, rhetoric studies, and related fields, this chapter provides an introduction to the issues of lying and deception in politics in three stages. Section 41.1 traces these phenomena back to ancient Greece. It identifies key interventions on the questions of the legitimacy and necessity of lying in politics, and assesses major contemporary contributions to this age-old debate. This section introduces central arguments as to when deception might be justified and associated concerns over its impact upon the democratic process. The second section links the concept of deception to abiding concerns in research on political communication, propaganda, and *organized persuasive communication*. Here, we discuss in more depth the politics of deception and the ways in which attempts are made to exercise political power through deceptive communications. The concluding section maps new directions for enquiry, including understanding the relationship between deception and coercion, and deception in the contemporary media environment.

Before continuing, it is necessary to briefly define our terms, 'lying' and 'deception'. Mahon (2015) asserts that the most common of the very many definitions of lying is 'to make a believed-false statement to another person with the intention that that other person believe that statement to be true'. Deception involves 'intentionally causing others to have false beliefs that one believes to be false or does not believe to be true' (Carson 2010: 49): as such deception does not necessarily involve lying, which requires a false statement to be made—although Mahon does suggest that it involves the deceiver 'bringing about evidence on the basis of which the other person has or continues to have that false belief'. Although the particular definition of and relationships between lying and deception are subject to unending debate, this chapter reflects the tendency amongst the scholarship discussed in the chapter to treat lying as a subset of the broader phenomenon of deception. Accordingly, in this chapter, attempts at deception involve intentionally trying to cause others to have false beliefs with or without lying (see also Cliffe, Ramsay, and Bartlett 2000).

41.2 Debating the Justifiability of Deception in Politics

The literature on deception in politics can be traced to Ancient Athens. Most notably Plato (360 BC: Book 3: 414b–415d), in *The Republic*, relaying the thinking of Socrates, described the importance of the 'noble lie', whereby grand myths or untruths might be necessary in order to maintain social order. At the same time, Plato critiqued the rhetoric of both the Sophists and Aristotle for its deceptive and manipulative aspects. In turn, Aristotle's *Rhetoric* (2010 [230 BC]) distinguished itself from sophistry on the grounds of moral purpose: sophistry involves winning an argument at all costs, whereas rhetoric has a moral purpose (Rawnsley 2005: 30). However, whilst Aristotle sought to counter harmful or damaging forms of rhetoric, his own articulation of the arts of persuasion often appears to advocate some level of deception (Corner 2007: 672). More generally, and as Hesk (2000: 4) argues, the emergence of ideas surrounding rhetoric and deceit 'can be located in political, legal and cultural discourses which defined Athenian democracy itself'. In particular, thinkers such as Aeschylus, Sophocles, Thucydides, and Plato distinguished 'persuasion brought about by deceit (*dolos*), false logic, coercion, and other forms of chicanery from persuasion (*peitho*)' (Lebow 2008: 28), achieved through sincere dialogue. In other words, the matter of lying and deception in politics has been there right from the start.

For the contemporary era, the clearest and most influential marker for starting discussion on lying in politics comes in the sixteenth-century text *The Prince* by Niccolo Machiavelli (2003 [1532]). Through its warranting of the necessity of both force and deception as essential components of successful governance, Machiavelli's treatise on how to govern has made his name a byword for what has become known as 'political realism'. Rooted in a decidedly pessimistic reading of humanity, Machiavelli advised that, because men are bad, 'and will not keep faith with you, you too are not bound to observe it with them'. Importantly, the 'Prince' (the person who governs) must and can:

> be a great pretender and dissembler; and men are simple, and so subject to present necessities, that he who seeks to deceive will always find someone who will allow himself to be deceived.
>
> (Machiavelli 2003 [1532]: ch. 18)

More broadly, *The Prince* is an endorsement of any means, including physical coercion and deception, providing they served useful ends, and the work is a touchstone for modern political realists. This can be seen in the publications of scholars such as Strauss (1958, 1975), Jay (2010), and Mearsheimer (2011) who, in different ways, make a virtue of mendacity in some circumstances, the key features of which are outlined in the following section.

41.2.1 Defenders of deception: elitism, realism, and scepticism about democracy

The elitist writings of Leo Strauss represent a twentieth-century manifestation of Plato's critique of democracy and the associated claim that governance by the wise is preferable to rule by the majority (Strauss 1975; see also Strauss 1958). Plato's advocacy of 'the noble lie' was based upon the idea that, in order to maintain harmony in the context of a social hierarchy, myths needed to be created in order to help people accept their location in the hierarchy: God made some to rule (the golden race), others to build (iron and bronze workers) and still others to fight (soldiers). Many see in Strauss the continuation of the Platonic idea that democratic politics is too idealistic and that the greater good can only be achieved by deferring to wise and enlightened elites. Strauss's concern is that, at times, the truth would threaten political stability and, consequently, deception becomes essential to political order and stability. Strauss has come to be associated with, and deployed by, those making anti-democratic and elitist arguments, most recently regarding neoconservatism in the US (for analysis of this use see Norton 2005), though such use of his work has been disputed (Smith 1997; Zuckert and Zuckert 2006). Strauss-inspired neoconservatives are said to have manipulated US public fears over Iraq in order to advance their political objectives (Sniegoski 2008: 322).

Other contemporary advocates of deception do not necessarily imply an elitist mindset. For realists such as the international relations theorist John Mearsheimer (2011), the threatening realm of international politics demands that leaders sometimes lie for reasons of state. Specifically, he argues that, whilst lying between state leaders is comparatively rare, leaders do often deceive their own publics in order to further what they see as, or claim to be, the national interest. Specifically, leaders might fearmonger when they 'see a threat emerging but think that they cannot make the public see the wolf at the door without resorting to a deception campaign' (Mearsheimer 2011: 45). A good example of this form of deception, now often seen as justified, are Franklin Delano Roosevelt's lies to the American public to try to get the US involved in WWII (Dallek 1979). In addition, lies might be used to cover up strategic failures if they think that it would serve the national interest (Mearsheimer 2011: 67). Furthermore, Mearsheimer (2011: ch. 7) describes how leaders of liberal democratic states lie when their behaviour falls short of liberal ideological claims regarding the law-abiding and war-averse nature of liberal democracies. Harking back to Plato's 'Noble Lie', he also notes how nationalist myths, designed to foster social cohesion and support for the state, frequently involve lies and half-truths (Mearsheimer 2011: 75).

Whilst Strauss and Mearsheimer present the case for deception with respect to particular circumstances, i.e., deception when social stability demands it or with respect to the realm of international politics, Jay (2010) argues that mendacity is part and parcel of democratic politics, and necessarily so. In part this is because democracy itself is underpinned by lies regarding common interests, in part because excessive truth within the public sphere might lead to the thwarting of healthy and pluralistic debate, but also because of the aesthetic nature of politics which, for Jay, means that the art of politics naturally involves dramatic performance of which deception is an integral part.

Deception in politics, then, can be justified in different ways: For Strauss we see this in the elitist idea that the masses need to be deceived in order to ensure their compliance with the existing social order; for Mearsheimer it is the dangers of an international politics that demands that leaders lie so as to protect the interests of their people; for Jay it is based upon a belief that democracy, in its idealized form, is simply not achievable. Although underpinned by different rationales, these positions all gravitate towards a conservative and status quo orientation in which considerable power and trust are left to elites.

41.2.2 Critics of deception: idealism and the valuing of democracy

In contrast to the advocates of lying, there are few Kantian absolutists who maintain that deception is always problematic. There are, however, those who have attempted to think through more precisely when deception might be justified and what the limits to it should be (e.g., Bok 1999; Cliffe, Ramsay, and Bartlett 2000). These scholars are more sceptical of elite power and hold a greater commitment to democratic politics and the importance of public involvement in political decision-making.

For example, Ramsay (2000a, b) acknowledges the consequentialist arguments made by theorists such as Walzer (1973) that moral ends can justify immoral means. But she also maintains that defenders of consequentialism fail to put sufficiently clear limits on what is 'morally permissible' (Ramsay 2000a: 17). Much of Ramsay's case against deception is rooted in what she claims is its incompatibility with democratic politics. Specifically, she argues that deception and secrecy by definition inhibit the free flow of information about 'the decisions and actions of political leaders and hamper both public participation' and accountability (Ramsay 2000b: 36). In these circumstances democratic notions regarding consent and representation are inevitably undermined when political actors are untruthful. So, even if deception might achieve beneficial ends in some circumstances, the cost with respect to the erosion of the democratic process may be too high. Ramsay (2000b: 37) also challenges advocates of deception on their own ground by arguing that, even if one might subscribe to the idea that elites are best placed to decide on certain political issues, deception and secrecy may undermine effective decision-making:

> Because information is only available to a small number of people, this limits debate and hinders communication between those who need to know the facts in order to ensure that sound decisions are made. It also narrows the range of perspectives and opinions brought to bear on solving problems, restricts consideration of all the implications of a course of action and prevents criticism and dissenting views from being heard.

Indeed, it is the idea of an elite cut off from reality owing to deceptive and self-deceptive groups of insulated 'professional problem solvers' that formed one aspect of Hannah Arendt's (1973: 9) seminal commentary on *The Pentagon Papers*. These official documents, commissioned by US Secretary of Defense Robert McNamara and leaked to the *New York Times* in 1971, revealed the disjuncture between the pessimistic intelligence assessments regarding the Vietnam War and official claims regarding both the course of the war and the reasons for US involvement (Sheehan 1971; Ellsberg 2003). For Arendt (1973: 12), whilst the raw intelligence reports were accurate, the professional problem-solvers sought to erase inconvenient facts to such an extent that their assessment became detached from reality. Arendt (1973: 8) concludes that, because a US President is so reliant upon advisers as a source of information as to what is going on, he or she may become the most vulnerable to 'complete manipulation'.

Critics of deception such as Ramsay (2000a, b) and Bok (1999) also tend to adopt a more questioning stance towards some of the assumptions made by defenders of deception. For example, Mearsheimer's appeal to the national interest in his defence of deception is disputed by Ramsay (2000b: 30–42) on the grounds that it is far too nebulous a concept, open to widely differing interpretations, to provide firm grounds for the justification of deception. She makes the same point about the idea of 'public interest'. She suggests the vagueness inherent to such concepts means that they are vulnerable to manipulation and exploitation by Plato's supposedly wise and noble elite. Bok's (1999: 13) influential work on lying in public and private life is initially sympathetic towards the idea that crises, frequently encountered in the realm of international politics and involving threats to survival posed by enemies, may well demand deception. However, she is quick to highlight the dangers inherent in deciding that action must be conducted without due scrutiny. For example, she argues that policy can end up being underpinned by a group-think mentality which leads to a tendency to perceive enemies in oversimplified and exaggerated terms and to see them as much more dangerous than they are. She explains how 'governments build up enormous, self-perpetuating machineries of deception in adversary contexts' (Bok 1999: 42), the consequence of which is that lies, 'whilst occasionally excusable, ... are weighted with very special dangers; dangers of bias, self-harm, proliferation, and severe injuries to trust' (Bok 1999: 143). Like Ramsay, Bok is unconvinced by political elites when they claim to be lying for the public good. In her final analysis, all acts of deception need to be tightly controlled via the test of public justification. Where deception has already occurred, this can obviously happen only after the event: but it should be applied in advance to deceptive practices. She concludes that 'only those deceptive practices which can be openly debated and consented to in advance are justifiable in a democracy' (Bok 1999: 181).

The debates discussed above reflect deep divisions over what is politically necessary, possible, and desirable when it comes to lying and deception. They also highlight recognition that communication, whether non-deceptive or deceptive, justified or unjustified, is integral to the exercise of power and influence. This brings us to the subject of *organized persuasive communication* and its various namesakes such as *propaganda*, *spin*, and *political marketing*.

41.3 Political power and deception: propaganda, spin, and political marketing

Over the course of the twentieth century, the rise of mass society and mass communication has been accompanied by organized and systematic approaches to persuasion. In the early part of the twentieth century, these activities were frequently referred to as *propaganda* (Lippman 1922; Lasswell 1927). In the contemporary era euphemisms such as *public relations (PR), political marketing, strategic communication*, and *public diplomacy* are frequently used. We see them as particular examples of a more general category that we label *organized persuasive communication* (OPC) (Bakir et al. 2015). Briefly, OPC refers to all organized activities aimed at influencing beliefs, attitudes, and behaviour and includes all of the activities historically described as propaganda and those now described as PR, strategic communication, and so on. We further subcategorize OPC into consensual and non-consensual forms. Consensual OPC involves combinations of rational persuasion and/or appeals to emotion whereby the persuadee is persuaded in a free and informed manner. For example, anti-smoking campaigns fit the definition of consensual OPC. Non-consensual forms involve combinations of deception, incentivization, and coercion whereby persuasion operates through either misleading the persuadee or subjecting them to some kind of incentive or physical threat. The value of the category of OPC is that it helps avoid using the confusing array of often euphemistic and value-laden terms now in circulation and helps to illuminate the fact that OPC can sometimes be consensual and truthful, as well as at other times manipulative.

For commentators such as Arendt (1973) and Corner (2007), the ubiquity of deceptive OPC activities has elevated the problem of deception and politics to new levels for decades now. In discussing *The Pentagon Papers*, Arendt (1973: 7–12) argues that it was a combination of the deceptive 'problem-solvers', mentioned earlier, and the 'apparently innocuous' PR managers that worked to create such a fundamental mismatch between the factually accurate intelligence reports and the deceptive claims and beliefs of policy-makers during the Vietnam War (see also Arendt 1958: 74–6). For Corner (2007), picking up on Wernick's (1991) idea of *promotional culture* and Arendt's notions of *organized lying* and *bureaucratic deceit*, patterns of deception and manipulation have become integral to contemporary society such that 'almost all types of promotional behaviour slide—perhaps sometimes plunge—into forms of deceit' (Corner 2007: 57). In short, the issue of deception needs to be understood in the context of the extensive OPC activities, and their propensity for deceptiveness, that have now permeated politics for many years.

41.3.1 Organized persuasive communication, deception, and modern politics

Whilst deceptive OPC has become integral to contemporary politics, as Arendt (1973) and Corner (2007) amongst others argue, much of the scholarship on OPC activities has failed to get to grips with the issue of how these practices can involve deception and lying. Part of the problem has been the tendency amongst a large body of scholars to perceive OPC activities as benign and non-deceptive. For example, Moloney argues that *Public Relations* scholarship has deceived itself into over-emphasizing 'PR as a practice of virtuous messaging, known as two-way communications between equal, listening, negotiating, mutually respectful message senders and receivers' (Moloney 2006: xiii). At the same time, some of the literature on propaganda has worked with a poorly developed conceptualization of what deceptive OPC looks like and frequently associates it only with blatant lying (e.g., Jowett and O'Donnell 2014: 17). Consequently, other forms of deception, such as omission (half-truths) and distortion (spin), are routinely ignored and, in line with much of the literature, deceptive and nefarious OPC is portrayed as occurring only in other contexts (conducted by official enemies of Western states) and times (e.g., wartime) or both, as in examples of Nazi or Soviet 'propaganda'. As discussed next, on the relatively rare occasions when scholars have engaged directly with the issue of deception, the conclusions have frequently suggested what Corner (2007: 674) refers to as a 'major and permanent adjustment or displacement of reality'. The critical point across these studies engaging with deceptive OPC is that it is a key component of how political and economic power is wielded in modern society (e.g., Miller and Dinan 2008). Moreover, the deceptive OPC campaigns described by these scholars are fundamentally anti-democratic because they tamper with the evidence base of information needed by the public to take meaningful democratic decisions.

To illustrate, the *propaganda model* advanced by Herman and Chomsky (1988), describes how mainstream US media relay the deceptive OPC of US political and business elites. The media are critical and adversarial, but mostly only within bounds that define the limits of legitimate, responsible criticism. Criticisms are frequently framed in terms of well-intentioned mistakes made in pursuit of legitimate goals. Questioning the motives of elites and the legitimacy of the system is rare, while the illegitimacy and nefarious motives of official enemies are regularly rehearsed. So, for example, US military action in Vietnam is described as a defensive *intervention* to protect democracy whilst Soviet military action in Afghanistan is described as an aggressive *invasion*. As a result the US public is left profoundly deceived as to the reality of US political and business activities. More recently, the 2003 invasion of Iraq has been accompanied by widespread debate over whether or not the US and UK governments engaged in deception with respect to intelligence on the alleged WMD (Weapons of Mass Destruction) threat from Iraq. Herring and Robinson demonstrate that UK officials intentionally deceived both by presenting available intelligence on Iraqi WMD as much more certain and threatening (Herring and Robinson 2014–15), and by claiming that diplomacy at the UN was motivated by a desire to avoid war when in fact it was aimed at smoothing the path to war (Herring and Robinson 2014). Similarly, Mearsheimer (2011) argues that the US and British governments lied to their publics and the world in this case. These major deceptions were all integral to the strategy of mobilizing publics to support war. Western involvement in torture has also been sustained through deceptive OPC. Following '9/11', the Bush administration proclaimed that Enhanced Interrogation Techniques (EITs) of al-Qa'eda suspects legally did not constitute torture while securing life-saving intelligence. To bolster their claim regarding torture, under the Bush administration the Office of Legal Counsel of the US Department of Justice created secret legal memoranda to advise the CIA, the US Department of Defense, and President Bush on the legality of the use of EITs: these memos redefined what constitutes torture, so that EITs would fall outside this definition. While these secret legal memos have since been exposed and rescinded and EITs recognized as constituting torture, the claim about EITs' effectiveness was at first left hanging, as the intelligence agencies and politicians kept secret the evidence on which their claims were based (Bakir 2013). Only in 2014 was this claim regarding effectiveness refuted by the long-awaited partial declassification of a US Senate Intelligence Committee study which concluded that the CIA lied to the White House, Congress, and media about EITs' efficacy and avoidance of brutality (US Senate Intelligence Committee 2012). Despite this, the CIA continues to try to dispute these conclusions (CIA 2013).

Deception in the context of OPC also raises the key issues of *self-deception* and modes of deception that avoid blatant, unambiguous lies. With respect to the former, whilst intentional deception may be the initial impulse of any given OPC strategy, the organized and extensive nature of campaigns also involves a high degree of internalization of the deceptive OPC whereby those involved may well come to believe the deceptions that they are involved in propagating. Of course, this can occur at the level of the individual when he or she elects to lie about something. But the organized and sustained nature of deception campaigns is likely to result in many officials coming to believe their deceptive messages. The other aspect of this dynamic is that multiple individuals, manipulating information in order to serve a particular political objective, can end up generating a profound degree of deception but without being fully aware of their part in it. As Arendt puts it: 'they will be tempted to fit their reality—which, after all, was man-made to begin with and thus could have been otherwise—into their theory, thereby mentally getting rid of its disconcerting contingency' (Arendt 1973: 12). Ellul (1965: 41) also draws attention to the importance of 'a general system of false claims' whereby falsehoods become so widely accepted that people believe in a general claim:

> When the United States poses as the defender of liberty—of all—everywhere and always—it uses a system of false representation. When the Soviet Union poses as the defender of true democracy, it is also employing a system of false representation. But the lie is not always deliberately set up; it may be an expression of a belief, of good faith—which leads to a lie regarding intentions because the belief is only a rationalization, a veil drawn deliberately over a reality one wishes not to see.

Ellul highlights how "Propaganda feeds, develops, and spreads the system of false claims—lies aimed at the complete transformation of minds, judgements, values, and actions (and constituting a frame of reference for systematic falsification)" (Ellul 1965: 61). Indeed, in long-term political deceptions, deceptive OPC (or propaganda) narratives become part of the cultural memory of a society, as seen with the German stab-in-the-back legend of WW1. Here the myth emerged that the loss of WW1 was caused, not by military failure, but by lack of support on the 'home front' (Carson 2010: 232–40). Corner's (2007) invocation of the notion of *promotional culture* also implies that deception is so ingrained in Western consumerist societies that it has become naturalized and unnoticed. In many respects this takes us close to questions of ideology (as an interest-linked perspective) (Miller 2001).

Connected with this is the matter of what form deception takes. Deception through lying, where a political actor makes a statement that is known or suspected to be untrue in order to mislead, is comparatively rare. Communicators know that lies are costly to credibility if exposed and so have an incentive to find other ways to mislead. As such, lying is generally seen as a last resort: 'Every propagandist worth his mettle will use the truth in preference to lies whenever he can; ... "Lies have short legs," a German proverb says' (Friedrich 1943: 78–9; see also Ellul 1965: 53–7). However, lying is still used in order to deceive. To support lies, *misinformation* may be used, whereby forgeries and staged events are deployed in order to deceive (Martin 1982; Lashmar and Oliver 1998). For example, immediately before WWII, Germany staged a bogus attack on a German radio station to use as a pretext for invading Poland. More commonly in the political world, deception can be achieved through withholding information to make the viewpoint being promoted more persuasive: this can be labelled as deception through omission (Corner 2007; Mearsheimer 2011; Herring and Robinson 2014, 2014–15) or 'half-truths' (Carson 2010) (see also Chapter 13 'Lying and omissions' by Don Fallis). It is deceptive because those involved know people would not be persuaded if they knew the full picture. Deception can also occur through distortion (Corner 2007; Mearsheimer 2011; Herring and Robinson 2014, 2014–15) or 'spin' (Carson 2010). This involves presenting a statement in a deliberately misleading way to support the viewpoint being promoted. One form of distortion is *exaggeration* but it can also involve de-emphasizing information, for example by releasing controversial information on busy news days. A further category is *deception through misdirection* (Bakir 2013), which entails producing and disseminating true information but which is intended to direct public attention away from problematic issues. To these categories might also be added the concept of 'bullshit', whereby persuasion is attempted by presenting a misleading impression of the persuader's knowledge of the facts but without any knowledge of, or regard to, the actual truth (Hardcastle and Reisch 2006; Seymour 2014).

When looking at deception in these terms, i.e., as a part of deceptive OPC strategies designed to influence public support for major policies involving patterns of self-deception and multiple deceptive techniques, we start to understand the extent to which it is a substantial part of, and problem for, contemporary democracies that have become so accustomed to the ubiquity of promotional activities. A world in which information is systematically manipulated via omission, distortion, exaggeration, and misdirection, leading to high levels of deception and self-deception, is dysfunctional in democratic terms because it makes it very difficult for publics to hold to account those engaged in the deception and suggests that true *consent* has not been given. Importantly, these issues only intensify in importance given the rise of new and social media where the possibilities of deception both in the content of messages and in terms of the sources of messages have proliferated. The use of public relations techniques such as the 'front group', where vested interests are disguised by ostensibly independent groups has become more complex in the age of 'mass self-communication' (Castells 2009: 55). Online identities can be assumed and used deceptively—a phenomena known as the 'sock puppet'. Though they can be used playfully, they are also used in economic and political influence strategies by, for example, Stella Artois (Watson 2012) and the Special Operations Command of the US military (Fielding and Cobain 2011). Conversely, developments such as wearable technologies (e.g., Google Glass smart glasses), which provide biometric data and physiological signs, and apps which claim to enable detection of the mood and emotional state of a speaker, may provide new forms of lie detection, useful for assessing veracity in the hyperconnected digital world (McStay 2018), and perhaps even help counter deceptive OPC strategies.

41.4 CONCLUSION: FUTURE RESEARCH AGENDAS

Summing up the key points, political philosophers who debate the ethics of deception fall, broadly speaking, into two camps: defenders of deception and critics of deception. To its defenders, lying and other forms of deception are necessary parts of political life, whilst for critics they should be exceptional practices that are justifiable only in very limited circumstances. For defenders, elites can and must be trusted to decide the public or national interest and to determine when deception is necessary to defend it. For critics, this leads to abuse of power and poor decision-making. While defenders find it acceptable that democracy is compromised by permitting elites to deceive, critics argue that democracy must be strengthened in order to check what they see as this abuse of power so that democratic consent is valid and democratic accountability possible. Examination of the social scientific and historical literature on OPC reveals the extent to which both OPC and deceptive OPC have become part of the political environment and central to the exercise of power, even in contemporary democracies.

A number of concerns arise from this and suggest important research agendas for future work. First, the literature on politics and lying would benefit from greater cross-fertilization with relevant literatures. For example, the expansive philosophy and psychology literatures, some of which is documented in this handbook edition, provide detailed investigations of the nature of deception and lying, as well as the circumstances in which they might be justified. The literature on lying in politics and OPC could be enriched through a closer engagement with this literature. Such an engagement would further the development of more sophisticated conceptualizations of deception for those studying deceptive OPC and contribute to the ongoing normative arguments between the defenders and the critics of deception in politics. Second, although the study of OPC is extensive, it was noted that engagement with deceptive OPC is comparatively rare and certainly underdeveloped. Given the gravity of those relatively few cases that have been explored from the point of view of deception, and the contemporary ubiquity of OPC activities, far greater empirical case-study analysis by academics is needed. This necessarily involves empirical exploration of OPC activities, major political issues, and the role that deception might be playing. There is no shortage of political issues demanding attention, including climate change and the organized strategies of denial, and current major conflicts including those in Iraq, Syria, Ukraine, and the Democratic Republic of Congo, and their promotion. In doing so, increasing attention needs to be paid to the way in which OPC and deception work through the contemporary media environment characterized by digital communication, where the potential for transparency of institutions may be overridden by ever more targeted and personalized deceptive communications. Opportunities provided by new technology to counter deceptive OPC also need to be explored. Third, and finally, as we have argued, deception in politics frequently works through OPC and can involve a variety of deceptive practices, all of which raise the question of how much *consent* there is in contemporary democracies. Two matters arise here: the first concerns the need for fuller engagement with forms of OPC that go beyond deception to include more clearly incentivizing and coercive strategies. For example, propaganda has always been understood to involve *bribes* and *threats of physical coercion* as well as linguistic-based deceptions. A fuller understanding of coercive OPC, and how it might interplay with deception, is necessary in order to more fully grasp the ways in which power is being exercised in the political realm and the extent to which democracy is being undermined. The second concerns finding ways of thinking about political communication that avoid deception and, conversely, allow informed consent. Here, a critical ethics of communication, perhaps linking with Habermasian notions of undistorted and dialogical communication, would enable a fuller understanding of OPC that avoids deception and coercion and succeeds in persuading via a consensual process. Such a development might inform moves towards a more democratic and less deceptive mode of communication than the one which currently dominates.

In conclusion, there is a wide spectrum of positions on the nature of lying and deception and whether they are integral and unavoidable aspects of politics. Further conceptual development, including that of deceptive and non-deceptive OPC, and empirical case studies are necessary to advance further our understanding of these issues.

Acknowledgements

Thanks to Jörg Meibauer, the two anonymous reviewers, and Stefanie Haueis for feedback on earlier drafts.

CHAPTER 42

LYING AND HISTORY

THOMAS L. CARSON

I begin by discussing views about the permissibility of lying by political leaders. Sections 42.2 and 42.3 address historically important lies and lies about history and the historical record. These two categories overlap—some lies about the historical record were historically important events. In section 42.4, I discuss the related notion of half-truths and give examples of misleading/deceptive half-truths about history. In the final section of this chapter, I briefly discuss the obligations of historians to give truthful accounts of historical events.

42.1 Views about the Permissibility of Lying by Leaders

In *The Republic*, Plato famously says that in an ideal society the guardians/leaders of a state will frequently need to make use "of falsehood and deception for the benefit of those they rule" (*The Republic* 2006:, 459c). He justifies leaders telling "useful falsehoods" and calls them "noble lies" (*The Republic* 2006: 414 b–c). Plato was a bitter opponent of democracy. He thought that the great majority of people were much too ignorant, intemperate, and irrational for democracy to be a good form of government (see *The Republic* 2006: 560e–2 and 435a). Plato holds that states should be ruled by wise, intelligent philosopher kings who will sometimes need to deceive the common people for their own good. He thinks that the wise, knowledgeable, and virtuous should rule the foolish, ignorant, and intemperate.[1]

Another defender of the frequent use of lying by leaders is Averroes, who writes the following in his commentary on Plato's *Republic*:

> The chiefs' lying to the multitude will be appropriate for them in the respect in which a drug is appropriate for a disease ... That is true because untrue stories are necessary

---

[1] On Plato's views see Lane (1999) and Schofield (2007).

for the teaching of the citizens ... this is something necessary for the multitude to reach their happiness.

(quoted in Melzer 2014: 122)

For references to other defenders of political lying, see Melzer (2014: 122-3). Melzer says that, because almost all societies have their origins in conquest and the displacement of other peoples, this "harsh reality ... must be covered over by a myth of just origins ... it is the Promised Land given to us by God, or we are owed it by Manifest Destiny" (Melzer 2014: 193).[2]

Lies told by leaders to the public about important matters relevant to public policy are contrary to the ideals of democratic societies. Democracies are unlikely to accurately express the will of the people unless the people have information adequate for them to vote in ways that further the goals and policies that they support. In democracies, lies told by leaders to members of their own societies are great betrayals of trust that subvert the will of the people. Given that democracy or government by the people is a worthy ideal to which societies should aspire, there is a very strong moral presumption against lying and deception by the leaders of democratic societies.[3] Deceiving other countries or the leaders of other countries is rarely a comparable breach of trust or harm to democratic ideals, but lies told to other countries often deceive one's own people as well (Mearsheimer 2011: 21). Lies told by the leaders of non-democratic societies are also often morally wrong; they are often used to manipulate people into supporting immoral policies that are contrary to their best interests.

But leaders can be justified in lying to their own people to protect vital state and military secrets. Mearsheimer gives several examples:

During WW I, Britain secretly developed the tank to help break the stalemate on the Western front. To help conceal that weapon from the Germans ... British leaders told a series of lies ... they said it was a water tank designed to transport water to the front lines ... this is how the tank got its name.

(Mearsheimer 2011: 33)

In 1980 President Carter's press secretary was asked whether the US was planning a military operation to free the American hostages held in Iran. He lied and said that this was not true to avoid tipping off the Iranian government about US plans to try to free the hostages (Mearsheimer 2011: 35). In principle, such lies can be morally justified (assuming that the actions and policies that they protect are morally permissible). And surely lying could be morally permissible if it were necessary to prevent a nuclear war or

---

[2] Comment: such myths might be necessary for national pride, but they have the potential to aggravate conflicts with other peoples.

[3] Cf. Lynch (2004: ch. 10), Carson (2010: 209), and Mearsheimer (2011: 55, 64, 69–70). Bok (1999: 175) discusses the indirect bad consequences of lying by politicians.

some other very great catastrophe (see Mearsheimer 2011: 31).[4] If we grant that nations are sometimes morally justified in fighting wars that kill large numbers of people in order to protect the lives of their citizens, it seems very implausible to say that lying and deception can never be justified for the purpose of saving lives (cf. Sidgwick 1966: 315 and Carson 2010: 85–6).

42.2 HISTORICALLY IMPORTANT LIES (TOLD BY LEADERS)

Sometimes leaders lie and deceive the public in order to gain support for wars when they believe that the public is unwilling to give adequate support for the wars unless it is deceived. During 1940–1941, President Franklin Roosevelt lied to the American public in order to try to get the US involved in a war with Germany. During the 1940 presidential campaign and on many other occasions, he assured the public that their sons would not be sent off to fight in "foreign wars." Just before the election on November 2, 1940, Roosevelt declared "Your president says your country is not going to war" (Dallek 1979: 250). Later he privately expressed very different intentions.

When he met Roosevelt in August 1941, Winston Churchill requested that the US declare war on Germany. Citing concern about public opinion and the US Congress, Roosevelt said that he could not accede to this request, but, according to Churchill:

> The President... said that he would wage war but not declare it... and that he would become more and more provocative. If the Germans did not like it, they could attack American forces... Everything was to be done to force an 'incident' that could lead to war.
>
> (LaFeber 1989: 381–2; LaFeber's source is the British War Cabinet Minutes of August 19, 1941, which were not made public for more than thirty years)

This does not prove that Roosevelt was lying about his intentions concerning war with Germany before the 1940 election. Perhaps he changed his mind between the times of those two statements. However, if he did change his mind, he never informed the public about this. So, even on the assumption that he changed his mind, he deceived the public by letting his assurance that he was trying to avoid a war with Germany stand on the record (since that was politically expedient for him).

On September 4, 1941, the US Navy warship the *Greer* followed a German submarine for three hours and signaled its location to the British Navy. A British airplane dropped depth charges on the submarine. After this, the German submarine turned and fired a torpedo at the *Greer* (Mearsheimer 2011: 46). A week later, on September 11, 1941,

---

[4] But for a dissenting view see Griffiths (2004: 229–30).

Roosevelt gave a radio address to the American people. He denounced the German attack on the *Greer* and claimed that the fact that the Greer was an American ship was "unmistakable" to the German submarine (Mearsheimer 2011: 47). Roosevelt said:

> We have sought no shooting war with Hitler. We do not seek it now ... But when you see a rattlesnake poised to strike, you do not wait until he has struck before you crush him.
> These Nazi submarines and raiders are the rattlesnakes of the Atlantic ...
> In the waters which we deem necessary for our defense, American naval vessels and American planes will no longer wait until Axis submarines lurking under the water, or Axis raiders on the surface of the sea, strike their deadly blow—first ... Let this warning be clear. From now on, if German or Italian vessels of war enter the waters, the protection of which is necessary for American defense, they do so at their own peril.
>
> (Dallek 1979: 288)

Roosevelt's radio address included two lies and two other deceptive statements. Roosevelt lied when he claimed that the crew of the German submarine knew that the *Greer* was an American ship. "In fact, Navy officials had told Roosevelt two days earlier that there was 'no positive evidence that [the] submarine knew [the] nationality of [the] ship at which it was firing'" (Mearsheimer 2011: 47). He also lied when he said "we have sought no shooting war with Hitler and we do not seek it now." He wanted the US to provoke the German Navy into an incident which would lead to war. He expressed this intention to Churchill less than a month before the Greer incident.

Roosevelt said that the German submarine "fired first" on the *Greer* and implied that the attack on the *Greer* was unprovoked. This was very deceptive because he failed to mention that the *Greer* was tracking the German submarine together with the British Navy and that the submarine had been attacked by a British airplane before it fired on the *Greer* (Mearsheimer 2011: 46–7). Roosevelt's order that the US attack German and Italian submarines on sight "in the waters which we deem necessary for our defense" was deceptively worded. This order did not just apply to waters off the coast of the US. It applied to all of the Atlantic Ocean west of Iceland and a significant area east of Iceland stretching to within 400 miles of Scotland (Reynolds 1982: 216). Roosevelt had declared most of the North Atlantic Ocean "waters which we deem necessary for our defense" (see LaFeber 1989: 377).

Robert Dallek claims that Roosevelt's lying and deception were justified:

> In light of the national unwillingness to face up fully to the international dangers facing the country, it is difficult to fault Roosevelt for building a consensus by devious means. Had he directly presented his view to the public of what it must do ... it would have won him few converts and undermined his popularity and ability to lead by confronting ambivalent Americans with choices they did not want to make. Further, if he advised the public of the fact that the U-boat had fired in defense and that Hitler did not then seem intent on attacking America's Atlantic traffic, as Churchill had

reported, he would have risked having to wait for the collapse of Russia and Britain's near demise before gaining broad national support for a call to arms ... that would have been a failure of his responsibility as Commander in Chief.

(Dallek 1979: 289; also see 530)

It is likely that Roosevelt's dishonesty helped to make the US better prepared for the war when it came. Roosevelt's fears of German victory without US entry into the war were quite reasonable. During the summer of 1941, most people thought that the Soviet Union was on the verge of collapse because of the German invasion. A German conquest of the Soviet Union would have been a tremendous catastrophe. With all of Russia and almost all of the rest of Europe at his disposal, Hitler could have created a huge empire that would have been invulnerable to invasion by any conceivable adversaries and that, together with Japan, could threaten the security of the rest of the world.

It is widely believed that George W. Bush, Richard Cheney, and other members of the Bush administration lied to and deceived the American public in order to gain support for the 2003 Iraq War. The charges against the Bush Administration include the following:

1. On the basis of very little evidence, members of the administration falsely claimed that there were close ties between Iraq and al Qaeda. Among other things, they said that there was "'bulletproof' evidence that Saddam was closely allied with Osama bin Laden" (Mearsheimer 2011: 50).[5]
2. The Bush administration made numerous false claims to the effect that it was *certain* that Iraq possessed weapons of mass destruction. In August 2002 Cheney said "there is no doubt that Saddam Hussein now has weapons of mass destruction. There is no doubt that he is amassing them to use against our friends, against our allies, and against us" (Mearsheimer 2011: 51). On February 5, 2003, Secretary of State Powell told the UN "There can be no doubt that Saddam Hussein has biological weapons and the capability to produce many many more" (Mearsheimer 2011: 51). On September 20, 2002, Cheney claimed that there was "irrefutable evidence" that Saddam Hussein was trying to build a nuclear bomb (Carson 2010: 212).

---

[5] Mearsheimer clearly shows that the Bush administration deceived the public by encouraging the false belief that Iraq was involved in the 9-11 attacks on the US. "The Bush administration made numerous statements before the war that were designed to imply that Saddam was in part responsible for the attacks on September 11 ... The aim ... was to lead the American public to draw a false conclusion. It is no accident that when the war began in mid-March 2003, about half of the American people believed that the Iraqi dictator had helped bring down the World Trade Center" (Mearsheimer 2011: 52). Mearsheimer's evidence is as follows. In his letter to Congress on March 18, 2003, just before he started the 2003 Iraq War, Bush stated that it was necessary to take action against nations "... who planned, authorized, committed, or aided the terrorist attacks that occurred on September 11, 2001" (Mearsheimer 2011: 53). In September 2003, Cheney said that if the US prevails in Iraq "we will have struck a major blow right at the heart of the base, if you will, the geographic base of the terrorists who have had us under assault for many years, but most especially on 9/11" (Mearsheimer 2011: 53-4).

3. In early 2003, Bush and Rumsfeld falsely claimed that they were seeking peace and that it might still be possible to avoid a war when, in fact, Bush had already decided to go to war (Mearsheimer 2011: 55; also see Carson 2010: 218).[6]

For additional evidence and details supporting these three charges see Korn (2003), Rich (2006), Carson (2010), and Mearsheimer (2011). Carson and Mearsheimer stress that claims to the effect that it was *certain* that Iraq possessed or was actively seeking to acquire nuclear weapons and other weapons of mass destruction were lies. In fact, the evidence was mixed and members of the administration knew of many reasons to question the factual claims that they made with such confidence (see Rich 2006: 187, 190, 216–17, 246–7, 249–54, 256–7, 264; Carson 2010: 216–17; Mearsheimer 2011: 50–2; Roberts 2015). To take just one example, while it might not have been a lie for Cheney to say that Iraq was actively seeking to acquire nuclear weapons (he might have believed this), his repeated claim that this *was certain* was a lie. He was aware of reasons to question these claims and his evidence for them. Further, many people in the intelligence community reported being pressured by Cheney and other members of the Bush Administration to give reports favorable to the case for war (Korn 2003: 213–14).[7]

Carson also argues that members of the Bush administration were guilty of deception by failing to correct false claims (including claims in Bush's 2003 State of the Union

---

[6] Herring and Robinson (2014) claim that the British government deceived the British public in much the same way. They contend that, contrary to what it said publicly, the British government had no intention of avoiding war when it took complaints about Iraq's WMD (weapons of mass destruction) to the UN in early 2003. A leaked British Cabinet office briefing from July 2002 titled *Iraq: Conditions for Military Action* said the following:

> It is just possible that an ultimatum could be cast in terms which Saddam would reject (because he is unwilling to accept unfettered access) and which would not be regarded as unreasonable by the international community, but failing that (or an Iraqi attack) we would be most unlikely to have a legal basis for military action by January 2003 (Herring and Robinson 2014: 224).

Herring and Robinson tartly observe "This framing is not what one would expect from a sincere effort at disarming Iraq peacefully through the UN" (Herring and Robinson 2014: 224).

[7] According to Herring and Robinson (2014–15), the British government of Tony Blair was involved in a similar kind of deception in its manipulation of intelligence reports about Iraq's WMD to gain support for its participation in the 2003 invasion of Iraq. The British government thought that the only legal basis for initiating a war with Iraq was Iraq's alleged development of WMD in defiance of the UN (Herring and Robinson 2014: 223, and (2014–15: 564). For this reason it thought that intelligence reports needed to make a case for saying that Iraq was actively developing WMD (Herring and Robinson 2014–15: 559). But Herring and Robinson give careful and detailed evidence that the key intelligence document, Dossier X, which was made public in September 2002 and used to justify the war to the British public, was deliberately modified to deceive the public and provide a justification for attacking Iraq. Here is one particularly striking example. An earlier draft of the document listed Iran, Libya, North Korea, and Iraq as WMD threats. On March 11, 2002, British Foreign Secretary Jack Straw said, "the paper has to show why there is exceptional threat from Iraq. It does not quite do this yet." Four days later a minute from John Scarlet (Chair of the Joint Intelligence Committee) suggested that the document omit mention of the other countries saying, "This would have the benefit of obscuring the fact that in terms of WMD, Iraq is not that exceptional" (Herring and Robinson 2014–15: 561–2).

Address) that they later had reason to think were false (Carson 2010: 216–17). Most people frequently make statements that they later discover to be false. This does not necessarily involve either lying or deception if one believes what one says when one says it. However, if one later discovers that what one said is false, failing to correct one's earlier mistakes sometimes constitutes deception. Suppose that I make an honest mistake and tell you something that I later discover to be false. Further, I know that you now accept and rely on what I told you earlier. If I realize my mistake and clearly have the opportunity to correct it, then by failing to correct it, I am intentionally causing you to persist in believing something that is false. This is especially clear in cases in which I state something important *on the record* and ask others to rely on it for making very important decisions about matters of life or death. These conditions are clearly satisfied in the case of some of the false claims that the Bush administration used to generate support for the 2003 Iraq War (Carson 2010: 216–17).

Bush's memoirs very briefly address the charge that he lied as a pretext for the 2003 invasion of Iraq. He admits that after the war "the WMD stockpiles everyone expected were not found" (Bush 2010: 292). He continues:

> The left trotted out a new mantra: "Bush Lied, People Died." The charge was illogical. If I wanted to mislead the country into war, why would I pick an allegation that was certain to be disproven publicly shortly after we invaded that country? The charge was dishonest. Members of the previous administration, John Kerry, John Edwards, and the vast majority of Congress had all read the same intelligence that I had and concluded that Iraq had WMD. So had intelligence agencies all around the world.
>
> (Bush 2010: 262)

Bush did *not* lie when he said that Iraq had WMD (as he used this term). He and many others believed that Iraq still possessed some of the chemical weapons that it had used earlier against Iran and the Kurds. But *he and his administration lied and deceived the public about many other things*, e.g., that it was *certain* that Iraq was actively seeking to acquire nuclear weapons and that Iraq helped to bring about the September 11 attacks on the US. So, his memoirs give a plausible answer to the charge that he lied when he said that Iraq had WMD but he completely (and misleadingly) ignores numerous other charges of lying and deception and gives no reason whatever for thinking they are ill-founded or dishonest.

I choose these two examples of lying as a pretext for war because of their historical importance. There are many cases of lying by leaders for other reasons. Leaders often lie to gain support for other policies they support. Sometimes leaders lie to deny blame for their own failed or immoral policies. In 1960, President Eisenhower and other members of his administration lied when they said that the U-2 spy plane shot down over the Soviet Union was a weather reconnaissance plane that had flown off course. They said this thinking that the pilot of the plane had been killed. Their lies were exposed when the pilot was put on trial in the Soviet Union. In response to harsh international criticism of the Israeli's Army's massacre of more than sixty civilians (mostly women and children) in the West Bank village of Qibya in October 1953, Israeli Prime Minister Ben Gurion lied and blamed the massacre on vigilante Jewish civilians who lived near Qibya (Morris 1997: 257–9).[8]

42.3 Lying and deception about the historical record

In 1939 Hitler lied and claimed that Poland had attacked Germany as a pretext for Germany's invasion of Poland on September 1, 1939. He went beyond lying about it and ordered the SS to fabricate phony evidence of a Polish attack on Germany and a German radio station in Gleiwitz near the Polish border. Concentration-camp inmates dressed in Polish Army uniforms were murdered and left as "casualties" of the alleged attack. A Polish-speaking German gave a brief anti-German speech on the radio in Polish to give credibility to the story. This fabrication was designed to deceive the German people into thinking that Germany had justification for its war with Poland. It was claimed that Poland had earlier rejected the Führer's "generous peace offer" (Shirer 1960: 518–20, 594–5).

Lying about history often poisons relations between peoples and nations and can generate and aggravate hatreds and conflicts.

Lying and deception by German leaders during and after WW I helped to create the *Dolchstoßlegende*—the myth that the German military was defeated by traitors on the home front who "stabbed their country in the back." This myth denies the plain facts of history. Germany was defeated because it was overwhelmed by a large coalition of enemies whose population and economic power greatly exceeded its own. The widespread acceptance of the myth of the stab in the back by the German people was one of the principal causes of the rise of Nazism and the Holocaust; indeed Hitler's fervent belief in the myth (and his belief that Jews were largely responsible for the stab in the back) were arguably the principal causes of his murderous anti-Semitism. By Hitler's own account, his acceptance of the *Dolchstoß* story was a decisive event in his life that caused him to passionately hate Jews and Marxists (Carson 2010: 238–40).

---

[8] This attack was a reprisal for a series of attacks from Jordan between May and October 1953 which resulted in the death of six Israelis (Morris 1997: 244). The attack on Qibya was led by Ariel Sharon (later Prime Minister of Israel) and approved by the Israeli government. The Israeli military units in question were ordered "to attack and temporarily occupy the village, carry out the destruction and maximum killing, in order to drive out the inhabitants of the village from their homes" (Morris 1997: 245).

Lying by German leaders whose press reports flatly denied the disastrous military defeats suffered by Germany in August 1918[9] made Hitler and many other Germans completely unprepared for the news of Germany's defeat in November 1918, just four months after the seemingly victorious German army was advancing on Paris after having defeated Russia. Learning the news of Germany's defeat while convalescing in a military hospital was a shattering and life-altering experience for Hitler—he describes this experience vividly in *Mein Kampf* (see Carson 2010: 238 and Hitler 1943: 204–6).

In addition, evasive and deceptive testimony by the greatly loved and revered war leader Field Marshal von Hindenburg to the Reichstag Commission of Inquiry on the causes of Germany's defeat lent support to his claim that Germany was not defeated on the battlefield but rather defeated by traitors on the home front. In the eyes of public opinion, he successfully shifted blame from himself and other leaders of the wartime government and military to leftists on the home front. Hindenburg refused to answer questions about the German government's disastrous decision to begin unrestricted submarine warfare in 1917 which caused the United States to enter the war—a decision that Hindenburg supported and helped to make (von der Goltz 2009: 67–8 and Carson 2010: 233–7).

Sometimes people lie about history to defend the honor of their countries and paint an inspiring view of their history. Two clear examples of this are Turkey's denial of its genocide against the Armenians in the early twentieth century and the lies and fabrications by the Daughters of the Confederacy in trying to put the Confederate States of America in a favorable light. Among other things, they claimed that the Confederacy did not fight the American Civil War to defend slavery and that it was planning to end slavery (see Carson 2010: 243–8). The total fabrications of the Protocols of the Elders of Zion (a document created in Czarist Russia) were intended to justify and incite hatred and animus against the Jewish people.

42.4 HALF-TRUTHS OR PARTIAL TRUTHS

Half-truths or partial truths are narratives consisting of true statements or sets of true statements that selectively emphasize facts that support a particular assessment of an issue and selectively ignore or minimize other relevant facts that support contrary assessments. For example, a politician might "spin" the interpretation of recent events to support the claim that her policies were successful if she describes the good consequences of those policies in considerable detail and omits any mention of the bad

---

[9] As early as August 10, 1918, the German high command realized that these defeats meant that Germany no longer had any hope of winning the war and communicated this to the Kaiser (Carson 2010: 233–4).

consequences. A man's description of his marriage is a half-truth or partial truth if it contains a long and accurate account of unkind and hurtful things that his wife has said and done to him but mentions only a few of the equal (or greater) number of unkind and hurtful things he has said and done to her. The use of half-truths that selectively omit certain information to make a particular view seem more plausible than it would otherwise is a very common way of making deceptive/misleading claims about history (cf. Herring and Robinson 2014: 558–9). Those who espouse half-truths frequently intend to deceive others, but not always or necessarily.

The public discussion of the conflict between Israel and the Palestinian people includes many partial truths. Many of the parties to this conflict and their supporters in other countries endorse partial truths. They are able to cite a long list of injuries inflicted by one of the parties on the other, but, at the same time, they downplay, ignore, or deny injuries caused by the party with whom they sympathize. Here are some salient truths that are downplayed, ignored, or denied by many Palestinian critics of Israel who have a detailed knowledge of Palestinian grounds for complaint against Israel: the numerous Arab riots and murders of Jewish residents of Palestine in the 1920s and 1930s, including the massacre of sixty-four Jews in Hebron in August 1929, the killing of sixty-nine other Jews in Palestine during the same week, the 143 different attacks on Jewish settlements in 1937 (Morris 1999: 114, 116, 145), the killing of roughly 200 Israeli civilians and scores of Israeli soldiers in Arab attacks across Israel's borders from 1948 to 1956 (Morris 1999: 271), widespread violence against and persecution of Jews in many Arab/Islamic countries after 1948 (850,000 Jews left Arab/Islamic countries after 1948—many of them fled violence and persecution, many were expelled, and many were dispossessed of their property; in 1948 seventy-six Jews were slaughtered in Aden, dozens were killed in Morocco, thirteen were killed in Libya, and anti-Jewish riots in Cairo killed at least fifty people[10]), and the pronouncements of many Arab and Islamic leaders calling for the destruction of Israel. At the time of this writing (Fall 2015), some Palestinian leaders are inciting people to violence against Israeli Jews by propounding the lie that the Israeli government is planning to tear down the Dome of the Rock Mosque in Jerusalem (one of the holiest sites in Islam). This has led to the murder of many Israeli civilians in a series of knife attacks.

Some salient truths ignored, downplayed, or denied by many Israelis and supporters of Israel are the following: the terrorist attacks by the Jewish groups the Irgun and Lehi against Arabs, the British, and UN officials prior to the independence of Israel, the leadership role of Menachem Begin (who was later Israeli Prime Minister) in the Irgun and the leadership of Yitzhak Shamir (who was also later Prime Minister of Israel) in Lehi, the massacre of 254 Arab villagers in Deir Yassin by the Israeli Army in 1948,[11] the slaughter of more than 200 Arab civilians in the town of Lydda in July 1948 (Shavit

---

[10] Wikipedia, and Morris (2008: 412–15).
[11] See Morris (1999: 207–9). The number of victims is in dispute. Morris puts the number of Arabs murdered at 100 to 110.

2013: 107), the Israeli army's massacre of more sixty civilians in the Arab village of Qibya in 1953 (Morris 1997: 227–62), the fact that Israel did not allow the 700,000 Arabs who left what is now Israeli territory during the 1948 war to return to their homes or retain their property,[12] and the large number of Arab civilians killed by the Israeli military in retaliation for Arab attacks on Israel.

Both of these lists of could be greatly expanded. The anti-Palestinian partial truths are widely accepted in the US. The anti-Israel partial truths are widely accepted in much of the rest of the world.

I do not venture a view as to the overall balance of injuries and grounds for complaint among the two parties to this conflict. I claim only that the facts I have listed are salient truths the knowledge of which is necessary for a well-informed moral assessment of this conflict. Clearly, many people have very strong views about the conflict that are based on ignorance or denial of one set of these salient facts. Their views and attitudes are ill-informed and based on a one-sided knowledge of relevant information.

Many examples of half-truths can be found in Lerone Bennett's book *Forced into Glory* (Bennett 2007), a harsh indictment of Abraham Lincoln which alleges that he was a racist who cared little about slavery and, contrary to popular belief, was not a good or admirable person. Bennett cites many facts that are prima facie evidence that Lincoln was a racist who was not sufficiently concerned with ending slavery or promoting the welfare of African Americans. But his book abounds with half-truths and what would be more aptly called one quarter-truths or one eighth-truths that are very unfair to Lincoln.[13]

Here is one example. Bennett claims that Lincoln always favored the immediate deportation of freed slaves (Bennett 2007: 415).[14] He attributes this to Lincoln's racism and dislike of blacks and says that Lincoln wanted to carry out an "ethnic cleansing" of America (Bennett 2007: ch. 10).

Lincoln was a long-time supporter of colonization. Bennett documents this, but he fails to report any of the abundant evidence that Lincoln changed his mind and did not actively support colonization during the latter part of his presidency. Bennett also fails to mention the very strong grounds for thinking that Lincoln's support for colonization was motivated largely by his desire to stem opposition to the Emancipation Proclamation (see Carson 2015: 95–110). One very important piece of evidence of his waning enthusiasm for colonization is that, although the preliminary version of the Emancipation Proclamation (September 22, 1862) states that "the effort to colonize persons of African descent, with their consent . . . will be continued" (Lincoln 1989: II,

---

[12] There is considerable controversy about how many of the 700,000 were forcibly expelled by Israel, but many of them were expelled (see Morris 1999: 252–7 and Shavit 2013: 108). On the most charitable interpretation, Israel dispossessed 700,000 Palestinians of their homes and property without due process of law and has never compensated them or their descendants.

[13] See Barr (2014: 277–82) for evidence of Bennett's use of partial truths and selective omissions.

[14] Bennett's use of the word "deportation" is misleading—Lincoln only supported the voluntary colonization of freed slaves. On this point see Carson (2015: 97–100).

368) the final version of the proclamation 100 days later (January 1, 1863) makes no mention of any plans for colonization. After his proposed Constitutional Amendment in December 1862,[15] he never again publicly proposed any measures calling for large-scale colonization. Bennett also fails to mention the fact that, as President, Lincoln did *almost nothing* to implement colonization apart from a small settlement on an island off the coast of Haiti and that he soon abandoned this venture (Carson 2015: 105). Late in his life, Lincoln made preliminary statements about the place of blacks in the postwar United States (including statements about education and voting rights) that *clearly* presuppose that they would remain in the country after the end of slavery (see Carson 2015: 106, 118). Bennett also fails to acknowledge John Hay's well-known diary entry from 1864 which reports that Lincoln had "sloughed off the idea of colonization" (Carson 2015: 100).[16]

42.5 OBLIGATIONS OF HISTORIANS TO BE TRUTHFUL AND ACCURATE

Historians have very serious obligations to be truthful, accurate, and fair in their accounts of the historical past. Public opinion and public policy need to be informed by full and accurate understandings of the historical past. Historical knowledge and understanding arguably also possess intrinsic value. Because academic history is a highly specialized field, progress in overall historical understanding depends on the honesty of individual historians who do primary research and help explain parts of the larger historical narrative. People debate the possibility or desirability of historians being completely objective and unbiased, but clearly lying, deception, and the fabrication of evidence by historians are prima facie very wrong. They violate the public trust and authority that their status as historians accords them (for discussions of these issues see Hoffer 2007 and Jaeger 2015).

---

[15] This amendment included plans for ending slavery and the voluntary colonization of freed slaves in tropical lands outside of the United States.
[16] Hay was Lincoln's personal secretary.

CHAPTER 43

LYING AND THE ARTS

BETTINA KÜMMERLING-MEIBAUER

43.1 INTRODUCTION

At a meeting of the Historical and Antiquarian Club of Hartford, Connecticut, the author Mark Twain presented a short essay, "On the Decay of the Art of Lying" (1880), in which he laments in a tongue-in-cheek manner the decline of the fashion of lying:

> Lying is universal—we all do it. Therefore, the wise thing is for us diligently to train ourselves to lie thoughtfully, judiciously; to lie with a good object, and not an evil one; to lie for others' advantage, and not our own; (...) to lie firmly, frankly, squarely, with head erect, not haltingly, tortuously, with pusillanimous mien, as being ashamed of our high calling.
>
> (Twain 1882: 217)

Nine years later, Oscar Wilde tied in with Twain's ideas in his famous essay "The Decay of Lying" (1889) by claiming that "Lying, the telling of beautiful untrue things, is the proper aim of Art" (Wilde 1891: 36). Both authors agree that lying is a universal human capacity which demands certain intellectual and moral reflections. Consequently, they express the opinion that successful lying is comparable to the creation of art. Twain's and Wilde's essays started a dispute that was continued in the twentieth century and stimulated different authors and philosophers, such as Jacques Derrida, Umberto Eco, Karl Kraus, and Friedrich Nietzsche, to reflect on the close relationship between literature, art, and lying. They call attention to the observation that literature has always stood in a vexed relation to lying. Literature and other forms of media are heavily populated with liars, child as well as adult characters whose lies propel the plots of the stories and are vital to the moral dimensions of the texts. Hence, the telling of lies is a central issue in literature and other art forms, be it single acts of lying, lying characters, or an entire web of lies in which almost all of the fictional characters are entangled. A web or network of lies includes at least three persons who are lying to one another and beyond that to other people so that the single lies are inextricably linked.

Despite some scholarly monographs and edited volumes that paid tribute to this intriguing topic, it is surprisingly underrated in academia. Moreover, comprehensive studies on this subject from a historical and/or comparative perspective are almost non-existent. Against this background, this chapter aims at highlighting the great significance of the topic of lying in the arts with an emphasis on a) the potential connection of lying with specific literary genres and the related question whether fiction can be understood as a specific form of lying, b) the depiction of liars, and c) the representation of standard situations of lying. The major examples are drawn from literary texts and films, with a brief outlook on d) painting and photography by addressing the often disputed issue of whether pictures are capable of lying.

43.2 LYING AND LITERARY GENRES

Although lying characters and situations of lying are observable across all literary genres and over all times, from classical antiquity to the present, some literary genres are intimately associated with the topic of lying, in particular the tall tale, the detective story, the dystopian novel, and the travelogue. The tall tale originates in oral folklore and centers on the figure of the trickster who outsmarts other people by inventing sophisticated cooked-up stories. Trickster tales have spread all over the world and influenced a variety of literary works, such as Homer's classical poems *Iliad* and *Odyssey* (both eighth century BC), in which Odysseus represents the lying character per se who is even praised by Athena, the goddess of wisdom, for his ingenious lies, Rudolf Erich Raspe's mocking *Baron Munchausen's Narrative of His Marvelous Travels and Campaigns in Russia* (1786), and Joel Chandler Harris' collection of stories *Uncle Remus. His Songs and His Sayings* (1902 [1880]). What these works have in common is that the main characters manage to survive by using their wits. They apply their skills in deceiving friends and foes alike whenever it seems appropriate and serves their own advantages (Bloom 2010). The interest in tall tales and related genres results from their non-compliance with societal norms and the reader's pleasure in seeing right through the speaker's lies.

While the literary works connected with the trickster figure serve mainly to amuse the reader, the detective story enmeshes the readers in a web of lies and entices them to follow the footsteps of the investigating detective in order to decipher the clues that finally solve the criminal case. By comprehending the reasons why a person is lying to other persons and under which circumstances, readers are invited to analytically consider how one lie is connected with another, but also to reflect on the moral implications of lying. The same applies to the dystopian novel, in which the characters are typically tangled in a web of propagandistic lies, and also forced to tell lies in order to protect themselves and others. Prominent examples are George Orwell's *1984* (1949) and Yevgeny Zamyatin's *My* (We) (Zamyatin 1924 [1920]).

Another popular genre associated with lying is the travelogue. Ever since the appearance of Lucian's parody *Vera Historia* (A True History, 2nd century) (Lucian 1905), travel tales have come under suspicion of only exaggerating the perils and wonders experienced during travels and also of lacking in veracity. This suspicion had an impact on the reception of subsequent travel tales, which have then in turn been accused of mixing truth and lies. This debate also referred to related genres and reached a peak in England in the seventeenth and early eighteenth centuries, when jest books captured the book market. The subtitles, which include expressions such as "lie," "improbability," and "probable improbable story," alert readers of the jest books' potential untruthfulness. Moreover, many readers at that time had a great interest in lying contests and banter shows, and those events typically took place in coffee houses and taverns, and they propagated the development of hoaxes, shams, and railleries. The most ambitious hoax back then was *A True and Exact Relation of the Strange Finding out of Moses His Tomb* (Anon 1657), a combination of a traveler's tale, a pamphlet, and a Jesuit plot-narrative (Loveman 2008: 47ff.). Distinguished by ironic humor and witty remarks, their main task was to feign credulity in order to involve the audience in a guessing game: A successful sham had to be recognized as such, implying that a sufficient number of readers was actually able to understand that the account was purposefully designed as a hoax. Consequently, the author was to be praised for his skills of deception. In addition, many shams turned out to be subversive narratives, as they were used as a cover for political satire.

The popularity of these narrative forms impacted on the assessment of the novels written by Daniel Defoe, Samuel Richardson, and Jonathan Swift that were released in the first half of the eighteenth century. As readers and critics mocked the stories' inconsistencies and ridiculed the authors' truth-claims, they provoked a fierce debate on the crucial question of whether the novel as such should be evaluated on the same level as the acclaimed hoaxes and shams or whether it should be regarded as a genre in its own right, thereby pushing the discussion of the relationship between fiction and lie into new directions (Loveman 2008: 199). The origin of this dispute goes back to Plato's attack on the status of poetry as a falsification of reality and has continued over the centuries. Among those authors who reflected on the impact of lying and its relationship to fiction were Giovanni Boccaccio, Daniel Defoe, John Locke, Michel de Montaigne, and Jonathan Swift, amongst others (Steinbrenner 2007).

The conundrum of fiction versus lie is one of the salient topics in their works, as is, for instance, evident in Defoe's novel *Robinson Crusoe* (3 vols, 1719–20), in which the author discusses the relation between fiction and lying in the third volume, *The Serious Reflections of Robinson Crusoe* (1720). Two of the chapters in this volume, "Of Lewd and Immodest Discourse" and "Of Talking Falsely," are an attack on those critics who claim that the first volume is telling a lie. Defoe makes no effort to hide the fact that a part of the story is pure invention, however, he defends his use of "random lies" that occur at the level of the allegoric explanation of the otherwise realistic story (Defoe 2008 [1719–20]; Smyth 2002).

Jonathan Swift even goes a step further with his masterpiece *Gulliver's Travels* (Swift 2001 [1726]) that he dubs "lying tales" by introducing a fictive editor who claims that censorship has mutilated the body of text and who accuses the narrative of Gulliver's travels of being a lie (Chase 1993: 341). Within the story, the relationship of fiction versus lie is picked up when Gulliver resides in the Houyhnhnm country where the inhabitants cultivate friendship, reason, and civility. In contrast to the Yahoos who represent mankind, these people are not able to lie (Swift 2001 [1726]: 246). The concepts of disbelief and deception are unheard of in the Houyhnhnm country, therefore, the Houyhnhnm master cannot comprehend Gulliver's reasoning when pointing out the probable fact that his own people will not believe his stories. The cognitive naivety of the Houyhnhnms comes to the fore when the master condemns lies as an offense against the belief that language should be used to transmit only true information. This principle would be flouted whenever words convey falsehoods or when pure imaginative stories are presented that cannot be proven as truthful (Terry 1994). By juxtaposing these different positions in relation to language and fiction, Swift triggered a debate which still continues today and simmers in the dispute on literary hoaxes and bogus texts.

In this regard a distinction is made between literary fakes concealing their origin and those that discreetly point to their own art of invention by means of ironic clues that help the reader recognize the deception. Julia Abramson (2005) suggests classifying literary works that fall under the latter category as "mystification" (13). A prime example of this type of deception is Marcel Schwob's *Vies imaginaires* (Imaginary Lives), (Schwob 1924 [1896]), a collection of twenty-two semi-biographical short stories about historical figures whose private lives are pretty much unknown. Schwob retells their biographies by substantially complementing them with invented stories. Interestingly, those episodes which seem to be authentic and true are fictional, while others which seem unreliable are true. The revealing of the faked passages provokes a reflection on the part of the readers, who are requested to reconsider their expectations concerning genre conventions.

In contrast, faked autobiographies and memoirs usually do not include clear hints inviting readers to demystify the allegedly authentic life story. A case in point for such literary forgery is the award-winning fictional memoir *Bruchstücke: Aus einer Kindheit 1939-1948* (Fragments. Memories of a Wartime Childhood) by Swiss author Binjamin Wilkomirski aka Bruno Dösseker (Wilkomirski 1995). As a son of Swiss parents he took on the identity of a Jewish child and Holocaust survivor, claiming to describe his wartime experiences, which he was finally able to retrieve after a long-lasting amnesia. Within a few years, the author was debunked as being a fraud, his book withdrawn from the stores, awards retracted. Wilkomirski was not the first author to write a faked autobiography telling of his sufferings caused by the Holocaust; however, it is his name that became synonymous with this phenomenon (Worth 2015: 99f.).

43.3 Lying Characters

One of the earliest famous lying characters appears in Aesop's fable "The Shepherd's Boy and the Wolf" (sixth century BC), also known as "The Boy Who Cried Wolf" (Aesop 1972). This story is an example of the risk of deception: A shepherd is bored with looking after his flock and tells the villagers that a wolf is attacking the sheep, and so they all come running. After several false alarms, nobody believes in the shepherd's truthfulness any longer, and so the herd gets destroyed when a real wolf attack finally happens. The universal message of Aesop's fable ("A liar will not be believed, even when he tells the truth") is obviously the main reason why it has endured for centuries in anthologies and schoolbooks for children and is still present in contemporary picturebook adaptations. Since this fable is regarded as a prototypical stance of a specific human demeanor, the English expression *to cry wolf* entered the lexicon as a synonym for 'to give a false alarm'.

The most popular lying character, however, stems from an Italian children's classic: the wooden puppet Pinocchio from Carlo Collodi's *Le avventure di Pinocchio* (The Adventures of Pinocchio), (Collodi 1988 [1881]) has become an international icon whose portrait frequently decorates covers of books that deal with the topic of lying. Pinocchio's telling of three lies to his guardian about the whereabouts of some gold coins is only a minor episode in the original text; however, his severe punishment—with every lie, his nose is growing longer and longer—has been memorized by generations of readers. While the first part of Collodi's book stresses the dishonesty of lying and its negative impact on Pinocchio, the second part focuses on the protagonist's moral development, which leads to his final redemption.

These two examples demonstrate that lying characters already appear in stories targeted at children, typically at the ages of four and up. This observation matches with studies in developmental psychology that have demonstrated that the capability to lie is not innate but usually acquired in a basic form at four years of age (Lee 2013). Since the acquisition of lying is closely connected to the theory of mind, that is, the capability to understand other people's thoughts, feelings, and imaginations, the representation of lying characters in fictional works requires the reader's ability to develop an emotional and empathic attitude toward the characters (Zunshine 2006; Vermeule 2010). In order to achieve this goal, readers may get access to the lying characters' motivations as well as to their mental dispositions and inner feelings. These processes are already mirrored in children's books, where the depiction of lying characters and the moral evaluation of lying are adjusted to the prospective child readers' cognitive, epistemic, emotional, and moral development.

While many picturebooks for younger children follow a didactic purpose when highlighting that lying is morally reprehensible and has to be punished, crossover picturebooks such as Margaret Wild's *Fox* (2006) and children's novels targeted at older children address the multiple types and functions of lying, thus inviting the child reader to consider the potential reasons that force people into lies (Ringrose 2006;

Kümmerling-Meibauer and Meibauer 2015; Silva-Díaz 2015). *Pippi Långstrump* (Pippi Longstocking, 1945) by Astrid Lindgren, on the other hand, is a good example of those children's books that focus on nonsensical lies, i.e., lies that serve not to harm anyone but to entertain through the imaginative power of the lie-telling characters.

Yet other children's books concentrate on the moral consequences of lies for both the lying characters and the deceived persons, as is evident in Mark Twain's *The Adventures of Tom Sawyer* (1876) and its sequel *The Adventures of Huckleberry Finn* (1884) (see Twain 2010a, b). The protagonists in both novels routinely tell lies, whose outcome has either a comical or serious effect. They lie in order to avoid punishment, to protect others and themselves, but also for the pure joy of confusing other people. Furthermore, both novels focus on a moral dilemma, which forces the protagonists to make serious decisions. Tom, as a secret witness of the doctor's murder by Injun Joe, is torn between fear of Injun Joe's revenge and the craving to save the life of the drunkard Potter, who is falsely accused of murder. Huckleberry Finn, by contrast, is torn between his attachment to the runaway slave Jim and the obligation to follow the societal laws. In both cases, the boys take a courageous decision by overcoming their fear and turning against the society's norms. In the first case, Tom unmasks the deceptive behavior of Injun Joe by telling the actual truth, whereas Huck is forced to consistently lie in order to save Jim from being captured. This complementary presentation emphasizes that telling a truth and telling a lie might both be considered adequate reactions, depending on the situational context.

Justine Larbalestier's young adult novel, *Liar* (2009), even goes a step further as the main protagonist, a 17-year old girl called Micah, is a notorious liar. Since the whole story is exclusively told from her point of view, the reader is totally dependent on the girl's report. Although she promises in the beginning to tell nothing but the truth, she confesses later that she had in fact lied. This happens only after one third of the story is already told and Micah promises here to stick to the true story henceforward. In the end, she finally blames the readers' credulity, offering them four different versions of the story, none of which can be unequivocally authenticated owing to the first-person narrator's unreliability. Since Micah is involved in a murder case and suspected of being a potential serial killer, readers are trapped in a web of lies, which they cannot entangle unambiguously (Mallan 2013).

This overview illustrates that the topic of lying in children's literature is gradually becoming more complex, apparently mirroring the different developmental stages in the acquisition of lying (Kümmerling-Meibauer and Meibauer 2011). In this respect, children's and young adult novels may be considered as precursors for the understanding of more complex lying characters in literature written for adults.

World literature is teeming with lying characters, but ever since his creation Iago—a main character in William Shakespeare's play *Othello* (1604)—is regarded as the prototypical liar, who blends the essential features of a wicked person empowered by the capacity to manipulate other people. Skilled in fooling other persons by playing diverse roles and distorting truths, Iago uses elaborated rhetorical tricks to deceive various characters, but above all, Othello. The famous temptation scene (act III, 3) reveals

Iago's perfidious strategy when raising suspicions about Desdemona's honesty. He ostensibly presents incontestable facts but misleads the listener into drawing wrong conclusions. By echoing words pronounced by Othello, he suggests that they carry some second meaning that he dares not to express frankly: "Indeed?—Othello: Indeed? Ay, indeed. Discern'st thou aught in that? Is he not honest?—Iago: Honest, my lord?—Othello: Honest? Ay, honest..." (Shakespeare, *Othello*, III, 3, 104–8).

The rhetorical figure of repetition displays how Othello interprets Iago's echoes as an attempt to communicate an unspoken message (Keller 2009: 169). As a consequence, Othello attempts to get more information from Iago and finally believes he has discovered Iago's hidden message: Desdemona is unfaithful to him. Iago has planned this entire conversation and pretends to mirror Othello's turns and to cooperate with him. But in reality, Iago obscures his real intentions and insinuates something he knows to be false. In the temptation scene, Iago uses arguments based on probabilities to prepare Othello for the report of Cassio talking about Desdemona in his sleep. He provides these insinuations in the form of two lies: the narrative of Cassio's dream and the assertion that he has seen Cassio with the handkerchief that Othello had given Desdemona as a present. Iago's capacity to deceive Othello becomes obvious another two scenes later when he juggles with Othello's credulity by increasing his doubts about Desdemona's innocence. The innocuous word play on "lie," "Lie with her? Lie on her? We say 'lie on her', when they belie her" (Shakespeare, *Othello*, IV, 1, 34–5), visualizes Iago's strategy of switching between abstract and concrete statements on the one hand, and declining all responsibility by giving vague answers, on the other. He uses fallacious arguments to distort the facts so that his conclusions seem to result from the conditions he has indicated (Porter 1991). As a result, Iago's lies start to totally capture Othello's mind, leading to the tragedy of Desdemona's murder and Othello's suicide. Although Iago seems to be driven by envy and vengefulness, these feelings alone do not explain his devilish comportment. Most often, he is in the position of a bystander, enjoying his manipulative game, which enables him to exploit other people's weaknesses like an almighty player. Since Iago has no personal gains from his wicked lies and refuses any explanations by making a vow of silence at the very end, he has often been regarded as the incarnation of evil per se (Raatzsch 2009).

Whether liars may be rated as bad or good, considering the reasons and moral implications of their acts of lying is key in literary works and has spawned remarkable lying characters in world literature. The same applies to the depiction of liars in films. In contrast to written texts, films may reveal both verbal and visual cues associated with lying. Such cues are often connected to emotional reactions evoked by the lies and their consequences for the liars and the persons they have lied to.

A notorious liar is center stage in the award-winning American TV series *Mad Men* (various directors, USA 2007–15), which focuses on the advertising milieu of the 1960s in New York and follows the main character's development over the course of thirty years. Don Draper, aka Dick Whitman, a creative director and philanderer, leads a second-hand life as a renegade, who fights to protect his status in the community while hiding his true identity from everybody. Situated in a social milieu and a professional field where telling lies seems to be quite convenient, Don Draper is cautious about being caught as a liar and is better at avoiding this than most people in his environment (South, Carveth, and Irwin 2010). As the archetype of the "man in the gray flannel suit"—an icon of businessmen in the 1960s—he is permanently lying about who he is to everyone, including his wife. By doing this, he constructs a tissue of lies that prevents his social position from being put in jeopardy. In addition, Don Draper is skilled in manipulating other people's perception of him and trained in using ruses and different types of lies, including bald-faced lies to his spouse (Meibauer 2014b). He only confesses the truth when he is faced with evidence, which rarely happens. Although he is mostly ruthless in order to improve his self-esteem and social position, he is torn between hubris and self-contempt, drowning his bad conscience in alcohol. Even though he is an irritating character, Don Draper gradually reveals some positive character traits as well, such as tolerance, generosity, and solidarity. Moreover, flashbacks into the past reveal his difficult childhood and his struggles to overcome the suppressive atmosphere at his parental home, contributing to a shift in the viewer's perception of him. In the course of time, Don Draper eventually understands that his private and professional success is illusory, built on a foundation of deceit. After several failed romantic relationships, two divorces, and summary dismissal by his advertising company, Don Draper is finally prepared to leave all behind and start anew, renouncing his former status as a prosperous businessman.

43.4 LYING SITUATIONS

A large number of literary texts and films display standard situations of lying, which impact on the moral evaluation of the characters and the progress of the plot. Very often these situations mirror the 'little lies' that can be found in ordinary communication in order to save one's own or other people's faces. However, the range of these standard situations also encompasses conversations and events that go beyond commonplace experiences, such as interrogations, rumors, and the aspiration to protect oneself or others from dangerous circumstances. A prime example is the German novel *Jakob der Lügner* (Jacob the Liar) (Becker 1999 [1969]) by Jurek Becker. The title character Jacob is trying to give hope to the Jews in the ghetto by providing news about the approach of the Red Army. But the news is not true, since the radio that Jacob pretends to possess does not exist. When he first passes on this information, he is able to save his best friend's life. Since his friend is circulating the news among the ghetto community, Jacob has to continue with his lies about the radio and the news he overheard. Despite the increasing suspicion of the ghetto inhabitants, he succeeds in raising hope among the Jewish people. In order to achieve this goal, Jacob uses different forms of lies, ranging from prosocial lies and noble lies to antisocial lies (toward the German guards). The answer to the question whether Jacob's strategy of lying is actually fit to save the Jews is left to the readers, who are offered both a happy ending—Russian soldiers free the Jews in the ghetto—and a desperate ending—the Jews are deported to Auschwitz. Furthermore, the relationship between telling lies and telling stories crops up on a meta level, as the narrator of the novel deceives the reader by claiming to tell a true story, even though the narrative is purely fictional (White and White 1978). In a nutshell, *Jacob the Liar* assembles different forms and functions of lying, even picking up the crucial issue of how fiction and lying are potentially intertwined.

In relation to lying, literature and film also address other possible topics, such as the origin of the human capacity of lying and the development of airtight methods for the detection of lies. The former aspect is addressed in the British movie *The Invention of Lying* (directed by Ricky Gervais, UK 2009). This film represents a world without lies, where everyone tells the truth, to the extent of brutal honesty. By happenstance, the main protagonist, Mark Bellison, tells a lie at the bank counter, when he claims that he owns more money than he actually has in his account. When the clerk assumes that this false information must be based on a computer error, Mark realizes that he has actually achieved a skill with which to outsmart other people. He uses this capacity to console his dying mother by inventing a story about the afterlife and the "man in the sky." Unintentionally overheard by the medical staff in the hospital, this lie is spread among the people, finally leading to the emergence of religion and the installment of the Ten Commandments that were to determine social life from then on.

While *The Invention of Lying* is a humorous proposal on how lying might have come into being, the American TV series *Lie to Me* (various directors, USA 2009–10) deals with the scientific detection of lies. The script is based on the investigations of Paul Ekman, who became famous for his studies on micro expressions (Ekman 2009). Such expressions are spontaneous changes of the facial muscles that can be linked to feasible emotional processes. In the TV series, the main character Dr. Cal and his colleagues from the Lightman Group are commissioned by the FBI and other institutions to debunk suspected criminals' lies. As a complement to the polygraph, Dr. Cal and his staff members analyze the micro expressions of people when being debriefed in interrogations in order to find possible stress indicators for insincerity and deception.

43.5 CAN PICTURES LIE?

The topical issue of whether pictures are actually capable of lying is a thread running through art history and philosophy of art. Although it is evident that pictures can refer to factual reality, the question whether they can convey a truth or a lie remains disputed. Ernest Gombrich argues that the inherent meanings and messages of pictures have a polysemic character and that they are quite vague in relation to verbal statements, thus implying that they cannot convey falsehood or truth per se (Gombrich 1968: 330f.). Ludwig Wittgenstein even points to the pragmatic indeterminacy of pictures (Wittgenstein 1953: 22), supporting those critics who question the assertive quality of pictures. As a result, they aver that textual signifiers or labels are necessary as indicators of the truth-claim of pictures (Horák 2007: 356f.). However, as the often-discussed painting "La trahison des images" (The Treachery of Images, 1929) by surrealist artist René Magritte shows, captions to pictures may result in an ambiguous message: the painting shows a tobacco pipe, so that the label 'ceci n'est pas un pipe' (this is not a pipe) seems to provide a false statement at first glance. On closer consideration, however, the textual information is also truthful, since a painting of a tobacco pipe is only a pictorial representation of the object, but not the object itself (Harris 2005).

While this debate points to the contextual incompleteness of pictures, there is evidence that visuals can also depict standard situations of lying and deception. A prime example is the famous painting "The Cardsharp with the Ace of Clubs" (c. 1635) by French painter Georges de la Tour, in which a professional cardsharper cheats a wealthy young man with the help of two pretty-looking women, who distract the infatuated fellow. Although pictures of this kind exist, researchers show a deeper interest in the manipulative power of pictorial messages, interrogating their inherent semiotic potential to lie. On the visual level, the creation of untrue pictorial statements can either originate from the artist's intention to deceive the viewer or lead to a visual play of imagination, which demands the capacity on the part of the viewer to deduce the actual sources of reference. The discussion of the veracity of paintings, drawings, and other kinds of images has been dependent on contemporary views on art.

The emergence of photography in the middle of the nineteenth century, however, changed the attitude toward the reality potential of visual representations. Henceforth, paintings and drawings have been generally perceived as artifacts, which allowed for a certain amount of freedom concerning their reproduction of the depicted world. Photographs, in contrast, were initially regarded as authentic and objective presentations of reality by reference to their indexical and iconic nature, as is evident in family photos, press photos, and scientific photos as prototypical examples of indexical reference and iconic correspondence between the object/person and the photo. However, this view was soon countermanded by the development of further techniques, such as retouch, color filtering, and double exposure, paving the way for the possible manipulation of photos. At the same time, the so-called Robinson–Emerson controversy came to the fore. In the treatise *Pictorial Effect in Photography* (1869), the photographer Henry Peachum Robinson expressed his view that "photography is an art because it can lie" (42) by pointing to the facility to manipulate photos. Opposing Robinson's view was the naturalist Peter Henry Emerson, who hailed photography as a medium to create untouched imagery straight from nature (1889: 13). While this controversy is still simmering in photographic communities, the seminal issue of intended counterfeiting in photography gathered momentum at the beginning of the twentieth century.

A notorious example is the famed photo of the purported 'Cottingley Fairies', taken by two young girls in 1917. The girls successfully provided the photographic illusion of a non-existing object by using paper figures that looked like little fairies. Although some experts expressed doubt about the photos' authenticity, Sir Arthur Conan Doyle, who was a fervent supporter of spiritualism, published an enthusiastic article in *The Strand Magazine* in 1920, in which he praised the photos as a proof of the existence of fairies.

The fact that Doyle and others were actually tricked by a forgery was not revealed until the 1980s, when better examination methods were provided. Fraudulent falsifications of photographs abound in photographic history, particularly in the realm of documentary photography, which should attest the authenticity of specific historical and political events (Brugioni 1999). The blotting out of persons from the official register as a sign that they had been disgraced led to their disappearance from official photographic documents. An often-referenced case is a photograph of Lenin with thirty-three members of his party taken in 1918, of which a new version was released in 1970 with Lenin and just three members left (King 1997). By using the strategies of retouching and montage, figures and objects could be added to or removed from a scene, thus cheating the inexperienced viewer.

The recent developments in computer graphics, with the possibilities of shape blending, simulation, and other modes of digital image manipulation, have led to the increasing creation of hoaxes on the internet. Just like fakes, manipulated photos are visuals which exemplify the pictorial potential to lie. Against Kendall Walton's claim of the photograph's "transparency" (1984: 126), technology's ability to change images has destroyed the idea of the photograph as a reliable record of reality, thus demanding the viewer's epistemic vigilance to debunk the manipulative power of allegedly authentic photos. The same applies to films, as the much discussed "Rodney King case" (Los Angeles, 1992) elucidates. A video taken by an eyewitness showed a black motorcyclist being severely beaten by some police officers. At the trial, this video was shown in slow-motion only, which transformed the brutal attack into soft, almost caressing body movements. As a consequence, the indicted policemen were acquitted, which led to violent protests, especially in the black communities in Los Angeles (Rogers 2013: 155ff.).

43.6 Conclusion: research topics lying ahead

The investigation of the representation of lying characters and standard situations of lying in literature and other art forms is a promising topic for different fields, such as literary studies, cultural studies, film studies, media studies, picture theory, and children's literature research. Such an undertaking would help to get an insight into the ongoing changes in the depiction of lying characters and standard situations of lying in fiction over time. This approach might be complemented by comparative studies that investigate the multifarious conceptualizations of lying in different literatures and cultures, as has been done in the studies by Reid (1993) on the struggle between fictional invention and fact-oriented description in the French realist novel of the nineteenth century, and by Kucich (1994) on the interest in lies in Victorian fiction of the nineteenth century. Since lies can surface on the level of action, characterization, and themes, it is definitely a promising endeavor to analyze the artful play of deceptions and intrigues in literature and other works of art.

This perspective could be smoothly connected with a cognitive-narratological analysis of lying in the arts by focusing on the question of how the acquisition of lying affects the representation of lying in fictional works targeted at different age groups. An approach that focuses on the epistemological and moral dimensions of the depiction of lying in literature may provide an insight into the inherent value systems and the ethical inferences, thus opening pathways for the understanding of literary characters' behavior and moral decisions. On the other hand, the philosophical reflection on truth and lie as well as on the authenticity of fiction engenders scholarly studies that focus either on narratological issues, such as multiperspectivity and unreliable narration and their connection to truthfulness, honesty, and lying (Ferenz 2008; Nünning 2015), or on metadiscursive features, such as the relationship between fiction and lying and its connection to metafictional considerations (Frangipane 2016). Finally, the potential connection between lying and different forms of propaganda used in literature, films, and other media formats is a subject worthy of academic investigation, particularly in relation to the increasing emergence of fakes, hoaxes, and bogus texts, which surely call for epistemic vigilance on the part of the recipients.

Chapter 44

Lying in Different Cultures

Fumiko Nishimura

44.1 Introduction

The purpose of this chapter is to reveal, within a cross-cultural context, key issues that relate to our understanding of lying. After briefly referring to important notions and frameworks of cross-cultural studies, I shall firstly consider various definitions of lying in different cultures. Studies such as Yoshimura (1995) suggest that people with different cultural backgrounds tend to place different weights on key elements of lying. Differing cultural norms also lead us to different perspectives on lying. Secondly, the motivations underlying the acceptability of lies will be examined. Finally, this chapter examines conversational data to see how people might use lies in everyday situations. The data to be examined derive from invitation–refusal conversations in English and Japanese. I compare data sets to focus on the nature of lies as well as the reactions to those lies.

44.2 Different cultures

There is no universally accepted definition of culture (Geertz 2000, as cited in Smith, Fischer, Vignoles, and Bond 2013). Sapir writes that "culture may be defined as what a society does and thinks" (Sapir 1949: 218). A more specific definition is due to Reiche, Carr, and Pudelko (2010: 131) who state that culture is "a system of shared, underlying values that explain but may also potentially vary from behavioural practice." Other definitions are possible (e.g., Ting-Toomey and Chung 1996; Smith, Fischer, Vignoles, and Bond 2013; Jackson 2014) and these typically feature common keywords such as 'shared', 'system', 'patterns', 'values', etc.

In the current global era, many of us are likely to be exposed to foreign cultures (Reiche et al. 2010). Therefore, we need to understand cultural differences. As Meibauer (2014a) points out, lying is no exception. Barnes (1994) and Vincent Marrelli (1997, 2004) also describe the potential for, and the danger of, skewed intercultural perceptions of lies or other types of deception. Simpson-Herbert (1987: 26, as cited in Barnes 1994) mentions a case of meal invitations: "in urban Iran, in the days of the Shah, invitations to a meal were extended frequently; these were almost always insincere" (Barnes 1994: 67). Anyone not familiar with Iranian culture is likely to take this invitation seriously. Miscommunication of this nature occurs owing to the lack of a shared system (i.e., a way of inviting people to meals) or values (i.e., it is worth giving an 'insincere' invitation in a certain situation).

Cross-cultural studies often employ value-orientation frameworks to interpret their data. Hofstede (1980) provides one of the most-cited publications in the social science area (Gerhart and Fang 2005). In order to explain cultural patterns, Hofstede (1980) introduces four 'dimensions', namely power distance, femininity/masculinity, uncertainty avoidance, and individualism/collectivism. In this section, I focus on Individualism/collectivism (henceforth I/C) since this dimension has played an important role in many cross-cultural studies.

The description of I/C is as follows:

> Individualism refers to the broad value tendencies of people in a culture to emphasize individual identity over group identity, individual rights over group obligations, and individual achievements over group concerns. In contrast, collectivism refers to the broad value tendencies of people in a culture to emphasize group identity over the individual identity, group obligations over individual rights, and in-group-oriented concerns over individual wants and desires.
>
> (Ting-Toomey and Chung 1996: 239)

To take an example from studies of lying, collectivistic people might use a lie to maintain harmony in the group they belong to. This lie might be accepted by the group (but not so by individualistic people) if the lie is considered to be for the greater good (Kim, Kam, Sharkey, and Singelis 2008).

There are several critiques on I/C (Chuang 2003; McSweeney 2002; Gerhart and Fang 2005; Brewer and Chen 2007; Takano 2008, etc.). For instance, it is unlikely that all members of a society share exactly the same values. Also, as mentioned above, ethnic diversity has almost become a norm and such diversity can no longer be captured by dichotomous concepts. However, Jackson (2014) explains that patterns of behaviour have been developed in groups, and people learn them through interactions; specifically, 'values... are thought to be transmitted from one generation to another. Thus, at the heart of most cultural difference studies is the conviction that we need to identify core values or "shared values orientations"' (Jackson 2014: 285). Wierzbicka (2010) also acknowledges such core values:

> In different societies there are different culture-specific speech practices and interactional norms, and ... the different ways of speaking prevailing in different societies

are linked with, and make sense in terms of, different local cultural values, or at least, different cultural priorities as far as values are concerned.

(Wierzbicka 2010: 47)

Certain values live in a culture and those are identified in specific patterns and systems shared by the majority in a society. We cannot completely deny frameworks such as the concepts of I/C as they provide vital clues to interpreting cross-cultural data. We should however, utilize these concepts judiciously referring to the specific cultural contexts (Kim 1994).

44.3 Definitions of lying

This section begins by discussing definitions of lying from the viewpoint of semantics. I present contributions from the areas of prototype semantics (Coleman and Kay 1981) and cognitive semantics (Sweetser 1987). A pragmatics perspective in the form of Grice's Cooperative Principle (henceforth CP) will also be considered (Grice 1989c). The CP is particularly relevant to lying in cross-cultural contexts. Specifically, one of the maxims of the CP, in referring to falsehood, can be used as a theoretical framework to examine deception in comparative studies (e.g., Yeung, Levine, and Nishiyama 1999).

44.3.1 Definition of lying from prototype semantics

Coleman and Kay (1981) initiated a study of lying based on prototype semantics. It is useful to look at their findings in the context of American versus Japanese lying (Yoshimura 1995). In prototype semantics, words can be defined by a list of elements or properties with which they are associated. In the case of the word *lie*, Coleman and Kay postulate the following three elements traditionally associated with lying:

> The speaker (S) asserts some proposition (P) to an addressee (A), where:
>
> (a) P is false.
> (b) S believes P to be false.
> (c) In uttering P, S intends to deceive A.
>
> (Coleman and Kay 1981: 28)

In this definition, three key elements are identified: factual falsehood ((a) above), belief of falsity (b), and deceptive intention (c). Coleman and Kay drew on these elements and created eight scenarios for a questionnaire survey. Each scenario included an utterance which could potentially be judged as a lie. Some utterances had all three elements, (a), (b), and (c); some others had only (a) and (b); and some others had (b) and (c) or (a) and (c). Their research respondents were asked to judge the utterances on a seven-point scale. Coleman and Kay used the survey to extract which element was the most important, and therefore, how respondents construed a prototypical lie.

The results indicated that any utterances that fulfilled these three elements were recognised as a prototype *lie* and that element (b) was the most important component. This means, for example, that the utterance that displays elements (a) and (b) does not represent the prototype, but is closer to it than the utterance that fulfils elements (a) and (c), as the former has the most important element (b) but the latter does not.

The importance of the speaker's belief, (b), was also supported by another study which attempted to define 'deception' (not 'lie') using a questionnaire survey based on lexical terms for deception. Hopper and Bell (1984) asked American respondents to classify each word from a selection of forty-six words such as 'lie', 'fib', and 'hoax' in an attempt to discover the definitive notions of deception. They found that evaluation, detectability, and premeditation were important in deceptive communication. The third element, premeditation, was similar to Coleman and Kay's (b) component, namely, the speaker's belief.

These findings, however, appear not to apply in the case of Japanese lying. Yoshimura (1995) investigated the word *lie* in Japanese using a translation of Coleman and Kay's question sheets with his Japanese respondents. Yoshimura found that element (a), the factual falsehood, was the most important. Yoshimura's finding coincides with the definition of *lie* in Japanese provided by the Kojien dictionary (Shinmura 1991). This Japanese dictionary defines *lie* only by referring to falsehood.

The findings from the above studies indicate that some utterances may be taken as a lie by Americans but not by the Japanese. Suppose, for instance, somebody stated that 'the weather forecast said it would be fine this afternoon' after hearing a prediction of rain. If the forecast was wrong (which occasionally happens) and the day turned out to be fine, the findings of Yoshimura (1995) suggested that this case would *not* be considered as a lie by Japanese people because the weather fortuitously turned out to be exactly what the speaker stated. On the other hand, Coleman and Kay's (1981) American subjects would consider it a lie, because what the speaker said was believed by him or her to be untrue at the time of the utterance.

Cole (1996) and Hardin (2010) also investigated Makkan Arabic *lie* and Ecuador Spanish *lie* respectively, following the method of Coleman and Kay (1981). Cole (1996) found remarkable similarity between Arabic and American English *lie*. Hardin, however, did not see such similarity in her Spanish data, although the importance of the speaker's belief, which Coleman and Kay found in their American data, was observed in Hardin's data as well. On the other hand, the Ecuadorian respondents did not acknowledge the speaker's intention to deceive in some given scenarios and this brought different results. Hardin explains this difference referring to a concept *calor humano* (meaning 'warmth, friendliness, doing good to others'); if somebody gives false information for the sake of *calor humano*, "many Ecuadorians understand this to be a culturally common type of lie that may not involve an intent to deceive" (Hardin 2010: 3207). This kind of different 'rule' can also be found in other cultures. In this case, we could state that Coleman and Kay's framework is not sufficiently adequate to explain *lie* universally.

The next section discusses Sweetser's (1987) cognitive model, which attempts to explain *lie* in cultural contexts. Hardin (2010) mentions Sweetser's model as a way to partially explain discrepancies which are observed in Ecuadorians' social lies, as mentioned.

44.3.2 Definition of lying from cognitive semantics

To define *lie*, Sweetser (1987) discusses two issues: the definition of truth and the simplified discourse setting required for *lie*. Sweetser says, "belief is normally taken as having adequate justification, and hence as equivalent to knowledge, which would entail truth" (Sweetser 1987: 47). This further implies that "a factually false statement must be known to be false by the speaker" as "a speaker's belief constitutes evidence of truth" (Sweetser 1987: 49). If a speaker does not believe that what he or she says is true, the speaker should consider his or her utterance a falsehood.

Falsehood, however, would not be automatically acknowledged as *lie*; *lie* needs a particular discourse setting for its existence; Sweetser describes this setting as where 'truth value is relevant, knowledge is beneficial and informing helpful' (Sweetser 1987: 49–50). Falsehood is labelled as *lie* only under this setting. In other words, any falsehood is not taken as *lie* if the above conditions of the setting are not met.

To take a simple example: people almost always say "I'm fine" in answer to "How are you?" even when they feel rotten (Sacks 1975). Sacks concludes that "everyone has to lie," using this example, but Sweetser's model determines this as a typical example of a non-lie whose proposition is false. People do not particularly focus on the truthfulness of daily small talk. When it comes to cultural contexts, each culture has different assumptions. Thus, an utterance acknowledged as a lie in one culture might not be regarded as a lie in others.

As another instance, consider somebody asking for a mother's whereabouts. If this inquiry occurs in Madagascar, traditional Malagasy village people generally avoid a straight answer (as reported and discussed in Ochs Keenan (1976), and cited in Sweetser (1987)). They would typically answer "she is in the kitchen or the living room," even if they know she is in the kitchen. This does not seem odd if we consider their situation; the traditional small villages hardly encounter visitors from outside and the village people do not share with strangers such private information (i.e., family members' whereabouts). From the Malagasy viewpoint, this type of utterance does not contain a blameworthy intent to deceive. However, non-Malagasy visitors might be puzzled at this response and take it as a lie. The cases Hardin (2010) mentions, that is, false information provided for the sake of *calor humano*, can be interpreted similarly in the Malagasy case.

Brown (2002) examines cases related to 'lying' amongst the Tzeltal people in the rural community of Tenejapa in southern Mexico. Tzeltal people give false information in certain situations; more precisely, Tzeltal adults threaten punishment or promise a reward in order to control their children's behaviour where, in fact, the adults have no intention of following through. For example, a mother might promise an ice lolly for a reward and/or punishment with a whip to make her child behave. Brown describes these types of communication as "the kind of speech that is not expected by anyone to be true" (Brown 2002: 269). As with the Malagasy cases, the Tzeltal adults' utterances might look dubious to outsiders but people in the community know exactly what is going on; therefore, within the Sweetser's model, the Tzeltal's false threats and promises should not be taken as *lies*. Sweetser explains that these cultural differences around lying necessarily involve a detailed understanding of the layers of cultural assumptions in defining lies.

44.3.3 Definition of lying from pragmatics

Gricean pragmatics offers a further framework. This section considers how the 'Cooperative Principle', as proposed originally by Grice (1975), can provide a baseline to give an account of lying.

The CP is an underlying principle for communication. Grice "subdivided it [= the CP] into nine maxims of conversation classified into four categories: Maxims of Quality, Quantity, Relation, and Manner" (Huang 2010: 608). Gricean pragmatics proposes that adherence to these maxims enables our communication to work smoothly, in other words, to understand each other's intended meanings even when expressed indirectly. However, people sometimes deliberately flout one or more maxims in conversation to achieve a certain communicative goal.

Consider the first maxim of Quality (i.e., do not say what you believe to be false) in the context of a sarcastic remark. For example, a university professor says "what a hard working student you are!" to a student who is playing a computer game. Nobody regards this remark as a lie, since the student is clearly not working; therefore, the meaning of the professor's words is effectively conveyed.

When it comes to intercultural situations, to properly understand cases which deviate from the maxims we should consider the speakers' cultural norms and expectations. People normally adhere to the maxims but the interpretation of the adherence seems different among cultures. For instance, Japanese and Hong Kong Chinese often leave certain things unsaid and this could be regarded as deviation from the second maxim of Manner (i.e., avoid ambiguity) or the first maxim of Quantity (i.e., make your contribution as informative as required). Wierzbicka (1997) points out that Japanese tend to refrain from expressing opinions and do not necessarily appreciate the frankness of Americans. Likewise, an utterance without sufficient or clear information would sound suspicious to those who do not share such practices, as if the speaker was trying to hide something. The level of 'sufficiency' and 'clarity' of information are, therefore, expected to vary among cultures.

McCornack (1992) examines deceptive messages referring to the Gricean maxims. He claims that "messages that are commonly thought of as deceptive derive from covert violations of the conversational maxims" (McCornack 1992: 5) and calls this theory *Information Manipulation Theory* (henceforth IMT). McCornack, Levine, Solowczuk, Torres, and Campbell (1992) carried out a test of IMT with American respondents and found deviation from any maxims to be taken as deceptive by the respondents. Yeung et al. held a test of IMT with Hong Kong Chinese and found that only violations of the maxims of Quality and Relevance (which result in 'falsification' and 'evasion' respectively, according to the labelling given by the researchers in the IMT paradigm) appear deceptive (Yeung et al. 1999). Yeung et al. suggested that fundamental differences in the appropriateness of maxims between American English and Hong Kong Chinese might explain the results of their study.

Shigemitsu (2005) suggested that the tendency of Japanese, which is akin to the Chinese tendency mentioned above, came from the high-context nature of Japanese culture. People from high-context cultures rely heavily on context for communication. Therefore, they often do not say everything but they can still achieve the message using contextual information (Hall 2000). Shigemitsu also mentioned that the Japanese tendency to leave things unsaid seemed to make American people uncomfortable.

Danziger (2010) examines Grice's maxim of Quality using data collected from Mopan Maya of Eastern Central America and found the maxim did not fit the Mopan Maya's culture. A supermaxim under the category of Quality says 'try to make your contribution one that is true' (Grice 1975: 46). However, one of the Mopan Maya's cultural philosophies is to "disregard utterer's belief and desire states" (Danziger 2010: 212). Mopan Maya are concerned only with the factual truth and not with what a speaker *tries* to say.

Besnier (1994) and Duranti (1993) report the different ways of determining the truthfulness of utterances in Polynesian communities. Their fieldwork revealed that a certain type of formal community gathering did not permit speakers to claim the right to the meaning of their own utterances. In such situations, the speakers' intentions (what they tried to say) were disregarded, as only the authority figure had the right to determine the meaning of the utterances.

These (and other) previous studies suggest that we should not automatically assume that a distinction between what people say and what people try to say is made in every culture. The Gricean maxims might need to be rewritten or at least recalibrated to take this difference into account in an intercultural context.

In summary, the different uptakes of Gricean maxims among different cultures lead to different interpretations of the same utterance. This implies, among other things, different definitions of 'lie' that could easily cause intercultural misunderstanding.

44.4 Motivations for lying

Motivations for lying have been associated with different weightings of cultural values. Several authors (Lee, Cameron, Xu, Fu, and Board 1997; Fu, Lee, Cameron, and Xu 2001) made a comparison between Chinese and Canadian people and revealed the relation between lying and the culturally motivated reasons behind it. Lee et al. set a questionnaire for children and found that "the particular trend with Chinese children suggests that the emphasis on self-effacement and modesty in Chinese culture increasingly asserts its impact on Chinese children's moral judgement" (Lee et al. 1997: 930). They reported that Chinese tended to lie when they thought that telling the truth would conflict with their morality. Fu et al. (2001) found similar results among Chinese adults.

Blum (2007) reported motivations for lying from her personal observation in China; she says Chinese sometimes lie in order to avoid potential unpleasantness in the future. Such lies seem rare in English-speaking countries. Shibuya and Shibuya (1993) also find a similar tendency in Japanese people.

Aune and Walters (1994) carried out a questionnaire survey and interpreted the data using the concepts of I/C. They asked Samoan and North American respondents about their thoughts on possible motivations for deception and concluded that Samoans, who are more collectivistic, were more readily prepared to accept deception for the benefit of their group. Americans, being more individualistic, tended to put more priority on their individual advantage.

Kim et al. (2008) also studied the motivations related to the concepts of I/C using data collected from respondents in Hong Kong, Hawaii, and the mainland United States. The respondents were asked to rate, using a seven-point scale, their willingness to use deception in certain situations. They showed that individualistic cultures encouraged people not to tell lies in general whereas collectivistic cultures, while not necessarily encouraging lying, allowed people to tell lies for the greater good—typically to maintain harmony within the group.

Another comparative study of lying is that of Nishimura (2005) who asked Japanese and New Zealanders to describe their experiences of lies. She found that Japanese people were not comfortable to talk about personal matters; therefore, Japanese might tend to lie rather than reveal personal details. Nishimura also mentions that lies of this nature are unlikely to be used by New Zealanders as they are more relaxed in terms of sharing personal information. Her argument is supported by cross-cultural studies such as Barnlund (1973) and Gudykunst and Nishida (1983). As a general tendency, Japanese people appear to be more private; and therefore less forthcoming than English speakers to talk on any personal matters.

44.5 ACCEPTABILITY OF LYING

The extent to which lies are considered acceptable is likely to vary significantly among cultures. Seiter, Bruschke, and Bai (2002) and Mealy, Walter, and Urrutia (2007) carried out comparative studies on the acceptability of lies. The former compared Chinese and American respondents and the latter compared Euro-American and Ecuadorian respondents. Both of them ask the respondents to rate acceptability of lying on given scenarios; Seiter et al. uses a nine-point scale and Mealy et al. a six-point scale for rating.

Both studies employed the concepts of I/C to interpret their results. Mealy et al. (2007) recognized that many of their findings were similar to the results of Seiter et al.'s (2002) study; for example, altruistic lies were more acceptable than egoistic lies. A similar finding was also reported in Nishimura (1997), who collected data from Australian and Japanese respondents.

Kim et al. (2008) reported that highly interdependent people (collectivists) did not necessarily see all deceptive communication as a condemnable action, while people in cultures oriented towards independence (individualists) were unlikely to share this attitude to the same degree. Individualistic cultures value the literal truth highly, regardless of the condition or circumstance (Kim 2002).

Nishimura (2005) also reported cultural differences between Japanese and New Zealanders in their acceptance of lies. The (collectivist) Japanese recipients in her study were relatively lenient towards lies, whereas the New Zealand recipients (individualists) were notably angry or resentful overall. The contrast between these two was significant, particularly in the case of lies told for the benefit of others. Nobody in the Japanese cases reacted negatively, but the New Zealand recipients claimed that even altruistic lies hurt—because using them implies that the recipients are not deserving of the truth.

Chen, Hu, and He (2013) also include an element of 'benefit' in their study of *lie*. They carried out a survey about objectionability of lying which asked Chinese and American English speakers to indicate where on a six-point scale they would place the utterances given in scenarios. Their findings suggest that lying for the benefit of others is more acceptable for Chinese than for American respondents. In other words, (individualist) Americans tended to find lies considerably more objectionable than (collectivist) Chinese respondents.

There is however, a significant inconsistency among the studies. While Seiter et al. found a higher acceptability rate in the answers from the Chinese (collectivists) than those from the American (individualists) participants, Mealy et al. (2007) noted that Euro-Americans (individualists) considered lies to be more acceptable than Ecuadorians (collectivists) did. Therefore, we cannot conclude definitively, at least from the above studies, that either collectivists or individualists are more likely to accept lies. Mealy et al. (2007: 700) suggested three areas that might offer an alternative explanation: (1) the different attitude towards uncertainty—whether people are afraid of uncertainty; (2) the different time orientation—whether long-term or short-term consequences are more important; and (3) different religious contexts. For example, in terms of religious viewpoints, Cole (1996) mentioned three cases of lying which were overtly permitted in Islam: in war or battle situations; for bringing reconciliation amongst persons; and the narration of the words of a wife to her husband (in order to bring reconciliation between them) (Cole 1996: 482). Such lies also exist in the Talmud (Bok 1999: 73–4). These religious values could conceivably overcome any other cultural tendencies.

Nishida (2006) points out the importance of attention to detail in cultural contexts. In his study, interpersonal closeness is mentioned as having impact. Nishida found that Japanese people tended to be more influenced by interpersonal closeness in their social behaviour than North American people. This implies that the Japanese could behave differently in terms of truth-telling depending on the closeness of the people involved. Americans on the other hand, pay less regard to whom they address.

In short, collectivists might be more prepared to accept lying for a greater social good. We need, however, to explore more micro aspects of culture to determine each case.

44.6 LIES IN THE CASE OF REFUSAL CONVERSATIONS

In this section, I shall look, as a case study, into lies used as excuses in the refusal of an invitation. Refusals are not desirable as they are acts against inviters' wishes. In particular, refusals could be detrimental to the inviters' ability to maintain a positive face, which is "the desire to be approved of" (Brown and Levinson 1987: 13). Thus, refusals are face-threatening acts. An excuse is important in refusals because it not only mitigates the 'threat' but also helps the inviter understand the invitee's situation. People might tell a lie if, for example, they decide the truth would not work as an appropriate excuse. This section examines such lies to figure out what kind of cultural factors influence a choice of lie in everyday communication.

I consider lies collected specifically from New Zealanders in English and Japanese people in Japanese using the role-play technique set up by Nishimura (2011). The role-play technique was employed as it is the most realistic and effective way to collect data under similar conditions to 'draw reasonable generalizations' (Mackey and Gass 2005: 86). Role-play conversations are based on a fictional situation but 'seem the closest to what we might expect to reflect naturally occurring speech events' (Gass and Houck 1999: 7).

Data were collected from thirty-two pairs of Japanese and thirty pairs of New Zealanders. The participants were friends in real life and came forward voluntarily to participate in this research project. The average age of the participants was 21.9 years old (Japanese) and 24.28 years old (New Zealanders). The participants were asked to construct a conversation based on the following situation: Role A invites Role B to go to a bar for a drink together; Role B does not have any particular plan that night but feels like having a quiet night at home; Role B declines the invitation with an untruthful excuse as he or she does not think the true reason would be adequate. Here is an example from Nishimura (2011):

(1) (JPN pair 1):
   A: kyoo wa chotto paatto nomi ni ikitai na toka omotteita n da kedo
      today TOP little cheerfully drink to want to go PTCP QUOT thought NOM COP but
      B san doo
      Ms B WH
      "I want to go out today and have a drink. How about you?"

→B: *atama itai*
　　head hurt
　　"I have a headache."

The line indicated by → contains an untruthful excuse to decline the invitation. The instructions given to the participants only said "make up something and decline the invitation" and the excuses that appeared in the data were created by the speakers.

The following sections examine the data focusing on the types of excuses and the reactions to those excuses with reference to the relevant cultural norms and protocols.

44.6.1 Types of excuses

Table 44.1 identifies six types of initial excuses based on the original invitation. The table also shows how many people used those excuses.

As observed below, the favoured excuse for Japanese is their physical condition and a lot more Japanese used this response than New Zealanders. A possible explanation for this tendency derives from culturally favourable topics for conversation. Mentioning one's physical condition is emphasised in Kinjo's (1987) study. Kinjo carried out a cross-cultural study of refusals between Japanese and American people and reported the Japanese tendency to mention their physical condition for refusals. In addition to Kinjo's study, some cross-cultural studies have revealed favourite conversational topics (Gudykunst and Nishida 1983; Nishimura 2011).

Another explanation behind the choice of the majority of Japanese people is the incontestable nature of the excuse (nobody can judge for sure if somebody actually has a headache). This could prevent further negotiation or uncertainty (i.e., being uncertain whether or not an invitee is to accept an invitation), which would be a favourable situation for Japanese (Hofstede 2001).

Like the Japanese, the New Zealand participants seemed to follow their cultural protocols for refusals, which means using a prior engagement to decline an invitation.

Table 44.1 The first excuse that appeared in the data

	Prior engagement	Physical condition	Relaxation at home	Too busy	Lack of money	Others	Total
Japan	10	11	3	3	1	4	32
NZ	14	5	4	1	2	4	30

According to Neustupny (1982), a prior engagement is the only acceptable reason for refusal in English-speaking societies, since socializing with people is regarded as an obligation (Neustupny 1982: 73). The rationale for this explanation probably derives from the premise that 'contracts' carry a lot of weight in many English-speaking societies. That is, when natives in English-speaking countries are committed to attending a social activity or event, this can be regarded as a type of contract which has priority over later offers (Nishimura 2011).

44.6.2 Expected patterns of conversation

To interpret the excuses in context, the sequence, namely, how the various types of excuses were received, should be looked at. Table 44.2 shows Role A's response to Role B's initial refusal.

Table 44.2 shows that around one third of Role A participants in both groups accepted the initial refusal. However, two thirds kept asking. The majority of Japanese participants either sought more information of Role B's circumstances or dismissed Role B's excuse. On the other hand, the New Zealand participants sought more information or offered an amended plan.

A marked difference is apparent in the second most popular response. The dismissal is definitive for Japanese but New Zealanders are willing to negotiate the initial plan. I present an example of each case.

(2) (NZ Pair 21):
  →B: I've got about six hours' work to do, I think. Ah, I'll probably get home at midnight, I should imagine.
  →→A: Oh, really. Would you want to go out then?

Table 44.2 Role A's responses to Role B's excuses

	Japan	NZ
Seeking more information	11	6
Dismissing the excuse	7	1
Amending the plan	0	6
Giving the reasons for going to the pub that night	2	2
Emphasizing the pleasure of his or her company	0	2
Simply asking again	1	1
Suggesting a change of date	0	1
Accepting the excuse	11	11
TOTAL	32	30

(3) (JPN Pair 13):
→ B: *a gomen anne ima ne tenkai kenkyu yattoru ja n hoide ne kakan*
Ah sorry well now PTCP tenkai-research doing NOM COP and PTCP write-NEG
to iken non yo un senseitoka ni suggoi damedashi sareto tte
if go-NEG NOM yes teacher etc. by terribly rejection do-PASS QUOT
"Oh, sorry. I have been doing *tenkai* research at the moment, you know, and I have to write up an essay. I have been told by the lecturer to work harder."
→→ A: *e son'nan tekitoo de ee tte*
Oh that kind slovenly COP good QUOT
"Oh, you can rustle up something."

Role A in Example 2 showed his respect for Role B's plan, which could be explained as a negative politeness strategy (Brown and Levinson 1987). Role A in Example 3 could be interpreted as a strategy for negotiation-avoidance, as it was a little too ridiculous to take the suggestion seriously and it would not lead to discussion in depth. Nisbett (2003) and Kondo (2007) report that Japanese people often avoid conflict situations, say by changing the topic, in an effort to diffuse conflict.

44.6.3 Lying to excuse themselves in cultural contexts

Previous studies suggest that lies are strongly influenced by cultural protocols. To respect the other's wants and to prepare for negotiation (New Zealand) and to avoid negotiation (Japanese) are cultural protocols central to the present refusal data. Application of these protocols allows us to understand the differing refusal structures and the nature of lies in the Japanese and New Zealand data sets.

44.7 CONCLUSIONS

This chapter examined various aspects of lying in cultural contexts. The definitions of, motivations for, and acceptability of lying vary considerably among different cultures. A case study of lies showed that Japanese and New Zealanders chose different kinds of lie in similar situations owing to their differences with respect to preferred conversational protcols and readiness for negotiation.

When it comes to lying in intercultural situations, we should always remember that lying is beyond mere falsehood. Failure to do this could lead to serious intercultural misunderstanding, friction, and all sorts of negative consequences.

References

Aarnio, Maria Losonen (2010). 'Unreasonable knowledge', *Philosophical Perspectives* 24: 1–21.
Abe, Nobuhito (2009). 'The neurobiology of deception: evidence from neuroimaging and loss-of-function studies', *Current Opinion in Neurology* 22 (6): 594–600.
Abe, Nobuhito (2011). 'How the brain shapes deception: an integrated review of the literature', *The Neuroscientist: A Review Journal Bringing Neurobiology, Neurology and Psychiatry* 17 (5): 560–74.
Abe, Nobuhito, Maki Suzuki, Etsuro Mori, Masatoshi Itoh, and Toshikatsu Fujii (2007). 'Deceiving others: distinct neural responses of the prefrontal cortex and amygdala in simple fabrication and deception with social interactions', *Journal of Cognitive Neuroscience* 19 (2): 287–95.
Abney, Steven (1996). 'Statistical Methods and Linguistics', in Judith L. Klavans and Philip Resnik (eds), *The Balancing Act: Combining Symbolic and Statistical Approaches to Language*. Cambridge, MA: MIT Press, 1–26.
Abraham, Anna (2013). 'The promises and perils of the neuroscience of creativity', *Frontiers in Human Neuroscience* 7: 246.
Abramson, Julia (2005). *Learning from Lying. Paradoxes of the Literary Mystification*. Newark, DE: University of Delaware Press.
Ackerman, Brian P. (1981). 'Young children's understanding of a speaker's intentional use of a false utterance', *Developmental Psychology* 17: 472–80.
Adams, Susan and John Jarvis (2006). 'Indicators of Veracity and Deception: An Analysis of Written Statements Made to Police', *The International Journal of Speech, Language, and the Law* 13 (1): 1–22.
Adenzato, Mauro and Rita Bianca Ardito (1999). 'The role of theory of mind and deontic reasoning in the evolution of deception', in Martin Hahn and Scott C. Stoness (eds), *Proceedings of the Twenty-First Annual Conference of the Cognitive Science Society*. Mahwah, NJ: Lawrence Erlbaum, 7–12.
Adler, Jonathan (1997). 'Lying, Deceiving, or Falsely Implicating', *The Journal of Philosophy* 94: 435–52.
Aesop (1972). *Fables*. London: Blackwell.
Agronin, Marc E. (2011). *How We Age: A Doctor's Journey Into the Heart of Growing Old*. Cambridge, MA: Da Capo Press.
Ahern, Elizabeth C., Thomas D. Lyon, and Jodi A. Quas (2011). 'Young children's emerging ability to make false statements', *Developmental Psychology* 47 (1): 61–6.
Aitchison, Jean (1996). *The Seeds of Speech. Language Origin and Evolution*. Cambridge: Cambridge University Press.
Akimoto, Yoritaka, Shiho Miyazawa, and Toshiaki Muramoto (2012). 'Comprehension processes of verbal irony: The effects of salience, egocentric context, and allocentric theory of mind', *Metaphor and Symbol* 27 (3): 217–42.

Allan, Keith and Kate Burridge (1991). *Euphemism and Dysphemism: Language Used as Shield and Weapon.* Oxford: Oxford University Press.

Allan, Keith and Kasia M. Jaszczolt (eds) (2012). *The Cambridge Handbook of Pragmatics.* Cambridge: Cambridge University Press.

Allen, John J., William G. Iacono, and Kurt D. Danielson (1992). 'The identification of concealed memories using the event-related potential and implicit behavioral measures: a methodology for prediction in the face of individual differences', *Psychophysiology* 29 (5): 504–22.

Allhoff, Fritz (2003). 'Business Bluffing Reconsidered', *Journal of Business Ethics* 45: 283–9.

Alston, William P. (1964). *Philosophy of Language.* Englewood Cliffs, NJ: Prentice-Hall.

Alston, William P. (2000). *Illocutionary Acts and Sentence Meaning.* Ithaca, NY and London: Cornell University Press.

Alterman, Eric (2004). *When Presidents Lie: A History of Official Deception and Its Consequences.* New York, NY: Viking Books.

Alxatib, Sam and Francis Jeffry Pelletier (2011). 'The psychology of vagueness: Borderline cases and contradictions', *Mind & Language* 26 (3): 287–326.

Amati, Franco, Hanna Oh, Virgina S. Y. Kwan, Kelly Jordan, and Julian P. Keenan (2010). 'Overclaiming and the medial prefrontal cortex: A transcranial magnetic stimulation study', *Cognitive Neuroscience* 1 (4): 268–76.

Ambach, Wolfgang, Rudolf Stark, and Dieter Vaitl (2011). 'An interfering n-back task facilitates the detection of concealed information with EDA but impedes it with cardiopulmonary physiology', *International Journal of Psychophysiology* 80 (3): 217–26.

Amir. (6 July 2008). A comment (in Hebrew). http://www.calcalist.co.il/Ext/Comp/ArticleLayout/Proc/TalkBacks_iframe/0,9657,L-3087502-68--2,00.html (Retrieved 17 February 2015).

Anolli, Luigi, Michela Balconi, and Rita Ciceri (2003). 'Linguistic Styles in Deceptive Communication: Dubitative Ambiguity and Elliptical Eluding in Packaged Lies', *Social Behavior and Personality* 31 (7): 687–710.

Anon. (1657). *A True and Exact Relation of the Strange Finding out of Moses His Tomb.* London: Richard Lowndes.

Anscombe, G. E. M. (1958). 'Modern Moral Philosophy', *Philosophy* 33: 1–19.

Aquinas, Thomas (1897 [c.1265–73]). *Summa theologiae IIaIIae,* 110, in S. Thomae de Aquino, Opera Omnia iussu Leonis XIII edita cura et studio Fratrum Praedicatorum ('Editio Leonina'), vol. IX. Roma 1897.

Arciuli, Joanne, David Mallar, and Gina Villar (2010). '"Um, I can tell you're lying": Linguistic markers of deception versus truth-telling in speech', *Applied Psycholinguistics* 31: 397–411.

Arendt, Hannah (1958). *The Human Condition.* Chicago: Chicago University Press.

Arendt, Hannah (1967). 'Truth and Politics', *The New Yorker,* 25 February.

Arendt, Hannah (1973). 'Lying in Politics', in Hannah Arendt, *Crises of the Republic.* San Diego, CA: Harcourt, Brace & Co., 1–48.

Arico, Adam J. and Don Fallis (2013). 'Lies, damned lies, and statistics. An empirical investigation of the concept of lying', *Philosophical Psychology* 26 (6): 790–816.

Ariel, Mira (2002). 'The demise of a unique concept of literal meaning', *Journal of Pragmatics* 34: 361–402.

Ariel, Mira (2010). *Defining Pragmatics.* Cambridge: Cambridge University Press.

Aristotle (1971). *Metaphysics, Book* Γ, Λ, E. Trans. C. Kirwan. Oxford: Clarendon Press.

Aristotle (1985). *Nicomachean Ethics.* Trans. Terence Irwin. Cambridge: Hackett.

Aristotle (2010 [230 BC]). *Rhetoric*. Trans. W. Rhys Roberts. ReadaClassic.com.
Armstrong, D. M. (2004). 'Going through the Open Door Again', in John Collins, Ned Hall, and Laurie A. Paul (eds), *Causation and Counterfactuals*. Cambridge, MA: MIT Press, 445–58.
Aron, Adam R., Trevor W. Robbins, and Russell A. Poldrack (2004). 'Inhibition and the right inferior frontal cortex', *Trends in Cognitive Sciences* 8 (4): 170–7.
Aron, Adam R., Trevor W. Robbins, and Russell A. Poldrack (2014). 'Inhibition and the right inferior frontal cortex: One decade on', *Trends in Cognitive Sciences* 18 (4): 177–85.
Asher, Nicholas and Alex Lascarides (2013). 'Strategic conversation', *Semantics and Pragmatics* 6, Article 2: 1–62.
Ashton, Michael C. and Kibeom Lee (2007). 'Empirical, Theoretical, and Practical Advantages of the HEXACO Model of Personality Structure', *Personality and Social Psychology Review* 11: 150–66.
Astington, Janet Wilde and Jennifer M. Jenkins (1999). 'A longitudinal study of the relationship between language and theory-of-mind development', *Developmental Psychology* 35: 1311–20.
Attardo, Salvatore (1994). *Linguistic Theories of Humor*. New York, NY: Mouton.
Attardo, Salvatore (2001). *Humorous Texts: A Semantic and Pragmatic Analysis*. New York, NY: De Gruyter.
Attardo, Salvatore and Victor Raskin (1991). 'Script Theory Revis(it)ed: Joke Similarity and Joke Representation Model', *Humor* 4: 293–348.
Augustine (1952a). 'Against lying', in Roy J. Deferrari (ed.), *Treatises on Various Subjects* (Vol. 16). Washington, DC: Catholic University of America Press, 125–79.
Augustine (1952b). 'Lying', in Roy J. Deferrari (ed.), *Treatises on Various Subjects* (Vol. 16). Washington, DC: Catholic University of America Press, 53–120.
Augustine (1961). *Enchiridion*, Henry Paoluccci (ed.). Chicago, IL: Regnery.
Aune, R. Kelly and Linda L. Walters (1994). 'Cultural Differences in Deception: Motivations to Deceive in Samoans and North Americans', *International Journal of Intercultural Relations* 18 (2): 159–72.
Austin, J. L. (1946). Other Minds. Aristotelian Society Supplementary Volume. 20:1.
Austin, John L. (1950). 'Truth', *Proceedings of the Aristotelian Society*, Supplementary Volume 24 (1): 111–28.
Austin, John L. (1958). 'Pretending', *Proceedings of the Aristotelian Society*, Supplementary Volume 32. London: Harrison and Sons, 261–78.
Austin, John L. ([1962a] 1976). *How to Do Things with Words*. Oxford: Oxford University Press. 2nd edn 1976.
Austin, John L. (1962b). *Sense and Sensibilia*. Oxford: Oxford University Press.
Ayasse, Manfred, Johannes Stökl, and Wittko Francke (2011). 'Chemical ecology and pollinator-driven speciation in sexually deceptive orchids', *Phytochemistry* 72 (13): 1667–77.
Bach, Kent (2001). 'You don't say?', *Synthese* 128: 15–44.
Bach, Kent (2013). 'Odds & Ends (loose/deep/dead)', Expanded handout for the New Work on Speech Acts Conference, Columbia University, 27–29 Sept, 2013.
Bach, Kent and Robert M. Harnish (1979). *Linguistic Communication and Speech Acts*. Cambridge, MA: MIT Press.
Backbier, Esther, Johan Hoogstraten, and Katharina M. Terwogt-Kouwenhoven (1997). 'Situational determinants of the acceptability of telling lies', *Journal of Applied Social Psychology* 27 (12): 1048–62.
Bacon, Francis (2015 [1612]). 'On Simulation and Dissimulation', in Alfred S. West (ed.), *Essays*. Cambridge: Cambridge University Press, 13–17.

Baddeley, Alan D. (1986). *Working Memory*. Oxford: Clarendon Press.
Bagley, Janice and Leon Manelis (1979). 'Effect of awareness on an indicator of cognitive load', *Perceptual and Motor Skills* 49: 591–4.
Baier, Annette (1986). 'Trust and Anti-Trust', *Ethics* 96 (2): 231–60.
Baima, Nicholas (2017). '*Republic* 382a–d: On the Dangers and Benefits of Falschood', *Classical Philology* 112: 1–19.
Baker-Hytch, Max and Matthew A. Benton (2015). 'Defeatism Defeated', *Philosophical Perspectives* 29 (1): 40–66.
Bakir, Vian (2010). *Sousveillance, Media and Strategic Political Communication: Iraq, USA, UK*. London: Bloomsbury Academic.
Bakir, Vian (2013). *Torture, Intelligence and Sousveillance in the War on Terror: Agenda-building Struggles*. London: Routledge.
Bakir, Vian and David M. Barlow (eds) (2007). *Communication in the Age of Suspicion: Trust and the Media*. London: Palgrave Macmillan.
Bakir, Vian, David Miller, Eric Herring, and Piers Robinson (2015). 'Rethinking propaganda as a sub-set of organised persuasive communication'. Unpublished working paper, Bangor, UK.
Balliet, Daniel (2010). 'Communication and Cooperation in Social Dilemmas: A Meta-Analytic Review', *Journal of Conflict Resolution* 54 (1): 39–57.
Bandler, Richard and John Grinder (1979). *Frogs into Princes*. Moab, UT: Real People Press.
Barbe, Katharina (1993). ' "Isn't it ironic that . . . ?": explicit irony markers', *Journal of Pragmatics* 20: 578–90.
Barker, Stephen (2004). *Renewing Meaning*. Oxford: Oxford University Press.
Barnes, Annette (1997). *Seeing through Self-deception*. Cambridge: Cambridge University Press.
Barnes, John A. (1994). *A Pack of Lies: Towards a Sociology of Lying*. Cambridge: Cambridge University Press.
Barnlund, Dean C. (1973). *Public and Private Self in Japan and the United States*. Tokyo: The Simul Press Inc.
Baron-Cohen, Simon (1992). 'The theory of mind hypothesis of autism: History and prospects of the idea', *The Psychologist* 5: 9–12.
Baron-Cohen, Simon (1999). 'The evolution of a theory of mind?', in Michael Corballis and Stephen E. G. Lea (eds), *The Descent of Mind: Psychological Perspectives on Hominid Evolution*. Oxford: Oxford University Press, 261–83.
Baron-Cohen, Simon, Alan M. Leslie, and Uta Frith (1985). 'Does the autistic child have a "theory of mind"?', *Cognition* 21 (1): 37–46.
Barr, Dale J. and Boaz Keysar (2002). 'Anchoring comprehension in linguistic precedents', *Journal of Memory and Language* 46 (2): 391–418.
Barr, Dale J. and Boaz Keysar (2006). 'Perspective taking and the coordination of meaning in language use', in Matthew J. Traxler and Morton A. Gernsbacher (eds), *Handbook of Psycholinguistics*, 2nd edn. Amsterdam: Elsevier, 901–38.
Barr, John McKee (2014). *Loathing Lincoln*. Baton Rouge, LA: Louisiana State University Press.
Barrios, Veronica, Virginia S. Y. Kwan, Giorgio Ganis, Jaime Gorman, Jennifer Romanowski, and Julian P. Keenan (2008). 'Elucidating the neural correlates of egoistic and moralistic self-enhancement', *Consciousness and Cognition* 17 (2): 451–6.
Bauer, Matthias and Sigrid Beck (2014). 'On the Meaning of Fictional Texts', in Daniel Gutzmann, Jan Köpping, and Cécile Meier (eds), *Approaches to Meaning*. Leiden: Brill, 250–75.

Baumgartner, Thomas, Lorena R. Gianotti, and Daria Knoch (2013). 'Who is honest and why: Baseline activation in anterior insula predicts inter-individual differences in deceptive behavior', *Biological Psychology* 94 (1): 192–7.

Baumgartner, Thomas, Urs Fischbacher, Anja Feierabend, Kai Lutz, and Ernst Fehr (2009). 'The neural circuitry of a broken promise', *Neuron* 64 (5): 756–70.

Bavelas, Janet Beavin (1983). 'Situations that lead to disqualifications', *Human Communication Research* 9: 130–45.

Bavelas, Janet Beavin, Alex Black, Nicole Chovil, and Jennifer Mullett (1990). *Equivocal Communication*. Thousand Oaks: Sage.

Bazzanella, Carla (2009). 'Approssimazioni pragmatiche e testuali alla menzogna' (Pragmatic and textual approaches to the concept of lying), in Federica Venier (ed.), *Tra Pragmatica e Linguistica testuale. Ricordando Maria-Elisabeth Conte*. Alessandria: Dell'Orso, 67–90.

Bazzanella, Carla, Claudia Caffi, and Marina Sbisà (1991). 'Scalar dimensions of illocutionary force', in Igor Ž. Žagar (ed.), *Speech Acts: Fiction or Reality*. Antwerp, Ljubljana: IPrA Distribution Center for Yugoslavia and Institute for Social Sciences, 63–76.

Beach, John (1985). 'Bluffing: Its Demise as a Subject into Itself', *Journal of Business Ethics* 4: 191–6.

Beardsley, Monroe Curtis (1958). *Aesthetics*. New York, NY: Harcourt, Brace and World.

Beaver, David and Bart Geurts (2011). 'Presupposition', in Edward N. Zalta (ed.), *Stanford Encyclopedia of Philosophy*. Online publication [https://plato.stanford.edu/entries/presupposition].

Becker, Jurek (1999 [1969]). *Jacob the Liar*. Trans. Leila Vennewitz. London: Penguin (original German edn *Jakob der Lügner*. 1969).

Beebee, Helen (2004). 'Causing and Nothingness', in John Collins, Ned Hall, and Laurie A. Paul (eds), *Causation and Counterfactuals*. Cambridge, MA: MIT Press, 291–308.

Beeman, William O. (1986). *Language, Status, and Power in Iran*. Bloomington, IN: Indiana University Press.

Beier, Kathi (2010). *Selbsttäuschung*. Berlin and New York, NY: De Gruyter.

Belfiore, Elizabeth (1985). ' "Lies Unlike the Truth": Plato on Hesiod, Theogony 27', *Transactions of the American Philological Association* 115: 47–57.

Bell, Kathy L. and Bella M. DePaulo (1996). 'Liking and Lying', *Basic and Applied Social Psychology* 18: 243–66.

Belot, Michèle and Jeroen van de Ven (2017). 'How private is private information? The ability to spot deception in an economic game', *Experimental Economics* 20 (1): 19–43.

Bennett, Lerone (2007). *Forced Into Glory: Abraham Lincoln's White Dream*. Chicago, IL: Johnson Publishing Company.

Ben-Shakhar, Gershon and Eitan Elaad (2003). 'The validity of psychophysiological detection of information with the Guilty Knowledge Test: A meta-analytic review', *Journal of Applied Psychology* 88 (1): 131–51.

Ben-Shakhar, Gershon and John J. Furedy (1990). *Theories and Applications in the Detection of Deception: A Psychophysiological and International Perspective*. New York, NY: Springer.

Benton, Matthew A. (2011). 'Two More for the Knowledge Account of Assertion', *Analysis* 71: 684–7.

Benton, Matthew A. (2014). 'Knowledge Norms', *Internet Encyclopedia of Philosophy*. Online. Available at http://www.iep.utm.edu/kn-norms/.

Benton, Matthew A. (2016). 'Gricean Quality', *Noûs* 50 (4), 689–703.

Benton, Matthew A. (2018). Lying, Accuracy, and Credence. *Analysis*.

Benton, Matthew A. (Forthcoming). *Knowledge and Language.* Unpublished ms., Seattle, WA.

Benton, Matthew A. and John Turri (2014). 'Iffy Predictions and Proper Expectations', *Synthese* 191: 1857–66.

Berger, Lee R., John Hawks, Darryl J. de Ruiter, Steven E. Churchill, Peter Schmid, Lucas K. Delezene, et al. (2015). 'Homo naledi, a new species of the genus Homo from the Dinaledi Chamber, South Africa', *eLife* 4.

Bermúdez, José Luis (2000). 'Self-deception, intentions, and contrary beliefs', *Analysis* 60: 309–19.

Berry, Dianne C., Peter R. Knapp, and Theo Raynor (2002). 'Is 15% very common? Informing people about the risk of medication side effects', *International Journal of Pharmacy Practice* 10: 145–51.

Bertucelli Papi, Marcella (2014). 'The pragmatics of insinuation', *Intercultural Pragmatics* 11 (1): 1–29.

Besnier, Niko (1994). 'Christianity, Authority, and Personhood: Sermonic Discourse on Nukulaelae Atoll', *Journal of the Polynesian Society* 103 (4): 339–378.

Bhatt, Meghana A., Terry Lohrenz, Colin F. Camerer, and P. Read Montague (2010). 'Neural Signatures of Strategic Types in a Two-Person Bargaining Game', *Proceedings of the National Academy of Sciences* 107: 19720–5.

Bibas, Stephanos (2004). 'Plea Bargaining Outside the Shadow of the Trial', *Harvard Law Review* 117: 2463–547.

Birch, Susan A. J., Nazanin Akmal, and Kristen L. Frampton (2010). 'Two-Year-Olds Are Vigilant of Others' Non-Verbal Cues to Credibility', *Developmental Science* 13 (2): 363–9.

Birner, Betty J. and Gregory Ward (1998). *Information Status and Noncanonical Word Order in English.* Amsterdam: John Benjamins.

Bittner, Rüdiger (1988). 'Understanding a Self-deceiver', in Brian P. McLaughlin and Amélie Oksenberg Rorty (eds), *Perspectives on Self-deception.* Berkeley, CA: University of California Press, 535–51.

Black, Max (1983). 'The prevalence of humbug', in his *The Prevalence of Humbug and Other Essays.* Ithaca, NY: Cornell University Press, 115–46.

Blackwell, Natalia and Jean E. Fox Tree (2012). 'Social factors affect quotative choice', *Journal of Pragmatics* 44: 1150–62.

Blommaert, Jan (2005). 'Why we are as good or bad as our language', *Guardian Weekly, Learning English Supplement* (21 Oct., 7).

Bloom, Harold (2010). *The Trickster.* New York, NY: Bloom's Literary Criticism.

Bloomquist, Jennifer (2009). 'Lying, Cheating, and Stealing: A Study of Categorical Misdeeds', *Journal of Pragmatics* 42 (6): 1595–605.

Blum, Susan D. (2005). 'Five Approaches to Explaining "Truth" and "Deception" in Human Communication', *Journal of Anthropological Research* 61 (3): 289–315.

Blum, Susan, D. (2007). *Lies that Bind: Chinese Truth, Other Truths.* Lanham, MD: Rownan & Littlefield.

Blume, Andreas, Douglas V. DeJong, Yong Gwan Kim, and Geoffrey B. Sprinkle (1998). 'Experimental Evidence on the Evolution of the Meaning of Messages in Sender-Receiver Games', *American Economic Review* 88: 1323–40.

Blume, Andreas, Douglas V. DeJong, Yong Gwan Kim, Geoffrey B. Sprinkle (2001). 'Evolution of Communication with Partial Common Interest', *Games and Economic Behavior* 37: 79–120.

BNC = *British National Corpus*. (2001). Version 2. Distributed by Oxford University Computing Services on behalf of the BNC Consortium.
Bok, Sissela (1999). *Lying. Moral Choice in Public and Private Life*. New York, NY: Vintage Books.
Bolhuis, Johan J. (2015). 'Evolution cannot explain how minds work', *Behavioural Processes* 117: 82–91.
Bolinger, Dwight (1980). *Language, the Loaded Weapon*. New York, NY: Longman.
Bond, Charles F. and Bella M. DePaulo (2006). 'Accuracy of deception judgments', *Personality and Social Psychology Review* 10 (3): 214–34.
Bond, Gary D. (2008). 'Deception detection expertise', *Law and Human Behavior* 32 (4): 339–51.
Bonomi, Andrea and Sandro Zucchi (2003). 'A pragmatic framework for truth in fiction', *Dialectica* 57 (2): 103–20.
Borg, Emma (2012). *Pursuing Meaning*. Oxford: Oxford University Press.
Borge, Steffen (2003). 'The Myth of Self-deception', *Southern Journal of Philosophy* 41: 1–28.
Börjesson, Kristin (2014). *The Semantics-Pragmatics Controversy*. Berlin and Boston, MA: De Gruyter.
Bosco, Francesca M. and Monica Bucciarelli (2008). 'Simple and Complex Deceits and Ironies', *Journal of Pragmatics* 40: 583–607.
Boxer, Diana and Florencia Cortés-Conde (1997). 'From Bonding and Biting: Conversational Joking and Identity Display', *Journal of Pragmatics* 27: 275–95.
Bradac, James J., Evan Friedman, and Howard Giles (1986). 'A social approach to propositional communication. Speakers lie to hearers', in Graham McGregor (ed.), *Language for Hearers*. Oxford: Pergamon Press, 127–51.
Bradlee, Ben (1995). *A Good Life: Newspapering and Other Adventures*. New York, NY: Simon and Schuster.
Brandom, Robert B. (1994). *Making it Explicit: Reasoning, Representing, and Discursive Commitment*. Cambridge, MA: Harvard University Press.
Brandom, Robert B. (2000). *Articulating Reasons: An Introduction to Inferentialism*. Cambridge, MA: Harvard University Press.
Brandt, Richard (1979). *A Theory of the Good and the Right*. Oxford: Oxford University Press.
Bratman, Michael (1993). 'Shared Intention', *Ethics* 104: 97–113.
Braun, David (2005). 'Empty names, fictional names, mythical names', *Noûs* 39 (4): 596–631.
Brewer, Gayle and Loren Abell (2015). 'Machiavellianism and Sexual Behavior: Motivations, Deception, and Infidelity', *Personality and Individual Differences* 74: 186–91.
Brewer, Marilynn and Ya-Ru Chen (2007). 'Where (who) are collectives in collectivism? Toward conceptual clarification of individualism and collectivism', *Psychological Review* 114 (1): 133–51.
Brickhouse, Thomas C. and Nicholas D. Smith (1983). 'Justice and Dishonesty in Plato's Republic', *Southern Journal of Philosophy* 21: 79–96.
Brickhouse, Thomas C. and Nicholas D. Smith (2000). *The Philosophy of Socrates*. Boulder, CO: Westview Press.
Brooks, D. (1989, October 5). 'Journalists and others for saving the planet', *The Wall Street Journal*, A28: 3.
Brown, Jessica and Herman Cappelen (2011). 'Assertion: An Introduction and Overview', in Jessica Brown and Herman Cappelen (eds), *Assertion. New Philosophical Essays*. Oxford: Oxford University Press, 1–17.

Brown, Penelope (2002). 'Everyone Has to Lie in Tzeltal', in Shoshana Blum-Kulka and Catherine E. Snow (eds), *Talking to Adults: The Contribution of Multiparty Discourse to Language Acquisition*. Mahwah, NJ: Lawrence Erlbaum, 241–75.

Brown, Penelope and Stephen C. Levinson (1987). *Politeness: Some Universals in Language Usage*. Cambridge: Cambridge University Press.

Brown, Peter, Thomas Sutikna, Michael J. Morwood, Raden P. Soejono, Jatmiko, E. Wayhu Saptomo, et al. (2004). 'A new small-bodied hominin from the Late Pleistocene of Flores, Indonesia', *Nature* 431 (7012): 1055–61.

Brown, Roger (1958). *Words and Things*. New York, NY: Free Press.

Brown, Stephen Rex (2014). 'Upstate NY Man Wrongly Convicted of Rape wins $41.6M Lawsuit; Lawyers Say It's Largest Sum in U.S. History. *New York Daily News*. Retrieved from: nydn.us/1FKZieS. Thursday, October 23, 2014.

Brown-Schmidt, Sarah, Christine Gunlogson, and Michael K. Tanenhaus (2008). 'Addressees distinguish shared from private information when interpreting questions during intercative conversation', *Cognition* 107 (3): 1122–34.

Brugioni, Dino A. (1999). *Photo Fakery. A History of Deception and Manipulation*. Dulles, VA: Brassey's Inc.

Bryan, Christopher J., Gabrielle S. Adams, and Benoît Monin (2013). 'When Cheating Would Make You a Cheater: Implicating the Self Prevents Unethical Behavior', *Journal of Experimental Psychology: General* 142 (4): 1001–5.

Bryant, Erin (2008). 'Real lies, white lies and gray lies: Towards a typology of deception', *Kaleidoscope* 7: 23–50.

Bryant, Gregory A. and Jean E. Fox Tree (2002). 'Recognizing verbal irony in spontaneous speech', *Metaphor and Symbol* 17: 99–117.

Buckwalter, Wesley and John Turri (2014). 'Telling, Showing, and Knowing: A Unified Theory of Pedagogical Norms', *Analysis* 74: 16–20.

Buller, David B. and Judee K. Burgoon (1996). 'Interpersonal deception theory', *Communication Theory* 6 (3): 203–42.

Burge, Tyler (1993). 'Content Preservation', *Philosophical Review* 101: 457–488.

Burkett, James P., Elissar Andari, Zachary V. Johnson, Daniel Curry, Frans B. M. de Waal, and Larry J. Young (2016). 'Oxytocin-dependent consolation behavior in rodents', *Science* 351 (6271): 375–8.

Burks, Arthur W. (1946). 'Empiricism and vagueness', *The Journal of Philosophy* 43 (18): 477–86.

Burnett, Heather (2016). *Gradability in Natural Language: Logical and Grammatical Foundations*. Oxford: Oxford University Press.

Burnyeat, Myles F. (1997). 'The Impiety of Socrates', *Ancient Philosophy* 17: 1–12.

Bursztyn, Leonardo, Florian Ederer, Bruno Ferman, and Noam Yuchtman (2014). 'Understanding peer effects in financial decisions: Evidence from a field experiment', *Econometrica* 82 (4): 1273–301.

Burton-Roberts, Noël (2010). 'Cancellation and Intention', in Belén Soria and Esther Romero (eds), *Explicit Communication. Robyn Carston's Pragmatics*. Basingstoke: Palgrave Macmillan, 138–55.

Burton-Roberts, Noël (2013). 'On Grice and cancellation', *Journal of Pragmatics* 48 (1): 17–28.

Bush, George W. (2010). *Decision Points*. New York, NY: Crown.

Bussey, Kay (1992). 'Lying and truthfulness: Children's definitions, standards, and evaluative reactions', *Child Development* 63 (1): 129–37.

Bussey, Kay (1999). 'Children's categorization and evaluation of different types of lies and truths', *Child Development* 70 (6): 1338–47.

Butterfill, Stephen A. and Ian A. Apperly (2013). 'How to Construct a Minimal Theory of Mind', *Mind & Language* 28: 606–37.
Byrne, Christopher C. and Jeffrey A. Kurland (2001). 'Self-deception in an evolutionary game', *Journal of Theoretical Biology* 212 (4): 457–80.
Byrne, Richard W. and Nadia Corp (2004). 'Neocortex size predicts deception rate in primates', *Proceedings. Biological Sciences/The Royal Society* 271 (1549): 1693–9.
Caffi, Claudia (2007). *Mitigation*. London: Elsevier.
Cai, Hongbin and Joseph Tao-Yi Wang (2006). 'Overcommunication in strategic information transmission games', *Games and Economic Behavior* 56: 7–36.
Caldwell, H. Mitchell (2012). 'Coercive Plea Bargaining: The Unrecognized Scourge of the Justice System', *Catholic University Law Review* 61: 63–96.
Call, Josep and Michael Tomasello (1999). 'A nonverbal false belief task: the performance of children and great apes', *Child Development* 70 (2): 381–95.
Call, Josep and Michael Tomasello (2008). 'Does the chimpanzee have a theory of mind? 30 years later', *Trends in Cognitive Sciences* 12 (5): 187–92.
Callaway, Ewen, Thomas Sutikna, Richard Roberts, Wahyu Saptomo, Peter Brown, Henry Gee, et al. (2014). 'The discovery of Homo floresiensis: Tales of the hobbit', *Nature* 514 (7523): 422–6.
Camden, Carl, Michael T. Motley, and Ann Wilson (1984). 'White Lies in Interpersonal Communication: A Taxonomy and Preliminary Investigation of Social Motivations', *The Western Journal of Speech Communication* 48 (4): 309–25.
Camerer, Colin F., Jonathan D. Cohen, Ernst Fehr, Paul W. Glimcher, and David Laibson. (2016). 'Neuroeconomics', in John Kagel and Alvin Roth (eds), *Handbook of Experimental Economics, Vol. 2*. Princeton, NJ: Princeton University Press, 153–216.
Cameron-Faulkner, Thea, Elena Lieven, and Michael Tomasello (2003). 'A construction based analysis of child directed speech', *Cognitive Science* 27 (6): 843–73.
Campbell, John D. and Albert N. Katz (2012). 'Are there necessary conditions for inducing a sense of sarcastic irony?', *Discourse Processes* 49: 459–80.
Cano Mora, Laura (2006). *'How to Make a Mountain out of a Molehill': A Corpus-Based Pragmatic and Conversational Analysis Study of Hyperbole in Interaction*. Doctoral Thesis. Universitat de Valencia: Servei de Publicacions.
Caplan, Jason P., Jonathan F. Borus, Grace Chang, and William E. Greenberg (2008). 'Poor Intentions or Poor Attention: Misrepresentation by Applicants to Psychiatry Residency', *Academic Psychiatry* 32: 225–9.
Cappelen, Alexander, Erik Ø. Sørensen, and Bertil Tungodden (2013). 'When do we lie?', *Journal of Economic Behavior & Organization* 93: 258–65.
Cappelen, Herman and Jessica Brown (eds) (2009). *Assertion*. Oxford: Oxford University Press.
Cappelen, Herman and Ernie Lepore (1997). 'Varieties of quotation', *Mind* 106 (423): 429–50.
Carenini, Giuseppe and Johanna D. Moore (2006). 'Generating and Evaluating Evaluative Arguments', *Artificial Intelligence* 170: 925–52.
Carlson, Stephanie M., Louis J. Moses, and Laura J. Claxton (2004). 'Individual differences in executive functioning and theory of mind: An investigation of inhibitory control and planning ability', *Journal of Experimental Child Psychology* 87 (4): 299–319.
Carlson, Stephanie M., Louis J. Moses, and Hollie R. Hix (1998). 'The role of inhibitory processes in young children's difficulties with deception and false belief', *Child Development* 69 (3): 672–91.
Carmola, Kateri (2003). 'Noble Lying: Justice and Intergenerational Tension in Plato's Republic', *Political Theory* 31: 39–62.

Carr, Albert Z. (1968). 'Is Business Bluffing Ethical?', *Harvard Business Review* 46: 143–53.
Carrión, Ricardo E., Julian P. Keenan, and Natalie Sebanz (2010). 'A truth that's told with bad intent: an ERP study of deception', *Cognition* 114 (1): 105–10.
Carson, Thomas L. (1993). 'Second Thoughts about Bluffing', *Business Ethics Quarterly* 3: 317–41.
Carson, Thomas L. (2006). 'The Definition of Lying', *Noûs* 40 (2): 284–306.
Carson, Thomas L. (2010). *Lying and Deception: Theory and Practice*. Oxford: Oxford University Press.
Carson, Thomas L. (2015). *Lincoln's Ethics*. New York, NY: Cambridge University Press.
Carson, Thomas L. (2016). 'Frankfurt and Cohen on Bullshit, Bullshitting, Deception, Lying, and Concern with the Truth of What One Says', *Pragmatics & Cognition* 23: 54–68.
Carson, Thomas L., Richard E. Wokutch, and Kent F. Murrmann (1982). 'Bluffing in Labor Negotiations: Legal and Ethical Issues', *Journal of Business Ethics* 1: 13–22.
Carston, Robyn (1996). 'Metalinguistic negation and echoic use', *Journal of Pragmatics* 25 (3): 309–30.
Carston, Robyn (2002). *Thoughts and Utterances. The Pragmatics of Explicit Communication*. Oxford: Blackwell.
Carston, Robyn and Catherine Wearing (2011). 'Metaphor, hyperbole and simile: A pragmatic approach', *Language and Cognition* 3 (2): 283–312.
Carter, C. Sue, Jessie R. Williams, Danie M. Witt, and Thomas R. Insel (1992). 'Oxytocin and social bonding', *Annals of the New York Academy of Sciences* 652: 204–11.
Carter, Cameron S. and Vincent van Veen (2007). 'Anterior cingulate cortex and conflict detection: an update of theory and data', *Cognitive, Affective and Behavioral Neuroscience* 7 (4): 367–79.
Caso, Letizia, Augusto Gnisci, Aldert Vrij, and Samantha Mann (2005). 'Processes underlying deception: an empirical analysis of truth and lies when manipulating the stakes', *Journal of Investigative Psychology and Offender Profiling* 2 (3): 195–202.
Castelfranchi, Cristiano and Isabella Poggi (1994). 'Lying as pretending to give information', in H. Parret (ed.), *Pretending to Communicate*, Berlin and New York, NY: De Gruyter, 276–90.
Castells, Manuel (2009). *Communication Power*. Oxford: Oxford University Press.
Caucci, Gina M. and Roger J. Kreuz (2012). 'Social and paralinguistic cues to sarcasm', *Humor* 25: 1–22.
Cecílio, Pedro, Begoña Pérez-Cabezas, Nuno Santarém, Joana Maciel, Vasco Rodrigues, and Anabela Cordeiro-da-Silva (2014). 'Deception and manipulation: the arms of leishmania, a successful parasite', *Frontiers in Immunology* 5: 480.
Chan, Timothy and Guy Kahane (2011). 'The trouble with being sincere', *Canadian Journal of Philosophy* 41(2): 215–34.
Channell, Joanna (1985). 'Vagueness as a conversational strategy', *Nottingham Linguistic Circular* 14: 3–24.
Channell, Joanna (1994). *Vague Language*. Oxford: Oxford University Press.
Chapman, Robert M. and Henry R. Bragdon (1964). 'Evoked Responses to Numerical and Non-Numerical Visual Stimuli While Problem Solving', *Nature* 203: 1155–7.
Chapman, Siobhan (1993). 'Metalinguistic negation, sentences and utterances', *Newcastle and Durham Working Papers in Linguistics* 1: 74–94.
Chapman, Siobhan (1996). 'Some observations on metalinguistic negation', *Journal of Linguistics* 32: 387–402.
Charness, Gary and Martin Dufwenberg (2006). 'Promises and Partnership', *Econometrica* 74: 1579–601.

Charteris-Black, Jonathan (2005). *Politicians and Rhetoric: The Persuasive Power of Metaphor.* London: Palgrave Macmillan.

Chase, Jefferson S. (1993). 'Lying in Swift's "Gulliver's Travels" and Heine's "Atta Troll"', *Comparative Literature* 45: 330–45.

Chen, Rong, Chunmei Hu, and Lin He (2013). '*Lying* between English and Chinese: An intercultural comparative study', *Intercultural pragmatics*: 10 (3): 375–401.

Cheney, Karen L. and Isabelle M. Côté (2005). 'Frequency-dependent success of aggressive mimics in a cleaning symbiosis', *Proceedings. Biological Sciences/The Royal Society* 272 (1581): 2635–9.

Cherry, E. Colin (1953). 'Some experiments on the recognition of speech, with one and with two ears', *Journal of Acoustic Society of America* 25: 975–9.

Chisholm, Roderick M. and Thomas D. Feehan (1977). 'The intent to deceive', *The Journal of Philosophy* 74 (3): 143–59.

Chouliaraki, Lilie and Norman Fairclough (1999). *Discourse in Late Modernity.* Edinburgh: Edinburgh University Press.

Christ, Shawn E., David C. Van Essen, Jason M. Watson, Lindsay E. Brubaker, and Kathleen B. McDermott (2009). 'The contributions of prefrontal cortex and executive control to deception: evidence from activation likelihood estimate meta-analyses', *Cerebral Cortex* 19 (7): 1557–66.

Christian, Sue Ellen (2013). 'Cognitive biases and errors as cause—and Journalistic best practices as effect', *Journal of Mass Media Ethics* 28: 160–74.

Chuang, Rueyling (2003). 'A postmodern critique of cross-cultural and intercultural communication research', in William J. Starosta and Guo-ming Chen (eds), *Ferment in the intercultural field.* Thousand Oaks, CA: Sage, 24–53.

CIA (US Central Intelligence Agency) (2013). *Memorandum for The Honorable Dianne Feinstein, The Honorable Saxby Chambliss. CIA Comments on the Senate Select Committee on Intelligence Report on the Rendition, Detention, and Interrogation Program*, 27 June.

Cialdini, Robert B. and Noah J. Goldstein (2004). 'Social influence: Compliance and conformity', *Annual Review of Psychology* 55 (1): 591–621.

Cialdini, Robert B., Jessica Li, and Adriana Samper (2015). The varied internal costs of unethical leadership: Performance decrements, turnover intentions, and the selective attrition effect. Unpublished ms.

Claridge, Claudia (2011). *Hyperbole in English.* Cambridge: Cambridge University Press.

Clark, Herbert H. (1996). *Using Language.* Cambridge: Cambridge University Press.

Clark, Herbert H. and Brennan, Susan E. (1991). 'Grounding in Communication', in Lauren B. Resnick, John M. Levine, and Stephanie D. Teasley (eds), *Perspectives on Socially Shared Cognition.* Washington, DC: APA Books, 127–49.

Clark, Herbert H. and Jean E. Fox-Tree (2002). 'Using *uh* and *um* in spontaneous speaking', *Cognition* 84 (1): 73–111.

Clark, Herbert H. and Richard J. Gerrig (1984). 'On the pretense theory of irony', *Journal of Experimental Psychology: General* 113: 121–6.

Clark, Herbert H. and Richard J. Gerrig (1990). 'Quotations as demonstrations', *Language* 66: 764–805.

Clark, Herbert H. and Gregory L. Murphy (1982). 'Audience design in meaning and reference', in Jean-Francois Le Ny and Walter Kintsch (eds), *Language and Comprehension.* Amsterdam: North Holland Publishing, 287–99.

Clément, Fabrice, Melissa A. Koenig, and Paul L. Harris (2004). 'The Ontogenesis of Trust', *Mind & Language* 19 (4): 360–79.

Clements, Wendy A. and Josef Perner (1994). 'Implicit understanding of belief', *Cognitive Development* 9: 377–95.
Cliffe, Lionel, Maureen Ramsay, and Dave Bartlett (2000). *The Politics of Lying. Implications for Democracy.* Basingstoke: Macmillan.
Coady, Cecil Anthony John (1992). *Testimony.* Oxford: Oxford University Press.
Coates, Jennifer (1987). 'Epistemic modality and spoken discourse', *Transactions of the Philological Society* 85 (1): 110–31.
Cobreros, Pablo, Paul Egré, David Ripley, and Robert van Rooij (2012). 'Tolerant, Classical, Strict', *The Journal of Philosophical Logic* 41 (2): 347–85.
Cobreros, Pablo, Paul Egré, David Ripley, and Robert van Rooij (2015). 'Pragmatic interpretations of vague expressions: Strongest meaning and nonmonotonic consequence', *Journal of Philosophical Logic* 44 (4): 375–93.
Cohen, Gerald A. (2002). 'Deeper into bullshit', in Sarah Buss and Lee Overton (eds), *Contours of Agency: Essays on Themes from Harry Frankfurt.* Cambridge, MA: MIT Press, 321–39.
Cohen, Jonathan D., Kevin Dunbar, and James L. McClelland (1990). 'On the control of automatic processes: A parallel distributed processing account of the Stroop effect', *Psychological Review* 97: 332–61.
Colb, Sherry F. (2013). 'Rape by Deception, Rape by Impersonation, and a New California Bill', *Justia.com* May 1.
Cole, Shirley A. N. (1996). 'Semantic Prototypes and the Pragmatics of *Lie* Across Cultures', *The LACUS Forum* 23: 475–83.
Coleman, Linda (2007). 'True Lies: Collusion, Evasion, and the Assignment of Responsibility in Cases of Misrepresentation', in Jochen Mecke (ed.), *Cultures of Lying: Theories and Practice of Lying in Society, Literature, and Film.* Berlin–Madison, WI: Galda + Wilch, 47–68.
Coleman, Linda and Paul Kay (1981). 'Prototype Semantics: The English Word *lie*,' *Language* 57 (1): 26–44.
College of William and Mary (1736). 'Statutes of the College of William and Mary in Virginia', *Bulletin of the College of William and Mary* 7: 13–14.
Collodi, Carlo (1988 [1881]). *The Adventures of Pinocchio.* Trans. Carol della Chiesa. New York, NY: Knopf (original Italian ed.: *Le avventure di Pinocchio*, 1881).
Colston, Herbert L. and Raymond W. Gibbs, Jr (2002). 'Are irony and metaphor understood differently?', *Metaphor and Symbol* 17 (1): 57–80.
Colston, Herbert L. and Shana B. Keller (1998). 'You'll Never Believe This: Irony and Hyperbole in Expressing Surprise', *Journal of Psycholinguistic Research* 27: 499–513.
Colston, Herbert L. and Jennifer O'Brien (2000). 'Contrast of Kind Versus Contrast of Magnitude: The Pragmatic Accomplishments of Irony and Hyperbole', *Discourse Processes* 30: 179–99.
Cook, Amy E. and Antje S. Meyer (2008). 'Capacity demands of phoneme selection in word production: New evidence from dual-task experiments', *Journal of Experimental Psychology: Learning, Memory, and Cognition* 34 (4): 886.
Coons, Christian and Michael Weber (eds) (2014). *Manipulation. Theory and Practice.* Oxford: Oxford University Press.
Corner, John (2007). 'Mediated Politics, Promotional Culture and the Idea of Propaganda', *Media, Culture and Society* 29 (3): 669–77.
Corriveau, Kathleen and Paul L. Harris (2009). 'Preschoolers Continue to Trust a More Accurate Informant 1 Week After Exposure to Accuracy Information', *Developmental Science* 12 (1): 188–93.

Corriveau, Kathleen and Paul L. Harris (2010). 'Young Children's Trust in What Other People Say', in Ken J. Rotenberg (ed.), *Interpersonal Trust During Childhood and Adolescence.* Cambridge: Cambridge University Press, 87–109.

Coupland, Nicolas (2004). 'Stylised Deception', in Adam C. Jaworski, Nicolas Coupland, and Dariusz Galasiński (eds), *Metalanguage: Social and Ideological Perspectives.* Berlin: De Gruyter, 259–74.

Crawford, Vincent P. (1998). 'A survey of experiments on communication via cheap talk', *Journal of Economic Theory* 78 (2): 286–98.

Crawford, Vincent P. and Joel Sobel (1982). 'Strategic Information Transmission', *Econometrica* 50 (6): 1431–51.

Culbertson, Hugh M. and Nancy Somerick (1976). 'Quotation marks and bylines—what do they mean to readers?', *Journalism Quarterly* 53: 463–9, 508.

Cummings, Louise (ed.) (2012). *The Pragmatics Encyclopedia.* London: Routledge.

Cuneo, Terence (2015). *Speech and Morality: On the Metaethical Implications of Speaking.* Oxford: Oxford University Press.

Currie, Gregory (1990). *The Nature of Fiction.* Cambridge: Cambridge University Press.

D'Agostini, Franca (2012). *Menzogna* (Lying). Turin: Bollati Boringhieri.

Dale, Anders M. (1999). 'Optimal experimental design for event-related fMRI', *Human Brain Mapping* 8: 109–14.

Dallek, Robert (1979). *Franklin D. Roosevelt and American Foreign Policy 1932-1945.* New York, NY: Oxford University Press.

Dalrymple, Mary, Makoto Kanazawa, Yookyung Kim, Sam Mchombo, and Stanley Peters (1998). 'Reciprocal expressions and the concept of reciprocity', *Linguistics and Philosophy* 21(2): 159–210.

Danks, Joseph H. (1970). 'Encoding of novel figures for communication and memory', *Cognitive Psychology* 1 (2): 171–91.

Danziger, Eve (2010). 'On trying and lying: Cultural configurations of Grice's Maxim of Quality', *Intercultural Pragmatics* 7 (2): 199–219.

Darwin, Charles (1877). 'A biographical sketch of an infant', *Mind* 2 (7): 285–94.

Dasgupta, Purnamita, John Morton, David Dodman, Barış Karapinar, Francisco Meza, Marta G. Rivera-Ferre, et al. (2014). 'Rural areas', in Christopher B. Field, Vincente R. Barros, David Jon Dokken, Katharine J. Mach, Michael D. Mastrandrea, T. Eren Bilir, et al. (eds), *Climate Change 2014: Impacts, Adaptation, and Vulnerability. Part A: Global and Sectoral Aspects. Contribution of Working Group II to the Fifth Assessment Report of the Intergovernmental Panel on Climate Change.* Cambridge: Cambridge University Press, 613–57.

Da Silva, Cayla S. and Amy-May Leach (2013). 'Detecting Deception in Second-Language Speakers', *Legal and Criminological Psychology* 18: 115–27.

Davatzikos, Christos, Kosha Ruparel, Yong Fan, Dinggang Shen, Mausumi Acharyya, James W. Loughead, et al. (2005). 'Classifying spatial patterns of brain activity with machine learning methods: application to lie detection', *NeuroImage* 28 (3): 663–8.

Davidson, Donald (1973). 'Radical Interpretation', *Dialectica* 27: 314–28.

Davidson, Donald (1978). 'What metaphors mean', *Critical Inquiry* 5 (1): 31–47.

Davidson, Donald (1985). 'Deception and Division', in Jon Elster (ed.), *The Multiple Self.* Cambridge: Cambridge University Press, 79–92.

Davidson, Donald (1989). 'A Coherence Theory of Truth and Knowledge', in Ernie LePore (ed.), *Truth and Interpretation: Perspectives on the Philosophy of Donald Davidson.* New York, NY: Blackwell, 307–19.

Davidson, Donald (2004a). 'Paradoxes of Irrationality', in Donald Davidson, *Problems of Rationality*. Oxford: Clarendon Press, 169–88.

Davidson, Donald (2004b). 'Deception and Division', in Donald Davidson, *Problems of Rationality*. Oxford: Clarendon Press, 199–212.

Davidson, Donald (2004c). 'Who is Fooled?', in Donald Davidson, *Problems of Rationality*. Oxford: Clarendon Press, 213–30.

Davis, Wayne (1998). *Implicature: Intention, Convention, and Principle in the Failure of Gricean Theory*. Cambridge: Cambridge University Press.

Debey, Evelyne, Jan De Houwer, and Bruno Verschuere (2014). 'Lying relies on the truth', *Cognition* 132 (3): 324–34.

Debey, Evelyne, Bruno Verschuere, and Geert Crombez (2012). 'Lying and executive control: An experimental investigation using ego depletion and goal neglect', *Acta Psychologica* 140 (2): 133–41.

De Brabanter, Philippe and Patrick Dendale (2008). 'Commitment: The Term and the Notions', *Belgian Journal of Linguistics* 22: 1–14.

Defoe, Daniel (2008 [1719–20]). *Robinson Crusoe*. 3 vols. Oxford: Oxford University Press (first British ed. 1719–20).

Dell, Gary S. (1984). 'The representation of serial order in speech: Evidence from phoneme effect in speech errors', *Journal of Experimental Psychology: Memory & Cognition* 10: 222–33.

Delorme, Arnaud and Scott Makeig (2004). 'EEGLAB: an open source toolbox for analysis of single-trial EEG dynamics including independent component analysis', *Journal of Neuroscience Methods* 134 (1): 9–21.

Demos, Raphael (1960). 'Lying to oneself', *The Journal of Philosophy* 57: 588–95.

Dennett, Daniel (2013). *Intuition Pumps and Other Tools for Thinking*. London: Penguin Books.

DePaulo, Bella M. and Kathy L. Bell (1996). 'Truth and Investment: Lies Are Told to Those Who Care', *Journal of Personality and Social Psychology* 71: 703–16.

DePaulo, Bella M. and Deborah A. Kashy (1998). 'Everyday Lies in Close and Casual Relationships', *Journal of Personality and Social Psychology* 74 (1): 63–79.

DePaulo, Bella M. and Susan E. Kirkendol (1989). 'The motivational impairment effect in the communication of deception', in John C. Yuille (ed.), *Credibility Assessment*. Dordrecht: Kluwer, 51–70.

DePaulo, Bella M. and Roger L. Pfeifer (1986). 'On-the-Job Experience and Skill at Detecting Deception', *Journal of Applied Social Psychology* 16: 249–67.

DePaulo, Bella M., Miron Zuckerman, and Robert Rosenthal (1980). 'Humans as lie detectors', *The Journal of Communication* 30 (2): 129–39.

DePaulo, Bella M., Matthew E. Ansfield, Susan E. Kirkendol, and Joseph M. Boden (2004). 'Serious Lies', *Basic and Applied Social Psychology* 26: 147–67.

DePaulo, Bella M., Deborah A. Kashy, Susan E. Kirkendol, Melissa M. Wyer, and Jennifer A. Epstein (1996). 'Lying in everyday life', *Journal of Personality and Social Psychology* 70 (5): 979–95.

DePaulo, Bella M., James J. Lindsay, Brian E. Malone, Laura Muhlenbruck, Kelly Charlton, and Harris Cooper (2003). 'Cues to deception,' *Psychological Bulletin* 129 (1): 74–118.

DeRose, Keith (1991). 'Epistemic possibilities', *The Philosophical Review* 100 (4): 581–605.

DeRose, Keith (2002). 'Assertion, Knowledge, and Context', *The Philosophical Review* 111: 167–203.

DeRose, Keith (2009). *The Case for Contextualism*. Oxford: Clarendon Press.

Descartes, René (1984). 'Meditations on First Philosophy', in John Cottingham (ed.), *The Philosophical Writings of Descartes, Volume II*. Cambridge: Cambridge University Press, 12–65.

de Villiers, Jill G. and Peter A. de Villiers (2000). 'Linguistic determinism and false belief', in Peter Mitchell and Kevin J. Riggs (eds), *Children's Reasoning and the Mind*. Hove: Psychology Press.

de Waal, Frans B. M. and Pier Francesco Ferrari (2010). 'Towards a bottom-up perspective on animal and human cognition', *Trends in Cognitive Sciences* 14 (5): 201–7.

Deweese-Boyd, Ian (2006). 'Self-deception', in Edward N. Zalta (ed.), *Stanford Encyclopedia of Philosophy*. Online. Available at https://plato.stanford.edu/entries/self-deception//.

De Witt Huberts, Jessie C., Catharine Evers, and Denise T. D. De Ridder (2014). ' "Because I am worth it": A theoretical framework and empirical review of a justification-based account of self-regulation failure', *Personality and Social Psychology Review* 18: 119–38.

Dews, Shelly and Ellen Winner (1999). 'Obligatory processing of the literal and nonliteral meanings of ironic utterances', *Journal of Pragmatics* 31: 1579–99.

Dickhaut, John W., Kevin A. McCabe, and Arijit Mukherji (1995). 'An experimental study of strategic information transmission', *Economic Theory* 6: 389–403.

Dietrichson, Paul (1969). 'Kant's Criteria of Universalizability', in Robert Paul Wolff (ed.), *Kant: Foundations of the Metaphysics of Morals*. Indianapolis, IN: Bobbs-Merrill, 163–207.

Dietz, Simone (2002). *Der Wert der Lüge. Über das Verhältnis von Sprache und Moral*. Paderborn: Mentis.

Dietz, Simone (2003). *Die Kunst des Lügens. Eine sprachliche Fähigkeit und ihr moralischer Wert*. Reinbek: Rowohlt.

Dilmon, Rakefet (2009). 'Between Thinking and Speaking—Linguistic Tools for Detecting a Fabrication', *Journal of Pragmatics* 41 (6): 1152–70.

Dirks, Paul H. G. M., Lee R. Berger, Eric M. Roberts, Jan D. Kramers, John Hawks, Patrick S. Randolph-Quinney, et al. (2015). 'Geological and taphonomic context for the new hominin species Homo naledi from the Dinaledi Chamber, South Africa', *eLife* 4. Online. Available at https://elifesciences.org/articles/09561.

Doherty-Sneddon, Gwyneth, Vicki Bruce, Lesley Bonner, Sarah Longbotham, and Caroline Doyle (2002). 'Development of gaze aversion as disengagement of visual information', *Developmental Psychology* 38: 438–45.

Donagan, Alan (1977). *The Theory of Morality*. Chicago, IL: University of Chicago Press.

Dong, Guangheng, Yanbo Hu, Qilin Lu, and Haiyan Wu (2010). 'The presentation order of cue and target matters in deception study', *Behavioral and Brain Functions* 6: 1–9.

Doran, Ryan, Gregory Ward, Meredith Larson, Yaron McNabb, and Rachel E. Baker (2012). 'A novel experimental paradigm for distinguishing between what is said and what is implicated', *Language* 88 (1), 124–54.

Douglass, John G. (2007). 'Can Prosecutors Bluff? Brady v. Maryland and Plea Bargaining', *Case Western Law Review* 57: 581–92.

Dover, Kenneth J. (1974). *Greek Popular Morality in the Time of Plato and Aristotle*. Indianapolis, IN: Hackett.

Dowe, Phil (2004). 'Why Preventers and Omissions are Not Causes', in Christopher Hitchcock (ed.), *Contemporary Debates in Philosophy of Science*. Malden, MA: Blackwell, 189–96.

Dreber, Anna and Magnus Johannesson (2008). 'Gender differences in deception', *Economics Letters* 99 (1): 197–99.

Du Bois, W. John (2014). 'Towards a dialogic syntax', *Cognitive Linguistics*, 25 (3): 359–410.
Dummett, Michael (1978). *Truth and Other Enigmas*. Cambridge, MA: Harvard University Press.
Dummett, Michael (1981). *Frege: Philosophy of Language*, 2nd edn. London: Duckworth.
Duran, Nicholas D., Rick Dale, and Danielle S. McNamara (2010). 'The action dynamics of overcoming the truth', *Psychonomic Bulletin and Review* 17 (4): 486–91.
Duranti, Alessandro (1993). 'Intentions, self, and responsibilities: an essay in Samoan Ethnopragmatics', in Jane H. Hill and Judith T. Irvine (eds), *Responsibility and Evidence in Oral Discourse* Cambridge: Cambridge University Press, 24–47.
Dyas, Julie Diane (2002). Linguistic Features of Lying under Oath: An Experimental Study of English and French. Doctoral dissertation. The University of Texas at Austin.
Dynel, Marta (2009). *Humorous Garden-Paths: A Pragmatic-Cognitive Study*. Newcastle: Cambridge Scholars Publishing.
Dynel, Marta (2011a). 'A Web of Deceit: A Neo-Gricean View on Types of Verbal Deception', *International Review of Pragmatics* 3 (2): 137–65.
Dynel, Marta (2011b). 'Joker in the Pack: Towards Determining the Status of Humorous Framing in Conversations', in Marta Dynel (ed.), *The Pragmatics of Humour across Discourse Domains*. Amsterdam: John Benjamins, 217–41.
Dynel, Marta (2011c). '"You Talking to Me?" The Viewer as a Ratified Listener to Film Discourse', *Journal of Pragmatics* 43: 1628–44.
Dynel, Marta (2012). 'Garden-Paths, Red Lights and Crossroads: On Finding our Way to Understanding the Cognitive Mechanisms Underlying Jokes', *Israeli Journal of Humor Research: An International Journal* 1: 6–28.
Dynel, Marta (2013a). 'Humorous Phenomena in Dramatic Discourse', *The European Journal of Humor Research* 1: 22–60.
Dynel, Marta (2013b). 'Impoliteness as Disaffiliative Humour in Film Talk', in Marta Dynel (ed.), *Developments in Linguistic Humour Theory*. Amsterdam: John Benjamins, 105–44.
Dynel, Marta (2013c). 'When Does Irony Tickle the Hearer? Towards Capturing the Characteristics of Humorous Irony', in Marta Dynel (ed.), *Developments in Linguistic Humour Theory*. Amsterdam: John Benjamins, 298–320.
Dynel, Marta (2014). 'Isn't it Ironic? Defining the Scope of Humorous Irony', *HUMOR: International Journal of Humor Research* 27: 619–39.
Dynel, Marta (2015). 'Intention to deceive, bald-faced lies, and deceptive implicature: Insights into Lying at the semantics-pragmatics interface', *Intercultural Pragmatics* 12 (3): 309–32.
Dynel, Marta (2016a). 'Comparing and combining covert and overt untruthfulness: On lying, deception, irony and metaphor', *Pragmatics & Cognition* 23 (1): 174–208.
Dynel, Marta (2016b). 'Conceptualizing Conversational Humour as (Im)Politeness: The Case of Film Talk', *Journal of Politeness Research*, 2/2: 117–47.
Dynel, Marta (2018a). *Irony, deception and humour. Seeking the truth about overt and covert untruthfulness*. Berlin and Boston, MA: De Gruyter.
Dynel, Marta (2018b). 'No child's play: A philosophical pragmatic view of overt pretence as a vehicle for conversational humour', in Villy Tsakona and Jan Chovanec (eds), *The Dynamics of Interactional Humour: Creating and Negotiating Humour in Everyday Encounters*. Amsterdam: John Benjamins, 205–28.
Dynel, Marta and Jörg Meibauer (2016). 'Introduction: Everything you Always Wanted to Know about the Pragmatics of Deception but were Afraid to Test', *International Review of Pragmatics* 8: 163–78.

Eckardt, Regine (2014). *The Semantics of Free Indirect Speech. How Texts Let You Read Minds and Eavesdrop*. Leiden: Brill.
Eelen, Gino (2001). *A Critique of Politeness Theories*. Manchester: St. Jerome.
Egan, Andy and Brian Weatherson (eds) (2011). *Epistemic Modality*. Oxford: Oxford University Press.
Egan, Andy, John Hawthorne, and Brian Weatherson (2005). 'Epistemic modals in context', in Gerhard Preyer and Georg Peter (eds), *Contextualism in Philosophy: Knowledge, Meaning and Truth*. Oxford: Clarendon Press, 1–48.
Egré, Paul (2017). 'Vague judgment: a probabilistic account', *Synthese* 194 (10): 3837–65.
Egré, Paul and Florian Cova (2015). 'Moral asymmetries and the semantics of *many*', *Semantics and Pragmatics* 8 (13): 1–45.
Egré, Paul and Nathan Klinedinst (eds) (2011). *Vagueness and Language Use*. Basingstoke: Palgrave Macmillan.
Eichelberger, Julie (2012). A Semantic and Pragmatic Analysis of the Spanish Word Lie: Implications and Applications for the Second Language Learner. Master's thesis. Baylor University.
Eisler, Frieda G. (1968). *Psycholinguistics: Experiments in spontaneous speech*. New York, NY: Academic Press.
Ekman, Paul (1997). 'Deception, lying and demeanor', in Diane F. Halpern and Alexander E. Voiskounsky (eds), *States of Mind: American and Post-Soviet Perspectives on Contemporary Issues in Psychology*. New York, NY: Oxford University Press, 93–105.
Ekman, Paul (2009). *Telling Lies. Clues to Deceit in the Marketplace, Politics, and Marriage*. New York, NY: W.W. Norton.
Ekman, Paul and Maureen O'Sullivan (1991). 'Who Can Catch a Liar?', *American Psychologist* 46: 913–20.
Elaad, Eitan (1998). 'The challenge of the concealed knowledge polygraph test', *Expert Evidence* 6 (3): 161–87.
Ellsberg, Daniel (2003). *Secrets: A Memoir of Vietnam and the Pentagon Papers*. London: Penguin.
Ellul, Jacques (1965). *Propaganda: the Formation of Men's Attitudes*. New York, NY: Alfred Knopf.
El Nakkouzi, Rania (2011). White Lies Telling in Lebanese Discourse. Master's thesis. Lebanese American University.
Emerson, Peter Henry (1889). *Naturalistic Photography for Students of the Art*. London: Sampson Low, Marston, Searle and Rivington.
Ennis, Edel, Aldert Vrij, and Claire Chance (2008). 'Individual Differences and Lying in Everyday Life', *Journal of Social and Personal Relationships* 25: 105–18.
Erat, Sanjiv and Uri Gneezy, Uri (2012). 'White lies', *Management Science* 58 (4): 723–33.
Eriksson, John (2011). 'Straight Talk: Conceptions of Sincerity in Speech', *Philosophical Studies* 153 (2): 213–34.
Erman, Britt and Beatrice Warren (2000). 'The idiom principle and the open choice principle', *Text* 20 (1): 29–62.
Eslami, Zoreh R. (2005). 'Invitations in Persian and English: ostensible or genuine?', *Intercultural Pragmatics* 2 (4): 453–80.
Estrich, Susan (1986). 'Rape', *Yale Law Journal* 95: 1087–184.
Evans, Angela D. and Kang Lee (2011). 'Verbal deceptions from late childhood to middle adolescence and its relation to executive functioning skills', *Developmental Psychology* 47: 39–49.

Evans, Angela D. and Kang Lee (2013). 'Emergence of lying in very young children', *Developmental Psychology* 49: 1958–63.

Evans, Angela D., Fen Xu, and Kang Lee (2011). 'When all signs point to you: Lies told in the face of evidence', *Developmental Psychology* 47: 39–49

Fabiani, Monica, Demetrios Karis, and Emanuel Donchin (1986). 'P300 and recall in an incidental memory paradigm', *Psychophysiology* 23 (3): 298–308.

Fagin, Ronald, Joseph Halpern, Yoram Moses, and Moshe Vardi (1995). *Reasoning About Knowledge*. Cambridge, MA: MIT Press.

Fairclough, Norman (1992). *Discourse and Social Change*. Oxford: Polity Press.

Fairclough, Norman and Ruth Wodak (1997). 'Critical Discourse Analysis', in Teun A. van Dijk (ed.), *Discourse as Social Interaction*. London: Sage, 258–84.

Falk, Dean, Charles Hildebolt, Kirk Smith, Michael J. Morwood, Thomas Sutikna, Peter Brown, et al. (2005). 'The brain of LB1, Homo floresiensis', *Science* 308 (5719): 242–5.

Falk, Dean, Charles Hildebolt, Kirk Smith, Michael J. Morwood, Thomas Sutikna, Jatmiko, et al. (2009). 'LB1's virtual endocast, microcephaly, and hominin brain evolution', *Journal of Human Evolution* 57 (5): 597–607.

Falk, Patricia J. (1998). 'Rape by Fraud and Rape by Coercion', *Brooklyn Law Review* 64: 44–180.

Falkenberg, Gabriel (1980). 'Lying and Truthfulness', in Rudolf Haller and Wolfgang Grassl (eds), *Language, Logic, and Philosophy. Proceedings of the fourth international Wittgenstein Symposium 1979*, Wien: Hölder-Pichler-Temsky, 328–31.

Falkenberg, Gabriel (1982). *Lügen. Grundzüge einer Theorie sprachlicher Täuschung*. Tübingen: Niemeyer.

Falkenberg, Gabriel (1988). 'Insincerity and disloyalty', *Argumentation* 2 (1): 89–97.

Falkenberg, Gabriel (1990). 'Searle on sincerity', in Armin Burkhardt (ed.), *Speech Acts, Meaning and Intentions. Critical Approaches to the Philosophy of J. R. Searle*. Berlin and New York, NY: De Gruyter, 129–46.

Fallis, Don (2009). 'What is Lying?', *The Journal of Philosophy* 106 (1): 29–56.

Fallis, Don (2010a). 'Lying and Deception', *Philosopher's Imprint* 10 (11): 1–22.

Fallis, Don (2010b). 'What is Deceptive Lying?', Paper presented at the *Pacific Division Meeting of the American Philosophical Association*. Online. Available at: https://papers.ssrn.com/sol3/papers.cfm?abstract_id=1702023.

Fallis, Don (2010c). Bayesians Don't Tell Knowledge-Lies (and probably nobody else does either), ms. University of Arizona.

Fallis, Don (2011). 'What liars can tell us about the knowledge norm of practical reasoning', *The Southern Journal of Philosophy* 49 (4): 347–67.

Fallis, Don (2012). 'Lying as a Violation of Grice's First Maxim of Quality', *Dialectica* 66 (4): 563–81.

Fallis, Don (2013a). 'Privacy and Lack of Knowledge', *Episteme* 10, Special Issue 2: 153–66.

Fallis, Don (2013b). 'Davidson was Almost Right About Lying', *Australasian Journal of Philosophy* 91: 337–53.

Fallis, Don (2015a). 'Are Bald-Faced Lies Deceptive After All?' *Ratio* 28: 81–96.

Fallis, Don (2015b). 'Frankfurt wasn't bullshitting!', *Southwest Philosophical Studies* 37, 11–20.

Fara, Delia (2000). 'Shifting Sands: an Interest-Relative Theory of Vagueness', *Philosophical Topics* 28 (1): 45–81. [Originally published under the name "Delia Graff".]

Farah, Martha J., J. Benjamin Hutchinson, Elizabeth A. Phelps, and Anthony D. Wagner (2014). 'Functional MRI-based lie detection: scientific and societal challenges', *Nature Reviews. Neuroscience* 15 (2): 123–31.

Farkas, Donka and Kim Bruce (2009). 'On Reacting to Assertions and Polar Questions', *Journal of Semantics* 27 (1): 81–118.
Farrell, Joseph (1993). 'Meaning and Credibility in Cheap-Talk Games', *Games and Economic Behavior* 5 (4): 514–31.
Farrell, Joseph and Matthew Rabin (1996). 'Cheap Talk', *Journal of Economic Perspectives* 10 (3): 103–18.
Farrow, Tom F. D., Jenny Burgess, Iain D. Wilkinson, and Michael D. Hunter (2015). 'Neural correlates of self-deception and impression-management', *Neuropsychologia* 67: 159–74.
Farrow, Tom F. D., Marie-Clare Hopwood, Randolph Parks, Michael D. Hunter, and Sean A. Spence (2010). 'Evidence of mnemonic ability selectively affecting truthful and deceptive response dynamics', *The American Journal of Psychology* 123 (4): 447–53.
Farwell, Lawrence A. and Emanuel Donchin (1991). 'The truth will out: interrogative polygraphy ("lie detection") with event-related brain potentials', *Psychophysiology* 28 (5): 531–47.
Fauconnier, Gilles (1994). *Mental Spaces: Aspects of Meaning Construction in Natural Language.* Cambridge: Cambridge University Press.
Faulkner, Paul (2007). 'What is wrong with lying?', *Philosophy and Phenomenological Research* 75 (3): 535–57.
Faulkner, Paul (2013). 'Lying and Deceit,' in Hugh LaFollette (ed.), *International Encyclopedia of Ethics*. Hoboken, NJ: Wiley-Blackwell, 3101–9.
Fawcett, Tom (2006). 'An introduction to ROC analysis', *Pattern Recognition Letters* 27: 861–74.
Fein, Ofer, Menahem Yeari, and Rachel Giora (2015). 'On the priority of salience-based interpretations: The case of irony', *Intercultural Pragmatics* 12 (1): 1–32.
Feldman, Richard and Earl Conee (2001). 'Internalism Defended', *American Philosophical Quarterly* 38 (1): 1–18.
Feldman, Robert S., James A. Forrest, and Benjamin R. Happ (2002). 'Self-Presentation and Verbal Deception: Do Self-Presenters Lie More?', *Basic and Applied Social Psychology* 24: 163–70.
Ferenz, Volker (2008). *Don't Believe His Lies. The Unreliable Narrator in Contemporary American Cinema*. Trier: WVT.
Ferguson, Heather J. and Richard Breheny (2011). 'Eye movements reveal the time-course of anticipating behavior based on complex, conflicting desires', *Cognition* 119 (2): 179–96.
Ferreira, Victor S. and Harold Pashler (2002). 'Central bottleneck influences on the processing stages of word production', *Journal of Experimental Psychology: Learning, Memory, and Cognition* 28 (6): 1187.
Field, Hartry (1994). 'Deflationist Views of Meaning and Content', *Mind* 103 (411): 249–85.
Fielding, Nick and Ian Cobain (2011). 'Revealed: US spy operation that manipulates social media', *The Guardian*, 17 March.
Filik, Ruth and Linda M. Moxey (2010). 'The on-line processing of written irony', *Cognition* 116: 421–36.
Filik, Ruth, Hartmut Leuthold, Katie Wallington, and Jemma Page (2014). 'Testing theories of irony processing using eye-tracking and ERPs', *Journal of Experimental Psychology: Learning, Memory, and Cognition* 40 (3): 811–28.
Fine, Kit (1975). 'Vagueness, Truth, and Logic', *Synthese* 30, 265–300.
Fingarette, Herbert (2000). *Self-deception*. Berkeley, CA: University of California Press.
Finkenauer, Catrin, Peter Kerkhof, Francesca Righetti, and Susan Branje (2009). 'Living Together Apart: Perceived Concealment as a Signal of Exclusion in Marital Relationships', *Personality and Social Psychology Bulletin* 35: 1410–22.

Fintel, Kai von and Anthony Gillies (2008). 'CIA leaks', *Philosophical Review* 117(1): 77–98.

Fischbacher, Urs and Franziska Heusi (2008). 'Lies in disguise: an experimental study on cheating', *Journal of the European Economic Association* 11 (3): 525–47.

Fleck, Ludwik (1980): *Entstehung und Entwicklung einer wissenschaftlichen Tatsache. Einführung in die Lehre vom Denkstil und Denkkollektiv*. Frankfurt am Main: Suhrkamp.

Foley, Richard (2001). *Intellectual Trust in Oneself and Others*. Cambridge: Cambridge University Press.

Foley, Richard (2005). 'Universal Intellectual Trust', *Episteme* 2 (1): 5–12.

Folstein, Jonathan R. and Cyma Van Petten (2008). 'Influence of cognitive control and mismatch on the N2 component of the ERP: a review', *Psychophysiology* 45 (1): 152–70.

Forabosco, Giovannantonio (1992). 'Cognitive Aspects of the Humour Process: The Concept of Incongruity', *Humor* 5: 9–26.

Forabosco, Giovannantonio (2008). 'Is the Concept of Incongruity Still a Useful Construct for the Advancement of Humor Research?', *Lodz Papers in Pragmatics* 4: 45–62.

Foreign Policy (July 21, 2015) 'There's Still Hope for the Legacy of Tunisia's Arab Spring', by Paul Bonicelli. Available at https://www.foreignpolicyjournal.com.

Fowler, Roger (1996). 'On critical linguistics', in Carmen Rosa Caldas-Coulthard and Malcolm Coulthard (eds), *Texts and Practices*. London: Routledge, 3–14.

Fox, Danny (2014). 'Cancelling the Maxim of Quantity: Another challenge for a Gricean theory of scalar implicatures', *Semantics and Pragmatics* 7 (5): 1–20.

Fox-Tree, Jean E. and Josef C. Schrock (1999). 'Discourse markers in spontaneous speech: Oh what a difference an *oh* makes', *Journal of Memory and Language* 40 (2): 280–95.

Frangipane, Nicholas (2016). 'Lockwood the Liar: A Call to Reconsider "Wuthering Heights" as a Metafictional Work on the Limits of Narrative', *Brontë Studies: The Journal of the Brontë Society* 41 (1): 29–38.

Franke Michael, Tikitu de Jager, and Robert van Rooij (2009). 'Relevance in Cooperation and Conflict', *Journal of Logic and Computation* 22 (1): 23–54.

Frankfurt, Harry G. (1986). 'On Bullshit', *Raritan* 6 (1986): 81–100.

Frankfurt, Harry G. (1988). *The Importance of What we Care About*. Cambridge: Cambridge University Press.

Frankfurt, Harry G. (2002). 'Reply to G.A. Cohen', in Sarah Buss and Lee Overton (eds), *Contours of Agency: Essays on Themes from Harry Frankfurt*. Cambridge, MA: MIT Press, 340–4.

Frankfurt, Harry G. (2005). *On Bullshit*. Princteon, NJ: Princeton University Press.

Frankish, Keith (2009). 'Partial belief and flat-out belief', in Franz Huber and Christoph Schmidt-Petri (eds), *Degrees of Belief*. Berlin: Springer, 75–93.

Franklin, Benjamin (1789). 'Letter to Jean-Baptiste Leroy' (13/11/1789), in *Bartlett's Familiar Quotations*, tenth edn (1919/2002), New York, NY: Bartleby.

Fraser, Bruce (1980). 'Conversational mitigation', *Journal of Pragmatics* 4: 341–50.

Fraser, Bruce (1994). 'No Conversation without Misrepresentation', in Herman Parret (ed.), *Pretending to Communicate*. New York, NY: De Gruyter, 143–53.

Frazee, Joey and David Beaver (2010). 'Vagueness Is Rational under Uncertainty', in Maria Aloni, Harald Bastiaanse, Tikitu de Jager, and Katrin Schulz (eds), *Logic, Language and Meaning. Lecture Notes in Computer Science*. Lecture Notes in Computer Science. Vol. 6042. Berlin, Heidelberg, and New York, NY: Springer, 153–62.

Frege, Gottlob (1892). 'Über Sinn und Bedeutung', *Zeitschrift für Philosophie und philosophische Kritik* 100 (1): 25–50.

Frege, Gottlob (1997 [1918–19]). 'Thought/Der Gedanke', in Michael Beaney (ed.), *The Frege Reader*. Oxford: Blackwell, 325–45.

Frege, Gottlob (1952). 'On Sense and Reference', in Peter Geach and Max Black (eds), *Translations from the Philosophical Writings of Gottlob Frege*. Oxford: Blackwell, 56–78.

Freud, Sigmund (1938). *The Basic Writings of Sigmund Freud* (Modern Library Edition). New York, NY: Random House.

Fricker, Elizabeth (1994). 'Against Gullibility', in Bimal K. Matilal and Arindam Chakrabarti (eds), *Knowing from Words: Western and Indian Philosophical Analysis of Understanding and Testimony*. London: Kluwer Academic Publishers, 125–61.

Fricker, Elizabeth (1995). 'Telling and Trusting: Reductionism and Anti-Reductionism in the Epistemology of Testimony', *Mind* 104: 393–411.

Fricker, Elizabeth (2006). 'Varieties of Anti-Reductionism About Testimony: A Reply to Goldberg and Henderson', *Philosophy and Phenomenological Research* 72 (3): 618–28.

Fricker, Elizabeth (2012). 'Stating and Insinuating', *Proceedings of the Aristotelian Society, Supplementary Volume* 86: 61–94.

Fricker, Elizabeth (2014). 'Epistemic Trust in Oneself and Others—An Argument from Analogy?', in Laura Frances Goins and Timothy O'Connor (eds), *Religious Faith and Intellectual Virtue*. Oxford: Oxford University Press, 174–203.

Fricker, Elizabeth (2016a). 'Doing what comes naturally: Zagzebski on rationality and epistemic self-trust', *Episteme* 13 (2): 151–66.

Fricker, Elizabeth (2016b). 'Unreliable Testimony', in Brian McLaughlin and Hilary Kornblith (eds), *Goldman and his Critics*. Oxford: Wiley-Blackwell, 88–120.

Fried, Charles (1978). *Right and Wrong*. Cambridge, MA: Harvard University Press.

Friedrich, Carl Joachim (1943). 'Issues of Informational Strategy', *Public Opinion Quarterly* 7 (1): 77–89.

Friend, Stacie (2007). 'Fictional Characters', *Philosophy Compass* 2 (2): 141–56.

Fu, Genyue, Angela D. Evans, Lingfeng Wang, and Kang Lee (2008). 'Lying in the name of the collective good: A developmental study', *Developmental Science* 11: 495–503.

Fu, Genyue, Kang Lee, Catherine Ann Cameron, and Fen Xu (2001). 'Chinese and Canadian adults' categorization and evaluation of lie- and truth-telling about prosocial and antisocial behaviours', *Journal of Cross-Cultural Psychology* 32 (6): 720–7.

Fu, Genyue, Fen Xu, Catherine A. Cameron, Gail Heyman, and Kang Lee (2007). 'Cross-cultural differences in children's choices, categorizations, and evaluations of truths and lies', *Developmental Psychology* 43: 278–93.

Fullam, Rachael S., Shane McKie, and Mairead C. Dolan (2009). 'Psychopathic traits and deception: functional magnetic resonance imaging study', *British Journal of Psychiatry* 194 (3): 229–35.

Furedy, John J., Caroline Davis, and Maria Gurevich (1988). 'Differentiation of deception as a psychological process: a psychophysiological approach', *Psychophysiology* 25 (6): 683–8.

Furedy, John J., Francesca Gigliotti, and Gershon Ben-Shakhar (1994). 'Electrodermal differentiation of deception: The effect of choice versus no choice of deceptive items', *International Journal of Psychophysiology* 18 (1): 13–22.

Furedy, John J., Ruth T. Posner, and Alex Vincent (1991). 'Electrodermal differentiation of deception: perceived accuracy and perceived memorial content manipulations', *International Journal of Psychophysiology* 11 (1): 91–7.

Galanxhi, Holtjona and Fiona Fui-Hoon Nah (2007). 'Deception in Cyberspace: A Comparison of Text-only vs. Avatar-supported Medium', *International Journal of Human-Computer Studies* 65: 770–83.

Galasiński, Dariusz (2000). *The Language of Deception: A Discourse Analytical Study.* Thousand Oaks, CA: Sage.
Galasiński, Dariusz (2004). 'Restoring the order. Metalanguage in the press coverage of Princess Diana's "Panorama" interview', in Adam Jaworski, Nikolas Coupland, and Dariusz Galasinski (eds), *Metalanguage.* Berlin: De Gruyter, 131–45.
Galasiński, Dariusz and Justyna Ziółkowska (2013). 'Managing information. Misrepresentation in the patient's notes', *Qualitative Inquiry* 19: 589–99.
Gallant, Tricia Bertram (2008). 'Revisiting the past: The historical context of academic integrity', *ASHE Higher Education Report* 33: 13–31.
Gamer, Matthias (2011). 'Detection of deception and concealed information using neuroimaging techniques', in Bruno Verschuere, Gershon Ben-Shakhar, and Ewout H. Meijer (eds), *Memory Detection: Theory and Application of the Concealed Information Test.* Cambridge: Cambridge University Press, 90–114.
Gamer, Matthias (2014). 'Mind reading using neuroimaging. Is this the future of deception detection?', *European Psychologist* 19 (3): 172–83.
Gamer, Matthias and Stefan Berti (2010). 'Task relevance and recognition of concealed information have different influences on electrodermal activity and event-related brain potentials', *Psychophysiology* 47 (2): 355–64.
Gamer, Matthias, Thomas Bauermann, Peter Stoeter, and Gerhard Vossel (2007). 'Covariations among fMRI, skin conductance, and behavioral data during processing of concealed information', *Human Brain Mapping* 28: 1287–301.
Ganis, Giorgio (2015). 'Deception detection using neuroimaging', in Pär Anders Granhag, Aldert Vrij, and Bruno Verschuere (eds), *Detecting Deception.* New York, NY: John Wiley, 105–22.
Ganis, Giorgio and Pooja Patnaik (2009). 'Detecting concealed knowledge using a novel attentional blink paradigm', *Applied Psychophysiology and Biofeedback* 34 (3): 189–96.
Ganis, Giorgio and Haline E. Schendan (2012). 'Concealed semantic and episodic autobiographical memory electrified', *Frontiers in Human Neuroscience* 6: 354.
Ganis, Giorgio, Robert R. Morris, and Stephen M. Kosslyn (2009). 'Neural processes underlying self- and other-related lies: An individual difference approach using fMRI', *Social Neuroscience* 4 (6): 539–53.
Ganis, Giorgio, J. Peter Rosenfeld, John Meixner, Rogier A. Kievit, and Haline E. Schendan (2011). 'Lying in the scanner: covert countermeasures disrupt deception detection by functional magnetic resonance imaging', *NeuroImage* 55 (1): 312–19.
Ganis, Giorgio, Stephen M. Kosslyn, S. Stose, William Lee Thompson, and Deborah A. Yurgelun-Todd (2003). 'Neural correlates of different types of deception: an fMRI investigation', *Cerebral Cortex* 13 (8): 830–6.
Garber, Marjorie (1999). ' " " (Quotation Marks)', *Critical Inquiry* 25: 653–64.
García-Carpintero, Manuel (2015). 'Contexts as Shared Commitments', *Frontiers in Psychology* 22 (6): 1932.
Gardiner, Patrick (1970). 'Error, faith, and self-deception', *Proceedings of the Aristotelian Society* 70: 221–43.
Gardner, Roy and Morris, Molly R. (1989). 'The Evolution of Bluffing in Animal Contests: An ESS Approach', *Journal of Theoretical Biology* 137: 235–43.
Gaskett, Anne C. (2011). 'Orchid pollination by sexual deception: pollinator perspectives', *Biological Reviews of the Cambridge Philosophical Society* 86 (1): 33–75.
Gass, Robert H. and John S. Seiter (2014). *Persuasion, Social Influence, and Compliance Gaining,* 5th edn. Boston, MA: Pearson/Allyn & Bacon.

Gass, Susan M. and Noel Houck (1999). *Interlanguage Refusals*. Berlin: De Gruyter.
Gehring, William J. and Robert T. Knight (2000). 'Prefrontal-cingulate interactions in action monitoring', *Nature Neuroscience* 3 (5): 516–520.
Gehring, William J. and Adrian R. Willoughby (2002). 'The medial frontal cortex and the rapid processing of monetary gains and losses', *Science* 295 (5563): 2279–82.
Geis, Michael L. (1982). *The Language of Television Advertising*. New York, NY: Academic Press.
George, Joey F. and Alastair Robb (2008). 'Deception and Computer-Mediated Communication in Daily Life', *Communication Reports* 21: 92–103.
Gerhart, Barry and Meiyu Fang (2005). 'National culture and human resource management: assumptions and evidence', *International Journal of Human Resource Management* 16(6): 971–86.
Gerken, Mikkel (2013). 'Internalism and Externalism in the Epistemology of Testimony', *Philosophy and Phenomenological Research* 87 (3): 532–57.
Gervais, Jean, Richard E. Tremblay, Lyse Desmarais-Gervais, and Frank Vitaro (2000). 'Children's persistent lying, gender differences, and disruptive behaviors: A longitudinal perspective', *International Journal of Behavioral Development* 24 (2): 213–21.
Geuss, Raymond (2014). 'A Note on Lying', in Raymond Geuss, *A World Without Why*. Princeton, NJ: Princeton University Press, 135–43.
Geyer, Naomi (2010). 'Teasing and Ambivalent Face in Japanese Multi-Party Discourse', *Journal of Pragmatics* 42: 2120–30.
Gibbs, Raymond W. Jr (1980). 'Spilling the beans on understanding and memory for idioms in conversation', *Memory and Cognition* 8: 449–56.
Gibbs, Raymond W. Jr (1981). 'Your wish is my command: Convention and context in interpreting indirect requests', *Journal of Verbal Learning and Verbal Behavior* 20: 431–44.
Gibbs, Raymond W. Jr (1986a). 'Comprehension and memory for nonliteral utterances: The problem of sarcastic indirect requests', *Acta Psychologica* 62: 41–57.
Gibbs, Raymond W. Jr (1986b). 'On the psycholinguistics of sarcasm', *Journal of Experimental Psychology: General* 115: 3–15.
Gibbs, Raymond W. Jr (1994). *The Poetics of Mind: Figurative Thought, Language, and Understanding*. Cambridge: Cambridge University Press.
Gibbs, Raymond W. Jr (1999). *Intentions in the Experience of Meaning*. Cambridge: Cambridge University Press.
Gibbs, Raymond W. Jr (2002). 'A new look at literal meaning in understanding what is said and implicated', *Journal of Pragmatics* 34: 457–86.
Gibbs, Raymond W. Jr and Herbert L. Colston (2012). *Interpreting Figurative Meaning*. Cambridge: Cambridge University Press.
Gibson, Rhonda and Dolf Zillmann (1993). 'The impact of quotation in news reports on issue Perception', *Journalism Quarterly* 70: 793–800.
Gibson, Rajna, Carmen Tanner, and Alexander F. Wagner (2013). 'Preferences for Truthfulness: Heterogeneity among and within Individuals', *American Economic Review* 103 (1): 532–48.
Gil, Armande (2005). 'Repressing distress in childhood: a defense against health-related stress', *Child Psychiatry and Human Development* 36 (1): 27–52.
Gilbert, Daniel T. and Edward E. Jones (1986). 'Perceiver-induced constraint: Interpretations of self-generated reality', *Journal of Personality and Social Psychology* 50 (2): 269–80.
Gilbert, Daniel T. and Patrick S. Malone (1995). 'The correspondence bias', *Psychological Bulletin* 117: 21–38.

Gilbert, Daniel T., Douglas S. Krull, and Patrick S. Malone (1990). 'Unbelieving the Unbelievable: Some Problems in the Rejection of False Information', *Journal of Personality and Social Psychology* 59 (4): 601–13.

Gilbert, Margaret (1989). *On Social Facts*. London and New York, NY: Routledge.

Giles, Howard and Tania Ogay (2007). 'Communication accommodation theory', in Bryan B. Whaley and Wendy Samter (eds), *Explaining Communication: Contemporary Theories and Exemplars*. Mahwah, NJ: Lawrence Erlbaum, 293–310.

Gill, Christopher (1993). 'Plato on Falsehood—not Fiction', in Christopher Gill and T. P. Wiseman (eds), *Lies and Fiction in the Ancient World*. Austin, TX: University of Texas, 38–87.

Gillath, Omri, Amanda K. Sesko, Philip R. Shaver, and David S. Chun (2010). 'Attachment, Authenticity, and Honesty: Dispositional and Experimentally Induced Security Can Reduce Self- and Other-Deception', *Journal of Personality and Social Psychology* 98: 841–55.

Gilovich, Thomas, Kenneth Savitsky, and Victoria H. Medvec (1998). 'The illusion of transparency: Biased assessments of others' ability to read our emotional states', *Journal of Personality and Social Psychology* 75: 332–46.

Giora, Rachel (1994). 'On the Political Message: Pretending to Communicate', in Herman Parret (ed.), *Pretending to Communicate*. New York, NY: De Gruyter, 104–23.

Giora, Rachel (1995). 'On irony and negation', *Discourse Processes* 19: 239–64.

Giora, Rachel (1997). 'Understanding figurative and literal language: The graded salience hypothesis', *Cognitive Linguistics* 7: 183–206.

Giora, Rachel (1999). 'On the priority of salient meanings: Studies of literal and figurative language' *Journal of Pragmatics* 31: 919–29.

Giora, Rachel (2003). *On our Mind: Salience, Context, and Figurative Language*. New York, NY: Oxford University Press.

Giora, Rachel (2011). 'Will anticipating irony facilitate it immediately?', in Marta Dynel (ed.), *The Pragmatics of Humour across Discourse Domains*. Amsterdam: John Benjamins, 19–31.

Giora, Rachel (2015). 'Default nonliteral interpretations: The case of negation as a low-salience marker', in Ewa Dąbrowska and Dagmar Divjak (eds), *Handbook of Cognitive Linguistics* (Handbooks of Linguistics and Communication Science 39), Berlin, Boston, MA: De Gruyter Mouton, 593–615.

Giora, Rachel and Ofer Fein (1999b). 'Irony: Context and salience', *Metaphor and Symbol* 14: 241–57.

Giora, Rachel and Inbal Gur (2003). 'Irony in conversation: salience and context effects', in Brigitte Nerlich, Zazie Todd, Vimala Herman, and David Clarke (eds), *Polysemy: Flexible Patterns of Meanings in Language and Mind*. Berlin: De Gruyter, 297–316.

Giora, Rachel, Ari Drucker, and Ofer Fein (2014). 'Resonating with default nonsalient interpretations: A corpus-based study of negative sarcasm', *Belgian Journal of Linguistics* 28: 3–18.

Giora, Rachel, Ofer Fein, and Tamir Schwartz (1998). 'Irony: Graded salience and indirect negation', *Metaphor and Symbol* 13: 83–101.

Giora, Rachel, Shir Givoni, and Ofer Fein (2015). 'Defaultness reigns: The case of sarcasm', *Metaphor and Symbol* 30 (4): 290–313.

Giora, Rachel, Ari Drucker, Ofer Fein, and Itamar Mendelson (2015). 'Default sarcastic interpretations: On the priority of nonsalient interpretations', *Discourse Processes* 52 (3): 173–200.

Giora, Rachel, Moshe Raphaely, Ofer Fein, and Elad Livnat (2014). 'Resonating with contextually inappropriate interpretations in production: The case of irony', *Cognitive Linguistics* 25(3): 443–55.

Giora, Rachel, Ofer Fein, Ronie Kaufman, Dana Eisenberg, and Shani Erez (2009). 'Does an "ironic situation" favor an ironic interpretation?', in Geert Brône and Jeroen Vandaele (eds), *Cognitive Poetics: Goal, Gain and Gaps*. Berlin: De Gruyter, 383–99.

Giora, Rachel, Ofer Fein, Nili Metuki, and Pnina Stern, P. (2010). 'Negation as a metaphor-inducing operator', in Laurence R. Horn (ed.), *The Expression of Negation*. Berlin and New York, NY: De Gruyter, 225–56.

Giora, Rachel, Inbal Jaffe, Israela Becker, and Ofer Fein (2018). 'Strongly attenuating highly positive concepts: The case of default sarcastic interpretations', *Review of Cognitive Linguistics*. 6 (1): 19–47.

Giora, Rachel, Eran Zaidel, Nachum Soroker, Gila Batori, and Asa Kasher (2000). 'Differential Effect of Right and Left Hemispheric Damage on Understanding Sarcasm and Metaphor', *Metaphor and Symbol* 15: 63–83.

Giora, Rachel, Elad Livnat, Ofer Fein, Anat Barnea, Rakefet Zeiman, and Iddo Berger (2013). 'Negation generates nonliteral interpretations by default', *Metaphor and Symbol* 28: 89–115.

Giora, Rachel, Ofer Fein, Dafna Laadan, Joe Wolfson, Michal Zeituny, Ran Kidron, et al. (2007). 'Expecting irony: Context vs. salience-based effects', *Metaphor and Symbol* 22: 119–46.

Givoni, Shir, Rachel Giora, and Dafna Bergerbest (2013). 'How speakers alert addressees to multiple meanings', *Journal of Pragmatics* 48 (1): 29–40.

Glaser, Wilhelm R. and Franz-Josef Düngelhoff (1984). 'The time course of picture-word interference'. *Journal of Experimental Psychology: Human Perception and Performance* 10 (5): 650–4.

Gneezy, Uri (2005). 'Deception: The role of consequences', *American Economic Review* 95 (1): 384–94.

Gneezy, Uri (ed.) (2013). 'Special Issue: Deception, Incentives and Behavior', *Journal of Economic Behavior & Organization* 93: 196–413.

Gneezy, Uri, Bettina Rockenbach, and Marta Serra-Garcia (2013). 'Measuring lying aversion', *Journal of Economic Behavior & Organization* 93: 293–300.

Gneezy, Uri, Silvia Saccardo, Marta Serra-Garcia, and Roel van Veldhuizen (2015). 'Bribing the self'. Mimeo.

Goatly, Andrew (1997). *The Language of Metaphors*. London and New York, NY: Routledge.

Goffman, Erving (1974). *Frame Analysis: An Essay in the Organization of Experience*. Cambridge, MA: Harvard University Press.

Goldberg, Sanford C. (2008). 'Testimonial Knowledge in Early Childhood, Revisited', *Philosophy and Phenomenological Research* 76 (1): 1–36.

Goldberg, Sanford C. (2011). '"If That Were True I Would Have Heard about It by Now"', in Alvin Goldman and Dennis Whitcomb (eds), *Social Epistemology*. Oxford: Oxford University Press, 92–108.

Goldberg, Sanford C. (2015). *Assertion. On the Philosophical Significance of Assertoric Speech*. Oxford: Oxford University Press.

Goldman, Alvin I. (1979). 'What Is Justified Belief?', in George Sotiros Pappas (ed.), *Justification and Knowledge*. Philosophical Studies Series, Vol 17. Dordrecht: Springer, 1–25.

Goldman-Eisler, Frieda (1968). *Psycholinguistics: Experiments in Spontaneous Speech*. London: Academic Press.

Gombrich, Ernst H. (1968). *Art and Illusion*. London: Phaidon.

Gordon, Nathan J., William L. Felisher, and C. Donald Weinberg (2002). *Effective Interviewing and Interrogation Techniques*. San Diego, CA: Academic Press.

Gore, Al (1992). *Earth in the Balance*. New York, NY: Houghton Mifflin.

Graham, Peter J. (2006). 'Liberal Fundamentalism and Its Rivals', in Jennifer Lackey and Ernest Sosa (eds), *The Epistemology of Testimony*. Oxford: Clarendon Press, 93–115.

Gramzow, Richard H. and Greg Willard (2006). 'Exaggerating Current and Past Performance: Motivated Self-Enhancement Versus Reconstructive Memory', *Personality and Social Psychology Bulletin* 32: 1114–25.

Granhag, Pär Anders, Franziska Clemens, and Leif A. Strömwall (2009). 'The Usual and the Unusual Suspects: Level of Suspicion and Counter-Interrogation Tactics', *Journal of Investigative Psychology and Offender Profiling* 6: 129–37.

Granhag, Pär Anders, Aldert Vrij, and Bruno Verschuere (eds) (2015). *Detecting Deception. Current Challenges and Cognitive Approaches*. Chichester: Wiley.

Granhag, Pär Anders, Lars O. Andersson, Leif A. Strömwall, and Maria Hartwig (2004). 'Imprisoned knowledge: Criminals' beliefs about deception', *Legal and Criminological Psychology* 9: 103–19.

Grant, Colin King (1958). 'Pragmatic implication', *Philosophy* 33 (127): 303–24.

Greely, Henry T., and Judy Illes (2007). 'Neuroscience-based lie detection: The urgent need for regulation', *American Journal of Law and Medicine* 33: 377–431.

Green, Stuart P. (2001). 'Lying, Misleading, and Falsely Denying: How Moral Concepts Inform the Law of Perjury, Fraud, and False Statements', *Hastings Law Journal* 53: 157–212.

Green, Stuart P. (2006). *Lying, Cheating, and Stealing. A Moral Theory of White-Collar Crime*. Oxford: Oxford University Press.

Green, Stuart P. (2015). 'Lies, Rape, and Statutory Rape', in Austin Sarat (ed.), *Law and Lies: Deception and Truth Telling in the American Legal System*. New York, NY: Cambridge University Press, 194–253.

Greer, Kristen A. (2014). 'Extensionality in natural language quantification: the case of *many* and *few*', *Linguistics and Philosophy* 37 (4): 315–51.

Grice, H. Paul (1957). 'Meaning', *The Philosophical Review* 66: 377–88.

Grice, H. Paul (1975). 'Logic and Conversation', in Peter Cole and Jerry L. Morgan (eds), *Syntax and Semantics 3: Speech Acts*. New York, NY: Academic Press, 41–58.

Grice, Paul (1989a). 'Logic and Conversation', in Paul Grice, *Studies in the Way of Words*, Cambridge, MA: Harvard University Press, 22–40.

Grice, Paul (1989b). 'Further Notes on Logic and Conversation', in Paul Grice, *Studies in the Way of Words*. Cambridge, MA: Harvard University Press, 41–57.

Grice, Paul (1989c). *Studies in the Way of Words*. Cambridge, MA: Harvard University Press.

Griffiths, Paul (2004). *Lying: An Augustinian Theology of Duplicity*. Grand Rapids, MI: Brazos Press.

Groenendijk, Jeroen and Martin Stokhof (1982). 'Semantic analysis of *wh*-complements', *Linguistics and Philosophy* 5(2): 175–233.

Gronau, Nurit, Gershon Ben-Shakhar, and Asher Cohen (2005). 'Behavioral and physiological measures in the detection of concealed information', *Journal of Applied Psychology* 90: 147–58.

Grotius, Hugo (1925 [1625]). *On the Law of War and Peace (De jure belli ac pacis)*. Trans. Francis Kelsey. Indianapolis, IN: Bobbs-Merrill.

Gudykunst, William B. and Tsukasa Nishida (1983). 'Social penetration in Japanese and American close friendships', in Robert N. Bostrom (ed.), *Communication Yearbook 7*. New Brunswick, NJ: International Communication Association: 592–610.

Guidice, Rebecca M., G. Stoney Alder, and Steven E. Phelan (2009). 'Competitive Bluffing: An Examination of a Common Practice and its Relationship with Performance', *Journal of Business Ethics* 87: 535–53.

Guise, Kevin, Karen Kelly, Jennifer Romanowski, Kai Vogeley, Steven M. Platek, Elizabeth Murray, et al. (2007). 'The Anatomical and Evolutionary Relationship between Self-awareness and Theory of Mind', *Human Nature* 18 (2): 132–42.

Gupta, Swati, Kayo Sakamoto, and Andrew Ortony (2012). 'Telling it like it isn't: A comprehensive approach to analyzing verbal deception', in Fabio Paglieri, Luca Tummolini, Rino Falcone, and Maria Miceli (eds), *The Goals of Cognition: Essays in Honor of Cristiano Castelfranchi*. London: College Publications, 579–610.

Gur, Ruben C. and Sackheim, Harold A. (1979). 'Self-deception: A Concept in Search of a Phenomenon', *Journal of Personality and Social Psychology* 37: 147–69.

Hadar, Aviad A., Stergios Makris, and Kielan N. Yarrow (2012). 'The truth-telling motor cortex: Response competition in M1 discloses deceptive behaviour', *Biological Psychology* 89 (2): 495–502.

Haight, Mary Rowland (1980). *A Study of Self-deception*. Brighton: Harvester Press.

Hala, Suzanne and James Russell (2001). 'Executive Control within Strategic Deception: A Window on Early Cognitive Development?', *Journal of Experimental Child Psychology* 80 (2): 112–41.

Hala, Suzanne, Michael Chandler, and Anna S. Fritz (1991). 'Fledgling theories of mind: Deception as a marker of three-year-olds' understanding of false belief', *Child Development* 62 (1): 83–97.

Hall, Edward Twitchell (2000). 'Context and meaning', in Larry A. Samovar and Richard E. Porter (eds), *Intercultural Communication*, 9th edn. Belmont, CA: Wadsworth, 34–43.

Hall, Granville Stanley (1891). 'Children's lies', *Pedagogical Seminary* 1: 211–18.

Hall, Jeffrey A., Namkee Park, Hayeon Song, and Michael J. Cody (2010). 'Strategic Misrepresentation in Online Dating: The Effects of Gender, Self-Monitoring, and Personality Traits', *Journal of Social and Personal Relationships* 27: 117–35.

Hall, Stuart (1981). 'Encoding/Decoding', in Stuart Hall, Dorothy Hobson, Andrew Lowe, and Paul Willis (eds), *Culture, Media, Language*. London: Hutchinson, 128–38.

Hall, Stuart (1996). 'The problem of ideology: Marxism without guarantees', in David Morley and Kuan-Hsing Chen (eds), *Stuart Hall: Critical Dialogues in Cultural Studies*. London: Routledge, 24–45.

Hall, Stuart (1997). 'The Work of Representation', in Stuart Hall (ed.), *Representation: Cultural Representation and Signifying Practices*. London and Thousand Oaks, CA: Sage, 13–74.

Hample, Dale (1980). 'Purposes and effects of lying', *Southern Speech Communication Journal* 46: 33–47.

Hancock, Jeffrey T. (2007). 'Digital deception. Why, when and how people lie online', in Adam Joinson, Katelyn McKenna, Tom Postmes, and Ulf-Dietrich Reips (eds), *The Oxford Handbook of Internet Psychology*. Oxford: Oxford University Press, 289–330.

Hancock, Jeffrey T. and Amy Gonzalez (2013). 'Deception in computer-mediated communication', in Susan Herring, Dieter Stein, and Tuija Virtanen (eds), *Pragmatics of Computer-Mediated Communication*. Berlin: De Gruyter, 363–85.

Hancock, Jeffrey T., Lauren E. Curry, Saurabh Goorha, and Michael Woodworth (2008). 'On Lying and Being Lied To: A Linguistic Analysis of Deception in Computer-Mediated Communication', *Discourse Processes* 45 (1): 1–23.

Hanna, Joy E., Michael K. Tanenhaus, and John C. Trueswell (2003). 'The effects of common ground and perspective on domains of referential interpretation', *Journal of Memory and Language* 49 (1): 43–61.

Hansson, Sten (2015). 'Calculated overcommunication: Strategic uses of prolixity, irrelevance, and repetition in administrative language', *Journal of Pragmatics* 84: 172–88.

Hardcastle, Gary L. and George A. Reisch (eds) (2006). *Bullshit and Philosophy. Guaranteed to Get Perfect Results Every Time*. Chicago, IL: Open Court.

Hardin, Karol J. (2010). 'The Spanish notion of *Lie*: Revisiting Coleman and Kay', *Journal of Pragmatics* 42 (12): 3199–213.

Hare, Brian, Josep Call, and Michael Tomasello (2006). 'Chimpanzees deceive a human competitor by hiding', *Cognition* 101 (3): 495–514.

Harman, Gilbert H. (1973). *Thought*. Princeton, NJ: Princeton University Press.

Harnish, Robert M. (2005). 'Commitment and speech act', *Philosophica* 75: 11–41.

Harrington, Brooke (ed.) (2009). *Deception. From Ancient Empires to Internet Dating*. Stanford, CA: Stanford University Press.

Harris, Joel Chandler (1902 [1880]). *Uncle Remus. His Songs and His Sayings*. New York, NY: Appleton (first American edn 1880).

Harris, Roy (2005). 'Visual and verbal ambiguity, or why ceci was never a pipe', *Word & Image* 21 (2): 182–7.

Harry, Joseph C. (2014). 'Journalistic quotation: Reported speech in newspapers from a semiotic-linguistic perspective', *Journalism* 15: 1041–58.

Hartshorne, Hugh and Mark A. May (1928). *Studies in the Nature of Character: Vol. I. Studies in Deceit*. New York, NY: Macmillan.

Hartwig, Maria and Charles F. Bond, Jr (2011). 'Why do lie-catchers fail? A lens model meta-analysis of human lie judgments', *Psychological Bulletin* 137 (4): 643–59.

Hartwig, Maria, Pär Anders Granhag, and Leif A. Strömwall (2007). 'Guilty and innocent suspects' strategies during police interrogations', *Psychology, Crime & Law* 13: 213–27.

Haselton, Martie G., David M. Buss, Viktor Oubaid, and Alois Angleitner (2005). 'Sex, Lies, and Strategic Interference: The Psychology of Deception between the Sexes', *Personality and Social Psychology Bulletin* 31: 3–23.

Hasson, Uri, Joseph P. Simmons, and Alexander Todorov (2005). 'Believe It or Not', *Psychological Science* 16 (7): 566–71.

Haugh, Michael (2010). 'Jocular Mockery, (Dis)affiliation, and Face', *Journal of Pragmatics* 42: 2106–19.

Haverkate, Henk (1990). 'A Speech Act Analysis of Irony', *Journal of Pragmatics* 14: 77–109.

Hawthorne, John (2004). *Knowledge and Lotteries*. Oxford: Oxford University Press.

Hawthorne, John (2012). 'Some Comments on Fricker's 'Stating and Insinuating'', *Proceedings of the Aristotelian Society, Supplementary Volumes* 86: 95–108.

Haxby, James V., M. Ida Gobbini, Maura L. Furey, Alumit Ishai, Jennifer L. Schouten, and Pietro Pietrini (2001). 'Distributed and overlapping representations of faces and objects in ventral temporal cortex', *Science* 293 (5539): 2425–30.

Hee, Sun Park and Ji Young Ahn (2007). 'Cultural Differences in Judgment of Truthful and Deceptive Messages', *Journal of Western Communication* 71 (4): 294–315.

Heller, Daphna H., Daniel Grodner, and Michael K. Tanenhaus (2008). 'The role of perspective in identifying domains of reference', *Cognition* 108 (3): 831–6.

Hempfer, Klaus W. (2004). 'Some Problems Concerning a Theory of Fiction(ality)', *Style* 38 (3): 302–23.

Herf, Jeffrey (2006). *The Jewish Enemy. Nazi Propaganda During World War II and the Holocaust*. Cambridge, MA: Harvard University Press.

Herman, Barbara (1993). *The Practice of Moral Judgment*. Cambridge, MA: Harvard University Press.
Herman, Edward S. and Noam Chomsky (1988). *Manufacturing Consent: The Political Economy of the Mass Media*. New York, NY: Pantheon Books.
Herring, Eric and Piers Robinson (2014). 'Deception and Britain's Road to War in Iraq', *International Journal of Contemporary Iraqi Studies*, 8 (2, 3): 213–32.
Herring, Eric and Piers Robinson (2014–15). 'Report X Marks the Spot: The British Government's Deceptive Dossier on Iraq and WMD', *Political Science Quarterly* 129 (4): 551–84.
Herring, Jonathan (2005). 'Mistaken Sex', *Criminal Law Review*, 511–524. Online. Available at: http://ssrn.com/abstract=1287130.
Hersh, Richard H. (1997, March-April). 'Intentions and perceptions: A national survey of public attitudes toward liberal arts education', *Change* 29: 16–23.
Hesk, Jon (2000). *Deception and Democracy in Classical Athens*. Cambridge: Cambridge University Press.
Heyman, Gail D. and Kang Lee (2012). 'Moral development: Revisiting Kohlberg's stages', in Paul C. Quinn and Alan Slater (eds), *Developmental Psychology: Revisiting the Classic Studies*. London: Sage, 164–75.
Hickey, Neil (1999). 'Handling corrections', *Columbia Journalism Review* 38 (2): 42–3.
Higgins, E. Tory (1997). 'Beyond Pleasure and Pain', *American Psychologist* 52 (12): 1280–300.
Hilbig, Benjamin E., Morten Moshagen, and Ingo Zettler (2015). 'Truth Will Out: Linking Personality, Morality, and Honesty through Indirect Questioning', *Social Psychology and Personality Science* 62: 140–7.
Hill, Thomas E. Jr (1984). 'Autonomy and Benevolent Lies', in *Journal of Value Inquiry* 18: 251–67.
Hillman, Jackie (2014). 'How much does it hurt? Detecting deceptive motion using point light displays', Paper presented at the Annual Conference of the European Association of Psychology and Law, St. Petersburg, 25 June 2014.
Hirata, Satoshi (2009). 'Chimpanzee social intelligence: Selfishness, altruism, and the mother-infant bond', *Primates* 50 (1): 3–11.
Hirata, Satoshi and Tetsuro Matsuzawa (2001). 'Tactics to obtain a hidden food item in chimpanzee pairs (Pan troglodytes)', *Animal Cognition* 4 (3–4): 285–95.
Hirstein, William (2005). *Brain Fiction. Self-Deception and the Riddle of Confabulation*. Cambridge, MA: MIT Press.
Hitler, Adolf (1939 [1924]). *Mein Kampf*. Trans. James Murphy. London: Hurst and Blackett.
Hitler, Adolf (1943). *Mein Kampf*. Trans. Ralph Manheim. Boston, MA: Houghton Mifflin Company.
Hockett, Charles (1972). 'Jokes', in M. Estellie Smith (ed.), *Studies in Linguistics in Honor of George L. Trager*. New York, NY: Mouton, 153–78.
Hodge, Robert, and Gunther Kress (1993). *Language as Ideology*. London: Routledge.
Hoffer, Peter (2007). *Past Imperfect: Facts, Fictions, Fraud—American History from Bancroft and Parkman to Ambrose, Bellesiles, Ellis, and Goodwin*. New York, NY: PublicAffairs.
Hofstede, Gerard Hendrik (1980). *Culture's Consequences: International Differences in Work-Related Values*. Beverly Hills, CA: Sage.
Hofstede, Gerard Hendrik (2001). *Culture's Consequences: Comparing Values, Behaviors, Institutions, and Organizations across Nations*, 2nd edn. Thousand Oaks, CA: Sage.
Holmes, Janet (1984). 'Modifying illocutionary force', *Journal of Pragmatics* 8: 345–65.

Holmstrom, Bengt (1979). 'Moral Hazard and Observability', *Bell Journal of Economics* 10 (1): 74–91.
Hooker, Brad (2000). *Ideal Code, Real World*. Oxford: Oxford University Press.
Hopper, Robert and Robert Bell (1984). 'Broadening the Deception Construct', *Quarterly Journal of Speech* 70 (3): 288–302.
Horák, Vitezslav (2007). 'On Lying with Pictures', in Jochen Mecke (ed.), *Cultures of Lying. Theories and Practice of Lying in Society, Literature, and Film*. Berlin: Galda + Wilch, 351–60.
Horn, Laurence R. (1984). 'A new taxonomy for pragmatic inference: Q-based and R-based implicature', in Deborah Schiffrin (ed.), *Meaning, Form and Use in Context* (GURT '84). Washington, DC: Georgetown University Press, 11–42.
Horn, Laurence R. (1985). 'Metalinguistic negation and pragmatic ambiguity', *Language* 61(1): 121–74.
Horn, Laurence R. (1989). *A Natural History of Negation*. Chicago, IL: The University of Chicago Press.
Horn, Laurence (2017a). 'What lies beyond: Untangling the web', in Rachel Giora and Michael Haugh (eds), *Doing Pragmatics Interculturally: Cognitive, Philosophical and Sociopragmatic Perspectives on Language Use*. Berlin and Boston, MA: De Gruyter, 151–74.
Horn, Laurence R. (2017b). 'Telling it slant: Toward a taxonomy of deception', in Dieter Stein and Janet Giltrow (eds), *The Pragmatic Turn. Inference and Interpretation in Legal Discourse*. Berlin, Boston, MA: De Gruyter, 23–55.
Hornung, Melanie (2016). 'Classifying Prosocial Lies. An Empirical Approach', *International Review of Pragmatics* 8: 219–46.
Horton, William S. and Boaz Keysar (1996). 'When do speakers take into account common ground?', *Cognition* 59: 91–117.
Horwich, Paul (1998). *Truth*. Oxford: Oxford University Press.
Howard-Snyder, Frances (2011). 'Doing vs. Allowing Harm', in Edward N. Zalta (ed.), *Stanford Encyclopedia of Philosophy*. Online. Available at https://plato.stanford.edu./entries/doing-allowing/.
Hoye, Leo (1997). *Adverbs and Modality in English*. London and New York, NY: Longman.
Hu, Xiaoqing, Angela Evans, Haiyan Wu, Kang Lee, and Genyue Fu (2013). 'An interfering dot-probe task facilitates the detection of mock crime memory in a reaction time (RT)-based concealed information test', *Acta Psychologica* 142 (2): 278–85.
Huang, Yan (2010). 'Neo-Gricean pragmatic theory', in Bernd Heine and Heiko Narrog (eds), *The Oxford Handbook of Linguistic Analysis*. Oxford: Oxford University Press, 607–31.
Huang, Yan (ed.) (2017). *The Oxford Handbook of Pragmatics*. Oxford: Oxford University Press.
Hume, David (1902 [1777]). *Enquiry concerning the Principles of Morals*. Oxford: Clarendon Press.
Hunter, Jim, Yvonne Freer, Albert Gatt, Ehud Reiter, Somayajulu Sripada, and Cindy Sykes (2012). 'Automatic generation of natural language nursing shift summaries in neonatal intensive care: BT-Nurse', *Artificial Intelligence in Medicine* 56: 157–72.
Hurka, Thomas (2015). *British Ethical Theorists from Sidgwick to Ewing*. Oxford: Oxford University Press.
Hyde, Dominic (1997). 'From heaps and gaps to heaps of gluts', *Mind* 106 (424): 641–60.
Iacono, William G. (2011). 'Encouraging the use of the Guilty Knowledge Test (GKT): what the GKT has to offer law enforcement', in Bruno Verschuere, Gershon Ben-Shakharm Ewout Meijer (eds), *Memory Detection: Theory and Application of the Concealed Information Test*. Cambridge: Cambridge University Press, 12–23.

Ikuenobe, Polycarp (2002). 'The meta-ethical issue of the nature of lying: Implications for moral education', *Studies in Philosophy and Education* 21: 37–63.

Indefrey, Peter and Willem J. M. Levelt (2000). 'The neural correlates of language production', in Michael S. Gazzaniga (ed.), *The New Cognitive Neurosciences*, second edn. Cambridge, MA: MIT Press, 845–65.

Innes, Robert and Arnab Mitra (2013). 'Is Dishonesty Contagious?', *Economic Inquiry* 51 (1): 722–34.

Intachakra, Songthama (2011). 'Politeness Motivated by the 'Heart' and 'Binary Rationality' in Thai Culture', *Journal of Pragmatics* 44 (5): 619–35.

Isenberg, Arnold (1964). 'Deontology and the Ethics of Lying,' *Philosophy and Phenomenological Research* 24 (4): 463–80.

Ivanko, Stacey L. and Penny M. Pexman (2003). 'Context incongruity and irony processing', *Discourse Processes* 35: 241–79.

Izadi, Ahmad (2015). 'Persian honorifics and im/politeness as social practice', *Journal of Pragmatics* 85: 81–91.

Jackson, Elizabeth. forthcoming. Belief and Credence: Why the Attitude-Type Matters. *Philosophical Studies.*

Jackson, Jane (2014). *Introducing Lnguage and Intercultural Communication*. London: Routledge.

Jaeger, Stephan (2015). 'Unreliable Narration in Historical Studies', in Vera Nünning (ed.) *Unreliable Narration and Trustworthiness*. Berlin: De Gruyter, 371–94.

James, William (1975a [1907]). Pragmatism. A New Name for Some Old Ways of Thinking. The Work of William James, I. Cambridge, MA: Harvard University Press.

James, William (1975b [1909]). The Meaning of Truth: A Sequel to 'Pragmatism'. The Works of William James, II. Cambridge, MA: Harvard University Press.

Jamieson, Kathleen Hall (1992). *Dirty Politics: Deception, Distraction and Democracy.* Oxford: Oxford University Press.

Jang, Su Ahn, Sandi W. Smith, and Timothy R. Levine (2002). 'To Stay or To Leave? The Role of Attachment Styles in Communication Patterns and Potential Termination of Romantic Relationships Following Discovery of Deception', *Communication Monographs* 69: 236–52.

Jankélévitch, Vladimir (1942). 'Du Mensonge', in Vladimir Jankélévitch (1998), *Philosophie morale*, Paris: Flammarion, 213–88.

Jary, Mark (2010a). *Assertion*. Basingstoke: Palgrave.

Jary, Mark (2010b). 'Assertion and false-belief attribution', *Pragmatics & Cognition* 18: 17–39.

Jay, Martin (2010). *The Virtues of Mendacity: On Lying in Politics*. Charlottesville, VA: University of Virginia Press.

Jentzsch, Ines and Werner Sommer, W. (2002). 'Functional localization and mechanisms of sequential effects in serial reaction time tasks', *Perception and Psychophysics*, 64 (7): 1169–88.

Jersáková, Jana, Steven D. Johnson, and Pavel Kindlmann (2006). 'Mechanisms and evolution of deceptive pollination in orchids', *Biological Reviews of the Cambridge Philosophical Society* 81 (2): 219–35.

John, Carolyn and Guy Dodgson (1994). 'Inductive reasoning in delusional thought', *Journal of Mental Health* 3: 31–49.

Johnson, Eric (2005). 'WAR in the media: Metaphors, ideology, and the formation of language policy', *Bilingual Research Journal* 29: 621–40.

Johnson, Ray, Jr, Jack Barnhardt, and John Zhu (2003). 'The deceptive response: effects of response conflict and strategic monitoring on the late positive component and episodic memory-related brain activity', *Biological Psychology* 64 (3): 217–53.

Johnson, Ray, Jr, Jack Barnhardt, and John Zhu (2004). 'The contribution of executive processes to deceptive responding', *Neuropsychologia* 42 (7): 878–901.

Johnson, Ray, Jr, Heather Henkell, Elizabeth Simon, and John Zhu (2008). 'The self in conflict: The role of executive processes during truthful and deceptive responses about attitudes', *NeuroImage* 39 (1): 469–82.

Johnson, Zachary V., Hasse Walum, Yaseen A. Jamal, Yao Xiao, Alaine C. Keebaugh, Kiyoshi Inoue, et al. (2015). 'Central oxytocin receptors mediate mating-induced partner preferences and enhance correlated activation across forebrain nuclei in male prairie voles', *Hormones and Behavior* 79: 8–17.

Johnston, Mark (1988). 'Self-deception and the Nature of Mind', in Brian P. McLaughlin and Amélie Oksenberg Rorty (eds), *Perspectives on Self-deception*. Berkeley, CA: University of California Press, 63–91.

Johnston, Mark (1992). 'How to Speak of the Colors', *Philosophical Studies* 68: 221–63.

Jonason, Peter K., Minna Lyons, Holly M. Baughman, and Philip A. Vernon (2014). 'What a Tangled Web We Weave: The Dark Triad Traits and Deception', *Personality and Individual Differences* 70: 117–19.

Jones, Edward E. and Victor A. Harris (1967). 'The attribution of attitudes', *Journal of Experimental Social Psychology* 3: 1–24.

Jongman, Suzanne R., Ardi Roelofs, and Antje S. Meyer (2015). 'Sustained attention in language production: An individual differences investigation', *The Quarterly Journal of Experimental Psychology* 68 (4): 710–30.

Jordan, August E. (2003). 'Implications of academic dishonesty for teaching in psychology', *Psychology of Teaching* 30: 216–19.

Jowett, Garth S. and Victoria J. O'Donnell (2014). *Propaganda and Persuasion*, 6th edn. London: Sage.

Judges, A. V. (1969). 'The evolution of examinations', in Joseph A. Lauwerys and David G. Scanlon (eds), *Examinations*. New York, NY: Harcourt, Brace & World, 18–31.

Kaakinen, Johanna K., Henri Olkoniemi, Taina Kinnari, and Jukka Hyönä (2014). 'Processing of written irony: An eye movement study', *Discourse Processes*, 51 (4): 287–311.

Kahn, Itamar, Yehezkel, Yeskurun, Pia Rotshtein, Itzak Fried, Dafna Ben-Bashat, and Talma Hendler (2002). 'The role of the amygdala in signaling prospective outcome of choice', *Neuron* 33 (6): 983–4.

Kahneman, Daniel and Tversky, Amos (1979). 'Prospect Theory: An Analysis of Decision under Risk', *Econometrica* 47 (2): 263–91.

Kalbfleisch, Pamela J. (1994). 'The Language of Detecting Deceit', *Journal of Language and Social Psychology* 13: 469–96.

Kamp, Hans (1975). 'Two theories about adjectives', in Edward Keenan (ed.), *Formal Semantics of Natural Language*. Cambridge: Cambridge University Press.

Kant, Immanuel (1949 [1797]). 'On a supposed right to lie from altruistic motives', in his *Critique of Practical Reason and Other Writings in Moral Philosophy*. Edited and translated by Lewis White Beck. Chicago, IL: University of Chicago Press.

Kant, Immanuel (1993a). 'On a Supposed Right to Tell Lies Because of Philanthropic Concerns', in Immanuel Kant, *Grounding for the Metaphysics of Morals*. Trans. James Ellington, 3rd edn. Indianapolis, IN: Hackett.

Kant, Immanuel (1993b). *Grounding for the Metaphysics of Morals*, trans. James Ellington, 3rd edn. Indianapolis, IN: Hackett.

Kant, Immanuel (1996a). *Metaphysics of Morals*. Trans. Mary Gregor. Cambridge: Cambridge University Press.

Kant, Immanuel (1996b). On a Supposed Right to Lie from Philanthropy, in his *Practical Philosophy*, ed. Mary J. Gregor and Allen W. Wood. Cambridge: Cambridge University Press, 605–16.

Kant, Immanuel (1996c): The Metaphysics of Morals, in his *Practical Philosophy*, trans. and ed. Mary J. Gregor. Cambridge: Cambridge University Press, 353–603.

Kant, Immanuel (1997). *Lectures on Ethics*, ed. Peter Heath and Jerome B. Schneewind. Cambridge: Cambridge University Press.

Kaplar, Mary E. and Anne K. Gordon (2004). 'The Enigma of Altruistic Lying: Perspective Differences in What Motivates and Justifies Lie Telling within Romantic Relationships', *Personal Relationships* 11: 489–507.

Kartik, Navin (2009). 'Strategic Communication with Lying Costs', *Review of Economic Studies* 76 (4): 1359–95.

Kartik, Navin, Marco Ottaviani, and Francesco Squintani (2007). 'Credulity, Lies, and Costly Talk', *Journal of Economic Theory* 134: 93–116.

Karton, Inga and Talis Bachmann (2011). 'Effect of prefrontal transcranial magnetic stimulation on spontaneous truth-telling', *Behavioural Brain Research* 225 (1): 209–14.

Kashy, Deborah A. and Bella M. DePaulo (1996). 'Who Lies?', *Journal of Personality and Social Psychology* 70: 1037–51.

Kassin, Saul M. (2005). 'On the Psychology of Confessions: Does Innocence Put Innocents at Risk?', *American Psychologist* 60: 215–328.

Kassin, Saul M. and Katherine L. Kiechel (1996). 'The Social Psychology of False Confessions: Compliance, Internalization, and Confabulation', *Psychological Science* 7: 125–8.

Katz, Albert N. and Todd R. Ferretti (2003). 'Reading proverbs in context: The role of explicit markers', *Discourse Processes* 36 (1): 19–46.

Katz, Albert N., Dawn G. Blasko, and Victoria A. Kazmerski (2004). 'Saying what you don't mean: Social influences on sarcastic language processing', *Current Directions in Psychological Science* 13: 186–9.

Kecskés, Istvan (1999). 'The use of situation-bound utterances from an interlanguage perspective', in Jef Verschueren (ed.), *Pragmatics in 1998: Selected Papers from the 6th International Pragmatics Conference, Vol. 2*. Antwerp: International Pragmatics Association, 299–310.

Kecskés, Istvan (2000). 'A cognitive-pragmatic approach to situation-bound utterances', *Journal of Pragmatics* 32: 605–25.

Keefe, Rosanna (2000). *Theories of Vagueness*. Cambridge: Cambridge University Press.

Keenan, Julian P. (2002). *The Face in the Mirror*. New York, NY: HarperCollins Ecco.

Keenan, Julian P., Jennifer Rubio, Connie Racioppi, Amanda Johnson, and Allyson Barnacz (2005). 'The right hemisphere and the dark side of consciousness', *Cortex. A Journal Devoted to the Study of the Nervous System and Behavior* 41 (5): 695–704; discussion 731–4.

Keiser, Jessica (2016). 'Bald-faced lies: how to make a move in a language game without making a move in a conversation', *Philosophical Studies* 173 (2): 461–77.

Keller, Daniel (2009). *The Development of Shakespeare's Rhetoric. A Study of Nine Plays*. Tübingen: Narr.

Kelley, Thomas M. (2014). 'Paltering', in Timothy R. Levine (ed.), *The Encyclopedia of Deception*. Los Angeles, CA: Sage, 745–7.

Kelly, Anita E. and S. E. Maxwell (2016). Bolstering psychology's capacity to advance scientific knowledge. Unpublished ms.

Keltner, Dacher, Randall Young, Erin Heerey, Carmen Oemig, and Natalie Monarch (1998). 'Teasing in Hierarchical and Intimate Relations', *Journal of Personality and Social Psychology* 75: 1231–47.

Kemp, Kenneth W. and Thomas Sullivan (1993). 'Speaking Falsely and Telling Lies,' *Proceedings of the American Catholic Philosophical Association* 67: 151–70.

Kennedy, Christopher (2007). 'Vagueness and grammar: The semantics of relative and absolute gradable adjectives', *Linguistics and Philosophy* 30 (1): 1–45.

Kennedy, Christopher (2013). 'Two sources of subjectivity: Qualitative assessment and dimensional uncertainty', *Inquiry* 56 (2–3): 258–77.

Kenyon, Tim (2003). 'Cynical assertion: Convention, Pragmatics, and Saying 'Uncle', *American Philosophical Quarterly* 40 (3): 241–8.

Kenyon, Tim (2010). 'Assertion and Capitulation', *Pacific Philosophical Quarterly* 91: 352–68.

Kerchner, Kathy (2001). *SoundBites: A Business Guide to Working with the Media*. Indianapolis, IN: Savage Press.

Kessler, Greg (2010). 'Virtual Business: An Enron Email Corpus Study', *Journal of Pragmatics* 42 (1): 262–70.

Khan, Imtiaz, Kees van Deemter, and Graeme Ritchie (2012). 'Managing ambiguity in reference generation: the role of surface structure', *Topics in Cognitive Science* 4 (2): 211–31.

Kim, Min-Sun (2002). *Non-western Perspectives on Human Communication*. Thousand Oaks, CA: Sage.

Kim, Min-Sun, Karadeen Y. Kam, William F. Sharkey, and Theodore M. Singelis (2008). 'Deception: Moral transgression or social necessity?: Cultural-relativity of deception motivations and perceptions of deceptive communication', *Journal of International and Intercultural Communication*, 1 (1): 23–50.

Kim, Uichol (1994). 'Individualism and collectivism: Conceptual clarification and elaboration', in Uichol Kim, Harry Charalambos Triandis, Çigdem Kâğitçibaşi, Sang-Chin Choi, and Gene Yoon (eds), *Individualism and Collectivism*. Thousand Oaks, CA: Sage, 19–40.

Kimball, Bruce A. (1986). *Orators & Philosophers: A History of the Idea of Liberal Education*. New York, NY: Teachers College Press.

Kimball, Bruce A. (1997). 'Naming pragmatic liberal education', in Robert Orrill (ed.), *Education and Democracy: Re-Imagining Liberal Learning in America*. New York, NY: College Entrance Examination Board, 45–67.

Kimbrough, Scott (2006). 'On letting it slide', in Gary Hardcastle and George Reich (eds), *Bullshit and Philosophy. Guaranteed to Get Perfect Results Every Time*. Chicago, IL: Open Court, 3–18.

King, David (1997). *Stalins Retuschen. Foto- und Kunstmanipulationen in der Sowjetunion*. Hamburg: Hamburger Edition.

Kinjo, Hitomi (1987). 'Oral refusals of invitations and request in English and Japanese', *Journal of Asian Culture* 11: 83–106.

Kipp, David (1980). 'On Self-deception', *The Philosophical Quarterly* 30: 305–17.

Kircher, John C., Steven W. Horowitz, and David C. Raskin (1988). 'Meta-analysis of mock crime studies of the control question polygraph technique', *Law and Human Behavior* 12 (1): 79–90.

Kitamura, Tasaku and Michio Imafuku (2015). 'Behavioural mimicry in flight path of Batesian intraspecific polymorphic butterfly Papilio polytes', *Proceedings. Biological Sciences/The Royal Society* 282 (1809): 20150483.

Kittredge, Richard and John Lehrberger (1982). *Sublanguage: Studies of Language in Restricted Semantic Domains*. Berlin: De Gruyter.

Klein, Ewan (1980). 'A semantics for positive and comparative adjectives', *Linguistics and Philosophy* 4 (1), 1–45.

Klein, Peter (1998). 'Certainty', in Edward Craig (ed.), *Routledge Encyclopedia of Philosophy*. London: Routledge, 264–7.

Klockars, Carl B. (1984). 'Blue lies and police placebos: The moralities of police lying', *American Behavioral Scientist* 27: 529–44.

Knapp, Mark L. and Mark E. Comadena (1979). 'Telling it like it isn't: A review of theory and research on deceptive communication', *Human Communication Research* 5: 270–85.

Knapp, Mark L., Roderick P. Hart, and Harry S. Dennis (1974). 'An Exploration of Deception as a Communication Construct', *Human Communication Research* 1 (1): 15–29.

Koehn, Daryl (1997). 'Business and Game-Playing: The False Analogy', *Journal of Business Ethics* 16: 1447–552.

Koenig, Melissa A. and Paul L. Harris (2007). 'The Basis of Epistemic Trust: Reliable Testimony or Reliable Sources?', *Episteme* 4 (3): 264–84.

Koenig, Melissa A., Fabrice Clément, and Paul L. Harris (2004). 'Trust in Testimony: Children's Use of True and False Statements', *Psychological Science* 15 (10): 694–8.

Kohlberg, Lawrence (1971). 'Stages of moral development as a basis of moral education', in Clive M. Beck, Brian S. Crittenden, and Edmund V. Sullivan (eds), *Moral Education: Interdisciplinary Approaches*. Toronto: University of Toronto Press, 23–92.

Kölbel, Max (2004). 'Faultless disagreement'. *Proceedings of the Aristotelian Society. New Series* 104: 53–73.

Kondo, Aya (2007). *Nihonjin to gaikokujin no bijinesu komyunikeshon ni kansuru jisho kenkyu* [The analysis of problems among Japanese and foreign business-people: Aiming at new "business communication in Japanese"]. Tokyo: Hituzi Shobo.

Korsgaard, Christine M. (1986). 'The Right to Lie: Kant on Dealing with Evil', *Philosophy and Public Affairs* 15: 325–49.

Korsgaard, Christine M. (1996a). *Creating the Kingdom of Ends*. Cambridge: Cambridge University Press.

Korsgaard, Christine M. (1996b). 'Two arguments against lying', in Christine M. Korsgaard, *Creating the Kingdom of Ends*. Cambridge: Cambridge University Press, 335–62.

Korn, David (2003). *The Lies of George W. Bush*. New York, NY: Crown Books.

Kotthoff, Helga (2003). 'Responding to irony in different contexts: cognition and conversation', *Journal of Pragmatics* 35: 1387–411.

Koutlaki, Sofia A. (1997). The Persian system of politeness and the Persian folk concept of face, with some reference to EFL teaching to Iranian native speakers. Unpublished PhD diss., University of Wales.

Kovach, Bill and Tom Rosenstiel (2007). *The Elements of Journalism*. New York, NY: Three Rivers Press.

Kovaz, David, Roger J. Kreuz, and Monica A. Riordan (2013). 'Distinguishing sarcasm from literal language: Evidence from books and blogging', *Discourse Processes* 50 (8): 598–615.

Kozel, F. Andrew, Kevin A. Johnson, Qiwen Mu, Emily L. Grenesko, Steven J. Laken, and Mark S. George (2005). 'Detecting deception using functional magnetic resonance imaging', *Biological Psychiatry* 58 (8): 605–13.

Kozel, F. Andrew, Steven J. Laken, Kevin A. Johnson, Bryant Boren, Kimberly S. Mapes, Paul S. Morgan, et al. (2009). 'Replication of Functional MRI Detection of Deception', *Open Forensic Science Journal* 2: 6–11.

Kozel, F. Andrew, Kevin A. Johnson, Emily L. Grenesko, Steven J. Laken, Samet Kose, Xinghua Lu, et al. (2009). 'Functional MRI detection of deception after committing a mock sabotage crime', *Journal of Forensic Sciences* 54 (1): 220–31.

Kozel, F. Andrew, Letty J. Revell, Jeffrey P. Lorberbaum, Ananda Shastri, Jon D. Elhai, Michael D. Horner, et al. (2004). 'A pilot study of functional magnetic resonance imaging brain correlates of deception in healthy young men', *Journal of Neuropsychiatry and Clinical Neuroscience* 16: 295–305.

Kratzer, Angelika (1981). 'The notional category of modality', in Hans-Jürgen Eikmeyer and Hannes Rieser (eds), *Worlds, Words, and Contexts*. Berlin: De Gruyter, 38–74.

Krauss, Robert M. (1981). 'Impression formation, impression management, and nonverbal behaviors', in E. Tory Higgins, C. Peter Herman, and Mark P. Zanna (eds), *Social Cognition: The Ontario Symposium. Vol. 1*. Hillsdale, NJ: Erlbaum, 323–41.

Krauss, Sam (2017). Lying, risk and accuracy. *Analysis*. 77 (4).

Kress, Gunther and Theo van Leeuwen (1996). *Reading Images. The Grammar of Visual Design*. London: Routledge.

Kreuz, Roger J. and Gina M. Caucci (2007). 'Lexical influences on the perception of sarcasm', in *Proceedings of the Workshop on Computational Approaches to Figurative Language*. Rochester, NY: Association for Computational Linguistics, 1–4.

Krifka, Manfred (2007). 'Approximate interpretation of number words', in Gerlof Bouma, Irene Krämer, and Joost Zwarts, J. (eds), *Cognitive Foundations of Interpretation*. Amsterdam: Koninklijke Nederlandse Akademie van Wetenschapen, 111–26.

Kripke, Saul (1980). *Naming and Necessity*. Cambridge, MA: Harvard University Press.

Kripke, Saul (2011). 'Vacuous names and fictional entities', in Saul A. Kripke, *Philosophical Troubles. Collected Papers, Vol. 1*. Oxford: Oxford University Press, 52–74.

Krishna, Daya (1961). '"Lying" and the Compleat Robot', *The British Journal for the Philosophy of Science* 12 (46): 146–9.

Kritsky, Gene (2008). 'Entomological reactions to Darwin's theory in the nineteenth century', *Annual Review of Entomology* 53: 345–60.

Kucich, John (1994). *The Power of Lies. Transgression, Class and Gender in Victorian Fiction*. Ithaca, NY: Cornell University Press.

Kümmerling-Meibauer, Bettina and Jörg Meibauer (2011). 'Lügengeschichten und Geschichten vom Lügen', *Zeitschrift für Literaturwissenschaft und Linguistik* (LiLi) 162: 118–38.

Kümmerling-Meibauer, Bettina and Jörg Meibauer (2015). 'Beware of the Fox! Emotion and Deception in "Fox" by Margaret Wild and Ron Brooks', in Janet Evans (ed.), *Challenging and Controversial Picturebooks: Creative and Critical Responses to Visual Texts*. London: Routledge, 144–59.

Künne, Wolfgang (2003). *Conceptions of Truth*. Oxford: Clarendon Press.

Kupfer, Joseph (1982). 'The Moral Presumption against Lying', *Review of Metaphysics* 36 (1): 103–26.

Kutlak, Roman (2014). *Generation of referring expressions for an unknown audience*. PhD thesis, University of Aberdeen.

Kwan, Virginia S. Y., Veronica Barrios, Giorgio Ganis, Jamie Gorman, Claudia Lange, Monisha Kumar, et al. (2007). 'Assessing the neural correlates of self-enhancement bias: a transcranial magnetic stimulation study', *Experimental Brain Research* 182 (3): 379–85.

Labinaz, Paolo and Marina Sbisà (2014). 'Certainty and Uncertainty in Assertive Speech Acts', in Ilaria Riccioni, Carla Canestrari, Andrzej Zuczkowski, and Ramona Bongelli (eds), *Communicating Certainty and Uncertainty in Medical, Supportive and Scientific Contexts*. Amsterdam: John Benjamins, 31–58.

Labov, William (1972). 'Rules for ritual insults', in Thomas Kochman (ed.), *Rappin' and Stylin' Out: Communication in Urban Black America*. Champaign-Urbana, IL: University of Illinois Press, 265–314.

Labov, William (1984). 'Intensity', in Deborah Schiffrin (ed.), *Meaning, Form and Use in Context: Linguistic Applications*. Washington, DC: Georgetown University Press, 43–70.

Lackey, Jennifer (1999). 'Testimonial Knowledge and Transmission', *The Philosophical Quarterly* 49 (197): 471–90.

Lackey, Jennifer (2005). 'Testimony and the Infant/Child Objection', *Philosophical Studies* 126 (2): 163–90.

Lackey, Jennifer (2007a). 'Norms of Assertion', *Noûs* 41: 594–626.

Lackey, Jennifer (2007b). 'Why We Don't Deserve Credit for Everything We Know', *Synthese* 158 (3): 345–61.

Lackey, Jennifer (2008). *Learning from Words. Testimony as a Source of Knowledge*. Oxford: Oxford University Press.

Lackey, Jennifer (2013). 'Lies and Deception: An Unhappy Divorce', *Analysis* 73 (2): 236–48.

Lackey, Jennifer (2015). 'Group Lies', forthcoming in Andreas Stocke and Eliot Michaelson (eds), *Lying: Language, Knowledge, Ethics, and Politics*. Oxford: Oxford University Press.

LaFeber, Walter (1989). *The American Age*. New York, NY: Norton.

Lakoff, George (1973). 'Hedges: A study in meaning criteria and the logic of fuzzy concepts', *Journal of philosophical logic* 2 (4): 458–508.

Lakoff, George and Mark Johnson (1980). *Metaphors We Live By*. Chicago, IL: The University of Chicago Press.

Lakoff, Robin T. (1982). 'Persuasive Discourse and Ordinary Conversation, with Examples from Advertising', in Deborah Tannen (ed.), *Analyzing Discourse: Text and Talk*. Washington, DC: Georgetown University Press, 25–42.

Lakoff, Robin T. (1973). Language and Woman's Place. *Language in Society* 2: 45–80.

Lamers, Martijn J. and Ardi Roelofs (2011). 'Attentional control adjustments in Eriksen and Stroop task performance can be independent of response conflict', *The Quarterly Journal of Experimental Psychology* 64 (6): 1056–81.

Landweer, Hilge (2001). 'Selbsttäuschung', *Deutsche Zeitschrift für Philosophie* 49 (2): 209–27.

Lane, Liane W., Michelle Groisman, and Victor S. Ferreira (2006). 'Don't talk about pink elephants! Speakers' control over leaking private information during language production', *Psychological Science* 17 (4): 273–7.

Lane, Melissa (1999). 'Plato, Popper, Strauss, and Utopianism: Open Secrets', *History of Philosophy Quarterly* 16: 119–42.

Langevoort, Donald C. (1999). 'Half-Truths: Protecting Mistaken Inferences by Investors and Others', *Stanford Law Review* 52: 87–125.

Langleben, Daniel D., James W. Loughead, Warren B. Bilker, Kosha Ruparel, Anna R. Childress, Samantha I. Busch, and Ruben C. Gur (2005). 'Telling truth from lie in individual subjects with fast event-related fMRI', *Human Brain Mapping* 26 (4): 262–72.

Langleben, Daniel D., Lee F. Schroeder, Joseph A. Maldjian, Ruben C. Gur, S. McDonald, John D. Ragland, et al. (2002). 'Brain Activity during Simulated Deception: An Event-Related Functional Magnetic Resonance Study', *NeuroImage* 15: 727–32.
Langton, Rae (1992). 'Duty and Desolation', *Philosophy* 67: 481–505.
Lappin, Shalom (2000). 'An intensional parametric semantics for vague quantifiers', *Linguistics and Philosophy* 23 (6): 599–620.
Larbalestier, Justine (2009). *Liar*. New York, NY: Bloomsbury.
Larson, Jane E. (1993). 'Women Understand So Little, They Call My Good Nature "Deceit": A Feminist Rethinking of Seduction', *Columbia Law Review* 93: 374–472.
Lasersohn, Peter (1999). 'Pragmatic halos', *Language* 75: 522–51.
Lashmar, Paul and James Oliver (1998). *Britain's Secret Propaganda War: Foreign Office and the Cold War, 1948-77*. Stroud: Sutton Publishing.
Lassiter, Daniel (2011). 'Vagueness as Probabilistic Linguistic Knowledge', in Rick Nouwen, Uli Sauerland, Hans-Christian Schmitz, Robert van Rooij (eds), *Vagueness in Communication*. Berlin, Heidelberg: Springer, 127–50.
Lassiter, Daniel and Noah D. Goodman (2017). 'Adjectival vagueness in a Bayesian model of interpretation', *Synthese* 194 (10): 3801–36.
Lasswell, Harold (1927). *Propaganda Technique in the World War*. Cambridge, MA: MIT Press.
Lave, Jean and Etienne Wenger (1991). *Situated Learning: Legitimate Peripheral Participation*. Cambridge: Cambridge University Press.
Lavoie, Jennifer, Karissa Leduc, Angela M. Crossman, and Victoria Talwar (2016). 'Do as I say and not as I think: Parent socialization of lie-telling behaviour', *Children & Society* 30 (4): 253–64.
Leal, Sharon, Aldert Vrij, Ronald P. Fisher, and Hannie van Hooff (2008). 'The time of the crime: cognitively induced tonic arousal suppression when lying in a free recall context', *Acta Psychologica* 129 (1): 1–7.
Leal, Sharon, Aldert Vrij, Lara Warmelink, Zarah Vernham, and Ronald P. Fisher (2015). 'You cannot hide your telephone lies: providing a model statement as an aid to detect deception in insurance telephone calls', *Legal and Criminological Psychology* 20: 129–46.
Lebow, Richard Ned (2008). 'The Ancient Greeks and Modern Realism: Ethics, Persuasion, and Power', *Philosophy and Social Science* 9 (1): 2–16.
Lee, James and Steven Pinker (2010). 'Rationales for indirect speech: the theory of strategic speaker', *Psychological Review* 117(3): 785–807.
Lee, Kang (2013). 'Little Liars. Development of Verbal Deception in Children,' *Child Development Perspectives* 7 (2): 91–6.
Lee, Kang and Hollie J. Ross (1997). 'The Concept of Lying in Adolescents and Young Adults: Testing Sweetser's Folkloristic Model', *Merrill-Palmer Quarterly* 43 (2): 255–70.
Lee, Kang, Catherine Ann Cameron, Fen Xu, Genyao Fu, and Julie Board (1997). 'Chinese and Canadian children's evaluation of lying and truth telling: Similarities and differences in the context of pro- and antisocial behaviours', *Child Development* 68 (5): 924–34.
Lee, Peter M. (2012). *Bayesian Statistics: An Introduction*. New York, NY: John Wiley.
Leech, Geoffrey (1969). *A Linguistic Guide to English Poetry*. London: Longman.
Leech, Geoffrey (1981). *Semantics: The Study of Meaning*, 2nd edn. Cambridge: Cambridge University Press.
Leech, Geoffrey (1983). *Principles of Pragmatics*. London: Longman.
Leekam, Susan (1991). 'Jokes and Lies: Children's Understanding of Intentional Falsehood', in Andrew Whiten (ed.), *Natural Theories of Mind. Evolution, Development and Simulation of Everyday Mindreading*. Oxford: Blackwell, 159–74.

Lehrer, Adrienne (1989). 'Between quotation marks', *Journalism Quarterly* 66: 902–6.
Leland, Patrick R. (2015). 'Rational responsibility and the assertoric character of bald-faced lies', *Analysis* 75 (4): 550–4.
Lenartowicz, Agatha, Donald J. Kalar, Eliza Congdon, and Russel A. Poldrack (2010). 'Towards an ontology of cognitive control', *Top Cogn Sci* 2 (4): 678–92.
Levashina, Julia and Michael A. Campion (2009). 'Expected Practices in Background Checking: Review of the Human Resource Management Literature', *Employee Responsibilities and Rights Journal* 21: 231–49.
Levelt, Willem J. M. (1989). *Speaking: From Intention to Articulation*. Cambridge, MA: MIT Press.
Levin, Nili (February 9, 2014). *"Intelligence"*: Smart it is not. (In Hebrew). http://www.ynet.co.il/articles/0,7340,L-4485714,00.html.
Levine, Emma and Maurice M. Schweitzer (2014). 'Are liars ethical? On the tension between benevolence and honesty', in *Journal of Experimental Social Psychology* 53: 107–17.
Levine, Emma and Maurice M. Schweitzer (2015). 'Prosocial lies. When deception breeds trust', in *Organizational Behavior and Human Decision Processes* 126: 88–106.
Levine, Timothy R. (ed.) (2014). *Encyclopedia of Deception*. Los Angeles, CA: Sage.
Levine, Timothy R., Kim B. Serota, Hillary Shulman, David D. Clare, Hee Sun Park, Allison S. Shaw, et al. (2011). 'Sender Demeanor: Individual Differences in Sender Believability Have a Powerful Impact on Deception Detection Judgments', *Human Communication Research* 37: 377–403.
Levinson, Stephen C. (1983). *Pragmatics*. Cambridge: Cambridge University Press.
Levinson, Stephen C. (2000). *Presumptive Meanings. The Theory of Generalized Conversational Implicature*. Cambridge, MA: MIT Press.
Lewicki, Roy J. and Robert J. Robinson (1998). 'Ethical and Unethical Bargaining Tactics: An Empirical Study', *Journal of Business Ethics* 17: 665–82.
Lewis, David (1969). *Convention*. Cambridge, MA: Harvard University Press.
Lewis, David (1970). 'General semantics', *Synthese* 22 (1): 18–67.
Lewis, David (1978). 'Truth in fiction', *American Philosophical Quarterly* 15 (1): 37–46.
Lewis, David (1979). 'Score-keeping in a language game', *Journal of Philosophical Logic* 8 (1): 339–59.
Lewis, David (1982). 'Logic for equivocators', *Noûs* 16: 431–41.
Lewis, David (2000). 'Causation as Influence', *The Journal of Philosophy* 97: 182–97.
Lewis, Michael, Catherine Stanger, and Margaret Sullivan (1989). 'Deception in 3-year olds', *Developmental Psychology* 25 (3): 439–43.
Li, Annie S., Elizabeth A. Kelley, Angela D. Evans, and Kang Lee (2011). 'Exploring the ability to deceive in children with autism spectrum disorders', *Journal of Autism and Developmental Disorders* 41 (2): 185–95.
Libet, Benjamin (1995). 'Necessary brain', *Nature* 375 (6527): 100.
Libet, Benjamin (2006). 'Reflections on the interaction of the mind and brain', *Progress in Neurobiology* 78 (3–5): 322–6.
Libet, Benjamin, Elwood W. Wright, and Curtis A. Gleason (1983). 'Preparation- or intention-to-act, in relation to pre-event potentials recorded at the vertex', *Electroencephalography and Clinical Neurophysiology* 56 (4): 367–72.
Lincoln, Abraham (1989). *Abraham Lincoln: Speeches and Writings*. New York, NY: The Library of America.
Lindgren, Astrid (2007). *Pippi Longstocking*, trans. Tiina Nunnally. Oxford: Oxford University Press. (Original Swedish edn: Pippi Långstrump, 1945.)

Lindley, Foster T. (1971). 'Lying and Falsity', *Australasian Journal of Philosophy* 49 (1971): 152–7.
Lippman, Walter (1922). *Public Opinion*. New York, NY: Harcourt, Brace.
Lisofsky, Nina, Philipp Kazzer, Hauke R. Heekeren, and Kristin Prehn (2014). 'Investigating socio-cognitive processes in deception: a quantitative meta-analysis of neuroimaging studies', *Neuropsychologia* 61: 113–22.
Locke, John (1996). *An Essay Concerning Human Understanding*. Edited by Kenneth P. Winkler. Indianapolis, IN: Hackett.
Loewenstein, George, Elke U. Weber, Christopher K. Hsee, and Ned Welch (2001). 'Risks As Feelings', *Psychological Bulletin* 127 (2): 267–86.
Loftus, Elizabeth F. and John C. Palmer (1974). 'Reconstruction of automobile destruction: An example of the interaction between language and memory', *Journal of Verbal Learning and Verbal Behavior* 13: 585–9.
Logothetis, Nikos K. and Brian A. Wandell (2004). 'Interpreting the BOLD signal', *Annual Review of Physiology* 66: 735–69.
Lohmann, Heidemarie and Michael Tomasello (2003). 'The role of language in the development of false belief understanding: A training study', *Child Development* 74: 1130–44.
Löhrer, Guido (2012). 'Ist es manchmal richtig, unaufrichtig zu sein? Zur moralischen Valenz der Lüge', *Allgemeine Zeitschrift für Philosophie* 37 (1): 5–22.
Lopez, Jason K. and Matthew Fuxjager (2012). 'Self-deception's adaptive value: effects of positive thinking and the winner effect', *Consciousness and Cognition* 21 (1): 315–24.
Louise, Patty (2013). 'Mistakes happen, but how do we tell readers?', *Gateway Journalism Review* 43: 14–20.
Loveman, Kate (2008). *Reading Fictions, 1660-1740: Deception in English Literary and Political Culture*. New York, NY: Routledge.
Loving, Bill and Brady Teufel (2012). 'False impressions: How digital editing is altering public discourse', *International Journal of Law and Social Sciences* 2(1): 167–72.
Löw-Beer, Martin (1990). *Selbsttäuschung. Philosophische Analyse eines psychischen Phänomens*. Freiburg, Munich: Verlag Karl Alber.
Lucian (1905) *The True History*. Transl. H. W. Fowler. Oxford: Clarendon Press (original Greek edn 2nd century).
Luck, Steven J. (2014). *An Introduction to the Event-Related Potential Technique*. Cambridge, MA: MIT Press.
Lundquist, Tobias, Tore Ellingsen, Erik Gribbe, and Magnus Johannesson (2009). 'The Aversion to Lying', *Journal of Economic Behavior and Organization* 70: 81–92.
Lutz, William (1987). *Doublespeak: From "Revenue Enhancement" to "Terminal Living": How Government, Business, Advertisers, and Others Use Language to Deceive You*. New York, NY: Harper & Row.
Lykken, David T. (1959). 'The GSR in the detection of guilt', *Journal of Applied Psychology* 43 (6): 385–8.
Lykken, David T. (1998). *A Tremor in the Blood: Uses and Abuses of the Lie Detector*. New York, NY: Plenum Press.
Lynch, Michael (2004). *True to Life: Why Truth Matters*. Cambridge, MA: MIT Press.
Lyons, John (1977). *Semantics*. Cambridge: Cambridge University Press.
MacFarlane, John (2011). 'What Is Assertion?' in Jessica Brown and Herman Cappelen (eds), *Assertion. New Philosophical Essays*. Oxford: Oxford University Press, 76–96.
Machiavelli, Niccolo (2003 [1532]). *The Prince*. Trans. George Bull. London: Penguin.

MacIntyre, Alasdair (1995). 'Truthfulness, Lies, and Moral Philosophers: What Can We Learn from Mill and Kant?', in Grethe B. Peterson (ed.), *The Tanner Lectures on Human Values, Vol. 16*. Salt Lake City, UT: The University of Utah Press, 308–61.

Mackey, Alison and Susan M. Gass (2005). *Second Language Research: Methodology and Design*. Mahwah, NJ: Lawrence Erlbaum.

MacLaren, Vance V. (2001). 'A quantitative review of the guilty knowledge test', *Journal of Applied Psychology* 86 (4): 674–83.

Mahamood, Saad and Ehud Reiter (2011). 'Generating Affective Natural Language for Parents of Neonatal Infants', *Proceedings of the 13th European Workshop on Natural Language Generation (ENLG), Nancy, France*: 12–21.

Mahon, James Edwin (2006). 'Kant and Maria von Herbert: Reticence vs. Deception', *Philosophy* 81: 417–44.

Mahon, James Edwin (2007). 'A Definition of Deceiving', *International Journal of Applied Philosophy* 21: 181–94.

Mahon, James Edwin (2008a). 'The definition of lying and deception', in Edward N. Zalta (ed.), *The Stanford Encyclopedia of Philosophy*. Online. Available at https://plato.stanford.edu/entries/lying-definition/.

Mahon, James Edwin (2008b). 'Two Definitions of Lying', *International Journal of Applied Philosophy* 22 (2): 211–30.

Mahon, James Edwin (2008c). 'An Analysis of Lying'. Unpublished ms.

Mahon, James Edwin (2009). 'The Truth about Kant on Lies,' in Clancy Martin (ed.), *The Philosophy of Deception*. Oxford: Oxford University Press, 201–24.

Mahon, James Edwin (2014a). 'Deception, Characteristics of', in Timothy R. Levine (ed.), *The Encyclopedia of Deception*. Los Angeles, CA: Sage, 246–50.

Mahon, James Edwin (2014b). 'Saint Augustine', in Timothy R. Levine (ed.), *The Encyclopedia of Deception*. Los Angeles, CA: Sage, 827–9.

Mahon, James Edwin (2015). 'The definition of lying and deception', in Edward N. Zalta (ed.), *The Stanford Encyclopedia of Philosophy*. Online. Available at https://plato.stanford.edu/entries/lying-definition/.

Mahon, James Edwin (2018). 'Secrets vs. Lies: Is There a Moral Asymmetry?', in Eliot Michaelson and Andreas Stokke (eds), *Lying. Language, Knowledge, Ethics, and Politics*. Oxford: Oxford University Press, 161–82.

Maier, Emar (2017). 'Fictional names in psychologistic semantics', *Theoretical Linguistics* 43 (1–2): 1–42.

Makinson, David C. (1965). 'The Paradox of the Preface', *Analysis* 25: 205–7.

Malcicka, Miriama, T. Martijn Bezemer, Bertanne Visser, Mark Bloemberg, Charles J. P. Snart, Ian C. Hardy, et al. (2015). 'Multi-trait mimicry of ants by a parasitoid wasp', *Scientific Reports* 5: 8043.

Mallan, Kerry (2013). *Secrets, Lies, and Children's Fiction*. Basingstoke: Palgrave.

Malone, Brian E. and Bella M. DePaulo (2001). 'Measuring Sensitivity to Deception', in Judith A. Hall and Frank Bernieri (eds), *Interpersonal Sensitivity: Theory, Measurement, and Application*. Hillsdale, NJ: Lawrence Erlbaum, 103–24.

Mameli, Francesca, Simona Mrakic-Sposta, Maurizio Vergari, Manuela Fumagalli, Margherita Macis, Roberta Ferrucci, et al. (2010). 'Dorsolateral prefrontal cortex specifically processes general—but not personal—knowledge deception: Multiple brain networks for lying', *Behavioural Brain Research* 211 (2): 164–8.

Mann, Michael E., Raymond S. Bradley, and Malcolm K. Hughes (1998). 'Global-scale temperature patterns and climate forcing over the past six centuries', *Nature* 392: 779–87.
Mann, Samantha, Aldert Vrij, and Ray Bull. (2002). 'Suspects, lies, and videotape: An analysis of authentic high-stake liars', *Law and Human Behavior* 36: 365–76.
Mann, Samantha, Aldert Vrij, and Ray Bull (2004). 'Detecting True Lies: Police Officers' Ability to Detect Suspects' Lies', *Journal of Applied Psychology* 89: 137–49.
Mann, Samantha, Aldert Vrij, Sharon Leal, Pär Anders Granhag, Lara Warmelink, L., and Dave Forrester (2012). 'Windows to the soul? Deliberate eye contact as a cue to deceit', *Journal of Nonverbal Behavior* 36: 205–15.
Mann, Samantha, Aldert Vrij, Erika Nasholm, Lara Warmelink, Sharon Leal, and Dave Forrester (2012). 'The direction of deception: Neuro-Linguistic Programming as a lie detection tool', *Journal of Police and Criminal Psychology* 27: 160–6.
Mann, Samantha, Aldert Vrij, Dominic J. Shaw, Sharon Leal, Sarah Ewens, Jackie Hillman, et al. (2013). 'Two heads are better than one? How to effectively use two interviewers to elicit cues to deception', *Legal and Criminological Psychology* 18: 324–40.
Mannison, Don (1969). 'Lying and Lies', *Australasian Journal of Philosophy* 47: 132–44.
Marelich, William D., Jessica Lundquist, Kimberly Painter, and Mindy B. Mechanic (2008). 'Sexual Deception as a Social-Exchange Process: Development of a Behavior-Based Sexual Deception Scale', *Journal of Sex Research* 45: 27–35.
Marsili, Neri (2014). 'Lying as a scalar phenomenon: insincerity along the certainty-uncertainty continuum', in Sibilla Cantarini, Werner Abraham, and Elisabeth Leiss (eds), *Certainty-Uncertainty and the Attitudinal Space in Between*. Amsterdam: John Benjamins, 154–73.
Marsili, Neri (2016). Lying by Promising. *International Review of Pragmatics* 8(2). Brill: 271–313.
Martin, Clancy (ed.) (2009). *The Philosophy of Deception*. Oxford: Oxford University Press.
Martin, L. John (1982). 'Disinformation: An Instrumentality in the Propaganda Arsenal', *Political Communication* 2 (1): 47–64.
Martin, Mike W. (1986). *Self-deception and Morality*. Lawrence, KS: University Press of Kansas.
Martin, Rod (2007). *The Psychology of Humor. An Integrative Approach*. Burlington, MA: Elsevier.
Martineau, Harriet (1989 [1838]). *How to Observe Morals and Manners* (Sesquicentennial edition). New Brunswick: Transaction Books.
Martinich, Al (2010). 'The Total Content of What a Speaker Means', in Klaus Petrus (ed.), *Meaning and Analysis. New Essays on Grice*. Basingstoke: Palgrave, 252–67.
Mas, Alexandre and Enrico Moretti (2009). 'Peers at work', *American Economic Review* 99 (1): 112–45.
Mascaro, Olivier and Dan Sperber (2009). 'The moral, epistemic, and mindreading components of children's vigilance towards deception', *Cognition* 112: 367–80.
Mason, John E. (1935). *Gentlefolk in the Making: Studies in the History of English Courtesy Literature and Related Topics from 1531 to 1774*. Philadelphia, PA: University of Pennsylvania Press.
Mateo, José and Francisco Yus (2013). 'Towards a Cross-cultural Pragmatic Taxonomy of Insults', *Journal of Language Aggression & Conflict* 1 (1): 87–114.
Mathiesen, Kay (2006). 'The Epistemic Features of Group Belief', *Episteme* 2 (3): 161–75.
Matsuda, Izumi, Hiroshi Nittono, and John J. B. Allen (2012). 'The current and future status of the concealed information test for field use', *Frontiers in Psychology* 3: 532.

Matsuda, Izumi, Hiroshi Nittono, and John J. B. Allen (2013). 'Detection of concealed information by P3 and frontal EEG asymmetry', *Neuroscience Letters* 537: 55–9.

Maunsell, John H., Gary Sclar, Tara A. Nealey, and Derryl D. DePriest (1991). 'Extraretinal representations in area V4 in the macaque monkey', *Visual Neuroscience* 7 (6): 561–73.

Mayer, Milton (1966). *They Thought They Were Free: The Germans, 1933-45*. Chicago, IL: University of Chicago Press.

Mazar, Nina, On Amir, and Dan Ariely (2008). 'The dishonesty of honest people: a theory of self-concept maintenance', *Journal of Marketing Research* 45: 633–44.

McCarthy, Michael J. and Ronald A. Carter (2004). "'There's millions of them': hyperbole in everyday conversation', *Journal of Pragmatics* 36: 149–84.

McCloskey, Michael E. and Sam Glucksberg (1978). Natural categories: Well defined or fuzzy sets? *Memory & Cognition*, 6(4), 462–72.

McCollam, Douglas (2010). 'A distant echo'. *Columbia Journalism Review*, 48 (5): 55–7.

McCornack, Steven A. (1992). 'Information manipulation theory', *Communication Monographs* 59 (1): 1–16.

McCornack, Steven A. (1997). 'The generation of deceptive messages: laying the groundwork for a viable theory of interpersonal deception', in John O. Greene (ed.), *Advances in Communication Theory*. Mahwah, NJ: Lawrence Erlbaum, 91–126

McCornack, Steven A., Timothy R. Levine, Kathleen A. Solowczuk, Helen I. Torres, and Dedra M. Campbell (1992). 'When the Alteration of Information is Viewed as Deceptive: An Empirical Test of Information Manipulation Theory', *Communication Monographs* 59: 17–29.

McCornack, Steven A., Kelly Morrison, Jihyun E. Paik, Amy M. Wisner, and Xun Zhu (2014). 'Information manipulation theory 2: A propositional theory of deceptive discourse production', *Journal of Language and Social Psychology* 33 (4): 348–77.

McDonald, William F. (1985). *Plea Bargaining: Critical Issues and Common Practices*. Washington, DC: Government Printing Office.

McDonald, William F., James A. Cramer, and Henry H. Rossman (1980). 'Prosecutorial Bluffing and the Case Against Plea Bargaining', in William F. McDonald and James A. Cramer (eds), *Plea Bargaining*. Lexington, MA: D. C. Heath, ch. 1, 1–23.

McDonough, Kevin (1995). 'The importance of examples for moral education: An Aristotelian perspective', *Studies in Philosophy and Education* 14: 77–103.

McFadden, Charles (1967). *Medical Ethics*, 6th edn. Philadelphia, PA: F. A. Davis.

McGinn, Colin (2008). *Mindfucking. A Critique of Mental Manipulation*. Stocksfield: Acumen.

McGlone, Matthew S. (2005). 'Quoted out of context: Contextomy and its consequences', *Journal of Communication* 55: 330–46.

McGlone, Matthew S. (2010). 'Deception by selective quotation', in Matthew S. McGlone and Mark L. Knapp (eds), *The Interplay of Truth and Deception*. New York, NY: Routledge, 54–65.

McGlone, Matthew S. and Mark L. Knapp (eds) (2010). *The Interplay of Truth and Deception. New Agendas in Communication*. New York, NY: Routledge.

McGrath, Sarah (2005). 'Causation by Omission: A Dilemma', *Philosophical Studies* 123: 125–48.

McKinnon, Rachel (2015). *The Norms of Assertion. Truth, Lies, and Warrant*. Basingstoke: Palgrave Macmillan.

McLeod, Beverly A. and Randy L. Genereux (2008). 'Predicting the Acceptability and Likelihood of Lying', *Personality and Individual Differences* 45: 591–6.

McNally, Louise and Isidora Stojanovic (2017). 'Aesthetic adjectives', in James O. Young, (ed.), *The Semantics of Aesthetic Judgment*. Oxford: Oxford University Press, 17–37.

McNaughton, David (1996). 'An Unconnected Heap of Duties?', *The Philosophical Quarterly* (46): 433–47.

McRae, Ken, Michael J. Spivey-Knowlton, and Michael K. Tanenhaus (1998). 'Modeling the influence of thematic fit (and other constraints) in on-line sentence comprehension', *Journal of Memory and Language* 38 (3): 283–312.

McStay, Andrew (2018). *Emotional AI: The Rise of Empathic Media*. London: Sage.

McSweeney, Brendan (2002). 'Hofstede's model of national cultural differences and their consequences: A triumph of faith—a failure of analysis', *Human Relations* 55 (1): 89–118.

Mead, Nicole L., Roy F. Baumeister, Francesca Gino, Maurice E. Schweitzer, and Dan Ariely (2009). 'Too Tired to Tell the Truth: Self-control Resource Depletion and Dishonesty', *Journal of Experimental Social Psychology* 45: 594–7.

Mealy, Marisa, Stephan Walter, and I. Carolina Urrutia (2007). 'The Acceptability of Lies: A Comparison of Ecuadorians and Euro-Americans', *International Journal of Intercultural Relations* 31: 689–702.

Mearsheimer, John (2011). *Why Leaders Lie. The Truth about Lying in International Politics*. Oxford: Oxford University Press.

Mehlberg, Henry (1958). *The Reach of Science*. Toronto: University of Toronto Press.

Meibauer, Jörg (2005). 'Lying and falsely implicating', *Journal of Pragmatics* 37: 1373–99.

Meibauer, Jörg (2011). 'On lying: intentionality, implicature and imprecision'. *Intercultural Pragmatics* 8: 277–92.

Meibauer, Jörg (2014a). *Lying at the Semantic-Pragmatics Interface*. Berlin and Boston, MA: De Gruyter.

Meibauer, Jörg (2014b). 'Bald-faced lies as acts of verbal aggression', *Journal of Language Aggression and Conflict* 2 (1): 127–50.

Meibauer, Jörg (2014c). 'A Truth that's Told with Bad Intent: Lying and Implicit Content', *Belgian Journal of Linguistics* 28: 97–118.

Meibauer, Jörg (2016a). 'Understanding bald-faced lies. An empirical approach', *International Review of Pragmatics* 8 (2): 247–70.

Meibauer, Jörg (2016b). 'Aspects of a Theory of Bullshit', *Pragmatics & Cognition* 23 (1): 69–92.

Meibauer, Jörg (2017). '"Western" Grice? Lying in a cross-cultural dimension', in Istvan Kecskes and Stavros Assimakopoulos (eds), *Current Issues in Intercultural Pragmatics*. Amsterdam, Philadelphia, PA: Benjamins, 33–52.

Meibauer, Jörg (2018): 'The Linguistics of Lying', *Annual Review of Linguistics* 4: 357–75.

Meijer, Ewout H. and Bruno Verschuere (2015). 'The Polygraph: Current Practice and New Approaches', in Pär Anders Granhag, Aldert Vrij, and Bruno Verschuere (eds), *Detecting Deception. Current Challenges and Cognitive Approaches*. Chichester: Wiley, 59–80.

Meijer, Ewout H., Nathalie Klein-Selle, Lotem Elber, and Gershon Ben-Shakhar (2014). 'Memory detection with the Concealed Information Test: A meta analysis of skin conductance, respiration, heart rate, and P300 data', *Psychophysiology* 51 (9): 879–904.

Meijer, Ewout H., Bruno Verschuere, Aldert Vrij, Harald Merckelbach, Fren Smulders, Sharon Leal, et al. (2009). 'A call for evidence-based security tools', *Open Access Journal of Forensic Psychology* 1: 1–4.

Mele, Alfred R. (1987). *Irrationality. An Essay on Akrasia, Self-deception, and Self-control*. New York, NY: Oxford University Press.

Mele, Alfred R. (1998). 'Two Paradoxes of Self-deception', in Jean-Pierre Dupuy (ed.), *Self-deception and Paradoxes of Rationality*. Stanford, CA: CSLI Publications, 37–58.

Mele, Alfred R. (2001). *Self-deception Unmasked*. Princeton, NJ, Oxford: Princeton University Press.
Melzer, Arthur (2014). *Philosophy Between the Lines*. Chicago, IL: University of Chicago Press.
Menz, Florian (1989). 'Manipulation Strategies in Newspapers: A program for Critical Linguistics', in Ruth Wodak (ed.), *Language, Power and Ideology*. Amsterdam: John Benjamins, 227–50.
Merriam-Webster Online Dictionary (2015). https://merriam-webster.com.
Mey, Jacob (1985). *Whose Language? A Study in Linguistic Pragmatics*. Philadelphia, PA: John Benjamins.
Michaelian, Kourken (2013). 'The Evolution of Testimony: Receiver Vigilance, Speaker Honesty, and the Reliability of Communication', *Episteme* 10 (1): 37–59.
Mill, John Stuart (1987 [1861]). 'Utilitarianism', in John Stuart Mill and Jeremy Bentham, *Utilitarianism and other Essays*, ed. Alan Ryan. London: Penguin.
Mill, John Stuart (2001). *Utilitarianism*, 2nd edn. Indianapolis, IN: Hackett.
Miller, Corey, Rachel D. Strong, Mark Vinson, and Claudia Brugman (2014). *Ritualized indirectness: Explaining the language practice taarof as a reflection of Persian speakers' cultural values*. Technical Report. Center for Advanced Study of Language. University of Maryland.
Miller, David (2001). 'Media Power and Class Power: Overplaying Ideology', in Leo Panitch and Colin Leys (eds), *Socialist Register 2002*. London: Merlin Press.
Miller, David and William Dinan (2008). *A Century of Spin: How Public Relations Became the Cutting Edge of Corporate Power*. London: Pluto.
Miller, Gerald R. and James B. Stiff (1993). *Deceptive Communication*. Newbury Park: Sage.
Miller, Scott A. (2012). *Theory of Mind: Beyond the Preschool Years*. New York, NY: Psychology Press.
Millikan, Ruth G. (1987). *Language, Thought, and Other Categories*. Cambridge, MA: MIT Press.
Moeschler, Jacques (2013). 'Is a speaker-based pragmatics possible? Or how can a hearer infer a speaker's commitment?', *Journal of Pragmatics* 48: 84–97.
Moloney, Kevin (2006). *Rethinking Public Relations: PR Propaganda and Democracy*, 2nd edn. London: Routledge.
Moncur, Wendy, Judith Masthoff, and Ehud Reiter (2009). 'Facilitating Benign Deceit in Mediated Communication', *CHI EA '09, Extended Abstracts on Human Factors in Computing Systems, Boston*: 3383–8.
Moncur, Wendy, Judith Masthoff, Ehud Reiter, Yvonne Freer, and Hien Nguyen (2013). 'Providing Adaptive Health Updates Across the Personal Social Network', *Human Computer Interaction* 29 (3): 256–309.
Montaigne, Michel (1595) (E). *Essais*. Verdun: P. Villey et Saulnier.
Monteleone, George T., K. Luan Phan, Howard C. Nusbaum, Daniel Fitzgerald, John-Stockton Irick, Stephen E. Fienberg, et al. (2009). 'Detection of deception using fMRI: better than chance, but well below perfection', *Social Neuroscience* 4 (6): 528–38.
Moore, George Edward (1962). *Commonplace Book: 1919–1953*. London: George Allen & Unwin.
Moore, George Edward (1965). *Ethics*. Oxford: Oxford University Press.
Moore, Joseph G. (2000). 'Did Clinton lie?', *Analysis* 60 (267): 250–4.
Moran, Richard (2005). 'Problems with sincerity', *Proceedings of the Aristotelian Society* 105: 325–45.

Morency, Patrick, Steve Oswald, and Louis de Saussure (2008). 'Explicitness, implicitness and commitment attribution: A cognitive pragmatic approach', *Belgian Journal of Linguistics* 22: 197–220.

Morgan, Charity J., Julia B. LeSage, and Stephen M. Kosslyn (2009). 'Types of deception revealed by individual differences in cognitive abilities', *Social Neuroscience* 4 (6): 554–69.

Morgenstern, Joe (2009). 'Reaching for the sky, "Up" fails to soar', *Wall Street Journal*, May 14, p. E4.

Morreall, John (1983). *Taking Laughter Seriously*. Albany, NY: State University of New York Press.

Morreall, John (1987). 'Introduction', in John Morreall (ed.), *The Philosophy of Laughter and Humour*. Albany, NY: State University of New York Press.

Morreall, John (1989). 'Enjoying Incongruity', *Humor* 2: 1–18.

Morreall, John (2009). *Comic Relief: A Comprehensive Philosophy of Humor*. Oxford: Wiley-Blackwell.

Morris, Benny (1997). *Israel's Border Wars*. Oxford: Oxford University Press.

Morris, Benny (1999). *Righteous Victims: A History of the Zionist Arab Conflict, 1881-1999*. New York, NY: Alfred A. Knopf.

Morris, Benny (2008). *1948*. New Haven, CT: Yale University Press.

Morris, John (1976). 'Can Computers Ever Lie?', *Philosophy Forum* 14: 389–401.

Morris, Wendy L., R. Weylin Sternglanz, Matthew E. Ansfield, D. Eric Anderson, Jillian L. H. Snyder, and Bella M. DePaulo (2016). 'A Longitudinal Study of the Development of Emotional Deception Detection Within New Same-Sex Friendships', *Personality & Social Psychology Bulletin* 42 (2): 204–18.

Morwood, Michael J., Radien P. Soejono, Richard G. Roberts, Thomas Sutikna, Chris S. M. Turney, Kira Westaway, et al. (2004). 'Archaeology and age of a new hominin from Flores in eastern Indonesia', *Nature* 431 (7012): 1087–91.

Mullaney, Steven (1980). 'Lying like truth: riddle, representation and treason in Renaissance England', *English Literary History*, 47 (1): 32–47.

Müller, Gregor (1962). *Die Wahrhaftigkeitspflicht und die Problematik der Lüge*. Freiburg, Basel, Wien: Herder.

Nahari, Galit, Aldert Vrij, and Ronald P. Fisher (2014). 'The verifiability approach: Countermeasures facilitate its ability to discriminate between truths and lies', *Applied Cognitive Psychology* 28: 122–8.

Naquin, Charles E., Terri R. Kurtzberg, and Liuba Y. Belkin (2010). 'The Finer Points of Lying Online: E-Mail Versus Pen and Paper', *Journal of Applied Psychology* 95: 387–94.

National Research Council (2003). *The Polygraph and Lie Detection*. Washington, DC: National Academies Press.

Neale, Stephen (1992). 'Paul Grice and the philosophy of language', *Linguistics and Philosophy* 15: 509–59.

Neu, Jerome (2008). *Sticks and Stones. The Philosophy of Insults*. Oxford: Oxford University Press.

Neustupny, Jiří Václav (1982). *Gaikokujin to no komyunikeshon* [Communication with foreigners]. Tokyo: Iwanami Shoten.

Newey, Glen (1997). 'Political Lying: A Defense', *Public Affairs Quarterly* 11: 93–116.

Newman, Matthew L., James W. Pennebaker, Diane S. Berry, and Jane M. Richards (2003). 'Lying Words: Predicting Deception from Linguistic Styles', *Personality and Social Psychology Bulletin* 29 (5): 665–75.

Newton, Paul, Vasudevi Reddy, and Ray Bull (2000). 'Children's everyday deception and performance on false-belief tasks', *British Journal of Developmental Psychology* 18 (2): 297–317.
Ng, Sik Hung and James J. Bradac (1993). *Power in Language*. Newbury Park, CA: Sage.
Nichols, Shaun and Stephen Stich (2000). 'A Cognitive Theory of Pretense', *Cognition* 74: 115–47.
Nisbett, Richard E. (2003). *The Geography of Thought: How Asians and Westerners Think Differently... and Why*. New York, NY: The Free Press.
Nishida, Tsukasa (2006). 'Taijin komyunikeshon kodo no tokucho' [The characteristics of behaviour in interpersonal communication], *Studies in International Relations* 27 (2): 139–61.
Nishimura, Fumiko (1997). 'Koi toshite no uso: Hanashite no doki toiu kanten kara no Kosatsu' [Lying as an action: Analysis from the speaker's perspective], *Bulletin of the Department of Teaching Japanese as Second Language, Hiroshima University* 7: 165–71.
Nishimura, Fumiko (2005). 'Nani wo uso to kanjiruka [what do you think a lie]', in Sachiko Ide and Masako Hiraga (eds), *Ibunka to komyumikeshon* [Different cultures and communication], Tokyo: Hituzi shobo, 238–54.
Nishimura, Fumiko (2011). Lying: Strategies to manage undesirable communicative situations in Japan and New Zealand. Doctoral thesis. University of Waikato.
Norman, Laurence (2014). 'EU moves to temper Putin "two weeks to Kiev" row; EU official says comments were made public out of context', *The Wall Street Journal*, September 4. Avaialable at https://www.wsj.com/articles/eu-moves-to-temper-pution-two-weeks-to-kiev-row-1409831828.
Norton, Anne (2005). *Leo Strauss and the Politics of American Empire*. New Haven, CT: Yale University Press.
Norton, Helen (2013). 'Lies and the Constitution,' *Supreme Court Review* 2012: 161–201.
Nose, Izuru, Jun'ichiro Murai, and Masato Taira (2009). 'Disclosing concealed information on the basis of cortical activations', *NeuroImage* 44 (4): 1380–6.
Nünning, Vera (ed.) (2015). *Unreliable Narration and Trustworthiness*. Berlin: De Gruyter.
Nussbaum, Martha (1988). 'Love's Knowledge', in Brian P. McLaughlin and Amélie Oksenberg Rorty (eds), *Perspectives on Self-deception*. Berkeley, CA: University of California Press, 487–514.
Nyberg, David (1993). *The Varnished Truth*. Chicago, IL: University of Chicago Press.
Oborne, Peter (2005). *The Rise of Political Lying*. London: Simon and Schuster, Free Press.
Ochs Keenan, Elinor (1976). 'The Universality of Conversational Implicature', *Language in Society* 5 (1): 67–80.
Onishi, Kristine H. and Renée Baillargeon (2005). 'Do 15-month-old infants understand false-beliefs?', *Science* 308: 255–8.
Orwell, George (1949). *1984*. London: Warburg.
Osugi, Akemi (2011). 'Daily application of the concealed information test: Japan', in Bruno Verschuere, Gershon Ben-Shakhar, and Ewout H. Meijer (eds), *Memory Detection: Theory and Application of the Concealed Information Test*. Cambridge: Cambridge University Press, 253–75.
Osvath, Mathias, and Elin Karvonen (2012). 'Spontaneous innovation for future deception in a male chimpanzee', *PloS One* 7 (5): e36782.
Page, Carl (1991). 'The Truth about Lies in Plato's *Republic*', *Ancient Philosophy* 11: 1–33.
Pagin, Peter (2015). 'Assertion', in Edward N. Zalta (ed.), *The Stanford Encyclopedia of Philosophy*. Spring 2015 edition. Online. Available at https://plato.stanford.edu/entries/assertion/.
Pagin, Peter (2016). 'Problems with Norms of Assertion', *Philosophy and Phenomenological Research* 93 (1): 178–207.

Paolazzi, Caterina (2013). ' "Do you really think it?": Testing hypotheses on nonliteral default interpretations', University of Trento, Italy. Unpublished ms.
Papafragou, Anna (2006). 'Epistemic modality and truth conditions', *Lingua* 116 (10): 1688–702.
Parikh, Rohit (1994). 'Vagueness and utility: The semantics of common nouns', *Linguistics and Philosophy* 17 (6): 521–35.
Parisi, Domenico and Castelfranchi, Cristiano (1977). 'The discourse as a hierarchy of goals', *Signs of Change* 1 (2): 31–67.
Parisi, Domenico and Castelfranchi, Cristiano (1981). 'A Goal Analysis of Some Pragmatic Aspects of Language', in Herman Parret, Marina Sbisà and Jef Verschueren (eds), *Possibilities and Limitations of Pragmatics. Proceedings of the Conference on Pragmatics, Urbino July 8-14, 1979*. Amsterdam: John Benjamins, 551–67.
Parkhurst, John L. (1825). *Elements of Moral Philosophy*. Concord, NH: J. B. Moore & J. W. Shepard.
Partee, Barbara (1989). 'Binding Implicit Variables in Quantified Contexts', in Caroline Wiltshire, Randolph Graczyk, and Bradley Music (eds), *Papers from the 25th Annual Regional Meeting of the Chicago Linguistic Society*. Chicago Linguistic Society, 342–65.
Partington, Alan (2011). 'Phrasal irony: Its form, function and exploitation', *Journal of Pragmatics* 43 (6): 1786–800.
Paton, Herbert James (1954). 'An Alleged Right to Lie: A Problem in Kantian Ethics', *Kant-Studien* 45: 190–203.
Patrick, Christopher J. and William G. Iacono (1989). 'Psychopathy, threat, and polygraph test accuracy', *Journal of Applied Psychology* 74 (2): 347–55.
Pavlidis, Ioannis, Norman L. Eberhardt, and James A. Levine (2002). 'Seeing through the face of deception', *Nature* 415 (6867): 35.
Pears, David (1984). *Motivated Irrationality*. Oxford: Clarendon Press.
Pears, David (1986). 'The goals and strategies of self-deception', in Jon Elster (ed.), *The multiple self*. Cambridge: Cambridge University Press, 59–77.
Pecorari, Diane (2008). *Academic Writing and Plagiarism: A Linguistic Analysis*. New York, NY: Continuum Books.
Peirce, Charles S. (1902). 'Vague', in James Mark Baldwin (ed.), *Dictionary of Philosophy and Psychology*. New York, NY, London: Macmillan.
Peirce, Charles S. (1958 [1931–5]): *Collected Papers*. Cambridge, MA: Harvard University Press.
Penn, Derek C. and Daniel J. Povinelli (2007). 'On the lack of evidence that non-human animals possess anything remotely resembling a "theory of mind"', *Philosophical Transactions of the Royal Society of London. Series B, Biological Sciences* 362 (1480): 731–44.
Penn, Derek C., Keith J. Holyoak, and Daniel J. Povinelli (2012). 'So, are we the massively lucky species?', *The Behavioral and Brain Sciences* 35 (4): 236–7.
Pennebaker, James W., Martha E. Francis, and Roger J. Booth (2001). *Linguistic Inquiry and Word Count (LIWC): LIWC 2001 Manual*. Mahwah, NJ: Lawrence Erlbaum.
Pennesi, Karen (2013). 'Predictions as Lies in Ceará, Brazil: The Intersection of Two Cultural Models', *Anthropological Quarterly* 86 (3): 759–89.
Pepp, Jessica (2020). 'Assertion, Lying, and Untruthfully Implicating', in: Sanford C. Goldberg (ed.): *The Oxford Handbook of Assertion*. Oxford: Oxford University Press, 829–50.
Perillo, Jennifer Torkildson and Saul M. Kassin (2011). 'Inside Interrogation: The Lie, the Bluff, and False Confessions', *Law and Human Behavior* 35: 327–37.
Perkins, Serena A. and Elliot Turiel (2007). 'To lie or not to lie: To whom and under what circumstances', *Child Development* 78 (2): 609–21.

Perner, Josef and Heinz Wimmer (1985). "'John thinks that Mary thinks that ... ': Attribution of second-order false beliefs by 5- to 10-year old children', *Journal of Experimental Child Psychology* 39 (3): 437–71.

Perner, Josef, Sandra Stummer, Manuel Sprung, and Martin J. Doherty (2002). 'Theory of mind finds its Piagetian perspective: why alternative naming comes with understanding belief', *Cognitive Development* 17: 1451–72.

Peskin, Joan (1992). 'Ruse and representations: On children's ability to conceal information.' *Developmental Psychology* 28: 84–9.

Petersen, Steven E., Peter T. Fox, Michael I. Posner, Mark A. Mintun, and Marcus E. Raichle (1988). 'Positron emission tomographic studies of the cortical anatomy of single-word processing', *Nature* 331 (6157): 585–9.

Peterson, Candida C. (1995). 'The role of perceived intention to deceive in children's and adults' concepts of lying', *British Journal of Developmental Psychology* 13 (3): 237–60.

Peterson, Candida C., James L. Peterson, and Diane Seeto (1983). 'Developmental changes in ideas about lying', *Child Development* 54 (6): 1529–35.

Peth, Judith, Tobias Sommer, Martin N. Hebart, Gerhard Vossel, Christian Buchel, and Matthias Gamer (2015). 'Memory detection using fMRI—Does the encoding context matter?', *NeuroImage* 113: 164–74.

Petrie, H. (1987). 'The psycholinguistics of speaking', in John Lyons, Richard Coates, Margaret Deuchar, and Gerald Gazdar (eds), *New Horizons in Linguistics 2*. London, Harmondsworth: Penguin, 336–66.

Pexman, Penny M., Todd Ferretti, and Albert N. Katz (2000). 'Discourse factors that influence on-line reading of metaphor and irony', *Discourse Processes* 29: 201–22.

Pfennig, David W. and Sean P. Mullen (2010). 'Mimics without models: causes and consequences of allopatry in Batesian mimicry complexes', *Proceedings. Biological Sciences/The Royal Society* 277 (1694): 2577–85.

Piaget, Jean (1965 [1932]). *The moral judgment of the child*. New York, NY: Free Press.

Pickel, Kerri L. (2004). 'When a Lie Becomes the Truth: The Effects of Self-generated Misinformation on Eyewitness Memory', *Memory* 12: 14–26.

Picornell, Isabel (2013). *Cues to deception in a textual narrative context*. PhD thesis. Aston University. [http://eprints.aston.ac.uk/19316/1/Studentthesis-2013.pdf] Accessed 12.08.2015.

Pinkal, Manfred (1995). *Logic and Lexicon: The Semantics of the indefinite*. Dordrecht: Kluwer Academic Publishers.

Pinker, Steven (1994). *The Language Instinct*. New York, NY: Harper Perennial Modern Classics.

Pinker, Steven (2011). 'Indirect speech, politeness, deniability, and relationship negotiation: Comment on Marina Terkourafi's "The puzzle of indirect speech"', *Journal of Pragmatics* 43: 2866–8.

Pinker, Steven, Martin Nowak, and James Lee (2008). 'The logic of indirect speech', *Proceedings of the National Academy of Sciences* 105 (3): 833–8.

Plantiga, Alvin (1993). *Warrant and Proper Function*. Oxford: Oxford University Press.

Plato (360 BC) *The Republic*, trans. B. Jowett, The Internet Classics Archive.

Plato (1997). 'Theaetetus', in John M. Cooper (ed.) *Complete Works*. Indianapolis, IN: Hackett, 137–234.

Plato (2002). *Five Dialogues: Euthyphro, Apology, Crito, Meno, Phaedo*, trans. G. M. A. Grube, rev. John Cooper. Indianapolis, IN: Hackett.

Plato (2006). *The Republic*, trans. R. E. Allen. New Haven, CT: Yale University Press.

Plessner, Helmuth (1999 [1924]). *The Limits of Community: A Critique of Social Radicalism*. Amherst, NY: Humanity Books.

Poggi, Isabella, Francesca D'Errico, and Laura Vincze (2011). 'Discrediting moves in Political Debates', in Francesco Ricci et al. (eds), *Proceedings of Second International Workshop on User Models for Motivational Systems: The Affective and the Rational Routes to Persuasion* (UMMS 2011) (Girona), LNCS. Heidelberg: Springer, 84–99.

Polak, Alan and Paul L. Harris (1999). 'Deception by young children following noncompliance', *Developmental Psychology* 35 (2): 561–8.

Poldrack, Russell A. (2011). 'Inferring mental states from neuroimaging data: from reverse inference to large-scale decoding', *Neuron* 72 (5): 692–7.

Poole, Steven (2006). *Unspeak: How Words Become Weapons, How Weapons Become a Message, and How that Message Becomes Reality*. London: Little Brown.

Popper, Karl R. (1959). *The Logic of Scientific Discovery*. London: Hutchinson.

Popper, Karl R. (1963). *Conjectures and Refutations: The Growth of Scientific Knowledge*. New York, NY: Basic Books.

Popper, Karl R. (1971). *The Open Society and Its Enemies, Vol. I: The Spell of Plato*. Princeton, NJ: Princeton University Press.

Porat, Ariel and Omri Yadlin (2014). 'Valuable Lies', *Coase-Sandor Institute for Law and Economics Working Paper 706/Public Law and Legal Theory Working Paper 491*. University of Chicago. [http://ssrn.com/abstract=2506309]

Porat, Ariel and Omri Yadlin (2016). 'A Welfarist Perspective on Lies', *Indiana Law Journal* 91(3), Article 1.

Porter, Joseph A. (1991). 'Complement Extern: Iago's Speech Acts', in Virginia M. Vaughan and Ken Cartwright (eds), *Othello. New Perspectives*. Rutherford, NJ: Fairleigh Dickinson University Press, 74–88.

Porter, Stephen, Naomi L. Doucette, Michael Woodworth, Jeff Earle, and Bonnie MacNeil (2008). 'Halfe the world knows not how the other halfe lies: Investigation of verbal and non-verbal signs of deception exhibited by criminal offenders and non-offenders', *Legal and Criminological Psychology* 13: 27–38.

Portet, Francois, Ehud Reiter, Albert Gatt, Jim Hunter, Somayajulu Sripada, Yvonne Freer, et al. (2009). 'Automatic Generation of Textual Summaries from Neonatal Intensive Care Data', *Artificial Intelligence* 173: 789–816.

Povinelli, Daniel J. (1993). 'Reconstructing the evolution of mind', *The American Psychologist* 48 (5): 493–509.

Povinelli, Daniel J. and D. Richard Davis (1994). 'Differences between chimpanzees (Pan troglodytes) and humans (Homo sapiens) in the resting state of the index finger: implications for pointing', *Journal of Comparative Psychology* 108 (2): 134–9.

Powell, Scott, Kleber Del-Claro, Rodrigo M. Feitosa, and Carlos R. F. Brandão (2014). 'Mimicry and eavesdropping enable a new form of social parasitism in ants', *The American Naturalist* 184 (4): 500–9.

Premack, David and Guy Woodruff (1978). 'Does the chimpanzee have a theory of mind?', *Behavioral and Brain Sciences* 1 (4): 515–26.

Primoratz, Igor (1984). 'Lying and "The Methods of Ethics"', *International Studies in Philosophy* 16 (1): 35–57.

Prince, Ellen F. (1981). 'Topicalization, focus-movement, and Yiddish-movement: A pragmatic differentiation', *Proceedings of the Seventh Annual Meeting of the Berkeley Linguistics Society* 7: 249–64.

Priori, Alberto, F. Mameli, Filippo Cogiamanian, Sara Marceglia, Marco Tiriticco, S. Mrakic-Sposta, et al. (2008). 'Lie-specific involvement of dorsolateral prefrontal cortex in deception', *Cerebral Cortex* 18 (2): 451–5.
Pritchard, Duncan (2005). *Epistemic Luck*. Oxford: Oxford University Press.
Pritchard, Duncan (2008). 'Sensitivity, Safety, and Anti-Luck Epistemology', in John Greco (ed.), *The Oxford Handbook of Skepticism*. Oxford: Oxford University Press, 437–55.
Pruss, Alexander (2012). 'Sincerely asserting what you do not believe,' *Australasian Journal of Philosophy* 90: 541–6.
Pulvermüller, Friedemann, Max Garagnani, and Thomas Wennekers (2014). 'Thinking in circuits: toward neurobiological explanation in cognitive neuroscience', *Biological Cybernetics* 108 (5): 573–93.
Putnam, Hilary (1981). *Reason, Truth and History*. Cambridge: Cambridge University Press.
Quine, Willard V.O. (1960). *Word and Object*. Cambridge, MA: Harvard University Press.
Quintilianus, Marcus Fabius (95 AD/1953ff). *The Institutio Oratoria of Quintilian*, ed./trans. H. E. Butler, Cambridge, MA: Harvard University Press (Loeb Classical Library).
Raatzsch, Richard (2009). *The Apologetics of Evil: The Case of Iago*. Princeton, NJ: Princeton University Press.
Rabab'ah, Ghaleb and Ali M. Al-Qarni (2012). 'Euphemism in Saudi Arabic and British English', *Journal of Pragmatics* 44: 730–43.
Radford, Colin (1975). 'How can we be moved by the fate of Anna Karenina?', *Proceedings of the Aristotelian Society* 49: 67–93.
Raffman, Diana (2013). *Unruly words: a study of vague language*. Oxford: Oxford University Press.
Ramsey, Frank (1927). 'Facts and Propositions', *Aristotelian Society Supplementary Volume* 7: 153–70.
Ramsay, Maureen (2000a). 'Justifications for Lying in Politics', in Lionel Cliffe, Maureen Ramsay, and Dave Bartlett (eds), *The Politics of Lying*. London: Macmillan, 3–26.
Ramsay, Maureen (2000b). 'Democratic Dirty Hands', in Lionel Cliffe, Maureen Ramsay, and Dave Bartlett (eds). *The Politics of Lying*. London: Macmillan, 27–42.
Ransom, Keith, Wouter Voorspoels, Amy Perfors, and Daniel J. Navarro (2017). 'A cognitive analysis of deception without lying', in *Proceedings of the 39th Annual Conference of the Cognitive Science Society*, 992–7.
Raskin, David C. and Charles R. Honts, C. (2002). 'The comparison question test', in Murray Kleiner (ed.), *Handbook of Polygraph Testing*. San Diego, CA: Academic Press, 1–47.
Raskin, David C., Charles R. Honts, and John C. Kircher (2014). *Credibility Assessment*. Oxford: Academic Press.
Rasmussen, Carmen, Victoria Talwar, Carly Loomes, and Gail Andrew (2007). 'Lie-telling in children with Fetal Alcohol Spectrum Disorder', *Journal of Pediatric Psychology* 33 (2): 220–5.
Rasmussen, Eric (2001). *Games & Information: An Introduction to Game Theory*, 3rd edn. Oxford: Blackwell.
Raspe, Rudolf Erich (1786). Baron Munchausen's Narrative of His Marvelous Travels and Campaigns in Russia. Oxford: n. publ.
Rawnsley, Gary D. (2005). *Political Communication and Democracy*. Basingstoke: Palgrave Macmillan.
Ray, Dixy Lee and Louis R. Guzzo (1990). *Trashing the Planet*. Washington, DC: Regnery Gateway.

Reboul, Anne (1994). 'The description of lies in speech acts theory', in Herman Parret (ed.), *Pretending to Communicate*. Berlin and New York, NY: De Gruyter, 292–8.

Recanati, François (2004). *Literal Meaning*. Cambridge: Cambridge University Press.

Rees, Clea F. (2014). '"Better Lie!"', *Analysis* 74: 59–64.

Reiche, B. Sebastian, Chris Carr, and Markus Pudelko (2010). 'The role of culture at different levels of analysis', *International Journal of Cross Cultural Management* 10 (2): 131–6.

Reid, James H. (1993). *Narration and Description in the French Realist Novel. The Temporality of Lying and Forgetting*. Cambridge: Cambridge University Press.

Reid, John E. (1947). 'A revised questioning technique in lie-detection tests', *Journal of Criminal Law and Criminology* (1931–1951): 542–7.

Reid, Thomas (2000). *Inquiry into the Human Mind*. Edited by T. Duggan. Chicago, IL: University of Chicago Press.

Reimer, Marga (2004). 'What malapropisms mean: A reply to Donald Davidson', *Erkenntnis* 60 (3): 317–34.

Reiner, Laura (1996). 'Why movie blurbs avoid newspapers', *Editor & Publisher: The Fourth Estate* 129, 123.

Reiss, Nira (1985). *Speech Act Taxonomy as a Tool for Ethnographic Description: An Analysis Based on Videotapes of Continuous Behavior in Two New York Households*. Philadelphia, PA: John Benjamins.

Reiter, Ehud (2007). 'An Architecture for Data-to-Text Systems', *Proceedings of ENLG-2007*: 97–104.

Reiter, Ehud and Robert Dale (2000). *Building Natural Language Generation Systems*. Cambridge: Cambridge University Press.

Reiter, Ehud, Roma Robertson, and Liesl M. Osman (2003). 'Lessons from a Failure: Generating Tailored Smoking Cessation Letters', *Artificial Intelligence* 144: 41–58.

Reynolds, David (1982). *The Creation of the Anglo-American Alliance 1937-41: A Study in Competitive Cooperation*. Chapel Hill, NC: University of North Carolina Press.

Rich, Frank (2006). *The Greatest Story Ever Sold*. New York, NY: Penguin.

Richards, Jane M. and Gross, James J. (1999). 'Composure at Any Cost? The Cognitive Consequences of Emotion Suppression', *Personality and Social Psychology Bulletin* 25: 1033–44.

Ridderinkhof, K. Richard, Markus Ullsperger, Eveline A. Crone, and Sander Nieuwenhuis (2004). 'The role of the medial frontal cortex in cognitive control', *Science* 306 (5695): 443–7.

Ridenour, D. (1998). 'How would Gore fare if he were called on to serve?', *Austin American-Statesman*: August 16: A15.

Ringrose, Christopher (2006). 'Lying in Children's Fiction', *Children's Literature in Education* 37: 229–36.

Ritchie, Graeme (1999). 'Developing the Incongruity-Resolution Theory', in *Proceedings of AISB Symposium on Creative Language: Stories and Humour*. Edinburgh, April 1999, 78–85.

Ritchie, Graeme (2004). *The Linguistic Analysis of Jokes*. London: Routledge.

Roberts, Craige (2004). 'Context in dynamic interpretation', in Laurence Horn and Gregory Ward (eds), *The Handbook of Pragmatics*. Oxford: Blackwell, 197–220.

Roberts, Craige (2012). 'Information structure in discourse: Towards an integrated formal theory of pragmatics', *Semantics & Pragmatics* 5, Article 6: 1–69.

Roberts, Richard M. and Roger J. Kreuz (1994). 'Why Do People Use Figurative Language?', *Psychological Science* 5 (3): 159–63.

Roberts, Sam (2015). 'Obituary for Tyler Drumheller', *New York Times*, August 9, 2015.
Robertson, Thomas S., Jehoshua Eliashberg, and Talia Rymon (1995). 'New Product Announcement Signals and Incumbent Reactions', *Journal of Marketing* 59: 1–15.
Robinson, Henry Peachum (1869). *Pictorial Effect in Photography*. Philadelphia, PA: Edward L. Wilson.
Robison, Adam (2005). 'Waiver of Plea Agreement Statements: A Glimmer of Hope to Limit Plea Statement Usage to Impeachment', *South Texas Law Review* 46: 661–93.
Rockwell, Patricia (2000). 'Lower, slower, louder: Vocal cues of sarcasm', *Journal of Psycholinguistic Research* 29: 483–93.
Rockwell, Patricia (2007). 'Vocal features of conversational sarcasm: A comparison of methods', *Journal of Psycholinguistic Research* 36: 361–9.
Rogers, Sheena (2013). 'Truth, Lies and Meaning in Slow Motion Images', in Arthur P. Shimamura (ed.), *Psychocinematics. Exploring Cognition at the Movies*. Oxford: Oxford University Press, 149–64.
Rolf, Eckard (2005). *Metaphertheorien. Typologie, Darstellung, Bibliographie*. Berlin and New York, NY: De Gruyter.
Ronan, Jehnna L., Wei Wu, and Gerald R. Crabtree (2013). 'From neural development to cognition: unexpected roles for chromatin', *Nature Reviews. Genetics* 14 (5): 347–59.
Rosenfeld, J. Peter, Matthew Soskins, Gregory Bosh, and Andrew Ryan (2004). 'Simple, effective countermeasures to P300-based tests of detection of concealed information', *Psychophysiology* 41 (2): 205–19.
Rosenfeld, J. Peter, Bradley Cantwell, Victoria T. Nasman, Valerie Wojdac, Suzana Ivanov, and Lisa Mazzeri (1988). 'A modified, event-related potential-based guilty knowledge test', *International Journal of Neuroscience* 42 (1-2): 157–61.
Rosenfeld, J. Peter, Elena Labkovsky, Michael Winograd, Ming A. Lui, Catherine Vandenboom, and Erica Chedid (2008). 'The Complex Trial Protocol (CTP): a new, countermeasure-resistant, accurate, P300-based method for detection of concealed information', *Psychophysiology* 45 (6): 906–19.
Ross, Jacqueline. (2008). 'Do Rules of Evidence Apply (Only) in the Courtroom? Deceptive Interrogation in the United States and Germany', *Oxford Journal of Legal Studies* 28: 443–74.
Ross, Lee (1977). 'The intuitive psychologist and his shortcomings: Distortions in the attribution process', in *Advances in Experimental Social Psychology* 10: 173–220.
Ross, William David (2002 [1930]). *The Right and the Good*. Edited by Philip Stratton-Lake. Oxford: Oxford University Press.
Ross, William David (1939). *Foundations of Ethics*. Oxford: Clarendon Press.
Ross, William T. and Diana C. Robertson (2000). 'Lying: The Impact of Decision Context', *Business Ethics Quarterly* 10: 409–40.
Rossnagel, Christian (2000). 'Cognitive load and perspective taking: Applying the automatic-controlled distinction to verbal communication', *European Journal of Social Psychology* 30: 429–45.
Rothbart, Mary (1976). 'Incongruity, Problem-Solving and Laughter', in Antony J. Chapman and Hugh C. Foot (eds), *Humour and Laughter: Theory, Research and Applications*. London: Wiley, 37–54.
Rott, Hans (2003). 'Der Wert der Wahrheit', in Matthias Mayer (ed.), *Kulturen der Lüge*. Cologne, Weimar: Böhlau, 7–34.
Rubio-Fernández, Paula and Bart Geurts (2013). 'How to Pass the False-Belief Task Before Your Fourth Birthday', *Psychological Science* 24: 27–33.

Rubio-Fernández, Paula, Catherine Wearing, and Robyn Carston (2013). 'How metaphor and hyperbole differ: An empirical investigation of the relevance-theoretic account of loose use', *UCL Working Papers in Linguistics*: 46–65.

Rubio-Fernández, Paula, Catherine Wearing, and Robyn Carston (2015). 'Metaphor and Hyperbole: Testing the Continuity Hypothesis', *Metaphor and Symbol* 30: 24–40.

Ruddick, William (1988). 'Social self-deception', in Brian P. McLaughlin and Amélie Oksenberg Rorty (eds), *Perspectives on Self-deception*. Berkeley, CA: University of California Press, 380–9.

Rudolph, Frederick and John R. Thelin (1990). *The American College and University: A History* (rev. edn). Athens, GA: University of Georgia Press.

Ruedy, Nicole E., Celia Moore, Francesca Gino, and Maurice E. Schweitzer (2013). 'The cheater's high: The unexpected affective benefits of unethical behavior', *Journal of Personality and Social Psychology* 105 (4): 531–48.

Rusconi, Elena and Timothy Mitchener-Nissen, T. (2013). 'Prospects of functional magnetic resonance imaging as lie detector', *Frontiers in Human Neuroscience* 7: 594.

Russano, Melissa B., Christian A. Meissner, Fadia M. Narchet, and Saul M. Kassin (2005). 'Investigating True and False Confessions Within a Novel Experimental Paradigm', *Psychological Science* 16: 481–6.

Russell, Bertrand (1923). 'Vagueness', *The Australasian Journal of Psychology and Philosophy* 1 (2): 84–92.

Russell, Bertrand (1967). *The Problems of Philosophy*. Oxford: Oxford Paperbacks.

Russell, James, Christofer Jarrold, and Deborah Potel (1995). 'What Makes Strategic Deception Difficult for Children: The Deception or the Strategy', *British Journal of Developmental Psychology* 12: 301–14.

Rutschmann, Ronja and Alex Wiegmann (2017). 'No need for an intention to deceive: Challenging the traditional definition of lying', *Philosophical Psychology* 30 (4): 434–53.

Ryan, Michael and Dorothea Owen (1977). 'An accuracy survey of metropolitan newspaper coverage of social issues', *Journalism Quarterly* 54: 27–32.

Rycyna, Caroline C., Crystal D. Champion, and Anita E. Kelly (2009). 'First impressions after various types of deception: Less favorable following expectancy violation', *Basic and Applied Social Psychology* 31: 40–8.

Ryle, Gilbert (1949). *The Concept of Mind*. London: Hutchinson.

Sacerdote, Bruce (2001). 'Peer effects with random assignment: Results for Dartmouth roommates', *Quarterly Journal of Economics* 116 (2): 681–704.

Sacks, Harvey (1975). 'Everyone Has to Lie', in Mary Sánches and Ben G. Blount (eds), *Sociocultural Dimensions of Language Use*. New York, NY: Academic Press, 57–80.

Sagarin, Brad J., Kelton v. L. Rhoads, and Robert B. Cialdini (1998). 'Deceiver's Distrust: Denigration as a Consequence of Undiscovered Deception', *Personality and Social Psychology Bulletin* 24: 1167–76.

Sainsbury, Mark (2005). *Reference without Referents*. Oxford: Oxford University Press.

Sainsbury, Mark (2011). 'Fiction and Acceptance-Relative Truth, Belief and Assertion', in Franck Lihoreau (ed.), *Truth in Fiction*. Berlin: De Gruyter, 38–137.

Sakama, Chiaki, Martin Caminada, and Andreas Herzig (2014). 'A Formal Account of Dishonesty', *Logic Journal of the IGPL* 23 (2): 259–94.

Sánchez-Pagés, Santiago and Marc Vorsatz (2007). 'An experimental study of truth-telling in sender-receiver games', *Games and Economic Behavior* 61: 86–112.

Santos, Fernanda (2006, September 20). 'DNA evidence frees a man imprisoned for half his life', *The New York Times*, A1.
Sapir, Edward (1944). 'Grading, a study in semantics', *Philosophy of Science* 11 (2): 93–116.
Sapir, Edward (1949). *Language: An Introduction to the Study of Speech*. New York, NY: Harcourt, Brace and Company.
Sarat, Austin (ed.) (2015). *Law and Lies. Deception and Truth-Telling in the American Legal System*. Oxford: Oxford University Press.
Sartre, Jean-Paul (2003). *Being and Nothingness*. Trans. Hazel E. Barnes. London, New York, NY: Routledge.
Sassoon, Galit W. (2012). 'A Typology of Multidimensional Adjectives', *Journal of Semantics* 30: 335–80.
Saul, Jennifer Mather (2000). 'Did Clinton say something false?', *Analysis* 60 (267): 255–7.
Saul, Jennifer Mather (2012a). *Lying, Misleading, and What is Said. An Exploration in Philosophy of Language and in Ethics*. Oxford: Oxford University Press.
Saul, Jennifer Mather (2012b). 'Just go ahead and lie!', *Analysis* 72 (1): 3–9.
SBC = *Santa Barbara Corpus of Spoken American English* (2000ff). By John W. Du Bois, Wallace L. Chafe, Chrales Meyer, and Sandra A. Thompson. Philadelphia, PA: Linguistic Data Consortium.
Sbisà, Marina (2001). 'Illocutionary force and degrees of strength in language use', *Journal of Pragmatics* 33: 1791–814.
Schaffer, Deborah (2012). 'The Language of Scam Spams: Linguistic Features of "Nigerian Fraud" E-Mails', *ETC: A Review of General Semantics* 69 (2): 157–79.
Schauer, Frederick and Richard Zeckhauser (2009). 'Paltering', in Brooke Harrington (ed.), *Deception: From Ancient Empires to Internet Dating*. Stanford, CA: Stanford University Press, 38–54.
Scheffler, Israel (1973). *Reason and Teaching*. London: Routledge.
Schiestl, Florian P. (2005). 'On the success of a swindle: pollination by deception in orchids', *Die Naturwissenschaften* 92 (6): 255–64.
Schmidt, Rosemarie and Joseph F. Kess (1985). 'Persuasive Language in the Television Medium: Contrasting Advertising and Televangelism', *Journal of Pragmatics* 9: 287–308.
Schmitt, Frederick F. (1994). 'The Justification of Group Beliefs', in Frederik F. Schmitt (ed.), *Socializing Epistemology: The Social Dimensions of Knowledge*. Lanham, MD: Rowman & Littlefield, 257–87.
Schofield, Malcomb (2007). 'The Noble Lie', in Giovanni R. F. Ferrari (ed.), *The Cambridge Companion to Plato's Republic*. Cambridge: Cambridge University Press, 138–64.
Schopenhauer, Arthur (1903 [1840]). *On the Basis of Morality*, trans. Arthur Brodrick Bullock. http://onlinebooks.library.upenn.edu/webbin/book/lookupname?key=Schopenhauer%2C%20Arthur%2C%201788%2D1860.
Schopenhauer, Arthur (1969 [1859]). *The World as Will and Representation*, trans. E. F. J. Payne. New York, NY: Dover.
Schwartz, A. (2010, June 14). Netanyahu—smart he is not. [in Hebrew]. Retrieved from http://www.facebook.com/topic.php?uid=120300104673132andtopic=146.
Schwartz, Beth M., Holly E. Tatum, and Jerry W. Wells (2012). 'The honor system: Influences on attitudes, behaviors, and pedagogy', in R. Eric Landrum and Maureen A. McCarthy (eds), *Teaching Ethically: Challenges and Opportunities*. Washington, DC: American Psychological Association, 89–98.

Schwob, Marcel (1924 [1896]). *Imaginary Lives*. Transl. Lorimer Hammond. New York, NY: Boni and Liveright (original French ed. *Vies imaginaires*. 1896).

Schwoebel, John, Shelly Dews, Ellen Winner, and Kavitha Srinivas (2000). 'Obligatory processing of the literal meaning of ironic utterances: Further evidence', *Metaphor and Symbol* 15 (1–2): 47–61.

Scott, Gini G. (2010). *Playing the Lying Game*. Santa Barbara, CA: Praeger.

Searle, John (1969). *Speech Acts: An Essay in the Philosophy of Language*. Cambridge: Cambridge University Press.

Searle, John R. (1975). 'The Logical Status of Fictional Discourse', *New Literary History* 6 (2): 319–32.

Searle, John R. (1979a). *Expression and Meaning: Studies in the Theory of Speech Acts*. Cambridge: Cambridge University Press.

Searle, John R. (1979b). 'Indirect Speech Acts', in: John R. Searle (1979), *Expression and Meaning. Studies in the Theory of Speech Acts*. Cambridge: Cambridge University Press, 30–57.

Searle, John R. (1979c). 'The logical status of fictional discourse', in John R. Searle, *Expression and Meaning. Studies in the Theory of Speech Acts*. Cambridge: Cambridge University Press, 58–75.

Searle, John R. and Daniel Vanderveken (1985). *Foundations of Illocutionary Logic*. Cambridge: Cambridge University Press.

Searle, John R. and Daniel Vanderveken (2005). 'Speech acts and illocutionary logic', Daniel Vanderveken (ed.), *Logic, Thought and Action*. Dordrecht: Springer, 109–32.

Seiter, John S., Jon Bruschke, and Chunsheng Bai (2002). 'The acceptability of deception as a function of perceivers' culture, deceiver's intention, and deceiver-deceived relationship', *Western Journal of Communication* 66 (2): 158–88.

Serota, Kim B., Timothy R. Levine, and Franklin J. Boster (2010). 'The Prevalence of Lying in America: Three Studies of Self-Reported Lies', *Human Communication Research* 36 (1): 2–25.

Serra-Garcia, Marta, Jan Potters, and Eric van Damme (2013). 'Lying About What You Know or About What You Do?', *Journal of the European Economic Association* 11 (5): 1204–29.

Seth, Anil K., John R. Iversen, and Gerald M. Edelman (2006). 'Single-trial discrimination of truthful from deceptive responses during a game of financial risk using alpha-band MEG signals', *NeuroImage* 32 (1): 465–76.

Seymour, Lee J. M. (2014). 'Let's Bullshit! Arguing, Bargaining and Dissembling Over Darfur', *European Journal of International Relations*, 20 (3): 571–95.

Seymour, Travis L. and Jess R. Kerlin (2008). 'Successful detection of verbal and visual concealed knowledge using an RT-based paradigm', *Applied Cognitive Psychology* 22: 475–90.

Seymour-Ure, Colin (1968). *The Press, Politics and the Public: An Essay on the Role of the National Press in the British Political System*. London: Methuen.

Shakespeare, William (2006). *Othello, the Moor of Venice*. Ed. Michael Neill. Oxford: Oxford University Press (first performance 1604; first British edn 1622).

Shalvi, Shaul and Carsten K. W. De Dreu (2014). 'Oxytocin promotes group-serving dishonesty', *Proceedings of the National Academy of Sciences of the United States of America* 111 (15): 5503–7.

Shao, Zeshu, Ardi Roelofs, and Antje S. Meyer (2012). 'Sources of individual differences in the speed of naming objects and actions: The contribution of executive control', *The Quarterly Journal of Experimental Psychology* 65 (10): 1927–44.

Shapiro, Debra L. and Robert J. Bies (1994). 'Threats, Bluffs, and Disclaimers in Negotiations', *Organizational Behavior and Human Decision Processes* 60: 14–35.

Shapiro, Ivor, Colette Brin, Isabelle Bédard-Brûlé, and Kasia Mychajlowycz (2013). 'Verification as a strategic ritual', *Journalism Practice* 7: 657–73.
Shavit, Ari (2013). *My Promised Land*. New York, NY: Random House.
Shaw, Dominic J., Aldert Vrij, Sharon Leal, Samantha Mann, Jackie Hillman, Pär Anders Granhag, et al. (2015). 'Mimicry and investigative interviewing: Using deliberate mimicry to elicit information and cues to deceit', *Journal of Investigative Psychology and Offender Profiling* 12 (3): 217–30.
Shaw, John C., Eric Wild, and Jason A. Colquitt (2003). 'To justify or excuse? A meta-analytic review of the effects of explanations', *Journal of Applied Psychology* 88: 444–58.
Sheehan, Neil (1971). *The Pentagon Papers*. New York, NY: Bantam.
Shen, Dan (2011). 'Unreliability', in Peter Hühn (ed.), *The Living Handbook of Narratology*. Hamburg: Hamburg University Press.
Shen, Helen (2015). 'Neuroscience: The hard science of oxytocin', *Nature* 522 (7557): 410–12.
Sherzer, Joel (2002). *Speech Play and Verbal Art*. Austin, TX: University of Texas Press.
Shibata, Mikihito, Forrest O. Gulden, and Nenad Sestan (2015). 'From trans to cis: transcriptional regulatory networks in neocortical development', *Trends in Genetics: TIG* 31 (2): 77–87.
Shibles, Warren (1985). *Lying: A Critical Analysis*. Whitewater, WI: The Language Press.
Shibuya, Shozo and Sonoe Shibuya (1993). 'The deception in personal relations', *Bulletin of Yamanashi Medical University* 10: 57–68.
Shiffrin, Seana Valentine (2014). *Speech Matters. On Lying, Morality, and the Law*. Princeton, NJ: Princeton University Press.
Shigemitsu, Yuka (2005). 'Nani wo kokochiyoi to kanjiru ka: Kaiwa no sutairu to ibunkakan komyunikeshon' [What do they feel comfortable: Conversational styles and intercultural communication], in Sachiko Ide and Masako Hiraga (eds), *Ibunka to komyunikeshon* [Different cultures and communication]. Tokyo: Hituzi Shobo, 216–37.
Shinmura, Izuru (ed.) (1991). *Kojien*. 4th edn. Tokyo: Iwanami Shoten.
Shirer, William (1960). *The Rise and Fall of the Third Reich*. New York, NY: Simon and Schuster.
Shu, Lisa L., Francesco Gino, and Max H. Bazerman (2011). 'Dishonest Deed, Clear Conscience: When Cheating Leads to Moral Disengagement and Motivated Forgetting', *Personality and Social Psychology Bulletin* 37: 330–49.
Shu, Lisa L., Nina Mazar, Francesca Gino, Dan Ariely,and Max H. Bazerman (2012). 'Signing at the beginning makes ethics salient and decreases dishonest self-reports in comparison to signing at the end', *Proceedings of the National Academic of Sciences*, 15197–200.
Shulman, David (2009). 'Accounts as social loopholes: reconciling contradictions between culture and conduct', in Matthew S. McGlone and Mark L. Knapp (eds), *The Interplay of Truth and Deception: New Agendas in Communication*. London: Routledge, 120–35.
Shuy, Roger W. (1993). *Language Crimes*. Oxford: Blackwell.
Shuy, Roger W. (1998). *The Language of Confession, Interrogation, and Deception*. Thousand Oaks, CA: Sage.
Sidgwick, Henry (1966). *The Methods of Ethics*. New York, NY: Dover.
Sidgwick, Henry (1981 [1874]). *Methods of Ethics*. (7th Hackett reprint edn.) Indianapolis, IN: Hackett.
Sidnell, Jack and Tanya Stivers (eds) (2012). *Handbook of Conversation Analysis*. Boston, MA: Wiley-Blackwell.

Siegal, Michael and Candida C. Peterson (1996). 'Breaking the mold: A fresh look at children's understanding of questions about lies and mistakes', *Developmental Psychology* 32 (2): 322–34.
Siegler, Frederick A. (1962). 'Demos on Lying to Oneself', *The Journal of Philosophy* 59: 469–75.
Siegler, Frederick A. (1966). 'Lying', *American Philosophical Quarterly* 3: 128–36.
Silva-Díaz, Cecilia (2015). 'Picturebooks, Lies and Mindreading', *BLFT. Nordic Journal of Childlit Aesthetics* 6.
Simons, Herbert W. and Jean Jones (2011). *Persuasion in Society*. New York: Routledge.
Simpson, David (1992). 'Lying, Liars and Language', *Philosophy and Phenomenological Research* 52: 623–39.
Simpson, David (2007). "Truth, Truthfulness and Philosophy in Plato and Nietzsche," *British Journal for the History of Philosophy* 15: 339–60.
Sing, Christine Simone (2007). 'The Linguistics of Lying—the State of the Art', in Jochen Mecke (ed.), *Cultures of Lying: Theories and Practice of Lying in Society, Literature, and Film*. Madison, WI: Galda + Wilch, 115–26.
Sinkeviciute, Valeria (2013). 'Decoding Encoded (Im)Politeness: "Cause on my Teasing you Can Depend"', in Marta Dynel (ed.), *Developments in Linguistic Humour Theory*. Amsterdam: John Benjamins, 263–88.
Sip, Kamila E., Andreas Roepstorff, William McGregor, and Chris D. Frith (2008). 'Detecting deception: the scope and limits', *Trends in Cognitive Sciences* 12 (2): 48–53.
Sip, Kamila E., Morten Lynge, Mikkel Wallentin, William B. McGregor, Christopher D. Frith, and Andreas Roepstorff (2010). 'The production and detection of deception in an interactive game', *Neuropsychologia* 48 (12): 3619–26.
Skyrms, Brian (2010). *Signals*. New York, NY: Oxford University Press.
Smiley, Marion (2010). 'Collective Responsibility', in Edward N. Zalta (ed.), *Stanford Encyclopedia of Philosophy*. Online. Available at https://plato.stanford.edu/entries/collective-responsibility/.
Smith, David Livingstone (2004). *Why We Lie: The Evolutionary Roots of Deception and the Unconscious Mind*. New York, NY: St. Martins.
Smith, Gregory Bruce (1997). 'Leo Strauss and the Straussians: An Anti-Democratic Cult?' *PS: Political Science and Politics* 30 (2): 180–9.
Smith, John Cyril and Brian Hogan (1988). *Criminal Law*, 6th edn. London: Butterworths.
Smith, Madeleine E., Jeffrey T. Hancock, Lindsay Reynolds, and Jeremy Birnholtz (2014). 'Everyday Deception or a Few Prolific Liars? The Prevalence of Lies in Text Messaging', *Computers in Human Behavior* 41: 220–7.
Smith, Peter B., Ronald Fischer, Vivian L. Vignoles, and Michael Harris Bond (2013) *Understanding social psychology across cultures*, 2nd edn. London: Sage.
Smyth, John Vignaux (2002). *The Habit of Lying: Sacrifical Studies in Literature, Philosophy, and Fashion Theory*. Durham, NC: Duke University Press.
Sniegoski, Stephen J. (2008). *The Transparent Cabal: The Neoconservative Agenda, War in the Middle East, and the National Interest of Israel*. Norfolk, VA: Enigma Editions.
Snow, Catherine E. (1972). 'Mothers' speech to children learning language', *Child Development* 43: 549–65.
Snyder, Jon R. (2009). *Dissimulation and the Culture of Secrecy in Early Modern Europe*. Berkeley, CA: University of California Press.
Snyder, Leslie C., Peter J. McQuillan, William L. Murphy, and Richard Joselson (June 2007). *Report on the conviction of Jeffrey Deskovic*. [http://www.westchesterda.net/jeffrey%20deskovic%20comm%20rpt.pdf]

Sodian, Beate (1991). 'The development of deception in young children', *British Journal of Developmental Psychology* 9 (1): 173–88.
Sodian, Beate and Uta Frith (1992). 'Deception and sabotage in autistic, retarded and normal children', *Journal of Child Psychology and Psychiatry* 33 (3): 591–605.
Sodian, Beate, Catherine Taylor, Paul L. Harris, and Josef Perner (1991). 'Early deception and the child's theory of mind: False trails and genuine markers', *Child Development* 62 (3): 468–83.
Sokol, Daniel K. (2006a). 'Dissecting "deception"', *Cambridge Quarterly of Healthcare Ethics* 15: 457–64.
Sokol, Daniel K. (2006b). 'Truth-telling in the doctor-patient relationship: a case analysis', *Clinical Ethics* September 1: 130–4.
Sokolov, Evgeniĭ Nikolaevich (1963). *Perception and the Conditioned Reflex*. New York, NY: Macmillan.
Solan, Lawrence M. and Peter M. Tiersma (2005). *Speaking of Crime: The Language of Criminal Justice*. Chicago, IL: The University of Chicago Press.
Solt, Stephanie (2015). 'Vagueness and imprecision: Empirical foundations', *Annual Review of Linguistics* 1 (1): 107–27.
Sorensen, Roy (2007). 'Bald-faced lies! Lying without the intent to deceive,' *Pacific Philosophical Quarterly* 88 (2): 251–64.
Sorensen, Roy (2010). 'Knowledge-Lies', *Analysis* 70 (4): 608–15.
Sorensen, Roy (2011). 'What lies behind misspeaking', *American Philosophical Quarterly* 48 (4): 399–409.
Sosa, Ernest (1994). 'Testimony and Coherence', in Bimal K. Matilal and Arindam Chakrabarti (eds), *Knowing from Words: Western and Indian Philosophical Analysis of Understanding and Testimony*. Oxford: Kluwer Academic Publishers, 59–67.
South, James, Rod Carveth, and William Irwin (eds) (2010). *Mad Men and Philosophy: Nothing Is as It Seems*. Oxford: Blackwell.
Southgate, Victoria, Coralie Chevallier, and Gergely Csibra (2010). 'Seventeen-month-olds appeal to false beliefs to interpret others' referential communication', *Developmental Science* 13: 907–12.
Spector, Benjamin (2013). 'Bare numerals and scalar implicatures', *Language and Linguistics Compass* 7 (5): 273–94.
Spence, Katelyn, Gina Villar, and Joanne Arciuli (2012). 'Markers of Deception in Italian Speech', *Frontiers in Psychology* 3: 1–9.
Spence, Sean A., Tom F. D. Farrow, Amy E. Herford, Iain D. Wilkinson, Ying Zheng, and Peter W. R. Woodruff (2001). 'Behavioural and functional anatomical correlates of deception in humans', *Neuroreport* 12 (13): 2849–53.
Sperber, Dan and Deirdre Wilson (1986). *Relevance: Communication and Cognition*. Oxford: Blackwell.
Sperber, Dan, Fabrice Clément, Christophe Heintz, Olivier Mascaro, Hugo Mercier, Gloria Origgi, et al. (2010). 'Epistemic vigilance', *Mind & Language* 25 (4): 359–93.
Spidel, Alicia, Hugues Hervé, Caroline Greaves, and John C. Yuille (2011). '"Wasn't Me!" A Field Study of the Relationship between Deceptive Motivations and Psychopathic Traits in Young Offenders', *Legal and Criminological Psychology* 16: 335–47.
Sporer, Siegfried L. (2004). 'Reality monitoring and detection of deception', in Pär Anders Granhag and Leif A. Strömwall (eds), *Deception Detection in Forensic Contexts*. Cambridge: Cambridge University Press, 64–102.

Sporer, Siegfried L. and Barbara Schwandt (2007). 'Moderators of nonverbal indicators of deception: A meta-analytic synthesis', *Psychology, Public Policy, and Law* 13 (1): 1–34.
Staffel, Julia (2011). 'Reply to Roy Sorenson, "Knowledge-lies"', *Analysis* 71 (2): 300–2.
Stalnaker, Robert (1970). 'Pragmatics', *Synthese* 22 (1–2): 272–89.
Stalnaker, Robert (1978). 'Assertion', in Peter Cole (ed.), *Syntax and Semantics 9: Pragmatics*, New York, NY: Academic Press, 315–32.
Stalnaker, Robert (1984). *Inquiry*. Cambridge, MA: MIT Press.
Stalnaker, Robert (1998). 'On the representation of context', in Robert Stalnaker, *Context and Content*. Oxford: Oxford University Press, 96–114.
Stalnaker, Robert (1999). 'Assertion', in Robert Stalnaker, *Context and Content*. Oxford: Oxford University Press, 78–95.
Stalnaker, Robert (2002). 'Common Ground', *Linguistics and Philosophy* 25 (5-6): 701–21.
Stanley, Jason (2015). *How Propaganda Works*. Princeton, NJ: Princeton University Press.
Steinbrenner, Jakob (2007). 'Can Fiction Lie?', in Jochen Mecke (ed.), *Cultures of Lying. Theories and Practice of Lying in Society, Literature, and Film*. Berlin: Galda + Wilch, 263–78.
Steller, Max and Günter Köhnken (1989). 'Criteria-based statement analysis. Credibility assessment of children's statements in sexual abuse cases', in David C. Raskin (ed.), *Psychological Methods in Criminal Investigation and Evidence*. New York, NY: Springer, 217–45.
Stern, Clara, William Stern, and James T. Lamiell (1909 [1999]). *Recollection, Testimony and Lying in Childhood*. Washington, DC: American Psychological Association.
Sternglanz, R. Weylin (2009). 'Exoneration of Serious Wrongdoing via Confession to a Lesser Offence', in Matthew S. McGlone and Mark L. Knapp (eds), *The Interplay of Truth and Deception*. New York, NY: Routledge, 165–92.
Stevenson, Leslie (1993). 'Why Believe What People Say?', *Synthese* 94 (3): 429–51.
Stokke, Andreas (2013a). 'Lying and Asserting', *The Journal of Philosophy* 110 (1): 33–60.
Stokke, Andreas (2013b). 'Lying, Deceiving, and Misleading'. *Philosophy Compass* 8 (4): 348–59.
Stokke, Andreas (2013c). 'Saying too Little and Saying too Much. Critical Notice of *Lying, Misleading, and What is Said* by Jennifer Saul', *Disputatio* V (35): 81–91.
Stokke, Andreas (2014). 'Insincerity', *Noûs* 48 (3): 496–520.
Stokke, Andreas (2016a). 'Lying and Misleading in Discourse', *Philosophical Review* 125 (1): 83–134.
Stokke, Andreas (2016b). 'Truthfulness and Gricean Cooperation'. *Grazer Philosophische Studien* 93 (3): 489–510.
Stokke, Andreas and Don Fallis (2016). 'Bullshitting, Lying, and Indifference toward Truth', *Ergo* (4) 10. http://dx.doi.org/103998/ergo.12405314.0004.010.
Stokke, Andreas (2018). *Lying and insincerity*. Oxford: Oxford University Press.
Stouthamer-Loeber, Magda (1986). 'Lying as a problem behavior in children: A review', *Clinical Psychology Review* 6 (4): 267–89.
Stratton-Lake, Philip (2002). 'Introduction', in William David Ross, *The Right and the Good*, ed. Philip Stratton-Lake. Oxford: Oxford University Press, ix–l.
Strauss, Leo (1958). *Thoughts on Machiavelli*. Chicago, IL: University of Chicago Press.
Strauss, Leo (1975). *The Argument and the Action of Plato's Laws*. Chicago, IL: University of Chicago Press.
Strawson, Peter F. (1950). 'Truth', *Proceedings of the Aristotelian Society* 24: 111–56.
Strichartz, Abigail F. and Roger V. Burton (1990). 'Lies and truth: A study of the development of the concept', *Child Development* 61 (1): 211–20.

Strömwall, Leif A., Maria Hartwig, and Pär Anders Granhag (2006). 'To act truthfully: Nonverbal behavior and strategies during a police interrogation', *Psychology Crime and Law* 12: 207–19.
Strudler, Alan (2005). 'Deception Unraveled', *The Journal of Philosophy* 102 (9): 458–73.
Suchotzki, Kristina, Geert Crombez, Evelyne Debey, Kim van Oorsouw, and Bruno Verschuere (2015). 'In Vino Veritas? Alcohol, Response Inhibition and Lying', *Alcohol and Alcoholism* 50 (1): 74–81.
Suchotzki, Kristina, Geert Crombez, Fren T. Y. Smulders, Ewout H. Meijer, and Bruno Verschuere (2015). 'The cognitive mechanisms underlying deception: An event-related potential study', *International Journal of Psychophysiology* 95 (3): 395–405.
Sullivan, Kate, Ellen Winner, and Natalie Hopfield (1995). 'How children tell a lie from a joke: The role of second-order mental attributions', *British Journal of Developmental Psychology* 13 (2): 191–204.
Sullivan, Kate, Deborah Zaitchik, and Helen Tager-Flusberg (1994). 'Preschoolers Can Attribute Second-Order Beliefs', *Developmental Psychology* 30: 395–402.
Suls, Jerry (1972). 'A Two-Stage Model for the Appreciation of Jokes and Cartoons: An Information Processing Analysis', in Jeffrey H. Goldstein and Paul E. McGhee (eds), *The Psychology of Humor*. New York, NY: Academic Press, 81–100.
Suls, Jerry (1983). 'Cognitive Processes in Humor Appreciation', in Paul E. McGhee and Jeffrey H. Goldstein (eds), *Handbook of Humor Research*, Vol. I. New York, NY: Springer Verlag, 39–57.
Sundali, James and Darryl A. Seale (2004). 'The value of cheap talk and costly signals in coordinating market entry decision', *Journal of Business Strategies* 21 (1): 69–94.
Surian, Luca, Stefania Caldi, and Dan Sperber (2007). 'Attribution of beliefs by 13-month-old infants', *Psychological Science* 18: 580–6.
Sutter, Matthias (2009). 'Deception through telling the truth?! Experimental evidence from individuals and teams', *The Economic Journal* 119: 47–60.
Sutton, Samuel, Margery Braren, Joseph Zubin, and E. R. John (1965). 'Evoked-potential correlates of stimulus uncertainty', *Science* 150 (3700): 1187–8.
Swanson, Eric (2011). 'How not to theorize about the language of subjective uncertainty', in Andy Egan and Brian Weatherson (eds), *Epistemic Modality*. Oxford: Oxford University Press, 249–69.
Sweet, Monica A., Gail D. Heyman, Genyue Fu, and Kang Lee (2010). 'Are there limits to collectivism? Culture and children's reasoning about lying to conceal a group transgression', *Infant and Child Development* 19: 422–42.
Sweetser, Eve V. (1987). 'The definition of *lie*: An examination of the folk models underlying a semantic prototype', in Dorothy Holland and Naomi Quinn (eds), *Cultural Models in Language and Thought*. Cambridge: Cambridge University Press, 43–66.
Swift, Jonathan (1710). 'The Art of Political Lying', *The Examiner*, 10.
Swift, Jonathan (2001 [1726]). *Gulliver's Travels*. New York, NY: W.A. Norton (first British edn 1726).
Swinney, David A. (1979). 'Lexical access during sentence comprehension: (Re)consideration of context effects', *Journal of Verbal Learning and Verbal Behavior* 18 (6): 645–59.
Takano, Yotaro (2008). *Shudan shugi to iu sakkaku* [Misunderstanding of Collectivism]. Tokyo: Shin'yosha.
Talbott, William J. (1995). 'Intentional self-deception in a single coherent self', *Philosophy and Phenomenological Research* 55: 27–74.

Talwar, Victoria and Angela Crossman (2011). 'From little white lies to filthy liars: the evolution of honesty and deception in young children', *Advances in Child Development and Behavior* 40: 139–79.

Talwar, Victoria and Kang Lee (2002a). 'Development of lying to conceal a transgression: Children's control of expressive behavior during verbal deception', *International Journal of Behavioral Development* 26 (5): 436–44.

Talwar, Victoria and Kang Lee (2002b). 'Emergence of white-lie telling in children between 3 and 7 years of age', *Merrill-Palmer Quarterly* 48 (2): 160–81.

Talwar, Victoria and Kang Lee (2008). 'Social and cognitive correlates of children's lying behavior', *Child Development* 79 (4): 866–81.

Talwar, Victoria, Heidi M. Gordon, and Kang Lee (2007). 'Lying in the elementary school years: Verbal deception and its relation to second-order belief understanding', *Developmental Psychology* 43 (3): 804–10.

Talwar, Victoria, Susan M. Murphy, and Kang Lee (2007). 'White lie-telling in children for politeness purposes', *International Journal of Behavioral Development* 31 (1), 1–11.

Talwar, Victoria, Lonnie Zwaigenbaum, Keith J. Goulden, Shazeen Manji, Carly Loomes, and Carmen Rasmussen (2012). 'Lie-telling behavior in children with autism and its relation to false belief understanding', *Focus on Autism and Other Developmental Disabilities* 27 (2): 122–9.

Tartter, Vivien, Hilary Gomes, Boris Dubrovsky, Sophie Molholm, and Rosemarie Vala Stewart (2002). 'Novel metaphors appear anomalous at least momentarily: Evidence from N400', *Brain and Language* 80: 488–509.

Terkourafi, Marina (2010). 'What is said from different points of view', *Language and Linguistics Compass* 4 (8): 705–18.

Terkourafi, Marina (2011a). 'The puzzle of indirect speech', *Journal of Pragmatics* 43: 2861–5.

Terkourafi, Marina (2011b). 'Why indirect speech is not a natural default: Rejoinder to Steven Pinker's "Indirect Speech, Politeness, Deniability, and Relationship Negotiation"', *Journal of Pragmatics* 43: 2869–71.

Terkourafi, Marina (2014). 'The importance of being indirect: A new nomenclature for indirect speech acts', *Belgian Journal of Linguistics* 28: 45–70.

Terry, Richard (1994). 'Swift and Lying', *Philological Quarterly* 73: 243–65.

Thomas Aquinas (1266/72). *Summa theologica*, translated by Fathers of the English Dominican Province. Online Library of Liberty: http://oll.libertyfund.org/people/father-of-the-english-dominican-province.

Thomas, George C. III (2007). 'Regulating Police Deception During Interrogation', *Texas Tech Law Review* 39: 1293–319.

Thomason, Richmond (1990). 'Accommodation, meaning, and implicature: Interdisciplinary foundations for pragmatics', in Philip Cohen, Jerry Morgan, and Martha Pollack (eds), *Intentions in Communication*. Cambridge, MA: MIT Press, 325–63.

Thomasson, Amie (1999). *Fiction and Metaphysics*. Cambridge: Cambridge University Press.

Tiersma, Peter M. (2004). 'Did Clinton Lie: Defining "Sexual Relations"', *Chicago-Kent Law Review* 79 (3), Article 24.

Tiersma, Peter M. and Lawrence M. Solan (2012). 'The Language of Crime', in Peter M. Tiersma and Lawrence M. Solan (eds), *The Oxford Handbook of Language and Law*. Oxford: Oxford University Press, 340–53.

Ting-Toomey, Stella and Leeva Chung (1996). 'Cross-cultural interpersonal communication', in William B. Gudykunst, Stella Ting-Toomey, and Tsukasa Nishida (eds), *Communication in Personal Relationships across Cultures*. London: Sage, 237–61.

Tollefsen, Christopher (2014). *Lying and Christian Ethics*. Cambridge: Cambridge University Press.
Tollefsen, Deborah (2007). 'Group Testimony', *Social Epistemology* 21: 299–311.
Tollefsen, Deborah (2009). 'Wikipedia and the Epistemology of Testimony', *Episteme* 6: 8–24.
Toma, Catalina L. and Jeffrey T. Hancock (2010). 'Looks and Lies: The Role of Physical Attractiveness in Online Dating Self-Presentation and Deception', *Communication Research* 37: 335–51.
Toma, Catalina L. and Jeffrey T. Hancock (2012). 'What Lies Beneath: The Linguistic Traces of Deception in Online Dating Profiles', *Journal of Communication* 62: 78–97.
Toma, Catalina L., Jeffrey T. Hancock, and Nicole B. Ellison (2008). 'Separating Fact from Fiction: An Examination of Deceptive Self-Presentation in Online Dating Profiles', *Personality and Social Psychology Bulletin* 34: 1023–36.
Tong, Frank and Michael S. Pratte (2012). 'Decoding patterns of human brain activity', *Annual Review of Psychology* 63: 483–509.
Toogood, J. H. (1980). 'What do we mean by *usually?*', *The Lancet* 1 (8177): 1094.
Tooke, William and Lori Camire (1991). 'Patterns of Deception in Intersexual and Intrasexual Mating Strategies', *Ethology and Sociobiology* 12: 345–64.
Travis, Catherine E. (2006). 'The Communicative Realisation of *Confianza* and *Calor Humano* in Colombian Spanish', in Cliff Goddard (ed.), *Ethnopragmatics: Understanding Discourse in Cultural Context*. Berlin: De Gruyter, 199–229.
Trivers, Robert (2000). 'The elements of a scientific theory of self-deception', *Annals of the New York Academy of Sciences* 907: 114–31.
Trivers, Robert (2010). *The Folly of Fools: The Logic of Deceit and Self-Deception in Human Life*. New York, NY: Basic Books.
Tsohatzidis, Savas L. (1990). 'A Few Untruths about Lie', in Savas L. Tsohatzidis (ed.), *Meanings and Prototypes: Studies in Linguistics Categorization*. New York, NY: Routledge, 438–46.
Tuckett, Anthony (1998). '"Bending the Truth": Professionals' Narratives about Lying and Deception in Nursing Practice', *International Journal of Nursing Studies* 35: 292–302.
Tuomela, Raimo (1992). 'Group Beliefs', *Synthese* 91: 285–318.
Turner, Ross E., Charles Edgley, and Glen Olmstead (1975). 'Information Control in Conversations: Honesty is not Always the Best Policy', *Kansas Journal of Sociology* 11 (1): 69–89.
Turner, Ross E., Somayajulu Sripada, and Ehud Reiter (2010). 'Generating Approximate Geographic Descriptions', in Emiel Krahmer and Mariet Theune (eds), *Empirical Methods in Natural Language Generation*. Berlin, Heidelberg: Springer, 121–40.
Turri, John (2010). 'Prompting Challenges', *Analysis* 70: 456–62.
Turri, John (2011). 'The Express Knowledge Account of Assertion', *Australasian Journal of Philosophy* 89: 37–45.
Turri, John (2014a). 'Knowledge and Suberogatory Assertion', *Philosophical Studies* 167: 557–67.
Turri, John (2014b). 'You Gotta Believe', in Clayton Littlejohn and John Turri (eds), *Epistemic Norms: New Essays on Action, Belief, and Assertion*. Oxford: Oxford University Press, 193–200.
Turri, John (2015). 'Selfless assertions: some empirical evidence', *Synthese* 192 (4): 1221–33.
Turri, John (2016). *Knowledge and the Norm of Assertion: An Essay in Philosophical Science*. Cambridge: Open Book Publishers.
Turri, John and Angelo Turri (2015). 'The Truth About Lying', *Cognition* 138 (1): 161–8.

Twain, Mark (1882). 'On the Decay of the Art of Lying', in Mark Twain, *The Stolen White Elephant and Other Detective Stories*. Boston, MA: James R. Osgood & Comp., 217–25.

Twain, Mark (1996 [1899]). 'My First Lie, and How I Got Out of It', in Shelley Fisher Fishkin (ed.), *The Man That Corrupted Hadleyburg*. Oxford: Oxford University Press, 167–80.

Twain, Mark (2010a). *The Adventures of Tom Sawyer*. New York, NY: Oxford University Press (first American edn 1876).

Twain, Mark (2010b). *The Adventures of Huckleberry Finn*. New York, NY: Oxford University Press (first American edn 1884).

Tyler, James M. and Robert S. Feldman (2005). 'Deflecting Threat to One's Image: Dissembling Personal Information as a Self-Presentation Strategy', *Basic and Applied Social Psychology* 27: 371–8.

Tyler, James M., Robert S. Feldman, and Andreas Reichert (2006). 'The price of deceptive behavior: Disliking and lying to people who lie to us', *Journal of Experimental Social Psychology* 42 (1): 69–77.

Tynan, Matthew (2011). 'Tour de farce!: Misblurb marketing in film and publishing', *Cardoza Arts and Entertainment Law Journal* 29: 793–826.

Ullsperger, Markus and D. Yves von Cramon (2001). 'Subprocesses of performance monitoring: a dissociation of error processing and response competition revealed by event-related fMRI and ERPs', *NeuroImage* 14 (6): 1387–401.

Uma, Divya, Caitlin Durkee, Gudrun Herzner, and Martha Weiss (2013). 'Double deception: ant-mimicking spiders elude both visually- and chemically-oriented predators', *PloS One* 8 (11): e79660.

Underwood, Jean D. M., Lianne Kerlin, and Lee Farrington-Flint (2011). 'The Lies We Tell and What They Say About Us: Using Behavioural Characteristics to Explain Facebook Activity', *Computers in Human Behavior* 27 (5): 1621–6.

Undeutsch, Udo (1967). *Forensische Psychologie* [*Forensic Psychology*]. Göttingen: Verlag für Psychologie.

Unger, Peter (1975). *Ignorance: A Defense of Skepticism*. Oxford: Clarendon Press.

US Senate Select Committee on Intelligence (2012). *Executive Summary: Committee Study of the Central Intelligence Agency's Detention and Interrogation Program*, 13 December. Updated for Release 3 April 2014. Declassified 3 December 2014.

Utsumi, Akira (2000). 'Verbal irony as implicit display of ironic environment: Distinguishing ironic utterances from nonirony', *Journal of Pragmatics* 32: 1777–806.

Van Bockstaele, Bram, Bruno Verschuere, Thomas Moens, Kristina Suchotzki, Evelyne Debey, and Adriaan Spruyt (2012). 'Learning to lie: Effects of practice on the cognitive cost of lying', *Frontiers in Psychology* 3: 1–8.

van Deemter, Kees (2009). 'Utility and language generation: the case of vagueness', *Journal of Philosophical Logic* 38 (6): 607–32.

van Deemter, Kees (2010). *Not Exactly: in Praise of Vagueness*. Oxford: Oxford University Press.

van der Henst, Jean-Baptiste and Laure Carles and Dan Sperber (2002). 'Truthfulness and Relevance in Telling the Time', *Mind & Language* 17 (5): 457–66.

Van Leeuwen, Theo and Ruth Wodak (1999). 'Legitimising immigration: a discourse-historical approach', *Discourse Studies* 1: 83–119.

Van Swol, Lyn M., Michael T. Braun, and Deepak Malhotra (2012). 'Evidence for the Pinocchio Effect: Linguistic Differences between Lies, Deception by Omissions, and Truths', *Discourse Processes* 49: 79–106.

Vannucci, Robert C., Todd F. Barron, and Ralph L. Holloway (2013). 'Frontal brain expansion during development using MRI and endocasts: relation to microcephaly and Homo floresiensis', *Anatomical Record* 296 (4): 630–7.

Varden, Helga (2010). 'Kant and Lying to the Murderer at the Door... One more Time: Kant's Legal Philosophy and Lies to Murderers and Nazis', *Journal of Social Philosophy* 41: 403–21.

Varelius, Jukka (2006). 'Allhoff on Business Bluffing', *Journal of Business Ethics* 65: 163–71.

Vendemia, Jennifer M. C., Robert F. Buzan, and Stephanie L. Simon-Dack (2005). 'Reaction time of motor responses in two-stimulus paradigms involving deception and congruity with varying levels of difficulty', *Behavioral Neurology* 16: 25–36.

Vergis, Nikolaos (2015). *The interplay of pragmatic inference, face and emotion.* Unpublished PhD diss. Department of Linguistics, University of Illinois at Urbana-Champaign.

Verheyen, Steven, Sabrina Dewil, and Paul Egré (2017). 'Subjective meaning in gradable adjectives: The case of *tall* and *heavy*', ms, Institut Jean Nicod, Paris, France.

Vermeule, Blakey (2010). *Why Do We Care about Literary Characters?* Baltimore, MD: The Johns Hopkins University Press.

Vernham, Zarah and Aldert Vrij (2015). 'A review of the collective interviewing approach to detecting deception in pairs', *Crime Psychology Review* 1: 43–58.

Vernham, Zarah, Aldert Vrij, Samantha Mann, Sharon Leal, and Jackie Hillman (2014). 'Collective interviewing: Eliciting cues to deceit using a turn-taking approach', *Psychology, Public Policy, and Law* 20: 309–24.

Verschuere, Bruno and Gershon Ben-Shakhar (2011). 'Theory of the Concealed Information Test', in Bruno Verschuere, Gershon Ben-Shakhar, and Ewout H. Meijer (eds), *Memory Detection: Theory and Application of the Concealed Information Test.* Cambridge: Cambridge University Press, 128–48.

Verschuere, Bruno, Gershon Ben-Shakhar, and Ewout H. Meijer (eds) (2011). *Memory Detection: Theory and Application of the Concealed Information Test.* Cambridge: Cambridge University Press.

Verschuere, Bruno, Teresa Schuhmann, and Alexander T. Sack (2012). 'Does the inferior frontal sulcus play a functional role in deception? A neuronavigated theta-burst transcranial magnetic stimulation study', *Frontiers in Human Neuroscience* 6: 284.

Verschuere, Bruno, Kristina Suchotzki, and Evelyne Debey (2015). 'Detecting Deception through Reaction Times', in Pär Anders Granhag, Aldert Vrij, and Bruno Verschuere (eds), *Detecting Deception. Current Challenges and Cognitive Approaches.* Chichester: Wiley, 269–91.

Verschuere, Bruno, Adriaan Spruyt, Ewout H. Meijer, and Henry Otgaar (2011). 'The ease of lying', *Consciousness and Cognition* 20 (3): 908–11.

Verschueren, Jef (1985). *What People Say They Do with Words: Prolegomena to an Empirical-Conceptual Approach to Linguistic Action.* New York, NY: Ablex.

Viebahn, Emanuel (2017). 'Non-literal lies', *Erkenntnis* 82: 1367–80.

Vincent Marrelli, Jocelyne (1997). 'On non-serious talk: cross-cultural remarks on the (un)importance of (not) being earnest', in Herman Parret (ed.), *Pretending to Communicate.* Amsterdam: John Benjamins, 253–75.

Vincent Marrelli, Jocelyne (2003). 'Truthfulness', in Jef Verschueren, Jan-Ola Östman, Jan Blommaert, and Chris Bulcaen (eds), *Handbook of Pragmatics.* Amsterdam: John Benjamins, 1–48.

Vincent Marrelli, Jocelyne (2004). *Words in the Way of Truth. Truthfulness, Deception, Lying across Cultures and Disciplines.* Naples: Edizione Scientifiche Italiane.

Vincent, Jocelyne M. and Cristiano Castelfranchi (1981). 'On the art of deception: How to lie while saying the truth', in Herman Parret, Marina Sbisà and Jef Verschueren (eds), *Possibilities and Limitations of Pragmatics. Proceedings of the Conference on Pragmatics, Urbino, July 8-14*. Amsterdam: John Benjamins, 749–77.

Visu-Petra, George, Mircea Miclea, and Laura Visu-Petra (2012). 'Reaction time-based detection of concealed information in relation to individual differences in executive functioning', *Applied Cognitive Psychology* 26 (3): 342–51.

Visu-Petra, George, Mihai Varga, Mircea Miclea, and Laura Visu-Petra (2013). 'When interference helps: increasing executive load to facilitate deception detection in the concealed information test', *Frontiers in Psychology* 4: 146.

Vitell, Scott J., Erin Baca Dickerson, and Troy A. Festervand (2000). 'Ethical Problems, Conflicts and Beliefs of Small Business Professionals', *Journal of Business Ethics* 28: 15–24.

Vlastos, Gregory (1991). *Socrates: Ironist and Moral Philosopher*. Ithaca, NY: Cornell University Press.

von der Goltz, Anna (2009). *Hindenburg*. Oxford: Oxford University Press.

von Hippel, William and Robert Trivers (2011). 'The evolution and psychology of self-deception', *The Behavioral and Brain Sciences* 34 (1): 1–16; discussion 16–56.

von Neumann, John and Oskar Morgenstern (1944). *The Theory of Games and Economic Behavior*. Princeton, NJ: Princeton University Press.

Voyer, Daniel and Cheryl Techentin (2010). 'Subjective acoustic features of sarcasm: Lower, slower, and more', *Metaphor and Symbol* 25: 1–16.

Vrij, Aldert (1993). 'Credibility judgements of detectives: the impact of nonverbal behavior, social skills, and physical characteristics on impression formation', *The Journal of Social Psychology* 133 (5): 601–10.

Vrij, Aldert (2000). *Detecting Lies and Deceit: The Psychology of Lying and Implications for Professional Practice*. Chichester: John Wiley.

Vrij, Aldert (2004). 'Why Professionals Fail to Catch Liars and How They Can Improve', *Legal and Criminal Psychology* 9: 159–83.

Vrij, Aldert (2005). 'Criteria-based content analysis: A qualitative review of the first 37 studies', *Psychology, Public Policy, and Law* 11: 3–41.

Vrij, Aldert (2008). *Detecting Lies and Deceit. Pitfalls and Opportunities*, 2nd edn. Chichester: Wiley.

Vrij, Aldert (2015). 'Verbal Lie Detection Tools: Statement Validity Analysis, Reality Monitoring and Scientific Content Analysis', in Pär Anders Granhag, Aldert Vrij, and Bruno Verschuere (eds), *Detecting Deception. Current Challenges and Cognitive Approaches*. Chichester: Wiley, 3–35.

Vrij, Aldert and Michelle Holland (1998). 'Individual Differences in Persistence in Lying and Experiences While Deceiving', *Communication Research Reports* 15: 299–308.

Vrij, Aldert and Samantha Mann (2001). 'Telling and detecting lies in a high-stake situation: The case of a convicted murderer', *Applied Cognitive Psychology* 15: 187–203.

Vrij, Aldert, Katherine Edward, and Ray Bull (2001a). 'Police officers' ability to detect deceit: The benefit of indirect deception detection measures', *Legal and Criminological Psychology* 6 (2): 185–96.

Vrij, Aldert, Katherine Edward, and Ray Bull (2001b). 'People's insight into their own behaviour and speech content while lying', *British Journal of Psychology* 92 Part 2: 373–89.

Vrij, Aldert, Pär Anders Granhag, and Stephen Porter (2010). 'Pitfalls and Opportunities in Nonverbal and Verbal Lie Detection', *Psychological Science in the Public Interest* 11: 89–121.

Vrij, Aldert, Gun R. Semin, and Ray Bull (1996). 'Insight into behavior displayed during deception', *Human Communication Research* 22 (4): 544–62.

Vrij, Aldert, Pär Anders Granhag, Samantha Mann, and Sharon Leal (2011). Outsmarting the liars: Toward a cognitive lie detection approach. *Current Directions in Psychological Science* 20 (1): 28–32.

Vrij, Aldert, Samantha Mann, Susanne Kristen, and Ronald P. Fisher (2007). 'Cues to deception and ability to detect lies as a function of police interview styles', *Law and Human Behavior* 31 (5): 499–518.

Vrij, Aldert, Sharon Leal, Samantha Mann, Lara Warmelink, Pär Anders Granhag, and Ronald P. Fisher (2010). 'Drawings as an innovative and successful lie detection tool', *Applied Cognitive Psychology* 24: 587–94.

Vrij, Aldert, Samantha Mann, Ronald P. Fisher, Sharon Leal, Rebecca Milne, and Ray Bull (2008). 'Increasing cognitive load to facilitate lie detection: the benefit of recalling an event in reverse order', *Law and Human Behavior* 32 (3): 253–65.

Vrij, Aldert, Shyma Jundi, Lorraine Hope, Jackie Hillman, Esther Gahr, Sharon Leal, et al. (2012). 'Collective interviewing of suspects', *Journal of Applied Research in Memory and Cognition* 1: 41–4.

Wade, Elizabeth and Herbert H. Clark (1993). 'Reproduction and demonstration in quotations', *Journal of Memory and Language* 32: 805–19.

Waismann, Friedrich (1945). 'Verifiability', Proceedings of the Aristotelian Society, Supplementary Volumes 19: 119–50.

Walczyk, Jeffrey J., Laura L. Harris, Terri K. Duck, and Devyani Mulay (2014). 'A Social-cognitive Framework for Understanding Serious Lies: Activation-Decision-Construction-Action Theory', *New Ideas in Psychology* 34: 22–36.

Walczyk, Jeffrey J., Frank P. Igou, Alexa P. Dixon, and Talar Tcholakian (2013). 'Advancing lie detection by inducing cognitive load on liars: a review of relevant theories and techniques guided by lessons from polygraph-based approaches', *Frontiers in Psychology* 4: 14.

Walczyk, Jeffrey J., Karen S. Roper, Eric Seemann, and Angela M. Humphrey (2003). 'Cognitive mechanisms underlying lying to questions: Response time as a cue to deception', *Applied Cognitive Psychology* 17: 755–74.

Walczyk, Jeffrey J., Jonathan P. Schwartz, Rayna Clifton, Barett Adams, Min Wei, and Peijia Zha (2005). 'Lying person-to-person about life events: A cognitive framework for lie detection', *Personnel Psychology* 58: 141–70.

Wall Street Journal Editorial Board (2014). Second climate thoughts, *The Wall Street Journal*, April 7.

Walper, Sabine, and Renate Valtin (1992). 'Children's understanding of white lies', in Richard Watts, Sachiko E. Ide, and Konrad Ehlich (eds), *Politeness in Language: Studies in its History, Theory and Practice*. Berlin: De Gruyter, 231–51.

Walsh, Richard (2007). *The Rhetoric of Fictionality: Narrative Theory and the Idea of Fiction*. Ohio, OH: The Ohio State University Press.

Walton, Douglas and Fabrizio Macagno (2009). 'Wrenching from context: The manipulation of commitments', *Argumentation* 24 (3): 283–317.

Walton, Kendall L. (1984). 'Transparent pictures: On the nature of photographic realism', *Critical Enquiry* 11 (2): 246–77.

Walton, Kendall L. (1990). *Mimesis as Make-Believe: On the Foundations of the Representational Arts*. Cambridge, MA: Harvard University Press.

Walzer, Michael (1973). 'Political Action and the Problem of Dirty Hands', *Philosophy and Public Affairs* 2 (2): 160–80.

Wang, Joseph Tao-Yi, Michael Spezio, and Colin F. Camerer (2010). 'Pinocchio's Pupil: Using Eyetracking and Pupil Dilation to Understand Truth-Telling and Deception in Sender-Receiver Games', *American Economic Review* 100 (3): 984–1007.

Wang, Xiao-Lei, Ronan Bernas, and Philippe Eberhard (2011). 'When a lie is not a lie: Understanding Chinese working-class mothers' moral teaching and moral conduct', *Social Development* 21: 68–87.

Ward, Gregory (1984). 'A pragmatic analysis of epitomization: Topical ization it's not', *Papers in Linguistics* 17: 145–61.

Ward, Gregory and Betty J. Birner (2006). 'Information structure', in Bas Aarts and April McMahon (eds), *Handbook of English Linguistics*. Oxford: Basil Blackwell, 291–317.

Warmelink, Lara, Aldert Vrij, Samantha Mann, Shyma Jundi, and Pär Anders Granhag (2012). 'The effect of question expectancy and experience on lying about intentions', *Acta Psychologica* 141: 178–83.

Warren, Donald I. and David Warren (1996). *Radio Priest: Charles Coughlin, the Father of Hate Radio*. New York, NY: Free Press.

Wason, Peter C. (1966). 'Reasoning', *New Horizons in Psychology* 1: 135–51.

Waterman, Richard J. and Martin I. Bidartondo (2008). 'Deception above, deception below: linking pollination and mycorrhizal biology of orchids', *Journal of Experimental Botany* 59 (5): 1085–96.

Watson, Tom (2012). 'The Lobbyists, the Russians, Google and "Wife Beater"', *Tom-Watson.co.uk*, 2 February. Online. Available at http://socialistunity.com/the-lobbyists-the-russians-google-and-wife-beater.

Webber, Jonathan (2013). 'Liar!', *Analysis* 73 (4): 651–9.

Wegner, Daniel M. (1994). 'Ironic processes of mental control', *Psychological Review* 101 (1): 34.

Weiner, Matthew (2006). 'Are all conversational implicatures cancellable?', *Analysis* 66: 127–30.

Weinrich, Harald (2005). 'The Linguistics of Lying', in Harald Weinrich, *The Linguistics of Lying and Other Essays*, trans. Jane K. Brown and Marshall Brown. Seattle, WA: University of Washington Press, 3–80.

Weiss, Brent and Robert S. Feldman (2006). 'Looking Good and Lying to Do It: Deception as an Impression Management Strategy in Job Interviews', *Journal of Applied Social Psychology* 36: 1070–86.

Weissman, Benjamin and Marina Terkourafi (2016). 'Are false implicatures lies? An experimental investigation', in Fabienne Salfner and Uli Sauerland (eds), *Pre-proceedings of 'Trends in Experimental Pragmatics'*. Berlin: XPRAG, 162–9.

Welling, Sarah N. et al. (1998). *Federal Criminal Law and Related Actions: Crimes, Forfeiture, the False Claims Act and RICO*. Vol. 2. St. Paul, MN: West Group.

Wellman, Henry M., David Cross, and Julanne Watson (2001). 'Meta-analysis of theory-of-mind development: The truth about false belief', *Child Development* 72 (3): 655–84.

Welsh, David T., Lisa D. Ordonez, Deidre G. Snyder, and Michael S. Christian (2015). 'The Slippery Slope: How Small Ethical Transgressions Pave the Way for Larger Future Transgressions', *Journal of Applied Psychology* 100: 114–27.

Wernick, Andrew (1991). *Promotional Culture: Advertising, Ideology and Symbolic Expression*. London: Sage.

Werth, Paul (1999). *Text Worlds: Representing Conceptual Space in Discourse*. Harlow: Longman.

Wetlaufer, Gerald B. (1990). 'The Ethics of Lying in Negotiations', *Iowa L. Rev.* 75: 1219–72.

Wheeler, Mark A. and Donald T. Stuss (2003). 'Remembering and knowing in patients with frontal lobe injuries', *Cortex; a Journal Devoted to the Study of the Nervous System and Behavior* 39 (4-5): 827-46.

Wheeler, Mark A., Donald T. Stuss, and Endel Tulving (1995). 'Frontal lobe damage produces episodic memory impairment', *Journal of the International Neuropsychological Society: JINS* 1 (6): 525-36.

Wheeler, Mark A., Donald T. Stuss, and Endel Tulving (1997). 'Toward a theory of episodic memory: the frontal lobes and autonoetic consciousness', *Psychological Bulletin* 121 (3): 331-54.

White, I. A. and J. J. White (1978). 'Wahrheit und Lüge in Jurek Beckers Roman "Jakob der Lügner"', in Gerd Labroisse (ed.), *Zur Literatur und Literaturwissenschaft der DDR*. Amsterdam: Rodopi, 207-31.

Whitley, Bernard E. (1998). 'Factors associated with cheating among college students: A review', *Research in Higher Education* 39: 235-74.

Whitty, Monica T. and Adam N. Joinson (2009). *Truth, Lies and Trust on the Internet*. London: Routledge.

Wiegmann, Alex and Pascale Willemsen (2017): 'How the truth can make a great lie: An empirical investigation of lying by falsely implicating', *CogSci 2017*: 3516-21.

Wiegmann, Alex, Jana Samland, and Michael R. Waldmann (2016). 'Lying despite telling the truth', *Cognition* 150: 37-42.

Wierzbicka, Anna (1985). 'Different Cultures, Different Languages, Different Speech Acts: Polish vs. English', *Journal of Pragmatics* 9: 145-78.

Wierzbicka, Anna (1997). *Understanding Cultures through their Key Words: English, Russian, Polish, German, and Japanese*. Oxford: Oxford University Press.

Wierzbicka, Anna (2010). 'Cultural scripts and intercultural communication', in Anna Trosborg (ed.), *Pragmatics across Languages and Cultures*, Berlin: De Gruyter, 43-78.

Wild, Margaret (2006). *Fox*. Illus. Ron Brooks. St. Leonards, NSW: Allen & Unwin.

Wilde, Oscar (1891). 'The Decay of Lying', in Oscar Wilde, *Intentions*. London: James R. Osgood, 1-36.

Wilkomirski, Binjamin (1996). *Fragments. Memories of a Wartime Childhood*. Trans. Carole Brown Janeway. New York: Schocken (original German ed. *Bruchstücke. Aus einer Kindheit 1939-1948*. 1995).

Willer, Stefan (2009). '"Imitation of similar beings": social mimesis as an argument in evolutionary theory around 1900', *History and Philosophy of the Life Sciences* 31 (2): 201-13.

Williams, Bernard (1996). 'Truth, Politics, and Self-deception', *Social Research* 63/3, 603-17.

Williams, Bernard (2002). *Truth and Truthfulness. An Essay in Genealogy*. Princeton, NJ: Princeton University Press.

Williams, Emma J., Lewis A. Bott, John Patrick, and Michael B. Lewis (2013). 'Telling lies: the irrepressible truth?', *PLoS ONE*, 8, 4: e60713.

Williams, Kaylene C., Edward H. Hernandez, Alfred R. Petrosky, and Robert A. Page (2009). 'The Business of Lying', *Journal of Leadership, Accountability, and Ethics* 7: 1-20.

Williams, Shanna, Karissa Leduc, Angela M. Crossman, and Victoria Talwar (2017). 'Young deceivers: The identification of lying, executive functions and antisocial lies in preschool aged children', *Infant and Child Development* 26 (1): e1956.

Williams, Shanna, Kelsey Moore, Angela M. Crossman, and Victoria Talwar (2016). 'The role of executive functions and theory of mind in children's prosocial lie-telling', *Journal of Experimental Child Psychology* 141: 256-66.

Williamson, Timothy (1996). 'Knowing and asserting', *The Philosophical Review* 105: 489–523.
Williamson, Timothy (2000). *Knowledge and its Limits*. Oxford: Oxford University Press.
Wilmington, M. (2007). 'The 3 faces of Eddie', *Chicago Tribune*, September 9: D5.
Wilson, Anne E., Melissa D. Smith, and Hildy S. Ross (2003). "The nature and effects of young children's lies', *Social Development* 12 (1): 21–45.
Wilson, Deirdre (1995). 'Is there a maxim of truthfulness?', *UCL Working Papers in Linguistics* 7: 197–212.
Wilson, Deirdre and Dan Sperber (2002). 'Truthfulness and Relevance', *Mind* 111: 583–632.
Wilson, Deirdre and Dan Sperber (2004). 'Relevance theory', in Laurence R. Horn and Gregory Ward (eds), *The Handbook of Pragmatics*. Oxford: Blackwell, 607–32.
Wilson, Woodrow (1905). 'The honor system in school and college', *The New York Times* August 12: ES1.
Wimmer, Heinz and Josef Perner (1983). 'Beliefs about beliefs: Representation and constraining function of wrong beliefs in young children's understanding of deception', *Cognition* 13 (1): 103–28.
Witt, Diane M., Carol S. Carter, and Dawn M. Walton (1990). 'Central and peripheral effects of oxytocin administration in prairie voles (Microtus ochrogaster)'. *Pharmacology, Biochemistry, and Behavior* 37 (1): 63–9.
Wittgenstein, Ludwig (1953). *Philosophical Investigations*. Oxford: Blackwell.
Wolfsdorf, David (2007). 'The Irony of Socrates', *The Journal of Aesthetics and Art Criticism* 65: 175–87.
Wolterstorff, Nicholas (1995). *Divine Discourse: Philosophical Reflections on the Claim that God Speaks*. Cambridge: Cambridge University Press.
Wood, Allen (2008). *Kantian Ethics*. Cambridge: Cambridge University Press.
Woodward, Bob and Carl Bernstein (1974). *All the President's Men*. New York, NY: Simon & Schuster.
Woody, William D., Krista D. Forrest, and Sarah Yendra (2014). 'Comparing the Effects of Explicit and Implicit False-Evidence Ploys on Mock Jurors' Verdicts, Sentencing Recommendations, and Perceptions of Police Interrogation', *Psychology, Crime & Law* 20: 603–17.
Woolf, Raphael (2009). 'Truth as a Value in Plato's Republic', *Phronesis* 54: 9–39.
Worth, Sara E. (2015). 'Narration, Representation, Memoir, Truth and Lies', in Alexander Bareis and Lene Nordrum (eds), *How to Make Believe. The Fictional Truths of the Representational Arts*. Berlin: De Gruyter, 95–111.
Wreen, Michael (2013). 'A P.S. on B.S.: Some remarks on humbug and bullshit', *Metaphilosophy* 44: 105–15.
Wright, Crispin (1995). 'The epistemic conception of vagueness', *The Southern Journal of Philosophy* 33(S1): 133–60.
Wrighter, Carl P. (1984). *I Can Sell You Anything*. New York, NY: Ballantine Books.
Wyatt, Tristram D. (2014). 'Introduction to Chemical Signaling in Vertebrates and Invertebrates', in Carla Mucignat-Caretta (ed.), *Neurobiology of Chemical Communication*. Boca Raton, FL: CRC Press, 1–21.
Xenophon (1990). *Memoirs of Socrates*, in Xenophon, *Conversations of Socrates*, ed. Robin Waterfield. London: Penguin, 68–216.
Yalcin, Seth (2007). 'Epistemic Modals', *Mind* 116 (464): 983–1026.

Yalcin, Seth (2011). 'Nonfactualism about epistemic modality', in Andy Egan and Brian Weatherson (eds), *Epistemic Modality*. Oxford: Oxford University Press, 295–332.

Yamaguchi, Haruhiko (1988). 'How to Pull Strings with Words: Deceptive Violations in the Garden-Path Joke', *Journal of Pragmatics* 12: 323–37.

Yang, Jia (2008). 'How to Say "No" in Chinese: A Pragmatic Study of Refusal Strategies in Five TV Series', in Marjorie K. M. Chan and Hana Kang (eds), *Proceedings of the 20th North American Conference on Chinese Linguistics* (NACCL-20) 2, 1041–58. Columbus, OH: The Ohio State University.

Yarkoni, Tal, Russel A. Poldrack, Thomas E. Nichols, David C. Van Essen, and Tor D. Wager (2011). 'Large-scale automated synthesis of human functional neuroimaging data', *Nature Methods* 8 (8): 665–70.

Yeung, Lorrita N. T., Timothy R. Levine, and Kazuo Nishiyama (1999). 'Information Manipulation Theory and Perceptions of Deception in Hong Kong', *Communication Reports* 12 (1): 1–11.

Yin, Lijun, Martin Reuter, and Bernd Weber (2015). 'Let the man choose what to do: Neural correlates of spontaneous lying and truth-telling', *Brain and Cognition* 102: 13–25.

Yoshimura, Kimihiro. (1995). *Ninchi imiron no hoho* [Methods of cognitive semantics]. Tokyo: Jinbun shobo.

Zagorin, Perez (1990). *Ways of Lying: Dissimulation, Persecution and Conformity in Early Modern Europe*. Cambridge, MA: Harvard University Press.

Zagzebski, Linda Trinkaus (1996). *Virtues of the Mind*. Cambridge: Cambridge University Press.

Zagzebski, Linda Trinkaus (2012). *Epistemic Authority*. Oxford: Oxford University Press.

Zalta, Edward (1983). *Abstract Objects: An Introduction to Axiomatic Metaphysics*. Berlin, Heidelberg: Springer.

Zamyatin, Yevgeny (1924 [1920]). *We*. Trans. Gregory Zilboorg. New York, NY: Dutton (original Russian ed. *My*; written 1920).

Zelazo, Philip D. and Ulrich Müller (2002). 'Executive function in typical and atypical development', in Usha Goswami (ed.), *Blackwell Handbook of Childhood Cognitive Development*. Malden, MA: Blackwell, 445–70.

Zembaty, Jane S. (1988). "Plato's Republic and Greek Morality on Lying," *Journal of the History of Philosophy* 26: 517–45.

Zembaty, Jane S. (1993). 'Aristotle on Lying', *Journal of the History of Philosophy* 31: 7–29.

Zhang, Fenghui (2008). 'Conversational constraint of truthfulness on presuppositions', *Intercultural Pragmatics* 5 (1): 367–88.

Zillmann, Dolf and Joanne Cantor (1972). 'Directionality of Transitory Dominance as a Communication Variable Affecting Humor Appreciation', *Journal of Personality and Social Psychology* 24: 191–8.

Zillmann, Dolf and Joanne Cantor (1976). 'A Disposition Theory of Humor and Mirth', in Antony J. Chapman and Hugh C. Foot (eds), *Humor and Laughter: Theory, Research and Applications*. New York, NY: Wiley and Sons, 93–116.

Zipfel, Frank (2011). 'Unreliable Narration and Fictional Truth', *Journal of Literary Theory* 5 (1): 109–30.

Ziv, Yael (2013). 'Staam': Šmirat ʕikviyut ba-siax (Hebrew 'staam': Maintaining consistency in discourse), in Moshe Florentin (ed.), *Mexkarim ba-ʕivrit ha-xadašah u-ve-mekoroteha le-zexer Shaul Aloni (Studies in Modern Hebrew and its Origins in Memory of Shaul Aloni)*. Jerusalem: The Academy of the Hebrew Language [in Hebrew], 151–9.

Zuanazzi, Arianna (2013). Italian affirmative rhetorical questions generate ironic interpretations by default. University of Trento, Italy. Unpublished ms.

Zuckerman, Miron, Bella M. DePaulo, and Robert Rosenthal (1981). 'Verbal and nonverbal communication of deception', in Leonard Berkowitz (ed.), *Advances in Experimental Social Psychology*. Vol. 14. New York, NY: Academic Press, 1–59.

Zuckert, Catherine H. and Michael P. Zuckert (2006). *The Truth about Leo Strauss: Political Philosophy and American Democracy*. Chicago, IL: University of Chicago Press.

Zunshine, Lisa (2006). *Why We Read Fiction. Theory of Mind and the Novel*. Columbus, OH: The Ohio State University Press.

Index

absolutism 469–77, 480–1
acceptability 66–8, 388, 390, 565, 572–4
acceptance 110, 112, 117, 309–10. *See also* joint acceptance
act-utilitarianism 477–8, 480–1. *See also* utilitarianism
Activation-Decision-Construction-Action-Theory (ADCAT) 443
Adler, Jonathan 53, 57, 142, 191, 193–4, 197, 198–202
Adventures of Huckleberry Finn, The by Mark Twain 558
Adventures of Tom Sawyer, The by Mark Twain 558
advertising 69, 318, 325, 329, 355, 367, 376, 378, 522, 559–60
affective correlates of lying 451–2
akrasia 127, 213
ambiguity 64, 69, 187, 318, 324, 329–30, 368, 429
 covert ambiguity 329–30
amphiboly 376. *See also* mental reservation
ancient Greece 13–31, 506
Anna Karenina by Leo Tolstoy 204
ant 85
anti-realist theories 95. *See also* realist theories
anxiety 299, 410–11, 418, 427, 429, 439, 451
ape 89
approximation 356–8, 360, 364
Aquinas, Thomas 13–14, 150, 203–4, 295
Arabic. *See* Makkan Arabic
Arendt, Hannah 533
Aristotle 13–31, 208, 213, 530
arts 553–64
asserting/assertion 2, 4, 33–43, 46, 50–4, 56, 59, 64, 67, 102, 105, 107, 109–19, 121–33, 135, 138, 144–9, 155, 157, 159, 161, 163–5, 170, 172, 174, 176–80, 182, 195, 197–8, 200–3, 232, 234, 239, 242–51, 253, 255–7, 259–63, 276, 281, 289, 292–3, 298, 303–5, 307–10, 313–14, 332, 335–6, 354–5, 361, 400, 423, 474, 477, 483–4, 486, 512, 515, 519–20, 559. *See also* cynical assertion; selfless assertion
 (epistemic) norm of assertion 121–3, 126, 129–30
 graded assertion 177
 insincere assertion 2, 4, 38–40, 59, 123, 135, 144–8, 195, 197, 263
 knowledge norm of assertion (KNA) 123, 129–30 (*see also* knowledge-assertion norm)
 negligently asserting 128
 reasonably asserting 128
 untruthful assertion 34–7
 vicious assertion 127–9, 131–2
assumption 6, 8, 42, 52, 96, 127, 143, 145, 152, 161, 176–7, 187–8, 194, 200, 253, 262, 285, 311, 313, 323, 325, 332, 364, 373–4, 378, 411, 495, 497–8, 522, 526, 534, 543, 569–70
attitude 30, 63, 68, 103–4, 113, 171, 200, 207, 243, 266, 276, 298, 310, 313, 316–17, 323–5, 341, 378, 439, 448, 525, 535, 551, 557, 562, 573
attribution 113–14, 324
audience design hypothesis 76
Augustine 142, 252, 274, 288–9, 326, 469–71, 480, 511
Austin, John L. 144, 200, 291–2, 358
Autism Spectrum Disorder (ASD) 404
autonomy 293–4, 488
Avventure di Pinocchio, Le by Carlo Collodi 557

Babytalk systems 420–35
bald-faced lie 3, 36–47, 60, 107–8, 116, 125, 129, 136, 137–8, 140, 143–4, 147–8, 199, 244–5, 252–63, 291, 304–5, 392, 560

banter 126, 394–5, 555
bargaining game 279
Baron Munchausen's Narrative of his Marvelous Travels and Campaigns in Russia by Rudolf Erich Raspe 544
being deceptive 107, 159, 187, 189–90, 235, 247–8, 258–9, 263
being economical with the truth 383, 394–5, 522
belief 1–2, 6–8, 18–19, 26, 33–4, 37–42, 51, 57, 60, 66, 68, 96, 98, 105, 107, 110, 112–19, 120–33, 135, 140, 149–67, 168, 171–82, 183–7, 189–91, 195, 199, 204–15, 219, 224, 227, 233–5, 242, 248–54, 259–60, 264–5, 268, 271–6, 280, 285, 295, 305–14, 317, 324–9, 331–9, 370, 374–5, 378, 381, 391, 394, 400–4, 409, 445, 447–8, 451, 476, 478, 481, 484, 508, 519, 530, 532, 535, 537, 548, 551, 567–9, 571
    biased belief 211–12
    coverage-supported belief 189
    first-order belief 7–8, 403–4, 508
    second-order belief 7–8, 403–4
bluffing/bluff 33, 87, 277–87
boaster 27–9
Bok, Sissela 1–2, 32, 57, 170, 224, 290, 367, 384–5, 388–9, 475–6, 512–13, 534, 573
brain 7, 83–94, 410, 413, 449, 456–68
Brandom, Robert 110–11, 114–19
brazenness 263
Brodmann area (BA) 90, 280, 461
Bronston case (Bronston v. United States) 201, 485
Bruchstücke: Aus einer Kindheit 1939–1948 by Binjamin Wilkomirski 556
bullshitting/bullshit 128, 175, 260, 264–76, 281, 430, 538
    evasive bullshit 269
Bush, George W. 545–7
butt 335–6
butterfly 85

canned joke 329, 338
capitulation 263
Carson, Thomas L. 43–5
central resources 80–1
certainty 170–82, 200–1, 432, 484, 521, 529. See also uncertainty
    certainty-uncertainty continuum 172

Charlie the gambler case 258–9
cheating student case 137, 147–8, 254, 260–1, 263
children's lie-telling behavior 399–407
children's literature 558
chilling deceptive speech 484
Chinese 66–7, 388, 392, 570–3
Chisholm, Roderick M. and Thomas D. Feehan 1, 34–7, 40–2, 44–6, 51–3, 103–5, 109–10, 117, 151–2, 162, 167, 181, 186, 191, 198, 236, 260, 291–2, 328
classroom 249, 507, 515
clinical communication. See doctor-patient communication
Clinton, Bill 51, 194, 365–6, 395, 485
cognition 84, 86–9, 91, 294, 402, 407, 462
    cognitive abilities 6, 7, 83, 86–9, 399–407
    cognitive load 64–5, 78, 410–11, 413–14, 418, 441–4, 450, 452, 461
    cognitive neuroscience findings 459–67
    cognitive neuroscience methods 458–9
coherence theories 95–6
Coleman, Linda and Paul Kay 4, 59–60, 62, 66–68, 195–6, 384–5, 567–9
collective interviewing 417–18. See also forced turn-taking
Collodi, Carlo 557
commission 149–69, 186
commitment 178–80, 198–9, 200–1, 383
common ground 48–9, 109, 148, 164, 308–13, 336
community week case 196–7
computational linguistics 420–35
concealed-information paradigms 457–60, 466
Concealed Information Test (CIT) 6, 454. See also Guilty Knowledge Test
concealing 57, 142, 155, 157, 247–8, 409, 445, 478, 556
concealment 29, 67, 184, 191, 260, 278, 299, 370
confidence 170–5, 178, 181, 219, 236–7, 293, 490, 513, 546
confirmation bias 355
consequences of lying 443–4
context 43–5, 47, 56, 58, 60, 62–3, 68–9, 75, 95, 118, 137, 142, 154, 157, 163–4, 199–201, 226, 246–7, 249, 255, 257–8, 260–2, 266, 269,

278, 282, 284–6, 292, 295–305, 308, 315–25, 327, 340–53, 355–61, 364, 367, 370–3, 376–8, 386, 388, 391–2, 417–18, 426, 428, 436, 439, 443, 448, 451, 462, 476, 483, 487, 489–91, 517–18, 522, 525–6, 531, 534, 536, 558, 562, 565–78. *See also* warranting context
contextomy 315–25
contrived distraction 155, 162–3, 168
Control Question Test (CQT) 411
conversational norm 129, 187–9, 191, 246, 269. *See also* maxim
cooperation 6, 61, 83, 295, 361, 363, 491, 502, 511, 519, 524
cooperative principle 3, 60–1, 134–5, 140, 145–6, 148–9, 373, 392, 567, 570
corpus/corpus-based evidence 344, 350–3, 373, 393. *See also* empirical evidence
correspondence theories 95–6
Cottingley Fairies 562–3
creationist teacher case 248, 250, 260, 271, 273
criminal offense 484–9
Criteria Based Content Analysis (CBCA) 412
culture 62, 65–7, 264, 374, 383, 388, 391, 517, 535, 565–77
Cuneo, Terence 50
cynical assertion 2, 255, 259

data-to-text generation 421–4
Davidson, Donald 96, 210–11, 372
Decay of Lying, The by Oscar Wilde 553
deceit 247, 259–60. *See also* deceive/deception
  benign deceit 427–8, 430
  bureaucratic deceit 535
  playful deceit 327
deceive/deception 1–3, 6–9, 13–21, 32–3, 35–6, 38–9, 42–3, 51–94, 109–10, 118–19, 136, 142, 149–69, 181, 183–8, 191, 194–5, 198–9, 233, 235–8, 246–50, 253–4, 257–60, 274, 280–1, 287–8, 291, 294–5, 298, 303–4, 317, 326–39, 356, 370–2, 374, 392, 394, 399–403, 411, 439, 443–70, 479, 481–4, 486–90, 512, 517–25, 529–40, 541–8, 552, 555–7, 561–2, 564, 566–8, 572. *See also* deceit; intention to deceive
deception by the police 483, 489–90
deception paradigms 449–50, 457–8
prevention-motivated deception 154, 156, 168
strategies of deception 155–69

deceptionists/non-deceptionists 33, 41–2, 46, 50, 53, 198–9, 252, 258–63, 518
deceptive false praise 18
declarative mood 114, 117
declarative sentence 59–60, 111–14, 179, 197
default interpretation 62, 329, 340–53
defaultness hypothesis 344–53
defaultness rules 353
definition of lie/lying 1, 14, 32–3, 35–8, 40–50, 65, 109, 115–16, 125–6, 174, 195, 198, 202–6, 244–7, 252–3, 288–92, 299, 384–6, 389, 446, 473, 476, 481–2, 518, 567–71
deflationary approaches 96–7, 212
degree-vagueness 358–60
development of lying 399–400
developmental psychology 399–407, 557
diary studies 409, 437, 439, 440, 444
discourse 4, 8, 22, 33, 39–40, 43, 60–1, 63–5, 117–18, 255, 265–6, 272, 289, 309, 311, 314, 323, 325, 328–9, 344, 346, 350, 352, 378, 517–28, 531, 569
discourse analysis 518
discourse marker 345
discourse types 69–70
dishonesty 474, 495, 503–5, 545, 557
  academic dishonesty 260, 268, 506–9
disposition theory of humour 338
dissimulation 141, 184
distortion 69, 294, 316, 323, 520, 523–4, 536, 538
division 209–12
doctor-patient communication 523–5
doctrine of the infelicities 144
Dolchstoßlegende (stab-in-the-back legend) 548–9
drawings 416–17
Dummett, Michael 110–14, 117
duping delight 441, 451–2
dynamic paradox 209
dystopian novel 554

economics 150, 495–505
education 150, 290, 378, 391, 438, 445, 506–16, 552
effect condition 206
Ekman, Paul 5, 57, 64, 184–6, 219, 410, 441, 451–4, 527, 561

electroencephalography (EEG) 458–61
elitism about democracy 531–3
emotion 64, 69, 79, 277, 304–6, 378, 391, 410, 418, 440, 448, 451–4, 478, 488, 535, 539, 557, 559, 561
empirical evidence 80, 195, 222, 257–9, 263, 341–4, 347–50, 452, 514, 541
empty names 307
English 4, 60, 62, 64, 66–8, 196, 247, 351, 373, 378, 421, 424, 557, 565, 568, 571–2, 574, 576
Enhanced Interrogation Techniques (EIT) 536
epistemic justification 122
epistemic modals 178–80
epistemic vigilance 214–228
equivocation 60, 156, 159, 164, 167–8, 476–7
ethics 8–9, 191–2, 282–302, 469–82, 540
euphemism 376, 394–5, 535
event-related potentials (ERP) 459
evolution 83–94, 217, 441, 444, 497, 505
exaggeration 538
ex-boyfriend case 195
excuse 289, 371, 375, 393, 408, 575–6
executive functioning (EF) 8, 400, 402, 404–6, 508
expected utility 432–3
exploitation of maxims 197, 257, 373
exploitation of vagueness 354, 365

fabrication 155, 158, 160–1, 163, 165–6, 168, 390, 409, 548–9, 552
　benign fabrication 327
face 384, 388, 393–4
　face-enhancement 392, 395
　face-threat 392, 395
faked autobiography 556
Fallis, Don 35, 47–8, 103–5, 138–9, 141, 143–5, 236–7, 246, 257–8, 260, 270, 272, 280, 291–2, 392
false-belief task 118–19, 403–4, 447–8. See also Sally-Anne task
falsehood 19–31, 46–9, 59, 66, 68, 125, 133, 136, 194, 199, 228, 236, 257, 265, 272, 281, 289, 305, 371–2, 376, 377–8, 379, 384, 389, 401, 420, 428, 447, 511, 519, 523, 537, 541, 556, 561, 567–9

false response 155, 159, 161, 166, 168
falsification 69, 520, 523, 537, 555, 563, 571
falsity 3, 8, 18, 46, 56, 60, 98–108, 110, 117–18, 131, 153, 160, 170–2, 174–5, 194, 203, 205, 209, 248, 264–5, 267, 271, 273–5, 281, 305, 354–6, 359, 362, 367, 373–4, 391, 395, 429, 484, 486, 567
Faulkner, Paul 41–2, 52–3
fiction 20, 270, 303–14, 327–8, 333–4, 336–8, 553–7, 561, 563–4, 574
flouting of maxims 66, 139–40, 197, 355, 373, 377, 385
forced turn-taking 417–18. See also collective interviewing
fraud 486–81
　Nigerian fraud emails 69
freedom 30, 293–4, 299
Frege, Gottlob 4, 35, 113, 307
French 64, 290
Fried, Charles 37–8, 184
functional magnetic resonance imaging (fMRI) 413, 451, 458–59, 462, 464, 467

game-theoretic model 430–3
garden-path joke 328–30. See also witticism
generality 356–7, 360, 363
goal 56–7, 61, 116, 149–60, 180, 193–4, 197–8, 272, 274, 280, 286–7, 327, 333, 335, 337, 339, 387–8, 395, 407, 425, 428, 439–41, 447–9, 508, 512–13, 515, 519–21, 524, 536, 542, 570
　acquire goal 152, 156–9, 167–8
　cease goal 152, 155, 165, 167
　continue goal 152, 159–60, 162–3
　prevent goal 152–5, 168
graded belief 171–80
graded salience hypothesis 341, 344, 353
Grice, Paul 3–4, 47, 60–1, 75, 109–11, 113, 122, 134–5, 139–49, 151–6, 187–8, 191, 194–5, 197, 199, 200–2, 257, 262, 266, 269, 292, 304, 314, 340, 355, 361–3, 368, 373, 385–6, 433–4, 517, 567, 570–1
ground truth 409
group intention 242
group lie 231–43
Guilty Knowledge Test (GKT) 6, 411, 454. See also concealed information test
Gulliver's Travels by Jonathan Swift 555–6

half-truth 1, 61, 155, 159, 161–2, 164, 167–8, 170, 185, 188, 191, 196, 356, 364–8, 376, 430, 532, 536, 538, 541, 549–52
Hebrew 326–39
hedge 381, 385
hiding information 361–4
historically important lies 543–8
history 1, 83, 197, 224, 541–52, 561, 563
Hitler, Adolf 529, 544–5, 548–9
hoax 327, 555–6, 563–4, 568
Homo Sapiens 88–92
Hooker, Brad 479
How-many-cars? case 197
humorous frame 327–8, 331, 335
humour 326–39
    put-on humour 330–3
hyperbole 45, 61, 106–7, 125, 158, 262, 370–81

idealism and the valuing of democracy 533–4
illocution/illocutionary act/illocutionary force 2, 6, 61–2, 178–80, 193, 200, 262–3, 315, 520
illusion of transparency 413
implicating/implicature
    conversational implicature 3, 54, 69, 123, 130, 139–41, 143, 146–7, 155, 194–6, 200–2, 254–5, 257, 262, 373
    deceptive implicature 196
    false implicature/falsely implicating 53, 61, 109, 141–5, 155, 157, 160, 165, 168, 193–4, 196, 198–9, 368, 373–4
    generalized implicature 196, 200
    particularized implicature 139, 196
    untruthful implicature 194–5, 197–8
imprecision 355–6
impression management 6–7, 410, 418, 427, 429, 439
incongruity-resolution model 338
indeterminacy 355–8, 361, 364, 366, 368, 561
indirectness 202, 394
individualism/collectivism 566
inference 77, 115, 121, 140, 191, 197, 200, 218, 256, 329, 335, 373, 423, 430, 433–4, 462–4, 509, 564
    logic of forward and reverse inference 463
Information Manipulation Theory 66, 457, 571
information transmission 496–7, 504

informativeness 355
inhibitory control 81, 400, 405–7, 462
inquiry 272–3
insincerity condition 173–5, 177
insinuating/insinuation 1, 194, 559
intention 8, 14, 32–3, 39–40, 44, 47–8, 52, 61, 66–7, 72, 77, 80, 89–90, 97, 105, 111, 133, 140, 149, 158, 163, 181, 191, 194, 200–3, 205, 209–10, 231–3, 239, 242, 251, 266, 273, 278, 284, 289–91, 293–5, 297, 315, 321–3, 325, 331, 333, 335–7, 364, 371, 374–5, 381, 386, 388–400, 403, 425, 433, 447, 469, 481, 496, 503, 511, 519, 521, 530, 537, 543–4, 559, 562, 570–1. *See also* group intention
intentionality condition 38, 205–7
intention to deceive 3, 17, 37–8, 40–2, 46, 116, 136, 180–1, 199, 203, 233, 235, 244–6, 251–4, 256, 258–63, 265, 288, 291, 299, 340, 391, 429, 447, 512, 518, 521–2, 562, 568. *See also* deceive/deception
interviewing. *See* collective interviewing
intralinguistic studies 67–8
Invention of Lying, The, movie 561
irony 17–19, 34, 45, 48, 57, 60, 65, 68, 125, 138–41, 197, 201, 247, 262, 291, 295, 326–7, 340–53, 370, 384
    affirmative irony 341–4
    negative irony 344–53

Jakob der Lügner by Jurek Becker 560
Japanese 565–78
joint acceptance 241–2
joke 7, 34, 50–1, 57, 138, 164, 247, 326–7, 328–30, 333, 335, 338, 385, 512
justifiability of deception 530–4
justification 1, 116, 237, 282, 292, 294–9, 385, 509–14, 534, 548, 569

Kant, Immanuel 8, 13–14, 36, 51, 150, 183, 186, 191, 195, 204, 262, 288, 291–2, 299, 471–5, 480–1, 497, 533
knowledge 17–18, 20–1, 26, 46, 48, 53, 60–1, 66, 72, 76, 120–33, 177–8, 181, 198, 205–7, 209–10, 214–28, 231–44, 260–1, 278, 284, 293, 310–13, 325, 336, 371, 377, 400, 402–3, 412, 422–3, 428, 447, 460, 463–4, 475, 506–7, 510, 514–16, 538, 550–2, 569

knowledge-action norm 233
knowledge-assertion norm 234. *See also* knowledge norm of assertion (KNA)
knowledge condition 205–7, 210
knowledge lie 2, 125, 129, 180–2, 231–43, 245, 254–7, 259

Lackey, Jennifer 104, 107, 116, 215–16, 218–19, 220, 223, 225, 235, 239–43, 254, 259–60, 271
law 9, 65, 69, 127, 142, 189, 192, 291, 297–8, 471–3, 483–94, 532
law of contradiction 208
leader 173, 255, 297–8, 321–4, 502, 514, 529, 532–3, 541–9, 550
learning 111–12, 223–5, 228, 506–7, 513–16
   learning environment 224, 228
   machine learning 468
leaving someone in the dark 190
lexical studies 58–9
Liar by Justine Larbalestier 558
lie/lying. *See also* bald-faced lie; definition of lie/lying; group lie; knowledge lie; lie detection
   acquisition of lying 7–8, 399–407, 557–8, 564
   altruistic lie 290, 296, 298, 449, 573
   aversion to lying 499
   benevolent lie 15, 288, 290, 294, 296–9
   blatant lie 331, 337, 354, 439, 444
   blue lie 68, 391–2
   categorization of lies 390
   coercion-lie 244–5, 254, 259
   collaborative lie 288, 290, 296, 298–9
   educational lie 297
   embedded lie 409
   evaluation of lying 8–9, 291, 400, 510, 557
   execution of the lie 78–80
   good lie 24–5
   green lie 339
   hard lie vs. soft lie 178, 180
   indirect lying 1, 193–4, 202
   lie construction 74–8
   low-stake lie vs. high-stake lie 446
   lying as pretexts for war 538, 543–8
   lying by lawyers and clients 490–1
   lying by the police 483, 489–90
   lying character 557–60
   lying in politics 491–3, 529–30
   lying in the media 491–3
   lying situations 560–1
   lying to oneself 205–7
   noble lie 23, 297, 530–2, 541, 560
   organized lying 535
   paternalistic lie 2, 25–6, 502
   pure lie 20–1
   red lie 392
   regular lie 20–2, 24
   self-defending lie 296
   shameful lie 27–8
   yellow lie 393
lie detection 5, 56, 58, 63–5, 78, 80, 91, 408–19, 452–5, 539. *See also* lie detector
lie detector 219, 409, 411, 453. *See also* polygraph
Lincoln, Abraham 551–2
linguistic cue 6, 58, 63–5
Linguistic Inquiry and Word Count (LIWC) 412
linguistics 2, 4, 56–70, 372–4, 420–35
literary genre 554–6
locution/locutionary act 61, 262, 396
lover of truth 26–7, 29

Machiavelli, Niccolo/machiavellism 439, 529, 531
magnanimous person 29–31
magnetoencephalography (MET) 458
Magritte, René 562
Makkan Arabic 66, 68, 568
Malagasy 68, 569–70
malapropism 45, 384
manipulation 2, 69, 526, 533–5, 562–3. *See also* Information Manipulation Theory
market-entry game 279, 284
maxim. *See also* exploitation of maxims; flouting of maxims; violation of maxims
   maxim of Manner 196, 256, 368, 570
   of Quality 3, 60, 66, 109–10, 122, 134–48, 187, 191, 197, 256–7, 269–72, 304, 355, 361, 373, 570–1
   of Quantity 143, 188, 191, 196–7, 355, 362, 570
   of Relation 146–7, 163, 196, 256
   of Truthfulness 135, 137, 139, 292, 373

Mearsheimer, John 297–8, 529, 531–2, 534, 536, 538, 542–6
media language 69
meiosis 61, 262
mendacity 332, 336, 411, 531–2
mental reservation 367, 476. *See also* amphiboly
meta-ethical analysis 510–11
metaphor 45, 59–60, 69, 106–7, 125, 139, 197, 262, 291, 295, 304, 327, 345, 370–81, 384–5, 512
microexpression 5, 451
Mill, John Stuart 13, 293, 297, 470, 477, 480
mimicking/mimicry 84–7, 416. *See also* pretending
misinformation 538
misleading 3, 45–6, 51–4, 57, 59–60, 105, 130, 133, 142, 173, 175, 177–8, 180, 185, 194, 197–201, 215, 242, 282, 290, 340, 344, 350, 354, 363–4, 367–8, 374, 376, 385, 405, 427, 442, 476, 483–6, 492, 535, 538, 541, 547, 550
misunderstanding 194, 199, 434, 571
modal statement 416
monitoring 6, 76–7, 443, 449, 456, 460. *See also* response monitoring
Moore, George Edward 480
Mopan Maya 66, 68, 571
moral education 391, 509–10
moral judgment 509–11
morality 13–16, 19–26, 31, 36, 50, 197, 200, 282–4, 469–82, 495, 572
　ordinary morality 14–16, 19, 26, 31
motivation 5–9, 27, 29, 67, 117, 150–2, 168, 205, 210–12, 273, 325, 388–9, 408, 440–1, 508, 557, 565, 571–2
multi-party interaction 331, 336–7
murderer-at-the-door case 8, 36–7, 193, 292, 298, 473
myth 21–4, 530–2, 537, 542, 548
　bad myth 21–4
　good myth 21–4
Myth of Autochthony 23–4
Myth of the Metals 23–4

Natural Language Generation (NLG) 420–35
near-infrared spectroscopy (NIRS) 458
Neuro-Linguistic Programming (NLP) 410–11

neuroimaging results 461–6
neuroscience 88, 456–68
New Zealand 572–7
non-deceptionists. *See* deceptionists/non-deceptionists
nonsense 266–7
nonverbal behavior 410–12, 418
nonverbal deception 418
normality 190, 522
norm of conversation 47, 139, 143, 246, 249, 257, 270
novelty 339, 347–8

obfuscation 1
omission 1, 51, 57, 78, 151–3, 161–2, 196, 243, 260, 321, 423–4, 426–7, 456, 536, 538
online dating 445
On the Decay of the Art of Lying by Mark Twain 553
open-texture 356, 359–60
orchid 84–7
organized persuasive communication (OPC) 530, 534–9
Othello by William Shakespeare 410, 454, 558–9
Othello error 410, 454
overlap analysis 465–6
overstatement 155, 158, 163–4, 166–8, 178–80, 370

paltering/palter 51, 194
partial or incorrect information 425–30
partial truth 390, 549–52
partitioning strategy 209
paternalistic lie 2, 25–6, 502
patterns of conversation 576–7
perjury 484–6
　literal truth defense 201
Persian 387
personality 413, 418, 438–40
perspective-taking 76–8, 118–19, 447, 510. *See also* Theory of Mind (ToM)
photography 562–3
picture 561–3
Pippi Långstrump by Astrid Lindgren 558
plagiarism 69. *See also* dishonesty: academic dishonesty

Plato 13–17, 19–26, 297, 506, 529–34, 541, 555
playings 327
police 391, 408–9, 413, 415, 417, 439, 441, 451, 483, 489–90, 496, 563
   police interrogations 285, 287
   police investigation 441–2
Polish 524, 527–8
politeness 9, 58, 60, 62, 67–8, 149, 158, 289, 295–6, 298–9, 309, 331, 365, 375, 382–98, 445, 577
political communication 529–30, 540
political marketing 534–9
political power 530, 534–9
political realism 531
politics 9, 39, 69, 181, 297, 319, 378, 491–2, 522, 529–40
polygraph 5, 277, 410–11, 453–4, 561
positron emission tomography (PET) 458–9
practical wisdom 510
pragmatics 60–3, 307–9, 310–14, 570–1
   cross-cultural pragmatics 65–7
   experimental pragmatics 70 (*see also* empirical evidence)
   intercultural pragmatics 65–7
   variational pragmatics 67–8
pragmatist theories 95
predicates of personal taste 359
presupposing/presupposition 49, 123, 193–202, 308–9, 330, 520
pretending 1, 49, 69, 84, 86, 156, 159, 164, 167–8, 177, 197, 255, 327, 335, 470, 519. *See also* mimicking/mimicry
pretending to lie 156, 159, 164, 167–8
pretense theories 313
prevention-motivated deception. *See* deception
prevention motivation 150–1
probability 175–6, 362, 432, 463–4, 495
processes versus outcomes 414–15
processing 6–7, 74, 76, 79–81, 200, 279, 344, 353, 405, 407, 451, 460, 462, 468
promise 2, 37–8, 43, 52, 61, 179, 187–8, 246, 253, 292–3, 386, 472, 474, 478–82, 486, 501–3, 519, 551, 558, 570
promotional culture 535, 537
promotion motivation 150
propaganda 2, 69, 268, 529–30, 534–40, 564
   propaganda model 536
proposition 1, 2, 33–55, 59–61, 72, 77, 95, 103, 109–19, 120–33, 139, 149–60, 170–82, 189, 193, 198–200, 208, 218–19, 236, 238, 244–51, 252–63, 270–6, 298, 303, 303–14, 328, 345, 354, 356, 520, 522–3, 556, 569
prosocial lie 128, 260, 288–302, 375, 404, 560
Prospect Theory 150
prototype semantics 567–9
psycholinguistics 7, 71–82
psychology 2, 5, 56, 63, 91–2, 150, 216, 219, 290, 297, 399–407, 409–10, 436–55, 462, 495, 518, 521, 526, 539, 557. *See also* developmental psychology; social psychology

Quintilian 372
quotation 315–25, 522–3
   selective quotation 318

rape by deception 483, 487–9
rate of lying 437–8
realism about democracy 531–2
realist theories. *See also* anti-realist theories
Reality Monitoring 5, 412
recontextualizing 323
redundancy theories 96–7
referential multiplicity 360
refusal 47, 375, 388, 565, 574–7
Regulatory Focus Theory 150
Reid, Thomas 216–18, 224
relationships 62, 89, 130, 279, 284, 388, 406, 436–7, 440, 444–6, 448–9, 512, 525–6, 530, 560
   close relationships 448–9
Relevance Theory 372–3
religion 56, 66, 69, 249, 561
response inhibition 7, 449–50, 456
response monitoring 449, 457, 460
rhetoric 321, 372, 529–30
   rhetorical figure 197, 262, 559
   rhetorical relation 423
Robinson Crusoe by Daniel Defoe 555–6
Rodney King case 563
Roosevelt, Franklin 532, 543–5
Ross, William David 52, 262, 478–81
rule consequentialism 479

salience 77, 340–53, 461
Sally-Anne task 7. *See also* false-belief task
Saul, Jennifer 3, 45–6, 51, 54, 97, 101, 103, 121, 142, 144, 148, 173, 175, 184–6, 191–2, 194, 199–200, 326, 384–6, 389, 512–13, 515

Schopenhauer, Arthur 290, 293–4, 296–7
Searle, John R. 2–3, 50, 61, 144, 172, 193, 200, 253, 291–2, 313, 520
second-language (L2) learner 65
selective excerpt 317–23
self-deception 86, 90–1, 203–13, 255, 260, 393, 444, 505, 537–8
self-deprecator 29
selfless assertion 2, 244–51, 259–61
self-regulation 8, 400, 405, 514
semantics 3–4, 58–63, 79, 306–7, 567, 569–70
    cognitive semantics 306, 567, 569–70
    truth-conditional semantics 59, 305–7
sentence 41, 45, 58–60, 63, 74, 77–80, 95, 110–14, 176, 179, 193, 197–9, 266, 305–7, 310, 322, 354–9, 365–8, 372, 426–7, 429, 434
sex differences 440, 444
sham 555
Shiffrin, Seana 42, 51, 53
Sidgwick, Henry 293, 297–8, 477, 480, 543
simple summativism 240
Simpson, David 20, 24, 33, 38–42, 44, 52–3
simulation 184, 284, 563
sincerity 2–3, 18, 38–9, 134–48, 171–2, 174, 176, 179, 212, 332, 382, 385, 440, 445. *See also* insincerity
sincerity condition 2, 3, 122, 144, 173–4, 180. *See also* insincerity condition
skepticism about democracy 531–3
social interaction 388, 430, 436–40, 444, 448, 457, 501, 503
social psychology 5, 150, 436–45, 521, 526
social situation 298–9, 447–9
Socrates 14–19, 24, 29, 530
Sorensen, Roy 2, 3, 46–8, 48, 53, 106, 116, 121, 125, 144, 175, 180, 231–8, 245–6, 254–7, 259, 261–3
Spanish 62, 65, 67–8, 378
    Colombian Spanish 58
    Ecuadorian Spanish 66, 196, 568
Spartacus case 231–2, 235–7, 245, 256–7, 263
speaker meaning 2–3, 194–5, 202
speech act 2–4, 59–62, 110, 112, 114, 118, 121–3, 125, 132, 139, 149–52, 163, 179, 200, 261–2, 288, 292, 295, 298–9, 303, 305, 309
    first-order and second-order speech act 295
    indirect speech act 193

speech act theory 2, 6, 61–2, 96, 144–5, 253, 291–2
speech production process 72, 74, 80
spin 319, 534–5
statement 6, 21, 29, 32–4, 36–8, 43–8, 51–2, 57, 59, 62–6, 68–9, 96–108, 112, 138, 141, 143, 149, 170, 172–9, 184–5, 194, 203, 222, 233, 241–2, 245–6, 249–50, 253–4, 257–8, 260, 264, 267, 270, 272–3, 275, 281–2, 293, 303–4, 307–8, 310–16, 320, 322–3, 326, 366–7, 380, 384–5, 391–2, 395, 399–400, 401–5, 412–13, 416, 424, 428, 443, 472–3, 475–6, 481, 484–7, 489–92, 496, 508–9, 512–13, 521, 524, 530, 538, 544, 547, 549, 552, 559, 561–2, 569
Statement Validity Analysis 412
static paradox 207–9. *See also* dynamic paradox
Stokke, Andreas 2–3, 48–9, 103–4, 109, 121, 173, 196–7, 199, 252, 309–11
strategic communication 5, 535
Strategic Use of Evidence (SUE) 415
subjectivity 359
success condition 206
suggestion 152–3
superiority theory of humour 338
supervaluation 360, 362, 365–7
supportive interviewer 416
suppression of relevant information 73–5
surprise 329, 331, 334, 338, 339
syntax 58, 64, 76, 79, 118, 305, 307, 518

taarof (Persian) 387–8
taking words out of context 69, 520–1
task switching 450, 462, 464–5
taxonomy 2, 132–3, 177–8, 243–4, 289, 294–9, 448
teasing 57, 327, 330–3, 335
temptation resistance paradigm 401, 404–5
testimony 44, 53, 104–5, 130, 214–30, 236, 254, 316, 325, 484–6, 549
Theory of Mind (ToM) 7, 8, 77, 83–4, 86, 89, 400, 402, 403–4, 443, 447, 464–5, 508, 557
total signification of an utterance (TSU) 195, 202
Tour, Georges de la 562
transcranial electrical stimulation (TES) 458
transcranial magnetic stimulation (TMS) 450, 458

travelogue/travel tale 554–5
trickster tale 554
trust 6, 28, 33, 38–46, 51–2, 53–4, 130, 141, 191, 202, 215–18, 221–8, 253, 256, 281–2, 288, 292, 293–5, 299, 388–9, 445, 472, 474, 477, 482, 502, 511–12, 532, 534, 542, 552
  betrayal of trust 38–9, 41–2, 44, 52, 54, 191, 542
  loss of social trust 293
trustworthiness 216, 221–3, 293
truth 2–8, 14–16, 18, 20–3, 26–7, 29–33, 36–9, 40–6, 53, 56, 58–82, 87, 90, 91, 95–108, 110–15, 117, 120–2, 130–1, 133, 137, 142, 148, 151, 153, 155, 157, 160, 162–3, 170–2, 174, 176, 178, 181, 183, 191, 193, 195, 200–1, 204–6, 208–9, 217, 219, 233, 246–9, 253–4, 256, 260–1, 264–5, 267–8, 271–6, 278, 281–2, 292–3, 297–9, 305–7, 310–12, 331, 355, 361, 365–7, 370–2, 376, 382–3, 385, 390–1, 394–5, 400–2, 405, 408–10, 412–13, 420, 424–7, 429–34, 441–4, 446, 449–59, 470, 471, 475, 481–2, 484–7, 490, 493, 502, 504, 506, 508, 510, 512–13, 517, 519, 521–2, 531–2, 538, 549–51, 555, 557–8, 560–1, 564, 569, 571–4
  concept of truth 20, 95, 117
  deviation from the truth 424–9
  fictional truth 304–5, 310
  property of truth 95
  truth predicate 95
truthfulness 13, 15, 26, 33, 40, 40–2, 51–2, 60, 64–5, 67, 135, 137, 139, 198–9, 201, 212, 253, 288–98, 331–2, 340, 355–6, 364, 373–4, 384–6, 390, 420, 472, 504, 512, 515, 521, 557, 564, 569, 571. See also *untruthfulness*
  lessened demands of truthfulness 199–200
  maxim of truthfulness 292, 373
truthmaker theories 95–6
TV series
  House, M.D. 326–39
  Lie to me 521
  Mad Men 559–60
Twain, Mark 120, 184, 553, 558
types of deviation from the truth 424–9
Tzeltal 68, 385, 387, 569–70

Ulbricht, Walter 232
uncertainty 170–82, 200–1, 278, 362, 364, 566, 573, 575. See also certainty
unclarity 266

understatement 158, 178–80, 262, 370, 409
unexpected questions 414
untruthfulness, 106, 204, 206, 262, 288, 293, 295, 299, 327, 332, 335–6, 385–6, 395, 555. See also truthfulness
  covert vs. overt untruthfulness 262, 327
  deceptive autotelic overt untruthfulness 335–6
  untruthfulness condition 206
utilitarianism 469, 477–81. See also act-utilitarianism

vagueness 354–69, 429, 534
  varieties of linguistic vagueness 356
verifiable details 415
violation of maxims 3, 60–1, 67, 69, 109, 135–46, 163, 196, 257, 263, 270, 304, 373, 571
violation of moral norms 50–1
virtue theory 210, 212–13
Vrij, Aldert 5–6, 57, 63–4, 78, 408–10, 412–18, 430, 441, 443–4, 447–50, 452, 455–6

warranting context 3, 43–5, 384–5
warranting the truth 43–4, 179, 200, 253, 255, 269, 481
what is implicated 3–4, 141, 202. See also what is said
what is said 3–4, 17, 29, 136, 139, 144, 197, 202, 260, 272–3, 308, 340–1, 370, 373, 376–7, 381, 385–6, 399, 409, 411, 518, 521–4. See also what is implicated
Williams, Bernard 40–1, 141–2, 212, 473, 512
withholding information 51, 184, 188, 192, 248, 394, 434, 538
witness case 44–5, 47–8, 60, 245, 254, 261–3, 304
Wittgenstein, Ludwig 360, 561
witticism 328–30. See also garden-path joke
word 4, 17–22, 33, 58–9, 63–4, 69, 71, 75, 77–8, 80–1, 239, 306, 315–21, 325, 345, 348, 356, 360, 372–3, 375, 378, 383, 385, 387, 394, 423–5, 429, 453, 458, 476, 559, 567–8
working memory 280, 400, 405–6, 443, 449–50, 457, 462–5
world knowledge 221, 225, 311–13, 377

Xenophon 14–15

OXFORD HANDBOOKS IN LINGUISTICS

THE OXFORD HANDBOOK OF AFRICAN AMERICAN LANGUAGE
Edited by Sonja Lanehart

THE OXFORD HANDBOOK OF APPLIED LINGUISTICS
Second edition
Edited by Robert B. Kaplan

THE OXFORD HANDBOOK OF ARABIC LINGUISTICS
Edited by Jonathan Owens

THE OXFORD HANDBOOK OF CASE
Edited by Andrej Malchukov and Andrew Spencer

THE OXFORD HANDBOOK OF CHINESE LINGUISTICS
Edited by William S-Y Wang and Chaofen Sun

THE OXFORD HANDBOOK OF COGNITIVE LINGUISTICS
Edited by Dirk Geeraerts and Hubert Cuyckens

THE OXFORD HANDBOOK OF COMPARATIVE SYNTAX
Edited by Gugliemo Cinque and Richard S. Kayne

THE OXFORD HANDBOOK OF COMPOSITIONALITY
Edited by Markus Werning, Wolfram Hinzen, and Edouard Machery

THE OXFORD HANDBOOK OF COMPOUNDING
Edited by Rochelle Lieber and Pavol Štekauer

THE OXFORD HANDBOOK OF COMPUTATIONAL LINGUISTICS
Edited by Ruslan Mitkov

THE OXFORD HANDBOOK OF CONSTRUCTION GRAMMAR
Edited by Thomas Hoffman and Graeme Trousdale

THE OXFORD HANDBOOK OF CORPUS PHONOLOGY
Edited by Jacques Durand, Ulrike Gut, and Gjert Kristoffersen

THE OXFORD HANDBOOK OF DERIVATIONAL MORPHOLOGY
Rochelle Lieber and Pavol Štekauer

THE OXFORD HANDBOOK OF DEVELOPMENTAL LINGUISTICS
Edited by Jeffrey Lidz, William Snyder, and Joe Pater

THE OXFORD HANDBOOK OF ELLIPSIS
Edited by Jeroen van Craenenbroeck and Tanja Temmerman

THE OXFORD HANDBOOK OF ERGATIVITY
Edited by Jessica Coon, Diane Massam, and Lisa deMena Travis

THE OXFORD HANDBOOK OF EVIDENTIALITY
Edited by Alexandra Y. Aikhenvald

THE OXFORD HANDBOOK OF GRAMMATICALIZATION
Edited by Heiko Narrog and Bernd Heine

THE OXFORD HANDBOOK OF HISTORICAL PHONOLOGY
Edited by Patrick Honeybone and Joseph Salmons

THE OXFORD HANDBOOK OF THE HISTORY OF ENGLISH
Edited by Terttu Nevalainen and Elizabeth Closs Traugott

THE OXFORD HANDBOOK OF THE HISTORY OF LINGUISTICS
Edited by Keith Allan

THE OXFORD HANDBOOK OF INFLECTION
Edited by Matthew Baerman

THE OXFORD HANDBOOK OF INFORMATION STRUCTURE
Edited by Caroline Féry and Shinichiro Ishihara

THE OXFORD HANDBOOK OF JAPANESE LINGUISTICS
Edited by Shigeru Miyagawa and Mamoru Saito

THE OXFORD HANDBOOK OF LABORATORY PHONOLOGY
Edited by Abigail C. Cohn, Cécile Fougeron, and Marie Hoffman

THE OXFORD HANDBOOK OF LANGUAGE AND LAW
Edited by Peter Tiersma and Lawrence M. Solan

THE OXFORD HANDBOOK OF LANGUAGE EVOLUTION
Edited by Maggie Tallerman and Kathleen Gibson

THE OXFORD HANDBOOK OF LEXICOGRAPHY
Edited by Philip Durkin

THE OXFORD HANDBOOK OF LINGUISTIC ANALYSIS
Second edition
Edited by Bernd Heine and Heiko Narrog

THE OXFORD HANDBOOK OF LINGUISTIC FIELDWORK
Edited by Nicholas Thieberger

THE OXFORD HANDBOOK OF LINGUISTIC INTERFACES
Edited by Gillian Ramchand and Charles Reiss

THE OXFORD HANDBOOK OF LINGUISTIC MINIMALISM
Edited by Cedric Boeckx

THE OXFORD HANDBOOK OF LINGUISTIC TYPOLOGY
Edited by Jae Jung Song

THE OXFORD HANDBOOK OF LYING
Edited by Jörg Meibauer

THE OXFORD HANDBOOK OF MODALITY AND MOOD
Edited by Jan Nuyts and Johan van der Auwera

THE OXFORD HANDBOOK OF NAMES AND NAMING
Edited by Carole Hough

THE OXFORD HANDBOOK OF PERSIAN LINGUISTICS
Edited by Anousha Sedighi and Pouneh Shabani-Jadidi

THE OXFORD HANDBOOK OF POLYSYNTHESIS
Edited by Michael Fortescue, Marianne Mithun, and Nicholas Evans

THE OXFORD HANDBOOK OF PRAGMATICS
Edited by Yan Huang

THE OXFORD HANDBOOK OF SOCIOLINGUISTICS
Second Edition
Edited by Robert Bayley, Richard Cameron, and Ceil Lucas

THE OXFORD HANDBOOK OF TENSE AND ASPECT
Edited by Robert I. Binnick

THE OXFORD HANDBOOK OF THE WORD
Edited by John R. Taylor

THE OXFORD HANDBOOK OF TRANSLATION STUDIES
Edited by Kirsten Malmkjaer and Kevin Windle

THE OXFORD HANDBOOK OF UNIVERSAL GRAMMAR
Edited by Ian Roberts